CONTENTS

What's Wrong?

WHAT'S WRONG?

Applied Ethicists and Their Critics

David Boonin
University of Colorado at Boulder

Graham Oddie
University of Colorado at Boulder

New York   Oxford
OXFORD UNIVERSITY PRESS
2005

Oxford University Press

Oxford   New York
Auckland   Bangkok   Buenos Aires   Cape Town   Chennai
Dar es Salaam   Delhi   Hong Kong   Istanbul   Karachi   Kolkata
Kuala Lumpur   Madrid   Melbourne   Mexico City   Mumbai
Nairobi   São Paulo   Shanghai   Taipei   Tokyo   Toronto

Published by Oxford University Press, Inc.
198 Madison Avenue, New York, New York, 10016
http://www.oup-usa.org

Oxford is a registered trademark of Oxford University Press

Library of Congress Cataloging-in-Publication Data
Boonin, David.
   What's wrong?: applied ethicists and their critics / by David Boonin, Graham Oddie.
      p. cm.
   Includes bibliographical references.
   ISBN 0-19-516761-9 (pbk.)
1. Applied ethics—Textbooks. I. Oddie, Graham, 1954– II. Title.
BJ1031.B66 2004
170—dc22
                                                            2004049545

Printing number: 9   8   7   6   5   4   3   2   1

Printed in the United States of America
on acid-free paper

ACKNOWLEDGMENTS

The editors wish to thank Julie van Camp, Kenneth Henly, Lawrence Pasternak, and Russ Shafer-Landau for their useful suggestions and to express particular gratitude to Ben Eggleston for his especially careful and probing comments and criticisms.

What's Wrong?

INTRODUCTION

What's Wrong with Arguing?

1 THE IMPORTANCE OF BEING ARGUMENTATIVE

The word *philosophy* derives from the Greek words *philein,* meaning "to love," and *sophia,* meaning "wisdom." Philosophy is therefore often defined as the love of wisdom. But if one examines the actual practice of people who call themselves philosophers, this common definition might well seem mistaken. The behavior of such people suggests that philosophy is not so much the love of wisdom as the love of argument. Philosophers are people who love to argue.

Ethics is that branch of philosophy concerned with both the content and the nature of morality, and applied ethics is that branch of ethics that concerns itself with practical moral questions. Is abortion morally permissible? Is it wrong to keep animals in zoos or to slaughter them for food? What, if anything, do children owe their parents? Should the descendents of slave owners pay reparations to the descendents of slaves? Applied ethicists are people who love to argue about these sorts of questions. (Theoretical ethicists, by contrast, treat questions about the nature of morality: What do moral claims mean or refer to? Are moral properties, such as *moral permissibility, moral obligatoriness, and moral goodness,* something over and above the properties that seem more familiar and straightforward, such as *redness, hardness, and sweetness*?)

That applied ethicists are people who love to argue about practical moral questions should be clear from even a quick look at almost any anthology in the field. Such works typically contain articles in which philosophers examine a particular moral controversy and make a point of not simply taking a stand on it, but attempting to offer an argument in defense of a position on the issue, or an argument against some rival position. Typically, in presenting an argument, a philosopher will identify some plausible claims from which to argue and then provide reasoning to show that if those claims are true, then a certain position on the issue must be the right one, or some rival position must be wrong. The claims *from* which philosophers argue we call the premises of their argument. The claim *for* which they argue we call the conclusion of their argument. Although philosophers do not always explicitly identify the premises and conclusion of each argument, those elements are present nonetheless. This much should be clear from reading any good piece of work in applied ethics or from perusing any anthology in the field.

But philosophers are not simply people who love to argue. They are people who love to *argue with one another,* to engage in a dialogue, discussing the merits and demerits of a single line of argument. When one person offers an argument in defense of abortion, say, and another counters with an argument against abortion, the two are arguing about abortion, but they are not arguing with each other in the way that is characteristic of philosophers. In order for them to be arguing with each other as philosophers do, one of them must offer an argument in defense of a particular *conclusion* about abortion, and the other must then offer, not a second argument in defense of a different conclusion about abortion, but rather *an argument about the first argument about abortion.* For people to argue with each other is for them to participate in a shared dialogue about a single argument, to work together to clarify that argument's content and structure, to probe its strengths and weaknesses, to discuss its merits, to uncover its implications, and to debate whether or not it should be accepted or rejected. This, above all else, is what philosophers do. And this is the most important thing that philosophers do.

That philosophers love not simply to argue but to argue with each other should be clear to anyone who has ever spent time in a room with more than one philosopher (and sometimes even one philosopher is enough!). It should be especially clear to anyone who has ever attended a convention of the American Philosophical Association. Almost every paper presented at that convention is immediately followed by a second, shorter paper that directly addresses the argument made in the first paper, typically by making some criticism of it. The author of the first paper will then typically respond to the commentator's criticisms, and toward the end of the discussion, members of the audience will raise additional questions and offer yet more comments as a way of advancing the dialogue still further. In addition, many of the featured papers at such conventions are themselves attempts to comment on arguments proposed in still earlier papers. The titles of papers that philosophers present to address other philosophers' arguments are routinely filled with such phrases as "a reply to" this philosopher, "a response to" that one, and "why" a third philosopher "is wrong."

Someone unfamiliar with the habits of philosophers would be likely to walk away from such a scene wondering what the point was of all of the bickering. Isn't it a foolish waste of time and energy to argue endlessly about pressing practical problems, problems for which we need good solutions to act on right now? And isn't foolishness the very opposite of the wisdom that philosophers are traditionally supposed to love?

This reaction to the seemingly endless arguments and counterarguments generated by philosophers is understandable, but it is mistaken. For philosophers do not argue merely for the sake of arguing (even though one might be forgiven for sometimes thinking that they do!). Arguing, the true philosopher understands, is not an end in itself. Rather, philosophers argue because they are interested in determining whether or not a particular view is more or less reasonable than its rivals. A reason for adopting a moral view can be best formulated as an argument in defense of that view. To evaluate the reasonableness of a moral view is thus to evaluate the reasons in favor of adopting that view, which in turn is to evaluate the arguments that people have found persuasive for embracing the view. Argumentation is thus valuable because evaluating reasons is valuable. The wise person would surely want to avoid unreasonable, inconsistent, or badly thought out moral views. So, argument is valuable precisely because it is our best tool, indeed our only tool, for attaining a consistent and reasonable moral outlook. In addition, by arguing with others who recognize the value of reason and argument, we are much more likely to discover both the weaknesses and strengths of our arguments than we would be if we simply contemplated our own arguments in isolation from others. For creatures such as we are, then, the love of arguing with others who love to argue is an indispensable asset in the pursuit of wisdom. Wisdom may be our ultimate goal, but we make progress toward it only by engaging in honest and open argument.

2 THE STRUCTURE OF THIS ANTHOLOGY

Arguing with each other is thus an essential feature of what it is to practice philosophy in general and applied ethics in particular. This much is clear to those who work in the field, but this crucial aspect of the discipline is all too often rendered invisible to students who learn about philosophy in the classroom. For example, virtually every anthology used in applied ethics courses includes philosophers presenting a variety of arguments on a single issue, but virtually none is devoted to philosophers presenting a variety of analyses of a single *argument*. Philosophers in most such anthologies argue, but they do not argue with one another.

To present philosophers arguing with one another about important questions in applied ethics is the central purpose of this book. To accomplish this, we've organized each chapter of the book not simply around a particular moral issue, but around a particular moral *argument*—an argument that has been developed in an attempt to help resolve a particular moral issue, and one that has been recognized as sufficiently important to merit the critical attention of other philosophers. This central argument is contained in what we refer to as the "featured article," the article that initiates and is the focal point of the set of readings for each chapter. The featured article is then followed by one or more critical-response pieces. The vast majority of these pieces are direct responses to the featured article in question, but even those that are not still address the argument (or arguments) contained in the featured article. By studying the featured article along with the critical responses to it, the reader will develop a clearer and more thorough understanding of some of the important ways in which the argument contained in the featured article can be subjected to critical scrutiny.

In addition, each chapter in this anthology is preceded by an extensive introduction. These introductions clarify the thesis defended in the featured article, outline the structure of the argument presented in defense of that thesis, and help the reader to see clearly and specifically just how the critical-response pieces relate to the original argument. A typical introduction to a chapter will show how the argument contained in the featured article can be stated clearly and explicitly by representing it as a set of premises leading to a conclusion. The introduction will go on to explain how the critical-response pieces can then be read as criticisms of that particular argument (e.g., showing which critical-response pieces attack which premises), thereby helping the reader to see clearly and specifically just how the critical-response pieces relate to the original argument. Finally, for those who wish to "follow the trail" of the argument still further, many of the chapters conclude with suggestions for further reading, including additional articles written in response to the featured article and, whenever possible, subsequent works by the authors of the featured articles in which they attempt to address some of the objections that have been raised against their original pieces.

3 ARGUMENTS IN GENERAL

The best way to learn about philosophical argumentation is simply to engage in it. Thus, the best way to learn from this volume is not simply to read the articles it contains, but to discuss them critically with others who have also read them (and even with those who have not). Before jumping into the fray by looking in detail at a particular moral controversy, however, it may be useful to consider a few features of moral argument in general, and a few kinds of moral argument in particular. Doing so is the principal goal of the remainder of this introduction.

3.1 What Arguments Are

It is important to begin by being very clear about just what it means to offer an argument in defense of a conclusion. A person might be opposed to a particular practice because the very thought of that practice makes him upset, for example, or disgusted. But basing one's opposition to a practice on the experience of such feelings is not the same as basing it on an argument. As we have noted already, an argument always involves a conclusion, the thesis that is being argued for or supported. The claims that are used to support the conclusion are the premises. The premises are supposed to entail the conclusion. The argument will constitute a reason for adopting the conclusion if two things are true: First, the premises are all plausible, and second, they really do jointly entail the conclusion. Any argument can thus be subjected to two different kinds of criticism. The first kind of criticism attacks the plausibility of one or more of the premises. The second kind attacks the claim that the premises entail the conclusion.

3.2 Evaluating Entailment Claims

What does it mean for some premises to entail a conclusion? It may help to begin with a simple single-premise example, where P is shorthand for *premise* and C for *conclusion* (a convention we apply throughout this book). A line is drawn to separate the premise or premises from the conclusion.

P   Any action that results in the death of a person is morally wrong.

C   Abortion is morally wrong.

One might criticize this argument, of course, by taking issue with the premise itself. It does not take much imagination, after all, to come up with at least a few cases in which an act resulted in the death of a person but in which we nonetheless believe that the act was not morally wrong. But even before we consider the question of whether or not we should accept the argument's premise, we might well wonder if the premise would be enough to justify the conclusion, even if the premise turned out to be true. We might wonder, in short, whether or not the premise really entailed the conclusion. The idea of entailment that we would employ in such a case, and the sense of entailment that is most relevant to our purposes here, runs as follows: For C to follow from P, the truth of P would have to guarantee the truth of C. Anyone who accepted P but rejected C would be implicitly endorsing incompatible claims. If P entailed C, anyone who accepted P would thereby be rationally obliged to accept C as well.

Is that the case with this argument? Grant, for the moment, that the premise is correct. That is to say, imagine that P really does articulate a correct moral principle. Granting that P is correct, can you think of any way in which the conclusion might still be incorrect? If you can, then that shows that even if you accept P, you are not thereby rationally obliged to accept C as well. So, to show that C does not follow from P, all you have to do is describe *one possible way* in which the premise might be correct while the conclusion is nevertheless incorrect.

Here is one slightly artificial way. First, note that a human embryo, for example, might be aborted—that is to say, expelled from the womb—as the result of human intervention, but that it might also abort spontaneously, without any human action precipitating the expulsion. In the case of a spontaneous abortion, the embryo is aborted, but the abortion was not an action. And it might well not be the result of any action at all. For example, it might have been an expulsion triggered by a genetic defect in the embryo itself. In such a case, no action is performed to bring the abortion about. So, even granted the correctness of P, if no action is performed, then no *wrong* action is performed. Accepting P does not, therefore, make it obligatory to accept C. And thus, as a result, there is no entailment between P and C. The argument is logically invalid, and this is so regardless of whether or not we ought to accept the argument's premise.

The kind of case we have just outlined is called a counterexample to the validity of an argument. A counterexample is a case in which the premise or premises of an argument are true but the conclusion of the argument is nonetheless false. One might suspect that this particular counterexample involves some kind of trick. After all, one might insist, anyone who seriously advanced the argument in question would have been thinking only of the class of induced abortions, abortions that are brought about by an intentional human act. That is, they would have been tacitly assuming that the term *abortion* as it appears in C does not embrace all cases of abortion and, in particular, does not embrace cases of spontaneous abortion. However, even if this is what a proponent of the argument was assuming, it is nonetheless a defect of the argument that it fails to make this assumption explicit. In argumentation, it is important to make explicit what one has in mind, and not leave it to your opponent to fill in the gaps. After all, the whole point of making your argument public, whether through speaking or writing, is to *communicate* to another what you have in mind. Good argumentation avoids ambiguities where ambiguities might be important to the validity of the argument.

Let us eliminate somewhat contrived counterexamples by agreeing to mean by *abortion* the intentional act of expelling an embryo or fetus from the womb. We will save the word *miscarriage* for spontaneous abortions. Even if we do agree to use words in this way, there are other, less artificial counterexamples that count against the validity of this argument. For example, many people deny that a human fetus—or at least a human fetus at relatively early stages of gestation—is a person. It is a *potential* person, they might concede, but not yet an actual person. Suppose they are right about this. Then, it would turn out that some (or many, or all) abortions do not result in the death of a person at all, even though they do result in the death of a human embryo or fetus. You yourself might not agree with this position. You might firmly believe that every human fetus is a person from the moment of conception onward. But even if you do believe this, you will still have to acknowledge that the premises of the argument presented above do not explicitly say this. It would be invalid to move from the claim that bringing about the death of a person is wrong to the conclusion that bringing about the death of a human fetus is wrong without relying on a further claim that *all human fetuses are persons*. Without this additional premise, the argument above is, once again, shown to be invalid. Granting the premise that any action that results in the death of a person is wrong does not, in and of itself, rationally oblige one to accept the conclusion that abortion is wrong. And that is just to say that P does not entail C.

3.3 Evaluating Premises

The sample argument we used in the previous section is a poor one, not just because the conclusion does not follow from the premise, but also because the premise itself is clearly defective. Hardly anyone would be willing to grant that it is a correct moral principle. For a start, hardly anyone thinks that it is always and everywhere wrong to kill a person, no matter what the circumstances. For example, most people consider killing in self-defense to be morally permissible. Also, most people think that it would have been morally permissible, indeed, morally praiseworthy, to have killed Hitler at various stages of his career. But even if one thought that it was always and everywhere wrong to kill someone, *P* might still be false. For we can make a distinction between intentionally doing something that leads directly to the death of a person (say, deliberately and intentionally administering a lethal dose of poison to your son) and doing something that unintentionally happens to bring about a person's death (say, accidentally administering a dose of lethal poison to your son believing it to be his daily dose of vitamins). Now, a case of accidentally poisoning someone might be a morally wrong action under certain conditions—you might have been negligent, or careless, for example—but not under others. We can certainly imagine cases in which bringing about a person's death would not be morally wrong, but a genuine and forgivable accident, one that happens to produce a terrible unintended consequence. The premise of our sample argument is thus implausible.

We have said, "hardly anyone thinks that it is always and everywhere wrong to kill a person, no matter what the circumstances." It does not follow from the fact that most people *think* that something is morally permissible, however, that it actually *is* morally permissible. People can get things wrong in moral matters just as they can in factual matters. Most people in the United States in the eighteenth century, for example, thought that slavery was permissible; but that fact didn't make slavery permissible. This should be clear for the following reason. A minority of people can clearly endorse immoral practices. And those practices hardly become more moral if the minority recruits further adherents to its immoral point of view. Moreover, since there is nothing morally magical about the figure 50 percent, when an immoral minority manages to recruit more than half of a given population, its immoral outlook does not thereby become magically transformed into a moral one. The fact that a majority of people hold a particular moral view, therefore, does not guarantee that that moral view is the correct one.

So, it might well be asked, why do we bother citing that most people believe there are circumstances in which it is permissible to kill a person? If this fact does not in itself entail that there actually are circumstances in which it is permissible to kill a person, of what possible value can it be in a critical analysis of the simple argument we have been looking at here?

The answer to this question is perhaps best framed in terms of a particular debate taking place between a particular pair of people. So, suppose that Pam and Dan are having an argument about the simple one-premise argument noted above. And suppose that in the course of this argument, Dan endorses the principle that any action that results in the death of a person is morally wrong. Pam decides to challenge Dan by citing the case of a nonnegligent, forgivable accident that results in someone's death. In citing this case, Pam is assuming that Dan will agree with her that there was nothing morally wrong about the person who accidentally killed someone. If Dan does agree with Pam about this case, then if he wants to be rational he will have to give up his principle, because his judgment on the case is inconsistent with an endorsement of that principle. To be rational, one must have consistent beliefs. If, on the other hand, Dan disagrees with Pam about the case, then Pam will have to find another case on which she and Dan do agree and use that other case as a means of forcing Dan to abandon his commitment to the general principle. In order for two people to argue profitably with each other they have to appeal to at least some cases and judgments on which they both agree. If they agree on absolutely nothing (and that is highly unlikely) then it will be virtually impossible for them to engage in a profitable philosophical exchange. So, the point of saying "hardly anyone thinks such and such" is to emphasize the enormous size of the class of people who will make a certain moral judgment on a particular case, and who will thus have to take the case seriously. If their considered judgment on that case is inconsistent with a principle they endorse, then, if they want to be rational participants in their quest for wisdom, they will have to give up the principle in question. The more people who agree about a particular case, therefore, the more powerful that case will be as a means of advancing public debate over a particular argument.

This first argument we examined, of course, was a very simple one. A somewhat more complex version of an argument against abortion might be represented in the following multi-premise manner (where *P1* is short for "premise 1," and so on).

P1   Abortion kills a fetus or an embryo.
P2   A fetus or an embryo is an innocent human being.
P3   Killing an innocent human being is murder.
P4   Murder is morally wrong.

C   Abortion is morally wrong.

Although the authors of the various articles in this anthology rarely present their views using this format (*P1, P2*, etc.), their arguments can be reconstructed in this more formal manner. The introductions to most of the featured articles in this text provide such reconstructions.

Reconstructing an argument in this illustrative premise-and-conclusion format is useful, in part because it can help one visualize the overall structure of an author's reasoning. In the case of the argument against abortion outlined above, for example, the reconstruction helps to make explicit the manner in which the argument attempts to show that abortion is wrong by subsuming it under a broader class of actions that are generally recognized to be wrong— the killing of innocent human beings. But representing arguments in this formal manner is also important as a means of thinking clearly about the various ways in which an argument might be productively criticized.

The argument above is indeed valid. The premises really do jointly entail the conclusion. To see this, note that P1 and P2 together entail that abortion is the killing of an innocent human being. Together with P3, this entails that abortion is murder. That abortion is murder, together with P4, entails that abortion is morally wrong, the conclusion. *If* the premises are all true, then the conclusion is *also* true. So, in looking for possible ways to criticize this argument, we will not waste time trying to construct a counterexample to the validity of the argument (although it might be an informative exercise to do so).

The fact that this argument is valid does *not* mean that the conclusion is true. A valid argument may have a false premise, and if it does have a false premise then it does not provide a good reason for endorsing its conclusion. Any good criticism of this argument will therefore have to take issue with one or more of the premises. Breaking the argument down into a series of clear, specific premises like this enables us to see more clearly that objecting to some of the assumptions made by the argument will be relatively less promising than objecting to others. In the argument under consideration here, for example, one premise that looks fairly unassailable is P4; the claim that murder is morally wrong. Indeed, by *murder* we generally *mean* "a wrongful killing of a person." So P4 comes very close to being not only true, but true by definition, and therefore there is not much to be gained by spending time on that premise.

Someone who thought this argument is defective might therefore instead turn their attention to P3 (the claim that killing an innocent human being is murder). Is the killing of an innocent human being always and everywhere a case of murder, or a wrongful killing? Is anyone who kills an innocent human being a murderer? Suppose someone has suffered severe and irreparable brain damage an automobile in accident, has gone into an irreversible coma, and is being kept alive on a heart-lung machine. To switch the machine off would be to do something intentionally to cause that person to die—in other words, to kill him. Let us also suppose that this comatose person is innocent (that is, prior to his accident, he had not, for example, done anything to deserve the death penalty). He is also a human being. Is it a case of murder to turn off the heart-lung machine? This case may be controversial, as we will see in chapter 2, on euthanasia, but most of us would judge it not to be a case of murder. Those who judged the case in this manner would then find that this was a reason to reject the argument's third premise.

Perhaps you think that switching the machine off is not really *killing* the patient. You might think that it is merely *letting him die,* and you might think that *letting die* is sometimes morally permissible. This is a controversial issue, which we will also address (in chapter 2). But in the meantime, think about this: Imagine you are the person on the heart-lung machine and that, unlike the man in the story above, you are conscious. Imagine also that if someone unplugs your machine you will die. An intruder, someone who happens to be an enemy of yours, climbs in the hospital window and pulls out the plug in order to ensure your death. Would that not be a case of killing? And if that is a case of killing, why is the case above not also a killing?

Of course, when we are asked to imagine cases involving the killing of human beings, we typically imagine cases of murder. When we think of the killing of human beings, we are generally not thinking of unusual human beings, such as irreversibly comatose patients. So, we might initially be inclined to assent to P3 uncritically, until we are presented with an unusual case such as the one involving the intruder. But when we initially think of the killing of human beings, we do not think about other, nonstandard cases of human beings, such as a newly fertilized ovum or a four-week-old fetus either. We tend to assent to general moral principles on the basis of typical, rather than atypical, cases. And so the extension of a principle from these typical cases (killing people like you or me) to atypical cases (killing irreparably brain-damaged and irreversibly comatose people or killing embryos and fetuses) might turn out to be unjustified. In such cases, what initially seems to be a plausible and acceptable premise turns out, upon reflection, to represent an unwarranted generalization.

Sometimes an adherent to a general principle such as that contained in P3 will try to rescue that principle from the apparent force of such potential counterexamples by reinterpreting a key term in the principle. For example, they might say, "My agreeing that it isn't wrong to turn off the life-support machine for the irreversibly comatose guy is not a violation of the principle I'm defending because the irreversibly comatose guy isn't a real human being anymore. And since he isn't a human being, in my sense of the term, it doesn't matter if I agree with you that killing him is not murder. The general moral principle I support in P3 does not say that all killings are murder, just that all killings of innocent human beings are. And since I don't think this guy is a human being, the fact that killing him is not murder can't count as a counterexample to my general principle."

The problem with this line of defense is that it appears to make use of one sense of the term *human being* to protect the general moral principle from these counterexamples, while making use of quite another sense of the term in order to apply the principle to, say, the killing of human embryos. If we retain a broad conception of *human being*—an organism of a particular biological species, *Homo sapiens*—then both the human embryo and the irreversibly comatose patient count as human beings. That much they both have in common with a fully grown, fully functioning, non-comatose human. If it is wrong to kill human beings in that broad sense, then of course it is wrong to kill any one of the three, and the argument succeeds. But on the broad conception, as we have seen, it is not at all clear that the principle in P3 is correct. Once we agree that it is not wrong to turn off the life-support machine on the permanently comatose patient, then it is not always wrong to kill innocent human beings in the broad sense. To maintain adherence to P3, we have to employ a narrower conception of *human,* one that excludes the being on the life-support machine. But then we as yet have no reason to accept that it does not also exclude the blastocyst (or the embryo or the fetus) as well, in which case P2 cannot be maintained. So whatever meaning of *human being* we choose, at least one of the two premises we are looking at here will prove to be unacceptable. Whenever an argument contains the same term in two different premises—as in the case of the argument above, which contains the term *human being* in both P2 and P3—the argument's validity depends crucially on the term's being used to mean precisely the same thing in both premises. If, as in this example, it turns out that P2 is true in one sense of the term and P3 is true in another sense of the term but that there is no one sense in which both P2 and P3 are true, then the argument must be rejected. This problem is commonly referred to as *equivocation,* and readers should be alert to the possibility of equivocations lurking in many of the arguments contained in this work.

4 ARGUMENTS IN PARTICULAR

While the notion of logical entailment applies across the board to arguments whatever their form, arguments come in a great variety of shapes and sizes. We cannot provide an exhaustive discussion here of all existing argument forms or of all the critical strategies most promising for each one of them. However, it is worth examining in some detail a few particularly important argument structures that recur at a number of points in this anthology.

4.1 Arguments from Analogy

Arguments from analogy are among the most common kind of argument found in applied ethics. Careful readers will notice the important role that arguments from analogy play in the featured articles in chapters 1, 3, 14, 16, 23, 24, 25, and in many of the response pieces to these and other articles.

4.1.1 Understanding Arguments from Analogy

An argument from analogy attempts to justify our accepting a moral assessment of a particular practice by comparing it with a second practice about which most people are already in agreement. Such an argument can be represented more formally (the argument is cashed out here in terms of a practice's being wrong, although everything that is said here would apply equally to cases involving a practice's being permissible, obligatory, bad, good, etc.):

P1   Practice 1 is wrong.
P2   Practice 2 is morally analogous to (morally on a par with) practice 1.
_____

C   Practice 2 is wrong.

In the article "Famine, Affluence, and Morality," for example, which serves as the featured article in chapter 23, Peter Singer appeals to an analogy between refraining from donating money to a famine-relief effort and refraining from wading into a shallow pond to rescue a small child who will otherwise drown. Virtually everyone would agree that it would be morally wrong not to wade in and save the child, especially in the case where doing so posed no risk of harm to the rescuer and resulted only in his getting his clothes dirty. Singer argues that the two cases are morally analogous because in each case one person can prevent something very bad from happening to another at only a trivial cost to himself. But if we agree that it would be wrong not to save the child in the shallow-pond case, and that the shallow-pond case is morally analogous to the famine-relief case, then Singer's quite strong conclusion seems to follow: that when people refrain from sending money to famine-relief efforts, they behave in a manner that is positively and seriously immoral. This argument in defense of the moral obligation to contribute to famine-relief efforts can be represented as follows:

P1   Refraining from saving the child in the shallow-pond case is wrong.
P2   Refraining from saving the child in the shallow-pond case is morally on a par with refraining from sending money to famine relief.
_____

C   Refraining from sending money to famine relief is wrong.

Reasoning by analogy is one of the most important argumentative tools that moral philosophers have available to them. When used effectively, it can help resolve a controversial issue by framing it in terms of a less controversial one. A large number of the readings that follow make use of appeals to such analogies. Readers should keep a sharp eye out for these throughout this anthology.

When examining an argument from analogy, it is important to understand as clearly as possible precisely what the argument is meant to establish and precisely why the analogy is supposed to help to establish it. In the case of Singer's argument, for example, one would first have to clarify the argument's thesis: Is it simply that it is a good thing to give money to famine relief, or that it is positively wrong *not* to give? One would then need to focus in some detail on the analogy itself: What exactly is involved in the story Singer tells? Why does he think it is relevantly analogous to the famine-relief case? And why is he so confident that we will share his assessment of it? When all of these questions can be answered, one can reasonably say that one has a fair and accurate understanding of the argument itself.

4.1.2 Criticizing Arguments from Analogy

After one has attained a clear grasp of an argument, the next step is to subject that argument to critical scrutiny. Since arguments from analogy can almost always be expressed in the simple two-premise format used above, there are typically two options available to the argument's critics: They can challenge the assessment of the example offered by the argument's author, or they can accept the assessment of the example but deny that it is relevantly analogous to the problem the argument is designed to resolve. Using Singer's argument, for example, the critic could either maintain that it would not be wrong to let the child in the shallow pond drown, or agree that doing so would be wrong but deny that this was relevantly analogous to the case of declining to contribute money to famine-relief efforts. Since most of the analogies to which the arguments in this text appeal involve cases about which most people seem to agree (for example, most people seem to agree that it would be wrong not to save the child in Singer's shallow-pond case), the more promising strategy in developing a thoughtful, critical response to such arguments will typically involve trying to identify a disanalogy between the example the author appeals to and the issue to which he or she compares it.

In order to be successful in identifying a disanalogy, the critic of an argument from analogy must establish two things: that there is a difference between the two cases and that the difference is a morally relevant one. Merely identifying a difference is not, in and of itself, sufficient to undermine an argument from analogy. Suppose, for example, that a critic of Singer's argument pointed out that the child drowning in the shallow pond was wet, while the children dying of hunger were dry. This would, indeed, identify a difference between the two cases. Being wet is not the same thing as being dry. But since the difference between a wet child dying and a dry child dying does not seem to be morally relevant, this difference would fail to undermine Singer's argument. If there are no other differences between the two cases—differences that do seem to be morally relevant—then Singer would be justified in maintaining that if it is wrong not to help in one case then it is (equally) wrong not to help in the other.

In the case of the difference between wet and dry, it is fairly clear and uncontroversial that the difference is not in itself a morally relevant one. But there are other kinds of differences that might be pointed to in which things might not be so clear. For example, a critic of Singer's argument could point out that in one case the child is very near us while in the other the child is very far, or that one child is a member of our community and the other is not, or that the help one can offer in one case is direct and in the other indirect, and so on. An excellent first step in critiquing an argument from analogy is to try to come up with a list of as many differences between the two cases as possible. But once we have found differences between the two cases, how do we decide if the differences are relevant ones?

4.1.3 The Technique of Variant Cases

One useful procedure involves the appeal to what are often referred to as variant cases. To illustrate this technique let us focus on the simple case of the wet/dry difference as an objection to Singer's shallow-pond argument. (What is said here will apply equally to many other objections to Singer's argument and to many objections to many other arguments from analogy.)

Suppose you were genuinely uncertain about whether or not to treat the difference between wet and dry as a morally relevant one. The technique of variant cases would tell you to begin by constructing a case that is just like the shallow-pond/famine-relief pair but that has been altered to correct for the wet/dry variable. What is required, then, is a case in which we have a child who is about to die, as is in the shallow-pond story, but who is dry, as would be the situation in the famine-relief case. And, ideally, we want a case that is in every other respect just like the shallow-pond case. In this way, we can ensure that we are focusing clearly and precisely on the exact question at hand: Is the wet/dry difference itself a morally relevant one? There are many possible scenarios that might be imagined here. Readers will become more adept at case construction the more such arguments they encounter, but as an illustration of the technique, we will provide one possibility here. Suppose that the child who is drowning is drowning in quicksand rather than in water, so that although he is drowning, he is not getting wet. You know that you are easily tall and strong enough to wade into the quicksand in order to rescue him without any risk of harm to yourself, although doing so will cause you to get your clothes dirty, just as it would in the original version of the shallow-pond case.

After you have arrived at a suitable variant case—such as the case of the child drowning in quicksand—the technique of variant cases adds a second step: Consider the variant case and ask if your intuitive reaction to it is any different from what it was to the original, non-variant case. Is it now okay to let the (dry) child drown, for example, or do you find that prospect just as wrong as you did in the original (wet) version of the story? Finally, assuming that you can give a fairly definitive answer to this question, the technique permits you to draw a conclusion about the merits of the objection under consideration. If the change from original case to variant case makes no difference to your assessment of the case, then this is evidence that that difference between the two cases (wet versus dry) is not a morally relevant one; if the change from original case to variant case *does* make a difference to your assessment, then this counts as some evidence that the difference between the two is a morally relevant one. If the change from wet drowning child to dry drowning child did not make any difference to your intuition about whether it is wrong not to prevent the child from drowning, for example, this would be a good reason to deny that the difference between wet and dry was a morally relevant one. But if in the case of some other, more promising objection, you found that the change from original case to variant case did make a difference to your intuitive reaction to the case, this would count as good evidence that you have succeeded in identifying a cogent objection to the original argument.

Critically assessing an argument from analogy will not always be as simple and tidy as this discussion suggests. There are many kinds of differences, which can be combined in various ways, and people's intuitions are not always as clear or as forceful as they would likely be in the easy case we have just focused on. When you encounter an argument from analogy, we suggest that you begin your critical deliberations about it by looking for disanalogies and then trying to use variant cases as one (though not necessarily the only) way to test their merits. Though not always effective, such an approach is often an excellent strategy to try.

4.2 Bare-Difference Arguments

The strategy of using variant cases to test for moral relevance when criticizing an argument from analogy is an instance of a somewhat more general argumentative technique, one that has been dubbed the method of bare differences. This method is closely related to the technique of variant cases, but has much wider application. It can be used not simply as a device for critically responding to an argument, but also as a method for generating an argument on its own. It therefore merits attention as a form of argument in its own right.

4.2.1 Understanding Bare-Difference Arguments

Consider, as an example, the debate over the moral permissibility of euthanasia. When suffering from very painful, debilitating, and probably incurable diseases, some people come to regard death as a welcome release. In such cases life can often be prolonged—that is, doing so is technically possible—but, generally speaking, most people do not believe that it ought to be prolonged. What most people seem to believe is that it is sometimes morally permissible to allow a person to die in such circumstances, or, put the other way around that it is not morally obligatory to continue to keep them alive. Sometimes, however, a person in such a situation wants more than simply that others discontinue keeping him alive, and it is this something more that tends to generate controversy. What he prefers, in such cases, is that others take active steps to end his life and his suffering immediately, rather than simply discontinue his treatment so that he dies a slower (and often more painful) death later. This further request generates controversy because many people who believe that it is morally permissible to to allow a person to die in such circumstances maintain that it would nonetheless be morally impermissible to kill him under the same circumstances, while many others maintain that it would be permissible not only to let such a person die, but also to carry out his request to kill him.

This important debate is often carried out in terms of the distinction between active and passive euthanasia. *Euthanasia* is derived from the Greek phrase for "a good death." A person's death can be a good one when it is better for him than the only available alternative, that is, continuing to live under intolerable circumstances. And this "good death" can come about in one of two ways. "Active euthanasia" refers to the practice of killing a person under such circumstances. "Passive euthanasia" refers to the practice of letting a person die under such circumstances by withholding treatment that would be necessary for him to go on living. The debate over euthanasia, therefore, is a debate about whether or not active euthanasia is worse than passive euthanasia.

Why should it be the case—as many people believe—that active euthanasia is always and everywhere wrong while passive euthanasia is sometimes permissible, and perhaps even obligatory? Presumably, the central idea behind such a position is this: Deliberately killing a person is bad, much worse than merely letting a person die. Even when death is good for the person who dies, and even when the person who dies wants to die, killing is itself so bad a thing that its badness outweighs whatever good or desired effects it brings about. On this account, active euthanasia is always and everywhere morally wrong (since active euthanasia involves killing a person), while passive euthanasia may sometimes be morally justified (since passive euthanasia involves merely letting someone die). In order for this position to be acceptable, therefore, it must be the case that killing is worse—indeed, much worse—than letting die.

How could we find out whether there really was such a morally important difference between killing and letting die? One way to do this would be to look at pairs of cases other than those involving suffering and terminally ill patients, pairs of cases that also differ only with respect to the distinction between killing and letting die, and then to see if the difference between killing and letting die seems to make a (big enough) moral difference in those cases. The basic idea is as follows: If killing really is much worse, in itself, than letting die, then it would entail that—given *any* pair of cases, one of which is a killing and the other of which is a letting die, and that differ only this one respect, the case of the killing must be much worse than the case of the letting die. Pairs of cases that differ in only one respect are called "barely different cases." And the principle articulated here suggests a potentially powerful argumentative strategy that may be constructed from them: We can test the relative moral weight of killing and letting die by considering various pairs of cases that differ only in this one respect.

In the featured article in chapter 2, for example, James Rachels applies precisely this technique. Indeed, Rachels's article made the technique of bare-difference argument famous. Rachels considers a pair of stories that differ in only one respect—one is a killing and the other is a letting-die. (In this respect they resemble a pair of variant cases.) But Rachels's pair of barely different cases is quite unrelated to the euthanasia issue. (In this Rachels's strategy differs from the technique of variant cases, which produces barely different pairs of cases analogous to the case at hand.) Rachels considers two people, Smith and Jones, each of whom stands to gain an inheritance from the death of his very rich six-year-old cousin. Each plans to drown his cousin in a bathtub and to make the death look like an accident. Smith does precisely this. Jones, however, comes into the bathroom to find that his cousin is already drowning from a genuine accident (having slipped on the soap and hit his head on the side of the tub). Jones could easily save his cousin, but instead he stands idly by, prepared to shove his cousin's head back underwater if he happens to surface. Much to Jones's delight, he does not need to do this. After thrashing about a bit, Jones's cousin dies without Jones having to kill him. While Smith kills his cousin, Jones merely lets his cousin die. And this is apparently the only difference between the two cases. Everything else that might be morally relevant is the same in both cases. This is what make the Smith and Jones pair of cases a set of "bare-difference" cases.

Now, is the Smith case worse than the Jones case? If you judge that it is not worse, that they are morally on a par, then it seems that you cannot affirm that killing is worse, in itself, than letting die. Of course, no one wants to say that letting die is, in itself, worse than killing, so the only alternative left seems to be that killing and letting die are on an equal footing, and that it is other features of such cases that determine both their badness and their wrongness.

Rachels's argument can be reconstructed in a number of different ways. Let us consider here a simple two-premise version:

P1   The Smith case is a case of killing, and the Jones case is exactly like the Smith
case in every respect except that it is a case of letting die.
P2   The Smith case is morally on a par with the Jones case.

C   Killing is, in itself, morally on a par with letting die.

The general form of this argument is something like this:

P1   Case A has feature P, and case B is exactly like case A except that it has feature Q
rather than feature P.
P2   Case A is morally on a par with case B.

C   P is, in itself, morally on a par with Q.

In chapter 2, we will see exactly how Rachels goes on to argue from his application of these
strategies to the permissibility of active euthanasia. What is important at this point, however,
is not to decide whether or not we agree with Rachels's position, but to ensure that we are
clear about the nature and structure of the kind of argument he offers in its defense.

First, we must be clear what the conclusion of the argument is supposed to be. Rachels
is not saying that every killing is morally equivalent to every letting die. He concedes that,
as it happens, most cases of killing are probably worse than most cases of letting someone
die. However, most cases of killing differ from most cases of letting die in many others
other ways, not just in the fact that one involves bringing about a preventable death and the
other involves allowing a preventable death to occur. Most killing/letting-die pairs are
not barely different. Most killings, for example, are violent affairs; most are done without
the consent of the one killed; most cause considerable harm both to the one killed and to
his loved ones; most are done with the intention of harming the person killed; and so on.
Many, perhaps most, cases of letting die do not have these features. Rachels's point is that
it is the badness of these other nasty features of killings that make most killings worse
than most cases of letting die. Those other features may frequently, but do not necessarily,
accompany killing. Furthermore, a letting-die might have those bad features, whereas a killing might lack them, and in that case the letting-die may well be much worse than the
killing.

Second, we must be clear about the grounds for the validity of the argument. Indeed, as
it stands it might not be at all clear that the argument is valid. What exactly establishes the
connection between the premises and the conclusion? Why should the fact that killing does
not make the Smith case worse than the Jones case mean that killing is not in itself worse
than letting die? Perhaps a bad feature, such as its being a killing, will make a difference in
some cases but not in others. Maybe it does not make a difference for the worse in the Smith
case, but it does make a difference for the worse in the case of euthanasia.

An answer to this question lies in a feature that moral reasons share with reasons in general, a feature that is often called their *universalizability*. Suppose some one objects to a certain practice—for example, the practice of sending children of different races to different
schools and giving the schools with white children more resources than the schools with
black children. One objection to such a practice might be that it is racist, that it involves
assigning resources to schools on the basis of racial characteristics. Another might be that it
is simply not fair because it gives some children more resources than other, equally deserv-

ing children. Note that these are two different reasons for rejecting the practice. We can imagine an arrangement that is not racist but is still unfair (mixed-race schools with differential resource allocations), and cases that may be racist although they do not distribute resources to children unequally (racially segregated schools with the same funding formula, for example). Now, if the fact that a practice is racist is a good reason to reject it, then it is an equally good reason for rejecting any other practice that involves racism to the same degree. If racism is bad, then it cannot count against some racist practices while not counting against other racist practices. For example, one cannot consistently object to the racism that currently favors black farmers over white farmers in Zimbabwe, say, without similarly objecting to the racism that used to favor white farmers over black farmers in South Africa (and vice versa). If racism is an evil, it is an evil wherever and whenever it crops up. And that is what it means to say that racism is itself a bad thing. The basic principle that guarantees the validity of the bare-difference strategy is thus captured in the old adage: What's sauce for the goose is sauce for the gander. As long as one accepts this principle, the inference made by bare-difference arguments should seem well grounded.

4.2.2 *Criticizing Bare-Difference Arguments*

As we have formalized both the bare-difference strategy of argumentation in general, and Rachels's application of it in particular, such arguments can be conceived of in terms of a conclusion that follows from two distinct premises. Assuming, therefore, that the two premises do, in fact, entail the conclusion, a critic of any particular bare-difference argument has two options available to him: He can attack the first premise or he can attack the second.

The first premise of any bare-difference argument involves the construction of two cases that are supposed to differ in only one respect. The first thing to do is to determine if this is true for the case at hand, or if there might be other respects in which they differ, respects that might at first lie hidden, and that might be doing some moral work. That is to say, in any bare-difference argument, one might argue that cases presented as being only *barely* different are not barely different after all and that there is a further difference that has gone unnoticed and is morally relevant. A good example of this sort of strategy can be found in the article by Winston Nesbitt, reprinted as part of chapter 2, in which he criticizes Rachels's Smith/Jones pair on precisely these grounds. (Roy W. Perrett, in his critique of Nesbitt's argument, then attempts to come to the defense of Rachels's original argument.)

The second premise of any bare-difference argument endorses a certain judgment on the cases that the argument presents: the claim that the two cases are morally equivalent. But a critic of a particular bare-difference argument might attempt to reject this claim as well. In the case of Rachels's argument, for example, he might maintain that the Smith case (the killing) really is worse than the Jones case (the letting-die). If most people have an initial intuitive reaction in favor of the claim that P2 is true, it will do the critic of the argument little good simply to insist that P2 is false. An argument that simply boils down to a competing set of conflicting assertions is barely an argument at all. But there might be more subtle ways for a critic of P2 of a particular bare-difference argument to attempt to press his case. Such a critic might point out, for example, that P2 embodies a very precise claim—that the two cases are morally on a par—and he might therefore maintain that we are really not in a position to affirm such a precise judgment even though we may not detect any difference in our response to the cases. Maybe we are inclined to judge that they are exactly equivalent morally simply because the they are both so bad that we do not really notice the relatively small additional badness involved in the killing. (Relatively small does not mean it is small; it is just small relative to the enormous evil involved in both cases.)

In his article "Killing and Letting Die: From Bare-Differences to Clear Differences" (see chapter 2), Graham Oddie takes seriously this kind of objection to Rachels's argument. In response to the objection, he provides an alternative way of arguing for the same conclusion (that killing is morally on a par with letting die) by substituting a series of judgments involving only fairly obvious inequalities of value, for the single disputed claim of exact equality. Still other, more general objections to the bare-difference argument strategy have been suggested by other writers. Readers who are interested in pursuing this question further should consult the suggested readings listed at the conclusion of chapter 2. In the meantime, however, we will assume that enough has been said about bare-difference arguments here to make their most basic features clear, and will therefore turn next to a third kind of argument structure.

4.3 Arguments from Inference to the Best Explanation

A third argument structure that merits preliminary consideration involves an application of what is often referred to as an inference to the best explanation. This kind of argument attempts to resolve a controversial issue not by comparing it with a single uncontroversial case, as arguments from analogy do, or by focusing exclusively on one pair of cases, as bare-difference arguments do, but rather by extracting a general lesson from a variety of uncontroversial cases and then applying this general lesson to a controversial case.

4.3.1 Understanding Arguments from Inference to the Best Explanation

Arguments from inference to the best explanation are generally somewhat complex. In order to grasp their overall structure, it may help to begin by picturing them as the result of combining two smaller, simpler sub-arguments. We can begin by specifying the purpose of each of these sub-arguments if we adopt a few abbreviations.

Consider a controversy in which K is some kind of action (e.g., the act of killing). Suppose we have a controversial case—call it C—in which people disagree about whether or not doing K is wrong (e.g., killing a cow or killing a fetus). Suppose also that there is a wide range of uncontroversial cases about which people on both sides of the debate over doing K in (controversial) case C generally agree (e.g., that it is wrong to kill you or me in ordinary circumstances). Let M be the moral principle that *best explains* the judgments about the uncontroversial cases, the ones that people on both sides of the debate generally agree on. (For examples, see the principles defended by Don Marquis in chapter 3 and Tom Regan in chapter 5.) In this situation, we can picture two separate arguments that, when combined, yield an overall argument in defense of a particular conclusion about the controversial case C. The first sub-argument is an argument that goes from an assumption about the uncontroversial cases to the conclusion that it is reasonable to believe that principle M is true. The second sub-argument is an argument going from the truth of principle M in general to the truth of a conclusion about doing K in the controversial case C.

The first sub-argument can be represented as follows:

Sub-argument 1

P1 Doing K is wrong in a range of uncontroversial cases.
P2 The best explanation for the fact that doing K is wrong in the uncontroversial cases is that principle M is true.
P3 It is reasonable to believe the best explanation of a given set of facts.

C   It is reasonable to believe that principle M is true.

The second sub-argument can then be pictured as an argument that builds on the result of the first. Since the result of the first sub-argument is that it is reasonable to believe that principle M is true, the second begins by simply assuming that principle M is, indeed, true and then proceeds to apply this general principle to the specific controversial case at issue. The second sub-argument can thus be represented as follows:

Sub-argument 2

P1 Principle M is true.
P2 If principle M is true, then doing K is wrong in case C.

C   Doing K is wrong in case C.

The result of combining these two sub-arguments is therefore an overall argument for the claim that doing K is wrong in case C.

This initial presentation of the manner in which arguments proceed from inference to the best explanation is admittedly abstract. Now that we have broken this structure of argument down into its constituent parts, let us look briefly at a few specific, concrete examples. In his article "Why Abortion Is Immoral," which serves as one of two featured articles about abortion in chapter 3, Don Marquis begins by focusing on cases that both sides of the abortion debate generally agree about (e.g., killing you or me, a young child, or someone in a temporary coma). He goes on to claim that the best explanation of why it is wrong to kill people in these cases is that a particular moral principle is true. The principle is that it is wrong to kill individuals who have futures that are relevantly like our futures. Marquis dubs this having a "future like ours." He then claims that this moral principle, in turn, entails that killing a typical human fetus is also wrong, because a fetus, according to Marquis, also has a future like ours.

In the article "The Case for Animal Rights" (chapter 5), Tom Regan also uses inference to the best explanation. He begins with a set of cases of killing about which people on both sides of the animal-rights debate generally agree—for example, killing a severely retarded or severely brain-damaged (but not permanently comatose) human being. He argues that the best explanation for our judgments on these cases is that it is wrong to kill individuals who have a certain set of mental capacities that make them, in Regan's terminology, a "subject of a life." He then uses this principle to argue that killing some species of nonhuman animals, namely all those whose members are subjects of a life, is also wrong.

When examining an argument from inference to the best explanation, one must begin by understanding as clearly as possible the nature of the argument itself, beginning with the argument's conclusion and then working through its various premises: Is Marquis's argument meant to apply to abortion in every context? Is Regan's argument supposed to apply to all species of animals? In some instances the answers may be fairly clear from the texts; in other cases, one may merely have to note levels of unclarity. What, specifically, is involved in the relatively uncontroversial cases to which the arguments appeal? Here, for example, one would have to take care to note that Marquis's case is about a person in a temporary coma rather than a permanent one, and that Regan's cases involving brain-damaged people do not involve people who have lost consciousness. Next, what does the author take to be the best explanation of the judgments we generally accept in the uncontroversial cases? That is, what is it about what all these cases are said to have in common that explains our judgments on them? What exactly is meant by a "future like ours" or a "subject of a life"? What is the basis for saying that the various cases have such properties in common? Why does the author think that their having such properties in common serves as an effective explanation of the wrongness of the actions in question? And, finally, why does the author think that this explanation helps to resolve the controversial case on which he is focusing? Why, in the end, does Marquis think that the best account of the wrongness of killing in general applies to human fetuses? Why does Regan think that it applies to (at least some) non-human animals?

4.3.2 *Criticizing Arguments from Inference to the Best Explanation*

After one has answered these essentially clarificatory questions, one is again in a position to move on to a more critical examination. As in the case of arguments from analogy and bare-difference arguments, arguments from inference to the best explanation vary considerably from case to case. However, it may be useful to keep in mind a few generalizations as you work your way through some of the readings that follow.

To being with, there are three general options for confronting any argument from inference to the best explanation. You can: (1) disagree with the judgments about the core cases to which the argument appeals (e.g., say that it is okay to kill someone if they are in a temporary coma); (2) agree with the judgments about the core cases but argue that the author's moral principle fails to provide a satisfactory explanation of them (e.g., deny that what Marquis calls his "future like ours" principle is an acceptable moral principle or that it accurately captures our shared judgments); or (3) agree that the author's moral principle provides a satisfactory explanation of the core cases but deny that it has the implication that the author claims it has (e.g., deny that the future-like-ours principle implies that killing a human fetus is wrong, perhaps because fetuses do not have have a future like ours).

The first option is, generally speaking, the least promising. Just as most arguments from analogy are constructed from cases that most people agree about, so most arguments from inference to the best explanation are constructed from sets of cases that most people agree about. This is not to say that one should accept the foundations of such arguments blindly; indeed, you should always begin by checking to see if you have the kind of intuitive reactions that the author presumes you to have. Rather, it is simply to emphasize that if one agrees with the author's assessment of the core cases, this is only the beginning of one's critical options.

In many instances, much of the sustained critical discussion of an argument from inference to the best explanation will revolve around the second option. Here the key question is: Has the author really given a compelling account of our judgments in the core cases about which we generally share the same moral judgments? Such a discussion may end up going in many different directions, but a few suggestions may help to get things started.

First, why does the author think that his explanation is the best? If the principle is claimed to be simple, what is simple about it? If it is claimed to be accurate, why, precisely, does he think it generates the right answers in the uncontroversial cases? If there are other features of the explanation that the author appeals to, what are they and why does he think they make his principle a powerful one?

Second, there are two distinct ways in which a principle might run into trouble with particular cases: It may fail to get the answer right in one of the cases it aims to address. (For example, some people may argue that the moral principle that Regan appeals to can not successfully account for all of the cases of brain-damaged human beings.) It may get the answer right in the core cases it addresses but then fail in a further case. (For example, some have argued that Marquis's future-like-ours principle gets the right results in the case of killing you or me, but gets it wrong in the case of killing sperm or eggs; see, for example, the critical response by Alastair Norcross near the end of the first half of chapter 3.)

Finally, there is the third option. On this approach, one accepts the author's general principle but denies that it supports his particular conclusion. In one of the critical responses to Marquis's article, for example, Peter K. McInerney argues that the human fetus does not yet have the future-like-ours property that Marquis appeals to in explaining the wrongness of killing. And in one of the critical responses we provide to Regan's article, R. G. Frey argues that nonhuman animals lack some of the properties that Regan says are required in order for one to be a subject of a life. If one can make a case for such a response, then one can reject a given author's specific conclusion about the controversial case without having to argue against his general explanation of the core cases about which most people agree. As with the case of arguments from analogy, what has been said here should be taken only as a suggestion, and not as a foolproof technique or blueprint, for how to initiate and organize an exhaustive critical discussion. Still, these are good ways to begin working through the articles in this anthology that have such a structure (the featured articles in chapters 13 and 32 are two further examples).

4.4 Arguments by Process of Elimination

While many of the arguments in this anthology are constructive in ways such as those we have identified and explained above, others are essentially destructive. They provide not so much a positive argument for the claim that, say, *X is not wrong,* as they do a negative argument *against* other arguments that have been made for the claim that *X is wrong.*

4.4.1 Understanding Arguments by Process of Elimination

Simply showing that one argument for a particular conclusion is a bad argument does little to demonstrate that the conclusion itself is false. The argument "four is my favorite number, therefore two plus two equals four," for example, is a bad argument for the conclusion that two plus two equals four, but this does not mean that two plus two does not equal four, or that there are not other, much better reasons for believing that two plus two equals four. The fact that there exists one bad argument for a given conclusion does not mean that there might not be other, better arguments for it. But if you can show that all of the seemingly plausible arguments for a given conclusion are bad arguments, this can at the least establish a much stronger presumption against the conclusion. In order to do this, such arguments must eliminate not just one argument, but a number of arguments. The manner in which those arguments proceed is thus typically referred to as an argument by process of elimination.

In his article "Charges Against Prostitution" (chapter 10), Lars O. Ericsson offers a defense of prostitution by trying to show that the various charges that have been raised against prostitution can be successfully overcome. And Ernest van den Haag's defense of capital punishment in "Refuting Reiman and Nathanson" (chapter 25) can, as the title suggests, be understood in a similar manner. It seeks support for the death penalty by trying to undermine a variety of arguments against it. (Further examples of arguments that utilize the process of elimination can be found in featured articles throughout this work, including those in chapters 8, 17, 27, and 31.)

4.4.2 Criticizing Arguments by Process of Elimination

Argument by process of elimination is not fully distinct from the other kinds of arguments we discuss in this introduction. In attempting to rebut some of the arguments that have been made against prostitution, for example, Ericsson appeals to a variety of analogies comparing prostitution with other professions, so that a complete critical analysis of his position will in the end involve much of the kind of thinking we discuss in the context of arguments from analogy. Once one has determined that a particular writer is proceeding by means of an argument by process of elimination, one must keep in mind that arguments by process of elimination can fail in one of two distinct ways: They can fail to eliminate one of the arguments they attempt to address, and they can fail to notice a further argument that should have been addressed. Some readers may feel that Ericsson's attempt to overcome what he calls the "feminist charge" against prostitution is unsuccessful (as do two of the critical-response pieces we provide after Ericsson's article, those by Carole Pateman and Laurie Shrage), but others may feel that prostitution is wrong for reasons that Ericsson has not really confronted in the first place (as Karen Green does, for example, in a final response to Ericsson's article).

4.5 Arguments by Reduction to Absurdity

Often known by its Latin label *reductio ad absurdum,* meaning "reduction to absurdity," and frequently by the abbreviation *reductio,* this strikingly simple and very effective argumentation strategy is popular in mathematical demonstrations; philosophers are very fond of it as well. The basic idea is nicely described in the label. In order to establish that a certain assumption is false we may derive an absurdity from the claim. Any assumption that implies something absurd is itself absurd, and so we can reject the assumption.

4.5.1 Understanding Reductio

The clearest instance of an absurdity is an explicit contradiction. A contradiction is a claim of the form:

B is true and B is not true.

Let us abbreviate "B is not true" to not-B and abbreviate "B is true" and "B is not true" to (B and not-B). Now, a claim of (B and not-B) cannot be true whatever claim B is. Whether

B is true or false, the conjunction (B and not-B) contains at least one false claim, and so the whole conjunction is false. (B and not-B) is thus *absurd* because it cannot possibly be true, whatever way the world happens to be.

Now, suppose that a claim A logically *entails* a conjunction of the form (B and not-B). Then it follows from the notion of entailment, and the fact that (B and not-B) *cannot* be true, that A also cannot be true. A, like (B and not-B) is also absurd. So we might lay out the general form of a reductio as follows:

P1   If A were true, then both B and not-B would have to be true
       (i.e., A entails (B and not-B)).
P2   (B and not-B) is absurd
       (i.e., it cannot be true).
_____

C   A is absurd (i.e., A cannot be true).

Sometimes a reductio will use a consequence *B* of some assumption or theory that, while not actually contradictory is *wildly implausible* or known to conflict with known facts. This is a weaker notion of an absurdity than a contradiction, but many arguments that philosophers call reductio use such consequences. If claim A entails a wildly implausible claim B, then A must also be wildly implausible. So, we might summarize the form of such an argument thus:

P1   A entails B.
P2   B is absurd (i.e., B is wildly implausible).
_____

C   A is absurd (i.e., A is wildly implausible).

Examples of reductio can be found in many of the selections. In chapter 5, Alan White, for example, uses a reductio against Regan's claim that nonhuman animals can be the subject of rights. In chapter 7, Stramel uses a reductio against Mohr's claim that it is wrong not to "out" a homosexual. In chapter 2, Shelly Kagan endeavors to show that a principle connected with bare-difference arguments (the "ubiquity" principle) would lead to contradictory judgments. (Strictly speaking, Kagan shows that an ubiquity principle in conjunction with two apparently obvious judgments generates a contradiction. Another example of this is found in chapters 11 and 14.)

4.5.2 Criticizing a Reductio

We have two kinds of reductio. The first kind involves the claim that some theory has as a consequence an explicit contradiction. The second kind involves the claim that some theory entails a wildly implausible consequence. Let us deal with these in this order.

Note that there is no disputing the absurdity of a claim of the form (B and not-B). Further, if A entails (B and not-B) then A, too, is absurd in the same sense—it cannot *possibly* be true. So, the only way of criticizing the first kind of *reductio* is to show that the first premise of the *reductio* is false. That is to say, one must show that A really does *not* lead to a contradiction after all. So, either A does not entail B, or else A does not entail not-B, the negation of B.

Now consider the *reductio* that involves a consequence that while not logically contradictory is held to be wildly implausible. Here we can also attack the first premise: the supposed entailment relation between A and the supposedly absurd consequence. But, in addition, the second premise of the *reductio* (that B is wildly implausible) might also be challenged. Lots of claims that people once *thought* to be wildly implausible (that the earth moves, that humans descended from amoeba, that mass is energy) have turned out to be true after all. So, while it is never a mistake to think that an explicit contradiction is absurd, it might be a mistake to think that the consequence of our theory really is wildly implausible. Maybe the reasons we had for thinking B implausible are themselves defective. Maybe it only seems wildly implausible, but we can explain why it seems that way even if it is true.

5 CONCLUSION

There are many different ways in which the readings in this anthology can fruitfully be analyzed and discussed. Readers should take the specific suggestions we have offered in this introduction not as a substitute for applying their own critical thinking, but rather as a first step toward thinking critically about the readings on their own.

PART 1

WHAT'S WRONG WITH KILLING?

One of the oldest and most familiar moral principles runs as follows: "Thou shalt not kill." Virtually everyone recognizes an element of truth to this ancient edict. The deliberate murder of an innocent human being is almost universally treated as among the most serious moral transgressions. At the same time, virtually no one truly accepts this principle in its unqualified form. A gardener, for example, might kill hundreds of weeds in tending to a garden. A doctor might kill millions of cancer cells in treating a patient. Consumers buy special cleaners aimed at killing mold and mildew, wash their hands with soaps specifically designed to kill bacteria, and buy their pets special collars that promise to kill ticks and fleas. Therefore, while killing is taken to be seriously immoral in some contexts, it is not seen as the least bit immoral in many others.

There is very little debate among moral philosophers about whether or not killing is wrong in these extreme cases. Virtually all would agree that it would be wrong for me to kill you, for example, but not wrong for me to kill the mold and mildew in my bathroom. In between these two extremes, however, lies an important range of cases that are much more difficult to resolve and, as a result, much more controversial. Part 1 of this book is devoted to such cases. We begin, in chapter 1, with the question of whether it is morally permissible to kill enemy noncombatants in wartime, and if not, whether this is compatible with the view that it is morally permissible to kill enemy combatants. We move on to consider cases of killing that many people do consider justified—euthanasia, or the killing of people who are suffering from terminal, debilitating, or very painful illnesses (chapter 2). We then turn to the subject of killing at the very early stages of human life: Is it wrong to kill a human fetus (chapter 3) or a human neonate (chapter 4)? Finally, chapter 5 concludes Part 1 by considering the question of whether or not it is wrong to kill nonhuman animals. In most cases, those who are opposed to a particular form of killing try to justify their opposition to it by trying to show that it is relevantly similar to killing innocent adult human beings, while those who support a particular form of killing attempt to justify their support of it by trying to show that it differs from such cases. That is, the investigation of the morality of killing in these controversial cases, typically involves, at least in part, an investigation into the morality of killing in uncontroversial cases as well.

1

Is Killing in War Wrong?

Fullinwider and His Critics

On March 16, 1968, the soldiers of Charlie Company, Eleventh Brigade, American Division, entered the village of My Lai, in the South Vietnamese district of Son My, an area with strong Vietcong sympathies. During the preceding weeks, several members of Charlie Company had been maimed or killed by Vietcong mines in the area. Under the command of Lieutenant William Calley, the soldiers entered the village ready to engage with the elusive Vietcong. However, instead of encountering enemy fire, they encountered a village full of noncombatants. Their mission quickly degenerated into a massacre of more than three hundred apparently unarmed civilians, including women, children, and the elderly. According to eyewitnesses, old men were bayoneted, praying women and children were shot in the back of the head, and at least one young girl was raped and then killed. When it became public knowledge, the massacre caused a storm of protest in the United States and was instrumental in crystallizing public opinion against the war.

War might seem a strange domain in which to be examining the morality of killing. After all, killing is the business of war. Soldiers are decorated for doing it. And yet we also recognize strong moral differences even in wartime killing. Killing enemy combatants is widely regarded not just as morally permissible, but even as morally commendable. But killing enemy noncombatants is nearly as widely condemned. The My Lai massacre, for example, was widely regarded as a moral outrage because it was a blatant case of the killing of noncombatants.

What justifies this difference in moral judgment on the killing of combatants and the killing of noncombatants? For it to be justified there must be some morally significant difference between a combatant and a noncombatant, and that difference must be sufficient to make it permissible to kill one but not the other. What is that difference?

Fullinwider begins his article by considering one traditional and influential answer to this question: the principle that to intentionally kill an innocent human being is seriously morally wrong, and that noncombatants, even enemy noncombatants, are clearly innocent human beings. Thus it is seriously morally wrong to kill enemy noncombatants. Enemy combatants, however, are not clearly innocent in the way that noncombatants are, so it may be permissible to kill them.

Fullinwider notes that lying behind this justification is something like a principle of punishment: It is morally permissible to kill someone if and only if he has done something to *deserve* death as some sort of *punishment*. Presumably, what it is that combatants are guilty of is intentionally prosecuting a war against your country, whereas noncombatants are not guilty of this. Fullinwider considers these a pair of dubious claims. A very reluctant conscripted combatant who serves in the army only under threat of punishment may be much less responsible for the prosecution of the war than, say, an influential and enthusiastic noncombatant.

Fullinwider nevertheless goes on to defend the traditional view—that whereas combatants may be killed, noncombatants may not. But he thinks that the difference rests on considerations that have to do with *self-defense,* not on considerations that have to do with guilt, desert, and punishment. Fullinwider begins with a short story (involving the ubiquitous Smith and Jones, a pair who seem to be perennially involved in morally messy situations):

> Jones is walking down a street. Smith steps from behind the corner of a nearby building and begins to fire a gun at Jones, with the appearance of deliberate intent to kill Jones. Surrounded by buildings, Jones is afforded no means of escape. Jones, who is carrying a gun himself, shoots at Smith and kills him.

Fullinwider asks us to share his judgment that in killing Smith, Jones is justified by the Principle of Self-Defense: that is, it is morally permissible to kill someone whose actions put your life directly and immediately in mortal danger if that is what is necessary to end the threat. Further, the facts as stated alone constitute a sufficient justification for Jones's killing of Smith. Now Fullinwider adds some further details to the story, details that he claims do not undermine the permissibility of Jones's killing of Smith. (In fact he considers three different additions; we will consider just one of them here.)

> . . . suppose Smith, through heavy gambling losses, is in debt to the mob for $100,000. The mobsters propose to Smith that if he will kill Jones (a crusading district attorney, say), they will forgive his debt. Unable to pay the debt, and knowing what will happen to him if he fails to pay it, Smith seeks out Jones and begins firing.

Fullinwider claims that this additional information does not undermine the permissibility of Jones's killing of Smith. The Principle of Self-Defense still endows Jones with the moral permission to kill. Furthermore, it licenses *only* the killing of Smith.

> . . . suppose the mobsters were parked across the street to observe Smith. After killing Smith, Jones could not turn his gun on them (assuming they were unarmed). No matter how causally implicated the . . . mobsters were in Smith's assault on Jones, in the situation it was only Smith who was the agent of immediate threat to Jones; the . . . mobsters were not posing a direct and immediate danger. From the point of view of justifiably killing in self-defense, they are not justifiably liable to be killed by Jones; they are immune.

It should be clear now that Fullinwider is drawing an analogy between Smith and the enemy combatants on the one hand, and the unarmed mobsters and enemy noncombatants who support the war on the other. We can construct an argument from analogy to justify the two different moral judgments.

P1   In the street scenario, it is morally permissible for Jones to kill Smith, but it would be morally wrong for Jones to kill the mobsters.

P2   Jones's killing Smith is morally on a par with a soldier's killing an enemy combatant; and Jones's killing the mobsters would be morally on a par with a soldier's killing enemy noncombatants.

C   It is morally permissible for a soldier to kill enemy combatants but morally wrong for a soldier to kill enemy noncombatants.

Alternatively, we might construct a direct, non-analogical argument for the different pair of judgments, using a broadened *principle of self-defense:* that it is morally permissible to kill someone who makes a direct and immediate threat either to one's own survival or to the survival of the nation of which one is a citizen.

P1* Principle of self-defense: It is only morally permissible to kill someone, in self-defense, who is the agent of a direct and immediate threat to one's survival (or one's nation's survival.)

P2* Enemy combatants are agents of a direct and immediate threat to one's survival or one's nation's survival, and enemy noncombatants are not.

C*   It is morally permissible to kill enemy combatants in self-defense, but it is morally wrong to kill enemy noncombatants in self-defense.

In his response to Fullinwider, Lawrence A. Alexander begins by elaborating on Fullinwider's story.

> Suppose the situation is the same except that Jones has not yet killed Smith. May Jones invoke the Principle of Self-Defense to kill the mobsters instead of Smith if by doing so he will cause Smith to relent? Of course he may. If the mobsters had a gun trained on Smith and had ordered him to kill Jones, and he were about to comply, Jones not only could, but should, kill the mobsters rather than Smith if killing them would be no riskier than killing Smith and would remove the threat to Jones by removing Smith's motive for killing him. Jones should kill the mobsters in such a situation even if the mobsters could not kill Jones directly (say, because the range of their guns was sufficient to reach Smith but not Jones, who carried a longer-range gun).

Clearly this is also an analogical argument. Alexander has tried to make the mobsters more like, for example, the noncombatant civilian leaders of the enemy country. Since Smith could remove the threat to himself just as easily by killing the mobsters as by killing Jones, it seems he should be just as entitled, by the principle of self-defense, to kill them instead. But if so, that means that either the principle of self-defense is false (i.e. P1* of Fullinwider's direct argument is false), or P2* of the direct argument is false, because the enemy noncombatants are correctly regarded as agents of a direct and immediate threat. Alexander goes on to draw some further analogies to illustrate his claim that noncombatants may be killed in self-defense. Furthermore, he goes on to argue that sometimes when one has to choose between killing combatants and certain noncombatants, one is morally obliged to kill the noncombatants rather than the combatants.

QUESTIONS FOR CONSIDERATION

In thinking about this issue, consider the following questions:

• What version of the principle of self-defense does each of our two authors use? Is there some other version that might be superior to both?

• Is the principle of self-defense (in any of the versions you are considering) actually true? Try to think of a possible case in which Jones poses an immediate threat to Smith through no fault of Jones, where Smith can avert the threat that Jones poses only by killing Jones, but where it does not seem immediately obvious that Smith is entitled to kill Jones.

• Does the principle of self-defense entitle Smith to kill a whole host of Joneses who are collectively posing a threat to Smith, through no fault of their own?

• What actually is an enemy combatant? Is an army cook, for example, a combatant? Does it make a difference whether the cook is an enlisted soldier or a contract laborer? If the cook is an enemy combatant, is the truck driver who delivers oatmeal (for the soldiers' breakfast) also a combatant? If not, why is he any different from the cook? After all, both help keep the combatants combat ready. But if so, what is the difference between the truck driver and the soldiers' wives (or husbands) and girlfriends (or boyfriends)?

FURTHER READING

MacKinnon, C. "Crimes of War, Crimes of Peace." In *On Human Rights,* edited by S. Shute and S. Hurley. New York: Basic Books, 1993.
Nagel, T. "War and Massacre." *Philosophy and Public Affairs* 1, no. 2 (1971): 123–44.

Robert K. Fullinwider | War and Innocence

I

In a war, is it morally permissible intentionally to kill noncombatants? Elizabeth Anscombe and Paul Ramsey argue that noncombatants may not be intentionally killed.[1] We are obligated to refrain from such killing because it is murder; and it is murder because noncombatants are innocent.

George Mavrodes questions the grounds for asserting that in war noncombatants are "innocent" and combatants are "guilty." If immunity of noncombatants from killing is to be established this way, he says, then we must find a "sense of 'innocence' such that all noncombatants are innocent and all combatants are guilty," and "this sense must be morally relevant." Mavrodes fears, however, that immunity theorists such as Anscombe and Ramsey are actually using "innocent" and "noncombatant" synonymously. He believes that the sense of "innocence" used in their arguments has no moral content.[2]

Mavrodes' main argument is this. There are noncombatants who may enthusiastically endorse and support the war their nation is waging, while there are combatants who may be under arms unhappily and unwillingly, who may not support the war but are unable to resist conscription. It is odd to claim that the enthusiastically supportive noncombatant is innocent and the reluctant conscript guilty. "Is it not clear," Mavrodes asks, "that 'innocence,' as used here, leaves out entirely all morally relevant considerations . . . ?"[3]

Anscombe and Ramsey both invite this sort of counterargument by the way they defend their immunity thesis. Anscombe implies that the thesis is rooted in the Principle of Punishment: no man is to be punished except for his own crime.[4] Ramsey, too, employs the model of the criminal in defending the

thesis.[5] But, from the point of view of punishment, it is odd, if not perverse, to view the enthusiastically supportive noncombatant as innocent and the reluctant combatant as guilty. Mavrodes, in my judgment, is right in believing this defense fails to establish the immunity of noncombatants from intentional killing.

Mavrodes believes that the obligation not to kill noncombatants intentionally can rest only on a convention among nations. Such an obligation, if it exists, is at best contingent, conditioned as it is on the existence of such a convention in force. Anscombe and Ramsey believe the obligation to refrain from intentionally killing noncombatants is noncontingent. It is not convention-dependent.[6]

In this paper I shall briefly sketch an argument for the immunity of noncombatants which avoids Mavrodes' criticisms. It will establish that in warfare there is a morally relevant distinction between noncombatants and combatants which prohibits the intentional killing of the former at the same time as it justifies the intentional killing of the latter. My argument will appeal to a nonconventional principle, and thus the obligation deriving from the principle will not be convention-dependent (or anyway not wholly so). I will then go on to show that even if certain considerations undercut drawing the line of immunity between combatants and noncombatants, a weaker version of the immunity thesis is still viable.

II

To set the scene, first consider an example. Jones is walking down a street. Smith steps from behind the corner of a nearby building and begins to fire a gun at Jones, with the appearance of deliberate intent

From Robert K. Fullinwider, "War and Innocence," *Philosophy and Public Affairs* 5, no. 1 (Autumn 1975): 90–97. Some notes have been deleted. Reprinted by permission of Princeton University Press.

to kill Jones. Surrounded by buildings, Jones is afforded no means of escape. Jones, who is carrying a gun himself, shoots at Smith and kills him.

Jones is morally justified in killing Smith by the Principle of Self-Defense. Smith's actions put Jones' life directly and immediately in mortal jeopardy, and Jones' killing Smith was necessary to end that threat. From the point of view of self-defense, these facts about Smith's actions are the *only* relevant ones. The moral justification of the killing rests on them alone given the legitimacy of self-defense.

But let me now sketch in some possible background circumstances to Smith's assault on Jones. Suppose Smith's wife, spurned by Jones when she made advances toward him, tells Smith she has been raped by Jones. Furious, and egged on by his wife, Smith seeks out Jones and begins firing. Or, suppose Smith, through heavy gambling losses, is in debt to the mob for $100,000. The mobsters propose to Smith that if he will kill Jones (a crusading district attorney, say), they will forgive his debt. Unable to pay the debt, and knowing what will happen to him if he fails to pay it, Smith seeks out Jones and begins firing. Or, suppose the mobsters kidnap Smith's children and threaten to kill them unless he kills Jones. Driven by the threat, Smith seeks out Jones and begins firing.

None of this background information alters the situation from the point of view of self-defense. Whatever prompted Smith to fire at Jones, the justification for Jones' killing Smith lies solely in the fact that Smith was the direct and immediate agent of a threat against Jones' life. From the point of view of self-defense, this fact justifies Jones in killing Smith—and *only* Smith.

Again, suppose that Smith's wife was standing across the street egging Smith on as he fired at Jones. Jones, though he justifiably shot Smith in self-defense, could not justifiably turn his gun on the wife in self-defense. Or suppose the mobsters were parked across the street to observe Smith. After killing Smith, Jones could not turn his gun on them (assuming they were unarmed). No matter how causally implicated the wife or the mobsters were in

Smith's assault on Jones, in the situation it was only Smith who was the agent of immediate threat to Jones; the wife and the mobsters were not posing a direct and immediate danger. From the point of view of justifiably killing in self-defense, they are not justifiably liable to be killed by Jones; they are immune.

There is a point of view from which these background features I have drawn in become morally relevant, namely the point of view of retribution or punishment. Smith's wife and the mobsters would be viewed as morally culpable for their contribution to Smith's assault on Jones' life. They ought to be punished. Perhaps Jones might be justified in taking his own retribution, and killing the wife or mobsters in revenge; but even if he is justified in killing them in retribution, he still cannot justify killing them on the grounds of self-defense.

In these cases of killing and attempted killing there are two points of view: the point of view of self-defense and the point of view of punishment. Some considerations that become morally relevant from the second point of view in justifying killing are not relevant from the first point of view. We use the notions of guilt and innocence almost always in connection with the second point of view, the perspective of punishment. From that point of view, Smith's wife and the mobsters are as guilty as Smith. In the instance where the mobsters cause Smith to act under duress, perhaps they are more guilty.

If we were to speak of innocence and guilt as categories applying in cases of self-defense, then for the purpose of justifiably killing in self-defense and from that point of view we would say that Smith alone was guilty (justifiably liable to killing) and his wife and the mobsters were innocent (not justifiably liable to killing), though all are guilty from the point of view of punishment.

It should be obvious now how my argument for the immunity thesis is going to run. The moral relevance of the distinction in war between combatants and noncombatants will be derived from the Principle of Self-Defense. Because we most commonly speak of innocence in connection with crime and punishment and because we also speak of innocent victims of war, Anscombe and Ramsey have been led to defend the innocents in war by appeal to the wrong model. For these same reasons, Mavrodes has failed to see an alternative to his conventionalism.

III

I shall now sketch an argument for the moral immunity of noncombatants from intentional killing.

The question at hand is the killing in war and its justifiability. Why is any killing at all justified? I claim that a nation may justifiably kill in self-defense. From the point of view of self-defense, only those are justifiably liable to be killed who pose the immediate and direct jeopardy. In the case of war, it is nations' armed forces which are the agents of the jeopardy. In a war, the armed forces of nation *A* stand to opponent nation *B* as Smith stood to Jones. It is against them that *B* may defend itself by the use of force. The active combatants, their arms, ammunition, war machines and facilities, are the legitimate targets of intentional destruction.

Though *A*'s civilian population may support its war against *B* and contribute to it in various ways, they stand to *B* as Smith's wife or the mobsters stood to Jones. For the purpose of justifiably killing in self-defense and from that point of view, the civilian population is morally immune—it is "innocent." To intentionally kill noncombatants is to kill beyond the scope of self-defense. It is to kill unjustifiably from the point of view of self-defense.

This, in brief, is my argument. It provides for drawing a line between combatants and noncombatants, and prohibits intentionally killing the latter. This is just where the immunity theorists want to draw the line of prohibition. Furthermore, they see the prohibition as "natural," not convention-dependent. My argument supports them in this. The distinction between combatants and noncombatants derives from the operation of the Principle of Self-Defense. Our obligation not to kill noncombatants stems from our obligation not to kill without justification; and the Principle of Self-Defense justifies killing only combatants. Since both the obligation to

not kill without justification and the Principle of Self-Defense are "natural" rather than conventional, the moral immunity of noncombatants does not rest (solely) upon the existence of appropriate conventions among nations.

IV

From the point of view of killing in self-defense in war, Mavrodes' reluctant conscript is "guilty" (justifiably liable to killing), and his noncombatant partisan is "innocent" (not justifiably liable to killing). To say that the reluctant conscript is guilty and the noncombatant partisan is innocent is to stand the matter on its head, claims Mavrodes. So it is—from the point of view of punishment. This, I have urged, is not the fundamentally governing point of view when it comes to justifying killing in war. The innocence of the noncombatant seems inexplicable to Mavrodes because he takes up the wrong point of view for evaluating killing in war. He is, of course, encouraged to take up this view by Anscombe's and Ramsey's own arguments in defense of the innocence of noncombatants. Viewing killing in war from this evaluative standpoint, and finding it incapable of explaining the prohibition against killing combatants, Mavrodes turns to conventionalism.

Might it not be contended against my defense of the immunity thesis that the point of view of self-defense is not the sole governing point of view when it comes to killing in war? Nations, it might be argued, exist in a state of nature, and thus possess the right to exact their own punishments on transgressors. Thus, in war, justifying deliberate killing may be done by appeal to both the Principle of Self-Defense *and* the Principle of Punishment. Finally, to the extent that retribution justifies some of the killing in war, it will justify killing some noncombatants.

I have two answers to this challenge. The first answer preserves the strong immunity thesis, but it requires an assumption of fact which may, theoretically, not obtain. The second answer, dropping the assumption, requires me to weaken the immunity thesis.

For purposes of argument, I will concede that nations have the right to exact their own punishment in war. Even so, the Principle of Punishment justifies punishing *only* the *morally guilty* (culpable from the point of view of punishment), not the *morally innocent* (innocent from the point of view of punishment). Techniques of warfare—combat, bombing, shelling, burning—are too indiscriminate in their destruction to serve as legitimate instruments of punishment. They cannot be used discriminatingly between the morally guilty and the morally innocent. It is not justified by the Principle of Punishment intentionally to kill the morally innocent. If a nation claims punitive rights in war, it must adopt mechanisms of punishment which will discriminate between those who deserve punishment and those who do not. Bombing, shelling, and other such techniques kill guilty and innocent alike. Consequently, if we wish to justify killing during war by the means of war, the only applicable perspective is self-defense.[7]

If, however, contrary to the facts, there were some perfectly discriminating techniques of warfare, then, since I have conceded the right of nations to exact their own punishment, I see no argument against a nation legitimately taking up both points of view in its prosecution of a war. Some of the justified killing will be justified by self-defense, some by merited punishment. This would require a weakening of the immunity thesis, since the Principle of Punishment would justify some intentional killing of noncombatants, namely those that were morally guilty. Nevertheless, a version of the immunity thesis can be preserved: some line prohibiting intentional killing would still be mandated. The Principle of Self-Defense will justify intentionally killing combatants, even the morally innocent among them. The Principle of Punishment will justify killing (if this is proportional to the crime) the morally guilty noncombatant. But neither principle will sanction or permit the intentional killing of the morally innocent noncombatant, many of whom will be found in any nation at war. There will thus be a line of immunity required to be drawn around a certain class in war, the class of morally innocent noncombatants. We shall be morally obliged to refrain from intentionally killing members of this class, and this moral obliga-

tion will not disappear in the absence of any particular convention among nations.

Because of the indiscriminate nature of modern techniques of destruction, I see two reasons why the line of immunity is to be maintained between combatants and noncombatants. First, if nations recognize the Principle of Punishment, they may nevertheless be required to refrain from attempting to use it as a justification for killing because they shall not be able to meet the discrimination requirement. Second, nations may find it collectively beneficial to agree to forgo the exercise of their punishment rights during war (the exercise of which is morally ruled out anyway). They might thus, as Mavrodes suggests, adopt conventions confirming the line of immunity during warfare between combatant and noncombatant. To this extent, Mavrodes' conventionalism has support. The obligation not to kill noncombatants may be partly conventional; but if my arguments have been correct, it is not wholly so.

NOTES

1. Elizabeth Anscombe, "War and Murder," in *War and Morality,* ed. Richard Wasserstrom (Belmont, Ca., 1970); Paul Ramsey, *The Last War* (New York, 1968). See also John C. Ford, "The Morality of Obliteration Bombing," in *War and Morality.*

2. George I. Mavrodes, "Conventions and the Morality of War," *Philosophy & Public Affairs* 4, no. 2 (Winter 1975): 121, 123.

3. Mavrodes, pp. 122–123.

4. Anscombe, p. 49; Mavrodes, pp. 120, 123.

5. Ramsey, p. 144; Mavrodes, p. 123.

6. For Mavrodes' definition of convention-dependent obligation, see p. 126 of his article.

7. The Principle of Self-Defense also requires discrimination—between combatants and noncombatants. Since usually combatants are in uniform, with weapons, on battlefields, instruments of war can be used in a way which (roughly) avoids the death of noncombatants. However, instruments which cannot be used in a discriminating way, and whose use entails extensive noncombatant casualties (e.g. hydrogen bombs), are ruled out for use even in self-defense. See Richard Wasserstrom, "On the Morality of War: A Preliminary Inquiry," in *War and Morality,* pp. 100–101. (See also pp. 89 ff. where Wasserstrom discusses the justification of self-defense; and pp. 94–96, where he discusses the meaning of innocence in war.)

Critics

Lawrence A. Alexander

Self-Defense and the Killing of Noncombatants

A Reply to Fullinwider

In a recent article[1] Robert Fullinwider argued that the distinction between combatants and noncombatants is morally relevant (in a sense unrelated to the existence of a specific convention among nations)[2] to the question of who among the enemy may be intentionally killed by a nation acting in self-defense. He concedes that the distinction is not based on the relative moral guilt or innocence of the two groups in connection with the prosecution of the war, recognizing that many combatants might be morally innocent (for example, reluctant conscripts) and many noncombatants morally guilty (for example, the governmental officials who launched the war). Moreover, he admits that guilt or innocence is relevant to the question of who should be punished by the defending nation. However, says Fullinwider, punishment of the guilty is not the only justification for intentional killing in war. Under the Principle of Self-Defense, innocent combatants, but not innocent noncombatants, may also justifiably be killed.

I do not intend to deny the widely held view that morally innocent persons may be intentionally killed in self-defense (although I believe a case can be made against it).[3] Rather, I intend to show that the permissibility of killing innocents in self-defense does not, as Fullinwider maintains, justify the moral distinction between combatants and noncombatants.

The heart of Fullinwider's argument is the following passage:

> ... [S]uppose Smith, through heavy gambling losses, is in debt to the mob for $100,000. The mobsters propose to Smith that if he will kill Jones (a

crusading district attorney, say), they will forgive his debt. Unable to pay the debt, and knowing what will happen to him if he fails to pay it, Smith seeks out Jones and begins firing. Or, suppose the mobsters kidnap Smith's children and threaten to kill them unless he kills Jones. Driven by the threat, Smith seeks out Jones and begins firing.

> None of this background information alters the situation from the point of view of self-defense. Whatever prompted Smith to fire at Jones, the justification for Jones' killing Smith lies solely in the fact that Smith was the direct and immediate agent of a threat against Jones' life. From the point of view of self-defense, this fact justifies Jones in killing Smith—and *only* Smith.

> Again ... suppose the mobsters were parked across the street to observe Smith. After killing Smith, Jones could not turn his gun on them (assuming they were unarmed). No matter how causally implicated ... the mobsters were in Smith's assault on Jones, in the situation it was only Smith who was the agent of immediate threat to Jones; ... the mobsters were not posing a direct and immediate danger. From the point of view of justifiably killing in self-defense, they are not justifiably liable to be killed by Jones; they are immune.[4]

Fullinwider is correct that *after* killing Smith, Jones may not invoke the Principle of Self-Defense to then turn and kill the mobsters. *The threat to his life has been removed.* At most the mobsters may be punished for their guilt in instigating the attempted murder.

However, Fullinwider's hypothetical is inapposite when we are discussing whether noncombatants

From Lawrence A. Alexander, "Self-Defense and the Killing of Noncombatants: A Reply to Fullinwider," *Philosophy and Public Affairs* 5, no. 4 (Summer 1976): 408–15. Some notes have been deleted. Reprinted by permission of Princeton University Press.

along with combatants may be killed in an on-going war. Surely no one has contended that after surrender, the point analogous to the killing of Smith by Jones, innocent noncombatants may still be killed in self-defense. (Indeed, no one has contended as much for innocent combatants either.) Fullinwider has constructed a straw man.

Let us amend Fullinwider's hypothetical to make it relevant to the issue he is addressing. Suppose the situation is the same except that Jones has not yet killed Smith. May Jones invoke the Principle of Self-Defense to kill the mobsters instead of Smith if by doing so he will cause Smith to relent? Of course he may. If the mobsters had a gun trained on Smith and had ordered him to kill Jones, and he were about to comply, Jones not only could, but should, kill the mobsters rather than Smith if killing them would be no riskier than killing Smith and would remove the threat to Jones by removing Smith's motive for killing him. Jones should kill the mobsters in such a situation even if the mobsters could not kill Jones directly (say, because the range of their guns was sufficient to reach Smith but not Jones, who carried a longer-range gun). From the standpoint of the Principle of Self-Defense, both the mobsters and Smith are necessary causes of the danger to Jones because killing either the mobsters or Smith removes the danger. Jones should, therefore, kill the ones who are morally guilty, not the one who is morally innocent. Such an interpretation of the Principle of Self-Defense is consistent with its application in the law, and any interpretation that permitted only the killing of Smith would be morally perverse.

Indeed, it would be morally perverse to limit Jones' right of self-defense to the killing of Smith, even where the mobsters have not threatened Smith's life. Suppose the chief mobster has merely offered Smith money. The mobster, unarmed, is across the street from Smith and Jones, so that if Jones kills the mobster, Smith will realize that he will not get paid for killing Jones. Jones should be able to kill the mobster instead of Smith if the mobster is morally as guilty or guiltier than Smith (who might have been driven to the wall financially).

What I propose as the correct formulation of the Principle of Self-Defense is that X (a person or persons) may be killed in self-defense, regardless of X's moral innocence, if the defender perceives (reasonably) that: (1) there exists the requisite threshold level of danger or greater; (2) killing X will reduce that danger; (3) more desirable courses of action, such as killing fewer or guiltier persons, or not killing at all, will not eliminate condition (1); and (4) more desirable courses of action will not reduce the danger as much as killing X.

In war, many noncombatants, guilty and innocent, are threats to the defending nation. Many of them are greater threats than many combatants. A combatant at a camp miles behind the lines is often less a threat than a noncombatant delivering arms and ammunition to combatants at the front. Indeed, the combatants at the front individually will quite likely be less of a threat than the noncombatant supplier. In such a case the Principle of Self-Defense would demand that the noncombatant be killed in preference to the combatants, especially if he is no less guilty than they. Consider, also, two alternative courses of action in fighting a hypothetical unjust aggressor: (1) killing millions of enemy soldiers, most of whom are morally innocent (indeed, many are children); or (2) killing a handful of noncombatant enemy leaders, all of whom are morally innocent because of insanity. If either course would end the war, the latter would have to be preferred. Similarly, if one madman is about to deliver bombs to a thousand other madmen, who in turn will throw them, the Principle of Self-Defense demands that we end the danger by killing the former if we are going to be forced to kill in self-defense in any event.

Fullinwider's error could have resulted from assuming that one whose activity or existence is a remote cause (in terms of space, time, or intervening mechanisms or acts) of a threat to another's life is immune from being killed in self-defense, even though he is a necessary or sufficient cause of that threat. In the domestic context, causal remoteness will usually mean that the threat is insufficient to permit killing in self-defense. For in the domestic context, the more remote the cause of the threat, the more likely it is that factors such as the intervention of the police will prevent the harm from occurring, thus obviating the need to kill the cause of the threat.

In the context of international warfare, remoteness, although relevant to the degree of the threat, is less significant, for there is less reason to assume that other factors short of killing will intervene and prevent the threat's materializing.

Although causal remoteness is relevant to the questions of whether a threat exists and whether a person is a necessary or sufficient cause of it, it is irrelevant to the right of self-defense once the threat, the necessary or sufficient causal relation, and the lack of superior alternatives to remove the threat are posited. Moreover, even if causal remoteness were the source of immunity from being killed in self-defense, it would not be the source of an immunity for noncombatants vis-à-vis combatants. As the example of the noncombatants front-line supplier and the rear guard combatants illustrates, some combatants are at any time more remote threats than some noncombatants. Fullinwider could, of course, respond that killing rear guard combatants is not consistent with the Principle of Self-Defense, or, what amounts to the same thing, that only front-line combatants are truly combatants. I do not take him to be making such a claim, which would be an indictment of widely accepted norms of warfare.

There is one other possible source of Fullinwider's error. He may hold the view that one is immune from being killed in self-defense if any further choice of a human agent is necessary for the harm to materialize. This view, he might believe, leads to the conclusion that only those who are sufficiently likely themselves to pull triggers (the infantry, but not the top generals, the ordnance personnel) or release bombs (the bombardiers, but not the pilots or navigators) may be killed. Although this view would not necessarily result in a distinction between combatants and noncombatants, because the likelihood of being killed in the future by one who is presently a noncombatant may exceed both the threshold required for self-defense and also the likelihood of being killed by particular combatants, it deserves a short comment. One cannot hold the view forbidding intervention before the last choice necessary for the harm as an absolute and at the same time accept the Principle of Self-Defense. Most acts sanctioned by the Principle of Self-Defense occur at a point when at least one choice still remains before someone is actually harmed—that is, they occur when the aggressor can still choose to cease his aggression. The fact that further choices are necessary to bring about the harm affects the likelihood of that harm's materializing; and the greater the number of choices required, the less likely it is that the harm will result. Under the Principle of Self-Defense, however, only the likelihood of harm, not the number of choices required to bring it about, is directly relevant.

In some of the hypotheticals I have used, only one choice is required for the harm to result. The mobsters, if they are out of range of Smith's hearing, cannot through any choice affect, in the short run, the likelihood of Smith's killing Jones. Only Smith can.

In other hypotheticals, more than once choice is required. Either the noncombatant munitions supplier or the combatants could through their choices reduce or eliminate the danger. Both must choose to aid the war effort to create the danger.

Whether one or more choices is required, however, is morally irrelevant (so long as the threshold probability of danger has been reached) and in any event is irrelevant to the combatant-noncombatant distinction. Suppose the noncombatant supplier is driving a truck full of munitions under the watchful eyes of his armed countrymen. If he attempts to turn the truck around, he will be stopped, and someone else will drive it. At that point only the choices of those whose hands are on the triggers, not the choice of the supplier, can be considered necessary or sufficient to bring about the harm to the defending nation. The supplier is in a situation analogous to that of a pilot of a bomber which also carries a bombardier. Once the bomber is over the target, no further choice *by the pilot* (at least no choice which would not lead to his death anyway) is necessary or sufficient to cause the bombing to commence. No one who accepts the Principle of Self-Defense could argue that the plane may not be shot down because the bombardier still has a choice to make and might decide not to release the bombs. And I cannot imagine that anyone would argue that the Principle of Self-Defense permits killing *only* the bombardier, not the pilot, where the most effective means of preventing the bombing is shooting down the plane (which, let us suppose, presents a far greater risk of death to the pilot than to the bombardier). But if the pilot, normally thought of as a combatant, may be killed in self-defense, so may the supplier, a noncombatant, perhaps by bombing the truck in order to blow up the munitions.

Finally, if noncombatants (say, children) were involuntarily harnessed with bombs and pushed down a slippery slope towards the troops of the defending nation, the bombs to be released automatically once the children were halfway down the slope, *no* further choice would be necessary to bring about the threatened harm. If the bombs could not be safely shot and detonated once they were released, self-defense would permit shooting the bombs before they were released and blowing up them and their noncombatant carriers, just as it would permit such an act if the carriers were morally innocent conscripted soldiers.

It is apparent, therefore, that neither the number of choices required to bring about the harm nor combatant-noncombatant status is morally relevant to the right to kill in self-defense.

In summary, punishment requires guilt, but guilt, even relative guilt, does not mark the distinction between combatants and noncombatants. On the other hand, the right to kill in self-defense requires only that the person killed be a necessary or sufficient cause of a danger, not that he be morally guilty. Again, however, being a cause of danger does not mark the distinction between combatants and noncombatants. Moreover, noncombatants are not necessarily more remote causes of danger than are combatants; nor is the danger noncombatants pose necessarily more dependent upon further choices than is the danger posed by combatants. Finally, neither causal remoteness nor the necessity of further choices is per se relevant to the Principle of Self-Defense. I conclude, therefore, that the intentional killing of innocent noncombatants is not necessarily immoral if one accepts the Principle of Self-Defense.

NOTES

1. Robert K. Fullinwider, "War and Innocence," *Philosophy & Public Affairs* 5, no. 1 (Fall 1975): 90.

2. See George I. Mavrodes, "Conventions and the Morality of War," *Philosophy & Public Affairs* 4, no. 2 (Winter 1975): 121, 126.

3. The formulation I shall give of the principle that allows the killing of innocent persons in self-defense can, for example, logically be extended to cover acts of terrorism, atomic bombings of cities, etc.

4. Fullinwider, "War and Innocence," pp. 92–93.

2

Is Euthanasia Wrong?

Rachels and His Critics

Imagine you have been diagnosed with cancer, which has spread to your vital organs, including your brain, and it is certain that your death is just a matter of days, or at most weeks, away. Your remaining time is going to be painful, and probably excessively undignified, and you may have no desire to live through all that. You have come to regard your own death not as the ultimate evil but rather as a welcome release from intolerable suffering, suffering that infuses your entire being. You would prefer that someone take active steps to end your life, rather than simply allow an indifferent Nature to take its dreadfully slow and humiliating course. What then, if anything, would be wrong with my giving you a dose of some drug powerful enough to bring about your death? What, in other words, would be wrong with my killing you?

Many people think that it would be morally wrong for me to kill you even in these circumstances. Now suppose that, as often happens with bedridden patients, you contract pneumonia. The pneumonia could easily be cured with antibiotics, but if left untreated it would bring about your death—probably a far less unpleasant death than the one that otherwise awaits you. In a case like this, many people would think it morally permissible for me to withhold the antibiotics. In other words they would think it morally permissible for me to let you die an easily preventable death.

Killing a terminally ill patient who wants to die, and whose death would be a blessing for him, is a case of active euthanasia. Allowing a terminally ill patient who wants to die to die and whose death would be a blessing for her but whose imminent death is preventable, is a case of passive euthanasia. Many people think that passive euthanasia can sometimes be morally permissible, whereas active euthanasia is always morally impermissible. Their reason for endorsing this moral difference is that they think that killing someone is morally worse, in itself, than letting die.

In our featured article, James Rachels argues that one cannot rationally maintain this pair of judgments. Killing, Rachels claims, is morally equivalent to letting die. Let us call this the equivalence thesis. Rachels argues for the equivalence thesis by means of a bare-difference argument. (Indeed, it was Rachels who coined the term "bare-difference argument" in connection with this very issue.)

The strategy is this: We are interested in what features make a moral difference, and whether they make a difference for the better or for the worse. A good-making feature should, other things being equal, make a situation better, and a bad-making feature should, other things being equal, make a situation worse. If killing is morally worse, in itself, than letting die, then a case of killing should be worse than a case of letting die, provided other things are equal. Suppose you take a pair of cases, case A and case B, where case A is a killing and case B is a letting-die, and suppose that case A, say, is morally on a par with case B. Does that mean that killing is not worse than letting die? No. This comparison of cases might not be enough, because case A might differ from case B in other ways, and one or more of those other features might make up for the moral difference between killing and letting die. In order to know that the killing/letting-die difference does not make a moral difference, you have to eliminate any other differences that might make a moral difference. Suppose, then, that the only difference between case A and case B is that case A is a killing and case B is a letting-die, and it turns out that case A is morally on a par with case B. Then killing is not worse than letting die, and given the plausible assumption that killing is not better, in itself, than letting die, it seems to follow that killing and letting die are morally on a par.

Rachels considers a pair of stories that differ in only one respect—one is a killing and the other is a letting-die.

Smith case

Smith stands to gain a large inheritance if anything should happen to his six-year-old cousin. One evening while the child is taking his bath, Smith sneaks into the bathroom and drowns the child, and then arranges things so that it will look like an accident.

Jones case

Jones also stands to gain if anything should happen to his six-year-old cousin. Like Smith, Jones sneaks in planning to drown the child in his bath. However, just as he enters the bathroom, Jones sees the child slip and hit his head and fall face down in the water. Jones is delighted; he stands by, ready to push the child's head back under if necessary, but it is not necessary. With only a little thrashing about, the child drowns all by himself, "accidentally," as Jones watches and does nothing.

The following is a general schema for establishing the moral equivalence of the features of each case.

P1   Case A has feature P and case B is exactly like case A except that it has feature Q rather than feature P.

P2   Case A is morally on a par with case B.

_____

C   P is (in itself) morally on a par with Q.

Ask yourself if the Smith case is worse than the Jones case. If your answer is no, then Rachels has given the following instance of this argument schema.

P1   The Smith case is a case of killing and the Jones case is exactly like the Smith case in every respect except that it is a case of letting die.

P2   The Smith case is morally on a par with the Jones case.

C   Killing is (in itself) morally on a par with letting die.

In his contribution to this debate, Winston Nesbitt does not question the bare-difference strategy itself. Nor does he take issue with Rachels's judgment on the two cases (the second premise). But he rejects Rachels's conclusion, and so, given that Nesbitt accepts the bare-difference strategy, he is obliged to take issue with P1. And that is precisely what he does.

Nesbitt argues that there is a crucial difference between the two cases, one that is morally relevant. Thus, he attacks P1. Further, he argues that if one removed this variable, the crucial difference, and constructed a modified Jones story, then our judgments would actually undermine the equivalence thesis.

What is this difference, according to Nesbitt? Nesbitt questions what our grounds are for condemning Smith. The answer: presumably that he "drowned his [cousin] for motives of personal gain." What are our grounds for condemning Jones? While it is true that Jones "let his [cousin] die for motives of personal gain," this is not, according to Nesbitt, our actual grounds for condemning him. This is because we also take into account the fact that Jones was "fully prepared to kill his [cousin], and would have done so had it proved necessary." So, our grounds for condemning Jones are different from our grounds for condemning Smith, and as a result there is a morally relevant difference between the two cases. Consequently Rachels's two cases cannot be used in a bare-difference argument.

Nesbitt goes on to argue that we can modify the Jones case, so that Jones is happy to let his cousin die but is not prepared to kill him if letting-die proves insufficient. In this case, Nesbitt claims, we would not think as badly of Jones as we would of Smith. And that, Nesbitt says, supports the thesis that the killing/letting-die distinction is morally relevant after all.

Roy Perrett counters that Nesbitt has changed the subject by shifting from moral evaluation of the two *acts* to moral evaluation of the two *agents*. But, regardless of this, Perrett goes on to defend the bare-difference argument by criticizing both of Nesbitt's claims. He argues, first, that Nesbitt is wrong to claim that he has identified a difference between the two cases. Rachels's cases can be spelled out a bit more fully so that it is true of both Smith and Jones that each goes in prepared "to kill his cousin if the option of letting him die is not feasible." Thus, with a little tweaking, this supposed difference between the two cases can be removed. Further, Perrett argues that Nesbitt's modified cases do not attract different moral judgments.

Finally, there is the question of the status of the bare-difference strategy itself. Suppose we accept Rachels's judgment on the Smith and Jones case, and accept also that the cases differ only in the one respect. Are we entitled to infer from this one case to the general claim that killing and letting die are morally on a par? In the excerpt from "the Additive Fallacy," Shelly Kagan argues that the bare-difference strategy (what he calls the "contrast" strategy) contains the "ubiquity assumption": If a factor makes a difference anywhere, it makes that difference everywhere, regardless of the configuration of other factors. So, if there is just one case of killing that is on a par with a barely different case of letting die, then any case of killing must be morally equivalent to a barely different case of letting die. Kagan goes on to argue that this principle presupposes the additivity of value—that the overall value of a situation is a simple sum of the values of the various individual factors. Kagan questions this additive assumption in two ways. First, he asks what grounds we have for thinking it is true. He acknowledges that the assumption is a natural one to make but finds that the arguments for it are less than compelling. Second, he adduces arguments against the additivity of value. For example, suppose we grant the judgment on the Smith-Jones cases and conclude that killing is morally on a par with letting die. But then we find another pair of barely different cases. One is a killing and the other is a letting-die, but this time the killing seems intuitively far worse than the letting-die. If these two cases were genuinely barely different, then the bare-difference strategy would enable us to prove that killing was worse than letting die. Then we would have two bare-difference arguments generating contradictory conclusions— that killing was both worse than letting die and that killing was morally on a par with (and therefore not worse than) letting die. Since these judgments are logically incompatible, we have to reject something, and we might be tempted to lay the blame at the feet of the bare-difference strategy itself. (There are two other candidates for blame: the intuitions about the relative merits of the two sets of cases and the claim that we are really dealing with genuine instances of bare difference.)

In the excerpt from his article "Killing and Letting Die: From Bare Differences to Clear Differences," Graham Oddie argues that there are at least two different ubiquity principles (together delivering Kagan's *ubiquity assumption*) that might be involved in a bare-difference argument. (The two principles are logically independent. First, the *bottom-up* ubiquity principle says that if a certain factor is, say), bad in itself then its presence will make a difference for the worse in every barely-different pair that differ only over that factor. (For example, if killing is worse in itself than letting die, then the Smith case must be worse than the Jones case.) That is to say, the value or disvalue of an individual factor transfers to the complex wholes of which it is a component. Second, there is the *top-down* ubiquity principle, which says that if there is a single pair of cases that differ in only one factor and the one in which the factor present is worse than the one in which the factor absent, then that factor is bad in itself. (For example, if the Smith case is worse than the Jones case then killing is worse, in itself, than letting die.) That is to say, the moral relations between the barely different wholes transfer to the factor over which they differ. Together the two ubiquity principles entail Kagan's ubiquity assumption—a difference in any one barely different pair entails that difference in every barely different pair.

There are different ways of refining Rachels's argument in light of Oddie's distinction. Rachels could be in the business of establishing the equivalence thesis by means of the Smith Jones pair and the top-down ubiquity principle. The argument would then go like this:

P1   The Smith case (a killing) is morally on a par with the barely different Jones case (a letting-die).
P2   If there is one killing that is morally on a par with one barely different letting-die, then killing is morally on a par with letting die (top-down ubiquity principle).

C   Killing is morally on a par with letting die (equivalence thesis).

However, we could also regard Rachels as *refuting* the claim that killing is worse, in itself, than letting die. Then his argument could be read as a reductio of the claim that killing is worse than letting die:

P1* That killing is, in itself, worse than letting die entails that the Smith case is worse than the Jones case (by the bottom-up ubiquity principle).

P1* It is absurd that the Smith case is worse than the Jones case (because the Smith case, a killing), is morally on a par with the Jones case, a letting die.

C*   Killing is not worse in itself than letting die.

Reading the argument in this way, Rachels is simply refuting the claim that killing is worse than letting die. In that case, all he needs is the bottom-up ubiquity principle and the standard judgment on the Smith Jones pair of cases. If he can refute the claim that killing is worse than letting die, then he may not have an argument *for* the moral equivalence of active and passive euthanasia, but he has refuted the key premise in one major argument (perhaps *the* major argument) against active euthanasia. This would constitute rational progress in the debate and would deprive those in favor of passive euthanasia but against active euthanasia of the strongest principled reason for maintaining their differential attitude.

QUESTIONS FOR CONSIDERATION

There are certain kinds of differences between the two cases that even Rachels would not deny. For example, Jones is a different person from Smith. Jones's cousin dies at a moment different from that at which Smith's cousin dies. The drownings take place in different bathtubs, and so on.

• Are any of these differences morally relevant? Can you show that they are morally irrelevant by means of bare-difference arguments?

• For example, take the issue of timing. Can you construct a pair of cases that differ only over the time of occurrence—same location, same participants, same mental states in the same order? What can you conclude about timing from a consideration of two such cases?

• Does Nesbitt misconstrue the structure of a bare-difference argument (as Perrett maintains)?

• What, if anything, does Nesbitt's modified Jones story tell us? Does it tell us that the only thing that matters in the evaluation of character is intention?

FURTHER READING

Haslett, D. W. "Moral Taxonomy and Rachels' Thesis." *Public Affairs Quarterly* 10, no. 4 (1996): 291–306.

James Rachels | Active and Passive Euthanasia

The distinction between active and passive euthanasia is thought to be crucial for medical ethics. The idea is that it is permissible, at least in some cases, to withhold treatment and allow a patient to die, but it is never permissible to take any direct action designed to kill the patient. This doctrine seems to be accepted by most doctors, and it is endorsed in a statement adopted by the House of Delegates of the American Medical Association on December 4, 1973:

> The intentional termination of the life of one human being by another—mercy killing—is contrary to that for which the medical profession stands and is contrary to the policy of the American Medical Association.
>
> The cessation of the employment of extraordinary means to prolong the life of the body when there is irrefutable evidence that biological death is imminent is the decision of the patient and/or his immediate family. The advice and judgment of the physician should be freely available to the patient and/or his immediate family.

However, a strong case can be made against this doctrine. In what follows I will set out some of the relevant arguments, and urge doctors to reconsider their views on this matter.

To begin with a familiar type of situation, a patient who is dying of incurable cancer of the throat is in terrible pain, which can no longer be satisfactorily alleviated. He is certain to die within a few days, even if present treatment is continued, but he does not want to go on living for those days since the pain is unbearable. So he asks the doctor for an end to it, and his family joins in the request.

Suppose the doctor agrees to withhold treatment, as the conventional doctrine says he may. The justification for his doing so is that the patient is in terri-

ble agony, and since he is going to die anyway, it would he wrong to prolong his suffering needlessly. But now notice this. If one simply withholds treatment, it may take the patient longer to die, and so he may suffer more than he would if more direct action were taken and a lethal injection given. This fact provides strong reason for thinking that, once the initial decision not to prolong his agony has been made active euthanasia is actually preferable to passive euthanasia, rather than the reverse. To say otherwise is to endorse the option that leads to more suffering rather than less, and is contrary to the humanitarian impulse that prompts the decision not to prolong his life in the first place.

Part of my point is that the process of being "allowed to die" can be relatively slow and painful, whereas being given a lethal injection is relatively quick and painless. Let me give a different sort of example. In the United States about one in 600 babies is born with Down's syndrome. Most of these babies are otherwise healthy—that is, with only the usual pediatric care, they will proceed to an otherwise normal infancy. Some, however, are born with congenital defects such as intestinal obstructions that require operations if they are to live. Sometimes, the parents and the doctor will decide not to operate, and let the infant die. Anthony Shaw describes what happens then:

> ... When surgery is denied the doctor must try to keep the infant from suffering while natural forces sap the baby's life away. As a surgeon whose natural inclination is to use the scalpel to fight off death, standing by and watching a salvageable baby die is the most emotionally exhausting experience I know. It is easy at a conference, in a theoretical discussion, to decide that such infants should be allowed to die. It is altogether different to stand by in the nursery and watch as dehydration and infec-

Reprinted by permission of *The New England Journal of Medicine* 292 (January 9, 1975): 78–80.

tion wither a tiny being over hours and days. This is a terrible ordeal for me and the hospital staff—much more so than for the parents who never set foot in the nursery.

I can understand why some people are opposed to all euthanasia, and insist that such infants must be allowed to live. I think I can also understand why other people favor destroying these babies quickly and painlessly. But why should anyone favor letting "dehydration and infection wither a tiny being over hours and days?" The doctrine that says that a baby may be allowed to dehydrate and wither, but may not be given an injection that would end its life without suffering, seems so patently cruel as to require no further refutation. The strong language is not intended to offend, but only to put the point in the clearest possible way.

My second argument is that the conventional doctrine leads to decisions concerning life and death made on irrelevant grounds.

Consider again the case of the infants with Down's syndrome who need operations for congenital defects unrelated to the syndrome to live. Sometimes, there is no operation, and the baby dies, but when there is no such defect, the baby lives on. Now, an operation such as that to remove an intestinal obstruction is not prohibitively difficult. The reason why such operations are not performed in these cases is, clearly, that the child has Down's syndrome and the parents and doctor judge that because of that fact it is better for the child to die.

But notice that this situation is absurd, no matter what view one takes of the lives and potentials of such babies. If the life of such an infant is worth preserving, what does it matter if it needs a simple operation? Or, if one thinks it better that such a baby should not live on, what difference does it make that it happens to have an unobstructed intestinal tract? In either case, the matter of life and death is being decided on irrelevant grounds. It is the Down's syndrome, and not the intestines, that is the issue. The matter should be decided, if at all, on that basis, and not be allowed to depend on the essentially irrelevant question of whether the intestinal tract is blocked.

What makes this situation possible, of course, is the idea that when there is an intestinal blockage,

one can "let the baby die," but when there is no such defect there is nothing that can be done, for one must not "kill" it. The fact that this idea leads to such results as deciding life or death on irrelevant grounds is another good reason why the doctrine should be rejected.

One reason why so many people think that there is an important moral difference between active and passive euthanasia is that they think killing someone is morally worse than letting someone die. But is it? Is killing, in itself, worse than letting die? To investigate this issue, two cases may be considered that are exactly alike except that one involves killing whereas the other involves letting someone die. Then, it can be asked whether this difference makes any difference to the moral assessments. It is important that the cases be exactly alike, except for this one difference, since otherwise one cannot be confident that it is this difference and not some other that accounts for any variation in the assessments of the two cases. So, let us consider this pair of cases:

In the first, Smith stands to gain a large inheritance if anything should happen to his six-year-old cousin. One evening while the child is taking his bath, Smith sneaks into the bathroom and drowns the child, and then arranges things so that it will look like an accident.

In the second, Jones also stands to gain if anything should happen to his six-year-old cousin. Like Smith, Jones sneaks in planning to drown the child in his bath. However, just as he enters the bathroom, Jones sees the child slip and hit his head, and fall face down in the water. Jones is delighted; he stands by, ready to push the child's head back under if it is necessary, but it is not necessary. With only a little thrashing about, the child drowns all by himself, "accidentally," as Jones watches and does nothing.

Now Smith killed the child, whereas Jones "merely" let the child die. That is the only difference between them. Did either man behave better, from a moral point of view? If the difference between killing and letting die were in itself a morally important matter, one should say that Jones's behavior was less reprehensible than Smith's. But does one really want to say that? I think not. In the first place, both men acted from the same motive, personal gain, and both had exactly the same end in view when they acted. It may be inferred from Smith's conduct that he is a bad man, although that judgment may be withdrawn or modified if certain further facts are learned about him—for example, that he is mentally deranged. But would not the very same thing be inferred about Jones from his conduct? And would not the same further considerations also be relevant to any modification of this judgment? Moreover, suppose Jones pleaded, in his own defense, "After all, I didn't do anything except just stand there and watch the child drown. I didn't kill him; I only let him die." Again, if letting die were in itself less bad than killing, this defense should have at least some weight. But it does not. Such a "defense" can only be regarded as a grotesque perversion of moral reasoning. Morally speaking, it is no defense at all.

Now, it may be pointed out, quite properly, that the cases of euthanasia with which doctors are concerned are not like this at all. They do not involve personal gain or the destruction of normal healthy children. Doctors are concerned only with cases in which the patient's life is of no further use to him, or in which the patient's life has become or will soon become a terrible burden. However, the point is the same in these cases: the bare difference between killing and letting die does not, in itself, make a moral difference. If a doctor lets a patient die, for humane reasons, he is in the same moral position as if he had given the patient a lethal injection for humane reasons. If his decision was wrong—if, for example, the patient's illness was in fact curable—the decision would be equally regrettable no matter which method was used to carry it out. And if the doctor's decision was the right one, the method used is not in itself important.

The AMA policy statement isolates the crucial issue very well; the crucial issue is "the intentional termination of the life of one human being by another." But after identifying this issue, and forbidding "mercy killing," the statement goes on to deny that the cessation of treatment is the intentional termination of a life. This is where the mistake comes in, for what is the cessation of treatment, in these circumstances, if it is not "the intentional termination of the life of one human being by another?" Of course it is exactly that, and if it were not, there would be no point to it.

Many people will find this judgment hard to accept. One reason, I think, is that it is very easy to conflate the question of whether killing is, in itself, worse than letting die, with the very different question of whether most actual cases of killing are more reprehensible than most actual cases of letting die. Most actual cases of killing are clearly terrible (think, for example, of all the murders reported in the newspapers), and one hears of such crises every day. On the other hand, one hardly ever hears of a case of letting die, except for the actions of doctors who are motivated by humanitarian reasons. So one learns to think of killing in a much worse light than of letting die. But this does not mean that there is something about killing that makes it in itself worse than letting die, for it is not the bare difference between killing and letting die that makes the difference in these cases. Rather, the other factors—the murderer's motive of personal gain, for example, contrasted with the doctor's humanitarian motivation—account for different reactions to the different cases.

I have argued that killing is not in itself any worse than letting die; if my contention is right, it follows that active euthanasia is not any worse than passive euthanasia. What arguments can be given on the other side? The most common, I believe, is the following:

> The important difference between active and passive euthanasia is that, in passive euthanasia, the doctor does not do anything to bring about the patient's death. The doctor does nothing, and the patient dies of whatever ills already afflict him. In active euthanasia, however, the doctor does something to bring about the patient's death: he kills him. The doctor who gives the patient with cancer a lethal injection has himself caused his patient's death; whereas if he merely ceases treatment, the cancer is the cause of the death.

A number of points need to be made here. The first is that it is not exactly correct to say that in passive euthanasia the doctor does nothing, for he does do one thing that is very important: he lets the patient die. "Letting someone die" is certainly different, in some respects, from other types of action—mainly in that it is a kind of action that one may perform by way of not performing certain other actions. For example, one may let a patient die by way of not giving medication, just as one may insult someone by way of not shaking his hand. But for any purpose of moral assessment, it is a type of action nonetheless. The decision to let a patient die is subject to moral appraisal in the same way that a decision to kill him would be subject to moral appraisal: it may be assessed as wise or unwise, compassionate or sadistic, right or wrong. If a doctor deliberately let a patient die who was suffering from a routinely curable illness, the doctor would certainly be to blame for what he had done, just as he would be to blame if he had needlessly killed the patient. Charges against him would then be appropriate. If so, it would be no defense at all for him to insist that he didn't "do anything." He would have done something very serious indeed, for he let his patient die.

Fixing the cause of death may be very important from a legal point of view, for it may determine whether criminal charges are brought against the doctor. But I do not think that this notion can be used to show a moral difference between active and passive euthanasia. The reason why it is considered bad to be the cause of someone's death is that death is regarded as a great evil—and so it is. However, if it has been decided that euthanasia—even passive euthanasia—is desirable in a given case, it has also been decided that in this instance death is no greater an evil than the patient's continued existence. And if this is true, the usual reason for not wanting to be the cause of someone's death simply does not apply.

Finally, doctors may think that all of this is only of academic interest—the sort of thing that philosophers may worry about but that has no practical bearing on their own work. After all, doctors must be concerned about the legal consequences of what they do, and active euthanasia is clearly forbidden by the law. But even so, doctors should also be concerned with the fact that the law is forcing upon them a moral doctrine that may well be indefensible, and has a considerable effect on their practices. Of course, most doctors are not now in the position of being coerced in this matter, for they do not regard themselves as merely going along with what the law requires. Rather, in statements such as the AMA policy statement that I have quoted, they are endorsing this doctrine as a central point of medical ethics. In that statement, active euthanasia is condemned not merely as illegal but as "contrary to that for which the medical profession stands," whereas passive euthanasia is approved. However, the preceding considerations suggest that there is really no moral difference between the two, considered in themselves (there may be important moral differences in some cases in their *consequences,* but, as I pointed out, these differences may make active euthanasia, and not passive euthanasia, the morally preferable option). So, whereas doctors may have to discriminate between active and passive euthanasia to satisfy the law, they should not do any more than that. In particular, they should not give the distinction any added authority and weight by writing it into official statements of medical ethics.

Critics

Winston Nesbitt | Is Killing No Worse Than Letting Die?

I want in this paper to consider a kind of argument sometimes produced against the thesis that it is worse to kill someone (that is, to deliberately take action that results in another's death) than merely to allow someone to die (that is, deliberately to fail to take steps which were available and which would have saved another's life). Let us, for brevity's sake, refer to this as the "difference thesis," since it implies that there is a moral difference between killing and letting die. . . .

2

It might seem at first glance a simple matter to show at least that common moral intuitions favour the difference thesis. Compare, . . . the case in which I push someone who I know cannot swim into a river, thereby killing her, with that in which I come across someone drowning and fail to rescue her, although I am able to do so, thereby letting her die. Wouldn't most of us agree that my behaviour is morally worse in the first case?

However, it would be generally agreed by those involved in the debate that nothing of importance for our issue, not even concerning common opinion, can be learned through considering such an example. . . . [W]ithout being told any more about the cases mentioned, we are inclined to assume that there are other morally relevant differences between them, because there usually would be. We assume, for example, some malicious motive in the case of killing, but perhaps only fear or indifference in the

case of failing to save. James Rachels and Michael Tooley, both of whom argue against the difference thesis, make similar points.[1] . . . Tooley, for example, notes that as well as differences in motives, there are also certain other morally relevant differences between typical acts of killing and typical acts of failing to save which may make us judge them differently. Typically, saving someone requires more effort than refraining from killing someone. Again, an act of killing necessarily results in someone's death, but an act of failing to save does not—someone else may come to the rescue. Factors such as these, it is suggested, may account for our tendency to judge failure to save (i.e., letting die) less harshly than killing. Tooley concludes that if one wishes to appeal to intuitions here, "one must be careful to confine one's attention to pairs of cases that do not differ in these, or other significant respects."[2]

Accordingly, efforts are made by opponents of the difference thesis to produce pairs of cases which do not differ in morally significant respects (other than in one being a case of killing while the other is a case of letting die or failing to save). In fact, at least the major part of the case mounted by Rachels and Tooley against the difference thesis consists of the production of such examples. It is suggested that when we compare a case of killing with one which differs from it *only* in being a case of letting die, we will agree that either agent is as culpable as the other; and this is then taken to show that any inclination we ordinarily have to think killing worse than letting die is attributable to our tending, illegitimately, to think of typical cases of killing and of let-

Winston Nesbitt, "Is Killing No Worse Than Letting Die?" *Journal of Applied Philosophy,* 12, no. 1 (1995): 101–5. Notes have been deleted. Reprinted by permission of Blackwell Publishing Ltd.

ting die, which differ in other morally relevant respects. I want now to examine the kind of example usually produced in these contexts.

3

I will begin with the examples produced by James Rachels in the article mentioned earlier, which is fast becoming one of the most frequently reprinted articles in the area. Although the article has been the subject of a good deal of discussion, as far as I know the points which I will make concerning it have not been previously made. Rachels asks us to compare the following two cases. The first is that of Smith, who will gain a large inheritance should his six-year-old nephew die. With this in mind, Smith one evening sneaks into the bathroom where his nephew is taking a bath, and drowns him. The other case, that of Jones, is identical, except that as Jones is about to drown his nephew, the child slips, hits his head, and falls, face down and unconscious, into the bath water. Jones, delighted at his good fortune, watches as his nephew drowns.

Rachels assumes that we will readily agree that Smith, who kills his nephew, is no worse, morally speaking, than Jones, who merely lets his nephew die. Do we really want to say, he asks, that either behaves better from the moral point of view than the other? It would, he suggests, be a "grotesque perversion of moral reasoning" for Jones to argue, "After all, I didn't do anything except just stand and watch the child drown. I didn't kill him; I only let him die." Yet, Rachels says, if letting die were in itself less bad than killing, this defence would carry some weight.

There is little doubt that Rachels is correct in taking it that we will agree that Smith behaves no worse in his examples than does Jones. Before we are persuaded by this that killing someone is in itself morally no worse than letting someone die, though, we need to consider the examples more closely. We concede that Jones, who merely let his nephew die, is just as reprehensible as Smith, who killed his nephew. Let us ask, however, just what is the ground of our judgement of the agent in each case. In the case of Smith,

this seems to be adequately captured by saying that Smith drowned his nephew for motives of personal gain. But can we say that the grounds on which we judge Jones to be reprehensible, and just as reprehensible as Smith, are that he let his nephew drown for motives of personal gain? I suggest not—for this neglects to mention a crucial fact about Jones, namely that he was fully prepared to kill his nephew, and would have done so had it proved necessary. It would be generally accepted, I think, quite independently of the present debate, that someone who is fully prepared to perform a reprehensible action, in the expectation of certain circumstances, but does not do so because the expected circumstances do not eventuate, is just as reprehensible as someone who actually performs that action in those circumstances. Now this alone is sufficient to account for our judging Jones as harshly as Smith. He was fully prepared to do what Smith did, and would have done so if circumstances had not turned out differently from those in Smith's case. Thus, though we may agree that he is just as reprehensible as Smith, this cannot be taken as showing that his letting his nephew die is as reprehensible as Smith's killing his nephew—for we would have judged him just as harshly, given what he was prepared to do, even if he had not let his nephew die. To make this clear, suppose that we modify Jones' story along the following lines—as before, he sneaks into the bathroom while his nephew is bathing, with the intention of drowning the child in his bath. This time, however, just before he can seize the child, *he* slips and hits his head on the bath, knocking himself unconscious. By the time he regains consciousness, the child, unaware of his intentions, has called his parents, and the opportunity is gone. Here, Jones neither kills his nephew *nor* lets him die—yet I think it would be agreed that given his preparedness to kill the child for personal gain, he is as reprehensible as Smith.

The examples produced by Michael Tooley, . . . suffer the same defect as those produced by Rachels. Tooley asks us to consider the following pair of scenarios, as it happens also featuring Smith and Jones. In the first, Jones is about to shoot Smith when he sees that Smith will be killed by a bomb unless Jones warns him, as he easily can. Jones does not warn him, and he is killed by the bomb—i.e., Jones lets Smith die. In the other, Jones wants Smith dead, and shoots him—i.e., he kills Smith.

Tooley elsewhere produces this further example: two sons are looking forward to the death of their wealthy father, and decide independently to poison him. One puts poison in his father's whiskey, and is discovered doing so by the other, who was just about to do the same. The latter then allows his father to drink the poisoned whiskey, and refrains from giving him the antidote, which he happens to possess.

Tooley is confident that we will agree that in each pair of cases, the agent who kills is morally no worse than the one who lets die. It will be clear, however, that his examples are open to criticisms parallel to those just produced against Rachels. To take first the case where Jones is saved the trouble of killing Smith by the fortunate circumstance of a bomb's being about to explode near the latter: it is true that we judge Jones to be just as reprehensible as if he had killed Smith, but since he was fully prepared to kill him had he not been saved the trouble by the bomb, we would make the same judgement even if he had neither killed Smith nor let him die (even if, say, no bomb had been present, but Smith suffered a massive and timely heart attack). As for the example of the like-minded sons, here too the son who didn't kill was prepared to do so, and given this, would be as reprehensible as the other even if he had not let his father die (if, say, he did not happen to possess the antidote, and so was powerless to save him).

Let us try to spell out more clearly just where the examples produced by Rachels and Tooley fail. What both writers overlook is that what determines whether someone is reprehensible or not is not simply what he in fact does, but what he is prepared to do, perhaps as revealed by what he in fact does. Thus, while Rachels is correct in taking it that we will be inclined to judge Smith and Jones in his examples equally harshly, this is not surprising, since both are judged reprehensible for precisely the same reason, namely that they were fully prepared to kill for motives of personal gain. The same, of course, is true of Tooley's examples. In each exam-

ple he gives of an agent who lets another die, the agent is fully prepared to kill (though in the event, he is spared the necessity). In their efforts to ensure that the members of each pair of cases they produce do not differ in any morally relevant respect (except that one is a case of killing and the other of letting die), Rachels and Tooley make them *too* similar—not only do Rachels' Smith and Jones, for example, have identical motives, but both are guilty of the same moral offence.

4

Given the foregoing account of the failings of the examples produced by Rachels and Tooley, what modifications do they require if they are to be legitimately used to gauge our attitudes towards killing and letting die, respectively? Let us again concentrate on Rachels' examples. Clearly, if his argument is to avoid the defect pointed out, we must stipulate that though Jones was prepared to let his nephew die once he saw that this would happen unless he intervened, he was not prepared to kill the child. The story will now go something like this: Jones stands to gain considerably from his nephew's death, as before, but he is not prepared to kill him for this reason. However, he happens to be on hand when his nephew slips, hits his head, and falls face down in the bath. Remembering that he will profit from the child's death, he allows him to drown. We need, however, to make a further stipulation, regarding the explanation of Jones's not being prepared to kill his nephew. It cannot be that he fears untoward consequences for himself, such as detection and punishment, or that he is too lazy to choose such an active course, or that the idea simply had not occurred to him. I think it would be common ground in the debate that if the only explanation of his not being prepared to kill his nephew was one of these kinds, he would be morally no better than Smith, who differed only in being more daring, or more energetic, whether or not fate then happened to offer him the opportunity to let his nephew die instead. In that case, we must suppose that the reason Jones is prepared to let his nephew die, but not to kill him, is a moral one—not intervening to save the child, he holds, is one thing, but actually bringing about his death is another, and altogether beyond the pale.

I suggest, then, that the case with which we must compare that of Smith is this: Jones happens to be on hand when his nephew slips, hits his head, and falls unconscious into his bath water. It is clear to Jones that the child will drown if he does not intervene. He remembers that the child's death would be greatly to his advantage, and does not intervene. Though he is prepared to let the child die however, and in fact does so, he would not have been prepared to kill him, because, as he might put it, wicked though he is, he draws the line at killing for gain.

I am not entirely sure what the general opinion would be here as to the relative reprehensibility of Smith and Jones. I can only report my own, which is that Smith's behaviour is indeed morally worse than that of Jones. What I do want to insist on, however, is that, for the reasons I have given, we cannot take our reactions to the examples provided by Rachels and Tooley as an indication of our intuitions concerning the relative heinousness of killing and of letting die.

So far, we have restricted ourselves to discussion of common intuitions on our question, and made no attempt to argue for any particular answer. I will conclude by pointing out that, given the fairly common view that the raison d'être of morality is to make it possible for people to live together in rea-sonable peace and security, it is not difficult to provide a rationale for the intuition that in our modified version of Rachels' examples, Jones is less reprehensible than Smith. For it is clearly preferable to have Jones-like persons around rather than Smith-like ones. We are not threatened by the former— such a person will not save me if my life should be in danger, but in this he is no more dangerous than an incapacitated person, or for that matter, a rock or tree (in fact he may be better, for he *might* save me as long as he doesn't think he will profit from my death). Smith-like persons, however, *are* a threat— if such a person should come to believe that she will benefit sufficiently from my death, then not only must I expect no help from her if my life happens to be in danger, but I must fear positive attempts on my life. In that case, given the view mentioned of the point of morality, people prepared to behave as Smith does are clearly of greater concern from the moral point of view than those prepared only to behave as Jones does; which is to say that killing is indeed morally worse than letting die.

NOTES

1. James Rachels (1979) Active and passive euthanasia in James Rachels (ed.), *Moral Problems* (NY, Harper and Row), pp. 490–497; Michael Tooley (1983) *Abortion and Infanticide* (Oxford, Clarendon Press), pp. 187–188.

2. Tooley, op. cit., p. 189.

Roy W. Perrett

Killing, Letting Die, and the Bare Difference Argument

I

In company with many other philosophers, I believe that there is no intrinsic moral difference between killing and letting die. That is, there is no difference that depends solely on the distinction between an act and an omission. I shall call this (following James Rachels) the Equivalence Thesis. I also believe that we can reasonably establish this thesis by appeal to what Rachels calls the Bare Difference Argument. The form of this argument involves considering two imaginary cases in which there are no morally rele-

From Roy W. Perrett, "Killing, Letting Die and the Bare Difference Argument," *Bioethics* 10, no. 2 (1996): 131–39. Some notes and some parts of the text have been deleted. Reprinted by permission of Blackwell Publishing Ltd.

vant differences present, save the bare difference that one is a case of killing and one a case of letting die. But in the pair of cases under consideration this bare difference makes no moral difference. Hence it cannot be that the bare difference between killing and letting die is in itself a morally important difference.

Winston Nesbitt has recently argued that the Bare Difference Argument fails because "the examples produced typically possess a feature which makes their use in this context illegitimate, and that when modified to remove this feature, they provide support for the view which they were designed to undermine". I shall argue that Nesbitt misunderstands the logic of the Bare Difference Argument and that accordingly his objections to the Equivalence Thesis are mistaken. . . .

III

Nesbitt . . . claims that (i) Rachels' two cases . . . are not in fact exactly similar in all morally relevant respects save that one is a case of killing and one a case of letting die; and (ii) if we modify the two cases so as to remove the extra morally relevant feature, the modified cases instead support the *denial* of the Equivalence Thesis.

It is not that Nesbitt disagrees with Rachels' claim that we should judge that Smith behaves no worse than Jones. However, he believes this should not lead us to embrace the Equivalence Thesis, for there is a crucial, morally relevant feature that is ignored in Rachels' treatment of the two cases:

> Let us ask . . . just what is the ground of our judgement of the agent in each case. In the case of Smith, this seems to be adequately captured by saying that Smith drowned his [cousin] for motives of personal gain. But can we say that the grounds on which we judge Jones to be reprehensible, and just as reprehensible as Smith, are that he let his [cousin] drown for motives of personal gain? I suggest not—for this neglects to mention a crucial fact about Jones, namely that he was fully prepared to kill his [cousin], and would have done so had it proved necessary.

Nesbitt goes on to claim that the following moral principle is generally accepted: "someone who is fully prepared to perform a reprehensible action, in the expectation of certain circumstances, but does not do so because the expected circumstances do not eventuate, is just as reprehensible as someone who actually performs that action in those circumstances." From this he concludes that our condemnation of Jones's action as morally equivalent to Smith's derives not from the moral equivalence of killing and letting die, but from Jones's violation of the above principle.

To bring this out Nesbitt suggests we modify the original Jones story along the following lines:

> . . . as before, he sneaks into the bathroom while his [cousin] is bathing, with the intention of drowning the child in his bath. This time, however, just before he can seize the child, *he* slips and hits his head on the bath, knocking himself unconscious. By the time he regains consciousness, the child, unaware of his intentions, has called his parents, and the opportunity is gone. Here Jones neither kills his [cousin] *nor* lets him die—yet I think it would be agreed that given his preparedness to kill the child for personal gain, he is as reprehensible as Smith.[1]

IV

So far as I can see, all of this argumentation is a complete ignoratio elenchi and badly misconstrues the logical structure of the Bare Difference Argument. First, note that in Nesbitt's modified case we are now concerned with *agent* evaluation ("Jones is as morally reprehensible as Smith"), not the *act* evaluation relevant to determining whether there is an intrinsic moral difference between *acts* of killing and letting die (i.e. whether the Equivalence Thesis is true). Secondly, in fact many would dispute that Jones now is as morally reprehensible as Smith, given the way things turned out in Nesbitt's example (this is the problem of moral luck). Thirdly, and most importantly, it is clear that Rachels' original Smith and Jones stories can easily accommodate the supposed moral significance of Jones's willingness to kill the boy if a strategy of letting die proves insufficient to achieve his ends. For insofar as this willingness is morally significant, we can assume it constant in both of Rachels' cases. That is, it is true of Jones (as Rachels makes explicit) that he intends to kill his cousin if the option of letting him die is not feasible. But presumably exactly the same is true of Smith: he also intends to kill his cousin if the option of letting die is not feasible. True, Rachels does not make this explicit about Smith (though perhaps he thought it implicit). However, we can easily stipulate that this is indeed true of Smith, in which case both Smith's and Jones's actions are exactly alike with respect to this supposedly morally relevant intention. Thus the only difference between their actions that now remains is that one is an act of killing and one is an act of letting die. But if we then agree we should still judge the actions of Smith and Jones to be morally equivalent (as presumably Nesbitt does), we must conclude that the bare difference between killing and letting die cannot be in itself a morally relevant difference.

Having thus misunderstood the point of the examples Rachels (and others) offer in support of the Bare Difference Argument, Nesbitt goes on to suggest that we need to modify their examples to avoid the defect he (mis)perceives himself to have uncovered. In the Jones case the story should now go something like the following (call this "the modified-Jones case"):

> Jones happens to be on hand when his [cousin] slips, hits his head, and falls unconscious into his bath water. It is clear to Jones that the child will drown if he does not intervene. He remembers that the child's death would be greatly to his advantage, and does not intervene. Though he is prepared to let the child die however, and in fact does so, he would not have been prepared to kill him, because, as he might put it, wicked though he is, he draws the line at killing for gain.

Nesbitt reports that when he compares the cases of Smith and modified-Jones he judges that Smith's behaviour is indeed morally worse than modified-Jones's. Whether or not we agree with this judgement is, of course, irrelevant to the central issue here: i.e. the soundness of the Bare Difference Argu-

ment. The Argument requires that the two cases invoked are alike in all morally relevant respects, save that one is a case of killing and one is a case of letting die. If we suppose with Nesbitt that an intention to kill the boy if letting die is not a feasible option is itself a morally relevant feature which is not present in both cases, then the original case of Smith and the case of modified-Jones obviously cannot be paired in a Bare Difference Argument. This is because they do not share, as the Argument's structure requires, all morally relevant features save that one is a case of killing and one a case of letting die. But this does not show the Bare Difference Argument fails, only that *this* pair of cases cannot be used to mount such an argument. On the other hand, Rachels' original pair of cases do satisfy this logical requirement on the Bare Difference Argument (provided we assume both Smith and Jones are willing to kill the boy if letting die is not a feasible option). Moreover we do judge the actions of Smith and Jones in *those* circumstances to be morally equivalent, notwithstanding that one is an act of killing and one is an act of letting die. Thus that bare difference in itself makes no moral difference.

Note further that in order to flesh out his (irrelevant) modified-Jones case Nesbitt thinks we need to say more about why his Jones is unwilling to kill the boy:

> It cannot be that he fears untoward consequences for himself, such as detection and punishment, or that he is too lazy to choose such an active course, or that the idea simply had not occurred to him. I think it would be common ground in the debate that if the only explanation of his not being prepared to kill his [cousin] was one of these kinds, he would be morally no better than Smith, who differed only in being more daring, or more energetic, whether or not fate then happened to offer him the opportunity to let his [cousin] die instead. In that case, we must suppose that the reason Jones is prepared to let his [cousin] die, but not to kill him, is a moral one—not intervening to save the child, he holds, is one thing, but actually bringing about his death is another, and altogether beyond the pale.

Once again, Nesbitt confuses the issue by sliding from *act* evaluation to *agent* evaluation. The real issue here is not whether modified-Jones is or is not morally better than Smith, or even whether agents who perform acts of letting die are generally morally better or worse than those who perform acts of killing. The real issue, the issue the Bare Difference Argument directly addresses, is whether the bare difference between an act of killing and an act of letting die in itself makes a moral difference. Rachels' original pair of cases show that this bare difference does not in itself make a moral difference. For (provided we make the tiny modification I suggested) those two cases do share all morally relevant properties, save that one is a case of killing and one a case of letting die. Yet we judge the two *acts* involved to be morally equivalent. Hence the Equivalence Thesis is true.

Of course, it is unsurprising that Nesbitt's own modified-Jones case fails to support the Equivalence Thesis if paired with the Smith case. In the first place we have already seen that he stipulates that the two cases no longer share all morally relevant features save that one is a killing and one a letting die. Hence it is trivially impossible for that pair of cases to satisfy the demands of the logical structure of the Bare Difference Argument. In the second place he insists that not only is modified-Jones (unlike Smith) not prepared to kill the boy, but that Jones's reluctance to do so is based on a *moral* reason: viz. that while killing the boy is morally wrong, letting him die is not. This latter stipulation, however, admits of both weak and strong construals. Construed weakly it is just the stipulation that modified-Jones's reluctance to kill the boy is based on his moral belief (mistaken or otherwise) that killing is morally wrong. Construed strongly the stipulation is that Jones's reluctance is based on his (correct) moral belief that killing is morally wrong. But this strong construal of what it is for Jones to act on a moral reason would assume the truth of precisely what is in dispute, namely whether the bare difference between killing and letting die is a morally relevant difference. In other words, on the strong construal introducing the modified-Jones case begs the very question such cases are being invoked to settle. If Nesbitt intends the strong rather than the weak construal, then it is no wonder the modified-Jones case lends no support

to the Equivalence Thesis when the case is stipulated in a way that presupposes the falsity of that thesis.

I conclude, then, that the Bare Difference Argument is indeed sound and that the Equivalence Thesis is true. The pair of cases Rachels offers do support this conclusion since (with a tiny modification I consider already implicit in Rachels' argument) we have two cases alike in all morally relevant respects, save that one is a case of killing and one a case of letting die. But the *acts* Smith and Jones perform are morally equivalent. Hence the bare difference that one of those acts is a killing and one a letting die is not in itself a morally relevant difference. In other words, the Bare Difference Argument does reasonably establish the Equivalence Thesis: there is no intrinsic moral difference between acts of killing and acts of letting die. Of course, there may be *extrinsic* factors which make various particular cases of killing worse than various particular cases of letting die (or vice versa). But this is not just because some of these cases are killings and some are cases of letting die.

It is perhaps worth saying a little more about this last point, for surely much of the resistance to the Equivalence Thesis that one so frequently encounters is generated by a confusion about this feature of it. It is perfectly consistent to affirm the Equivalence Thesis and also to concede that, in some cases, it may be permissible to let die but not to kill, while in other cases it may be permissible to kill but not to let die. All that is required is that, in such cases, it is some feature other than the bare difference between killing and letting die that makes the moral difference. These other, extrinsic features are often present and do justify differential moral judgements. For instance, it is clearly morally worse to kill an elderly relative without her consent in order to inherit her money than it is to allow her to die of pneumonia at her request from a desire to relieve her sufferings from terminal cancer. But it is the *extrinsic* factors here (permission, motive) that are morally relevant, not the mere fact that one is a killing and one a letting die. And the presence or absence of these same extrinsic features can also on occasion make it morally worse to let die than to kill. For instance, it is plausibly morally worse to let an elderly relative die of pneumonia without her consent in order to inherit her money than it is to kill her at her own request from a desire to relieve her sufferings from terminal cancer. What the Equivalence Thesis tells us is just that the bare difference between killing and letting die is not in itself a morally significant difference, not that every case of killing is morally equivalent to every case of letting die. However, if there is a moral difference, it is due to extrinsic features of the cases; there is no *intrinsic* moral difference between killing and letting die. And the Bare Difference Argument demonstrates that this is so.

NOTE

1. I have changed Nesbitt's references to a "nephew" to a "cousin" throughout to make it consistent with the cases as described in the version from Rachels I cited earlier. (It is also a "cousin" in the original paper by Rachels that Nesbitt cites.)

Shelly Kagan | # The Additive Fallacy

Much moral philosophy is concerned with defending or attacking the moral relevance of various distinctions. Thus consequentialists disagree with deontologists, and deontologists disagree among themselves, over whether any moral weight should be given to such distinctions as that between what one does and what one merely allows, or to the distinction between what one intends as a means, and what one merely foresees as a side-effect, and so on. Similarly, there is disagreement over the moral relevance of such factors as the motive of the agent, the consequences of a given act, or the guilt of those who may be harmed. (On some matters, perhaps, there is widespread agreement: there seems to be a contemporary consensus, e.g., that skin color is of no intrinsic moral importance.) . . .

A very common form of argument proceeds by offering a pair of cases that differ only in terms of the factor in question. If we judge the two cases to be morally different, it is argued, this difference must arise from the different values of the given factor (everything else being held constant), and so the factor is shown to be morally relevant. If we judge the cases to be similar, on the other hand, despite the variation in the given factor, this shows that the fac-

tor is not actually morally relevant after all. Let us call the pair of cases offered for comparison *contrast cases* (since the argument turns on the presence or absence of a contrast in our judgments about the cases), and let us call arguments of this sort *contrast arguments.*

By way of example, consider the distinction between what I do and what I (merely) allow. If I take out my gun and shoot you, I have brought about your death, killed you: I have done harm. In contrast, if I merely come upon you drowning, and fail to throw you the life preserver, I have not *done* any harm to you, even if you drown: I have only allowed harm. Most of us not only draw this distinction, we give it moral weight, holding that doing harm is worse than merely allowing harm. Now it is not easy to make the do/allow distinction precise, but this need not concern us here. Assuming that we *can* make the distinction, we still need to ask: is it morally relevant?

A critic of the do/allow distinction might argue as follows: "The issue of whether I brought about a given harm or merely allowed it is not itself of intrinsic moral importance. No doubt the distinction is typically correlated with other factors which do

From Shelly Kagan, "The Additive Fallacy," *Ethics* 99, no. 1 (1988): 5–31. Notes and some parts of the text have been deleted. Reprinted by permission of University of Chicago Press.

make a difference morally, and this has perhaps blinded us to the irrelevance of the do/allow distinction itself. For example, cases of doing harm are typically also cases of harming as a means, or cases where the agent has a repugnant motive, or cases where the consequences would be better if the act in question were avoided, and so on; cases of allowing harm, on the other hand, typically do not display these features. [Different critics will, of course, offer different lists of factors.] For this reason, cases of doing harm typically *are* worse than cases of allowing harm. But this does not show that the distinction between doing and allowing *itself* affects the moral status of an act. For if the distinction *were* morally relevant, it should make a difference even when all of these other factors are held constant. We can see that this isn't so, however, by considering this pair of contrast cases:

a) Gertrude pushes Bertrand into a deep pit, hoping that the fall will kill him so that she will inherit the family fortune;

b) Seeing that Bertrand is about to fall into a deep pit, Gertrude deliberately refrains from warning him, hoping that the fall will kill him so that she will inherit the family fortune.

These cases display the same morally relevant features (e.g., motive, outcome, etc.); they differ only with regard to the doing or allowing of harm. If the do/allow distinction were itself of genuine moral importance, there should be some difference in the moral status of the two acts. But surely Gertrude's behavior in the second case is quite as bad as in the first, despite the fact that in the first case she kills Bertrand, while in the second she merely allows him to die. Since the difference between doing and allowing harm does not make a difference in this case, we can see that the do/allow distinction is not itself of any intrinsic moral importance."

Armed with this conclusion, the critic may go on to derive moral implications concerning other cases. He might, for example, argue that our failure to make significant contributions to famine relief is roughly the moral equivalent of murder. For although we are only allowing the starving to die,

given the moral irrelevance of the do/allow distinction, our failure to aid is morally as bad as if we were killing them. (Other differences, of course, e.g., our lack of ill will toward the starving, may ameliorate the badness of our act somewhat in comparison with typical cases of murder.)

. . . [F]irst it is important to see that contrast arguments can be used to advocate as well as to criticize a distinction. Thus the advocate of the do/allow distinction might argue as follows: "Admittedly, cases of doing harm typically differ from cases of allowing harm in terms of *several* morally relevant factors. But of course this does not show that the do/allow distinction lacks moral importance in its own right. If it *were* morally irrelevant, then in contrast cases where the only difference was whether harm was done or merely allowed, all other features being held constant, no moral difference between the cases should remain. But we can see that this is not so, by considering the following pair of cases:

c) Ludwig sees Sylvia drowning, but since the rocks beneath the water would do extensive damage to his boat, he decides not to rescue her;

d) Ludwig sees that his boat is about to hit Sylvia, but since avoiding her would mean steering into the rocks, which would do extensive damage to his boat, he decides not to change course.

Certainly there is something morally unacceptable about Ludwig's behavior in the first case; but surely his action is even worse in the second. Yet how could there be this moral difference in the status of the two cases if the do/allow distinction were morally irrelevant? After all, all of the other relevant features of the two cases are the same. So it must be that the do/allow distinction *is* of intrinsic moral importance, and what we have just established is that doing harm is morally more significant than merely allowing harm."

Armed with *this* conclusion, the advocate may go on to suggest that negative duties (not to do harm) are more strict than positive duties (to provide aid). Or she might use her conclusion in defense of the claim that an innocent person may not be harmed, even if this is the only way to save several other people from equivalent harms. And so on.

This time it is the critic of the distinction who must try to disarm the contrast argument. But it should be clear that although the two sides may disagree about the use of particular instances of contrast arguments, they share a common belief in the general strategy behind such arguments. Both sides believe that with a properly constructed pair of contrast cases, the moral status of the cases will differ if and only if the do/allow distinction is morally relevant.

Obviously enough, additional contrast arguments concerning doing and allowing can be offered using other pairs of cases. It is equally obvious that contrast arguments can also be constructed (and have been constructed) concerning other disputed factors. It is worth noting, however, that contrast arguments can be used not only to test the relevance of various factors for the moral status of *acts,* but also to test the relevance of factors for *other* categories of moral concern, such as the moral character of the agent, or the moral value of states of affairs. (There is, as it were, more than one dependent variable in ethics.) In principle, a factor which is irrelevant for one category might well be relevant for some other category. For simplicity, however, I will limit our examples to arguments concerning the relevance of factors for the moral status of acts.

It should also be noted that in actual practice, contrast arguments are rarely spelled out as explicitly as in the examples I have given. Indeed, in many cases, we are not actually presented with a pair of contrast cases at all: the argument may simply draw our attention to the overall moral status of a single case with some salient feature; it may then conclude that the given feature has made a difference to the status of that case. Such arguments are apt to be unintelligible unless we assume that there is an implied reference to the missing member of the contrast pair: it is taken to be so obvious that the moral status would differ in the corresponding case in which all other features are held constant except for the given factor, that there is no need to explicitly state this fact.

Contrast arguments, then, are an important and widely used method of tackling questions about the relevance of disputed factors. Both advocates and critics of the factor in question propose appropriate contrast cases, in the shared belief that examination of such cases will indicate whether or not the given factor has genuine moral weight. And since both sides accept the validity of the general strategy behind contrast arguments, each side is troubled by the existence of contrast cases that appear to support the other side. For example, as already noted, the advocate of the do/allow distinction must do something to impugn the negative argument based on cases *a* and *b;* and the critic of the distinction must do something to undermine the positive argument based on cases *c* and *d.* In such disputes, each side must attempt to disarm the contrast arguments offered by the other side. . . .

The account of contrast arguments I have just given normally lies mostly implicit in our use of such arguments; but I believe most will recognize it as a reasonable portrayal of the thinking that lies behind our common practice. I have spent a fair amount of space developing this account in order to draw attention both to the wide use of such arguments and to their plausibility. Contrast arguments are based on a clear and plausible strategy, and that strategy can be accompanied by a well-articulated set of considerations that must be met if the strategy is to be properly applied.

Nonetheless, I believe that our in-principle acceptance of contrast arguments must be mistaken. Despite its plausibility, the strategy relies on an underlying assumption concerning the role of factors—an assumption that is questionable and should probably be rejected. Yet without this assumption, contrast arguments cannot be used to derive the conclusions we draw from them. . . .

The contrast strategy clearly assumes that if a factor has genuine moral relevance, then for *any* pair of cases, where the given factor varies while others are held constant, the cases in that pair will differ in moral status. (The difference, of course, need not be so extreme as to make, e.g., one act permissible and the other act impermissible; the point is simply that *some* difference in moral status should exist.) That is, putting aside difficulties with proper construction and assessment, in principle *any one pair of cases* should be sufficient to settle the question of whether the given factor is of intrinsic moral relevance. In effect, the contrast strategy must be assuming that if variation in a given factor makes a difference *anywhere,* it makes a difference *everywhere.* Let us call this the *ubiquity thesis.*

Contrast arguments presuppose the ubiquity thesis. Without this assumption, after all, from the mere fact that some particular pair of contrast cases did not differ in moral status, critics of the given factor could not go on to conclude that the factor must lack intrinsic moral significance—for it might well make a difference in other cases, even though it did not make one here. Similarly, without this assumption, from the mere fact that some particular pair of contrast cases *did* differ in moral status, advocates of the given factor could not go on to conclude that the factor must make a difference in other cases where it is present—for it might well fail to do so someplace else even though it did make a difference here. Indeed, recognizing that the contrast argument makes this assumption—that if the factor makes a difference anywhere it must make one everywhere—helps to explain why both critics and advocates are at such pains to disarm the contrast cases offered by the other side: if the assumption is correct, a single well-constructed and properly assessed pair of cases from either side must be decisive.

The ubiquity thesis is in need of some defense. Why must a factor make a difference everywhere if it makes one anywhere? There is a strong temptation to think that this must follow (indeed, follow trivially) from the fact that the fundamental principles of morality are universal, that is, that the basic principles that determine the moral status of an act do not vary from case to case. Admittedly, the applicability of derivative principles may change with the situation, but the underlying principles of morality do not. But this means that the role that a given genuine moral factor plays in determining the moral status of an act must be universal as well: it too cannot vary from case to case. Therefore—or so it seems to follow—if a factor makes a difference *somewhere* it must make a difference *everywhere.*

Despite the seductiveness of this line of thought, I believe it is mistaken. I do find it plausible to think

that the universal nature of fundamental moral principles implies that the role a genuine factor plays must be universal as well. But I do not think that we can infer the ubiquity thesis from this. That thesis asserts that if a factor ever makes a difference to the overall moral status of an act, it must always do so. That is, it asserts that a particular kind of *effect* must be universal. Obviously, however, the universality of that particular effect will only follow from the universality of the role that the factor plays, if it is part of that role that it have that effect. Once again, it may seem trivial to assert that every effect that a factor has is part of its role (or, at the very least, that this particular effect must be part of its role); but in fact this depends on substantive claims about the roles of genuine moral factors.

An analogy may be helpful here. The presence or absence of oxygen has a role in determining chemical reactions. This role is presumably universal— that is, the fundamental laws of chemistry do not vary from case to case. Yet, obviously enough, the particular effects of oxygen's presence or absence do vary: in some cases, for example, the presence of oxygen makes a difference to whether or not a compound burns; but it would be a mistake to think that it must make this difference in every case. This is because making a difference to whether compounds burn is not, strictly speaking, part of the role of oxygen in the laws of chemistry. Rather, it is a consequence of that role in particular cases. The mere fact that the role of oxygen in the laws of chemistry is universal does not imply that some particular kind of effect must be universal. Similarly, the mere fact that the role of some factor in the fundamental principles of morality must be universal does not automatically imply that some particular effect must be universal. Whether the ubiquity thesis is true depends on taking a substantive position on the role of genuine moral factors.

Talk of the role of moral factors seems to naturally suggest the following general model: the moral status of an act is a function of the various (genuinely relevant) factors that come into play in the given situation. Different moral theories will, of course, hold different views about which factors are of intrinsic moral importance; but whatever the particular list, all theories agree that the overall status of an act in a given situation depends on the values that the genuine factors (whatever they are) have in that situation. This agreement, however, is limited to the view that there is a function of *some* sort connecting the values of the factors to the overall status of the act. Exactly *how* the status of the act is thought to be affected by the factors depends on what *particular* function is accepted by the given moral theory.

Let us call the function (whatever it is) that is taken to determine the overall status of the act on the basis of the values of the factors the *governing function.* In principle, even theories that agree about the list of relevant factors might disagree about what the governing function is like, and thus disagree about how the factors combine and interact in determining the act's overall moral status.

When we say that the role of a given moral factor is universal, we are saying that the governing function remains the same from case to case. That is, the rules governing the interaction of the various moral factors in determining the moral status of an act remain constant.

But this does not yield the ubiquity thesis. Depending on the particular governing function accepted by a theory, it might well be that variation in a given factor would make a difference to the moral status of the act in certain situations, but not in others—because of differences in the interactions of the various moral factors arising from the differences in the values of the *other* factors. Only for particular kinds of governing functions will the ubiquity thesis hold true. What I want to suggest is that those who offer contrast arguments presuppose a particular view of the nature of the governing function.

The view which underlies the use of contrast arguments seems to be this: the function that determines the overall status of the act given the values of the particular factors is an *additive* one. That is, the status of the act is the net balance or sum which is the result of adding up the separate positive and negative effects of the individual factors. On this view, each factor makes a contribution, whether positive or negative, to the moral status of the act. (The strength of the contribution will depend on the particular value of the factor in the given situation, e.g., how *much* good will be done by the act.) The overall

status is the sum of these positive and negative contributions.

In effect, each of the positive factors provides a reason *for* performing the act (the strength of the reason depending on the value of the factor), and each of the negative factors provides a reason for *not* performing the act. The moral status of the act depends on whether the combined weight of the reasons for performing the act is greater or less than the combined weight of the reasons for not performing the act—and by how much.

It is worth stressing that the view that the governing function is additive is more than the mere suggestion that the overall status is the sum of two amounts—that is, the joint positive contribution and the joint negative contribution. Rather, each of these amounts is in turn taken to be the sum of the individual contributions of the individual factors. Each factor makes its own contribution to the status of the act, and the overall status is the sum of these separate contributions.

It is certainly not obvious that the contrast argument assumes that the governing function is additive. Yet I think that something like this assumption must be made for there to be any reason to believe that a well-constructed pair of contrast cases will differ in moral status if and only if the given factor has intrinsic moral relevance.

It is easy to see why one will believe in the ubiquity thesis—and thus in the strategy behind contrast arguments—if one believes that the governing function is additive. For if the overall status of an act is the sum of the separate contributions made by the individual factors, then if one holds all but one of those contributions fixed (by holding all but one of the factors constant) and varies the remaining contribution (by varying the factor under examination), the sum will have to vary as well. The mathematical analogy should make this clear. If $S = x + y + z,$ then if we hold x and y constant, but vary z, S will have to vary as well. *Any* genuine difference in z will have to make a difference to S, no matter *what* the values of x and y—provided only that x and y are kept constant. (The same is true, of course, for each of the other variables.) Similarly, then, if the governing moral function is additive, if we hold all but one factor constant, no matter what contributions those particular factors make, varying the remaining factor will have to vary the remaining contribution, and thus will have to make a difference to the sum.

Now for some purported factors, no doubt, variations in the factor will make no difference to the contribution the factor makes. But this is just to say that the factor is not of any genuine moral relevance. Since it will contribute equally to the moral status of all acts, it can just as easily—and less misleadingly—be dropped from consideration altogether. (Consider, e.g., the claim that being performed in time makes a positive contribution to the moral status of the act, a contribution whose size is constant, no matter what the time of performance.) For any genuine factor, variations will affect the contribution, and thus the sum. . . .

My claim, then, is that one should accept the strategy behind contrast arguments only if one accepts the additive assumption. It is not so much that contrast arguments *could* not be sound if the additive assumption is false, but rather that there is no plausible reason to think that they *are* sound if the additive assumption is false.

The view that the moral status of an act is the sum of individual positive and negative contributions—the particular reasons for and against performing the act—is, I have suggested, a familiar and attractive one. Nonetheless, I believe that the additive assumption should be rejected. More exactly, I believe that the assumption is a controversial one, likely to be false on most moral theories. To assume the truth of the additive model without defense, therefore, is unacceptable: it begs the question against most plausible theories, and it may well be incompatible with one's own considered views.

One or two examples should be sufficient to show that most theorists will need to reject the additive assumption. Consider, first, the issue of self-defense. Most of us believe that in some situations killing someone in self-defense can be morally permissible. Imagine such a situation, and compare these two cases:

  e) In order to defend myself against the aggressor, I push him into a pit, expecting the fall to kill him;

  f) In order to defend myself against the aggressor, I refrain from warning him about the pit into which he is about to fall, and I expect the fall to kill him.

Most of us will certainly want to claim that the moral status of these two cases is the same, even though, obviously enough, in the first case I do harm, while in the second case I merely allow it. Not everyone will accept this judgment: some may insist that there is a slight difference, but it is lost on our insufficiently sensitive intuitions; others (e.g., pacifists) may claim the difference is rather significant. Nonetheless, most of us will want to maintain that the distinction between doing harm and allowing harm makes *no* difference in such legitimate cases of self-defense. The crucial point to see is that even the *advocate* of the do/allow distinction may well want to make this claim, and surely it is coherent for her to do so. In fact, this view—that although the difference between doing harm and allowing it typically has a great effect on the moral status of an act, in cases of self-defense it makes no difference whatsoever—is not only coherent: most of us want to claim that it is true.

Yet if the additive assumption is correct, then the view I have just described *must* be false, since it violates the ubiquity thesis to claim that although the do/allow distinction normally makes a difference, in cases of self-defense it does not. Thus, if we make the additive assumption (thereby justifying the ubiquity thesis), this view can be ruled out a priori. Obviously, however, such a move would simply beg the question. On the other hand, if we want at the very least to allow for the possibility of such views—we cannot simply presuppose that the governing function is additive. The example of self-defense suggests that most of us (unwittingly, perhaps) are committed to the rejection of the additive assumption.

It seems a mistake to treat the factor of self-defense as though it made an independent contribution to the overall moral status of the act—a contribution to be added to that made by other factors. A more natural interpretation, one closer to our intuitive understanding of the situation, would be to view the factor of self-defense as acting more like a zero multiplier.

Recall the earlier mathematical example where $S = x \cdot y + z$, and suppose for simplicity that x can equal only zero or one. When x is equal to one, differences in y will make a difference to S; but when x is equal to zero, differences in y will not matter at all. The self-defense/non-self-defense factor seems to act somewhat like x in this example: normally, with a value of one, it allows the do/allow distinction to make a difference; but in cases of self-defense, it takes on the value of zero, and so differences between doing and allowing harm do not affect the moral status of the act at all.

I would not want to put too much weight on this mathematical analogy; I certainly do not think it captures all that we intuitively want to say about the interaction of self-defense and the do/allow distinction. But it clearly comes closer than viewing the governing function in strictly additive terms. It seems reasonable to suspect that intuitively adequate representations of most views in this area would have to stray even further from the additive path. This does not prove, of course, that the correct governing function is nonadditive. But it does, I think, show that most will want to accept this conclusion, and that arguments that presuppose the opposite will tend to beg the question.

A second example suggests that even in some areas where we may initially seem able to give an additive formulation, we may nonetheless require a nonadditive one if we are to capture more of what we want to say. Most of us believe that the alleviation of suffering is a morally relevant factor: the fact that an act will relieve suffering provides a reason for performing that act (although the reason can, of course, be outweighed by other considerations). Thus, when all things are equal, if we can aid only one of two people in pain, there is greater reason to help the one whose suffering is greater. Suppose, however, that all things are not equal, and a second factor comes into play: imagine that the person whose pain is greater—Trixie—is partially responsible for the plight of both, while the other person—Fritz—is not responsible at all. Most of us want to say of such situations that there is somewhat less reason to aid Trixie than there would be were she free from responsibility; and if her responsibility is significant enough, we may judge it better

to aid Fritz, even though he is in considerably less pain.

Now we could, I suppose, view this in an additive manner. The magnitude of Trixie's suffering makes an independent, positive contribution to the moral status of aiding her. This is offset by her partial responsibility, which makes an independent negative contribution—that is, provides a reason for not aiding her. The sum of these two contributions may well be less than the corresponding sum for aiding Fritz, where the admittedly smaller positive contribution is not offset by any negative factor.

Such a model may seem plausible so long as we imagine Trixie morally blameless, despite her partial responsibility. The problem is that the additive assumption requires this same model even when Trixie is morally to blame for having performed the act which created the situation. Perhaps, for example, Trixie had attempted to harm Fritz, but her scheme had gone awry, harming them both, and her more significantly. The additive model can point to her guilt as a reason for not helping Trixie, but it is forced to maintain that the magnitude of her suffering provides just as strong a reason to aid her as if she were innocent. Yet many would want to reject exactly this latter claim: the suffering of the guilty simply does not count as much as the suffering of the innocent.

Obviously, not all will share this judgment; but those who do will find it plausible to reject the additive assumption. It will seem more appropriate to view the factor of innocence/guilt not as making an independent contribution, but rather as a multiplier—this one able to range from one to zero. Fritz is innocent, so the multiplier has the value of one, and his suffering can take on its full potential weight. Trixie is guilty, so the multiplier is less than one, and her suffering counts less. Potentially, with significant enough guilt, the multiplier would be equal to zero, and so one's suffering would not count at all. (A more pronounced version of this view might allow the multiplier to range between positive one and negative one. If the wicked deserve to be unhappy, then the presence of suffering and desert should together sometimes yield a positive contribution.)

Once again, I certainly would not want to claim that this alternative model captures all that we want to say about the interplay of desert and well-being. But it seems a more natural fit than the additive model, and it suggests that those sympathetic to such views should reject the additive assumption. . . .

Reflection on such examples, I believe, should support two conclusions. First, since a great number of moral views are incompatible with the additive assumption, it is unacceptable to criticize such views through the use of arguments that simply presuppose that assumption: to do so merely begs the question. Second, since one's own moral views are likely to be incompatible with the additive assumption, it is dan-

gerous to defend those views through the use of arguments that presuppose that assumption: to do so may render one's position incoherent.

I suspect, in fact, that for most views the additive model is grossly inadequate. It is not merely that the claim that the *entire* governing function is additive is false. Rather, on most views, *most* of the governing function will fail to be additive. For most factors, their role in determining the overall moral status of an act simply cannot be adequately captured in terms of separate and independent contributions that merely need to be added in.

Graham Oddie

Killing and Letting Die

From Bare Differences to Clear Differences

The method of bare-differences . . . involves a controversial ubiquity thesis. However, there are two quite different ubiquity theses which are not always clearly distinguished and disentangled. The first, which I will call *bottom-up* ubiquity is the modest assumption that if B is worse in itself than A, then merely replacing A by B (holding all else fixed) will make the overall situation worse. Slightly more formally let S(B/A) be the situation which is just like S except that A has been replaced by B:

> *Bottom-up ubiquity:* If B is worse (in itself) than A then (for any situation S) S (B/A) is worse than S.

What could it mean that B is *in itself* worse than A if merely replacing A with B did not make things worse? Another quite different principle, which I will call *top-down ubiquity,* says that if merely replacing B with A makes things worse in *any* single case, then B in itself is worse than A

> *Top-down ubiquity:* If (for some situation S) S(B/A) is worse than S, then B is worse in itself than A.

The ubiquity principle that is sometimes criticized is the conjunction of both bottom-up and top-down ubiquity. The conjunction is by no means a modest principle. The two principles are naturally useful for establishing quite different theses. Using bottom-up ubiquity we can refute the thesis that B is, in itself, worse than A, by means of a single counterexample. All we need is a single situation S, such that replacing B for A in S does not make things worse. Refutation of claims of intrinsic value are thus rather easy.

Suppose we want to establish the thesis that B is, in itself, worse than A. We cannot do so using the bottom-up principle. However, with the top-down principle we can establish the thesis in one swift blow. A single pair of barely different situations, S

From Graham Oddie, "Killing and Letting-Die: From Bare Differences to Clear Differences," *Philosophical Studies* 88 (1997): 267–87. Notes and some parts of the text have been deleted. Reprinted by permission of Kluwer Academic Publishers.

and S(B/A), is sufficient to order A and B. Thus top-down ubiquity is an incredibly powerful principle, even in isolation, but especially when employed in conjunction with bottom-up ubiquity. Given both principles, a single barely different pair has implications for all barely-different pairs of that kind.

Judith Jarvis Thomson [in her 1976 article (p. 9)] thinks that chopping off a person's head is, in itself, worse than punching a person on the nose—and the rest of us are naturally inclined to agree. But imagine that Jones has a strange nasal condition such that punching him on the nose would kill him. This makes a barely different pair out of punching Jones on the nose and chopping off Jones's head. In these conditions it seems that punching Jones on the nose would be just as bad as chopping off Jones's head. Thomson suggests, however, that this one case should not force us to revise our judgement that chopping off a person's head is, in itself, worse than punching a person on the nose. If Thomson is right then even bottom-up ubiquity fails, and the existence of a single value-identical barely-different A/B-pair is not sufficient to refute a claim of intrinsic worseness.

Thomson's judgement on the pair is not obvious to me. There are bad aspects of a head chopping which are absent from a nose-punching, even when both kill the victim. For example, the former displays less respect for the integrity of the victim's body. (Hanging, drawing and quartering is worse than hanging.) But if we do grant Thomson's particular comparative judgement then I think we should indeed give up the idea that *in itself* head-chopping is worse than nose-punching. However, this conclusion is not nearly as counter-intuitive as it first might sound. What survives such examination by barely-different pairs is the claim that chopping off a *normal* person's head is, in itself, worse than punching a *normal* person on the nose. That is, a *normal* head-chopping is worse than a *normal* nose-punching— and that is surely what was intended all along. The unstated condition of normality builds in various important features of noses and necks. However, it would not do to try and rescue the traditional judgement on killing and letting-die in this way, because there is no comparable notion of a *normal* killing or

a *normal* letting-die in the sense in which there are normal noses and normal necks.

Although there is no such notion as that of a normal killing, perhaps a related point can be made about *typical* killings. Just as a normal A may be worse than a normal B, as it happens so too a *typical* A may be worse than a *typical* B, because of typical concomitants of A and B. As it happens, a typical killing, for instance, has horrible features which a typical letting-die lacks—malicious intent, unnecessary suffering, acting without the person's informed consent, perhaps violation of certain rights, and so forth. But, according to the equivalence thesis, it is those other horrible features which make killing typically worse than letting-die. And it is precisely in those situations in which the badness of killing humans is controversial—in the case of the terminally or congenitally ill, say—that these other horrible features may well be absent from a killing and present in a letting-die. The point of the bare-difference arguments is to force us to abstract from the typical concomitants of killing or letting-die and focus on the possible value-contribution of killing and letting-die in themselves.

Note that some have been tempted to cite a single barely-different, value-equivalent A/B-pair as a refutation of the claim that the A/B-distinction is evaluatively *significant* or *relevant*. Such a conclusion is indeed unwarranted but that is because evaluative significance is a relatively weak condition. Compare the situation with causal relevance or significance. Suppose a wet, oxygen-surrounded match fails to burn when struck, and so too does a wet, oxygen-deprived match. It would clearly be absurd to take this as a refutation of the causal relevance of oxygen to burning. Being oxygen-surrounded is causally relevant to burning if the bare shift from being oxygen-deprived to being oxygen surrounded *can* (rather than *must*) make a difference to burning. Similarly the moral or evaluative significance of the A/B-distinction is guaranteed if substituting B for A can make a difference to value. The existence of a single case S in which S(B/A) is worse than S makes the A/B distinction evaluatively significant, but provided top-down ubiquity is false, the evaluative significance of A/B is quite compatible with other cases in which the substitution of B for A makes no difference to value.

The upshot is that bottom-up ubiquity is a necessary constraint on intrinsic value and given this we can refute a claim of intrinsic worseness . . . by means of a single barely-different, value-equivalent pair. . . .

Another problem emerges. Without top-down ubiquity, a bare-difference refutation of the claim that A is worse than B, even in conjunction with the assumption that B is not worse than A, does not establish the intrinsic value-equivalence of A and B, or the evaluative-insignificance of the A/B-distinction. Similarly, demonstrating that in a certain class of cases the shift from letting-die to killing does not makes things worse does not show that they have exactly the same intrinsic value. . . .

One way of filling the gap would be, of course, to employ top-down ubiquity, but this is a very strong and controversial principle. Another would be to assume, simply, that killing and letting-die are *comparable* for intrinsic value. Then if killing is no worse than letting-die either killing is evaluatively equivalent to letting-die, or killing is worse than letting die. The argument then proceeds by refuting the last disjunct. To summarize then, the argument establishes the following interesting and rather important result:

> If killing and letting-die are comparable for intrinsic value, then they are . . . evaluatively equivalent.

The condition here is by no means a trivial one. However, to justify a strong presumption against active euthanasia while retaining a soft spot for passive euthanasia, one would need to invoke the thesis that killing is, in itself, worse than letting-die. If it is not worse to kill then each case will have to be assessed on other merits and demerits. But the thesis that killing is worse, in itself, than letting die implies that killing and letting-die are comparable for value. And that's all we need to establish the equivalence thesis. . . .

3

Is Abortion Wrong?

Marquis and His Critics

The moral problem of abortion is really two distinct moral problems. The first problem concerns the moral status of the human fetus, and the second concerns the moral significance of the relationship between the fetus and the pregnant woman whose body the fetus inhabits. Critics of abortion typically respond to the first problem by maintaining that the fetus has the same right to life that you or I have, that killing a human fetus is morally on a par with killing a typical adult human being. They then respond to the second problem by maintaining that a pregnant woman's right to control her own body is not strong enough to outweigh this consideration. Defenders of abortion typically respond to this position by attempting to show either that the human fetus does not have this high moral standing in the first place or that, if it does, the woman's interest in ending an unwanted pregnancy is strong enough to outweigh it. The standard argument about the moral permissibility of abortion, therefore, can be construed in terms of a simple argument with two premises and a conclusion that follows directly from them:

P1 The human fetus has the same right to life as an adult human being.
P2 If the human fetus has the same right to life as an adult human being, then abortion is morally impermissible.

C   Abortion is morally impermissible.

The critic of abortion maintains that both of these premises are true, and the defender of abortion maintains that at least one of them is false.

This chapter is organized around two featured articles, each of which focuses exclusively on one of these two key premises. In "Why Abortion Is Immoral," Don Marquis provides what many philosophers believe to be the most powerful argument in defense of P1. And in "A Defense of Abortion," Judith Jarvis Thomson defends what has become the most famous (or infamous) argument against P2. In arguing for P1, Marquis simply assumes that P2 is true, and in arguing against P2, Thomson assumes, at least for the sake of the argument, that

P1 is true. Although Marquis and Thomson represent diametrically opposing views on the morality of abortion, their arguments do not directly address each other, and therefore must be investigated separately.

Marquis's argument in defense of the rights of the human fetus (or, at least, of what he refers to as the "standard" or typical human fetus) has the logical structure that we refer to in the introduction as "inference to the best explanation" (see section 4.3). That is, he begins by looking at cases about which virtually everyone agrees, regardless of their stance on abortion. We all agree, for example, that it is immoral to kill a typical (innocent) adult human being, and agree that this is so even if the human being in question is an unloved hermit, a suicidal teenager, or a temporarily comatose adult. Marquis then asks what account of the wrongness of killing in general would do the best job of explaining the wrongness of killing in these cases. The answer he defends turns crucially on the claim that in all of these cases, the individual killed is deprived of what Marquis refers to as a "future like ours": the set of experiences that constitute their personal futures and that they would otherwise have been able to enjoy had they not been killed. The account of the wrongness of killing in general that best accounts for the beliefs with which both defenders and critics of abortion agree is the one that states that it is wrong to kill someone if killing them would deprive them of a future like ours that they either currently value or would come to value. Marquis then points out that the typical human fetus has just such a future. So the feature that is sufficient to make killing wrong in the uncontroversial cases and equally so in the controversial ones, shows that killing is also wrong. Put more formally (and using some of the terms that Marquis frequently employs in defending his position), the argument can therefore be represented as follows:

P1   It is prima facie seriously immoral to kill an individual *if both*
       (a) that individual has a future like ours, *and*
       (b) that individual values *or* will come to value its future like ours.
P2   A standard human fetus has a future like ours and will come to value it.

C   It is prima facie seriously immoral to kill a standard human fetus.

The first premise of this argument is grounded in the claim that it provides the best explanation for the various judgments that defenders and critics of abortion agree upon. The second premise arises from the claim that the future of a standard human fetus contains the same sorts of experiences as are contained in the future of a typical adult human being. And the conclusion is Marquis's way of stating what we referred to earlier as P1 of the standard argument against abortion, the claim that the human fetus has the same right to life that you or I have.

Marquis's argument is among the most prominent in the literature on abortion. It is also, perhaps not surprisingly, one of the arguments for which the most commentary has been generated. In the excerpted critical responses following Marquis's article, three philosophers offer three distinct strategies for attempting to rebut Marquis's future-like-ours argument. In the first reading, Gerald H. Paske argues that Marquis has misidentified the property that renders killing wrong in the cases in which it is uncontroversially wrong. Rather than appealing to facts about the victims' futures in such cases, Paske suggests that a more satisfying account of the wrongness of killing them focuses exclusively on facts about their *present* condition, facts that turn out not to apply in the case of the human fetus. This amounts to rejecting P1 of Marquis's argument on the grounds that it does not, in fact, provide the best account of the wrongness of killing in those cases in which killing is clearly immoral.

Alastair Norcross also argues against P1 of Marquis's argument, but on very different grounds. Norcross claims that P1 is unacceptable because it has an implication that is itself unacceptable: that contraception is morally on a par with killing an adult human being. Marquis briefly attempts to fend off this *reductio ad absurdum* objection to his argument in section V of his article, but Norcross argues that he is ultimately unsuccessful in this attempt.

Finally, Peter K. McInerney raises a challenge to P2 of Marquis's argument. Although it is true that the fetus will eventually develop into an adult human being, McInerney maintains that this fact does not suffice to establish that a future like ours is something that the fetus already has. If the future experiences of the future adult are not psychologically connected to the current fetus in a certain manner, McInerney argues, then they are not yet future experiences of the fetus. And if they are not yet future experiences of the fetus, then the fetus cannot be deprived of them by being killed. If McInerney is right, then even if P1 of Marquis's argument can overcome the objections to it raised by Paske and Norcross, it will still fail to support the conclusion that it is prima facie seriously immoral to kill a standard human fetus.

QUESTIONS FOR CONSIDERATION

In thinking critically about the exchange between Marquis and his critics, it may be useful to keep some of the following questions in mind.

• Is Paske right in thinking that our current properties account better for the wrongness of killing us than do facts about our futures?

• What advantages does Marquis's account of the wrongness of killing have over Paske's? What advantages does Paske's have over Marquis's?

• Is Norcross right in thinking that Marquis has failed to overcome the contraception objection? How does Marquis try to rebut that objection in section V of his article? Where, specifically, does Norcross think he goes wrong? Is there a way that Marquis could modify his position to overcome the objection without losing his ability to defend his anti-abortion conclusion?

• Why does McInerney believe that the fetus does not yet have a future like ours? Are his reasons good enough? Based on the kinds of examples that Marquis gives in response to other possible accounts of the wrongness of killing, how might he try to respond to McInerney's central contention?

FURTHER READING

Cudd, Ann E. "Sensationalized Philosophy: A Reply to Marquis's 'Why Abortion Is Immoral.' " *Journal of Philosophy* 87, no. 5 (1990): 262–64.

Daniels Charles B. "Having a Future." *Dialogue* 31 (2003): 661–65.

Marquis, Don. "A Future Like Ours and the Concept of Person: A Reply to McInerney and Paske." In *The Abortion Controversy: 25 Years After Roe v. Wade,* edited by Louis Pojman and Francis J. Beckwith. Belmont, Calif.: Wadsworth, 1998, pp. 372–85.

———. "Shirley's 'Marquis' Argument Against Abortion.' " *Southwest Philosophy Review* 6, no. 2 (1995): 263–65.

Shirley, Edward S. "Marquis' Argument Against Abortion: A Critique." *Southwest Philosophy Review* 6, no. 1 (1995): 79–89.

Sinnott-Armstrong, Walter. "You Can't Lose What You Ain't Never Had: A Reply to Marquis on Abortion." *Philosophical Studies* 96, no. 1 (1999): 59–72.

Don Marquis | Why Abortion Is Immoral

The view that abortion is, with rare exceptions, seriously immoral has received little support in the recent philosophical literature. No doubt most philosophers affiliated with secular institutions of higher education believe that the anti-abortion position is either a symptom of irrational religious dogma or a conclusion generated by seriously confused philosophical argument. The purpose of this essay is to undermine this general belief. This essay sets out an argument that purports to show, as well as any argument in ethics can show, that abortion is, except possibly in rare cases, seriously immoral, that it is in the same moral category as killing an innocent adult human being.

The argument is based on a major assumption. Many of the most insightful and careful writers on the ethics of abortion—such as Joel Feinberg, Michael Tooley, Mary Anne Warren, H. Tristram Engelhardt, Jr., L. W. Sumner, John T. Noonan, Jr., and Philip Devine[1]—believe that whether or not abortion is morally permissible stands or falls on whether or not a fetus is the sort of being whose life it is seriously wrong to end. The argument of this essay will assume, but not argue, that they are correct.

Also, this essay will neglect issues of great importance to a complete ethics of abortion. Some anti-abortionists will allow that certain abortions, such as abortion before implantation or abortion when the life of a woman is threatened by a pregnancy or abortion after rape, may be morally permissible. This essay will not explore the casuistry of these hard cases. The purpose of this essay is to develop a general argument for the claim that the overwhelming majority of deliberate abortions are seriously immoral.

I

... [A] necessary condition of resolving the abortion controversy is a more theoretical account of the wrongness of killing. After all, if we merely believe, but do not understand, why killing adult human beings such as ourselves is wrong, how could we conceivably show that abortion is either immoral or permissible?

II

In order to develop such an account, we can start from the following unproblematic assumption concerning our own case: it is wrong to kill *us*. Why is it wrong? Some answers can be easily eliminated. It might be said that what makes killing us wrong is that a killing brutalizes the one who kills. But the brutalization consists of being inured to the performance of an act that is hideously immoral; hence, the brutalization does not explain the immorality. It might be said that what makes killing us wrong is the great loss others would experience due to our absence. Although such hubris is understandable, such an explanation does not account for the wrongness of killing hermits, or those whose lives are relatively independent and whose friends find it easy to make new friends.

A more obvious answer is better. What primarily makes killing wrong is neither its effect on the murderer nor its effect on the victim's friends and relatives, but its effect on the victim. The loss of one's life is one of the greatest losses one can suffer. The loss of one's life deprives one of all the experiences, activities, projects, and enjoyments that would otherwise have constituted one's future. Therefore,

From Don Marquis, "Why Abortion Is Immoral," *Journal of Philosophy* 86, no. 4 (1989): 183–202. Some notes and some text have been deleted. Reprinted by permission of The Journal of Philosophy.

killing someone is wrong, primarily because the killing inflicts (one of) the greatest possible losses on the victim. To describe this as the loss of life can be misleading, however. The change in my biological state does not by itself make killing me wrong. The effect of the loss of my biological life is the loss to me of all those activities, projects, experiences, and enjoyments which would otherwise have constituted my future personal life. These activities, projects, experiences, and enjoyments are either valuable for their own sakes or are means to something else that is valuable for its own sake. Some parts of my future are not valued by me now, but will come to be valued by me as I grow older and as my values and capacities change. When I am killed, I am deprived both of what I now value which would have been part of my future personal life, but also what I would come to value. Therefore, when I die, I am deprived of all of the value of my future. Inflicting this loss on me is ultimately what makes killing me wrong. This being the case, it would seem that what makes killing *any* adult human being prima facie seriously wrong is the loss of his or her future.[2]

How should this rudimentary theory of the wrongness of killing be evaluated? It cannot be faulted for deriving an "ought" from an "is," for it does not. The analysis assumes that killing me (or you, reader) is prima facie seriously wrong. The point of the analysis is to establish which natural property ultimately explains the wrongness of the killing, given that it is wrong. A natural property will ultimately explain the wrongness of killing, only if (1) the explanation fits with our intuitions about the matter and (2) there is no other natural property that provides the basis for a better explanation of the wrongness of killing. This analysis rests on the intuition that what makes killing a particular human or animal wrong is what it does to that particular human or animal. What makes killing wrong is some natural effect or other of the killing. Some would deny this. For instance, a divine-command theorist in ethics would deny it. Surely this denial is, however, one of those features of divine-command theory which renders it so implausible.

The claim that what makes killing wrong is the loss of the victim's future is directly supported by two considerations. In the first place, this theory explains why we regard killing as one of the worst of crimes. Killing is especially wrong, because it deprives the victim of more than perhaps any other crime. In the second place, people with AIDS or cancer who know they are dying believe, of course, that dying is a very bad thing for them. They believe that the loss of a future to them that they would otherwise have experienced is what makes their premature death a very bad thing for them. A better theory of the wrongness of killing would require a different natural property associated with killing which better fits with the attitudes of the dying. What could it be?

The view that what makes killing wrong is the loss to the victim of the value of the victim's future gains additional support when some of its implications are examined. In the first place, it is incompatible with the view that it is wrong to kill only beings who are biologically human. It is possible that there exists a different species from another planet whose members have a future like ours. Since having a future like that is what makes killing someone wrong, this theory entails that it would be wrong to kill members of such a species. Hence, this theory is opposed to the claim that only life that is biologically human has great moral worth, a claim which many anti-abortionists have seemed to adopt. This opposition, which this theory has in common with personhood theories, seems to be a merit of the theory.

In the second place, the claim that the loss of one's future is the wrong-making feature of one's being killed entails the possibility that the futures of some actual nonhuman mammals on our own planet are sufficiently like ours that it is seriously wrong to kill them also. Whether some animals do have the same right to life as human beings depends on adding to the account of the wrongness of killing some additional account of just what it is about my future or the futures of other adult human beings which makes it wrong to kill us. No such additional account will be offered in this essay. Undoubtedly, the provision of such an account would be a very difficult matter. Undoubtedly, any such account would be quite controversial. Hence, it surely should not reflect badly on this sketch of an elementary theory of the wrongness of killing that it is indeterminate with respect to some very difficult issues regarding animal rights.

In the third place, the claim that the loss of one's future is the wrong-making feature of one's being killed does not entail, as sanctity of human life theories do, that active euthanasia is wrong. Persons who are severely and incurably ill, who face a future of pain and despair, and who wish to die will not have suffered a loss if they are killed. It is, strictly speaking, the value of a human's future which makes killing wrong in this theory. This being so, killing does not necessarily wrong some persons who are sick and dying. Of course, there may be other reasons for a prohibition of active euthanasia, but that is another matter. Sanctity-of-human-life theories seem to hold that active euthanasia is seriously wrong even in an individual case where there seems to be good reason for it independently of public policy considerations. This consequence is most implausible, and it is a plus for the claim that the loss of a future of value is what makes killing wrong that it does not share this consequence.

In the fourth place, the account of the wrongness of killing defended in this essay does straightforwardly entail that it is prima facie seriously wrong to kill children and infants, for we do presume that they have futures of value. Since we do believe that it is wrong to kill defenseless little babies, it is important that a theory of the wrongness of killing easily account for this. Personhood theories of the wrongness of killing, on the other hand, cannot straightforwardly account for the wrongness of killing infants and young children.[3] Hence, such theories must add special ad hoc accounts of the wrongness of killing the young. The plausibility of such ad hoc theories seems to be a function of how desperately one wants such theories to work. The claim that the primary wrong-making feature of a killing is the loss to the victim of the value of its future accounts for the wrongness of killing young children and infants directly; it makes the wrongness of such acts as obvious as we actually think it is. This is a further merit of this theory. Accordingly, it seems that this value of a future-like-ours theory of the wrongness of killing shares strengths of both sanctity-of-life and personhood accounts while avoiding weaknesses of

both. In addition, it meshes with a central intuition concerning what makes killing wrong.

The claim that the primary wrong-making feature of a killing is the loss to the victim of the value of its future has obvious consequences for the ethics of abortion. The future of a standard fetus includes a set of experiences, projects, activities, and such which are identical with the futures of adult human beings and are identical with the futures of young children. Since the reason that is sufficient to explain why it is wrong to kill human beings after the time of birth is a reason that also applies to fetuses, it follows that abortion is prima facie seriously morally wrong.

This argument does not rely on the invalid inference that, since it is wrong to kill persons, it is wrong to kill potential persons also. The category that is morally central to this analysis is the category of having a valuable future like ours; it is not the category of personhood. The argument to the conclusion that abortion is prima facie seriously morally wrong proceeded independently of the notion of person or potential person or any equivalent. Someone may wish to start with this analysis in terms of the value of a human future, conclude that abortion is, except perhaps in rare circumstances, seriously morally wrong, infer that fetuses have the right to life, and then call fetuses "persons" as a result of their having the right to life. Clearly, in this case, the category of person is being used to state the *conclusion* of the analysis rather than to generate the *argument* of the analysis.

The structure of this anti-abortion argument can be both illuminated and defended by comparing it to what appears to be the best argument for the wrongness of the wanton infliction of pain on animals. This latter argument is based on the assumption that it is prima facie wrong to inflict pain on me (or you, reader). What is the natural property associated with the infliction of pain which makes such infliction wrong? The obvious answer seems to be that the infliction of pain causes suffering and that suffering is a misfortune. The suffering caused by the infliction of pain is what makes the wanton infliction of pain on me wrong. The wanton infliction of pain on other adult humans causes suffering. The wanton infliction of pain on animals causes suffering. Since causing suffering is what makes the wanton infliction of pain wrong and since the wanton infliction of pain on animals causes suffering, it follows that the wanton infliction of pain on animals is wrong.

This argument for the wrongness of the wanton infliction of pain on animals shares a number of structural features with the argument for the serious prima facie wrongness of abortion. Both arguments start with an obvious assumption concerning what it is wrong to do to me (or you, reader). Both then look for the characteristic or the consequence of the wrong action which makes the action wrong. Both recognize that the wrong-making feature of these immoral actions is a property of actions sometimes directed at individuals other than postnatal human beings. If the structure of the argument for the wrongness of the wanton infliction of pain on animals is sound, then the structure of the argument for the prima facie serious wrongness of abortion is also sound, for the structure of the two arguments is the same. The structure common to both is the key to the explanation of how the wrongness of abortion can be demonstrated without recourse to the category of person. In neither argument is that category crucial.

This defense of an argument for the wrongness of abortion in terms of a structurally similar argument for the wrongness of the wanton infliction of pain on animals succeeds only if the account regarding animals is the correct account. Is it? In the first place, it seems plausible. In the second place, its major competition is Kant's account. Kant believed that we do not have direct duties to animals at all, because they are not persons. Hence, Kant had to explain and justify the wrongness of inflicting pain on animals on the grounds that "he who is hard in his dealings with animals becomes hard also in his dealing with men."[4] The problem with Kant's account is that there seems to be no reason for accepting this latter claim unless Kant's account is rejected. If the alternative to Kant's account is accepted, then it is easy to understand why someone who is indifferent to inflicting pain on animals is also indifferent to inflicting pain on humans, for one is indifferent to what makes inflicting pain wrong in both cases. But, if Kant's account is accepted, there is no intelligible reason why one who is hard in his dealings with animals (or crabgrass or stones) should also be hard in his dealings with men. After all, men are persons: animals are no more persons than crabgrass or stones. Persons are Kant's crucial moral category. Why, in short, should a Kantian accept the basic claim in Kant's argument?

Hence, Kant's argument for the wrongness of inflicting pain on animals rests on a claim that, in a world of Kantian moral agents, is demonstrably false. Therefore, the alternative analysis, being more plausible anyway, should be accepted. Since this alternative analysis has the same structure as the anti-abortion argument being defended here, we have further support for the argument for the immorality of abortion being defended in this essay.

Of course, this value of a future-like-ours argument, if sound, shows only that abortion is prima facie wrong, not that it is wrong in any and all circumstances. Since the loss of the future to a standard fetus, if killed, is, however, at least as great a loss as the loss of the future to a standard adult human being who is killed, abortion, like ordinary killing, could be justified only by the most compelling reasons. The loss of one's life is almost the greatest misfortune that can happen to one. Presumably abortion could be justified in some circumstances, only if the loss consequent on failing to abort would be at least as great. Accordingly, morally permissible abortions will be rare indeed unless, perhaps, they occur so early in pregnancy that a fetus is not yet definitely an individual. Hence, this argument should be taken as showing that abortion is presumptively very seriously wrong, where the presumption is very strong—as strong as the presumption that killing another adult human being is wrong.

III

How complete an account of the wrongness of killing does the value of a future-like-ours account have to be in order that the wrongness of abortion is a consequence? This account does not have to be an account of the necessary conditions for the wrongness of killing. Some persons in nursing homes may lack valuable human futures, yet it may be wrong to kill them for other reasons. Furthermore, this account does not obviously have to be the sole reason killing is wrong where the victim did have a valuable future. This analysis claims only that, for any killing where the victim did have a valuable future like ours, having that future by itself is sufficient to create the strong presumption that the killing is seriously wrong.

One way to overturn the value of a future-like-ours argument would be to find some account of the wrongness of killing which is at least as intelligible and which has different implications for the ethics of abortion. Two rival accounts possess at least some degree of plausibility. One account is based on the obvious fact that people value the experience of living and wish for that valuable experience to continue. Therefore, it might be said, what makes killing wrong is the discontinuation of that experience for the victim. Let us call this the *discontinuation account*.[5] Another rival account is based upon the obvious fact that people strongly desire to continue to live. This suggests that what makes killing us so wrong is that it interferes with the fulfillment of a strong and fundamental desire, the fulfillment of which is necessary for the fulfillment of any other desires we might have. Let us call this the *desire account*.[6]

Consider first the desire account as a rival account of the ethics of killing which would provide the basis for rejecting the anti-abortion position. Such an account will have to be stronger than the value of a future-like-ours account of the wrongness of abortion if it is to do the job expected of it. To entail the wrongness of abortion, the value of a future-like-ours account has only to provide a sufficient, but not a necessary, condition for the wrongness of killing. The desire account, on the other hand, must provide us also with a necessary condition for the wrongness of killing in order to generate a pro-choice conclusion on abortion. The reason for this is that presumably the argument from the desire account moves from the claim that what makes killing wrong is interference with a very strong desire to the claim that abortion is not wrong because the fetus lacks a strong desire to live. Obviously, this inference fails if someone's having the desire to live

is not a necessary condition of its being wrong to kill that individual.

One problem with the desire account is that we do regard it as seriously wrong to kill persons who have little desire to live or who have no desire to live or, indeed, have a desire not to live. We believe it is seriously wrong to kill the unconscious, the sleeping, those who are tired of life, and those who are suicidal. The value-of-a-human-future account renders standard morality intelligible in these cases; these cases appear to be incompatible with the desire account.

The desire account is subject to a deeper difficulty. We desire life, because we value the goods of this life. The goodness of life is not secondary to our desire for it. If this were not so, the pain of one's own premature death could be done away with merely by an appropriate alteration in the configuration of one's desires. This is absurd. Hence, it would seem that it is the loss of the goods of one's future, not the interference with the fulfillment of a strong desire to live, which accounts ultimately for the wrongness of killing.

It is worth noting that, if the desire account is modified so that it does not provide a necessary, but only a sufficient, condition for the wrongness of killing, the desire account is compatible with the value of a future-like-ours account. The combined accounts will yield an anti-abortion ethic. This suggests that one can retain what is intuitively plausible about the desire account without a challenge to the basic argument of this paper.

It is also worth noting that, if future desires have moral force in a modified desire account of the wrongness of killing, one can find support for an anti-abortion ethic even in the absence of a value of a future-like-ours account. If one decides that a morally relevant property, the possession of which is sufficient to make it wrong to kill some individual, is the desire at some future time to live—one might decide to justify one's refusal to kill suicidal teenagers on these grounds, for example—then, since typical fetuses will have the desire in the future to live, it is wrong to kill typical fetuses. Accordingly, it does not seem that a desire account of the wrongness of killing can provide a justification of a pro-choice ethic of abortion which is nearly as adequate as the value of a human-future justification of an anti-abortion ethic.

The discontinuation account looks more promising as an account of the wrongness of killing. It seems just as intelligible as the value of a future-like-ours account, but it does not justify an anti-abortion position. Obviously, if it is the continuation of one's activities, experiences, and projects, the loss of which makes killing wrong, then it is not wrong to kill fetuses for that reason, for fetuses do not have experiences, activities, and projects to be continued or discontinued. Accordingly, the discontinuation account does not have the anti-abortion consequences that the value of a future-like-ours account has. Yet, it seems as intelligible as the value of a future-like-ours account, for when we think of what would be wrong with our being killed, it does seem as if it is the discontinuation of what makes our lives worthwhile which makes killing us wrong.

Is the discontinuation account just as good an account as the value of a future-like-ours account? The discontinuation account will not be adequate at all, if it does not refer to the *value* of the experience that may be discontinued. One does not want the discontinuation account to make it wrong to kill a patient who begs for death and who is in severe pain that cannot be relieved short of killing. (I leave open the question of whether it is wrong for other reasons.) Accordingly, the discontinuation account must be more than a bare discontinuation account. It must make some reference to the positive value of the patient's experiences. But, by the same token, the value of a future-like-ours account cannot be a bare future account either. Just having a future surely does not itself rule out killing the above patient. This account must make some reference to the value of the patient's future experiences and projects also. Hence, both accounts involve the value of experiences, projects, and activities. So far we still have symmetry between the accounts.

The symmetry fades, however, when we focus on the time period of the value of the experiences, etc., which has moral consequences. Although both accounts leave open the possibility that the patient in our example may be killed, this possibility is left

open only in virtue of the utterly bleak future for the patient. It makes no difference whether the patient's immediate past contains intolerable pain, or consists in being in a coma (which we can imagine is a situation of indifference), or consists in a life of value. If the patient's future is a future of value, we want our account to make it wrong to kill the patient. If the patient's future is intolerable, whatever his or her immediate past, we want our account to allow killing the patient. Obviously, then, it is the value of that patient's future which is doing the work in rendering the morality of killing the patient intelligible.

This being the case, it seems clear that whether one has immediate past experiences or not does no work in the explanation of what makes killing wrong. The addition the discontinuation account makes to the value of a human future account is otiose. Its addition to the value-of-a-future account plays no role at all in rendering intelligible the wrongness of killing. Therefore, it can be discarded with the discontinuation account of which it is a part.

IV

The analysis of the previous section suggests that alternative general accounts of the wrongness of killing are either inadequate or unsuccessful in getting around the anti-abortion consequences of the value of a future-like-ours argument. A different strategy for avoiding these anti-abortion consequences involves limiting the scope of the value of a future argument. More precisely, the strategy involves arguing that fetuses lack a property that is essential for the value-of-a-future argument (or for any anti-abortion argument) to apply to them.

One move of this sort is based upon the claim that a necessary condition of one's future being valuable is that one values it. Value implies a valuer. Given this one might argue that, since fetuses cannot value their futures, their futures are not valuable to them. Hence, it does not seriously wrong them deliberately to end their lives.

This move fails, however, because of some ambiguities. Let us assume that something cannot be of value unless it is valued by someone. This does not entail that my life is of no value unless it is valued by me. I may think, in a period of despair, that my future is of no worth whatsoever, but I may be wrong because others rightly see value—even great value—in it. Furthermore, my future can be valuable to me even if I do not value it. This is the case when a young person attempts suicide, but is rescued and goes on to significant human achievements. Such young people's futures are ultimately valuable to them, even though such futures do not seem to be valuable to them at the moment of attempted suicide. A fetus's future can be valuable to it in the same way. Accordingly, this attempt to limit the anti-abortion argument fails.

Another similar attempt to reject the anti-abortion position is based on Tooley's claim that an entity cannot possess the right to life unless it has the capacity to desire its continued existence. It follows that, since fetuses lack the conceptual capacity to desire to continue to live, they lack the right to life. Accordingly, Tooley concludes that abortion cannot be seriously prima facie wrong (op. cit., pp. 46–7).

What could be the evidence for Tooley's basic claim? Tooley once argued that individuals have a prima facie right to what they desire and that the lack of the capacity to desire something undercuts the basis of one's right to it (op. cit., pp. 44–5). This argument plainly will not succeed in the context of the analysis of this essay, however, since the point here is to establish the fetus's right to life on other grounds. Tooley's argument assumes that the right to life cannot be established in general on some basis other than the desire for life. This position was considered and rejected in the preceding section of this paper.

One might attempt to defend Tooley's basic claim on the grounds that, because a fetus cannot apprehend continued life as a benefit, its continued life cannot be a benefit or cannot be something it has a right to or cannot be something that is in its interest. This might be defended in terms of the general proposition that, if an individual is literally incapable of caring about or taking an interest in some X, then one does not have a right to X or X is not a benefit or X is not something that is in one's interest.[7]

Each member of this family of claims seems to be open to objections. As John C. Stevens[8] has pointed out, one may have a right to be treated with a certain medical procedure (because of a health insurance policy one has purchased), even though one cannot conceive of the nature of the procedure. And, as Tooley himself has pointed out, persons who have been indoctrinated, or drugged, or rendered temporarily unconscious may be literally incapable of caring about or taking an interest in something that is in their interest or is something to which they have a right, or is something that benefits them. Hence, the Tooley claim that would restrict the scope of the value of a future-like-ours argument is undermined by counterexamples.[9]

Finally, Paul Bassen[10] has argued that, even though the prospects of an embryo might seem to be a basis for the wrongness of abortion, an embryo cannot be a victim and therefore cannot be wronged. An embryo cannot be a victim, he says, because it lacks sentience. His central argument for this seems to be that, even though plants and the permanently unconscious are alive, they clearly cannot be victims. What is the explanation of this? Bassen claims that the explanation is that their lives consist of mere metabolism and mere metabolism is not enough to ground victimizability. Mentation is required.

The problem with this attempt to establish the absence of victimizability is that both plants and the permanently unconscious clearly lack what Bassen calls "prospects" or what I have called "a future life like ours." Hence, it is surely open to one to argue that the real reason we believe plants and the permanently unconscious cannot be victims is that killing them cannot deprive them of a future life like ours; the real reason is not their absence of present mentation.

Bassen recognizes that his view is subject to this difficulty, and he recognizes that the case of children seems to support this difficulty, for "much of what we do for children is based on prospects." He argues, however, that, in the case of children and in other such cases, "potentiality comes into play only where victimizability has been secured on other grounds" (ibid., p. 333).

Bassen's defense of his view is patently question-begging, since what is adequate to secure victimizability is exactly what is at issue. His examples do not support his own view against the thesis of this essay. Of course, embryos can be victims: when their lives are deliberately terminated, they are deprived of their futures of value, their prospects. This makes them victims, for it directly wrongs them.

The seeming plausibility of Bassen's view stems from the fact that paradigmatic cases of imagining someone as a victim involve empathy, and empathy requires mentation of the victim. The victims of flood, famine, rape, or child abuse are all persons with whom we can empathize. That empathy seems to be part of seeing them as victims.[11]

In spite of the strength of these examples, the attractive intuition that a situation in which there is victimization requires the possibility of empathy is subject to counterexamples. Consider a case that Bassen himself offers: "Posthumous obliteration of an author's work constitutes a misfortune for him only if he had wished his work to endure" (op. cit., p. 318). The conditions Bassen wishes to impose upon the possibility of being victimized here seem far too strong. Perhaps this author, due to his unrealistic standards of excellence and his low self-esteem, regarded his work as unworthy of survival, even though it possessed genuine literary merit. Destruction of such work would surely victimize its author. In such a case, empathy with the victim concerning the loss is clearly impossible.

Of course, Bassen does not make the possibility of empathy a necessary condition of victimizability; he requires only mentation. Hence, on Bassen's actual view, this author, as I have described him, can be a victim. The problem is that the basic intuition that renders Bassen's view plausible is missing in the author's case. In order to attempt to avoid counterexamples, Bassen has made his thesis too weak to be supported by the intuitions that suggested it.

Even so, the mentation requirement on victimizability is still subject to counterexamples. Suppose a severe accident renders me totally unconscious for a month, after which I recover. Surely killing me while I am unconscious victimizes me, even though I am incapable of mentation during that time. It follows that Bassen's thesis fails. Apparently, attempts to restrict the value of a future-like-ours argument so that fetuses do not fall within its scope do not succeed.

V

In this essay, it has been argued that the correct ethic of the wrongness of killing can be extended to fetal life and used to show that there is a strong presumption that any abortion is morally impermissible. If the ethic of killing adopted here entails, however, that contraception is also seriously immoral, then there would appear to be a difficulty with the analysis of this essay.

But this analysis does not entail that contraception is wrong. Of course, contraception prevents the actualization of a possible future of value. Hence, it follows from the claim that futures of value should be maximized that contraception is prima facie immoral. This obligation to maximize does not exist, however; furthermore, nothing in the ethics of killing in this paper entails that it does. The ethics of killing in this essay would entail that contraception is wrong only if something were denied a human future of value by contraception. Nothing at all is denied such a future by contraception, however.

Candidates for a subject of harm by contraception fall into four categories: (1) some sperm or other, (2) some ovum or other, (3) a sperm and an ovum separately, and (4) a sperm and an ovum together. Assigning the harm to some sperm is utterly arbitrary, for no reason can be given for making a sperm the subject of harm rather than an ovum. Assigning the harm to some ovum is utterly arbitrary, for no reason can be given for making an ovum the subject of harm rather than a sperm. One might attempt to avoid these problems by insisting that contraception deprives both the sperm and the ovum separately of a valuable future like ours. On this alternative, too many futures are lost. Contraception was supposed to be wrong, because it deprived us of one future of value, not two. One might attempt to avoid this problem by holding that contraception deprives the combination of sperm and ovum of a valuable future like ours. But here the definite article misleads. At the time of contraception, there are hundreds of millions of sperm, one (released) ovum and millions of possible combinations of all of these. There is no actual combination at all. Is the subject of the loss to be a merely possible combination? Which one? This alternative does not yield an actual subject of harm either. Accordingly, the immorality of contraception is not entailed by the loss of a future-like-ours argument simply because there is no nonarbitrarily identifiable subject of the loss in the case of contraception.

VI

The purpose of this essay has been to set out an argument for the serious presumptive wrongness of abortion subject to the assumption that the moral permissibility of abortion stands or falls on the moral status of the fetus. Since a fetus possesses a property, the possession of which in adult human beings is sufficient to make killing an adult human being wrong, abortion is wrong. This way of dealing with the problem of abortion seems superior to other approaches to the ethics of abortion, because it rests on an ethics of killing which is close to self-evident, because the crucial morally relevant property clearly applies to fetuses, and because the argument avoids the usual equivocations on "human life," "human being," or "person." The argument rests neither on religious claims nor on Papal dogma. It is not subject to the objection of "speciesism." Its soundness is compatible with the moral permissibility of euthanasia and contraception. It deals with our intuitions concerning young children.

Finally, this analysis can be viewed as resolving a standard problem—indeed, *the* standard problem— concerning the ethics of abortion. Clearly, it is wrong to kill adult human beings. Clearly, it is not wrong to end the life of some arbitrarily chosen single human cell. Fetuses seem to be like arbitrarily chosen human cells in some respects and like adult humans in other respects. The problem of the ethics of abortion is the problem of determining the fetal property that settles this moral controversy. The thesis of this essay is that the problem of the ethics of abortion, so understood, is solvable.

NOTES

1. Feinberg, "Abortion," in *Matters of Life and Death: New Introductory Essays in Moral Philosophy,* Tom Regan, ed. (New York: Random House, 1986), pp. 256–293; Tooley, "Abortion and Infanticide," *Philosophy and Public Affairs,* ii, 1 (1972):37–65, Tooley, *Abortion and Infanticide* (New York: Oxford, 1984); Warren, "On the Moral and Legal Status of Abortion," *The Monist,* l.vii, 1 (1973):43–61; Engelhardt, "The Ontology of Abortion," *Ethics,* l.xxxiv, 3 (1974):217–234; Sumner, *Abortion and Moral Theory* (Princeton: University Press, 1981); Noonan, "An Almost Absolute Value in History," in *The Morality of Abortion: Legal and Historical Perspectives,* Noonan, ed. (Cambridge: Harvard, 1970); and Devine, *The Ethics of Homicide* (Ithaca: Cornell, 1978).

2. I have been most influenced on this matter by Jonathan Glover, *Causing Death and Saving Lives* (New York: Penguin, 1977), ch. 3; and Robert Young, "What Is So Wrong with Killing People?" *Philosophy,* l.iv, 210 (1979):515–528.

3. Feinberg, Tooley, Warren, and Engelhardt have all dealt with this problem.

4. "Duties to Animals and Spirits," in *Lectures on Ethics,* Louis Infeld, trans. (New York: Harper, 1963), p. 239.

5. I am indebted to Jack Bricke for raising this objection.

6. Presumably a preference utilitarian would press such an objection. Tooley once suggested that his account has such a theoretical underpinning. See his "Abortion and Infanticide," pp. 44–5.

7. Donald VanDeVeer seems to think this is self-evident. See his "Whither Baby Doe?" in *Matters of Life and Death,* p. 233.

8. "Must the Bearer of a Right Have the Concept of That to Which He Has a Right?" *Ethics,* xcv, 1 (1984):68–74.

9. See Tooley again in "Abortion and Infanticide," pp. 47–49.

10. "Present Sakes and Future Prospects: The Status of Early Abortion," *Philosophy and Public Affairs,* xi, 4 (1982):322–326.

11. Note carefully the reasons he gives on the bottom of p. 316.

Critics

Gerald H. Paske

Abortion and the Neo-Natal Right to Life

A Critique of Marquis's Futurist Argument

In an influential but misleadingly entitled paper, Don Marquis has presented a serious challenge to the pro-choice position.[1] Although the paper is entitled "Why Abortion Is Immoral," Marquis's argument actually allows for abortions of severely mentally defective fetuses. Marquis, thus, is on the conservative end of the prochoice spectrum.

Marquis's challenge remains serious, however, because his argument, if sound, would show that from conception onward all abortions of normal fetuses are seriously immoral. Marquis's argument is based on the following three claims: (1) Personhood is an inadequate foundation for the right to life. (2) The right to life is based on having a future-like-ours. (3) Normal fetuses have a future-like-ours and, hence, normal fetuses have a right to life. Marquis also claims that the personhood concept provides an inadequate basis for the right to life of infants and children, and he takes this to constitute an additional serious challenge to the standard prochoice position.

I shall argue (a) that Marquis's own position presupposes the concept of personhood, (b) that having a future-like-ours is neither a sufficient nor a necessary condition for having a right to life, and (c) that given the concept of personhood, neonates, infants, and children have a right to life.

Marquis summarizes his argument as follows:

> In order to develop (my) account, we can start from the following unproblematic assumption concerning our own case: It is wrong to kill *us*. . . . The loss of one's life is one of the greatest losses one can suffer. The loss of one's life deprives one of all the experiences, activities, projects, and enjoyments that would otherwise have constituted one's future. . . . To describe this as the loss of life can be misleading, however. The change in my biological state does not by itself make killing me wrong. The effect of the loss of my biological life is the loss to me of all those activities, projects, experiences, and enjoyments that would otherwise have constituted my future personal life. . . . Therefore, when I die I am deprived of all of the value of my future. Inflicting this loss on me is ultimately what makes killing me wrong. This being the case, it would seem that what makes killing *any* adult human being prima facie seriously wrong is the loss of his or her future. [189–90]

Marquis applies this "deprivation argument" to the abortion issue as follows:

> The claim that the primary wrong-making feature of a killing is the loss to the victim of the value of its future has obvious consequences for the ethics of abortion. The future of a standard fetus includes a set of experiences, projects, activities, and such that are identical with the futures of adult human beings and are identical with the futures of young children. Since the reason that is sufficient to explain why it is wrong to kill human beings after the time of birth is a reason that also applies to fetuses, it follows that abortion is prima facie seriously morally wrong. [192]

While granting the appeal of Marquis's argument, I shall nevertheless attack it at its foundation: the claim that having a future-like-ours is a sufficient condition for a right to life. Since Marquis's positive

From Gerald H. Paske. "Abortion and the Neo-Natal Right to Life: A Critique of Marquis's Futurist Argument," in *The Abortion Controversy: 25 Years After Roe. v. Wade: A Reader,* 2nd. ed., ed. Louis P. Pojman and Francis J. Beckwith (Belmont, CA: Wadsworth, 1998), pp. 361–71.

argument is entwined with his negative claims about personhood, I shall begin with the concept of personhood.

Marquis is correct when he offers the "unproblematic assumption" that "it is wrong to kill *us*." But though the assumption is unproblematic, it requires explication. Indeed, if we are to avoid "human chauvinism" and "species bias," this unproblematic assumption must be explicated. Why is it that a future-like-ours is the one that counts and not—say—the future of a pig or a cow? The answer lies in the concept of personhood.

The concept of personhood is both complex and controversial. I will discuss it in some detail later, but first I shall appeal to intuitions. Given the popularity of the television show *Star Trek* and of the movie *E.T.,* most of us are comfortable with the notion of nonhuman rational beings and it is easy to ascribe a right to life to such beings. We do so because, no matter how much they differ physically, their mental lives are very similar to ours. Intuitively, then, personhood is that set of mental characteristics which hypothetical nonhuman rational beings share with humans, but which neither they nor humans share with pigs and cows. It is this personhood which makes a future-like-ours possible and it is, hence, personhood which underlies Marquis's right to life. This becomes quite clear when one examines Marquis's defense of his own position. He offers the following as points in support of his thesis:

> In the first place, (my theory) is incompatible with the view that it is wrong to kill only human beings who are biologically human. . . . In the second place, the claim that the loss of one's future is the wrong-making feature of one's being killed entails the possibility that the futures of some actual nonhuman mammals on our own planet are sufficiently like ours that it is seriously wrong to kill them also. . . . In the third place, the claim that the loss of one's future is the wrong-making feature of one's being killed does not entail . . . that active euthanasia is wrong. [190–191]

Since Marquis offers these points in support of his thesis, one assumes that these points are more basic than the thesis itself. But, in response to his first point, if we ask what differentiates those nonhumans who have a right to life from those nonhumans who lack such a right, the answer is clear. Those nonhumans who have a right to life are persons, as are we, and those nonhumans who lack a right to life also lack personhood. With regard to Marquis's second point, the nonhuman mammals on our own planet that have something like a future-like-ours are the higher apes, and they come closest to being persons. And finally, what could justify active euthanasia except that the human *person* is either gone (comatose) or overwhelmed by excruciating pain?

Despite the fact that the Marquis thesis presupposes personhood, Marquis explicitly rejects the personhood criterion when he says that those who accept the personhood criteria are "left with the problem of explaining why *psychological* characteristics should make a *moral* difference." Insofar as this is offered as an argument it commits the *ad ignorantiam* fallacy. One is tempted, therefore, to offer the *ad hominem* response that Marquis has exactly the same problem with regard to explaining why human futures are more important than other futures. But I will not base my case on fallacies. Rather, I will provide an explanation of why certain psychological characteristics make a moral difference.

It is a basic moral principle that harming sentient life requires justification. It is also an empirical fact that different kinds of harm can be done to various forms of sentient life depending on the nature of their consciousness. For example, you can cause a snake physical pain, but you cannot cause it psychological pain by insulting it. Persons can grasp and use many concepts that cannot be understood by nonpersons. Such concepts can generate attitudes and expectations that can be frustrated. Since such frustrations constitute an emotional harm, persons can be harmed in ways that nonpersons cannot. Some of these harms are the most serious that can be done to humans. Thus, what is special about human or person consciousness is that persons are capable of experiencing *conceptually based emotions*.

Conceptually based emotions are feeling states that can be experienced only if one is capable of understanding a variety of quite abstract concepts. Some examples of conceptually based emotions are the feelings of moral guilt, regret, indignation, hope, and pride. We can feel moral guilt only if we have a concept of moral wrong. We can feel indignant only if we have a concept of justice and fairness. We can feel hope only if we can foresee a variety of possible futures.

The conceptually based emotions are the basis of the demand that human beings be treated differently from other animals. For example, the desire to be an autonomous individual is a desire that can be had only by persons, and thus it is only persons whose autonomy can be violated. Also, there is nothing wrong with taking a cat's kittens away from her because, after a brief period, the cat will not and cannot miss the kittens. This is because she has no significant sense of self, nor does she have any prolonged memory of her kittens. If she were able to look forward to raising her kittens, to anticipate eventual grandkittens, and to feel a lifelong despair over the loss of her kittens, then to take her kittens from her would be immoral. But then she would be a person, a cat-person to be sure, but a person nonetheless.

Persons, and only persons, can conceptualize a distant future in which they are a participant. Only persons can anticipate and deliberately shape their own future. Only persons can desire and possess the freedom to shape their own self, their own life, their own future. Only persons can have their long-term plans frustrated by their untimely death. One aspect of the seriousness of death for a person is the loss of an anticipated, intended, longed-for future. No non-person can be harmed in this way. It is the loss of this sort of a future that constitutes a common—but not a universal—harm arising from death. Thus, the harm constituted by the loss of *our* future presupposes that we are persons. This, in brief, is the explanation of why psychological states have moral importance.

But, for a person, what is an even more serious loss than the loss of a possible future is the loss of the actual, existent person. It is this immediate loss of personhood which constitutes the basic harm in killing. It is this loss that makes the murder of persons even on their deathbeds a serious harm. One

more minute of being a living person is of great value—even if that minute is an innocuous one—and taking that minute is a great harm. The loss of a future increases the harm of a killing, but the primary harm of a killing is the loss of the life of the person. This is a serious harm even when the person has no future.

It might be replied that even if one's future amounts to no more than one more minute, it is nevertheless the loss of that minute, and not the loss of personhood, that constitutes the harm. This reply is certainly plausible, but it gets its plausibility from confusing two distinct harms that result from murder: the loss of one's personhood and the loss of one's future. If, as the reply suggests, the loss of one's future is the only harm, then the badness of the murder under discussion would arise from the harm done by the loss of the last minute of life. But surely, the difference between a life of—say—89 years and a life of 89 years and one minute, given that the minute is an innocuous one, is not sufficient to account for the serious wrongness of a deathbed murder.

Were we to derive the wrongness of a murder solely from the loss of one's future, the degree of wrongness would vary inversely with life expectancy. Murdering the elderly would be less wrong than murdering the young. While such a consequence might be appealing to some, it goes against legal practice and, I believe, it goes against moral intuition. Thus, if all murders, *qua* murder, are equally bad, it is the loss of personhood that accounts for the intrinsic wrongness of murder, and it is the failure to recognize this that constitutes the basic error involved in Marquis's deprivation thesis. However, this error is both understandable and alluring.

Having a future-like-ours and being a person are conceptually independent but empirically related properties. All persons, insofar as they retain their personhood, have a future-like-ours. Thus, whenever a person is killed, there is the simultaneous destruction of a future-like-ours. This empirical entwining of personhood and having a future-like-ours makes it difficult to ascertain whether it is the loss of personhood, the loss of a future-like-ours, or the loss of both that constitutes the definitive harm done by the killing of a person.

However, consider a situation where, because of limited resources, one must choose between saving the life of a 9-year-old and saving the life of an 89-year-old. The differences in their expected futures (as well as their pasts) is surely relevant with regard to who should be saved. Surely one ought to save the child. This indicates that the value of a future-like-ours can vary in degree, one parameter being the expected length of the specific future-like-ours. It is this that makes premature death sadder than death at the end of a normal life-span.

Contrast the difference between premature and "normal" death with the difference between the murders of a 9-year-old and an 89-year-old. It is *not* the case that one murder is less wrong than the other. Both are equally wrong *qua* murder. The murders are equally wrong even though the murder of the 9-year-old causes a greater loss of a future-like-ours than does the murder of an 89-year-old. The degree of loss, the degree of harm, is not relevant to the wrongness of the murder per se. Rather, it is the destruction of personhood that makes all murders, *qua* murder, equally wrong.

Given that we can detach the harm of the loss of personhood from the harm of the loss of a future-like-ours, we can now consider the importance of the loss of a future-like-ours when the entity undergoing the loss has not attained personhood.

Imagine that a kitten is injected with a serum that will have no significant effect on the kitten for nine months but that will, after nine months, instantaneously cause the kitten to become a person and hence, to have both a present and a future-like-ours. Suppose further that an antidote to the serum is available. Would it be morally permissible to give the antidote before the kitten becomes a person? More important, would there be any moral difference between giving the antidote before the kitten becomes a person and giving the antidote after the kitten becomes a person (assuming that the antidote will then return the kitten to a normal cat state)? Giving the antidote before the acquisition of personhood changes the biological state of the kitten, but giving the antidote after the acquisition of personhood destroys an existing person. Marquis, presumably, would have to conclude that the antidote should never be given. I, on the other hand, believe that the antidote could be given before the kitten becomes a person, but not after.

Perhaps this difference merely reduces to a difference in intuitions, but I think not. It is appropriate to ask what underlies the different intuitions. Marquis and I agree that—for normal adult humans—the loss of a future-like-ours is a tragic loss. But—for normal adult humans—such a loss is simultaneous with the loss of personhood. That is, it is the simultaneous loss of personhood that underlies the tragedy of the loss of a future.

Insofar as this is correct, and insofar as killing a dying patient against their conscious will is wrong, having a future-like-ours is not a necessary condition for having a right to life. Furthermore, insofar as giving our hypothetical kitten the antidote before it becomes a person is morally permissible, having a future-like-ours is not a sufficient condition for having a right to life. What is a sufficient condition for having a right to life is *being* a person. What is wrong with killing us is not the destruction of a future but the destruction of a person.

Marquis recognizes this possibility and he discusses it under the rubric of the "discontinuation account" of the wrongness of killing. This account, he says, seems just as intelligible as the value of a future-like-ours account, but, since it does not justify an anti-abortion position, Marquis feels compelled to argue against it. His argument is as follows:

> The discontinuation account will not be adequate at all, if it does not refer to the *value of* the experience that may be discontinued. One does not want the discontinuation account to make it wrong to kill a patient who begs for death and who is in severe pain that cannot be relieved short of killing. . . . If the patient's future is a future of value, we want our account to make it wrong to kill the patient. If the patient's future is intolerable, whatever his or her immediate past, we want our account to allow killing the patient. Obviously, then, it is the value of that patient's future that is doing the work

in rendering the morality of killing the patient intelligible.

This being the case, it seems clear that whether one has immediate past experiences or not does no work in the explanation of what makes killing wrong. The addition the discontinuation account makes to the value of a human future account is otiose. Its addition to the value-of-a-future account plays no role at all in rendering intelligible the wrongness of killing. [197]

Contrary to Marquis, what the discontinuation account is asserting is that the immediate existence of a person has great value. It is significant that in his purported refutation of this account Marquis refers to both the past and future of a person, but says absolutely nothing about the value of the instantaneous present. Thus he says: "If the patient's future is intolerable, whatever his or her immediate past, we want our account to allow killing the patient." But this is surely a mistake. Even if one is faced with a future life of intolerable pain, one ought not be killed *now*. If possible, euthanasia should be postponed until one's life *is* intolerable. Ideally, euthanasia should not be performed merely because one's life will become intolerable in the future.

In summary, Marquis's deprivation thesis acquires some initial plausibility because a full explanation of all the harms involved in a killing usually must refer to the future, for the loss of a future is *usually* part of the harm. But even if one has no (significant) future, killing one is still wrong. It is the immediate death of a person, the immediate snuffing out of personhood, that constitutes the evil of killing. The loss of a valuable future, when it accompanies the loss of personhood, is a significant *additional* loss. But it is not the loss of the future that is crucial vis-à-vis the killing. What is crucial is the loss of personhood.

The personhood account of the wrongness of killing, explicated by the concept of the conceptually based emotions, can explain the wrongness of killing, including the killing of persons who have no significant future. It is therefore superior to the future-like-ours account. However, the personhood account is still vulnerable to Marquis's claim that it cannot adequately account for the right to life of neonates. This is so, he argues, because neonates are not persons and hence would have no right to life.

Marquis's argument is unsound. His argument rests on the false assumption that a neonatal right to life must arise from the same source that generates an adult right to life. But there are many types of right. Human, or more accurately *person* rights are those rights that each person has by virtue of being a person. Social rights are those rights that are fundamental to the well functioning of a morally acceptable society. The right to life (of persons) is a human or person right. The right to—say—property is a social right. Both types of rights can be important enough to justify sacrificing one's life in their defense.

All persons have a right to life as a result of being persons. But other entities might also have a right to life, a social right to life. Indeed, I shall argue that neonates should have a social right to life. This is not a right that springs *de novo* into existence. It is rather a right that grows out of a specific fetal right, the right to care (to be cared for).

The recognition that the right to care is an increasing, dynamic right makes possible a rational defense of the widespread intuition that late abortions require more justification than early abortions. In addition, the right to care accounts for and is compatible with the equally widespread intuition that some moral significance should be attributed to conception since it is at conception that each of us as a unique biological entity first came into being.

The right to care has four sources that can be divided into two groups: those *intrinsic* to the developing entity and those that relate the entity to others, the *relational* sources. The intrinsic sources are genetic humanness and potentiality of personhood. The relational sources are both the degree to which the fetus is cared about and whether or not a decision has been made to allow it to develop.

Genetic humanness is instantaneously present at conception, and the potentiality for personhood (for normal fetuses) is generated at conception also. This is what underlies the intuition that conception is a morally significant point. Nevertheless, conception is not sufficient to generate a right to life. Conception is the beginning of a biological entity that, after extensive development, may result in the beginnings of a person, but the beginning of personhood is better thought of as occurring when sentience begins and not with mere biological existence.

The concept of brain death is relevant to this point. Brain death clearly indicates that mere genetic humanness does not generate a right to life. Indeed, biologically alive genetic human beings are humanly dead if lacking the possibility of consciousness. Brain dead individuals are biologically living human organisms, but since they permanently lack consciousness they are not living *persons*. They are biological living organisms that, because they have been persons, are now dead people.

Of course the brain dead not only lack consciousness, they also lack the potential for consciousness and, hence, are crucially different from fetuses. It is the fact that most human fetuses are potential persons that generates a minimal right to care at conception. This right is generated as follows: First, we are human and, hence, have both a right and an obligation to treat human entities in a special way even if those entities are not persons. In a sense this is species bias, but if it is thought of on the analogy of a family—the human family—it is quite plausible. If the right to care is kept within legitimate bounds, the species bias that underlies it is quite reasonable. We may legitimately treat the members of our own family in special ways so long as our doing so does not violate the rights of other entities. Family members have claims on one another that others do not. So too with the human family. Exactly what claims our family members have on us, and what responsibilities we have toward them, is a subject for another paper. Nevertheless, if human beings exist whose conceptual abilities are no more than those of a cat, we should not treat them just as we treat cats. They are one of ours, and on that basis we may and ought to treat them as one of ours. We ought to care for them.

The role of *potentiality,* though significant, is minimal. It is significant enough so that the loss of the entity is at least unfortunate, but since a potential person is not a person, its loss is not equivalent to the loss of a person. The loss of an early fetus is less sad than the loss of a more developed fetus because more of the potential becomes actualized as time passes. But at no stage is the fetus a person, and hence its loss is never the equivalent of the loss of a person. The two intrinsic properties of fetuses, therefore, generate a minimal right to care. This right can be strengthened by the relational properties of the fetus.

This first relational property is that of being cared about. Reflection dispels any doubt that merely caring about something can give it value. If we think of a family heirloom we can recognize that the objective value of the heirloom can be quite small compared with the subjective value family members attach to it. This difference in value does not mean that the family members do not know the heirloom's objective value. Its value to the family, however, grows out of the history of the object, a history that they as family members share. This subjective value transcends the mere objective value of the object.

A conceptus, like an heirloom, can acquire a great deal of relational value depending on the response to it by others, primarily its biological progenitors. If the biological progenitors want to have a child the relational value of the fetus can be enormous. Yet this relational value is contingent on the attitude of the biological progenitors. If the pregnancy is not wanted, then the conceptus gains no relational value from this source.

The second source of relational value is possible only in situations where abortions are legally permissible. In such cases, the continuation of a pregnancy is a matter of choice and the decision to continue the pregnancy increases the responsibility of the woman and thereby increases the right to care of the fetus. If a woman decides to continue her pregnancy even though she does not really want a child, that decision nevertheless increases her responsibility towards the fetus. If she decides to continue the pregnancy, the fetus will (most likely) become a person. Hence the woman's support for the continuation of the pregnancy increases the fetal right to care since the well-being of the person-to-be depends on the care given to the fetus. If you allow a process that will result in a person to continue, you acquire some responsibility toward that future person and, hence, for the fetus which will become that person. The woman's decision to continue the pregnancy gives the fetus an additional degree of the right to care. She cannot morally continue the pregnancy and neglect the fetus. If she decides to remain pregnant, she has an obligation to take care of herself for the good of the fetus, and the fetus has a right to such care.

The right to care increases throughout the pregnancy because the woman's voluntary assumption of responsibility increases the longer she continues the pregnancy and the potentiality of the fetus becomes more actualized. Thus late term abortions are justifiable only to prevent the death of or serious harm to the woman. Since this final "threat" ends with birth, the neonate has a full (social) right to life.

In conclusion, personhood is the primary source of the right to life. Until a human passes through the fetal and neonatal stages and develops personhood its rights depend on the other four sources of rights. Those sources generate a range of rights beginning with a minimal and easily defeasible right to care during the early stages of the pregnancy, through an increasingly significant right to care, and culminating in a full social right to life for neonates.

NOTE

1. [Don Marquis, "Why Abortion Is Immoral," *Journal of Philosophy,* 86, no. 4 (April 1989): 183–202.]

Killing, Abortion, and Contraception

Alastair Norcross

A Reply to Marquis

Don Marquis, in "Why Abortion Is Immoral,"[1] argues that "abortion is, except possibly in rare cases, seriously immoral, that it is in the same moral category as killing an innocent human being" (183). His argument for this is that abortions share with killings the central feature that makes them wrong. "Killing someone is wrong, primarily because the killing inflicts (one of) the greatest possible losses on the victim . . . the loss . . . of all those activities, projects, experiences, and enjoyment which would otherwise have constituted [the victim's] future personal life" (189). Marquis argues that, since fetuses have futures that include a set of "experiences, projects, activities and such which are identical with the futures of adult human beings," it follows that abortion is "prima facie seriously morally wrong" (192). Marquis answers several possible objections to his account. In this paper, I shall discuss the one objection to which his answer is clearly inadequate. I shall claim not only that his answer is inadequate, but that an adequate answer is not available to him, and thus that his account fails to support the claim that the overwhelming majority of abortions are seriously immoral.

I

Marquis admits that, if his account of the wrongness of killing and of abortion entails that contraception is also seriously immoral, "then there would appear to be a difficulty with the analysis of [the] essay" (201). He claims that his analysis would entail that contraception is wrong "only if something were denied a

Alastair Norcross, "Killing, Abortion, and Contraception: A Reply to Marquis," *Journal of Philosophy* 87, no. 5 (1990): 268–77. Reprinted by permission of the Journal of Philosophy.

human future of value by contraception. Nothing at all is denied such a future by contraception, however" (201). Marquis considers and rejects four candidates for the role of subject of harm by contraception: (1) some sperm or other, (2) some ovum or other, (3) a sperm and an ovum separately, (4) a sperm and an ovum together. I shall concentrate on his treatment of (4), since I think it is clearly the most promising candidate.

Marquis offers the following argument in response to the suggestion that contraception deprives the combination of sperm and ovum of a valuable future-like-ours:

> At the time of contraception, there are hundreds of millions of sperm, one (released) ovum and millions of possible combinations of all of these. There is no actual combination at all. Is the subject of the loss to be a merely possible combination? Which one? This alternative does not yield an actual subject of harm either. Accordingly, the immorality of contraception is not entailed by the loss of a future-like-ours argument simply because there is no nonarbitrarily identifiable subject of the loss in the case of contraception. (202)

I do not think it is clear from this passage what Marquis is claiming. It is all we get by way of argument against candidate (4), however, so we will have to work with it. I take it that Marquis does not mean that we could never tell which combination of sperm and ovum is the subject of loss in the case of successful contraception. I do not see how such an epistemic difficulty could rescue contraception from the charge of wrongdoing that Marquis's account levels against abortion. Consider the following two scenarios: (i) London is struck by a series of freak accidents involving power plants, which result in the deaths of almost everyone within a twenty-mile radius of Whitehall. The Prime Minister, Mrs. Butcher, is informed that there are a handful of survivors. She orders the army to round up the survivors, make a record of their names, and kill them. (ii) In response to the same information as in the previous example, Mrs. Butcher orders a hydrogen bomb to be detonated in London, thereby eliminating the possibility of discovering who survived the

initial accidents. I hope it is clear that at least part of what is morally wrong with Mrs. Butcher's actions in each case is that some people are killed who would otherwise have lived. It makes no difference that in case (ii) it is impossible to tell which people were killed by the nuclear explosion.

It might be objected that contraception differs crucially from my example (ii) in that one cannot say of every use of contraception that it prevents conception. In most cases pregnancy would not have resulted anyway. One response to this would be to modify (ii) so that Mrs. Butcher is only told that there is a small but significant possibility that there are survivors. More importantly, though, I think it would be small comfort to the proponent of the moral acceptability of contraception to be told that contraception is morally permissible in all those cases in which it does not actually prevent conception. The intuition that contraception is morally permissible is the intuition that it is permissible even, or perhaps especially, in those cases in which it fulfills its purpose.

Perhaps Marquis is not simply making an epistemic claim when he says that there is no nonarbitrarily identifiable subject of loss in the case of contraception. When he says that there are millions of possible combinations of sperm and ovum, but no actual combination, perhaps he means that there is no fact of the matter as to which sperm, if any, would have fertilized the ovum. It may be that the behavior of sperm is not strictly deterministic. Does this distinguish contraception from abortion and killing?

Consider the following scenario: two prisoners of conscience, Smith and Jones, are slated for execution in a small totalitarian republic. The president, Shrub, troubled by the effect of an Amnesty International campaign on his public image, decides to spare one of the prisoners. He cannot make up his mind whose life to spare, so he devises the following apparatus: Smith and Jones are placed in separate cells, each with air vents leading to a cannister of poison gas, which is set to release its contents at noon. A computer is programmed to select a three-digit number at random at one second before noon. If the number is even or zero, the computer will close the air vent in Smith's cell; if the number is odd, the computer will close the air vent in Jones's cell. The random-number selection process is truly indeterministic. The vice-president of the republic, Fowl, does not approve of Shrub bowing to liberal pressure. Fowl unplugs the computer at one minute before noon. The gas is released at noon, and both Smith and Jones die. I hope it is clear that Fowl has done something bad in this example. Two people have died instead of one. It is also clear that there is no fact of the matter as to which prisoner has been deprived of a valuable future by Fowl's actions. I do not think that the moral status of Fowl's action would change if the number of condemned prisoners was increased, but the number to be saved was kept at one. Even if Fowl's action makes it the case that a million and one die, instead of a million, he would have been responsible for the occurrence of one more death than would otherwise have occurred. In both of these cases, it seems that there is no nonarbitrarily identifiable subject of the loss of a valuable future. In both of these cases, Fowl's action is morally on a par with killing one person.

Let us return to the two-person case. We might still want to say that Fowl has harmed both Smith and Jones. We might say that the harm consists in lowering, from fifty percent to zero, their chances of surviving. (Indeed, given uncertainty about the length and quality of anyone's life, we should probably give a similar account of the harm involved in killing anyone.) If we increase the numbers, we can still say that Fowl has harmed all the prisoners. In the case of a million and one prisoners, Fowl has reduced each of their chances of survival from just under one ten thousandth of one percent to zero. However we describe the immorality of Fowl's action, it is clear that what he does is wrong for precisely the same reason as a standard killing is wrong. Either Fowl harms all the prisoners, or the lack of a nonarbitrarily identifiable subject of loss does not provide a morally relevant distinction between this case and a standard case of killing.

The similarities between contraception and the example discussed above are clear in terms of the loss of a valuable future. Either contraception harms all the combinations of sperm and ovum, or the lack of a nonarbitrarily identifiable subject of loss does

not provide a morally relevant distinction between contraception and abortion.

II

It might be claimed that there is a significant difference between the case of contraception and my poison-gas examples. In the poison-gas example, all the candidates for subject of the loss of a valuable future were things, people, in fact. In the case of contraception, the candidates I have been considering—combinations of sperm and ovum—are nonstarters, not because there is no nonarbitrarily identifiable subject of loss, but because a combination of sperm and ovum cannot be a subject of anything, because "it" is not a thing.[2] I do not know whether Marquis would be prepared to make this claim, but it is worth considering on its own merits.

It might be instructive at this point to consider what could be meant by "a combination of sperm and ovum." What has to be the case for such a thing to exist? It might be natural to assume that, for such a thing to exist, a sperm and an ovum would have to be combined. What would have to be the case for a sperm and ovum to be combined? Perhaps a sperm and an ovum would have had to have joined to form a zygote. Marquis might be taken to be espousing this reading of "a combination of sperm and ovum" when he claims that there is no actual combination at the time of contraception. If this is his position, then he is, of course, right to say that there is no actual combination at the time of contraception (in the case of those forms of contraception which prevent a zygote from being formed, that is; it is an interesting question what Marquis would say about those forms of contraception which prevent the zygote from developing). If this is his position, though, why should we agree that his four categories of candidates for subject of harm are exhaustive? Why can we not say that the subject of harm is the mereological sum of a sperm and an ovum? Indeed, this is what I understand "a combination of sperm and ovum" to mean. So what is the response to the claim that a combination of sperm and ovum, understood as a mereological sum, is not a thing?

Perhaps the most obvious answer to the charge that a combination of sperm and ovum is not a thing is simply to deny it. I am inclined to pursue this option. To the extent that I am prepared to admit that a zygote or a fetus is a thing, I would claim that a combination of sperm and ovum is also a thing.

Let us assume, for the sake of argument, that a combination of a sperm and an ovum is not a thing. In that case, either the sperm and ovum, taken separately, *are* things, or neither is (I cannot imagine a plausible metaphysic that would classify one as a thing, but not the other). Consider the former alternative first. If both the sperm and the ovum are things, but the combination of the two is not, why can we not say that contraception harms both, because it deprives each one of the valuable future it would have had as a result of causal interaction with the other? This would appear to be Marquis's candidate (3), "a sperm and an ovum separately." Marquis rejects (3), because, "on this alternative, too many futures are lost. Contraception was supposed to be wrong, because it deprived us of one future of value, not two" (201). The obvious reply to this is that, on the assumption that a sperm and an ovum are both things, there *is* only one future lost as a result of contraception. It is the *same* future for both the sperm and the ovum. It is a shared future. Consider the possibility of human fusion. Imagine that it is possible for two people to fuse physically, so that a single person results, who has, among other things, some of the memories of both of the original people.[3] Imagine further that two people, Smith and Jones, will die, if they do not fuse with each other. Hector, an enemy of both Smith and Jones, knows of their predicament and of their plan to fuse. He locks them in adjoining rooms and waits until their anguished cries die out before gloating over their dead bodies. Given that Smith and Jones would have fused, if Hector had not locked the connecting door, it seems that Hector has deprived both Smith and Jones of a valuable future—the same valuable future. It might be objected that Hector has not deprived Smith and Jones of a valuable future, because they would have ceased to exist after they had fused, and a third person would have come into existence.[4] In this case, Hector has simply prevented the existence of something with a valuable future. I do not think that such a distinction could possibly ground a judgment that Hector has not behaved at least as badly as if he had killed one person, who would otherwise have lived. However we describe Hector's action, it is clear that what he has done is morally on a par with killing. Could anyone honestly insist that it would be permissible for Hector to shoot Smith and Jones as they are running toward each other, about to fuse, but impermissible for him to shoot the person who results from the fusion a few seconds later?

III

The case of contraception, it might be argued, differs from my fusion example, because the sperm and the ovum are not things themselves. Before conception, goes the claim, there is just some stuff—fundamental particles or metaphysical simples or whatever—arranged in such a way that we are inclined to say that there is a sperm and an ovum. At conception, or thereabouts, all this stuff interacts in such a way that a thing comes into existence. This may seem like a drowning metaphysician clutching at straws, but I do not think that this, even if it is a good account of what there is, will ground a moral distinction between contraception and abortion.

Let us say, what is perhaps natural, that, in order to deprive something of a valuable future, that thing must at some time exist. So let us define an intransitive verb, "to deprave" (not to be confused with the transitive verb "to deprave"): to deprave is to act in such a way that some stuff, which would otherwise have interacted in such a way that a thing with a valuable future would have resulted, does not so interact. There would seem to be pairs of cases of contraception and abortion such that the contraception is a case of depraving, and the abortion is a case of depriving something of a valuable future. Some pairs of a depraving and a depriving differ only in that the hostile environment created by the contraceptive/abortifacient has the desired effect on the stuff before a thing comes into existence, in the case of the depraving, but on the thing after it has come into existence, in the case of the depriving. If there is a moral difference between a depraving and a depriving, it must be grounded in the fact that there is just some stuff that would otherwise have resulted in the existence of a thing, in the case of a depraving, but there actually *is* a thing, in the case of a depriving.

If we are to defend Marquis's position on the morality of abortion and contraception by appealing to the distinction between depriving and depraving, we must investigate further the category of "thing," which is at the heart of the distinction. It might be instructive to remind ourselves of Marquis's treatment of the anti-abortionist's attempt to base an argument on the category "human being":

> If "human being" is taken to be a biological category, then the anti-abortionist is left with the problem of explaining why a merely biological category should make a moral difference. Why, it is asked, is it any more reasonable to base a moral conclusion on the number of chromosomes in one's cells than on the color of one's skin? If "human being," on the other hand, is taken to be a moral category, then the claim that the fetus is a human being cannot be taken to be a premise in the anti-abortion argument, for it is precisely what needs to be established. (186)

A similar argument can be used against an attempt to distinguish morally between contraception and abortion by appealing to the category "thing." Consider a case of depraving and a case of depriving something of a valuable future, which differ as little as is consistent with the former being definitely a case of depraving and the latter being definitely a case of depriving (the category of "thing" might have vague boundaries). In each case, there is some stuff that is affected by the contraceptive/abortifacient. In the latter case, but not in the former, there is also a thing that is the result of the interaction of the stuff. How might we establish that there is a thing in the latter case, but not in the former? If Marquis's position is to be defended, whatever makes the difference between thing and nothing must be definable without help from moral judgments on abortion and contraception, because those judgments are supposed to arise out of the difference between thing and no-thing. The most likely option would be to appeal to biological facts about the arrangement and interac-

tion of the stuff in each case. But if our explanation of the difference between thing and no-thing depends simply on biological facts, it seems that we will still have to argue that the difference between a depraving and a depriving is morally significant.

IV

Marquis might object at this point that he does not have to argue that the difference between a depriving and a depraving is morally significant, because it is just obvious that there is a morally important difference between depriving a thing of its potentialities and preventing it from coming about that there is a thing with potentialities. It is difficult to know what to say to this, except to point out that it is far from obvious to me. Perhaps we could point out that a similar line of defense could be used by the pro-abortionists who argue that fetuses (at least in the early stages) cannot be victims. It is just obvious, we might claim, that an early fetus cannot be a victim, because it lacks sentience. Alternatively, we might claim that it is just obvious that there is a morally significant difference between depriving a sentient victim of a valuable future, on the one hand, and depriving a presentient victim of a valuable future, on the other. Of course, we might also claim that it is obvious that there is a morally significant difference between depriving something that has not been born yet of a valuable future and depriving something that has been born of a similar future. We might disagree with Marquis's claim that the central wrong-making feature of a killing is that it deprives something of a valuable future. On the one hand, we might claim instead that the central wrong-making feature of a killing is that it deprives a certain specified sort of something of a valuable future. On the other hand, we might claim that the central wrong-making feature of a killing is what a depriving and a depraving have in common. I have tried to show that the distinction between thing and no-thing is no more morally significant than the distinction between sentient thing and presentient thing. Of course, one can always claim that a particular intuition is just rock-bottom. But if that is Marquis's claim about the distinction between thing and no-thing, then I would claim that he has given no arguments against abortion that would appeal to any of those who do not share his intuitions. My argument is not, however, that we should simply pick whichever distinction we feel most strongly about, and then base our position around that; at least not with respect to the question of what is bad about depriving something of a valuable future. I would claim that a consideration of the various distinctions—between postnatal and prenatal thing, between sentient and presentient thing, between thing and no-thing—should lead us to reject the claim that any of them makes a moral difference with respect to what is bad about depriving something of a valuable future (and, of course, what is bad about preventing it from coming about that there is a thing with a valuable future).

V

Another approach to the question of whether we should imbue the distinction between thing and nothing with moral significance would be to ask why it is bad to deprive something of a valuable future. As far as I can see, there are two broad approaches that can be taken to answer this question (other than simply insisting that it *is* bad). On the one hand, we could claim that it is bad to deprive something of a valuable future, because it is bad, other things being equal, to prevent the occurrence of the valuable experiences and the like that constitute a valuable future. I hope it is clear why this approach will militate against drawing a morally significant line between depraving and depriving. On the other hand, we could claim that it is bad to deprive something of a valuable future, because the victim is, in some sense, entitled to her valuable future. We might say that she has a right to her valuable future. This would seem to allow us to draw a line between depraving and depriving. Depriving something of a valuable future violates certain rights of that thing. A depraving, on the other hand, involves no violations of rights, because there is no victim. The right to life, though, is far from unproblematic. Why does anything have a right to a valuable future, as opposed to, say, a very bad future, or no future at all? Why does

this fetus have a right to the future that would ensue if I do not perform the abortion, rather than the future that would ensue if I do?[5] We cannot answer that question with an appeal to the supposed immorality of performing an abortion, since it is that very immorality that we are seeking to establish by appeal to the right to a valuable future. How, in general, can we explain why something has a right to the good aspects of its future, but not to the bad ones? Perhaps we could appeal to the goodness of such good aspects obtaining (goodness, that is, that is not dependent on the claim that the possessor of such a future has a right to those good aspects). If my right to a valuable future is grounded in the value of the occurrence of those experiences and the like that constitute such a future, however, the very same grounding will apply to the immorality of a depraving.

Perhaps it could be argued that my right to a certain sort of future is not restricted to a valuable future. In fact, I have a right to all the unpleasantness that might be in my future, too. It is a common feature of rights that they can be waived, and so I am taken to have waived my rights to the unpleasant aspects of my future. Thus, it is not true to say of a doctor, who has deprived me of much pain and suffering, that she has violated my rights. If we take this line, it is very hard to see what is being claimed as the content of something's right to a future. If my right is not restricted to valuable aspects of my future, just what do I have a right to? I presume the claim is not that I have a right to my *actual* future, because, if that were the case, no actual behavior that affected me could violate such a right. Perhaps the content of my right varies, according to the situation I am in. Perhaps, in general, I have a right to whatever future would ensue, if the agent who might act so as to affect me does not so act. But this clearly will not do. If an agent's action will affect me, then his not performing the action will also affect me, since my future will be different from how it would otherwise have been.

Perhaps we will have to postulate a distinction between *doing* and *allowing,* and claim that I have a right to the future that would have ensued, if the agent had not done the thing in question. Quite apart from the difficulty of drawing a distinction between doing and allowing (or anything remotely resembling such a distinction), and the much greater difficulty, if not impossibility, of establishing that such a distinction can bear any moral weight, this distinction does not accord with our normal intuitions about rights. Any version of the doing/allowing distinction will have to place the neglect of a newborn baby, so that it starves to death, on the side of allowing. But it would be a strange position indeed that condemned abortion as the violation of the fetus's right to a valuable future, but did not render the same judgment about allowing a new-born to starve to death. Perhaps Marquis could claim that a thing that might have a valuable future just does have a right to a valuable future, and that is all there is to it. I would claim that, if we are disinclined to accept such a right as a basic intuition and seek some grounding for the right, we will have a hard time finding grounding for such a right which will not also ground the immorality of contraception.

VI

I have attempted to give reasons why we should be, at the very least, uncomfortable with allowing moral weight to the distinction between thing and no-thing, and thus the distinction between abortion and contraception. Lest I be taken to be arguing against contraception (and, indeed, sexual abstinence), I should add that I do not consider the deprivation of a valuable future to be the only, or even the central, wrong-making feature of a standard killing. Thus, although what is bad about depriving someone of a valuable future is shared by abortion, regular use of contraception, and sexual abstinence, there are many morally significant factors that distinguish standard killings from abortions, and abortions from contraception. But they are the subject of another paper.[6]

I have argued in this paper that Marquis fails to distinguish morally between contraception and abortion. I have also argued that an attempt to distinguish between contraception and abortion by appeal to a parsimonious ontology does not provide a morally relevant distinction. I conclude that Marquis is unable to distinguish morally between contraception and abortion without appealing to morally relevant features other than what he calls the "wrong-making feature of one's being killed." I conjecture that any appeal to morally relevant features sufficient to ground a moral distinction between abortion and contraception will also ground a moral distinction between abortion and standard cases of killing.

NOTES

1. Don Marquis, "Why Abortion Is Immoral," *Journal of Philosophy* LXXXVI, 4 (April 1989): 183–202.

2. This argument was suggested to me by Frances Howard.

3. It might be objected that one cannot have a memory of, say, doing *x*, if one did not, oneself, do *x*. So, to say that the resulting person has some of the memories of both original persons might entail that the resulting person *is* both original persons. My argument does not require any such claim, so it is acceptable to modify the story so that it is merely claimed that the resulting person *seems* to have some of the memories of both original persons.

4. It is important to note that, for Marquis, the central wrong-making feature of killing is that it deprives the victim of those valuable experiences which she would otherwise have had. A killing of someone who was about to die is not, therefore, morally bad, or at least does not share the central wrong-making feature of killings of people who would otherwise have lived long happy lives.

5. It might sound strange to talk of the future that would ensue for the fetus if I perform an abortion. The fetus, it would seem, will have no future if I perform an abortion. I think it is clear, however, that the option of nonexistence for a fetus, or an adult human being, can be compared with other possible futures. It is also clear that nonexistence is preferable to some futures, futures filled with unmitigated pain and misery, for example. If we ask what sort of a future a fetus (or any other being) has a right to, it would be strange to exclude nonexistence from the options being considered.

6. Although I do not wish to wade into this topic here, I shall say that I consider the main weakness of Marquis's account of the wrongness of a standard killing to be that it does not take into consideration the full range of consequences of such an act.

Does a Fetus Already Have a Future-Like-Ours?

Peter K. McInerney

Some of the most interesting and underexplored issues in philosophy are those of how human beings are in time. A person's relationship to her future is very complex, particularly if time passes, as we commonsensically believe that it does. In "Why Abortion Is Immoral," Don Marquis[1] argues that what makes killing a person wrong is that it deprives the person of her future. He concludes that abortion is wrong because it deprives the fetus of a "future-like-ours." The line of argument is clear.

> The future of a standard fetus includes a set of experiences, projects, activities, and such which are identical with the futures of adult human beings and are identical with the futures of young children. Since the reason that is sufficient to explain why it is wrong to kill human beings after the time of birth is a reason that also applies to fetuses, it follows that abortion is prima facie seriously morally wrong. (192)

The unexamined premise in the argument is that a fetus *already* has a future-like-ours of which it can be deprived.[2] For the argument to be convincing, it is necessary that a fetus *at its time* "possess" or be related to a future-like-ours in a way that allows the transfer from the wrongness of killing us persons to the wrongness of killing fetuses.

Fetuses are very different from normal adult humans. The connections between a fetus at an earlier time and a person (or person stage) at a significantly later time are very different from the connections between the person stages at different times which compose one person. Philosophical investigations of personal identity through time have revealed the complexity of the biological and psychological connections between the earlier and later stages of one person. These significant differences invalidate the claim that a fetus has a personal future in the same way that a normal adult human has a personal future.

The differences between a person's relationship to her future and a fetus's relationship to its future are striking even when the passage of time is ignored. In B-series time (a time that is composed entirely of earlier and later temporal locations with their occupants), an earlier person stage has many relations with later person stages which make these later person stages be "her future." The most widely considered relations in contemporary discussions of personal identity are those of memory, continuity of character, and intention-to-action.[3] Memory relations are from later person stages to earlier person stages. The later person stages are able to remember the experiences of the earlier person stages or there is an overlapping chain of such memory connections (memory continuity). The relation of continuity of character is that in which later person stages either have a character similar to the earlier person stages or are different in ways that are explicable by the operation of normal causes.[4] The relation of intention-to-action is that between an earlier intention and a later action that carries out that intention. Normal adult humans have all sorts of plans and projects for their short- and long-term futures which take time to implement.

There are other relations that connect earlier and later person stages. Some of the "mental processing" that ordinarily goes on in normal humans, such as forming generalizations from repeated observations

Peter K. McInerney, "Does a Fetus Already Have a Future-Like-Ours?" *Journal of Philosophy* 87, no. 5 (1990): 264–68. Reprinted by permission of the Journal of Philosophy.

or "digesting" an emotionally charged experience, takes a significant amount of time and so can be considered to include relations between person stages. In addition, there are all of the neurophysiological relations that underlie the ordinary continuation of mental life in persons. That a person has pretty much the same beliefs, wants, skills, and habits that she had 30 minutes (or 30 days) earlier depends upon a similarity of neurophysiological conditions between the earlier and later person stages.

Most of these relations to later person stages exist even when the earlier person is asleep or temporarily unconscious. Even intentions to perform later actions might be considered to continue through periods of unconsciousness. Since a temporarily unconscious person is still strongly related to her future, to kill her while she is unconscious is to deprive her of her future.

Young infants do not have all of the psychological complexity that adult persons have. Nevertheless, young infants are commonsensically understood to have perceptions, beliefs, desires, and emotions (whether or not the experimental data confirms this) and to learn from experience. For this reason, the neurophysiological states and processes of young infants can be understood to underlie something like the ordinary continuation of mental life in persons. A good case can be made that young infants are related in some (though not all) ways to a personal future.

The situation of a fetus at an early stage of development is very different.[5] A fetus at an early stage of development has neither a mental life of feelings, beliefs, and desires nor a developed brain and nervous system. There are none of the main relations with a personal future which exist in persons. Although there is some biological continuity between them so that there is a sense in which the later person stages "are the future" of the fetus, the fetus is so little connected to the later personal life that it can not be deprived of that personal life. At its time the fetus does not already "possess" that future personal life in the way that a normal adult human already "possesses" his future personal life.

Our commonsense views about time and entities in time involve a past that is fixed and determinate, a future that includes alternative possibilities whose actualization may be affected by action, and a process of what is future becoming present and past. In a time of this sort, how an entity "has a future" is more complex because when some temporal part (stage) of the entity is present, there is not a fixed and fully determinate future to which that entity can now be related. With respect to persons, a present person stage is not now related to a specific determinate later person stage that will become present. A person's future includes a branching range of possibilities (including his death) from which only one life course can become present. The branching of possibilities is such that most outcomes can become present only if certain earlier possibilities have become present. The actualization of one possibility makes available those later possibilities which presuppose it. This is particularly pronounced for the acquisition of skills, abilities, and capacities, which open up new ranges of possibilities that would otherwise not be available.

Many factors external to the person affect which of the person's possibilities become present. A normal adult human has only limited control over which of his possibilities become present. This control which a person exercises and attempts to exercise over his future is the most important connection that now exists with a specifically personal future. This control also depends upon the person's wants, skills, abilities, and capacities. The person wants various things for his future (including wanting himself to act) and exercises his powers to affect what happens.

A fetus is separated from a personal future by many "layers" of possibility. The possibilities that are available to a person or even to a young infant are not now available to the fetus. Only if the fetus develops in the right ways (favorable possibilities become present) will it acquire the capacities that make available the infant's possibilities. A great deal of favorable development would be necessary before the fetus could control its future in the way that persons do. The fetus does not now have a personal future.

Marquis has succeeded in formulating an important feature of people's opposition to abortion: the notion that abortion "cuts off" the fetus's future. A close examination of what it is "to have a future" reveals that at its time a fetus does not have a personal future of which it can be deprived. A living human cell that might be stimulated to develop into a clone of a person does not now have a personal future. A fetus similarly has only the potentiality to develop a personal future. For this reason, killing a fetus is morally very different from killing a normal adult human.

NOTES

1. *Journal of Philosophy,* LXXXVI, 4 (April 1989): 183–202.

2. "Since a fetus possesses a property, the possession of which in adult human beings is sufficient to make killing an adult human being wrong, abortion is wrong" (202).

3. See Derek Parfit, *Reasons and Persons* (New York: Oxford, 1984), pp. 205–7.

4. See *Reasons and Persons,* p. 207, for a brief discussion of "normal causes."

5. As the fetus develops, it becomes more similar to a young infant, and so progressively acquires more of a relationship to a personal future.

Thomson and Her Critics

Marquis's argument is aimed at establishing what we referred to earlier as P1 of the standard argument against abortion, the claim that the fetus has the same right to life that you or I have. Let us now suppose that Marquis is correct about this. The claim that the fetus has this important right to life will serve to establish that abortion is impermissible only if what we referred to above as P2 of the standard argument is also accepted, the claim that if the fetus has this right to life, then abortion is morally impermissible. Most people on both sides of the abortion debate tend to assume that this is true. As a result, the debate over the morality of abortion tends to focus largely, if not exclusively, on the moral status of the fetus. But in her seminal 1971 article "A Defense of Abortion," Judith Jarvis Thomson argues that this widely accepted assumption is false. Even if the fetus is granted to be a person with the same right to life as any other human being, she argues, abortion is still morally permissible.

Thomson's article touches on a number of distinct points, but her argument is, at its core, what we refer to in the introduction to this volume as an argument from analogy (see section 4.1). Specifically, Thomson compares the situation of a woman burdened by an unwanted pregnancy to you in the following hypothetical scenario:

> You wake up in the morning and find yourself back to back in bed with an unconscious violinist. A famous unconscious violinist. He has been found to have a fatal kidney ailment, and the Society of Music Lovers has canvassed all the available medical records and found that you alone have the right blood type to help. They have therefore kidnapped you, and last night the violinist's circulatory system was plugged into yours, so that your kidneys can be used to extract poisons from his blood as well as your own. The director of the hospital now tells you, "Look, we're sorry the Society of Music Lovers did this to you—we would never have permitted it if we had known. But still, they did it, and the violinist is now plugged into you. To unplug you

would be to kill him. But never mind, it's only for nine months. By then he will have recovered from his ailment, and can safely be unplugged from you.

Thomson takes it that you will agree that, morally speaking, you have the right to unplug yourself from the famous unconscious violinist, even though this means that he will die. This is not because she thinks your right to control your body is more important than the violinist's right to life, although Thomson has often mistakenly been interpreted in this way. Rather, Thomson's central contention is that it would be permissible for you to unplug yourself in this situation because doing so would not violate the violinist's right to life in the first place. That is, he has a right to life, but he does not have a right to be kept alive. By unplugging yourself from the violinist, you refrain from making a considerable sacrifice in order to keep him alive, and on Thomson's account at least, this you are morally permitted to do. The crucial lesson of Thomson's violinist story, then, is that (according to her) the right to life does not include or entail the right to life support. But, Thomson then argues, if this is so in the case of the relationship between you and the violinist, why should it not also be true in the case of the relationship between a pregnant woman and the fetus she does not wish to carry to term? That is, even if we assume that the fetus has a right to life, Thomson claims that it does not have the right to be kept alive by the pregnant woman. And, if this is so, then abortion may prove to be morally permissible even if the fetus does have the same right to life as a typical adult human being. Put in the simple two-premise format, Thomson's argument in defense of abortion can be seen as follows:

P1   It is morally permissible for you to unplug yourself from the famous violinist.
P2   Unplugging yourself from the famous violinist is morally on a par with a woman aborting an unwanted pregnancy.

C   It is morally permissible for a woman to abort an unwanted pregnancy.

Although there is more to Thomson's article than this one analogy (readers should be particularly alert to the analogy involving a burglar coming into an open window), most of Thomson's critics have focused their responses on it. And since the vast majority of Thomson's readers seem to agree with her that you do have the moral right to unplug yourself from the violinist, virtually every critical response to Thomson's argument has turned on attempting to identify a morally relevant difference between the violinist scenario and the unwanted pregnancy scenario. Thomson's article has been called the most widely reprinted essay in contemporary philosophy, and it is certainly among the most widely discussed. The two response pieces that follow it in this anthology therefore, should be taken only as a representative sampling of the very large number of objections that have been raised against Thomson's argument. Readers are encouraged to consult some of the suggested further readings for still more objections worthy of discussion.

Baruch Brody's response piece, "Thomson on Abortion," is important for its clear and forceful statement of two potentially very powerful objections: that Thomson's argument neglects the importance of the distinction between killing someone and letting someone die, and the importance of the distinction between voluntary and involuntary actions. In both instances, Brody argues that the distinction in question can be used to undermine Thomson's analogy. Francis J. Beckwith's piece, "Arguments from Bodily Rights: A Critical Analysis," an excerpt of which follows Brody's, is valuable for the number and diversity of objections Beckwith is able to defend in a clear and concise manner. Beckwith raises too many points for us to summarize them here—readers are urged to work at seeing how many distinct criticisms Beckwith ultimately has to offer—but, at the very least, one should consider the force of his claims that Thomson's argument overlooks special obligations we can have to our own family members, and that it is in various ways inconsistent with a certain kind of feminist stance.

QUESTIONS FOR CONSIDERATION

In thinking about the various objections raised against Thomson's article in both of the critical-response pieces reprinted here, readers will find it useful to consider applying the technique of *variant cases* (see Introduction to this volume).

• For any particular disanalogy a critic of Thomson's offers, begin by considering why the difference is supposed to be *morally relevant*. Test the claim that the difference is relevant by modifying Thomson's violinist scenario so that it is more like the unwanted pregnancy scenario with respect to the particular factor identified by Thomson's critic. What happens, for example, if you have the violinist story involve a child or a relative? What difference, if any, does it make whether it is a killing or a letting-die, or a result of voluntary rather than involuntary behavior?

• When the violinist case is made to resemble an unwanted pregnancy case more closely, do you find that you now believe it would be impermissible to unplug yourself from the violinist? If so, this would tend to vindicate the position taken by Thomson's critics.

• Or do you, on the other hand, find that you still tend to think that you would be morally entitled to unplug yourself? If so, this would tend to vindicate the position taken by Thomson.

FURTHER READING

Boonin, David. *A Defense of Abortion.* Cambridge: Cambridge University Press, 2002, chap. 4.

Davis, Michael. "Foetuses, Famous Violinists and the Right to Continued Aid." *Philosophical Quarterly* 33 (1983): 259–78.

Finnis, John. "The Rights and Wrongs of Abortion: A Reply to Judith Thomson." *Philosophy and Public Affairs* 2 (1973): 117–45.

Fischer, John. "Abortion and Self-Determination." *Journal of Social Philosophy* 22, no. 2 (1991): 5–13.

Meyers, Christopher. "Maintaining the Violinist: A Mother's Obligations to the Fetus She Decides to Keep." *Journal of Social Philosophy* 23, no. 2, (1992): 52–64.

Pavlischek, Keith J. "Abortion Logic and Paternal Responsibility: One More Look at Judith Thomson's 'A Defense of Abortion.'" *Public Affairs Quarterly* 7, no. 4 (1993): 341–61.

Stone, Jim. "Abortion and the Control of Human Bodies." *Journal of Value—Inquiry* 17 (1983): 77–85.

Thomson, Judith. "Rights and Deaths." *Philosophy and Public Affairs* 2 (1973): 146–59.

Judith Jarvis Thomson | # A Defense of Abortion

Most opposition to abortion relies on the premise that the fetus is a human being, a person, from the moment of conception. The premise is argued for, but, as I think, not well. Take, for example, the most common argument. We are asked to notice that the development of a human being from conception through birth into childhood is continuous; then it is said that to draw a line, to choose a point in this development and say "before this point the thing is not a person, after this point it is a person" is to make an arbitrary choice, a choice for which in the nature of things no good reason can be given. It is concluded that the fetus is, or anyway that we had better say it is, a person from the moment of conception. But this conclusion does not follow. Similar things might be said about the development of an acorn into an oak tree, and it does not follow that acorns are oak trees, or that we had better say they are. Arguments of this form are sometimes called "slippery slope arguments"—the phrase is perhaps self-explanatory—and it is dismaying that opponents of abortion rely on them so heavily and uncritically.

I am inclined to agree, however, that the prospects for "drawing a line" in the development of the fetus look dim. I am inclined to think also that we shall probably have to agree that the fetus has already become a human person well before birth. Indeed, it comes as a surprise when one first learns how early in its life it begins to acquire human characteristics. By the tenth week, for example, it already has a face, arms and legs, fingers and toes; it has internal organs, and brain activity is detectable. On the other hand, I think that the premise is false, that the fetus is not a person from the moment of conception. A newly fertilized ovum, a newly implanted clump of cells, is no more a person than an acorn is an oak tree. But I shall not discuss any of this. For it seems to me to be of great interest to ask what happens if, for the sake of argument, we allow the premise. How, precisely, are we supposed to get from there to the conclusion that abortion is morally impermissible? Opponents of abortion commonly spend most of their time establishing that the fetus is a person, and hardly any time explaining the step from there to the impermissibility of abortion. Perhaps they think the step too simple and obvious to require much comment. Or perhaps instead they are simply being economical in argument. Many of those who defend abortion rely on the premise that the fetus is not a person, but only a bit of tissue that will become a person at birth; and why pay out more arguments than you have to? Whatever the explanation, I suggest that the step they take is neither easy nor obvious, that it calls for closer examination than it is commonly given, and that when we do give it this closer examination we shall feel inclined to reject it.

I propose, then, that we grant that the fetus is a person from the moment of conception. How does the argument go from here? Something like this, I take it. Every person has a right to life. So the fetus has a right to life. No doubt the mother has a right to decide what shall happen in and to her body; everyone would grant that. But surely a person's right to life is stronger and more stringent than the mother's right to decide what happens in and to her body, and so outweighs it. So the fetus may not be killed; an abortion may not be performed.

It sounds plausible. But now let me ask you to imagine this. You wake up in the morning and find yourself back to back in bed with an unconscious violinist. A famous unconscious violinist. He has been found to have a fatal kidney ailment, and the Society

Judith Jarvis Thomson, "A Defense of Abortion," *Philosophy and Public Affairs* 1, no. 1 (Fall 1971): 47–66. Some notes have been deleted. Reprinted by permission of Princeton University Press.

of Music Lovers has canvassed all the available medical records and found that you alone have the right blood type to help. They have therefore kidnapped you, and last night the violinist's circulatory system was plugged into yours, so that your kidneys can be used to extract poisons from his blood as well as your own. The director of the hospital now tells you, "Look, we're sorry the Society of Music Lovers did this to you—we would never have permitted it if we had known. But still, they did it, and the violinist now is plugged into you. To unplug you would be to kill him. But never mind, it's only for nine months. By then he will have recovered from his ailment, and can safely be unplugged from you." Is it morally incumbent on you to accede to this situation? No doubt it would be very nice of you if you did, a great kindness. But do you *have* to accede to it? What if it were not nine months, but nine years? Or longer still? What if the director of the hospital says, "Tough luck, I agree, but you've now got to stay in bed, with the violinist plugged into you, for the rest of your life. Because remember this. All persons have a right to life, and violinists are persons. Granted you have a right to decide what happens in and to your body, but a person's right to life outweighs your right to decide what happens in and to your body. So you cannot ever be unplugged from him." I imagine you would regard this as outrageous, which suggests that something really is wrong with that plausible-sounding argument I mentioned a moment ago.

In this case, of course, you were kidnapped; you didn't volunteer for the operation that plugged the violinist into your kidneys. Can those who oppose abortion on the ground I mentioned make an exception for a pregnancy due to rape? Certainly. They can say that persons have a right to life only if they didn't come into existence because of rape; or they can say that all persons have a right to life, but that some have less of a right to life than others, in particular, that those who came into existence because of rape have less. But these statements have a rather unpleasant sound. Surely the question of whether you have a right to life at all, or how much of it you have, shouldn't turn on the question of whether or not you are the product of a rape. And in fact the people who oppose abortion on the ground I mentioned

do not make this distinction, and hence do not make an exception in case of rape.

Nor do they make an exception for a case in which the mother has to spend the nine months of her pregnancy in bed. They would agree that would be a great pity, and hard on the mother; but all the same, all persons have a right to life, the fetus is a person, and so on. I suspect, in fact, that they would not make an exception for a case in which, miraculously enough, the pregnancy went on for nine years, or even the rest of the mother's life.

Some won't even make an exception for a case in which continuation of the pregnancy is likely to shorten the mother's life; they regard abortion as impermissible even to save the mother's life. Such cases are nowadays very rare, and many opponents of abortion do not accept this extreme view. All the same, it is a good place to begin: a number of points of interest come out in respect to it.

1. Let us call the view that abortion is impermissible even to save the mother's life "the extreme view." I want to suggest first that it does not issue from the argument I mentioned earlier without the addition of some fairly powerful premises. Suppose a woman has become pregnant, and now learns that she has a cardiac condition such that she will die if she carries the baby to term. What may be done for her? The fetus, being a person, has a right to life, but as the mother is a person too, so has she a right to life. Presumably they have an equal right to life. How is it supposed to come out that an abortion may not be performed? If mother and child have an equal right to life, shouldn't we perhaps flip a coin? Or should we add to the mother's right to life her right to decide what happens in and to her body, which everybody seems to be ready to grant—the sum of her rights now outweighing the fetus' right to life?

The most familiar argument here is the following. We are told that performing the abortion would be directly killing[1] the child, whereas doing nothing would not be killing the mother, but only letting her die. Moreover, in killing the child, one would be killing an innocent person, for the child has committed no crime, and is not aiming at his mother's death. And then there are a variety of ways in which this might be continued. (1) But as directly killing an innocent person is always and absolutely impermissible, an abortion may not be performed. Or, (2) as directly killing an innocent person is murder, and murder is always and absolutely impermissible, an abortion may not be performed Or, (3) as one's duty to refrain from directly killing an innocent person is more stringent than one's duty to keep a person from dying, an abortion may not be performed. Or, (4) if one's only options are directly killing an innocent person or letting a person die, one must prefer letting the person die, and thus an abortion may not be performed.[2]

Some people seem to have thought that these are not further premises which must be added if the conclusion is to be reached, but that they follow from the very fact that an innocent person has a right to life. But this seems to me to be a mistake, and perhaps the simplest way to show this is to bring out that while we must certainly grant that innocent persons have a right to life, the theses in (1) through (4) are all false. Take (2), for example. If directly killing an innocent person is murder, and thus is impermissible, then the mother's directly killing the innocent person inside her is murder, and thus is impermissible. But it cannot seriously be thought to be murder if the mother performs an abortion on herself to save her life. It cannot seriously be said that she *must* refrain, that she *must* sit passively by and wait for her death. Let us look again at the case of you and the violinist. There you are, in bed with the violinist, and the director of the hospital says to you, "It's all most distressing, and I deeply sympathize, but you see this is putting an additional strain on your kidneys, and you'll be dead within the month. But you *have* to stay where you are all the same. Because unplugging you would be directly killing an innocent violinist, and that's murder, and that's impermissible." If anything in the world is true, it is that you do not commit murder, you do not do what is impermissible, if you reach around to your back and unplug yourself from that violinist to save your life.

The main focus of attention in writings on abortion has been on what a third party may or may not do in answer to a request from a woman for an abortion. This is in a way understandable. Things being as they are, there isn't much a woman can safely do

to abort herself. So the question asked is what a third party may do, and what the mother may do, if it is mentioned at all, is deduced, almost as an afterthought, from what it is concluded that third parties may do. But it seems to me that to treat the matter in this way is to refuse to grant to the mother that very status of person which is so firmly insisted on for the fetus. For we cannot simply read off what a person may do from what a third party may do. Suppose you find yourself trapped in a tiny house with a growing child. I mean a very tiny house, and a rapidly growing child—you are already up against the wall of the house and in a few minutes you'll be crushed to death. The child on the other hand won't be crushed to death; if nothing is done to stop him from growing he'll be hurt, but in the end he'll simply burst open the house and walk out a free man. Now I could well understand it if a bystander were to say, "There's nothing we can do for you. We cannot choose between your life and his, we cannot be the ones to decide who is to live, we cannot intervene." But it cannot be concluded that you too can do nothing, that you cannot attack it to save your life. However innocent the child may be, you do not have to wait passively while it crushes you to death. Perhaps a pregnant woman is vaguely felt to have the status of house, to which we don't allow the right of self-defense. But if the woman houses the child, it should be remembered that she is a person who houses it.

I should perhaps stop to say explicitly that I am not claiming that people have a right to do anything whatever to save their lives. I think, rather, that there are drastic limits to the right of self-defense. If someone threatens you with death unless you torture someone else to death, I think you have not the right, even to save your life, to do so. But the case under consideration here is very different. In our case there are only two people involved, one whose life is threatened, and one who threatens it. Both are innocent: the one who is threatened is not threatened because of any fault, the one who threatens does not threaten because of any fault. For this reason we may feel that we bystanders cannot intervene. But the person threatened can.

In sum, a woman surely can defend her life against the threat to it posed by the unborn child, even if doing so involves its death. And this shows not merely that the theses in (1) through (4) are false; it shows also that the extreme view of abortion is false, and so we need not canvass any other possible ways of arriving at it from the argument I mentioned at the outset.

2. The extreme view could of course be weakened to say that while abortion is permissible to save the mother's life, it may not be performed by a third party, but only by the mother herself. But this cannot be right either. For what we have to keep in mind is that the mother and the unborn child are not like two tenants in a small house which has, by an unfortunate mistake, been rented to both: the mother *owns* the house. The fact that she does adds to the offensiveness of deducing that the mother can do nothing from the supposition that third parties can do nothing. But it does more than this: it casts a bright light on the supposition that third parties can do nothing. Certainly it lets us see that a third party who says "I cannot choose between you" is fooling himself if he thinks this is impartiality. If Jones has found and fastened on a certain coat, which he needs to keep him from freezing, but which Smith also needs to keep him from freezing, then it is not impartiality that says "I cannot choose between you" when Smith owns the coat. Women have said again and again "This body is *my* body!" and they have reason to feel angry, reason to feel that it has been like shouting into the wind. Smith, after all, is hardly likely to bless us if we say to him, "Of course it's your coat, anybody would grant that it is. But no one may choose between you and Jones who is to have it."

We should really ask what it is that says "no one may choose" in the face of the fact that the body that houses the child is the mother's body. It may be simply a failure to appreciate this fact. But it may be something more interesting, namely the sense that one has a right to refuse to lay hands on people, even where it would be just and fair to do so, even where justice seems to require that somebody do so. Thus justice might call for somebody to get Smith's coat back from Jones, and yet you have a right to refuse to be the one to lay hands on Jones, a right to refuse to do physical violence to him. This, I think, must be granted. But then what should be said is not "no one

may choose," but only "*I* cannot choose," and indeed not even this, but "*I* will not *act*," leaving it open that somebody else can or should, and in particular that anyone in a position of authority, with the job of securing people's rights, both can and should. So this is no difficulty. I have not been arguing that any given third party must accede to the mother's request that he perform an abortion to save her life, but only that he may.

I suppose that in some views of human life the mother's body is only on loan to her, the loan not being one which gives her any prior claim to it. One who held this view might well think it impartiality to say "I cannot choose." But I shall simply ignore this possibility. My own view is that if a human being has any just, prior claim to anything at all, he has a just, prior claim to his own body. And perhaps this needn't be argued for here anyway, since, as I mentioned, the arguments against abortion we are looking at do grant that the woman has a right to decide what happens in and to her body.

But although they do grant it, I have tried to show that they do not take seriously what is done in granting it. I suggest the same thing will reappear even more clearly when we turn away from cases in which the mother's life is at stake, and attend, as I propose we now do, to the vastly more common cases in which a woman wants an abortion for some less weighty reason than preserving her own life.

3. Where the mother's life is not at stake, the argument I mentioned at the outset seems to have a much stronger pull. "Everyone has a right to life, so the unborn person has a right to life." And isn't the child's right to life weightier than anything other than the mother's own right to life, which she might put forward as ground for an abortion?

This argument treats the right to life as if it were unproblematic. It is not, and this seems to me to be precisely the source of the mistake.

For we should now, at long last, ask what it comes to, to have a right to life. In some views having a right to life includes having a right to be given at least the bare minimum one needs for continued life. But suppose that what in fact *is* the bare minimum a man needs for continued life is something he has no right at all to be given? If I am sick unto death, and the only thing that will save my life is the touch of Henry Fonda's cool hand on my fevered brow, then all the same, I have no right to be given the touch of Henry Fonda's cool hand on my fevered brow. It would be frightfully nice of him to fly in from the West Coast to provide it. It would be less nice, though no doubt well meant, if my friends flew out to the West Coast and carried Henry Fonda back with them. But I have no right at all against anybody that he should do this for me. Or again, to return to the story I told earlier, the fact that for continued life that violinist needs the continued use of your kidneys does not establish that he has a right to be given the continued use of your kidneys. He certainly has no right against you that *you* should give him continued use of your kidneys. For nobody has any right to use your kidneys unless you give him such a right; and nobody has the right against you that you shall give him this right—if you do allow him to go on using your kidneys, this is a kindness on your part, and not something he can claim from you as his due. Nor has he any right against anybody else that *they* should give him continued use of your kidneys. Certainly he had no right against the Society of Music Lovers that they should plug him into you in the first place. And if you now start to unplug yourself, having learned that you will otherwise have to spend nine years in bed with him, there is nobody in the world who must try to prevent you, in order to see to it that he is given something he has a right to be given.

Some people are rather stricter about the right to life. In their view, it does not include the right to be given anything, but amounts to, and only to, the right not to be killed by anybody. But here a related difficulty arises. If everybody is to refrain from killing that violinist, then everybody must refrain from doing a great many different sorts of things. Everybody must refrain from slitting his throat, everybody must refrain from shooting him—and everybody must refrain from unplugging you from him. But does he have a right against everybody that they shall refrain from unplugging you from him? To refrain from doing this is to allow him to continue to use your kidneys. It could be argued that he has a right against us that *we* should allow him to continue to use your kidneys. That is, while he had no right

against us that we should give him the use of your kidneys, it might be argued that he anyway has a right against us that we shall not now intervene and deprive him of the use of your kidneys. I shall come back to third-party interventions later. But certainly the violinist has no right against you that *you* shall allow him to continue to use your kidneys. As I said, if you do allow him to use them, it is a kindness on your part, and not something you owe him.

The difficulty I point to here is not peculiar to the right to life. It reappears in connection with all the other natural rights; and it is something which an adequate account of rights must deal with. For present purposes it is enough just to draw attention to it. But I would stress that I am not arguing that people do not have a right to life—quite to the contrary, it seems to me that the primary control we must place on the acceptability of an account of rights is that it should turn out in that account to be a truth that all persons have a right to life. I am arguing only that having a right to life does not guarantee having either a right to be given the use of or a right to be allowed continued use of another person's body— even if one needs it for life itself. So the right to life will not serve the opponents of abortion in the very simple and clear way in which they seem to have thought it would.

4. There is another way to bring out the difficulty. In the most ordinary sort of case, to deprive someone of what he has a right to is to treat him unjustly. Suppose a boy and his small brother are jointly given a box of chocolates for Christmas. If the older boy takes the box and refuses to give his brother any of the chocolates, he is unjust to him, for the brother has been given a right to half of them. But suppose that, having learned that otherwise it means nine years in bed with that violinist, you unplug yourself from him. You surely are not being unjust to him, for you gave him no right to use your kidneys, and no one else can have given him any such right. But we have to notice that in unplugging yourself, you are killing him; and violinists, like everybody else, have a right to life, and thus in the view we were considering just now, the right not to be killed. So here you do what he supposedly has a right you shall not do, but you do not act unjustly to him in doing it.

The emendation which may be made at this point is this: the right to life consists not in the right not to be killed, but rather in the right not to be killed unjustly. This runs a risk of circularity, but never mind: it would enable us to square the fact that the violinist has a right to life with the fact that you do not act unjustly toward him in unplugging yourself, thereby killing him. For if you do not kill him unjustly, you do not violate his right to life, and so it is no wonder you do him no injustice.

But if this emendation is accepted, the gap in the argument against abortion stares us plainly in the face: it is by no means enough to show that the fetus is a person, and to remind us that all persons have a right to life—we need to be shown also that killing the fetus violates its right to life, i.e., that abortion is unjust killing. And is it?

I suppose we may take it as a datum that in a case of pregnancy due to rape the mother has not given the unborn person a right to the use of her body for food and shelter. Indeed, in what pregnancy could it be supposed that the mother has given the unborn person such a right? It is not as if there were unborn persons drifting about the world, to whom a woman who wants a child says "I invite you in."

But it might be argued that there are other ways one can have acquired a right to the use of another person's body than by having been invited to use it by that person. Suppose a woman voluntarily indulges in intercourse, knowing of the chance it will issue in pregnancy, and then she does become pregnant; is she not in part responsible for the presence, in fact the very existence, of the unborn person inside her? No doubt she did not invite it in. But doesn't her partial responsibility for its being there itself give it a right to the use of her body? If so, then her aborting it would be more like the boy's taking away the chocolates, and less like your unplugging yourself from the violinist—doing so would be depriving it of what it does have a right to, and thus would be doing it an injustice.

And then, too, it might be asked whether or not she can kill it even to save her own life: If she voluntarily called it into existence, how can she now kill it, even in self-defense?

The first thing to be said about this is that it is something new. Opponents of abortion have been so concerned to make out the independence of the fetus, in order to establish that it has a right to life, just as its mother does, that they have tended to overlook the possible support they might gain from making out that the fetus is *dependent* on the mother, in order to establish that she has a special kind of responsibility for it, a responsibility that gives it rights against her which are not possessed by any independent person—such as an ailing violinist who is a stranger to her.

On the other hand, this argument would give the unborn person a right to its mother's body only if her pregnancy resulted from a voluntary act, undertaken in full knowledge of the chance a pregnancy might result from it. It would leave out entirely the unborn person whose existence is due to rape. Pending the availability of some further argument, then, we would be left with the conclusion that unborn persons whose existence is due to rape have no right to the use of their mothers' bodies, and thus that aborting them is not depriving them of anything they have a right to and hence is not unjust killing.

And we should also notice that it is not at all plain that this argument really does go even as far as it purports to. For there are cases and cases, and the details make a difference. If the room is stuffy, and I therefore open a window to air it, and a burglar climbs in, it would be absurd to say, "Ah, now he can stay, she's given him a right to the use of her house—for she is partially responsible for his presence there, having voluntarily done what enabled him to get in, in full knowledge that there are such things as burglars, and that burglars burgle." It would be still more absurd to say this if I had had bars installed outside my windows, precisely to prevent burglars from getting in, and a burglar got in only because of a defect in the bars. It remains equally absurd if we imagine it is not a burglar who climbs in, but an innocent person who blunders or falls in. Again, suppose it were like this: people-seeds drift about in the air like pollen, and if you open your windows, one may drift in and take root in your carpets or upholstery. You don't want children, so you fix up your windows with fine mesh screens, the very best you can buy. As can happen, however, and on very, very rare occasions does happen, one of the screens is defective; and a seed drifts in and takes root. Does the person-plant who now develops have a right to the use of your house? Surely not—despite the fact that you voluntarily opened your windows, you knowingly kept carpets and upholstered furniture, and you knew that screens were sometimes defective. Someone may argue that you are responsible for its rooting, that it does have a right to your house, because after all you *could* have lived out your life with bare floors and furniture, or with sealed windows and doors. But this won't do—for by the same token anyone can avoid a pregnancy due to rape by having a hysterectomy, or anyway by never leaving home without a (reliable!) army.

It seems to me that the argument we are looking at can establish at most that there are *some* cases in which the unborn person has a right to the use of its mother's body, and therefore *some* cases in which abortion is unjust killing. There is room for much discussion and argument as to precisely which, if any. But I think we should sidestep this issue and leave it open, for at any rate the argument certainly does not establish that all abortion is unjust killing.

5. There is room for yet another argument here, however. We surely must all grant that there may be cases in which it would be morally indecent to detach a person from your body at the cost of his life. Suppose you learn that what the violinist needs is not nine years of your life, but only one hour: all you need do to save his life is to spend one hour in that bed with him. Suppose also that letting him use your kidneys for that one hour would not affect your health in the slightest. Admittedly you were kidnapped. Admittedly you did not give anyone permission to plug him into you. Nevertheless it seems to me plain you *ought* to allow him to use your kidneys for that hour—it would be indecent to refuse.

Again, suppose pregnancy lasted only an hour, and constituted no threat to life or health. And suppose that a woman becomes pregnant as a result of rape. Admittedly she did not voluntarily do anything to bring about the existence of a child. Admittedly she did nothing at all which would give the unborn person a right to the use of her body. All the same it might well be said, as in the newly emended violinist story, that she *ought* to allow it to remain for that hour—that it would be indecent in her to refuse.

Now some people are inclined to use the term "right" in such a way that it follows from the fact that you ought to allow a person to use your body for the hour he needs, that he has a right to use your body for the hour he needs, even though he has not been given that right by any person or act. They may say that it follows also that if you refuse, you act unjustly toward him. This use of the term is perhaps so common that it cannot be called wrong; nevertheless it seems to me to be an unfortunate loosening of what we would do better to keep a tight rein on. Suppose that box of chocolates I mentioned earlier had not been given to both boys jointly, but was given only to the older boy. There he sits, stolidly eating his way through the box, his small brother watching enviously. Here we are likely to say "You ought not to be so mean. You ought to give your brother some of those chocolates." My own view is that it just does not follow from the truth of this that the brother has any right to any of the chocolates. If the boy refuses to give his brother any, he is greedy, stingy, callous—but not unjust. I suppose that the people I have in mind will say it does follow that the brother has a right to some of the chocolates, and thus that the boy does act unjustly if he refuses to give his brother any. But the effect of saying this is to obscure what we should keep distinct, namely the difference between the boy's refusal in this case and the boy's refusal in the earlier case, in which the box was given to both boys jointly, and in which the small brother thus had what was from any point of view clear title to half.

A further objection to so using the term "right" that from the fact that A ought to do a thing for B, it follows that B has a right against A that A do it for him, is that it is going to make the question of whether or not a man has a right to a thing turn on how easy it is to provide him with it; and this seems not merely unfortunate, but morally unacceptable. Take the case of Henry Fonda again. I said earlier that I had no right to the touch of his cool hand on my fevered brow, even though I needed it to save my life. I said it would be frightfully nice of him to fly in from the West Coast to provide me with it, but that I had no right against him that he should do so. But suppose he isn't on the West Coast. Suppose he has only to walk across the room, place a hand briefly on my brow— and lo, my life is saved. Then surely he ought to do it, it would be indecent to refuse. Is it to be said "Ah, well, it follows that in this case she has a right to the touch of his hand on her brow, and so it would be an injustice in him to refuse"? So that I have a right to it when it is easy for him to provide it, though no right when it's hard? It's rather a shocking idea that anyone's rights should fade away and disappear as it gets harder and harder to accord them to him.

So my own view is that even though you ought to let the violinist use your kidneys for the one hour he needs, we should not conclude that he has a right to do so—we should say that if you refuse, you are, like the boy who owns all the chocolates and will give none away, self-centered and callous, indecent in fact, but not unjust. And similarly, that even supposing a case in which a woman pregnant due to rape ought to allow the unborn person to use her body for the hour he needs, we should not conclude that he has a right to do so; we should conclude that she is self-centered, callous, indecent, but not unjust, if she refuses. The complaints are no less grave; they are just different. However, there is no need to insist on this point. If anyone does wish to deduce "he has a right" from "you ought," then all the same he must surely grant that there are cases in which it is not morally required of you that you allow that violinist to use your kidneys, and in which he does not have a right to use them, and in which you do not do him an injustice if you refuse. And so also for mother and unborn child. Except in such cases as the unborn person has a right to demand it—and we were leaving open the possibility that there may be such cases— nobody is morally *required* to make large sacrifices, of health, of all other interests and concerns, of all other duties and commitments, for nine years, or even for nine months, in order to keep another person alive.

6. We have in fact to distinguish between two kinds of Samaritan: the Good Samaritan and what we might call the Minimally Decent Samaritan. The story of the Good Samaritan, you will remember, goes like this:

> A certain man went down from Jerusalem to Jericho, and fell among thieves, which stripped him of his raiment, and wounded him, and departed, leaving him half dead.
>
> And by chance there came down a certain priest that way; and when he saw him, he passed by on the other side.
>
> And likewise a Levite, when he was at the place, came and looked on him, and passed by on the other side.
>
> But a certain Samaritan, as he journeyed, came where he was; and when he saw him he had compassion on him.
>
> And went to him, and bound up his wounds, pouring in oil and wine, and set him on his own beast, and brought him to an inn, and took care of him.
>
> And on the morrow, when he departed, he took out two pence, and gave them to the host, and said unto him, "Take care of him; and whatsoever thou spendest more, when I come again, I will repay thee." (Luke 10:30–35)

The Good Samaritan went out of his way, at some cost to himself, to help one in need of it. We are not told what the options were, that is, whether or not the priest and the Levite could have helped by doing less than the Good Samaritan did, but assuming they could have, then the fact they did nothing at all shows they were not even Minimally Decent Samaritans, not because they were not Samaritans, but because they were not even minimally decent.

These things are a matter of degree, of course, but there is a difference, and it comes out perhaps most clearly in the story of Kitty Genovese, who, as you will remember, was murdered while thirty-eight people watched or listened, and did nothing at all to help her. A Good Samaritan would have rushed out to give direct assistance against the murderer. Or perhaps we had better allow that it would have been a Splendid Samaritan who did this, on the ground that it would have involved a risk of death for himself. But the thirty-eight not only did not do this, they did not even trouble to pick up a phone to call the police. Minimally Decent Samaritanism would call for doing at least that, and their not having done it was monstrous.

After telling the story of the Good Samaritan, Jesus said "Go, and do thou likewise." Perhaps he meant that we are morally required to act as the Good Samaritan did. Perhaps he was urging people to do more than is morally required of them. At all events it seems plain that it was not morally required of any of the thirty-eight that he rush out to give direct assistance at the risk of his own life, and that it is not morally required of anyone that he give long stretches of his life—nine years or nine months—to sustaining the life of a person who has no special right (we were leaving open the possibility of this) to demand it.

Indeed, with one rather striking class of exceptions, no one in any country in the world is *legally* required to do anywhere near as much as this for anyone else. The class of exceptions is obvious. My main concern here is not the state of the law in respect to abortion, but it is worth drawing attention to the fact that in no state in this country is any man compelled by law to be even a Minimally Decent Samaritan to any person; there is no law under which charges could be brought against the thirty-eight who stood by while Kitty Genovese died. By contrast, in most states in this country women are compelled by law to be not merely Minimally Decent Samaritans, but Good Samaritans to unborn persons inside them. This doesn't by itself settle anything one way or the other, because it may well be argued that there should be laws in this country—as there are in many European countries—compelling at least Minimally Decent Samaritanism. But it does show that there is a gross injustice in the existing state of the law. And it shows also that the groups currently working against liberalization of abortion laws, in fact working toward having it declared unconstitutional for a state to permit abortion, had better start working for the adoption of Good Samaritan laws generally, or earn the charge that they are acting in bad faith.

I should think, myself, that Minimally Decent Samaritan laws would be one thing, Good Samaritan laws quite another, and in fact highly improper. But we are not here concerned with the law. What we should ask is not whether anybody should be compelled by law to be a Good Samaritan, but whether we must accede to a situation in which somebody is being compelled—by nature, perhaps—to be a Good Samaritan. We have, in other words, to look now at third-party interventions. I have been arguing that no person is morally required to make large sacrifices to sustain the life of another who has no right to demand them, and this even where the sacrifices do not include life itself; we are not morally required to be Good Samaritans or anyway Very Good Samaritans to one another. But what if a man cannot extricate himself from such a situation? What if he appeals to us to extricate him? It seems to me plain that there are cases in which we can, cases in which a Good Samaritan would extricate him. There you are, you were kidnapped, and nine years in bed with that violinist lie ahead of you. You have your own life to lead. You are sorry, but you simply cannot see giving up so much of your life to the sustaining of his. You cannot extricate yourself, and ask us to do so. I should have thought that—in light of his having no right to the use of your body—it was obvious that we do not have to accede to your being forced to give up so much. We can do what you ask. There is no injustice to the violinist in our doing so.

7. Following the lead of the opponents of abortion, I have throughout been speaking of the fetus merely as a person, and what I have been asking is whether or not the argument we began with, which proceeds only from the fetus' being a person, really does establish its conclusion. I have argued that it does not.

But of course there are arguments and arguments, and it may be said that I have simply fastened on the wrong one. It may be said that what is important is not merely the fact that the fetus is a person, but that it is a person for whom the woman has a special kind of responsibility issuing from the fact that she is its mother. And it might be argued that all my analogies are therefore irrelevant—for you do not have that special kind of responsibility for that violinist, Henry Fonda does not have that special kind of responsibility for me. And our attention might be drawn to the fact that men and women both *are* compelled by law to provide support for their children.

I have in effect dealt (briefly) with this argument in section 4 above; but a (still briefer) recapitulation now may be in order. Surely we do not have any such "special responsibility" for a person unless we have assumed it, explicitly or implicitly. If a set of parents do not try to prevent pregnancy, do not obtain an abortion, and then at the time of birth of the child do not put it out for adoption, but rather take it home with them, then they have assumed responsibility for it, they have given it rights, and they cannot *now* withdraw support from it at the cost of its life because they now find it difficult to go on providing for it. But if they have taken all reasonable precautions against having a child, they do not simply by virtue of their biological relationship to the child who comes into existence have a special responsibility for it. They may wish to assume responsibility for it, or they may not wish to. And I am suggesting that if assuming responsibility for it would require large sacrifices, then they may refuse. A Good Samaritan would not refuse—or anyway, a Splendid Samaritan, if the sacrifices that had to be made were enormous. But then so would a Good Samaritan assume responsibility for that violinist; so would Henry Fonda, if he is a Good Samaritan, fly in from the West Coast and assume responsibility for me.

8. My argument will be found unsatisfactory on two counts by many of those who want to regard abortion as morally permissible. First, while I do argue that abortion is not impermissible, I do not argue that it is always permissible. There may well be cases in which carrying the child to term requires only Minimally Decent Samaritanism of the mother, and this is a standard we must not fall below. I am inclined to think it a merit of my account precisely that it does *not* give a general yes or a general no. It allows for and supports our sense that, for example, a sick and desperately frightened fourteen-year-old schoolgirl, pregnant due to rape, may *of course* choose abortion, and that any law which rules this out is an insane law. And it also allows for and supports our sense that in other cases resort to abortion is even positively indecent. It would be indecent in

the woman to request an abortion, and indecent in a doctor to perform it, if she is in her seventh month, and wants the abortion just to avoid the nuisance of postponing a trip abroad. The very fact that the arguments I have been drawing attention to treat all cases of abortion, or even all cases of abortion in which the mother's life is not at stake, as morally on a par ought to have made them suspect at the outset.

Secondly, while I am arguing for the permissibility of abortion in some cases, I am not arguing for the right to secure the death of the unborn child. It is easy to confuse these two things in that up to a certain point in the life of the fetus it is not able to survive outside the mother's body; hence removing it from her body guarantees its death. But they are importantly different. I have argued that you are not morally required to spend nine months in bed, sustaining the life of that violinist; but to say this is by no means to say that if, when you unplug yourself, there is a miracle and he survives, you then have a right to turn round and slit his throat. You may detach yourself even if this costs him his life; you have no right to be guaranteed his death, by some other means, if unplugging yourself does not kill him. There are some people who will feel dissatisfied by this feature of my argument. A woman may be utterly devastated by the thought of a child, a bit of herself, put out for adoption and never seen or heard of again. She may therefore want not merely that the child be detached from her, but more, that it die. Some opponents of abortion are inclined to regard this as beneath contempt—thereby showing insensitivity to what is surely a powerful source of despair. All the same, I agree that the desire for the child's death is not one which anybody may gratify, should it turn out to be possible to detach the child alive.

At this place, however, it should be remembered that we have only been pretending throughout that the fetus is a human being from the moment of conception. A very early abortion is surely not the killing of a person, and so is not dealt with by anything I have said here.

NOTES

1. The term "direct" in the arguments I refer to is a technical one. Roughly, what is meant by "direct killing" is either killing as an end in itself, or killing as a means to some end, for example, the end of saving someone else's life. . . .

2. The thesis in (4) is in an interesting way weaker than those in (1), (2), and (3): they rule out abortion even in cases in which both mother *and* child will die if the abortion is not performed. By contrast, one who held the view expressed in (4) could consistently say that one needn't prefer letting two persons die to killing one.

Critics

Baruch Brody | Thomson on Abortion

There is a familiar argument that purports to show that it is always wrong for an expectant woman to have an abortion. It runs as follows: (1) from the moment of conception, a foetus is a human being with the same rights to life as any other human being; (2) it is always wrong to take (directly) the life of an innocent human being; (3) therefore, it is always wrong to have an abortion. Judith Jarvis Thomson, in her recent article, criticized the above argument by challenging (2). More importantly, she argued that (at least in most cases) a woman has the right to secure an abortion even if (1) is true, although there are cases in which it would be positively indecent to exercise this right. It seems to me, however, that her discussions of these points, as interesting as they are, are not entirely convincing. I would like in this note to explain why.

I

Professor Thomson unfortunately offers as her counterexample to (2) her very problematic account of the violinist, a case to which we will return below. There are, however, far more straightforward cases that show that (2) is false. One such case—another will be discussed briefly at the end of this note—is the one in which Y is about to shoot X and X can save his life only by taking Y's life. We would certainly want to say that, as part of his right of self-defense, X has the right to take Y's life, and he has that right even if Y is a perfectly innocent child. So the right of self-defense includes in some cases the taking of innocent lives, (2) is false, and the above argument against abortion collapses.

This point raises important theoretical issues and it is therefore worth elaborating upon. In a normal case of self-defense, the following three factors seem to be involved: (a) the continued existence of Y poses a threat to the life of X, a threat that can be met only by the taking of Y's life; (b) Y is unjustly attempting to take X's life; (c) Y is responsible for his attempt to take X's life and is therefore guilty of attempting to take X's life. There is, moreover, a very plausible argument that would seem to suggest

Baruch Brody, "Thomson on Abortion," *Philosophy and Public Affairs* 1, no. 3 (Spring 1972): 335–40. Notes have been deleted. Reprinted by permission of Princeton University Press.

that all three of these factors must be involved if X is to be justified in taking Y's life in self-defense. It runs as follows: Why is X justified in killing Y? Isn't it Y's guilt for his attempt to take X's life together with the threat that Y's continued existence poses for X's life that justifies X's killing Y? Or, to put it another way, Y's guilt makes X's life take precedence over Y's. But if this is the justification for taking a life in self-defense, then conditions (a), (b), and (c) must be satisfied. If (a) is not satisfied, then Y's living is no threat to X, and if (b) and (c) are not satisfied, then there is no relevant guilt on Y's part that makes X's life take precedence over his.

What our example of the child shows is that this plausible argument will not do. Even if conditions (a) and (b), but not (c), are satisfied, X has the right to take Y's life in self-defense. This means that the above justification is not the justification for acts of self-defense. And this raises two fundamental and interrelated questions: What is the justification for taking a life in self-defense, and what conditions are required for an act of self-defense to be justified? The answers to these questions are not clear. One thing is, however, certain. X is not justified in taking Y's life merely because condition (a) is satisfied, and the justification for acts of self-defense is not simply that one has the right to do anything one has to in order to save one's life. After all, if Z threatens to, and will, kill X unless X kills Y, then Y's continued existence poses a threat to the life of X that can only be met by the taking of Y's life. Nevertheless, X is not therefore justified in killing Y. We would understand X's killing Y, and we might even excuse the action, but he would certainly have killed Y unjustly.

All of this has great relevance to the problem of abortion. While our discussion has shown that Professor Thomson is right in claiming that step (2) of the standard argument against abortion is mistaken, it also casts considerable doubt upon a standard argument for abortion. It is often argued that, no matter what status we ascribe to the foetus, the woman has, as part of her right of self-defense, the right to abort the foetus if the continuation of the pregnancy threatens her life. Now the foetus certainly does not satisfy condition (c), but that, as we have seen, is not required for the woman's being

able to destroy it in self-defense. However, the foetus is not even attempting to take her life, and it therefore doesn't even satisfy condition (b). This must therefore cast doubt upon the claim that, no matter what the status of the foetus, abortions can sometimes be justified on grounds of self-defense.

II

Assuming that the foetus is human and that one should look at an abortion as a standard case of self-defense, we have seen that even when the foetus' continued existence poses a threat to the life of the woman, she probably has no right, as an act of self-defense, to an abortion. How then does Professor Thomson defend her claim that even if (1) is true the woman (at least in most cases) has the right to have an abortion, whether or not her life is threatened and whether or not she has consented to the act of intercourse in which the foetus is conceived? At one point, she makes the following strange suggestion: "In our case there are only two people involved, one whose life is threatened and one who threatens it. Both are innocent: the one who is threatened is not threatened because of any fault, the one who threatens does not threaten because of any fault. For this reason we may feel that we bystanders cannot intervene. But the person threatened can." But surely this description is equally applicable to the following case. X and Y are adrift in a lifeboat. Y has a disease which he can survive but which will kill X if he contracts it, and the only way X can avoid that is by killing Y and pushing him overboard. Surely, X has no right to do this. So there must be some other reason why the woman has, if she does, the right to abort the foetus.

There is, however, an important difference between our lifeboat case and an abortion, one that leads us to the heart of Professor Thomson's argument. In the case we envisaged, both X and Y had equal right to be in the lifeboat; but the woman's body is hers, not the foetus', and she has first rights to its use. This is why the woman has a right to an abortion if her life is threatened (and even if it is not). Professor Thomson summarizes this argument, which she illustrates by her violinist example, as follows: "I am arguing only that having a right to life does not guarantee having either a right to be given the use of or a right to be allowed continued use of another person's body—even if one needs it for life itself."

One part of this claim is clearly correct. I have no duty to X to save X's life by giving him the use of my body (or my life savings, my wife, etc.) and X has no right, even to save his life, to any of those things. Thus, if a foetus were conceived in a test tube and would die unless it were implanted in a woman's body, that foetus has no right to any woman's body. But all of this is irrelevant to the abortion issue, for what is at stake there is something else, the right of the woman to kill X to get back the sole use of her body, and that is an entirely different matter.

This point can also be put as follows: we must distinguish the taking of X's life from the saving of X's life, even if we assume that one has a duty not to do the former and to do the latter. Now that second duty, if it exists at all, is much weaker than the first duty; many things will relieve us of it which will not relieve us of the first one. Thus, I am certainly relieved of my duty to save X's life by the fact that fulfilling it means a loss of my life savings. It may be noble for me to save X's life at the cost of everything I have, but I certainly have no duty to do that. And the same thing is true in cases in which I can save X's life by giving him use of my body for an extended period of time. However, I am not relieved of my duty not to take X's life by the fact that fulfilling it means the loss of everything I have and not even by the mere fact that fulfilling it means the loss of my life. As the original example of Y threatening X shows, something more is required before rights like self-defense become applicable. A fortiori, it would seem that I am not relieved of my duty not to take X's life by the fact that its fulfillment means that some other person, who is innocently occupying it, continues to use my body. I cannot see, then, how the woman's right to her body gives her a right to take the life of the foetus.

Perhaps we are missing the point of Professor Thomson's argument. Could we perhaps view her argument as follows: consider the case (and only the case) in which the foetus threatens the life of the woman. Then don't we have a choice between saving the woman and saving the foetus, and doesn't the woman come first because it is her body? I think, once more, that there is a point to such a claim. When one has a choice between using all or part of a woman's body to save her or the foetus, the fact that it is her body gives her precedence. But that is not the choice in the case of an abortion. There one chooses between saving the woman by taking the life of the foetus and not taking the life of the foetus, thereby failing to save the woman. Given that choice, as we have seen, her rights to her body have no revelance.

I conclude, therefore, that Professor Thomson has not established the truth of her claims about abortion, primarily because she has not attended to the distinction between our duty to save X's life and our duty not to take it. Once one attends to that distinction, it would seem that if (1) is true, it is wrong to perform an abortion even to save the life of the woman.

III

What has been said above might seem to suggest that if (1) is true, then it is always wrong for a woman to secure an abortion. I think that this suggestion is a mistake, and I should like, in this final section, to propose that there is at least one case in which, even if (1) is true, the woman has the right to secure an abortion.

The general principle about the taking of human lives that lies behind this case is rather complicated. It can best be stated as follows: it is permissible for X to take Y's life in order to save his own life if Y is going to die anyway in a relatively short time, taking Y's life is the only way to save X's life, and either (i) taking X's life (or doing anything else) will not save Y's life or (ii) there is a way to save Y's life but it has been determined by a fair random method that X's life should be saved rather than Y's. The rationale for this principle is that, in such a case, there is everything to gain by X's taking Y's life and nothing to lose. After all, both X and Y will die soon anyway if nothing is done, so Y loses nothing by X's killing him. Moreover, there is a reason why X should be saved rather than Y; either Y's life cannot be saved or X won over Y in a fair random choice.

It should be noted that this is not a principle of self-defense, for in some of the cases that it covers Y is in no way attempting to take X's life and is doing no action that leads to X's death. It should also be noted that this principle has nothing to do with the objectionable principles that would allow one to save several lives by taking a single innocent life. All such maximization-of-lives-saved principles, but not our principle, fall prey to the same objection that destroys all standard maximization-of-happiness principles, viz., that they fail to insure that no one will be treated unjustly when we maximize the quantity in question.

If we apply this principle to the question of abortion, we see that an abortion would be justified if, were the abortion not performed, both the woman and foetus would die soon, and if we either cannot save the foetus or have determined by a fair random procedure that it is the woman that should be saved.

One important point should be noted about this argument. It makes no appeal to any special fact about the foetus, the woman, or their relation. It depends solely upon a general principle about the taking of some human lives to save others. It is for just this reason that there can be no doubt about its conclusion being perfectly compatible with the claim that the foetus is just another human being.

Arguments from Bodily Rights

Francis J. Beckwith

A Critical Analysis

There are at least nine problems with Thomson's argument. These problems can be put into three categories: ethical, legal, and ideological.

ETHICAL PROBLEMS WITH THOMSON'S ARGUMENT

1. *Thomson assumes volunteerism.* By using the story as a paradigm for all relationships, thus implying that moral obligations must be voluntarily accepted to have moral force, Thomson mistakenly infers that all true moral obligations to one's offspring are voluntary. But consider the following story. Suppose a couple has a sexual encounter that is fully protected by several forms of birth control short of surgical abortion (condom, the Pill, IUD), but nevertheless

results in conception. Instead of getting an abortion, the mother of the conceptus decides to bring it to term, although the father is unaware of this decision. After the birth of the child, the mother pleads with the father for child support. Because he refuses, she takes legal action. Although he took every precaution to avoid fatherhood, thus showing that he did not wish to accept such a status, according to nearly all child-support laws in the United States, he would still be obligated to pay support *precisely because* of his relationship to this child. . . .

But this obligatory relationship is not based strictly on biology, for this would make sperm donors morally responsible for children conceived by their seed. Rather, the father's responsibility for his offspring stems from the fact that he engaged in an act,

From Francis J. Beckwith, "Arguments from Bodily Rights: A Critical Analysis" in *The Abortion Controversy: 25 Years After Roe v. Wade: A Reader,* 2nd ed., ed. Louis P. Pojman and Francis J. Beckwith (Belmont, Calif.: Wadsworth, 1998), pp. 132–50. Some text and notes have been deleted. Reprinted by permission of Baker Book House Company.

sexual intercourse, that he fully realized could result in the creation of another human being, although he took every precaution to avoid such a result. This is not an unusual way to frame moral obligations, for we hold drunk people whose driving results in manslaughter responsible for their actions, even if they did not intend to kill someone prior to becoming intoxicated. Such special obligations, although not directly undertaken voluntarily, are necessary in any civilized culture to preserve the rights of the vulnerable, the weak, and the young, who can offer very little in exchange for the rights bestowed on them by the strong, the powerful, and the postuterine in Thomson's moral universe of the social contract. Thus, Thomson is wrong, in addition to ignoring the *natural* relationship between sexual intercourse and human reproduction,[1] when she claims that if a couple has "taken all reasonable precautions against having a child, they do not by virtue of their biological relationship to the child who comes into existence have a special responsibility for it." "Surely we do not have any such 'special responsibility' for a person unless we have assumed it, explicitly or implicitly." Hence, instead of providing reasons for rejecting any special responsibilities for one's offspring, Thomson simply dismisses the concept altogether.

2. *Thomson's argument is fatal to family morality.* It follows from the first criticism that Thomson's volunteerism is fatal to family morality, which has as one of its central beliefs that an individual has special and filial obligations to his offspring and family that he does not have to other persons. Although Thomson might not consider such a fatality as being all that terrible because she might accept the feminist dogma that the traditional family is "oppressive" to women, a great number of ordinary men and women, who have found joy, happiness, and love in family life, find Thomson's volunteerism to be counterintuitive. Christina Sommers has come to a similar conclusion:

> For it [the volunteerist thesis] means that there is no such thing as filial duty per se, no such thing as the special duty of mother to child, and generally no such thing as morality of special family or kinship relations. All of which is contrary to what people think. For most people think that we do owe special debts to our parents even though we have

not voluntarily assumed our obligations to them. Most people think that what we owe to our children does not have its origin in any voluntary undertaking, explicit or implicit, that we have made to them. And "preanalytically," many people believe that we owe special consideration to our siblings even at times when we may not *feel* very friendly to them . . . The idea that to be committed to an individual is to have made a voluntarily implicit or explicit commitment to that individual is generally fatal to family morality. For it looks upon the network of felt obligation and expectation that binds family members as a sociological phenomenon that is without presumptive moral force. The social critics who hold this view of family obligation usually are aware that promoting it in public policy must further the disintegration of the traditional family as an institution. But whether they deplore the disintegration or welcome it, they are bound in principle to abet it.[2]

3. *A case can be made that the unborn does have a prima facie right to her mother's body.* Assuming that there is such a thing as a special filial obligation, a principle that does not have to be voluntarily accepted to have moral force, it is not obvious that the unborn entity in ordinary circumstances (that is, with the exception of when the mother's life is in significant danger) does not have a natural prima facie claim to her mother's body. There are several reasons to suppose that the unborn entity does have such a natural claim.

a. Unlike Thomson's violinist, who is artificially attached to another person to save his life and is therefore not naturally dependent on any particular human being, the unborn entity is a human being who by her very nature is dependent on her mother, for this is how human beings are at this stage of their development.

b. This period of a human being's natural development occurs in the womb. This is the journey that we all must take and is a necessary condition for any human being's postuterine existence. And this fact alone brings out the most glaring difference between the violinist and the unborn: The womb is the unborn's natural environment whereas being artificially hooked up to a stranger is not the natural environment for the violinist. It would seem, then, that the unborn has a prima facie natural claim on her mother's body.

c. This same entity, when she becomes a newborn, has a natural claim on her parents to care for her, regardless of whether her parents wanted her (see the story of the irresponsible father). This is why we prosecute child abusers, people who throw their babies in trash cans, and parents who abandon their children. Although it should not be ignored that pregnancy and childbirth entail certain emotional, physical, and financial sacrifices by the pregnant woman, these sacrifices are also endemic of parenthood in general (which ordinarily lasts much longer than nine months) and do not seem to justify the execution of troublesome infants and younger children whose existence entails a natural claim to certain financial and bodily goods that are under the ownership of their parents. If the unborn entity is fully human, as Thomson is willing to grant, why should the unborn's natural prima facie claim to her parents' goods differ before birth? Of course, a court will not force a parent to donate a kidney to her dying offspring, but this sort of dependence on the parent's body is highly unusual and is not part of the ordinary obligations associated with the natural process of human development, just as in the case of the violinist's artificial dependency on the reluctant music lover.

As Stephen D. Schwarz points out: "So, the very thing that makes it plausible to say that the person in bed with the violinist has no duty to sustain him; namely, that he is a stranger unnaturally hooked up to him, is precisely what is absent in the case of the mother and her child." That is to say, the mother "does have an obligation to take care of her child, to sustain her, to protect her, and especially, to let her live in the only place where she can now be protected, nourished, and allowed to grow, namely the womb."[3]

If Thomson responds to this argument by saying that birth is the threshold at which parents become fully responsible, then she has begged the question, for her argument was supposed to show us why there is no parental responsibility before birth. That is to say, Thomson cannot appeal to birth as the decisive

moment at which parents become responsible to prove that birth is the time at which parents become responsible.

It is evident that Thomson's violinist illustration undermines the deep natural bond between mother and child by making it seem no different from that between two strangers artificially hooked up to each other so that one can "steal" the service of the other's kidneys. Never has something so human, so natural, so beautiful, and so wonderfully demanding of our human creativity and love been reduced to such a brutal caricature.

I am not saying that the unborn entity has an absolute natural claim to her mother's body, but simply that she has a prima facie natural claim. For one can easily imagine a situation in which this natural claim is outweighed by other important prima facie values, such as when a pregnancy significantly endangers the mother's life. Since the continuation of such a pregnancy would most likely entail the death of both mother and child, and since it is better that one human should live rather than two die, terminating such a pregnancy via abortion is morally justified.

Someone may respond to the three criticisms by agreeing that Thomson's illustration may not apply in cases of ordinary sexual intercourse, but only in cases in which pregnancy results from rape or incest, although it should be noted that Thomson herself does not press this argument. She writes, "Surely the question of whether you have a right to life at all, or how much of it you have, shouldn't turn on the question of whether or not you are the product of rape."

But those who do press the rape argument may choose to argue in the following way: Just as the sperm donor is not responsible for how his sperm is used or what results from its use (for example, it might be stolen, or an unmarried woman might purchase it, inseminate herself, and give birth to a child), the raped woman, who did not voluntarily engage in intercourse cannot be held responsible for the unborn human who is living inside her.

But there is a problem with this analogy: The sperm donor's relinquishing of responsibility does not result in the death of a human person. The following story should help illustrate the differences and similarities between these two cases.

Suppose that the sperm donated by the sperm donor was stolen by an unscrupulous physician and inseminated into a woman. Although he is not morally responsible for the child that results from such an insemination, the donor is nevertheless forced by an unjust court to pay a large monthly sum for child support, a sum so large that it may drive him into serious debt, maybe even bankruptcy. This would be similar to the woman who became pregnant as a result of rape. She was unjustly violated and is supporting a human being against her will at an emotional and financial cost. Is it morally right for the sperm donor to kill the child he is supporting to allegedly right the wrong that has been committed against him? Not at all, because such an act would be murder. Now if we assume, as does Thomson, that the raped woman is carrying a being who is fully human (or "a person"), her killing of the unborn entity by abortion, except if the pregnancy has a strong possibility of endangering her life, would be as unjust as the sperm donor killing the child he is unjustly forced to support. As the victimized man can rightly refuse to pay the child support, the raped woman can rightly refuse to bring up her child after the pregnancy has come to term. She can choose to put the child up for adoption. But in both cases, the killing of child is not morally justified. Although neither the sperm donor nor the rape victim might have the same special obligation to their biological offspring as does the couple who voluntarily engaged in intercourse with no direct intention to produce a child, it seems that the more general obligation not to directly kill another human person does apply.

4. *Thomson ignores the fact that abortion is indeed killing and not merely the withholding of treatment.* Thomson makes an excellent point: Namely, there are times when withholding or withdrawing medical treatment is morally justified. For instance, I am not morally obligated to donate my kidney to Fred, my next-door neighbor, simply because he needs a kidney to live. In other words, I am not obligated to risk my life so that Fred can live

a few years longer. Fred should not expect that of me. If, however, I donate one of my kidneys to Fred, I will have acted above and beyond the call of duty because I will have performed a supererogatory moral act. But this case is not analogous to pregnancy and abortion.

Levin argues that there is an essential difference between abortion and the unplugging of the violinist. In the case of the violinist (as well as my relationship to Fred's welfare), "the person who withdraws [or withholds] his assistance is not completely responsible for the dependency on him of the person who is about to die, while the mother *is* completely responsible for the dependency of her fetus on her. When one is completely responsible for dependence, refusal to continue to aid is indeed killing." For example, "if a woman brings a newborn home from the hospital, puts it in its crib and refuses to feed it until it has starved to death, it would be absurd to say that she simply refused to assist it and had done nothing for which she should be criminally liable."[4] In other words, just as the withholding of food kills the child after birth, in the case of abortion, the abortion kills the child. In neither case is there any ailment from which the child suffers and for which highly invasive medical treatment, with the cooperation of another's bodily organs, is necessary to cure this ailment and save the child's life.

Or consider the following case, which can be applied to the case of pregnancy resulting from rape or incest. Suppose a person returns home after work to find a baby at his doorstep. Suppose that no one else is able to take care of the child, but this person has only to take care of the child for nine months (after that time a couple will adopt the child). Imagine that this person, because of the child's presence, will have some bouts with morning sickness, water retention, and other minor ailments. If we assume with Thomson that the unborn child is as much a person as you or I, would "withholding treatment" from this child and its subsequent death be justified on the basis that the homeowner was only "withholding treatment" of a child he did not ask for to benefit himself? Is any person, born or unborn, obligated to sacrifice his life because his death would benefit another person? Consequently, there is no doubt that such "withholding" of treatment (and it seems totally false to call ordinary shelter and sustenance "treatment") is indeed murder. . . .

IDEOLOGICAL PROBLEMS
WITH THE USE
OF THOMSON'S ARGUMENT

There are at least three ideological problems in the use of Thomson's argument by others. The latter two problems are usually found in the books, speeches, articles, or papers of those in the feminist or abortion-rights movements who sometimes uncritically use Thomson's argument or ones similar to it. In fact, Thomson might agree with most or all of the following critique.

1. *Inconsistent use of the burden of pregnancy.* Thomson has to paint pregnancy in the most horrific of terms to make her argument seem plausible. Dr. Bernard Nathanson, an obstetrician/gynecologist and former abortion provider, objects "strenuously to Thomson's portrayal of pregnancy as a ninemonth involuntary imprisonment in bed. This casts an unfair and wrongheaded prejudice against the consideration of the state of pregnancy and skews the argument." Nathanson points out that "pregnancy is not a 'sickness.' Few pregnant women are bedridden and many, emotionally and physically, have never felt better. For these it is a stimulating experience, even for mothers who originally did not 'want' to be pregnant." Unlike the person who is plugged into Thomson's violinist, "alpha [the unborn entity] does not hurt the mother by being 'plugged in' . . . except in the case of well-defined medical indications." And "in those few cases where pregnancy is a medical penalty, it is a penalty lasting nine months."[5]

Compare and contrast Thomson's portrayal of pregnancy with the fact that researchers have recently discovered that many people believe that a pregnant woman cannot work as effectively as a nonpregnant woman who is employed to do the same job in the same work place. This has upset a number of feminists, and rightfully so. They argue that a pregnant woman is not incapacitated or ill, but can work just as effectively as a nonpregnant

woman.[6] But why then do feminists who use Thomson's argument argue, when it comes to abortion, that pregnancy is similar to being bedridden and hooked up to a violinist for nine months? When it comes to equality in the workplace (with which I agree with the feminists), there is no problem. But in the case of morally justifying abortion rights, pregnancy is painted in the most horrific of terms. Although not logically fatal to the abortion-rights position, this sort of double-mindedness is not conducive to good moral reasoning.

2. *The libertarian principles underlying Thomson's case are inconsistent with the State-mandated agenda of radical feminism.* If Thomson's illustration works at all, it works contrary to the statist principles of radical feminism (of course, a libertarian feminist need not be fazed by this objection). Levin points out that "while appeal to an absolute right to the disposition of one's body coheres well with other strongly libertarian positions (laissez-faire in the marketplace, parental autonomy in education of their children, freedom of private association), this appeal is most commonly made by feminists who are antilibertarian on just about every other issue." For example, "feminists who advocate state-mandated quotas, state-mandated comparable worth pay scales, the censorship of 'sexist' textbooks in the public schools, laws against 'sexually harassing speech' and legal limitations on private association excluding homosexuals, will go on to advocate abortion on the basis of an absolute libertarianism at odds with every one of those policies."[7] Although this criticism is ad hominem, as was the previous one, it underscores the important political fact that many abortion-rights advocates are more than willing to hold and earnestly defend contrary principles for the sake of legally mandating their ideological agenda.

This sort of inconsistency is evident in abortion-rights activity throughout the United States. In the state of Nevada, those who supported an abortion-rights referendum in November of 1990 told the voting public that they wanted to "get the government off of our backs and out of the bedrooms." But when the state legislature met in January these same abortion-rights supporters, under the auspices of the Nevada Women's Lobby, proposed legislation that asked for the taxpayers of the state to fund school-based sex clinics (which will refer teenage girls to abortion services and are euphemistically called health clinics) and assorted other programs. Forgetting that many of us keep our wallets in our back pockets and place them in the evening on our dressers in our bedrooms, the members of the Nevada Women's Lobby did not hesitate to do in January what they vehemently opposed in November: to get the government on our backs and *in* our bedrooms. The libertarians of November became the social engineers of March.

3. *Thomson's argument implies a macho view of bodily control, a view inconsistent with true feminism.* Some have pointed out that Thomson's argument or the reasoning behind it is actually quite antifeminist.[8] In response to a similar argument from a woman's right to control her own body, one feminist publication asks, "What kind of control are we talking about? A control that allows for violence against another human being is a macho, oppressive kind of control. Women rightly object when others try to have that kind of control over them, and the movement for women's rights asserts the moral right of women to be free from the control of others." After all, "abortion involves violence against a small, weak and dependent child. It is macho control, the very kind the feminist movement most eloquently opposes in other contexts."[9]

Celia Wolf-Devine observes that "abortion has something . . . in common with the behavior eco-feminists and pacifist feminists take to be characteristically masculine; it shows a willingness to use violence in order to take control. The fetus is destroyed by being pulled apart by suction, cut in pieces, or poisoned." Wolf-Devine goes on to point out that "in terms of social thought . . . it is the masculine models which are most frequently employed in thinking about abortion. If masculine thought is naturally hierarchical and oriented toward power and control, then the interests of the fetus (who has no power) would naturally be suppressed in favor of the interests of the mother. But to the extent that feminist social thought is egalitarian, the question must be raised of why the mother's interests should prevail over the child's . . . Feminist thought about abortion

has . . . been deeply pervaded by the individualism which they so ardently criticize."[10]

NOTES

1. The lengths to which Thomson will go to deny the natural relationship between sex, reproduction, and filial obligations is evident in her use of the following analogy: "If the room is stuffy, and I therefore open a window to air it, and a burglar climbs in, it would be absurd to say. 'Ah, now he can stay, she's given him a right to use her house—for she is partially responsible for his presence there, having voluntarily done what enabled him to get in, in full knowledge that there are such things as burglars, and that burglars burgle.'" Because there is no natural dependency between burglar and homeowner, as there is between child and parent, Thomson's analogy is way off the mark. Burglars don't belong in other people's homes; whereas pre-born children belong in no other place except their mother's wombs.

2. Christina Hoff Sommers, "Philosophers Against the Family," in *Person to Person,* ed. Hugh LaFollette and George Graham (Philadelphia: Temple University Press, 1989). [Reprinted in chapter 12 of this volume.] this volume, chapter 12.

3. Stephen D. Schwarz, *The Moral Question of Abortion.* Chicago: Loyola University Press, 1990, 118.

4. Michael Levin, *Feminism and Freedom.* New Brunswick, N.J.: Transaction, 1987, 288–289.

5. Bernard Nathanson, M.D., *Aborting America.* New York: Doubleday, 1979, 220.

6. Michelle Healy "At Work: Maternity Bias," *USA Today* (30 July 1990): 1A. Conducted by researcher Hal Gruental of State University of New York, Albany, this survey found that 41 percent of those interviewed (133 women and 122 men at eight businesses in the Northeast) "said they think pregnancy hurts a woman's job performance."

7. Michael Levin, review of *Life in the Balance* by Robert Weinberg, *Constitutional Commentary* 3 (Summer 1986): 507–508.

8. Although not dealing exclusively with Thomson's argument, Celia Wolf-Devine's article is quite helpful: "Abortion and the 'Feminine Voice,'" *Public Affairs Quarterly* 3 (July 1989): 181–197. See also Doris Gordon, "Abortion and Thomson's Violinist," a paper published by Libertarians for Life, 1991 (13424 Hathaway Drive, Wheaton, Md. 20906; 301-460-4041); Janet Smith, "Abortion as a Feminist Concern," in *The Zero People,* ed. Jeffe

Lane Hensley, Ann Arbor, Mich.: Servant, 1983, 77–95; and John T. Wilcox, "Nature as Demonic in Thomson's Defense of Abortion," *The New Scholasticism* 63 (Autumn 1989). 463–484.

9. N.a., *Sound Advice for all Prolife Activists and Candidates Who Wish to Include a Concern for Women's Rights in Their Prolife Advocacy: Feminists for Life Debate Handbook.* Kansas City, Mo.: Feminists for Life of America, n.d., 15–16.

10. Wolf-Devine, "Abortion," 86, 87.

4

Is Infanticide Wrong?

Tooley and His Critics

Infanticide is the killing of a human newborn (or neonate). Those who think that abortion is morally impermissible typically think that there cannot be any morally significant difference between abortion and infanticide. They argue that whatever it is that endows the human neonate with a right to life also endows the human fetus with the same right to life. Those who think that abortion is morally permissible typically agree with their opponents that infanticide is morally impermissible. Hence they typically resist the claim that the fetus and the neonate have exactly the same right to life.

Michael Tooley is an exception. Tooley agrees with the opponents of abortion that the permissibility of abortion stands or falls with the permissibility of infanticide. Furthermore, he argues for the claim that infanticide is morally permissible, and that it is morally permissible for the same reason that abortion is morally permissible: They are both permissible because neither the human fetus nor the human neonate has a right to life.

If a being has a right to something, then others are under an obligation not to deprive the right-bearer of that something. So, if a being has a right to life, then others have an obligation not to kill it. What does it take for a being to have a right to life? Tooley argues that for a being to have a right to life it must satisfy a certain condition: "An organism possesses a serious right to life only if it possesses the concept of a self as a continuing subject of experiences and other mental states, and believes that it is itself such a continuing entity." Let us abbreviate everything that follows "only if" by the following short summary: "it possesses the concept of self." Tooley's main argument can be summarized thus:

P1   An organism has a serious right to life only if it possesses the concept of self.
P2   A human neonate does not possess the concept of self.
P3   Killing an organism is, *in itself*, seriously immoral only if the organism has a serious right to life.

C   Infanticide is not, *in itself*, seriously immoral.

It is easy to see that a parallel argument can be run for abortion, for if the neonate does not possess the concept of self, then a fetus surely lacks that concept.

The bulk of Tooley's article is devoted to establishing the first premise—that an organism has a right to life only if it has the concept of self. Offering a simplified version of his argument, Tooley begins with the following observation: "To ascribe a right to an individual is to assert something about the prima facie obligations of other individuals to act, or to refrain from acting, in certain ways." Tooley talks here of a prima facie obligation, and we need to spell out quickly what that is. You have an obligation to fulfill your promise to meet me for lunch, but you are running late and can make the lunch date only by driving recklessly and endangering the lives of others on the road. Clearly, you also have an obligation not to endanger the lives of other drivers. Your obligations thus conflict. You clearly cannot fulfill both of them. Clearly, you do not have an absolute obligation to keep your lunch promise. You have an obligation to keep your lunch promise only conditionally: you are obligated to do so provided that fulfilling that obligation does not involve the violation of other, weightier obligations (or other, weightier considerations). An obligation that is conditional on a proviso is a "prima facie obligation." Once the condition is satisfied, then the prima facie obligation ceases to be conditional and becomes absolute.

Tooley goes on to claim that the obligation that a right to X imposes on others is conditional upon the right-bearer having a certain desire, the desire for X. He continues:

> However, the obligations in question are conditional ones, being dependent upon the existence of certain desires of the individual to whom the right is ascribed. Thus if an individual asks one to destroy something to which he has a right, one does not violate his right to that thing if one proceeds to destroy it. This suggests the following analysis: "A has a right to X" is roughly synonomous with "If A desires X, then others are under a prima facie obligation to refrain from actions that would deprive him of it."

The crucial point here is that the obligation that A's right to X imposes on others is conditional upon A's actually desiring X. If A lacks that desire, then others have no corresponding obligation not to deprive A of X. Further, A cannot be said to desire X unless he possesses the appropriate concepts. Consider property rights. Part of a property right is the right not to have your property stolen. According to Tooley, then, for you to have the right not to have your property stolen, you must desire not to have your property stolen, and to desire not to have your property stolen, you must possess the concept of property and the concept of stealing. So a right to X requires the right-bearer's possession of the desire for X, and the desire for X requires possession of the requisite concepts.

Let us turn now to the right to life. What exactly is that a right to? Tooley argues that what we value in continuing to live is the continuation of our life as a self-conscious subject of experience. If I were to put you into a deep and irreversible coma, your body would go on functioning biologically but your mental life would come to an end; you would cease to be a self-conscious subject of experiences, and what I had done to you would be just as bad as having killed you. This suggests that your right to life is not a right to continued biological functioning but rather to continued existence as a self-conscious subject of experiences. For your right to life to impose obligations on me, you must desire life—that is to say, to desire to continue as a self-conscious subject of experiences. And to desire that, you must possess the concept of a self-conscious subject of experience. You must possess the concept of self.

We can now summarize Tooley's subsidiary argument for P1 of his main argument:

P1* A has a right to X only if A desires X.
P2* A desires X only if A possesses the concept of X.
P3* The right to life is the right to continue as a self-conscious subject of experiences.

C   A has the right to life only if A possesses the concept of self.

This is the simplified version of Tooley's argument. The more sophisticated version deals with cases of beings who do not *currently* have the requisite desires but to whom we nevertheless ascribe rights, including the right to life. For example, the temporarily comatose person may currently lack the desire to continue as a self-conscious subject of experiences, but it would still be wrong to kill him. The same applies to those who are asleep, drugged, or depressed. For these cases, Tooley substitutes a conditional—that they would desire X if they were not comatose, asleep, depressed, or drugged. The important point, Tooley argues, is that to have an effective right to life, one that imposes obligations on others not to kill you, you must have the capability of possessing the concept of self.

Alan Carter attacks the first premise, P1*, of Tooley's subsidiary argument: that one cannot possess a right to X without desiring X. Carter considers two cases. The first concerns the rights of the dead. Suppose someone promises her dying father that she will take good care of his cat after he dies. The daughter now has a prima facie obligation to feed the cat after her father's demise, and her father has the correlative right to have his cat fed by his daughter. Clearly neither the father's right nor his daughter's obligation ceases with his death; rather, they are activated by his death. But after he is dead, the man has no desires at all. So, neither the actual desire to have his cat fed nor the capability of desiring that is necessary for the father to possess the right to have the cat fed by his daughter.

But perhaps the dead are problematic in various ways, and ascribing rights to them does seem odd. Carter makes a more direct attack on Tooley's claim with some less controversial rights, namely property rights. Suppose you own a coat but no longer want it. Does it follow that I can now take it out of your wardrobe and make off with it? Carter answers no. That would be theft, a clear infringement of your property rights. You must explicitly waive your property rights before I am entitled to take the coat: "You must express your desire that I take your coat before I can take it permissibly. To take it permissibly I must have your express permission." What this suggests is that "A has a right to X" is roughly equivalent to something different from Tooley's suggestion: that unless A clearly expresses his desire not to have or retain X, others are under a prima facie obligation not to deprive A of X. Carter continues:

> One ramification of such an alternative analysis is that it provides no reason to think that desiring X is a necessary condition for having a right to X. Hence, it provides no reason to think that desiring to continue as a subject of experiences is a necessary condition for having a serious right to life.

Carter suggests that one enjoys a right unless one desires to waive it and in addition explicitly expresses one's desire to waive it. So, anyone who was incapable of expressing his desire to waive a right could not waive it. This provides a simpler explanation of why it would be wrong to kill the man in a temporary coma than Tooley's account gives us.

John Stevens also launches an attack on Tooley's subsidiary argument, but his paper is primarily an attack on the premises one and two (P1* and P2*) taken together. For these jointly entail what Stevens calls the "conceptual possession requirement"; that in order to possess a right to X one must possess the concept of X. This requirement can be validly inferred directly from P1* and P2*:

P1* A has a right to X only if A desires X.
P2* A desires X only if A possesses the concept of X.

C   A has a right to X only if A possesses the concept of X.

Note that this argument is valid. It is an instance of the following valid schema, every instance of which is a valid argument:

P1 E only if F.
P2 F only if G.

C   E only if G.

Given that the argument is valid, the only question is whether the premises are true. Stevens shows that they cannot both be true, by providing the following counterexample to the principle stated in the conclusion.

Mr. Smith has a very comprehensive medical insurance plan, one that guarantees him the best available treatment for any medical condition. But Smith never bothers to bone up on medical conditions. Consequently, he knows nothing about the immune system, let alone what an autoimmune disease is or what immunosuppressive therapy amounts to. That is, he lacks the concept of immunosuppressive therapy. Then Smith discovers that he is sick. He goes to the clinic and asks for the best treatment available for whatever it is he has. As it happens, he has an autoimmune disease. According to his contract, he has a right to the best treatment available, and in fact the best treatment available is immunosuppressive therapy, so he has a right to immunosuppressive therapy. But he has no concept of immunosuppressive therapy. We can state Stevens's argument thus:

P1 Smith has a right to the best available treatment for his autoimmune disease.
P2 The best available treatment for his autoimmune disease is immunosuppressive therapy.
P3 Smith does not possess the concept of immunosuppressive therapy.

C   Smith has a right to X and Smith does not possess the concept of X.

What is interesting about Stevens's article is that he does not stop with this apparent refutation of the conceptual-possession requirement. Rather, he goes on to consider various possible responses that someone defending Tooley's main argument might try, and for each such response he argues that Tooley's main argument will run into deep trouble.

QUESTIONS FOR CONSIDERATION

In thinking about Tooley's argument, and those of his critics, explore some of the following questions.

• First, what is Tooley's reason for asserting that "'A has a right to X' is roughly synonymous with 'If A desires X then others have a prima facie obligation not to deprive A of X.'" Is the reason a good one?

• Consider Carter's example of the daughter's promise to her dying father. Does her father have a right to have his cat fed? Do the dead have any rights? Does Tooley's simple analysis deprive the dead of all rights?

• Go back to the article and read carefully Tooley's more sophisticated account of what it is to have a right. Apply that account to the dead. Does it give plausible results? Does it, too, deprive the dead of rights?

• Consider the reply that Stevens calls "possible reply A." Does it make sense to say that someone desires X even though he lacks the concept of X? (Does Smith desire immunosuppressive therapy even though he has no idea that immunosuppressive therapy is what he desires?) Consider Stevens's possible reply B: Can you have a right to X and not have a right to Y, even though X is identical to Y?

• Showing that Tooley's argument is defective is not tantamount to showing that newborns or fetuses have the same kind of right to life that adult human beings have. Nor does it discharge one of the responsibility of finding what it is that does ground a being's right to life. Rather, it moves the debate to fresh ground.

FURTHER READING

Goldman, Alan H. "Abortion and the Right to Life." *Personalist* 60 (1979): 402–06.
Jones, Gary. "Rights and Desires." *Ethics* 92 (1981): 52–56.

Michael Tooley | # Abortion and Infanticide

This essay deals with the question of the morality of abortion and infanticide. The fundamental ethical objection traditionally advanced against these practices rests on the contention that human fetuses and infants have a right to life. It is this claim which will be the focus of attention here. The basic issue to be discussed, then, is what properties a thing must possess in order to have a serious right to life. My approach will be to set out and defend a basic moral principle specifying a condition an organism must satisfy if it is to have a serious right to life. It will be seen that this condition is not satisfied by human fetuses and infants, and thus that they do not have a right to life. So unless there are other substantial

objections to abortion and infanticide, one is forced to conclude that these practices are morally acceptable ones. In contrast, it may turn out that our treatment of adult members of other species—cats, dogs, polar bears—is morally indefensible. For it is quite possible that such animals do possess properties that endow them with a right to life.

I. ABORTION AND INFANTICIDE

One reason the question of the morality of infanticide is worth examining is that it seems very difficult to formulate a completely satisfactory liberal posi-

From Michael Tooley, "Abortion and Infanticide," *Philosophy and Public Affairs* 2 (1972): 37–65. Some notes and some parts of the text have been deleted. Reprinted by permission of Princeton University Press.

tion on abortion without coming to grips with the infanticide issue. The problem the liberal encounters is essentially that of specifying a cutoff point which is not arbitrary: at what stage in the development of a human being does it cease to be morally permissible to destroy it? It is important to be clear about the difficulty here. The conservative's objection is not that since there is a continuous line of development from a zygote to a newborn baby, one must conclude that if it is seriously wrong to destroy a newborn baby it is also seriously wrong to destroy a zygote or any intermediate stage in the development of a human being. His point is rather that if one says it is wrong to destroy a newborn baby but not a zygote or some intermediate stage in the development of a human being, one should be prepared to point to a *morally relevant* difference between a newborn baby and the earlier stage in the development of a human being.

Precisely the same difficulty can, of course, be raised for a person who holds that infanticide is morally permissible. The conservative will ask what morally relevant differences there are between an adult human being and a newborn baby. What makes it morally permissible to destroy a baby, but wrong to kill an adult? So the challenge remains. But I will argue that in this case there is an extremely plausible answer.

Reflecting on the morality of infanticide forces one to face up to this challenge. In the case of abortion a number of events—quickening or viability, for instance—might be taken as cutoff points, and it is easy to overlook the fact that none of these events involves any morally significant change in the developing human. In contrast, if one is going to defend infanticide, one has to get very clear about what makes something a person, what gives something a right to life.

One of the interesting ways in which the abortion issue differs from most other moral issues is that the plausible positions on abortion appear to be extreme positions. For if a human fetus is a person, one is inclined to say that, in general, one would be justified in killing it only to save the life of the mother.[1] Such is the extreme conservative position. On the other hand, if the fetus is not a person, how can it be

seriously wrong to destroy it? Why would one need to point to special circumstances to justify such action? The upshot is that there is no room for a moderate position on the issue of abortion such as one finds, for example, in the Model Penal Code recommendations.

Aside from the light it may shed on the abortion question, the issue of infanticide is both interesting and important in its own right. The theoretical interest has been mentioned: it forces one to face up to the question of what makes something a person. The practical importance need not be labored. Most people would prefer to raise children who do not suffer from gross deformities or from severe physical, emotional, or intellectual handicaps. If it could be shown that there is no moral objection to infanticide the happiness of society could be significantly and justifiably increased.

Infanticide is also of interest because of the strong emotions it arouses. The typical reaction to infanticide is like the reaction to incest or cannibalism, or the reaction of previous generations to masturbation or oral sex. The response, rather than appealing to carefully formulated moral principles, is primarily visceral. When philosophers themselves respond in this way, offering no arguments, and dismissing infanticide out of hand, it is reasonable to suspect that one is dealing with a taboo rather than with a rational prohibition. I shall attempt to show that this is in fact the case.

II.   TERMINOLOGY: "PERSON" VERSUS "HUMAN BEING"

How is the term "person" to be interpreted? I shall treat the concept of a person as a purely moral concept, free of all descriptive content. Specifically, in my usage the sentence "X is a person" will be synonymous with the sentence "X has a (serious) moral right to life."

This usage diverges slightly from what is perhaps the more common way of interpreting the term "person" when it is employed as a purely moral term, where to say that X is a person is to say that X has rights. If everything that had rights had a right to life, these interpretations would be extensionally equivalent. But I am inclined to think that it does not follow from acceptable moral principles that whatever has any rights at all has a right to life. My reason is this. Given the choice between being killed and being tortured for an hour, most adult humans would surely choose the latter. So it seems plausible to say it is worse to kill an adult human being than it is to torture him for an hour. In contrast, it seems to me that while it is not seriously wrong to kill a newborn kitten, it is seriously wrong to torture one for an hour. This *suggests* that newborn kittens may have a right not to be tortured without having a serious right to life. For it seems to be true that an individual has a right to something whenever it is the case that, if he wants that thing, it would be wrong for others to deprive him of it. Then if it is wrong to inflict a certain sensation upon a kitten if it doesn't want to experience that sensation, it will follow that the kitten has a right not to have sensation inflicted upon it. I shall return to this example later. My point here is merely that it provides some reason for holding that it does not follow from acceptable moral principles that if something has any rights at all, it has a serious right to life.

There has been a tendency in recent discussions of abortion to use expressions such as "person" and "human being" interchangeably. B. A. Brody, for example, refers to the difficulty of determining "whether destroying the foetus constitutes the taking of a human life," and suggests it is very plausible that "the taking of a human life is an action that has bad consequences for him whose life is being taken."[2] When Brody refers to something as a human life he apparently construes this as entailing that the thing is a person. For if every living organism belonging to the species homo sapiens counted as a human life, there would be no difficulty in determining whether a fetus inside a human mother was a human life.

The same tendency is found in Judith Jarvis Thomson's article, which opens with the statement: "Most opposition to abortion relies on the premise that the fetus is a human being, a person, from the moment of conception."[3] The same is true of Roger Wertheimer, who explicitly says: "First off I should note that the expressions 'a human life,' 'a human being,' 'a person' are virtually interchangeable in this context."[4]

The tendency to use expressions like "person" and "human being" interchangeably is an unfortunate one. For one thing, it tends to lend covert support to antiabortionist positions. Given such usage, one who holds a liberal view of abortion is put in the position of maintaining that fetuses, at least up to a certain point, are not human beings. Even philosophers are led astray by this usage. Thus Wertheimer says that "except for monstrosities, every member of our species is indubitably a person, a human being, at the very latest at birth."[5] Is it really *indubitable* that newborn babies are persons? Surely this is a wild contention. Wertheimer is falling prey to the confusion naturally engendered by the practice of using "person" and "human being" interchangeably. Another example of this is provided by Thomson: "I am inclined to think also that we shall probably have to agree that the fetus has already become a human person well before birth. Indeed, it comes as a surprise when one first learns how early in its life it begins to acquire human characteristics. By the tenth week, for example, it already has a face, arms and legs, fingers and toes; it has internal organs, and brain activity is detectable."[6] But what do such physiological characteristics have to do with the question of whether the organism is a person? Thomson, partly, I think, because of the unfortunate use of terminology, does not even raise this question. As a result she virtually takes it for granted that there are some cases in which abortion is "positively indecent."[7]

There is a second reason why using "person" and "human being" interchangeably is unhappy philosophically. If one says that the dispute between pro- and anti-abortionists centers on whether the fetus is a human, it is natural to conclude that it is essentially a disagreement about certain facts, a disagreement about what properties a fetus possesses. Thus, Wertheimer says that "if one insists on using the raggy fact-value distinction, then one ought to say that the dispute is over a matter of fact in the sense in which it is a fact that the Negro slaves were human beings."[8] I shall argue that the two cases are not parallel, and that in the case of abortion what is primarily at stake is what moral principles one should accept. If one says that the central issue between conservatives and liberals in the abortion question is whether the fetus is a person, it is clear that the dispute may be either about what properties a thing must have in order to be a person, in order to have a right to life—a moral question—or about whether a fetus at a given stage of development as a matter of fact possesses the properties in question. The temptation to suppose that the disagreement must be a factual one is removed.

It should now be clear why the common practice of using expressions such as "person" and "human being" interchangeably in discussions of abortion is unfortunate. It would perhaps be best to avoid the term "human" altogether, employing instead some expression that is more naturally interpreted as referring to a certain type of biological organism characterized in physiological terms, such as "member of the species Homo sapiens." My own approach will be to use the term "human" only in contexts where it is not philosophically dangerous.

III.   THE BASIC ISSUE: WHEN IS A MEMBER OF THE SPECIES HOMO SAPIENS A PERSON?

Settling the issue of the morality of abortion and infanticide will involve answering the following questions: What properties must something have to be a person, i.e., to have a serious right to life? At what point in the development of a member of the species Homo sapiens does the organism possess the properties that make it a person? The first question raises a moral issue. To answer it is to decide what basic[9] moral principles involving the ascription of a right to life one ought to accept. The second question raises a purely factual issue, since the properties in question are properties of a purely descriptive sort.

Some writers seem quite pessimistic about the possibility of resolving the question of the morality of abortion. Indeed, some have gone so far as to suggest that the question of whether the fetus is a person is in principle unanswerable: "we seem to be stuck with the indeterminateness of the fetus' humanity."[10] An understanding of some of the sources of

this pessimism will, I think, help us to tackle the problem. Let us begin by considering the similarity a number of people have noted between the issue of abortion and the issue of Negro slavery. The question here is why it should be more difficult to decide whether abortion and infanticide are acceptable than it was to decide whether slavery was acceptable. The answer seems to be that in the case of slavery there are moral principles of a quite uncontroversial sort that settle the issue. Thus most people would agree to some such principle as the following: No organism that has experiences, that is capable of thought and of using language, and that has harmed no one, should be made a slave. In the case of abortion, on the other hand, conditions that are generally agreed to be sufficient grounds for ascribing a right to life to something do not suffice to settle the issue. It is easy to specify other, purportedly sufficient conditions that will settle the issue, but no one has been successful in putting forward considerations that will convince others to accept those additional moral principles.

I do not share the general pessimism about the possibility of resolving the issue of abortion and infanticide because I believe it is possible to point to a very plausible moral principle dealing with the question of *necessary* conditions for something's having a right to life, where the conditions in question will provide an answer to the question of the permissibility of abortion and infanticide.

There is a second cause of pessimism that should be noted before proceeding. It is tied up with the fact that the development of an organism is one of gradual and continuous change. Given this continuity, how is one to draw a line at one point and declare it permissible to destroy a member of Homo sapiens up to, but not beyond, that point? Won't there be an arbitrariness about any point that is chosen? I will return to this worry shortly. It does not present a serious difficulty once the basic moral principles relevant to the ascription of a right to life to an individual are established.

Let us turn now to the first and most fundamental question: What properties must something have in order to be a person, i.e., to have a serious right to life? The claim I wish to defend is this: An organism possesses a serious right to life only if it possesses the concept of a self as a continuing subject of experiences and other mental states, and believes that it is itself such a continuing entity.

My basic argument in support of this claim, which I will call the self-consciousness requirement, will be clearest, I think, if I first offer a simplified version of the argument, and then consider a modification that seems desirable. The simplified version of my argument is this. To ascribe a right to an individual is to assert something about the prima facie obligations of other individuals to act, or to refrain from acting, in certain ways. However, the obligations in question are conditional ones, being dependent upon the existence of certain desires of the individual to whom the right is ascribed. Thus if an individual asks one to destroy something to which he has a right, one does not violate his right to that thing if one proceeds to destroy it. This suggests the following analysis: "A has a right to X" is roughly synonymous with "If A desires X, then others are under a prima facie obligation to refrain from actions that would deprive him of it."[11]

Although this analysis is initially plausible, there are reasons for thinking it not entirely correct. I will consider these later. Even here, however, some expansion is necessary, since there are features of the concept of a right that are important in the present context, and that ought to be dealt with more explicitly. In particular, it seems to be a conceptual truth that things that lack consciousness, such as ordinary machines, cannot have rights. Does this conceptual truth follow from the above analysis of the concept of a right? The answer depends on how the term "desire" is interpreted. If one adopts a completely behavioristic interpretation of "desire," so that a machine that searches for an electrical outlet in order to get its batteries recharged is described as having a desire to be recharged, then it will not follow from this analysis that objects that lack consciousness cannot have rights. On the other hand, if "desire" is interpreted in such a way that desires are states necessarily standing in some sort of relationship to states of consciousness, it will follow from the analysis that a machine that is not capable of being conscious, and consequently of having de-

sires, cannot have any rights. I think those who defend analyses of the concept of a right along the lines of this one do have in mind an interpretation of the term "desire" that involves reference to something more than behavioral dispositions. However, rather than relying on this, it seems preferable to make such an interpretation explicit. The following analysis is a natural way of doing that: "A has a right to X" is roughly synonymous with "A is the sort of thing that is a subject of experiences and other mental states, A is capable of desiring X, and if A does desire X, then others are under a prima facie obligation to refrain from actions that would deprive him of it."

The next step in the argument is basically a matter of applying this analysis to the concept of a right to life. Unfortunately the expression "right to life" is not entirely a happy one, since it suggests that the right in question concerns the continued existence of a biological organism. That this is incorrect can be brought out by considering possible ways of violating an individual's right to life. Suppose, for example, that by some technology of the future the brain of an adult human were to be completely reprogrammed, so that the organism wound up with memories (or rather, apparent memories), beliefs, attitudes, and personality traits completely different from those associated with it before it was subjected to reprogramming. In such a case one would surely say that an individual had been destroyed, that an adult human's right to life had been violated, even though no biological organism had been killed. This example shows that the expression "right to life" is misleading, since what one is really concerned about is not just the continued existence of a biological organism, but the right of a subject of experiences and other mental states to continue to exist.

Given this more precise description of the right with which we are here concerned, we are now in a position to apply the analysis of the concept of a right stated above. When we do so we find that the statement "A has a right to continue to exist as a subject of experiences and other mental states" is roughly synonymous with the statement "A is a subject of experiences and other mental states, A is capable of desiring to continue to exist as a subject of experiences and other mental states, and if A does desire to continue to exist as such an entity, then others are under a prima facie obligation not to prevent him from doing so."

The final stage in the argument is simply a matter of asking what must be the case if something is to be capable of having a desire to continue existing as a subject of experiences and other mental states. The basic point here is that the desires a thing can have are limited by the concepts it possesses. For the fundamental way of describing a given desire is as a desire that a certain proposition be true. Then, since one cannot desire that a certain proposition be true unless one understands it, and since one cannot understand it without possessing the concepts involved in it, it follows that the desires one can have are limited by the concepts one possesses. Applying this to the present case results in the conclusion that an entity cannot be the sort of thing that can desire that a subject of experiences and other mental states exist unless it possesses the concept of such a subject. Moreover, an entity cannot desire that it itself *continue* existing as a subject of experiences and other mental states unless it believes that it is now such a subject. This completes the justification of the claim that it is a necessary condition of something's having a serious right to life that it possess the concept of a self as a continuing subject of experiences, and that it believe that it is itself such an entity.

Let us now consider a modification in the above argument that seems desirable. This modification concerns the crucial conceptual claim advanced about the relationship between ascription of rights and ascription of the corresponding desires. Certain situations suggest that there may be exceptions to the claim that if a person doesn't desire something, one cannot violate his right to it. There are three types of situations that call this claim into question: (i) situations in which an individual's desires reflect a state of emotional disturbance; (ii) situations in which a previously conscious individual is temporarily unconscious; (iii) situations in which an individual's desires have been distorted by conditioning or by indoctrination.

As an example of the first, consider a case in which an adult human falls into a state of depression

which his psychiatrist recognizes as temporary. While in the state he tells people he wishes he were dead. His psychiatrist, accepting the view that there can be no violation of an individual's right to life unless the individual has a desire to live, decides to let his patient have his way and kills him. Or consider a related case in which one person gives another a drug that produces a state of temporary depression; the recipient expresses a wish that he were dead. The person who administered the drug then kills him. Doesn't one want to say in both these cases that the agent did something seriously wrong in killing the other person? And isn't the reason the action was seriously wrong in each case the fact that it violated the individual's right to life? If so, the right to life cannot be linked with a desire to live in the way claimed above.

The second set of situations are ones in which an individual is unconscious for some reason—that is, he is sleeping, or drugged, or in a temporary coma. Does an individual in such a state have any desires? People do sometimes say that an unconscious individual wants something, but it might be argued that if such talk is not to be simply false it must be interpreted as actually referring to the desires the individual *would* have if he were now conscious. Consequently, if the analysis of the concept of a right proposed above were correct, it would follow that one does not violate an individual's right if one takes his car, or kills him, while he is asleep.

Finally, consider situations in which an individual's desires have been distorted, either by inculcation of irrational beliefs or by direct conditioning. Thus an individual may permit someone to kill him because he has been convinced that if he allows himself to be sacrificed to the gods he will be gloriously rewarded in a life to come. Or an individual may be enslaved after first having been conditioned to desire a life of slavery. Doesn't one want to say that in the former case an individual's right to life has been violated, and in the latter his right to freedom?

Situations such as these strongly suggest that even if an individual doesn't want something, it is still possible to violate his right to it. Some modification of the earlier account of the concept of a right thus seems in order. The analysis given covers, I believe, the paradigmatic cases of violation of an individual's rights, but there are other, secondary cases where one also wants to say that someone's right has been violated which are not included.

Precisely how the revised analysis should be formulated in unclear. Here it will be sufficient merely to say that, in view of the above, an individual's right to X can be violated not only when he desires X, but also when he *would* now desire X were it not for one of the following: (i) he is in an emotionally unbalanced state; (ii) he is temporarily unconscious; (iii) he has been conditioned to desire the absence of X.

The critical point now is that, even given this extension of the conditions under which an individual's right to something can be violated, it is still true that one's right to something can be violated only when one has the conceptual capability of desiring the thing in question. For example, an individual who would now desire not to be a slave if he weren't emotionally unbalanced, or if he weren't temporarily unconscious, or if he hadn't previously been conditioned to want to be a slave, must possess the concepts involved in the desire not to be a slave. Since it is really only the conceptual capability presupposed by the desire to continue existing as a subject of experiences and other mental states, and not the desire itself, that enters into the above argument, the modification required in the account of the conditions under which an individual's rights can be violated does not undercut my defense of the self-consciousness requirement.[12]

To sum up, my argument has been that having a right to life presupposes that one is capable of desiring to continue existing as a subject of experiences and other mental states. This in turn presupposes both that one has the concept of such a continuing entity and that one believes that one is oneself such an entity. So an entity that lacks such a consciousness of itself as a continuing subject of mental states does not have a right to life.

It would be natural to ask at this point whether satisfaction of this requirement is not only necessary but also sufficient to ensure that a thing has a right to life. I am inclined to an affirmative answer. However, the issue is not urgent in the present context, since as long as the requirement is in fact a necessary

one we have the basis of an adequate defense of abortion and infanticide. If an organism must satisfy some other condition before it has a serious right to life, the result will merely be that the interval during which infanticide is morally permissible may be somewhat longer. Although the point at which an organism first achieves self-consciousness and hence the capacity of desiring to continue existing as a subject of experiences and other mental states may be a theoretically incorrect cutoff point, it is at least a morally safe one: any error it involves is on the side of caution. . . .

V. REFUTATION OF THE CONSERVATIVE POSITION

Many have felt that the conservative's position is more defensible than the liberal's because the conservative can point to the gradual and continuous development of an organism as it changes from a zygote to an adult human being. He is then in a position to argue that it is morally arbitrary for the liberal to draw a line at some point in this continuous process and to say that abortion is permissible before, but not after, that particular point. The liberal's reply would presumably be that the emphasis upon the continuity of the process is misleading. What the conservative is really doing is simply challenging the liberal to specify the properties a thing must have in order to be a person, and to show that the developing organism does acquire the properties at the point selected by the liberal. The liberal may then reply that the difficulty he has meeting this challenge should not be taken as grounds for rejecting his position. For the conservative cannot meet this challenge either; the conservative is equally unable to say what properties something must have if it is to have a right to life.

Although this rejoinder does not dispose of the conservative's argument, it is not without bite. For defenders of the view that abortion is always wrong have failed to face up to the question of the basic moral principles on which their position rests. They have been content to assert the wrongness of killing any organism, from a zygote on, if that organism is a member of the species Homo sapiens. But they have overlooked the point that this cannot be an acceptable *basic* moral principle, since difference in species is not in itself a morally relevant difference. The conservative can reply, however, that it is possible to defend his position—but not the liberal's—*without* getting clear about the properties a thing must possess if it is to have a right to life. The conservative's defense will rest upon the following two claims: first, that there is a property, even if one is unable to specify what it is, that (i) is possessed by adult humans, and (ii) endows any organism possessing it with a serious right to life. Second, that if there are properties which satisfy (i) and (ii) above, at least one of those properties will be such that any organism potentially possessing that property has a serious right to life even now, simply by virtue of that potentiality, where an organism possesses a property potentially if it will come to have that property in the normal course of its development. The second claim—which I shall refer to as the potentiality principle—is critical to the conservative's defense. Because of it he is able to defend his position without deciding what properties a thing must possess in order to have a right to life. It is enough to know that adult members of Homo sapiens do have such a right. For then one can conclude that any organism which belongs to the species Homo sapiens, from a zygote on, must also have a right to life by virtue of the potentiality principle.

The liberal, by contrast, cannot mount a comparable argument. He cannot defend his position without offering at least a partial answer to the question of what properties a thing must possess in order to have a right to life.

The importance of the potentiality principle, however, goes beyond the fact that it provides support for the conservative's position. If the principle is unacceptable, then so is his position. For if the conservative cannot defend the view that an organism's having certain potentialities is sufficient grounds for ascribing to it a right to life, his claim that a fetus which is a member of Homo sapiens has a right to life can be attacked as follows. The reason an adult member of Homo sapiens has a right to life, but an infant ape does not, is that there are certain psychological properties which the former possesses

and the latter lacks. Now, even if one is unsure exactly what these psychological properties are, it is clear that an organism in the early stages of development from a zygote into an adult member of Homo sapiens does not possess these properties. One need merely compare a human fetus with an ape fetus. What mental states does the former enjoy that the latter does not? Surely it is reasonable to hold that there are no significant differences in their respective mental lives—assuming that one wishes to ascribe any mental states at all to such organisms. (Does a zygote have a mental life? Does it have experiences? Or beliefs? Or desires?) There are, of course, physiological differences, but these are not in themselves morally significant. *If* one held that potentialities were relevant to the ascription of a right to life, one could argue that the physiological differences, though not morally significant in themselves, are morally significant by virtue of their causal consequences: they will lead to later psychological differences that are morally relevant, and for this reason the physiological differences are themselves morally significant. But if the potentiality principle is not available, this line of argument cannot be used, and there will then be no differences between a human fetus and an ape fetus that the conservative can use as grounds for ascribing a serious right to life to the former but not to the latter.

It is therefore tempting to conclude that the conservative view of abortion is acceptable if and only if the potentiality principle is acceptable. But to say that the conservative position can be defended if the potentiality principle is acceptable is to assume that the argument is over once it is granted that the fetus has a right to life, and, as was noted above, Thomson has shown that there are serious grounds for questioning this assumption. In any case, the important point here is that the conservative position on abortion is acceptable *only if* the potentiality principle is sound.

One way to attack the potentiality principle is simply to argue in support of the self-consciousness requirement—the claim that only an organism that conceives of itself as a continuing subject of experiences has a right to life. For this requirement, when taken together with the claim that there is at least one property, possessed by adult humans, such that any organism possessing it has a serious right to life, entails the denial of the potentiality principle. Or at least this is so if we add the uncontroversial empirical claim that an organism that will in the normal course of events develop into an adult human does not from the very beginning of its existence possess a concept of a continuing subject of experiences together with a belief that it is itself such an entity.

I think it best, however, to scrutinize the potentiality principle itself, and not to base one's case against it simply on the self-consciousness requirement. Perhaps the first point to note is that the potentiality principle should not be confused with principles such as the following: the value of an object is related to the value of the things into which it can develop. This "valuation principle" is rather vague. There are ways of making it more precise, but we need not consider these here. Suppose now that one were to speak not of a right to life, but of the value of life. It would then be easy to make the mistake of thinking that the valuation principle was relevant to the potentiality principle—indeed, that it entailed it. But an individual's right to life is not based on the value of his life. To say that the world would be better off if it contained fewer people is not to say that it would be right to achieve such a better world by killing some of the present inhabitants. *If* having a right to life were a matter of a thing's value, then a thing's potentialities, being connected with its expected value, would clearly be relevant to the question of what rights it had. Conversely, once one realizes that a thing's rights are not a matter of its value, I think it becomes clear that an organism's potentialities are irrelevant to the question of whether it has a right to life.

But let us now turn to the task of finding a direct refutation of the potentiality principle. The basic issue is this. Is there any property J which satisfies the following conditions: (1) There is a property K such that any individual possessing property K has a right to life, and there is a scientific law L to the effect that any organism possessing property J will in the normal course of events come to possess property K at some later time. (2) Given the relationship between property J and property K just described,

anything possessing property J has a right to life. (3) If property J were not related to property K in the way indicated, it would not be the case that anything possessing property J thereby had a right to life. In short, the question is whether there is a property J that bestows a right to life on an organism *only because* J stands in a certain causal relationship to a second property K, which is such that anything possessing that property ipso facto has a right to life.

My argument turns upon the following critical principle: Let C be a causal process that normally leads to outcome E. Let A be an action that initiates process C, and B be an action involving a minimal expenditure of energy that stops process C before outcome E occurs. Assume further that actions A and B do not have any other consequences, and that E is the only morally significant outcome of process C. Then there is no moral difference between intentionally performing action B and intentionally refraining from performing action A, assuming identical motivation in both cases. This principle, which I shall refer to as the moral symmetry principle with respect to action and inaction, would be rejected by some philosophers. They would argue that there is an important distinction to be drawn between "what we owe people in the form of aid and what we owe them in the way of non-interference,"[13] and that the latter, "negative duties," are duties that it is more serious to neglect than the former, "positive" ones. This view arises from an intuitive response to examples such as the following. Even if it is wrong not to send food to starving people in other parts of the world, it is more wrong still to kill someone. And isn't the conclusion, then, that one's obligation to refrain from killing someone is a more serious obligation than one's obligation to save lives?

I want to argue that this is not the correct conclusion. I think it is tempting to draw this conclusion if one fails to consider the motivation that is likely to be associated with the respective actions. If someone performs an action he knows will kill someone else, this will usually be grounds for concluding that he wanted to kill the person in question. In contrast, failing to help someone may indicate only apathy, laziness, selfishness, or an amoral outlook: the fact that a person knowingly allows another to die will not normally be grounds for concluding that he desired that person's death. Someone who knowingly kills another is more likely to be seriously defective from a moral point of view than someone who fails to save another's life.

If we are not to be led to false conclusions by our intuitions about certain cases, we must explicitly assume identical motivations in the two situations. Compare, for example, the following: (1) Jones sees that Smith will be killed by a bomb unless he warns him. Jones's reaction is: "How lucky, it will save me the trouble of killing Smith myself." So Jones allows Smith to be killed by the bomb, even though he could easily have warned him. (2) Jones wants Smith dead, and therefore shoots him. Is one to say there is a significant difference between the wrongness of Jones's behavior in these two cases? Surely not. This shows the mistake of drawing a distinction between positive duties and negative duties and holding that the latter impose stricter obligations than the former. The difference in our intuitions about situations that involve giving aid to others and corresponding situations that involve not interfering with others is to be explained by reference to probable differences in the motivations operating in the two situations, and not by reference to a distinction between positive and negative duties. For once it is specified that the motivation is the same in the two situations, we realize that inaction is as wrong in the one case as action is in the other.

There is another point that may be relevant. Action involves effort, while inaction usually does not. It usually does not require any effort on my part to refrain from killing someone, but saving someone's life will require an expenditure of energy. One must then ask how large a sacrifice a person is morally required to make to save the life of another. If the sacrifice of time and energy is quite large it may be that one is not morally obliged to save the life of another in that situation. Superficial reflection upon such cases might easily lead us to introduce the distinction between positive and negative duties, but again it is clear that this would be a mistake. The point is not that one has a greater duty to refrain from killing others than to perform positive actions that will save them. It is rather that positive actions

require effort, and this means that in deciding what to do a person has to take into account his own right to do what he wants with his life, and not only the other person's right to life. To avoid this confusion, we should confine ourselves to comparisons between situations in which the positive action involves minimal effort.

The moral symmetry principle, as formulated above, explicitly takes these two factors into account. It applies only to pairs of situations in which the motivations are identical and the positive action involves minimal effort. Without these restrictions, the principle would be open to serious objection; with them, it seems perfectly acceptable. For the central objection to it rests on the claim that we must distinguish positive from negative duties and recognize that negative duties impose stronger obligations than positive ones. I have tried to show how this claim derives from an unsound account of our moral intuitions about certain situations.

My argument against the potentiality principle can now be stated. Suppose at some future time a chemical were to be discovered which when injected into the brain of a kitten would cause the kitten to develop into a cat possessing a brain of the sort possessed by humans, and consequently into a cat having all the psychological capabilities characteristic of adult humans. Such cats would be able to think, to use language, and so on. Now it would surely be morally indefensible in such a situation to ascribe a serious right to life to members of the species Homo sapiens without also ascribing it to cats that have undergone such a process of development: there would be no morally significant differences.

Secondly, it would not be seriously wrong to refain from injecting a newborn kitten with the special chemical, and to kill it instead. The fact that one could initiate a causal process that would transform a kitten into an entity that would eventually possess properties such that anything possessing them ipso facto has a serious right to life does not mean that the kitten has a serious right to life even before it has been subjected to the process of injection and transformation. The possibility of transforming kittens into persons will not make it any more wrong to kill newborn kittens than it is now.

Thirdly, in view of the symmetry principle, if it is not seriously wrong to refrain from initiating such a causal process, neither is it seriously wrong to interfere with such a process. Suppose a kitten is accidentally injected with the chemical. As long as it has not yet developed those properties that in themselves endow something with a right to life, there cannot be anything wrong with interfering with the causal process and preventing the development of the properties in question. Such interference might be accomplished either by injecting the kitten with some "neutralizing" chemical or simply by killing it.

But if it is not seriously wrong to destroy an injected kitten which will naturally develop the properties that bestow a right to life, neither can it be seriously wrong to destroy a member of Homo sapiens which lacks such properties, but will naturally come to have them. The potentialities are the same in both cases. The only difference is that in the case of a human fetus the potentialities have been present from the beginning of the organism's development, while in the case of the kitten they have been present only from the time it was injected with the special chemical. This difference in the time at which the potentialities were acquired is a morally irrelevant difference.

It should be emphasized that I am not here assuming that a human fetus does not possess properties which in themselves, and irrespective of their causal relationships to other properties, provide grounds for ascribing a right to life to whatever possesses them. The point is merely that if it is seriously wrong to kill something, the reason cannot be that the thing will later acquire properties that in themselves provide something with a right to life.

Finally, it is reasonable to believe that there are properties possessed by adult members of Homo sapiens which establish their right to life, and also that any normal human fetus will come to possess those properties shared by adult humans. But it has just been shown that if it is wrong to kill a human fetus, it cannot be because of its potentialities. One is therefore forced to conclude that the conservative's potentiality principle is false.

In short, anyone who wants to defend the potentiality principle must either argue against the moral symmetry principle or hold that in a world in which kittens could be transformed into "rational animals" it would be seriously wrong to kill newborn kittens. It is hard to believe there is much to be said for the latter moral claim. Consequently one expects the conservative's rejoinder to be directed against the symmetry principle. While I have not attempted to provide a thorough defense of that principle, I have tried to show that what seems to be the most important objection to it—the one that appeals to a distinction between positive and negative duties—is based on a superficial analysis of our moral intuitions. I believe that a more thorough examination of the symmetry principle would show it to be sound. If so, we should reject the potentiality principle, and the conservative position on abortion as well.

VI.   SUMMARY AND CONCLUSIONS

Let us return now to my basic claim, the self-consciousness requirement: An organism possesses a serious right to life only if it possesses the concept of a self as a continuing subject of experiences and other mental states, and believes that it is itself such a continuing entity. My defense of this claim has been twofold. I have offered a direct argument in support of it, and I have tried to show that traditional conservative and liberal views on abortion and infanticide, which involve a rejection of it, are unsound. I now want to mention one final reason why my claim should be accepted. Consider the example mentioned in section II—that of killing, as opposed to torturing, newborn kittens. I suggested there that while in the case of adult humans most people would consider it worse to kill an individual than to torture him for an hour, we do not usually view the killing of a newborn kitten as morally outrageous, although we would regard someone who tortured a newborn kitten for an hour as heinously evil. I pointed out that a possible conclusion that might be drawn from this is that newborn kittens have a right not to be tortured, but do not have a serious right to life. If this is the correct conclusion, how is one to explain it? One merit of the self-consciousness requirement is that it provides an explanation of this situation. The reason a newborn kitten does not have a right to life is explained by the fact that it does not possess the concept of a self. But how is one to explain the kitten's having a right not to be tortured? The answer is that a desire not to suffer pain can be ascribed to something without assuming that it has any concept of a continuing self. For while something that lacks the concept of a self cannot desire that a self not suffer, it can desire that a given sensation not exist. The state desired—the absence of a particular sensation, or of sensations of a certain sort—can be described in a purely phenomenalistic language, and hence without the concept of a continuing self. So long as the newborn kitten possesses the relevant phenomenal concepts, it can truly be said to desire that a certain sensation not exist. So we can ascribe to it a right not to be tortured even though, since it lacks the concept of a continuing self, we cannot ascribe to it a right to life.

This completes my discussion of the basic moral principles involved in the issue of abortion and infanticide. But I want to comment upon an important factual question, namely, at what point an organism comes to possess the concept of a self as a continuing subject of experiences and other mental states, together with the belief that it is itself such a continuing entity. This is obviously a matter for detailed psychological investigation, but everyday observation makes it perfectly clear, I believe, that a newborn baby does not possess the concept of a continuing self, any more than a newborn kitten possesses such a concept. If so, infanticide during a time interval shortly after birth must be morally acceptable.

But where is the line to be drawn? What is the cutoff point? If one maintained, as some philosophers have, that an individual possesses concepts only if he can express these concepts in language, it would be a matter of everyday observation whether or not a given organism possessed the concept of a continuing self. Infanticide would then be permissible up to the time an organism learned how to use certain expressions. However, I think the claim that acquisition of concepts is dependent on acquisition of language is mistaken. For example, one wants to ascribe mental states of a conceptual sort—such as

beliefs and desires—to organisms that are incapable of learning a language. This issue of prelinguistic understanding is clearly outside the scope of this discussion. My point is simply that *if* an organism can acquire concepts without thereby acquiring a way of expressing those concepts linguistically, the question of whether a given organism possesses the concept of a self as a continuing subject of experiences and other mental states, together with the belief that it is itself such a continuing entity, may be a question that requires fairly subtle experimental techniques to answer.

If this view of the matter is roughly correct, there are two worries one is left with at the level of practical moral decisions, one of which may turn out to be deeply disturbing. The lesser worry is where the line is to be drawn in the case of infanticide. It is not troubling because there is no serious need to know the exact point at which a human infant acquires a right to life. For in the vast majority of cases in which infanticide is desirable, its desirability will be apparent within a short time after birth. Since it is virtually certain that an infant at such a stage of its development does not possess the concept of a continuing self, and thus does not possess a serious right to life, there is excellent reason to believe that infanticide is morally permissible in most cases where it is otherwise desirable. The practical moral problem can thus be satisfactorily handled by choosing some period of time, such as a week after birth, as the interval during which infanticide will be permitted. This interval could then be modified once psychologists have established the point at which a human organism comes to believe that it is a continuing subject of experiences and other mental states.

The troubling worry is whether adult animals belonging to species other than Homo sapiens may not also possess a serious right to life. For once one says that an organism can possess the concept of a continuing self, together with the belief that it is itself such an entity, without having any way of expressing that concept and that belief linguistically, one has to face up to the question of whether animals may not possess properties that bestow a serious right to life upon them. The suggestion itself is a familiar one, and one that most of us are accustomed to dismiss very casually. The line of thought advanced here suggests that this attitude may turn out to be tragically mistaken. Once one reflects upon the question of the *basic* moral principles involved in the ascription of a right to life to organisms, one may find himself driven to conclude that our everyday treatment of animals is morally indefensible, and that we are in fact murdering innocent persons.

NOTES

1. Judith Jarvis Thomson, in her article, "A Defense of Abortion," *Philosophy & Public Affairs* 1, no. 1 (Fall 1971): 47–66, has argued with great force and ingenuity that this conclusion is mistaken. I will comment on her argument later in this paper.

2. B. A. Brody, "Abortion and the Law," *Journal of Philosophy,* LXVIII, no. 12 (17 June 1971): 357–369. See pp. 357–358.

3. Thomson, "A Defense of Abortion," p. 47.

4. Roger Wertheimer, "Understanding the Abortion Argument," *Philosophy and Public Affairs* 1, no. 1 (1971):69.

5. Ibid.

6. Thomson, "A Defense of Abortion," pp. 47–48.

7. Ibid., p. 65.

8. Wertheimer, "Understanding the Abortion Argument," p. 78.

9. A moral principle accepted by a person is *basic for him* if and only if his acceptance of it is not dependent upon any of his (nonmoral) factual beliefs. That is, no change in his factual beliefs would cause him to abandon the principle in question.

10. Wertheimer, "Understanding the Abortion Argument," p. 88.

11. Again, compare the analysis defended by Brandt in *Ethical Theory*, pp. 434–441.

12. There are, however, situations other than those discussed here which might seem to count against the claim that a person cannot have a right unless he is conceptually capable of having the corresponding desire. Can't a young child, for example, have a right to an estate, even though he may not be conceptually capable of wanting the estate? It is clear that such situations have to be carefully considered if one is to arrive at a satisfactory account of the concept of a right. My inclination is to say that the correct description is not that the child now has a right to the estate, but that he will come to have such a right when he is mature, and that in the meantime no one else has a right to the estate. My reason for saying that the child does not now have a right to the estate is that he cannot now do things with the estate, such as selling it or giving it away, that he will be able to do later on.

13. Philippa Foot, "The Problem of Abortion and the Doctrine of the Double Effect," *The Oxford Review* 5 (1967): 5–15. See the discussion on pp. 11ff.

Critics

Alan Carter | # Infanticide and the Right to Life

Most people in the industrially advanced countries today would view infanticide with abhorrence. Yet several influential philosophers have argued in favour of it—none more influential in the field than Michael Tooley.[1] Tooley's seminal justification of infanticide continues to dominate the discussion; but is it really incapable of rebuttal, as some would appear to believe?

I

If infanticide is morally permissible, what morally significant difference is there between young infants and adults? Murdering adults is morally impermissible and yet killing young infants is not, Tooley argues, because adults possess a serious right to life while young infants lack such a right. But what would justify ascribing such a right to adults and not to young infants? Tooley's answer is that "it is a necessary condition of something's having a serious right to life that it possess the concept of a self as a continuing subject of experiences, and that it believe that it is itself such an entity."[2] Adults satisfy this condition, while it is Tooley's contention that young infants do not. But why should possessing the concept of a self as a continuing subject of experiences be relevant to the question of whether or not something has a serious right to life? In order to answer this, it is necessary to analyze conceptually what it means to have a right.

What does it mean for someone to have a right? According to the conceptual analysis proposed by Tooley:

> To ascribe a right to an individual is to assert something about the prima-facie obligations of other individuals to act, or to refrain from acting, in certain ways. However, the obligations in question are conditional ones, being dependent upon the existence of certain desires of the individual to whom the right is ascribed. Thus if an individual asks one to destroy something to which he [or she] has a right, one does not violate his [or her] right to that thing if one proceeds to destroy it. This suggests the following analysis: "*A* has a right to *X*" is roughly synonymous with "If *A* desires *X*, then others are under a prima-facie obligation to refrain from actions that would deprive him [or her] of it."[3]

But as "the desires a thing can have are limited by the concepts it possesses,"[4] and as Tooley thinks that a young infant lacks any conceptual capacity for desiring to continue existing (for he or she has no conception of being a continuing subject of experiences), then the infant cannot have any desire to continue existing. But if having a right is conditional upon what one desires, then, lacking any desire to continue existing, a young infant cannot have a right to continue existing. In short, a young infant cannot possibly have a serious right to life. Hence, infanticide is morally permissible.

Tooley would appear to be subscribing to a particular theory of rights—a variant of the "choice the-

From Alan Carter, "Infanticide and the Right to Life," *Ratio* 10, no 1 (1997): 1–9. Some notes have been deleted. Reprinted by permission of Blackwell Publishing Ltd.

ory" made famous by H.L.A. Hart.[5] Hart takes promising as the clearest illustration of obligations and rights. If *X* promises *Y* to do something, *X* (the promisor) is then under an obligation to *Y* (the promisee). *Y*, correlatively has a right against *X* that he or she perform the action promised. What Hart sees as crucial is the right-holder's (the promisee's) ability either to keep the promisor to the promise or to waive his or her right to the performance of the promised action. As to whether or not *X* (the promisor) remains bound to perform the action is *Y*'s (the promisee's) choice. The promisor is bound to the right-holder—the promisee—but, as Hart points out, "the precise figure is not that of two persons bound by a chain, but of *one* person bound, the other end of the chain lying in the hands of another to use if he [or she] chooses."[6] In other words, a core feature of having a right is the choice of forgoing what one is entitled to.

One implication that might be drawn from Hart's argument is that if one is not the sort of entity that can exercise such a choice, then one cannot, in principle, be the sort of entity that can have rights. On such an approach, animals couldn't possibly have rights (for they couldn't understand what waiving a right consisted in), future generations cannot now have rights (for they cannot now make choices) and, of course, young infants couldn't possibly have rights.

II

But need we draw any of these conclusions? Is the ability to waive one's right a necessary feature of having that right or is it merely an ability that right-holders usually have, but which is not an essential feature of possessing a right? An unconscious human adult cannot, at that time, waive his or her rights, but we would not conclude that he or she thereby lost all rights as a result of becoming unconscious. In order to deal with this kind of objection, Tooley argues that it is the conceptual capacity for desiring whatever a right confers that is a necessary condition for having that right. But whereas a conceptual analysis of rights might plausibly suggest that having a desire for what

a right confers is a condition for having that right, it is far from clear that the mere conceptual capacity for having such a desire is either a necessary or a sufficient condition for having the right in question. And if the mere conceptual capacity for having such a desire is not a sufficient condition for having the right in question, adult humans who are not conscious (for example, those asleep) would lack rights. In an attempt to seek some clarification, we might more fruitfully focus on duty-holders, rather than on right-holders.

Consider someone who makes a promise to her dying father to make sure that, after his death, his cat will be well cared for. The father has a right against his daughter that, after his death, his cat will be looked after. His daughter has, after so promising, acquired an obligation to her father to care for his cat after he has died. Before he dies, he could release her from that promise. He could waive his right. But after he has died he cannot do so. His daughter would, after her father's death, appear to be under an obligation that she cannot be released from. Does the dead father have a right that his daughter look after his cat? That is not a question that all of us, at first glance at least, would be able to get any clear sense out of. But this notwithstanding, most of us would feel that the daughter remained under a prima facie obligation, even though it was one which she could not, in principle, be released from.

Moreover, the practice of making promises to dying people to carry out their wishes after their deaths would be unintelligible were such promises not binding after their deaths. This would suggest that being under an obligation is not dependent upon the present desires, nor the present capacity to desire, of whomever one has an obligation towards. Consequently, one could, in principle, be under an obligation to a young infant not to kill him or her, even if, at present, he or she lacked the capacity to desire continuing as a subject of experiences.

III

However, it is possible to mount a more direct attack on Tooley's justification of infanticide. Tooley, it will be recalled, concludes that "*A* has a right to *X*" is roughly synonymous with "If *A* desires *X*, then others are under a prima facie obligation to refrain from actions that would deprive him or her of it." And his purported justification for this analysis is that "if an individual asks one to destroy something to which he [or she] has a right, one does not violate his [or her] right to that thing if one proceeds to destroy it."[7] But a consideration of rights does not, in fact, suggest the synonymity Tooley claims, as I now proceed to show.

Consider a property right—for many, the archetypal right. On widely held views of property, I cannot just help myself to your coat simply because you no longer desire to keep it. That would be theft. That would be an infringement of property rights. It is not sufficient that you no longer desire what you have a right to for another's correlative (or, alternatively, grounded) obligation to be justifiably considered no longer binding. You must *express* your desire that I take your coat before I can take it permissibly. To take it permissibly, I must have your express permission.

This does not suggest, as Tooley assumes, that "*A* has a right to *X*" is roughly synonymous with "If *A* desires *X,* then others are under a prima facie obligation to refrain from actions that would deprive him or her of it." Rather, it suggests something slightly more subtle, where the replacement for Tooley's if-clause contains a double negative—namely, that "*A* has a right to *X*" is roughly extensionally equivalent with "Unless *A* expresses his or her desire that not-*X*, then others are under a prima facie obligation to refrain from actions that would deprive him or her of *X.*" One ramification of such an alternative analysis is that it provides no reason to think that desiring *X* is a necessary condition for having a right to *X*. Hence, it provides no reason to think that desiring to continue as a subject of experiences is a necessary condition for having a serious right to life.

IV

However, it might be objected that this alternative analysis must be flawed because it seems, on the face of it, to be incompatible with inalienable rights. The analysis implies that "*A* has a right to *X,* and that right is inalienable" is roughly extensionally equivalent with "Unless *A* expresses his or her desire that not-*X*, then others are under a prima facie obligation to refrain from actions that would deprive him or her of *X,* and they are under that obligation irrespective of whether or not *A* expresses his or her desire that not-*X*." But this might appear to be contradictory, for it might be thought to suggest that if *A* expresses his or her desire that not-*X,* then others could *not* be under an obligation, while they simultaneously *are* under an obligation, to refrain from actions which would deprive *A* of *X*. Hence, the objector would conclude, the alternate analysis is mistaken.

But such an objection confuses necessary and sufficient conditions. On the alternative analysis, while *A*'s not expressing his or her desire that not-*X* is a sufficient condition for others to be under a prima facie obligation to refrain from actions that would deprive him or her of *X, A*'s expressing his or her desire that not-*X* is only a necessary condition for it not to be the case that others remain under such an obligation. In the case of an inalienable right, for the right to be waived, it would be necessary for the right-holder to express his or her desire not to benefit from that right, but such an expressed desire would not be sufficient. In fact, nothing singly or jointly would constitute a sufficient condition for the waiving of an inalienable right. But as the alternative analysis does not presume the right-holder's expressed desire that the right be waived *is* a sufficient condition for its being waived, then inalienable rights pose no problem for the alternative analysis.

Moreover, either there are such things as inalienable rights or there are not. If there are no such things as inalienable rights, the objection to the alternative analysis is empty. If there are inalienable rights, then there are rights which cannot be waived. In which case, any analysis like Tooley's, which rests upon the choice theory of rights, would appear to be false, for the choice theory presupposes that all rights are conditional upon the right-holder being able to forgo the benefit of whatever the right confers, whereas certain inalienable rights could not be waived even if the right-holder did not desire to benefit from them. (Possible examples of such mooted inalienable rights are the right to a fair trial or the right not to be sold into slavery.) And if Tooley's analysis of rights is false, then his justification of infanticide, which relies upon that analyis, falls.

V

Let us, then, set aside the assumption that there are inalienable rights. What can we say about rights which can, perhaps, be waived? On Tooley's analysis, one may only enjoy a right if one desires what that right confers; whereas on the alternative analysis, one may enjoy what a right confers unless one desires otherwise (assuming that any expression of a desire to forgo the benefits of a right presupposes such a desire). Given Tooley's analysis, one must possess the conceptual capability necessary to desire what the right in question confers if the right is to obtain. On the alternative analysis, however, no such conceptual capability is required. If one may enjoy what a right confers unless one desires otherwise, then the conceptual incapacity to desire otherwise would not prevent one from enjoying what the right in question confers, and would not prevent the right from obtaining. If one may only enjoy a right if one desires what it confers, and if one can only desire what it confers if one possesses the conceptual capacity required to desire it, then one's possessing that conceptual capacity is a necessary condition for one's enjoying the right in question. But if, on the other hand, one may enjoy what a right confers unless one desires otherwise, and if one can only desire otherwise if one possesses the conceptual capacity required to desire otherwise, then one's possessing that conceptual capacity is, instead, a necessary condition for others' justifiably regarding the right in question as having been waived.

This is especially interesting when viewed from the standpoint of the duty-holder. If one can only be released from a prima facie obligation by means of the individual to whom one is under that obligation expressing the desire that one no longer remain under that obligation, then if he or she is incapable of expressing such a desire, one cannot be released from the obligation. In Tooley's opinion, a young infant cannot conceive of himself or herself as a continuing subject of experiences. If that is so, then he or she cannot desire to remain such a subject. Hence, on Tooley's analysis, he or she cannot desire what is required in order to possess a serious right to life. But if a young infant cannot conceive of himself or herself as a continuing subject of experiences, then the infant cannot desire that he or she not remain such a subject. In which case, on the alternative analysis, as a young infant lacks the conceptual capacity for expressing the desire that he or she cease as a continuing subject of experiences, then one could not be released from any obligation one might have not to kill the infant (a duty not to commit infanticide) until, at the very least, he or she became capable of expressing such a desire. Consequently, whereas infanticide would be impermissible, voluntary euthanasia might not be.

However, I should add that I do not intend the alternative analysis employed here to be taken as a correct account of rights. I have merely drawn out some of the implications of Tooley's key example of forgoing the benefit of a right. Nor do I believe that the issue of whether or not infanticide is morally permissible can be settled by a conceptual analysis of how we currently employ the term 'rights'. It is an issue that must be settled by substantive moral arguments.

NOTES

1. See Michael Tooley, "Abortion and Infanticide," in Peter Singer (ed.), *Applied Ethics* (Oxford: Oxford University Press, 1986).
2. Tooley, "Abortion and Infanticide," p. 64.
3. Ibid.
4. Ibid., p. 66.
5. See H. L. A. Hart, "Are There Any Natural Rights?," in Jeremy Waldron (ed.), *Theories of Rights* (Oxford: Oxford University Press, 1984).
6. Hart, "Are there any natural rights?" p. 82.
7. Tooley, "Abortion and infanticide," p. 64.

John C. Stevens

Must the Bearer of a Right Have the Concept of That to Which He Has a Right?

I

In his well-known article "Abortion and Infanticide," Michael Tooley commits himself to the claim that a thing has a right to something only if it has the concept of that thing.[1] I shall call this the conceptual possession requirement. In this article I shall criticize the conceptual possession requirement and Tooley's argument for it.

Although Tooley does not explicitly state the conceptual possession requirement, he is committed to it. The considerations below show this. Tooley gives the following analysis of having a right. "'A has a right to X' is roughly synonymous with 'A is the sort of thing that is a subject of experience and other mental states, A is capable of desiring X, and if A does desire X, then others are under a prima facie obligation to refrain from actions that would deprive him of it.'"[2] This analysis entails

1. A has a right to X only if A is capable of desiring X.

Tooley goes on to explain what must be the case for someone to be capable of desiring something. He says, "The basic point here is that the desires a thing can have are limited by the concepts it possesses. For the fundamental way of describing a given desire is as a desire that a certain proposition be true. Then, since one cannot desire that a certain proposition be true unless one understands it, and since one cannot understand it unless one possesses the concepts involved in it, it follows that the desires one can have are limited by the concepts one possesses."[3] It also follows from the premises Tooley here asserts that one cannot have a certain desire, which he takes to be a desire that a certain proposition be true, unless one has the concepts involved in that proposition. If someone desires an apple, Tooley would hold that the proposition in terms of which this desire should be described would be a proposition involving the concept of an apple. Similarly, if someone desires to eat an apple, Tooley would hold that the proposition in terms of which this desire should be described would be a proposition involving the concept of eating an apple. Thus it would be fair to say that, on Tooley's view, if one desires X, then one must have the concept of X. Tooley thus is committed to the view that

2. A is capable of desiring X only if A has the concept of X.

From 1 and 2 it logically follows that

3. A has a right to X only if A has the concept of X.

But this is the conceptual possession requirement. Hence, Tooley is committed to the conceptual possession requirement.

II

I shall argue that the conceptual possession requirement is not true and that the argument from 1 and 2 to 3 is not sound. I begin with a counterexample to the conceptual possession requirement.

Mr. Smith is a man who is quite ignorant of human anatomy and physiology and of medical

John C. Stevens, "Must the Bearer of a Right Have the Concept of That to Which He Has a Right?" *Ethics* 95 (1984): 68–74. Some notes have been deleted. Reprinted by permission of University of Chicago Press.

practice. He does not know what an immune response is; he has no idea what an autoimmune disease is; he has no idea what immunosuppressive therapy—the use of immunosuppressive agents to suppress the body's immune response for some therapeutic reason—would be. But Mr. Smith is fortunate to have a complete health maintenance insurance policy with a certain clinic. The policy guarantees Mr. Smith that the clinic will provide him with the best medical treatment that money can buy for whatever illness he gets. Suppose Mr. Smith comes down with an autoimmune disease. He doesn't know what is wrong with him, but he knows he feels bad. He goes to the clinic and asks for the best medical treatment for his disease that money can buy. Given the conditions of his insurance policy, I would say that Mr. Smith has a right to the best medical treatment for his illness that money can buy. But suppose that the best medical treatment that money can buy for his particular disease is immunosuppressive therapy. It follows, I would think, that Mr. Smith has a right to immunosuppressive therapy. But remember that Mr. Smith has no concept of immunosuppressive therapy; he has no idea what it is. Thus, we have here a counterexample to Tooley's conceptual possession requirement. Mr. Smith has a right to immunosuppressive therapy, but he does not have the concept of immunosuppressive therapy. Thus, having the concept of X is not necessary for having a right to X.

How might Tooley reply to this counterexample?

A. Tooley might hold that Mr. Smith does desire the best medical treatment for his illness that money can buy, that the best medical treatment for his illness that money can buy is immunosuppressive therapy, and that it follows from this that Mr. Smith does desire, without realizing it, immunosuppressive therapy, even though he lacks the concept of immunosuppressive therapy. I doubt that this conclusion follows. But even if the conclusion did follow and the reply were correct, it would not help Tooley. If this reply were correct, it would show that my example is not a counterexample to Tooley's claim (proposition 1) that A has a right to X only if A is capable of desiring X. But this will not help

Tooley. For Tooley is committed to the view that "the desires one can have are limited by the concepts one possesses."[4] In other words, Tooley holds (proposition 2) that A is capable of desiring X only if A has the concept of X. But since Mr. Smith lacks the concept of immunosuppressive therapy, one cannot consistently hold that 2 is true and that Mr. Smith desires immunosuppressive therapy.

B. Tooley might grant that Mr. Smith has the right to the best medical treatment for his illness that money can buy, that the best medical treatment for his illness that money can buy is immunosuppressive therapy, but that it does not follow that Mr. Smith has a right to immunosuppressive therapy.

It would, I think, be absurd to hold that Mr. Smith has a right to the best medical treatment for his illness that money can buy, that immunosuppressive therapy is that best medical treatment, and that denying Mr. Smith immunosuppressive therapy would not violate his rights. For to deny this therapy would be to deny him the best medical treatment for his illness that money can buy, which would be to deny him what he has a right to and so would be to violate one of his rights. Tooley could, however, insist that while denying Mr. Smith immunosuppressive therapy would violate one of Mr. Smith's rights—his right to the best medical treatment for his illness that money can buy—Mr. Smith does not, in the technical sense, have a right to the immunosuppressive therapy, for he does not have the concept of immunosuppressive therapy. This point of view would insist that it could be that someone has a right to X, that X is identical with Y, and that the person does not have a right to Y. Taking this line would not necessarily reduce the number of things that would violate a person's rights. This defense would hold that we don't need to appeal to the right to Y to explain why certain acts are wrong, for the acts that deprive the person of Y also deprive him of X and so violate the right to X.

The main problem that I see with this line of thought is that, if we adopt it, then establishing that someone does not have a right to something will not show very much. For example, the fact that Mr. Smith does not have a right to immunosuppressive therapy would not show that it is permissible to deprive Mr. Smith of this therapy or that depriving him of it would not violate one of his rights. For perhaps immunosuppressive therapy can be described, in the situation, in some other way, as F, such that he does have a right to F, and so depriving him of immunosuppressive therapy does violate his right to F.

This consequence of this particular defense against my counterexample would be particularly troublesome for Tooley. Tooley, in his article, argues that infants and fetuses do not have a serious right to life. He argues for this conclusion in order to show that abortion and infanticide are morally permissible. But if an entity can lack a serious right to life because it lacks certain concepts but have another right that amounts to the same thing in the circumstances, then the fact that fetuses and infants lack a serious right to life will not go very far toward showing that it is permissible to kill fetuses and infants.

Tooley makes clear in the following passage that he thinks that, if an infant lacks a serious right to life, that is very strong evidence that it is permissible to kill that infant if it is desirable to do so: "In the vast majority of cases in which infanticide is desirable, its desirability will be apparent within a short time after its birth. Since it is virtually certain that an infant at such a stage of development does not possess the concept of a continuing self, and thus does not possess a serious right to life, there is excellent reason to believe that infanticide is morally permissible in most cases where it is otherwise desirable."[5] Clearly, Tooley is at least assuming here that from the fact that a newborn infant lacks a serious right to life it follows that there is excellent reason to believe that killing such an infant is morally permissible provided that it is desirable to kill it. But this inference would be invalid in the view we are examining, for from the fact that an entity lacks a certain right nothing can be inferred about what it is permissible to do to it. There might be another right that amounts to the same thing in the circumstances. Thus Tooley cannot consistently adopt this defense against my counterexample.

Furthermore, it seems to me that it would be much less misleading to say, and thus much better to say, that Mr. Smith, in my example, does have a right to immunosuppressive therapy. Otherwise, we would have to be very careful to distinguish A's lacking a right to X on the technical ground that A does not have the concept of X, even though A's rights do imply that it is prima facie wrong to deprive A of X, and A's lacking a right to X where there are no reasons based on A's rights that imply that it is prima facie wrong to deprive A of X.

C. Tooley might argue that my example does not present a counterexample to the conceptual possession requirement because, even though Mr. Smith has a right to immunosuppressive therapy, he does not lack the concept of immunosuppressive therapy, despite all the appearances to the contrary. Tooley might argue as follows:

> Mr. Smith has the concept of the best medical treatment for his illness that money can buy. The best medical treatment for his illness that money can buy is immunosuppressive therapy. Thus, Mr. Smith has the concept of immunosuppressive therapy.

On the face of it, this seems absurd. "A has the concept of __" is an intensional context; in this context we cannot substitute descriptions that refer to the same thing and expect to preserve the truth value of the sentence. A might have the concept of the morning star without having the concept of the planet Venus, even though the morning star is the planet Venus. Thus, the inference in the above argument is invalid.

We could interpret the context "A has a concept of __" extensionally, of course, so that the above argument would be valid. We could stipulate such an extensional sense for "has the concept of" so that, if A has the concept of X and X is identical with Y, then A has the concept of Y. Let us use the word "concept$_e$" to convey this stipulated sense of the word. Will this help Tooley to avoid the counterexample? Mr. Smith has the concept$_e$ of the best medical treatment for his illness that money can buy; the best medical treatment for his illness that money can buy is immunosuppressive therapy; therefore Mr. Smith has the concept$_e$ of immunosuppressive therapy. The fact that Mr. Smith is ignorant about what immunosuppressive therapy is does not show that he lacks the concept$_e$ of that therapy. Thus, the example is not a counterexample to the conceptual possession requirement.

The problem with this line of thought is that it will now be very difficult to establish that anyone lacks a certain concept$_e$. Tooley, however, thinks that everyday observation can establish that certain beings lack certain concepts. For example, he says, "Everyday observation makes it perfectly clear, I believe, that a newborn baby does not possess the concept of a continuing self."[6] But if the concept of a continuing self were a concept$_e$ of a continuing self, then if the baby had the concept of anything that was in fact a continuing self the baby would have the concept$_e$ of a continuing self. For example, if the two-day-old infant had a rudimentary concept of its mother, based on its perceptions, as the thing that holds it or the thing that feeds it or even "this thing here" which it sees, then, since the mother is a continuing self and the mother is also the thing that holds the baby, the thing that feeds the baby, and the thing that it sees, the baby, in having these rudimentary concepts, has a concept$_e$ of a continuing self. Everyday observations do not make it perfectly clear that the newborn infant has no such rudimentary concepts of the things that are in fact continuing selves. Tooley, then, cannot consistently interpret "concept" to mean "concept$_e$." We should, then, take Tooley to be using the term "concept" in the intensional sense, which I take to be the ordinary sense. In this sense, if someone has the concept of X and $X = Y$, it does not follow that he has the concept of Y. Hence Tooley cannot consistently employ the above strategy to avoid my counterexample.

If the term "concept" is used in the intensional sense in the statement of the conceptual possession requirement, then my counterexample refutes that requirement. As I mentioned, I take this intensional sense to be the ordinary sense and to be Tooley's sense. Hence, I conclude that my counterexample refutes Tooley's conceptual possession requirement.

Would the conceptual possession requirement be correct if, in the statement of that requirement, the term "concept$_e$" were interpreted to mean "concept"? The argument I have given would not refute this extensional version of the conceptual possession

requirement. My argument relies on the possibility that someone has the concept of X and the right to X, that $X = Y$, and that he not have the concept of Y. This would be impossible if we took concepts to be concepts$_e$. For if $X = Y$ and the person had the concept of X, he would therefore have the concept$_e$ of Y.

We can, however, refute this extensional version of the conceptual possession requirement by means of a direct counterexample. Consider the following. Mr. and Mrs. Brown, parents of a six-month-old son, could easily give their child nutritious meals but never do. They feed their son on a diet that prevents starvation but does not supply adequate nutrition for the proper mental and physical development of the child. It is possible that, while the child has the concept of food, he does not have the concept of nutritious food. Furthermore, it is possible that he has no concept of nutritious food. He has never experienced anything that is nutritious food and has never had the thought of anything that is in fact nutritious food. The child, nevertheless, has a right to be given nutritious food even though he has no concept of being given nutritious food. Hence the extensional version of the conceptual possession requirement is also false.

III

Since the argument from 1 and 2 to 3 for the conceptual possession requirement has a false conclusion, that argument is not sound. The argument is valid. Hence at least one of the premises is false. The second premise, 2, seems to be true; a person is not capable of desiring something if he lacks the concept of that thing. Thus, the other premise, 1, must be false. In other words, it is not true that A has a right to X only if A is capable of desiring X. Our first example confirms this: Mr. Smith is not capable of desiring immunosuppressive therapy, but he does have a right to it in the circumstances.

Proposition 1, however, is a direct consequence of Tooley's analysis of the concept of a right: "'A has a right to X' is roughly synonymous with 'A is the sort of thing that is a subject of experiences and other mental states, *A is capable of desiring X,* and if

A does desire X, then others are under a prima facie obligation to refrain from actions that would deprive him of it'" (my emphasis).[7] But since 1 is false, it follows that Tooley's analysis of the concept of a right is mistaken.

The problem with Tooley's analysis of the concept of a right can be diagnosed as follows. The term "right" is an extensional term; if A has a right to X and X is identical to Y, it follows that A has a right to Y. The phrase "is capable of desiring" is a nonextensional phrase; if A is capable of desiring X and X is identical to Y, it does not follow that A is capable of desiring Y. Tooley's analysis goes wrong because it asserts as a necessary condition for the application of an extensional term, "right," to an object that a nonextensional term apply to that same object. But, provided that there are possible cases in which the extensional term does apply to some object, no such necessary condition could possibly hold. The application of the extensional term to the object will not vary, no matter how the object is described; the application of the nonextensional term to the object will vary depending on how the object is described. Hence there will be possible cases in which the extensional term applies and the nonextensional term does not apply to the object in question. Hence the application of the nonextensional term will not be a necessary condition for the application of the extensional term. To give this fault a name, we could call it the fallacy of defining an extensional term by means of intensional terms. Tooley's definition of rights commits this fallacy and so is bound to fail.

We see then that Tooley's analysis of the concept of a right is mistaken. Tooley's argument for the claim that fetuses and infants lack a right to life crucially depended on this analysis.[8] Thus Tooley's argument to show that fetuses and infants lack a right to life is unsound. We see also that the conceptual possession requirement is false. We cannot, then, use this requirement to argue that things without concepts can have no rights, nor can we use it to argue that things which lack a certain concept cannot have a right to that thing.

NOTES

1. Michael Tooley, "Abortion and Infanticide," *Philosophy & Public Affairs* 2 (Fall 1972): 37–65.
2. Ibid., p. 45.
3. Ibid., pp. 46–47.
4. Ibid., p. 47.
5. Ibid., p. 64.
6. Ibid., p. 63.
7. Ibid., p. 45.
8. Ibid., pp. 44–49.

5

Is Killing Nonhuman Animals Wrong?

Regan and His Critics

One of the most important recent public developments within the area of applied ethics that concerns the morality of killing has been the rise of the animal-rights movement, a movement that opposes, among other things, the killing of nonhuman animals for sport, for food, and for science. Tom Regan's 1983 book *The Case for Animal Rights* is widely recognized as the most philosophically powerful defense of this animal-rights position. In his 1985 essay of the same title, reprinted here in its entirety, Regan provides a summary version of the core argument of that book.

The overall structure of Regan's argument in his essay is, like that of Marquis's argument in defense of the rights of the human fetus, one of inference to the best explanation (see section 4.3 of the Introduction). Like Marquis, Regan begins by identifying a set of moral beliefs that he assumes most people, regardless of their views on the issue at hand, are likely to share. In the case of Regan's argument, these include beliefs about what morality permits us to do to one another and, more specifically, to those human beings whose mental lives are considerably less developed than those of typical human beings. Such people are often referred to as "marginal humans." They include severely retarded or brain-damaged adults, for example. Again like Marquis, Regan then proceeds by attempting to uncover the general moral theory that best accounts for these commonly held beliefs. In the course of his discussion, he considers a variety of views, but perhaps most important are what he refers to as the *contractarian view,* the *utilitarian view* and the *rights view.* Regan argues that the contractarian view must be rejected because it fails to account for our duties to the very young and severely retarded; the utilitarian view must be rejected because it fails to account for our duties not to harm one another merely to produce beneficial consequences; and the rights view succeeds where both of these alternatives fail. He argues, in short, that the rights view in general should be accepted on the grounds that it "surpasses all other theories in the degree to which it illuminates and explains the foundation of our duties to one another—the domain of human morality."

Finally, once again like Marquis, Regan turns to the question of what the general theory that he has defended implies about the particular case with which he is concerned. That is, having defended the claim that human beings have important moral rights, he turns to the question of what this implies about the moral standing of nonhuman animals. Here Regan argues that attributing rights to all human beings while withholding them from at least some nonhuman animals would be morally arbitrary. For example, if we attribute rights to a severely brain-damaged human being, despite the fact that he is not rational, then we cannot consistently appeal to the claim that a cow is not rational as a basis for denying the cow rights. The best account of why we have the rights we have, Regan therefore concludes, rests on the claim that each of us is what he calls an "experiencing subject of a life, a conscious creature having an individual welfare that has importance to us whatever our usefulness to others." Regan describes this notion in a bit more detail and maintains that it applies as well to the sorts of nonhuman animals with which his work is concerned. If we have these important moral rights, Regan concludes, then so do they. Put formally, then, Regan's overall argument can be understood as follows:

P1   Typical human beings have the right not to be treated as a mere resource for others.
P2   If typical human beings have the right not to be treated as a mere resource for others, then any individual that is the experiencing subject of a life has a right not to be treated as a mere resource for others.
P3   Many nonhuman animals are the experiencing subjects of a life.

C   Many nonhuman animals have the right not to be treated as a mere resource for others.

The first premise arises from Regan's rejection of utilitarianism, the second arises from his claim that his subject-of-a-life principle provides the best explanation of why we have the right identified in the first premise, and the third premise rests on what he takes to be commonsense empirical claims about at least some nonhuman animals.

Regan's argument for animal rights is complex, and his conclusion is controversial. Because of the former, his argument can be attacked from a number of directions. Because of the latter, it has been. The four excerpts that follow Regan's essay help to represent the great variety of distinct strategies that critics have followed in arguing against Regan's essay and his book. In the first piece, Jan Narveson argues that Regan has failed to justify his rejection of the contractarian approach to morality as an alternative to the rights view. At a general level, Narveson argues that the moral principles we have the best reason to adopt are those whose adoption makes us better off. Applied more specifically to the case of animals, Narveson then argues that such an approach can justify both a minimal set of restrictions on our treatment of (at least some) nonhuman animals and stopping well short of adopting the various sorts of rights-based prohibitions Regan defends. At the same time, Narveson argues—again, contrary to Regan—that the contractarian approach can overcome the argument from marginal cases and explain why we have much stronger duties to, say, a severely retarded child than to a nonhuman animal possessing comparable mental capacities. In all of this, Narveson can be understood as in effect challenging P1 of Regan's overall argument, the claim that the rights view in general is the best moral theory in general.

In the years since Regan's essay and book were first published, perhaps the most frequent and most prominent critic of Regan has been R. G. Frey. In the excerpts from two different works that appear following Narveson's, Frey develops two very different kinds of objections to Regan's position. In the first, Frey argues that because animals do not possess language, they lack beliefs; and because they lack beliefs, they lack desires, and because they lack desires, they fail to have interests in the sense that is relevant to their having moral rights. In terms of Regan's position, this amounts to denying that animals have some of the important qualities Regan attributes to them when he claims that they are "subjects of a life," and thus denying P3 of Regan's argument. In the second piece, Frey responds specifically to the use Regan makes of cases involving so-called "marginal" humans, argueing that Regan is unsuccessful. In particular, Frey rejects Regan's insistence that all human beings have the same moral value, and in doing so challenges the basis for Regan's defense of P2 of his argument.

Finally, in a short excerpt from his book *Rights,* Alan White presents a brief argument that amounts to a *reductio ad absurdum* objection aimed directly at Regan's conclusion (See section 4.5 of the Introduction). White claims that whether or not a particular subject is "logically capable of having a right" depends upon whether or not it is the kind of subject about which it makes sense to use, in White's words, "the full language of rights." Further, White maintains that since animals cannot, for example, claim, assert, or waive rights, they are not the kinds of things that can have rights in the first place. Only a person can have rights, on White's account, and thus Regan's conclusion is not true because it cannot be true.

QUESTIONS FOR CONSIDERATION

The debate between Regan and his critics ultimately touches on a wide variety of potentially difficult issues; it would be impossible to summarize all of them here. As a good start, however, readers may find it useful to consider the following questions:

• First, how successful is Narveson's attempt to defend contractarian moral theory from Regan's attack? Does he succeed in showing that contractarianism can give a credible account of our duties to one another?

• If Narveson is successful, does he also succeed in showing that such an account can give us at least some duties with respect to animals without giving us what he would regard as too many?

• Second, how credible is Regan's claim that at least some nonhuman animals are what he calls a subject of a life? Is Regan naively anthropomorphizing when he pictures animals as having the requisite mental abilities? Or is Frey simply refusing to acknowledge that such animals may be fairly sophisticated?

• Third, how powerful is the argument from "marginal" cases? Is Regan right that we must admit that some animals have much greater moral standing than has been thought? Or should we agree with Frey that perhaps some human beings have less moral standing than has been thought?

• Is Regan right that marginal humans and comparably equipped nonhuman animals must stand or fall together? And, if he is right, should they stand, or fall?

• Finally, is White right to maintain that animals can't have rights because they don't participate in the "full language of rights" in other ways? Is Regan's position even coherent?

FURTHER READING

Luke, Brian. "Justice, Caring, and Animal Liberation" *Between the Species* 8, no. 2 (1992): 100–108.

Machan, Tibor. "Do Animals Have Rights?" *Public Affairs Quarterly* 5 (1991): 163–73.

Paske, Gerald. "Why Animals Have No Right to Life: A Response to Regan." *Australasian Journal of Philosophy* 66 (1988): 498–511.

Pojman, Louis. "Do Animal Rights Entail Moral Nihilism?" *Public Affairs Quarterly* 7, no. 2 (1993): 165–85.

Tom Regan | # The Case for Animal Rights

I regard myself as an advocate of animal rights—as a part of the animal rights movement. That movement, as I conceive it, is committed to a number of goals, including:

- the total abolition of the use of animals in science;
- the total dissolution of commercial animal agriculture;
- the total elimination of commercial and sport hunting and trapping.

There are, I know, people who profess to believe in animal rights but do not avow these goals. Factory farming, they say, is wrong—it violates animals' rights—but traditional animal agriculture is all right. Toxicity tests of cosmetics on animals violates their rights, but important medical research—cancer research, for example—does not. The clubbing of baby seals is abhorrent, but not the harvesting of adult seals. I used to think I understood this reasoning. Not any more. You don't change unjust institutions by tidying them up.

What's wrong—fundamentally wrong—with the way animals are treated isn't the details that vary from case to case. It's the whole system. The forlornness of the veal calf is pathetic, heart wrenching; the pulsing pain of the chimp with electrodes planted deep in her brain is repulsive; the slow, tortuous death of the racoon caught in the leg-hold trap is agonizing. But what is wrong isn't the pain, isn't the suffering, isn't the deprivation. These compound what's wrong. Sometimes—often—they make it much, much worse. But they are not the fundamental wrong.

The fundamental wrong is the system that allows us to view animals as *our resources,* here for *us*—to be eaten, or surgically manipulated, or exploited for sport or money. Once we accept this view of animals—as our resources—the rest is as predictable as it is regrettable. Why worry about their loneliness, their pain, their death? Since animals exist for us, to benefit us in one way or another, what harms them really doesn't matter—or matters only if it starts to bother us, makes us feel a trifle uneasy when we eat our veal escalope, for example. So, yes, let us get veal calves out of solitary confinement, give them more space, a little straw, a few companions. But let us keep our veal escalope.

But a little straw, more space and a few companions won't eliminate—won't even touch—the basic wrong that attaches to our viewing and treating these animals as our resources. A veal calf killed to be eaten after living in close confinement is viewed and treated in this way: but so, too, is another who is raised (as they say) "more humanely." To right the wrong of our treatment of farm animals requires more than making rearing methods "more humane"; it requires the total dissolution of commercial animal agriculture.

How we do this, whether we do it or, as in the case of animals in science, whether and how we abolish their use—these are to a large extent political questions. People must change their beliefs before they change their habits. Enough people, especially those elected to public office, must believe in change—must want it—before we will have laws that protect the rights of animals. This process of change is very complicated, very demanding, very exhausting, calling for the efforts of many hands in education, publicity, political organization and activity, down to the licking of envelopes and stamps. As a trained and practising philosopher, the sort of

Tom Regan, "The Case for Animal Rights," in *In Defense of Animals,* ed. Peter Singer (New York: Blackwell Publishers, 1985), pp. 13–26. Reprinted by permission of Blackwell Publishing Ltd.

contribution I can make is limited but, I like to think, important. The currency of philosophy is ideas—their meaning and rational foundation—not the nuts and bolts of the legislative process, say, or the mechanics of community organization. That's what I have been exploring over the past ten years or so in my essays and talks and, most recently, in my book, *The Case for Animal Rights*. I believe the major conclusions I reach in the book are true because they are supported by the weight of the best arguments. I believe the idea of animal rights has reason, not just emotion, on its side.

In the space I have at my disposal here I can only sketch, in the barest outline, some of the main features of the book. It's main themes—and we should not be surprised by this—involve asking and answering deep, foundational moral questions about what morality is, how it should be understood and what is the best moral theory, all considered. I hope I can convey something of the shape I think this theory takes. The attempt to do this will be (to use a word a friendly critic once used to describe my work) cerebral, perhaps too cerebral. But this is misleading. My feelings about how animals are sometimes treated run just as deep and just as strong as those of my more volatile compatriots. Philosophers do—to use the jargon of the day—have a right side to their brains. If it's the left side we contribute (or mainly should), that's because what talents we have reside there.

How to proceed? We begin by asking how the moral status of animals has been understood by thinkers who deny that animals have rights. Then we test the mettle of their ideas by seeing how well they stand up under the heat of fair criticism. If we start our thinking in this way, we soon find that some people believe that we have no duties directly to animals, that we owe nothing to them, that we can do nothing that wrongs them. Rather, we can do wrong acts that involve animals, and so we have duties regarding them, though none to them. Such views may be called indirect duty views. By way of illustration: suppose your neighbour kicks your dog. Then your neighbour has done something wrong. But not to your dog. The wrong that has been done is a wrong to you. After all, it is wrong to upset people, and your neighbour's kicking your dog upsets you. So you are the one who is wronged, not your dog. Or again: by kicking your dog your neighbour damages your property. And since it is wrong to damage another person's property, your neighbour has done something wrong—to you, of course, not to your dog. Your neighbour no more wrongs your dog than your car would be wronged if the windshield were smashed. Your neighbour's duties involving your dog are indirect duties to you. More generally, all of our duties regarding animals are indirect duties to one another—to humanity.

How could someone try to justify such a view? Someone might say that your dog doesn't feel anything and so isn't hurt by your neighbour's kick, doesn't care about the pain since none is felt, is as unaware of anything as is your windshield. Someone might say this, but no rational person will, since, among other considerations, such a view will commit anyone who holds it to the position that no human being feels pain either—that human beings also don't care about what happens to them. A second possibility is that though both humans and your dog are hurt when kicked, it is only human pain that matters. But, again, no rational person can believe this. Pain is pain wherever it occurs. If your neighbour's causing you pain is wrong because of the pain that is caused, we cannot rationally ignore or dismiss the moral relevance of the pain that your dog feels.

Philosophers who hold indirect duty views—and many still do—have come to understand that they must avoid the two defects just noted: that is, both the view that animals don't feel anything as well as the idea that only human pain can be morally relevant. Among such thinkers the sort of view now favoured is one or other form of what is called *contractarianism*.

Here, very crudely, is the root idea: morality consists of a set of rules that individuals voluntarily agree to abide by, as we do when we sign a contract (hence the name contractarianism). Those who understand and accept the terms of the contract are covered directly; they have rights created and recognized by, and protected in, the contract. And these contractors can also have protection spelled out for others who, though they lack the ability to under-

stand morality and so cannot sign the contract themselves, are loved or cherished by those who can.
Thus young children, for example, are unable to sign
contracts and lack rights. But they are protected by
the contract none the less because of the sentimental
interests of others, most notably their parents. So we
have, then, duties involving these children, duties
regarding them, but no duties to them. Our duties in
their case are indirect duties to other human beings,
usually their parents.

As for animals, since they cannot understand contracts, they obviously cannot sign; and since they
cannot sign, they have no rights. Like children, however, some animals are the objects of the sentimental
interest of others. You, for example, love your dog
or cat. So those animals that enough people care
about (companion animals, whales, baby seals, the
American bald eagle), though they lack rights themselves, will be protected because of the sentimental
interests of people. I have, then, according to contractarianism, no duty directly to your dog or any
other animal, not even the duty not to cause them
pain or suffering; my duty not to hurt them is a duty
I have to those people who care about what happens
to them. As for other animals, where no or little sentimental interest is present—in the case of farm animals, for example, or laboratory rats—what duties
we have grow weaker and weaker, perhaps to van-
ishing point. The pain and death they endure, though
real, are not wrong if no one cares about them.

When it comes to the moral status of animals'
contractarianism could be a hard view to refute if it
were an adequate theoretical approach to the moral
status of human beings. It is not adequate in this latter respect, however, which makes the question of its
adequacy in the former case, regarding animals,
utterly moot. For consider: morality, according to
the (crude) contractarian position before us, consists
of rules that people agree to abide by. What people?
Well, enough to make a difference—enough, that is,
collectively to have the power to enforce the rules
that are drawn up in the contract. That is very well
and good for the signatories but not so good for anyone who is not asked to sign. And there is nothing in
contractarianism of the sort we are discussing that
guarantees or requires that everyone will have a

chance to participate equally in framing the rules of
morality. The result is that this approach to ethics
could sanction the most blatant forms of social, economic, moral and political injustice, ranging from a
repressive caste system to systematic racial or sexual
discrimination. Might, according to this theory, does
make right. Let those who are the victims of injustice
suffer as they will. It matters not so long as no one
else—no contractor, or too few of them—cares
about it. Such a theory takes one's moral breath
away . . . as if, for example, there would be nothing
wrong with apartheid in South Africa if few white
South Africans were upset by it. A theory with so little to recommend it at the level of the ethics of our
treatment of our fellow humans cannot have anything more to recommend it when it comes to the
ethics of how we treat our fellow animals.

The version of contractarianism just examined is,
as I have noted, a crude variety, and in fairness to
those of a contractarian persuasion it must be noted
that much more refined, subtle and ingenious varieties are possible. For example, John Rawls, in his *A
Theory of Justice,* sets forth a version of contractarianism that forces contractors to ignore the accidental
features of being a human being—for example,
whether one is white or black, male or female, a
genius or of modest intellect. Only by ignoring such
features, Rawls believes, can we ensure that the principles of justice that contractors would agree upon
are not based on bias or prejudice. Despite the
improvement a view such as Rawls's represents over
the cruder forms of contractarianism, it remains
deficient: it systematically denies that we have direct
duties to those human beings who do not have a
sense of justice—young children, for instance, and
many mentally retarded humans. And yet it seems
reasonably certain that, were we to torture a young
child or a retarded elder, we would be doing something that wronged him or her, not something that
would be wrong if (and only if) other humans with a
sense of justice were upset. And since this is true in
the case of these humans, we cannot rationally deny
the same in the case of animals.

Indirect duty views, then, including the best
among them, fail to command our rational assent.
Whatever ethical theory we should accept rationally,

therefore, it must at least recognize that we have some duties directly to animals, just as we have some duties directly to each other. The next two theories I'll sketch attempt to meet this requirement.

The first I call the cruelty-kindness view. Simply stated, this says that we have a direct duty to be kind to animals and a direct duty not to be cruel to them. Despite the familiar, reassuring ring of these ideas, I do not believe that this view offers an adequate theory. To make this clearer, consider kindness. A kind person acts from a certain kind of motive—compassion or concern, for example. And that is a virtue. But there is no guarantee that a kind act is a right act. If I am a generous racist, for example, I will be inclined to act kindly towards members of my own race, favouring their interests above those of others. My kindness would be real and, so far as it goes, good. But I trust it is too obvious to require argument that my kind acts may not be above moral reproach—may, in fact, be positively wrong because rooted in injustice. So kindness, notwithstanding its status as a virtue to be encouraged, simply will not carry the weight of a theory of right action.

Cruelty fares no better. People or their acts are cruel if they display either a lack of sympathy for or, worse, the presence of enjoyment in another's suffering. Cruelty in all its guises is a bad thing, a tragic human failing. But just as a person's being motivated by kindness does not guarantee that he or she does what is right, so the absence of cruelty does not ensure that he or she avoids doing what is wrong. Many people who perform abortions, for example, are not cruel, sadistic people. But that fact alone does not settle the terribly difficult question of the morality of abortion. The case is no different when we examine the ethics of our treatment of animals. So, yes, let us be for kindness and against cruelty. But let us not suppose that being for the one and against the other answers questions about moral right and wrong.

Some people think that the theory we are looking for is utilitarianism. A utilitarian accepts two moral principles. The first is that of equality: everyone's interests count, and similar interests must be counted as having similar weight or importance. White or black, American or Iranian, human or animal—

everyone's pain or frustration matter, and matter just as much as the equivalent pain or frustration of anyone else. The second principle a utilitarian accepts is that of utility: do the act that will bring about the best balance between satisfaction and frustration for everyone affected by the outcome.

As a utilitarian, then, here is how I am to approach the task of deciding what I morally ought to do: I must ask who will be affected if I choose to do one thing rather than another, how much each individual will be affected, and where the best results are most likely to lie—which option, in other words, is most likely to bring about the best results, the best balance between satisfaction and frustration. That option, whatever it may be, is the one I ought to choose. That is where my moral duty lies.

The great appeal of utilitarianism rests with its uncompromising *egalitarianism:* everyone's interests count and count as much as the like interests of everyone else. The kind of odious discrimination that some forms of contractarianism can justify—discrimination based on race or sex, for example—seems disallowed in principle by utilitarianism, as is speciesism, systematic discrimination based on species membership.

The equality we find in utilitarianism, however, is not the sort an advocate of animal or human rights should have in mind. Utilitarianism has no room for the equal moral rights of different individuals because it has no room for their equal inherent value or worth. What has value for the utilitarian is the satisfaction of an individual's interests, not the individual whose interests they are. A universe in which you satisfy your desire for water, food and warmth is, other things being equal, better than a universe in which these desires are frustrated. And the same is true in the case of an animal with similar desires. But neither you nor the animal have any value in your own right. Only your feelings do.

Here is an analogy to help make the philosophical point clearer: a cup contains different liquids, sometimes sweet, sometimes bitter, sometimes a mix of the two. What has value are the liquids: the sweeter the better, the bitterer the worse. The cup, the container, has no value. It is what goes into it, not what they go into, that has value. For the utilitarian you and I are like the cup; we have no value as individuals and thus no equal value. What has value is what goes into us, what we serve as receptacles for; our feelings of satisfaction have positive value, our feelings of frustration negative value.

Serious problems arise for utilitarianism when we remind ourselves that it enjoins us to bring about the best consequences. What does this mean? It doesn't mean the best consequences for me alone, or for my family or friends, or any other person taken individually. No, what we must do is, roughly, as follows: we must add up (somehow!) the separate satisfactions and frustrations of everyone likely to be affected by our choice, the satisfactions in one column, the frustrations in the other. We must total each column for each of the options before us. That is what it means to say the theory is aggregative. And then we must choose that option which is most likely to bring about the best balance of totalled satisfactions over totalled frustrations. Whatever act would lead to this outcome is the one we ought morally to perform—it is where our moral duty lies. And that act quite clearly might not be the same one that would bring about the best results for me personally, or for my family or friends, or for a lab animal. The best aggregated consequences for everyone concerned are not necessarily the best for each individual.

That utilitarianism is an aggregative theory—different individuals' satisfactions or frustrations are added, or summed, or totalled—is the key objection to this theory. My Aunt Bea is old, inactive, a cranky, sour person, though not physically ill. She prefers to go on living. She is also rather rich. I could make a fortune if I could get my hands on her money, money she intends to give me in any event, after she dies, but which she refuses to give me now. In order to avoid a huge tax bite, I plan to donate a handsome sum of my profits to a local children's hospital. Many, many children will benefit from my generosity, and much joy will be brought to their parents, relatives and friends. If I don't get the money rather soon, all these ambitions will come to naught. The once-in-a-lifetime opportunity to make a real killing will be gone. Why, then, not kill my Aunt Bea? Oh, of course I *might* get caught. But I'm no fool and, besides, her doctor can be counted on to co-operate (he has an eye for the same investment

and I happen to know a good deal about his shady past). The deed can be done . . . professionally, shall we say. There is *very* little chance of getting caught. And as for my conscience being guilt-ridden, I am a resourceful sort of fellow and will take more than sufficient comfort—as I lie on the beach at Acapulco—in contemplating the joy and health I have brought to so many others.

Suppose Aunt Bea is killed and the rest of the story comes out as told. Would I have done anything wrong? Anything immoral? One would have thought that I had. Not according to utilitarianism. Since what I have done has brought about the best balance between totalled satisfaction and frustration for all those affected by the outcome, my action is not wrong. Indeed, in killing Aunt Bea the physician and I did what duty required.

This same kind of argument can be repeated in all sorts of cases, illustrating, time after time, how the utilitarian's position leads to results that impartial people find morally callous. It *is* wrong to kill my Aunt Bea in the name of bringing about the best results for others. A good end does not justify an evil means. Any adequate moral theory will have to explain why this is so. Utilitarianism fails in this respect and so cannot be the theory we seek.

What to do? Where to begin anew? The place to begin, I think, is with the utilitarian's view of the value of the individual—or, rather, lack of value. In its place, suppose we consider that you and I, for example, do have value as individuals—what we'll call *inherent value*. To say we have such value is to say that we are something more than, something different from, mere receptacles. Moreover, to ensure that we do not pave the way for such injustices as slavery or sexual discrimination, we must believe that all who have inherent value have it equally, regardless of their sex, race, religion, birthplace and so on. Similarly to be discarded as irrelevant are one's talents or skills, intelligence and wealth, personality or pathology, whether one is loved and admired or despised and loathed. The genius and the retarded child, the prince and the pauper, the brain surgeon and the fruit vendor, Mother Teresa and the most unscrupulous used-car salesman—all have inherent value, all possess it equally, and all have an equal right to be treated with respect, to be treated in ways that do not reduce them to the status of things, as if they existed as resources for others. My value as an individual is independent of my usefulness to you. Yours is not dependent on your usefulness to me. For either of us to treat the other in ways that fail to show respect for the other's independent value is to act immorally, to violate the individual's rights.

Some of the rational virtues of this view—what I call the rights view—should be evident. Unlike (crude) contractarianism, for example, the rights view *in principle* denies the moral tolerability of any and all forms of racial, sexual or social discrimination; and unlike utilitarianism, this view *in principle* denies that we can justify good results by using evil means that violate an individual's rights—denies, for example, that it could be moral to kill my Aunt Bea to harvest beneficial consequences for others. That would be to sanction the disrespectful treatment of the individual in the name of the social good, something the rights view will not—categorically will not—ever allow.

The rights view, I believe, is rationally the most satisfactory moral theory. It surpasses all other theories in the degree to which it illuminates and explains the foundation of our duties to one another—the domain of human morality. On this score it has the best reasons, the best arguments, on its side. Of course, if it were possible to show that only human beings are included within its scope, then a person like myself, who believes in animal rights, would be obliged to look elsewhere.

But attempts to limit its scope to humans only can be shown to be rationally defective. Animals, it is true, lack many of the abilities humans possess. They can't read, do higher mathematics, build a bookcase or make baba ghanoush. Neither can many human beings, however, and yet we don't (and shouldn't) say that they (these humans) therefore have less inherent value, less of a right to be treated with respect, than do others. It is the *similarities* between those human beings who most clearly, most non-controversially have such value (the people reading this, for example), not our differences, that matter most. And the really crucial, the basic similarity is simply this: we are each of us the experiencing subject of a life, a conscious creature having an individual welfare that has importance to us what-

ever our usefulness to others. We want and prefer things, believe and feel things, recall and expect things. And all these dimensions of our life, including our pleasure and pain, our enjoyment and suffering, our satisfaction and frustration, our continued existence or our untimely death—all make a difference to the quality of our life as lived, as experienced, by us as individuals. As the same is true of those animals that concern us (the ones that are eaten and trapped, for example), they too must be viewed as the experiencing subjects of a life, with inherent value of their own.

Some there are who resist the idea that animals have inherent value. "Only humans have such value," they profess. How might this narrow view be defended? Shall we say that only humans have the requisite intelligence, or autonomy, or reason? But there are many, many humans who fail to meet these standards and yet are reasonably viewed as having value above and beyond their usefulness to others. Shall we claim that only humans belong to the right species, the species Homo sapiens? But this is blatant speciesism. Will it be said, then, that all—and only—humans have immortal souls? Then our opponents have their work cut out for them. I am myself not ill-disposed to the proposition that there are immortal souls. Personally, I profoundly hope I have one. But I would not want to rest my position on a controversial ethical issue on the even more controversial question about who or what has an immortal soul. That is to dig one's hole deeper, not to climb out. Rationally, it is better to resolve moral issues without making more controversial assumptions than are needed. The question of who has inherent value is such a question, one that is resolved more rationally without the introduction of the idea of immortal souls than by its use.

Well, perhaps some will say that animals have some inherent value, only less than we have. Once again, however, attempts to defend this view can be shown to lack rational justification. What could be the basis of our having more inherent value than animals? Their lack of reason, or autonomy, or intellect? Only if we are willing to make the same judgement in the case of humans who are similarly deficient. But it is not true that such humans—the retarded child, for example, or the mentally deranged—have less inherent value than you or I. Neither, then, can we rationally sustain the view that animals like them in being the experiencing subjects of a life have less inherent value. *All* who have inherent value have it *equally,* whether they be human animals or not.

Inherent value, then, belongs equally to those who are the experiencing subjects of a life. Whether it belongs to others—to rocks and rivers, trees and glaciers, for example—we do not know and may never know. But neither do we need to know, if we are to make the case for animal rights. We do not need to know, for example, how many people are eligible to vote in the next presidential election before we can know whether I am. Similarly, we do not need to know how many individuals have inherent value before we can know that some do. When it comes to the case for animal rights, then, what we need to know is whether the animals that, in our culture, are routinely eaten, hunted and used in our laboratories, for example, are like us in being subjects of a life. And we do know this. We do know that many—literally, billions and billions—of these animals are the subjects of a life in the sense explained and so have inherent value if we do. And since, in order to arrive at the best theory of our duties to one another, we must recognize our equal inherent value as individuals, reason—not sentiment, not emotion—reason compels us to recognize the equal inherent value of these animals and, with this, their equal right to be treated with respect.

That, *very* roughly, is the shape and feel of the case for animal rights. Most of the details of the supporting argument are missing. They are to be found in the book to which I alluded earlier. Here, the details go begging, and I must, in closing, limit myself to four final points.

The first is how the theory that underlies the case for animal rights shows that the animal rights movement is a part of, not antagonistic to, the human rights movement. The theory that rationally grounds the rights of animals also grounds the rights of humans. Thus those involved in the animal rights movement are partners in the struggle to secure respect for human rights—the rights of women, for example, or minorities, or workers. The animal rights movement is cut from the same moral cloth as these.

Second, having set out the broad outlines of the rights view, I can now say why its implications for farming and science, among other fields, are both clear and uncompromising. In the case of the use of animals in science, the rights view is categorically abolitionist. Lab animals are not our tasters; we are not their kings. Because these animals are treated routinely, systematically as if their value were reducible to their usefulness to others, they are routinely, systematically treated with a lack of respect, and thus are their rights routinely, systematically violated. This is just as true when they are used in trivial, duplicative, unnecessary or unwise research as it is when they are used in studies that hold out real promise of human benefits. We can't justify harming or killing a human being (my Aunt Bea, for example) just for these sorts of reason. Neither can we do so even in the case of so lowly a creature as a laboratory rat. It is not just refinement or reduction that is called for, not just larger, cleaner cages, not just more generous use of anaesthetic or the elimination of multiple surgery, not just tidying up the system. It is complete replacement. The best we can do when it comes to using animals in science is—not to use them. That is where our duty lies, according to the rights view.

As for commercial animal agriculture, the rights view takes a similar abolitionist position. The fundamental moral wrong here is not that animals are kept in stressful close confinement or in isolation, or that their pain and suffering, their needs and preferences are ignored or discounted. All these *are* wrong, of course, but they are not the fundamental wrong. They are symptoms and effects of the deeper, systematic wrong that allows these animals to be viewed and treated as lacking independent value, as resources for us—as, indeed, a renewable resource. Giving farm animals more space, more natural environments, more companions does not right the fundamental wrong, any more than giving lab animals more anaesthesia or bigger, cleaner cages would right the fundamental wrong in their case. Nothing less than the total dissolution of commercial animal agriculture will do this, just as, for similar reasons I won't develop at length here, morality requires nothing less than the total elimination of hunting and trapping for commercial and sporting ends. The rights view's implications, then, as I have said, are clear and uncompromising.

My last two points are about philosophy, my profession. It is, most obviously, no substitute for political action. The words I have written here and in other places by themselves don't change a thing. It is what we do with the thoughts that the words express—our acts, our deeds—that changes things. All that philosophy can do, and all I have attempted, is to offer a vision of what our deeds should aim at. And the why. But not the how.

Finally, I am reminded of my thoughtful critic, the one I mentioned earlier, who chastised me for being too cerebral. Well, cerebral I have been: indirect duty views, utilitarianism, contractarianism—hardly the stuff deep passions are made of. I am also reminded, however, of the image another friend once set before me—the image of the ballerina as expressive of disciplined passion. Long hours of sweat and toil, of loneliness and practice, of doubt and fatigue: those are the discipline of her craft. But the passion is there too, the fierce drive to excel, to speak through her body, to do it right, to pierce our minds. That is the image of philosophy I would leave with you, not "too cerebral" but *disciplined passion.* Of the discipline enough has been seen. As for the passion: there are times, and these not infrequent, when tears come to my eyes when I see, or read, or hear of the wretched plight of animals in the hands of humans. Their pain, their suffering, their loneliness, their innocence, their death. Anger. Rage. Pity. Sorrow. Disgust. The whole creation groans under the weight of the evil we humans visit upon these mute, powerless creatures. It *is* our hearts, not just our heads, that call for an end to it all, that demand of us that we overcome, for them, the habits and forces behind their systematic oppression. All great movements, it is written, go through three stages: ridicule, discussion, adoption. It is the realization of this third stage, adoption, that requires both our passion and our discipline, our hearts and our heads. The fate of animals is in our hands. God grant we are equal to the task.

Critics

Jan Narveson | On a Case for Animal Rights

. . . [W]hy should the fact that a certain being would feel pain if I were to perform action x constitute a reason why I should refrain from x?

One evident possibility is that I dislike pain—not only my own, but that of others. But unfortunately, not everyone is constituted that way. They may care little or nothing for the pains of others as such. And what do we say to those people? They may not be impressed by the answer that their view of the matter is morally below par. They'd like to know why it's wrong to inflict pain on other creatures, apart from the fact that Tom Regan and quite a few other people have a unique and apparently inexplicable intuition that it is.

I am assuming, of course, that something's being wrong either constitutes or at least implies that there is a reason for not doing it. And I am also assuming that for an agent, A, to "have a reason" for not doing x is for it to be the case that among *A*'s values is a negative value attached to x or to something con-

From Jan Narveson, "On a Case for Animal Rights," *The Monist* 70, no. 1 (January 1987): 31–49. Some notes and some parts of the text deleted. Reprinted by permission of the Monist.

nected with x. What might this be, however, if our information thus far is only that x would cause pain to individual D, where D is not one of the individuals A has any particular interest in or affection for? (Whether D is a human or, say, a dog, is thus far unspecified.)

Suppose we add that D also registers the information that it was A who *did* x. Will this matter? Again, not necessarily. So let us add that D also is able to react to the information in various ways. Perhaps, for instance, that D is able to give A a reproachful look. This might indeed help. A could be sensitive to reproaches, even if they come from a nonmember of Homo sapiens. A might, for that matter, care more about such reproaches from D than from E, who is a member of that species. (It's unusual, but it's quite possible. One has seen it happen!)

If we add still another item, viz., that D is able to react to x by tearing A to shreds, we can well imagine that A will sit up and take notice. But what kind of notice? Avoiding D, shooting D, trying to make friends with D, are all possibilities. But we don't as yet have the particular set of information which will surely supply A with a reason for adopting a *moral* aversion to doing x. When do we have that?

To answer this question, we need two things: first, a reasonably clear characterization of what constitutes having a "moral" aversion to something, as distinct from any other sort of aversion one might have; and second, a characterization of the sort of facts or circumstances which would constitute good reasons for A to adopt such an aversion.

There is a good deal of confusion about the first one. By this I do not mean either that people in general or philosophers in particular are greatly confused about it, but rather, that their various uses of this segment of our vocabulary is confusing. I shall adopt some of the main features of common usage, but I don't suppose that any single analysis would capture all of those that are frequently associated with these terms. I shall seize on these: A morality is a set of prescriptions—requirements, prohibitions, recommendations, rules—with the following features: (1) Overridingness, (2) Universal application, (3) Internalization, (4) Interpersonal Reinforcement; and (5) Decentralization, or Informality.

Brief explications: (1) Overridingness: A moral rule is *meant to* overrule contrary inclinations or interests, as such. "But I didn't feel like it," or "it wasn't in my interest" cannot be an acceptable justification for doing what morality forbids. (2) Moral rules apply to everyone, or at any rate, everyone in the relevant group whose morality it purports to be. We will assume for present purposes that we are considering rules meant to apply to every moral agent. (3) Part of the idea of a moral rule is that A will apply it to A: e.g., by making A feel uncomfortable for breaking it. An individual, A, is immoral if A does what a (true) moral rule requires, even if A can "get away with" it. Persons disposed to do those things under those circumstances are necessarily to be rated immoral; they lack the degree of internalization that is aimed at, and essential if the system is to work. And (4) people are *not* to "let people get away with it" if they can do something about it (at least, without appreciable cost or risk to themselves). Everybody is to "enforce" morality, especially by the relevant verbal means, just as everyone is subject to its rules. (5) Decentralization: Finally, morality is not a system imposed by force of declared law from without. Everyone is to enforce it, and no central authority can alter its content by fiat. This characterization, it should be noted, does not include the philosophically fancier properties favored by many theorists. A morality could, on this analysis, be clannish, biased, or full of what seem to us arbitrary distinctions without ceasing to be a morality. It could, logically: but if we are addressing ourselves to the question what morality *ought* to be as distinct from what it merely is in this or that group, then we can readily find strong internal reasons why a rationally acceptable morality would not have any of those characteristics. The reason is that morality is informal, and to be universally inculcated and enforced, including self-enforced. But rational individuals will not accept as restrictions on themselves and will not assist in the informal reinforcement of restrictions on behavior that is contrary to reason, restrictions they see no reason to submit to and to induce all others to submit to. Now there are lots of imaginable rules that would be very much in the interest of Group A to advocate and self-apply, but very much contrary to the interest of another group, B, to do so: aristocratic moralities, master/slave moralities, or moralities in which some group's religion is to be enforced on all, and so on. Such rules are non-starters for general morality, although they certainly could be elements in the more restricted morality of some particular group.

Will anything pass all these rquirements? Morality, I have said, is to override individual inclinations and even interests. But how can an individual have a rational interest in overriding his or her own inclinations and interests? The answer is now well known.[1] There are plenty of acts with the interesting property that an individual, A, will want to do them, but they will only be in A's interest *provided that others don't*. However, the others will be in the same boat. And if all act as they wish, all will be worse off than if all were to agree to act in certain ways. A necessary part of making it worth A's while to act on R is that A can reasonably expect that all others will too (and vice versa). Under these circumstances, there will be a temptation for any individual to cheat; but there will be a strong inducement for others not to let him cheat, and everyone knows both of these things. It is, then, in their interest to adopt collective rules overriding any particular interest. Such rules will be components of a rational morality.

But if some individuals are only patients and not agents, then no such schema can apply. It will not necessarily be in the interests of others to adopt and assist in the reinforcement of rules requiring agents to have regard for patients as such. Many will, of course, be interested in many patients, and it will indeed be in everyone's interest to have rules which enable *such* patients to be free from harm and perhaps to share in certain benefits. But rules benefiting patients simply as such, or calling upon everyone to refrain from harming them simply as such, have no fundamental appeal. The fact, for instance, that if I were a pig, I would want pigs (or at least that one) to be treated well is of no interest, so far as it goes. I'm not a pig, and never will be; and the pig himself has no rational clout. He is not able to address himself to the question of what he can do to make life difficult for us if we don't cater to his needs, or of how much better he could make it for us if we do. If we want

something out of the pig, and treating the pig well is necessary for getting it, then we shall have reason to treat him well. If we don't, however, or if it isn't, then why should we go to the trouble?

Thus, consider the idea of "relevant" differences and similarities. Is the fact that individual A and individual B are identical in some respect in which they have an interest a good enough reason for having a moral rule which calls upon everyone to treat them alike? It is *not*. Only if they are alike in some respect which there is antecedent reason to insist upon everyone's paying attention to will the identity of their cases in other respects have any weight as such.

It certainly could be that owing to some feature of human psychology, we will have a sympathetic involvement with individuals having certain experiences, quite irrespective of the capacity of those individuals to do anything about it or to enter into arrangements whereby we will do something about it. (Such, very nearly, is the case with human adults in relation to human children.) Or it could be that if agents characteristically treat certain sorts of patients in certain ways, that will induce a habit or a cast of mind likely to work ill for other agents in future. But we would need facts to support those claims; they can't be taken to be true a priori; any more than can the claim that humans, *qua* human, take a sympathetic interest in other humans or in rational beings generally.

This characterization of reasons and of morality sets the stakes for establishing that some principle belongs to general human morality very high. Does it set them too high? If we are busy trying to shore up Reganian intuitions, it certainly does, so far as I can see. The suggestion that we, as rational beings, should forego the many benefits available from extensive animal experimentation, not to mention those to be got from eating meat, merely because those benefits are got at considerable cost to the animals themselves is one that looks to have no chance of passing muster.

As it happens, intuition here seems to be on my side, not Regan's. For one who professes so much respect for our ordinary intuitions, he is surely pressing a most unintuitive program. To most humans, it is surely just obvious that we do no wrong in raising animals for their meat, chickens for their eggs, and so on, even though those animals suffer and die as a result. However, there is also the belief that we shouldn't be cruel to animals, and the belief that it is wrong to mistreat or take the lives of human infants and idiots. Indeed, it is perhaps not going too far to suggest that the "argument from marginal cases," as I once called it, is the main intuition-based argument in Regan's armoury. The argument has it that some humans to whom we are inclined to extend the benefits of morality are less qualified for them (on "our" normal view of what qualifies one for the benefits of morality) than are some animals. Yet there is some overlap between the human and some animal species in respects we are currently inclined to ask people to have moral regard for. How, then, can we maintain this disparity?

At this point, many people would simply invoke the fact that the one set of individuals are human and the other are not as quite relevant enough, all by itself. Species membership is, undoubtedly, *a* characteristic; it does, undoubtedly, distinguish the two sets of cases; and ordinary people's morality does pay heed to it. Nor can they be accused of any purely logical incoherence or contradiction in the process. Were we to accept appeals to intuition as of fundamental significance to moral theory, we could stop right here, simply denying Regan's case outright.

But I, for one, am disinclined to do this. I agree with him that "speciesism" looks a poor candidate for moral relevance. There are various reasons one might give for this. But the best way to show it would be to come up with a list of the characteristics of individuals that *are* relevant to morality and then point out that membership in a particular species isn't on the list. This requires that we have a good theory of morality handy. But I claim to have such a theory (or, more modestly, a start at one): moral relevance is established when it is shown that there is good reason for moral agents to have a principle in which the characteristic in question figures significantly, i.e., that distinguishes the way we should behave toward individuals having it and those lacking it. And that good reason is provided by showing that there is good reason to think that moral agents

will be better off having such a principle than they would not having one. This in turn requires that we find an interest on the part of all such agents, an interest commonly shared and such that there is an individual/collective contrast of the kind depicted above. And I take it as obvious that there is no such fact about the property of being a member of any species, simply as such.

Humans are interested creatures, and formidable in their ability to pursue their interests, including in the means by which they do so the use of force, lethal and otherwise. Some moral theories would put a proscription on the use of force for any such purposes other than that of defending persons against the initial use of force by others. Whether or not that can be made out, it is clear that we have a great and enduring interest in not having force used against ourselves. The "social contract," as we may refer to the general articles of morality on the conception being pressed here, will doubtless be very negative on the use of force for other than defensive purposes. But then, there is the question what "defensive purposes" will include. Consider people inclined to use force to defend their ways of life, where such ways include extensive cultural involvements with many other people. Do they come properly within the scope of such principles? And what about the case where some moral agents identify strongly, in comparable ways, with a group of individuals which are not moral agents: animals, for instance? Take the sacred cows of the Hindus, for example. There are many good reasons for not having their attitude. But while we are in India, will we not respect the customs of the Hindus even though we find them not only strange but perhaps downright irrational? And so, on the present conception, we should.

Similarly, we have good reason to place restrictions on the treatment of some particular animals, such as household pets. People who have no special feelings about animals in general may well develop intense affection for certain particular ones, and these they can, in current circumstances, buy or otherwise appropriate and take under their care. The rest of us are then to treat those animals with due respect. But there is a special problem about persons, such as the members of Greenpeace, who propose to identify with the higher animals *generally,* claiming that animals are members of oppressed groups, comparable to minority groups of humans in various countries. Those people may be inclined to press their claims by force (and sometimes have done do, recently.) Groups might attempt to proselytize elsewhere by force, as did the Moors in the 7th–9th Centuries, giving their victims the choice between subscribing to the Koran or losing their heads. But it must surely be obvious that the members of such groups have no moral leg to stand on, if a morality applicable to moral agents generally is our aim. The only principle that will pass muster among rational agents is an agreement to disagree about such matters: which means, a proscription on the use of force as a means of promoting assent to doctrines lacking the support of fact ascertainable by publicly confirmable procedures.

And such, I suggest, is substantially the current situation in regard to "animal rights." Such commitments to animals, given current knowledge, is comparable to (though not, of course, an actual case of) religious belief. In particular, it is comparable to the moral content of such beliefs, in a different sense of the term *moral* from that employed here. In this sense of the term, a morality is what Mill called a "theory of life": a doctrine about what makes a life a good life, a life worth living in preference to other possible types of life. Those, like Regan, who think to extend the protections of ordinary morality to individuals lacking the usual claims to it, find it intolerable to contemplate, say, the eating of meat when those who "supply" it are defenseless creatures lacking the sophisticated cognitive equipment of persons. Their case, from the point of view of the rest of us, may be accounted a personal one: how, they put it to us, can we *live with* ourselves if we continue to treat some feeling beings badly when we would object strongly to such treatment in the case of others (such as ourselves)?

A fair number of peope do feel like Regan in these respects, and certainly the rest of us, especially if we wish to engage in friendly dealings with them, will wish to consider how much deference to their views we should pay. And this, in turn, seems to me not a matter on which a very definite uniform rule is required. Some vegetarians would be discomfited greatly if their dinner companions in restaurants ordered meat dishes; some nonvegetarians would as a matter of course refrain from ordering such dishes when in company with vegetarians; and so on. But it is clear, I think, that our deference need not extend to taking up vegetarianism ourselves, nor to supporting legislative changes that would deprive everyone of the right to employ animals for laboratory experiments or as sources of food—any more than it need extend to the making of animal sacrifices out of deference to the many religious groups which insist on such practices.

Apart from the case of special sympathizers, as we may refer to the current supporters of rights for animals, we may also point to considerations that underwrite, I think, a claim to public-interest status on the part of some animals. One is ecological. We have come to appreciate that there are interconnections among various elements of our biological environment which make it imprudent to hunt wantonly, for instance. And there is a general sense of curiosity, an intellectual interest, in the continued existence of different species of animals. There is, I think, no special claim by, say, would-be hunters on the members of any hunted species strong enough to outweigh this enduring interest. If the hunters have their way, humankind in general may be deprived of *any* further contact with the species that would succumb to their uninhibited pursuit of that interest (and hunter-kind is deprived of all future quarries of that species). But as Regan rightly observes, this interest is not at all equivalent to a moral claim for the rights of individual members of any of those species. He thinks, for instance, that we would not be justified in killing some innocent animals in order that others may flourish, as an interest in species survival could possibly do. That interest is, for example, quite compatible with controlled hunting, which ensures both that the species will flourish and that individual members of it will on frequent occasions be, in Regan's view, murdered. Or we might engage in involuntary artificial insemination, which Regan might object to as comparable to rape! Thus public interest arguments give some support to protections of animals of various kinds and degrees; but nothing like the sweeping restrictions imposed by Regan's principles.

Let us, finally, return to the Argument from Marginal Cases. The view that emerges from the Contractarian theory of morality must, of course, classify those humans who are so far below the standard for our species as to be unable to communicate effectively or react in a rational way to the actions of the rest of us as not inherently qualified for basic rights. Such individuals are, necessarily, wards of someone, since they cannot care for themselves. Why, then, should we be as concerned for their wellbeing as we mostly are? Why not allow people to hunt *them?* Or what about infants? All of these are important cases—though it is well to remember that they are also cases concerning which there has been tremendous variation in approved treatment in the de facto moralities of different ages and cultures Exposure of unpromising infants, for instance, was routine in many cultures. Nevertheless, I wish to stand my ground, despite the criticisms advanced by Regan in *The Case for Animal Rights*. The question of how to treat such cases is to be answered by reference to two strongly supporting sets of considerations. First, that essentially every subnormal or infant human individual is the offspring, and often the sibling, of persons who take a close sympathetic interest in its welfare; and second, that there simply is no appreciable general interest in treating such individuals adversely.[2] If we compare the case here with that of animals, we find, of course, a striking contrast. Various animals have much to offer us which motivates impositions on them: the culinary interest, of course, but also that in furs, etc. Apart from the special case of medical experimentation, there is no comparable systematic interest in marginal humans. And there is one special "interest" that properly rates special negative attention: viz., that of cruelty for its own sake. An interest in seeing animals suffer is psychologically very comparable to an interest in seeing people suffer: indeed, since humans are much more capable of expressing their pains than animals, one would expect sadists to prefer human victims—and experience, to my limited knowledge, bears this out. There is certainly a public interest in exterminating attitudes such as that. Thus the standard attitude toward animals, which is that they are not to be wantonly misused, though they certainly can be used for human purposes in ways that will undoubtedly be uncomfortable or fatal to them, has some basis in commonsense psychology.

But there is no need to defend in detail prevailing attitudes in our culture. Why should there be? We are, I take it, trying to find a rational basis for giving animals a particular moral status, one that is compelling and conceptually coherent with our case for moral rights of humans. Cases of overlap—the "marginal cases," as I call them—are grey areas. There is an overwhelming case for not classifying these cases identically with normal humans, and there is a good case for generally regarding the higher animals as eligible for minimally decent treatment. And since there is strong support, arising from the special attachments to other individual humans that marginal humans have but animals lack, for cultivating a general attitude of care for those cases, we arrive at the reasonable conclusion that marginal humans are, in general, to be given an intermediate status. *Given* is the crucial term here. Marginals are not, so to speak, charter members of the moral club; normal adults are. (Children are still a distinct special case, for children are our only source of future adults, and our duties to them stem overwhelmingly from that special consideration, and not from their current repertoire of psychological attributes.)

CONCLUSION

The de facto morality of any particular time and place is bound to be the product of many factors, some of them quite independent of reason. Philosophical critics who, like Regan, wish to invoke the aid of "intuition," face the formidable task of discerning beneath the surface of the welter of received moral views which of them are due to philosophically respectable causes and which not. They don't come stamped with "Genuine" and "Culturally Biased" labels—especially in view of the fact that the very notion of a bias is itself a part of the conceptual package we are trying to scrutinize. So too, as I have tried to make clear above, is the notion of consistency: rarely do we get an out-and-out case of two principles one of which is the negation or the contrary of the other. Instead, we get groups of cases that are similar in some respects and dissimilar in others, leaving us to decide whether the similarities are what matter, thus leaving us with conflicting judgments stemming from intuited principles telling us to treat them differently, or the dissimilarities, thus leaving those judgments nonconflicting after all. Such is the nature of a terrain ripe for philosophical theorizing. But to propose to avail oneself of the fact that something is intuited as a recourse for theoretical validation is to leave oneself open to the charge that a different selection of those intuitions would have left one with a wholly differing but equally well-grounded theory. In the view of this writer, the only solution to this problem is to jettison appeals to intuition for those purposes. What we must do is to hold that an intuition is just that: an unanalyzed sense, hunch, or feeling, *that* a certain finding is the right one, without quite knowing why. The job of the theorist is then to find out the "why." But if we take the hunch as itself a legitimate part of the explanation, muddle is the almost inevitable result. Or, if one came from a particular cultural milieu happening to be possessed of an exceptionally articulate and coherent set of intuitions (as did, apparently, Oxbridge philosophers of the first decade of this century), one will come up with a beautiful theory the total groundlessness of which is singularly unapt to be noticed by one's fellow theorists from that same culture—and singularly unlikely to persuade anybody else.

Regan, in *Animal Rights,* takes on the job of disavowing very substantial parts of our received morality—he is not far from being a starry-eyed radical by current standards. His weapons on behalf of this rather revolutionary project consist of a judicious selection of (1) logic, (2) intuitions taken from the very set of received beliefs from which he is so considerably dissenting, and (3) higher-level, "meta-ethical" intuitions got from the standard practice of recent Anglo-American philosophy. Those eager for something new to feel guilty about will be impressed. The rest will not. I side with the latter, personally. And philosophically, I should like to know why we should accept the particular selection Regan has come up with on behalf of his rather unintuitive results, rather than another selection which would not at all support those results. Until we have compelling argument for that selection, this writer, at any rate, will continue to eat meat in good conscience.

NOTES

1. David Gauthier's impressive new book, *Morals by Agreement* (New York: Oxford University Press, 1986) is the major source now, but see also, for instance, Kurt Baier's "Justification in Ethics," in J. Roland Pennock and John W. Chapman, eds., *Justification* (NOMOS XXIII, New York University Press, 1985), or the author's "Contractarian Ethics," in R. G. Frey, ed., *Utility and Rights* (Minneapolis, MN: University of Minnesota Press, 1984).

2. Cf. the author's "Abortion and Infanticide: A Defense of the Liberal View on Abortion and the Wrongness of Infanticide," forthcoming in Bowling Green Studies in Philosophy, vol. VI, 1986.

R. G. Frey | Why Animals Lack Beliefs and Desires

Do animals . . . have interests in the . . . sense of having wants which can be satisfied or left unsatisfied? In this sense, of course, it appears that tractors do not have interests; for though being well-oiled may be conducive to tractors being good of their kind, tractors do not *have an interest* in being well-oiled, since they cannot *want* to be well-oiled, cannot, in fact, have any wants whatever. But farmers can have wants, and they certainly have an interest in their tractors being well-oiled.

What, then, about animals? Can they have wants? By "wants" I understand a term that encompasses both needs and desires, and it is these that I shall consider.

If to ask whether animals can have wants is to ask whether they can have needs, then certainly animals have wants. A dog can need water. But *this* cannot be the sense of "want" on which having interests will depend, since it does not exclude things from the class of want-holders. Just as dogs need water in order to function normally, so tractors need oil in order to function normally; and just as dogs will die unless their need for water is satisfied, so trees and grass and a wide variety of plants and shrubs will die unless their need for water is satisfied. Though we should not give the fact undue weight, someone who in ordinary discourse says "The tractor wants oiling" certainly means the tractor needs oiling, if it is not to fall away from those standards which make tractors good of their kind. Dogs, too, need water, if they are not to fall away from the standards which make them good of their kind. It is perhaps worth emphasizing, moreover, as the cases of the tractor, trees, grass, etc., show, that needs do not require the presence either of consciousness or of knowledge of the lack which makes up the need. If, in sum, we are to agree

that tractors, trees, grass, etc., do not have wants, and, therefore, interests, it cannot be the case that wants are to be construed as needs.

This, then, leaves desires, and the question of whether animals can have wants as desires. I may as well say at once that I do not think animals can have desires. My reasons for thinking this turn largely upon my doubts that animals can have beliefs, and my doubts in this regard turn partially, though in large part, upon the view that having beliefs is not compatible with the absence of language and linguistic ability. I realize that the claim that animals cannot have desires is a controversial one; but I think the case to be made in support of it, complex though it is, is persuasive. . . .

Suppose I am a collector of rare books and desire to own a Gutenberg Bible: my desire to own this volume is to be traced to my belief that I do not now own such a work and that my rare book collection is deficient in this regard. By "to be traced" here, what I mean is this: if someone were to ask *how* my belief that my book collection lacks a Gutenberg Bible is connected with my desire to own such a Bible, what better or more direct repy could be given than that, without this belief, I would not have this desire? For if I believed that my rare book collection *did* contain a Gutenberg Bible and so was complete in this sense, then I would not desire a Gutenberg Bible in order to make up what I now believe to be a notable deficiency in my collection. (Of course, I might desire to own more than one such Bible, but this contingency is not what is at issrue here.)

Now what is it that I believe? I believe that my collection lacks a Gutenberg Bible; that is, I believe that the sentence "My collection lacks a Gutenberg Bible" is true. In constructions of the form "I believe

From R. G. Frey, "Rights, Interests, Desires, and Beliefs," *American Philosophical Quarterly* 16 (July 1979): 233–39. Notes and some parts of text deleted. Reprinted by permission of North American Philosophical Publications.

that . . . ," what follows upon the "that" is a declarative sentence; and *what* I believe is that that sentence is true. The same is the case with constructions of the form "He believes that . . .": what follows upon the "that" is a declarative sentence, and what the "he" in question believes is that that sentence is true. The difficulty in the case of animals should be apparent: if someone were to say, e.g., "The cat believes that the door is locked," then that person is holding, as I see it, that the cat holds the declarative sentence "The door is locked" to be true; and I can see no reason whatever for crediting the cat or any other creature which lacks language, including human infants, with entertaining declarative sentences and holding certain declarative sentences to be true.

Importantly, nothing whatever in this account is affected by changing the example, in order to rid it of sophisticated concepts like "door" and "locked," which in any event may be thought beyond cats, and to put in their place more rudimentary concepts. For the essence of this account is not about the relative sophistication of this or that concept but rather about the relationship between believing something and entertaining and regarding as true certain declarative sentences. If what is believed is that a certain declarative sentence is true, then no creature which lacks language can have beliefs; and without beliefs, a creature cannot have desires. And this is the case with animals, or so I suggest; and if I am right, not even in the sense, then, of wants as desires do animals have interests . . .

But is what is believed that a certain declarative sentence is true? I think there are three arguments of sorts that shore up the claim that this *is* what is believed.

First, I do not see how a creature could have the concept of belief without being able to distinguish between true and false beliefs. When I believe that my collection of rare books lacks a Gutenberg Bible, I believe that it is true that my collection lacks a Gutenberg Bible; put another way, I believe that it is false that my collection contains a Gutenberg Bible. I can distinguish, and do distinguish, between the sentences "My collection lacks a Gutenberg Bible" and "My collection contains a Gutenberg Bible," and it is only the former I hold to be true. According to my view, what I believe in this case is that this sentence is true; and sentences are the sorts of things we regard as or hold to be true. As for the cat, and leaving aside now all questions about the relative sophistication of concepts, I do not see how it could have the belief that the door is locked unless it could distinguish this true belief from the false belief that the door is unlocked. But what is true or false are not states of affairs which correspond to or reflect or pertain to these beliefs; states of affairs are not true or false but either are or are not the case, either do or do not obtain. If, then, one is going to credit cats with beliefs, and cats must be able to distinguish true from false beliefs, and states of affairs are not true or false, then what exactly is it that cats are being credited with distinguishing as true or false? Reflection on this question, I think, forces one to credit cats with language, in order for there to be something that can be true or false in belief; and it is precisely because they lack language that we cannot make this move.

Second, if in order to have the concept of belief a creature must be possessed of the difference between true and false belief, then in order for a creature to be able to distinguish true from false beliefs that creature must—simply must, as I see it—have some awareness of, to put the matter in the most general terms, how language connects with, links up with the world; and I see no reason to credit cats with such an awareness. My belief that my collection lacks a Gutenberg Bible is true if and only if my collection lacks a Gutenberg Bible; that is, the *truth* of this belief cannot be entertained by me without it being the case that I am aware that the truth of the sentence "My collection lacks a Gutenberg Bible" is *at the very least* partially a function of how the world is. However difficult to capture, it is this relationship between language and the world a grasp of which is necessary if a creature is to grasp the difference between true and false belief, a distinction which it must grasp, if it is to possess the concept of belief at all.

Third, I do not see how a creature could have an awareness or grasp of how language connects with, links up with the world, to leave the matter at its most general, unless that creature was itself possessed of language; and cats are not possessed of language. If it were to be suggested, for example, that the sounds that cats make do amount to a language, I should deny it. This matter is far too large and complex to be tackled here; but the general line of argument I should use to support my denial can be sketched in a very few words. Can cats lie? If they cannot, then they cannot assert anything; and if they lack assertion, I do not see how they could possess a language. And I should be strict: I do not suggest that, lacking assertion, cats possess a language in some attenuated or secondary sense; rather, I suggest that, lacking assertion, they do not possess a language *at all.*

R. G. Frey | # The Case Against Animal Rights

Regan is convinced that animals have *rights*. Of his rights view, he says that "of course, if it were possible to show that only human beings are included within its scope, then a person like myself, who believes in animal rights, would be obliged to look elsewhere."[1] Presumably, Regan so believes in animal *rights* that any theory whatever that failed to accord them *rights* would, even if it condemned all the practices he condemned and found wrong the maltreatment of animals, be unsatisfactory. It is difficult to know, therefore, how arguments stand that try to weaken his faith in the *rights* of animals. Are they as it were, bound to go awry, a priori? I am unsure exactly how Regan would respond to such questions; that is, I do not know what counts as, indeed, whether anything at all counts as, a challenge to his intuitions on this score. In any event, nothing that follows turns upon Regan's intuition that animals have *rights,* that they are rights-holders; *this* intuition, though I do not share it, is not here at issue.

What *is* at issue is Regan's reliance upon variants of the argument from marginal cases to *support* his claims. In each case, I do not believe these variants do support his claims, do not believe, that is, that appeal to the cases of defective humans does the work on behalf of animals that Regan supposes it does.

First, then, there is Regan's claim of the equal inherent worth of human and animal life:

> Well, perhaps some will say that animals have some inherent value, only less than we have. Once again, however, attempts to defend this view can be shown to lack rational justification. What could be the basis of our having more inherent value than animals? Their lack of reason, or autonomy, or intellect? Only if we are willing to make the same judgment in the case of humans who are similarly deficient. But it is not true that such humans—the retarded child, for example, or the mentally deranged—have less inherent value than you or I.[2]

This affirmation turns entirely upon our agreeing that all human life, however deficient, has the same value; and I, as the reader will know, do not agree. For me, the value of life is a function of its quality, its quality a function of its richness, and its richness a function of its scope or potentiality for enrichment; and the fact is that many humans lead lives of a very much lower quality than ordinary normal lives, lives which lack enrichment and where the potentialities for enrichment are severely truncated or absent. If, then, we confront the fact that not all human life has, not merely the same enrichment, but also the same scope for enrichment, then it follows that not all human life has the same value. (Anyone who thinks that we do not use this argument in order to trade off

R. G. Frey, "The Case Against Animal Rights," in *Animal Rights and Human Obligations,* 2nd ed., ed. Tom Regan and Peter Singer (Englewood Cliffs, NJ: Prentice-Hall, Inc.), pp. 115–18. Reprinted by permission of R. G. Frey.

lives of very low quality would do well to read some of the contributions by health care professionals to many of the contemporary debates in medical ethics over death and dying.) If not all human life has the same value, then Regan's claim of the equal inherent worth of animals collapses; for we do judge some human lives of less value than others.

Second, there is Regan's claim, not of equal inherent worth, but of inherent worth in the first place:

> Some there are who resist the idea that animals have inherent value. "Only humans have such value", they profess. How might this narrow view be defended? Shall we say that only humans have the requisite intelligence, or autonomy, or reason? But there are many, many humans who fail to meet these standards and yet are reasonably viewed as having value above and beyond their usefulness to others.[3]

Again, the case of deficient humans is being appealed to, this time to cede animal life inherent value at all. But I do not regard all human life as of equal value; I do not accept that a very severely mentally-enfeebled human or an elderly human fully in the grip of senile dementia or an infant born with only half a brain has a life whose value is equal to that of normal, adult humans. The quality of human life can plummet, to a point where we would not wish *that* life on even our worst enemies; and I see no reason to pretend that a life I would not wish upon even my worst enemies is nevertheless as valuable as the life of any normal, adult human. As the quality of human life falls, trade-offs between it and other things we value become possible; and if this is what one is going to mean by the phrase "usefulness to others," then I see no reason to deny that that label can be applied to me and my views. (But so, too, can it be applied to countless other people. Regan's book is littered with warnings against utilitarianism; but any of the numerous textbooks on medical ethics now on offer will show in, e.g., their sections on death and dying that all kinds of people, utilitarians and non-utilitarians alike, are no longer prepared to concede all human life, irrespective of quality, equal value.) Accordingly, Regan's claim of the inherent

worth of animals is compromised; for there are good reasons not to judge deficient human life either of equal value to normal, adult human life or, in extreme cases, even of much value at all.

By lives of not much value at all, I have in mind lives whose quality is so low that they are no longer worth living. I concede the difficulty of determining in many cases when a life is no longer worth living; but in other cases, including cases quite apart from those involving the irreversibly comatose, the matter seems far less problematic. Work recently done in Oxford by Ronald Dworkin on some of the policy implications of the prevalence of Altzheimer's disease leaves me in little doubt that a life wholly and irreversibly in the grip of senile dementia is a life not worth living; and the case of infants born without any brain whatever seems an even clearer instance.

Third, there is Regan's claim that attempts to limit the scope of his rights view to humans come unstuck:

> Animals, it is true, lack many of the abilities humans possess. They can't read, do higher mathematics, build a bookcase or make *baba ghanoush*. Neither can many human beings, however, and yet we don't (and shouldn't) say that they (these humans) therefore have less inherent value, less of a right to be treated with respect, than do others.[4]

Perhaps Regan is right, that a human who cannot build a bookcase does not per se have a less valuable life than other humans; but what about very severely mentally-enfeebled humans or elderly people fully in the grip of senile dementia or infants born without a brain? I think *these* lives have less value than ordinary human life. What is the difference between these cases and the bookcase example? It is that the inability to build a bookcase is unlikely, bizarre circumstances apart, drastically to affect the quality of one's life, whereas severe mental-enfeebledness, senile dementia, and the absence of a brain quite obviously have a seriously negative effect on the quality of life. But one need not go so far afield to find such negative effects: some of the patients in the final stages of AIDS come to the view, I gather, that life is no longer worth living, as first one illness and then another ravages their bodies.

A word on Regan's point about treating deficient humans with respect is necessary. He ties talk of respect in the passage above to some right to respect, without explaining what justifies this linkage; but the real problem is that the use of some right to respect in the present context begs the question. A doctor friend recently described to me the case of a very severely handicapped child who managed to be kept alive to the age of four through a series of eleven operations; the doctor's wife described the case as one of "keeping the child alive long enough for nature to kill it," which nature duly did. How exactly does one show respect to this child? By yet another operation, to extend its life a few weeks longer? It is all well and good to advocate treating deficient humans with respect; in the absence of some statement in a particular case about what constitutes respect, however, such talk does not come to much. How, for example, does one show respect for an individual with AIDS, who has thought long and hard about suicide and decided to kill himself? By intervening and stopping him? Or by not intervening and permitting him to carry on?

NOTES

1. Tom Regan, "The Case for Animal Rights," in P. Singer (ed.), *In Defence of Animal Rights* (Oxford: Blackwell, 1985), p. 22.
2. Ibid., p. 23.
3. Ibid., p. 22.
4. Ibid., p. 22; italics in original.

Alan White | # Rights

Most discussions about the kinds of things which can possess rights centre on the kinds of capacities either necessary or sufficient for their possible possession, whether it be interests, rationality, sentience, the ability to claim, etc. Advocates of the various capabilities are usually torn between making them so strong, for example rationality or the ability to sue, that they exclude subjects to which they wish to allow rights, whether they be children, the feebleminded, unborn generations, etc., and making them so weak that they include almost anything, whether they be inanimate objects, artefacts, abstract conceptions etc.

I have tried to show that no criterion couched in terms of substantive characteristics is logically either sufficient or necessary in itself for the possible—or, indeed, the actual—possession of a right. What I would suggest is that such characteristics are at most a mark of a certain type of subject of which the question is whether that type of subject is logically capable of having a right. And the answer to that question depends on whether it is the sort of subject of which it makes sense to use what may be called "the full language of rights."

A right is something which can be said to be exercised, earned, enjoyed, or given, which can be claimed,[1] demanded, asserted, insisted on, secured, waived, or surrendered; there can be a right to do so and so or have such and such done for one, to be in a certain state, to have a certain feeling or adopt a certain attitude. A right is related to and contrasted with a duty, an obligation, a privilege, a power, a liability. A possible possessor of a right is, therefore, whatever can properly be spoken of in such language; that is, whatever can intelligibly, whether truly or falsely, be said to exercise, earn, etc. a right, to have a right to such logically varied things, to have duties, privileges, etc. Furthermore, . . . a necessary condition of something's being capable of having a right to V is that it should be something which logically can V.

Excerpted from Alan White, *Rights* (Oxford: Oxford University Press, 1984). Reprinted by permission of Oxford University Press.

In the full language of "a right" only a *person* can logically have a right because only a person can be the subject of such predications. Rights are not the sorts of things of which non-persons can be the subjects, however right it may be to treat them in certain ways. Nor does this, as some contend, exclude infants, children, the feeble-minded, the comatose, the dead, or generations yet unborn.[2] Any of these may be for various reasons empirically unable to fulfil the full role of a right-holder. But so long as they are persons—and it is significant that we think and speak of them as young, feeble-minded, incapacitated, dead, unborn *persons*—they are logically possible subjects of rights to whom the full language of rights can significantly, however falsely, be used. It is a misfortune, not a tautology, that these persons cannot exercise or enjoy, claim, or waive, their rights or do their duty or fulfil their obligations. The law has always linked together the notions of a person and of the bearer of rights, duties, privileges, powers, liberties, liabilities, immunities, etc., so that a change in application of one notion has accompanied a parallel change in application of the other.[3] Thus, at various times in the law, gods, idols, unborn and dead human beings, animals, inanimate things, corporations, and governments, have been treated as persons because they were conceived as possible subjects of such jural relations as rights, duties, etc. who can commit or be the victims of torts and crimes. In Roman law slaves were things, not persons, and, hence, had no rights. The attitudes of various legal systems to the possible rights of an unborn child depend on how far they are regarded as legal persons.[4]

What this legal practice brings out is the importance of using a set of concepts, for example rights, duties, privileges, obligations, etc. together and not isolating one of them, for example rights, so that, as Wittgenstein might put it, the lone concept is only "idling." The concept of a right can, of course, be stretched—as when Trollope, for example talks of a house with certain grandiose features as having "the right" to be called a castle—and debates about the rights of foetuses, animals, works of art, or of nature can become merely terminological. What is important is to ask what job, if any, is being done in such

contexts by the notion of "a right" as contrasted with that of "right" when it is isolated from such normal companions as the notions of duty, obligation, power, etc.

Something capable only of sentience or of suffering would not necessarily be capable of exercising, owning, or enjoying a right, much less of claiming, asserting, insisting on, or fighting for its rights or of waiving or relinquishing them. Nor of having obligations, duties, privileges, etc. And though it would be capable of having something done for it or of being in a certain state, it would not necessarily be capable of performing tasks, assuming attitudes, or having emotions. Hence, its possible rights, if any, would be confined to the right to have something done for it, such as to be well treated or protected, or to be in a certain state, such as to be happy or free or to remain alive. Moreover, though sentience or capacity to suffer would be necessary for the possible possession of a right to anything relevant to these, such as a right to protection from suffering—because a right to V implies being logically able to V—they would not be sufficient. The fact that an animal can suffer from growing pains or a man suffer from doubt does not in itself prove that it or he is capable of a right to protection from these.

It is a misunderstanding to object to this distinction between the kinds of things which can have rights and those which cannot on the ground that it constitutes a sort of speciesism. For it is not being argued that it is right to treat one species less considerately than another, but only that one species, that is, a person, can sensibly be said to exercise or waive a right, be under an obligation, have a duty, etc., whereas another cannot, however unable particular members of the former species may be to do so.

NOTES

1. The fact that a right can be claimed is no evidence for the mistaken thesis (e.g., Joel Feinberg, "Duties, Rights and Claims." *American Philosophical Quarterly* 64 [1966], pp. 137–44) that a right is a claim.

2. E.g., W. D. Lamont, *The Principles of Moral Judgement* (Oxford, 1946), pp. 83–85.

3. R. Pound, *Jurisprudence* (St. Paul, MN, 1959), IV. ch. 25 and references on p. 191, n. 1.

4. P.D. Lasok, "The Rights of the Unborn" in *Fundamental Rights*, ed. J. W. Bridge, D. Lasok, *et al.* (London, 1973), pp. 18–30; and D. W. Louisell, "Abortion, the Practice of Medicine and the Due Process of Law." *U.C.L.A. Law Review* 16 (1969), 233–54. M. Tooley goes too far in making "is a person" and "has a moral right to life" synonymous. See his "Abortion and infanticide." *Philosophy and Public Affairs* 2 (1972), pp. 37–65.

PART 2

WHAT'S WRONG WITH SEX?

Some sexual acts generate little moral opposition. Procreative, heterosexual intercourse that takes place within a healthy and loving marriage, for example, is widely taken to be an instance of morally acceptable behavior. Other sexual acts are considered as clearly wrong. The violent rape of a young child is surely an example. But many forms of sexual behavior lie between these two extremes. They are freely engaged in by consenting adults, but differ from the case of marital, heterosexual intercourse in ways that many people find morally troubling.

Part 2 is devoted to a critical examination of some of these cases. We begin with the morality of homosexual acts. In chapter 6 we look at the question of whether or not homosexual behavior is itself morally objectionable, and in chapter 7 we turn to the question of whether publicly revealing the sexual orientation of people who have attempted to conceal their homosexuality is morally objectionable. In chapter 8 we ask what if anything is wrong with adultery. We then consider two quite different questions that involve issues of freedom and consent: the question of the moral appropriateness of campus sexual-conduct codes, and the question of whether consenting adults may freely buy and sell sexual services.

6

Is Homosexuality Wrong?

Levin and His Critics

There is widespread antagonism both to homosexual behavior and to homosexual tendencies, and often along with that antagonism comes a presumption of immorality. It is only relatively recently that laws against homosexual acts have been repealed, and in many countries, and in some states in the U.S., those acts are still illegal. Even some of those who support the repeal of those laws think that homosexual acts are immoral. They just think that such acts—like adulterous acts, for example—while immoral, are not the sort of immoral acts which the State should concern itself with discouraging, policing, or punishing.

How might one argue for such a view? A popular and rather simple argument is based on the feeling that there is something "unnatural" about homosexual acts, that it is this "unnaturalness" that makes them wrong. Let's spell out this rather popular argument:

P1 Homosexual acts are unnatural.
P2 Unnatural acts are morally wrong.

C Homosexual acts are morally wrong.

As soon as the popular view is spelled out in this formal argument, however, it becomes obvious that it is rather weak. (Note that this popular argument is not the argument that Levin puts forward in the feature article of this section, although the two arguments are related.) While this popular argument is valid, both its premises are problematic. Exactly what does it take it for an act to be *natural* or *unnatural?* And why should the *unnatural* be deemed *morally wrong?* Consider eyeglasses, for example. It seems that wearing eye glasses is unnatural. Eyeglasses are not naturally occurring objects, but rather human artifacts manufactured to correct for what are typically naturally occurring problems people have with their eyesight. But we do not consider it morally wrong for someone to improve his vision by wearing eyeglasses. By contrast, urinating is clearly a natural act, and most animals in their natural state unabashedly urinate in public, so urinating in public seems very much a natural act. But despite its apparent naturalness, urinating in public is not highly regarded among human beings, and in at least some circumstances (say, during a lecture) would be regarded as morally improper. So, to the extent that we have a clear idea of what acts are natural, the natural and the moral do not line up. Natural acts can be morally wrong, and unnatural acts can be morally permissible. So, either premise 2 is false or else these apparently intuitive judgments of what is natural are false. But if these intuitive judgments are false, then we don't really have a firm grasp of what it takes for something to count as *natural*. Therefore, we really don't know how to tell whether premise 1 is true or false. Either way it seems that at least one of the premises of the popular argument fails.

Levin's argument has its origin in the same hunch—that homosexual acts are in some morally relevant sense *unnatural*—but he makes a number of interesting variations on the intuitive argument. First, he argues that homosexual acts are *abnormal*. They are abnormal because they involve a *misuse* of bodily parts. He goes on to argue that misusing bodily parts is very likely to lead to unhappiness. And finally he argues that because homosexuality is very likely to lead to unhappiness, not only is it imprudent for individuals to indulge in homosexual acts, but it is also wrong for the State to give homosexuality legitimacy by extending to homosexuals the kinds of rights and protections that have been extended to other protected classes. Such legislation is likely to increase the prevalence of homosexuality, and hence spread unhappiness.

Levin observes that "the erect penis fits the vagina, and fits it better than any other natural orifice; penis and vagina seem made for each other. . . . the penis is not *for* inserting into the anus of another man . . ." What sense can be made of the idea that a certain body part has one purpose, but not another? One theological tradition maintains that God, in creating men and women with their respective sexual organs, clearly intended them to use those organs for sex with each other for the purpose of procreation of the species. If God exists, and that was God's intention, then there is some content to the idea that any other use of the sexual organs is a misuse, much as it would be a misuse of a screwdriver to use it to hammer in nails. But suppose the theological account of our origins or of God's intentions were false. Suppose, for example, that biological organisms such as ourselves evolved without supernatural supervision. Would it still make sense to attribute purposes or functions to bits and pieces of our bodies?

Even if there is no God, intuitively the purpose or function of the eye is to enable its possessor to see. The purpose or function of the nose is to enable its possessor to breathe and smell. The purpose or function of the heart is to pump blood. And the purpose of an erect penis is for it to be inserted into a vagina, with the clear biological purpose of insemination and subsequent reproduction of the species. Levin argues that we can flesh out this idea of a biological purpose as follows: That people have penises or vaginas today is because our ancestors used them for heterosexual reproduction. We wouldn't be here today, equipped with penises and vaginas, if those ancestors had instead diverted themselves into homosexual activity. As Levin puts it: "an organ is for a given activity if the organ's performing that activity helps its host or organisms suitably related to its host, *and* if this contribution is how the organ got and stays where it is." Thus it is, for example, that teeth are for *chewing* and not for turning into necklaces for ornamentation.

Armed with this notion of *purely biological* function or purpose, we can classify acts as *natural* to the extent that they are in accord with biological purposes or functions; otherwise they are *unnatural*. As noted, Levin does not argue that homosexual acts are immoral or sinful, but rather that because they are abnormal in this biological sense they are "likely to lead to unhappiness." And the reason for this is quite general. One way in which evolution ensures that the use of an organ for a certain end becomes widespread is to reward that use by making it enjoyable, and to make misuse of it unenjoyable. This would ensure that our inclinations, in general, were toward those activities conducive to the survival and well-being of the species.

> Nature has consequently made this use of the penis [viz. inserting it in vaginas and depositing semen in them] rewarding. It is clear enough that any proto-human males who found unrewarding the insertion of penis into vagina have left no descendents. In particular, proto-human males who enjoyed inserting their penises into each other's anuses have left no descendents. This is why homosexuality is abnormal, and why its abnormality counts prudentially against it. Homosexuality is likely to cause unhappiness because it leaves unfulfilled an innate and innately rewarding desire.

Levin does not claim that homosexuals are all unhappy, but that happy practicing homosexuals are rather rare.

Levin's argument has three parts. The first part seeks to establish that homosexual activity is (evolutionarily and biologically) abnormal. The second seeks to show that, because of this, homosexual activity conduces to unhappiness. And the third part seeks to show that this abnormality justifies legal sanctions against homosexual activity, or at least a rolling back of legislation that ensures that homosexuals enjoy all civil rights.

Timothy Murphy criticizes Levin on all three counts. First, he argues that Levin fails to show that the evolutionary origins of sexual behavior have any significant normative force. That our organs evolved in a certain way cannot in itself oblige us to use them in one way rather than another. Thus, saying that a certain use of an organ, given its evolutionary history, is a *misuse* or is *abnormal* does not entail that it is *wrong* in any moral sense.

Murphy thus concludes that an activity's being evolutionarily abnormal in Levin's sense has no implications for its wrongness. But that is presumably one reason why Levin does not stop with the assertion that homosexual activity is abnormal, but rather goes on to argue that abnormal behavior is prone to make one unhappy. Homosexual behavior is no exception, and Levin adduces some empirical evidence that homosexuals are generally unhappy, and unhappier than heterosexuals.

Murphy claims, first, that Levin tries to make this claim invulnerable to any possible empirical refutation. A homosexual's protestation of happiness will not count as evidence against Levin's thesis because, no matter how happy the homosexual is, he cannot be as happy as any comparable heterosexual. (Why? What is Levin's reason for claiming that?) Second, Murphy attacks the kind of evidence that Levin cites as "anecdotal and trivial." Further, much of the unhappiness of homosexuals can be traced to the hostile social conditions that homophobic societies construct. Murphy outlines the kind of evidence that would be required—via a controlled large-scale social experiment—to determine if homosexuals were, by their very nature, unhappier than heterosexuals or if their unhappiness were attributable to social causes.

Finally, Murphy argues that even if it were true that, for various biological reasons, homosexuals had a greater tendency toward unhappiness than heterosexuals, it does not follow that the State should impose extra burdens on people who engage in homosexual activity. Suppose it is a fact that atheists tend to be less happy than theists. Does it follow, then, that the State should discourage atheism by imposing burdens on atheists or that atheists should not enjoy the same rights as theists?

QUESTIONS FOR CONSIDERATION

• Suppose a certain activity was once essential for the survival and reproduction of humanity (say, killing animals and eating their flesh) and that various organs evolved to enable us to do exactly that. Does it follow that it would be wrong for a particular human being to desist from killing animals in order to eat their flesh? Are we morally obliged to be meat-eaters? Suppose that although we evolved by eating meat, we no longer needed to eat meat to survive and reproduce (which, as it happens, is the case). Might there not be good moral arguments for becoming vegetarians despite our evolutionary history?

• Suppose an activity had the following feature: that *not everyone* engaged in it played an essential role in our evolution and our survival, and that it was essential, for our future survival, that not everyone engage in that activity. (Being completely celibate is clearly an example of this.) Would it follow, then, that *no one* should engage in that activity? (Is it true that *no one* should remain celibate?) If we do not deem it immoral for people to take on a vow of life-long chastity, what implications does that have for Levin's argument?

• Recently a new fad has emerged among those who like piercing their bodies: tongue splitting. Would tongue-splitting count as a misuse of an organ, according to Levin's theory? Should there be laws discouraging tongue-splitting and body-piercing? Perhaps tongue-splitting, though abnormal, is not a very drastic misuse of an organ. A far more drastic misuse of organs, as reported in the December 2000 issue of *Atlantic Monthly* (C. Elliot, "A New Way to Be Mad"; also available online at http://www.theatlantic.com/issues/2000/12/elliott.htm) involves the following:

> In January of this year British newspapers began running articles about Robert Smith, a surgeon at Falkirk and District Royal Infirmary, in Scotland. Smith had amputated the legs of two patients at their request, and he was planning to carry out a third amputation when the trust that runs his hospital stopped him. These patients were not physically sick. Their legs did not need to be amputated for any medical reason. Nor were they incompetent, according to the psychiatrists who examined them. They simply wanted to have their legs cut off. In fact, both the men whose limbs Smith amputated have declared in public interviews how much happier they are, now that they have finally had their legs removed.

• Apotemnophilia, or the desire to be an amputee, is a strange and disturbing phenomenon. An apotemnophiliac desires to have one or more of his own healthy limbs amputated, and evidently is sometimes able to persuade others to fulfill this desire. Cases are not as uncommon as one might think. Elliot reports several, including that of a seventy-nine-year-old New Yorker who, in May 1998, traveled to Mexico, paid $10,000 for a leg amputation on the black market, and subsequently died of gangrene. Those of us who do not suffer such desires judge them to be perverse, and we feel extremely uncomfortable about Dr. Smith's helping his patients satisfy them. Does Levin's account capture what we think of as abnormal in such desires? And could Murphy's defense of homosexual acts also be used as a defense of apotemnophiliac acts of amputation? If not, why not?

FURTHER READING

Ruse, Michael. "Homosexuality: Right or Wrong?" *Free Inquiry* 13, no. 2. (1993): 35–37.

Michael Levin | # Why Homosexuality Is Abnormal

1. INTRODUCTION

This paper defends the view that homosexuality is abnormal and hence undesirable—not because it is immoral or sinful, or because it weakens society or hampers evolutionary development, but for a purely mechanical reason. It is a misuse of bodily parts. Clear empirical sense attaches to the idea of *the use* of such bodily parts as genitals, the idea that they are *for* something, and consequently to the idea of their misuse. I argue on grounds involving natural selection that misuse of bodily parts can with high probability be connected to unhappiness. I regard these matters as prolegomena to such policy issues as the rights of homosexuals, the rights of those desiring not to associate with homosexuals, and legislation concerning homosexuality, issues which I shall not discuss systematically here. However, I do in the last section draw a seemingly evident corollary from my view that homosexuality is abnormal and likely to lead to unhappiness.

I have confined myself to male homosexuality for brevity's sake, but I believe that much of what I say applies *mutatis mutandis* to lesbianism. There may well be significant differences between the two: the data of [4], for example, support the popular idea that sex per se is less important to women and in particular lesbians than it is to men. On the other hand, lesbians are generally denied motherhood, which seems more important to women than is fatherhood—normally denied homosexual males—to men. On this matter,[4] offers no data. Overall, it is reasonable to expect general innate gender differences to explain the major differences between male homosexuals and lesbians.

Despite the publicity currently enjoyed by the claim that one's "sexual preference" is nobody's business but one's own, the intuition that there is something unnatural about homosexuality remains vital. The erect penis fits the vagina, and fits it better than any other natural orifice; penis and vagina seem made for each other. This intuition ultimately derives from, or is another way of capturing, the idea that the penis is not *for* inserting into the anus of another man—that so using the penis is not the way it is *supposed, even intended,* to be used. Such intuitions may appear to rest on an outmoded teleological view of nature, but recent work in the logic of functional ascription shows how they may be explicated, and justified, in suitably naturalistic terms. Such is the burden of Section 2, the particular application to homosexuality coming in Section 3. Furthermore, when we understand the sense in which homosexual acts involve a misuse of genitalia, we will see why such misuse is bad and not to be encouraged. (The case for this constitutes the balance of Section 3.) Clearly, the general idea that homosexuality is a pathological violation of nature's intent is not shunned by scientists. Here is Gadpille:

> The view of cultural relativity seems to be without justification. Cultural judgment is collective human caprice, and whether it accepts or rejects homosexuality is irrelevant. Biological intent . . . is to differentiate male and female both physiologically and psychologically in such a manner as to insure species survival, which can be served only through heterosexual union ([7], 193).

Gadpille refers to homosexuality as "an abiological maladaptation." The novelty of the present paper is to link adaptiveness and normality via the notion of happiness.

But before turning to these issues, I want to make four preliminary remarks. The first concerns the

From Michael Levin, "Why Homosexuality Is Abnormal," *The Monist* 67 (1984): 251–83. Notes and some parts of text deleted. Reprinted by permission of the Monist.

explicitness of my language in the foregoing paragraph and the rest of this paper. Explicit mention of bodily parts and the frank description of sexual acts are necessary to keep the phenomenon under discussion in clear focus. Euphemistic vagary about "sexual orientation" or "the gay lifestyle" encourage one to slide over homosexuality without having to face or even acknowledge what it really is. Such talk encourages one to treat "sexual preference" as if it were akin to preference among flavors of ice cream. Since unusual taste in ice-cream is neither right nor wrong, this usage suggests, why should unusual taste in sex be regarded as objectionable? Opposed to this usage is the unblinkable fact that the sexual preferences in question are such acts as mutual fellation. Is one man's taste for pistachio ice cream really just like another man's taste for fellation? Unwillingness to call this particular spade a spade allows delicacy to award the field by default to the view that homosexuality is normal. Anyway, such delicacy is misplaced in a day when "the love that dare not speak its name" is shouting its name from the rooftops.

My second, related, point concerns the length of the present paper, which has a general and a specific cause. The general cause is that advocates of an unpopular position—as mine is, at least in intellectual circles—assume the burden of proof. My view is the one that needs defending, my presuppositions the ones not widely shared. I would not have entertained so many implausible and digressive objections had not so many competent philosophers urged them on me with great seriousness. Some of these objections even generate a dialectic among themselves. For example, I have to defend my view on two sociobiological fronts—against the view that what is innate is polymorphous sexuality shaped by culture, and against the incompatible view that not only are the details of sexual behavior innate, but homosexuality is one such behavior, and hence "normal."

The third point is this. The chain of intuitions I discussed earlier has other links, links connected to the conclusion that homosexuality is bad. They go something like this: Homosexual acts involve the use of the genitals for what they aren't for, and it is

a *bad* or at least *unwise* thing to use a part of your body for what it isn't for. Calling homosexual acts "unnatural" is intended to sum up this entire line of reasoning. "Unnatural" carries disapprobative connotations, and any explication of it should capture this. One can, stipulatively or by observing the ordinary usage of biologists, coin an evaluatively neutral use for "normal," or "proper function," or any cognate thereof. One might for example take the normal use of an organ to be what the organ is used for 95% of the time. But there is a normative dimension to the concept of abnormality that all such explications miss. To have anything to do with our intuitions—even if designed to demonstrate them groundless—an explication of "abnormal" must capture the analytic truth that the abnormality of a practice is a reason for avoiding it. If our ordinary concept of normality turns out to be ill-formed, so that various acts are at worst "abnormal" in some non-evaluative sense, this will simply mean that, as we ordinarily use the expression, *nothing is abnormal.* (Not that anyone really believes this—people who deny that cacophagia or necrophilia are abnormal do so only to maintain the appearance of consistency.)

Fourth, I should mention Steven Goldberg's defense of a position similar to mine ([8]). Goldberg's first approximation to a definition of abnormality runs as follows: behavior is abnormal when it is emitted in circumstances in which it is highly negatively sanctioned. This captures the insight that even if there is nothing *intrinsically* wrong with a bit of behavior, there probably must be something wrong with anyone who persists in doing it when he knows he will be punished. There may be nothing wrong with eating beef per se, but there must be something wrong with a Hindu who invites death by walking the streets of Calcutta eating a hamburger. The trouble with this definition is that as it stands it brands as abnormal a highly-sanctioned behavior done to make a moral point. To exclude such cases Goldberg adds a second clause: person A's doing act B is abnormal if A is caused to do B by conditions one would intuitively judge to be abnormal. This excludes high-minded sacrifices but does include homosexuality if, as Freudians believe, homosexuality results from maternal dominance and paternal indifference, conditions most people regard as abnormal. Goldberg is aware that defining "abnormal" via "abnormal cause" is circular, but he finds the circularity benign. He contends that the definition does capture a definite reality people have in mind when they label homosexuality or necrophilia abnormal, and that anyone who brings the charge of circularity must also take this circularity to prevent us from viewing necrophilia as abnormal. Goldberg assumes that no reasonable person would carry the charge of circularity that far.

Goldberg's analysis is persuasive, and the first clause should be preserved, even if the circular second clause is jettisoned. My own analysis—which I believe to be even clearer than Goldberg's, as well as more formally adequate—is indeed compatible with Goldberg's. It turns out that what Goldberg has correctly analyzed is not what "abnormal" means, but the *evidence* on which ordinary judgements of abnormality are based. That something is abnormal in Goldberg's sense is good evidence that it is abnormal in the central sense I explicate below. I will have occasion to use this lemma.

2. ON "FUNCTION" AND ITS COGNATES

To bring into relief the point of the idea that homosexuality involves a misuse of bodily parts, I will begin with an uncontroversial case of misuse, a case in which the clarity of our intuitions is not obscured by the conviction that they are untrustworthy. Mr. Jones pulls all his teeth and strings them around his neck because he thinks his teeth look nice as a necklace. He takes pureéd liquids supplemented by intravenous solutions for nourishment. It is surely natural to say that Jones is misusing his teeth, that he is not using them for what they are for, that indeed the way he is using them is incompatible with what they are for. Pedants might argue that Jones's teeth are no longer part of him and hence that he is not misusing any bodily parts. To them I offer Mr. Smith, who likes to play "Old MacDonald" on his teeth. So devoted is he to this amusement, in fact, that he never uses his teeth for chewing—like Jones, he takes nourishment intravenously. Now, not only do

we find it perfectly plain that Smith and Jones are misusing their teeth, we predict a dim future for them on purely physiological grounds; we expect the muscles of Jones's jaw that are used for—that *are* for—chewing to lose their tone, and we expect this to affect Jones's gums. Those parts of Jones's digestive tract that are for processing solids will also suffer from disuse. The net result will be deteriorating health and perhaps a shortened life. Nor is this all. Human beings enjoy chewing. Not only has natural selection selected in muscles for chewing and favored creatures with such muscles, it has selected in a tendency to find the use of those muscles reinforcing. Creatures who do not enjoy using such parts of their bodies as deteriorate with disuse, will tend to be selected out. Jones, product of natural selection that he is, descended from creatures who at least tended to enjoy the use of such parts. Competitors who didn't simply had fewer descendants. So we expect Jones sooner or later to experience vague yearnings to chew something, just as we find people who take no exercise to experience a general listlessness. Even waiving for now my apparent reification of the evolutionary process, let me emphasize how little anyone is tempted to say "each to his own" about Jones or to regard Jones's disposition of his teeth as simply a deviation from a statistical norm. This sort of case is my paradigm when discussing homosexuality.

The main obstacle to talk of what a process or organic structure is for is that, literally understood, such talk presupposes an agent who intends that structure or process to be used in a certain way. Talk of function derives its primitive meaning from the human use of artifacts, artifacts being for what purposive agents intend them for. Indeed, there is in this primitive context a natural reason for using something for what it is for: to use it otherwise would frustrate the intention of some purposeful agent. Since it now seems clear that our bodily parts were not emplaced by purposeful agency, it is easy to dismiss talk of what they are for as "theologically" based on a faulty theory of how we came to be built as we are:

The idea that sex was designed for propagation is a theological argument, but not a scientific one. . . .

To speak of the "fit" of penis and vagina as proof of nature's intention for their exclusive union is pure theological reasoning—imposing a meaning or purpose upon a simple, natural phenomenon ([9], 63).

Barash—who elsewhere uses its cognates freely—dismisses "unnatural" as a mere term of abuse: "people with a social or political axe to grind will call what they don't like 'unnatural' and what they do, 'natural'" ([1], 237). Hume long ago put the philosopher's case against the term 'natural' with characteristic succinctness: "'Tis founded on final Causes; which is a consideration, that appears to me pretty uncertain & unphilosophical. For pray, what is the End of Man? Is he created for Happiness or for Virtue? For this Life or the next? For himself or for his Maker?" ([20], 134).

Until recently, philosophers of science half-countered, half-conceded such doubts by "rationally reconstructing" the locution "structure S is for function F in organism O" as—omitting inessential refinements—"S's doing F in O is necessary for the integrity or prosperity of O". This, the classical analysis, suffers from two weaknesses. First, it quite severs the link stressed earlier between a structure's having a function and the inadvisability of using that structure in a way inconsistent with its function. An organism may not be interested in survival, or prosperity, or the prosperity of some genetically defined group that contains the organism. The classical analysis provides no clue as to why Jones should desist from stringing his teeth on a necklace. It must be supplemented with the premise that survival or fitness are desirable, and however strong the desire to survive may be as a de facto motive, there are too many cogent arguments against survival as a basic norm for this supplement to be plausible.

None of this will disturb proponents of the classical analysis, since their very aim was, in part, to remove the teleological and normative connotations of "function" as unscientific ideas. So what if the classical analysis obstructs the inference from "Jones is not using his teeth for what they are for" to "Jones is misusing his teeth"? That is one of its virtues. However, the more decisive second objection to the classical analysis is the existence of clear counter-examples—counter-examples that turn out, on reflection, to be connected to the first objection. An accidentally incurred heart lesion might be necessary for the heart's pumping blood if it is otherwise diseased; but the lesion is not *for* pumping blood. A patient's heartbeat might be the only way his doctor can diagnose a disease that would be fatal if undiagnosed; but the beat of his heart is not *for* diagnosis. Such cases suggest that the classical analysis pays insufficient attention to how structures come to be in organisms and why they persist in reproductive cohorts. In light of this, a more adequate explication of "S is for F in O" runs:

(i) S conduces to F in O,
(ii) O's being F is necessary for the maintenance of O or O's genetic cohort, and
(iii) (i) and (ii) are part of the causal explanation of the existence or persistence of S in O and member's of O's genetic cohort (see [5], sec. 23; [15]; and esp. [33]).

In rougher and plainer English: an organ is for a given activity if the organ's performing that activity helps its host or organisms suitably related to its host, *and* if this contribution is how the organ got and stays where it is. This disqualifies the fortuitous heart lesion and the symptomatic heartbeat, which did not arise or persist by increasing (inclusive) fitness. This definition also distinguishes what something is for from what it may be *used* for on some occasion. Teeth are for chewing—we have teeth because their use in chewing favored the survival of organisms with teeth—whereas Jones is using his teeth for ornamentation.

Counter-examples to this explication have appeared in the literature, but none administer more than superficial wounds. What if S's being F once was, but is no longer, necessary? What if, for example, implanting semen in the vagina is no longer necessary for propagation because of artificial insemination? The overall shape of my reply will become clearer only a bit later on, but, roughly speaking, if S is for F in O in my sense, O will find the use of S to F reinforcing. This is the point behind the popular observation that whatever modern society is like, humans still carry a heritage of traits evolved by lower mammals and by their tenure as hunter-gatherers. Anyway, such evolutionary lags tend to be unstable. For example, elaborate but clumsy plumage *for* mating displays would likely disappear from a population of birds whose mating was controlled by human breeders uninterested in bright feathers. After, say, 1000 generations, all surviving structures would be used for what, *per* my definition, they *are* for.

Notice that my definition refers to an organism's "genetic cohort" rather than its species. Dawkins [6] and others have argued that species-selection does not actually occur in nature. Taking the natural unit of replication, the "gene," as whatever bit of chromosome can retain its identity through enough generations to matter, a gene will most fecundly copy itself if either the organism that contains it, or organisms with a good chance of containing it—relatives of the gene's organism—reproduce prolifically. A gene is not helping itself reproduce if it instructs the body housing it to assist unrelated members of that body's species; it helps itself reproduce by instructing the body housing it to assist the organisms that might have reproducible copies of itself. So natural selection selects for "inclusive fitness": for traits that benefit an organism taken together with some group of relatives (see [31], 343). How wide the group should be is a matter of some debate, and will indeed be different for different kinds of organisms. Nor has species-selection lost all its defenders. For this reason, I am using "genetic cohort" to name whatever degree of relatedness turns out to be most appropriate for evolutionary theory.

One might well ask how my analysis of "function" can be what people meant before Darwin was ever heard of, even if people did have some inchoate notion of "minimum chain of emplacement" in mind. Doesn't "function" inherently refer to someone with a purpose—or, if not, what is simply de facto beneficial to organisms? No. What happened, I believe, was that before Darwin people thought that the only way S's aptness for F could cause S's existence was for someone, namely God, to notice that S is apt for F and for this reason choose to put S in O. We now know this is false; we now know of another way S's aptness for F can result in S's implantation—mutational

emergence and subsequent natural selection. The core meaning of "function" was always (i)–(iii), the idea that God put organs in organisms being merely a theory about how (iii) was or had to be realized. This theory was so "obvious," however, that it appeared to be part of the meaning of "function" itself. Perhaps in concession to our ancestor's ignorance of causes, "reproductive" ought to replace "genetic" in (iii); beyond that, the present definition does capture what people meant by "function" even before Darwin was ever heard of.

Within a Darwinian setting, the function of bodily parts can be linked to normative notions in a way that imputes no extrinsic direction to evolution. The empirical sense coaxed from "S is for F in O" explains our intuition that, since their efficacy in chewing got them selected in, teeth are for masticating and Jones is preventing his teeth from doing their proper job. To begin, it is clear that "Man has teeth because teeth grind food" cannot mean that the power of teeth to grind food is literally what provided Jones or anyone else with teeth. Causal powers aren't causes, and anyway the causal powers an object would have can hardly be what brings the object into existence. Rather, the presence or persistence of S in O's cohort is better understood in more general evolutionary terms. Genetic mutation brought forth the first S in one of our ancestors. There is a mechanism, the coding of the DNA, that transmits S. Here is where S's causal powers come in. Possession of S aided its first possessor and his cohorts in the struggle for survival, and since S is transmissible, this initial possessor survived to transmit S to his descendants, who, in turn, were better fitted than their S-less competitors to reproduce and transmit S . . . We, the descendants of S's original possessors, possess S as a result of this filtration. And it is just here that a eudaimonistic normative link begins to appear.

Consider this first-approximation guess about one of the mechanisms of natural selection. Imagine for a moment that S is for F in the sense explained, and that exercise of S does not lie wholly within the province of O's autonomic nervous system. It is, loosely speaking, up to O whether to use S, or use S for F. Imagine as well two subpopulations O_1 and

O_2. Members of O_1 *enjoy* using S to F, while members of O_2 do not. Since O_2's do not enjoy using S to F, they will use S to F less frequently than do O_1's. Since S favors the survival of possessors of S precisely because S conduces to F, it is the members of O_1 who are more likely to reproduce themselves and transmit, in addition to S, a desire to use S to F. It is thus likely that present-day O's will enjoy using S to F, because they are more probably descendants of the O_1 than of the O_2. Nature is interested in making its creatures like what is (inclusively) good for them. A creature that does not enjoy using its teeth for chewing uses them less than does a toothed competitor who enjoys chewing. Since the use of teeth for chewing favors the survival of an individual with teeth, and, other things being equal, traits favorable to the survival of individuals favor survival of the relevant cohort, toothed creatures who do not enjoy chewing tend to get selected out. We today are the filtrate of this process, descendants of creatures who liked to chew.

To be sure, the best evolutionary strategy might be a mix of O_1-ness and O_2-ness, so that the filtrate of evolution will be creatures with alleles for enjoying, and alleles for not enjoying, the use of S. Constant use of S might be too much of a good thing. The filtrate would be a population mixing O_1's and O_2's. We will consider in due course whether this model is applicable to homosexuality. But even in its simplified form, the present analysis does suggest that a gene for enjoying the use of S to F would at least tend to spread rapidly through O. It is hard to imagine how the enjoyment of the use of such things as human teeth could not take over, and there seems to be no current benefit associated with the absence of this enjoyment. And here—to return to the main strand of the argument—is why it is advisable to use your organs for what they are for: you will enjoy it. Jones's behavior is ill-advised not only because of the avertible objective consequences of his defanging himself, but because he will feel that something is missing. Similarly, this is why you should exercise. It is not just that muscles are for running. We have already heard the sceptic's reply to that: "So what? Suppose I don't mind being flabby? Suppose I don't give a hang about what will propagate my genetic cohort?" Rather, run-

ning is good because nature made sure people like to run. This is, of course, the prudential "good," not the moral "good"—but I disavowed at the outset the doctrine that misuse of bodily parts is *morally* bad, at least in any narrow sense. You ought to run because running was once necessary for catching food: creatures who did not enjoy running, if there ever were any, caught less food and reproduced less frequently than competitors who enjoyed running. These competitors passed on their appetites along with their muscles *to you*. This is not to say that those who suffer the affective consequences of laziness must recognize them as such, or even be able to identify them against their general background feeling-tone. They may not realize they would feel better if they exercised. They may even doubt it. They may have allowed their muscles to deteriorate beyond the point at which satisfying exercise is possible. For all that, evolution has decreed that a life involving regular exercise is on the whole more enjoyable than a life without. The same holds for every activity that is the purpose of an organ.

My loose talk of "enjoyment" can be tightened by appeal to the notion of reinforcement. Psychologists define "R is a reinforcer or reward" as: "R makes more probable the repetition of any behavior R follows." Contrary to a surprisingly wide misconception, this definition allows internal states to be rewards, even unconditioned rewards. We can say that organism O enjoys emitting behavior B without explicitly appealing to O's feeling-tone by saying that O's emission of B puts O in a rewarding internal state. In these terms, my general evolutionary hypothesis holds that nature tends to make rewarding behavior that favors cohort survival, and to make unrewarding behavior that does not. More specifically, it holds that if S is for F, using S to F will be rewarding, while using S for something incompatible with F will be unrewarding. I should add that this standard definition of "reinforcer" does not trivialize the law of effect—the law that the probability of behavior increases as it is reinforced. What saves the law, in its usual uses, is some antecedent and independent specification of what in fact is reinforcing.

Positing an inherited tendency to find the use of S for F rewarding coheres well with the present evolutionary hypothesis. It may not be clear how so nebulous a state as enjoyment can be transmitted, but prospects for a transmission mechanism are improved by replacing talk of enjoyment with talk of an as-yet unidentified internal state that increases the probability of behavior it follows. Even if the internal state itself is nonphysical, its presence is doubtless correlated with some physical state, and it is easy to imagine DNA instructions for building a nervous system that lapses into the physical correlate of the reinforcing state when some selected behavior is emitted. It is these instructions that transmit "a tendency to enjoy" the behavior. Indeed, its genes would "tell" an organism to emit some bit of behavior by so constructing it that emission of the behavior would be followed by the reinforcing state. It becomes nearly, but not quite fatally, analytic that, if using S to F increases fitness, cohorts or strains that are reinforced by using S to F are more likely to survive, and produce offspring that produce offspring. Finally, construing enjoyment behaviorally renders more natural the idea that one may not know that one's sense of well-being is being impaired by failure to perform certain actions. It is a commonplace that an organism need not be consciously aware of what is reinforcing it, and this holds for internal and external, conditioned and unconditioned rewards. An internal state can be reinforcing even if its subject fails to discriminate it against a general affective background, or to notice its absence.

These speculations are much in the spirit of Barash's, especially if one recalls that by the fitness of an organism Barash means the relative number of copies of that organism's genotype that appear in the next generation:

> Just as we find sugar sweet, we find certain behavior to be sweet as well. This means that, at least in part because of evolution's handiwork, we are inclined to do certain things rather than others, and it should be no surprise that in general our inclinations are those that contribute to our fitness. ([1], 39)

Put this way, it is surprising that anyone denies that evolution can shape behavior, even "social" behavior. We are all sociobiologists. Obviously, physical structures like hearts and earlobes are selected in. But physical structures do things. The line between structure and behavior is further blurred by the heritability of time-dependent phenomena. Stanislaw Ulam reports in his autobiography that John von Neumann's two-year-old grandson, who had never seen his grandfather, had von Neumann's distinctive walk. And who can draw a fixed line between simple patterns of behavior like a characteristic gait, and complex patterns of behavior like altruism? And who will draw a sharp line between either kind of behavior, and physical structure?

3. APPLICATIONS TO HOMOSEXUALITY

The application of this general picture to homosexuality should be obvious. There can be no reasonable doubt that one of the functions of the penis is to introduce semen into the vagina. It does this, and it has been selected in because it does this. (Sexual intercourse itself can probably be explained by the evolutionary value of bisexual reproduction. For $n > 2$, n-sexual reproduction would increase genetic variety at the cost of hardly ever occurring: (see e.g., [3].) The advantages accruing to relatively motile gametes seems to account for the emergence of bisexual reproduction itself.) Nature has consequently made this use of the penis rewarding. It is clear enough that any proto-human males who found unrewarding the insertion of penis into vagina have left no descendants. In particular, proto-human males who enjoyed inserting their penises into each other's anuses have left no descendants. This is why homosexuality is abnormal, and why its abnormality counts prudentially against it. Homosexuality is likely to cause unhappiness because it leaves unfulfilled an innate and innately rewarding desire. And should the reader's environmentalism threaten to get the upper hand, let me remind him again of an unproblematic case. Lack of exercise is bad and even abnormal not only because it is unhealthy but also because one feels poorly without regular exercise. Nature made exercise rewarding because, until recently, we had to exercise to survive. Creatures who found running after game unrewarding were eliminated. Laziness leaves unreaped the rewards nature has planted in exercise, even if the lazy man cannot tell this introspectively. If this is a correct description of the place of exercise in human life, it is by the same token a correct description of the place of heterosexuality.

It hardly needs saying, but perhaps I should say it anyway, that this argument concerns tendencies and probabilities. Generalizations about human affairs being notoriously "true by and large and for the most part" only, saying that homosexuals are bound to be less happy than heterosexuals must be understood as short for "Not coincidentally, a larger proportion of homosexuals will be unhappy than a corresponding selection of the heterosexual population." There are, after all, genuinely jolly fat men. To say that laziness leads to adverse affective consequences means that, because of our evolutionary history, the odds are relatively good that a man who takes no exercise will suffer adverse affective consequences. Obviously, some people will get away with misusing their bodily parts. Thus, when evaluating the empirical evidence that bears on this account, it will be pointless to cite cases of well-adjusted homosexuals. I do not say they are non-existent; my claim is that, of biological necessity, they are rare.

My argument might seem to show at most that heterosexual behavior is (self-) reinforcing, not that homosexuality is self-extinguishing—that homosexuals go without the built-in rewards of heterosexuality, but not that homosexuality has a built-in punishment. This distinction, however, is merely verbal. They are two different ways of saying that homosexuals will find their lives less rewarding than will heterosexuals. Even if some line demarcated happiness from unhappiness absolutely, it would be irrelevant if homosexuals were all happily above the line. It is the comparison with the heterosexual life that is at issue. A lazy man might count as happy by some mythic absolute standard, but he is likely to be less happy than someone otherwise like him who exercises.

Another objection to my argument, or conjectural evolutionary scenario, is that heterosexuality might have been selected in not because it favors survival, but as a by-product of some other inclusively fit structure or behavior. A related suggestion is that what really has been selected in is some blend of dominant heterosexual and recessive homosexual genes. As for the former, it seems extraordinarily unlikely, given how long life has reproduced itself by sexual intercourse, that the apparently self-reinforcing character of heterosexuality is a by-product of some other fitness-enhancing trait. If heterosexual intercourse is not *directly* connected to propagation, what is? Biologists have no trouble determining when bird plumage is there to attract mates, and hence favors survival. It would be astounding if the same could not be said for heterosexual intercourse.

The sophisticate might complain that I am not giving "by-product" hypotheses their due. And indeed at this point sociobiological hypotheses come thick and fast. I will be discussing some others later in this paper, and making some overall observations about sociobiology and homosexuality. Here it is appropriate to examine one hypothesis of the "by-product" school, that of Hutchinson (see [13]). Fact: there can be recessive genes for a trait that inhibits the reproduction of and even kills organisms which exhibit it, but which, when co-occurring with the dominant trait-suppressing allele, give rise to an organism or phenotype more inclusively fit than a comparable organism with two of the dominant alleles. In such cases, the "bad" allele will be passed along in fit heterozygous organisms and its associated trait will occasionally surface. For example, sickle-cell anemia persists because the heterozygote Cc (Non-sickle-cell C, sickle-cell c) confers resistance to malaria. Perhaps a recessive gene predisposing to homosexuality persists in this way. Organisms of genotype Hh—a dominant allele H for heterosexuality, a recessive allele h for homosexuality— might be most fit, and then of course organisms with hh genotype will surface with some regularity.

Without even considering the empirical likelihood of this elegant hypothesis, it is clearly consistent with my chief claim. For as it stands it represents sickle-cell anemia and the perpetuation of the c allele as *unfortunate by-products* of a process that selects in resistance to malaria; and, presumably, the same would go for homosexuality. For what does it mean to say that sickle-cell anemia is a by-product?

Precisely this: had immunity to malaria not been associated with the Cc genotype, the "gene" for malarial immunity would have been selected in anyway; however, had the Cc genotype and hence sickle-cell anemia not been associated with malarial immunity or some other inclusive-fitness-enhancing trait, the c allele would have disappeared. Recurring to our definition of "function," the cause of the persistence of the c allele and the Cc genotype, what that genotype is for, is fending off malaria. Sickle-cell anemia is a maladaptive by-product of the Cc genotype since, had it not been associated with what is in fact the function of the Cc genotype, sickle-cell anemia would have caused the disappearance of the Cc genotype. Nothing, not even the c allele, has sickle-cell anemia as its function. The key question, of course, is whether a maladaptive by-product, so understood, is reinforcing. On the present model, it is not. For suppose sickle-cell anemia could be contracted voluntarily, and there were a gene which (a) made contracting or becoming vulnerable to it reinforcing, but (b) was not connected with malarial immunity. A strain with the tastes this gene confers would soon be selected out. Therefore, surviving humans who get sickle-cell anemia do not find it in any way reinforcing. So the "heterozygote fitness" hypothesis (and the kin-selection hypothesis: see below) predict, consistently with my view, that homosexuality is associated with unhappiness; and, conversely, wide-spread homosexual unhappiness would confirm that homosexuality is a maladaptive by-product.

An important methodological corollary of this discussion is that a trait or tendency may be "in the genes" but still be abnormal. It is normal only if it is in the genes because it itself enhances fitness, not because it is associated with something else that enhances fitness on independent grounds. Sickle-cell anemia is a malfunction of its victims' blood, which was selected in to oxygenate the muscles. A comparable story for homosexuality would involve a gene that instructed its organism to make just a little testosterone. This might have survival value by raising phenotypic verbal sensitivity, and perhaps low testosterone is the only way nature has figured out to secure this inclusively fit trait. Suppose, too, that a

disposition to homosexuality was a causal consequence, a by-product, of low testosterone—but not so disadvantageous a by-product that the gene was selected out. Homosexuality would then be a necessary condition for advantageous verbal ability, but it would not follow that homosexuality was selected in because it conduced to verbal ability, or for any other reason. It would not follow that homosexuality is the least reinforcing. Unhappy homosexuals might be the price nature pays for verbal ability, homosexuality being no more a cause of verbal ability than sickle-cell anemia is a cause of malarial resistance.

Talk of what is "in the genes" inevitably provokes the observation that we should not blame homosexuals for their homosexuality if it is "in their genes." True enough. Indeed, since nobody decides what he is going to find sexually arousing, the moral appraisal of sexual object "choice" is entirely absurd. However, so saying is quite consistent with regarding homosexuality as a misfortune, and taking steps—this being within the realm of the will—to minimize its incidence, especially among children. Calling homosexuality involuntary does not place it outside the scope of evaluation. Victims of sickle-cell anemia are not blameworthy, but it is absurd to pretend that there is nothing wrong with them. Homosexual activists are partial to genetic explanations and hostile to Freudian environmentalism in part because they see a genetic cause as exempting homosexuals from blame. But surely people are equally blameless for indelible traits acquired in early childhood. And anyway, a blameless condition may still be worth trying to prevent. (Defenders of homosexuality fear Freud at another level, because his account removes homosexuality from the biological realm altogether and deprives it of whatever legitimacy adheres to what is "in the genes.")

My sociobiological scenario also finds no place for the fashionable remark that homosexuality has become fitness-enhancing in our supposedly overpopulated world. Homosexuality is said to increase our species' chances by easing the population pressure. This observation, however correct, is irrelevant. Even if homosexuality has lately come to favor species survival, this is no part of how homosexuality is created. Salvation of the human species would be at best a fortuitous by-product of behavior having other causes. It is not easy, moreover, to see how this feature of homosexuality could get it selected in. If homosexuality enhances inclusive fitness precisely because homosexuals don't reproduce, the tendency to homosexuality cannot get selected for by a filtering process when it is passed to the next generation—it doesn't get passed to the next generation at all. The same applies, of course, to any tendency to find homosexuality rewarding.

The whole matter of the survival advantage of homosexuality is in any case beside the point. Our organs have the functions and rewards they do because of the way the world was, and what favored survival, many millions of years ago. *Then,* homosexuality decreased fitness and heterosexuality increased it; an innate tendency to homosexuality would have gotten selected out if anything did. We today have the tendencies transmitted to us by those other ancestors, whether or not the race is going to pay a price for this. That 50 years ago certain self-reinforcing behavior began to threaten the race's future is quite consistent with the behavior remaining self-reinforcing. Similarly, widespread obesity and the patent enjoyment many people experience in gorging themselves just show that our appetites were shaped in conditions of food scarcity under which gorging oneself when one had the chance was good policy. Anyway, the instability created by abundance is, presumably, temporary. If the current abundance continues for 5,000 generations, natural gluttons will almost certainly disappear through early heart disease and unattractiveness to the opposite sex. The ways in which the populous human herd will be trimmed is best left to speculation.

I should also note that nothing I have said shows bisexuality or sheer polymorphous sexuality to be unnatural or self-punishing. One might cite the Greeks to show that only exclusive homosexuality conflicts with our evolved reinforcement mechanism. But in point of fact bisexuality seems to be a quite rare phenomenon—and animals, who receive no cultural conditioning, seem instinctively heterosexual in the vast majority of cases. Clinicians evidently agree that it is possible for a person to be homosexual at one period of his life and heterosex-

ual at another, but not at the same time. Some statistics in [4] confirm this. 18% of the male homosexuals interviewed had been married; while 90% reported having intercourse with their wives during the first year of marriage, 72% reported having homosexual fantasies during intercourse, and 33% reported this "often" ([4], tables 17.1–17.7). So only 4.5% of the sample had "reciprocal" heterosexual intercourse. This coheres well with table 22.4 in [4], which indicates that roughly 95% of male homosexuals in the Bell-Weinberg sample were "exclusively homosexual." But one mustn't move too quickly or dogmatically here. On the face of it, telling its host body "Put your penis in any reasonably small, moist opening" is a sufficiently adaptive gene strategy to ensconce a gene that follows it in the gene pool. A body controlled by such a gene would reproduce itself and hence the gene often enough. The flaw in the plan is that a competitor gene might evolve to tell its body: "Put your penis only in vaginas, i.e., moist openings with a certain feel and which are accompanied by such visual clues as breasts and wide hips." The second gene would reproduce itself even more often and—waiving by-products—would eventually displace the first. But our bisexual gene isn't finished. It might evolve the following strategy: "Body, insert your penis in vaginas most of the time, but insert your penis in male anuses frequently enough to keep other males, who are competing with you for females, occupied." A body with such a gene could keep a harem pregnant. A male who put other males out of commission for n hours by stimulating them to orgasm might himself seem vulnerable to exhausting himself, but he can avoid this by refraining from orgasm during homosexual acts. The fly in *this* ointment is the counter-strategy that purely heterosexual genes could evolve: "Avoid erect penises heading for your anus." If even one such gene appeared in a population of bisexuals it would reproduce itself a little more readily, since it would never waste time spiking the guns of its competitors.

By now we are lost in speculation. There is no way to disprove the existence of a hardy bisexual gene, or to prove that heterosexual counter-measures always evolved. It is *possible,* but not likely and not suggested by anything currently known, that a bisexual gene has achieved stable existence in the human gene pool. It is also quite unlikely, on equivalent analytical grounds and the virtual nonexistence of polymorphous animal sexuality in the wild, that males are primed only for an undifferentiated enjoyment of sex that is shaped by culture into heterosexuality.

Utilitarians must take the present evolutionary scenario seriously. The utilitarian attitude toward homosexuality usually runs something like this even if homosexuality is in some sense unnatural, as a matter of brute fact homosexuals take pleasure in sexual contact with members of the same sex. As long as they don't hurt anyone else, homosexuality is as great a good as heterosexuality. But the matter cannot end here. Not even a utilitarian doctor would have words of praise for a degenerative disease that happened to foster a certain kind of pleasure (as sore muscles uniquely conduce to the pleasure of stretching them). A utilitarian doctor would presumably try just as zealously to cure diseases that feel good as less pleasant degenerative diseases. A pleasure causally connected with great distress cannot be treated as just another pleasure to be toted up on the felicific scoreboard. Utilitarians have to reckon with the inevitable consequences of pain-causing pleasure.

Similar remarks apply to the question of whether homosexuality is a "disease." A widely-quoted pronouncement of the American Psychiatric Association runs:

> Surely the time has come for psychiatry to give up the archaic practice of classifying the millions of men and women who accept or prefer homosexual object choices as being, by virtue of that fact alone, mentally ill. The fact that their alternative life-style happens to be out of favor with current cultural conventions must not be a basis in itself for a diagnosis.

Apart from some question-begging turns of phrase, this is right. One's taste for mutual anal intercourse is nothing "in itself" for one's psychiatrist to worry about, any more than a life of indolence is anything "in itself" for one's doctor to worry about. In fact, in itself there is nothing wrong with a broken arm or an occluded artery. The fact that my right ulna is now in two pieces is just a fact of nature, not a "basis for diagnosis." But this condition is a matter for medical science anyway, because it will lead to pain. Permitted to persist, my fracture will provoke increasingly punishing states. So if homosexuality is a reliable sign of present or future misery, it is beside the point that homosexuality is not "by virtue of that fact alone" a mental illness. High rates of drug addiction, divorce and illegitimacy are in themselves no basis for diagnosing social pathology. They support this diagnosis because of what else they signify about a society which exhibits them. Part of the problem here is the presence of germs in paradigm diseases, and the lack of a germ for homosexuality (or psychosis). I myself am fairly sure that a suitably general and germfree definition of "disease" can be extruded from the general notion of "function" exhibited in Section 2, but however that may be, whether homosexuality is a disease is a largely verbal issue. If homosexuality is a self-punishing maladaptation, it hardly matters what it is called.

4. EVIDENCE AND FURTHER CLARIFICATION

I have argued that homosexuality is "abnormal" in both a descriptive and a normative sense because— for evolutionary reasons—homosexuals are bound to be unhappy. In Kantian terms, I have explained how it is possible for homosexuality to be unnatural even if it violates no cosmic purpose or such purposes as we retrospectively impose on nature. What is the evidence for my view? For one thing, by emphasizing homosexual unhappiness, my view explains a ubiquitous fact in a simple way. The fact is the universally acknowledged unhappiness of homosexuals. Even the staunchest defenders of homosexuality admit that, as of now, homosexuals are not happy. A conspicuous exception to this is [4], which has been widely taken to show that homosexuals can be just as happy as heterosexuals. A look at their statistics tells a different story—an important matter I have dealt with in some detail in the Appendix.

The usual environmentalist explanation for homosexuals' unhappiness is the misunderstanding, contempt and abuse that society heaps on them. But this not only leaves unexplained why society has this attitude, it sins against parsimony by explaining a nearly universal phenomenon in terms of variable circumstances that have, by coincidence, the same upshot. Parsimony urges that we seek the explanation of homosexual unhappiness in the nature of homosexuality itself, as my explanation does. Having to "stay in the closet" may be a great strain, but it does not account for all the miseries that writers on homosexuality say is the homosexual's lot.

Incorporating unhappiness into the present evolutionary picture also smooths a bothersome ad-hocness in some otherwise appealing analyses of abnormality. Many writers define abnormality as compulsiveness. On this conception, homosexuality is abnormal because it is an autonomy-obstructing compulsion. Such an analysis is obviously open to the question, What if an autonomous homosexual comes along? To that, writers like van den Haag point out that homosexuality is, in fact, highly correlated with compulsiveness. The trouble here is that the definition in question sheds no light on why abnormal, compulsive, traits are such. The present account not only provides a criterion for abnormality, it encapsulates an explanation of *why* behavior abnormal by its lights is indeed compulsive and bound to lead to unhappiness.

One crucial test of my account is its prediction that homosexuals will continue to be unhappy even if people altogether abandon their "prejudice" against homosexuality. This prediction, that homosexuality being unnatural homosexuals will still find their behavior self-punishing, coheres with available evidence. It is consistent with the failure of other oppressed groups, such as American Negroes and European Jews, to become warped in the direction of "cruising," sado-masochism and other practices common in homosexual life (see [19]). It is consistent as well with the admission by even so sympathetic an observer of homosexuality as Rechy ([23]) that the immediate cause of homosexual unhappiness is a taste for promiscuity, anonymous encounters, and humiliation. It is hard to see how such tastes are related to the dim view society takes of them.

Such a relation would be plausible only if homosexuals courted multiple anonymous encounters *faute de mieux,* longing all the while to settle down to some sort of domesticity. But, again, Europeans abhorred Jews for centuries, but this did not create in Jews a special weakness for anonymous, promiscuous sex. Whatever drives a man away from women, to be fellated by as many different men as possible, seems independent of what society thinks of such behavior. It is this behavior that occasions misery, and we may expect the misery of homosexuals to continue.

In a 1974 study, Weinberg and Williams ([29]) found no difference in the distress experienced by homosexuals in Denmark and the Netherlands, and in the U.S., where they found public tolerance of homosexuality to be lower. This would confirm rather strikingly that homosexual unhappiness is endogenous, unless one says that Weinberg's and Williams's indices for public tolerance and distress—chiefly homosexuals' self-reports of "unhappiness" and "lack of faith in others"—are unreliable. Such complaints, however, push the social causation theory toward untestability. Weinberg and Williams themselves cleave to the hypothesis that homosexual unhappiness is entirely a reaction to society's attitudes, and suggest that a condition of homosexual happiness is positive endorsement by the surrounding society. It is hard to imagine a more flagrantly *ad hoc* hypothesis. Neither a Catholic living among Protestants nor a copywriter working on the great American novel in his off hours asks more of society than tolerance in order to be happy in his pursuits.

It is interesting to reflect on a natural experiment that has gotten under way in the decade since the Weinberg-Williams study. A remarkable change in public opinion, if not private sentiment, has occurred in America. For whatever reason—the prodding of homosexual activists, the desire not to seem like a fuddy-duddy—various organs of opinion are now hard at work providing a "positive image" for homosexuals. Judges allow homosexuals to adopt their lovers. The Unitarian Church now performs homosexual marriages. Hollywood produces highly sanitized movies like *Making Love* and *Personal Best* about homosexuality. Macmillan strongly urges its authors to show little boys using cosmetics. Homosexuals no longer fear revealing themselves, as is shown by the prevalence of the "clone look." Certain products run advertising obviously directed at the homosexual market. On the societal reaction theory, there ought to be an enormous rise in homosexual happiness. I know of no systematic study to determine if this is so, but anecdotal evidence suggests it may not be. The homosexual press has been just as strident in denouncing pro-homosexual movies as in denouncing Doris Day movies. Especially virulent venereal diseases have very recently appeared in homosexual communities, evidently spread in epidemic proportions by unabating homosexual promiscuity. One selling point for a presumably serious "gay rights" rally in Washington D.C. was an "all-night disco train" from New York to Washington. What is perhaps most salient is that, even if the changed public mood results in decreased homosexual unhappiness, the question remains of why homosexuals in the recent past, who suffered greatly for being homosexuals, persisted in being homosexuals.

But does not my position also predict—contrary to fact—that any sexual activity not aimed at procreation or at least sexual intercourse leads to unhappiness? First, I am not sure this conclusion is contrary to the facts properly understood. It is universally recognized that, for humans and the higher animals, sex is more than the insertion of the penis into the vagina. Foreplay is necessary to prepare the female and, to a lesser extent, the male. Ethologists have studied the elaborate mating rituals of even relatively simple animals. Sexual intercourse must therefore be understood to include the kisses and caresses that necessarily precede copulation, behaviors that nature has made rewarding. What my view does predict is that exclusive preoccupation with behaviors normally preparatory for intercourse is highly correlated with unhappiness. And, so far as I know, psychologists do agree that such preoccupation or "fixation" with, e.g., cunnilingus, is associated with personality traits independently recognized as disorders. In this sense, sexual intercourse really is virtually necessary for well-being. Only if one is antecedently convinced

that "nothing is more natural than anything else" will one confound foreplay as a prelude to intercourse with "foreplay" that leads nowhere at all. One might speculate on the evolutionary advantages of foreplay, at least for humans: by increasing the intensity and complexity of the pleasures of intercourse, it binds the partners more firmly and makes them more fit for child-rearing. In fact, such analyses of sexual perversion as Nagel's ([22]), which correctly focus on the interruption of mutuality as central to perversion, go wrong by ignoring the evolutionary role and built-in rewards of mutuality. They fail to explain why the interruption of mutuality is disturbing.

It should also be clear that my argument permits gradations in abnormality. Behavior is the more abnormal, and the less likely to be rewarding, the more its emission tends to extinguish a genetic cohort that practices it. The less likely a behavior is to get selected out, the less abnormal it is. Those of our ancestors who found certain aspects of foreplay reinforcing might have managed to reproduce themselves sufficiently to implant this strain in us. There might be an equilibrium between intercourse and such not directly reproductive behavior. It is not required that any behavior not directly linked to heterosexual intercourse lead to maximum dissatisfaction. But the existence of these gradations provides no entering wedge for homosexuality. As no behavior is more likely to get selected out than rewarding homosexuality—except perhaps an innate tendency to suicide at the onset of puberty—it is extremely unlikely that homosexuality can now be unconditionally reinforcing in humans to any extent.

Nor does my position predict, again contrary to fact, that celibate priests will be unhappy. My view is compatible with the existence of happy celibates who deny themselves as part of a higher calling which yields compensating satisfactions. Indeed, the very fact that one needs to explain how the priesthood can compensate for the lack of family means that people do regard heterosexual mating as the natural or "inertial" state of human relations. The comparison between priests and homosexuals is in any case inapt. Priests do not simply give up sexual activity without ill-effect; they give it up for a reason. Homosexuals have hardly given up the use of their sexual organs, for a higher calling or anything else. Homosexuals continue to use them, but, unlike priests, they use them for what they are not for.

I have encountered the thought that by my lights female heterosexuality must be abnormal, since according to feminism women have been unhappy down the ages. The datum is questionable, to say the least. Feminists have offered no documentation whatever for this extravagant claim; their evidence is usually the unhappiness of the feminist in question and her circle of friends. Such attempts to prove female discontent in past centuries as [11] are transparently anachronistic projections of contemporary feminist discontent onto inappropriate historical objects. An objection from a similar source runs that my argument, suitably extended, implies the naturalness and hence rewardingness of traditional monogamous marriage. Once again, instead of seeing this as a *reductio,* I am inclined to take the supposed absurdity as a truth that nicely fits my theory. It is not a theoretical contention but an observable fact that women enjoy motherhood, that failure to bear and care for children breeds unhappiness in women, and that the role of "primary caretaker" is much more important for women than men. However, there is no need to be dogmatic. This conception of the family is in extreme disrepute in contemporary America. Many women work and many marriages last less than a decade. Here we have another natural experiment about what people find reinforcing. My view predicts that women will on the whole become unhappier if current trends continue. Let us see. . . .

5. SOCIOBIOLOGY AGAIN

Several sociobiological hypotheses are currently under discussion about the possible function of a "gene for homosexuality," and how this function might have lodged such a gene in the human gene pool. We looked in an earlier section at Hutchinson's "by-product" hypothesis and will return to it. In this section I want to make a general point about current sociobiological speculation and homosexuality, and

it will be helpful to examine briefly another hypothesis: "kin selection." This hypothesis stresses that a gene is fit if it copies itself in the next generation, even if not through the organism that houses it. We all recognize the adaptive advantages in a mother's self-sacrifice for her brood; the same holds for a brother's regard for his siblings. So, the hypothesis goes, homosexuality's reproductive costs may be more than balanced by the aid a homosexual gives his close genetic cohort. Homosexuality in one offspring might mean more fecund siblings who have a good chance of carrying the "homosexual gene" (see [31], [32]). Testing this hypothesis would obviously be very difficult, requiring complete data on the relative fecundity of humans with homosexual siblings, nephews, etc., and a detailed and plausible mechanism to explain how an individual's homosexuality contributes to his cohort's fecundity. (Such demographic data would also be pertinent to the Freudian theory, which stresses the overbearing love of the homosexual's mother. A prediction of this theory would seem to be that homosexuality is higher among only children, and decreases as the number of siblings and birth-order increases.) No sociobiologist claims to have such data, and I know of no conjectures about the mechanism. The data of the last section and the appendix suggests that no such mechanism exists because homosexuality serves no inclusively adaptive function.

Where that leaves us is in the following position. Most of the sociobiological speculation about homosexuality known to me—particularly the influential writings of Wilson—simply *assumes* that homosexuality serves a function which accounts for its retention in the human population. Sociobiologists thus see their theoretical task as discovering what this function is. So far as I can tell, they rest this assumption on a single datum: Kinsey's finding that over 10% of the U.S. male population reported itself to be homosexual, by a reasonably strict criterion of homosexuality. Thus Wilson reasons (see [32], 143): given its sheer prevalence, homosexuality must be serving some fitness-enhancing purpose. My central point, in reply, is that there is not a single reason beyond this to think that homosexuality increases fitness or serves any purpose at all. The sociobiological models I've mentioned come into play only if we *already know* that homosexuality enhances fitness. Kinsey aside, we have no reason to think this, so the sociobiological hypotheses—kin-selection, parental manipulation and superior heterozygote fitness—currently stand as explanations in search of something to explain.

Still, there are the Kinsey data and certain twin studies which suggest some genetic component to homosexuality. What the latter would mean is, precisely, that there can be two males brought up in the same environment such that one becomes a homosexual and the other does not. However, as I noted in an earlier section, a giant chasm separates the existence of a genetic contribution to homosexuality and the existence of a function that homosexuality serves. The point bears amplifying, in terms of the homely example of broken bones. While on the face of it a broken arm seems purely an accident and one wholly caused by environment, at any time a significant proportion of the human race will have broken bones. This might prompt sociologists to think there is a fitness-enhancing gene for broken-bonedness. And in a sense they would be right. People's bones break because, in part, their genes have told the rest of them to hang their muscles on an armature of calcium. Had our genes told the rest of us to make our skeletons out of chrome steel, banging into walls would not break arms. A broken arm is really the result of an environmental cause triggering a genetically determined predisposition.

There is something of truth and something of parody in this account of broken bones. A calcium-based skeleton is adaptively advantageous because calcium is light. But calcium's lightness is inseparable from its softness. The frangibility of bones is genetically coded, but only as a byproduct of an otherwise adaptive process. And it is relatively easy to contrive mechanisms that yield a predisposition to homosexuality in males as a by-product. Low fetal testosterone might be good for organisms. Evolution might never have had to select in genotypes which insure enough testosterone for heterosexuality come what family life may. But this would not mean that

homosexuality is for anything or that the gene is for homosexuality, any more than broken arms are for anything. So even a strong form of the kin-selection hypothesis would not mean anything more than a genetic predisposition to homosexuality; the trait thus disposed to need be no more adaptive or reinforcing than the breakability of bones.

6. ON POLICY ISSUES

Homosexuality is intrinsically bad only in a prudential sense. It makes for unhappiness. However, this does not exempt homosexuality from the larger categories of ethics—rights, duties, liabilities. Deontic categories apply to acts which increase or decrease happiness or expose the helpless to the risk of unhappiness.

If homosexuality is unnatural, legislation which raises the odds that a given child will become homosexual raises the odds that he will be unhappy. The only gap in the syllogism is whether legislation which legitimates, endorses or protects homosexuality does increase the chances that a child will become homosexual. If so, such legislation is *prima facie* objectionable. The question is not whether homosexual elementary school teachers will molest their charges. Pro-homosexual legislation might increase the incidence of homosexuality in subtler ways. If it does, and if the protection of children is a fundamental obligation of society, legislation which legitimates homosexuality is a dereliction of duty. I am reluctant to deploy the language of "children's rights," which usually serves as one more excuse to interfere with the prerogatives of parents. But we do have obligations to our children, and one of them is to protect them from harm. If, as some have suggested, children have a right to protection from a religious education, they surely have a right to protection from homosexuality. So protecting them limits somebody else's freedom, but we are often willing to protect quite obscure children's rights at the expense of the freedom of others. There is a movement to ban TV commercials for sugar-coated cereals, to protect children from the relatively trivial harm of tooth decay. Such a ban would restrict the freedom of advertisers, and restrict it even though the last clear chance of avoiding the harm, and thus the responsibility, lies with the parents who control the TV set. I cannot see how one can consistently support such legislation and also urge homosexual rights, which risk much graver damage to children in exchange for increased freedom for homosexuals. (If homosexual behavior is largely compulsive, it is falsifying the issue to present it as balancing risks to children against the freedom of homosexuals.) The right of a homosexual to work for the Fire Department is not a negligible good. Neither is fostering a legal atmosphere in which as many people as possible grow up heterosexual.

It is commonly asserted that legislation granting homosexuals the privilege or right to be firemen endorses not homosexuality, but an expanded conception of human liberation. It is conjectural how sincerely this can be said in a legal order that forbids employers to hire whom they please and demands hours of paperwork for an interstate shipment of hamburger. But in any case legislation "legalizing homosexuality" cannot be neutral because passing it would have an inexpungeable speech-act dimension. Society cannot grant unaccustomed rights and privileges to homosexuals while remaining neutral about the value of homosexuality. Working from the assumption that society rests on the family and its consequences, the Judaeo-Christian tradition has deemed homosexuality a sin and withheld many privileges from homosexuals. Whether or not such denial was right, for our society to grant these privileges to homosexuals *now* would amount to declaring that it has rethought the matter and decided that homosexuality is not as bad as it had previously supposed. And unless such rethinking is a direct response to new empirical findings about homosexuality, it can only be a revaluing. Someone who suddenly accepts a policy he has previously opposed is open to the same interpretation: he has come to think better of the policy. And if he embraces the policy while knowing that this interpretation will be put on his behavior, and if he knows that others know that he knows they will so interpret it, he is acquiescing in this interpretation. He can be held to

have intended, meant, this interpretation. A society that grants privileges to homosexuals while recognizing that, in the light of generally known history, this act can be interpreted as a positive re-evaluation of homosexuality, is signalling that it now thinks homosexuality is all right. Many commentators in the popular press have observed that homosexuals, unlike members of racial minorities, can always "stay in the closet" when applying for jobs. What homosexual rights activists really want, therefore, is not access to jobs but legitimation of their homosexuality. Since this is known, giving them what they want will be seen as conceding their claim to legitimacy. And since legislators know their actions will support this interpretation, and know that their constituencies know they know this, the Gricean effect or symbolic meaning of passing anti-discrimination ordinances is to declare homosexuality legitimate (see [30]).

Legislation permitting frisbees in the park does not imply approval of frisbees for the simple reason that frisbees are new; there is no tradition of banning them from parks. The legislature's action in permitting frisbees is not interpretable, known to be interpretable, and so on, as the reversal of long-standing disapproval. It is because these Gricean conditions are met in the case of abortion that legislation—or rather judicial fiat—permitting abortions and mandating their public funding are widely interpreted as tacit approval. Up to now, society has deemed homosexuality so harmful that restricting it outweighs putative homosexual rights. If society reverses itself, it will in effect be deciding that homosexuality is not as bad as it once thought.

APPENDIX

The best case for inevitable homosexual unhappiness comes from [4], a study which received much attention when it appeared. As their subtitle suggests, Bell and Weinberg claim to have shown that there is no such thing as homosexuality per se; there are different types of homosexuals, some of whom can be as well-adjusted, on the average, as heterosexuals. Bell and Weinberg admit that demonstrating this was the aim of their study: "We are pleased at the extent to which the aims of our investigation of homosexual men and women have been realized. The tables . . . clearly show that homosexuals are a remarkably diverse group" (217). They always refer to commonly held beliefs about homosexuals as "myths" (15) and "stereotypes" (73), and blame society's "homoerotophobia" (188) on the preoccupation of Jews with survival and the Christian Church with sin (149, 195). Working on the principle that a position is seriously weakened if the evidence marshalled by its friends disconfirms it, let us look at the Bell-Weinberg data.

Bell and Weinberg studied 686 San Francisco Bay area male homosexuals (and 293 lesbians, whom I ignore as in the body of the paper). One might question their methods: apart from the nonrandomness of their sample (22), the authors are oddly credulous about their informants' reports. They determined the level of their informants' health, and that of the informants in their heterosexual control group, by simply asking them how their health was (484). Not surprisingly, 87% of the white homosexuals and 91% of the black homosexuals reported that they were in good to excellent health, about the same as for the heterosexuals. But this accords ill with their table 19.2, which shows that 58% of all homosexuals spend 3 or more nights a week out. Common sense agrees with Satchel Paige that the social whirl isn't restful, but in any case the authors use none of the standard objective measures of health—visits to the doctor, use of medication, drugs, average amount of sleep, and the like. This, incidental though it is, warrants scepticism about self-report methodology in a matter like homosexuality.

Of the 206 pages of tables, 3 entries are particularly noteworthy as measures of homosexual unhappiness. The first (337, 339) is that 27% of all homosexuals experience either some or a great deal of regret about being homosexual. Taken with the 24% who experience "very little" regret, this prompts one to ask if only 49% of a random sample of heterosexuals would report no regrets about their heterosexuality. Would 27% of heterosexuals agree or agree strongly that their condition is an emotional disorder? (cf. 339; the control group disappears at this junc-

ture). More strikingly, homosexuals are more than 6 times as likely as heterosexuals to attempt suicide—a criterion of unhappiness independent of the subject's report. The authors try to explain this statistic with an aside to the effect that the suicide rate in San Francisco is very high (211–12), a testimony to their faith in the explanatory power of nonprojectible predicates. (Perhaps not all philosophers would find this explanation defective. When I asked a well-known social philosopher critical of capital punishment why the murder rate had gone up in states where capital punishment had been abandoned, he said "the crime rate is going up everywhere.") In any case, the heterosexual sample was drawn from the same population, and homosexuals constitute a significant portion of San Francisco's population, so the San Francisco suicide rate is high, in part, because so many homosexuals commit suicide.

Perhaps the most striking trait revealed—or stereotype confirmed—is the extreme impersonality and frequency of homosexual contacts. Roughly speaking, 75% of the respondents reported having had more than 100 sexual partners, and 43% reported having had 500 or more (308). These numbers are not easy to believe. Even taken *cum grano,* they should be compared to the reader's own experience of sex as he tries to imagine what it would be like to move so promiscuously among anonymous encounters—79% of the respondents reported that more than half their partners were strangers. Surely having these many partners is a criterion for maladjustment and compulsivity, a chronic inability to find anyone satisfactory. A harder datum than these numbers is the report that 56% of the respondents usually spend several hours or less with a partner (305); in fact, the authors distinguish "several hours from "all night." Only 2% usually spend as much as a weekend with a partner successfully "cruised." (I interpret this statistic to make it consistent with the amount of "close-coupledness" reported: see below.) Incidentally, the authors say that "the largest numbers of our respondents spent all night with their partners" (77), but this is misleading. 41% of the respondents usually spent all night, and this is the modal number; but, as noted, *most* homosexuals spend considerably less than a whole night with a partner.

What Bell and Weinberg want to emphasize, however, is that their sample tended to cluster around five "types" of homosexual, one of which—the "close-coupled"—seem on the whole to be as well-adjusted as heterosexuals. The finding was duplicated for lesbians. Close-coupled homosexuals are those involved in a sort of marriage, living monogamously with a partner of the same sex, not cruising, not experiencing any extraordinary amount of "tension" or regret about homosexuality, and displaying much "joy and exuberance in their particular life-style" (231). This, the authors contend, shows that homosexuality "is not necessarily related to pathology" (ibid.).

The existence of close-coupled homosexuals by no means implies that homosexuality is not pathological. As I have noted, there are almost no significant exceptionless generalizations in human affairs. My evolutionary hypothesis implies only that homosexuals are more likely to be unhappy than their heterosexual counterparts. The pertinent questions are, how many "close-coupled" homosexuals are there, and how many homosexuals exhibit "stereotypic" personality disorders? In point of fact, [4] assigns only 67 homosexuals to the "close-coupled" category, less than 10% of the sample. By contrast, 12% fell into the "dysfunctional" category, tormented souls who regret their homosexuality, cruise frequently, and have many sexual partners. An additional 16% were "Asexuals," homosexuals who tend to live alone without lovers or friends, and whose suicide rate is the highest among homosexuals. On the evidence presented, sociopathic homosexuals outnumber well-adjusted ones 2.8 to 1. If one adds to these at least some of the "functionals"—"men and women [who] seem to organize their lives around their sexual experience" (223)—deeply troubled homosexuals outnumber happy ones by at least 3 to 1.

The authors mislead the reader when they say that close-coupled homosexuals are on the average as happy and well-adjusted as heterosexuals. For this is to compare the best-adjusted homosexual subtype with the homogeneous heterosexual control group, and that is special pleading. It would be more appropriate to compare close-coupled homosexuals to happily married men, something Bell and Weinberg admit in passing but for which they offer no statistics. Since a random sample of heterosexuals will include a number of lonely, twisted individuals, the adjustment level of happily "coupled" heterosexuals must be considerably higher than that of the best-adjusted homosexuals. So viewed, monogamous homosexual coupling looks like a vain attempt at marriage—and homosexual cruising looks perhaps like a realization, of sorts, of adolescent male fantasy. "Dysfunctionals and Asexuals have a difficult time of it, but there are certainly equivalent groups among heterosexuals" (231). Certainly. But do such groups make up 28% of all heterosexuals and 41% of all classifiable heterosexuals, as the Dysfunctionals and Asexuals jointly comprise 41% of all classifiable homosexuals in the Bell-Weinberg sample (346, table 13.5)? Moreover, the authors go only so far as to say that close-coupled men "did less cruising" than the homosexual average (132; also see table 13.7, p. 349), leaving the impression that even close-coupled men do sometimes cruise. No quantitative comparisons are offered between such cruising and extra-marital straying for heterosexual males. Table 22.4 shows that 1% of the coupleds cruise at least once a week, but there are no statistics on how many have cruised in, say, the preceding year. Incomplete though it is, this figure should be contrasted with the heterosexual case. It seems unlikely that 1% of the married male readership of this paper had anonymous sexual encounters last week.

Bell and Weinberg's peroration is a textbook example of circular reasoning:

> It would appear that homosexual adults who have come to terms with their homosexuality, who do not regret their sexual orientation, and who can function effectively sexually and socially, are no more distressed psychologically than are heterosexual men and women (216).

Obviously, anyone who can "function effectively sexually and socially" will not be especially "distressed psychologically." But even going by the Bell-Weinberg sample drawn from volunteers from the "good scene" (27) of the Bay area, the chances that a homosexual will fall into this category are rather low.

REFERENCES

[1] Barash, D. *The Whispering Within*. New York: Harper & Row, 1979.

[2] Beach, F. "Cross-Species Comparisons and the Human Heritage." *Archives of Sexual Behavior* 5 (1976): 469–85.

[3] Beadle, G. and M. *The Language of Life*. New York: Anchor, 1967.

[4] Bell, A. and M. Weinberg. *Homosexualities*. New York: Simon and Schuster, 1978.

[5] Bennett, J. *Linguistic Behavior*. Cambridge: Cambridge University Press, 1976.

[6] Dawkins, R. *The Selfish Gene*. Oxford: Oxford University Press, 1976.

[7] Gadpille, W. "Research into the Physiology of Maleness and Femaleness: Its Contribution to the Etiology and Psychodynamics of Homosexuality." *Archives of General Psychiatry* (1972): 193–206.

[8] Goldberg, S. "What is 'Normal'? Logical Aspects of the Question of Homosexual Behavior." *Psychiatry* (1975):

[9] Gould, R. "What We Don't Know about Homosexuality." *New York Times Magazine,* Feb. 24, 1974.

[10] Gary, R. "Sex and Sexual Perversion." *Journal of Philosophy* 74 (1978): 189–99.

[11] Greer, G. *The Obstacle Race*. New York: Farrar, Strauss & Giroux, 1979.

[12] Grice, H. "Utterer's Meaning, Sentence-Meaning, and Word-Meaning." *Foundations of Language* 4 (1968): 1–18.

[13] Hutchinson, G. "A Speculative Consideration of Certain Possible Forms of Sexual Selection in Man." *American Naturalist* 93 (1959): 81–91.

[14] Karlen, A. *Sexuality and Homosexuality: A New View*. New York: Norton, 1967.

[15] Levin, M. "On the Ascription of Functions to Objects." *Philosophy of the Social Sciences* 6 (1976): 227–34.

[16] Levin, M. "'Sexism' is Meaningless." *St. John's Review* XXXIII (1981): 35–40.

[17] Lewis, D. *Convention*. Cambridge, MA: Harvard University Press, 1970.

[18] Masters, W. and V. Johnson. *Homosexuality in Perspective*. Boston, MA: Little, Brown and Company, 1979.

[19] McCracken, S. "Replies to Correspondents." *Commentary,* April 1979.

[20] Mossner, E. *The Life of David Hume,* 1st. ed. New York: Nelson & Sons, 1954.

[21] Nagel, E. "Teleology Revisited." *Journal of Philosophy* 74 (1977): 261–301.

[22] Nagel, T. "Sexual Perversion." *Journal of Philosophy* 66 (1969): 5–17.

[23] Rechy, J. *The Sexual Outlaw*. New York: Grove Press, 1977.

[24] Sagarin, E. "The Good Guys, the Bad Guys, and the Gay Guys." *Contemporary Sociology* (1973): 3–13.

[25] Sagarin, E. and R. Kelley. "The Labelling of Deviance," in W. Grove, ed., *The Labelling of Deviance*. New York: Wiley & Sons, 1975.

[26] Sayre, K. *Cybernetics and the Philosophy of Mind*. Atlantic Highlands, NJ: Humanities Press, 1976.

[27] Schiffer, S. *Meaning*. Oxford: Oxford University Press, 1972.

[28] Singer, P. *Democracy and Disobedience*. Oxford: Oxford University Press, 1968.

[29] Weinberg, M. and C. Williams. *Male Homosexuals: Their Problems and Adaptations*. Oxford: Oxford University Press, 1974.

[30] Will, G. "How Far Out of the Closet?" *Newsweek,* 30 May 1977, p. 92.

[31] Wilson, E. *Sociobiology: The New Synthesis*. Cambridge, MA: Harvard University Press, 1975.

[32] Wilson, E. *On Human Nature*. Cambridge, MA: Harvard University Press, 1978.

[33] Wright, L. "Functions." *Philosophical Review* 82 (1973): 139–68.

Critics

Homosexuality and Nature

Timothy F. Murphy

Happiness and the Law at Stake

The nature and legitimacy of homosexual behaviour continue to generate considerable controversy. Since 1973, the American Psychiatric Association has formally professed that homosexuality per se is no disease entity, but one may still seek and find practitioners of sexual conversion therapy. While some religious thinkers have become more tolerant of it, others continue to conceptualize homosexuality as a sin of the first order, a sin said to be formally condemned in strong Old and New Testament language. While at present 26 states of the Union do *not* have criminal statutes for private consensual homosexual behaviour, the US Supreme Court recently held that states may criminalize such behaviour if they so choose.

There are many ways used to argue against the moral legitimacy of homosexual behaviour, whether such behaviour is transient or exclusive. Some seek recourse to concepts of sinfulness, disease or crime in order to flesh out objections. Others appeal to the argument that homosexuality, its religious, medical, and criminal implications apart, is a kind of unnatural aberration which undermines its practitioners' prospects for happiness. I will consider this kind of argument here and contend that such an argument fails to establish that homosexuality is any significant abnormality and that neither its purported abnormality nor the unhappiness said to be associated with such behaviour can constitute a basis for criminalizing consensual homosexual behaviour or for failing to provide equal protections under the law for homosexuals in the area of public housing, service, jobs, and so on. I consider Michael Levin's

"Why homosexuality is abnormal" as paradigmatic of the kind of argument I wish to investigate. Although I confine myself to his specific argument and frequently use its language, my position is applicable *a fortiori* to all similar kinds of positions.

THE ARGUMENT FROM NATURE

Levin says homosexuality is abnormal because it involves a misuse of body parts, that there is "clear empirical sense" of that misuse, and that homosexual behaviour is contrary to the evolutionary adaptive order. Homosexual behaviour is abnormal, he says, because it is not the kind of behaviour which brought us to be the kind of physically constituted persons that we are today. Persons who used their penises for *coitus per anum* presumably left no ancestors. (Levin does not accept sociobiological contentions that homosexuality plays a supporting role in adaptive success.) That there are penises and vaginas today is due to the fact that they *were* used for heterosexual coitus, and hence we can infer that heterosexual coitus is indeed what such organs are for. Levin says: "an organ is for a given activity if the organ's performing that activity helps its host or organisms suitably related to its host, *and* if this contribution is how the organ got and stays where it is." Homosexual behaviour constitutes, according to this line of thought, an abandonment of certain functions on which species survival depended, and that abandonment is said to imply the loss of naturally occurring rewards selected for by adaptive success. This latter point does not mean that there are *no* compen-

Timothy F. Murphy, "Homosexuality and Nature: Happiness and the Law at Stake," *Journal of Applied Philosophy* 4 (1987): 195–204. Some notes deleted. Reprinted by permission of Blackwell Publishing Ltd.

satory pleasures, for just as the obese person will find gustatory rewards in his or her food, the homosexual who misuses his or her body parts can find *some* compensatory sexual rewards. It is just that the wilful overeater or homosexual cannot reap the deepest rewards that nature has provided for in heterosexual usages and achievements.

Despite the effort which Levin takes to show that homosexual behaviour falls outside the behaviour upon which human adaptive success depended, I cannot say that I think this argument is even remotely convincing. Indeed, I believe it to be subject to a damning criticism. Even if it were certainly established that homosexuality was not part of originally adaptive behaviour, I do not see how that conclusion alone could establish the abnormality of homosexuality because there is neither a premise that natural selection has any kind of ultimate normative force nor a premise that human beings are bound to continue to be the kind of things that cosmic accident brought them to be. There is nothing in Levin's argument to sustain a claim that departures from a blind, accidental force of nature, or whatever metaphor of randomness is chosen, must be resisted. Without a logically prior and controlling premise that patterns of adaptive success possess ultimate, normative force, then it seems that human beings are completely at liberty to dispose of their world, their behaviour, and even such things as their anatomy and physiology as they see fit. H. Tristam Engelhardt has made an argument along similar lines: that we human beings may choose our futures and are in no metaphysically binding sense bound to continue being the kind of persons blind determinants of nature have brought us to be. Violations of a random order of nature carry no inherent penalty for there is no ultimate enforcer, or at least none is specified by this argument. Levin believes that he can show the abnormality of homosexuality without having to show that it violates some cosmic principle, by showing its inherent obstacles to adaptive success. But I think it is because no cosmic principle is invoked that we can judge that adaptive success itself is no binding force. The only guide available for human beings in respect of their lives, sexuality, and future is their will and imagination. Should the entire population of the planet choose to become exclusive homosexuals, for example, leaving the business of reproduction to ectogenesis, I cannot think of a reason *derived from nature* why they should not do so.

Levin's argument, and others like it, ignore the prospects of beneficial departures from the naturally adaptive order. His argument assumes that each departure from our adaptive heritage will be unhappy in result. The argument, too, assumes that *all* behaviour of *all* persons must serve the purpose of adaption. Clearly, it is possible that some departures from the adaptive order are possible which do not threaten a species survival as a whole. If a species can survive if only a majority of its members use their organs in a particular fashion, then it may enjoy a surplus of adaptive protection even for those who act in wholly non-procreative fashion. Homosexuality, then, might have served some beneficial advantage (as sociobiology asserts) or it may have been (and this is more important for my argument) no impediment to selective adaptation. If this is so, it is hard to see in what sense homosexuality would have to be reckoned as a natural aberration.

Even if one were to accept Levin's suggestions regarding the abnormality of homosexuality with respect to natural selection, it seems to me that his definition of homosexuality is highly problematic. He defines homosexuality behaviourally, i.e. as something one does with one's body, specifically with one's organs. It is *behaviour* which is said to be unnatural. Since there are, after all, self-identified gay men and lesbians who have never had sexual relations with a member of the same (or opposite) sex, this definition seems ill-advised. By their own lights, adolescents and closeted adults see themselves as homosexual, their sexual continence notwithstanding. How is one to understand the nature of their sexual dispositions if there is no overt behaviour? Is their homoerotic desire itself abnormal? Or is only behaviour abnormal? I believe that homosexuality is better defined as primarily a psychic phenomenon and that specific homosexual behaviour is virtually epiphenomenal, merely a matter of what biology makes possible (this claim would also apply to heterosexuality). Most psychiatric texts follow this approach. If one accepts the condition that homosexuality is primarily a psychic phenomenon, and if one wanted to argue its abnormality along the lines Levin has suggested, it would seem that one would have to argue that homoeroticism is somehow a misuse of the brain! There are arguments, of course, that attempt to show homosexuality as a result of some psychic disrepair, but even though these arguments are themselves the matter of much debate, that debate is only about psychical development, not about uses of the brain. It is hard to imagine that one could show homoeroticism as a misuse of the brain.

Finally, it is to be noted that Levin believes that homosexuality may be intuited as abnormal. He says that such an intuition "remains vital." Yet however profoundly felt and however psychologically convincing intuitions may be, still they can be conceptually shallow and more importantly even dead wrong. That is, the appeal to intuition is by itself no guarantee of the accuracy of the intuition, for presumably one would, for purposes of confirmation, have to check the intuition against some other external criterion of justification. I am hard-pressed to see how this intuition of homosexuality's abnormality is to be made available to others who do not already share it. Indeed, arguments from intuition are like issues said to be self-evident: precious little can be said on their behalf, they are either seen or not. Yet Levin seems to assume that the readers of his essay *already* share the intuition. For example, he apologizes for the allegedly graphic language that he must use in his essay. Of course, only persons who already share a revulsion *at the mere mention* of mutual fellation will find such terms in need of apology. Levin also says at one point that it is hard to believe the high number of sexual partners homosexual men report having. He then transfers this lack of imagination to all his readers; even when these figures, he says, are "taken *cum grano,* they should be compared to the reader's own experience as he tries to imagine what it would be like to move so promiscuously among anonymous encounters." Evidently, Levin believes that no promiscuous heterosexual or homosexual male (or that any female, promiscuous or not) will read this essay, their time being spent, I suppose, entirely on the prowl. It is clear from these examples, and others, that there is no accommodation of persons who do not find the mere mention of fellation an inherent degradation, who do not find a high number of sexual partners psychically repulsive, or who intuit homosexuality as erotic rather than repulsive. This kind of argument presupposes an audience which already shares Levin's conclusions, and I believe fails to show how another person, lacking these conclusions, could ever come to an appropriation of them. However, even if such a move were made, the position would remain open to the standard, incisive criticisms of intuitonistic moral philosophy.

PROSPECTS FOR HAPPINESS

Levin makes a great deal of the supposed link between homosexuality and unhappiness. One may assume that he would reply to my foregoing remarks by admitting that even if it were true that humans are not bound by any ultimate metaphysical sexual directive, then it would still remain true that prudential cautions obtain against homosexuality and that these cautions are sufficient to ground legal measures designed to minimize the occurrence of homosexuality. "Homosexuality," Levin says, "is likely to cause unhappiness because it leaves unfulfilled an innate and innately rewarding desire," a desire supposedly ingrained through millennia of evolutionary selection. One might find some happy homosexuals, but Levin believes that such exceptions are inconsequential and do not disable his argument. He does not say that happy homosexuals are non-existent, only that they are rare and that their lives will be inherently less rewarding than those of heterosexuals. Moreover, "Even if some line demarcated happiness from unhappiness absolutely, it would be irrelevant if homosexuals were all happily above that line. It is the comparison with the heterosexual life that is at issue." The happiest persons are practitioners of heterosexuality, therefore, even if, according to Levin, each and every homosexual was, by his or her own admission, happy. But homosexuals are not even proximately happy, Levin says. According to him, awash in the travails of their own self-punishing promiscuity, present-day homosexuals would like to believe that all their ills are the result of an ill-constructed society, that their unhappiness is merely artifactual and in principle eliminable by the appropriate cultural and political accommodations. Levin suggests that this belief is a self-serving rationalization. Happiness has not followed, he says, the Danish and Dutch abandonment of prejudice against homosexuals. Happiness has not followed the work of various American organs to provide a positive image of homosexuals, judges allowing homosexuals to adopt their lovers, the Hollywood production of "highly sanitized" movies about homosexuality, publishers urging their authors to show little boys using cosmetics, or advertisers appealing directly to the homosexual market. That there has not been a resultant rise in homosexual happiness is said to be evident from (a) the gay press not liking Hollywood's movies, (b) the appearance of especially virulent diseases in homosexual populations, and (c) gay men needing frivolous enticements to get them to support important political causes on their behalf.

By way of comment on all this, I would first note that Levin has formulated his position in terms that *in principle* do not admit of refutation. He said that in principle, however happy homosexuals may be, they still cannot be as happy as heterosexuals. Of course, it is possible that a claim is unfalsifiable because the claim is indeed true. On the other hand, I think one would do better to see a definitional fiat being asserted here: human happiness, *true* human happiness is said to be coextensive with the happiness of heterosexual behaviour. By definition there is nothing which could falsify this proposition, *not even* the self-asserted happiness of each and every homosexual person. I believe that this claim is no argument, avoiding as it does any potentially falsifying statement, and that it ought to be rejected as untestable rather than accepted as true by definition. As I have urged above, moreover, I do not believe that the accidental contingency of the primacy of heterosexual sexuality requires that all human happiness be sought there or that, perhaps, other kinds of happiness cannot be engineered.

Secondly, the kind of evidence that Levin uses to establish the unhappiness of homosexuals is alto-

gether anecdotal and trivial. That Hollywood continues to make bad movies, even when their subjects are "sanitized" gay men and lesbians, is no evidence that homosexuality per se leads to unhappiness. The existence of viral disease *is* a major concern of gay men, but it is not because they are gay that it is their concern; it is because these viral diseases happen by accident of fate to affect the gay population. Would one want to argue that heterosexuals qua heterosexuals are somehow intrinsically headed for unhappiness as AIDS expands into that population? Moreover, that homosexuals mix business with pleasure is no argument that they are any less serious about their political agenda (let alone unhappier) than others. There is a kind of unfair asymmetry being used here in adducing Levin's evidence. If one uses such issues as he conjures up as evidence of the continuing unhappiness of homosexuals, why couldn't one equally and legitimately use similar evidence against the supposed happiness of heterosexuals? Most wars, for example, are the doing of heterosexuals. Nuclear weapons are their products. Most bad movies are also theirs. Must one infer therefore the continuing unhappiness of heterosexuals and assert prudential cautions against heterosexuality? If Levin's use of anecdotal evidence is acceptable against homosexuals, then it ought to be equally acceptable as an indictment of heterosexuality. Ironically, the case against heterosexuality would probably have to be seen as more damaging.

As for Levin's claims that homosexuals ought to be happier these days than they were in the past, it is probably the case that this is true. Anecdotal evidence may be used here since Levin uses it. The increasing success of gay pride parades ought to be taken as an indicator of some measure of increased homosexual happiness. At the very least persons who participate in them have been freed of the fear of some of the unhappy consequences that could befall them following public identification of their being gay. It is not without significance that in Boston, for example, the 1986 gay pride parade attracted some 25,000–30,000 participants whereas the first parade of 1970 had but 50! Furthermore, the heady increase in the number of gay and lesbian organizations for social, business, and political and support services indicates that homosexuals are not much inclined to wallow in despair over their sexual fate. One could go on in this vein, but I think it is important to consider that a verdict about the happiness of homosexuals would be a one-sided verdict indeed if it were to follow only from the evidence Levin puts forward.

To put specific quarrels about evidence aside, it seems to me that Levin fails almost culpably to imagine what a society would have to be like in order to be free of the oppressive elements which contribute to the putative unhappiness of homosexuals. In order to see the extent to which homosexual unhappiness is caused by social repressions and to what extent it is intrinsic, society would have to be completely free at every significant level of bias against homosexuals. To begin with—let's call this Phase I of the agenda: there should be no gratuitous assumption of heterosexuality in education, politics, advertising, and so on, just as a gender-neutral society would not presume the priority, real and symbolic, of males. For example, in education, texts and films ought to incorporate the experiences of gay men and lesbians. Educational measures should attempt to reduce anti-homosexuality in the same ways and to the same extent they educate against racism. In a society reconstructed along these lines, moreover, there would also have to be no right of access or entitlement possessed by a heterosexual that could be denied to a homosexual. *Only* in such a radically restructured society would one be able to see if homosexual unhappiness were immune to social deconstruction. Even if it weren't, one could still argue that homosexuals are not necessarily unhappy but that their happiness requires social protections or accommodations unrequired by heterosexuals. That is, homosexuals might need, as Phase II of the agenda, entitlements which heterosexuals do not in the way, for example, that legally-mandated minority hiring quotas serve other specific populations. Of course, one might want to argue that such entitlements would be anti-democratic and therefore objectionable. This protestation however would not by itself diminish the point being made: that homosexual unhappiness is perhaps adventitious and that the only way of discovering this is to protect homosexuals in their lives, jobs, and interests in ways that are not presently served.

It is unlikely, of course, that the above-described experiment in social reconstruction is in any important sense immediately forthcoming. Nevertheless, that the experiment may be clearly formulated and seen as the definitive test of the social-reaction theory of homosexual unhappiness is sufficient ground to show that Levin's account of the unhappiness of homosexuals is unproved, its adduced evidence merely anecdotal. Even if it were true, I will argue later, since not all human unhappiness is tractable to social interventions, any residual unhappiness that was to survive Phase I and II of our social reformation agenda would still be no evidence against homosexuality.

ISSUES AT LAW

Levin believes that the abnormality of homosexuality and its attendant unhappiness are warrant enough to ground legal enactments against homosexuality and this is a matter of protecting citizens from lives impoverished by the loss of heterosexual rewards. Any legislation therefore that raises the odds that a child will become homosexual ought to be rejected as prima facie objectionable, as a dereliction of the duty of protecting children from the unhappy homosexual selves they might become. The US Supreme Court recently ruled in Bowers v. Hardwick that states may enact, if they choose, statutes proscribing private consensual homosexual behaviour since, according to the opinion, there is nothing in the Constitution making such behaviour a fundamental right. Levin's argument would presumably extend further since private consensual homosexual behaviour is socially invisible and unlikely as such to influence persons to become homosexual. Although he does not specifically mention what kinds of laws ought to be called for, or what kinds of laws ought to be rejected, presumably he means denying homosexuals protections in jobs, housing, foster-parenting, and so on. In short, the law would presumably have to serve the function of rendering homosexuality entirely invisible else there would continue to exist subtle promptings to homosexuality by virtue of degree of acceptance extended to it. Levin says he does not believe that this legal scenario would put any undue burden on any actual homosexual since, unlike members of racial minorities, he or she can always stay in the closet while applying for jobs, housing and the like. Therefore to give homosexuals protections they don't really need would have to be interpreted as a de facto social legitimation of homosexuality. This implied approval might be causally involved in the production of more homosexuals and therefore ought to be rejected.

I do not believe that this argument is convincing. First of all, the "cause" or "causes" of homosexuality are a matter of continuing controversy. There are metaphysical arguments that homosexuality is the result of some cosmic principle of world ordering; Plato's *Symposium* depicts homosexuals (and heterosexuals) as the result of an angry god's punishment. Biological theories hold homosexuality to be the result of some developmental variance or organismal dysfunction. Genetic theories try to locate the origins of homosexuality at the lowest level of biological causality, the gene. The most numerous kinds of theories are psychosocial theories which see homoeroticism as the result of either original psychical constitution or some developmental influences. Even the briefest perusal of the literature of the "cause" of homosexuality leaves one with the conclusion that the "cause" is an essentially disputed concept. There is not even agreement that homosexuality is a reifiable trait (any more than, say, courage) that can be explained by reference to a universally pre-existing set of conditions. This dispute is important to consider since Levin seems to hold, without justification (at least without explanation), a developmental theory of homosexuality, a theory that homosexuals are made not born. This may or may not be true, but it seems wrong-headed to establish legal policy on the basis of one particular speculative theory of the origins of homosexual behaviour. If homosexuality is primarily a function of biological variance, for example, such laws and forbearances that Levin would see as desirable would have no effect whatever on the production of more homosexuals. Even if the law diligently erased all

evidence of homosexual behaviour and persons from public view, one could not automatically assume a reduced number of homosexuals or a decrease in homosexual behaviour. I suspect that most persons are homosexual and become homosexual in ways completely immune to the written or enforced statutes of the various states. Children who never hear a word about homosexuality in their youth nevertheless become homosexuals. Children who walk past homosexual clubs and persons in the streets of certain American cities do not thereby automatically become homosexuals. Would it really be the case that there are more homosexuals spawned in West Virginia because there are no laws against private, consensual homosexual behaviour there than in Virginia where there are such laws? The net result of efforts to criminalize and reduce the visibility of homosexuality then would be to impose burdens on those who are perhaps involuntarily homosexual. At the very least, Levin's theory gratuitously supposes a developmental theory of homosexuality, a theory which has its insistent critics. One should also point out that even if some developmental theory of homosexuality were true, it is not necessarily the case that changing statutes would halt the flow of homosexuals since there may be other pathways to homosexuality. It is also the suspicion of many psychologists that homosexual tendencies are established very early on in childhood, in which case one presumes fairly that statutes criminalizing sodomy and lacks of protection in housing on the basis of sexual orientation have little to do with either ingraining or stifling homosexual dispositions.

If the reason that Levin suggests anti-homosexual measures is to contain human unhappiness, then his argument may be turned on its head. If the reason, or part of the reason that homosexuals are unhappy is because of the existence of certain legally permissible discriminations (or what comes to the same thing: fear of such), then it can certainly be suggested that laws ought to be changed in order to protect and enlarge the happiness of homosexuals, whether their homosexuality is elective or involuntary. In the name of their happiness, they ought to be afforded protections under the law, freedom from fear of prosecution for their private consensual behaviour and freedom to occupy jobs as persons they are, not as the persons others would have them be. The law could further protect them by saving them from blackmailers who would expose their homosexuality to employers, landlords, and so on. It is eminently clear that the law could at least enlarge the happiness of gay men and lesbians in these respects even if it cannot vouchsafe them absolute satisfaction in their lives.

Interestingly enough, even if all the unhappiness said to be associated with being homosexual were not eliminated by a dogged social reconstruction that achieved full parity between homosexuality and heterosexuality, it would still not follow that the law ought to be put to the purpose of eliminating homosexuality (assuming it could). Life, sad to say, is in some of its aspects inherently tragic. For example, in some important ways, law or society could never fully compensate the atheist for the lost rewards of religion. Atheism can discover in the world no incentives to conduct, no promise of the eventual recompense for injustices borne, and no guarantee that the heart's desires will be met.[1] Society might provide such consolations as it can, but it is certainly the case that a certain tragedy antagonistic to human happiness is an irreducible element of atheistic thought. That atheism leads to this measure of unhappiness would certainly not be a reason for instituting social and legal barriers to atheism on the theory that children ought to be glowingly happy (if self-deceived) theists rather than unhappy atheists. Human dignity is not automatically overthrown by a position of atheism; the atheist accepts and honours those satisfactions that are within his or her power. That homosexuality too might lead to a certain amount of unhappiness does not thereby overthrow the dignity of homosexual persons. One realizes merely that the law is no unfailing conduit to human happiness.

Levin's conclusions that legal measures ought to be taken to minimize the possibility that children become themselves the sad new recruits of homosexuality therefore cannot stand. I believe, on the contrary, that the law ought to do what it can to protect homosexuals from socially inflicted unhappiness. Levin's point that to decriminalize homosexual behaviour and to provide legal protections for homosexual persons would be seen as social legitimization of homosexuality (and not just tolerance) is correct. But this is no point over which to despair, for this inference is precisely compatible with the underlying metaphysics of gay activism, that homosexuality is no degrading impoverishment of human life. On the contrary, it has an integrity of its own apart from invidious comparisons with heterosexuality. Therefore, lest society be a political enforcer of sexual ideology, homosexuals ought to be afforded equal standing and protections under the law, and this in the name of serving human happiness.

CONCLUSIONS

Levin has argued that homosexuality is a self-punishing maladaption likely to cause unhappiness since homosexuals do not use their organs for what they are for. Human happiness is said to attend that behaviour which follows out the natural paths plotted by evolutionary selection: As homosexuality has not thus far been shown to have contributed (*pace* sociobiology) to the kind of beings we are today, it may be assumed that homosexual behaviour is abnormal. As such behaviour, too, is linked with unhappiness it is to be rejected as both abnormal and unrewarding. The law ought to follow this conclusion through and reject any inducements to homosexuality.

I have argued against this position on a number of grounds. The most important is this: nature is represented here by Levin as without guiding or controlling force. Therefore, as pathways of evolutionary adaptation are themselves only a matter of metaphysical blind accident, nature lacks normative force and human beings are completely at liberty to dipose of the world, their behaviour, and their bodies as they see fit. One could still try to argue against homosexuality on prudential grounds, on grounds that it causes unhappiness, but I have argued that conclusions from claims about unhappiness are inconclusive because it is not clear how much homosexual unhappiness is adventitious and how much intrinsic. Levin's evidence that such unhappiness is intrinsic is anecdotal evidence of the most unconvincing kind. A complete reconstruction of society such that homosexuality was on a par with hetero-sexuality would be required in order to distinguish adventitious from intrinsic unhappiness and make the argument conclusive. But even if there were residual unhappiness attaching to homosexuality under socially liberating conditions of this grand experiment, such unhappiness might be likened to the irreducible tragic aspects of atheism. Such an unhappiness is no writ for legal and social measures designed to stem the genesis of either atheists or homosexuals.

On the contrary, rather than using the law as an instrument of enforcing invisibility on homosexuals, the law should, I think, be used to afford what measure of happiness it can. How far the law ought to serve the needs of gay men and lesbians is, of course, a matter of debate. But it seems to follow that at the very least, the law ought to protect gay men and lesbians from unhappiness caused by victimization and social exclusions which it is within the law's power to reject.

NOTE

1. Ernest Nagel (1965) A defense of atheism, in: P. Edwards & A. Pap *A Modern Introduction to Philosophy*, pp. 460–472, rev edn (New York, Free Press).

7

Is "Outing" Homosexuals Wrong?

Mohr and His Critics

"Outing" refers to the practice of publicly revealing the sexual orientation of people who have attempted to conceal their homosexuality. Richard Mohr has been called "perhaps its most eloquent and persuasive advocate." His extensive 1992 essay, "The Outing Contro-versy: Privacy and Dignity in Gay Ethics," helped initiate the philosophical debate on the subject and has served as a focal point for many subsequent discussions of the issue. In "The Case for Outing," which appears this chapter in its entirely, Mohr presents a much briefer, more recent version of his central argument. The critical responses that follow it refer at times to claims made in Mohr's earlier essay, "The Outing Controversy," but the substan-tive points they raise can all be brought to bear on the essay reprinted here.

Outings are sometimes defended on punitive grounds. If a gay public official, for exam-ple, has successfully concealed his homosexuality while pursuing a legislative agenda harm-ful to the interests of homosexuals, then he may be viewed as guilty of hypocrisy and thus deserving of being revealed publicly as homosexual.

More often, those who support the practice of outing appeal to a more utilitarian argu-ment, urging that the long-term benefits of outing outweigh its costs and that this fact suf-fices to render it morally permissible

What is most important about Mohr's argument is that it embraces neither of these approaches. Instead, Mohr appeals to the value of dignity, maintaining that a person who refrains from revealing the sexual orientation of those he knows to be gay is, in effect, guilty of perpetuating the view that there is something reprehensible about homosexuality. That is, going along with a closeted gay person's decision to remain in the closet is, in Mohr's words, "a commitment to viewing gayness as disgusting, horrible, unspeakably gross, in short, as abjection." Of course, many people may be willing simply to endorse the view that homo-sexuality is all of these things. But Mohr's argument is not aimed at such readers, and so, for the purposes of considering the merits of Mohr's argument, we must assume that this view of homosexuality is misguided. Indeed, Mohr's argument is perhaps most forcefully aimed at the reader who is himself or herself openly gay but who respects the privacy of closeted homosexuals by helping them to keep their secret. Many gay people adopt this stance and view the practice of outing as a morally objectionable violation of the privacy of others. But such an attitude, Mohr maintains, amounts to complicity with the enemy. Put more formally, Mohr's argument can be represented as follows:

P1 To refrain from outing a closeted gay person is to reinforce the convention of the closet.

P2 To reinforce the convention of the closet is to degrade homosexuality as subhuman.

P3 It is morally wrong to degrade homosexuality as subhuman.

C It is morally wrong to refrain from outing a closeted gay person.

The result of Mohr's argument, therefore, is not merely that outing is morally *permissible,* but that it can be morally *obligatory.* It is not merely that it is not wrong to out, but that it is wrong *not* to out.

In his response to Mohr's argument, James S. Stramel raises several concerns, but most of them point to the same general conclusion: that P1 of Mohr's argument is false because it fails to take into account the ways in which outing a person can also reinforce the degrading convention of the closet. That is, outing a closeted homosexual causes even worse consequences from the standpoint of dignity than does refraining from outing him, then given that outing is the only alternative to not outing, the choice to refrain from outing someone is the best choice to make in terms of fighting the degrading convention of the closet. Stramel offers two distinct arguments for the claim that outing is more degrading than not outing. The first turns on the contention that what matters most in determining whether or not outing degrades the "outee" is not the motivation and intention of the person who does the outing, but rather the way the outing is generally received by the public. And given that much of the public regards homosexuality as "bad or immoral," Stramel argues, the result is that the outing degrades the outed person even if this was not what the "outer" intended. Stramel's second argument turns on the claim that Mohr's defense of P1 overlooks the importance of autonomy to dignity. A person who is outed is deprived of the ability to control his public identity, and if such a violation of autonomy amounts to an infringement on his dignity as a human being, then this counts as a reason to conclude that outing is worse than not outing from the standpoint of dignity. Finally, Stramel presents what amounts to a *reductio ad absurdum* objection to Mohr's argument: just as there is an undeserved stigma attached to homosexuals, so is there an undeserved stigma attached to rape victims. If Mohr's argument justifies outing closeted homosexuals, therefore, it would seem also to justify "outing" rape victims who wish to keep this fact about their lives private. Stramel takes it that this would be an objectionable result, and this in turn is meant to count as a final reason to reject Mohr's argument.

In their article, "Privacy and the Ethics of Outing," Mayo and Gunderson raise two further objections to Mohr's position. The first amounts, in effect, to an objection to P2. Even if not outing a closeted homosexual does strengthen the convention of the closet, and even if the convention of the closet itself is degrading, Mayo and Gunderson argue that a gay person's decision to respect the decision of another gay person to remain in the closet need not be a manifestation of a negative attitude toward (his or the other person's) homosexuality. It may, for example, simply be a matter of protecting that person's physical well-being or honoring a commitment one has made to them. If one can refrain from outing a person without in any way committing oneself to the view that homosexuality is undignified, then Mohr's argument would seem to be defeated. The second objection that Mayo and Gunderson raise amounts to a rejection of P3. It can certainly be prima facie wrong to contribute to the view of homosexuality as disgusting, they acknowledge, but the third premise of Mohr's argument, they charge, requires a much stronger claim: the claim that considerations of dignity override any other considerations when it comes to deciding what the morally right thing to do is. That is, P3, maintains not just that an act's being degrading counts as a moral reason against doing it, but that it always counts as a *decisive* moral reason against doing it. And that, Mayo and Gunderson maintain, is unreasonable. There are other morally relevant values, including the promotion of human happiness and well-being, and they question whether Mohr has justified his insistence that dignity always trumps these other values when they come into conflict.

QUESTIONS FOR CONSIDERATION

• In considering the relative merits of the positions of Mohr and Stramel, it may prove useful to begin by assessing the relative significance of the intention of the "outer" versus the beliefs of the public at large. Stramel maintains that what matters most is that an outing will be perceived as degrading even if it is not intended to be, and it is therefore worth considering whether or not Mohr might be in a position to counter this contention. Could a defender of Mohr's position sustain the claim that the dignified thing to do is that which you believe to be right even if it is likely to be misunderstood by others? Indeed, might Mohr argue that Stramel's objection would only perpetuate the stigma associated with the closet, rendering the objection a self-fulfilling prophecy? Or can Mohr's critic vindicate the contention that since what the closet is is itself a matter of convention what matters most is how outings are conventionally received?

• In addition, one should consider the merits of Stramel's argument about autonomy. Does outing a person violate his autonomy or does it simply exercise the autonomy of the outer? Should autonomy include control over one's public identity? Why or why not?

• Finally, it is worth considering the merits of Stramel's rape-based objection: is the analogy between the closeted homosexual and the rape victim strong enough for Stramel's purposes? What sorts of differences might there be between the two cases, and do any of those differences suffice to overcome the objection? Or should Mohr be willing simply to bite the bullet and accept the implication: that helping rape victims conceal their status as rape victims is also morally objectionable? Many newspapers, for example, publish the names of crime victims in general, but refrain from publishing the names of victims of rape in particular. Is that a praiseworthy policy or a criticizable one?

• In turning next to the objections raised by Mayo and Gunderson, one might begin by returning to the question of intent versus perception. But in this case, the roles seem to be reversed: It is Mohr's critics who maintain that what matters is the intent of the non-outer, which on their account may be perfectly benign. Mohr's defender may, then, have to justify the claim that what matters is that leaving someone in the closet perpetuates a degrading view of homosexuality, regardless of the non-outer's intention.

• In addition, one should consider whether Mayo and Gunderson are correct in their objection to the very strong claim that considerations of dignity must morally trump all other considerations. Does Mohr's position require him to rely on this seemingly extreme claim, or could he modify it and still reach the conclusion he wishes to reach? Can Mohr show that dignity is important enough to justify outing without making it so important that it would justify acts that most people would think unjustified?

FURTHER READING

Broach, Ronald J. "Does Human Dignity Require Outing Homosexuals?" *Journal of Social Philosophy* 29, no. 23 (1998): 2–45.
Mohr, Richard. "The Outing Controversy: Privacy and Dignity in Gay Ethics." In *Gay Ideas: Outing and Other Controversies.* Boston: Beacon Press, 1992, pp. 11–48.

Richard D. Mohr | # The Case for Outing

The disclosure on the Internet in July 1996 that Arizona Republican Congressman Jim Kolbe is gay and his public acknowledgment of this fact the next month—just as the national gay news magazine *The Advocate* was going to press with the story—catapulted the issue of outing back into national headlines. Gays outed Kolbe in response to his voting for the insidiously anti-gay Defense of Marriage Act. Gays deemed that the socially liberal Republican was not liberal enough. But two can play that game. In 1994, far-right Congressman Robert Dornan outed fellow-Republican Congressman Steve Gunderson on the floor of the House. Dornan deemed Gunderson too liberal. In both cases, the outing was vindictive—aimed at punishing and incapacitating its target.

Such outings are of dubious political worth. In the November 1996 elections, Kolbe was reelected, Dornan was not. More important, such outings are morally reprehensible. In order for vindictive outing to be effective, the outer counts upon the amassed anti-gay forces in society to strike out against the person outed. Such outing legitimates the use of anti-gay forces as a political tool and, in that very use, strengthens them.

Vindictive outings are not limited to the political realm. In January 1996, gay novelist and wit Armistead Maupin outed comedienne Lily Tomlin in the *Village Voice* for her failure to come out in her role as the narrator for the movie *The Celluloid Closet,* a history of gay cinema. And a number of gay military court cases have resulted from vindictive outings, as when a disgruntled "roommate" outed her Air Force major "girlfriend" to the military police. But such illegitimate, vindictive outings are not the only form of outing. Not all outing points fingers. Not all outing recriminates. Not all outing shouts from soapboxes to stir up the homophobic crowds.

Some outing is simply news—the letting come to light of a person's sexual orientation in relevant contexts. Take 1995's biggest outing story. After twenty-six years of marriage, *Rolling Stone* founder Jann Wenner left his wife and three sons to move into a Manhattan hotel with a former male model who now works as a designer for Calvin Klein. Despite Wenner's and his wife's efforts to have the story suppressed, it ran anyway—not in the tabloids and tattlers, but in *Newsweek, New York* magazine, *Advertising Age,* the *Boston Herald,* and the *Wall Street Journal.* What made the story particularly

Richard Mohr, "The Case for Outing," in *Same Sex: Debating the Ethics, Science, and Culture of Homosexuality,* ed. John Corvino (New York: Rowman & Littlefield, 1997), pp. 281–83. Reprinted by permission of Rowman & Littlefield Publishers, Inc.

newsworthy was that in 1993 Wenner had jumped on the "family values" bandwagon and had begun publishing a yuppie magazine, *Family Life,* to portray the glories of the heterosexual nuclear family. What was missing from this portrait? The editor himself.

The American press is no longer creating "beards" nor assuring silences for would-be closet cases in order to deflect attention away from gay issues and gay lives as though gayness were just too embarrassing to mention. To its credit, the press is gradually abandoning both its past policy of "don't ask, don't tell" when it comes to gayness and its phony belief that to discuss unasked someone's sexual *orientation* (as opposed to his or her sexual acts) is to violate that person's privacy. It is time that gays carry over these trends into their daily lives as well.

People need to let the gayness of individuals come up when it is relevant, rather than along with the shaming social convention of the closet, the demand that every gay person is bound to keep every other gay person's secret secret. For the closet is the site where anti-gay loathing and gay self-loathing mutually reinforce each other. Even people who are out of the closet demean themselves when they maintain other people's closets. For the closet's secret is a dirty little secret that degrades all gay people.

To put the point systematically, living by the convention of the closet—whether one is closeted oneself or not—is a commitment to viewing gayness as disgusting, horrible, unspeakably gross, in short, as abjection. Core cases of abjection are excrement, vomit, pus, and the smells associated with these. It is exactly around just these (only ever half-acknowledged) abject matters that society sets up

rituals requiring that one may neither inquire nor report about them—rituals of the form "don't ask, don't tell." Take, for example, the case of flatulence in a crowded elevator: no one tells; no one asks; everyone acts as though nothing is amiss, and so this behavior reinforces the abject thing's status as loathsome. This daunting effort to repress knowing and acknowledgment requires a blanket of silence to be cast over the abject thing. To tell of the abject is to break a taboo, for names, like scents, are enough to bring the abject back to full consciousness. And to ask about the abject is to be reminded of its constantly recurring, lurking, louring presence just beyond oneself.

The chief problem of the closet as a social institution, then, is not that it promotes hypocrisy, requires lies, sets snares, blames the victim when snared, and causes unhappiness—though it does have all these results. No, the chief problem with the closet is that it treats gays as less than human, less than animal, less even than vegetable—it treats gays as reeking scum, the breath of death.

Therefore, each time a gay person finds the closet morally acceptable for himself or others, he degrades himself as gay and sinks to the level of abjection dictated for gays by the dominant culture. No gay person with sufficient self-respect and dignity can be required to view himself or other gays in this way. In consequence, the openly gay person, in order to live morally, must not play along with the convention of the closet, lest he degrade himself. He must allow gayness to come up in conversations when it is relevant.

Moral outing is simply living in the truth and withdrawing from the social conventions that degrade gay existence.

Critics

Outing, Ethics, and Politics

James S. Stramel

A Reply to Mohr

In place of more common utilitarian defenses of outing, Mohr claims that by not outing others one knows to be gay, the openly gay person is participating in "the secret of the closet." He thereby degrades himself by "commit[ting] his life to the very values that keep him oppressed" and trades his own dignity for the happiness of the closet case. So, in defense of their dignity and the dignity of all gays, out gays living in the truth may—are even expected to—"out nearly everyone he or she knows to be gay."

If there is a prima facie privacy right against outing, then (as Mohr admits) even dignity-based outing would not be justified; but I also find Mohr's position troubling on its own terms. Outing may diminish gay dignity, both individual and collective, because the public regards homosexuality as bad or immoral and sees outing as punishment. Rather than serving to dismantle antigay attitudes, outing utilizes and reinforces the notion that homosexuality is shameful. Even when conscientiously motivated, the practice can look petty and vindictive.

Perhaps the most repugnant feature of all outing is that it steals from the outee a major opportunity to take control of and assume responsibility for his identity, integrity and dignity—to come out on his own principles. Mohr complains that this argument—"dressed up in the finery of liberal cant"—misunderstands the scope and possible materials of dignity and the complexity of coming out. Shifting attention to the outee, Mohr says the relevant questions are: (1) Can a person, though outed, still have access to enough dignity to be highly dignified? (2) Are conditions such that individuals can achieve a

rich life of their own making given the cussedness of their social and material circumstances? (3) Can the outee still have a positive, robust, dignifying relation to his sexual orientation? I agree that the answer to each question is yes. But none of this refutes the claim that outing wrongly diminishes the dignity of the outee.

It is certainly possible to imagine situations in which a failure to identify a person as gay would involve the loss of one's own dignity. But it is simply not plausible to claim that a person who decides not to out another out of respect for her autonomy and dignity necessarily regards homosexuality as shameful or has committed her life to the oppression of gays. Except in unusual circumstances, the threat to my dignity of your closetude—and my leaving you there—is negligible. As Mohr observes, dignity has many sources, and I can still be highly dignified despite forgoing the opportunity to out you. To see this, we can stand Mohr's questions on their heads to inquire whether a gay person can have access to enough dignity to be highly dignified, a rich life of his own making, and a robust dignifying relation to his sexual orientation—all without engaging in outing. Here too, the answer is yes.

Like many other groups, gay people are faced with a situation in which society unfairly and severely stigmatizes them for having a particular characteristic. One's dignity as a given type of person does not require outing every person one knows to share the relevant characteristic. Compare again the situation of gays to that of women who have been raped. Through no fault of their own rape victims are sad-

From James S. Stramel, "Outing, Ethics, and Politics: A Reply to Mohr." In *Same Sex: Debating the Ethics, Science, and Culture of Homosexuality,* ed. John Corvino, (New York: Rowman & Littlefield, 1997), pp. 284–88. Some parts of the text have been deleted. Reprinted by permission of Rowman & Littlefield Publishers, Inc.

dled with a status that is not inherently disre-spectable, but that often prompts disrespectful treat-ment. Suppose that Anne was a victim of rape but has been able to rid herself of the shame and stigma rape victims often internalize; she now works actively in rape-prevention programs, counseling women and giving public talks in which she "comes out" as her-self a victim of rape. If Anne knows that Brenda was also raped but remains "closeted," how does Anne's failure to out her cause a loss of Anne's dignity?

Mohr grants that outing can diminish the outee's dignity, but he holds that this will rarely outweigh the dignity gained for all gays by outing because the indignity bred by the secret of the closet is so great and pervasive. I think Mohr too readily trades con-crete and significant individual harms and indigni-ties for a hypothetical and incremental increase in the abstract quantity of overall dignity.

It is important to realize that objecting to outing does not require defending the closet. Lesbians and gays should certainly be encouraged to come out as a matter of moral virtue. But as long as homosexual-ity is stigmatized in ways that heterosexuality is not, being publicly gay will be personally dangerous and politically volatile. Except in unusual circum-stances, individuals should have the freedom to de-cide for themselves whether to join the sociopolitical fray, rather than being made political footballs by others professing to know better the proper course for their lives.

There is no one way—certainly no correct way—to be gay, although some gays speak as if there were. What being gay means to a person and whether, when, and to what extent one shall be publicly iden-tified as gay are decisions properly left to the indi-vidual. Tyranny takes many forms—wherever a per-son is victimized by coercive power. Outers, who know well that information is power, commit a tyranny of the few. In doing so, they betray one of gay activism's fundamental values: the right to pur-sue one's life free from domination and interference by others.

David J. Mayo
Martin Gunderson | # Privacy and the Ethics of Outing

DIGNITY AND THE CLOSET

According to Mohr, the closet is an institution which is so evil and insidious that the moral individual, as a matter of dignity, cannot participate in its existence or continuation. Mohr's non-utilitarian defense of outing involves rich and complex arguments which we cannot treat fully here. Instead, we will isolate several important threads of his defense of outing in order to assess their success.

Mohr agrees with utilitarian critics that the closet is the primary mechanism by which gays and les-bians are oppressed. Moreover, Mohr grants that gays within the gay community do generally recog-nize a code of secrecy regarding sexual orientation. He refers to this code or convention of honoring each other's secrecy as "The Secret.". Indeed, Mohr sees The Secret as "*the* gay social convention . . . the structuring element, the DNA, the constitutive convention of the gay community" (29–30). The

From David J. Mayo and Martin Gunderson, "Privacy and the Ethics of Outing," in *Gay Ethics: Outing, Civil Rights, and Sexual Science,* ed. Timothy F. Murphy (New York: The Haworth Press, 1994), pp. 47–65. Some parts of the text have been deleted. Reprinted by permission of the Haworth Press, Inc.

closet and The Secret are especially insidious, he thinks, for two reasons. Borrowing from the account offered by Jeremiah McCarthy in this volume, Mohr insists that the closet doesn't merely oppress gays. Through the convention of The Secret, it also recruits them as willing agents of their own oppression. This dual tyranny is possible only so long as they cooperate and respect The Secret. The second reason is that the gay person who respects The Secret "accept[s] insult so that one avoids harm" (31), and in so doing "commits to the view of gays that the convention presupposes: that gays are loathsome and disgusting, to be kept from sight, nauseating if touched or seen, filth always to be flushed away" (33). Mohr views this as "a complete capitulation to the general social belief that the only good gay is a nonexistent one" (30). Any gay respecting The Secret, regarding himself or another, "commit[s] his life to the very values that keep him oppressed" (31). Mohr concludes that *as a matter of dignity* gays must renounce The Secret, neither remaining closeted themselves, nor participating in the closet on behalf of others.

We take exception to two of these claims. The first is that those who respect The Secret not only pay lip service to the values which oppress them but actually share, embrace, and even "commit their lives" to them. While some persons doubtless remain in the closet out of a sense of shame, it simply doesn't follow that *any* gay or lesbian who remains closeted shares or accepts homophobic values. This is true even if one acknowledges he is indirectly contributing to homophobia. Shame is not the only possible motivation for remaining closeted. Concern for either individual welfare or individual rights might also provide such motivation. For instance, a gay man may believe that remaining closeted himself, or not outing a lesbian, will reduce the risk of very real harms in a homophobic world. But even if he believes a closeted lesbian's fears are irrational and she would be better off if she were out, he may keep The Secret out of obligation, knowing that another had revealed herself to him in light of the convention and expected benefits of The Secret:

trusting others to keep her sexual orientation confidential. He *might* even keep The Secret (again for himself or another) out of love or compassion for a homophobic straight. Imagine a gay man who is comfortable with himself, who loves a frail, elderly parent who is of another age and homophobic. In the abstract, it is easy enough to claim that we shouldn't humor others' hateful prejudices. However, there *are* competing values, and it seems either dogmatic or naive to insist in advance that there are *never* circumstances in which competing values should prevail. Mohr quotes Steve Berry approvingly: "The principle is really very simple. Either being gay is OK or it isn't" (37). But for most of us things really *aren't* that simple.

Second, we take issue with Mohr's claim that consideration of dignity alone should dictate the morality of actions, and that happiness (for oneself or others) is irrelevant to the morality of outing. Having grounded his case for outing squarely in considerations of dignity, Mohr is willing to let the utilitarian chips fall where they may: "It is not one's happiness that one is seeking through outing—it is the avoidance of being an instrument of insult to one's own dignity, the avoidance of complicity in one's own degradation" (43). He does acknowledge that many gays remain closeted for economic reasons or even to retain custody of their children, but he finds this morally irrelevant: "the closet case . . . barter[s] away his self-respect, his worthiness for respect, his dignity, for happiness, regard, and nonrespectful love . . . accepts insult to avoid harm . . . [and thus] becomes a simulacrum—a deceptive substitute . . . of a person" (31–32). Moreover, the indignity is not confined merely to the closeted person alone. The openly gay person who keeps The Secret for others commits himself "to a similar vision of gay people and so commit[s] him[self] to give up his own dignity for the happiness of the closeted gay person. To do that," Mohr adds, "is the very inversion of the moral life" (33). At one point, Mohr acknowledges "*if* it were the case . . . that the government was shooting gays, I would morally be expected to suspend my dignity temporarily. . . ."

But he then goes on to insist that even this would not be a matter of the protection of happiness but done "so that the current and prospective dignity of others is made possible" (34).

We believe Mohr is simply mistaken in holding that dignity simply outweighs all other values here—that "a dignity may outweigh a dignity, as a pleasure or measure of happiness may not" (34). We would hope, moreover, that Mohr would lie not only to save another's life but that he would be willing to do so simply as a matter of compassion, without having to reconstruct it as a matter of dignity. Again, life is not as simple as Steve Berry suggests it is. In any event, it is not simple enough that one can always put dignity first. Life is morally complicated: along with dignity, we believe morality sometimes requires us to take account of both human welfare and individual rights.

8

Is Adultery Wrong?

Wasserstrom and His Critics

According to traditional Western morality, sex is permissible only between a man and a woman who are married to each other. With the revolution in attitudes toward sex that occurred in the second half of the twentieth century, however, many of the tenets of traditional sexual morality were abandoned. Now few people outside deeply religious circles pronounce all sex outside monogamous marital relationships immoral. Various relaxations of the traditional view have been widely accepted. Nevertheless, as Bonnie Steinbock points out in her contribution to this section, attitudes toward *adultery* have remained fairly stable throughout these changes.

In the feature article of this chapter, Richard Wasserstrom raises the question of whether adultery really is immoral, and his answer is negative. His strategy, for the most part, is one of process of elimination. He considers what he takes to be the plausible arguments *for* the immorality of adultery and finds each one wanting. (He does briefly consider arguments *against* the immorality of adultery, but these are largely dependent on his consideration of the arguments for the immorality of adultery.)

To have an *argument* for the immorality of adultery (as opposed to, say, simply adopting it as self-evident) one must appeal to some feature that adultery necessarily possesses and about which there are already some plausible, or at least agreed upon, moral principles. Two features adultery appears to have and about the morality of which we are generally agreed are promise-breaking and deception. Both promise-breaking and deception are, in themselves, immoral. That is not to say that it is always and everywhere immoral to break a promise or to deceive someone. We can imagine circumstances in which it is permissible to break a promise. I might promise to meet you at noon for lunch, but in my haste to make that appointment I knock over a pedestrian with my car, injuring him seriously. Clearly, I would be morally obliged to give the injured pedestrian assistance, even at the cost of breaking my lunch promise to you. The obligation to lend assistance here outweighs the wrongness of my promise-breaking. If an action involves breaking a promise, that is definitely a moral consideration against the action, but there may be strong reasons in favor of the action that out-weigh the wrongness of the promise-breaking, making it morally permissible, all things con-sidered. Promise-breaking is thus what Wasserstrom calls prima facie immoral, and the immorality of breaking a promise depends in part on how serious or important the promise is. The more important the promise the more seriously immoral it is to break it, and the harder it is to override the obligation to keep the promise. This suggests a quick argument for the immorality of adultery.

P1   Married people promise to abstain from sex with third parties.
P2   Adultery necessarily involves breaking this deep and important promise.
P3   Breaking a deep and important promise is prima facie seriously immoral.

C   Adultery is prima facie seriously immoral.

A second argument appeals to the immorality of deception. Since marriage involves the promise to abstain from sex with third parties, those who indulge in extramarital affairs typ-ically try to hide them from their spouses. This typically involves lying and other forms of deception on a fairly large scale. Again, there is at least an implicit agreement that in mar-rying someone you will not systematically deceive them about important matters.

P1   Adultery necessarily involves widespread deception.
P2   Widespread deception about an important matter is prima facie seriously immoral.

C   Adultery is prima facie seriously immoral.

Wasserstrom develops a subsidiary argument for the idea that adultery necessarily involves deception of *someone,* even if not one's spouse. There is, in Western culture at least, a strong tie between sexual intimacy and the expression of romantic love and devotion. Sexual inti-macy is one of the main ways to convey romantic attachment to another. To engage in sex with someone, under normal conditions, is thus to appear to inform them that you are in love with them. If we conjoin this with the widespread idea that one cannot really be in love with two different people at once, then we have an argument that the adulterer must be deceiving *someone*—either the spouse or the partner in adultery. (This argument must assume that the adulterer is still having sex with his or her spouse.)

Wasserstrom grants that both promise-breaking and deception are prima facie immoral. But he disputes the first premise of each argument. First, consider a married couple who agree to a so-called "open marriage." Neither promises sexual exclusivity to the other, and each gives the other permission to have extramarital sex. Both would be adulterous, because both would indulge in extramarital sex, but no promises would be broken and no deception would be perpetrated. If Wasserstrom is right that an agreement to have an open marriage is possible, then the promise-breaking argument is unsound. It would be entirely possible for a married person to have extramarital sex without breaking any promises. What about decep-tion? Our couple might have a policy of "don't ask, don't tell," which would probably involve a certain amount of deception. But they might agree instead that when one or the other has an extramarital affair, he or she will not try to hide it, but rather will discuss it openly with his or her marital partner. If such a relationship could be sustained, then the deception argument also fails.

The simple version of the deception argument—that by indulging in an affair one will be deceiving one's spouse—is thus exposed as unsound if such a marriage is genuinely possible. What about Wasserstrom's subsidiary deception argument? Recall that that involves some further assumptions: that to have sex with someone is thereby to present yourself as being in love with them; that one cannot love two people at once; and that the adulterer has an active sexual relationship with two people—not only his (her) partner in adultery but also his (her) spouse. It follows from all this that the adulterer must be deceiving the one or the other. This argument has more premises than the simple deception argument, and provided it is possible to detach sex from expressions of love, at least one premise is false. Further, the argument assumes that the kind of love expressed through sex can only be directed at one other person. Wasserstrom argues that this premise is also likely to be false.

Wasserstrom considers a third and quite different kind of argument for the immorality of adultery, one that involves the desirability of maintaining an institution of marriage in which sexual exclusivity is the norm.

P1   Strong, stable nuclear families are required if children are to be raised successfully.

P2   Sexual exclusivity between married people supports strong, stable nuclear families, and lack of sexual exclusivity tends to undermine that.

C   Adultery is prima facie immoral.

There may well be evidence that children tend to fare better in stable nuclear families, and that the higher divorce rates in the last half of the twentieth century were at least in part a result of increased extramarital sex. But even supposing both premises to be true, does the conclusion *follow* from them? Is the argument *valid?* Wasserstrom argues that it might not be, and he does so by constructing a parody of the argument—a parallel argument that is both invalid and, if and only if this first argument is valid. Suppose we found that the following rule enhanced the strength and stability of nuclear families: One is permitted to eat a pleasurable meal only with one's spouse, and with all others one may only consume bread and water. Wasserstrom argues that if this rule were enforced it would provide a very strong incentive for people to get married, and stay married, because one large important class of pleasures would be available only to those who were married. Let us call this institution "marital gustatory exclusivity." Imagine a situation in which the institution of gustatory exclusivity was in operation and in which the accepted moral code allowed only married couples to enjoy gustatory pleasure with each other. (Something like this does prevail in various non-Western cultures.) Then, in such a situation it might well be that loosening that prohibition would tend to make it less attractive for people to stay in their marriages. But would it be *immoral* to go out to dinner with someone other than one's spouse?

Wasserstrom does not outline this parody explicitly. However, he does claim that it shows that even if sexual exclusivity in marriage is a good way to maintain the institution (just as gustatory pleasure would be such a way), it does not follow that adultery is *morally* wrong. Once the prohibition is in place, it might be a good thing if people *generally* conformed to it, even though it is not *morally* impermissible for anyone to violate it.

Ween, in his critique, claims that Wasserstrom's enumeration of arguments against adultery overlooks the central and most important of these. Ween gives a rather simpleminded argument at first, but he hints at a more developed one. The simpleminded argument is this: To be willing to commit adultery one has to be married. Marriage involves a promise of, and commitment to, sexual fidelity, while adultery involves a violation of sexual fidelity. The adulterer thus endorses a contradiction: committing himself to sexual fidelity while intending to commit adultery. On the face of it, this simpleminded argument does not sound much different from the promise-breaking argument Wasserstrom outlines and criticizes. As we will see, Don Marquis, in his contribution, faults Wreen's argument along just these lines.

Wreen's claim that a promise of sexual fidelity is essential to marriage denies one of the main assumptions that Wasserstrom employs in his critique of the deception and promise-breaking arguments: the real possibility of an open marriage. In Wreen's account an open marriage is like a false friend, and a false friend is no friend at all. Similarly, according to Wreen, an "open marriage" is no marriage at all.

Bonnie Steinbock, in her contribution, reviews both the deception and promise-breaking arguments, and agrees with Wasserstrom's conclusion that neither establishes the moral impermissibility of adultery. Also, like Wasserstrom, but unlike Wreen, Steinbock finds nothing *inconsistent* in the notion of an open marriage. However, she presents a rather different kind of argument in favor of marital fidelity. First, she claims that it is entirely natural to link sex with expressions of affection and intimacy, and for feelings of love or affection to occur between people enjoying sexual intercourse. "People naturally have feelings of affection for those who make them happy, and sex is a very good way of making someone extraordinarily happy." This does not establish an ideal of fidelity, though, without the presumption that sexual love should be reserved for exactly one other person. Here Steinbock offers only a sketch of an argument, noting that the "logistics of multiple involvement are certainly daunting. Having an affair (as opposed to a roll in the hay) requires time and concentration; it will almost inevitably mean neglecting one's spouse, one's children, one's work." This is still not quite enough to establish the ideal of marital fidelity as a desirable one, however, since it requires the additional assumption that one can love only one person. Steinbock goes on to plug this logical gap: ". . . exclusivity seems to be an intrinsic part of 'true love.' . . . In our ideal of romantic love, one chooses to forgo pleasure with other partners in order to have a unique relationship with one's beloved." Steinbock's conclusion is summarized in the following passage:

> . . . open marriages are not *immoral,* although they deviate from a valued ideal of what marriage should be. While this is not the only ideal, or incumbent on all rational agents, it is a moral view in that it embodies a claim about a good way for people to live. The prohibition of adultery, then, is neither arbitrary nor irrational.

Steinbock's conclusion is thus that, although it is not obligatory for married partners to impose on themselves an obligation to be faithful, if they want to pursue the worthy and reasonable ideal of romantic love, to be romantically in love with their married partner, then they are justified, morally and rationally, in imposing that obligation on themselves.

Marquis finds the accounts of the wrongness of adultery in the articles by Wasserstrom, Wreen, and Steinbock "inadequate or oversimplified," while nevertheless granting that there is some aspect of truth buried in each. The wrongness of adultery has to have something to do with promise-breaking, the nature of marriage, and an ideal of married love. However, with Wasserstrom, Marquis thinks that the promise-breaking account fails to explain why adultery is typically considered a *serious* wrong. Breaking promises is not always considered as bad as adultery. In Wreen's account, Marquis takes issue with what we have called Wreen's simpleminded argument. The adulterer need not be involved in any kind of contradiction by both committing himself to fidelity and intending to break that very commitment. She commits to fidelity at one time (on her wedding day, say), but later on she changes her mind and abandons the commitment. There is nothing *logically* incoherent in that. But Marquis also has an objection to any account, such as the one we have sketched on Wreen's behalf that would entail that *every* instance of adultery was morally wrong. Marquis claims that this is simply implausible. Finally, Marquis argues that Steinbock's account suffers a different kind of defect: it does not entail that adultery is *ever* really wrong. To fail to adopt a very worthy ideal or to fail to live up to an ideal once adopted is typically not considered morally wrong. (We do not criticize someone who is less perfect than Mother Theresa for failing to embody fully the worthy ideal Mother Theresa espouses, even if we think that Mother Theresa's ideal is a praiseworthy one.)

Marquis goes on to offer an account of what makes adultery wrong, when it is wrong, and what would make it permissible—an account that he claims captures whatever truth there is in the preceding three accounts.

He contrasts what he calls the "covenant model" of marriage with the "contract model." In the covenant model, two people make *unconditional* promises (of sexual fidelity, among others). They promise to be faithful and stick with each other "for better or for worse, until death do us part." But in the contract model, marriage is a contract involving various *conditional* promises.

A contract is an agreement that two or more people enter into, and in which they typically promise to do various things for the other party to the contract. But the promises involved in a contract are typically conditional upon the other party's fulfilling various conditions. Each party promises to comply with the terms of the contract on the condition that other party does so. For example, I have entered into a labor contract with a university. I promise to perform various teaching, research, and administrative duties, conditional upon the university paying me a monthly salary. The university promises to pay me a monthly salary, conditional upon my carrying out those duties to a certain standard. Neither I nor the university makes an *unconditional* promise (to work, or to pay) *come what may*. If one party to the contract fails to satisfy those conditions, that can release the other party from a duty to carry out *their* conditional. So, if I fail to perform all the duties I promised (I fail to turn up to class, say), I cannot justly complain if the university fails to pay me. And if the university fails to pay me, it cannot complain if I don't show up to teach my classes.

What kind of a contract is marriage, according to Marquis? In marrying, two close friends make a large number of quite substantial promises—promises that involve altering their life plans—including one to love each other and to find sexual fulfillment through each other and only with each other. They make these promises, and organize their life plans around them, because each believes that marriage to the other will enhance his or her own well-being. A marriage is a good one if it turns out that, by fulfilling his or her promises, each helps to make the other happy. But in the nature of a contract, these promises contain various conditions.

Suppose your spouse keeps up her end of the bargain, and thereby provides you with a reasonable level of well-being, and as a consequence you judge your marriage to be a good one. Then, in the contract model, it would be wrong for you to go out and commit adultery. Your partner has kept up her side of the bargain, so in committing adultery you are breaking the promises you made to her. But not all marriages are good. Some marriages are bad. One response to a bad marriage is divorce, but that can be extremely difficult or ill-advised. There may be overriding reasons (finances, the upbringing of children, and so on) for someone to stay in a bad marriage. Suppose we confine our attention to bad marriages that, for various reasons, should nevertheless be maintained. Marquis outlines a series of cases in which a husband fails to fully comply with the implicit conditions on the wife's promise to remain sexually faithful, thereby releasing his wife from that promise. If a wife discovers that her husband is having sex with someone else, for example, that releases her from her conditional obligation to remain sexually faithful to him. Or suppose her husband no longer loves her or he fails to satisfy her sexually, even though it would be within his power to do so, thus denying her the level of sexual satisfaction he implicitly promised her. These might also be plausibly regarded as the husband's failure to comply with the implicit conditions of her pledge to sexual fidelity, thereby releasing her from the burden of sexual fidelity to him.

We can illustrate this formally.

P1   Marriage is a contract involving various conditional promises.

P2   The marital pledge of sexual fidelity is conditional upon one's spouse's satisfying certain conditions (including, among other things, sexual fidelity, contributing appropriately to your well-being, and so on).

P3   It is morally wrong to violate a conditional promise if the conditions are satisfied, but it is morally permissible if the conditions are not satisfied.

C   If the conditions of the marital promise of sexual fidelity are satisfied, then it is morally wrong for you to commit adultery, but if the conditions of the promise of sexual fidelity are not satisfied, then adultery is morally permissible.

Inspired by Kant's moral theory, Wreen's argument that there is some kind of contradiction involved in adultery is not well articulated, as Marquis points out. But it could be developed in a much more interesting way, utilizing an insight made famous by Kant. This provides us with an opportunity to give a brief background introduction to Kant's central insight, which is appealed in many of the articles in this volume.

Philosopher Immanuel Kant claimed that all moral laws could be derived from one general principle, which he called the Categorical Imperative: "Act only on that maxim by which you can at the same time will that it should become a universal law."

The central idea behind Kant's quite simple but also quite profound principle is based on a phenomenon with which everyone is familiar. The standard objection people often make to any morally dubious behavior is, "What if *everyone* did that?" For example, suppose you want to see the first screening of a movie but when you get to the cinema, the line at the ticket booth is so long that you are not going to get a seat if you take your place at the back of the line. Then you see that there is a place close to the front of the line, beside a column, where you could cut in the line without being noticed. You proceed to do so. Intuitively we feel this is wrong. If someone spied you cutting in line they might ask, "What if *everyone* did that?" What exactly is the force of that rebuke? Why would it miss the point to reply: "Well, lucky for me, everyone is not doing it. In fact I am the only one doing it, and so if I can get away with it, that suits me just fine thank you!"?

Kant has an interesting way of answering this question. He would ask: what maxim (policy, or rule) are you implicitly acting on when you decide to cut in line in these circumstances? You are implicitly acting on, and in some sense endorsing, the maxim: Whenever it suits my purposes to do so, I will cut in line. Kant points out that there is nothing special about you. If it is permissible for you to act on this maxim, it must be permissible for anyone else, similarly situated, to so act. So, in effect, by your action you are *recommending* this maxim as a general policy that everyone should follow. You are effectively willing that everyone follow this rule. Does that make sense? Can you coherently will that your maxim become a universally followed rule? Can you consistently require that everyone act as you are acting? This is called the universalization of this maxim, and it generates the following universal principle: Whenever it suits a person to do so, he should cut in line.

If everybody were prepared to cut in line, there would be no lines left to cut into. You cannot cut into a line if there is no line in the first place. So, the universalization of your maxim generates a certain logical problem, one that Kant calls a "contradiction". To cut in line, there must be lines. For there to be lines, people must be prepared to stay in line. If everyone acted on your maxim, however, no one would be prepared to stay in line and so there would be no lines at all to cut into. It is thus irrational to recommend your maxim to everyone, and hence irrational even for you to adopt it.

According to Kant, all correct moral principles are like this. Morally permissible acts are instances of maxims or rules that can be consistently universalized, whereas morally impermissible acts are instances of maxims that cannot be so universalized. The attempt to universalize them involves a kind of logical incoherence—the incoherence of recommending a course of action that it would be impossible to carry out if everyone followed that recommendation.

Wreen claims that the adulterer is implicitly involved in a violation of Kant's Categorical Imperative, but as Wreen states his argument it is not clear how it fits the Kantian model. But let us suppose that Smith is married (say, to Mrs. Smith) but that one day he finds himself sexually attracted to the beguiling Ms Jones. Ms Jones also fancies Smith and indicates that she is sexually available, and straight away they have sex. What maxim is Smith acting on? Maybe it is this: Whenever I am sexually attracted to a person who is not my spouse, I will commit adultery with her/him provided she/he is willing.

Can Smith recommend that everyone follow this rule to commit adultery whenever the opportunity presents itself? Well, suppose everybody were to follow this policy, and everyone were to accept that everyone else is acting on this rule. Would that mean the end of the institution of marriage? Would it be just like the line-cutting maxim? You are able to cut in line when there is an institution of line formation on which people agree and that they regard as placing legitimate constraints on what they would otherwise like to do. But if everyone were to cut in line whenever it suited them, there would be no lines at all, and cutting in line would be *impossible*. When there is an institution of marriage, you are certainly able to commit adultery. But if everyone were primed to commit adultery with anyone with whom they felt a sufficient mutual sexual attraction, then would there still be such a thing as marriage? If the answer to that is "No, there would be no such institution if everyone behaved like *that*," then in such a situation it would be impossible to commit adultery, and so the adulterer's maxim could not be coherently universalized.

Why would there be no such thing as marriage in such a situation? Why would it not just be a situation in which married people commited adultery all the time? Wreen may have an answer to this. He disagrees with Wasserstrom about the essential features of marriage. He claims that the promise of sexual fidelity is essential to being married. He claims that marriage necessarily involves a promise of sexual fidelity. Thus, you cannot be married without having promised, implicitly or explicitly, to be sexually faithful to your marriage partner (or partners; Wreen does not endorse sexual exclusivity as part of marriage, because he wants to leave open the possibility that polygamy is still genuine marriage). You have to be married to commit adultery, and marriage has to be understood as involving a commitment to sexual fidelity. But in a society in which people universally adopt Smith's maxim, no one would have sincerely promised sexual fidelity, no one would be married, and so the institution of marriage would not exist.

The would-be adulterer is thus implicitly involved in logical incoherence. He advocates a policy (that of committing adultery when it seems attractive to do so) that, if everyone adopted it, would make it impossible to commit adultery—because no one would be married in the first place.

QUESTIONS FOR CONSIDERATION

• It is striking that none of the first three articles in this chapter consider that the threat of sexually transmitted diseases or the possibility of unwanted pregnancy raises any moral problems. In fact, both Wasserstrom and Steinbock are even dismissive of the moral importance of these. (Note also that the first three articles were written after contraception became regarded as morally acceptable, reliable, and widespread, but before the HIV/AIDS epidemic took hold.) Does the possibility of contracting a life-threatening and highly contagious disease have a bearing on the morality of sexual fidelity? If adultery exposes your marital partner to a chance of acquiring a fatal condition does that make it wrong? If not, why not?

• Suppose you agree that the risk of infecting your marital partner with a fatal or debilitating illness does make adultery wrong. Does it follow that taking your marital partner on a surprise rock-climbing adventure or a downhill skiing vacation, is morally wrong for the same reason? If not, what is the morally relevant difference between these two?

• Is Marquis right that the *contract* model is the preferred model for marriage? Does his argument fail if the correct model for marriage is the covenant? What could adjudicate between these two models? Is it just a matter of choice?

• Should those who are getting married make it explicit whether it is a contract or a covenant that they are entering into?

• Are there arguments for preferring the covenant model? Would those who thought of themselves as in a covenant be more motivated to keep their promises than those who thought of themselves as in a contract?

• If marriage is a contract, then why do we not regard the contract as simply *voided* once one of the parties to it violates its conditions? That is to say, if each party promises sexual fidelity to the other (conditional upon various provisos), then once one of the parties is adulterous, has not the contract been broken? Is not the marriage actually over? Compare this situation with other contracts with which you are familiar.

• Does the contract account capture what makes adultery wrong? Why, for example, is the discovery of adultery typically so much more painful for the faithful spouse than the discovery of violations of other contracts?

• In the introduction to this chapter we attempt to rescue Wreen's Kantian objection to adultery—that the adulterer is involved in a contradiction in the same sense in which a line-cutter is involved in a contradiction. That is to say, the adulterer's maxim cannot be universalized without rendering the maxim inapplicable. But is this rescue successful? The line-cutter cannot recommend that everyone cut in line without destroying the practice he wants to exploit—the fact that other people are patiently waiting in line. Is this the same with adultery? Suppose the compulsive adulterer says something like this: "You haven't correctly identified the maxim I am operating with. All I want is to have sex with willing partners wherever and whenever they are willing. Suppose everyone were to act on my maxim. That wouldn't stop me having sex with whomever I want to have it with. Far from stopping me acting on the maxim, it would actually make it easier for me."

FURTHER READING

Halwani, Raja Fouad. "Virtue Ethics and Adultery." *Journal of Social Philosophy* 29, no. 3 (1998): pp. 5–18.

Richard Wasserstrom | Is Adultery Immoral?

Many discussions of the enforcement of morality by the law take as illustrative of the problem under consideration the regulation of various types of sexual behavior by the criminal law. It was, for example, the Wolfenden Report's recommendations concerning homosexuality and prostitution that led Lord Devlin to compose his now famous lecture, "The Enforcement of Morals." And that lecture in turn provoked important philosophical responses from H. L. A. Hart, Ronald Dworkin, and others.

Much, if not all, of the recent philosophical literature on the enforcement of morals appears to take for granted the immorality of the sexual behavior in question. The focus of discussion, at least, is whether such things as homosexuality, prostitution, and adultery ought to be made illegal even if they are immoral, and not whether they are immoral.

I propose in this paper to think about the latter, more neglected topic, that of sexual morality, and to do so in the following fashion. I shall consider just one kind of behavior that is often taken to be a case of sexual immorality—adultery. I am interested in pursuing at least two questions. First, I want to explore the question of in what respects adulterous behavior falls within the domain of morality at all: For this surely is one of the puzzles one encounters when considering the topic of sexual morality. It is often hard to see on what grounds much of the behavior is deemed to be either moral or immoral, for example, private homosexual behavior between consenting adults. I have purposely selected adultery because it seems a more plausible candidate for moral assessment than many other kinds of sexual behavior.

The second question I want to examine is that of what is to be said about adultery, without being especially concerned to stay within the area of morality.

I shall endeavor, in other words, to identify and to assess a number of the major arguments that might be advanced against adultery. I believe that they are the chief arguments that would be given in support of the view that adultery is immoral, but I think they are worth considering even if some of them turn out to be nonmoral arguments and considerations.

A number of the issues involved seem to me to be complicated and difficult. In a number of places I have at best indicated where further philosophical exploration is required without having successfully conducted the exploration myself. The paper may very well be more useful as an illustration of how one might begin to think about the subject of sexual morality than as an elucidation of important truths about the topic.

Before I turn to the arguments themselves there are two preliminary points that require some clarification. Throughout the paper I shall refer to the immorality of such things as breaking a promise, deceiving someone, etc. In a very rough way, I mean by this that there is something morally wrong that is done in doing the action in question. I mean that the action is, in a strong sense, of "prima facie" prima facie wrong or unjustified. I do not mean that it may never be right or justifiable to do the action; just that the fact that it is an action of this description always does count against the rightness of the action. I leave entirely open the question of what it is that makes actions of this kind immoral in this sense of "immoral."

The second preliminary point concerns what is meant or implied by the concept of adultery. I mean by "adultery" any case of extramarital sex, and I want to explore the arguments for and against extramarital sex, undertaken in a variety of morally relevant situations. Someone might claim that the con-

From Richard Wasserstrom, "Is Adultery Immoral?" in *Philosophy and Sex,* ed. Robert Baker and Frederick Elliston, pp. 207–21 (Buffalo, N.Y.: Prometheus Books, 1975). Reprinted by permission of the author.

cept of adultery is conceptually connected with the concept of immorality, and that to characterize behavior as adulterous is already to characterize it as immoral or unjustified in the sense described above. There may be something to this. Hence the importance of making it clear that I want to talk about extramarital sexual relations. If they are always immoral, this is something that must be shown by argument. If the concept of adultery does in some sense entail or imply immorality, I want to ask whether that connection is a rationally based one. If not all cases of extramarital sex are immoral (again, in the sense described above), then the concept of adultery should either be weakened accordingly or restricted to those classes of extramarital sex for which the predication of immorality is warranted.

One argument for the immorality of adultery might go something like this: what makes adultery immoral is that it involves the breaking of a promise, and what makes adultery seriously wrong is that it involves the breaking of an important promise. For, so the argument might continue, one of the things the two parties promise each other when they get married is that they will abstain from sexual relationships with third persons. Because of this promise both spouses quite reasonably entertain the expectation that the other will behave in conformity with it. Hence, when one of the parties has sexual intercourse with a third person he or she breaks that promise about sexual relationships which was made when the marriage was entered into, and defeats the reasonable expectations of exclusivity entertained by the spouse.

In many cases the immorality involved in breaching the promise relating to extramarital sex may be a good deal more serious than that involved in the breach of other promises. This is so because adherence to this promise may be of much greater importance to the parties than is adherence to many of the other promises given or received by them in their lifetime. The breaking of this promise may be much more hurtful and painful than is typically the case.

Why is this so? To begin with, it may have been difficult for the non-adulterous spouse to have kept the promise. Hence that spouse may feel the unfairness of having restrained himself or herself in the absence of reciprocal restraint having been exercised by the adulterous spouse. In addition, the spouse may perceive the breaking of the promise as an indication of a kind of indifference on the part of the adulterous spouse. If you really cared about me and my feelings—the spouse might say—you would not have done this to me. And third, and related to the above, the spouse may see the act of sexual intercourse with another as a sign of affection for the other person and as an additional rejection of the non-adulterous spouse as the one who is loved by the adulterous spouse. It is not just that the adulterous spouse does not take the feelings of the spouse sufficiently into account, the adulterous spouse also indicates through the act of adultery affection for someone other than the spouse. I will return to these points later. For the present, it is sufficient to note that a set of arguments can be developed in support of the proposition that certain kinds of adultery are wrong just because they involve the breach of a serious promise which, among other things, leads to the intentional infliction of substantial pain by one spouse upon the other.

Another argument for the immorality of adultery focuses not on the existence of a promise of sexual exclusivity but on the connection between adultery and deception. According to this argument, adultery involves deception. And because deception is wrong, so is adultery.

Although it is certainly not obviously so, I shall simply assume in this paper that deception is always immoral. Thus the crucial issue for my purposes is the asserted connection between extramarital sex and deception. Is it plausible to maintain, as this argument does, that adultery always does involve deception and is on that basis to be condemned?

The most obvious person on whom deceptions might be practiced is the nonparticipating spouse; and the most obvious thing about which the nonparticipating spouse can be deceived is the existence of the adulterous act. One clear case of deception is that of lying. Instead of saying that the afternoon was spent in bed with A, the adulterous spouse asserts that it was spent in the library with B, or on the golf course with C.

There can also be deception even when no lies are told. Suppose, for instance, that a person has sexual intercourse with someone other than his or her spouse and just does not tell the spouse about it. Is that deception? It may not be a case of lying if, for example, the spouse is never asked by the other about the situation. Still, we might say, it is surely deceptive because of the promises that were exchanged at marriage. As we saw earlier, these promises provide a foundation for the reasonable belief that neither spouse will engage in sexual relationships with any other persons. Hence the failure to bring the fact of extramarital sex to the attention of the other spouse deceives that spouse about the present state of the marital relationship.

Adultery, in other words, can involve both active and passive deception. An adulterous spouse may just keep silent or, as is often the fact, the spouse may engage in an increasingly complex way of life devoted to the concealment of the facts from the nonparticipating spouse. Lies, half-truths, clandestine meetings, and the like may become a central feature of the adulterous spouse's existence. These are things that can and do happen, and when they do they make the case against adultery an easy one. Still, neither active nor passive deception is inevitably a feature of an extramarital relationship.

It is possible, though, that a more subtle but pervasive kind of deceptiveness is a feature of adultery. It comes about because of the connection in our culture between sexual intimacy and certain feelings of love and affection. The point can be made indirectly at first by seeing that one way in which we can, in our culture, mark off our close friends from our mere acquaintances is through the kinds of intimacies that we are prepared to share with them. I may, for instance, be willing to reveal my very private thoughts and emotions to my closest friends or to my wife, but to no one else. My sharing of these intimate facts about myself is from one perspective a way of making a gift to those who mean the most to me. Revealing these things and sharing them with those who mean the most to me is one means by which I create, maintain, and confirm those interpersonal relationships that are of most importance to me.

Now in our culture, it might be claimed, sexual intimacy is one of the chief currencies through which gifts of this sort are exchanged. One way to tell someone—particularly someone of the opposite sex—that you have feelings of affection and love for them is by allowing to them or sharing with them sexual behaviors that one doesn't share with the rest of the world. This way of measuring affection was certainly very much a part of the culture in which I matured. It worked something like this. If you were a girl, you showed how much you liked someone by the degree of sexual intimacy you would allow. If you liked a boy only a little, you never did more than kiss—and even the kiss was not very passionate. If you liked the boy a lot and if your feeling was reciprocated, necking, and possibly petting, was permissible. If the attachment was still stronger and you thought it might even become a permanent relationship, the sexual activity was correspondingly more intense and more intimate, although whether it would ever lead to sexual intercourse depended on whether the parties (and particularly the girl) accepted fully the prohibition on non-marital sex. The situation for the boy was related, but not exactly the same. The assumption was that males did not naturally link sex with affection in the way in which females did. However, since women did, males had to take this into account. That is to say, because a woman would permit sexual intimacies only if she had feelings of affection for the male and only if those feelings were reciprocated, the male had to have and express those feelings, too, before sexual intimacies of any sort would occur.

The result was that the importance of a correlation between sexual intimacy and feelings of love and affection was taught by the culture and assimilated by those growing up in the culture. The scale of possible positive feelings toward persons of the other sex ran from casual liking at the one end to the love that was deemed essential to and characteristic of marriage at the other. The scale of possible sexual behavior ran from brief, passionless kissing or handholding at the one end to sexual intercourse at the other. And the correlation between the two scales was quite precise. As a result, any act of sexual intimacy carried substantial meaning with it, and no act of sexual intimacy was simply a pleasurable set of bodily sensations. Many such acts were, of course, more pleasurable to the participants because they were a way of saying what the participants feelings were. And sometimes they were less pleasurable for the same reason. The point is, however, that in any event sexual activity was much more than mere bodily enjoyment. It was not like eating a good meal, listening to good music, lying in the sun, or getting a pleasant back rub. It was behavior that meant a great deal concerning one's feelings for persons of the opposite sex in whom one was most interested and with whom one was most involved. It was among the most authoritative ways in which one could communicate to another the nature and degree of one's affection.

If this sketch is even roughly right, then several things become somewhat clearer. To begin with, a possible rationale for many of the rules of conventional sexual morality can be developed. If, for example, sexual intercourse is associated with the kind of affection and commitment to another that is regarded as characteristic of the marriage relationship, then it is natural that sexual intercourse should be thought properly to take place between persons who are married to each other. And if it is thought that this kind of affection and commitment is only to be found within the marriage relationship, then it is not surprising that sexual intercourse should only be thought to be proper within marriage.

Related to what has just been said is the idea that sexual intercourse ought to be restricted to those who are married to each other as a means by which to confirm the very special feelings that the spouses have for each other. Because the culture teaches that sexual intercourse means that the strongest of all feelings for each other are shared by the lovers, it is natural that persons who are married to each other should be able to say this to each other in this way. Revealing and confirming verbally that these feelings are present is one thing that helps to sustain the relationship; engaging in sexual intercourse is another.

In addition, this account would help to provide a framework within which to make sense of the notion that some sex is better than other sex. As I indicated

earlier, the fact that sexual intimacy can be meaningful in the sense described tends to make it also the case that sexual intercourse can sometimes be more enjoyable than at other times. On this view, sexual intercourse will typically be more enjoyable where the strong feelings of affection are present than it will be where it is merely "mechanical." This is so in part because people enjoy being loved, especially by those whom they love. Just as we like to hear words of affection, so we like to receive affectionate behavior. And the meaning enhances the independently pleasurable behavior.

More to the point, moreover, an additional rationale for the prohibition on extramarital sex can now be developed. For given this way of viewing the sexual world, extramarital sex will almost always involve deception of a deeper sort. If the adulterous spouse does not in fact have the appropriate feelings of affection for the extramarital partner, then the adulterous spouse is deceiving that person about the presence of such feelings. If, on the other hand, the adulterous spouse does have the corresponding feelings for the extramarital partner but not toward the nonparticipating spouse, the adulterous spouse is very probably deceiving the nonparticipating spouse about the presence of such feelings toward that spouse. Indeed, it might be argued, whenever there is no longer love between the two persons who are married to each other, there is deception just because being married implies both to the participants and to the world that such a bond exists. Deception is inevitable, the argument might conclude, because the feelings of affection that ought to accompany any act of sexual intercourse can only be held toward one other person at any given time in one's life. And if this is so, then the adulterous spouse always deceives either the partner in adultery or the nonparticipating spouse about the existence of such feelings. Thus extramarital sex involves deception of this sort and is for this reason immoral even if no deception vis-à-vis the occurrence of the act of adultery takes place.

What might be said in response to the foregoing arguments? The first thing that might be said is that the account of the connection between sexual intimacy and feelings of affection is inaccurate. Not inaccurate in the sense that no one thinks of things that way, but in the sense that there is substantially more divergence of opinion than that account suggests. For example, the view I have delineated may describe reasonably accurately the concepts of the sexual world in which I grew up, but it does not capture the sexual *weltanschauung* of today's youth at all. Thus, whether or not adultery implies deception in respect to feelings depends very much on the persons who are involved and the way they look at the "meaning" of sexual intimacy.

Second, the argument leaves to be answered the question of whether it is desirable for sexual intimacy to carry the sorts of messages described above. For those persons for whom sex does have these implications, there are special feelings and sensibilities that must be taken into account. But it is another question entirely whether any valuable end—moral or otherwise—is served by investing sexual behavior with such significance. That is something that must be shown and not just assumed. It might, for instance, be the case that substantially more good than harm would come from a kind of demystification of sexual behavior: one that would encourage the enjoyment of sex more for its own sake and one that would reject the centrality both of the association of sex with love and of love with only one other person.

I regard these as two of the more difficult, unresolved issues that our culture faces today in respect to thinking sensibly about the attitudes toward sex and love that we should try to develop in ourselves and in our children. Much of the contemporary literature that advocates sexual liberation of one sort or another embraces one or the other of two different views about the relationship between sex and love.

One view holds that sex should be separated from love and affection. To be sure sex is probably better when the partners genuinely like and enjoy each other. But sex is basically an intensive, exciting sensuous activity that can be enjoyed in a variety of suitable settings with a variety of suitable partners. The situation in respect to sexual pleasure is no different from that of the person who knows and appreciates fine food and who can have a very satisfying meal in any number of good restaurants with any number of congenial companions. One question that must be settled here is whether sex can be so demystified; another, more important question is whether it would be desirable to do so. What would we gain and what might we lose if we all lived in a world in which an act of sexual intercourse was no more or less significant or enjoyable than having a delicious meal in a nice setting with a good friend? The answer to this question lies beyond the scope of this paper.

The second view seeks to drive the wedge in a different place. It is not the link between sex and love that needs to be broken; rather, on this view, it is the connection between love and exclusivity that ought to be severed. For a number of the reasons already given, it is desirable, so this argument goes, that sexual intimacy continue to be reserved to and shared with only those for whom one has very great affection. The mistake lies in thinking that any "normal" adult will only have those feelings toward one other adult during his or her lifetime—or even at any time in his or her life. It is the concept of adult love, not ideas about sex, that, on this view, needs demystification. What are thought to be both unrealistic and unfortunate are the notions of exclusivity and possessiveness that attach to the dominant conception of love between adults in our and other cultures. Parents of four, five, six, or even ten children can certainly claim and sometimes claim correctly that they love all of their children, that they love them all equally, and that it is simply untrue to their feelings to insist that the numbers involved diminish either the quantity or the quality of their love. If this is an idea that is readily understandable in the case of parents and children, there is no necessary reason why it is an impossible or undesirable ideal in the case of adults. To be sure, there is probably a limit to the number of intimate, "primary" relationships that any person can maintain at any given time without the quality of the relationship being affected. But one adult ought surely be able to love two, three, or even six other adults at any one time without that love being different in kind or degree from that of the traditional, monogomous, lifetime marriage. And as between the individuals in these relationships, whether within a marriage or without, sexual intimacy is fitting and good.

The issues raised by a position such as this one are also surely worth exploring in detail and with care. Is there something to be called "sexual love" which is different from parental love or the nonsexual love of close friends? Is there something about love in general that links it naturally and appropriately with feelings of exclusivity and possession? Or is there something about sexual love, whatever that may be, that makes these feelings especially fitting here? Once again the issues are conceptual, empirical, and normative all at once: What is love? How could it be different? Would it be a good thing or a bad thing if it were different?

Suppose, though, that having delineated these problems we were now to pass them by. Suppose, moreover, we were to be persuaded of the possibility and the desirability of weakening substantially either the links between sex and love or the links between sexual love and exclusivity. Would it not then be the case that adultery could be free from all of the morally objectionable features described so far? To be more specific, let us imagine that a husband and wife have what is today sometimes characterized as an "open marriage." Suppose, that is, that they have agreed in advance that extramarital sex is—under certain circumstances—acceptable behavior for each to engage in. Suppose, that as a result there is no impulse to deceive each other about the occurrence or nature of any such relationships, and that no deception in fact occurs. Suppose, too, that there is no deception in respect to the feelings involved between the adulterous spouse and the extramarital partner. And suppose, finally, that one or the other or both of the spouses then has sexual intercourse in circumstances consistent with these understandings. Under this description, so the agreement might conclude, adultery is simply not immoral. At a minimum, adultery cannot very plausibly be condemned either on the ground that it involves deception or on the ground that it requires the breaking of a promise.

At least two responses are worth considering. One calls attention to the connection between marriage and adultery; the other looks to more instru-

mental arguments for the immorality of adultery. Both issues deserve further exploration.

One way to deal with the case of the "open marriage" is to question whether the two persons involved are still properly to be described as being married to each other. Part of the meaning of what it is for two persons to be married to each other, so this argument would go, is to have committed oneself to have sexual relationships only with one's spouse. Of course, it would be added, we know that that commitment is not always honored. We know that persons who are married to each other often do commit adultery. But there is a difference between being willing to make a commitment to marital fidelity, even though one may fail to honor that commitment, and not making the commitment at all. Whatever the relationship may be between the two individuals in the case described above, the absence of any commitment to sexual exclusivity requires the conclusion that their relationship is not a marital one. For a commitment to sexual exclusivity is a necessary although not a sufficient condition for the existence of a marriage.

Although there may be something to this suggestion, as it is stated it is too strong to be acceptable. To begin with, I think it is very doubtful that there are many, if any, *necessary* conditions for marriage; but even if there are, a commitment to sexual exclusivity is not such a condition.

To see that this is so, consider what might be taken to be some of the essential characteristics of a marriage. We might be tempted to propose that the concept of marriage requires the following: a formal ceremony of some sort in which mutual obligations are undertaken between two persons of the opposite sex; the capacity on the part of the persons involved to have sexual intercourse with each other; the willingness to have sexual intercourse only with each other; and feelings of love and affection between the two persons. The problem is that we can imagine relationships that are clearly marital and yet lack one or more of these features. For example, in our own society, it is possible for two persons to be married without going through a formal ceremony, as in the common-law marriages recognized in some jurisdictions. It is also possible for two persons to get married even though one or both lacks the capacity to engage in sexual intercourse. Thus, two very elderly persons who have neither the desire nor the ability to have intercourse can, nonetheless, get married, as can persons whose sexual organs have been injured so that intercourse is not possible. And we certainly know of marriages in which love was not present at the time of the marriage, as, for instance, in marriages of state and marriages of convenience.

Counterexamples not satisfying the condition relating to the abstention from extramarital sex are even more easily produced. We certainly know of societies and cultures in which polygamy and polyandry are practiced, and we have no difficulty in recognizing these relationships as cases of marriages. It might be objected, though, that these are not counterexamples because they are plural marriages rather than marriages in which sex is permitted with someone other than with one of the persons to whom one is married. But we also know of societies in which it is permissible for married persons to have sexual relationships with persons to whom they were not married, for example, temple prostitutes, concubines, and homosexual lovers. And even if we knew of no such societies, the conceptual claim would still, I submit, not be well taken. For suppose all of the other indicia of marriage were present: suppose the two persons were of the opposite sex. Suppose they had the capacity and desire to have intercourse with each other, suppose they participated in a formal ceremony in which they understood themselves voluntarily to be entering into a relationship with each other in which substantial mutual commitments were assumed. If all these conditions were satisfied, we would not be in any doubt about whether or not the two persons were married even though they had not taken on a commitment of sexual exclusivity and even though they had expressly agreed that extramarital sexual intercourse was a permissible behavior for each to engage in.

A commitment to sexual exclusivity is neither a necessary nor a sufficient condition for the existence of a marriage. It does, nonetheless, have this much to do with the nature of marriage: like the other indicia enumerated above, its presence tends to establish the existence of a marriage. Thus, in the absence of a formal ceremony of any sort, an explicit commitment to sexual exclusivity would count in favor of regarding the two persons as married. The conceptual role of the commitment to sexual exclusivity can, perhaps, be brought out through the following example. Suppose we found a tribe which had a practice in which all the other indicia of marriage were present but in which the two parties were *prohibited* ever from having sexual intercourse with each other. Moreover, suppose that sexual intercourse with others was clearly permitted. In such a case we would, I think, reject the idea that the two were married to each other and we would describe their relationship in other terms, for example, as some kind of formalized, special friendship relation—a kind of heterosexual "blood-brother" bond.

Compare that case with the following. Suppose again that the tribe had a practice in which all of the other indicia of marriage were present, but instead of a prohibition on sexual intercourse between the persons in the relationship there was no rule at all. Sexual intercourse was permissible with the person with whom one had this ceremonial relationship, but it was no more or less permissible than with a number of other persons to whom one was not so related (for instance, all consenting adults of the opposite sex). Although we might be in doubt as to whether we ought to describe the persons as married to each other, we would probably conclude that they were married and that they simply were members of a tribe whose views about sex were quite different from our own.

What all of this shows is that *a prohibition* on sexual intercourse between the two persons involved in a relationship is conceptually incompatible with the claim that the two of them are married. The *permissibility* of intramarital sex is a necessary part of the idea of marriage. But no such incompatibility follows simply from the added permissibility of extra-marital sex.

These arguments do not, of course, exhaust the arguments for the prohibition on extramarital sexual relations. The remaining argument that I wish to consider—as I indicated earlier—is a more instrumental one. It seeks to justify the prohibition by virtue of the role that it plays in the development and maintenance of nuclear families. The argument, or set of arguments, might, I believe, go something like this.

Consider first a farfetched nonsexual example. Suppose a society were organized so that after some suitable age—say, 18, 19, or 20—persons were forbidden to eat anything but bread and water with anyone but their spouse. Persons might still choose in such a society not to get married. Good food just might not be very important to them because they have underdeveloped taste buds. Or good food might be bad for them because there is something wrong with their digestive system. Or good food might be important to them, but they might decide that the enjoyment of good food would get in the way of the attainment of other things that were more important. But most persons would, I think, be led to favor marriage in part because they preferred a richer, more varied, diet to one of bread and water. And they might remain married because the family was the only legitimate setting within which good food was obtainable. If it is important to have society organized so that persons will both get married and stay married, such an arrangement would be well suited to the preservation of the family, and the prohibitions relating to food consumption could be understood as fulfilling that function.

It is obvious that one of the more powerful human desires is the desire for sexual gratification. The desire is a natural one, like hunger and thirst, in the sense that it need not be learned in order to be present within us and operative upon us. But there is in addition much that we do learn about what the act of sexual intercourse is like. Once we experience sexual intercourse ourselves—and in particular once we experience orgasm—we discover that it is among the most intensive, short-term pleasures of the body.

Because this is so, it is easy to see how the prohibition upon extramarital sex helps to hold marriage together. At least during that period of life when the enjoyment of sexual intercourse is one of the desirable bodily pleasures, persons will wish to enjoy those pleasures. If one consequence of being married is that one is prohibited from having sexual intercourse with anyone but one's spouse, then the spouses in a marriage are in a position to provide an

important source of pleasure for each other that is unavailable to them elsewhere in the society.

The point emerges still more clearly if this rule of sexual morality is seen as of a piece with the other rules of sexual morality. When this prohibition is coupled, for example, with the prohibition on non-marital sexual intercourse, we are presented with the inducement both to get married and to stay married. For if sexual intercourse is only legitimate within marriage, then persons seeking that gratification which is a feature of sexual intercourse are furnished explicit social directions for its attainment; namely marriage.

Nor, to continue the argument, is it necessary to focus exclusively on the bodily enjoyment that is involved. Orgasm may be a significant part of what there is to sexual intercourse, but it is not the whole of it. We need only recall the earlier discussion of the meaning that sexual intimacy has in our own culture to begin to see some of the more intricate ways in which sexual exclusivity may be connected with the establishment and maintenance of marriage as the primary heterosexual, love relationship. Adultery is wrong, in other words, because a prohibition on extramarital sex is a way to help maintain the institutions of marriage and the nuclear family.

Now I am frankly not sure what we are to say about an argument such as this one. What I am convinced of is that, like the arguments discussed earlier, this one also reveals something of the difficulty and complexity of the issues that are involved. So, what I want now to do—in the brief and final portion of this paper—is to try to delineate with reasonable precision what I take several of the fundamental, unresolved issues to be.

The first is whether this last argument is an argument for the *immorality* of extramarital sexual intercourse. What does seem clear is that there are differences between this argument and the ones considered earlier. The earlier arguments condemned adulterous behavior because it was behavior that involved breaking of a promise, taking unfair advantage, or deceiving another. To the degree to which the prohibition on extramarital sex can be supported by arguments which invoke considerations such as these, there is little question but that violations of the prohibition are properly regarded as immoral. And such a claim could be defended on one or both of two distinct grounds. The first is that things like promise-breaking and deception are just wrong. The second is that adultery involving promisebreaking or deception is wrong because it involves the straightforward infliction of harm on another human being—typically the nonadulterous spouse—who has a strong claim not to have that harm so inflicted.

The argument that connects the prohibition on extramarital sex with the maintenance and preservation of the institution of marriage is an argument for the instrumental value of the prohibition. To some degree this counts, I think, against regarding all violations of the prohibition as obvious cases of immorality. This is so partly because hypothetical imperatives are less clearly within the domain of morality than are categorical ones, and even more because instrumental prohibitions are within the domain of morality only if the end they serve or the way they serve it is itself within the domain of morality.

What this should help us see, I think, is the fact that the argument that connects the prohibition on adultery with the preservation of marriage is at best seriously incomplete. Before we ought to be convinced by it, we ought to have reasons for believing that marriage is a morally desirable and just social

institution. And this is not quite as easy or obvious a task as it may seem to be. For the concept of marriage is, as we have seen, both a loosely structured and a complicated one. There may be all sorts of intimate, interpersonal relationships which will resemble but not be identical with the typical marriage relationship presupposed by the traditional sexual morality. There may be a number of distinguishable sexual and loving arrangements which can all legitimately claim to be called *marriages*. The prohibitions of the traditional sexual morality may be effective ways to maintain some marriages and ineffective ways to promote and preserve others. The prohibitions of the traditional sexual morality may make good psychological sense if certain psychological theories are true, and they may be purveyors of immense psychological mischief if other psychological theories are true. The prohibitions of the traditional sexual morality may seem obviously correct if sexual intimacy carries the meaning that the dominant culture has often ascribed to it, and they may seem equally bizarre when sex is viewed through the perspective of the counterculture. Irrespective of whether instrumental arguments of this sort are properly deemed moral arguments, they ought not to fully convince anyone until questions like these are answered.

Critics

Michael J. Wreen | ## What's Really Wrong with Adultery

While philosophers are probably as interested in adultery as everyone else is—and that's pretty interested—philosophical literature on the topic is somewhat scarcer than that on golden mountains or unicorns. To my knowledge, only one paper devoted exclusively to the topic, Richard Wasserstrom's "Is Adultery Immoral?" has appeared in print thus far. In this paper I will argue that, contrary to Wasser-

Michael J. Wreen, "What's Really Wrong with Adultery," in *The Philosophy of Sex: Contemporary Readings,* ed. Alan Soble (Savage, Md.: Rowman & Littlefield, 1991).

strom's admittedly well-considered views, we do in fact have good grounds for thinking that adultery is prima facie wrong.

Before I present my argument, though, a definition of adultery is in order. Wasserstrom defines adultery as "any case of extramarital sex" with "case" here apparently referring to a particular act of sexual intercourse, whether heterosexual or homosexual. My disagreement with this definition is a minor one, though one which, as will be seen, will make a difference in the argument which follows. A given "case" of adultery could involve extramarital sex on the part of one partner but not on the part of the other, namely if the second partner isn't married at all. So, I prefer to define adultery in terms of a particular individual's engaging in a particular act of sexual intercourse with another:

> X's engaging in sexual intercourse with Y at time t is an act of adultery if and only if either X or Y is married at time t, and X and Y are not married to each other at that time.

Why then is adultery wrong? Wasserstrom argues that although many, many cases of adultery involve promise breaking, deception, or hurting others, not all do, and so none can serve as a reason for thinking that adultery per se is immoral. He is undoubtedly correct about this. Indeed, other reasons for thinking that adultery as such is immoral—that it involves a breach in the relations between two individuals respecting sex and feelings of deep affection (love), or love and exclusivity, or that it threatens the development and maintenance of the nuclear family—all fare little better, according to Wasserstrom, since in each case the argument is incomplete. Sex without love may be not only possible but desirable, and so adultery not immoral (the proper place for love being assumed here, for the sake of argument, to be within, and only within, the confines of marriage). Or, sex without love not being possible or desirable, love with more than one person, or more than the permissible number of marital partners, may be both possible and desirable, and so adultery not immoral. And, as for the preservation of the nuclear family: this argument is predicated on the nuclear family's

being desirable, but whether it really is such is far from clear.

The reason that I think that adultery is wrong, however, focuses on what adultery itself is. The key concept is *marriage*. Marriage, on my view, is living together (or at least a commitment to do so), plus a commitment to at least occasional sexual intercourse if possible—and if not possible, the fact known to both (or however many) marital partners—plus a commitment to exclusivity as far as sexual intercourse is concerned. This definition allows the newly wedded, elderly couples incapable of sexual intercourse, and those married for convenience's sake all to be married. It captures the common view that marriage is commitment, specifically the commitment to be and love as one, and explains why non-consummation is a legally sufficient ground for annulment. But it is the commitment to sexual exclusivity that is important here.

Let us assume for the present, then, that marriage involves a commitment to exclusivity as far as sexual intercourse is concerned. If so, then there does seem to be something wrong with adultery. For, first, such a commitment is, or at least entails, the adoption of a policy, namely the policy to have sexual congress only with a single, particular person of the opposite sex (the example of standard monogamy being used here for simplicity's sake). And secondly, the concept of adultery is logically parasitic on that of marriage; it is defined in terms of marriage, and adulterous behavior logically impossible in the absence of marriage. Given these facts, and given what adultery is, adultery necessarily involves a contradiction in the will—or, to be more accurate (and Kantian), a contradiction in conception. For marriage involves the adoption of a policy of sexual exclusivity; and adultery, by definition, is a violation of that policy, an attack on one of the conceptual cornerstones of marriage itself. The contradiction consists in adopting policies which cannot be consistently acted upon, or universalized. It is inconsistent to adopt both a policy of sexual exclusivity and a policy of engaging in sexual intercourse with a person not specified in the original policy when, for whatever reason, that seems to be a good idea. Let me put the point this way. To be married is, in part, to adopt the maxim "Whenever I engage in sexual intercourse I shall do so with person X," while to commit adultery is, in part, to adopt the maxim 'Whenever I engage in sexual intercourse I shall do so for such-and-such or so-and-so reasons, regardless of my sexual commitments.' The policies represented by these maxims are internally inconsistent. The immorality—irrationality, in Kant's terms—lies in the contradictoriness of the policies, indeed, the necessary contradictoriness of the policies, not in some other fact.

A succinct way to put this point is the following. Adultery is and must be wrong because, by definition, it involves the violation of a defining commitment of the very institution on which it itself is parasitic. Adultery may not be, as jealousy is, a "green-eyed monster," but it does, conceptually speaking, "mock the meat which it feeds on."

It will be noticed that this is a formalistic, Kantian objection to adultery. If a good objection, it holds even if the spouse of an adulterer knows of and condones his/her spouse's adulterous behavior. The fact that they are married is sufficient for such behavior to be wrong. (But, it could be replied, a spouse who knows of and condones adulterous behavior is a spouse only in the legal sense of the term. Morally speaking, it could be argued that he/she is no longer married at all, since he/she has released his/her spouse from a commitment to exclusivity. Whether the commitment to exclusivity is so easily banished, however, is a difficult question.)

The above argument, however, would seem to apply only to married adulterers; and, as I've noted, not all adulterers are married. What of the nonmarried person who engages in adultery? Does he/she do anything wrong? I think so; I think the above argument applies at one remove to non-married adulterers, at least in most cases. For *if* such a person accepts the institution of marriage at all, then his/her act of adultery involves a similar contradiction in conception, one between a policy which accepts marriage, and so is committed to honoring the marital commitments of others, and a policy which permits him/her to engage in sexual intercourse whenever such-and-such or so-and-so reasons obtain, regardless of the sexual commitments of his/her

partner. The first policy here commits one to respecting marriage commitments; the second allows one to disregard them; and the result is a contradiction in conception similar to that of a married adulterer. But, of course, a non-married adulterer may not accept the institution of marriage at all; it is possible to reject the institution altogether. In that case, then, there would seem to be nothing wrong with adultery as such. Rebels of the above sort, though, are, like Cartesian madmen, more the product of the philosopher's imagination than the stuff of flesh and blood people.

One objection to the above argument is that it depends on a false premise; viz., that a commitment to sexual exclusivity is a necessary condition of marriage. Wasserstrom, for instance, holds that "it is doubtful that there are many, if any, *necessary* conditions for marriage; but even if there are, a commitment to sexual exclusivity is not such a condition." Why? Because "counterexamples not satisfying [such a] condition are . . . easily produced." Societies in which "polygamy and polyandry are practiced" are no such counterexamples, as Wasserstrom himself recognizes, because these are not societies in which "sex is permitted with someone other than one of the persons to whom one is married." Genuine counterexamples do exist, though, according to Wasserstrom: there are societies "in which it is permissible for married persons to have sexual relations with persons to whom they are not married, for example, temple prostitutes, concubines, and homosexual lovers." And secondly, if "all of the other indcia of marriage were present[—if] the two persons were of the opposite sex . . . and had the capacity and desire to have intercourse with each other . . . and participated in a formal ceremony in which they understood themselves to be entering into a relationship with each other in which substantial mutual commitments were assumed [—*then*] we would not be in any doubt as to whether the two person were married, even though they had not taken on a commitment to sexual exclusivity and even though they had agreed that extramarital sexual intercourse was permissible behavior for each to engage in."

Neither of these counterarguments convinces me, however. To take the second one first: I *do* doubt that such a couple is married. From Wasserstrom's description, what I would conclude is that the two people have entered in a public, formalized contractual agreement, one *apparently* regarding sexual intercourse, i.e., that they had agreed to have sexual intercourse with each other, and, apparently, regarding important business matters as well—at least "business matters" is what comes to mind most readily, given that the "substantial mutual commitments" assumed don't include a commitment to sexual exclusivity. Wasserstrom's description, in short, is one of contractual sex plus other mutual services. A formalized, extended prostitute/ "John" relationship, one which also included, say, health care in exchange for extensive home repair, as well as sex for money, satisfies his description, as does any other formalized, sex-plus contractual relationship.

As for societies "in which it is permissible for married persons to have sexual relations with persons to whom they are not married . . . temple prostitutes, concubines, and homosexual lovers"—and, perhaps, geisha girls: in and of itself this does not show that marriage does not involve a commitment to sexual exclusivity in such societies. What it does show is that even if marriage does involve a commitment to sexual exclusivity, such societies permit, and may even promote, to some extent, extramarital sex. In point of fact, in the United States, there exist states in which prostitution is legal—and legal not just for the unmarried. There might be any number of reasons why a society condones or even encourages extramarital sex. Legal moralism might be thought objectionable; there might be laws against adultery, but society might, for whatever reason, "look the other way" whenever violations occur, e.g., violations might be pervasive but not harm the society to any appreciable extent (as is the case with widespread violations of anti-jay-walking laws in the United States); tax revenues might be needed (as is the case with legalized, state regulated prostitution in Mexico and Nevada); the general populace might be indifferent to the practice of adultery; and so on.

As a matter of fact, there are even sub-sectors of societies in which, for cultural reasons, the practice of "the big house" and "the little house" obtains and is enthusiastically supported by members of those

sub-sectors. In some Latin American countries—or at least parts of those countries— a man is not only expected to marry and maintain a "big house" for his wife and legitimate offspring; he is also expected—and virtually socially required—to have at least one mistress and to maintain a "little house," which may include supporting illegitimate offspring. The practice may not be publicly proclaimed and applauded, but it is as obvious to, and as accepted by, everyone in such subsectors as the sky. Indeed, the practice is so deeply entrenched that if a husband does not have a mistress, his wife is likely to badger and insult him until he acquires one—*machismo* is *that* important, and that accepted, a cultural concept in such subsectors. Societies, like people, are complex—far too complex to infer, as Wasserstrom apparently does, that because extramarital sexual intercourse is permitted in some societies, marriage does not involve a commitment to sexual exclusivity in those societies.

A seemingly stronger counterexample, though not one mentioned by Wasserstrom, is provided by "certain cultures [which] permit extramarital sexuality [sexual intercourse, I take it] by married persons with friends, guests, or in-laws." Although the author of this passage does not provide any details, or cite any sources, regarding friends or inlaws—or guests, for that matter—stories of guests being granted the privilege of sleeping with his/her host's spouse—always *his* host's *wife,* in the tales I've been told—are at least as old as European exploration of (and imperialism in) the South Pacific. Supposing the stories true, do we have a genuine counterexample of the sort Wasserstrom requires?

Is *marriage* a family resemblance concept, then, as he has it? I still think not. Although the point is not generally recognized, the notion of a family resemblance concept can be interpreted, and so can cut, in either of two ways: to show that a given concept, C, has no necessary conditions, this being based on the (alleged) fact that Cs resemble each other only in there being strands of similarity, but nothing common, among Cs; or—and this is the road not taken—to show that C does have necessary conditions, but bears a family resemblance to other concepts, C', C'', C''', and so on, which are in the near vicinity and may well be known, for that reason, by the same sobriquet as *C*. Which of the two routes is best to take in a given case may well depend on a number of factors, but among them are undoubtedly the conceptual entrenchment of a putatively necessary condition, *N,* for *C*, the strength of our intuitions regarding *N,* the place of *N* in binding *C* to other concepts, and the importance of *N* and *C* in the social, scientific, moral, and personal orders. It seems to me that all of these factors argue for the second alternative as far as *marriage* is concerned; that is, they argue for saying, Yes, the South Sea Islanders in question are married—but not in our sense of the term. Family resemblance concepts, in the second sense of the term, are, like relatives, frequently spread far and wide; and again like relatives, they may well bear the same name. But lacking the necessary blood connections, they succeed to no thrones.

Two other objections to my argument can be more briefly stated and answered. First, it might be objected that there is nothing particularly immoral about conduct which entails a contradiction in conception. Contradictions in conception can arise in relation to purely prudential behavior; hence, the question of whether adultery is immoral remains unanswered. Second, it could be argued that there are many imaginable circumstances in which adultery would seem to be morally permissible or even obligatory (or at least an "ought to engage in adultery" judgment would seem to be true). For example,

a married man or woman might be experiencing sexual dysfunction, and the couple might realize that the dysfunctional partner's engaging in sexual intercourse with another would help remedy the dysfunction and, in the long run, strengthen the marriage and make them both happier. Adultery would seem to be at least permissible in such circumstances, if the husband, wife, and third party knowingly and voluntarily agree to its occurrence.

The proper answer to the first of these objections, I think, is that adultery is immoral not just because a contradiction in conception is involved, but because the contradiction essentially includes a social, as well as personal, commitment to a second party. Such relationships are, or at least are close to, the paradigm of moral relationships.

The second objection is adequately answered by noting that if my argument is successful, all that it establishes is the prima facie wrongness of adultery. Failure of universalizability seems to me, and to most moral philosophers (but not to Kant, of course), to establish no more than the prima facie wrongness of a course of behavior. And prima facie wrongness can be overridden in some circumstances, such as, in the case of adultery, those indicated above.

So, as I can think of no other objections to my argument, I conclude that adultery is indeed prima facie immoral.

Bonnie Steinbock | # Adultery

According to a 1980 survey in *Cosmopolitan,* 54 percent of American wives have had extramarital affairs; a study of 100,000 married women by the considerably tamer *Redbook* magazine found that 40 percent of the wives over 40 had been unfaithful. While such surveys are, to some extent, self-selecting—those who do it are more likely to fill out questionnaires about it—sexual mores have clearly changed in recent years. Linda Wolfe, who reported

the results of the *Cosmopolitan* survey, suggests that "this increase in infidelity among married women represents not so much a deviation from traditional standards of fidelity as a break with the old double standard." Studies show that men have always strayed in significant numbers.

Yet 80 percent of "*Cosmo* girls" did not approve of infidelity and wished their own husbands and lovers would be faithful. Eighty-eight percent of

Bonnie Steinbock, "Adultery," *QQ: Report from the Center for Philosophy and Public Policy* 6, no. 1 (Winter 1986): 12–14.

respondents to a poll taken in Iowa in 1983 viewed "coveting your neighbor's spouse" as a "major sin." It seems that while almost nobody approves of adultery, men have always done it, and women are catching up.

The increase in female adultery doubtless has to do with recent and radical changes in our attitudes toward sex and sexuality. We no longer feel guilty about enjoying sex; indeed, the capacity for sexual enjoyment is often regarded as a criterion of mental health. When sex itself is no longer intrinsically shameful, restraints on sexual behavior are loosened. In fact, we might question whether the abiding disapproval of infidelity merely gives lip service to an ancient taboo. Is there a rational justification for disapproving of adultery which will carry force with everyone, religious and nonreligious alike?

TRUST AND DECEPTION

Note first that adultery, unlike murder, theft, and lying, is not universally forbidden. Traditional Eskimo culture, for example, regarded sharing one's wife with a visitor as a matter of courtesy. The difference can be explained by looking at the effects of these practices on social cohesiveness. Without rules protecting the lives, persons, and property of its members, no group could long endure. Indeed, rules against killing, assault, lying, and stealing seem fundamental to having a morality at all.

Not so with adultery. For adultery is a *private* matter, essentially concerning only the relationship between husband and wife. It is not essential to morality like these other prohibitions: there are stable societies with genuine moral codes which tolerate extra-marital sex. Although adultery remains a criminal offense in some jurisdictions, it is rarely prosecuted. Surely this is because it is widely regarded as a private matter: in the words of Billie Holiday, "Ain't nobody's business if I do."

However, even if adultery is a private matter, with which the state should not interfere, it is not a morally neutral issue. Our view of adultery is connected to our thoughts and feelings about love and marriage, sex and the family, the value of fidelity,

sexual jealousy, and exclusivity. How we think about adultery will affect the quality of our relationships, the way we raise our children, the kind of society we have and want to have. So it is important to consider whether our attitudes toward adultery are justifiable.

Several practical considerations militate against adultery: pregnancy and genital herpes immediately spring to mind. However, unwanted pregnancies are a risk of all sexual intercourse, within or without marriage; venereal disease is a risk of all non-exclusive sex, not just adulterous sex. So these risks do not provide a reason for objecting specifically to adultery. In any event, they offer merely pragmatic, as opposed to moral, objections. If adultery is wrong, it does not become less so because one has been sterilized or inoculated against venereal disease.

Two main reasons support regarding adultery as seriously immoral. One is that adultery is an instance of promise-breaking, on the view that marriage involves, explicitly or implicitly, a promise of sexual fidelity: to forsake all others. That there is this attitude in our culture is clear. Mick Jagger, not noted for sexual puritanism, allegedly refused to marry Jerry Hall, the mother of his baby, because he had no intention of accepting an exclusive sexual relationship. While Jagger's willingness to become an unwed father is hardly mainstream morality, his refusal to marry, knowing that he did not wish to be faithful, respects the idea that *marriage* requires such a commitment. Moreover, the promise of sexual fidelity is regarded as a very serious and important one. To cheat on one's spouse indicates a lack of concern, a willingness to cause pain, and so a lack of love. Finally, one who breaks promises cannot be trusted. And trust is essential to the intimate partnership of marriage, which may be irreparably weakened by its betrayal.

The second reason for regarding adultery as immoral is that it involves deception, for example, lying about one's whereabouts and relations with others. Perhaps a marriage can withstand the occasional lie, but a pattern of lying will have irrevocable consequences for a marriage, if discovered, and probably even if not. Like breaking promises, lying is regarded as a fundamental kind of wrongdoing, a failure to take the one lied to seriously as a moral person entitled to respect.

OPEN MARRIAGE

These two arguments suffice to make most cases of adultery wrong, given the attitudes and expectations of most people. But what if marriage did not involve any promise of sexual fidelity? What if there were no need for deception, because neither partner expected or wanted such fidelity? Objections to "open marriage" cannot focus on promise-breaking and deception, for the expectation of exclusivity is absent. If an open marriage has been freely chosen by both spouses, and not imposed by a dominant on a dependent partner, would such an arrangement be morally acceptable, even desirable?

The attractiveness of extramarital affairs, without dishonesty, disloyalty, or guilt, should not be downplayed. However satisfying sex between married people may be, it cannot have the excitement of a new relationship. ("Not *better*," a friend once said defensively to his wife, attempting to explain his infidelity, "just *different*.") Might we not be better off, our lives fuller and richer, if we allowed ourselves the thrill of new and different sexual encounters?

Perhaps the expectation of sexual exclusivity in marriage stems from emotions which are not admirable: jealousy and possessiveness. That most people experience these feelings is no reason for applauding or institutionalizing them. Independence in marriage is now generally regarded as a good thing: too much "togetherness" is boring and stifling. In a good marriage, the partners can enjoy different activities, travel apart, and have separate friends. Why draw the line at sexual activity?

The natural response to this question invokes a certain conception of love and sex: sex is an expression of affection and intimacy and so should be reserved for people who love each other. Further, it is assumed that one can and should have such feelings for only one other person at any time. To make love with someone else is to express feelings of affection and intimacy that should be reserved for one's spouse alone.

This rejection of adultery assumes the validity of a particular conception of love and sex, which can be attacked in two ways. We might divorce sex from love and regard sex as a pleasurable activity in its own right, comparable to the enjoyment of a good meal. In his article "Is Adultery Immoral?" Richard Wasserstrom suggests that the linkage of sex with love reflects a belief that unless it is purified by a higher emotion, such as love, sex is intrinsically bad or dirty.

But this is an overly simplistic view of the connection between sex and love. Feelings of love occur between people enjoying sexual intercourse, not out of a sense that sexual pleasure must be purified, but precisely because of the mutual pleasure they give one another. People naturally have feelings of affection for those who make them happy, and sex is a very good way of making someone extraordinarily happy. At the same time, sex is by its nature intimate, involving both physical and psychological exposure. This both requires and creates trust, which is closely allied to feelings of affection and love. This is not to say that sex necessarily requires or leads to love; but a conception of the relation between love and sex that ignores these factors is inadequate and superficial.

Alternatively, one might acknowledge the connection between sex and love, but attack the assumption of exclusivity. If parents can love all their children equally and if adults can have numerous close friends, why should it be impossible to love more than one sexual partner at a time? Perhaps we could learn to love more widely and to accept that a spouse's sexual involvement with another is not a sign of rejection or lack of love.

The logistics of multiple involvement are certainly daunting. Having an affair (as opposed to a roll in the hay) requires time and concentration; it will almost inevitably mean neglecting one's spouse, one's children, one's work. More important, however, exclusivity seems to be an intrinsic part of "true love." Imagine Romeo pouring out his heart to both Juliet *and* Rosalind! In our ideal of romantic love, one chooses to forgo pleasure with other partners in order to have a unique relationship with one's beloved. Such "renunciation" is natural in the first throes of romantic love; it is precisely because this stage does *not* last that we must promise to be faithful through the notoriously unromantic realities of married life.

FIDELITY AS AN IDEAL

On the view I have been defending, genuinely open marriages are not *immoral,* although they deviate from a valued ideal of what marriage should be. While this is not the only ideal, or incumbent on all rational agents, it is a moral view in that it embodies a claim about a good way for people to live. The prohibition of adultery, then, is neither arbitrary nor irrational. However, even if we are justified in accepting the ideal of fidelity, we know that people do not always live up to the ideals they accept and we recognize that some failures to do so are worse than others. We regard a brief affair, occasioned by a prolonged separation, as morally different from installing a mistress.

Further, sexual activity is not necessary for deviation from the ideal of marriage which lies behind the demand for fidelity. As John Heckler observed during his bitter and public divorce from former Health and Human Services Secretary Margaret Heckler, "In marriage, there are two partners. When one person starts contributing far less than the other person to the marriage, that's the original infidelity. You don't need any third party." While this statement was probably a justification of his own infidelities, the point is valid. To abandon one's spouse, whether to a career or to another person, is also a kind of betrayal.

If a man becomes deeply involved emotionally with another woman, it may be little comfort that he is able to assure his wife that "Nothing happened." Sexual infidelity has significance as a sign of a deeper betrayal—falling in love with someone else. It may be objected that we cannot control the way we feel, only the way we behave; that we should not be blamed for falling in love, but only for acting on the feeling. While we may not have direct control over our feelings, however, we are responsible for getting ourselves into situations in which certain feelings naturally arise. "It just happened" is rarely an accurate portrayal of an extramarital love affair.

If there can be betrayal without sex, can there be sex without betrayal? In the novel *Forfeit,* by Dick Francis, the hero is deeply in love with his wife, who was paralyzed by polio in the early days of their marriage. Her great unspoken fear is that he will leave her; instead, he tends to her devotedly. For several years, he forgoes sex, but eventually succumbs to an affair. While his adultery is hardly praiseworthy, it is understandable. He could divorce his wife and marry again, but it is precisely his refusal to abandon her, his continuing love and tender care, that makes us admire him.

People do fall in love with others and out of love with their spouses. Ought they to refrain from making love while still legally tied? I cannot see much, if any, moral value in remaining physically faithful, on principle, to a spouse one no longer loves. This will displease those who regard the wrongness of adultery as a moral absolute, but my account has nothing to do with absolutes and everything to do with what it means to love someone deeply and completely. It is the value of that sort of relationship that makes sexual fidelity an ideal worth the sacrifice.

Neither a mere religiously based taboo, nor a relic of a repressive view of sexuality, the prohibition against adultery expresses a particular conception of married love. It is one we can honor in our own lives and bequeath to our children with confidence in its value as a coherent and rational ideal.

Don Marquis | What's Wrong with Adultery?

The ethics of adultery has received surprisingly little attention from philosophers.[1] On the one hand, many believe that the serious wrongness of adultery is utterly uncontroversial. On the other hand, adultery is hardly uncommon. The adulteries of leading politicians have been widely reported. Almost everyone of a certain age has friends who, they know, have committed adultery and who are not bad people. This suggests that the ethics of adultery is more difficult and subtle than often thought.

The subject of this essay is the morality of extramarital sex by persons in typical marriages in our culture. I shall first argue that accounts of the wrongness of adultery in the philosophical literature are inadequate or oversimplified. I shall then propose an account of the wrongness of adultery that, I hope, is superior to, and incorporates the best features of, other accounts. Many may believe this account is excessively permissive. I shall suggest that this thought results from a tension in our concepts of marriage.

I. SOME ACCOUNTS OF THE WRONGNESS OF ADULTERY

Many believe that adultery is wrong because it involves breaking a promise. This, by itself, does not account for the seriousness of the wrong of adultery. This is why Richard Wasserstrom said

> The breaking of this promise may be more hurtful and painful than is typically the case [with other promises]. Why is this so? To begin with . . . [the] spouse may feel the unfairness of having restrained himself or herself in the absence of reciprocal restraint having been exercised by the adulterous spouse. In addition, the spouse may perceive the breaking of the promise as an indication of a kind of indifference on the part of the adulterous spouse . . . And third, and related to the above, the spouse may see the act of sexual intercourse with another as a sign of affection for the other person and as an additional rejection of the non-adulterous spouse as the one who is loved by the adulterous spouse . . . [Thus] certain kinds of adultery are wrong just because they involve the breach of a serious promise which, among other things, leads to the intentional infliction of substantial pain by one spouse upon the other.[2]

Although Wasserstrom believed that adultery in a standard marriage also typically involves the wrong of deception, evaluation of Wasserstrom's account of the promise-breaking aspect of the wrong is useful. Two main difficulties are apparent. The less serious difficulty concerns his claim that adultery involves the *intentional* infliction of substantial pain. This seems clearly false, for most adulterers attempt to hide their adulteries. If they intended to inflict pain on their spouses, then they would not, of course, hide their adulteries. However, dealing with this difficulty requires only a minimal alteration in Wasserstrom's account. The more serious difficulty is that, on Wasserstrom's account, the promise-breaking is seriously wrong only if the adultery is discovered. This would have the consequence that adulteries that stay hidden—and surely many do—are not seriously wrong for the promise-breaking reason. Almost no one believes this. In particular, persons who discover that their spouses have been committing adultery do not believe this. When the adulteries are discovered, they believe that they were seriously wronged when the adulteries took place. They do not believe that the seriousness of the wrong begins only when adultery is discovered and the emotional pain

This paper is published here for the first time with the permission of Don Marquis.

begins. Wasserstrom's order of explanation is backwards. Someone who discovers her spouse's adultery suffers because she believes that she *was seriously betrayed;* it is not the case that she believes that the seriousness of the betrayal is due to the fact that she now suffers. The trouble with Wasserstrom's account is that he attempted to account for the seriousness of a deontological wrong in consequentialist terms.

Those who are wedded to consequence-based wrongs might object that, because the adultery might be discovered and because the discovery would cause one's spouse severe pain, the chance that the adultery will cause the spouse severe pain accounts for the serious wrong of breaking this promise. The trouble with this objection is that, from the considerations to which it appeals, it could be replaced with an even better argument for the adulterer's stringent duty to be exceedingly careful to hide his adultery from his spouse.

Michael Wreen's deontological account of the wrong of adultery avoids the difficulty with Wasserstrom's account. His account is quite simple. To be married is to be committed to having sexual intercourse with no one other than one's spouse. Adulterers have a policy of having sexual intercourse with someone other than their spouses. Therefore, adulterers are committed to rules of conduct that are inconsistent. Wreen says that adultery is wrong because it involves what Kant called "a contradiction in conception."[3]

This account has implications that are, to say the least, unacceptable. According to Wreen, "a commitment to sexual exclusivity is a necessary condition for being married."[4] Since an adulterer is not committed to sexual exclusivity, it follows that an adulterer is not married. Since being married is a necessary condition for committing adultery, Wreen's view entails that adultery is logically impossible. It follows that there are no adulterous acts and therefore, no immoral adulterous acts. The contradiction in conception in Wreen's account is not the adulterer's but Wreen's.

What went so terribly wrong? Wreen's claim that a commitment to sexual exclusivity is a necessary condition of being married is a corollary of his belief that open marriage is logically impossible and his view that the concept of open marriage involves an equivocation on the concept of marriage.[5] Although I disagree, this disagreement is irrelevant to the analysis of this essay because that analysis concerns typical marriages in our culture. In the ceremonies establishing such marriages, couples do commit themselves to sexual exclusivity. (The possibility that the bride or groom might lie complicates matters, but raises issues that would only divert us from the analysis of this essay.) Nevertheless, changing one's mind is not logically impossible. This is what the adulterer does. The contradiction in conception vanishes.

This suggests nothing problematic about Kant's ethics, for Wreen's view is not really Kantian. Kant's "contradiction in conception" requires universalizing a maxim. (I also waive difficult issues concerning the difference between Kantian contradictions in conception and contradictions in the will.) Wreen's contradiction in conception does not essentially involve universalization. Thus, for another reason, Wreen's contradiction in conception is Wreen's, not Kant's.

Wreen might object that the adulterer vowed at his wedding that on no future occasion would he have sex with anyone else. However, he did have sex with someone else on at least one future occasion. This certainly looks like a contradiction. It isn't. There is nothing whatsoever contradictory about my promise that I shall do X at t and my not doing X at t. It may be wrong, of course, to say that and not to do that, but it is not wrong because it is self-contradictory. The ethics of promising is not that easy.

Of course, adultery would be condemned on Kantian grounds if the maxim of the adulterer's action failed Kant's universalization test. Treating this issue well involves complications that would divert us from adultery. Suffice it to say here that it is not at all difficult to imagine *some* circumstances in which one chooses to commit adultery and wills at the same time that everyone similarly situated chooses to commit adultery without a trace of contradiction. Of course, it does not follow that adultery in *any* circumstance passes the Kantian universalization test. Neither Wreen's view, nor any Kantian universalization view, supports the universal wrongness of adultery.

It is safe to conclude that both an account of the serious wrongness of adultery in terms of the consequences of its discovery and a deontological account of the universal wrongness of adultery are unsatisfactory. A virtue ethics account of adultery avoids the difficulties of these other accounts. On such accounts a major good and a major purpose of a marriage is the establishment and the preservation of a loving relationship. Sexual fidelity is a virtue because it promotes this good.[6] Two positive features of this account are that, as compared with Wasserstrom's account, it seems to explain why undiscovered adultery is seriously wrong and, as compared with Wreen's account it does not imply that adultery is always wrong. On a virtue ethics account, adultery is not a vice in a loveless marriage.[7]

Sexual fidelity promotes the good of a loving relationship because sexual infidelity often will lead to, and perhaps already involve, falling in love with someone else. Falling in love with someone else can lead to loving one's spouse less. Loving one's spouse less departs from a, and perhaps the, valued ideal of marriage.[8] This virtue ethics account is based upon the consequences of the actual adultery, even if it remains undiscovered.

The truth of each of the claims on which the virtue ethics account is based is questionable. First of all, departure from a valued ideal of a marriage is not, *by itself,* a wrong-making feature of an action. Many actions, other than adultery, depart from this valued ideal. Some individuals, because of their career commitments, spend more hours at their jobs than would be optimal if their sole goal were a loving relationship with their spouse. Some marriage partners find themselves more tied up in their children's activities than tied to one another. Often hobbies interfere with optimizing a love relationship. A good life has many aspects. Given the limited number of hours in a day, not all aspects can be pursued to an ideal extent. If the virtue ethics account were correct too *many* activities would be wrong.

Second, as the following excerpt from a story in *The New Yorker* shows, falling in love with someone else does not always lead to loving one's spouse less.

Reclining in his EzeeGuy, he would puff a spliff and try to envision life without one or the other of them. He had always loved Gloria: Senegale had stomped into his life with her goofy belief in the divinity of Ethiopia just when he had started to get sour, making him aware of some motivating force in the world besides money. Until Senegale came along he had not known how much he loved Gloria, because falling in love with Senegale reminded him that he had love inside himself to give. So suddenly he also found himself in love with Gloria again.[9]

A third problem is that an extracurricular sexual relationship not involving love would not be wrong on the virtue ethics analysis. Imagine two people who enjoy friendship and a little more at annual professional conferences. Imagine an affair between two people who find each other great in bed, but who cannot, in their wildest dreams, imagine themselves married to each other. A virtue ethics account does not seem to be able to account for the wrongness of such adulteries. Yet, most think that they are wrong. In short, the truth of each of the claims on which the virtue ethics account is based is at least disputable. This is another instance of a common problem with accounts of wrongness based on consequences.

II. ADULTERY AS BREAKING A CONTRACT

In spite of the weaknesses of accounts of the wrongness of adultery found in the literature, at least one aspect of each is correct. Wasserstrom was right: When adultery is wrong, its serious wrongness is based upon breaking a promise. Wreen was right: The wrongness of adultery is deontological. The virtue ethicists are right in at least two ways: The wrongness of adultery is based upon the nature and value of marriage. Adultery is not always wrong. All of these virtues can be found in a contractual account of the wrongness of adultery.

When adultery is wrong it is wrong because it violates a marriage contract. A typical marriage in our culture is a complex arrangement between two friends in which they have pledged to continue their close friendship, to socialize with others, at least sometimes, as a unit, to have a common domicile which they jointly maintain and (generally) to raise a family together. These two people pledge to be fair in making contributions to their common projects. Their commitment is intended to be life long. They pledge to love one another and to find sexual fulfillment through each other and only with each other. These pledges are not made in a spirit of self-sacrifice, but because each of the partners sincerely believes that marriage to the other will enhance her well being.[10] Because of this, the partners are often willing to make major changes in their life trajectories to promote the ends of the marriage.[11]

This account of the marriage contract explains why adultery is wrong when it is wrong. Suppose that your marriage is a good marriage. If so, then adultery is wrong, for you have entered into a contract one of whose terms is sexual exclusivity. Indeed, adultery would be seriously wrong, not because it could be discovered, but because you would be breaking, not only a pledge but, a very solemn and public pledge, and not only such an important pledge, but a pledge on the basis of which your spouse has changed, or has been willing to change, his life plans. Your adultery would be a sign that you do not take the pledge seriously. Your good marriage is a sign that your partner does take the pledge seriously. Your partner has been prepared to alter his[12] life on the assumption that you did take the pledge seriously. Accordingly, adultery is a serious betrayal. Adultery is seriously wrong, not just because it is breaking a promise, or because it is breaking a promise the breaking of which may have serious consequences, but because it is breaking a contractually based, ceremonial, public, and potentially life altering promise.

III. WHEN ADULTERY IS MORALLY PERMISSIBLE

Not all marriages are good. When one's marriage is bad, divorce frequently is the best option. Nevertheless, a divorce often entails a profound upheaval for yourself, for your spouse and for your children. After all, the nature of the marriage contract is such that one often has altered the trajectory of one's life because of an anticipated lifetime commitment. You made

this lifetime commitment in the belief that this commitment would promote your own well being. When you begin to realize that your marriage is less than good, you may be left with the altered life trajectory without the justification for the alteration. This can leave a person in a very disadvantageous situation.

Accordingly, you may have good reasons for not getting a divorce even though your marriage is bad in important respects. Perhaps, you believe that the overall good of your marriage for you outweighs the bad.[13] Perhaps you believe that, because there are children or other relatives involved, it would be better for all concerned to continue the marriage. Perhaps, because you have radically altered your life plans on the basis of your marriage vows, divorce would be very disadvantageous to you. Perhaps you believe that you owe your spouse continued care in a continuing marriage. On the assumption that there are good reasons for not abandoning a marriage that is considerably less than good, is adultery ever morally permissible?

The contractual account of the wrongness of adultery can sometimes allow for a justification of adultery. There are two situations in which this is so. In the first, your spouse is committing adultery. In a traditional wedding, your pledge not to have sex with someone other than your spouse was made on the condition that your future spouse not have sex with someone other than you. Since that condition no longer obtains, then since your commitment not to commit adultery was conditional, adultery is not wrong when one's spouse is committing adultery.

It is not the case that a bride promises at her wedding that she will remain sexually faithful to her husband no matter how many other women he sleeps with. Her pledge not to commit adultery appears to be unconditional because she promises not to have sex with anyone else on the condition that her groom will not have sex with anyone else and he has indeed solemnly promised not to have sex with anyone else. Accordingly, her pledge is conditional. It does not follow that the bride has given the least bit of thought to what she is committed to if the condition does not obtain. Thus, it does not follow from this that the wedding pledge is about what it is permissible to do if one's spouse commits adultery. The wedding pledge omits that possibility entirely. Because this is so, one has not pledged not to commit adultery if one's spouse is committing adultery. Since your obligation not to commit adultery is based on your conditional wedding pledge, if your spouse commits adultery, your adultery is not a violation of your wedding vows.

The second situation requires a somewhat more elaborate analysis. One of the major purposes of marriage is a loving and sexually fulfilling relationship. People get married on the assumption that their marriage will fulfill that purpose. A loving and sexual fulfilling relationship is a presupposition of the pledge of sexual fidelity. No rational person, in a typical marriage ceremony, would pledge not to love a third party or not to have sexual relations with a third party if she did not anticipate, and if her soon-to-be spouse did not encourage her to anticipate, that within marriage she would find a sexually fulfilling relationship and a lifetime love partner. Not to love one's partner or not to offer one's partner a sexually fulfilling relationship is to negate the tacit conditions under which the partner's vow not to be sexually unfaithful was made. Brides and grooms get married in order to promote their well being. (If you don't believe this, ask them on their wedding day!) Plainly no one chooses to be married in order to be sexually unfulfilled or to be emotionally lonely. Thus, the only sensible way of understanding the vow of sexual fidelity is, again, as a conditional vow, as a vow conditioned upon one's partner's willingness to uphold his sex and love part of the marriage contract.

If this account of the love and sex aspect of the marriage contract is correct, then adultery can be morally permissible when your spouse does not love you or when your spouse does not offer you a sexual fulfilling relationship. If either of these conditions obtain, then your spouse is not fulfilling his part of the marriage contract in the sex and love department. Your pledge not to commit adultery presupposed that your spouse would fulfill his part of the contract in the sex and love department. He has not fulfilled the conditions that were presuppositions of your vow not to commit adultery. Therefore, adultery in such a situation may be morally permissible, for it is not a violation of the marriage contract at all.

An argument for the moral permissibility of adultery in this general situation can be developed in a slightly different way. You entered into marriage in order to promote your well being. In particular, you entered into the marriage contract in order to promote your well being in the sex and love department. Your spouse is not making it possible for you even minimally to flourish in this department. Therefore, your sexual fidelity is depriving you of important aspects of your well being, aspects of your well-being that it was a point of the marriage to nurture. Therefore, of course, adultery is permissible when your spouse is not satisfying the terms of the agreement in the sex and love department. It is not that the marriage contract explicitly gives you permission to commit adultery if you are not fulfilled in the sex and love department. Rather, the contract is not about your relationship under that condition at all. Therefore, it is not the case that sexual fidelity is a contractual obligation when you are married and your spouse does not offer you minimal fulfillment in the sex or love department.

Consideration of a superficially similar case will illuminate this analysis. Suppose that traveling is a very important part of what makes your life worthwhile. Suppose that your spouse either will not travel with you or, when he does, hates the travel so much that he makes your trip unpleasant for you both. He promised when you wed to make you happy. Has he violated your marriage contract? Does his behavior justify adultery?

Notice that this case differs from the sex or love case in several respects. In the first place, you can fulfill that aspect of your well being that your spouse does not promote by finding another traveling partner. In the second place, adultery will not promote that dimension of your well being of which you are deprived by not traveling. In the third place, there is no agreement, explicit or tacit, in a typical marriage ceremony that your spouse will promote *every* aspect of your well being. Accordingly, in this traveling case, the considerations based on contract and well being which justified adultery in the former case are absent.

Nevertheless, this contractual analysis may permit adultery in a fairly wide range of cases. In marriages in which one partner is interested in sexual relations and the other is not, adultery by the former partner may be morally permissible. In marriages in which one partner is unwilling (or unable) to satisfy sexually the other partner, adultery may be morally permissible. An example of this might be a case in which a wife has orgasms only with cunnilingus and her husband finds such a sexual act repulsive. A marriage in which a husband clearly cares for his job, his hobbies and his buddies, but not his wife is a marriage is which it may be morally permissible for his wife to take a lover.

Even if adultery is morally permissible with respect to contractual considerations, there may be good reasons not to commit adultery. Suppose that your husband discovers the affair, and he divorces you. Given that you have decided that there are good reasons not to get a divorce, such a consideration may be a good reason either not to commit adultery or to be very careful. Suppose that you acquire a sexually transmitted disease that you pass on to your husband. Adultery may be defensible (because it is not ruled out) on the basis of contractual considerations and may still not be in the interests of the parties who might be affected by it. Adultery can be wrong for good consequentialist reasons even if the adultery passes the contractual tests.

Those skeptical of this analysis will note that the deception of one's spouse has not yet played a role in the analysis of the conditions under which adultery is permissible. One might argue that if one is going to commit adultery, then one has an obligation to tell one's spouse, since otherwise the sexual infidelity is deceptive and one has an obligation not to be deceptive.

A good treatment of this issue requires more analysis than is possible in an essay of this length. However, a few rough and ready comments are relevant. There can be powerful reasons for maintaining some families even though the spouses' relationship with one another is dysfunctional in the sex and love department. If this is so, then there are good reasons for not telling one's spouse of one's adultery if one has good reasons for believing that one's spouse would break up one's family if he learned of it. Nevertheless, since adultery by one spouse makes adultery by the other spouse morally permissible, then your adultery released your spouse from his obligation not to commit adultery. Furthermore, when your relationship with your spouse is dysfunctional in the sex and love department, moral considerations suggest that you intimate to your spouse that he is under no obligation to live an emotionally lonely or sexually dissatisfied life. Finally, if your marriage is such that the adultery of your wife is morally permissible because you are prepared either not to love your wife or not to sexually satisfy her, then if your spouse has a need for love or sex, then the adultery of your spouse is a not unreasonable expectation. You are not justified in believing that your spouse has misled you by not telling you of her adultery.[14]

A virtue of this contractual account of the moral permissibility of adultery is that it is a unitary analysis. Your spouse at your wedding promised to love and sexually to fulfill you and only you. Violation of that pledge is the ground for the moral permissibility of your adultery.

IV. SOME CONCLUDING REMARKS

No doubt many will be disturbed by the thought that the analysis of this essay has rendered far too much adultery morally permissible. The conflict between this intuition and this analysis can be explained. Our culture endorses two different and incompatible concepts of marriage. On the one hand, we think of marriage as a covenant. When we marry, we marry for better or for worse. We arrange our lives and alter our life's plans on the assumption that marriage is a lifetime commitment. Given that one of the purposes of typical marriages is to raise children and given that the rearing of children is a long-term project, there are excellent reasons for thinking of marriage in terms of the concept of covenant.

On the other hand, we also think of marriage as a contract. Contracts are not unconditionally binding. If the other party does not fulfill his part of the bargain, it is not the case that you are obligated to fulfill yours. Contractual obligations are not "for better or for worse." Each person who enters into a typical marriage contract enters into it in order to promote her well being. Contracts can be broken. Someone who is contemplating divorce thinks of her marriage in these terms. If we thought of marriages exclusively as covenants and not as contracts, we would think that divorce is impermissible. But we don't think that way. These two concepts of marriage, when thought through, have incompatible consequences in some situations. When couples recite their marriage vows they, no doubt, are taking for granted both concepts. This explains two things.

Individuals who commit adultery may be taking for granted the contract concept. People who condemn that same adultery may presuppose the covenant concept. This explains our conflicting intuitions concerning the morally permissibility of adultery.

It also explains the need for adultery. Persons who shape their lives in accordance with the covenant concept may find themselves in unhappy marriages. When thinking of what to do, they think in terms of the contract concept. This can lead to adultery if the argument of this essay is close to the mark.

Two restrictions on the conditions under which adultery is permissible deserve mention. First, suppose, not that your spouse does not love you, but that you have fallen out of love with your spouse. Or suppose that you no longer desire to have sexual relations with your spouse. The contract analysis does not permit adultery in these cases. On the assumption that your spouse is willing to uphold his part of the marriage bargain, if you have fallen out of love with your spouse, you have a duty to do what you can do to develop an emotional bond again if you are going to continue in your marriage. If you are no longer interested in sexual relations with your spouse, then you need to do something about this. In these situations the contract analysis underwrites your obligation not to commit adultery. It is worth noting that it is far easier for us to change our own attitudes and behavior than the attitudes of others.

Notice also that if your spouse does not love you or if your spouse does not sexually satisfy you, the reason may be due to something that you can change. If this is so, then you have an obligation to make that change. The marriage contract contains at least an implicit promise that you will be someone your spouse will find both sexually desirable and lovable.

I regard this essay as a stab at some tough issues that have received little sustained systematic thought in the philosophical literature. The account of the moral permissibility of adultery I have offered is surely incomplete in many ways. The difficult issue of the degree to which a marriage must be unsatisfactory in the sex or love department in order for adultery to be morally permissible has not been explored. An individual's culpable failure to learn of her potential spouse's shortcomings before the wedding may override the moral permissibility of her adultery when those shortcomings become apparent. In addition, the conditions that make adultery morally permissible are nearly always matters of personal judgment rather than publicly verifiable states of affairs. This should not detract from the general philosophical interest in this topic.[15]

NOTES

1. An earlier version of this paper was read at the Mountain-Plains Philosophy Conference in October 1999 and at the meeting of the Pacific Division of the American Philosophical Association in Spring 2000. Eva Dadlez, Hugh LaFollette, Don Loeb, Raja Halwani, Lawrence Houlgate, Jenifer Dodd, Ben Eggleston, and Teresa Robertson have provided me with helpful comments. The comments of Ben Eggleston and Teresa Robertson have been especially helpful.

2. Richard Wasserstrom, "Is Adultery Immoral?" from Richard Wasserstrom ed. *Today's Moral Problems* 2nd ed. (New York: Macmillan, 1979) 290.

3. Michael J. Wreen, "What's Really Wrong with Adultery" from *Philosophy of Sex and Love: A Reader* Robert Trevas, Arthur Zucker, Donald Borchert (ed.) (Upper Saddle River, New Jersey: Prentice Hall, 1997) 176–181.

4. Wreen 177.

5. Wreen 178–179.

6. Raja Halwani, "Virtue Ethics and Adultery," *Journal of Social Philosophy* XXIX #3 (Winter, 1998) 5–18; Mike Martin, *Love's Virtues* (Lawrence, Kansas: University Press of Kansas) 1996 Chapter 4, Sexual Fidelity; and Bonnie Steinbock, "Adultery" *Philosophy and Public Policy* 6, #1 (Winter, 1986) 12–14.

7. See Martin, 81–82; Halwani, 14; and Steinbock, 14–15.

8. See Steinbock, 14, Halwani, 13 and Martin, 77.

9. William Melvin Kelley, "Carlyle Tries Polygamy" *The New Yorker* (August 4, 1997) I thank Teresa Robertson for suggesting this passage.

10. There are difficulties in giving an account of one's own well being in a marriage which can be a new unity. See Robert Nozick's discussion in "Love's Bond" from his *The Examined Life* (New York: Simon and Schuster, 1989).

11. This account is drawn from Lyla O'Driscoll's excellent discussion in "On the Nature and Value of Marriage" which first appeared in Mary Vetterling-Bragging, Frederick A. Elliston and Jane English, eds. *Feminism and Philosophy* (Totowa, New Jersey: Littlefield, Adams and Co. 1978) 249–263. This way of looking at the nature of marriage can accommodate deviations from the paradigm in special circumstances.

12. I shall assume that the person contemplating adultery is a woman because (1) I have to choose some singular pronoun and I prefer the traditionally less conventional one and (2) I have, in my own life, had more opportunity to think through this issue from a feminine than from a masculine perspective.

13. Ann Landers' famous question in these circumstances was: "Are you better off with him or without him?"

14. Consider the following passage from Michele Weiner Davis, *The Sex-Starved Marriage,* (New York: Simon and Schuster, 2003) 10–11. "I also urge you to consider the unfairness of the tacit agreement you have had with your spouse so clearly pointed out in Dr. Pat Love's excellent book, *The Truth About Love.* It goes something like this: 'I know you're sexually unhappy. Although I don't plan on doing anything about it, I still expect you to remain faithful.' Can you see what's wrong with this picture?"

15. I surmise, however, that a lack of philosophical interest in this topic may be explained by the fact that most philosophers are either married or in other serious long term relationships. This may make the topic difficult to write about if one's significant other takes an interest in one's philosophical projects.

9

Is Antioch's Sexual Offense Policy Wrong?

Soble and His Critics

Virtually everyone agrees that having sex with someone without that person's consent is morally wrong. But not everyone agrees about just what, precisely, constitutes consent. The result is the controversy surrounding date rape (also called "acquaintance rape"). In response to concerns about this problem, in the fall of 1990 and winter of 1991, students at Antioch College drafted the college's first Sexual Offense Policy. The policy aims to provide rules for determining what does and does not constitute consent for the purposes of sexual behavior by members of the campus community. The eventual implementation of the policy generated a nationwide debate and helped propel the issue of date rape into the forefront of discussions about sexuality on college campuses across the country. Critics of the policy charged that it was vague and paternalistic, while its defenders maintained that it was an effective, if imperfect, remedy for a serious problem. And while in the decade that followed, many campuses adopted policies that were comparable to that of Antioch, the Antioch policy has remained a focal point in the debate over how universities should respond to the problem of date rape.

Alan Soble is perhaps the leading philosopher writing on issues involving human sexuality. In 1997, he published a widely discussed critique of the Antioch policy (i.e., the version of the policy in effect in 1994; revisions to the policy have been made since then). In the reading that follows, Soble explains the basic motivation behind the policy and then raises a number of objections to it. Most important, he charges that the policy places insufficient weight on nonverbal forms of consent and significantly weakens the practice of consent itself. To support the first contention, Soble argues that verbal forms of communication are not always unequivocal—"no" sometimes means "maybe," and "yes" sometimes reveals only the lack of will to say "no"—and nonverbal forms of communication are sometimes virtually unambiguous. To support his second, contention, he argues that by requiring additional statements of consent at each additional level of intimacy, the policy prevents people from consenting ahead of time to an entire sexual experience and that this renders impossible a certain kind of valuable commitment that people should be able to make to each other.

In her reply to Soble's article, Eva Feder Kittay admits that she, too, was at first skeptical of the Antioch policy. But upon reflection, she now argues, the policy appears more sensible than it might at first seem, and more reasonable than Soble claims it to be. This is so, in part, Kittay believes, because Soble's explanation of the *content* of the policy is incomplete in a relevant respect. The content allows, she argues, more weight to be given to nonverbal communication than Soble recognizes, at least in some contexts. But, more important, Kittay argues that Soble's critique of the Antioch policy overlooks the importance of the *context* of the policy: its having come from, and stayed in place with the approval of, the student body of the college. This is relevant, Kittay argues, in part because it casts the policy's focus on verbal consent in a different light and in part because it suggests that Soble's concern about the policy's impact on long-term relationships is misplaced. As a result, while Soble's analysis maintains that the Antioch policy infringes on student autonomy in various respects, Kittay suggests that the policy reaffirms it.

QUESTIONS FOR CONSIDERATION

The debate about Antioch's Sexual Offense Policy in particular, and about date rape in general, is complex and highly charged, and touches upon a number of issues beyond those dealt with explicitly in these readings. As way of initiating a critical discussion of the debate that arises from the clash between Soble and Kittay, however, we would suggest at least beginning with the following questions:

• Is Soble right that the policy places insufficient weight on nonverbal forms of consent, or is Kittay right in thinking that it gives them as much weight as they merit?

• Is Soble right in thinking that the policy precludes a valuable kind of commitment, one that involves consenting ahead of time to everything that follows from the initiation of sexual activity, or is Kittay right to have serious reservations about the value of such open-ended forms of consent?

• Is Kittay justified in maintaining that the context of the Antioch policy helps to overcome some of the objections that might initially seem to warrant rejecting it? In particular, in what sense does the fact that students have generally embraced the policy make its focus on verbal consent more reasonable? Does it make it reasonable even for students who opposed the policy? And does it succeed in overcoming Soble's worry about the effect of the policy on the viability of long-term relationships, or is Kittay unjustifiably cynical about the desire that most students have for less stable interactions?

Antioch's "Sexual Offense Policy"

A Philosophical Exploration

Alan Soble

> She: For the last time, do you love me or don't you?
> He: I DON'T!
> She: Quit stalling, I want a *direct* answer.
> —Jane Russell and Fred Astaire[1]

1. "WHEN IN DOUBT, ASK"

Consider this seemingly innocuous moral judgment issued by philosopher Raymond Belliotti:

> "teasing" without the intention to fulfill that which the other can reasonably be expected to think was offered is immoral since it involves the nonfulfillment of that which the other could reasonably be expected as having been agreed upon.[2]

This might be right in the abstract; provocative and lingering flirtatious glances sometimes can reasonably be taken as an invitation to engage in sex; hence brazenly flirting and not fulfilling its meaning, or never intending to fulfill its meaning, is, like failing to honor other promises or invitations, *ceteris paribus* a moral defect—even if not a mortal sin. Abstractions aside, however, how are we to grasp "can *reasonably* be taken as"? A woman's innocent, inquisitive glance might be taken as a sexual invitation by an awfully optimistic fellow, and he and his peers might judge his perception "reasonable." This is the reason Catharine MacKinnon says that to use "reasonable belief as a standard without asking, on a substantive social basis, to whom the belief is reasonable and why—meaning, what conditions make it reasonable—is one-sided: male-sided."[3] Simi-

larly, a man's innocent, inquisitive glance might be taken as a sexual leer by an anxiously sensitive woman, and she and her peers might judge this perception "reasonable." Belliotti writes as if all were well with "reasonable":

> Although sexual contracts are not as formal or explicit as corporation agreements the rule of thumb should be the concept of reasonable expectation. If a woman smiles at me and agrees to have a drink I cannot reasonably assume . . . that she has agreed to spend the weekend with me.[4]

I suppose not. But why not? We do not now have in our culture a convention, a practice like the display of colored hankies, in which a smile before an accepted drink has that meaning. But nothing intrinsic to the action prevents its having, in the proper circumstances, that very meaning. And an optimistic fellow might say that the *special* sort of smile she, or another he, gave him constituted a sexual invitation. Belliotti continues his example:

> On the other hand if she did agree to share a room and bed with me for the weekend I could reasonably assume that she had agreed to have sexual intercourse.

Not true for many American couples as they travel through foreign lands together. Or maybe in accepting the invitation to share a room or sleeping car she agreed only to snuggle. Cues indicating the presence and kind of sexual interest are fluid; at one time in the recent past, a woman's inviting a man to her apartment or room carried more sexual meaning

Alan Soble, "Antioch's 'Sexual Offense Policy': A Philosophical Exploration," *Journal of Social Philosophy* 28, no. 1 (1997): 22–36. Some notes have been deleted. Reprinted by permission of Blackwell Publishing Ltd.

than it does now—even if that meaning still lingers on college campuses and elsewhere. To forestall such objections, Belliotti offers these instructions:

> If there is any doubt concerning whether or not someone has agreed to perform a certain sexual act with another, I would suggest that the doubting party simply ask the other and make the contract more explicit. . . . [W]hen in doubt assume nothing until a more explicit overture has been made.[5]

What could be more commonsensically true than this? But it is wrong. The man who thinks it reasonable in a given situation to assume that the woman has agreed to have sex will not have any doubt and so will have no motive to ask more explicitly what she wants. His failure to doubt, or his failure to imagine the bare possibility of doubting, whether the other has consented to engage in sex is brought about by the same factors that determine, for him, the reasonableness of his belief in her consent. It is silly to suggest *when* in doubt, ask," because the problem is that not enough doubt arises in the first place, i.e., the brief look is taken too readily as reasonable or conclusive evidence of a sexual invitation. A man touches the arm of a woman who briefly glanced at him; she pulls away abruptly; but he is not caused to have doubts about her interest. Even if he does not take her resistance as further evidence of her desire, the reasonableness, for him, of his belief that her earlier glance was intentionally sexual is enough to prevent doubt from taking root when it should—immediately.

2. " 'NO' MEANS 'NO' "

According to Susan Estrich, a man who engages in sex with a woman on the basis of an unreasonable belief in her consent should be charged with rape; only a genuinely reasonable belief in her consent should exculpate an accused rapist. Estrich wants it to be legally impossible for a man accused of rape to plead that he believed that the woman consented, when that belief was unreasonable, even though *he* thought it was reasonable. Estrich realizes that "reasonable belief" is a difficult notion. Still, she heroically proposes that "the reasonable man in the

1980s should be the one who understands that a woman's word is deserving of respect, whether she is a perfect stranger or his own wife." The reasonable man "is the one who . . . understands that 'no means no'."[6] The man pawing the arm of the woman who pulls abruptly away—the physical equivalent of "no"—had better immediately doubt the quality of his belief in her sexual interest. At the psychological level, this man might not doubt that she is sexually interested in him; Estrich's normative proposal is that he is to be held liable anyway, because he *should* be doubtful. Beyond this crude sort of case, I think Estrich means that, for the reasonable man, a woman's qualified locution ("Please, not tonight, I think I'd rather not"; "I don't know, I just don't feel like it") is not an invitation to continue trying, but "no." Her wish is expressed softly because she is tactful or frightened or because this is the women's language she has learned to speak. For the reasonable man, her "I'm not sure I want to" is either a tactful "no" or a request to back off while she autonomously makes up her own mind.

As congenial as Estrich's proposal is, she muddies the water with a tantalizing piece of logic:

> Many feminists would argue that so long as women are powerless relative to men, viewing a "yes" as a sign of true consent is misguided. . . . [M]any women who say yes to men they know, whether on dates or on the job, would say no if they could. I have no doubt that women's silence sometimes is the product not of passion and desire but of pressure and fear. Yet if yes may often mean no, at least from a woman's perspective, it does not seem so much to ask men, and the law, to respect the courage of the woman who does say no and to take her at her word.[7]

Estrich's reasoning seems to be: if something as antithetical to "no" as "yes" can mean "no," then surely something as consistent with "no," "no" itself, means "no." This argument has a curious consequence. If "yes" can mean "no," at least from a woman's *own* perspective (the woman who consents for financial reasons but whose heart and desire are not wrapped up in the act; a woman who agrees, but only after a barrage of pleading), then it will be difficult to deny that "no" spoken by some women can mean "maybe" or even "yes." From the perspective of some women, "no" can mean "try harder to convince me" or "show me how manly you are." Charlene Muehlenhard and Lisa Hollabaugh reported in 1988 that some women occasionally say "no" but do not mean it; 39.3 percent of the 610 college women they surveyed at Texas A&M University indicated that they had offered "token resistance" to sex "even though [they] had every intention to and [were] willing to engage in sexual intercourse."[8] Susan Rae Peterson partially explains these findings: "typical sexual involvement includes some resistance on the part of women . . . because they have been taught to do so, or they do not want to appear 'easy' or 'cheap'."[9]

Men cannot always tell when a woman's resistance is real or token, serious or playful; men are, moreover, often insensitive, even callous, as to what a woman does intend to communicate; and, after all, Muehlenhard and Hollabaugh's figure is only 39 percent and not 99 percent. For these reasons, as well as her own, Estrich's proposal is a wise suggestion. Men, and the courts, should always assume, in order to be cognitively, morally, and legally safe, that a woman's "no" means "no"—*even in those cases when it does or might not.* A man who takes "no" as "no" even when he suspects that a woman is testing his masculinity with token resistance is advised by Estrich to risk suffering a loss of sexual pleasure and a possible blow to his ego, in order to secure the greater good, for both him and her, of avoiding rape.

But if men are always to assume that "no" means "no," even though there is a nontrivial chance that it means "keep trying" or "yes," then Estrich, to be consistent, should permit men to assume that a woman's "yes" always means "yes"—even though, on her view, a woman's "yes" sometimes means "no." If, instead, Estrich wants men to sort out when a woman's "yes" really means "yes" and when it does not, in order that he be able to decide whether to take the "yes" at its face value and proceed with sex, she should propose some workable procedure for men to follow. Yet her description of the reasonable man mentions only what his response to "no" should be, and not what his response to "yes" should be. Encouraging women to abandon the token resistance maneuver, to give up saying "no" when they

mean "maybe" or "yes," is helpful. But it will not take theorists of sex, or men in the presence of an apparently consenting woman, very far in deciphering when "yes" means "no."

3. THE ANTIOCH POLICY

I propose that we understand Antioch University's "Sexual Offense Policy" as addressing the issues raised in our discussion of Belliotti and Estrich. The Policy's central provisions are these:[10]

A1. "Consent must be obtained verbally before there is any sexual contact or conduct."

A2. "[O]btaining consent is an on-going process in any sexual interaction."

A3. "If the level of sexual intimacy increases during an interaction . . . the people involved need to express their clear verbal consent before moving to that new level."

A4. "The request for consent must be specific to each act."

A5. "If you have had a particular level of sexual intimacy before with someone, you must still ask each and every time."

A6. "If someone has initially consented but then stops consenting during a sexual interaction, she/he should communicate withdrawal verbally and/or through physical resistance. The other individual(s) must stop immediately."

A7. "Don't ever make any assumptions about consent."

In an ethnically, religiously, economically, socially, and sexually diverse population, there might be no common and comprehensive understanding of what various bits of behavior mean in terms of expressing interest in or consenting to sex. In the absence of rigid conventions or a homogeneous community, a glance, either brief or prolonged, is too indefinite to be relied on to transmit information; an invitation to come to one's room, or sharing a room, or a bed, on a trip might or might not have some settled meaning; clothing and cosmetics in a pluralistic culture are equivocal. (Young men, more so than young women, take tight jeans and the absence of a bra under a top to signal an interest in sex.) Because physical movements and cues of various kinds can be interpreted in widely different ways, sexual activity entered into or carried out on the basis of this sort of (mis)information is liable to violate someone's rights or otherwise be indecent or offensive. Antioch insists that consent to sexual activity be verbal (A1) instead of behavioral.[11] Following this rule will minimize miscommunication and the harms it causes and encourage persons to treat each other with respect as autonomous agents.

Further, bodily movements or behaviors of a sexual sort that occur in the early stages of a possible sexual encounter can also be ambiguous and do not necessarily indicate a willingness to increase the intensity of, or to prolong, the encounter (hence A2, A3). Verbal communication is supposed to prevent misunderstandings rooted in indefinite body language; we should not assume consent on the basis of expressions of desire (lubrication, groans) or failures to resist an embrace (A1). Neither of these bodily phenomena—reacting with sexual arousal to a touch; not moving away when intimately touched— necessarily mean that the touched person welcomes the touch or wants it to continue. There are times when one's body responds with pleasure to a touch but one's mind disagrees with the body's judgment; Antioch's insistence on verbal consent after discussion and deliberation is meant to give the mind the decisive and autonomous say. Similarly, the verbal request for, and the verbal consent to, sexual contact must be not only explicit, but also specific for any sexual act that might occur (A4). Consenting to and then sharing a kiss does not imply consent to any other sexual act; the bodily movements that accompany the sexual arousal created by the kiss do not signal permission to proceed to some other sexual activity not yet discussed.

One provision (A7) is a rebuttal of Belliotti's advice, "when in doubt, ask." Antioch demands, more strictly than this, that the sexual partners entertain *universal* doubt and therefore *always* ask. Doubt about the other's consent must be categorical rather than hypothetical: not Belliotti's "when in doubt, assume nothing," but a Cartesian "doubt!" and "assume nothing!" To be on the cognitive, moral, and legal safe side, to avoid mistakes about desire or

intention, always assume "no" unless a clear, verbal, explicit "yes" is forthcoming (A1, A3, A4). Men no longer have to worry about distinguishing a woman's mildly seductive behavior from her "incomplete rejection strategy," about which men and boys are often confused; in the absence of an explicit "yes" on her part, he is, as demanded by Estrich, to assume a respectful "no." There's still the question of how a man is to know, when obvious consent-negating factors are lacking (e.g., she's had too much alcohol), whether a woman's "yes" truly means "yes." Antioch's solution is to rely on explicit, probing verbal communication that must occur not only before but also during a sexual encounter (A3, A5). The constant dialogue, the "on-going process" (A2) of getting consent in what Lois Pineau calls "communicative sexuality,"[12] is meant to provide the man with an opportunity to assess whether the woman's "yes" means "yes," to give her the opportunity to say a definite even if tactful "no," and to clear up confusions created by her silence or passive acquiescence. At the same time, there is to be no constant badgering—especially not under the rubric of "communicative sexuality"—of a woman by a man in response to her "no." A man's querying whether a woman's "no" really means "no" is to disrespect her "no" and fails to acknowledge her autonomy. It is also to embark on a course that might constitute verbal coercion.

It is illuminating to look at the Antioch policy from the perspective of the sadomasochistic subculture, in particular its use of "safe words." A set of safe words is a language, a common understanding, a convention jointly created (hence a Cartesian foundation) in advance of sex by the partners, to be used during a sexual encounter as a way to say "yes," "more," "no," to convey details about wants and dislikes, without spoiling the erotic mood. Thus the use of safe words attempts to achieve some of the goals of Antioch's policy without the cumbersome apparatus of explicit verbal consent at each level of sexual interaction (A3, A4). And a tactful safe word can gently accomplish an Antiochian withdrawal of consent to sex (A6). But there is a major difference between sadomasochism and Antiochian sex: a sadomasochistic pair want the activities to proceed smoothly, spontaneously, realistically, so one party grants to the other the right to carry on as she wishes, subject to the veto or modifications of safe words, which are to be used sparingly, only when necessary, as a last resort; the couple therefore eschew Antiochian constant dialogue. In dispensing with the incessant chatter of on-going consent to higher levels of sexual interaction (A2, A3), the sadomasochistic pair violate another provision (A7): consent is assumed throughout the encounter in virtue of the early granting of rights. No such prior consent to sex into an indefinite future is admissible by Antioch (A2, A3, A4).

4. PLEASURE

Does Antioch's policy make sex less exciting? Does it force a couple to slow down, to savor each finger and tooth, when they would rather be overwhelmed by passion? Sarah Crichton criticizes the Antioch policy on the grounds that "it criminalizes the delicious unexpectedness of sex—a hand suddenly moves to here, a mouth to there."[13] But this consideration is not decisive. One goal of the Policy is to decrease the possibility that a person will unexpectedly experience (i.e., without being warned by being asked) something unpleasant that he or she does not want to experience: a mouth sucking on the wrong toe, a finger too rudely rammed in the rectum. The risk of undergoing unwanted acts or sensations is especially great with strangers, and it is in such a context that the requirement that consent be obtained specifically for each act makes the most sense. Sometimes we do not want the unexpected but only the expected, the particular sensations we know, trust, and yearn for. So there is in the Antioch policy a trade off: we lose the pleasure, if any, of the unexpected, but we also avoid the unpleasantness of the unexpected. This is why Crichton's point is not decisive. Perhaps for young people, or for those more generally who do not yet know what they like, verbal consent to specifically described touches or acts might make less sense. But in this case, too, reason exists to insist, for the sake of caution, on such consent.

Julia Reidhead also attempts to rebut the objection that Antioch's policy begets dull sex.[14] She claims that the Policy gives the partners a chance to be creative with language, to play linguistically with a request to touch the breast or "kiss the hollow of your neck" and to "reinvent [sex] privately." But Antioch thinks that sexual language needs to be less, rather than more, private; more specific, not less.[15] Hence Reidhead's praise for Antioch's policy misses its point: common linguistic understandings cannot be assumed in a heterogenous population. To encourage the creative, poetic use of language in framing sexual requests to proceed to a new level of sex is to provoke the misunderstandings the Policy was designed to prevent. Thus, when Reidhead queries, "What woman or man on Antioch's campus, or elsewhere, wouldn't welcome . . . 'May I kiss the hollow of your neck'," her homogenizing "or elsewhere" betrays the insensitivity to cultural and social differences and their linguistic concomitants that Antioch is trying to overcome.

Reidhead defends Antioch also by arguing that vocalizing creatively about sex before we do it is a fine way to mix the pleasures of language with the pleasures of the body. Indeed, the pleasures of talk are themselves sensual. "Antioch's subtle and imaginative mandate is an erotic windfall: an opportunity for undergraduates to discover that wordplay and foreplay can be happily entwined." Reidhead is right that talking about sex can be sexy and arousing, but wrong that this fact is consistent with the Antioch policy and one of its advantages. This cute reading of communication as itself sex almost throws Antioch's procedure into a vicious regress: if no sexual activity is permissible without prior consent (A1), and consent must be spoken, then if a request for sexual activity is constructed to be a sexually arousing locution, it would amount to a sexual act and hence would be impermissible unless it, in turn, had already received specific consent (A1, A4). So Y's consent to nonverbal sexual activity must be preceded by X's request for that activity *and* by X's request to utter that request. Further, to try to get consent for the sexual act of kissing the neck by talking sensually about kissing the neck is to employ the pleasure elicited by one sexual act to bring about the occurrence of another sexual act. But obtaining consent for a sexual act by causing even mild sexual pleasure with a seductive request is to interfere with calm and rational deliberation—as much as a shot or two of whiskey would. This is why Antioch insists (A3) that between any two sexual levels there must be a pause, a sexual gap, that makes space for three things: (1) a thoughtful, verbal act of request, (2) deliberations about whether or not to proceed, and then (3) either consent or denial. A well-timed hiatus respected by both parties provides an obstacle to misreadings; Augustinian bodily perturbations are to be checked while the mind reconsiders.

5. BODY TALK

The body should not be dismissed. When two people in love embrace tightly, eyes glued to the other's eyes, bodies pulsating with pleasure, they often do know (*how,* is the mystery) without explicit verbalization, from the way they touch each other and respond to these touches, that each wants and consents to the sex that is about to occur. Other cases of successful communication—in and out of sexual contexts—are explicit and specific without being verbal. So even if the truth of the particular claim that the mouth can say "no" while the body exclaims an overriding "yes" is debatable, the general idea, that the body sometimes does speak a clear language, seems fine. Maybe this is why Antioch, even though it requires a verbal "yes" for proceeding with sex (A1), allows a nonverbal "no" to be sufficient for *withdrawing* consent (A6); nonverbal behavior can have a clear meaning. Certain voluntary actions, even some impulsive, reflex-like, bodily movements, do mean "no," and about these there should be no mistake, in the same Estrichian way that about the meaning of the simple verbal "no" there should be no mistake. But if such motions can be assumed or demanded to be understood in a pluralistic community—*pulling away when touched means "no"*—then some voluntary behaviors and involuntary bodily movements must reliably signal "yes."

According to the Policy, a verbal "yes" replaces any possible bodily movement or behavior as the one and only reliable sign that proceeding with sexual activity is permissible. If I ask, "may I kiss you?" I may not proceed on the basis of your bodily reply,

e.g., you push your mouth out at mine, or groan and open your mouth invitingly, because even though it seems obvious what these behaviors mean ("yes"), I might be making an interpretive mistake: I see your open mouth as presented "invitingly" because I have with undue optimism deceived myself into thinking that's what you mean. So I must wait for the words, "yes, you may kiss me,"[16] about which interpretive unclarity is not supposed to arise, else the problem Antioch set for itself is unsolvable. The verbal "yes," *after* communicative probing, is Antioch's Cartesian foundation. But can the ambiguities of the verbal be cleared up by language itself? How much communicative probing is *enough?* This question opens up a hermeneutic circle that traps Antioch's policy. Her "yes," repeated several times under the third-degree of communicative sex, can always be probed more for genuineness, if I wanted to *really* make sure. But, losing patience, she shows her "yes" to be genuine when she grabs me. The body reasserts itself.

My continuing to probe her "yes" over and over again, to make sure that her heart and desire are wrapped up in the act to which she is apparently consenting (must I ask her whether her agreement has been engineered for my benefit by "compulsory heterosexuality"?), is a kind of paternalism. Because the robust respect that Antioch's policy fosters for a woman's "no" is offset by the weaker respect it fosters for her "yes," conceiving of the Antioch policy not as attempting to foster respect for the autonomy of the other, but as attempting to prevent acquaintance rape, i.e., harmful behaviors, is more accurate. At best, the relationship between Antioch's policy and autonomy is unclear. One Antioch student, Suzy Martin, defends the Policy by saying that "It made me aware I *have* a voice. I didn't know that before."[17] Coming in the mid-90s from a college-age woman, the kind of person we expect to know better, this remark is astonishing. In effect, she admits that what Antioch is doing for her, at such an advanced age, is what her parents and earlier schooling should have done long ago, to teach her that she has a voice. Thus Antioch is employing an anti-autonomy principle in its treatment of young adults—in loco parentis—that my college generation had fought to eliminate.

6. CONSENT

The Policy lays it down that previous sexual encounters between two people do not relax or change the rules to be followed during their later encounters (A5); the casual sex of one-night stands and that of on-going relationships are governed by the same standards. Nor does a person's sexual biography (reputation) count for anything. No historical facts allow "assumptions about consent" (A7). Indeed, in requiring consent at each different level of a single sexual encounter, Antioch applies the same principle of the irrelevance of history to each sub-act within that encounter. Earlier consent to one sub-act within a single encounter creates no presumption that one may proceed, without repeating the procedure of obtaining explicit and specific consent, to later sub-acts in the same encounter, in the same way that one sexual encounter does not mean that consent can be assumed for later encounters. The history of the relationship, let alone the history of the evening, counts for nothing. The Antioch policy, then, implies that one cannot consent in advance to a whole night of sex, but only to a single atomistic act, one small part of an encounter. Similarly, in denying the relevance of the historical, Antioch makes a Pauline marriage contract impossible.[18] In such a marriage, one consents at the very beginning, in advance, to a whole series of sexual acts that might comprise the rest of one's sexual life; consent to sex is presumed after the exchange of vows and rings; each spouse owns the body and sexual powers of the other; and so marital rape is conceptually impossible, replaced by a notion of fulfilling the "marriage debt." In rejecting the possibility of such an arrangement, even if voluntarily contracted, Antioch cuts back on a traditional power of consent, its ability to apply to an indefinite, open future. For Antioch, consent is short-lived; it dies an easy death, and must always be replaced by a new generation of consents.

Antioch also cuts back on the power of consent by making it not binding: one can withdraw consent at any time during any act or sub-act (A6). Nothing in the Policy indicates that the right to withdraw is limited by the sexual satisfaction or other expectations of one's partner. Any such qualification would also run counter to the Policy's spirit. This is a difference between Antioch's policy and Belliotti's libertarianism, according to which breaking a sexual promise is at least a prima facie moral fault. It is also contrary to the indissolubility of Pauline marriage. But that Antioch would be indulgent about withdrawing consent makes sense, given Antioch's distrust of the historical. Consenting is an act that occupies a discrete location in place and time; it is a historical event, and that it has occurred is a historical fact; thus consent is itself precisely the kind of thing whose weight Antioch discounts. Consenting to a sexual act does not entail, for Antioch, that one ought to perform the act, and not even that one has a prima facie duty to do so; the act need not take place because the only justification for it to occur is the act of consenting that has already receded into the past and has become a mere piece of impotent history. When consent into the future, given today for tomorrow, is ruled out, so too is consent into the future, now for ten seconds from now. How could consent have the power to legitimize any subsequent sexual act? An air of paradox surrounds the Policy: it makes consent the centerpiece of valid sexual conduct, yet its concept of consent is emaciated. Of course, "unless refusal of consent or withdrawal of consent are real possibilities, we can no longer speak of 'consent' in any genuine sense."[19] But that withdrawing consent must be possible does not entail that we have carte blanche permission to do so. My guess is that Belliotti is right, that withdrawing consent to an act to which one has consented is prima facie wrong. The logical possibility that consent is binding in this way is necessary for taking consent seriously as a legitimizer of sexual activity.

Still, if X has promised a sexual act to Y, but withdraws consent and so reneges, it does *not* follow from libertarianism that Y has a right to compel X into compliance. Nor does it follow from the terms of Pauline marriage, in which the spouses consent to a lifetime of sexual acts. Neither the fact that each person has a duty, the marriage debt, to provide sexual pleasure for the other whenever the other wants it, nor the fact that in such a marriage the one initial act of consent makes rape conceptually impossible, imply that a spurned spouse may rightfully force himself upon the other. Pauline marriage is egalitar-ian; the wife owns the husband and his ability to perform sexually as much as he owns her capacity to provide pleasure. In patriarchal practice, the man expects sexual access to his wife in exchange for economic support, and even if rape is conceptually impossible he might extract the marriage debt: "if she shows unwillingness or lack of inclination to engage with him in sexual intercourse, he may wish to remind her of the nature of the bargain they struck. The act of rape may serve conveniently as a communicative vehicle for reminding her."[20] Neither violence nor abuse are legitimated by the principles of Pauline marriage; perhaps their possibility explains why Paul admonishes spouses to show "benevolence" to each other (1 Cor. 7:3).[21]

Finally, Antioch's policy also does not permit "metaconsent," or consent about (the necessity of) consent. Consent, in principle, should be able to alter the background presumption, in the relationship between two people, *from* "assume 'no' unless you hear an explicit 'yes' " *to* "assume 'yes' unless you hear an explicit 'no'," or *from* "don't you dare try without an explicit go-ahead" *to* "feel free to try but be prepared for a 'no'." This power of consent is abolished by Antioch's making history irrelevant; consent to prior acts creates no presumption in favor of "yes" tonight (A5). Further, to give consent into the future allows one's partner to make a prohibited assumption (A7). There is no provision in the Policy that empowers a couple to jettison the Policy by free and mutual consent; here is another way Antioch's policy is not designed to foster autonomy. In Pauline marriage, by contrast, one act of consent, the marriage vow, has the power to change presumptions from "no" to an ongoing "yes." Such is the power of consent for Paul, that it both applies to the future and is binding: we make our bed and then lie in it. Antioch's notion of consent has freed us from such stodgy concerns.

NOTES

1. The epigraph to chapter 9 of Susan Haack's *Evidence and Inquiry* (Oxford: Blackwell, 1993), 182. Professor Haack thanks David Stove for supplying it.

2. "A Philosophical Analysis of Sexual Ethics," *Journal of Social Philosophy* 10, no. 3 (1979): 8–11, at 11

3. *Toward a Feminist Theory of the State* (Cambridge: Harvard University Press, 1989), 183; see 181.

4. "A Philosophical Analysis of Sexual Ethics," 9.

5. Belliotti repeats the "when in doubt, ask" advice in his essay "Sex" (in Peter Singer, ed., *A Companion to Ethics* [Oxford: Blackwell, 1991], 315–26, at 325) and in his treatise *Good Sex: Perspectives on Sexual Ethics* (Lawrence, Kan.: University Press of Kansas, 1993), 106–107. See my "book note" in *Ethics* 105, no. 2 (1995): 447–48.

6. *Real Rape* (Cambridge: Harvard University Press, 1987), 97–98.

7. Ibid., 102.

8. "Do Women Sometimes Say No When They Mean Yes? The Prevalence and Correlates of Token Resistance to Sex," *Journal of Personality and Social Psychology* 54, no. 5 (1988): 872–79.

9. "Coercion and Rape: The State as a Male Protection Racket," in Mary Vetterling-Braggin, Frederick A. Elliston, and Jane English, eds., *Feminism and Philosophy* (Totowa, N.J.: Littlefield, Adams, 1977), 360–71, at 365. See also Muehlenhard and Hollabaugh on the wide variety of reasons women have for carrying out this sometimes "rational" strategy (875, 878).

10. I quote from a copy of the Policy and its introduction sent to me in 1994 by the Office of the President, Antioch University. The numbering of the provisions is my own. The Policy was intended to be gender- and sexual orientation-neutral, allowing the possibility of gay or lesbian acquaintance rape and the rape of a man by a woman.

11. At least seven times in the Policy and its introduction, it is stated that consent to sexual activity must be verbal. Only once does the Policy depart from this formula: "the person with whom sexual contact/conduct is initiated is responsible to express verbally and/or physically her/his willingness or lack of willingness when reasonably possible." Because the bulk of the Policy insists that consent be verbal, I discount this one awkward and *possibly* contradictory sentence. Further, "reasonably" here nearly destroys the power of the Policy to resolve issues *about* reasonableness.

The Policy also says, "If sexual contact . . . is *not* mutually and simultaneously initiated, then the person who initiates sexual contact . . . is responsible for getting the verbal consent of the other individuals(s) involved" (italics added). From the statement that when mutual and simultaneous initiation is absent, verbal consent is required, it does not follow (nor does the Policy ever assert) that when mutual and simultaneous initiation is present, verbal consent can be dispensed with. To claim otherwise—to deny that the Antioch policy always requires verbal consent—is to commit an elementary logical fallacy. (This mistake was made by my commentator at the APA session.) Anyway, if we are to construe the Antioch policy as an interesting and novel approach to the problems we are discussing, we should not read it as asserting that "mutual and simultaneous initiation," cancels the need for verbal consent. The aroused and optimistic person who subjectively has no doubt that the other person is consenting, but is mistaken about that, is a version of the aroused and optimistic person who assumes that his initiation is reciprocated mutually and simultaneously by the other, but is similarly mistaken. Thus the good intentions of the Antioch policy would fall prey to the same psychological and moral delusions that undermined Belliotti's principle, "when in doubt, ask."

12. A man "cannot know, except through the practice of communicative sexuality, whether his partner has any sexual reason for continuing the encounter"—or any other reason for doing so ("Date Rape: A Feminist Analysis," *Law and Philosophy* 8 [1989]: 217–43, at 239). The essays in Leslie Francis's anthology *Date Rape* (University Park: Penn State University Press, 1996) explore both the Antioch policy and Pineau's essay.

13. "Sexual Correctness. Has It Gone Too Far?" in Susan J. Bunting, ed., *Human Sexuality 95/96* (Guilford, Conn.: Dushkin, 1995), 208–211, at 209.

14. "Good Sex" [letter], *The New Yorker* (Jan. 10, 1994), 8.

15. Antioch, however, does very little to make specific the "specific" of A4. Thus the Policy is vulnerable to wisecracks:

> [*X* and *Y* sit on a couch, face-to-face.]
> *X:* May I kiss you?
> *Y:* Of course. Go ahead.
> [*Y* makes *Y*'s mouth available; *X* slides *X*'s tongue deeply into *Y*'s oral cavity. *Y* pulls sharply away.]
> *Y:* I didn't say you could *French* kiss me!

16. According to the Policy, "Consent must be clear and verbal (i.e., saying: yes, I want to kiss you also)."

17. Jennifer Wolf, "Sex By the Rules," *Glamour* (May 1994), 256–59, 290, at 258.

18. See 1 Cor. 7: [4]The wife hath not power of her own body, but the husband: and likewise also the husband hath not power of his own body, but the wife. [5]Defraud ye not one the other, except it be with consent for a time, that ye may give yourselves to fasting and prayer; and come together again, that Satan tempt you not for your incontinency.

19. Pateman, "Women and Consent," 150.

20. Carolyn Shafer and Marilyn Frye, "Rape and Respect," in Mary Vetterling-Braggin et al., *Feminism and Philosophy,* 333–46, at 342.

21. "It is in fact justly observed that a conjugal act imposed upon one's partner without regard for his or her condition and lawful desires is not a true act of love, and therefore denies an exigency of right moral order in the relationships between husband and wife" (Paul VI, "Humanac Vitae," in Robert Baker and Frederick Elliston, eds., *Philosophy and Sex,* 2nd ed. [Buffalo, N.Y.: Prometheus, 1984], 167–83, at 173).

Critics

ΛH! My Foolish Heart

Eva Feder Kittay

A Reply to Alan Soble's "Antioch's 'Sexual Offense Policy': A Philosophical Exploration"[1]

A sexual code occupies an uneasy position at the intersection of the public and private, the communal and intimate, the codifiable and spontaneous, the articulate and ineffable. And sexual conduct is located at the troubling interface of pleasure and offense; passion and power; freedom and submission; desire as an individual drive and desire as the epiphany of mutuality—the desiring of the other's desire. How do we regulate sexual conduct? How can any code legislate sexual desire or successfully thwart abusive sexuality? Here the wise say that only fools do tread. Since Antioch announced its Sexual Offense Policy, Antioch has, in the eyes of the media and some retro (and not so retro) feminists and academics, worn a dunce cap. Is it well-deserved?

After a clear, and seemingly sympathetic, discussion of the code that includes much of the motivation for the policy, Alan Soble weighs in with the wise. On three grounds: pleasure, body talk, and consent.[2]

Upon first learning of the Sexual Offense Policy, my romantic heart declared this was a silly, foolish code—though my feminist mind urged a more cautious judgment. To have to verbally consent to each level (and just what is a level anyway?) of sexual intimacy? each time? even with a partner with whom one had been intimate many times before? Many of us lose the capacity of articulate speech at these moments. Are we to be deprived of our hearts' desire since, unlike Molly Bloom, we don't utter an ecstatic "Yes! yes! yes!" at the appropriate moment?

Reading the harrowing accounts of date rapes recounted by Robin Warshaw,[3] I kept wondering if a code such as Antioch's would help in any of these cases. And if it would not, what *was* the point? Being on sabbatical, I was unable to canvas my classes for the student point of view. Fortunately, I had some private college-aged informants, my twenty-year-old son, his girlfriend (whom I questioned separately), and their friends. I also queried colleagues who had discussed the code with their students. There seemed to be a rather interesting response that came up again and again: "The code is silly, but I wouldn't mind it being there. It would be a way of opening up discussion on these issues." Only one young man I spoke to said it would encourage him to only have sex with himself—he always would know that the answer was "yes."

Taking a closer look at the code, I noticed some interesting phrases that are omitted in Alan Soble's summary. In the seven-point discussion of consent, the first point justifies Soble's claim that "verbal 'yes' . . . is Antioch's "Cartesian foundation":[4]

1. For the purpose of this policy, "consent" shall be defined as follows: "the act of willingly and verbally agreeing to engage in a specific sexual contact or conduct."[5]

And yet the next point has an antecedent clause that implies that verbal consent is not *always* demanded:

2. If sexual contact and/or conduct is not mutually and simultaneously initiated, then the person who initiates sexual contact/conduct is responsible for getting the verbal consent of the other individual(s) involved.[6]

From Eva Feder Kittay, "AH! My Foolish Heart: A Reply to Alan Soble's 'Antioch's "Sexual Offense Policy": A Philosophical Exploration,'" *Journal of Social Philosophy* 28, no. 2 (1997): 153–59. Some notes and some parts of the text have been deleted. Reprinted by permission of Blackwell Publishing Ltd.

"*If* sexual contact and/or conduct is *not mutually* and *simultaneously* initiated . . ." So, if my partner and I simultaneously are seized with the desire to kiss, we don't need to say a thing as our mouths spontaneously move toward each other. And if I am as passionately unbuttoning my partner and my partner unbuttons me, we can both remain undisturbed in our inarticulate bliss.

Therefore, contrary to Soble's reading, we are not always obliged to obtain verbal consent, not forced to "mix the pleasures of language with the pleasures of the body"[7] *if* the sex is mutually initiated.

Now consider the fourth point:

4. The person with whom sexual contact/conduct is initiated is responsible to express verbally and/or *physically* his/her willingness or lack of willingness when *reasonably* possible (emphasis mine).[8]

To express verbally *or physically* willingness or unwillingness, when *reasonably* possible. Aha! If the initiator asks, I can respond physically, I don't have to utter "yes" or even moan. And if the noninitiator is in a swoon of delight and tongue-tiedness, the whole sexual encounter can go on with a minimal amount of question and answer. But, if there is any ambiguity at all, the code protects both the noninitiator and the initiator alike by defining responsibilities for each.

Now this begins to sound less absurd. Under the heading of "Body Talk" Soble writes: "According to the policy, a verbal 'yes' replaces all bodily movements as the only reliable sign that proceeding with sex is permissible. If I ask, "may I kiss you?" I may not proceed on the basis of your bodily reply, e.g., you push your mouth out at mine and open it invitingly . . ."[9] A verbal yes may be the only fully *reliable* sign, but it's not at all clear from the passages cited above that the code *proscribes* sex based on such "body talk," or that it construes heeding (affirmative) body talk—in limited and unambiguous circumstances—as sexual offense.

Soble furthermore insists that the verbal "yes" is only a yes after sufficient probing. The probing requirement isn't explicit in the code, but arises from the possibility that women, because of their social-ization to be cooperative and nonconfrontational, may say "yes" when they mean "no," Rather than explicitly calling for the sort of probing Soble envisions, the code sets out a clear set of responsibilities for both initiator and noninitiator. The initiator is responsible for obtaining verbal consent; the noninitiator is responsible for responding verbally or physically whenever possible. As Soble points out, this privileges the physical withdrawal over the physical assent since consent is, both by definition and by explicit statement, verbal. But it also opens the window, when there is no ambiguity in the situation for the sexual activity to respond to body talk.

Two things are learned from considering the passages omitted in Soble's summary.

First: there are allowances for the body language so often more in tune with the heightened sexual state than articulate speech. Perhaps this is a contradiction in the policy. Or perhaps the policy only starts to make sense in a context where there is a great deal of discussion that helps to clarify its intent and purpose.

Second: The noninitiator has a responsibility in this interaction, along with the initiator. A young woman socialized in a stereotypical feminine way has a responsibility to work her way out of such constricting socializing influences. If the policy is more educative and preventative than proscriptive and punitive, as it declares itself to be, "The educational aspects of this policy are intended to prevent sexual offenses and ultimately to heighten community awareness,"[10] then this code serves to encourage previously unassertive partners to be more assertive and to encourage overly assertive partners to reign in their overbearing behavior. Rather than undermining autonomy and acting paternalistically in loco parentis, Antioch encourages autonomy in the form of more responsible and responsive sexuality.

These considerations mark a considerable change in my first reaction to the Antioch code. The clincher came when I located Antioch College on a websurfing night and read the home page addressed to prospective students: "Antioch believes it should be a single cohesive community based on principles of democracy and citizenship. . . . Because Antioch students are considered equal members of the community, they participate in major decision-making committees at the College and have responsibility for student organizations and activities on campus." Although many student handbooks read like this, Antioch has always had a very strong tradition of taking such words seriously. As Alan Guskin, President of Antioch at the time the policy was first formulated, writes,[11] and as discussions with Antioch alumnae confirmed,[12] the policy was arrived at through intensive campus discussion among students and faculty. Even more significant, the code is reviewed each year and each year students elect whether to retain it, modify it, or discard it.

This contextualization of the code is, I believe, crucial to evaluating it. If this policy were handed down from on high by the administration to a reluctant student body that had to puzzle its way through the sorts of unclarities and paradoxes Soble highlights, then I would continue to share his skepticism. Likewise, if this policy were to be adopted outside of a specific and close community in which the code serves as a prod to discussing consensual sex, then again, we should be swayed by Soble's arguments. Although there is a sense in which the policy is, as Matthew Silliman declares in the title of an article, "a community experiment in communicative sexuality,"[13] the policy is also a product of an understanding of a *particular* community. How does contextualizing the policy to the Antioch community help?

Consider first the question of pleasure. Those who mutually initiate sex, at all levels, can have pleasure non-interruptus. But when one initiates sex, then a verbal consent is necessary. Can the verbal question and the consent be less intrusive to the romance than it seems at first? Soble says no, because sexy speech (as MacKinnon likes to remind us) is already sex. So either we have a nonsexy way of asking or we have an infinite regress. When I raised this point with the president of the Alum Association, he responded that the permissibility of making the request a part of the sexual encounter is part of the social contract which established the code in the first place. That is to say, in the numerous workshops and discussions around the policy, the permissibility of this initiatory level of sexual contact is established. It forms part of the background

condition and is not explicitly stated in the code.[14] Take the Antioch out of "Antioch's Sexual Offense Policy" and you have a different policy. Of course, this understanding of the policy leaves the door open to a lascivious and unwanted sexual invitation of, say, a faculty member to a student. Such a sexual invitation/question has all the power imbalances in place that can, at worst, make refusal difficult, and, at best, be shocking and highly offensive to the more vulnerable party. Such a possibility exposes a limitation of the policy and the need for more than a code to insure fully consensual sex. But it doesn't vitiate the usefulness of the code.[15]

Second, consider the question of "body talk." We have already seen that in the situation in which all partners are mutually initiating at all points in the encounter, they can speak, moan, groan or remain silent—as long as everything is completely clear to both. For the rest of the cases, Soble argues that not only do we have to ask and reply, but the initiator has to probe for a sincere "yes." This, he suggests, is because the Antioch policy does not sufficiently respect the ways in which the body talks, not only in sexual affairs, but in all matters. This argument is premised on a sexual scenario of a "yes" meaning a "no," one common enough. Soble directs us to a Texas A&M study in which 39 percent of college women polled indicated that they have offered token "resistance" when they *intended* to engage in sex.[16] However, within a community that affirms the sexual offense policy in question each year anew, where the policy becomes the prod to open discussion of matters sexual, and where the responsibility for learning to say no when you mean no is understood as part of the educative purpose of the code, the probing is *de trop*. The demand for verbal consent is not about a disregard for body talk (when affirmative) but about setting forth the conditions for a communication sufficiently *unambiguous* to minimize the dangers and harm of date rape. So contextualized, Soble's claim that "the robust respect that Antioch's policy fosters for a woman's 'no' is offset by the weaker respect it fosters for her 'yes' " is false.

Finally let us consider the question of consent. It is true that "Antioch cuts back on a traditional power of consent, its ability to apply to an indefinite, open future."[17] But perhaps that is just right, when it comes to matters of sexual desire. A Pauline marriage, after all, makes marital rape on oxymoron, and any woman who has been raped by her husband will tell you that there is nothing oxymoronic about her trauma. Antioch's policy, however, is not meant to govern long-term relationships or marriages, Pauline or otherwise. In the context of the Antioch College, the code applies to an undergraduate population that does not, in general, have many long-term relationships. Probably most sexual encounters are first-, second-, thirdtime contacts.[18] It is to these transient relations that the policy is directed. In this context it is inappropriate to think that consent applies to "an indefinite, open future." This is not to say that a marriage or long term relation in which one could not make a transition from "assume 'no' unless you get a 'yes' " to "assume 'yes' unless you get a no" would be a sad affair.

Soble, however, raises a more difficult issue with respect to consent. He points out that Antioch cuts back on the power of consent by making it not binding: I agree to have so much sex with you and while halfway through I change my mind and want you to stop. Am I immoral? Is the policy fostering the immorality of the tease in countering the immorality of the rapist? If I agree to a sexual act in bad faith, then I am a tease. But if I agree in good faith, and if in the midst of the experience I find it unpleasant or unexciting and so ask my partner to stop, I am not *teasing* but responding to something important to my own self-respect. To continue sex past the point of my own desiring is to experience myself as a mere object for another's use. "But," says my partner, "you consented and you are obliged to let me continue." Why doesn't that work? There is a feature of sexuality that is not amenable to a notion of consent. Consent within policies or codes are generally understood through the model of contract: I voluntarily agree to a specified such and such, and you forming your expectations based on the agreement hold me to the contractual terms.

The contractual model, however, is inappropriate in many intimate domains. Consent in these contexts is less an agreement binding into the future that will override itinerant desires than the expression of a willing, wanting, desiring self that seeks fulfillment with and through another. So-called "surrogate mothering" falls into this category. If a birth mother gives up the child she has born as a gift, that is one thing; if she gives it up for payment, that is quite another. A contractual relation demands the action of an agreed-to giving, whether or not the desire to give continues to be present at the moment, past the time the contract is signed. If I promise you a gift and don't deliver on the promise, I will disappoint you, but you will not have a claim on that gift. While you can accuse me of breaking my promise, you cannot make a claim to that gift. The strong sense that surrogacy ought not to be bound to contract in the same way other transactions are arises from the nature of the act as a gift, that is a giving to which we attach a desire to give another satisfaction through our own actions. Sexual contact has a similar nature. If the sexual contact is not desired at *that* moment, then one makes of oneself a sexual object and not a sexual agent. One makes oneself into a thing, and the other who insists on the sexual act makes of the partner a means only, a means to one's own pleasure regardless of the desire of the partner.

Barbara Herman in a fascinating article argues that Kant's view of sexuality is remarkably akin to that of some radical feminists, in particular, Andrea Dworkin and MacKinnon. Kant's resolution to the problem of sexual love, which makes of the other an object of one's own sexual desire without regard to human nature but to sex alone, is marriage:

> The sole condition on which we are free to make use of our sexual desire depends upon the right to dispose over the person as a whole—over the welfare and happiness and generally over all the circumstances of that person . . . [I obtain these rights over the whole person (and so have the right of sexual use of that person)] only by giving the person the same rights over myself.[19]

But why not say instead: A sexual encounter with another, which has the recognition of the other's desire (and so the other's sexual agency) as a sine qua non, is the sole way in which we can engage in sex without reducing the other to an object—whether in marriage or in a one-night stand. In that case, consent cannot be understood on the contractual model, but on a model of mutual desiring, a desiring which must be alive at each moment. This, I believe, stands behind the model of communicative sex as better sex that is advocated by Lois Pineau.[20] To the extent that the Antioch policy's demand for consent is understood contractually, it will be a limitation of the policy. But if the policy is used as an educative tool, accompanied by discussion about its meaning and intent, then it can serve to instruct and train young persons for sexual encounters that promote mutuality and respect. In so doing, it can foster both good sex and the autonomy of the one who initiates and the one who responds.

Now I have made a full 180-degree turnabout from my first reactions to the policy. Of course, it seems that some things might be lost: That surprise (not yet consented to) touch that thrills beyond measure; the awakening of ardor through a kiss by someone who never before moved you; and doubtless much else. Then again it would also be fun to drive without seatbelts and road signs, and with only a watchful eye. But even with the road signs there are too many car accidents. Best to keep the seatbelts on.

Maybe the policy seen in context is not so foolish after all. And perhaps it teaches me that I do well to listen to my feminist mind before allowing my foolish heart the last word.

NOTES

1. This paper was first delivered as a commentary to Alan Soble's "Antioch's 'Sexual Offense Policy': A Philosophical Exploration," Dec. 1995, at the Eastern Division APA Meetings.

2. Alan Soble, "Antioch's 'Sexual Offense Policy': A Philosophical Exploration," *Journal of Social Philosophy* 28, no. 1 (Spring 1997): 22–36.

3. Robin Warshaw, *I Never Called It Rape: The Ms. Report on Recognizing, Fighting and Survroing Date Rape* (New York: Harper & Row, 1988).

4. Soble, 27.

5. Antioch College, "The Antioch College Sexual Offense Policy," in *Date Rape: Feminism Philosophy, and the Law,* ed. Leslie Francis (University Park, PA: The Pennsylvania University Press, 1992), 140.

6. Antioch, 140.

7. Soble, 28.

8. Antioch, 140.

9. Soble, 29.

10. Antioch, 139.

11. Alan E. Guskin, "The Antioch Response: Sex, You Just Don't Talk About It," in *Date Rape: Feminism Philosophy, and the Law,* 155–66.

12. My discussions included one with Eric Bates, president of Antioch's Alumnae Association.

13. "The Antioch Policy, a Community Experiment in Communicative Sexuality" in *Date Rape: Feminism Philosophy, and the Law,* 167–76.

14. Personal Communication with Eric Bates.

15. There is, however, a clause in the "Consent" discussion which covers situations of intimidation and coercion used for obtaining the verbal consent:

> 7. If someone verbally agrees to engage in specific contact or conduct, but it is not of her/his own free will due to any of the circumstances stated in (a) through (d) below, then the person initiating shall be considered in violation of this policy if: . . . (d) the person initiating has forced, threatened, coerced, or intimidated the other individual(s) into engaging in sexual contact and/or sexual conduct.

Antioch College, "The Antioch College Sexual Offense Policy," in *Date Rape: Feminism Philosophy, and the Law,* 141.

16. This study is cited in Soble, 24.

17. Soble, 31.

18. This point is emphasized in Guskin, 1996.

19. Kant, *Lectures on Ethics,* p. 167, quoted in Barbara Herman, "Thinking about Kant on Sex and Marriage," in Anthony and Witt, eds., *A Mind of One's Own: Feminist Essays on Reason and Objectivity* (Boulder: Westview Press, 1993), p. 60.

20. Lois Pineau, "Date Rape: A Feminist Analysis," in *Date Rape: Feminism Philosophy, and the Law,* 1–26.

10

Is Prostitution Wrong?

Ericsson and His Critics

Prostitution involves the exchange of money for sexual services. Although it can come in many forms, the standard case of prostitution involves a man paying a woman in exchange for her having sexual intercourse with him. Many people find this practice to be morally objectionable. Prostitution is forbidden by most religious traditions and by the laws of many nations, and even those who believe that criminal laws against prostitution are unjust still often agree that engaging in the practice is nonetheless itself morally objectionable. Although they might believe that it is none of the government's business, they would feel ashamed to work as a prostitute, to hire one, or even to be friendly with or related to one. Surely the view that prostitution is a morally objectionable profession in this sense is a widespread one.

But one can also regard prostitution as simply one further example of a free and voluntary commercial exchange for services provided. This is the way that Lars O. Ericsson conceives of the practice in his article "Charges Against Prostitution: An Attempt at a Philosophical Assessment." It is true, as Ericsson recognizes, that prostitution differs from the provision of other services in that the services a prostitute provides are sexual in nature. But, he maintains, this difference in itself is not morally relevant. If the general provision of nonsexual services on an open market is morally unobjectionable, Ericsson argues, then there is no reason to object to the similar provision of sexual services. Although Ericsson's article touches upon a number of considerations and attempts to rebut a number of charges against prostitution, the core of his position might therefore be represented as follows:

P1 It is morally unobjectionable for a consumer to purchase nonsexual services from a supplier in a free exchange on an open market.

P2 Purchasing sexual services is morally on a par with purchasing nonsexual services.

P3 Prostitution is the practice of a consumer purchasing sexual services from a supplier in a free exchange on an open market.

C   Prostitution is morally unobjectionable.

For the most part, Ericsson treats the first and third premises of this argument as uncontroversial and devotes most of the article to defending the second premise against various charges that could be leveled against it. This strategy is understandable. Most people who find prostitution objectionable would likely say that it is precisely the sexual nature of the service that the prostitute provides that makes the difference, that this is what explains why it is perfectly appropriate to pay a physical trainer to work out with you but completely unacceptable to pay a prostitute to have sex with you. The critical question therefore becomes: Why, exactly, should the sexual nature of the services provided make a difference?

In the text of his article, Ericsson considers several possible answers to this question, including, perhaps most important, what he calls "the sentimentalist charge" that the sexual nature of the services provided are appropriately linked to certain emotions and sentiments that are undermined by treating sex as an economic commodity (section III) and what he calls "the feminist charge" that the sexual nature of the services provided render their sale incompatible with the ideal of equality between men and women. His strategy in defending what we have here labeled as P2 of his argument, therefore, is the process of elimination, which we discuss in the introduction to this anthology. In each case, Ericsson maintains that the charges against prostitution must be rejected, that they ultimately fail to distinguish prostitution from other forms of economic exchange that most people accept as uncontroversially appropriate. Indeed Ericsson maintains that it is not that people object to prostitution because it has legitimate objectionable properties. Rather, it is that whatever undesirable properties prostitution has as it is currently practiced it has only because so many people misguidedly treat it as if it were something objectionable.

As the text and even the title of Ericsson's article suggests, his defense of the morality of prostitution can be attacked from a number of different sides. And, perhaps not surprising, it has been. One important line of criticism maintains that Ericsson has failed sufficiently to rebut what he calls "the feminist charge," that his defense of prostitution does not do full justice to the ways in which the practice may prove inconsistent with feminist values. This criticism is represented here in the critical responses by Carole Pateman and Laurie Shrage, each of whom maintain that Ericsson fails to understand the ways in which prostitution constitutes a form of male domination over women and contributes to the perpetuation of such domination. Pateman's and Shrage's critiques of Ericsson's argument can each be understood, at least in part, as an attack on his argument's crucial second premise. Sexual services, Pateman argues, are relevantly different from nonsexual services because sexual services are "inseparably connected to the body," which in turn is "integrally connected to conceptions of femininity and masculinity." Similarly, Shrage argues, reducing sex to a commodity provided by women to men according to economic demand "implies general acceptance of principles which perpetuate women's social subordination," including the belief that men are naturally the dominant members of society and that sexual experience "pollutes" women in a way that it does not pollute men. In addition to attempting to support a feminist objection to P2, Pateman's critique can also be understood in part as an attack on P3. In a patriarchical society, Pateman urges, the sale of sex cannot simply be assumed to take place on free and equal terms, and it is not a simple coincidence that the vast majority of prostitutes are women and the vast majority of customers men. In other words, it is not clear that these are perfectly voluntary exchanges.

While Pateman and Shrage each attack Ericsson's argument from the standpoint of feminist values, Karen Green attacks it from the standpoint of what she calls "the traditional ideal of the family." More specifically, while Green's objection can also be understood as a rejection of the second premise of Ericsson's argument, she is concerned with showing that Ericsson has failed to overcome what she calls "the sentimentalist charge" against that premise. Borrowing from the great social and political philosopher John Rawls, Green argues that a just and well-ordered society must preserve the foundations for the development of important moral sentiments such as justice and benevolence. A close connection between sex and love is essential to such development, on Green's account, and since prostitution involves distributing sexual acts according to economic demand rather than according to mutual love, its acceptance amounts to a severing of this connection. A market in sexual services is relevantly different from a market in nonsexual services, on this account, because the survival of important moral sentiments demands that sexual services be connected to mutual love in a way that nonsexual services need not be.

QUESTIONS FOR CONSIDERATION

In thinking about Ericcson and his critics the following questions can be considered.

- Has Ericsson in fact neglected some important ways in which the feminist challenge can undermine P2 of his argument? If he has not, then what, specifically, has he said that can counter the worries raised by Pateman and Shrage? If he has, then what might a defender of his position say in response to those worries?

- Is Shrage right to think that the patriarchal context in which prostitution takes place poses a problem for P3 of the argument?

- In what sense is the prostitute acting freely and in what sense is she acting unfreely? Is her behavior free in the sense that Shrage clearly thinks it is not free?

- Has Green found a way to vindicate the sentimentalist charge against prostitution? Does Green's claim about the importance of the moral sentiments justify objecting to prostitution as socially corrosive, or does Ericsson's discussion of the sentimentalist charge provide a basis for overcoming this objection?

FURTHER READINGS

Kupfer, Joseph H. "Prostitutes, Musicians, and Self-Respect." *Journal of Social Philosophy* 26, no. 3 (1995): 75–88.
Primoratz, Igor. "What's Wrong with Prostitution?" *Philosophy* 68, no. 264 (1993): 159–82.

Charges Against Prostitution

Lars O. Ericsson

An Attempt at a Philosophical Assessment

I. A NEGLECTED PHILOSOPHICAL TASK

. . . It is the purpose of this paper to undertake a critical assessment of the view that prostitution is an undesirable social phenomenon that ought to be eradicated. I shall do this by examining what seem to me (and to others) the most important and serious charges against prostitution. I shall try to show that mercenary love per se must, upon closer inspection, be acquitted of most of these charges. Instead, I shall argue, the major culprit is the hostile and punitive attitudes which the surrounding hypocritical society adopts toward promiscuous sexual relations in general and prostitution in particular.

II. THE CHARGE FROM CONVENTIONAL MORALITY

By far the most common ground for holding that prostitution is undesirable is that it constitutes a case of sexual immorality. Society and conventional morality condemn it. The law at best barely tolerates it; sometimes, as in most states in the United States, it downright prohibits it. In order to improve prostitution, we must first and foremost improve our attitudes toward it. Contrary to what is usually contended, I shall conclude that prostitution, although not in any way *ultimately* desirable, is still conditionally desirable because of certain ubiquitous and permanent imperfections of actual human societies.

The prostitute, according to the moralist, is a sinful creature who ought to be banned from civilized society. Whoredom is "the great social evil" representing a flagrant defiance of common decency. The harlot is a threat to the family, and she corrupts the young. The engage in prostitution signifies a total loss of character. To choose "the life" is to choose a style of living unworthy of any decent human being. And so on.

There is also a less crude form of moralism, which mixes moral disapproval with a more "compassionate" and "concerned" attitude. The fate of a whore is "a fate worse than death." The hustler is a poor creature who has to debase herself in order to gratify the lusts of immoral men. Prostitution is degrading for all parties involved, but especially for the woman.

It might seem tempting to say that the best thing to do with respect to the moralistic critique is to ignore it. But this is exactly what moral philosophers have been doing for far too long. It appears that many otherwise sophisticated persons more or less consciously adhere to views of a rather unreflectively moralistic kind where prostitution is concerned. More important, to ignore conventional moralism would be philosophically unsatisfactory for the simple reason that the mere fact that an idea is conventional does not constitute a disproof of its validity. Thus, arguments are what we need, not silence.

How are the hostile and punitive attitudes of society toward prostitution to be explained? It seems to be an anthropological fact that sexual institutions are ranked on the basis of their relation to reproduction. Hence, in virtue of its intimate relation to reproduc-

From Lars O. Ericsson, "Charges Against Prostitution: An Attempt at a Philosophical Assessment," *Ethics* 90 (1980): 335–66. Some notes and some parts of the text have been deleted. Reprinted by permission of University of Chicago Press.

tion, the monogamous marriage constitutes the sexual institution in society which is ranked the highest and which receives the strongest support from law and mores. On the other hand, the less a sexual practice has to do with the bearing and rearing of children, the less sanctioned it is. Therefore, when coitus is practiced for pecuniary reasons (the hooker), with pleasure and not procreation in mind (the client), we have a sexual practice that, far from being sanctioned, finds itself at the opposite extreme on the scale of social approval.[1]

Two other factors should be mentioned in this connection. First, wherever descent is reckoned solely through the male line, promiscuity in the female can hardly be approved by society. And the property relations associated with descent of course point in the same direction. Second, our Christian heritage—especially in its Lutheran and Calvinist versions—is both antisexual and antihedonistic. To indulge in sexual activities is bad enough, but to indulge in them for the sheer fun and pleasure of them is a major feat in the art of sin. Moreover, sex is time consuming and as such quite contrary to Protestant morals with respect to work.

An explanation of our antiprostitution attitudes and their probably prehistoric roots must not, however, be confused with a *rationale* for their continuation in our own time. That we understand why the average moralist, who is a predominantly unreflecting upholder of prevailing rules and values, regards prostitution and prostitutes as immoral gives us no good reason to shield those rules and values from criticism, especially if we find, upon reflection, that they are no longer adequate to our present social conditions.

That prostitution neither is nor ever was a threat to reproduction within the nuclear family is too obvious to be worth arguing for. Nor has it ever been a threat to the family itself. People marry and visit whores for quite different reasons. In point of fact, the greatest threat to the family is also the greatest threat to prostitution, namely, complete sexual liberty for both sexes. The conclusion we must draw from this is that neither the value of future generations nor the importance of the family (if it is important) warrants the view that prostitution is bad and undesirable.

It is hardly likely, however, that the moralist would be particularly perturbed by this, for the kernel of his view is rather that to engage in prostitution is *intrinsically* wrong. Both whore and customer (or at least the former) act immorally, according to the moralist, even if neither of them nor anyone else gets hurt. Mercenary love per se is regarded as immoral.

Personally, I must confess that I, upon reflection, am no more able to see that coition for a fee is intrinsically wrong than I am able to see that drunkenness is. There is something fanatic about both of these views which I find utterly repelling. If two adults voluntarily consent to an economic arrangement concerning sexual activity and this activity takes place in private, it seems plainly absurd to maintain that there is something intrinsically wrong with it. In fact, I very much doubt that it is wrong at all. To say that prostitution is intrinsically immoral is in a way to refuse to give any arguments. The moralist simply "senses" or "sees" its immorality. And this terminates rational discussion at the point where it should begin.

III. THE SENTIMENTALIST CHARGE

There is also a common contention that harlotry is undesirable because the relation between whore and customer must by the nature of things be a very poor relation to nonmercenary sex. Poor, not in a moral, but in a nonmoral, sense. Since the majority of the objections under this heading have to do with the quality of the feelings and sentiments involved or with the lack of them, I shall refer to this critique as "the sentimentalist charge."

Sex between two persons who love and care for one another can of course be, and often is, a very good thing. The affection and tenderness which exists between the parties tends to create an atmosphere in which the sexual activities can take place in such a way as to be a source of mutual pleasure and satisfaction. Sexual intercourse is here a way of becoming even more intimate in a relation which is already filled with other kinds of intimacies.

Now, according to the sentimentalist, mercenary sex lacks just about all of these qualities. Coitus between prostitute and client is held to be impoverished, cold, and impersonal. The association is regarded as characterized by detachment and emotional noninvolvement. And the whole thing is considered to be a rather sordid and drab affair.

In order to answer this charge, there is no need to romanticize prostitution. Mercenary sex usually *is* of poorer quality compared with sentimental sex between lovers. To deny this would be simply foolish. But does it follow from this that hustling is undesirable? Of course not! That would be like contending that because 1955 Ch. Mouton-Rothschild is a much better wine than ordinary claret, we should condemn the act of drinking the latter.

The sentimentalist's mistake lies in the comparison on which he relies. He contrasts a virtual sexual ideal with prostitutional sex, which necessarily represents an entirely different kind of erotic association and which therefore fulfills quite different social and individual functions. Only a minute share of all sex that takes place deserves to be described as romantic sex love. And if, in defending mercenary sex, we should beware of romanticizing *it*, the same caution holds for the sentimentalist when he is describing nonprostitutional sex. The sex lives of ordinary people often fall miles short of the sentimentalist's ideal. On the other hand, the sexual services performed by harlots are by no means always of such poor quality as we are conditioned to think. And we would most likely think better of them were we able to rid ourselves of the feelings of guilt and remorse that puritanism and conventional morality create in us.

In fact, the comparison between sex love and mercenary lovemaking is both pointless and naive. That lovers have very little need for the services of hustlers is at best a silly argument against prostitution. Most couples are not lovers. A great number of persons do not even have a sexual partner. And not so few individuals will, in any society, always have great difficulties in finding one. What is the point of comparing the ideal sex life of the sentimentalist with the sexual services of prostitutes in the case of someone whose only alternative to the latter is masturbation? Is there any reason to think that mercenary sex must be impersonal, cold, and impoverished compared with autosex?

By this I do not wish to contend that the typical customer is either unattractive, physically or mentally handicapped, or extremely shy. There is abundant empirical evidence showing that the prostitute's customers represent all walks of life and many different types of personalities.[2] That the typical "John" is a male who for some reason cannot find a sexual partner other than a prostitute is just one of the many popular myths about harlotry which empirical studies seem unable to kill. Approximately 75 percent of the customers are married men,[3] most of whom are "respectable" taxpaying citizens.

This brings us to another aspect of the sentimentalist charge. It is not seldom a tacit and insiduous presupposition of the sentimentalist's reasoning that good sex equals intramarital sex, and that bad sex equals extramarital—especially prostitutional—sex. This is just another stereotype, which deserves to be destroyed. Concerning this aspect, Benjamin and Masters make the following comment: "The experience with a prostitute is probably ethically, and may be esthetically, on a higher level than an affectionless intercourse between husband and wife, such as is all too common in our present society."[4] The demarcation line between marital and mercenary sex is not quality but the contrasting nature of the respective legal arrangements. Furthermore, we must not think that the quality—in terms of physical pleasure—of the sex services of prostitutes varies any less than the quality of "regular" sex. The best prostitutional sex available is probably much better from the customer's point of view than average marital sex.

The sentimentalistic critique of the prostitute-customer relationship, however, has also another side to it. This consists in the notion that sex without love or affection—sex "pure and simple"—is "no good." I have already admitted the obvious here—namely, that sex love is a beautiful thing. But this seems to me no reason for embracing the romantic notion that sex without love or mutual affection must be valueless. On the contrary, satisfaction of sexual desires is, qua satisfaction of a basic need, *intrinsically good,* love or no love.

The argument fails to show that prostitution is undesirable. If it shows anthing at all it shows lack of contact with reality. As I pointed out earlier, sex between lovers hardly dominates the scene of human sex quantitatively. Consequently, the argument entails that a major part of the sex that takes place between humans is worthless. And how interesting is this? Even if correct, it does not show that there is something *particularly* or *distinctively* bad about prostitution.

In conclusion, I would like to counter the charge that the prostitute-customer relationship is bad on the ground that it involves the selling of something that is too basic and too elementary in human life to be sold. This is perhaps not a sentimentalist charge proper, but since it seems to be related to it I shall deal with it here.

Common parlance notwithstanding, what the hustler sells is of course not her body or vagina, but sexual *services*. If she actually did sell herself, she would no longer be a prostitute but a sexual slave. I wish to emphasize this simple fact, because the popular misnomer certainly contributes to and maintains our distorted views about prostitution.

But is it not bad enough to sell sexual services? To go to bed with someone just for the sake of money? To perform fellatio on a guy you neither love nor care for? In view of the fact that sex is a fundamental need, is it not wrong that anyone should have to pay to have it satisfied and that anyone should profit from its satisfaction? Is it not a deplorable fact that in the prostitute-customer relationship sexuality is completely alienated from the rest of the personality and reduced to a piece of merchandise?

In reply to these serious charges I would, first, like to confess that I have the greatest sympathy for the idea that the means necessary for the satisfaction of our most basic needs should be free, or at least not beyond the economic means of anyone. We all need food, so food should be available to us. We all need clothes and a roof over our heads, so these things should also be available to us. And since our sexual desires are just as basic, natural, and compelling as our appetite for food, this also holds for them. But I try not to forget that this is, and probably for long time will remain, an *ideal* state of affairs.

Although we live in a society in which we have to pay (often dearly) for the satisfaction of our ap-

petites, including the most basic and natural ones, I still do not regard food vendors and the like with contempt. They fulfill an important function in the imperfect world in which we are destined to live. That we have to pay for the satisfaction of our most basic appetites is no reason for socially stigmatizing those individuals whose profession it is to cater to those appetites. With this, I take it, at least the non-fanatical sentimentalist agrees. But if so, it seems to me inconsistent to hold that prostitution is undesirable on the ground that it involves the selling of something that, ideally, should not be sold but freely given away. Emotional prejudice aside, there is on *this* ground no more reason to despise the sex market and those engaged in it than there is to despise the food market and those engaged in it.

But still, is there not an abyss between selling meat and selling "flesh"? Is there not something private, personal, and intimate about sex that makes it unfit for commercial purposes? Of course, I do not wish to deny that there are great differences between what the butcher does and what the whore does, but at the same time it seems to me clear that the conventional labeling of the former as "respectable" and the latter as "indecent" is not so much the result of these differences as of the influence of cultural, especially religious and sexual, taboos. That the naked human body is "obscene," that genitalia are "offending," that menstrual blood is "unclean," etc., are expressions of taboos which strongly contribute to the often neurotic way in which sex is surrounded with mysteriousness and secrecy. Once we have been able to liberate ourselves from these taboos we will come to realize that we are no more justified in devaluating the prostitute, who, for example, masturbates her customers, than we are in devaluating the assistant nurse, whose job it is to take care of the intimate hygiene of disabled patients. Both help to satisfy important human needs, and both get paid for doing so. That the harlot, in distinction to the nurse, intentionally gives her client pleasure is of course nothing that should be held against her!

As for the charge that in the prostitute-customer relationship sexuality is completely alienated from the rest of the personality—this is no doubt largely true. I fail to see, however, that it constitutes a very serious charge. My reason for this is, once again, that the all-embracing sex act represents an ideal with which it is unfair to compare the prostitutecustomer relationship, especially if, as is often the case, such an all-embracing sex act does not constitute a realizable alternative. Moreover, there is no empirical evidence showing that sex between two complete strangers must be of poor quality.

IV. THE PATERNALISTIC CHARGE

It is a well-established fact that the occupational hazards connected with prostitution constitute a serious problem. The prostitute runs the risk of being hurt, physically as well as mentally. On the physical side there is always the risk of getting infected by some venereal disease. Certain forms of urosis are known to be more common among harlots than among women in general. And then there is the risk of assault and battery from customers with sadistic tendencies. On the mental side we encounter such phenomena as depression and neurosis, compulsive behavior, self-degrading and self-destructive impulses, etc.

It is therefore not uncommon to find it argued that prostitution is undesirable because it is not in the best interest of the prostitute to be what she is. It is held that society should, for the prostitutes' own good, try to prevent people from becoming prostitutes and to try to "rehabilitate" those who already are. This type of criticism I shall refer to as "the paternalistic charge."

I shall not consider the question—discussed by Mill, Devlin, Hart, and others—of whether society has the *right* to interfere with a person's liberty for his own good. I shall limit my discussion to the question of whether the fact that the hustler runs the risks that she runs is a good reason for holding that prostitution is undesirable.

A comparison with other fields clearly shows that the fact that a certain job is very hazardous is not regarded as a good reason for the view that the type of job in question is undesirable. Take, for instance, a miner: he runs considerable risks in his job, but we hardly think that this warrants the conclusion that mining should be prohibited. What we do think (or

at least ought to think) is that, since the miner is doing a socially valuable job, everything possible should be done to minimize those risks by improving his working conditions by installing various safety devices, introducing shorter working hours, etc. It seems to me, therefore, that in cases like this—and there are many of them—paternalistic considerations carry no weight. The individual is not to be protected from himself (for wanting to take risks) but from certain factors in the environment. It is not the individual who should be changed but the milieu in which he has to place himself in order to be able to follow his occupational inclinations.

Unless the paternalist simply assumes what remains to be proven, namely, that what the prostitute does is of no value to society, a similar argument also applies in the case of prostitution. The individual whore does not need to be protected from herself if her hustling is voluntary in the same sense of "voluntary" as someone's choice of profession may be voluntary. What she does need protection from are detrimental factors in the social environment, especially the hostile, punitive, or condescending attitudes of so-called respectable citizens. It is not the hooker who should be changed, reformed, or rehabilitated but the social milieu in which she works.

The paternalistic charge is not an independent argument against prostitution. It only seems to work because it has already given in to conventional morality. To oppose prostitution by referring to the welfare, good, happiness, needs, or interests of the prostitute may seem very noble and humanitarian; but in reality it serves the status quo by leaving the norms and values of the surrounding society intact, viewing prostitution through the unreflected spectacles of a conservative public opinion, and placing the "blame" exclusively on the individual.

If public opinion accorded prostitutes the same status as, say, social workers, most of the hazards connected with hustling would probably disappear. And those that would remain would not be thought to make hustling undesirable. Society would try to minimize the risks rather than try to rehabilitate and reform those who run them.

The paternalist does not ask himself *why* depressions and neuroses are common among harlots, *why* they display self-degrading and self-destructive tendencies, *why* their behavior often is antisocial, and so on. Yet the answer should be obvious: the principal cause of these psychological and sociological "dysfunctions" is the social anathema attached to their way of life. Make people outcasts and they will behave like outcasts. It is thus the degradation in which the harlot is held, and as a result also often holds herself, that constitutes the greatest danger to her physical and mental health. In addition, as I shall hereafter argue, this constitutes the basis for her being exploited in various ways.

To sum up. The paternalistic charge rests on two assumptions, neither of which is valid. First, it rests on the assumption that society's scorn for whoredom is justified. Second, it rests on the assumption that the hooker is not doing a socially valuable job. From these assumptions together with the fact that harlotry is known to be a hazardous profession the paternalist jumps to the conclusion that prostitution is undesirable and that society should intervene against it for the prostitutes' own good. . . .

VI. THE FEMINIST CHARGE

In this essay I have deliberately desisted from trying to *define* "prostitution." I have simply relied upon the fact that we seem to know pretty well what we mean by this term. My reason for resisting the well-known predilection of philosophers for definitional questions is that ordinary usage seems to me sufficiently precise for my present purposes.[5] In consequence, I have up till now referred to the prostitute as "she" and to the customer as "he." For in ordinary parlance the whore is a woman and her customer a man. I do not think, however, that ordinary usage is such that this is true by definition. I rather suspect that our habit of thinking of the hustler as a *she* and her customer as a *he* simply reflects the empirical fact that most prostitutes are women and most customers men.

I shall in this section discuss a group of arguments in support of the thesis that prostitution is undesirable whose common feature is this fact. Prostitution is held to be undesirable on the ground that it constitutes an extreme instance of the inequality

between the sexes. Whoredom is regarded as displaying the male oppression of the female in its most naked form. It is contended that the relation between hooker and "John" is one of object to subject—the prostitute being reified into a mere object, a thing for the male's pleasure, lust, and contempt. The customer-man pays to use the whore-woman and consequently has the upper hand. He is the dominating figure, the master. It is the whore's task to oblige, to satisfy his most "perverse" and secret desires, desires that the male is unable to reveal to his wife or girl friend. Prostitution, it is argued, reduces the woman to a piece of merchandise that anyone who can pay the price may buy. The unequal nature of prostitution is also contended to consist in the fact that it represents a way out of *misère sexuel* only for men. Instead of trying to solve the sexual problems together with his wife, the married man can resort to the services of the hustler; but the married woman lacks the same advantage, since there are not so many male heterosexual prostitutes around. I shall refer to this group of arguments as "the feminist charge."

Like the moralist and the Marxist, the feminist is of the opinion that prostitution can and ought to be eradicated.[6] Some feminists, like the moralist, even want to criminalize prostitution. But unlike the moralist they want to criminalize both whore and customer.

The core of the feminist charge—that prostitution is unequal and disfavors the female sex—deserves to be taken seriously. For social in-equality is a serious matter both morally and politically. And inequalities based on differences with regard to race, color of skin, religious belief, sex, and the like are particularly serious. Thus, if valid, the feminist critique would constitute powerful support for the view that prostitution is undesirable.

Before I proceed to an attempt to counter the feminist charge, I would like to add a few nuancing facts to the prostitute-customer picture outlined at the beginning of this section.[7] No one denies that a majority of prostitutes are women, and no one denies that a majority of customers are men. But it is clear from the evidence that a large portion of the prostitutes, especially in metropolitan areas, are male homosexuals.[8] There is also lesbian prostitution, though this is not (at least not yet) sufficiently widespread to be of any great social importance. And finally, there is male heterosexual prostitution, the prevalence of which is also rather limited. We may sum up by saying that, rather than constituting a dichotomy between the sexes, prostitution has the characteristic that a considerable portion of the prostitutes are men, and a small minority of the customers are women. I mention this because I think that a rational assessment should not be based on an incomplete picture of the phenomenon under assessment and I consider these data to have some relevance with respect to the feminist charge against prostitution.

There are at least two types of inequalities. In the one, the inequality consists in the fact that some *benefit* is withheld from some group or individual. A typical example: only white members of a society are allowed to vote. In the other, the inequality consists in the fact that some *burden* is placed only on some group or individual. A typical example: a feudal society in which peasants and artisans are the only ones who have to pay taxes. We may also distinguish between unequal practices which, like racial discrimination, are best dealt with through a complete *abolition* of them, and unequal practices which, like male franchise, are best dealt with by *modifying* them (in the case of male franchise, by granting the franchise to women). The one type of unequal practice is always and under all conditions undesirable: there is no remedy to the inequality of apartheid but abolition. The other type of unequal practice is also undesirable, but it has the seed of something defensible or valuable in it: the franchise is something good, although the franchise restricted to males is not. Obviously, these two pairs of categories are not mutually exclusive. On the contrary, all combinations of them are possible.

After these preliminaries, we come to the question of how prostitution is to be classified. Is harlotry an unequal practice? And if so, in what precisely does its inequality consist?

If it is conceded that in exchange for his money the customer receives a service—something that at least the sentimentalist seems most reluctant to concede—it could be argued that harlotry is unequal in the sense that some benefit is withheld from or denied women that is not withheld from or denied men. This is perhaps how the argument that hustling represents a way out only for men should be understood. However, if this is what the feminist charge amounts to, two things appear to be eminently clear. The first is that prostitution is unequal in a less serious way than, for instance, male franchise. For in the latter the benefit (opportunity to vote) which is withheld from women is withheld from them in the strong sense that it is not legally possible for the women to vote, while in the former no such legal or formal obstacle stands in their way. In fact, instead of saying that the sex services of prostitutes are withheld or denied women, it would be more appropriate to say that centuries of cultural and social conditioning makes them desist from asking for them. It is after all only recently that women have begun to define their sexuality and require that their sexual needs and desires be recognized. Rowbotham reminds us that " 'Nymphomania' was actually used in the 1840s to describe any woman who felt sexual desire, and such women were seen as necessarily abandoned, women of the streets, women of the lower classes."[9] The second point is that if, through prostitution, a benefit is "withheld" the female sex, the best way to deal with this inequality would not be an attempt to stamp out the institution but an attempt to modify it, by making the benefit in question available to both sexes.

Could it be then that the inequality of whoredom consists in the fact that some burden is unequally placed on the two sexes and in disfavor of the female sex? This allegation can be interpreted in several different ways. And I shall in what follows consider those that seem to me the most important.

To begin with, this allegation can be understood in accordance with the view that it is women, and not men, who are in peril of becoming prostitutes. But first of all, this is largely untrue since, as I have argued earlier, a great many prostitutes are men. Moreover, the perils of being a prostitute, although existent today (due to factors discussed in Sec. IV), do not constitute a good reason for abolishing harlotry; rather they constitute a good reason for a social reform that will reduce the perils to a minimum tomorrow.[10]

Another way of interpreting this allegation is to say that prostitution constitutes exploitation of the female sex, since harlots are being exploited by, inter alia, sex capitalists and customers, and a majority of harlots are women. This interpretation of the allegation merits careful study, and I shall therefore in the first instance limit my discussion to the capitalist exploitation of prostitutes.

It is of course true that not all prostitutes can be described as workers in the sex industry. Some are in point of fact more adequately described as small-scale private entrepreneurs. Others are being exploited without being exploited by sex capitalists. Those who can be regarded as workers in the sex industry—the growing number of girls working in sex clubs and similar establishments for instance—are, of course, according to Marxist theory, being exploited in the same sense as any wage worker is exploited. But exploitation in this Marxist sense, although perhaps effective as an argument against wage labor in general, is hardly effective as an argument against prostitution.

There is no doubt, however, that practically all harlots—irrespective of whether they are high-class call girls, cheap streetwalkers, or sex-club performers—are being exploited, economically, in a much more crude sense than that in which an automobile worker at General Motors is being exploited. I am thinking here of the fact that all of them—there are very few exceptions to this—have to pay usury rents in order to be able to operate. Many are literally being plundered by their landlords—sex capitalists who often specialize in letting out rooms, flats, or apartments to people in the racket. Not a few prostitutes also have to pay for "protection" to mafiosi with close connections to organized crime.

What makes all this possible? And what are the implications of the existence of conditions such as these for the question of the alleged undesirability of prostitution? With respect to the first of these questions the answer, it seems to me, is that the major culprit is society's hypocritical attitude toward harlotry and harlots. It is this hypocrisy which creates the prerequisites for the sex-capitalist exploitation of the prostitutes. . . .

A third way of interpreting the charge that prostitution is unequal in the sense that it places a burden on women that it does not place on men is to say that whores are being oppressed, reified, and reduced to a piece of merchandise by their male customers. To begin with the last version of this charge first, I have already pointed out the obvious, namely, that whores do not sell themselves. The individual hooker is not for sale, but her sexual services are. One could therefore with equal lack of propriety say of any person whose job it is to sell a certain service that he, as a result thereof, is reduced to a piece of merchandise. I cannot help suspecting that behind this talk of reduction to a piece of merchandise lies a good portion of contempt for prostitutes and the kind of services they offer for sale.

As for the version according to which the whore is reified—turned into an object, a thing—it can be understood in a similar way as the one just dealt with. But it can also be understood as the view that the customer does not look upon the prostitute as a human being but as "a piece of ass." He is not interested in her as a person. He is exclusively interested in her sexual performance. As far as I can see, this version of the charge collapses into the kind of sentimentalistic critique that I discussed in Section III. Let me just add this: Since when does the fact that we, when visiting a professional, are not interested in him or her as a person, but only in his or her professional performance, constitute a ground for saying that the professional is dehumanized, turned into an object?

The "reification charge" may, however, be understood in still another way. It may be interpreted as saying that the whore is nothing but a means, a mere instrument, for the male customer's ends. This also comes rather close to the sentimentalist charge. Its Kantian character does perhaps deserve a few words of comment, however. First of all, that the customer treats the harlot as a means to his ends is only partly true. The other part of the truth is that the prostitute treats her customer as a means to *her* ends. Thus, the complete truth (if it deserves to be called that) is that prostitute and customer treat *one another* as means rather than as ends.

I have to say, however, that I do not find much substance in this Kantian-inspired talk about means and ends. The kind of relationship that exists between prostitute and customer is one that we find in most service professions. It is simply cultural blindness and sexual taboos that prevent so many of us from seeing this. Moreover, in virtue of the prevalence of this type of relationship—a contractual relation in which services are traded—I suspect that those who talk about the badness of it in the case of prostitute-customer relationship have in fact long before decided that the relationship is bad on some *other*—not declared—ground. The means-ends talk is just a way of rationalizing a preconceived opinion.

I shall conclude this section by considering the charge that harlotry constitutes oppression of the female sex. Prostitution is here regarded as displaying male oppression of the female in its most overt and extreme form. The seriousness of this charge calls, to begin with, for a clarification of the meaning of the word "oppression." If A oppresses B, I take it that B's freedom of choice and action is severely reduced, against his will, as a result of actions undertaken by A against B. In the case of political oppression, for example, A thwarts B's desire to form unions and political parties, prevents B from expressing his political opinions, throws B in jail if he refuses to comply, and so on.

It can hardly be disputed that prostitutes are oppressed in this sense. They would not have chosen to become hustlers if some better alternative had been open to them. They are very much aware of the fact that to be a prostitute is to be socially devalued; to be at the bottom of society. To become a hooker is to make just the reverse of a career. It should be observed, however, that none of this warrants the charge that prostitution means the oppression of the female by the male sex. The oppression just described is not an oppression on the basis of sex, as male franchise would be. The "oppressor" is rather those social conditions—present in practically all known social systems—which offer some individuals (both men and women) no better alternative than hustling.

But perhaps what the charge amounts to is that the male sex's oppression of the female sex consists in the oppression of the whore by her male customer. It certainly happens that customers treat prostitutes in ways which could motivate use of the term "oppression." But this does not mean that this term typically applies to the prostitute-customer relationship. Moreover, harlots usually develop a keen eye for judging people, and that helps them to avoid many of the (latently) dangerous customers. For it is just a myth that their freedom of choice and action is reduced to a point where they have to accept customers indiscriminately. This is not even true of prostitutes in the lowest bracket, and it certainly is not true of girls in the higher ones.

It is not seldom argued from feminist quarters that the liberation of women must start with the liberation of women from exploitation of their sex. Hence the crusade against prostitution, pornography, and the use of beautiful women in commercial advertising, etc. It is argued that women's lib must have as its primary goal the abolition of the (ab)use of the female sex as a commodity. As long as the female sex is up for sale, just like any other commercial object, there can be no true liberation from oppression.

To the reader who has read this far it should be obvious that, at least in part, this type of reasoning rests on or is misguided by such misnomers as "the whore sells her body," "to live by selling oneself," "to buy oneself a piece of ass," etc. So I need not say any more about that. Instead I wish to make a comparison between a typical middle-class housewife in suburbia and her prostitute counterpart, the moderately successful call girl. And I ask, emotional prejudice aside, which of them needs to be "liberated" the most? Both are doing fairly well economically, but while the housewife is totally dependent on her husband, at least economically, the call girl in that respect stands on her own two feet. If she has a pimp, it is she, not he, who is the breadwinner in the family. Is she a traitor to her own sex? If she is (which I doubt), she is no more a traitor to her own sex than her bourgeois counterpart. For, after all, Engels was basically right when he said that the major difference between the two is that the one hires out her body on piecework while the other hires it out once and for all.

All this does not mean that I am unsympathetic toward the aspirations of the feminist movement. It rather means that I disagree with its order of priorities.

Both men and women need to be liberated from the harness of their respective sex roles. But in order to be able to do this, we must liberate ourselves from those mental fossils which prevent us from looking upon sex and sexuality with the same naturalness as upon our cravings for food and drink. And, contrary to popular belief, we may have something to learn from prostitution in this respect, namely, that coition resembles nourishment in that if it can not be obtained in any other way it can always be bought. And bought meals are not always the worst.

VII. THE CHARGE OF COMMERCIALIZATION OF SOCIETY

Very few reflective persons would regard a totally commercialized society as a good society. Most of us think that there are certain areas of life that should be as exempt from commercialism as possible. We tend, for example, to take a dim view of people who use money to substitute true friendship with bought "friends." And we hardly consider it proper to buy moral or political beliefs as we buy beer or toothpaste.

In a previous section (Sec. III) I have already discussed the charge against prostitution that it involves the selling of something that ought not to be sold. Here I shall examine a different but related view, namely, the charge that prostitution contributes to the commercialization of society. The charge is that prostitution strengthens the commercial elements in society and that, by way of example, it encourages a commercialistic life-style.

To make this charge as strong as possible I shall assume that it is not inspired by the kind of puritanical anticommercialism which considers all business as dirty business. I shall regard it as an expression of the view, which I share, that a thoroughly commercialized society represents not a utopia but a dystopia.

It is, in my opinion, a deplorable fact that we are close to a point where almost any social activity presupposes that we act as consumers. And it gets increasingly difficult, especially for the young, to avoid the illusion that the solution to practically every problem in living lies in consumption.

My objection to the present charge against prostitution is, thus, not normative. It is rather of an empirical nature. I do not wish to exclude the possibility that prostitution, through the power of example, to some extent contributes to the commercialization of society. But I do wish to deny that its causal influence in this direction is more than utterly marginal.

First of all, this charge seems difficult to square with the historical fact that most societies which have seen harlotry flourish have been societies that hardly deserve to be described as commercialized. In no society has prostitution been more than a minor commercial and economic phenomenon.

Moreover, if there were a causal connection between prostitution and commercialization, one would expect the latter to be a contributing cause of the former rather than the reverse. For one would possibly expect a society in which practically everything is bought and sold to be more tolerant also to the buying and selling of sexual services.

However that may be, I think we have to look elsewhere for the real causes of the spreading of commerce to new areas of life. The core of any capitalist society is the production of commodities and services for profit. If a capitalist does not have a superior product to sell, if he does not have more effective methods of marketing at his disposal, or if he is otherwise unable to beat competition, he is likely to try to reach his goal—maximum profit—by introducing a new commodity or service. And in many cases this will of course result in a commercialization of previously noncommercial areas.

I have previously denied the Marxist claim that prostitution is based on and falls with capitalism. And what I just said is not inconsistent with this. For, to begin with, mercenary sex is not a capitalist invention. Furthermore, even in modern capitalist societies, most prostitutes work on their own. Unlike, for instance, porno models, they are typically not workers in the sex industry.

In saying this, I am denying something like the opposite of the Marxist claim, namely, that prostitution is one of the factors that generates a capitalistic commercialization of society. Capitalism is perfectly able to create commercialistic dystopias on its own. It hardly needs the aid of prostitution in the process.

If we want to fight against the increasing commercialization of society, we must fight against its capitalistic roots rather than against such loosely related symptoms of human dissatisfaction as prostitution.

VIII. THE CHARGE OF A DISTURBED EMOTIONAL LIFE

Most of the emotional problems that often afflict prostitutes can be traced back to the social stigma that we attach to their way of life. If our attitudes to sexuality, promiscuity, and mercenary sex were different—if for example, prostitutes were held in esteem instead of in degradation—I am convinced that they would display very little of the mental disturbances that not seldom haunt them today.

But is it not possible that certain emotional problems would always remain, no matter how the attitudes of the surrounding society changed? Is it not likely, for instance, that even a harlot whose occupation was held in esteem would find her own love life, her feelings for the man she loves, disturbed by her professional activities? Can one have a well-functioning sexual life if sex is what one lives by? Compulsive behavior apart, the sex drive is no more of an insatiable appetite than hunger. Must not, therefore, the repetitious performance of sexual acts always in the end result in nausea or total indifference? And if the prostitute tries to avoid this effect through a complete detachment, not allowing herself to feel anything when with a customer, will she be able to "switch on" her feelings when with her lover?

I must admit that I do not feel certain what to say about this charge, which we may call "the charge of a disturbed emotional life." Since those prostitutes who are active today are victims of our present scornful attitudes, we cannot but speculate what would happen to their emotional lives if those attitudes were changed in a positive direction. I am inclined to think, however, that some prostitutes, even under the best of circumstances, would run the risk of getting emotional problems. But on the other hand, some prostitutes seem capable of preserving their integrity and sensibility even under the adverse conditions of today.

Since we cannot but speculate, no definite conclusions can be drawn. I wish to add, however, that I think that if prostitution were to be reformed in accordance with the suggestions that I am presently about to make, no prostitute would have to continue in the profession, should she (or he) find that she (or he) was not suited for it. . . .

NOTES

1. Here I am indebted to Kingsley Davis (see his "The Sociology of Prostitution," reprinted in *Deviance, Studies in the Process of Stigmatization and Social Reaction,* ed. A. C. Clarke, S. Dinitz, and R. R. Dynes (New York: Oxford University Press, 1975).

2. See Harry Benjamin and R. E. L. Masters, *Prostitution and Morality* (New York: Julian Press, 1964), chap. 6.

3. Ibid.

4. Ibid., p. 208.

5. I should perhaps stress, however, that I use the term "prostitution" in a neutral, descriptive sense, disregarding the ordinary negative value association of the term. In a later section (X) a normative concept 'sound prostitution' will be developed.

6. The empirical part of this opinion will be examined critically in the next section.

7. My major source of information has here as elsewhere been Benjamin and Masters (n. 4 above), esp. chaps. 5, 6, and 10. I have also consulted the reports of Jersild (Jens Jersild, *Boy Prostitution* [Copenhagen: G. E. C. Gad, 1956]) and Butts (W. M. Butts, "Boy Prostitutes of the Metropolis," *Journal of Clinical Psychopathology* [1947], pp. 673–81).

8. A ratio of 60/40 has been mentioned for big city areas like New York and Los Angeles. I do not regard this (or any other) figure as completely reliable, however. The empirical material available does not seem to allow any exact conclusions.

9. Rowbotham, *Women, Resistance, and Revolution* (London: Penguin Press, 1972) p. 66.

10. To those who find this statement a bit too categorical I suggest a quick glance back to Sec. IV).

Critics

Defending Prostitution

Carole Pateman

Charges Against Ericsson

Ericsson's contractarian defense of prostitution[1] extends the liberal ideals of individualism, equality of opportunity, and the free market to sexual life. The real problem with prostitution, Ericsson claims, is the hypocrisy, prejudice, and punitive attitudes that surround it. Once unblinkered, we can see that prostitution is merely one service occupation among others and that, with some reforms, a morally acceptable, or "sound," prostitution could exist. This defense has its appeal at a time when strict control of sexual conduct is again being strenuously advocated. However, Ericsson's argument fails to overcome the general weaknesses of abstract contractarianism, and his claim that he has rebutted the feminist charge against prostitution cannot be granted. The central feminist argument is that prostitution remains morally undesirable, no matter what reforms are made, because it is one of the most graphic examples of men's domination of women.

Ericsson's argument illustrates nicely how liberal contractarianism systematically excludes the patriarchal dimension of our society from philosophical scrutiny. He interprets feminists as arguing that prostitution is "undesirable on the ground that it constitutes an extreme instance of the inequality between the sexes" (p. 348), and he then interprets inequality to be a matter of the distribution of benefits and burdens. It thus appears that a remedy can be found for the withholding of a benefit (access to prostitutes) from women by extending equality of opportunity to buy and sell sexual services on the market to both sexes. Ericsson ignores the fact that men earn a good deal more than women, so the lat-

ter would still have a greater incentive to be sellers than buyers (or would be confined to the cheaper end of the market as buyers; Ericsson pays no attention to the different categories of prostitution). Moreover, Ericsson notes that three-quarters of the men who are in the market for prostitutes are married. Any change in attitudes would have to be sufficient to make it acceptable that wives could spend what they save from housekeeping money, or spend part of their own earnings, on prostitutes. Second, Ericsson dismisses as meaningless the charge that prostitution unfairly burdens women because they are oppressed as prostitutes; properly understood, prostitution is an example of a free contract between individuals in the market in which services are exchanged for money. Ericsson's defense does not and cannot confront the feminist objection to prostitution. Feminists do not see prostitution as unacceptable because it distributes benefits and burdens unequally; rather, to use Ericsson's language of inequality, because prostitution is grounded in the inequality of domination and subjection. The problem of domination is both denied by and hidden behind Ericsson's assertion that prostitution is a free contract or an equal exchange.

The most striking feature of Ericsson's defense is that he makes no attempt to substantiate the key claim that prostitution *is* the sale of sexual services. His assertion relies on the conventional assumption that free wage labor stands at the opposite pole from slavery. The worker freely contracts to sell labor power or services for a specified period, whereas the person of the slave is sold for an unlimited time.

From Carole Pateman, "Defending Prostitution: Charges Against Ericsson," *Ethics* 93 (1983); 561–65. Some notes and some parts of the text have been deleted. Reprinted by permission of University of Chicago Press.

Ericsson comments that if a prostitute "actually did sell herself, she would no longer be a prostitute but a sexual slave" (p. 341). More exactly, since she has the civil and juridical status of a free individual in the capitalist market, she would be in a form of subjection that fell short of slavery. Ericsson avoids discussing whether this is indeed the position of the prostitute because he ignores the problems involved in separating the sale of services through contract from the sale of the body and the self. In capitalist societies it appears as if labor power and services are bought and sold on the market, but "labor power" and "services" are abstractions. When workers sell labor power, or professionals sell services to clients (and Ericsson regards some prostitutes as "small scale private entrepreneurs"),[2] neither the labor power nor services can in reality be separated from the person offering them for sale. Unless the "owners" of these abstractions agree to, or are compelled to, use them in certain ways, which means that the "owners" act in a specified manner, there is nothing to be sold. The employer appears to buy labor power; what he actually obtains is the right of command over workers, the right to put their capacities, their bodies, to use as he determines.

Services and labor power are inseparably connected to the body and the body is, in turn, inseparably connected to the sense of self. Ericsson writes of the prostitute as a kind of social worker, but the services of the prostitute are related in a more intimate manner to her body than those of other professionals. Sexual services, that is to say, sex and sexuality, are constitutive of the body in a way in which the counseling skills of the social worker are not (a point illustrated in a backhanded way by the ubiquitous use by men of vulgar terms for female sexual organs to refer to women themselves). Sexuality and the body are, further, integrally connected to conceptions of femininity and masculinity, and all these are constitutive of our individuality, our sense of self-identity. When sex becomes a commodity in the capitalist market so, necessarily, do bodies and selves. The prostitute cannot sell sexual services alone; what she sells is her body. To supply services contracted for, professionals must act in certain ways, or use their bodies; to use the labor power he has bought the employer has command over the worker's capacities and body; to use the prostitute's "services," her purchaser must buy her body and use her body. In prostitution, because of the relation between the commodity being marketed and the body, it is the body that is up for sale.

Critics of marriage have often claimed that wives are no different from prostitutes. Women who marry also contract away their bodies but (in principle) for life rather than for minutes or hours like the prostitute. However, a form of marriage in which the husband gains legal right of sexual use of his wife's body is only one possible form. The conjugal relation is not necessarily one of domination and subjection, and in this it differs from prostitution. Ericsson's defense is about prostitution in capitalist societies; that is, the practice through which women's bodies become commodities in the market which can be bought (contracted for) for sexual use. The questions his defense raises are why there is a demand for this commodity, exactly what the commodity is, and why it is *men* who demand it.

Ericsson cannot admit that the first two questions arise. The third he treats as unproblematic. He stands firmly in the patriarchal tradition which discusses prostitution as a problem about the women who are prostitutes, and our attitudes to them, not a problem about the men who demand to buy them. For Ericsson it is merely a contingent fact that most prostitutes are women and customers men.[3] He claims that the demand for prostitution could never disappear because of some "ubiquitous and permanent imperfections" (p. 337) of human existence arising from the sexual urge. In other words, prostitution is a natural feature of human life. Certainly, sexual impulses are part of our natural constitution as humans, but the sale of "sexual services" as a commodity in the capitalist market cannot be reduced to an expression of our natural biology and physiology. To compare the fulfillment of sexual urges through prostitution to other natural necessities of human survival, to argue from the fact that we need food, so it should be available, to the claim that "our sexual desires are just as basic, natural, and compelling as our appetite for food, [so] this also holds for them" (p. 341), is, to say the least, disingenuous. What counts as "food" varies widely, of course, in different cultures, but, at the most fundamental level of survival there is one obvious difference between sex and other human needs. Without a certain minimum of food, drink, and shelter, people die; but, to my knowledge, no one has yet died from want of sexual release. Moreover, sometimes food and drink are impossible to obtain no matter what people do, but every person has the means to find sexual release at hand.

To treat prostitution as a natural way of satisfying a basic human need, to state that "bought meals are not always the worst" (p. 355), neatly, if vulgarly, obscures the real, social character of contemporary sexual relations. Prostitution is not, as Ericsson claims, the same as "sex without love or mutual affection" (p. 341). The latter is morally acceptable *if* it is the result of mutual physical attraction that is freely expressed by both individuals. The difference between sex without love and prostitution is not the difference between cooking at home and buying food in restaurants; the difference is that between the reciprocal expression of desire and unilateral subjection to sexual acts with the consolation of payment: it is the difference for women between freedom and subjection.

To understand why men (not women) demand prostitutes, and what is demanded, prostitution has to be rescued from Ericsson's abstract contractarianism and placed in the social context of the structure of sexual relations between women and men. Since the revival of the organized feminist movement, moral and political philosophers have begun to turn their attention to sexual life, but their discussions are usually divided into a set of discrete compartments which take for granted that a clear distinction can be drawn between consensual and coercive sexual relationships. However, as an examination of consent and rape makes graphically clear,[4] throughout the whole of sexual life domination, subjection, and enforced submission are confused with consent, free association, and the reciprocal fulfillment of mutual desire. The assertion that prostitution is no more than an example of a free contract between equal individuals in the market is another illustration of the presentation of submission as freedom. Feminists have often argued that what is fundamentally at issue in relations between women and men is not sex but power. But, in the present circumstances of our sexual lives, it is not possible to separate power from sex. The expression of sexuality and what it means to be feminine and a woman, or masculine and a man, is developed within, and intricately bound up with, relations of domination and subordination.

Ericsson remarks that "the best prostitutional sex available is probably much better from the customer's point of view than average marital sex" (p. 340). It is far from obvious that it is either "quality" or the "need" for sex, in the commonsense view of "quality" and "sex," that explains why three-quarters of these customers are husbands. In the "permissive society" there are numerous ways in which men can find sex without payment, in addition to the access that husbands have to wives. But, except in the case of the most brutal husbands, most spouses work out a modus vivendi about all aspects of their lives, including the wife's bodily integrity. Not all husbands exercise to the full their socially and legally recognized right—which is the right of a master. There is, however, another institution which enables all men to affirm themselves as masters. To be able to purchase a body in the market presupposes the existence of masters. Prostitution is the public recognition of men as sexual masters; it puts submission on sale as a commodity in the market. . . .

NOTES

1. L. O. Ericsson, "Charges Against Prostitution: An Attempt at a Philosophical Assessment," *Ethics* 90, no. 3 (1980): 335–66. Page references to this paper are in parentheses in the text.

2. On workers as "petty entrepreneurs," their labor power or services, see R. P. Wolff, "A Critique and Reinterpretation of Marx's Labor Theory of Value," *Philosophy and Public Affairs* 10 (1981): 89–120, esp. 109–11.

3. In cities like Sydney, male homosexual prostitutes are not uncommon. Following Ericsson, I discuss only heterosexual (genitally oriented) prostitution. It is not immediately clear that homosexual prostitution has the same social significance.

4. See my "Women and Consent," *Political Theory* 8 (1980): 149–68.

Laurie Shrage | # Should Feminists Oppose Prostitution?

THE SOCIAL MEANING
OF PROSTITUTION

Let me begin with a simple analogy. In our society there exists a taboo against eating cats and dogs. Now, suppose a member of our society wishes to engage in the unconventional behavior of ingesting cat or dog meat. In evaluating the moral and political character of this person's behavior, it is somewhat irrelevant whether eating cats and dogs "really" is or isn't healthy, or whether it "really" is or isn't different than eating cows, pigs, and chickens. What is relevant is that, by including cat and dog flesh in one's diet, a person may really make others upset and, therefore, do damage to them as well as to oneself. In short, how actions are widely perceived and interpreted by others, even if wrongly or seemingly irrationally, is crucial to determining their moral status because, though such interpretations may not hold up against some "objective reality," they are part of the "social reality" in which we live.

I am not using this example to argue that unconventional behavior is wrong but, rather, to illustrate the relevance of cultural convention to how our outward behaviors are perceived. Indeed, what is wrong with prostitution is not that it violates deeply entrenched social conventions—ideals of feminine purity, and the noncommoditization of sex—but precisely that it epitomizes other cultural assumptions—beliefs which, reasonable or not, serve to legitimate women's social subordination. In other words, rather than subvert patriarchal ideology, the prostitute's actions, and the industry as a whole, serve to perpetuate this system of values. By contrast, lesbian sex, and egalitarian heterosexual economic and romantic relationships, do not. In short, female prostitution oppresses women, not because some women who participate in it "suffer in the eyes of society" but because its organized practice testifies to and perpetuates socially hegemonic beliefs which oppress all women in many domains of their lives.

What, then, are some of the beliefs and values which structure the social meaning of the prostitute's business in our culture—principles which are not necessarily consciously held by us but are implicit in our observable behavior and social practice? First, people in our society generally believe that human beings naturally possess, but socially repress, powerful, emotionally destabilizing sexual appetites. Second, we assume that men are naturally suited for dominant social roles. Third, we assume that contact with male genitals in virtually all contexts is damaging and polluting to women. Fourth, we assume that a person's sexual practice renders her or him a particular "kind" of person, for example, "a homosexual," "a bisexual," "a whore," "a virgin," "a pervert," and so on. I will briefly examine the nature of these four assumptions, and then discuss how they determine the social significance and impact of prostitution in our society. Such principles are inscribed in all of a culture's communicative acts and institutions, but my examples will only be drawn from a common body of disciplinary resources: the writings of philosophers and other intellectuals.

The Universal Possession
of a Potent Sex Drive

. . . The assumption of a potent "sex drive" is implicit in Lars Ericsson's relatively recent defense of prostitution: "We must liberate ourselves from those mental fossils which prevent us from looking upon sex and sexuality with the same naturalness as upon our

From Laurie Shrage, "Should Feminists Oppose Prostitution?" *Ethics* 99 (1989): 347–61. Some notes and some parts of the text have been deleted.

cravings for food and drink. And, contrary to popular belief, we may have something to learn from prostitution in this respect, namely, that coition resembles nourishment in that if it cannot be obtained in any other way it can always be bought. And bought meals are not always the worst."[1] More explicitly, he argues that the "sex drive" provides a noneconomic, natural basis for explaining the demand for commercial sex.[2] Moreover, he claims that because of the irrational nature of this impulse, prostitution will exist until all persons are granted sexual access upon demand to all other persons.[3] In a society where individuals lack such access to others, but where women are the social equals of men, Ericsson predicts that "the degree of female frustration that exists today . . . will no longer be tolerated, rationalized, or sublimated, but channeled into a demand for, inter alia, mercenary sex."[4] Consequently, Ericsson favors an unregulated sex industry, which can respond spontaneously to these natural human wants. Although Pateman, in her response to Ericsson, does not see the capitalist commoditization of sexuality as physiologically determined, she nevertheless yields to the assumption that "sexual impulses are part of our natural constitution as humans."[5] . . .

By contrast, consider a group of people in New Guinea, called the Dani, as described by Karl Heider: "Especially striking is their five year post-partum sexual abstinence, which is uniformly observed and is not a subject of great concern or stress. This low level of sexuality appears to be a purely cultural phenomenon, not caused by any biological factors."[6] The moral of this anthropological tale is that our high level of sexuality is also "a purely cultural phenomenon," and not the inevitable result of human biology. Though the Dani's disinterest in sex need not lead us to regard our excessive concern as improper, it should lead us to view one of our cultural rationalizations for prostitution as just that—a cultural rationalization.

The "Natural" Dominance of Men

One readily apparent feature of the sex industry in our society is that it caters almost exclusively to a male clientele. Even the relatively small number of male prostitutes at work serve a predominantly male consumer group. Implicit in this particular division of labor, and also the predominant division of labor in other domains of our society, is the cultural principle that men are naturally disposed to dominate in their relations with others. . . .

Sexual Contact Pollutes Women

To say that extensive sexual experience in a woman is not prized in our society is to be guilty of indirectness and understatement. Rather, a history of sexual activity is a negative mark that is used to differentiate kinds of women. Instead of being valued for their experience in sexual matters, women are valued for their "innocence." . . .

The Reification of Sexual Practice

Another belief that determines the social significance of prostitution concerns the relationship between a person's social identity and her or his sexual behavior.[7] For example, we identify a person who has sexual relations with a person of the same gender as a "homosexual," and we regard a woman who has intercourse with multiple sexual partners as being of a particular type—for instance, a "loose woman," "slut," or "prostitute." As critics of our society, we may find these categories too narrow or the values they reflect objectionable. If so, we may refer to women who are sexually promiscuous, or who have sexual relations with other women, as "liberated women," and thereby show a rejection of double (and homophobic) standards of sexual morality. However, what such linguistic iconoclasm generally fails to challenge is that a person's sexual practice makes her a particular "kind" of person.

I will now consider how these cultural convictions and values structure the meaning of prostitution in our society. Our society's tolerance for commercially available sex, legal or not, implies general acceptance of principles which perpetuate women's social subordination. Moreover, by their participation in an industry which exploits the myths of female social inequality and sexual vulnerability, the actions of the prostitute and her clients imply that they accept a set of values and beliefs which assign women to marginal social roles in all our cultural institutions, including marriage and waged employment. Just as an Uncle Tom exploits noxious beliefs about blacks for personal gain, and implies through his actions that blacks can benefit from a system of white supremacy, the prostitute and her clients imply that women can profit economically from patriarchy. Though we should not blame the workers in the sex industry for the social degradation they suffer, as theorists and critics of our society, we should question the existence of such businesses and the social principles implicit in our tolerance for them. . . .

NOTES

1. Lars O. Ericsson, "Charges Against Prostitution: An Attempt at a Philosophical Assessment," *Ethics* 90 (1980): 335–66.

2. Ibid., p. 347.

3. Ibid., pp. 359–60.

4. Ibid., p. 360.

5. Carole Pateman, "Defending Prostitution: Charges Against Ericsson," *Ethics* 93 (1983): 561–65.

6. Karl Heider, "Dani Sexuality: A Low Energy System," *Man* 11 (1976): 188–201.

7. In "Defending Prostitution," Pateman states: "The services of the prostitute are related in a more intimate manner to her body than those of other professionals. Sexual services, that is to say, sex and sexuality, are constitutive of the body in a way in which the counseling skills of the social worker are not. . . . Sexuality and the body are, further, integrally connected to conceptions of femininity and masculinity, and all these are constitutive of our individuality, our sense of self-identity" (p. 562). On my view, while our social identities are determined by our outward sexual practice, this is due to arbitrary, culturally determined conceptual mappings, rather than some universal relationship holding between persons and their bodies.

Karen Green | Prostitution, Exploitation, and Taboo

A simple free market liberalism would have it that the continuing community sentiment that prostitution is morally suspect is merely an archaic taboo.[1] But this observation can be turned on its head. Psychoanalysts suggest that the acquisition of a certain structure of emotional reactions is of a piece with the acquisition of a sense of oneself as a moral being. The sense that certain acts or objects are unclean or taboo is the reverse side of the sense of oneself as a clean or virtuous person. Sex, according to Ericsson, is just a natural instinctual drive like hunger. Yet, in hunter-gatherer societies, where a clan-member's sense of self involves identification with a sacred animal or food, eating of that food is taboo. This should alert us to the possibility that the taboo status of prostitution, in our society, is connected, at a fundamental level, with the psychological processes that result in the development, in a mature individual, of a structure of moral sentiments.

In the third part of *A Theory of Justice* John Rawls argues that his liberal theory of justice generates its own support within society and is hence stable. In arguing this he describes "how human beings in a well-ordered society might acquire a sense of justice and the other moral sentiments." It is the claim of this paper that when we consider the preconditions for the development of a liberal (or any other) sense of justice and the other moral sentiments, we are forced to recognize that these are incompatible with the conclusion that, on liberal grounds, there is nothing morally wrong with prostitution. Such sentiments are necessary in order for liberal societies to be stable and to reproduce themselves, but such sentiments could not be acquired in a society in which

From Karen Green, "Prostitution, Exploitation and Taboo," *Philosophy* 64, no. 250 (1989): 525–34. Some notes and some parts of the text have been deleted. Reprinted with the permission of Cambridge University Press.

prostitution was seriously considered morally on a par with marriage.

The argument depends on accepting, as at least roughly accurate, certain empirical theories about the development of a moral sense. There are a number of controversies in this area. However, for the sake of this argument all that needs to be accepted is that the preconditions for the development of the most basic set of moral sentiments are accurately outlined in the following passage from Rawls:

> . . . when the parents' love of the child is recognized by him on the basis of their evident intentions, the child is assured of his worth as a person. . . . He experiences parental affection as unconditional; they care for his presence and spontaneous acts, and the pleasure they take in him is not dependent upon disciplined performances that contribute to the well-being of others. . . . Gradually he acquires various skills and develops a sense of competence that affirms his self-esteem. It is in the course of this whole process that the child's affection for his parents develops. He connects them with the success and enjoyment that he has in sustaining his world, and with his sense of his own worth. And this brings about his love for them.
>
> . . . if he does love and trust his parents, then, once he has given in to temptation, he is disposed to share their attitude towards his misdemeanors. He will be inclined to confess his transgression and to seek reconciliation . . . given the nature of the authority situation and the principles of moral psychology connecting the ethical and natural attitudes, love and trust will give rise to feelings of guilt once the parental injunctions are disobeyed.[2]

The relationship between parent and child, that gives rise to a developed moral sense, is quite different from that which holds between mature equals. It is unconditional and in no way based on contract. Parents' love for their children is partly natural but is largely a result of their own childhood experiences and the development of their own moral sentiments. Particularly, the sentiment that parents have a duty to love their offspring, no matter how demanding and self-centred they may be in their earliest years. By a duty to love I mean a duty to provide for the well-being and self-esteem of another without this being

conditional on reciprocal benefits. Without such moral sentiments, the preconditions for the development of children into free rational individuals, imbued with a moral sense, would not be met. Self-esteem depends on the prior love of others, and self-esteem and the fear of its loss is the motive force of virtue.

It is at this juncture that the moral significance of the connection between sex and love arises. If parents are to provide the love their children require, they themselves need self-esteem. Sexual love between parents has moral value because, so long as Freud is at least roughly correct, such sexual love replaces in the adult psyche the infantile desire for satisfaction. Loved, the parent experiences a reflection of earlier parental love. Self-esteem is reinforced and the duty to love is less onerous. The picture of the ideal moral relationship between sex and love is that sex, which leads to procreation, should be accompanied by mutual love. The moral value of such love lies in the part it plays in the reproduction of social beings with a moral sense, a capacity to love and a belief in their own self-worth.

These observations show the moral value of the association of sex and love, where procreation is concerned. But, it might be objected, they fail to show that the existence of prostitution threatens this connection. Prostitution does not involve procreation, its existence is quite compatible with the existence of marriages within which the ideal is realized. In a sense, this is quite true. However, it fails to come to grips with the character of the moral judgment that these considerations imply. What is morally disturbing about prostitution is not its immediate consequences. Rather, it is the moral psychology, or structure of moral sentiments, that is intuitively recognized to accompany it. In the healthy psyche the intimacy of sex evokes the intimacy of earlier parental love, one's sexual self is private because it is felt to be closely linked to one's sense of oneself as a unique and lovable being. Exposing this self in an intimate relationship involves the risk of rebuff but also promises reinforcement of one's sense of self-worth. In order to prostitute oneself, these psychic connections have to be broken. Prostitutes deal with this problem in different ways. Some, like a young male prostitute and homeless youth, recently interviewed on ABC TV, feel that no one cares for them. The experience of the impersonality of prostitutional sex reinforces an attitude of worthlessness and moral anomy already well rooted in a sense of parental rejection.[3] Many others split their sexuality and draw the line between intimacy and indifference at a place different from the norm. Characteristically, they refuse to kiss their clients, disassociating vaginal sex from intimacy and retaining the privacy of their affective being by kissing only those who are close to them.[4] Often, such frigidity in a female prostitute's relationship to her clients is accompanied by a contrasting total dependence on the love of a boy-friend or pimp, who is then in a position to manipulate and abuse her.[5] Yet others, who seem to be the most stable and independent, have a reasonably small clientele of 'regulars' and have less need to suppress all connections between sexuality and feelings of affection. Given this, one can see that prostitution is morally suspect because its practice involves the suppression of a structure of moral sentiments which has its moral value in promoting the altruistic behaviour that is necessary if a just society is to reproduce itself.

This argument must not be interpreted as simply a claim that prostitution is immoral because society could not reproduce itself if we all felt and behaved like prostitutes. Society would not reproduce itself if we were all celibate but celibacy is not therefore immoral.[6] The difference between prostitution and celibacy lies in the fact that prostitution is an extreme which implies a moral psychology destructive even in its less extreme forms. The tendency to treat sex as an arena of self-gratification, divorced from love or duties of care, is destructive of family life, even in its milder forms. On the other hand, the capacity to suppress sexual desire, of which celibacy is an extreme form, is taken to be a moral virtue because its exercise is sometimes necessary in order to preserve the integrity of family life.

A critique of prostitution along these lines depends on a partial defence of the traditional ideal of the family. It need not go so far as to abjure all forms of promiscuity, nor fluid or extended families,

so long as these are not destructive of the psychic structures that facilitate parental love. It might turn out, for instance, that a measure of early promiscuity facilitates the later development of a stable relationship with spouse and children. But it sees prostitution as immoral because its practice does involve the suppression of these structures. The value of these structures and of the concept of a duty to love one's sexual partner arises, on this view, out of the need to maintain the duty to love one's children. Liberal society would suffer internal collapse if it did not supplement its rational egoism with sufficient rational altruism to ensure the reproduction of rational beings with a sense of justice.

Liberal feminists might object that the constraints of sexual fidelity have always fallen most heavily on women and that this indicates that their primary purpose has been to secure paternity rather than to facilitate parental altruism. But the following thought experiment shows that the situation is not so simple. Suppose that we were to accept that there is absolutely nothing morally wrong with prostitution. In a society that took such a view, free women, unhampered by patriarchal prudery, would, presumably, choose to have whatever sexual relations they desired. Some, who were particularly attractive, or particularly needy, might sell their services, others would have to pay for sex from male prostitutes but most, no doubt, would enter into open-ended relationships based on mutual attraction. This is not too different from the situation that is developing today. But the practical outcome of a situation in which sex relations are seen in terms of self-gratification is that, for children, the bonds of love with one or another parent, and often both, are loosened. Since mothers usually keep and want to keep their children, it is most often fathers who withdraw from the day-to-day attention to their children's physical and emotional well-being. The effect is that the duties of parenthood fall more heavily than ever on women. The point is not that families headed by women are necessarily defective at rearing children with a moral sense. There is little evidence that this is the case. The point is that a liberal society in which mothers contribute the greatest share of parental altruism is one which maintains, in a new form, Rousseau's double standard. Rousseau maintains the sphere of family relations by condemning women to a life of service in the interests of free, rational men. Liberal feminists have rightly objected that freedom must equally be granted to women. The danger is that by forgetting that human beings do not come into the world as rational individuals, endowed with a moral sense, we are in danger of falling into one or other of two unacceptable outcomes. Either, a society in which all relations are based on contracts in a free market and no one recognizes any duty to love. This would be one in which children were left to survive as best they could, whenever the strains of care conflicted too heavily with parental self-interest. Or, a society in which the constraints placed on self-interest by the duty to love one's children fall largely on women. Which would be one in which women would not have the same liberty as men to pursue their other interests. Neither outcome is such that a liberal feminist should happily rest with it. . . .

NOTES

1. Lars Ericsson, "Charges Against Prostitution: An Attempt at a Philosophical Assessment," *Ethics* 90 (1980): 342.

2. John Rawls, *A Theory of Justice* (Oxford University Press 1972), 464–465.

3. Dr Harold Greenwald, *The Elegant Prostitute* (New York: Ballatine Books, 1958), includes a number of cases of prostitutes who express similar sentiments of deprivation.

4. Eileen Mcleod, *Women Working: Prostitution Now* (London and Canberra: Croom Helm, 1982), 38–42.

5. Kate Millett, *The Prostitution Papers* (New York: Ballantine, 1973).

6. I am indebted to Peter Singer for this observation.

PART 3

What's Wrong with the Family?

Many of the questions that moral philosophers are concerned with concern the obligations we have to other people simply as people. My obligation not to commit murder, for example, extends equally to everyone: relative, friend, neighbor, stranger. But some of the most important moral questions that people confront in their everyday lives concern obligations they have not simply as one human being to another, but rather as one member of a particular family to another. The goal of Part 3 is to provide a basis for discussion of some of these questions. We begin by examining the obligations that adult children may have to their aging parents (chapter 11). We then raise questions about the traditional family and the obligations it undergirds (chapter 12). Married couples have traditionally been accorded the right to have children. Chapter 13 looks at the question of whether couples should be licensed by the state before embarking on that enterprise. Finally, we conclude with a look at one alternative to the traditional family union, that of same-sex marriage.

11

Is Neglecting One's Parents Wrong?

English and Her Critics

One of the Ten Commandments, which Moses reportedly received from God on Mount Sinai, is the injunction to "Honor the father and thy mother that thy days may be long upon the land which the LORD thy God giveth thee" (Exodus 20:12). In ancient Israel there wasn't very much in the way of Social Security for elderly people, so if a person's days turned out to be long, the honoring by his children would involve a pretty substantial commitment. Many people accept that adult children have serious moral obligations to their aging parents. In the featured article of this section, Jane English takes issue with this widespread view. To the question "What do grown children owe their parents?" her rather shocking reply is "Nothing."

As English notes, the sacrifices parents make for their children, in conjunction with a principle of reciprocity, are often appealed to in arguments for the standard view. The implicit argument for the standard view goes something like this:

P1 If someone makes sacrifices in order to promote another's well-being, then the recipient of the benefit is morally obliged to reciprocate by making comparable sacrifices to promote the benefactor's well-being (principle of reciprocity).

P2 Parents make very large sacrifices in order to promote their children's well being.

C   Children owe their aging parents reciprocal sacrifices comparable to those their parents made for them.

The argument has some nice features. For example, it helps explain why a person who was abandoned at birth by his natural parents owes his natural parents nothing. However, if he was saved from death and adopted by some compassionate couple, who go on to make a large contribution to his well-being, then he may owe his adoptive parents quite a lot. The idea explains why mere genetic relations as such do not generate debts, but familial relations, even non-genetic family relations from which one substantially benefits, do generate debts of obligation.

The problem with this argument is that the principle of reciprocity as stated runs up against an apparent counterexample. Take English's neighborly favor case. Max asks neighbor Nina to take in his mail for him while he is on vacation, and Nina agrees. She sacrifices some of her free time to benefit Max. Max thus incurs a debt to Nina, and if Nina now asks Max to reciprocate by taking in her mail while she is on vacation, Max owes it to her to do so. He owes her a reciprocal favor. Favors, requested and accepted, generate debts—debts of roughly the same order as the original favor. Further, once Max does something equivalent for Nina that particular debt has been "discharged." This is explained by the principle of reciprocity. Nina makes a sacrifice that benefits Max, and by that fact he becomes indebted to Nina. So far, so good.

Now consider English's neighborly sacrifice case. Max goes on vacation without asking Nina to take in his mail, but when he returns he finds, to his surprise and delight, that Nina has taken in his mail in his absence. Is Max now obligated to take Nina's mail in for her when she goes on vacation? Not according to English. English claims that Nina has made a *voluntary sacrifice* and that such unasked-for sacrifices do not generate debts of reciprocal sacrifice. If Nina now goes on vacation, she cannot demand that Max take in her mail while she is away.

What these two cases show is that while *favors* of the sort that Nina does for Max *when requested* generate reciprocal debts, *voluntary sacrifices* of the sort Nina makes without being asked do not. The principle of reciprocity as stated is thus refuted by the neighborly sacrifice case. A version of the Principle certainly applies in the neighborly favor case, but it incorporates a proviso that the first leaves out—the request for the favor:

Revised Principle of Reciprocity

If someone asks another for a favor, and the latter grants the favor, then the recipient of the favor is morally obliged to reciprocate with a comparable favor

Would this revised principle, in conjunction with premise 2, entail that grown children have acquired substantial obligations their parents? Obviously not, and the reason is that, as with Max in the voluntary sacrifice case, the child did not *ask* his parents to bring him into the world or to make those sacrifices necessary to promote his well-being. English concludes that parental sacrifices do not, in themselves, generate obligations on offspring to reciprocate with comparable sacrifices. This is the negative part of her paper, which also contains a positive part. She introduces a different model of filial obligation, *the friendship model.*

Return to the sacrifice case. Max might be so taken with Nina's gesture that he becomes friends with her. They may start making a habit of helping each other out, and he may very well be willing to make similar sacrifices for her while she is on vacation—which is the right and proper thing for him to do as Nina's friend. But Max is not *obligated* to become friends with Nina, and if they do not become friendly with each other, he is not obligated to reciprocate with a comparable sacrifice. Nina's sacrifice is thus best construed as an overture to friendship, one that Max is free to accept or reject. If he does accept it, then by entering into a friendship with Nina, he now must act according to the rules of friendship, which are quite different from the principle of reciprocity. Friendships are ruled by mutuality, rather than reciprocity. Reciprocity involves a kind of tit-for-tat accounting, whereas mutuality is characterized by mutual care and concern. This suggests a different point to parental sacrifices. They are not favors, which then guarantee that the recipients have reciprocal obligations.

Rather, like Nina's sacrifice, they are best construed as overtures to friendship. Let's call them "friendly overtures," and let's say that a friendly overture is successful if it leads to friendship. If a parent's friendly overtures are successful—her offspring becomes her friend—then as an adult, her offspring will bear those obligations to her that people generally bear to their friends. We might construct an argument for filial obligations on the friendship model:

P1 Parents make large sacrifices as friendly overtures to their children.
P2 If friendly overtures are successful then a friendship ensues.
P3 Friends have obligations of mutual support, care, and concern.

C   When parents' friendly overtures are successful, their adult children assume the obligations of support, care, and concern for their parents.

The friendship model explains a range of filial obligations, but only on the condition that parents and their children are friends. It thus suggests that if friendly overtures do not have their intended effect—if parents and children are not friends—then the children owe their parents nothing. Or, rather, they owe them nothing over and above the normal obligations humans have to one another. And that is precisely the radical and interesting conclusion English advertises in the first sentence of her article. Furthermore, English accepts the consequence that children who were once friends with their parents but are no longer friends also do not have any special obligations to their parents.

In "Can Parents and Children Be Friends?" Joseph Kupfer argues that parents and children cannot really be friends, because friendship presupposes a kind of equality that children cannot share with their parents. First, children lack a certain kind of autonomy with regard to their parents, because of the influence parents have in shaping and forming their character and identity. Second, children lack the kind of independence from their parents that is a necessary condition of true friendship. A friendship has to form between independent beings who grow to know, like, and appreciate one another, on equal terms. The asymmetries inherent in the parent-child relationship preclude that kind of development. Kupfer is effectively taking issue with premise 1 of our reconstructed argument. (Premises 2 and 3 do not mention the parent-child relationship, and what they say about friendship seems unassailable.) Since parents cannot be friends with their offspring, their sacrifices cannot sensibly be interpreted as friendly overtures. Furthermore, if there are filial obligations, they cannot be accounted for within the friendship model.

Nicholas Dixon defends a version of the friendship model against various attacks, including those of Kupfer. First, he argues that English was too quick to accept an unpleasant and implausible consequence: that once children cease to be friends with their parents, they no longer have any special filial duties toward them. He argues instead that the duties of friendship might persist even when the friendship dies. He does raise what is probably the most obvious objection to the friendship model. Suppose we have a pair of model parents who, in bringing up their child, go far beyond what is required of parents, providing their child, at huge cost to themselves, lots of opportunities to develop interests and talents. The child accepts all these advantages and, as a result, flourishes. However, the child remains cold and distant from his parents, never forming any friendly relationship with them at any time. Does the latter fact really release this rather unpleasant child from all special obligations to his benefactors? Is he not guilty of gross ingratitude, and does that not imply or at least suggest that he is failing in some of his obligations? Dixon is inclined to accept that the child has the obligation to *thank* his benefactors, but has no obligation to offer reciprocal sacrifices.

QUESTIONS FOR CONSIDERATION

• In thinking about this issue, it might be helpful to go back to the original cases and reexamine your reactions to them. What do you *now* think Max's obligations to Nina are, in the case where she makes the voluntary sacrifice? Does he simply owe her a thank-you or is there something more required of him?

• If you agree with English that in the neighborly sacrifice case Max does not have an obligation of reciprocity to Nina since he did not ask Nina to make the sacrifice, is this enough to show that unrequested sacrifices *never* generate obligations of reciprocity? Can you think of any cases in which a person helps another without that other person's request and in which such an obligation might well arise? What if a person helps you when you are unconscious? Does this mean that you owe them nothing in return since you did not ask them to help you? If there are some cases of unrequested sacrifice that do generate obligations and others that do not, which are more like the case of the child who did not ask his parents to make sacrifices on his behalf? Does this help or hurt English's position?

• Is it *possible* for parents to achieve friendship with their offspring? (Do you count your parents among your set of friends? Would you *like* to count them as friends?)

• Are there genuine friendships that do not satisfy Kupfer's criteria for friendship? What do you think are the essential features of a genuine friendship? (To answer this question you have to do some philosophical analysis of the notion of friendship.)

• Given the essential features of friendship you have identified, are parents precluded from ever becoming friends with their offspring?

• Are Dixon's examples of duties to ex-friends plausible? Are they analogous to the duties that children might have to parents they no longer like?

• Does Dixon adequately defuse the objection of the cold, unfriendly child? Does it follow from Dixon's account that you can minimize your obligations to your parents by remaining aloof and indifferent to them? Is it intuitively plausible that the more unpleasant you are to your parents, the less you owe them?

FURTHER READING

Li, Chenyang. "Shifting Perspectives: Filial Morality Revisited." *Philosophy East and West* 47, no. 2 (1997): 211–32.

Jane English

What Do Grown Children Owe Their Parents?

What do grown children owe their parents? I will contend that the answer is "nothing." Although I agree that there are many things that children *ought* to do for their parents, I will argue that it is inappropriate and misleading to describe them as things "owed." I will maintain that parents' voluntary sacrifices, rather than creating "debts" to be "repaid," tend to create love or "friendship." The duties of grown children are those of friends and result from love between them and their parents, rather than being things owed in repayment for the parents' earlier sacrifices. Thus, I will oppose those philosophers who use the word "owe" whenever a duty or obligation exists. Although the "debt" metaphor is appropriate in some moral circumstances, my argument is that a love relationship is not such a case.

Misunderstandings about the proper relationship between parents and their grown children have resulted from reliance on the "owing" terminology. For instance, we hear parents complain, "You owe it to us to write home (keep up your piano playing, not adopt a hippie lifestyle), because of all we sacrificed for you (paying for piano lessons, sending you to college)." The child is sometimes even heard to reply, "I didn't ask to be born (to be given piano lessons, to be sent to college)." This inappropriate idiom of ordinary language tends to obscure, or even to undermine, the love that is the correct ground of filial obligation.

1. FAVORS CREATE DEBTS

There are some cases, other than literal debts, in which talk of "owing," though metaphorical, is apt.

New to the neighborhood, Max barely knows his neighbor, Nina, but he asks her if she will take in his mail while he is gone for a month's vacation. She agrees. If, subsequently, Nina asks Max to do the same for her, it seems that Max has a moral obligation to agree (greater than the one he would have had if Nina had not done the same for him), unless for some reason it would be a burden far out of proportion to the one Nina bore for him. I will call this a *favor:* when A, at B's request, bears some burden for B, then B incurs an obligation to reciprocate. Here the metaphor of Max's "owing" Nina is appropriate. It is not literally a debt, of course, nor can Nina pass this IOU on to heirs, demand payment in the form of Max's taking out her garbage, or sue Max. Nonetheless, since Max ought to perform one act of similar nature and amount of sacrifice in return, the term is suggestive. Once he reciprocates, the debt is "discharged"—that is, their obligations revert to the condition they were in before Max's initial request.

Contrast a situation in which Max simply goes on vacation and, to his surprise, finds upon his return that his neighbor has mowed his grass twice weekly in his absence. This is a voluntary sacrifice rather than a favor, and Max has no duty to reciprocate. It would be nice for him to volunteer to do so, but this would be supererogatory on his part. Rather than a favor, Nina's action is a friendly gesture. As a result, she might expect Max to chat over the back fence, help her catch her straying dog, or something similar—she might expect the development of a friendship. But Max would be chatting (or whatever) out of friendship, rather than in repayment for mown grass. If he did not return her gesture, she might feel

Jane English, "What Do Grown Children Owe Their Parents?" in *Having Children,* ed. Onora O'Neill New York: Oxford University Press, 1979), pp. 174–78. Notes have been deleted. Used by permission of Oxford University Press, Inc.

rebuffed or miffed, but not unjustly treated or indignant, since Max has not failed to perform a duty. Talk of "owing" would be out of place in this case.

It is sometimes difficult to distinguish between favors and non-favors, because friends tend to do favors for each other, and those who exchange favors tend to become friends. But one test is to ask how Max is motivated. Is it "to be nice to Nina" or "because she did *x* for me"? Favors are frequently performed by total strangers without any friendship developing. Nevertheless, a temporary obligation is created, even if the chance for repayment never arises. For instance, suppose that Oscar and Matilda, total strangers, are waiting in a long checkout line at the supermarket. Oscar, having forgotten the oregano, asks Matilda to watch his cart for a second. She does. If Matilda now asks Oscar to return the favor while she picks up some tomato sauce, he is obligated to agree. Even if she had not watched his cart, it would be inconsiderate of him to refuse, claiming he was too busy reading the magazines. He may have had a duty to help others, but he would not "owe" it to her. But if she has done the same for him, he incurs an additional obligation to help, and talk of "owing" is apt. It suggests an agreement to perform equal, reciprocal, canceling sacrifices.

2. THE DUTIES OF FRIENDSHIP

The terms "owe" and "repay" are helpful in the case of favors, because the sameness of the amount of sacrifice on the two sides is important; the monetary metaphor suggests equal quantities of sacrifice. But friendship ought to be characterized by *mutuality* rather than reciprocity: friends offer what they can give and accept what they need, without regard for the total amounts of benefits exchanged. And friends are motivated by love rather than by the prospect of repayment. Hence, talk of "owing" is singularly out of place in friendship.

For example, suppose Alfred takes Beatrice out for an expensive dinner and a movie. Beatrice incurs no obligation to "repay" him with a goodnight kiss or a return engagement. If Alfred complains that she

"owes" him something, he is operating under the assumption that she should repay a favor, but on the contrary his was a generous gesture done in the hopes of developing a friendship. We hope that he would not want her repayment in the form of sex or attention if this was done to discharge a debt rather than from friendship. Since, if Alfred is prone to reasoning in this way, Beatrice may well decline the invitation or request to pay for her own dinner, his attitude of expecting a "return" on his "investment" could hinder the development of a friendship. Beatrice should return the gesture only if she is motivated by friendship.

Another common misuse of the "owing" idiom occurs when the Smiths have dined at the Joneses' four times, but the Joneses at the Smiths' only once. People often say, "We owe them three dinners." This line of thinking may be appropriate between business acquaintants, but not between friends. After all, the Joneses invited the Smiths not in order to feed them or to be fed in turn, but because of the friendly contact presumably enjoyed by all on such occasions. If the Smiths do not feel friendship toward the Joneses, they can decline future invitations and not invite the Joneses; they owe them nothing. Of course, between friends of equal resources and needs, roughly equal sacrifices (though not necessarily roughly equal dinners) will typically occur. If the sacrifices are highly out of proportion to the resources, the relationship is closer to servility than to friendship.[1]

Another difference between favors and friendship is that after a friendship ends, the duties of friendship end. The party that has sacrificed less owes the other nothing. For instance, suppose Elmer donated a pint of blood that his wife Doris needed during an operation. Years after their divorce, Elmer is in an accident and needs one pint of blood. His new wife, Cora, is also of the same blood type. It seems not only that Doris does not "owe" Elmer blood, but that she should actually refrain from coming forward if Cora has volunteered to donate. To insist on donating not only interferes with the newlyweds' friendship, but it belittles Doris and Elmer's former relationship by suggesting that Elmer gave blood in hopes of favors returned instead of simply out of love for Doris. It is one of the heartrending features of divorce that it attends to quantity in a relationship previously characterized by mutuality. If Cora could not donate, Doris's obligation is the same as that for any former spouse in need of blood; it is not increased by the fact that Elmer similarly aided her. It *is* affected by the degree to which they are still friends, which in turn may (or may not) have been influenced by Elmer's donation.

In short, unlike the debts created by favors, the duties of friendship do not require equal quantities of sacrifice. Performing equal sacrifices does not cancel the duties of friendship, as it does the debts of favors. Unrequested sacrifices do not themselves create debts, but friends have duties regardless of whether they requested or initiated the friendship. Those who perform favors may be motivated by mutual gain, whereas friends should be motivated by affection. These characteristics of the friendship relation are distorted by talk of "owing."

3. PARENTS AND CHILDREN

The relationship between children and their parents should be one of friendship characterized by mutuality rather than one of reciprocal favors. The quantity of parental sacrifice is not relevant in determining what duties the grown child has. The medical assistance grown children ought to offer their ill mothers in old age depends upon the mothers' need, not upon whether they endured a difficult pregnancy, for example. Nor do one's duties to one's parents cease once an equal quantity of sacrifice has been performed, as the phrase "discharging a debt" may lead us to think.

Rather, what children ought to do for their parents (and parents for children) depends upon (1) their respective needs, abilities, and resources and (2) the extent to which there is an ongoing friendship between them. Thus, regardless of the quantity of childhood sacrifices, an able, wealthy child has an obligation to help his needy parents more than does a needy child. To illustrate, suppose sisters Cecile and Dana are equally loved by their parents, even

though Cecile was an easy child to care for, seldom ill, while Dana was often sick and caused some trouble as a juvenile delinquent. As adults, Dana is a struggling artist living far away, while Cecile is a wealthy lawyer living nearby. When the parents need visits and financial aid, Cecile has an obligation to bear a higher proportion of these burdens than her sister. This results from her abilities, rather than from the quantities of sacrifice made by the parents earlier.

Sacrifices have an important causal role in creating an ongoing friendship, which may lead us to assume incorrectly that it is the sacrifices that are the source of obligation. That the source is the friendship instead can be seen by examining cases in which the sacrifices occurred but the friendship, for some reason, did not develop or persist. For example, if a woman gives up her newborn child for adoption, and if no feelings of love ever develop on either side, it seems that the grown child does not have an obligation to "repay" her for her sacrifices in pregnancy. For that matter, if the adopted child has an unimpaired love relationship with the adoptive parents, he or she has the same obligations to help them as a natural child would have.

The filial obligations of grown children are a result of friendship, rather than owed for services rendered. Suppose that Vance married Lola despite his parents' strong wish that he marry within their religion, and that as a result, the parents refuse to speak to him again. As the years pass, the parents are unaware of Vance's problems, his accomplishments, the birth of his children. The love that once existed between them, let us suppose, has been completely destroyed by this event and thirty years of desuetude. At this point, it seems, Vance is under no obligation to pay his parents' medical bills in their old age, beyond his general duty to help those in need. An additional, filial obligation would only arise from whatever love he may still feel for them. It would be irrelevant for his parents to argue, "But look how much we sacrificed for you when you were young," for that sacrifice was not a favor but occurred as part of a friendship which existed at the time but is now, we have supposed, defunct. A more appropriate message would be, "We still love you, and we would like to renew our friendship."

I hope this helps to set the question of what children ought to do for their parents in a new light. The parental argument, "You ought to do x because we did y for you," should be replaced by, "We love you and you will be happier if you do x," or "We believe you love us, and anyone who loved us would do x." If the parents' sacrifice had been a favor, the child's reply, "I never asked you to do y for me," would have been relevant; to the revised parental remarks, this reply is clearly irrelevant. The child can either do x or dispute one of the parents' claims: by showing that a love relationship does not exist, or that love for someone does not motivate doing x, or that he or she will not be happier doing x.

Seen in this light, parental requests for children to write home, visit, and offer them a reasonable amount of emotional and financial support in life's crises are well founded, so long as a friendship still exists. Love for others does call for caring about and caring for them. Some other parental requests, such as for more sweeping changes in the child's lifestyle or life goals, can be seen to be insupportable, once we shift the justification from debts owed to love. The terminology of favors suggests the reasoning, "Since we paid for your college education, you owe it to us to make a career of engineering, rather than becoming a rock musician." This tends to alienate affection even further, since the tuition payments are depicted as investments for a return rather than done from love, as though the child's life goals could be "bought." Basing the argument on love leads to different reasoning patterns. The suppressed premise, "If A loves B, then A follows B's wishes as to A's lifelong career" is simply false. Love does not even dictate that the child adopt the parents' values as to the desirability of alternative life goals. So the parents' strongest available argument here is, "We love you, we are deeply concerned about your happiness, and in the long run you will be happier as an engineer." This makes it clear that an empirical claim is really the subject of the debate.

The function of these examples is to draw out our considered judgments as to the proper relation between parents and their grown children, and to show how poorly they fit the model of favors. What is relevant is the ongoing friendship that exists between parents and children. Although that relationship developed partly as a result of parental sacrifices for the child, the duties that grown children have to their parents result from the friendship rather than from the sacrifices. The idiom of owing favors to one's parents can actually be destructive if it undermines the role of mutuality and leads us to think in terms of quantitative reciprocal favors.

Critics

Joseph Kupfer | Can Parents and Children Be Friends?

It is often said by layman and philosopher alike that ideally children should grow up to be friends with their parents. Growing up and out of the one-sided dependency characteristic of the early phases of their relationship, adult children should become companions to their parents. There ought to be a mutual caring and counsel. This emphasis on friendship reflects the fact that young children become adults able to contribute to their parents' lives in ways comparable to what their parents have done for them. It also reflects the undesirability of the apparent alternatives to friendship: estrangement, continued child-dependence, or mere civility.

Part of the difficulty is that we don't have a word or clear concept to capture the ideal parent-adult child relationship, and "friendship" does indeed come closest to what it should be. How else describe the affection, respect, and give and take into which the relationship should evolve? In what follows I argue that parents and their adult children cannot become the "true" or "complete" friends they might be with peers. Contrary to an increasingly popular view, it is a mistake to turn to friendship as an ideal by which parents and children should orient or govern their relationships (or philosophers should theorize about them). Fundamental features of the ideal parent-adult child relationship keep it from developing into full-blown friendship. While peers may fail to become ideal friends, it isn't for the same reasons that parents and their grown children can't. The obstacles between parents and children are built into the structure of the relationship.

On the other hand, parents and adult children can enjoy a relationship rich in qualities that are lacking in the best of friendships. As we shall see, the structural features which prevent complete friendship are also responsible for these goods unique to parents and their adult children. The ideal parent-adult child relationship and complete friendship complement one another because each possesses values and virtues which the other lacks. For the most part, I shall be neglecting the large areas of overlap, areas in which parents and adult children can enjoy a kind of friendship that is quite worthwhile in its own right. I will be purposely pressing the features which differentiate these two important relationships.

Obviously, the following discussion assumes certain parameters to the family structure; however, these wouldn't seem to make the remarks "historical" in a narrow sense. For certain historical periods such as Victorian England, a discussion such as this one would be unnecessary since the very idea of parents and adult children being friends would be laughable. It is precisely in a society such as ours where children have considerable freedom and rights, not to mention power, and where parents too often strive to be youthful, that the idea of their being friends can take hold. In showing that parents and adult children can't be ideal friends even in middle-class America, I do make assumptions which need not hold for all societies.

For one thing, I assume that the parents are primarily responsible for rearing their children. In a society where child-rearing responsibility is diffused throughout the community, as in a Kibbutz, parents and adult children might be able to establish a genuine friendship. In the idealization of the parent-adult child relationship presented here, I also assume that the parents do an excellent job of rearing their children. The thrust of this is that to the extent that par-

From Joseph Kupfer, "Can Parents and Children Be Friends?" *American Philosophical Quarterly* 27, no. 1 (January 1990): 15–21. All notes and some parts of the text have been deleted. Reprinted by permission of North American Philosophical Publications.

ents are ideal parents they cannot enter into an ideal friendship with their grown children. Since my claim is not a logical one it is of course *possible* for parents and adult children to form a complete friendship, just as it is possible to change one's voice pattern or handwriting. However, I hope that the analysis offered here of both the parent-child relationship and ideal friendship relegates that possibility to the merely logical.

I

Parents and adult children cannot become true friends for two reasons. Their relationship lacks the equality friendship requires, and they are not sufficiently independent or separate from one another. Both the inequality and lack of independence from one another result from the distinctive history of the relationship. Let's consider first the sort of equality missing from the ideal parent-adult child relationship. Aristotle thinks that equally good character is needed in order for true friends to esteem each other sufficiently for equal affection. Only if the friends are equally virtuous will they mutually strive for the other's good for his own sake. Someone who is morally better than another cannot care as much about that person's welfare as he does his own. Moreover, he can't receive enough of the benefits a virtuous friend can provide.

While I agree with Aristotle, inequality in virtue is not the obstacle to friendship between parents and adult children. The inequality which prevents their friendship is inequality in autonomy. By autonomy I mean the ability to be self-determining: to choose for oneself on the basis of one's own values and beliefs. The autonomous person takes into account the opinions and advice of others, but reaches conclusions and decisions based on critical reflection of the matters at hand. Adult children are not necessarily less autonomous than their parents per se, or in general. Rather, they are less autonomous than their parents in the relationship. Although a grown child may generally be more autonomous than her parents, in interaction with them she cannot be. Adult children can't quite "be themselves," at least not all of the selves they've become apart from their parents.

Adult children's thoughts and actions are not as free as their parents' *in the context of their relationship.* Moreover, adult children cannot affect their parents in as fundamental ways as parents influenced them when young. This claim about unequal autonomy is what I shall now try to develop and defend. First, let me briefly suggest why equal autonomy is characteristic of true friendship.

Ideal friendship requires equal autonomy in the relationship for several reasons. Without it, there will be unequal influence and power. One friend will be making more of the decisions or having more impact on the decisions at which they mutually arrive. The less autonomous friend will offer less of the resistance and counterpoise upon which the best friendships stay balanced. As a consequence, the friendship of unequal autonomy will tend toward inequality in dependency, with one friend needing or relying disproportionately on the other. The more autonomous party to the relationship will receive less from the friendship, at least in terms of advice, criticism, and alternative perspective. These are important goods inherent to friendship, and their unequal enjoyment is a detriment to complete friendship.

In addition, the lack of equality in autonomy is likely to constrain the mutual and full self-disclosure at work in ideal friendships. The less autonomous friend may be inhibited from revealing too much, lest he become too dependent on the other. The more autonomous friend may be reluctant to confide deeply out of lack of respect for the other friend's judgment or doubts about her willingness to respond with independent conviction. For these and related reasons, equality in autonomy seems ingredient to the best of friendships.

To see why grown children can't be as autonomous as their parents within the relationship we need to examine the unequal exercise of autonomy which characterizes the young child's upbringing. I shall then argue that this history of inequality prevents equality later on, when the child is an adult. The inequality in autonomy has two particularly powerful expressions—one ontological, the other epistemological. To begin with, we should make much of the obvious—the parent helps *shape* who and what the young child is. Where the parent developed into an adult independently of the child, the young child grows up under the parent's influence and care. The physical, psychological, and social dependence of the child translates into an ontological inequality; the parent simply is more responsible for the being or identity of the young child than the other way around. Bringing the child into the world, raising her, taking part in her successes and failures, the parent contributes to the young child's identity in ways which she cannot reciprocate. While the parent may be changed dramatically *as a result* of rearing a child, the parent is not shaped *by* the child. The parent authors change in the young child, exerting control, both intentional and unwitting, over her development.

Who the young child is, then, results in part from the parent's exercise of autonomy. Even the young child's character and degree of autonomy itself ideally are cultivated by parental industry. Their history together is a history of parents making decisions for the young child, provisionally exercising an autonomy on her behalf that the child will (should) eventually exercise for herself.

Two senses of "exercising autonomy" should be distinguished here. The weak sense indicates parents making their own decisions in rearing the young child. Their wishes and decisions with regard to the young child take precedence, and the child must respond to them. This means that the parents are "in charge," able to determine the young child's life in ways that the child is not. The strong sense of "exercising autonomy" indicates that parents deliberately and effectively shape the young child according to their goals for her. We might say that this is a more directed exercise of autonomy, exerted purposefully over the young child's nature rather than simply exerted over her. While the strong sense of "exercising autonomy" in rearing the young child no doubt contributes to a deeper inequality in autonomy, the more typical weak sense is enough to keep parents and adult children from the equality of autonomy needed for friendship.

The inequality in autonomy between parent and young child has an epistemological dimension as well as an ontological one. The parent witnesses the young child's coming-to-be. Consequently, he pos-

sesses intimate knowledge of the young child's development, including knowledge of the child before she knows herself. This gives the parent special access to the young child's personal identity which the child does not and can never enjoy with respect to the parent. The parent is, literally, an "authority" on the child, at least her childhood. When the young child is old enough to realize it, she knows that this person enjoys a unique knowledge of her. This epistemological disparity complements the ontological inequality in giving the parents greater autonomy in relation to the young child.

II/A

But why must this history of unequal autonomy in the relationship prevent equality later on, when the child is grown up? It is because this history endures in the identities of the parent and adult child in at least two ways: in their self-concepts, and in their habits and attitudes toward each other.

The adult child's self-concept includes different aspects of her history with the parent. The parent protecting, nurturing, encouraging, and letting go all figure in. Our degree of autonomy in general depends upon our self-concept. For example, people who see themselves as able to carry out choices effectively or who have strong body images, tend to exercise greater control over their lives than those who do not. Because it includes the history of the unequal relationship with the parent, the adult child's self-concept limits the degree to which she can function autonomously with the parent.

It might be objected here that such a self-concept reflects an immature adult child suffering from a pathological dependency on the parent. Plagued by memories of parental control, the grown child simply has not outgrown the infantile sense of inferiority. The role I ascribe to the history of the unequal exercise of autonomy, however, is not confined to adult children who can't grow up. The self-concept of the healthy, mature adult child has a place for the parent as one who has helped make her autonomous. As such, the parent should (in the best of cases) be seen as a moral authority: teaching right and wrong; exemplifying virtues; displaying moral judgment in helping the young child through quandaries and conflicts. The adult child's self-concept will then include awareness of those values and abilities the parent was instrumental in cultivating. We should bear in mind that the specifics of the history of unequal autonomy need not be remembered in order to influence the child's self-concept, and so its impact cannot be reduced simply to memory of dependency.

The history of the unequal autonomy affects the adult child in another way, besides informing her self-concept. It also fosters enduring habits and attitudes towards the parents which persist into the child's adulthood. Some of these enter into her self-concept, but not all. These habits and attitudes help constitute who we are. Such attitudes as respect and loyalty, as well as habits of deference and accommodation engendered in youth persist into adulthood. As a result, the adult child is less likely than her parent to press disagreements or criticism in their interaction; she is less likely to assert herself.

Because they receive continuous reinforcement in the ongoing interactions with parents, such basic habits and attitudes are self-perpetuating. Instigated by interaction, these habits and attitudes then beget the consonant behavior, which in turn further entrenches them. Of course, it may be *possible* to break the habits, dismantle our attitudes towards our parents, even rearrange our self-concept. But not without rebuilding our very selves. The self-concept, together with these habits and attitudes, critically defines who we are.

II/B

What has been said about the impact of unequal autonomy on the self-concept, habits, and attitudes of grown children reciprocally holds for parents as well. The parent's sense of self is informed in a complementary way by the history of unequal autonomy. The parent sees himself as provider and protector, teacher and guardian of the young child. Most people include the role of "parent" (but not child) in their self-concept. For it is, after all, something of an occupation: an arduous, rewarding job that becomes part of our self-understanding. A large component of

this self-concept hinges on the ontological and epistemological discrepancy discussed above.

The parent sees himself as partly responsible for the adult child's existence, growth, and well-being. He can reasonably take credit for some of her accomplishments as well as blame for various shortcomings. His epistemic superiority also enters into the parent's self-understanding. He is an expert on the formation of his adult child's temperament and tastes, aspirations and humiliations. The adult child, of course, knows that this particular individual (however much a "friend"), unlike all others, knew her and knew all about her before she had consciousness of herself as a person.

There is an irony in the parent's superior knowledge of the young child; too often it limits parental appreciation of the adult child—even in ideal relationships. Precisely because parents know their children so well qua children they may be kept from truly seeing and appreciating who the child is as an adult, the image of the young child coloring the parent's later perceptions. A poor childhood showing in mathematics, for example, may make it difficult for a parent to accept the adult child's achievements in computer programming. Conversely, a parent may be disconcerted by his adult child's failure to pursue a youthful interest in art or music. People who meet us as adults, however, can more readily appreciate who and what we are since unencumbered by childhood history or their role in who we've become.

As a result of interacting with their young children, parents also develop characteristic habits and attitudes. Such habits as solicitousness and helpfulness, as well as attitudes of concern and protectiveness live on in interactions with their grown children. While children should outlive their childhoods, they remain their parents' children. Even though these original parental habits and attitudes should be *modified* as the children mature, they are practically impossible to uproot. Because such habits and attitudes bespeak an inequality in autonomy, parents remain more autonomous in relation to their grown children, and this keeps them from becoming complete or true friends.

Before examining the second obstacle to friendship, lack of separateness, it may be helpful to consider a few of the ways in which inequality in autonomy is revealed in everyday life.

II/C

How does the inequality in autonomy between parents and their adult children manifest itself in less than complete friendship? A few examples of behavior that is appropriate in a peer friendship but not for a parent in relation to his grown child should vivify the position being advanced. Consider a parent complaining to his grown child about the other parent; telling sexual stories or jokes; or, an unmarried parent going with the adult child to socialize with others in sexually oriented ways. While usually acceptable in a peer friendship, these sorts of behavior seem somehow out of place in the parent-adult child relationship. But why?

The answer has to do with the authority enjoyed by the parent. As the "author of his being," the young child's parent possesses an authority over her which does not just disappear once the child is grown up. The parent is ideally a morally authority *for* the young child: one to whom the child looks for insight and advice. And this, too, is likely to carry over into the child's adulthood. In addition, the parent possesses de facto authority—influence or power to secure compliance—as a diffuse consequence of the inequality in autonomy. Due to both sorts of authority parental values and opinions carry disproportionate weight even when meeting filial disagreement. The adult child cannot act as freely in the presence of parents as she can with others. Parental authority, for example, inhibits grown children from expressing conflicting views or criticizing those of the parents. But authority works in different ways to account for what is wrong in the examples mentioned above.

When one parent complains about the other to the adult child, for instance, the second parent's status and authority as parent is jeopardized. If it were just a matter of weakening the other parent's de facto authority (henceforth, simply "power"), the critical behavior might not be wrong. But when the criticism undermines the other parent's credibility as a moral authority (simply "authority"), it seems untoward.

The complaining parent seems to be trying to make the child an ally against the other parent. The adult child's loyalties threaten to be divided. Which parent to credit or side with or talk to? The complaining might also make the adult child feel responsible, either to do something about the conflict or for the existence of the conflict in the first place. For these reasons, the adult child's autonomy is to some extent compromised. Divided loyalty, guilt, and confusion easily impede the adult child's ability to interact freely with the criticized parent.

The critical parent misuses his power and abuses his authority by compromising both the other parent's authority and the adult child's autonomy. The child is being subtly told that she is the parents' moral equal, someone fit to judge the criticized parent. But this message conflicts with both the complaining parent's power and authority as well as the threatened authority of the maligned parent. The authority of the criticized parent is still at work, accounting for the adult child's confusion and mixed feelings. It is ironic that the thrust of this apparently equalizing behavior is to inhibit the adult child's autonomy in interacting with the criticized parent. Such inhibition bespeaks a reduced rather than elevated status. It is just this tension between the appearance of equality and the reality of inequality, responsible for this irony, which accounts for the wrongness in the next two examples.

In both sexual banter and socializing, there is an apparent renunciation of parental authority. This can cause the adult child conflict in either of two opposite ways, depending on whether the parental authority or the camaraderie predominates. First, because the parent is nonetheless an authority, there is the imposition of parental values which interferes with the adult child's autonomous expression of herself. The adult child naturally feels deference toward or hemmed in by someone who has raised her. What results is a tension between the buddy-like behavior and the parent's implicit authority. With genuine peers, however, the adult child's autonomy is not restricted, as no special deference or constraint is dictated by the nature of the relationship. The adult child is thus free to engage in sexual banter or socializing as she sees fit.

On the other hand, the adult child may be discomfited by the parent's seeming renunciation of authority, by his stepping out of the role of parent. Why else is striving to be "one of the boys" or "girls" in dress, speech, or behavior so embarrassing? It isn't just a matter of age. I suggest that it has to do with the conflict between the (embarrassing) behavior and the parent's role.

If my earlier contentions are correct, the parent's role in rearing the young child leaves a profound residue in the grown child's persona and interaction with the parent. The parent's role places his or her sexual activity in a family context. After all, the parent's sexuality is realized within the family in the *person* of the child; the child herself embodies the parental union. When the parent, even though no longer married, engages in sexually oriented socializing, his or her role as parent is clouded. The parent's sexuality is isolated from family relationships and responsibility. Simply knowing of this behavior might disturb the grown child. But if the adult child is actually accompanying the parent in the socializing, then the child is implicated in the behavior as a witness and accomplice. She is then likely to feel conflict or resentment over her parent's refusal to act "like a parent" with her.

Perhaps sexual examples are most apt or spring most readily to mind because one important way an adult child demonstrates maturation and emancipation from the parent is in her own sexual activity. This may be partly due to the connection of sex with the adult child's emergence into the role, herself, of parent and householder, independent and on her own. When the parent steps into the adult child's sexual world as a cohort, narratively (as in storytelling) or literally (as in bar-hopping), either the adult child's autonomy is limited or the camaraderie undermines the parent's status as a moral authority for the adult child.

III

Let us now take up the second obstacle to complete friendship between parents and grown children: their lack of independence from one another. The parent and grown child cannot *enter into* the relationship as equally developed people, bringing to the relationship the independent histories that fuel and provide a healthy tautness to friendship. Where above we focused on the adult child's lack of autonomy in interacting with the parent, here the parent and grown child lack autonomy *from one another*: a lack of relational autonomy in the sense of independence from one another.

Neither the parent nor the adult child can meet or view the other as truly "other." To begin with, the union between infant and parent is primitive in the sense of primal. Theirs is an intimacy which begins on a pre-conscious level for the infant, and continues on both a conscious and subconscious level for both parent and child. They experience a pre-verbal and non-verbal sensuous bond, the intimacy of immediate, sensory communication. I suggest that this primitive union persists for both into the child's adulthood.

The young child grows up by means of the parent's help, in the shade of parental direction and protection. From earliest memory, the parent was "there." Much of the way the young child comes to understand herself and world is through her parent's eyes. They shape and color what the young child takes to be important or trivial, noble or banal. Moreover, this influence doesn't just disappear when the child reaches adulthood. Parental tastes and values, opinions and principles, inform the grown child's outlook.

On the other hand, a sizable portion of the parent's adult life is spent raising his young child. The energy and attention bestowed upon their young children, as much as physical resemblance, encourages parents to see their children as temporal extensions of themselves. As noted earlier, parents identify themselves *as* parents, like an occupation or religion. Seeing ourselves in our children, love of them is to some extent self-love (so argues Aristotle). Even though the parent is formed independently of the child, much of his identity is nonetheless tied to the adult child's.

Part of the delight in a complete friendship turns upon the way two people discover and grow into each other's lives, but parents and adult children cannot develop in quite this fresh way because their lives have been entwined since the child's beginning. Neither one can really "discover" an independently existing other. They are virtually too close to have the independence needed for friendship. Here it is not a matter of the independence of autonomy, of self-determination. Rather, it is the independence of identity. The union which characterizes true friendship presupposes separateness. Only the truly separate are capable of overcoming their separateness while yet remaining "other." The parent-adult child union precludes the degree of separateness needed.

I am not suggesting a persisting symbiotic relationship in which the participants really have a hard time seeing each other as separate. Each must see the other with needs, interests, and a life of her own. In the ideal relationship, the parent gradually lets go and the adult child finally fends for herself. However, although they may discover particular things about one another as they go their separate ways, neither brings the wholly separate baggage *to* the relationship the way friends do. As a result, they don't discover each other as beings with independent histories and different values to be learned. As a result, parents and adult children don't encounter one another as sufficiently *different*.

The intimacy we ought to enjoy with our parents keeps us too close. Not in a sick loss of identity or independence, but in the enmeshing of lived life: meals taken, plans hatched, disappointments suffered. Ours is a common history peopled with crises, stories, and other family members—all along, right from the child's beginning. Intimacy and love, sharing and caring, aren't won or earned between parents and children. They evolve. But they are earned with friends. Establishing and maintaining friendships are achievements at which we must work. We prove ourselves before and to prospective friends. We woo them.

A couple of analogies should clarify the sense of otherness I find lacking in the ideal parent-adult child relationship. Think of your home town. It is part of you, helps constitute you (and you it). You can still view it as separate from you, but not the way you do a *new* city, where you must forge a home. Or, consider the difference between learning a foreign language and discovering more about your own. We must work to make a foreign language familiar. On the other hand, the way we think of the world, envision the future, deliberate—all are conditioned by our native tongue in a unique way. And so are we formed by our parents as well. They are naturally familiar, like a first language; and we are naturally at home with them, as with our home town. . . .

Nicholas Dixon | ## The Friendship Model of Filial Obligations

To what extent, if any, are grown children obligated to help their parents? In the light of the immense sacrifices made by our parents as they raised us, should we reciprocate when our parents need our material or emotional assistance? According to Jane English, our duties to our parents are grounded in and vary according to the depth of our friendship with them.[1] The goal of this paper is to develop a more defensible version of English's view, which I will call the *friendship model* of filial obligations. I begin with a sketch of English's statement of the model.

Nicholas Dixon, "The Friendship Model of Filial Obligations," *Journal of Applied Philosophy* 12, no. 1 (1995): pp. 77–87. Some notes have been deleted. Reprinted by permission of Blackwell Publishing Ltd.

I

English rejects the notion that we owe our parents reciprocal sacrifices. The paradigm case of an obligation to return a favour is when the favour was *requested* in the first place. Since no child asks to be born and given the benefits of parental care, the notion of "repayment" seems inappropriate.[2] Another obstacle to filial duties to parents is that, once they had us, our parents were *obligated* to care for us. Their merely doing what was morally required does not seem to generate any reciprocal duties on our part.[3]

The innovation of English's approach is to argue that the question of what we owe our parents, in the light of what they did for us, is poorly formulated. It wrongly casts parental sacrifices as favours that create debts and the obligation to perform reciprocal favours. Such an approach, she argues, cheapens parent-child and other love relationships, which should be characterised instead by voluntary *friendly gestures* given without any expectation of repayment, parental sacrifices should be freely given, instead of being investments made in the hope of a future "return" from grateful children. However, the absence of reciprocal debts "owed" to parents does not exhaust all filial obligations. Friendly gestures are symptomatic of ongoing friendships, and ongoing friendships give rise to duties of friendship. A decent person, that is, will offer help when her friends are in need. Unlike favours, friendships cannot be "paid off"; and, again unlike favours, my duties of friendship depend on my friends' *needs,* and my ability to help, not on whether and how much they have helped me in the past. To the extent that a grown child enjoys an ongoing friendship with her parents, she has the same duties of friendship towards her parents as she would have toward people with whom she has a similar friendship.

Filial obligations, then, are not a repayment for parental sacrifices. Rather, they arise from the friendship that these sacrifices may have played a role in creating. However, argues English, just as duties of friendship in general are contingent on the continuation of the friendship, our special obligations to our parents would dissolve if we were to cease to be friends with our parents.[4]

English's account does justice to the intuition that we should help our parents when necessary, at least when we enjoy friendly relations with them. In contrast to the *repayment model* which she criticises, English places our obligations within the appealing context of voluntary, loving friendship with our parents.

II

Because of the voluntary nature of friendship, and the belief that we should do things for our friends freely and willingly, the idea of duties of friendship may sound odd. Indeed, the voluntariness and spontaneity of friendly gestures is one of the most appealing features of friendship. If we were to discover that a friend's kindness were motivated only by a sense of duty, we would begin to question our friendship. I have two responses.

First, the fact that our friends' actions towards us are typically motivated only by spontaneous affection does not preclude the existence of duties of friendship. That duty may coincide with inclination does not diminish its status as duty. Second, while many occasions exist for optional, supererogatory acts of generosity towards our friends, we can easily think of cases in which it is natural to say that we *should* help them. If a close friend is in desperate need of my help, which would cost me negligible effort, wouldn't I be *wrong,* in the light of our long-lasting and ongoing friendship, to refuse? I mean by "duties of friendship" that we ought to help friends in such circumstances. Such duties arise from the particular relationships I have with my friends, and go beyond any general obligation I have to help strangers.

The notion of duties of friendship would also be severely restricted in the hands of libertarians who restrict all obligations to duties of noninterference. If conjoined with a libertarian approach, the friendship model of filial obligations would require only that we refrain from harming our parents. Since I argue that the friendship model creates the obligation to help our parents in some cases, I am assuming both that there *are* duties of friendship, and that moral obligations in general go beyond mere noninterference with others.[5]

I offer the friendship model as both a justification of the view that we do have duties to our parents, and an explanation of the moral basis of these duties. The friendship model casts filial obligations as a special type of obligation or friendship. As in the case of duties of friendship in general, exactly what is required of us by the friendship model of filial duties depends on both the circumstances in each particular case, and on the broader social context. For example, filial duties will be more extensive in a society in which the government provides only minimally for the needs of older people than in a society with extensive welfare programmes for the elderly.

As long as grown children enjoy a friendly relationship with their parents, the friendship model and the more traditional repayment model will usually require similar filial duties.[6] However, in the absence of friendly relations, English's version of the friendship model imposes no filial obligation to help needy parents, since there is no longer any friendship to ground filial duties, no matter how caring the parents were when the children were younger. English's willingness to embrace this consequence of her view opens her up to the criticism that she is endorsing, or at least tolerating, filial ingratitude. If the end of friendship cancels duties of friendship, so the objection goes, then so much the worse for the friendship model of filial duties, since most people believe that we would still have duties to our parents, even if we were no longer friends with them.

I maintain, on the contrary, that an advocate of the friendship model should not insist that the end of friendship with one's parents signals the end of filial obligations. English has failed to realise that duties of friendship can in general outlive friendships, whether between peers or between children and parents. The reason why English has overlooked the "residual duties" that can remain even after the end of friendships is very likely the fact that many friendships are relatively short-lived and superficial,

and arguably create few if any residual duties. However, if we turn to peer friendships comparable in duration and depth to child-parent friendships, the notion of residual duties of friendship becomes much more plausible.

Consider, for instance, a stranger and a former long-term, close friend (who voluntarily made immense sacrifices throughout our friendship) who both urgently need a blood transfusion using my rare blood type. Any obligation I have to help is stronger in the case of my former friend than in the case of the stranger. It would require an overzealous commitment to impartiality to ignore the extra moral ties created by our former long-term, close friendship. These ties are not precipitately dissolved by our unfortunate estrangement. The longevity of our friendship, and depth of friendship indicated by the sacrifices my former friend made for me,[7] make this situation analogous to my relationship with my parents. The existence of filial duties even after my friendship with my parents is over can therefore be accounted for by the friendship model, and does not indicate that filial duties have a different basis.

An analogous situation in which a former friendship can exert a moral claim on us today is the practice of forgiving someone "for old times' sake." The key to forgiveness is being able to separate the sin from the sinner, and forgive the wrongdoer while continuing to condemn her action. One way in which this separation is facilitated is when she is a former friend, and we are able to forgive her in the light of our former friendship, even though we still regard her action as wrong.[8]

I suggest that the moral basis of residual duties to former friends is *respect* for our former friendships, our former friends and ourselves. To treat a former close friend as a stranger (e.g., by refusing to give priority to our former friend in the blood transfusion case) is to discount our former friendship, and indirectly devalues both of us, since we both invested part of ourselves in the friendship. When someone is genuinely unconcerned about the end of a romantic relationship, we suspect that she held no strong feelings for her former partner. Similarly, when someone treats a former friend as a stranger as soon as their friendship is over, we start to question the depth of her friendship in the first place. It may then be a psychological truth that the genuine moral concern for another which characterises friendship is inseparable from feeling residual duties of friendship even after friendship ends. Even if we allow the possibility of the person who genuinely cares about her friends while the friendship lasts, but whose moral concern completely evaporates when friendship ends, such a person exhibits the vice of *inconstancy.* Her concern for her friends seems to be fickle, and we would hesitate to trust her.

Another vice exhibited by the person who treats former friends as strangers is a form of *inauthenticity:* a desire to disown part of herself. It is comparable to the self-made millionaire who refuses any contact with his family or his former friends from the blue-collar neighbourhood in which he grew up. Aside from the disrespect he shows for others, in some sense he is disrespecting himself, by failing to acknowledge the connections between the person he is now and the earlier stages of his life.[9]

Any residual duties of friendship are of course normally far weaker than those we have toward our current friends. Moreover, if the reason for the end of our friendship was unforgivable behaviour on the part of our former friend, our residual duties may diminish to zero.

The moral ties created by decades of parent-child love, which often develops into friendship from the late teens onwards, are surely even stronger than those of all but the deepest long-term friendships. This is why English's claim that the end of friendship necessarily signals the end of filial obligations is unjust. Granted, the children of abusive parents are very unlikely to have established any friendly relations with their parents in the first place, and would have no obligation to help their parents under the friendship model. But in the case of children who enjoyed good relations with their parents into early adulthood, but then became estranged after a disagreement, respect for their former good relations arguably requires that they help their parents, when doing so would be easy, and would produce major benefits for the parents (e.g., providing for life-saving medical treatment.) Such residual duties are of course

far weaker than the filial duties of children who currently enjoy good friendships with their parents.

While seeking a formula that would determine the exact extent of filial obligations in various circumstances would be absurd, it is reasonable to regard three factors as central in the case of adult children no longer friendly with their parents: (1) The extent of parental need, and the cost to adult children of meeting it; (2) the depth and duration of their former friendly relations with their parents; and (3) the reason for and the severity of the argument that caused the estrangement. The adult child has to strike a balance between respect for her former good relations with her parents, and, on the other hand, self-respect in the case of parental misbehaviour.[10] Only in the most extreme limiting case will a child whose friendship with her parents is over have no residual duties to her parents.

III

Another criticism of the friendship model is to point out differences between parent-child relationships and typical friendships. The key question to decide is whether these differences invalidate the friendship model, or whether parent-child relationships can naturally be viewed as a special *kind* of friendship.

The sheer weight of sacrifices typically borne by parents in raising their children creates an inequality unlikely to be met by any services which adult children perform for their parents. Friendship might be a relationship only possible between people who are roughly equal. However, it might be said in defence of the friendship model that the inequality of sacrifices is quite natural, given the parents' superior ability to help, and is quite compatible with friendship.[11] We can easily imagine similarly unequal relationships that we would have no hesitation in calling friendships. For instance, a deep friendship can arise between a wheelchair-bound person and the able-bodied person who looks after her. The alleged inequality in such relationships may be only superficial, since the able-bodied person may gain just as much in terms of emotional satisfaction and intellectual stimulation as she gives in physical assistance.

Joseph Kupfer notes two more significant differences between parent-child relationships and peer friendships.[12] First, we will always lack autonomy *with regard to* our parents because of the immense influence they had in forming our character and creating our identity. Our self-concept, which "includes the history of the unequal relationship with the parent . . . limits the degree to which [we] can function autonomously with the parent."[13] An inequality in autonomy will inhibit the formation of an ideal friendship because it will create undue dependence in the less autonomous friend, for whom the more autonomous friend will consequently have less respect.[14] Second, parents and children lack the independence needed for one characteristic of deep friendships: a voluntary union between two *separate* people, who *achieve* a friendship by growing to know and appreciate each other.[15]

While Kupfer concludes that these two differences between typical friendship and parent-child relationships preclude parents and their adult children from becoming "true" or "ideal" friends, he also asserts that "parents and children can enjoy a kind of friendship that is quite worthwhile in its own right."[16] I will argue that Kupfer's discussion makes it natural for us to regard parent-adult child relationships as legitimate friendships, albeit different from peer friendships.

The positive side of adult children's lack of autonomy from their parents is the "mutual identification" that enables parents to share their children's successes. The parents know that they played a key role in making their children the kind of people likely to succeed, a point of which the children are gratefully aware.[17] However, our close peer friends also to a lesser extent, influence who we are. This may explain why our close friends, especially long-standing ones, often delight in our triumphs just as much as our parents do. It also indicates that we experience a similar, though less pronounced, lack of autonomy with regard to our close friends as we do toward our parents. What follows is that the lack of autonomy with regard to our parents that allegedly precludes parent-child relationships from being friendships is also present, to a lesser degree, in peer relationships we have no hesitation in calling

friendships. A similar point can be made about the lack of independence between parents and children. A comparable lack of independence will apply between childhood friends who continue their friendship, without our being tempted to deny to their relationship the status of friendship.[18]

The upshot of the discussion of the current section is that even peer friendships can to a lesser extent display the features alleged to disqualify parent-child relationships from the status of friendships. It would be wiser to recognise a multiplicity of types of friendship. Parent-child relationships may involve more dependence than peer friendships, but they are genuine friendships nonetheless.

If one insists that the differences pointed out by Kupfer prevent parent-child relations from being regarded as a type of friendship, only a minor modification of the friendship model will be required. The parent-child relationship described by Kupfer is a long-term, loving, voluntary relationship, and is consequently quite able to generate duties comparable to those of friendship. Just as in the case of friendship, this relationship creates moral ties that can outlive the relationship itself. Exactly what duties are left after the end of the relationship will depend, as in the case of friendship, on the strength of the former relationship and the reason for its dissolution. In other words, all that would be required would be to *rename* the model, since it would retain all the salient features of the friendship model.

IV

A more fundamental objection to the friendship model of filial obligations can be derived from the work of Christina Hoff Sommers.[19] Sommers dubs as *the volunteer theory of obligation* the view that all moral requirements fall into one of two categories: (1) universal duties owed to everyone, and (2) *voluntarily assumed* obligations to particular persons.[20] The friendship model, which makes filial obligations contingent on the voluntary continuation of friendly relations between parents and children, presupposes the volunteer theory. Theories that base moral obligations on the existence of feelings, such as love and affection for one's parents, are named by Sommers as *sentimentalist*.[21]

Sommers presents an account of filial obligation in direct opposition to the volunteer theory of obligation and sentimentalism. In contrast to the friendship model, according to which "there is no such thing as filial duty *per se*," Sommers points out that "most people think that we do owe special debts to our parents even though we have not voluntarily assumed our obligations to them."[22] Having rejected the "dogmatic" volunteer theory of obligation, "we are free to respect the commonsense views that attribute moral force to many obligations associated with kinship and other family relationships."[23]

Sommers grounds family obligations, including filial obligations, in our family members' negative right to pursue their "noninvasive" interests (i.e., those that do not violate those of other people.) The particular interests in question are their "legitimate expectations" of our performance of actions in accordance with traditional social roles.[24] The reason why my failure to help my parents is wrong, then, is not because I am violating duties of friendship. It is wrong because I am violating their legitimate (in the context of our society's practices) expectation that I will support them in their later years. It would be wrong even if I were not friends with them. Adherents of the volunteer theory of obligation, Sommers continues, make the mistake of taking the deliberate act of promising as the paradigm case of particular moral requirements. They ignore particular obligations, such as filial duties, that arise from social arrangements that may have developed without any voluntary commitment on our part.

Sommers concedes to sentimentalists that adult children who help their parents are often motivated by love and friendship. However, she points out that the *moral ground* of our obligations may be institutional expectations that are independent of our feelings.[25]

Sommers criticises sentimentalism as too flimsy a basis for filial obligations. Feelings of good will toward our parents are fickle, whereas the institutional expectations on which Sommers grounds filial

morality guarantee parents the support they deserve[26] Sentimentalism is "ethics without ethos," and has a "disintegrative effect on tradition."[27]

My strategy in responding to Sommers is to sidestep her main argument, by insisting that the friendship model provides a robust account of filial duty without reference to obligations created by institutional expectations. I remain neutral as to the existence of duties based on such expectations.

The very feature of the friendship model which Sommers attacks—i.e., that it makes filial obligations contingent on the *voluntary* establishment of friendship, as opposed to institutional expectations—is actually a strength. Sommers' use of the term "sentimentalism" to refer to theories such as the friendship model misleadingly casts them in a negative light which obscures this strength. It implies that "sentimentalists" base moral obligations on mere feelings, which are understood by her as more or less arbitrary *passions* over which we have minimal control. As applied to the so-called sentimentalist account of friendship, it de-emphasises the voluntariness of friendship, which is instead portrayed as a natural attraction with no moral significance.

In contrast to this caricature of theories of moral obligation that stress feelings and attitudes, friendship involves a *commitment* to our friends' well-being. Both the exercise of altruism, and the moral effort which is sometimes required to maintain and deepen friendships, are moral excellences.[28] The friendship model bases filial obligations on the voluntariness that makes this commitment and these excellences possible.

The extent of our friendship with and affection for our parents is undeniably limited by factors beyond anyone's control: the complex genetic and environmental factors that can sometimes cause a "personality conflict" even between reasonable and good-willed people. However, this should not blind us to the role of *choice* in parent-child relations. Especially as a child's moral awareness develops, and increasingly throughout adulthood, she appreciates the moral effort involved in parent-child relationships. She recognises, for instance, the need for patience in tolerating her parents' sometimes exasperating ways, and for compromise in reconciling her desire for freedom (both as a child and as an adult) with her parents' demands and needs. Perhaps more than all but the closest peer friendships parent-child relationships are *worked on,* usually over many decades. This sketch reveals parent-child friendship to be a far more substantial basis for filial obligations than one would be led to believe by Sommers' characterisation of it as a "sentimentalist" theory.

V

I complete my defence of the friendship model of filial obligations by considering some problem cases. Central to the friendship model is that the extent of filial obligations is determined by the extent of our friendly relations with our parents. Exactly the same holds in the case of peer friendships, where deeper friendships generate more extensive duties of friendship.

I have shown in section II how the friendship model makes more or less considerable demands on adult children, even when they are no longer friends with their parents. Among the few people who would escape filial duties under the model would be those who have *never* enjoyed friendly relations with their parents. Since this is most likely to occur when the parents have been uncaring and even abusive, this consequence of the model seems right.

A more troubling case for the friendship model as developed so far is the person whose parents were exemplary in providing her loving care, yet who fails to establish any kind of loving relationship with them. Should she fail to provide her parents with much needed financial or emotional support, when she could have easily afforded it, many would condemn her ingratitude. Since there is no friendship on which to build obligations, the friendship model seems unable to account for this condemnation.

Distinguishing the supererogatory benefits her parents have given her from those that they were morally obliged to give is important. Providing food, clothing, and shelter to children is a minimal responsibility that accompanies the decision to bring children into the world, and can hardly be said to require

gratitude on the part of the children. On the other hand, the love and support which go beyond the call of duty give rise, in the majority of cases, to the friendship relations that are, on this model, the basis of filial duties. The problem case for the friendship model, then, is the cold, ungrateful child who never responds to her loving parents' supererogatory actions by returning their love and by helping them when they are in need.

If her ingratitude upon further consideration should be considered blameless, then the friendship model's failure to condemn her is an advantage, not a weakness. If, on the other hand, it is culpable, I contend that whatever fault she has can be explained without reference to filial morality per se. The same vice of ingratitude, which she exhibits by her failure to thank her parents for their efforts and to offer them much-needed assistance, can also arise in the context of a peer friendship. More pertinently, since in the hypothetical case we are considering there *is* no friendship between the child and parents, the obligations of the cold child to her loving parents are based on the general duty to be grateful after a series of generous acts by an acquaintance or even a stranger.[29] We can thus explain the filial obligations of the cold, ungrateful child in a manner independent of but perfectly consistent with the friendship model. I leave open exactly what the general duty of gratitude requires of the child who has never had a friendship with her parents. Expressions of thanks are morally required, but it isn't clear that any reciprocal services are obligatory in return for unsolicited benefits.

My account of the filial obligations of the cold, ungrateful child in terms of the general duty of gratitude towards any generous person is open to the objection that I am ignoring crucial differences between the cold child's parents, and, on the other hand, acquaintances and strangers. In reality, the objection continues, the cold, ungrateful child has the same filial duties as any child with loving, generous parents. However, this objection begs the question against the friendship model. While the cold, ungrateful child is *biologically and socially* related to her parents in the same way that any child is, from an emotional point of view the cold child's parents *are* acquaintances or even strangers. If my theory is correct filial obligations are based primarily on friendship. And friendship is simply absent in this case.

A more serious objection is that my admission that duties to our parents exist which are not directly explicable by the friendship model shows that the model is at best incomplete. My response is that the fact that the cold child's filial duties are not grounded in friendship reflects her impoverished relationship with her parents, and not any inadequacy in the friendship model. The friendship model is an account of the moral basis of filial duties in the vast majority of cases, where adult children either currently enjoy or have enjoyed some degree of friendship with their parents. It is not refuted by the logical possibility of unlikely deviant cases in which filial obligations are based on the weaker general duty of gratitude that we owe to *anyone* who is extremely generous.

We are now in a position to see a deeper error in the repayment model of filial obligations. It bases all filial duties on the general duty to show gratitude toward generous people. This general duty is the only basis of the filial obligations of the cold, ungrateful child. However, the filial obligations of the vast majority of us have a far more congenial, extensive basis: the friendship which we enjoy or have enjoyed with our parents. The repayment model is an appropriate account of filial obligations only in a deviant, unrepresentative case.

This is not to deny that even those of us who enjoy friendships with our parents should be grateful for the generous things they have done for us. In this respect, we are like the cold child, and any other beneficiary of generous acts. However, the gratitude we should feel is not the basis of our filial duties, which are based instead on our friendship with our parents. Now there may be a contingent link between the amount of sacrifices our parents made and the depth of our friendship, since our gratitude for our parents' generosity may deepen our friendship. If so, the friendship model may forge a contingent link between the amount of sacrifices our parents made and the extent of our filial duties. But the link *is*

only contingent. Deep parent-child friendships, and hence extensive filial duties of friendship, can exist even though our parents have not needed to make great sacrifices in raising us. At the other extreme, parents who have made many sacrifices may be cold and emotionally distant, and fail to form a close friendship with their children, whose filial duties will hence be weaker than those of children who enjoy a loving relationship with their parents.[30] A second error that the repayment model makes, then, is basing filial duties on just one of the possible causes of friendship—parents' sacrifices, and their children's subsequent gratitude— instead of on the friendship itself. The friendship model, in contrast, recognises that the moral basis of our duty to help our parents is just that they are or have been our friends, they need help, and we are able to help them.

Is the child's failure to become friends with her parents in the first place, even though the are models of devoted care, morally blameworthy? We would not want to allow people to minimise their filial obligations by deliberately forming only a weak friendship, or none at all, with their parents. However, blaming someone for the failure to develop a friendship with someone else sounds odd, however loving and caring that other person may be. At worst, the unloving child is guilty of the vice of coldness. A more plausible analysis of the rare occasions when a child fails to develop affection for her loving, generous parents is that the child suffers from a personality disorder which prevents certain kinds of intimacy. While her parents may justly claim that they deserve better treatment from their child, her inability to love them is beyond her control, and hence blameless.

The friendship model of filial obligations accounts well for the obligations which are felt by most adult children who are friendly with their parents. It also explains how residual obligations can remain even after their friendship has ended. The main problem case for the friendship model of filial obligations is the child who never forms a friendship with her loving, caring parents. However, while the friendship model is unable to condemn her, and blameworthiness on her part can be explained by her violation of the general duty to show gratitude toward generous people. That the usual ground of filial obligations is absent in her case reflects only her deficient relationship with her parents, and indicates no flaw in the friendship model.

I conclude that my modified version of the friendship model provides a plausible, fair framework for determining the extent of our filial obligations. Like English's original statement of this model, it retains the advantage of stressing the voluntary, loving nature of sacrifices made by both parents and children, instead of regarding filial duties as repayments for services rendered.

NOTES

1. Jane English (1979) What do grown children owe their parents?, originally published in Onora O'Neill and William Ruddick (eds.) *Having Children: Philosophical and Legal Reflections on Parenthood* (New York, Oxford University Press); and reprinted in Christina Sommers and Fred Sommers (eds., 1993) *Vice and Virtue in Everyday Life,* 3rd edition (Fort Worth, Harcourt Brace Jovanovich), pp. 758–65. Page citations for 'What Do Grown Children Owe Their Parents?' will be from *Vice and Virtue in Everyday Life.*

2. English, op. cit., What Do Grown Children Owe Their Parents?, pp. 759–60. See also Michael Slote Obedience and Illusions, in O'Neill and Ruddick, op. cit., *Having Children,* p. 320; and Jeffrey Blustein (1982) *Parents and Children: The Ethics of the Family* (Oxford, Oxford University Press), excerpted in Joshua Halberstam (ed., 1988) *Virtues and Values* (Englewood Cliffs, NJ, Prentice-Hall), p. 197.

3. Blustein, in op. cit., *Virtues and Values,* p. 197.

4. English, op. cit., What Do Grown Children Owe Their Parents?, pp. 761–63.

5. For a defence of the view that the existence of rights between friends is perfectly compatible with friendship, see Michael J. Meyer (1992) Rights between Friends, *Journal of Philosophy,* Vol. LXXXIX, pp. 467–83. My paper depends on the weaker claim that, regardless of whether rights exist in friendships, obligations of friendship exist.

6. The models will diverge when the degree of parent-child friendship does not correspond to the extent of parental sacrifices. In section V, I will argue that these divergences show the superiority of the friendship model.

7. My residual duties to my former friend are not a repayment for the sacrifices he made for me, since this would be a return to the repayment model which I reject. Instead, his sacrifices are relevant to my duties of friendship only insofar as they deepened our friendship. Extensive residual duties may persist after the end of any deep friendship, even if it did not involve any great sacrifices. Respect for our former friendship (see text below for more detail), and not the repayment of moral debts incurred as a result of my former friend's generosity, is the basis of my residual duties to him.

8. See Jeffrie Murphy (1982) Forgiveness and Resentment, *Minnesota Studies in Philosophy,* Vol. VII, *Social and Political Philosophy;* reprinted in op. cit., *Virtues and Values,* p. 131.

9. Michael Meyer has suggested to me that the faults I have been describing can be characterised as a lack of integrity.

10. Cf., again, Murphy's account of forgiveness, op. cit., in which he stresses maintaining self-respect by avoiding forgiveness unless substantial reasons exist for it.

11. [F]riends offer what they can give and accept what they need, without regard for the total amounts of benefits exchanged, English, op. cit., What do Grown Children Owe Their Parents?, p. 761.

12. Joseph Kupfer (1990) Can parents and children be friends?, *American Philosophical Quarterly* 27:1, pp. 15–26.

13. Ibid., p. 17.

14. Ibid., p. 16.

15. Ibid., pp. 20–21.

16. Ibid., p. 15.

17. Ibid., pp. 21–23.

18. Kupfer, ibid., p. 20, note 11, mentions the lack of independence between adult friends who became friends in childhood.

19. Christina Hoff Sommers (1986) Filial morality, *Journal of Philosophy,* pp. 439–56; and Philosophers against the family, reprinted in Sommers and Sommers, op. cit., *Vice and Virtue in Everyday Life,* pp. 804–29.

20. Sommers, Philosophers against the family, p. 820.

21. Sommers, Filial morality, p. 448.

22. Sommers, Philosophers against the family, pp. 820–21. Sommers' assertion that the friendship mode recognises no filial duties per se is a little misleading. While the model treats filial duties as a special type of duty of friendship, it does not preclude recognition of the uniqueness of our duties to our parents.

23. Ibid., p. 822.

24. Sommers, op. cit., Filial morality, pp. 445–48.

25. Ibid., pp. 449–50.

26. Ibid., pp. 450–51.

27. Ibid., p. 455.

28. See Laurence Blum The Morality of Friendship, reprinted in Halberstam, op. cit., *Virtues and Values,* pp. 205–14.

29. In asserting that we have duties of gratitude after unsolicited acts of generosity, I depart from the volunteer theory of obligation, since I concede that there can be particular duties that are not voluntarily assumed. The main ground of duties of gratitude is that respect for generous people requires that we treat them as ends in themselves, and not merely as sources of benefit for us. See Fred R. Berger (1975) "Gratitude," *Ethics* 85:4, pp. 298–309.

30. The view that parental sacrifices do not in themselves create filial duties is supported by English's claim that the child who was adopted as a newborn has no obligation to repay her biological mother for the sacrifices she made to go through with pregnancy. Her only duties toward her birth mother arise from any friendship they may develop. See English, op. cit., What do grown children owe their parents?, p. 763.

12

Is the Traditional Family Wrong?

Sommers and Her Critics

Jane English's argument against the traditional conception of filial obligations, which we considered in the previous unit, is one of a set of arguments offered by contemporary philosophers concerning the obligations traditionally associated with familial relations. These arguments are the focus of this section's featured article, by Christina Hoff Sommers, entitled "Philosophers Against the Family." One obvious common feature of the arguments treated by Sommers is that they draw conclusions that depart radically from "traditional" and "commonsense" morality.

In the first part of her article (sections 2 and 3) Sommers considers what she calls "the direct attack" on the family. She focuses on feminist critiques of family life, of the traditional differentiation of family roles in particular, and of gendered obligations more generally. The authors she critiques espouse an ideal of *assimilation,* according to which gender differences should not in any way undergird differences in duties or obligations. Sommers cites Alison Jaggar, for example, as lauding "the transformation of biological functions" such as insemination, gestation, and lactation so that they are no longer the province of particular genders. Sommers notes that many people, including "most women," would find Jaggar's recommendations "bizarre." They would not want to promote insemination of women by other women or the conversion of men's bodies to make male gestation and lactation possible. Sommers notes that feminists are unimpressed by what, in fact, people, including women, *want.* Feminists maintain that the wants of "ordinary" women have been corrupted, in part because traditional morality has carved up duties along biological and gender lines. The wants of ordinary women need to be revised in the light of moral theory.

Sommers attributes something like the following argument to philosophers like Jaggar:

P1 Sexism is morally indefensible.
P2 The alternative to sexism is assimilationism.

C   Assimilationism is morally obligatory.

The trouble according to Sommers, is that there are two senses of *sexism*. In one sense of sexism, premise 1 is true, but premise 2 is false. In the other sense, premise 2 may be true, but on this reading premise 1 is false. What are these two senses?

> Literally and popularly *sexism* connotes unfair discrimination, period.
> But in its extended philosophical sense it connotes discrimination, period.

So Sommers's objection to the argument is that it trades on an ambiguity in the notion of sexism. In the "literal and popular" sense of *sexism*—that is to say, *unfair* discrimination on the basis of sex or gender—premise 1 is clearly and obviously true. But in that sense of *sexism* premise 2 is clearly false, because assimilationism is *not* the only alternative to it—unless we assume in addition that every instance of discrimination on the basis of sex or gender is impermissible. What about excluding men from women's bathrooms? What about universities enrolling students of only one gender? Sommers suggests that there are legitimate differences in roles and obligations based on gender, and she endorses sexism in the *philosophical* sense, but not in the *literal* sense. Suppose we could eliminate unfair cases of discrimination (say, in the allocation of jobs or salaries) while leaving untouched "the basic institutions that women want and support, i.e., marriage and motherhood." This would be sexism only in the philosophical sense, that of marking certain differences along gender lines. To simply assert that that all such discrimination is necessarily unfair or immoral would be to assume what we need to have proved.

An important part of Sommers's defense of gender roles is that women *want* them. By ignoring women's actual wants, feminists are not only being condescending, but they are violating Mill's principle to the effect that "there can be no appeal from a majority verdict of those who have experienced two alternatives." That is to say, if a majority of women who have experienced both an assimilationist society and a society based on gender roles prefer the latter, then the latter must be best for them, regardless of the abstract arguments to which feminists appeal.

In the second part of her article (sections 4 and 5) Sommers focuses on "indirect attacks" on the family, all of which she claims stem from a view that "subverts, ignores or denies the special moral relations that characterize the family and are responsible for its functioning." She takes issue with several of the protagonists we have included in this anthology—Thomson on abortion; Tooley on infanticide; Wasserstrom on adultery; English on filial obligations—arguing that all of these authors assume the *volunteer theory of obligation,* which she clearly finds wanting. The view is characterized in the following passage:

> Let us call a requirement a *duty* if it devolves on the moral agents whether or not they have voluntarily assumed it. (It is, for example, a duty to refrain from murder.) And let us call a requirement an *obligation* only if it devolves on certain moral agents but not necessarily on all moral agents. (One is, for example, morally obligated to keep a promise.) According to our three philosophers [*viz. those Sommers is criticizing*], all duties are general in the sense of being requirements on all moral agents. Any moral requirement that is *specific* to a given moral agent must be grounded in his or her voluntary commitment. Thus, there is no room for any special requirement on a moral agent that has not been assumed voluntarily by that agent. In other words, *there are no special duties.*

Consider the kinds of requirements we normally think apply to me *as a parent*—such as feeding and caring for those individuals who happen to be *my* children. On Sommers's characterization, these are *special* requirements of me—not everyone is required to feed and care for *my* children. However, are they special *duties* (requirements that apply to me irrespective of what commitments I have voluntarily entered into) or are they special *obligations* (requirements I have voluntarily imposed on myself). In this particular case it seems that they could be regarded as voluntarily self-imposed, since I tacitly consented to them by, say, having sexual intercourse with a fertile woman. But now consider the supposed requirement on my adult children to care for me when I become old, feeble, and incontinent. This would also be a special requirement (not everyone is required to care for me when I get old, feeble, and incontinent). But if my children *owe* it to me simply by virtue of being *my children,* then it would be a special duty of theirs, since at no time did they voluntarily consent to being my children. Sommers attributes to her opponents the following argument:

P1   Any special requirement that applies to an individual must derive from that individual's voluntarily agreements (either explicit or implicit).

P2   Special family duties are those requirements that apply to you simply by virtue of your being related to the various members of your family.

P3   People do not voluntarily agree to be related to the other members of their family.

C   There are no special family duties.

Sommers clearly accepts both that the argument is valid, and that premises 2 and 3 are true, but she does not accept the conclusion. She thus construes the argument as a *reductio ad absurdum* (reduction to absurdity) of premise 1, the volunteer theory of special obligations. (For an account of reductio see the Introduction.) But before adducing any reasons *against* the volunteer theory, she challenges her opponents to supply reasons *for* the theory. She speculates that most philosophers have accepted it "because of an uncritical use of the model of promises as the paradigm of obligations." They have tacitly subscribed to something like the following argument from analogy:

P1   One has an obligation to keep a promise only if one has made a voluntary commitment or agreement to do so.

P2   Special requirements are all analogous to promises.

C   Special requirements arise only if one has made a voluntary commitment or agreement.

The conclusion of the argument is the volunteer theory. The argument is defective, according to Sommers, because there is no reason to accept premise 1. "There is no reason to take promises as paradigmatic of obligation." But to criticize one argument *for* a theory (here, the volunteer theory) is *not* to provide a reason to *reject* the theory. Sommers is still rationally obliged to offer reasons for rejecting the volunteer theory. Her reasons are summarized in the following passage:

> I believe the defense of special duties is far more plausible than rival theories that reject special duties. My primary objective has been to raise the strong suspicion that the volunteer theory of obligation is a dogma that is very probably wrong and misconceived, a view that is certainly at odds with common opinion.

However, Sommers does not actually offer "the defense of special duties" (something she says would take too long in a single article) and rests her case against the volunteer theory on the evident incompatibility of its consequences with common moral opinions. However, the philosophers she takes to task for putting forward their radical conclusions were never in doubt that they were "certainly at odds with common opinion."

In her response, Marilyn Friedman considers Sommers's criticisms of both the direct and indirect attacks on the family. On the direct feminist attack, she disputes Sommers's claim that women really want obligations to be governed by the traditional gender roles that Sommers seems to be defending. Further, she disputes Sommers's application of Mill's principle (that "there can be no appeal from a majority verdict of those who have experienced two alternatives"). Even if we grant that the principle is true it is not clear that most women have adequately experienced the relevant alternatives.

On the indirect argument, Friedman notes that Sommers takes "common opinion," "what most people think," or "tradition" to constitute an important premise in her argument against the volunteer theory. The volunteer theory entails that there are no special family duties. But that conflicts with "what most people think," and so we should abandon the volunteer theory. Friedman notes that "common opinion" and "tradition" vary enormously from one generation to the next, as well as across cultures. To whose common opinions and to whose cultural traditions are we supposed to defer? Should we defer to the traditions of the antebellum South, in which it was the common opinion that slavery of blacks by whites was morally permissible? Should we defer to the common opinion of certain fundamentalist Islamic views of the place of women in society? Both of these traditions conflict with what most white Westerners currently regard as common opinion.

Claudia Mills, in her contribution "The Ties That Bind: Duties to Family Members," is ostensibly addressing the issue raised by Jane English in the featured article of the previous chapter—namely, what children owe their aging parents. However, Mills's goal is really more ambitious than that of determining the extent of one's obligations to one's aging parents. Rather, she aims to lay bare the distinctive nature of family relationships and of the obligations they generate. She addresses arguments put forward by both Sommers, in the featured article of this chapter, and English in the previous featured article. Unlike Friedman, Mills does not directly challenge Sommers's methodology—that of placing considerable weight on the judgments that most folk make about, for example, family relationships. With Sommers (and against English), Mills rejects the volunteer theory of obligations, along with the idea that family obligations can be reduced to the obligations of voluntary friendships. But she also finds Sommers's views of filial duties inadequate:

> Sommers's view is not without troubles of its own. The stress on social roles seems to make family relationships overly conventional and does not distinguish family relationship from any of the myriad other social roles we all occupy. Moreover, some of the duties Sommers proposes (gratitude, deference) echo traditional debt-based views of the source of filial obligation that most of us now reject.

Mills offers a new account of family relationship, and a new argument for their value and hence their binding nature, one based on an analogy with sibling relationships:

> I argue that family relationships are importantly different both from friendship (English's analogy) and from other social roles (Sommers's analogy) in their uniquely unchosen and unconditional nature. I suggest that we can shed light on what grown children owe their parents by looking first at a category of family relationships less shadowed by traditional encrustations of debt and gratitude: the relationship of siblings. I claim that we have strong reasons to participate in

unconditional, unchosen relationships and corresponding obligations not to deny others the good of participating in such relationships with us.

Mills argues that the analogy between sibling relationships and parent-child relationships is stronger and more illuminating than the analogies offered by English or Sommers. Further, she argues that the duties that one owes to a sibling are more extensive than those one owes to strangers, but different from those one owes to friends. They are generated by the unique value of being a participant in relationships that she characterizes as both "unchosen" and "unconditional." But the kinds of obligations that one has to one's siblings, and by extension to one's aging parents, are also different and less demanding than what that have traditionally been deemed to be.

QUESTIONS FOR CONSIDERATION

In thinking about this unit, the following questions might prove fruitful:
- Is Sommers right that the radical feminists ignore what women really want? Does she provide any evidence for her claims about "what women want"? What kind of evidence would suffice? Would a survey do the job? Who would be the appropriate subjects of the survey? Women in the United States? Women in Western democracies? Women in industrialized countries? All women everywhere? Would such a survey reveal what women *really* wanted or would it merely reveal what they have been socialized into believing they want?
- Do people always want what is in their own best interests? What weight should we put on the wants that people actually express as opposed to what might be in their best interests?
- Now consider Sommers's critique of the indirect attack on the family. Are there clear examples of special obligations that people have that they have not voluntarily agreed to? Take the example of a parent's special duties towards his offspring. Can this be explained by some theory other than the volunteer theory?
- Suppose you have offspring even though you didn't voluntarily agree to have them. Suppose, for example you are the victim of rape. Does your biological parentage of a child conceived during rape make you responsible for that child's welfare?
- Suppose you have deposited a sample of your sperm in a sperm bank, just in case you might need it at some stage. Suppose someone unknown to you steals that sample of your sperm, artificially inseminates herself with it, and brings your child into the world. Do you now have a special duty to care for and feed that child? Does that child have any special duties to you, like taking care of you in your old age? If, in these cases, the person in question has no special duties toward their respective family members, what does that suggest about the volunteer theory?
- Is the analogy introduced by Mills—that of sibling relationships and the obligations they entail—an illuminating one? Why does Mills think that we have special duties to our siblings? Why does she think that this model of family obligation can be extended to other family relationships?

FURTHER READING

Okin, Susan. "Feminism, Women's Human Rights, and Cultural Differences." *Hypatia,* 13, no. 2 (1998): 32–52.

Christina Hoff Sommers | Philosophers Against the Family

Much of what commonly counts as personal morality is measured by how well we behave within family relationships. We live our moral lives as son or daughter to this mother and that father, as brother or sister to this sister or brother, as father or mother, grandfather, granddaughter to this boy or girl or that man or woman. These relationships and the moral duties defined by them were once popular topics of moral casuistry; but when we turn to the literature of recent moral philosophy, we find little discussion of what it means to be a good son or daughter, a good mother or father, a good husband or wife, a good brother or sister.

Modern ethical theory concentrates on more general topics. Perhaps the majority of us who involve ourselves with ethics accept some version of Kantianism or utilitarianism, yet these mainstream doctrines are better designed for telling us about what we should do as persons in general than about our special duties as parents or children or siblings. We believe, perhaps, that such universal theories can account fully for the morality of special relations. In any case, modern ethics is singularly silent on the bread and butter issues of personal morality in everyday life. However, silence is only part of it. With the exception of marriage itself, family relationships are a biological given. The contemporary philosopher is, on the whole, actively unsympathetic to the idea that we have *any* duties defined by relationships into which we have not voluntarily entered. We do not, after all, choose our parents or siblings. And even if we do choose to have children, this is not the same as choosing, say, our friends. Because the special relationships that constitute the family as a social arrangement are, in this sense, not voluntarily assumed, many moralists feel bound in

principle to dismiss them altogether. The practical result is that philosophers are to be found among those who are contributing to an ongoing disintegration of the traditional family. In what follows I shall expose some of the philosophical roots of the current hostility to family morality. My own view that the ethical theses underlying this hostility are bad philosophy will be made evident throughout the discussion.

1. THE MORAL VANTAGE

Social criticism is a heady pastime to which philosophers are professionally addicted. . . .

Much contemporary social criticism is radical in temper. In particular, I shall suggest that the prevailing attitude toward the family is radical and not liberal. And the inability of mainstream ethical theory to come to grips with the special obligations that family members bear to one another contributes to the current disregard of the commonsense morality of the family cave. We find, indeed, that family obligations are criticized and discounted precisely because they do not fit the standard theories of obligation. If I am right, contemporary ethics is at a loss when it comes to dealing with parochial morality; but few have acknowledged this as a defect to be repaired. Instead the common reaction has been: if the family does not fit my model of autonomy, rights, or obligations, then so much the worse for the family.

To illustrate this, I cite without comment recent views on some aspects of family morality.

1. Michael Slote[1] maintains that any child capable of supporting itself is "morally free to opt

From Christina Hoff Sommers, "Philosophers Against the Family," in *Person to Person,* ed. Hugh LaFollette and George Graham (Philadelphia: Temple University Press), pp. 82–105. Some notes and some parts of the text have been deleted.

out of the family situation." To those who say that the child should be expected to help his needy parents for a year or two out of reciprocity or fair play, Slote responds:

> The duty of fair play presumably exists only where past benefits are voluntarily accepted . . . and we can hardly suppose that a child has voluntarily accepted his role in family . . . life.[2]

2. Virgina Held[3] wants traditional family roles to be abolished and she recommends that husbands and wives think of themselves as roommates of the same sex in assigning household and parental tasks. (She calls this the "Roommate Test.") To the objection that such a restructuring might injure family life, she replies that similar objections were made when factory workers demanded overtime pay.

3. The late Jane English[4] defended the view that adult children owe their parents no more than they owe their good friends. "[A]fter friendship ends, the duties of friendship end." John Simmons[5] and Jeffrey Blustein[6] also look with suspicion upon the idea that there is a debt of gratitude to the parents for what, in any case, they were duty-bound to do.

4. Where Slote argues for the older child's right to leave, Howard Cohen[7] argues for granting that right to young children who still need parental care. He proposes that every child be assigned a "trusted advisor" or agent. If the child wants to leave his parents, his agent will be charged with finding alternative caretakers for him.

The philosophers I have cited are not atypical in their dismissive attitude to commonsense morality or in their readiness to replace the parochial norms of the family cave with practices that would better approximate the ideals of human rights and equality. A theory of rights and obligations that applies generally to moral agents is, in this way, applied to the family with the predictable result that the family system of special relations and noncontractual special obligations is judged to be grossly unfair to its members.

2. FEMINISM AND THE FAMILY

I have said that the morality of the family has been relatively neglected. The glaring exception to this is, of course, the feminist movement. Although the movement is complex, I am confined primarily to its moral philosophers, of whom the most influential is Simone de Beauvoir. For de Beauvoir, a social arrangement that does not allow all its participants full autonomy is to be condemned. De Beauvoir criticizes the family as an unacceptable arrangement since, for women, marriage and childbearing are essentially incompatible with their subjectivity and freedom:

> The tragedy of marriage is not that it fails to assure woman the promised happiness . . . but that it mutilates her; it dooms her to repetition and routine . . . At twenty or thereabouts mistress of a home, bound permanently to a man, a child in her arms, she stands with her life virtually finished forever.[8]

For de Beauvoir the tragedy goes deeper than marriage. The loss of subjectivity is unavoidable as long as human reproduction requires the woman's womb. De Beauvoir starkly describes the pregnant woman who ought to be a "free individual" as a "stockpile of colloids, an incubator, an egg."[9] And as recently as 1977 she compared childbearing and nurturing to slavery.[10]

It would be a mistake to say that de Beauvoir's criticism of the family is outside the mainstream of Anglo-American philosophy. Her criterion of moral adequacy may be formulated in continental existentialist terms, but its central contention is generally accepted: who would deny that an arrangement that systematically thwarts the freedom and autonomy of the individual is *eo ipso* defective? What is perhaps a bit odd to Anglo-American ears is that de Beauvoir makes such scant appeal to ideals of fairness and equality. For her, it is the loss of autonomy that is decisive.

De Beauvoir is more pessimistic than most feminists she has influenced about the prospects for technological and social solutions. But implicit in her critique is the ideal of a society in which sexual differences are minimal or nonexistent. This ideal is shared by many contemporary feminist philosophers. The views of Richard Wasserstrom, Ann Ferguson, Carol Gould, and Alison Jaggar are representative.

[According to Wasserstrom,] the ideal society is nonsexist and "assimilationist."[11] Social reality is scrutinized for its approximation to this ideal and criticism is directed against all existing norms. Take the custom of having sexually segregated bathrooms: whether this is right or wrong "depends on what the good society would look like in respect to sexual differentiation." The key question in evaluating any law or arrangement in which sex difference figures is: "What would the good or just society make of (it)?"[12]

Thus the supernal light shines on the cave, revealing its moral defects. *There,* in the ideal society, gender in the choice of lover or spouse would be of no more significance than eye color. *There* the family would consist of adults but not necessarily of different sexes and not necessarily in pairs. *There* we find equality ensured by a kind of affirmative action which compensates for disabilities. If women are somewhat weaker than men, or if they are subject to lunar disabilities, then this must be compensated for. (Wasserstrom compares women to persons with congenital defects for whom the good society makes special arrangements.) Such male-dominated sports as wrestling and football will there be eliminated and marriage, as we know it, will not exist. "Bisexuality, not heterosexuality or homosexuality, would be the typical intimate, sexual relationship in the ideal society that was assimilationist in respect to sex."[13]

Other feminist philosophers are equally confident about the need for sweeping change. Ann Ferguson wants a "radical reorganization of child rearing." She recommends communal living and a deemphasis on biological parenting. In the ideal society "[l]ove relationships, and the sexual relationships developing out of them, would be based on the individual meshing-together of androgynous human beings."[14] Carol Gould argues for androgyny and for abolishing legal marriage. She favors single parenting, co-parenting and communal parenting. The only arrangement she opposes emphatically is the traditional one where the mother provides primary care

for the children.[15] Alison Jaggar, arguing for a "socialist feminism," wants a society that is both classless and genderless. She looks to the day of a possible transformation of such biological functions as insemination, lactation, and gestation "so that one woman could inseminate another . . . and . . . fertilized ova could be transplanted into women's or even men's bodies." This idea is partly illustrated in a science fiction story that Jaggar praises in which "neither sex bears children, but both sexes, through hormone treatments, suckle them . . ."[16] To those of us who find this bizarre, Jaggar replies that this betrays the depth of our prejudice in favor of the "natural" family.

Though they differ in detail, the radical feminists hold to a common social ideal that is broadly assimilationist in character and inimical to the traditional family. Sometimes it seems as if the radical feminist simply takes the classical Marxist eschatology of the Communist Manifesto and substitutes "gender" for "class." Indeed, the feminist and the old-fashioned Marxist do have much in common. Both see [society] as politically divided into two warring factions: one oppressing, the other oppressed. Both see the need of raising the consciousness of the oppressed group to its predicament and to the possibility of removing its shackles. Both look forward to the day of a classless or genderless society. Both deny the value and naturalness of tradition. Both believe that people and the institutions they inhabit are as malleable as Silly Putty. And both groups are zealots, paying little attention to the tragic personal costs to be paid for the revolution they wish to bring about. The feminists tell us little about that side of things. To begin with, how will the benighted myriads in the cave who do not wish to "mesh together" with other androgynous beings be reeducated? And how are children to be brought up in the genderless society? Plato took great pains to explain his methods: would the new methods be as thoroughgoing? Unless these questions can be given plausible answers, the supernal attack on the family must always be irresponsible. The appeal to the just society justifies nothing until it can be shown that the radical proposals do not have monstrous consequences. That has not been shown. Indeed, given the perennially dubious state of the social sciences, it is precisely what *cannot* be shown.

Any social arrangement that falls short of the assimilationist ideal is labeled "sexist." It should be noted that this characteristically feminist use of the term "sexist" differs significantly from its popular or literal sense. Literally, and popularly, "sexism" connotes unfair discrimination. But in its extended philosophical use it connotes discrimination, period. Wasserstrom and many feminists trade on the popular pejorative connotations of sexism when they invite us to be antisexist. Most liberals are antisexist in the popular sense. But to be antisexist in the technical, radical philosophical sense is not merely to be opposed to discrimination against women; it is to be *for* what Wasserstrom calls the assimilationist ideal. The antisexist philosopher opposes any social policy that is nonandrogynous, objecting, for example, to legislation that allows for maternity leave. As Alison Jaggar remarks: "We do not, after all, elevate 'prostate leave' into a special right of men."[17] From being liberally opposed to sexism, one may in this way be led insensibly to a radical critique of the family whose ideal is assimilationist and androgynous. For it is very clear that the realization of the androgynous ideal is incompatible with the survival of the family as we know it.

The neological extension of such labels as "sexism," "slavery," and "prostitution" is a feature of radical discourse. The liberal too sometimes calls for radical solutions to social problems. Some institutions are essentially unjust. To "reform" slavery or a totalitarian system of government is to eliminate them. Radicals trade on these extreme practices in characterizing other practices. They may, for example, characterize low wages as "slave" wages and the workers who are paid them as "slave" laborers. Taking these descriptions seriously may start one on the way to treating a free-labor market system as a "slave system" that, in simple justice, must be overthrown and replaced by an alternative system of production. The radical feminist typically explains that, "existentially," women, being treated by men as sex objects, are especially prone to bad faith and false consciousness. Marxist feminists see them as part of an unawakened and oppressed economic class. Clearly we cannot call on a deluded woman to cast off her bonds before we have made her aware of her bondage. So the first task of freeing the slave woman is dispelling the thrall of a false and deceptive consciousness. One must "raise" her consciousness to the "reality" of her situation. (Some feminists acknowledge that it may in fact be too late for many of the women who have fallen too far into the delusions of marriage and motherhood. But the educative process can save many from falling into the marriage and baby trap.)

In this sort of rhetorical climate nothing is what it seems. Prostitution is another term that has been subjected to a radical enlargement. Alison Jaggar believes that a feminist interpretation of the term "prostitution" is badly needed and asks for a "philosophical theory of prostitution." Observing that the average woman dresses for men, marries a man for protection, and so forth, she says: "For contemporary radical feminists, prostitution is the archetypal relationship of women to men."[18]

Of course, the housewife Jaggar has in mind might be offended at the suggestion that she herself is a prostitute, albeit less well paid and less aware of it than the professional street prostitute. To this the radical feminist reply is (quoting Jaggar):

> [I]ndividuals' intentions do not necessarily indicate the true nature of what is going on. Both men and women might be outraged at the description of their candlelit dinner as prostitution, but the radical feminist argues this outrage is due simply to the participants' failure or refusal to perceive the social context in which their dinner date occurs.[19]

Apparently, this failure or refusal to perceive affects most women. Thus we may even suppose that the majority of women who have been treated to a candlelit dinner by a man prefer it to other dining alternatives they have experienced. To say that these preferences are misguided is a hard and condescending doctrine. It would seem that most feminist philosophers are not overly impressed with Mill's principle that there can be no appeal from a majority verdict of those who have experienced two alternatives.

The dismissive feminist attitude to the widespread preferences of women takes its human toll. Most women, for example, prefer to have children and those who have them rarely regret having them. It is no more than sensible, from a utilitarian standpoint, to take note of such widespread preferences and to take it seriously in planning one's own life. But a significant number of women discount this general verdict as benighted, taking more seriously the idea that the reported joys of motherhood are exaggerated and fleeting, if not altogether illusory. These women tell themselves and others that having babies is a trap to be avoided. But for many women childlessness has become a trap of its own, somewhat lonelier than the more conventional traps of marriage and babies. Some come to find their childlessness regrettable; this sort of regret is common to those who flout Mill's reasonable maxim by putting the verdict of ideology over the verdict of human experience.

3.   FEMINISTS AGAINST FEMININITY

It is a serious defect of American feminism that it concentrates its zeal on impugning femininity and feminine culture at the expense of the grass roots fight against economic and social injustices to which women are subjected. As we have seen, the radical feminist attitude to the woman who enjoys her femininity is condescending or even contemptuous. Indeed, the contempt for femininity reminds one of misogynist biases in such philosophers as Kant, Rousseau, and Schopenhauer, who believed that femininity was charming but incompatible with full personhood and reasonableness. The feminists deny the charm, but they too accept the verdict that femininity is weakness. It goes without saying that an essential connection between femininity and powerlessness has not been established by *either* party.

By denigrating conventional feminine roles and holding to an assimilationist ideal in social policy, the feminist movement has lost its natural constituency. The actual concerns, beliefs, and aspirations of the majority of women are not taken seriously *except* as illustrations of bad faith, false consciousness, and successful brainwashing. What

women actually want is discounted and reinterpreted as to what they (have been led to) *think* they want ("a man," "children"). What most women *enjoy* (male gallantry, candlelit dinners, sexy clothes, makeup) is treated as an obscenity (prostitution).

As the British feminist, Janet Radcliffe Richards, says:

> Most women still dream about beauty, dress, weddings, dashing lovers, domesticity and babies . . . but if feminists seem (as they do) to want to eliminate nearly all of these things—beauty, sex conventions, families and all—for most people that simply means the removal of everything in life which is worth living for.[20]

Radical feminism creates a false dichotomy between sexism and assimilation, as if there were nothing in between. This view ignores completely the middle ground in which a woman can be free of oppression and nevertheless feminine in the sense abhorred by many feminists. For women are simply not waiting to be freed from the particular chains the radical feminists are trying to sunder. The average woman enjoys her femininity. She wants a man, not a roommate. She wants children and the time to care for them. When she enters the work force, she wants fair opportunity and equal treatment. These are the goals that women actually have, and they are not easily attainable. But they will never be furthered by an elitist radical movement that views the actual aspirations of women as the product of a false consciousness. There is room for a liberal feminism that would work for reforms that would give women equal opportunity in the workplace and in politics, but would leave unimpugned the basic institutions that women want and support, i.e., marriage and motherhood. Such a feminism is already in operation in some European countries. But it has been obstructed here in the United States by the ideologues who now hold the seat of power in the feminist movement.[21] . . .

4.   THE INDIRECT ATTACK

The philosophers I shall now discuss do not criticize the family directly; in some cases they do not even mention the family. However, each one holds a view that subverts, ignores, or denies the special moral relations that characterize the family and are responsible for its functioning. And if they are right, family morality is a vacuous subject.

Judith Thomson maintains that an abortion may be permissible even if the fetus is deemed a person from the moment of conception,[22] for in that case being pregnant would be like having an adult surgically attached to one's body. And it is arguable that if one finds oneself attached to another person, one has the right to free oneself even if such freedom is obtained at the price of the other person's death by, say, kidney failure. I shall, for purposes of this discussion, refer to the fetus as a prenatal child. I myself do not think the fetus is a person from the moment of conception. Nor does Thomson. But here we are interested in her argument for the proposition that abortion of a prenatal child/person should be permissible.

Many have been repelled by Thomson's comparison of pregnancy to arbitrary attachment. Thomson herself is well aware that the comparison may be bizarre. She says:

> It may be said that what is important is not merely the fact that the fetus is a person, but that it is a person for whom the woman has a special kind of responsibility issuing from the fact that she is its mother.[23]

To this Thomson replies: "Surely we do not have any such 'special responsibility' for a person unless we have assumed it, explicitly or implicitly." If the mother does not try to prevent pregnancy, does not obtain an abortion, but instead gives birth to it and takes it home with her, then, at least implicitly, she has assumed responsibility for it.

One might object that although pregnancy is a state into which many women do not enter voluntarily, it is nevertheless a state in which one has some responsibility to care for the prenatal child. Many pregnant women do feel such a prenatal responsibility, and take measures to assure the prenatal child's survival and future health. But here one must be grateful to Professor Thomson for her clarity. A mother who has not sought pregnancy deliberately bears *no* special responsibility to her prenatal child.

For she has neither implicitly nor explicitly taken on the responsibility of caring for it. For example, the act of taking the infant home from the hospital implies voluntary acceptance of such responsibility. By choosing to take it with her, the mother undertakes to care for the infant and no longer has the right to free herself of the burden of motherhood at the cost of the child's life.

The assumption, then, is that there are no non-contractual obligations or special duties defined by the kinship of mother to child. As for social expectations, none are legitimate in the morally binding sense unless they are underpinned by an implicit or explicit contract freely entered into. If this assumption is correct, sociological arrangements and norms have no moral force unless they are voluntarily accepted by the moral agent who is bound by them. I shall call this the "volunteer theory of moral obligation." It is a thesis that is so widely accepted today that Thomson saw no need to argue for it.

Michael Tooley's arguments in defense of infanticide provide another solid example of how a contemporary philosopher sidetracks and ultimately subverts the special relations that bind the family.[24] Tooley holds that being sentient confers the prima facie right not to be treated cruelly, and that possession of those characteristics that make one a person confers the *additional* right to life. Tooley then argues that infants lack these characteristics and so may be painlessly killed. In reaching this conclusion, Tooley's sole consideration is whether the infant intrinsically possesses the relevant "right-to-life-making characteristic" of personality—a consideration that abstracts from any right to care and protection that the infant's relation to its parents confers on it causally and institutionally. For Tooley, as for Thomson, the relations of family or motherhood are morally irrelevant. So it is perhaps not surprising that one finds nothing in the index under "family," "mother," or "father" in Tooley's book on abortion and infanticide.

Howard Cohen is concerned strictly with the rights of persons irrespective of the special relations they may bear to others.[25] Just as Thomson holds that the mother's right to the free unencumbered use of her body is not qualified by any special obligations to her child, so Cohen holds that the child's right to a no-fault divorce from its parents cannot be diminished because of the special relation it bears to them. Where Thomson is concerned with the overriding right of the mother, Cohen is concerned with the right of the child. Yet all three philosophers agree that the right of a child is not less strong than the right of any adult. Indeed, Thomson compares the unborn child to a fully grown adult and Tooley holds that any person—be it child, adult, or sapient nonhuman—is equal in rights.

Our three philosophers are typical in holding that any moral requirement is either a general duty incumbent on everyone or else a specific obligation voluntarily assumed. Let us call a requirement a *duty* if it devolves on the moral agents whether or not they have voluntarily assumed it. (It is, for example, a duty to refrain from murder.) And let us call a requirement an *obligation* only if it devolves on certain moral agents but not necessarily on all moral agents. (One is, for example, morally obligated to keep a promise.) According to our three philosophers, all duties are general in the sense of being requirements on all moral agents. Any moral requirement that is *specific* to a given moral agent must be grounded in his or her voluntary commitment. Thus, there is no room for any special requirement on a moral agent that has not been assumed voluntarily by that agent. In other words, *there are no special duties.* This is what I am calling the volunteer theory of obligation. According to the voluntaristic thesis, all duties are general and only those who volunteer for them have any obligations toward them.

This thesis underlies Cohen's view that the child can divorce its parents. For it is unnecessary to consider whether the child has any special duties to the parents that could conflict with the exercise of its right to leave them. It underlies Thomson's view that the woman who had not sought pregnancy has no special responsibility to her unborn child and that any such responsibility that she may later have is assumed implicitly by her voluntary act of taking it home with her. In underlies Tooley's psychobiological method for answering the moral question of infanticide by determining the right-making characteristics of personhood: all we need to know about the neonate is whether or not it possesses the psychological characteristics of personhood. If it does, then it has a right to life. If it does not, then it is not a person and thus may be killed painlessly. It is unnecessary to consider the question of whether the child has a special relation to anyone who may have a "special responsibility" to see to the child's survival.

What I am calling the volunteer thesis is a confidently held thesis of many contemporary Anglo-American philosophers. It is easy to see that the thesis is contrary to what Sidgwick called Common Sense. For it means that there is no such thing as filial duty per se, no such thing as the special duty of mother to child, and generally no such thing as a morality of special family or kinship relations. All of which is contrary to what people think. For most people think that we do owe special debts to our parents even though we have not voluntarily assumed our obligations to them. Most people think that what we owe to our own children does not have its origin in any voluntary undertaking, explicit or implicit, that we have made to them. And, "preanalytically," many people believe that we owe special consideration to our siblings even at times when we may not *feel* very friendly to them. But if there are no special duties, then most of these prima facie requirements are misplaced and without moral force, and should be looked upon as archaic survivals to be ignored in assessing our moral obligations.

The idea that to be committed to an individual is to have made a voluntarily implicit or explicit commitment to that individual is generally fatal to family morality. For it looks upon the network of felt obligation and expectation that binds family members as a sociological phenomenon that is without presumptive moral force. The social critics who hold this view of family obligation usually are aware that promoting it in public policy must further the disintegration of the traditional family as an institution. But whether they deplore the disintegration or welcome it, they are bound in principle to abet it.

It may be that so many philosophers have accepted the voluntaristic dogma because of an uncritical use of the model of promises as the paradigm for obligations. If all obligations are like the obligation to keep a promise, then indeed they could not be incumbent on anyone who did not undertake to perform in a specified way. But there is no reason to take promises as paradigmatic of obligation. Indeed, the moral force of the norm of promise-keeping must itself be grounded in a theory of obligations that moral philosophers have yet to work out.

A better defense of the special duties would require considerably more space than I can give it here.[26] However, I believe the defense of special duties is far more plausible than rival theories that reject special duties. My primary objective has been to raise the strong suspicion that the volunteer theory of obligation is a dogma that is very probably wrong and misconceived, a view that is certainly at odds with common opinion.

Once we reject the doctrine that a voluntary act by the person concerned is a necessary condition of special obligation, we are free to respect the commonsense views that attribute moral force to many obligations associated with kinship and other family relationships. We may then accept the family as an institution that defines many special duties but that is nevertheless imperfect in numerous respects. . . .

It should be said that the appeal to common sense or common opinion is not final. For common sense often delivers conflicting verdicts on behavior. But a commonsense verdict is strongly presumptive. For example, there is the common belief that biological mothers have a special responsibility to care for their children, even their unwanted children. One *takes* this as presumptive evidence of an *objective* moral responsibility on the part of the mother. Note that the "verdict" of common sense is not really a verdict at all. Rather, it is evidence of a moral consideration that *must* enter into the final verdict on what to do and how to behave. Thomson ignores common sense when she asserts that the mother of a child, born or unborn, has no special responsibility to it unless she has in some way voluntarily assumed responsibility for it. Now, to say that a pregnant woman may have a moral responsibility to her unborn child does not entail that abortion is impermissible. For there are other commonsense considerations that enter here and other responsibilities that the mother may have (to her other children, to herself) that may conflict and override the responsibility to the fetus. So com-

mon sense is often not decisive. One may say that a commonsense opinion is symptomatic of a prima facie duty or liberty, as the case may be. Yet it still remains for the casuist to determine the *weight* of the duty in relation to other moral considerations that also may have the support of common sense. Politically and morally, lack of respect for common sense fosters illiberalism and elitism. Here we have the radical temper that often advocates actions and policies wildly at odds with common opinion—from infanticide to male lactation, from non-fault divorce on demand for children to the "roommate test" for marital relationships.

5.   THE BROKEN FAMILY

In the final section we look at certain of the social consequences of applying radical theory to family obligation. I have suggested that, insofar as moral philosophers have any influence on the course of social history, their influence has recently been in aid of institutional disintegration. I shall now give some indication of how the principled philosophical disrespect for common sense in the area of family morality has weakened the family and how this affects the happiness of its members. Although much of what I say here is fairly well known, it is useful to say it in the context of an essay critical of the radical way of approaching moral philosophy. For there are periods in history when the radical way has great influence.

The most dramatic evidence of the progressive weakening of the family is found in the statistics on divorce. Almost all divorce is painful and most divorce affects children. Although divorce does not end but merely disrupts the life of a child, the life it disrupts is uncontroversially the life of a person who can be wronged directly by the actions of a moral agent. One might, therefore, expect that philosophers who carefully examine the morality of abortion also would carefully examine the moral ground for divorce. But here, too, the contemporary reluctance of philosophers to deal with the special casuistry of family relations is evidenced. For example, there are more articles on euthanasia or on recombinant DNA research than on divorce.

Each year there are another million and a quarter divorces in the United States affecting over one million children. The mother is granted custody in ninety percent of the cases, although legally it is no longer a matter of course. There is very persuasive evidence that children of divorced parents are affected seriously and adversely. Compared with children from intact families, they are referred more often to school psychologists, are more likely to have lower IQ and achievement test scores, are arrested more often, and need more remedial classes.[27] Moreover, these effects show little correlation to economic class. Children in the so-called latency period (between six and twelve) are the most seriously affected. In one study of children in this age group, one-half the subjects showed evidence of a "consolidation into troubled and conflicted depressive behavior patterns."[28] Their behavior patterns included "continuing depression and low self-esteem, combined with frequent school and peer difficulties."

One major cause for the difference between children from broken and intact families is the effective loss of the father. In the *majority* of cases the child has not seen the father within the past year. Only one child in six has seen his or her father in the past week; only 16 percent have seen their fathers in the past month; 15 percent see them once a year; the remaining 52 percent have had no contact at all for the past year. Although 57 percent of college educated fathers see their children at least once a month, their weekly contact is the same as for all other groups (one in six).[29]

It would be difficult to demonstrate that the dismissive attitude of most contemporary moral philosophers to the moral force of kinship ties and conventional family roles has been a serious factor in contributing to the growth in the divorce rate. But that is only because it is so difficult in general to demonstrate how much bread is baked by the dissemination of philosophical ideas. It is surely fair to say that the emphasis on autonomy and equality, when combined with the philosophical denigration of family ties, may have helped to make divorce both easy and respectable, thereby facilitating the rapid change from fault-based to no-fault divorce. If contemporary moralists have not caused the tide of family disintegration, they are avidly riding it. On the other side, it is not difficult to demonstrate that there is very little in recent moral philosophy that could be cited as possibly contributing to *stemming* the tide.

In the past two decades there has been a celebrated resurgence of interest in applied or practical ethics. It would appear, however, that the new enthusiasm for getting down to normative cases does not extend to topics of personal morality defined by family relationships. Accordingly, the children who are being victimized by the breakdown of the family have not benefited from this. Indeed, we find far more concern about the effect of divorce on children from philosophers a generation or two ago when divorce was relatively rare than we find today. Thus, Bertrand Russell writes:

> [H]usband and wife, if they have any love for their children, will so regulate their conduct as to give their children the best chance of a happy and healthy development. This may involve, at times, very considerable self-repression. And it certainly requires that both should realize the superiority of the claims of children to the claims of their own romantic emotions.[30]

And while Russell is not opposed to divorce, he believes that children place great contraints on it.

> ... parents who divorce each other, except for grave cause, appear to me to be failing their parental duty.[31]

Discerning and sensitive observers of a generation ago did not need masses of statistics to alert them to the effects of divorce on children. Nor did it take a professional philosopher (citing statistics gathered by a professional sociologist) to see that acting to dissolve a family must be evaluated morally primarily in terms of what such action means for the children.

Writing in the *London Daily Express* in 1930, Rebecca West says:

> The divorce of married people with children is nearly always an unspeakable calamity. It is only just being understood ... how much a child depends for its healthy growth on the presence in the home of both its parents. .... The point is that if

a child is deprived of either its father or its mother it feels that it has been cheated out of a right.[32]

West describes the harmful effects of divorce on children as effects of "a radiating kind, likely to travel down and down through the generations, such as few would care to have on their consciences."

I have quoted West in some fullness because her remarks contrast sharply with what one typically finds in contemporary college texts. In a book called *Living Issues in Ethics,* the authors discuss unhappy parents and the moral questions they face in contemplating divorce.

> We believe that staying together for the sake of the children is worse than the feelings and adjustment of separation and divorce.[33]

Further on the authors give what they feel to be a decisive reason for this policy:

> Remaining together in an irreconcilable relationship violates the norm of interpersonal love.

One of the very few philosophers to discuss the question of divorce and its consequences for children is Jeffrey Blustein in his book, *Parents and Children.* Blustein looks with equanimity on the priority of personal commitment to parental responsibility, pointing out that

> The traditional view . . . that the central duties of husband and wife are the . . . duties of parenthood is giving way to a conception of marriage as essentially involving a serious commitment between two individuals as individuals.[34]

Blustein also tells us (without telling us how he knows it) that children whose parents are unhappily married are worse off than if their parents were divorced.

> Indeed it could be argued that precisely on account of the children the parents' unhappy marriage should be dissolved. . . . [35]

The suggestion that parents who are unhappy should get a divorce "for the sake of the children" is *very* contemporary.

To my knowledge, no reliable study has yet been made that compares children of divorced parents to children from intact families whose parents do not get on well together. So I have no way of knowing whether the claims of these authors are true or not. Moreover, because any such study would be compromised by certain arbitrary measures of parental incompatibility, one should probably place little reliance on them. It is, therefore, easy to see that contemporary philosophers are anxious to jump to conclusions that do not render implausible the interesting view that the overriding question in considering divorce is the compatibility of the parents, and that marital ties should be dissolved when they threaten or thwart the personal fulfillment of one or both the marital partners.

These philosophers set aside special duties and replace them with an emphasis on friendship, compatibility, and interpersonal love among family members. However, this has a disintegrative effect. That is to say, if what one owes to members of one's family is largely to be understood in terms of feelings of personal commitment, definite limits are placed on what one owes. For as feelings change, so may one's commitments. The result is a structure of responsibility within the family that is permanently unstable.

I have, in this final section, illustrated the indifference of contemporary philosophers to the family by dwelling on their indifference to the children affected by divorce. Nevertheless, I hope it is clear that nothing I have said is meant to convey that I oppose divorce. I do not. Neither Russell nor West nor any of the sane and compassionate liberal thinkers of the recent past opposed divorce. They simply did not play fast and loose with family mores, did not encourage divorce, and pointed out that moralists must insist that the system of family obligations is only partially severed by a divorce that cuts the marital tie. Morally, as well as legally, the obligations to the children remain as before. Legally, this is still recognized. But in a moral climate where the system of family obligation is given no more weight than can be justified in terms of popular theories of deontic volunteerism, the obligatory ties are too fragile to survive the personal estrangements that result from divorce. It is, therefore, to be expected that parents (especially fathers) will be off and away doing their own thing. And the law is largely helpless.

I have no special solutions to the tragedy of economic impoverishment and social deprivation that results from the weakening of family ties. I believe in the right of divorce and do not even oppose no-fault divorce. I do not know how to get back to the good old days when moral philosophers had the common sense to acknowledge the moral weight of special ties and the courage to condemn those who failed in them—the days when, in consequence, the *climate* of moral approval and disapproval was quite different from what it is today. I do not know how to make fathers ashamed of their neglect and inadvertent cruelty. What I do know is that moral philosophers should be paying far more attention to the social consequences of their views than they are. It is as concrete as taking care that what one says will not affect adversely the students whom one is addressing. If what students learn from us encourages social disintegration, then we are responsible for the effects this may have on their lives and on the lives of their children. This then is a grave responsibility, even graver than the responsibility we take in being for or against something as serious as euthanasia or capital punishment—since most of our students will never face these questions in a practical way.

I believe then that responsible moral philosophers are liberal or conservative but not radical. They respect human relationships and traditions and the social environment in which they live as much as they respect the natural environment and its ecology. They respect the family. William James saw the rejection of radicalism as central to the pragmatist way of confronting moral questions.

> [Experience] has proved that the laws and usages of the land are what yield the maximum of satisfaction. . . . The presumption in cases of conflict must always be in favor of the conventionally recognized good. The philosopher must be a conservative, and in the construction of his casuistic scale must put things most in accordance with the customs of the community on top.[36]

A moral philosophy that does not give proper weight to the customs and opinions of the community is presumptuous in its attitude and pernicious in its consequences. In an important sense it is not a moral philosophy at all. For it is humanly irrelevant.

NOTES

1. Michael Slote, "Obedience and Illusions," in Onora O'Neill and William Ruddick, eds., *Having Children* (New York: Oxford, 1979), p. 320.

2. Slote, p. 230.

3. Virginia Held, "The Obligations of Mothers and Fathers," in Joyce Trebilcot, ed., *Mothering: Essays in Feminist Theory* (Totowa, NJ: Rowman and Allanheld, 1983), pp. 7–20.

4. Jane English, "What Do Grown Children Owe Their Parents?" in O'Neill and Ruddick, op. cit., pp. 351–56.

5. John Simmons, *Moral Principles and Political Obligation* (Princeton, NJ: Princeton University Press, 1979), p. 162.

6. Jeffrey Blustein, *Parents and Children: The Ethics of the Family* (New York: Oxford, 1982), p. 182.

7. Howard Cohen, *Equal Rights for Children* (Totowa, NJ: Rowman and Littlefield, 1980), p. 66.

8. Simone de Beauvoir, *The Second Sex,* tr. H. M. Parshley (New York: Random House 1952), p. 534.

9. De Beauvoir, p. 553.

10. De Beauvoir, "Talking to De Beauvoir," *Spare Rib* (March 1977), p. 2.

11. Richard Wasserstrom, *Philosophy and Social Issues* (Notre Dame, IN: University of Notre Dame Press, 1980), p. 26.

12. Wasserstrom, p. 23.

13. Wasserstrom, p. 26.

14. Ann Ferguson, "Androgyny as an Ideal for Human Development," in *Feminism and Philosophy,* eds. M. Vetterling-Braggin, F. Elliston and J. English (Totowa, NJ: Rowman and Littlefield, 1977), pp. 45–69.

15. Carol Gould, "Private Rights and Public Virtues: Woman, the Family and Democracy," in *Beyond Domination,* ed. Carol Gould (Totowa, NJ: Rowman and Allanheld, 1983), pp. 3–18.

16. Alison Jaggar, "Human Biology in Feminist Theory: Sexual Equality Reconsidered," in Gould, op. cit., p. 41. Jaggar is serious about the possibility and desirability of what she calls the "transformation of sexuality," which is elaborated in her book *Feminist Politics and Human Nature* (Totowa, NJ: Rowman and Allanheld, 1983), p. 132.

17. Alison Jaggar, "On Sex Equality," in *Sex Equality,* ed. Jane English (Englewood Cliffs, NJ: Prentice-Hall, 1977), p. 102.

18. Alison Jaggar, "Prostitution," in Marilyn Pearsell, ed., *Women and Values: Reading in Recent Feminist Philosophy* (Belmont, CA: Wadsworth, 1986), pp. 108–121.

19. Jaggar, "Prostitution," p. 117.

20. Janet Radcliffe Richards. *The Skeptical Feminist* (Middlesex, England: Penguin Books, 1980), pp. 341–42.

21. See Sylvia Ann Hewlett, *A Lesser Life: The Myth of Woman's Liberation in America* (New York: William Morrow, 1986).

22. Judith Thomson, "A Defense of Abortion," in *Philosophy and Public Affairs,* vol. 1, no. 1, 1972.

23. Thomson, p. 64.

24. Michael Tooley, "Abortion and Infanticide," in *Philosophy and Public Affairs,* vol. 2, no. 1, 1972.

25. Howard Cohen, *Equal Rights for Children,* chs. V and VI.

26. For a defense of the special duties not assumed voluntarily, see Christina Sommers, "Filial Morality," *The Journal of Philosophy,* no. 8, August 1986.

27. Lenore Weitzman, *The Divorce Revolution: The Unexpected Social and Economic Consequences for Women and Children in America* (New York: The Free Press, 1985).

28. A. Skolnick and J. Skolnick, eds., *Family in Transition* (Boston: Little Brown, 1929), p. 452.

29. Weitzman, p. 259.

30. Bertrand Russell, *Marriage and Morals* (New York: Liveright, 1929), p. 236.

31. Russell, p. 238.

32. Rebecca West, *London Daily Express,* 1930

33. R. Nolan and F. Kirkpatrick, eds., *Living Issues in Ethics* (Belmont, CA: Wadsworth, 1983), p. 147.

34. Blustein, *Parents and Children,* p. 230.

35. Blustein, p. 232.

36. William James, "The Moral Philosopher and the Moral Life", in *Essays in Pragmatism* (New York: Hafner, 1948), p. 80.

Critics

"They Lived Happily Ever After"

Marilyn Friedman

Sommers on Women and Marriage

1. In a series of papers which has recently appeared in several philosophical and general academic publications, Christina Sommers mounts a campaign against feminist philosophers and "American feminism" in general. Sommers blames feminists for contributing to the current divorce rate and the breakdown of the traditional family, and she repudiates feminist critiques of traditional forms of marriage, family, and femininity. In this paper, I explore Sommers's views in some detail. My aim is not primarily to defend her feminist targets, but to ferret out Sommers's own views of traditional marriage, family, and femininity, and to see whether or not they have any philosophical merit.

2. In her writings, Sommers generally defends what she claims that feminists have challenged. Whether or not she is actually discussing the same things is often open to question since she fails to define the key terms behind which she rallies. Sommers, for example, endorses "the family," the "traditional family," and "the family as we know it". These are not equivalent expressions. The so-called "traditional family"—a nuclear family consisting of a legally married heterosexual couple and their children, in which the man is the sole breadwinner and "head" of the household, and the woman does the domestic work and childcare—comprised only 16% of all U.S. households in 1977, according to the U.S.

Marilyn Friedman, " 'They Lived Happily Ever After': Sommers on Women and Marriage" *Journal of Social Philosophy* 21 (1990): 57–65. Some notes have been deleted. Reprinted by permission of Blackwell Publishing Ltd.

Census Bureau. Hence, the "traditional family" is no longer "*the* family" or "*the* family as we know it" (italics mine) but is only one sort of family that we know.

Sommers also rallies behind "femininity," "feminine culture," "conventional feminine roles," and "a primary gender role" (1989a, 90, 92). These expressions, as well, call for clarification; they do not necessarily refer to the same practices. In recent years, many feminists have defended various aspects of what might also be called "feminine culture." Sommers notes a few of these authors and works (Carol Gilligan, for example), but finds one reason or another for repudiating each one that she cites.

3. To see what Sommers is promoting under the banner of "feminine culture," we should look to Sommers's claims about what women value, want, and enjoy. First, there are wants, values, and enjoyments pertaining to men. Sommers claims that women want "a man," "marriage," and "to marry good providers." She asserts that "most women" enjoy "male gallantry," that the "majority of women" enjoy being "treated by a man to a candlelit dinner," and that "many women . . . swoon at the sight of Rhett Butler carrying Scarlett O'Hara up the stairs to a fate undreamt of in feminist philosophy."

Second, there are wants, values, and enjoyments having to do with children. Women, Sommers tells us, want children, motherhood, "*conventional* motherhood," "family," and "the time to care for children." In a revealing turn of phrase, Sommers also asserts that women are "willing to pay the price" for family and motherhood (1989b, B2). Sommers does not say, however, what she thinks the price is.

Third, there are wants, values, and enjoyments having to do with femininity. Women are said to enjoy their "femininity," makeup, "sexy clothes," and, even more specifically, "clothes that render them 'sex objects.' " On the topic of femininity, Sommers also quotes approvingly (1989a, 90–91) the words of Janet Radcliffe Richards who wrote that, "Most women still dream about beauty, dress, weddings, dashing lovers," and "domesticity," and that, for "most people," "beauty, sex conventions, families and all" comprise "everything in life which is worth living for."[1]

4. A very few of the wants which Sommers attributes to women do not fit into my three-part classification scheme (men, children, femininity). Sommers claims that women want "fair economic opportunities" (1989a, 91), and that they are "generally receptive to liberal feminist reforms that enhance their political and economic powers." (1989b, B2) Sommers, ironically, does not recognize that the enhanced economic and political power of women makes them less needful of traditional marriage to a "good provider," and when they are married, makes them less afraid to resort to divorce to solve marital and family problems. The economic concerns of liberal feminism directly threaten one colossal support for the "traditional family," namely, the extreme economic vulnerability of the non-income-earning woman and her concomitant material dependence on a "good provider."

Under traditional arrangements, most women did not merely *want* marriage; they *needed* it. It was by far a woman's most socially legitimated option for economic survival. Take away the need, as liberal feminism seeks to do, and at least some of the want also disappears. One otherwise very traditional aunt of mine became a wealthy widow in her late fifties when my rich uncle died. She never remarried. Now a dynamic woman of 82 who travels widely and lives well, she confesses that no man has interested her enough to make it worthwhile to give up her freedom a second time. "I'm lucky," she confides, "I don't need a meal-ticket." Even a nonfeminist can understand what she is getting at.

5. Before assessing Sommers's overall views, let us rescue Scarlett O'Hara. Sommers' remark that Scarlett O'Hara's rape by Rhett Butler is a fate undreamt of in feminist philosophy is . . . simply stunning. (Note that Sommers does not use the word "rape" here—one of many omissions in her writings.) Even a passing knowledge of feminist philosophy reveals that rape is hardly undreamt of in it. Rape, of course, is not a dream; it is a nightmare. Any form of sexual aggression can involve coercion, intimidation, degradation, physical abuse, battering, and, in extreme cases, death.

The reality of rape is rendered invisible by the many novels and films, such as *Gone with the Wind,* which romanticize and mystify it. They portray the rapist as a handsome man whose domination is pleasurable in bed, and portray women as happy to have their own sexual choices and refusals crushed by such men. In a culture in which these sorts of portrayals are routine, it is no surprise that this scene arouses the sexual desire of some women. However, the name of Richard Speck, to take one example, can remind us that real rape is not the pleasurable fantasy intimated in *Gone with the Wind.* To put the point graphically: would "many women" still swoon over Butler's rape of O'Hara if they knew that he urinated on her? When you're the victim of rape, you don't have much choice over what goes on.

6. Let us move on to femininity. Sommers never spells out exactly what she means by femininity. For guidance on this topic, we could turn to literature in social psychology which identifies the important traits of femininity and which explores the social devaluation of the feminine. However, it might be more revealing to turn to a different sort of "expert." By a lucky coincidence, I recently acquired a gem of a cultural artifact, a 1965 book entitled, *Always Ask a Man: Arlene Dahl's Key to Femininity,* written by a rather well-known actress and model of the 1960s, Arlene Dahl. I have learned a great deal from this femininity manifesto.

As you might guess from the title, one guiding theme of the book, and of the femininity it aims to promote, is utter deference to the opinions of men. Dahl instructs the female reader: "Look at Yourself Objectively (try to see yourself through a man's eyes)." (p.2) In Dahl's view, the "truly feminine" woman works "instinctively" at pleasing men and making men feel important. "When [a man] speaks to her, she listens with rapt attention to every word" (p. 5). Dahl believes that every woman has the capacity to measure up to men's ideals of femininity. This is because "Every woman is an actress. (Admit it!) Her first role is that of a coquette. (If you have any doubts just watch a baby girl with her father.)" (p. 6)

Dahl's book is laced with quotations from male celebrities who are treated as incontrovertible authorities on what women should be like. Yul Brynner, for example, wants women to be good lis-

teners who are not particularly logical (p. 3). Richard Burton likes women who are "faintly giggly" (p. 3). Tony Perkins thinks that a "girl should act like a girl and not like the head of a corporation—even if she is" (p. 8). The most revealing observation comes from George Hamilton: "A woman is often like a strip of film—obliterated, insignificant—until a man puts a light behind her." (pp. 5–6)

Surprisingly, some of the traits advocated for women by these male celebrities are actually valuable traits: honesty, straightforwardness, maturity, ingenuity, understanding, dignity, generosity, and humor. These traits are not distinctively feminine, however, and that may be the reason why they quickly disappear from Dahl's discussion. The twin themes that resound throughout this femininity manual are that of cultivating one's physical attractiveness and slavishly deferring to men. Instead of a chapter on honesty, a chapter on dignity, and so on, the book features chapters on every aspect of bodily grooming and adornment, including a separate chapter on each of the four basic categories of Caucasian hair color: blonde, redhead, "brownette," and brunette.

The slavish deference to men is crucial, since the whole point of the enterprise is to get a man. Thus, Dahl explains in the introduction that this book is written to counteract a tendency for women to dress to please other women, and it is also not for "women who want to be beautiful for beauty's sake. Such beauty serves no purpose, other than self-satisfaction, if that can be considered a purpose" (pp. x–xi).

The quintessential prohibition involved in femininity seems to be this: "NEVER upstage a man. Don't try to top his joke, even if you have to bite your tongue to keep from doing it. Never launch loudly into your own opinion on a subject—whether it's petunias or politics. Instead, draw out his ideas to which you can gracefully add your footnotes from time to time." (p. 12) Dahl is less sanguine than Sommers that the role of motherhood fits comfortably into a feminine life; she advises, " . . . don't get so involved with your role of MOTHER that you forget to play WIFE." (p. 9) Once married, your own interests should never override your husband's interests, job, and even hobbies, and, "There should be nothing that takes precedence in your day's schedule over making yourself attractive and appealing for the man in your life," not even your "children's activities"! (p. 175)

Voila, femininity. Such servility shows the dubiousness of Sommers's' claim that "a woman can be free of oppression and nevertheless feminine in the sense abhorred by many feminists" (1989a, 91).

7. Let us turn now to Sommers's overall philosophical defense of traditional marriage, family, and femininity. Having asserted that most women value or want all of these traditions, Sommers charges feminist views with a serious defect: they either dismiss or disparage these popular feminine wants and values. Sommers herself defers to these alleged views of most women as if they were as such authoritative: because "most women" (as she alleges) want traditional marriage and family, therefore these practices must be better than any alternatives. It is important to note that Sommers does not argue that traditional marriage and so on, on balance, promote important moral values better than any feminist alternatives. No comprehensive moral comparisons appear in her writings. Her argument begins (and ends, as I will argue) with an appeal to popular opinion.

8. Is Sommers right about what "most women" think? She refers to no studies, no representative samples whatsoever to support her generalizations. Whole categories of women are patently excluded from her reference group and are invisible in her writings. This is a fitting moment to mention the "L" word—and I don't mean "liberal." Obviously, no lesbians, unless seriously closeted, are among Sommers's alleged majority of women who want "a man," conventional marriage, or a traditional family.

Even among nonlesbians, a goodly number of women these days do not want a *traditional* marriage or a *traditional* family. Some heterosexual women simply do not want to marry or to have children at all, and many others want *non*-traditional marriages and *non*-traditional families. Surveys show that *this* attitude, and not the preference for tradition alleged by Sommers, is actually in the majority. In one 1983 study, 63% of women surveyed expressed preferences for non-traditional family arrangements (Sapiro, 1990, 355). Sommers's factual claims are, thus, debatable.

Even apart from questions of popularity, the wants, values, and enjoyments which Sommers attributes to "most women" are frankly suspicious as an ensemble. Candlelit dinners do not combine easily with babies. Dashing lovers (extra-marital!) can be disastrous for a marriage. This list of wants and values seems to show a failure to separate what is idealized and mythic from what is (to put it very advisedly) authentic and genuinely possible in the daily reality of marital and family relationships over the long haul. To hear Sommers tell it, women are blandly unconcerned about wife-battering, incest, marital rape, or the profound economic vulnerability of the traditional non-income-earning wife. This is hard to believe. What is more likely is that, for many women, " . . . they got married and lived happily ever after," is only a fairy tale—especially for those who have been married for awhile. Even the most traditional of women, I am convinced, has some sense of the risks involved in traditional heterosexual relationships. As an old saying goes, "When two hearts beat as one, someone is dead."

Sommers's list of women's wants and values is also woefully short. It suggests that this is *all* that "most women" want, that women's aspirations extend no farther than to being "feminine," getting a man—any man—and having babies. On the contrary, many women want meaningful and fulfilling work apart from childcare and domestic labor. Many women aspire to making a social contribution, or they have artistic impulses seeking expression, spiritual callings, deep friendships with other women, and abiding concerns for moral value and their own integrity. One foundational motivation for feminism has always been the aim to overcome the *constraints* on women's genuinely wide-ranging aspirations posed by traditional marital and family arrangements.

9. What philosophical difference would it make if Sommers were right about women's wants and values in general? The popularity of an opinion is hardly an infallible measure of its empirical or moral credibility. Even popular opinions may be based on misinformation, unfounded rumor, and so on. Sommers ignores these possibilities and recommends that we defer to popular opinion on the basis of " . . . Mill's principle that there can be no appeal

from a majority verdict of those who have experienced two alternatives" (1989a, 89–90). Sommers is evidently suggesting that feminist critiques of traditional family, marriage, and femininity should be judged by whether or not they conform to the "majority verdict of those who have experienced" the relevant alternatives. Now, carefully understood, this is actually not such a bad idea. However, rather than supporting Sommers's deference to popular opinion, this principle repudiates it.

First, there are more than just "two" feminist alternatives to any of the traditions in question. Consider, for example, the traditionally married, heterosexual couple comprised of dominant, breadwinning male and domestic, childrearing female. Feminists have recommended various alternative family arrangements, including egalitarian heterosexual marriage, communal living, lesbian relationships, and single parenting when economic circumstances are favorable. To decide the value of traditional marriage and family, one would have to try all the relevant alternatives—or at least *some* of them. And on Mill's view, merely experiencing alternatives is not enough; one must also be capable of "appreciating and enjoying" them (Mill, 1979, 9). If Sommers is right, however, most women want and choose traditional family, traditional marriage, and traditional femininity, and, thus, do not either experience or enjoy living according to any feminist alternatives. Women such as these are not what Mill calls "competent judges" of the value of those traditions since "they know only their own side of the question" (p. 10). And it is only from the verdict of *competent judges* that Mill believes that "there can be no appeal" (p. 11).

Second, of the "competent judges," in Mill's sense, that is, of the women who *have* experienced and enjoyed feminist alternatives to traditional marriage and family, most (I would wager) *prefer the feminist alternatives*. I am referring, among others, to women in lesbian relationships and women in genuinely egalitarian heterosexual relationships. If I am right about this, then by Mill's principle, we must reject "popular opinion" along with traditional marriage and the rest.

10. The truth of the matter is that, in the end, Sommers does not rest her case on Mill's principle.

Apparently without realizing that she changes her argument, she ends by appealing to something less vaulted than the majority verdict of those who have experienced and enjoyed *both* traditional family, etc., and various feminist alternatives. Her final court of appeal is simply to "what most people think," to so-called "commonsense," and to "tradition" itself (1989a, 95, 97). Sommers urges that "A moral philosophy that does not give proper weight to the customs and opinions of the community is presumptuous in its attitude and pernicious in its consequences" (1989a, 103). She speaks warmly of the Aristotelian conviction that "traditional arrangements have great moral weight and that common opinion is a primary source of moral truth" (1989a, 83). When it comes to tradition, Sommers would do well to consider Mill again. Mill often deferred to tradition, but it was not a deference from which he thought there was "no appeal," as he amply demonstrated in the important *indictment* of nineteenth century marital traditions on which he collaborated with Harriet Taylor (Mill & Taylor, 1970). (It would be interesting to know what "pernicious . . . consequences," to use Sommers's phrase, flowed from Mill's and Taylor's critique.)

Tradition is a fickle husband. He is constantly changing his mind. On the grounds of tradition, eighty years ago, Sommers would have opposed women's suffrage. One hundred and fifty years ago, she would have opposed women speaking in public (She would have had to do so in private!), opposed the rights of married women to property in their own names, opposed the abolition of slavery, and so on. She would have supported wife-battering since it was permitted by legal tradition—so long as the rod was no bigger around than the size of the husband's thumb.

Not only is tradition ever-changing, it is also plural, both within our own society and globally. Which tradition shall we follow when there is more than one from which to choose? Islam is the world's most widely practiced religion. Shall we non-Islamic women heed the most globally numerous of our sisters' voices and don the veil, retire from public life, and allow husbands to marry up to four wives? Within our own society, marital traditions also vary. Shall we follow the traditions of orthodox Jewish and orthodox Catholic women and avoid all contraceptives? My maternal grandmother did so; she had fourteen births. At nine months per gestation, she spent ten and a half years of her life being pregnant. Although she lingered on to the age of eighty-seven, she seemed even older than her age for the final sixteen, worn-out years of her life in which I knew her. Doubtless, that, too, was part of her tradition.

Why suppose that there is special merit to any of the alternative traditions that we happen to have at this historical moment in this particular geopolitical location? Why suppose that any of our current traditions are better or more deserving of loyalty and support than the traditions toward which we are evolving? And how will we ever evolve if we remain deadlocked in loyalty to all of the traditions we happen to have today?

11. Sommers allows that our traditions may need reform and even recommends "piecemeal social engineering" to deal with "imperfections" in the family (1989a, 97)—although it is noteworthy that she never specifies what these imperfections are, and, in a different passage, she inconsistently calls upon American feminism to leave marriage and motherhood simply "untouched and unimpugned" (1989a, 91). Nevertheless, she insists that her arguments are directed only against those radical feminists who seek the abolition of the family and the "radical reform of preferences, values, aspirations, and prejudices" (1990, 151, 148).

A serious concern to reform imperfections in the family should lead someone to consider the views of non-radical feminist reformers who also criticize marital and family traditions. Many feminists would be content with piecemeal family reform—so long as it was genuine reform (Thorne & Yalom, 1982; Okin, 1987; Okin, 1989). At any rate, this issue is a red herring. A dispute over the pace of reform does not show that radical feminist critiques of family traditions are wrong in substance. Most importantly, by allowing that change *is needed* in family traditions, Sommers effectively concedes that we should not automatically defer to tradition. To admit that reform of tradition is morally permissible is to reject tradition per se as an incontestable moral authority. The controversy can only be decided by directly

evaluating the conditions of life established by marital and family traditions—and their alternatives.

12. Sommers has one final twist to her argument which we should consider. She notes briefly—all too briefly—that traditions "have prima facie moral force" so long as they are not "essentially unjust" (1989a, 97). Sommers does not explain what she means by "essential injustice." Just how much injustice makes a traditional practice "essentially unjust?"

Despite its vagueness, this concession to injustice is critically important. It makes the merit of Sommers's own appeal to tradition contingent on the essential non-injustice of the particular traditions in question. Sommers, however, provides no argument to establish that traditional marriage practices and so forth are not essentially unjust. Nor does she respond substantively to those feminist arguments which claim to locate important injustices in these traditional practices. She rejects all feminist criticisms of the traditional family because they do not coincide with "popular opinion," "commonsense," or tradition. Traditional marriage and family are not essentially unjust, in Sommers's view, simply because most people allegedly do not *think* they are.

We seem to have come full circle. Sommers rejects feminist critiques of traditional marriage and so on because they are inconsistent with popular opinion, commonsense, and tradition. Tradition is to be relied on, in turn, so long as it is not essentially unjust. But Sommers rejects feminist arguments to show injustices in marital and family traditions simply on the grounds that those arguments are inconsistent with popular opinion, commonsense, and tradition itself. Sommers's defense of traditional marriage and family is, in the final analysis, circular and amounts to nothing more than simple *deference to tradition*—indeed, to particular traditions which are no longer so pervasive or popular as Sommers thinks.

13. One final concern: Sommers blames feminists for contributing to the growing divorce rate and the "disintegration of the traditional family." However, feminism could only contribute to the divorce rate if married women ended their marriages as a result of adopting feminist ideas. If Sommers is right, how-

ever, in thinking that "most women" reject non-liberal feminist values, then non-liberal feminists could not be having a significant impact on the divorce rate. Sommers cannot have it both ways. Either feminism *is* significantly contributing to the growing divorce rate, in which case it must be in virtue of the wide appeal of feminist ideas about marriage and family, or feminist ideas do *not* have wide appeal, in which case they cannot be significantly contributing to the growing divorce rate.

14. To conclude: My overall assessment of Sommers's views on marriage, family, and femininity is grim. Most importantly, Sommers rejects feminist views of marriage, family, and femininity ultimately on the basis of her own simple deference to (allegedly) popular opinion, commonsense, and tradition. This deference is defensible only if feminist views about injustices in those traditions can be shown, on *independent* grounds, to be misguided—and Sommers never provides this independent argument.

NOTE

1. Richards, 1980, 341–42. Quoted in Sommers, 1989a, 90–91.

REFERENCES

Dahl, Arlene. *Always Ask a Man: Arlene Dahl's Key to Femininity.* Englewood Cliffs, NJ: Prentice-Hall, 1965.

Mill, John Stuart. 1979. *Utilitarianism.* George Sher, ed. Indianapolis: Hackett.

Mill, John Stuart and Harriet Taylor. 1970. *Essays on Sex Equality.* Alice S. Rossi, ed. Chicago: University of Chicago Press.

Okin, Susan Moller. 1989. *Justice, Gender, and the Family.* New York: Basic Books.

Richards, Janet Radcliffe. 1980. *The Sceptical Feminist.* Harmondsworth: Penguin.

Sapiro, Virginia. 1990. *Women in American Society.* Mountain View, CA: Mayfield Publishing Co.

Sommers, Christina. 1988. "Should the Academy Support Academic Feminism." *Public Affairs Quarterly,* 2, 3 (July), 97–120.

———. 1989a. "Philosophers Against the Family." In: George Graham and Hugh LaFollette, eds. *Person to Person.* Philadelphia: Temple University Press, 82–105.

———. 1989b. "Feminist Philosophers Are Oddly Unsympathetic to the Women They Claim to Represent." *Chronicle of Higher Education,* October 11th, pp. B2–B3.

———. 1990. "The Feminist Revelation," *Social Philosophy and Policy Center,* 8, 1 (Autumn), 141–158.

The Ties That Bind

Claudia Mills

Duties to Family Members

"What do grown children owe their parents?" Over two decades ago philosopher Jane English asked this question and came up with the startling answer: nothing [ref. 1]. English joins many contemporary philosophers in rejecting the once-traditional view that grown children owe their parents some kind of fitting repayment for past services rendered. The problem with the traditional view, as argued by many, is, first, that parents have duties to provide fairly significant services to their growing children, and persons do not owe repayment for others' mere performance of duty; second, even where parents go above and beyond duty in their loving and generous rearing of their children, the benefits are bestowed,

Claudia Mills, "Duties to Aging Parents," in *Care of the Aged,* ed. James M. Humber and Robert F. Almeder (Totowa, N.J.: Humana Press, 2003). Notes have been deleted. Reprinted by permission of Humana Press, Inc.

at least on young children, without their voluntary acceptance and consent, and so, again, fail to generate any obligation of subsequent repayment on their part (*see* ref. 2, pp. 182–183). Moreover, the entire idiom of obligation and repayment, in English's words, "tends to obscure, or even to undermine, the love that is the correct ground of filial obligation" (ref. 1, p. 352).

English's alternative, however—that children strictly "owe" their parents nothing except what flows naturally from whatever love and affection exist between them—also strikes many as problematic. Sommers offers examples of what seem to be clearly delinquent adult children, who simply do not "feel" like sharing their lives with their aging parents, or providing any emotional or financial support to them, and so do not (ref. 3, pp. 440–441). Sommers points out that we need some talk of obligations in order to fill in the cracks in human relationships where love and affection fail: "The ideal relationship cannot be 'duty-free,' if only because sentimental ties may come unraveled, often leaving one of the parties at a material disadvantage" (ref. 3, pp. 450–451). Sommers proposes as her alternative to English that legitimate duties arise out of special relationships defined by social roles: Being a father or mother, a son or a daughter, "is socially as well as biologically prescriptive; it not only defines what one is; it also defines who one is and what one owes" (ref. 3, p. 447). According to Sommers, "The filial duties of adult children include such things as being grateful, loyal, attentive, respectful and deferential to parents (more so than to strangers)" (ref. 3, p. 447).

Sommers's view is not without troubles of its own. The stress on social roles seems to make family relationships overly conventional and does not distinguish family relationships from any of the myriad other social roles we all occupy. Moreover, some of the duties Sommers proposes (gratitude, deference) echo traditional debt-based views of the source of filial obligation that most of us now reject.

In what follows, I look at the duties of grown children to parents from a somewhat different angle. I begin with English's claim that the "duties" in question are merely "duties of friendship," duties situated within and made sense of through an ongoing mutual relationship, but then offer an argument that allows us to establish genuine filial obligations in a way that she is unable to do. I argue that family relationships are importantly different both from friendship (English's analogy) and from other social roles (Sommers's analogy) in their uniquely unchosen and unconditional nature. I suggest that we can shed light on what grown children owe their parents by looking first at a category of family relationships less shadowed by traditional encrustations of debt and gratitude: the relationship of siblings. I claim that we have strong reasons to participate in unconditional, unchosen relationships and corresponding obligations not to deny others the good of participating in such relationships with us. I conclude by trying to say something about exactly what grown children owe their parents: Grown children owe their parents those things that flow from participating together in an unconditional, unchosen relationship, and not (generally) material goods that can be otherwise obtained.

THE NATURE OF FAMILY RELATIONSHIPS

Many philosophers in the past few decades have turned their attention away from moral impartiality toward special relationships: friendship, membership in a community, family ties. I want to advance a claim about what makes family ties special even among other "special" relationships.

For a point of contrast, let us look first at nonfamilial friendship. As English characterizes friendship, certain "obligations" flow from friendship, but these are obligations only in an attenuated sense. What they are is, rather, defining features of friendship itself, features that, were they absent from A's interactions with B, we would say that A and B were not friends at all. So, friends care about each other, take an interest in each other's problems and successes, spend time together, help each other when needed, and so forth. Are these strictly speaking "obligations"? No, but were two people who claimed to be friends not to do any of these things for each other, we would question their claim to be friends in the first place. To be friends simply *is* to do these kinds of things for each other. We are given, as it were, the following choice: either be friends (and then do these sort of things for each other) or do not be friends (and so do not do such things for each other). The imperatives of friendship are, at bottom, hypothetical. One can escape the so-called obligations of friendship by declining to be a friend.

Families strike me as importantly different. When it comes to families, there is an imperative not only to fulfill whatever obligations are defined and generated by the underlying relationship but also to continue to participate in the relationship itself. We no longer have the same kind of choice: be a friend or walk away. In the case of families, I will argue, walking away is not the same kind of option.

Of course, there are many different kinds of family relationships: that of spouses to each other, of parents to children, of children to parents, and of siblings to siblings. In a liberal, modern society such as ours, which permits the initial choice of spouse and subsequent easy, no-fault, nonstigmatizing divorce, people may seem to marry each other, and to stay married to each other, through choice. The ideal, however, remains one of lasting commitment; in the vows that are still typical of most marriages, the partners to it pledge to remain with each other for better or worse, for richer or poorer, through sickness and health, as long as they both shall live. Few marriages begin with vows to stay together only as long as either party fails to find any other partner more eligible or attractive. Still, there is an undeniable element of choice in the initial mating.

Parents also seem to choose to have children in a way that children do not choose to have parents: I choose to give birth in a way that I did not choose to be born. However, this appearance of genuine, extensive parental choice cannot survive closer scrutiny. Certainly, the choice that I have of my children is much less than the choice that I have of my spouse, or any of my friends.

First, although one may choose to be a parent, to be the parent of some child or other, in the vast majority of cases, one has little or no choice of the identity of the actual child in question. Except in rare cases of adoption of older children with already revealed and well-established personalities, the choice of a child is

the choice of a pig in a poke. Gender, appearance, intelligence, talents, and temperament all appear to the parents as an unfolding surprise. Parents of two or more children are invariably astonished at the differences between individuals produced by the same parental genes and reared in the same family environment. We are still far away from the prospect of "designer" children, tailor-made to match parental expectations.

Second, even beyond one's initial lack of choice regarding the actual children to parent, the continuation of the relationship itself does not reflect parental choice to any significant degree, or so I will argue. Now, many philosophers seek to base parental obligations to children on other than bare biological grounds. In their view, I owe this or that to my children not because of the brute biological fact that I begat them (male) or bore them (female), but because I have voluntarily assumed such an obligation. I signaled my willingness to assume it by taking my child home with me from the hospital rather than exercising the option of giving him or her up, via adoption, to someone else to raise. In a society, like ours, that offers safe and legal abortion, the mother at least could have had an abortion and so declined to bring the child into existence in the first place. Thus, by not aborting, she chooses to give birth, and so, unless she surrenders her parental rights and obligations to another, chooses to become a parent, or so runs one common view.

This grounding of parental obligations in parental choice, however, is vulnerable to challenge on several points. What if I give birth and, as it turns out, there happens to be no one else available and willing to adopt my child? Surely, I have some extra responsibility for this child, *my* child, the child to whom I have just given birth, whether I assume it voluntarily or not. And, a more telling point: Suppose I do accept responsibility for some child, either by taking my own biological child home with me after its birth, or by agreeing to become an adoptive parent. What exactly have I committed myself to, in so doing? If we assimilate parenthood to friendship, then the answer would be that I have committed myself to taking care of the child as long as I feel like doing so; that taking care of a child is constitutive of being a parent, and I continue in the parental relationship as long as I feel like doing so. However, few would be ready to endorse this view of parenthood. If there is a basic choice involved, I submit, it is to take care of the child *forever,* come what may, whether I still want to or not. The choice of a biological parent to give up his or her child for adoption at birth is seldom criticized; the choice of a parent, biological or adoptive, to give up his or her child several years later would be almost uniformly criticized, and I would argue, rightly so. Now, parents may, and often do, subsequently delegate or transfer certain of the responsibilities of parenthood: They hire nannies, arrange for day care, send their children off to public or private schools, and allow other relatives to establish trust funds in their names. However, what (in most cases) they do not delegate or transfer is the relationship itself. They still, through all of these other alterations in their performed duties, remain parents, the persons unconditionally and permanently committed to the love and care of this particular child.

Why is this? Is the answer simply that this is what you promised in that initial act of assuming parental responsibility—to care for the child forever? Why should we understand the promise in such a sweeping and all-encompassing way? Where else in life do we promise such huge things extending over such a long duration of time? Well, as just noted, we promise them in marriage, understood as the foundation of a family, breaking such promises as often as we manage to keep them. Where else? Consent itself is insufficient to establish such deep and enduring duties. For who could ever consent, in an informed way, to such a thing? Whoever could do it?

My answer to the question of how parents end up in long-term committed relationships with their children instead is this. It is a great good to participate in a relationship that is enduring and unconditional. And because it is a great good for a child to be in that kind of relationship and a great harm to the child to be deprived of that kind of relationship, parents acquire an obligation to stick with the relationship, which means to fulfill the tasks that flow from it, through thick and thin. Indeed, as I will explain, it is a great good precisely to participate in a relationship

that is importantly *unchosen.* Thus, far from grounding the obligations of parenthood in a recognition of the importance of choice, my argument grounds these obligations in the recognition of the importance of that which is unchosen.

Now, is the great good here to participate in an unconditional and unchosen *relationship,* or to be the recipient of the unconditional *love* which usually—but not invariably—accompanies it? Some parents—only a few, I would speculate—do not love their children, or more properly, for some sad reason of their own history and constitution, cannot. However, most of us do love our children in this way. It is very odd that we do, that we love them before they were born, with no knowledge of a single fact about them except that in some sense they are *ours.* Biological parents love their children in this way; adoptive parents, waiting for the arrival of a child they have never seen from half the world away, love their children in this way. It is a love-based on nothing distinctive about the individual in question, nothing at all. One might wonder why we should even value love like this in the first place. I have heard some people devalue God's love in this way: God loves me? Yeah, well, big deal, God loves *everybody.* However, parents do not love everybody. They love this child, these (small number of) children. Why should I care about being loved if the love is not based on any trait or quality of mine, any distinctive feature, any uniqueness, anything that has to do with *me?* Well, love based on my distinctive uniqueness will come; parents do come to dwell lovingly, and sometimes despairingly, on all of their child's individual characteristics. However, the only answer I can come up with here is that it is simply a great good to have some reservoir of love that does not have to be earned and, more important, cannot be forfeited. As Elizabeth Barrett Browning wrote in one of her *Sonnets from the Portuguese,* love based on any particular trait or feature is vulnerable to altering when that trait or feature alters. So Browning writes, "If thou must love me, let it be for naught/Except for love's sake only." Love based on a choice can vary with changes in the features of the beloved that motivated and justified that choice. Unchosen love is, in this way, uniquely secure.

If this—unconditional, unchosen love—is the great good, is there any value to a continuing parental relationship in which such love is not present? I would argue that there is. One certainly cannot have love of this sort in the absence of the relationship, so the relationship at the least is the necessary precondition of the love; and the relationship itself can breed love over time—not love based on appreciation of any set of traits or characteristics, but love based simply on a shared history, of the passage of time in another's company. Minow notes that "duties and feelings interact in complicated ways" and that "feelings themselves can be educated as someone learns about and carries out responsibilities" (ref. 4, p. 267). Far from familiarity breeding contempt, I have found that familiarity breeds fondness, comfort in each other's presence, a quiet "growing accustomed" to the other's face. Sheer continuity, steadfastness over time, is itself a great good in one's life. Of course, I am assuming here that the parents are making a good-faith effort to love the child. I address the question of indifferent, neglectful, or even abusive parents later.

Now, this argument, appealing to the great good of unconditional and unchosen relationships, as I have stated it, is symmetrical between parents and children. While there may be some asymmetry in the choice involved on the part of parents and of children to enter into the relationship (although I have argued that the asymmetry is easily overstated, through overstating the presence of genuine parental choice), the good of being in the relationship itself is a good for all parties to it. As it is a great good for children to participate in such a relationship, so it is a great good for parents to participate in it as well. It may be a greater good for children, simply in that they are developing and forming their sense of their own identity and of their own self-worth, but for all persons, I submit, it is a great good to have at least some relationships in one's life that are unchosen and unconditional. This will lead me to make some speculations about what grown children owe their parents, but first I want to make a detour to look at the relationship of siblings to each other, for this is also an unchosen relationship. We do not choose our brothers and sisters, as we choose our friends.

Herein lies the distinctive good offered to us by this relationship, which will shape our expectations of what siblings owe to each other.

BROTHERS AND SISTERS

What, if anything, do grown brothers and sisters owe each other? Do they owe each other more or less than what they owe friends? How are we to understand their relationship and what flows from it? I would approach an answer to this question by saying that there is no way we can even begin to itemize duties of siblings to each other without first looking at the nature of the relationship they share. Again, the distinctive feature of this relationship, in contrast to most friendships, is that it is unchosen and, in some important sense, uncontingent on the merits, affinities, characters, virtues, and accomplishments of the parties to it. Brothers and sisters are simply born, or adopted, into the same family; they do not select each other; they may not even like each other all that well; it may be that if they were not siblings they would have little or nothing to do with each other. However, they are siblings. They are stuck with each other. Each one is a "given" in the other's life.

Now, if we were to follow English's model, we would say that siblings have only such "obligations" to each other as flow from their ongoing feeling of affection toward each other; insofar as they are friends, they should treat each other in the ways constitutive and definitive of friendship—and if they no longer want to be friends, so be it. If we were to follow Sommers's model, we would say that we would need to look at what flows from the social role of "brother" or "sister." However, I maintain that there is a great good in continuing the relationship and engaging in the activities characteristic of it, even in the absence of the appropriate underlying feelings. I would maintain that the social role of "brother" or "sister" is crucially undefined and largely beside the point. My sister is not special to me because we occupy a certain social role vis-à-vis each other.

So what do brothers and sisters owe each other? My claim is that they owe each other simply this: to continue in an ongoing relationship as brothers and sisters. This means sharing each others' lives to some extent—at the minimum, talking occasionally on the telephone or by e-mail, seeing each other sometimes at family gatherings, keeping each other somehow present in each other's lives. How often is often enough? I am not arrogant enough to prescribe that here; it can certainly vary from family to family. Siblings may be more or less "close," and I do not want to argue that closer is always better. However, all things equal, estrangement is always worse.

If this is what brothers and sisters owe each other, it follows that there are two things brothers and sisters do not owe each other. The first is, to put it in its most general terms, anything they can in principle get from somebody else, whether or not they can actually get it from them in the current state of affairs of their life. They owe each other only what they can get from nobody else: that is, the experience of being in an unchosen, unconditional relationship with a brother or sister. In particular, here I mean to exclude financial support. Money one can get from anywhere. In my view, one should get it from one's own efforts; failing that, one should get it from communally provided support for the indigent. What if the latter fails as well? Do I have any special responsibility to help an indigent brother or sister, more than I have to help an indigent stranger? Or an indigent friend? Is blood thicker than water here? My answer on this point is a bit uncertain. Usually, loving brothers and sisters will want to help each other when they can; at the same time, financial entanglements can deform even the most loving relationships. I have known more siblings estranged from each other for financial reasons than for any others. Thus, from my own admittedly anecdotal evidence, I think it is better if brothers and sisters do not depend on each other financially. Here, too, different families may have different expectations for what it means to participate in an ongoing family relationship. However, for the most part, I would continue to say: siblings do not owe each other what they can get from somebody else.

To put this same point another way, Donaldson distinguishes between what he calls "value-intrinsic" and "value-extrinsic" institutions, where an insti-

tution is "value intrinsic" to the "extent to which an institution's ends are logically unobtainable without the existence of the institution itself" and an institution is "value extrinsic" to "the extent to which an institution's ends conceivably could be achieved by other means" (ref. 5, p. 36). Recasting his point in the language of relationships rather than institutions, we can say that it is important that siblings give each other goods that are value intrinsic to their relationship, goods which simply cannot be acquired in any other way, and far less important that they give each other goods that are value extrinsic, even if conventional expectations, in a given society, may tie these goods in some way to the relationship. It is the value-intrinsic goods that are at the heart of family relationships. They are what brothers and sisters most fundamentally owe one another: the goods of being in the relationship itself.

The second, related thing that is not owed by siblings to each other, in my view, is sheer preference for one's siblings in giving out some benefit not directly tied to the relationship itself. Such preference has often been taken to be paradigmatic of "special" relationships and in direct challenge to the "impartiality" required by universal morality: to be in a special relationship just is to favor certain others in this way. However, I do not see that special relationships, such as family relationships, require this at all, in any mechanical way, except for the goods that are value intrinsic to that relationship, as discussed earlier. Siblings do not owe each other preference in hiring, for example. In fact, such preference is often (rightly) frowned on as nepotism. I owe my siblings some measure of preference only in how I spend my time, how I invest my affections, how I structure my days, but that is all. Philosophers at this point will want to introduce a range of hypothetical cases: If a trolley runs off the track and strikes both my sister and a stranger, whom do I help first? How serious of an injury to a stranger outweighs my duty to help my sister first? And so on. I am one who believes that in situations of dire emergency, philosophical argumentation runs out and real human emotion appropriately claims us. As Bernard Williams famously argues, in such cases "we just act, as a possibly confused result of the situation we are in.

That, I suspect, is very often an exceedingly good thing" (ref. 6, p. 118). When the trolley strikes, I will run to my sister's side. What I will do next will depend on the details of the situation in which I find myself. More than this I cannot specify in advance.

PARENTS AND CHILDREN

Let us now draw closer to the case at hand—the duties of grown children to their parents—by asking what parents owe their grown children. My answer here is the same as it was in the case of siblings. Parents do not owe their children what they could, and should, get from anyone else: a job, a place to live, money—either during their lives or in an inheritance after their death. In my view, children have no claim whatsoever on any inheritance of their parents' wealth; to the contrary, we would make great strides toward social justice by eliminating the practice of inheritance altogether (ref. 2, Appendix; ref. 7). Instead, our parents owe us only what we can get from parents alone (to the extent that they can provide it): unconditional love, abiding interest in our activities, pride in our accomplishments, worry over our problems, advice based on knowing us longer and better than anyone else, time, companionship— the continuation of the relationship itself.

What, then, do grown children owe their parents? The very same thing. Grown children do not owe their parents a home to live in, or money to live on, or day-to-day health care; nor, contrary to Sommers, do they owe their parents deference and gratitude. They owe them simply continuation in the relationship as their children, sharing their lives, caring about their lives, building an ongoing life together. Nothing more, nothing less.

Now, if we follow English, grown children may *want* to provide their parents with many other additional goods; they may want to offer them a home, pay their bills, and care for them physically when they are no longer able to care for themselves. If we follow Sommers, there may (or may not be) certain social expectations to do such things. However, this, in my view, goes beyond what is entailed simply by the continuation of the relationship itself. I do not see that such additional services are owed to parents by their grown children any more than they are owed to grown children by their parents, or to grown siblings by each other. All that is owed is the relationship itself. Thus, my view is more demanding than English's and less demanding than Sommers's. English seems to *require* essentially nothing, except what is defined by participation in a relationship of a certain kind, whereas I require participation in the relationship itself. Sommers requires whatever is specified by our social understandings of certain roles, whereas I want to reject certain common (although certainly not universally shared) understandings of what grown children owe their parents as unnecessarily burdensome. We do *not* owe our parents services that can easily be provided by others, such as basic physical care or financial support. I think it is a strength of my view that it identifies a plausible and livable middle ground between two untenable extremes.

OBJECTIONS AND REPLIES

Let me now clarify and further defend my view by considering a range of questions and objections that can be raised regarding it.

1. Can we really require people, morally, to be in a relationship when they do not want to? In part, this objection may be a restatement of the earlier question of whether the relationship itself has any real value in the absence of the unconditional love, which is the real good in question. My answer is the same as it was before: that there is some good in the relationship itself, especially if the parties to it make some real effort to cultivate the feelings that should accompany it. Of course, no one is out there enforcing this obligation. There can be laws mandating financial support of parents by children, laws that I would oppose, but no laws requiring children to visit their parents, or call them on their birthdays, let alone laws mandating love. However, I would say that there is an obligation here nonetheless: the obligation not to deny another a great good that one can supply at relatively modest cost to oneself. This obligation is supported by both prudential as well as moral reasons, for in providing this great good to another, I also provide it to myself.

2. What about dysfunctional, toxic families? What, if anything, do grown children owe parents, or parents owe grown children, or grown siblings owe each other, when the underlying relationship is seriously damaging to at least one of the individuals participating in it? Here, I would say two things. First, mutuality is an important part of the good of family relationships; it is what makes them *relationships* at all. It is hard, if not impossible, for me to have a relationship of a certain kind with you if you do not have a relationship of that kind with me. If a relationship is proving toxic, or too painful, it is fine to sever it; one is not required to sacrifice one's own personhood— one's identity, one's happiness, one's sanity—to provide some good for others, if one even *can* provide this good in such a setting. That said, second, it is worthwhile to try to mend and heal family relationships when possible, as much for one's own sake as for the sake of one's parents or siblings. Reconciliation and forgiveness are great goods in their own right, although, again, they can be purchased at too high a price. However, most people who reach out to parents, children, and siblings who have wronged them, I suspect, are not sorry for having done so.

3. Does my view give undue weight to biological ties? Does it just mask a fetish for the biological? Where, after all, do truly unchosen relationships come from, if not from our biological links to one another? Although I intend for my view to give equal consideration to adoptive and biological families, to families formed in both conventional and unconventional ways, we may have a clearer case of unchosen relationships in the standard, biological case. It is interesting that in one much discussed surrogacy case, when parties were disputing the custody of a child born with a serious disability, biological ties won out over contractual agreements: "when it was proved that the child was certainly biologically theirs, [the Stivers] accepted the child, named him Christopher Ray, and sought help for him" (ref. 8, p. 336). There may be some primacy given to the biological on my view, but I do not think it is excessive, or disturbing. It simply acknowledges, as Smith writes, that "in setting the boundaries of the composition of families, . . . in all times and places biology is central."

4. Along the same lines, does my view ignore or wrongly deny the extent to which families, at bottom, *are* chosen? As Minow argues, "family" as defined by law is hardly "natural or obvious" but reveals "the political, religious, and social choices embedded in that institution" (ref. 9, p. 250). Minow is, of course, correct that current family law reflects a long and sometimes confused series of societal choices regarding what should and should not be recognized as a family. However, I think that there is more disagreement at the margins than there is at the core. Moreover, even as Minow argues for an expansive definition of family membership, she argues for a stringent attitude toward family obligation. I read this as saying that although we may have some (fairly small degree of) choice regarding who counts as a family member, to recognize another as a family member is to recognize that one stands to another in a relationship where the concept of choice now ceases to apply.

5. This leads me to another, closely related question. Are family relationships indeed as "special" as I have said? Do not many of us have friends who are as close to us as our siblings, who become, in essence, "families of choice"? My answer here is yes, of course we can, but to treat friends as family is precisely to discard the idiom of "choice" in our interactions with them. A family by *choice,* I submit, is not a family at all. To have a friend who becomes a "sister" or a "brother" is to have a friend to whom one recognizes that one is irrevocably committed, committed come what may, from whom it would be inconceivable to walk away.

6. What if one has several brothers and sisters? Can one opt out of a continuing relationship with one's siblings then, or with one's parents, on the grounds that the great good of participating in an unchosen, unconditional relationship is available to them elsewhere? They do not need to be in such a relationship with *me;* they can enjoy it with *them.* In a very large family, family ties may be somewhat attenuated—this was Aristotle's objection to Plato's model of family relationships in *The Republic*—but, generally, it is a great good to have more than one such relationship in one's life. It is too much to expect any one relationship to provide the entire good avail-

able here. (Again, the good in question that I provide to another is equally, on my view, a good for me.) On a similar note, does my view establish obligations to participate in a continuing relationship not only with parents, children, and siblings, but with grandparents, aunts, uncles, cousins, second cousins twice removed? My answer here would be that this may well be so, depending on the particular configuration of the family. Some large, far-flung families have little interaction beyond the nuclear family, but, in others, such relationships may be an important part of one's participation in family life.

7. What does this view imply for relationships with aged parents who have become senile, who can no longer participate in an ongoing mutual relationship? One implication of my view, which some will view as welcome, some as unwelcome, is that the obligation to participate in an ongoing relationship continues only when the relationship itself remains possible. I do not have—cannot have—an obligation to be in a *relationship* with someone who cannot be in a relationship with me. It is one of the tragedies of senility that genuine relationships with other human beings are no longer possible. However, can't I continue to love, unconditionally, someone who is senile and manifest this love to him or her in various ways, even if he or she is not able to recognize it? Yes. Ideally, familial love continues through all alterations, but, again, the relationship that is in many ways the foundation of the love cannot. Heartless as it may seem to say this, I see little point in spending extensive time with someone who does not know me for who I am. To do so is to engage in a pretense that a relationship still continues that, tragically, is gone forever.

8. Do we generally have an obligation to provide others with a great good that they can get nowhere else? Can we generalize beyond the familial case to establish other obligations to provide others with goods of this sort—for example, to donate blood or bone marrow, if I have the only matching type? My answer here is "maybe." However, such cases will be very rare. My principle is not that I have an obligation to provide others with a great good that no one else *will* provide, but only with a great good that no one else *can* provide—if I can provide it at a relatively

modest cost to myself, and especially if I can provide it in a way that benefits me as well. In the family-relationship case, I benefit from benefiting you; we both gain equally from continuing in a mutual relationship with each other. In the bone marrow case, the benefit is almost completely one sided, which makes a difference to our assessment of the two cases.

9. This leads me to my final question. How far should we go in maintaining family relationships in our lives? How much do these relationships demand of us? This echoes our earlier discussion: How "close" a relationship is close enough? Here, we need to remember that although family relationships are a great good, in the view proposed here, they are not the only good that life offers to us, not by a long shot. The good of participating in an unchosen, unconditionally loving relationship needs to be balanced against the many other goods that make up a flourishing life: satisfying and meaningful work, spiritual growth, health and fitness, creative expression, and sheer fun. No mechanical guidelines can be offered here.

I have a friend who has done nothing of significance with her life for the past 10 years but take care of her completely senile and demented mother, including a daily battle over flossing her mother's few remaining teeth. I am fairly confident that this is too much—both because my friend has neglected every other good in her life and because her mother is no longer capable of engaging in a real relationship with her. She flosses her mother's teeth every day not as a daughter who has shared a long, complex, and enduring life with her mother, but as a total stranger. Most of us can also come up with cases where it seems that the relationship is valued and nurtured far too little—where months and years go by, without any effort at achieving a genuine connection. However, again, there is no simple algorithm that can give us all our answers here.

CONCLUSIONS

I have argued that family relationships are special in that they are, for the most part, unchosen and unconditional. Because it is a great good to participate in such relationships, one has prudential reasons to do so for the sake of oneself and moral reasons to do so for the sake of others; that is, one has some actual obligation to continue in family relationships. However, what one owes adult family members is only continuation in the relationship itself, and provision of the goods internal to that relationship, not any of a wide range of external goods that can be procured in other ways. Grown children, in my view, do not owe their parents financial support, or a home, or nursing services; they do owe them continuation in the relationship itself, insofar as the (nonsenile) parents are capable of participating in it, too. The great good they provide to their parents through doing this is a good that they equally provide to themselves.

REFERENCES

[1] English, J. (1979) "What Do Grown Children Owe Their Parents?" in *Having Children: Philosophical and Legal Reflections on Parenthood,* O'Neill, O. and Ruddick, W., eds., Oxford University Press, New York.

[2] Blustein, J. (1982) *Parents and Children: The Ethics of the Family,* Oxford University Press, New York.

[3] Sommers, C. H. (1986) "Filial morality." *J. Phil.* 83(8), 439–456.

[4] Minow, M. (1997) "All in the Family and in All Families: Membership, Loving, and Owing," in *Sex, Preference, and Family: Essays on Law and Nature,* Estlund, D. M. and Nussbaum, M. C., eds., Oxford University Press, New York.

[5] Donaldson, T. (1993) "Morally Privileged Relationships," in *Kindred Matters: Rethinking the Philosophy of the Family,* Meyers, D. T., et al., eds., Cornell University Press, Ithaca, NY.

[6] Williams, B. and Smart, J. J. C. (1973) "A Critique of Utilitarianism," in *Utilitarianism: For and Against,* Cambridge University Press, Cambridge.

[7] Haslett, D. W. (1986) "Is Inheritance Justified?" *Phil. Public Affairs* 15(2), 122–155.

[8] Alpern, K. D. (1992) "Parenting Through Contract When No One Wants the Child," in *The Ethics of Reproductive Technology,* Alpern, K. D., ed., Oxford University Press, New York.

[9] Smith, P. (1993) Family Responsibility and the Nature of Obligation, in *Kindred Matters: Rethinking the Philosophy of the Family,* Meyers, D. T., et al., eds., Cornell University Press, Ithaca, NY.

13

Is Licensing Parents Wrong?

LaFollette and His Critics

The thesis of Hugh LaFollette's widely discussed article "Licensing Parents" is as simple as it is shocking: Morally speaking, the State ought to require a license for someone to be a parent. LaFollette argues both that this claim is true in principle and that it can be implemented in a fair and workable manner in practice.

While LaFollette's thesis strikes most people as outrageous, the argument he offers in its defense is grounded in an assumption that most people are willing to accept: that there are many other cases of activities that people engage in, such as practicing medicine or driving an automobile, in which the State should require a license in order for people to engage in them. LaFollette's argument turns on the claim that if we are right in accepting the practice of licensing in such cases, then the best explanation of this practice (see section 4.3 in the Introduction for more on arguments from inference to the best explanation) must be that these activities have certain properties in common: They are potentially harmful to others; they require a certain amount of competence to be performed safely; and we have a reasonably reliable means of testing people for that competence. But, LaFollette adds, these things are all true of raising children as well: The harms caused by poor parenting are clear and sizeable, he maintains; some parents clearly seem to do a better job than others, he adds; and if we don't think we could figure out ahead of time who was more likely to be a competent parent, he asks, then why do we screen people ahead of time before we allow them to adopt children? The best explanation of why the State should require a license in order for someone to be a driver or a doctor (and of why the State should screen people ahead of time before allowing them to adopt children), therefore, also justifies the claim that the State should require a license for someone to be a mother or a father.

LaFollette's argument can be represented as follows:

P1 The State should require licenses for such activities as practicing medicine and driving an automobile.

P2 If the State should require licenses for such activities as practicing medicine and driving an automobile, then the State should require a license for engaging in any activity if (a) the activity is potentially harmful to others, (b) safe performance of the activity requires a certain competence, *and* (c) we have a moderately reliable procedure for determining that competence.

P3 The activity of parenting a child is such that (a) it is potentially harmful to others, (b) safe performance of it requires a certain competence, and (c) we have a moderately reliable procedure for determining that competence.

C   The State should require a license for parenting children.

It is not surprising that the proposal that the State license parents has generated a good deal of critical response. In the first response reprinted here, Lawrence E. Frisch raises two distinct objections to LaFollette's argument. The first can be construed as an argument against P2. While conceding that condition (a)–(c) of that premise do identify considerations relevant to regulatory licensing, Frisch denies that the conditions are jointly *sufficient* to justify such licensing. That is, even if a practice is such that it is potentially harmful and its safe performance requires a certain competence that can be determined in a moderately reliable manner, Frisch argues that licensing it will still not be justified unless a fourth condition is met: that licensing will actually succeed in significantly modifying the risk of harm inherent in the practice at issue. Since Frisch believes that this is not so in the case of parenting, this amounts to arguing that P2 as it stands is unsatisfactory and that modifying it so that it would be satisfactory—by adding a condition (d) to the effect that regulation would have a significant effect on the problem it aims to address—would render the argument as a whole unable to justify its conclusion. In addition to this objection, Frisch also raises a challenge to P3(c). Against LaFollette, Frisch argues that we do not possess even a moderately reliable procedure for determining which prospective parents are competent to be parents. If Frisch is correct about this, then the argument fails even if Frisch's objection to P2 can be overcome.

In the second critical reading, Pierre Lemieux presents a very different kind of objection to LaFollette's position, one that can best be understood as a slippery-slope argument: If we were to accept LaFollette's proposal, we would also have to accept a massive increase in the scope and power of government in all sorts of other areas. In particular, adopting the proposal to license parents would move society further in the direction of what Lemieux calls the "Sanitary State": away from the traditional limited-government model, in which the State serves only to protect our rights, and toward a much more paternalistic system, one in which the government attempts to satisfy our every want and desire. Lemieux argues there is no good reason to believe that a centralized authority can serve our interests better than a more open-market system. According to Lemieux, LaFollette's license system would ultimately do much more harm than good.

QUESTIONS FOR CONSIDERATION

In critically evaluating the debate between LaFollette and Frisch, readers should begin by getting clear about precisely where Frisch is attacking LaFollette's argument, and then consider ways in which a defender of LaFollette's position might attempt to reply to them.

• Why, for example, does Frisch think that licensing would not significantly reduce the risk of harm inherent in parenting? Could a defender of LaFollette come up with sufficiently specific examples of risky parenting behaviors that licensing could help to reduce? Could analogies with other widely accepted instances of licensing help LaFollette's position here or not?

• Why does Frisch deny that we could have an even moderately reliable means of determining which prospective parents were likely to be competent? Can LaFollette's focus on weeding out only the very bad parents (as opposed to selecting only the very good ones) help him to respond to this worry? Why or why not?

• Regarding LaFollette's analogy with the case of adoption; are the two cases sufficiently similar to help to support his claim, or are there differences between the two cases that are relevant? If so, what are those differences and how, specifically, would they undermine LaFollette's position?

• In critically assessing the objection that Lemieux aims at LaFollette's position, one should instead focus primarily on the slippery-slope argument that underlies his attack. Lemieux's argument turns on the claim that the licensing proposal would be a significant step in a more statist direction, and that this direction would itself be an undesirable one. One should therefore think about whether there are ways that LaFollette could respond to either of these claims. Is it true that following this proposal would lead to the kind of "Sanitary State" Lemieux finds so objectionable? Or would it be, as LaFollette seems to see it, merely a consistent application of the more traditional view that the State should protect the rights of its citizens (in this case, its young and newborn citizens)? Is what matters the intention behind the proposal or the practical consequences of adopting it? And if LaFollette were forced to concede that his proposal starts us down a slippery slope to a more paternalistic State, might he be able to deny that this counts as an objection to his proposal? How, for example, might he attempt to draw a line that would prevent us from reaching the kind of undesirable society Lemieux seems to fear? Or might he think that we should simply be willing to bite the bullet because the well-being of young children is of such vital importance?

FURTHER READING

LaFollette, Hugh. "A Reply to Frisch." *Philosophy and Public Affairs* 11, no. 2 (1982): 181–83.

Hugh LaFollette | Licensing Parents

In this essay I shall argue that the state should require all parents to be licensed. My main goal is to demonstrate that the licensing of parents is theoretically desirable, though I shall also argue that a workable and just licensing program actually could be established.

My strategy is simple. After developing the basic rationale for the licensing of parents, I shall consider several objections to the proposal and argue that these objections fail to undermine it. I shall then isolate some striking similarities between this licensing program and our present policies on the adoption of children. If we retain these adoption policies—as we surely should—then, I argue, a general licensing program should also be established. Finally, I shall briefly suggest that the reason many people object to licensing is that they think parents, particularly biological parents, own or have natural sovereignty over their children.

REGULATING POTENTIALLY HARMFUL ACTIVITIES

Our society normally regulates a certain range of activities; it is illegal to perform these activities unless one has received prior permission to do so. We require automobile operators to have licenses. We forbid people from practicing medicine, law, pharmacy, or psychiatry unless they have satisfied certain licensing requirements.

Society's decision to regulate just these activities is not ad hoc. The decision to restrict admission to certain vocations and to forbid some people from driving is based on an eminently plausible, though not often explicitly formulated, rationale. We require drivers to be licensed because driving an auto is an activity which is potentially harmful to others, safe performance of the activity requires a certain competence, and we have a moderately reliable procedure for determining that competence. The potential harm is obvious: incompetent drivers can and do maim and kill people. The best way we have of limiting this harm without sacrificing the benefits of automobile travel is to require that all drivers demonstrate at least minimal competence. We likewise license doctors, lawyers, and psychologists because they perform activities which can harm others. Obviously they must be proficient if they are to perform these activities properly, and we have moderately reliable procedures for determining proficiency.[1] Imagine a world in which everyone could legally drive a car, in which everyone could legally perform surgery, prescribe medications, dispense drugs, or offer legal advice. Such a world would hardly be desirable.

Consequently, any activity that is potentially harmful to others and requires certain demonstrated competence for its safe performance, is subject to regulation—that is, it is theoretically desirable that we regulate it. If we also have a reliable procedure for determining whether someone has the requisite competence, then the action is not only subject to regulation but ought, all things considered, to be regulated.

It is particularly significant that we license these hazardous activities, even though denying a license to someone can severely inconvenience and even harm that person. Furthermore, available competency tests are not 100 percent accurate. Denying someone a driver's license in our society, for example, would inconvenience that person acutely. In effect that person would be prohibited from working, shopping, or visiting in places reachable only by car. Similarly, people denied vocational licenses are inconvenienced, even devastated. We have all heard of individuals who had the "life-long dream" of becoming physicians or

Hugh Lafollette, "Licensing Parents," *Philosophy and Public Affairs* 9, no. 2 (1980): 182–97. Reprinted by permission of Princeton University Press.

lawyers, yet were denied that dream. However, the realization that some people are disappointed or inconvenienced does not diminish our conviction that we must regulate occupations or activities that are potentially dangerous to others. Innocent people must be protected even if it means that others cannot pursue activities they deem highly desirable.

Furthermore, we maintain licensing procedures even though our competency tests are sometimes inaccurate. Some people competent to perform the licensed activity (for example, driving a car) will be unable to demonstrate competence (they freeze up on the driver's test). Others may be incompetent, yet pass the test (they are lucky or certain aspects of competence—for example, the sense of responsibility—are not tested). We recognize clearly—or should recognize clearly—that no test will pick out all and only competent drivers, physicians, lawyers, and so on. Mistakes are inevitable. This does not mean we should forget that innocent people may be harmed by faulty regulatory procedures. In fact, if the procedures are sufficiently faulty, we should cease regulating that activity entirely until more reliable tests are available. I only want to emphasize here that tests need not be perfect. Where moderately reliable tests are available, licensing procedures should be used to protect innocent people from incompetents.[2]

These general criteria for regulatory licensing can certainly be applied to parents. First, parenting is an activity potentially very harmful to children. The potential for harm is apparent: each year more than half a million children are physically abused or neglected by their parents.[3] Many millions more are psychologically abused or neglected—not given love, respect, or a sense of self-worth. The results of this maltreatment are obvious. Abused children bear the physical and psychological scars of maltreatment throughout their lives. Far too often they turn to crime.[4] They are far more likely than others to abuse their own children.[5] Even if these maltreated children never harm anyone, they will probably never be well-adjusted, happy adults. Therefore, parenting clearly satisfies the first criterion of activities subject to regulation.

The second criterion is also incontestably satisfied. A parent must be competent if he is to avoid harming his children; even greater competence is required if he is to do the "job" well. But not everyone has this minimal competence. Many people lack the knowledge needed to rear children adequately. Many others lack the requisite energy, temperament, or stability. Therefore, child-rearing manifestly satisfies both criteria of activities subject to regulation. In fact, I dare say that parenting is a paradigm of such activities since the potential for harm is so great (both in the extent of harm any one person can suffer and in the number of people potentially harmed) and the need for competence is so evident. Consequently, there is good reason to believe that all parents should be licensed. The only ways to avoid this conclusion are to deny the need for licensing *any* potentially harmful activity; to deny that I have identified the standard criteria of activities which should be regulated; to deny that parenting satisfies the standard criteria; to show that even though parenting satisfies the standard criteria there are special reasons why licensing parents is not theoretically desirable; or to show that there is no reliable and just procedure for implementing this program.

While developing my argument for licensing I have already identified the standard criteria for activities that should be regulated, and I have shown that they can properly be applied to parenting. One could deny the legitimacy of regulation by licensing, but in doing so one would condemn not only the regulation of parenting, but also the regulation of drivers, physicians, druggists, and doctors. Furthermore, regulation of hazardous activities appears to be a fundamental task of any stable society.

Thus only two objections remain. In the next section I shall see if there are any special reasons why licensing parents is not theoretically desirable. Then, in the following section, I shall examine several practical objections designed to demonstrate that even if licensing were theoretically desirable, it could not be justly implemented.

THEORETICAL OBJECTIONS TO LICENSING

Licensing is unacceptable, someone might say, since people have a right to have children, just as they have rights to free speech and free religious expression. They do not need a license to speak freely or to worship as they wish. Why? Because they have a right to engage in these activities. Similarly, since people have a right to have children, any attempt to license parents would be unjust.

This is an important objection since many people find it plausible, if not self-evident. However, it is not as convincing as it appears. The specific rights appealed to in this analogy are not without limitations. Both slander and human sacrifice are prohibited by law; both could result from the unrestricted exercise of freedom of speech and freedom of religion. Thus, even if people have these rights, they may sometimes be limited in order to protect innocent people. Consequently, even if people had a right to have children, that right might also be limited in order to protect innocent people, in this case children. Secondly, the phrase "right to have children" is ambiguous; hence, it is important to isolate its most plausible meaning in this context. Two possible interpretations are not credible and can be dismissed summarily. It is implausible to claim either that infertile people have rights to be *given* children or that people have rights to intentionally create children biologically without incurring any subsequent responsibility to them.

A third interpretation, however, is more plausible, particularly when coupled with observations about the degree of intrusion into one's life that the licensing scheme represents. On this interpretation people have a right to rear children if they make good-faith efforts to rear procreated children the best way they see fit. One might defend this claim on the ground that licensing would require too much intrusion into the lives of sincere applicants.

Undoubtedly one should be wary of unnecessary governmental intervention into individuals' lives. In this case, though, the intrusion would not often be substantial, and when it is, it would be warranted. Those granted licenses would face merely minor intervention; only those denied licenses would encounter marked intrusion. This encroachment, however, is a necessary side-effect of licensing parents—just as it is for automobile and vocational

licensing. In addition, as I shall argue in more detail later, the degree of intrusion arising from a general licensing program would be no more than, and probably less than, the present (and presumably justifiable) encroachment into the lives of people who apply to adopt children. Furthermore, since some people hold unacceptable views about what is best for children (they think children should be abused regularly), people do not automatically have rights to rear children just because they will rear them in a way they deem appropriate.[6]

Consequently, we come to a somewhat weaker interpretation of this right claim: a person has a right to rear children if he meets certain minimal standards of child rearing. Parents must not abuse or neglect their children and must also provide for the basic needs of the children. This claim of right is certainly more credible than the previously canvassed alternatives, though some people might still reject this claim in situations where exercise of the right would lead to negative consequences, for example, to overpopulation. More to the point, though, this conditional right is compatible with licensing. On this interpretation one has a right to have children only if one is not going to abuse or neglect them. Of course the very purpose if licensing is just to determing whether people *are* going to abuse or neglect their children. If the determination is made that someone will maltreat children, then that person is subject to the limitations of the right to have children and can legitimately be denied a parenting license.

In fact, this conditional way of formulating the right to have children provides a model for formulating all alleged rights to engage in hazardous activities. Consider, for example, the right to drive a car. People do not have an unconditional right to drive, although they do have a right to drive if they are competent. Similarly, people do not have an unconditional right to practice medicine; they have a right only if they are demonstrably competent. Hence, denying a driver's or physician's license to someone who has not demonstrated the requisite competence does not deny that person's rights. Likewise, on this model, denying a parenting license to someone who is not competent does not violate that person's rights.

Of course someone might object that the right is conditional on actually being a person who will abuse or neglect children, whereas my proposal only picks out those we can reasonably predict will abuse children. Hence, this conditional right *would* be incompatible with licensing.

There are two ways to interpret this objection and it is important to distinguish these divergent formulations. First, the objection could be a way of questioning our ability to predict reasonably and accurately whether people would maltreat their own children. This is an important practical objection, but I will defer discussion of it until the next section. Second, this objection could be a way of expressing doubt about the moral propriety of the prior restraint licensing requires. A parental licensing program would deny licenses to applicants judged to be incompetent even though they had never maltreated any children. This practice would be in tension with our normal skepticism about the propriety of prior restraint.

Despite this healthy skepticism, we do sometimes use prior restraint. In extreme circumstances we may hospitalize or imprison people judged insane, even though they are not legally guilty of any crime, simply because we predict they are likely to harm others. More typically, though, prior restraint is used only if the restriction is not terribly onerous and the restricted activity is one which could lead easily to serious harm. Most types of licensing (for example, those for doctors, drivers, and druggists) fall into this latter category. They require prior restraint to prevent serious harm, and generally the restraint is minor— though it is important to remember that some individuals will find it oppressive. The same is true of parental licensing. The purpose of licensing is to prevent serious harm to children. Moreover, the prior restraint required by licensing would not be terribly onerous for many people. Certainly the restraint would be far less extensive than the presumably justifiable prior restraint of, say, insane criminals. Criminals preventively detained and mentally ill people forceably hospitalized are denied most basic liberties, while those denied parental licenses would be denied only that one specific opportunity. They could still vote, work for political candidates, speak on con-

troversial topics, and so on. Doubtless some individuals would find the restraint onerous. But when compared to other types of restraint currently practiced, and when judged in light of the severity of harm maltreated children suffer, the restraint appears *relatively* minor.

Furthermore, we could make certain, as we do with most licensing programs, that individuals denied licenses are given the opportunity to reapply easily and repeatedly for a license. Thus, many people correctly denied licenses (because they are incompetent) would choose (perhaps it would be provided) to take counseling or therapy to improve their chances of passing the next test. On the other hand, most of those mistakenly denied licenses would probably be able to demonstrate in a later test that they would be competent parents.

Consequently, even though one needs to be wary of prior restraint, if the potential for harm is great and the restraint is minor relative to the harm we are trying to prevent—as it would be with parental licensing—then such restraint is justified. This objection, like all the theoretical objections reviewed, has failed.

PRACTICAL OBJECTIONS TO LICENSING

I shall now consider five practical objections to licensing. Each objection focuses on the problems or difficulties of implementing this proposal. According to these objections, licensing is (or may be) theoretically desirable; nevertheless, it cannot be efficiently and justly implemented.

The first objection is that there may not be, or we may not be able to discover, adequate criteria of "a good parent." We simply do not have the knowledge, and it is unlikely that we could ever obtain the knowledge, that would enable us to distinguish adequate from inadequate parents.

Clearly there is some force to this objection. It is highly improbable that we can formulate criteria that would distinguish precisely between good and less than good parents. There is too much we do not know about child development and adult psychology. My proposal, however, does not demand that we make these fine distinctions. It does not demand that we license only the best parents; rather it is designed to exclude only the very bad ones.[7] This is not just a semantic difference, but a substantive one. Although we do not have infallible criteria for picking out good parents, we undoubtedly can identify bad ones—those who will abuse or neglect their children. Even though we could have a lively debate about the range of freedom a child should be given or the appropriateness of corporal punishment, we do not wonder if a parent who severely beats or neglects a child is adequate. We know that person isn't. Consequently, we do have reliable and useable criteria for determining who is a bad parent; we have the criteria necessary to make a licensing program work.

The second practical objection to licensing is that there is no reliable way to predict who will maltreat their children. Without an accurate predictive test, licensing would be not only unjust, but also a waste of time. Now I recognize that as a philosopher (and not a psychologist, sociologist, or social worker), I am on shaky ground if I make sweeping claims about the present or future abilities of professionals to produce such predictive tests. Nevertheless, there are some relevant observations I can offer.

Initially, we need to be certain that the demands on predictive tests are not unreasonable. For example, it would be improper to require that tests be 100 percent accurate. Procedures for licensing drivers, physicians, lawyers, druggists, etc., plainly are not 100 percent (or anywhere near 100 percent) accurate. Presumably we recognize these deficiencies yet embrace the procedures anyway. Consequently, it would be imprudent to demand considerably more exacting standards for the tests used in licensing parents.

In addition, from what I can piece together, the practical possibilities for constructing a reliable predictive test are not all that gloomy. Since my proposal does not require that we make fine line distinctions between good and less than good parents, but rather that we weed out those who are potentially very bad, we can use existing tests that claim to isolate relevant predictive characteristics—whether a person is violence-prone, easily frustrated, or unduly self-centered. In fact, researchers at Nashville Gen-

eral Hospital have developed a brief interview questionnaire which seems to have significant predictive value. Based on their data, the researchers identified 20 percent of the interviewees as a "risk group"—those having great potential for serious problems. After one year they found "the incidence of major breakdown in parent-child interaction in the risk group was approximately four to five times as great as in the low risk group."[8] We also know that parents who maltreat children often have certain identifiable experiences, for example, most of them were themselves maltreated as children. Consequently, if we combined our information about these parents with certain psychological test results, we would probably be able to predict with reasonable accuracy which people will maltreat their children.

However, my point is not to argue about the precise reliability of present tests. I cannot say emphatically that we now have accurate predictive tests. Nevertheless, even if such tests are not available, we could undoubtedly develop them. For example, we could begin a longitudinal study in which all potential parents would be required to take a specified battery of tests. Then these parents could be "followed" to discover which ones abused or neglected their children. By correlating test scores with information on maltreatment, a usable, accurate test could be fashioned. Therefore, I do not think that the present unavailability of such tests (if they are unavailable) would count against the legitimacy of licensing parents.

The third practical objection is that even if a reliable test for ascertaining who would be an acceptable parent were available, administrators would unintentionally misuse that test. These unintentional mistakes would clearly harm innocent individuals. Therefore, so the argument goes, this proposal ought to be scrapped. This objection can be dispensed with fairly easily unless one assumes there is some special reason to believe that more mistakes will be made in administering parenting licenses than in other regulatory activities. No matter how reliable our proceedings are, there will always be mistakes. We may license a physician who, through incompetence, would cause the death of a patient; or we may mistakenly deny a physician's license to someone who would be competent. But the fact that mistakes are made does not and should not lead us to abandon attempts to determine competence. The harm done in these cases could be far worse than the harm of mistakenly denying a person a parenting license. As far as I can tell, there is no reason to believe that more mistakes will be made here than elsewhere.

The fourth proposed practical objection claims that any testing procedure will be intentionally abused. People administering the process will disqualify people they dislike, or people who espouse views they dislike, from rearing children.

The response to this objection is parallel to the response to the previous objection, namely, that there is no reason to believe that the licensing of parents is more likely to be abused than driver's license tests or other regulatory procedures. In addition, individuals can be protected from prejudicial treatment by pursuing appeals available to them. Since the licensing test can be taken on numerous occasions, the likelihood of the applicant's working with different administrative personnel increases and therefore the likelihood decreases that intentional abuse could ultimately stop a qualified person from rearing children. Consequently, since the probability of such abuse is not more than, and may even be less than, the intentional abuse of judicial and other regulatory authority, this objection does not give us any reason to reject the licensing of parents.

The fifth objection is that we could never adequately, reasonably, and fairly enforce such a program. That is, even if we could establish a reasonable and fair way of determining which people would be inadequate parents, it would be difficult, if not impossible, to enforce the program. How would one deal with violators and what could we do with babies so conceived? There are difficult problems here, no doubt, but they are not insurmountable. We might not punish parents at all—we might just remove the children and put them up for adoption. However, even if we are presently uncertain about the precise way to establish a just and effective form of enforcement, I do not see why this should undermine my licensing proposal. If it is important enough to protect children from being maltreated by parents, then surely a reasonable enforcement procedure can be secured. At

least we should assume one can be unless someone shows that it cannot.

AN ANALOGY WITH ADOPTION

So far I have argued that parents should be licensed. Undoubtedly many readers find this claim extremely radical. It is revealing to notice, however, that this program is not as radical as it seems. Our moral and legal systems already recognize that not everyone is capable of rearing children well. In fact, well-entrenched laws require adoptive parents to be investigated—in much the same ways and for much the same reasons as in the general licensing program advocated here. For example, we do not allow just anyone to adopt a child; nor do we let someone adopt without first estimating the likelihood of the person's being a good parent. In fact, the adoptive process is far more rigorous than the general licensing procedures I envision. Prior to adoption the candidates must first formally apply to adopt a child. The applicants are then subjected to an exacting home study to determine whether they really want to have children and whether they are capable of caring for and rearing them adequately. No one is allowed to adopt a child until the administrators can reasonably predict that the person will be an adequate parent. The results of these procedures are impressive. Despite the trauma children often face before they are finally adopted, they are five times less likely to be abused than children reared by their biological parents.[9]

Nevertheless we recognize, or should recognize, that these demanding procedures exclude some people who would be adequate parents. The selection criteria may be inadequate; the testing procedures may be somewhat unreliable. We may make mistakes. Probably there is some intentional abuse of the system. Adoption procedures intrude directly in the applicants' lives. Yet we continue the present adoption policies because we think it better to mistakenly deny some people the opportunity to adopt than to let just anyone adopt.

Once these features of our adoption policies are clearly identified, it becomes quite apparent that there are striking parallels between the general licensing program I have advocated and our present adoption system. Both programs have the same aim—protecting children. Both have the same drawbacks and are subject to the same abuses. The only obvious dissimilarity is that the adoption requirements are *more* rigorous than those proposed for the general licensing program. Consequently, if we think it is so important to protect adopted children, even though people who want to adopt are less likely than biological parents to maltreat their children, then we should likewise afford the same protection to children reared by their biological parents.

I suspect, though, that many people will think the cases are not analogous. The cases are relevantly different, someone might retort, because biological parents have a natural affection for their children and the strength of this affection makes it unlikely that parents would maltreat their biologically produced children.

Even if it were generally true that parents have special natural affections for their biological offspring, that does not mean that all parents have enough affection to keep them from maltreating their children. This should be apparent given the number of children abused each year by their biological parents. Therefore, even if there is generally such a bond, that does not explain why we should not have licensing procedures to protect children of parents who do not have a sufficiently strong bond. Consequently, if we continue our practice of regulating the adoption of children, and certainly we should, we are rationally compelled to establish a licensing program for all parents.

However, I am not wedded to a strict form of licensing. It may well be that there are alternative ways of regulating parents which would achieve the desired results—the protection of children—without strictly prohibiting nonlicensed people from rearing children. For example, a system of tax incentives for licensed parents, and protective services scrutiny of nonlicensed parents, might adequately protect children. If it would, I would endorse the less drastic measure. My principal concern is to protect children from maltreatment by parents. I begin by advocating the more strict form of licensing since that is the standard method of regulating hazardous activities.

I have argued that all parents should be licensed by the state. This licensing program is attractive, not because state intrusion is inherently judicious and efficacious, but simply because it seems to be the best way to prevent children from being reared by incompetent parents. Nonetheless, even after considering the previous arguments, many people will find the proposal a useless academic exercise, probably silly, and possibly even morally perverse. But why? Why do most of us find this proposal unpalatable, particularly when the arguments supporting it are good and the objections to it are philosophically flimsy?

I suspect the answer is found in a long-held, deeply ingrained attitude toward children, repeatedly reaffirmed in recent court decisions, and present, at least to some degree, in almost all of us. The belief is that parents own, or at least have natural sovereignty over, their children.[10] It does not matter precisely how this belief is described, since on both views parents legitimately exercise extensive and virtually unlimited control over their children. Others can properly interfere with or criticize parental decisions only in unusual and tightly prescribed circumstances—for example, when parents severely and repeatedly abuse their children. In all other cases, the parents reign supreme.

This belief is abhorrent and needs to be supplanted with a more child-centered view. Why? Briefly put, this attitude has adverse effects on children and on the adults these children will become. Parents who hold this view may well maltreat their children. If these parents happen to treat their children well, it is only because they want to, not because they think their children deserve or have a right to good treatment. Moreover, this belief is manifestly at odds with the conviction that parents should prepare children for life as adults. Children subject to parents who perceive children in this way are likely to be adequately prepared for adulthood. Hence, to prepare children for life as adults and to protect them from maltreatment, this attitude toward children must be dislodged. As I have argued, licensing is a viable way to protect children. Furthermore, it would increase the likelihood that more children will be adequately prepared for life as adults than is now the case.

NOTES

1. "When practice of a profession or calling requires special knowledge or skill and intimately affects public health, morals, order or safety, or general welfare, legislature may prescribe reasonable qualifications for persons desiring to pursue such professions or calling and require them to demonstrate possession of such qualifications by examination on subjects with which such profession or calling has to deal as a condition precedent to right to follow that profession or calling." 50 SE 2nd 735 (1949). Also see 199 US 306, 318 (1905) and 123 US 623, 661 (1887).

2. What counts as a moderately reliable test for these purposes will vary from circumstance to circumstance. For example, if the activity could cause a relatively small amount of harm, yet regulating that activity would place extensive constraints on people regulated, then any tests should be extremely accurate. On the other hand, if the activity could be exceedingly harmful but the constraints on the regulated person are minor, then the test can be considerably less reliable.

3. The statistics on the incidence of child abuse vary. Probably the most recent detailed study (Saad Nagi, *Child Maltreatment in the United States,* Columbia University Press, 1977) suggests that between 400,000 and 1,000,000 children are abused or neglected each year. Other experts claim the incidence is considerably higher.

4. According to the National Committee for the Prevention of Child Abuse, more than 80 percent of incarcerated criminals were, as children, abused by their parents. In addition, a study in the *Journal of the American Medical Association* 168, no. 3: 1755–1758, reported that first-degree murderers from middle-class homes and who have "no history of addiction to drugs, alcoholism, organic disease of the brain, or epilepsy" were frequently found to have been subject to "remorseless physical brutality at the hands of the parents."

5. "A review of the literature points out that abusive parents were raised in the same style that they have recreated in the pattern of rearing children. . . . An individual who was raised by parents who used physical force to train their children and who grew up in a violent household has had as a role model the use of force and violence as a means of family problem solving." R. J. Gelles, "Child Abuse as Psychopathology—a Sociological Critique and Reformulations," *American Journal of Orthopsychiatry* 43, no. 4 (1973): 618–19.

6. Some people might question if any parents actually believe they should beat their children. However, that does appear to be the sincere view of many abusing parents.

See, for example, case descriptions in *A Silent Tragedy* by Peter and Judith DeCourcy (Sherman Oaks, CA.: Alfred Publishing Co., 1973).

7. I suppose I might be for licensing only good parents if I knew there were reasonable criteria and some plausible way of deciding if a potential parent satisfied these criteria. However, since I don't think we have those criteria or that method, nor can I seriously envision that we will discover those criteria and that method, I haven't seriously entertained the stronger proposal.

8. The research gathered by Altemeir was reported by Ray Helfer in "Review of the Concepts and a Sampling of the Research Relating to Screening for the Potential to Abuse and/or Neglect One's Child." Helfer's paper was presented at a workshop sponsored by the National Committee for the Prevention of Child Abuse, 3–6 December 1978.

9. According to a study published by the Child Welfare League of America, at least 51 percent of the adopted children had suffered, prior to adoption, more than minimal emotional deprivation. See A *Follow-up Study of Adoptions: Post Placement Functioning of Adoption Families,* Elizabeth A. Lawder et al., New York 1969.

According to a study by David Gil (*Violence Against Children,* Cambridge: Harvard University Press, 1970) only .4 percent of abused children were abused by adoptive parents. Since at least 2 percent of the children in the United States are adopted (*Encyclopedia of Social Work,* National Association of Social Workers, New York, 1977), that means the rate of abuse by biological parents is five time that of adoptive parents.

10. We can see this belief in a court case chronicled by DeCourcy and DeCourcy in *A Silent Tragedy.* The judge ruled that three children, severely and regularly beaten, burned, and cut by their father, should be placed back with their father since he was only "trying to do what is right." If the court did not adopt this belief would it even be tempted to so excuse such abusive behavior? This attitude also emerges in the all-too-frequent court rulings (see S. Katz, *When Parents Fail,* Boston: Beacon Press, 1971) giving custody of children back to their biological parents even though the parents had abandoned them for years, and even though the children expressed a strong desire to stay with foster parents.

In "The Child, the Law, and the State" (*Children's Rights: Toward the Liberation of the Child,* Leila Berg et al., New York: Praeger Publishers, 1971), Nan Berger persuasively argues that our adoption and foster care laws are comprehensible only if children are regarded as the property of their parents.

Critics

Lawrence E. Frisch

On Licentious Licensing

A Reply to Hugh LaFollette

In his essay "Licensing Parents," Hugh LaFollette fails to make a convincing case in large part because he assumes, without stating or proving, that licensing of parents and parenting is analogous to other societal licensing.[1] He comes close to stating this premise in suggesting that "one could deny the legitimacy of regulation by licensing, but in doing so one would condemn not only the regulation of parenting, but also the regulation of drivers, physicians, druggists, and doctors." Regulation of hazardous activities is indeed "a fundamental task of any stable society," and LaFollette has made a convincing case that parenting is an activity of potential hazard. But hazards may differ significantly in their accessibility to regulatory control, and parenting practices present hazards that cannot be significantly modified by current licensing techniques.

Societies undertake licensing, I believe, because there is reason to expect that the licensing process will exert some control over specific risks. These risks may be usefully divided into the following four categories:

1. Risks arising out of ignorance.
2. Risks arising through physical or mental incapacity.
3. Risks arising from willful misconduct.
4. Risks arising through negligence or inability to exert self-control over behavior.

LICENSING AND IGNORANCE

The assessment of knowledge plays a major role in most licensing procedures, and it is reasonable to assume that imposition of this form of licensing protects society against errors committed through ignorance. With licensed drivers on the roads we can anticipate fewer accidents caused by incorrect turns into one-way streets, and with licensed doctors in the operating theater we can reasonably anticipate fewer kidneys inadvertently removed at gallbladder operations. What could we expect if such an assessment were correspondingly extended to parents?

First, and most laudably, we would anticipate the thorough development of a body of parenting knowledge, the training of appropriate teachers of parenting skills, the promulgation of recognized parenting curricula, and certification for mastery of this knowledge. Second, we could hope for a change in prospective parents' appreciation of the difficulties of good and safe parenting. Some might learn enough about children's needs to decide to defer childrearing until they are ready to meet its challenge. However, there is no empirical reason to believe that making *knowledge of parenting* a prime criterion for licensing would reduce the incidence of child abuse, and such a practice risks denying licensure to potentially excellent parents possessing superior intuitive skills but lacking knowledge of "what the book says" concerning child behavior or development.[2]

PHYSICAL OR MENTAL INCAPACITY

Obviously, licensing procedures should exclude persons whose inherent incapacities make them unsafe practitioners of the activity we are licensing. For example, most states require a vision evaluation and

Lawrence E. Frisch, "On Licentious Licensing: A Reply to Hugh LaFollette," *Philosophy and Public Affairs* 11, no. 2 (1982): 173–80. Reprinted by permission of Princeton University Press.

disqualify from licensure a driver whose visual handicap cannot be optically corrected. If we were to pattern a parenting examination after driver's test, we might require a normative degree of vision, hearing, literacy, and physical mobility. Where impairments were severe we might license only with restrictions—for example, a deaf parent could care for an infant only if flashing lights were provided to alert the parent to the baby's crying.

I have no doubt that parental licensing procedures involving an assessment of physical and mental capacity would have some effect on the incidence of child abuse and neglect. However, we believe that it would be a minimal one because of the relatively small contribution made to child maltreatment by parents with physical and mental disabilities. Some handicapped, retarded, or mentally ill parents do abuse or neglect their children, but many manage to rear children at or above the minimum community standard.

WILLFUL MISCONDUCT

I take willful misconduct to mean purposive violations of accepted modes of behavior or performance in which there is no reason to doubt the wrongdoer's ability to act in accord with reasonable and accepted standards. No licensing procedure with which we are familiar would purposefully license persons who habitually engage in willful misconduct. Unfortunately, most persons do not blatantly announce their intention to violate those standards when applying for licensure and hence may be licensed without these intentions being considered. Just as current licensing of drivers and doctors stipulates forfeiture for wrongdoing, present child-care laws already allow for removal of maltreated children from a harmful environment. Thus licensing parents to prevent willful maltreatment even if it could succeed in this end, offers no *new* protection to abused children.

NEGLIGENT OR UNCONTROLLABLE BEHAVIOR

Many, if not most, traffic violations and mishaps occur because the driver is distracted, preoccupied, or under the influence of alcohol. They result from negligence rather than purposive wrongdoing. I suspect that most cases of child abuse and neglect fall into this category, particularly if we include in it those cases in which a parent, meaning to punish a child, loses control and in anger inflicts serious injury. Social and economic stresses may play an often unanticipated role. It is difficult to imagine a testing situation which duplicates that, for example, of a mother whose husband has just left her and whose baby, after two days of constant crying due to illness, refuses to go to sleep. Licensing has no traditional interest in determining how examinees react under extraordinary stress—other than that of the examination itself—and LaFollette has made no clear argument for striking out in new licensing directions for parents alone.

Licensing as currently practiced cannot, I submit, prevent either willful child maltreatment or maltreatment having its origins in parental behavior beyond ready control. This means quite simply that licensing, despite laudable intentions, cannot prevent most cases of child abuse and neglect.

LAFOLLETTE'S VIEW OF LICENSING

LaFollette is anxious to make sure that parents are competent, just as he is to make sure that his doctor and the driver in the oncoming car are safely capable. He rightly recognizes that we are at risk from incompetent drivers and doctors and, consequently, license their activities. In a leap, or perhaps a lapse, of logic, LaFollette peremptorily concludes that "the very purpose of licensing is just to determine whether people *are* going to abuse or neglect their children." Thus, without warning, he appears to have shifted the focus of licensing from its traditional purpose of assessing knowledge to the realm of predicting future behavior and confronting issues of negligence and misconduct—areas in which licensing has no historical interest.[3] Clearly, if we can accurately predict that someone will actually abuse a child we can usefully deny a parenting license to that person. There are many other matters in which such divine foreknowledge would be useful, but lacking divinity, we must rely on other methods. LaFollette falls back on statistics. He envisions tests capable of predicting future abusive behavior, while asking us to forgo our own serious doubts about sociologists' ability to prognosticate, because "even if such tests are not available we could undoubtedly develop them." Unlicensable parents can only be "identified" prior to an abusive incident by their mathematical resemblance on psychological or sociological scales to who, at the time the scales were validated, were thought to be guilty of maltreating their children. This is a most unusual approach to licensing, which he justifies by appealing to analogy with traditional licensing procedures. However, it is just wrong to imply that "the very purpose" of, for example, licensing drivers, is to predict which people will have an accident or violate the law. Licensing procedures, as currently employed, are designed to audit present performance, not to predict future practice.

As LaFollette suggests, his statistical prediction paradigm does "provide a model for formulating all alleged rights to engage in hazardous activities." We could (and perhaps should) try to deny driver's licenses to people who statistically resemble past or current violators. This might result in safer roads (if only because there would be fewer licensees), but it is emphatically not current licensing practice. We cannot exclude a class of potential child maltreaters from parenthood without invoking a new and untested theory of predictive licensure. For example, a recent survey of practicing women psychiatrists has revealed that 73 percent of them suffer from significant mental depression at some point during their working careers. If we believe (or could demonstrate) that a depressed psychiatrist potentially lacks judgment or empathy, would we be justified in refusing to license women to practice psychiatry? We could perhaps add other tests to improve predictive ability to, say, 90 percent, but no matter what numbers we supply, our current licensing procedures do not take such predictive measures into consideration in granting or denying the right to practice hazardous activities. Nor should they. As Davis wrote recently in a different context, "this utilitarian mentality, if pushed to its consistent extreme, would

require the identification and confinement of people who seemed to pose a high risk of criminal behavior soon after birth."[4]

PRACTICAL ISSUES

Fundamental to LaFollette's licensing scheme is the presumption that we will be able to predict future abusive behavior. "From what I can piece together," he says, "the practical possibilities for constructing a reliable predictive test are not all that gloomy." The world in which we and our children live is so gloomy that admittedly the least glimmer of light looks positively cheerful. However, it does nothing more than constitute assurance. Even if we accept LaFollette's optimism, there remain a number of practical obstacles which seem virtually insurmountable.

What, for instance, do we do about a situation in which one parent passes the licensing test but the other does not? What if testing shows that a given mother is an adequate parent (licensable) unless she lives with a man who abuses her—and then she moves in with such a man? What if she does this after a child is born? Is the child removed forthwith or only after abuse actually occurs? Should licensing examinations be repeated at intervals, or does a single passing score forever qualify one as a parent? By not retesting we would be ignoring the effect that mounting stresses have on people's abilities to cope. However, if we retest, we run the risk of delicensing parents who have never abused or neglected their children. Such a procedure, if it resulted in child removal, would have all the faults of our current foster-care system (multiple home placements for often arbitrary reasons), but might also place loved and wanted children who have never been abused because their parents were ill or ill-humored on their retest days. Accumulating evidence shows that not all children are alike in temperament; in the simplest terms some are "easy" and some are "difficult." It is plausible that some parents could safely care for an easy child but would be likely to abuse a difficult one. Do we remove a difficult child at six months of age because, no matter how they are actually getting on with him, his parents are licensed only to bring up an easy child?

LaFollette has presented us with a cleverly written and provocative argument which fails theoretically. He has mistakenly construed current licensing procedures for other social goods and has proposed licensing parents based on predictions of future behavior. By confusing competence (in the sense used in examining drivers or doctors and pronouncing them fit to license) with good judgment and acceptable response to stressful situations (qualities we at best consider only indirectly in our present licensing procedures), he is suggesting a licensing of parents which goes beyond forms of licensing that society conventionally employs. Furthermore, he appears to be far too sanguine about the practical difficulties such licensing would pose, relying on a naive faith in the ability of sociological technology to succeed against any obstacle if licensing is adopted.

However, the issue LaFollette raises is not silly even if the arguments he advances to support it (as he himself implies) may be. Should we license parents? Something about the question tells us it is an interesting one to ask, and no one has previously asked it with such good-natured verve.[5] "Parenting," he tells us "is an activity potentially very harmful to children . . . abused children bear the physical and psychological scars of maltreatment throughout their lives . . . even if these maltreated children never harm anyone, they will probably never be well-adjusted, happy adults." The freshness (some would say naivete) of LaFollette's approach is that he bases his argument on an implicit human right to be "well-adjusted and happy" as an adult, and he wants to give children claim on that right for their future.

Unlike LaFollette, most child abuse literature does not ask, How can we bring up the best and happiest children? Perhaps in posing this question he should have moved his argument one step further from the conventional and suggested, not that we license parents, but that we closely monitor the performance of families. When an examiner gives a practical driving test, he or she is observing not so much what the driver does, but how the car performs. The driver may be docked for failing to look

both ways at an intersection, but most demerits are given for crossing yellow lines, exceeding speed limits, parking ineptly, and failing to stop for school buses. Similarly, if our goal is successful childrearing, perhaps we would do better not to focus on parents, but to look at how their children are developing from early childhood. We could then offer services if deviations in behavior or development are observed, and remove children from their homes not just (or perhaps not at all) because they have been abused, but because their development is faltering despite offered services. Such an approach would not focus on determining whether parents are fit to raise children in general, but only on whether a given child is being raised to a defined community standard in the family in which he or she is living. If we adopted this approach, and like LaFollette's proposal, it is far from modest, our focus could be on promoting the child's development into a "well-adjusted" and fully realized adult.

The practical problems with monitoring families in this way are very great, the likelihood that social agencies can truly improve unsatisfactory families is not very high, and the idea represents an extraordinary and probably unconstitutional intrusion into family privacy. However, if we believe that childbearing is a privilege (or at least a highly qualifiable right) and that children have the claim right to "well-adjusted" adulthood, such family surveillance may offer an alternative rather more reasonable than licensing.

NOTES

1. "Licensing Parents," *Philosophy & Public Affairs,* 9, no. 2 (Winter 1980): 182–97.

2. This observation was made, en passant, in what remains the most comprehensive psychological study of abusive parenting. The authors conducted extended interviews with sixty families and concluded that "the central issue involved (in child maltreatment) concerns a breakdown in . . . 'mothering'—a disruption of the maternal affectional system." Lack of parenting knowledge was not a factor described in any of these families, although lack of appropriate parenting "intuitions" was pervasive. We might expect to be able to make similar observations about a num-

ber of unsafe (but still licensed) drivers: their knowledge base is acceptable but their intuitive skills are wanting. Brandt F. Steele and Carl B. Pollock, "A Psychiatric Study of Parents who Abuse Infants and Small Children," in Ray Helfer and C. Henry Kempe, *The Battered Child,* 2d ed. (Chicago: University of Chicago Press, 1974), pp. 89–135.

3. Excepting forfeiture of the license, earlier noted, in the case of misconduct.

4. David Brion Davis, "The Crime of Reform," *New York Review of Books 27* (26 June 1980):14–18.

5. Christopher Lasch credits both Judge Ben Lindsey and Margaret Mead with proposals to license parents. He suggests that both intended that the middle and upper classes would carry the major burden of childrearing with the poor largely unenfranchised. Neither, it appears, was as concerned with issues of practicality or fairness as LaFollette. For those who find LaFollette's enthusiasm for social engineering distressing, Lasch may prove a healthful antidote. See Lasch's *Haven in a Heartless World* (New York: Basic Books, 1977).

Pierre Lemieux | # Parent Licensing

In the Winter 1980 issue of *Philosophy and Public Affairs,* Hugh LaFollette, a philosophy professor at East Tennessee State University, published an article arguing for the need to license parents.[1] The argument is quite straightforward. "We," or "our society," understandably require licensing for automobile operators, physicians, lawyers, pharmacists, psychologists, and psychiatrists, all activities that require a certain competence and are "potentially harmful to others." The two criteria of potential harm and ascertainable competence apply even more to parenting, which is "an activity potentially very harmful to children." Therefore, would-be parents should be forced to demonstrate their competence, obtain a license, and perhaps be trained, before rearing their children, for the same reasons that we strictly regulate the adoption process. "Undoubtedly," LaFollette writes, "one should be wary of unnecessary government intervention in individuals' lives. In this case, though, the intrusion would not often be substantial, and when it is, it would be warranted."

Since it was originally published, this paradigmatic article has been reproduced in more than a dozen books of public policy, ethical philosophy, and "environmental ethics." The proposal has gained disciples in other countries, and these are often more

radical than LaFollette himself, who thought that alternative systems could perhaps protect children adequately. "For example," he wrote, "a system of tax incentives for licensed parents, and protective services scrutiny of nonlicensed parents, might adequately protect children." Two Canadian public health specialists argue that "[n]o one should be allowed to raise children until they have finished high school, completed a parenting course, and obtained a licence."[2] A famous British surgeon, Sir Roy Calne, argues that people should have to pass a parenting test and obtain a reproduction license before being allowed to have children.[3]

Note how narrow a conception of rights underlies Prof. LaFollette's argument. Prior restraint of the kind involved in licensing is justified "if the restriction is not terribly onerous and the restricted activity is one which could lead easily to serious harm." In this perspective, only a limited number of real rights exist: rights of free speech (which, coincidentally, apply mainly to intellectuals like LaFollette), religious rights, right to vote, and rights of association. Presumably, individuals will associate to talk and worship, for what else is there to do? Even the enumerated rights can be limited to protect third parties. And "rights" to engage in hazardous activities, like

Pierre Lemieux, "Parent Licensing," *Laissez Faire City Times* 5, no. 19 (May 7, 2001). Reprinted by permission of Pierre Lemieux.

parenting, are conditional on meeting minimal standards. Determination of the nature of harm and the cost of restraint, and definition of real and conditional rights, presumably belong to "society."

Also underlying the proposed scheme is an underestimation of the efficiency of free human interactions, combined with an overblown confidence in political and bureaucratic processes. Statists tend to compare imperfect markets with perfect government. In this perspective, LaFollette would certainly agree with the World Bank researchers who recently wrote: "A priori, parents would ideally always be willing and able to protect children from tobacco themselves. If this happened, there would be little need for government to duplicate such efforts . . . Perfect parents, however, are rare."[4]

LaFollette would probably add, in his usual cool way, that the parent licensing system will not be perfect, but just less imperfect than the harmful system of totally private parenting that we now have. This completely neglects the effect of the proposed system on the growth of state power. It is recommended not to laugh at slippery slope arguments when you are actually speeding on a very slippery one.

In evaluating the efficiency of a parent licensing system, we must factor in the impact it will have on the relations between the individual and the state. LaFollette argues that the system "would increase the likelihood that more children will be adequately prepared for life as adults." This is the standard argument for limiting everybody's liberty in the name of manufactured pubic health causes. Under this general umbrella, the goal of protecting children is especially attractive, since the exploited children cannot defend themselves.[5]

Gun control, the war on drugs, the witch-hunt against child pornographers, tobacco prohibitions, are all aspects of the same trend. Indeed, on all such issues, the same politically-correct, public-health crowd is usually on the statist side of the barricades. LaFollette wrote "Licensing Parents" before Jonesboro, Dunblane, and Littleton, and could not grasp the tragic irony of overly-protected children mass-killing their little classmates. The society being created is not exactly what LaFollette envisions for

when children will be adults. The point is that, in the eyes of the authorities, they will never be adults.

It is not clear if, in LaFollette's scheme, a license would be required before conceiving a child, or only for keeping and rearing the baby. LaFollette claims that enforcement problems are "not insurmountable." "We might not punish parents at all," he adds, "we might just remove the children and put them up for adoption." Of course, laws are ultimately enforced by armed men, and scenes similar to agents with fully automatic weapons seizing Elian Gonzalez would be repeated. Usually, though, parents would let a social worker "peacefully" take their children away because they know that they have no chance against the SWAT team. So, with a few exceptions, the tyranny would be soft and quiet—tyranny with an invisible hand.

The project of licensing parents is symptomatic of the rise of what we may call the "Sanitary State," large components of which have already been put in place with the apparent consent of the majority. The Sanitary State is the continuation of the Social State, whose mission was to maximize social welfare. The Social State itself followed the Redistributive State, whose official goal was to redistribute income from the rich to the poor, and which conveniently built up its electoral clienteles this way.

The Sanitary State's mission is to keep its subjects healthy, and cure them when their lifestyles do not correspond to public health diktats. It acts within the limits of the rule of law, which now means that there is a law for every situation, and that you are always free to explain yourself before a judge. The tyrant is nice, soft, and relentlessly pursues its wards' happiness. The majority has nothing to fear. The dissenting minority cannot do much, if only because the state has made sure to disarm ordinary citizens for public health reasons.

Unrealistic? The people will never accept this? Let's hope so. But consider what our ancestors would have said if they had been told that the driver's license would become an ID card, that the state would assign citizens unique identifying number that would become necessary for most private transactions (except for the most trivial), that people would need the government's permission to own or carry guns, that they would need to fill in forms when they deposit more than $10,000 in cash, etc.

Welcome to the 21st century.

NOTES

1. Hugh LaFollette, "Licensing Parents," *Philosophy and Public Affairs,* 9, no. 2 (Winter 1980): 182–197.

2. *National Post,* February 22, 1999.

3. *The Observer,* August 7, 1994.

4. Prabhat Jha et al., "The Economic Rationale for Intervention in the Tobacco Market," in *Tobacco Control in Developing Countries,* edited by Prabhat Jha and Frank Chaloupka (Oxford: Oxford University Press, 2000), p. 164.

5. See my "Why I Hate Children," *Laissez Faire City Times,* April 2, 2001; reproduced at http://www.pierrelemieux.org/artchildren.html.

14

Is Same-Sex Marriage Wrong?

Jordan and His Critics

Most arguments against same-sex marriage rest at least in part on the claim that homosexual behavior is morally objectionable. Readers interested in pursuing this sort of argument should refer to the discussion of the question "Is homosexuality wrong?" in section 2.1. In "Is It Wrong to Discriminate on the Basis of Homosexuality?" on the other hand, Jeff Jordan attempts to produce an argument against same-sex marriage that makes no such assumption. Rather than relying on claims about the morality of homosexuality per se, Jordan attempts to show that the state should refuse to sanction same-sex marriages by appealing to the idea that marriage is a public rather than a private institution, and to the fact that there is widespread public disagreement about the moral status of homosexuality.

Jordan's argument can be reconstructed formally once a few key terms are defined. Jordan defines an "impasse" over the moral status of X as a situation in which people hold "genuinely conflicting beliefs regarding the moral status of X," and a "public dilemma" as an impasse that has "public policy consequences." In cases of genuine public dilemmas, the State will have to act in a way that has some implications with respect to X, and as a result will not be able to satisfy fully the interests of everyone on both sides of the impasse. When it puts its power and authority squarely on one side of the impasse—as in the case of the federal government forcibly ending slavery—it in effect "declares that side of the impasse the correct side." Jordan refers to this as "resolution by declaration." When it finds a way to stake out some kind of middle ground "in a way that gives as much as possible to all sides of the impasse," it ensures that "there are no absolute victors and no absolute losers" in the impasse and that the views of all sides are respected. Jordan refers to this as "resolution by accommodation," and cites abortion as a possible example (pornography might be another): The government permits its use, but restricts its availability. Jordan then argues that whenever a public dilemma must be actively resolved, the State should institute a resolution by accommodation rather than by declaration, unless there is an "overriding reason" for it to take sides, such as for "the protection of generally recognized rights."

With this general framework in place, Jordan then makes the following claims about same-sex marriage: First, there is an impasse over the question of whether or not homosexual acts are morally permissible. Many people think they are, and many think they are not. Second, while engaging in homosexual conduct is essentially a private matter, entering into a relationship of marriage is essentially a public one. Marriage involves a public recognition of a personal relationship between two people, and people who are married become eligible for various sorts of public benefits that are unavailable to unmarried couples. As a result, the debate over same-sex marriage represents not merely a moral impasse, but a public dilemma. Third, for the government to sanction same-sex marriage is for it to resolve this public dilemma by declaration in favor of one side of the dispute, in a way that leaves no room for accommodation. If it does this, then members of one segment of the population "are faced with a public, state-sanctioned matter which they find seriously immoral." But, fourth, if the State instead refuses to sanction same-sex marriage, this counts as a resolution by accommodation, provided that the State permits private homosexual acts between consenting adults. In this case, each side of the impasse gets some but not all of what it wants and thus neither side is an absolute victor or an absolute loser. Fifth, and finally, there is no overriding reason for the State to take sides in this dispute. What is at stake is not comparable to what is at stake in cases such as the abolition of slavery, where there is plainly a reason for the State to resolve the issue by declaration.

The argument can be summarized as follows:

P1   If (a) there is a public dilemma about X *and* (b) resolution of the dilemma by accommodation is possible *and* (c) there is no overriding reason to prefer resolution of the dilemma by declaration, *then* (d) the state should resolve the public dilemma about X by accommodation.

P2   There is a public dilemma about same-sex marriage.

P3   It is possible for the State to resolve the dilemma by accommodation if it refuses to sanction same-sex marriage (provided that it permits private homosexual acts between consenting adults.)

P4   It is not possible for the State to resolve the dilemma by accommodation if it sanctions same-sex marriage (since that amounts to resolving the dilemma by declaration and leaves no room for accommodation).

P5   There is no overriding reason for the State to resolve the dilemma by declaration.

C   The state should refuse to sanction same-sex marriage (provided that it permits private homosexual acts between consenting adults).

This argument from public disagreement is not the most familiar kind of argument against same-sex marriage. But because it seems to allow the critic of same-sex marriage to avoid depending on controversial claims about the moral status of homosexuality itself, it is potentially among the most powerful. The two critical responses to this sort of argument reprinted here, however, maintain that it is not powerful enough. In the first selection, David Boonin raises two objections to Jordan's argument. The first objection maintains that P2 is importantly ambiguous and that either way of resolving the ambiguity renders the third and fourth premises of the argument false. This amounts to the claim that Jordan's argument is guilty of equivocation (see section 3.3 in the Introduction): Either the disagreement at issue is about homosexual marriage or it is about homosexual sexual behavior, but on either construal it is not true that refusing to sanction same-sex marriage amounts to a resolution by accommodation and on either construal it is not true that sanctioning same-sex marriage amounts to a resolution by declaration. Boonin's second objection maintains that Jordan's argument is undermined by a *reductio ad absurdum* (see section 45 in the Introduction) objection that Jordan tries, but fails, to overcome—the claim that if the argument succeeds in showing that the State should not sanction same-sex marriage, then it unacceptably implies that the same is true in the case of interracial marriage. This objection amounts to saying that if the general principle embodied by P1 is sufficient to justify the conclusion that Jordan wishes to justify, it is also sufficient to justify the further conclusion that he seeks to avoid.

The excerpt from Andrew Sullivan's book, *Virtually Normal,* which follows Boonin's critical response, does not directly refer to Jordan's article. But it is nonetheless clear that Sullivan means to respond to the kind of argument Jordan's article offers, one that focuses, in Sullivan's words, on "what the allegedly neutral liberal state should do" with respect to same-sex marriage given the understanding that marriage "is not simply a private contract; it is a social and public recognition of a private commitment." While Jordan argues that state neutrality counts as a consideration against instituting same-sex marriage, however, Sullivan argues that it is a crucial consideration in its favor. More specifically, Sullivan argues that marriage, understood as a public institution, is essentially about a certain kind of personal bond between two people, and is not in any way essentially about sexual reproduction. But if this is so, Sullivan maintains, then there is no publicly neutral way to justify extending marriage rights to heterosexuals while denying them to homosexuals. To do so would be to treat heterosexuals and homosexuals unequally in a context in which there was no value-neutral justification for doing so. In terms of the reconstruction of Jordan's argument outlined above, then, while Boonin's objections focus essentially on the first four premises of the argument, Sullivan's argument can be understood as directly challenging P5: There is, on Sullivan's account, an overriding reason for the State to take sides in the dilemma over same-sex marriage because failing to side with proponents of the institution would involve violating the fundamental principle of human equality under the law.

QUESTIONS FOR CONSIDERATION

In critically evaluating Boonin's critique of Jordan's argument, readers should focus on two distinct sets of questions.

• First, is Boonin correct in claiming that there are two importantly distinct issues involved—one concerning sexual behavior and one concerning marriage—or are the two so closely intertwined that his separating them is unwarranted? If the distinction is maintained, then Boonin's first objection may seem to be viable, but if it is not, then the objection may seem too contrived. In thinking about this problem, it may help to think about the reasons Boonin gives for trying to keep the two issues distinct, and the reasons Jordan seems to have for viewing them as part of a single controversy about homosexuality as a whole.

• Second, is Boonin correct that Jordan has failed to avoid the following result: That if his argument works against same-sex marriage then it works against mixed-race marriage as well? Here readers should focus on the three specific differences Jordan presents between the two cases. In each instance, one should identify the reason Boonin gives for denying that the difference is sufficiently relevant, and then consider how Jordan might attempt to respond to that reason.

• Finally, in considering the excerpt from Sullivan's book, it will help to understand exactly how Sullivan's argument can be taken as an attack on P5 of Jordan's argument. What is Sullivan's overriding reason for resolving the dilemma in favor of those who favor same-sex marriage? What does he mean by human equality in this context and why does he take it to be so important? Once Sullivan's position is clearly understood, one can then consider whether or not Jordan is in a position to respond to it effectively. Is refusing to recognize same-sex marriage denying equal rights to homosexuals or is it simply refraining from extending a further and publicly divisive privilege to them? If the former, then Sullivan's objection may seem to be well grounded, but if the latter, then Jordan's position may seem largely immune to it.

FURTHER READING

Wedgwood, Ralph. "The Fundamental Argument for Same-Sex Marriage." *Journal of Political Philosophy* 7, no. 3, (1999): 225–42.

Jeff Jordan | # Is It Wrong to Discriminate on the Basis of Homosexuality?

Much like the issue of abortion in the early 1970s, the issue of homosexuality has exploded to the forefront of social discussion. Is homosexual sex on a moral par with heterosexual sex? Or is homosexuality in some way morally inferior? Is it wrong to discriminate against homosexuals—to treat homosexuals in less favorable ways than one does heterosexuals? Or is some discrimination against homosexuals morally justified? These questions are the focus of this essay.

In what follows, I argue that there are situations in which it is morally permissible to discriminate against homosexuals because of their homosexuality. That is, there are some morally relevant differ-ences between heterosexuality and homosexuality which, in some instances, permit a difference in treatment. The issue of marriage provides a good example. While it is clear that heterosexual unions merit the state recognition known as marriage, along with all the attendant advantages—spousal insurance coverage, inheritance rights, ready eligibility of adoption—it is far from clear that homosexual couples ought to be accorded that state recognition.

The argument of this essay makes no claim about the moral status of homosexuality per se. Briefly put, it is the argument of this essay that the moral impasse generated by conflicting views concerning homosexuality, and the public policy ramifications

Jeff Jordan, "Is It Wrong to Discriminate on the Basis of Homosexuality?" *Journal of Social Philosophy* 26, no. 1 (1995): 39–52. Reprinted by permission of Blackwell Publishing Ltd.

of those conflicting views justify the claim that it is morally permissible, in certain circumstances, to discriminate against homosexuals.[1]

1. THE ISSUE

The relevant issue is this: does homosexuality have the same moral status as heterosexuality? Put differently, since there are no occasions in which it is morally permissible to treat heterosexuals unfavorably, whether because they are heterosexual or because of heterosexual acts, are there occasions in which it is morally permissible to treat homosexuals unfavorably, whether because they are homosexuals or because of homosexual acts?

A negative answer to the above can be termed the "parity thesis." The parity thesis contends that *homosexuality has the same moral status as heterosexuality.* If the parity thesis is correct, then it would be immoral to discriminate against homosexuals because of their homosexuality. An affirmative answer can be termed the "difference thesis" and contends that there are morally relevant differences between heterosexuality and homosexuality which justify a difference in moral status and treatment between homosexuals and heterosexuals. The difference thesis entails that *there are situations in which it is morally permissible to discriminate against homosexuals.*

It is perhaps needless to point out that the difference thesis follows as long as there is at least one occasion in which it is morally permissible to discriminate against homosexuals. If the parity thesis were true, then on no occasion would a difference in treatment between heterosexuals and homosexuals ever be justified. The difference thesis does not, even if true, justify discriminatory actions on every occasion. Nonetheless, even though the scope of the difference thesis is relatively modest, it is, if true, a significant principle which has not only theoretical import but important practical consequences as well.[2]

A word should be said about the notion of discrimination. To discriminate against *X* means treating *X* in an unfavorable way. The word "discrimination" is not a synonym for "morally unjustifiable treatment." Some discrimination is morally unjustifiable; some is not. For example, we discriminate against convicted felons in that they are disenfranchised. This legal discrimination is morally permissible even though it involves treating one person unfavorably different from how other persons are treated. The difference thesis entails that there are circumstances in which it is morally permissible to discriminate against homosexuals.

2. AN ARGUMENT FOR THE PARITY THESIS

One might suppose that an appeal to a moral right, the right to privacy, perhaps, or the right to liberty, would provide the strongest grounds for the parity thesis. Rights talk, though sometimes helpful, is not very helpful here. If there is reason to think that the right to privacy or the right to liberty encompasses sexuality (which seems plausible enough), it would do so only with regard to private acts and not public acts. Sexual acts performed in public (whether heterosexual or homosexual) are properly suppressible. It does not take too much imagination to see that the right to be free from offense would soon be offered as a counter consideration by those who find homosexuality morally problematic. Furthermore, how one adjudicates between the competing rights claims is far from clear. Hence, the bald appeal to a right will not, in this case anyway, take one very far.

Perhaps the strongest reason to hold that the parity thesis is true is something like the following:

1. Homosexual acts between consenting adults harm no one. And,
2. respecting persons' privacy and choices in harmless sexual matters maximizes individual freedom. And,
3. individual freedom should be maximized. But,
4. discrimination against homosexuals, because of their homosexuality, diminishes individual freedom since it ignores personal choice and privacy. So,
5. the toleration of homosexuality rather than discriminating against homosexuals is the

preferable option since it would maximize individual freedom. Therefore,

6. the parity thesis is more plausible than the difference thesis.

Premise (2) is unimpeachable: if an act is harmless and if there are persons who want to do it and who choose to do it, then it seems clear that respecting the choices of those people would tend to maximize their freedom.[3] Step (3) is also beyond reproach: since freedom is arguably a great good and since there does not appear to be any ceiling on the amount of individual freedom—no "too much of a good thing"—(3) appears to be true.

At first glance, premise (1) seems true enough as long as we recognize that if there is any harm involved in the homosexual acts of consenting adults, it would be harm absorbed by the freely consenting participants. This is true, however, only if the acts in question are done in private. Public acts may involve more than just the willing participants. Persons who have no desire to participate, even if only as spectators, may have no choice if the acts are done in public. A real probability of there being unwilling participants is indicative of the public realm and not the private. However, where one draws the line between private acts and public acts is not always easy to discern, it is clear that different moral standards apply to public acts than to private acts.[4]

If premise (1) is understood to apply only to acts done in private, then it would appear to be true. The same goes for (4): discrimination against homosexuals for acts done in private would result in a diminishing of freedom. So (1)–(4) would lend support to (5) only if we understand (1)–(4) to refer to acts done in private. Hence, (5) must be understood as referring to private acts; and, as a consequence, (6) also must be read as referring only to acts done in private.

With regard to acts which involve only willing adult participants, there may be no morally relevant difference between homosexuality and heterosexuality. In other words, acts done in private. However, acts done in public add a new ingredient to the mix; an ingredient which has moral consequence. Consequently, the argument (1)–(6) fails in supporting the parity thesis. The argument (1)–(6) may show that there are some circumstances in which the moral status of homosexuality and heterosexuality are the same, but it gives us no reason for thinking that this result holds for all circumstances.[5]

3. MORAL IMPASSES AND PUBLIC DILEMMAS

Suppose one person believes that X is morally wrong, while another believes that X is morally permissible. The two people, let's stipulate, are not involved in a semantical quibble; they hold genuinely conflicting beliefs regarding the moral status of X. If the first person is correct, then the second person is wrong; and, of course, if the second person is right, then the first must be wrong. This situation of conflicting claims is what we will call an "impasse." Impasses arise out of moral disputes. Since the conflicting parties in an impasse take contrary views, the conflicting views cannot all be true, nor can they all be false.[6] Moral impasses may concern matters only of a personal nature, but moral impasses can involve public policy. An impasse is likely to have public policy ramifications if large numbers of people hold the conflicting views, and the conflict involves matters which are fundamental to a person's moral identity (and, hence, from a practical point of view, are probably irresolvable) and it involves acts done in public. Since not every impasse has public policy ramifications, one can mark off "public dilemma" as a special case of moral impasses: those moral impasses that have public policy consequences. Public dilemmas, then, are impasses located in the public square. Since they have public policy ramifications and since they arise from impasses, one side or another of the dispute will have its views implemented as public policy. Because of the public policy ramifications, and also because social order is sometimes threatened by the volatile parties involved in the impasse, the state has a role to play in resolving a public dilemma.

A public dilemma can be actively resolved in two ways.[7] The first is when the government allies itself with one side of the impasse and, by state coercion and sanction, declares that side of the impasse the correct side. The American Civil War was an example of this: the federal government forcibly ended slavery by aligning itself with the Abolitionist side of the impasse.[8] Prohibition is another example. The 18th Amendment and the Volstead Act allied the state with the Temperance side of the impasse. State mandated affirmative action programs provide a modern example of this. This kind of resolution of a public dilemma we can call a "resolution by declaration." The first of the examples cited above indicates that declarations can be morally proper, the right thing to do. The second example, however, indicates that declarations are not always morally proper. The state does not always take the side of the morally correct; nor is it always clear which side is the correct one.

The second way of actively resolving a public dilemma is that of accommodation. An accommodation in this context means resolving the public dilemma in a way that gives as much as possible to all sides of the impasse. A resolution by accommodation involves staking out some middle ground in a dispute and placing public policy in that location. The middle ground location of a resolution via accommodation is a virtue since it entails that there are no absolute victors and no absolute losers. The middle ground is reached in order to resolve the public dilemma in a way which respects the relevant views of the conflicting parties and which maintains social order. The Federal Fair Housing Act and, perhaps, the current status of abortion (legal but with restrictions) provide examples of actual resolutions via accommodation.[9]

In general, governments should be, at least as far as possible, neutral with regard to the disputing parties in a public dilemma. Unless there is some overriding reason why the state should take sides in a public dilemma—the protection of innocent life, or abolishing slavery, for instance—the state should be neutral, because no matter which side of the public dilemma the state takes, the other side will be the recipient of unequal treatment by the state. A state which is partial and takes sides in moral disputes via declaration, when there is no overriding reason why it

should, is tyrannical. Overriding reasons involve, typically, the protection of generally recognized rights.[10] In the case of slavery, the right to liberty; in the case of protecting innocent life, the right involved is the negative right to life. If a public dilemma must be actively resolved, the state should do so (in the absence of an overriding reason) via accommodation and not declaration since the latter entails that a sizable number of people would be forced to live under a government which "legitimizes" and does not just tolerate activities which they find immoral. Resolution via declaration is appropriate only if there is an overriding reason for the state to throw its weight behind one side in a public dilemma.

Is moral rightness an overriding reason for a resolution via declaration? What better reason might there be for a resolution by declaration than that it is the right thing to do? Unless one is prepared to endorse a view that is called "legal moralism"—that immorality alone is a sufficient reason for the state to curtail individual liberty—then one had best hold that moral rightness alone is not an overriding reason. Since some immoral acts neither harm nor offend nor violate another's rights, it seems clear enough that too much liberty would be lost if legal moralism were adopted as public policy.[11]

Though we do not have a definite rule for determining *a priori* which moral impasses genuinely constitute public dilemmas, we can proceed via a case by case method. For example, many people hold that cigarette smoking is harmful and, on that basis, is properly suppressible. Others disagree. Is this a public dilemma? Probably not. Whether someone engages in an imprudent action is, as long as it involves no unwilling participants, a private matter and does not, on that account, constitute a public dilemma. What about abortion? Is abortion a public dilemma? Unlike cigarette smoking, abortion is a public dilemma. This is clear from the adamant and even violent contrary positions involved in the impasse. Abortion is an issue which forces itself into the public square. So, it is clear that, even though we lack a rule which filters through moral impasses designating some as public dilemmas, not every impasse constitutes a public dilemma.

4. CONFLICTING CLAIMS ON HOMOSEXUALITY

The theistic tradition, Judaism and Christianity and Islam, has a clear and deeply entrenched position on homosexual acts: they are prohibited. Now it seems clear enough that if one is going to take seriously the authoritative texts of the respective religions, then one will have to adopt the views of those texts, unless one wishes to engage in a demythologizing of them with the result that one ends up being only a nominal adherent of that tradition.[12] As a consequence, many contemporary theistic adherents of the theistic tradition, in no small part because they can read, hold that homosexual behavior is sinful. Though God loves the homosexual, these folk say, God hates the sinful behavior. To say that act X is a sin entails that X is morally wrong, not necessarily because it is harmful or offensive, but because X violates God's will. So, the claim that homosexuality is sinful entails the claim that it is also morally wrong. And, it is clear, many people adopt the difference thesis just because of their religious views: because the Bible or the Koran holds that homosexuality is wrong, they too hold that view.

Well, what should we make of these observations? We do not, for one thing, have to base our moral conclusions on those views, if for no other reason than not every one is a theist. If one does not adopt the religion based moral view, one must still respect those who do; they cannot just be dismissed out of hand.[13] And, significantly, this situation yields a reason for thinking that the difference thesis is probably true. Because many religious people sincerely believe homosexual acts to be morally wrong and many others believe that homosexual acts are not morally wrong, there results a public dilemma.[14]

The existence of this public dilemma gives us reason for thinking that the difference thesis is true. It is only via the difference thesis and not the parity thesis, that an accommodation can be reached. Here again, the private/public distinction will come into play.

To see this, take as an example the issue of homosexual marriages. A same-sex marriage would be a public matter. For the government to sanction same-sex marriages—to grant the recognition and reciprocal benefits which attach to marriage—would ally the government with one side of the public dilemma and against the adherents of religion-based moralities. This is especially true given that, historically, no government has sanctioned same-sex marriages. The status quo has been no same-sex marriages. If the state were to change its practice now, it would be clear that the state has taken sides in the impasse. Given the history, for a state to sanction a same-sex marriage now would not be a neutral act.

Of course, some would respond here that by not sanctioning same-sex marriages the state is, and historically has been, taking sides to the detriment of homosexuals. There is some truth in this claim. But one must be careful here. The respective resolutions of this issue—whether the state should recognize and sanction same-sex marriages—do not have symmetrical implications. The asymmetry of this issue is a function of the private/public distinction and the fact that marriage is a public matter. If the state sanctions same-sex marriages, then there is no accommodation available. In that event, the religion-based morality proponents are faced with a public, state sanctioned matter which they find seriously immoral. This would be an example of a resolution via declaration. On the other hand, if the state does not sanction same-sex marriages, there is an accommodation available: in the public realm the state sides with the religion-based moral view, but the state can tolerate private homosexual acts. That is, since homosexual acts are not essentially public acts; they can be, and historically have been, performed in private. The state, by not sanctioning same-sex marriages is acting in the public realm, but it can leave the private realm to personal choice.[15]

5. THE ARGUMENT FROM CONFLICTING CLAIMS

It was suggested in the previous section that the public dilemma concerning homosexuality, and in particular whether states should sanction same-sex marriages, generates an argument in support of the difference thesis. The argument, again using same-sex marriages as the particular case, is as follows:

7.   There are conflicting claims regarding whether the state should sanction same-sex marriages. And,
8.   this controversy constitutes a public dilemma. And,
9.   there is an accommodation possible if the state does not recognize same-sex marriages. And,
10. there is no accommodation possible if the state does sanction same-sex marriages. And,
11. there is no overriding reason for a resolution via declaration. Hence,
12. the state ought not sanction same-sex marriages. And,
13. the state ought to sanction heterosexual marriages. So,
14. there is at least one morally relevant case in which discrimination against homosexuals, because of their homosexuality, is morally permissible. Therefore,
15. the difference thesis is true.

Since proposition (14) is logically equivalent to the difference thesis, then, if (7)–(14) are sound, proposition (15) certainly follows.

Premises (7) and (8) are uncontroversial. Premises (9) and (10) are based on the asymmetry that results from the public nature of marriage. Proposition (11) is based on our earlier analysis of the argument (1)–(6). Since the strongest argument in support of the parity thesis fails, we have reason to think that there is no overriding reason why the state ought to resolve the public dilemma via declaration in favor of same-sex marriages. We have reason, in other words, to think that (11) is true.

Proposition (12) is based on the conjunction of (7)–(11) and the principle that, in the absence of an overriding reason for state intervention via declaration, resolution by accommodation is the preferable route. Proposition (13) is just trivially true. So, given the moral difference mentioned in (12) and (13), proposition (14) logically follows.

6. TWO OBJECTIONS CONSIDERED

The first objection to the argument from conflicting claims would contend that it is unsound because a similar sort of argument would permit discrimination against some practice which, though perhaps controversial at some earlier time, is now widely thought to be morally permissible. Take mixed-race marriages, for example. The opponent of the argument from conflicting claims could argue that a similar argument would warrant prohibition against mixed-race marriages. If it does, we would have good reason to reject (7)–(14) as unsound.

There are three responses to this objection. The first response denies that the issue of mixed-race marriages is in fact a public dilemma. It may have been so at one time, but it does not seem to generate much, if any, controversy today. Hence, the objection is based upon a faulty analogy.

The second response grants for the sake of the argument that the issue of mixed-race marriages generates a public dilemma. But the second response points out that there is a relevant difference between mixed-race marriages and same-sex marriages that allows for a resolution by declaration in the one case but not the other. As evident from the earlier analysis of the argument in support of (1)–(6), there is reason to think that there is no overriding reason for a resolution by declaration in support of the parity thesis. On the other hand, it is a settled matter that state protection from racial discrimination is a reason sufficient for a resolution via declaration. Hence, the two cases are only apparently similar, and, in reality, they are crucially different. They are quite different because, clearly enough, if mixed-race marriages do generate a public dilemma, the state should use resolution by declaration in support of such marriages. The same cannot be said for same-sex marriages.

One should note that the second response to the objection does not beg the question against the proponent of the parity thesis. Though the second response denies that race and sexuality are strict analogues, it does so for a defensible and independent reason: it is a settled matter that race is not a sufficient reason for disparate treatment; but, as we have seen from the analysis of (1)–(6), there is no overriding reason to think the same about sexuality.[16]

The third response to the first objection is that the grounds of objection differ in the respective cases: one concerns racial identity; the other concerns behavior thought to be morally problematic. A same-sex marriage would involve behavior which many people find morally objectionable; a mixed-race marriage is objectionable to some, not because of the participants' behavior, but because of the racial identity of the participants. It is the race of the marriage partners which some find of primary complaint concerning mixed-race marriages. With same-sex marriages, however, it is the behavior which is primarily objectionable. To see this latter point, one should note that, though promiscuously Puritan in tone, the kind of sexual acts that are likely involved in a same-sex marriage are objectionable to some, regardless of whether done by homosexuals or heterosexuals.[17] So again, there is reason to reject the analogy between same-sex marriages and mixed-race marriages. Racial identity is an immutable trait and a complaint about mixed-race marriages necessarily involves, then, a complaint about an immutable trait. Sexual behavior is not an immutable trait and it is possible to object to same-sex marriages based on the behavior which would be involved in such marriages. Put succinctly, the third response could be formulated as follows: objections to mixed-race marriages necessarily involve objections over status, while objections to same-sex marriages could involve objections over behavior. Therefore, the two cases are not analogues since there is a significant modal difference in the ground of the objection.

The second objection to the argument from conflicting claims can be stated so: if homosexuality is biologically based—if it is inborn[18]—then how can discrimination ever be justified? If it is not a matter of choice, homosexuality is an immutable trait which is, as a consequence, morally permissible. Just as it would be absurd to hold someone morally culpable for being of a certain race, likewise it would be absurd to hold someone morally culpable for being a homosexual. Consequently, according to this objection, the argument from conflicting claims "legitimizes" unjustifiable discrimination.

But this second objection is not cogent, primarily because it ignores an important distinction. No one could plausibly hold that homosexuals act by some sort of biological compulsion. If there is a biological component involved in sexual identity, it would incline but it would not compel. Just because one naturally (without any choice) has certain dispositions, is not in itself a morally cogent reason for acting upon that disposition. Most people are naturally selfish, but it clearly does not follow that selfishness is in any way permissible on that account. Even if it is true that one has a predisposition to do X as a matter of biology and not as a matter of choice, it does not follow that doing X is morally permissible. For example, suppose that pyromania is an inborn predisposition. Just because one has an inborn and, in that sense, natural desire to set fires, one still has to decide whether or not to act on that desire.[19] The reason that the appeal to biology is specious is that it ignores the important distinction between being a homosexual and homosexual acts. One is status; the other is behavior. Even if one has the status naturally, it does not follow that the behavior is morally permissible, nor that others have a duty to tolerate the behavior.

But, while moral permissibility does not necessarily follow if homosexuality should turn out to be biologically based, what does follow is this: in the absence of a good reason to discriminate between homosexuals and heterosexuals, then, assuming that homosexuality is inborn, one ought not discriminate between them. If a certain phenomenon X is natural in the sense of being involuntary and nonpathological, and if there is no good reason to hold that X is morally problematic, then that is reason enough to think that X is morally permissible. In the absence of a good reason to repress X, one should tolerate it since, as per supposition, it is largely nonvoluntary. The argument from conflicting claims, however, provides a good reason which overrides this presumption.

7. A SECOND ARGUMENT FOR THE DIFFERENCE THESIS

A second argument for the difference thesis, similar to the argument from conflicting claims, is what might be called the "no-exit argument." This argument is based on the principle that:

A. no just government can coerce a citizen into violating a deeply held moral belief or religious belief.

Is (A) plausible? It seems to be since the prospect of a citizen being coerced by the state into a practice which she finds profoundly immoral appears to be a clear example of an injustice. Principle (A), conjoined with there being a public dilemma arising over the issue of same-sex marriages, leads to the observation that if the state were to sanction same-sex marriages, then persons who have profound religious or moral objections to such unions would be legally mandated to violate their beliefs since there does not appear to be any feasible "exit right" possible with regard to state sanctioned marriage. An exit right is an exemption from some legally mandated practice, granted to a person or group, the purpose of which is to protect the religious or moral integrity of that person or group. Prominent examples of exit rights include conscientious objection and military service, home-schooling of the young because of some religious concern, and property used for religious purposes being free from taxation.

It is important to note that marriage is a public matter in the sense that, for instance, if one is an employer who provides health care benefits to the spouses of employees, one must provide those benefits to any employee who is married. Since there is no exit right possible in this case, one would be coerced, by force of law, into subsidizing a practice one finds morally or religiously objectionable.[20]

In the absence of an exit right, and if (A) is plausible, then the state cannot morally force persons to violate deeply held beliefs that are moral or religious in nature. In particular, the state morally could not sanction same-sex marriages since this would result in coercing some into violating a deeply held religious conviction.

8. A CONCLUSION

It is important to note that neither the argument from conflicting claims nor the no-exit argument

licenses wholesale discrimination against homosexuals. What they do show is that some discrimination against homosexuals, in this case refusal to sanction same-sex marriages, is not only legally permissible but also morally permissible. The discrimination is a way of resolving a public policy dilemma that accommodates, to an extent, each side of the impasse and, further, protects the religious and moral integrity of a good number of people. In short, the arguments show us that there are occasions in which it is morally permissible to discriminate on the basis of homosexuality.[21]

NOTES

1. The terms "homosexuality" and "heterosexuality" are defined as follows. The former is defined as sexual feelings or behavior directed toward individuals of the same sex. The latter, naturally enough, is defined as sexual feelings or behavior directed toward individuals of the opposite sex.

Sometimes the term "gay" is offered as an alternative to "homosexual." Ordinary use of "gay" has it as a synonym of a male homosexual (hence, the common expression, "gays and lesbians"). Given this ordinary usage, the substitution would lead to a confusing equivocation. Since there are female homosexuals, it is best to use "homosexual" to refer to both male and female homosexuals, and reserve "gay" to signify male homosexuals, and "lesbian" for female homosexuals in order to avoid the equivocation.

2. Perhaps we should distinguish the weak difference thesis (permissible discrimination on *some* occasions) from the strong difference thesis (given the relevant moral differences, discrimination on *any* occasion is permissible).

3. This would be true even if the act in question is immoral.

4. The standard answer is, of course, that the line between public and private is based on the notion of harm. Acts which carry a real probability of harming third parties are public acts.

5. For other arguments supporting the moral parity of homosexuality and heterosexuality, see Richard Mohr, *Gays/Justice: A Study of Ethics, Society and Law* (NY: Columbia, 1988); and see Michael Ruse, "The Morality of Homosexuality" in *Philosophy and Sex,* eds. R. Baker & F. Elliston, (Buffalo, NY: Prometheus Books, 1984), pp. 370–390.

6. Perhaps it would be better to term the disputing positions "contradictory" views rather than "contrary" views.

7. Resolutions can also be passive in the sense of the state doing nothing. If the state does nothing to resolve the public dilemma, it stands pat with the status quo, and the public dilemma is resolved gradually by sociological changes (changes in mores and in beliefs).

8. Assuming, plausibly enough, that the disputes over the sovereignty of the Union and concerning states' rights were at bottom disputes about slavery.

9. The Federal Fair Housing Act prohibits discrimination in housing on the basis of race, religion, and sex. But it does not apply to the rental of rooms in single-family houses, or to a building of five units or less if the owner lives in one of the units. See 42 U.S.C. Section 3603.

10. Note that overriding reasons involve *generally recognized* rights. If a right is not widely recognized and the state nonetheless uses coercion to enforce it, there is a considerable risk that the state will be seen by many or even most people as tyrannical.

11. This claim is, perhaps, controversial. For a contrary view see Richard George, *Making Men Moral* (Oxford: Clarendon Press, 1993).

12. See, for example, Leviticus 18:22, 21:3; and Romans 1:22–32; and Koran IV:13

13. For an argument that religiously-based moral views should not be dismissed out of hand, see Stephen Carter, *The Culture of Disbelief: How American Law and Politics Trivialize Religious Devotion* (NY: Basic Books, 1993).

14. Two assumptions are these: that the prohibitions against homosexuality activity are part of the religious doctrine and not just an extraneous addition; second, that if *X* is part of one's religious belief or religious doctrine, then it is morally permissible to hold *X*. Though this latter principle is vague, it is, I think, clear enough for our pur-

poses here (I ignore here any points concerning the rationality of religious belief in general, or in particular cases).

15. This point has implications for the moral legitimacy of sodomy laws. One implication would be this: the private acts of consenting adults should not be criminalized.

16. An *ad hominem* point: If this response begs the question against the proponent of the parity thesis, it does not beg the question any more than the original objection does by presupposing that sexuality is analogous with race.

17. Think of the sodomy laws found in some states which criminalize certain sexual acts, whether performed by heterosexuals or homosexuals.

18. There is some interesting recent research which, though still tentative, strongly suggests that homosexuality is, at least in part, biologically based. See Simon LeVay, *The Sexual Brain* (Cambridge, MA: MIT Press, 1993), pp. 120–122; and J.M. Bailey & R.C. Pillard "A Genetic Study of Male Sexual Orientation" *Archives of General Psychiatry* 48 (1991): 1089–1096; and C. Burr, "Homosexuality and Biology" *The Atlantic* 271/3 (March, 1993): 64; and D. Hamer, S. Hu, V. Magnuson, N. Hu, A. Pattatucci, "A Linkage Between DNA Markers on the *X* Chromosome and Male Sexual Orientation" *Science* 261 (16 July 1993): 321–327; and see the summary of this article by Robert Pool, "Evidence for Homosexuality Gene" *Science* 261 (16 July 1993): 291–292.

19. I do not mean to suggest that homosexuality is morally equivalent or even comparable to pyromania.

20. Is the use of subsidy here inappropriate? It does not seem so since providing health care to spouses, in a society where this is not legally mandatory, seems to be more than part of a salary and is a case of providing supporting funds for a certain end.

21. I thank David Haslett, Kate Rogers, Louis Pojman, and Jim Fieser for helpful and critical comments.

Critics

David Boonin

Same-Sex Marriage and the Argument from Public Disagreement

. . . Let me begin by raising a question about P2: the claim that there is a public dilemma about same-sex marriage. On the face of it, this might seem to be the clearest and least problematic of all of the premises in Jordan's argument. If anything at all about same-sex marriage is uncontroversial it is the fact that it is controversial. But what, exactly, does the claim made by P2 mean? Jordan, remember, defines a public dilemma as a special case of a moral impasse, and a moral impasse as a situation in which people "hold genuinely conflicting beliefs regarding the moral status of *x*." The question is: in the case of the public dilemma about same-sex marriage, what does the *x* stand for?

There are two possibilities: it can stand for acts of homosexual behavior, or it can stand for acts of participating in a same-sex marriage. Jordan at one point speaks of "*the* public dilemma concerning homosexuality, and in particular whether states should sanction same-sex marriages" (78, emphasis added), as if there is a single subject of dispute here, but these are in fact two distinct subjects of disagreement. The former concerns the moral permissibility of certain forms of sexual behavior, regardless of whether the people who engage in them are generally heterosexual or homosexual in their orientation. The latter concerns the moral permissibility of granting certain forms of social recognition and public benefits to same-sex couples, regardless of whether or not they engage in such (or any) sexual behavior.

Suppose that the genuinely conflicting beliefs that generate the dilemma referred to in P2 are beliefs regarding the moral status of acts of participating in a same-sex marriage. This seems to be the most natural interpretation, since the dilemma itself is about same-sex marriage and since a dilemma is simply a special case of an impasse, which is itself a case of conflicting beliefs about something. If this is what is meant by P2, then P3 and P4 are false. P3 says that if the state refuses to sanction same-sex marriages, then it resolves the public dilemma by accommodation (provided that it permits private homosexual acts between consenting adults). If we conflate the two distinct questions about private acts and public benefits into one issue, and think of it as "the" dispute over homosexuality, then this seems plausible enough. Each side gets some of what it wants, and neither side gets all of what it wants. But if the conflict is over the permissibility of same-sex *marriage* in particular, as opposed to about the complex cluster of issues relating to homosexuality taken as a whole, then this is no accommodation at all. It is simply a declaration that one side of the debate is entirely correct (those who oppose same-sex marriages) and the other side entirely incorrect (those who support them). It is as if one were to join together the distinct but related debates about whether or not the government should fund the arts and whether or not it should ban violent pornography, announce that the government will permit violent pornography but will not subsidize it, and declare that "the" debate in question had been settled in a way that accommodates both sides. This would not be a resolution by accommodation of one dilemma, but rather a resolution by declaration of two distinct but related dilemmas.

On this understanding of P2, P4 is also false, for similar but distinct reasons. P4 says that if the state sanctions same-sex marriage, then it resolves the public dilemma by declaration and leaves no room for accommodation. But if the dilemma is over

David Boonin, "Same-Sex Marriage and the Argument from Public Disagreement," *Journal of Social Philosophy* (Fall 1999): 251–59. Notes and some parts of the text have been deleted. Reprinted by permission of Blackwell Publishing Ltd.

same-sex marriage rather than over same-sex sex, this too is incorrect. If accommodation is reached in controversies such as that over pornography or abortion by permitting but discouraging the controversial practice, then the same would hold here as well. The state could sanction same-sex marriage, but make it more difficult to obtain a same-sex marriage license than to obtain an opposite-sex marriage license. For example, it could require proof that a homosexual couple had been engaged for two years before obtaining a same-sex marriage license, but not require such proof from heterosexual couples, or require extensive premarital counseling, or charge a greater licensing fee. And it could discourage homosexuals from marrying in other ways, such as by taxing married homosexuals at a higher rate (higher than married heterosexuals and/or higher than unmarried homosexuals), or making it more difficult for them to obtain divorces or to adopt children than it is for heterosexual couples.

None of these suggestions will be fully satisfactory to defenders of same-sex marriage, of course. What they demand is marriage for homosexuals that is on an equal footing with marriage for heterosexuals. Nor will any of these proposals be fully satisfactory to opponents of same-sex marriage. What they demand is that there be no such thing as same-sex marriage. But that is precisely the point. If Jordan is correct that dilemmas of this sort should be resolved by accommodation, and if the dilemma is understood to be one over marriage and not over sex, then following a proposal that is fully satisfactory to neither side is exactly what his argument demands that we do. As in other such cases, the state should find a way to allow those who wish to engage in the disputed behavior to engage in it while at the same time expressing society's disapproval or at least lack of approval of the behavior in question.

Suppose, on the other hand, that the genuinely conflicting beliefs that generate the dilemma referred to in P2 are beliefs regarding the moral status of acts of homosexual behavior. This seems to be what Jordan typically has in mind when he introduces his argument. When he supports the contention that there exists a public dilemma that needs some sort of resolution, for example, he cites the fact that "[t]he theistic tradition, Judaism and Christian-

ity and Islam, has a clear and deeply entrenched position on homosexual *acts:* they are prohibited" (77, emphasis added). And he concludes his argument for the claim by saying that "[b]ecause many religious people sincerely believe homosexual *acts* to be morally wrong and many others believe that homosexual *acts* are not morally wrong, there results a public dilemma" (77, emphasis added).

But if the genuinely conflicting beliefs that generate the dilemma referred to in P2 are beliefs regarding the moral status of acts of homosexual behavior, then P3 and P4 are again false, for different but parallel reasons. If the state sanctions same-sex marriage, it does not resolve the conflicting beliefs about the moral permissibility of acts of homosexual behavior in a way that leaves no room for accommodation. For example, the state could recognize both same-sex and opposite-sex marriage and make it illegal to have homosexual intercourse outside of such a relation while legal to have heterosexual intercourse outside of such a relation. This would have the effect of permitting but restricting the form of behavior whose moral status is the subject of genuinely conflicting beliefs. So if the conflicting beliefs referred to in P2 concern the permissibility of acts of homosexual behavior, then P4 is false. Similarly, if the state refuses to sanction same-sex marriage and permits private homosexual acts between consenting adults, it does not resolve the conflicting beliefs about the moral permissibility of acts of homosexual behavior by accommodation. Rather, it simply declares that one side of the conflict is the correct side, namely, the side that believes that such acts are permissible. Doing so thus renders P3 false as well. So either way that we specify the meaning of the claim made in P2, the argument as a whole proves to be unsound.

A second objection to Jordan's argument takes the form of a reductio ad absurdum: if the state should refuse to sanction same-sex marriage because it is the subject of a moral impasse, then it should also refuse to sanction mixed-race marriage on the same ground. But the claim that the state should refuse to sanction mixed-race marriage is surely intolerable. So, therefore, is Jordan's argument. Jordan provides three responses to this objection, but none of them are satisfactory.

His first response is that unlike the issue of same-sex marriage, the issue of mixed-race marriages "does not seem to generate much, if any, controversy today" (79). On this account, there is no such public dilemma in the first place, and so it does not matter that Jordan's position would justify forbidding mixed-race marriage if there were. This response is unsuccessful for two reasons. First, it is not at all clear that there is no such dilemma about mixed-race marriage. In many communities in the South, at least, there remains substantial opposition to interracial *dating,* let alone interracial marriage. And although such opposition is traditionally associated with white racists, there is a more recent and hardly less heated controversy within the black community in all parts of the country about whether or not black men, in particular, have an obligation to marry black women. Second, and more importantly, even if Jordan is right that there is no longer a moral impasse on this issue, this response makes the impermissibility of laws forbidding mixed-race marriage contingent on this fact. And surely such laws were impermissible even when many racists supported them.

Jordan's second response to the mixed-race objection is to say that even if it does represent a public dilemma, it is one in which there is an overriding reason in favor of resolution by declaration. The reason is that "it is a settled matter that state protection from racial discrimination is a reason sufficient for a resolution via declaration" while the same is not true of protection from discrimination according to sexual orientation (80). This response fails for the simple reason that a law banning mixed-race marriages does not discriminate against people on racial grounds. It says that *every* person, regardless of race, is free to marry anyone else of his or her race, and that *every* person, regardless of race, is prohibited from marrying anyone else of some other race. A white person who falls in love with a black person is adversely affected in just the same way as is black person who falls in love with a white person. And since every black-white couple consists of one black person and one white person, the total number of blacks and whites who are adversely affected in this way is the same. As a result, a law recognizing mixed-race marriage does not protect anyone from racial discrimination that would occur without such a law.

A law forbidding same-sex marriage, it is worth noting, is fundamentally different in this respect. It says that a heterosexual man can marry any member of the sex he is attracted to while a homosexual man can marry any member of the sex he is *not* attracted to, and that a heterosexual man is forbidden to marry any member of the sex that he is not attracted to while a homosexual man is forbidden to marry any member of the sex that he *is* attracted to. This law does discriminate by sexual orientation, since all of the people who are adversely affected by it (at least directly) are homosexuals. And thus a law recognizing same-sex marriage does protect people from discrimination on the basis of sexual orientation that would otherwise occur without such a law. In short, laws banning mixed-race marriage treat people of all races equally while laws banning same-sex marriage do not treat people of all sexual orientations equally. So Jordan has failed to show that there is an overriding reason for the state to resolve the mixed-race marriage issue by declaration that does not also apply to the case of same-sex marriages. Indeed, if anything, he has pointed to an overriding reason to resolve the same-sex marriage issue by declaration that does not apply to the mixed-race marriage issue.

Jordan's final response to the mixed-race marriage objection turns on his attempt to identify a second disanalogy between the two cases: "A same-sex marriage would involve behavior which many people find morally objectionable; a mixed-race marriage is objectionable to some, not because of the participants' behavior, but because of the racial identity of the participants" (80). And since objections based on a person's identity are different from objections based on a person's behavior, it does not follow from the fact that the objection to mixed-race marriage should be overruled by a resolution by declaration that the objection to same-sex marriage should also be overruled in this manner.

This response must be rejected because it rests on a misdescription of the view held by those who object to mixed-race marriage. It is not that they object to the *identity* of the individuals involved. White racists need not have anything against blacks marrying other blacks, and black separatists surely have nothing against white people marrying other whites. It is not the identity of the individuals that they object to, but the act they perform: the act of weakening the purity of the race, or of violating the obligation to put one's own community first. In this sense, they are no different from the antihomosexual people Jordan describes: they say they object not to what homosexuals are, but to what they do.

Virtually Normal

Andrew Sullivan

An Argument About Homosexuality

. . . Marriage is not simply a private contract; it is a social and public recognition of a private commitment. As such, it is the highest public recognition of personal integrity. Denying it to homosexuals is the most public affront possible to their public equality.

This point may be the hardest for many heterosexuals to accept. Even those tolerant of homosexuals may find this institution so wedded to the notion of heterosexual commitment that to extend it would be to undo its very essence. And there may be religious reasons for resisting this that, within certain traditions, are unanswerable. But I am not here discussing what churches do in their private affairs. I am discussing what the allegedly neutral liberal state should do in public matters. For liberals, the case for homosexual marriage is overwhelming. As a classic public institution, it should be available to any two citizens.

Some might argue that marriage is by definition between a man and a woman; and it is difficult to argue with a definition. But if marriage is articulated beyond this circular fiat, then the argument for its exclusivity to one man and one woman disappears. The center of the public contract is an emotional, financial, and psychological bond between two people; in this respect, heterosexuals and homosexuals are identical. The heterosexuality of marriage is intrinsic only if it is understood to be intrinsically procreative; but that definition has long been abandoned in Western society. No civil marriage license is granted on the condition that the couple bear children; and the marriage is no less legal and no less defensible if it remains childless. In the contemporary West, marriage has become a way in which the state recognizes an emotional commitment by two people to each other for life. And within that definition, there is no public way, if one believes in equal rights under the law, in which it should legally be denied homosexuals.

Of course, no public sanctioning of a contract should be given to people who cannot actually fulfill it. The state rightly, for example, withholds marriage from minors, or from one adult and a minor, since at least one party is unable to understand or live up to the contract. And the state has also rightly barred close family relatives from marriage because familial emotional ties are too strong and powerful to enable a marriage contract to be entered into freely by two autonomous, independent individuals; and because incest poses a uniquely dangerous threat to the trust and responsibility that the family needs to survive. But do homosexuals fall into a similar category? History and experience strongly suggest they don't. Of course, marriage is characterized by a kind of commitment that is rare—and perhaps declining—even among heterosexuals. But it isn't necessary to prove that homosexuals or lesbians are less—or more—able to form long-term relationships than straights for it to be clear that at least *some* are. Moreover, giving these people an equal right to affirm their commitment doesn't reduce the incentive for heterosexuals to do the same. . . .

Excerpted from Andrew Sullivan, *Virtually Normal: An Argument About Homosexuality* (New York: Alfred A. Knopf, 1995). Used by permission of Alfred A. Knopf, a division of Random House, Inc.

PART 4

What's Wrong with Race Relations?

Some of the deepest and most divisive debates in contemporary society concern race. While virtually everyone will agree that injustices based on race have been committed in the past, and while virtually no one would deny that there is still room for improvement in race relations, a variety of important debates persist over just what, if anything, should be done to make amends for past misdeeds and how the growing number of questions involving race should be handled.

Part 4 is devoted to an examination of some of these issues. We introduce the subject of race by focusing on questions about how we should respond to past injustices. Can affirmative-action programs be justified, at least in part, as a means of rectifying past harms to minorities (chapter 15)? Does the United States government, in particular, have a moral obligation to make reparations to black Americans for the wrongs inflicted as a part of the institution of slavery and its aftermath (chapter 16)? Then, in chapter 17 we consider the issue of "cultural appropriation," of one racial or ethnic group's taking on a cultural tradition that appears to belong to another. And finally, in chapter 18, we examine the extremely heated debate over the practice of racial profiling.

15

Is Affirmative Action Wrong?

Thomson and Her Critics

It is now quite generally accepted that it is wrong to prefer one job candidate over another simply because the first is a man and the second is a woman, or because the first is a white person and the second is a black person. The outlawing of racial and gender discrimination in hiring is widely considered as a big moral step forward, and it is striking to us just how recently this occurred. Now consider affirmative action in the form of a policy of preferential hiring for blacks and women. Doesn't such a policy violate the hard-won principle that it is wrong to discriminate, in hiring, on the basis of race or gender? Don't equally qualified candidates have a right to an equal chance at being hired regardless of their race or gender? In the lead article of this chapter, Judith Jarvis Thomson argues that even if we accept that everyone has this right, giving preference to black and female candidates does not violate that right.

Thomson focuses on justifying a particular kind of preferential hiring policy—that of allowing being black or female to tip the balance in those cases where two or more equally qualified candidates present themselves for a job. For if we cannot justify this fairly modest preferential hiring practice clearly we have no hope of justifying the more radical practice of allowing being black or female to outweigh other considerations. And if we can justify the modest practice then, as Thomson suggests, there may well be a possibility of extending that justification to the radical policy. Thomson focuses on one particular case of preferential hiring of this sort, namely, the hiring of professors into (publicly funded) university positions.

Arguments for affirmative action are often classified as those that are forward looking and those that are backward looking. The forward-looking arguments seek to justify the practices in terms of their good consequences—for example, raising the standard of living or self-esteem of members of traditionally disadvantaged groups. The backward-looking arguments seek to justify them in terms of the rectification of past injustices. For example, we need to compensate blacks and women for past discrimination against them in hiring practices, and one way of doing that is to discriminate in their favor both now and for some time into the future. Thomson briefly considers two forward-looking arguments for justifying preferential hiring (the learning-environment argument and the role-model argument), but finds both of them wanting.

Thomson's positive case for preferential hiring is backward looking and is a version of the compensatory argument. For the sake of the argument, Thomson concedes that everyone, including a white male, has a right to an equal chance at a university job. She argues that preferential hiring does not in fact violate this right although it might override it. Preferential hiring is one way of compensating traditionally disadvantaged groups for past injustices. Preferential hiring of those who have been traditionally discriminated against is not itself a simple case of discrimination on the basis of race or gender. The policy is not an endorsement of the claim that it is legitimate to prefer B over A for a job simply because B is black and A is white. Rather, the policy is an endorsement of the claim that it is legitimate to prefer B over A for this job because B is black, A is white, and because blacks have suffered from a history of discrimination on the part of whites.

Thomson illustrates her argument with a couple of analogies. Suppose there is a private eating club and its members are joint owners of it. Suppose two members turn up at the same time for dinner, but there is only one available table. The just thing to do, Thomson argues, is to give each an equal chance at being assigned the table, say, by tossing a coin. Or suppose the club receives a donation of a splendid apple tart. The just way to distribute the tart among the members is to give them all equal slices. We might add that if there are not not enough slices for everyone, then the club should distribute tickets for slices in a fair lottery.

> Consideration of these cases might suggest the following principle: every owner of a jointly owned property has a right to either an equal chance at, or an equal share in, any benefit which that property generates, and which is available for distribution amongst the owners— equal chance rather than equal share if the benefit is indivisible, or for some reason is best left undivided.

So far this goes against preferential hiring. A publicly funded university is owned by the community that funds it, and members of that community are like the joint owners of an eating club. The jobs that universities hand out are somewhat like the benefits the club distributes to its members. So among a group of equally qualified job applicants, each should have an equal chance at getting the job. We should not decide straightway that the job should go to a black or a woman if one happens to be in the top tier of the applicant pool.

Thomson goes on to consider cases in which this right to an equal chance can be overridden (not violated). Return to the eating club. Suppose Smith, a member of the club, has recently performed a series of magnificent favors for the club, favors that others have not performed. Then the club might adopt the following policy out of gratitude to Smith: For the next six months, if there is only one table left and Smith is among those waiting, then it will be given to him. (In other cases the headwaiter will toss a coin.) Or, if someone donates a splendid apple tart to the club, Smith can, if he wants, have a bigger piece than everyone else, and everyone else can have equal shares of what remains. Or if you and Smith turn up for dinner, and there is only one table left, and the headwaiter gives it to Smith, then your right to an equal chance at the table has been overridden, but no injustice has been done to you. Smith's favors have generated a debt of gratitude on the part of the club, of which you are a member, and there is no impropriety in the club's repaying its debt in this way.

Debts owed to a creditor are an even clearer case where the right to an equal chance of a benefit may be denied. Suppose Dickenson has lent the club $1000 and the club now owes him that sum. Suppose someone else donates a painting to the club worth $1000. The club cannot simply distribute the painting to one member or another by way of a fair lottery—as it might do if it had no particular debts. First it has an obligation to settle its debt to Dickenson, and it may do that by giving him the painting. Other club members cannot complain that they have been unjustly treated by being denied an equal chance at ownership of the painting. Their right has been overridden—because Dickenson was owed $1000—but it has not been violated.

Thomson applies this to the preferential hiring of war veterans. War veterans have done us a big favor by serving their country in dangerous situations (or even just by virtue of being willing to do so). The country therefore owes them a debt of gratitude, and giving them preference for jobs is one way of discharging that debt. We could reconstruct the argument thus:

P1   No one's right to an equal chance of a benefit is violated when the club gives Smith preferential treatment.
P2   The community's giving war veterans preference over non-veterans in hiring is morally on a par with the club's giving Smith preferential treatment.

C   No one's right to an equal chance of a benefit is violated when veterans are given preference in hiring over non-veterans.

Now let us turn to the case of blacks and women. If blacks and women have been badly treated in the past, then they are owed something by the community for those past injustices or injuries. We can amend Thomson's Dickenson story to make it more analogous. Suppose Dickenson did not lend the club $1000 but that the headwaiter clumsily dropped a bottle of wine on Dickenson' foot, causing him to incur medical expenses of $500 and the same amount in pain and discomfort. Then the club owes Dickenson $1000 and that debt is a first call on its resources.

P1   No one's right to an equal chance of a club benefit is violated when the club gives Dickenson preferential treatment in the gift of the painting in order to compensate him for his injuries.
P2   Giving blacks and women preference over white males in hiring is morally on a par with the club's giving Dickenson preferential treatment in the gift of the painting.

C   No one's right to an equal chance of a benefit is violated when blacks and women are given preference in hiring over white males.

Robert Simon develops three objections to Thomson's arguments. In his first objection he constructs a dilemma. Either the case of blacks and women is analogous to that of Dickenson, and we owe something to individuals who have been harmed; or it is like that of the veterans, and we owe compensation to a group of individuals. If compensation is owed to harmed individuals, then the current policy does not target those individuals precisely enough. Privileged members of the preferential group are getting benefits denied to white males who may well have suffered more harm. If compensation is owed to the group, then it is not clear that preferential hiring of individual members of the group actually achieves that. The argument for preferential hiring is seriously incomplete.

In his second objection, Simon raises a problem of arbitrariness in the distribution of compensation. University hiring is driven, at least in part, by market considerations. Universities need to pick from among the best-qualified candidates for teaching and researching subjects that are currently in demand. But there is a lot of luck involved in ending up in that group because which disciplines are currently in demand is itself a matter of luck. So, the compensation is restricted to those who have had the necessary good luck. And that is not a satisfactory method of compensation.

Finally Simon objects that preferential hiring distributes costs unevenly and arbitrarily. Those who pay the costs (young, white, male applicants for university posts) are not necessarily those who perpetrated the harms. Thomson also considers this objection and responds that it is not unfitting that young white males bear the costs, since they have probably indirectly profited from wrongs inflicted on women and blacks. (She also says that old, white males, in comfortable tenured positions, should also have to pay some of the cost.) Simon marshals several arguments against this claim. He argues that there is inequity in the distribution of the costs. Again this is to point to a disanalogy with cases like that of Dickenson. In that case every member of the club loses an equal chance to win the donated painting in a lottery. In the case of preferential university hiring, only a small contingent of university-trained, young, white males lose their equal chance in a job lottery among equally qualified applicants for university positions.

QUESTIONS FOR CONSIDERATION

• Why does Thomson think that a purely private university can institute preferential hiring policies without violating or overriding anyone's rights? If she is right about that, are laws against discrimination in hiring in the private sector morally unjustified?

• Is the prevention of the violation of moral rights the only grounds for outlawing discriminatory practices in the private sector? Might we have reasons to outlaw discrimination in hiring even if they would not necessarily violate anyone's rights?

• There is an obvious objection to the analogy claimed in the second premise of the last of Thomson's arguments—namely, that while most blacks and women indeed suffered from discriminatory practices in hiring in the past, the particular individual blacks and women who are applying for jobs now may not have suffered from that kind of discrimination. Indeed, they might have benefited from a series of affirmative-action programs. Is this disanalogous to the case of Dickenson? The community may owe compensation to those who were directly harmed by past discrimination (as the club owes a debt to Dickenson), but does it follow that the community owes compensation to each and every female or black person, regardless of whether or not that particular person actually suffered from discrimination? (Does the club owe anything to members of Dickerson's extended family?)

• Thomson counters this kind of objection by appealing to the legitimacy of preferences for veterans. Not every veteran has done more for the community than every non-veteran, but, still, we think it legitimate to accord veterans preference in hiring over non-veterans. Why? If this is legitimate, then we can use the group designation even if our policy compensates some members of the group more than they themselves deserve by virtue of their injuries. Is this rejoinder successful or does it cast doubt on the legitimacy of the veteran policy?

• Thomson's article was published in 1973, more than thirty years ago. Does this affect the soundness of her argument? For example, if compensation for past injustices is the main reason for a policy of preferential hiring, for how long should such compensation be paid? Ten years? Thirty years? As many years as there was discrimination against blacks and females in hiring? Are the cases of blacks and women sufficiently similar for them to be bundled together like this? How might we assess the strength of a claim for preferences of a black male applicant with respect to those of a white female applicant, or of a black female with respect to a black male?

   • Thomson mentions at the start of her article that she is arguing for race and gender as factors that might tip the balance in favor of one of two equally qualified candidates, but she also mentions that this kind of argument might be extended to justify using race and gender as factors that *override* other considerations. Can her argument be extended in this way?

FURTHER READING

Hajdin, Mane. "Affirmative Action, Old and New." *Journal of Social Philosophy* 33, no. 1 (2002): 83–96.

Kershnar, Stephen. "Strong Affirmative Action Programs and Disproportionate Burdens." *Journal of Value Inquiry* 33, no. 2 (1999): 201–209.

Judith Jarvis Thomson | # Preferential Hiring

Many people are inclined to think preferential hiring an obvious injustice.[1] I should have said "feel" rather than "think": it seems to me the matter has not been carefully thought out, and that what is in question, really, is a gut reaction.

I am going to deal with only a very limited range of preferential hirings: that is, I am concerned with cases in which several candidates present themselves for a job, in which the hiring officer finds, on examination, that all are equally qualified to hold that job, and he then straightway declares for the black, or for the woman, because he or she *is* a black or a woman. And I shall talk only of hiring decisions in the universities, partly because I am most familiar with them, partly because it is in the universities that the most vocal and articulate opposition to preferential hiring is now heard—not surprisingly, perhaps, since no one is more vocal and articulate than a university professor who feels deprived of his rights.

I suspect that some people may say, Oh well, in *that* kind of case it's all right, what we object to is preferring the less qualified to the better qualified. Or again, What we object to is refusing even to consider the qualifications of white males. I shall say nothing at all about these things. I think that the argument I shall give for saying that preferential hiring is not unjust in the cases I do concentrate on can also be appealed to to justify it outside that range of cases. But I won't draw any conclusions about cases outside it. Many people do have that gut reaction I mentioned against preferential hiring in *any* degree or form; and it seems to me worthwhile bringing out that there is good reason to think they are wrong to have it. Nothing I say will be in the slightest degree

Judith Jarvis Thomson, "Preferential Hiring," *Philosophy and Public Affairs* 2, no. 4 (Summer 1973): 364–384. Reprinted by permission of Princeton University Press.

novel or original. It will, I hope, be enough to set the relevant issues out clearly.

I

But first, something should be said about qualifications.

I said I would consider only cases in which the several candidates who present themselves for the job are equally qualified to hold it; and there plainly are difficulties in the way of saying precisely how this is to be established, and even what is to be established. Strictly academic qualifications seem at a first glance to be relatively straightforward: the hiring officer must see if the candidates have done equally well in courses (both courses they took, and any they taught), and if they are recommended equally strongly by their teachers, and if the work they submit for consideration is equally good. There is no denying that even these things are less easy to establish than first appears: for example, you may have a suspicion that Professor Smith is given to exaggeration, and that his "great student" is in fact less strong than Professor Jones's "good student"—but do you *know* that this is so? But there is a more serious difficulty still: as blacks and women have been saying, strictly academic indicators may themselves be skewed by prejudice. My impression is that women, white and black, may possibly suffer more from this than black males. A black male who is discouraged or down-graded for being black is discouraged or down-graded out of dislike, repulsion, a desire to avoid contact; and I suspect that there are very few teachers nowadays who allow themselves to feel such things, or, if they do feel them, to act on them. A woman who is discouraged or down-graded for being a woman is not discouraged or down-graded out of dislike, but out of a conviction she is not serious, and I suspect that while there are very few teachers nowadays who allow themselves to feel that women generally are not serious, there are many who allow themselves to feel of the particular individual women students they confront that Ah, this one isn't serious, and in fact that one isn't either, nor is that other one—women generally are, of course, one thing, but these particular women, really they're

just girls in search of husbands, are quite another. And I suspect that this will be far harder to root out. A teacher could not face himself in the mirror of a morning if he had down-graded anyone out of dislike; but a teacher can well face himself in the mirror if he down-grades someone out of a conviction that that person is not serious: after all, life is serious, and jobs and work, and who can take the unserious seriously? who pays attention to the dilettante? So the hiring officer must read very very carefully between the lines in the candidates' dossiers even to assess their strictly academic qualifications.

And then of course there are other qualifications besides the strictly academic ones. Is one of the candidates exceedingly disagreeable? A department is not merely a collection of individuals, but a working unit; and if anyone is going to disrupt that unit, and to make its work more difficult, then this counts against him—he may be as well qualified in strictly academic terms, but he is not as well qualified. Again, is one of the candidates incurably sloppy? Is he going to mess up his records, is he going to have to be nagged to get his grades in, and worse, is he going to lose students' papers? This too would count against him: keeping track of students' work, records, and grades, after all, is part of the job.

What seems to me to be questionable, however, is that a candidate's race or sex is itself a qualification. Many people who favor preferential hiring in the universities seem to think it is; in their view, if a group of candidates is equally well qualified in respect of those measures I have already indicated, then if one is of the right race (black) or of the right sex (female), then that being itself a qualification, it tips the balance, and that one is the best qualified. If so, then of course no issue of injustice, or indeed of any other impropriety, is raised if the hiring officer declares for that one of the candidates straightway.

Why does race or sex seem to many to be, itself, a qualification? There seem to be two claims in back of the view that it is. First, there is the claim that blacks learn better from a black, women from a woman. One hears this less often in respect of women; blacks, however, are often said to mistrust the whites who teach them, with the result that they simply do not learn as well, or progress as far, as they would if taught by blacks. Secondly, and this one hears in respect of women as well as blacks, what is wanted is *role models*. The proportion of black and women faculty members in the larger universities (particularly as one moves up the ladder of rank) is very much smaller than the proportion of blacks and women in the society at large—even, in the case of women, than the proportion of them amongst recipients of Ph.D. degrees from those very same universities. Black and women students suffer a constricting of ambition because of this. They need to see members of their race or sex who are accepted, successful, professionals. They need concrete evidence that those of their race or sex *can* become accepted, successful professionals.

And perhaps it is thought that it is precisely by virtue of having a role model right in the classroom that blacks do learn better from a black, women from a woman.

Now it is obviously essential for a university to staff its classrooms with people who can teach, and so from whom its students can learn, and indeed learn as much and as well as possible—teaching, after all, is, if not the whole of the game, then anyway a very large part of it. So if the first claim is true, then race and sex *do* seem to be qualifications. It obviously would not follow that a university should continue to regard them as qualifications indefinitely; I suppose, however, that it would follow that it should regard them as qualifications at least until the proportion of blacks and women on the faculty matches the proportion of blacks and women among the students.

But in the first place, allowing this kind of consideration to have a bearing on a hiring decision might make for trouble of a kind that blacks and women would not be at all happy with. For suppose it could be made out that white males learn better from white males? (I once, years ago, had a student who said he really felt uncomfortable in a class taught by a woman, it was interfering with his work, and did I mind if he switched to another section?) I suppose we would feel that this was due to prejudice, and that it was precisely to be discouraged, certainly not encouraged by establishing hiring ratios. I don't suppose it is true of white males generally that they learn better from white males; I am concerned only with the way in which we should take the fact, if it

were a fact, that they did—and if it would be improper to take it to be reason to think being a white male is a qualification in a teacher, then how shall we take its analogue to be reason to think being black, or being a woman, is a qualification in a teacher?

And in the second place, I must confess that, speaking personally, I do not find the claim we are looking at borne out in experience; I do not think that as a student I learned any better, or any more, from the women who taught me than from the men, and I do not think that my own women students now learn any better or any more from me than they do from my male colleagues. Blacks, of course, may have, and may have had, very different experiences, and I don't presume to speak for them—or even for women generally. But my own experience being what it is, it seems to *me* that any defense of preferential hiring in the universities which takes this first claim as premise is so far not an entirely convincing one.

The second claim, however, does seem to me to be plainly true: black and women students do need role models, they do need concrete evidence that those of their race or sex can become accepted, successful, professionals—plainly, you won't try to become what you don't believe you can become.

But do they need these role models right there in the classroom? Of course it might be argued that they do: that a black learns better from a black teacher, a woman from a woman teacher. But we have already looked at this. And if they are, though needed, not needed in the classroom, then is it the university's job to provide them?

For it must surely be granted that a college, or university, has not the responsibility—or perhaps, if it is supported out of public funds, even the right—to provide just *any* service to its students which it might be good for them, or even which they may need, to be provided with. Sports seem to me plainly a case in point. No doubt it is very good for students to be offered, and perhaps even required to become involved in, a certain amount of physical exercise; but I can see no reason whatever to think that universities should be expected to provide facilities for it, or taxpayers to pay for those facilities. I suspect others may disagree, but my own feeling is that it is the same with medical and psychiatric services: I am sure that at least some students need medical and psychiatric help, but I cannot see why it should be provided for them in the universities, at public expense.

So the further question which would have to be answered is this: granting that black and female students need black and female role models, why should the universities be expected to provide them within their faculties? In the case of publicly supported universities, why should taxpayers be expected to provide them?

I don't say these questions can't be answered. But I do think we need to come at them from a quite different direction. So I shall simply sidestep this ground for preferential hiring in the universities. The defense I give will not turn on anyone's supposing that of two otherwise equally well qualified candidates, one may be better qualified for the job by virtue, simply, of being of the right race or sex.

II

I mentioned several times in the preceding section the obvious fact that it is the taxpayers who support public universities. Not that private universities are wholly private: the public contributes to the support of most of them, for example by allowing them tax-free use of land, and of the dividends and capital gains on investments. But it will be the public universities in which the problem appears most starkly: as I shall suggest, it is the fact of public support that makes preferential hiring in the universities problematic.

For it seems to me that—other things being equal—there is no problem about preferential hiring in the case of a wholly private college or university, that is, one which receives no measure of public support at all, and which lives simply on tuition and (non-tax-deductible) contributions.

The principle here seems to me to be this: no perfect stranger has a right to be given a benefit which is yours to dispose of; no perfect stranger even has a right to be given an equal chance at getting a benefit which is yours to dispose of. You not only needn't give the benefit to the first perfect stranger who walks in and asks for it; you needn't even give him a chance at it, as, e.g., by tossing a coin.

I should stress that I am here talking about *benefits,* that is, things which people would like to have, which would perhaps not merely please them, but improve their lives, but which they don't actually *need.* (I suspect the same holds true of things people do actually need, but many would disagree, and as it is unnecessary to speak here of needs, I shall not discuss them.) If I have extra apples (they're mine: I grew them, on my own land, from my own trees), or extra money, or extra tickets to a series of lectures I am giving on How to Improve Your Life Through Philosophy, and am prepared to give them away, word of this may get around, and people may present themselves as candidate recipients. I do not have to give to the first, or to proceed by letting them all draw straws; if I really do own the things, I can give to whom I like, on any ground I please, and in so doing, I violate no one's *rights,* I treat no one *unjustly.* None of the candidate recipients has a right to the benefit, or even to a chance at it.

There are four caveats. (1) Some grounds for giving or refraining from giving are less respectable than others. Thus, I might give the apples to the first who asks for them simply because he is the first who asks for them. Or again, I might give the apples to the first who asks for them because he is black, and because I am black and feel an interest in and concern for blacks which I do not feel in and for whites. In either case, not merely do I do what it is within my rights to do, but more, my ground for giving them to that person is a not immoral ground for giving them to him. But I might instead give the apples to the sixth who asks, and this because the first five were black and I hate blacks—or because the first five were white and I hate whites. Here I do what I have a right to do (for the apples are *mine*), and I violate no one's rights in doing it, but my ground for disposing of the apples as I did was a bad one; and it might even, more strongly, be said that I ought not have disposed of the apples in the way I did. But it is important to note that it is perfectly consistent, on the one hand, that a man's ground for acting as he did was a bad one, and even that he ought not have done what he did, and, on the other hand, that he had a right to do what he did, that he violated no one's rights in doing it, and that no one can complain he was unjustly treated.

The second caveat (2) is that although I have a right to dispose of my apples as I wish, I have no right to harm, or gratuitously hurt or offend. Thus I am within my rights to refuse to give the apples to the first five because they are black (or because they are white); but I am not within my rights to say to them "I refuse to give you apples because you are black (or white) and because those who are black (or white) are inferior."

And (3) if word of my extra apples, and of my willingness to give them away, got around because I advertised, saying or implying First Come First Served Till Supply Runs Out, then I cannot refuse the first five because they are black, or white. By so advertising I have *given* them a right to a chance at the apples. If they come in one at a time, I must give out apples in order, till the supply runs out; if they come in together, and I have only four apples, then I must either cut up the apples, or give them each Ian equal chance, as, e.g., by having them draw straws.

And lastly (4), there may be people who would say that I don't really, or don't fully own those apples, even though I grew them on my own land, from my own trees, and therefore that I don't have a right to give them away as I see fit. For after all, I don't own the police who protected my land while those apples were growing, or the sunlight because of which they grew. Or again, wasn't it just a matter of luck for me that I was born with a green thumb?—and why should I profit from a competence that I didn't deserve to have, that I didn't earn? Or perhaps some other reason might be put forward for saying that I don't own those apples. I don't want to take this up here. It seems to me wrong, but I want to let it pass. If anyone thinks that I don't own the apples, or, more generally, that no one really or fully owns anything, he will regard what I shall say in the remainder of this section, in which I talk about what may be done with what is privately owned, as an idle academic exercise. I'll simply ask that anyone who does think this be patient: we will come to what is publicly owned later.

Now what was in question was a job, not apples; and it may be insisted that to give a man a job is not to give him a benefit, but rather something he needs. Well, I am sure that people do need jobs, that it does not fully satisfy people's needs to supply them only with food, shelter, and medical care. Indeed, I am sure that people need, not merely jobs, but jobs that interest them, and that they can therefore get satisfaction from the doing of. But on the other hand, I am not at all sure that any candidate for a job in a university needs a job in a university. One would very much like it if all graduate students who wish it could find jobs teaching in universities; it is in some measure a tragedy that a person should spend three or four years preparing for a career, and then find there is no job available, and that he has in consequence to take work which is less interesting than he had hoped and prepared for. But one thing seems plain: no one *needs* that work which would interest him most in all the whole world of work. Plenty of people have to make do with work they like less than other work—no economy is rich enough to provide everyone with the work he likes best of all—and I should think that this does not mean they lack something they *need*. We are all of us prepared to tax ourselves so that no one shall be in need; but I should imagine that we are not prepared to tax ourselves (to tax barbers, truck drivers, salesclerks, waitresses, and factory workers) in order that everyone who wants a university job, and is competent to fill it, shall have one made available to him.

All the same, if a university job is a benefit rather than something needed, it is anyway not a "pure" benefit (like an apple), but an "impure" one. To give a man a university job is to give him an opportunity to do work which is interesting and satisfying; but he will only *be* interested and satisfied if he actually does the work he is given an opportunity to do, and does it well.

What this should remind us of is that certain cases of preferential hiring might well be utterly irrational. Suppose we have an eating club, and need a new chef; we have two applicants, a qualified French chef, and a Greek who happens to like to cook, though he doesn't do it very well. We are fools if we say to ourselves "We like the Greeks, and dislike the French, so let's hire the Greek." We simply won't eat as well as we could have, and eating, after all, was the point of the club. On the other hand, it's *our* club, and so *our* job. And who shall say it is not within a man's rights to dispose of what really is his in as foolish a way as he likes?

And there is no irrationality, of course, if one imagines that the two applicants are equally qualified French chefs, and one is a cousin of one of our members, the other a perfect stranger. Here if we declare directly for the cousin, we do not act irrationally, we violate no one's rights, and indeed do not have a morally bad ground for making the choice we make. It's not a morally splendid ground, but it isn't a morally bad one either.

Universities differ from eating clubs in one way which is important for present purposes: in an eating club, those who consume what the club serves are the members, and thus the owners of the club themselves—by contrast, if the university is wholly private, those who consume what it serves are not among the owners. This makes a difference: the owners of the university have a responsibility not merely to themselves (as the owners of an eating club do), but also to those who come to buy what it offers. It could, I suppose, make plain in its advertising that it is prepared to allow the owners' racial or religious or other preferences to outweigh academic qualifications in its teachers. But in the absence of that, it must, in light of what a university is normally expected to be and to aim at, provide the best teachers it can afford. It does not merely act irrationally, but indeed violates the rights of its student-customers if it does not.

On the other hand, this leaves it open to the university that in case of a choice between equally qualified candidates, it violates no one's rights if it declares for the black because he is black, or for the white because he is white. To the wholly *private* university, that is, for that is all I have so far been talking of. Other things being equal—that is, given it has not advertised the job in a manner which would entitle applicants to believe that all who are equally qualified will be given an equal chance at it, and given it does not gratuitously give offence to those whom it rejects—the university may choose as it

pleases, and violates no one's rights in doing so. Though no doubt its grounds for choosing may be morally bad ones, and we may even wish to say, more strongly, that it ought not choose as it does.

What will have come out in the preceding is that the issue I am concerned with is a moral, and not a legal one. My understanding is that the law does prevent an employer wholly in the private sector from choosing a white rather than a black on ground of that difference alone—though not from choosing a black rather than a white on ground of that difference alone. Now if, as many people say, legal rights (or perhaps, legal rights in a relatively just society) create moral rights, then even a moral investigation should take the law into account; and indeed, if I am not mistaken as to the law, it would have to be concluded that blacks (but not whites) do have rights of the kind I have been denying. I want to sidestep all this. My question can be re-put: would a private employer's choosing a white (or black) rather than a black (or white) on ground of that difference alone be a violation of anyone's rights if there were no law making it illegal. And the answer seems to me to be: it would not.

III

But hardly any college or university in America is purely private. As I said, most enjoy some public support, and the moral issues may be affected by the extent of the burden carried by the public. I shall concentrate on universities which are entirely publicly funded, such as state or city universities, and ignore the complications which might arise in case of partial private funding.

The special problem which arises here, as I see it, is this: where a community pays the bills, the community owns the university.

I said earlier that the members, who are therefore the owners, of a private eating club may declare for whichever chef they wish, even if the man they declare for is not as well qualified for the job as some other; in choosing amongst applicants, they are *not* choosing amongst fellow members of the club who is to get some benefit from the club. But now suppose, by contrast, that two of us who are members arrive at the same time, and there is only one available table. And suppose also that this has never happened before, and that the club has not voted on any policy for handling it when it does happen. What seems to me to be plain is this: the headwaiter cannot indulge in preferential seating, he cannot simply declare for one or the other of us on just any ground he pleases. He must randomize: as it might be, by tossing a coin.

Or again, suppose someone arrives at the dining room with a gift for the club: a large and very splendid apple tart. And suppose that this, too, has never happened before, and that the club has not voted on any policy for handling it when it does happen. What seems to me plain is this: the headwaiter cannot distribute that tart in just any manner, and on any ground he pleases. If the tart won't keep till the next meeting, and it's impossible to convene one now, he must divide the tart amongst us equally.

Consideration of these cases might suggest the following principle: every owner of a jointly owned property has a right to either an equal chance at, or an equal share in, any benefit which that property generates, and which is available for distribution amongst the owners—equal chance rather than equal share if the benefit is indivisible, or for some reason is better left undivided.

Now I have all along been taking it that the members of a club jointly own the club, and therefore jointly own whatever the club owns. It seems to me possible to view a community in the same way: to suppose that its members jointly own it, and therefore jointly own whatever it owns. If a community is properly viewed in this way, and if the principle I set out above is true, then every member of the community is a joint owner of whatever the community owns, and so in particular, a joint owner of its university; and therefore every member of the community has a right to an equal chance at, or equal share in, any benefit which the university generates, which is available for distribution amongst the owners. And that includes university jobs, if, as I argued, a university job is a benefit.

Alternatively, one might view a community as an imaginary Person: one might say that the members of that community are in some sense participants in that Person, but that they do not jointly own what the Per-

son owns. One might in fact say the same of a club: that its members do not jointly own the club or anything which the club owns, but only in some sense participate in the Person which owns the things. And then the cases I mentioned might suggest an analogous principle: every "participant" in a Person (Community-Person, Club-Person) has a right to either an equal chance at, or an equal share in, any benefit which is generated by a property which that Person owns, which is available for distribution amongst the "participants."

On the other hand, if we accept any of this, we have to remember that there are cases in which a member may, without the slightest impropriety, be deprived of this equal chance or equal share. For it is plainly not required that the university's hiring officer decide who gets the available job by randomizing amongst *all* the community members, however well- or ill-qualified, who want it. The university's student-customers, after all, have rights too; and their rights to good teaching are surely more stringent than each member's right (if each has such a right) to an equal chance at the job. I think we do best to reserve the term "violation of a right" for cases in which a man is unjustly deprived of something he has a right to, and speak rather of "overriding a right" in cases in which, though a man is deprived of something he has a right to, it is not unjust to deprive him of it. So here the members' rights to an equal chance (if they have them) would be, not violated, but merely overridden.

It could of course be said that these principles hold only of benefits of a kind I pointed to earlier, and called "pure" benefits (such as apples and apple tarts), and that we should find some other, weaker, principle to cover "impure" benefits (such as jobs).

Or it could be said that a university job is not a benefit which is available for distribution amongst the community members—that although a university job is a benefit, it is, in light of the rights of the students, available for distribution only amongst those members of the community who are best qualified to hold it. And therefore that they alone have a right to an equal chance at it.

It is important to notice, however, that unless *some* such principle as I have set out is true of the publicly owned university, there is no real problem about preferential hiring in it. Unless the white male applicant who is turned away had a right that this should not be done, doing so is quite certainly not violating any of his rights. Perhaps being joint owner of the university (on the first model) or being joint participant in the Person which owns the university (on the second model), do not give him a right to an equal chance at the job; perhaps he is neither joint owner nor joint participant (some third model is preferable), and it is something else which gives him his right to an equal chance at the job. Or perhaps he hasn't a right to an equal chance at the job, but has instead some other right which is violated by declaring for the equally qualified black or woman straightway. It is here that it seems to me it emerges most clearly that opponents of preferential hiring are merely expressing a gut reaction against it: for they have not asked themselves precisely what right is in question, and what it issues from.

Perhaps there is lurking in the background some sense that everyone has a right to "equal treatment," and that it is this which is violated by preferential hiring. But what on earth right is this? Mary surely does not have to decide between Tom and Dick by toss of a coin, if what is in question is marrying. Nor even, as I said earlier, if what is in question is giving out apples, which she grew on her own land, on her own trees.

It could, of course, be argued that declaring for the black or woman straightway isn't a violation of the white male applicant's rights, but is all the same wrong, bad, something which ought not be done. As I said, it is perfectly consistent that one ought not do something which it is, nevertheless, no violation of anyone's rights to do. So perhaps opponents of preferential hiring might say that rights are not in question, and still argue against it on other grounds. I say they *might,* but I think they plainly do better not to. If the white male applicant has no rights which would be violated, and appointing the black or woman indirectly benefits other blacks or women (remember that need for role models), and thereby still more indirectly benefits us all (by widening the available pool of talent), then it is very hard to see how it could come out to be morally objectionable to declare for the black or woman straightway.

I think we should do the best we can for those who oppose preferential hiring: I think we should grant that the white male applicant has a right to an equal chance at the job, and see what happens for preferential hiring if we do. I shall simply leave open whether this right issues from considerations of the kind I drew attention to, and so also whether or not every member of the community, however well- or ill-qualified for the job, has the same right to an equal chance at it.

Now it is, I think, widely believed that we may, without injustice, refuse to grant a man what he has a right to only if *either* someone else has a conflicting and more stringent right, *or* there is some very great benefit to be obtained by doing so—perhaps that a disaster of some kind is thereby averted. If so, then there really is trouble for preferential hiring. For what more stringent right could be thought to override the right of the white male applicant for an equal chance? What great benefit obtained, what disaster averted, by declaring for the black or the woman straightway? I suggested that benefits are obtained, and they are not small ones. But are they large enough to override a right? If these questions cannot be satisfactorily answered, then it looks as if the hiring officer does act unjustly, and does violate the rights of the white males, if he declares for the black or woman straightway.

But in fact there are other ways in which a right may be overridden. Let's go back to that eating club again. Suppose that now it has happened that two of us arrive at the same time when there is only one available table, we think we had better decide on some policy for handling it when it happens. And suppose that we have of late had reason to be especially grateful to one of the members, whom I'll call Smith: Smith has done a series of very great favors for the club. It seems to me we might, out of gratitude to Smith, adopt the following policy: for the next six months, if two members arrive at the same time, and there is only one available table, then Smith gets in first, if he's one of the two; whereas if he's not, then the headwaiter shall toss a coin.

We might even vote that for the next year, if he wants apple tart, he gets more of it than the rest of us.

It seems to me that there would be no impropriety in our taking these actions—by which I mean to include that there would be no injustice in our taking them. Suppose another member, Jones, votes No. Suppose he says "Look. I admit we all benefited from what Smith did for us. But still, I'm a member, and a member in as good standing as Smith is. So I have a right to an equal chance (and equal share), and I demand what I have a right to." I think we may rightly feel that Jones merely shows insensitivity: he does not adequately appreciate what Smith did for us. Jones, like all of us, has a right to an equal chance at such benefits as the club has available for distribution to the members; but there is no injustice in a majority's refusing to grant the members this equal chance, in the name of a debt of gratitude to Smith.

It is worth noticing an important difference between a debt of gratitude and debts owed to a creditor. Suppose the club had borrowed $1000 from Dickenson, and then was left as a legacy, a painting appraised at $1000. If the club has no other saleable assets, and if no member is willing to buy the painting, then I take it that justice would precisely require *not* randomizing amongst the members who is to get that painting, but would instead require our offering it to Dickenson. Jones could not complain that to offer it to Dickenson is to treat him, Jones, unjustly: Dickenson has a right to be paid back, and that right is more stringent than any member's right to an equal chance at the painting. Now Smith, by contrast, did not have a right to be given anything, he did not have a right to our adopting a policy of preferential seating in his favor. If we fail to do anything for Dickenson, we do him an injustice; if we fail to do anything for Smith, we do *him* no injustice—our failing is, not injustice, but ingratitude. There is no harm in speaking of debts of gratitude and in saying that they are owed to a benefactor, by analogy with debts owed to a creditor; but it is important to remember that a creditor has, and a benefactor does not have, a right to repayment.

To move now from clubs to more serious matters, suppose two candidates for a civil service job have equally good test scores, but that there is only one job available. We could decide between them by coin-tossing. But in fact we do allow for declaring for A straightway, where A is a veteran, and B is not.[2] It may be that B is a nonveteran through no fault of his own: perhaps he was refused induction for flat feet, or

a heart murmur. That is, those things in virtue of which B is a non-veteran may be things which it was no more in his power to control or change than it is in anyone's power to control or change the color of his skin. Yet the fact is that B is not a veteran and A is. On the assumption that the veteran has served his country,[3] the country owes him something. And it seems plain that giving him preference is a not unjust way in which part of that debt of gratitude can be paid.

And now, finally, we should turn to those debts which are incurred by one who wrongs another. It is here we find what seems to me the most powerful argument for the conclusion that the preferential hiring of blacks and women is not unjust.

I obviously cannot claim any novelty for this argument: it's a very familiar one. Indeed, not merely is it familiar, but so are a battery of objections to it. It may be granted that if we have wronged A, we owe him something: we should make amends, we should compensate him for the wrong done him. It may even be granted that if we have wronged A, we must make amends, that justice requires it, and that a failure to make amends is not merely callousness, but injustice. But (a) are the young blacks and women who are amongst the current applicants for university jobs amongst the blacks and women who were wronged? To turn to particular cases, it might happen that the black applicant is middle class, son of professionals, and has had the very best in private schooling; or that the woman applicant is plainly the product of feminist upbringing and encouragement. Is it proper, much less required, that the black or woman be given preference over a white male who grew up in poverty, and has to make his own way and earn his encouragements? Again, (b), did we, the current members of the community, wrong any blacks or women? Lots of people once did; but then isn't it for them to do the compensating? That is, if they're still alive. For presumably nobody now alive owned any slaves, and perhaps nobody now alive voted against women's suffrage. And (c) what if the white male applicant for the job has never in any degree wronged any blacks or women? If so, *he* doesn't owe any debts to them, so why should *he* make amends to them?

These objections seem to me quite wrong-headed.

Obviously the situation for blacks and women is better than it was a hundred and fifty, fifty, twenty-five years ago. But it is absurd to suppose that the young blacks and women now of an age to apply for jobs have not been wronged. Large-scale, blatant, overt wrongs have presumably disappeared; but it is only within the last twenty-five years (perhaps the last ten years in the case of women) that it has become at all widely agreed in this country that blacks and women must be recognized as having, not merely this or that particular right normally recognized as belonging to white males, but all of the rights and respect which go with full membership in the community. Even young blacks and women have lived through down-grading for being black or female: they have not merely not been given that very equal chance at the benefits generated by what the community owns which is so firmly insisted on for white males, they have not until lately even been felt to have a right to it.

And even those were not themselves down-graded for being black or female have suffered the consequences of the down-grading of other blacks and women: lack of self-confidence, and lack of self-respect. For where a community accepts that a person's being black, or being a woman, are right and proper grounds for denying that person full membership in the community, it can hardly be supposed that any but the most extraordinarily independent black or woman will escape self-doubt. All but the most extraordinarily independent of them have had to work harder—if only against self-doubt—than all but the most deprived white males, in the competition for a place amongst the best qualified.

If any black or woman has been unjustly deprived of what he or she has a right to, then of course justice does call for making amends. But what of the blacks and women who haven't actually been deprived of what they have a right to, but only made to suffer the consequences of injustice to other blacks and women? *Perhaps* justice doesn't require making amends to them as well; but common decency certainly does. To fail, at the very least, to make what counts as public apology to all, and to take positive steps to show that it is sincerely meant, is, if not injustice, then anyway a fault at least as serious as ingratitude.

Opting for a policy of preferential hiring may of course mean that some black or woman is preferred to some white male who as a matter of fact has had a harder life than the black or woman. But so may opting for a policy of veterans' preference mean that a healthy, unscarred, middle class veteran is preferred to a poor, struggling, scarred, nonveteran. Indeed, opting for a policy of settling who gets the job by having all equally qualified candidates draw straws may also mean that in a given case the candidate with the hardest life loses out. Opting for any policy other than hard-life preference may have this result.

I have no objection to anyone's arguing that it is precisely hard-life preference that we ought to opt for. If all, or anyway all of the equally qualified, have a right to an equal chance, then the argument would have to draw attention to something sufficiently powerful to override that right. But perhaps this could be done along the lines I followed in the case of blacks and women: perhaps it could be successfully argued that we have wronged those who have had hard lives, and therefore owe it to them to make amends. And then we should have in more extreme form a difficulty already present: how are these preferences to be ranked? shall we place the hard-lifers ahead of blacks? both ahead of women? and what about veterans? I leave these questions aside. My concern has been only to show that the white male applicant's right to an equal chance does not make it unjust to opt for a policy under which blacks and women are given preference. That a white male with a specially hard history may lose out under this policy cannot possibly be any objection to it, in the absence of a showing that hard-life preference is not unjust, and, more important, takes priority over preference for blacks and women.

Lastly, it should be stressed that to opt for such a policy is not to make the young white male applicants themselves make amends for any wrongs done to blacks and women. Under such a policy, no one is asked to give up a job which is already his; the job for which the white male competes isn't his, but is the community's, and it is the hiring officer who gives it to the black or woman in the community's name. Of course the white male is asked to give up his equal chance at the job. But that is not something he pays to the black or woman by way of making amends; it is something the community takes away from him in order that *it* may make amends.

Still, the community does impose a burden on him: it is able to make amends for its wrongs only by taking something away from him, something which, after all, we are supposing he has a right to. And why should *he* pay the cost of the community's amends-making?

If there were some appropriate way in which the community could make amends to its blacks and women, some way which did not require depriving anyone of anything he has a right to, then that would be the best course of action for it to take. Or if there were anyway some way in which the costs could be shared by everyone, and not imposed entirely on the young white male job applicants, then that would be, if not best, then anyway better than opting for a policy of preferential hiring. But in fact the nature of the wrongs done is such as to make jobs the best and most suitable form of compensation. What blacks and women were denied was full membership in the community; and nothing can more appropriately make amends for that wrong than precisely what will make them feel they now finally have it. And that means jobs. Financial compensation (the cost of which could be shared equally) slips through the fingers; having a job, and discovering you do it well, yield—perhaps better than anything else—that very self-respect which blacks and women have had to do without.

But of course choosing this way of making amends means that the costs are imposed on the young white male applicants who are turned away. And so it should be noticed that it is not entirely inappropriate that those applicants should pay the costs. No doubt few, if any, have themselves, individually, done any wrongs to blacks and women. But they have profited from the wrongs the community did. Many may actually have been direct beneficiaries of policies which excluded or down-graded blacks and women—perhaps in school admissions, perhaps in access to financial aid, perhaps elsewhere; and even those who did not directly benefit in this way had, at any rate, the advantage in the competition which comes of confidence in one's full membership, and of one's rights being recognized as a matter of course.

Of course it isn't only the young white male ap-plicant for a university job who has benefited from the exclusion of blacks and women: the older white male, now comfortably tenured, also benefited, and many defenders of preferential hiring feel that he should be asked to share the costs. Well, presumably we can't demand that he give up his job, or share it. But it seems to me in place to expect the occupants of comfortable professorial chairs to contribute in some way, to make some form of return to the young white male who bears the cost, and is turned away. It will have been plain that I find the outcry now heard against preferential hiring in the universities objectionable; it would also be objectionable that those of us who are now securely situated should placidly defend it, with no more than a sigh of regret for the young white male who pays for it.

IV

One final word: "discrimination." I am inclined to think we so use it that if anyone is convicted of discriminating against blacks, women, white males, or what have you, then he is thereby convicted of acting unjustly. If so, and if I am right in thinking that preferential hiring in the restricted range of cases we have been looking at is *not* unjust, then we have two options: (a) we can simply reply that to opt for a policy of preferential hiring in those cases is not to opt for a policy of discriminating against white males, or (b) we can hope to get usage changed—e.g., by trying to get people to allow that there is discriminating against and discriminating against, and that some is unjust, but some is not.

Best of all, however, would be for that phrase to be avoided altogether. It's at best a blunt tool: there are all sorts of nice moral discriminations [*sic*] which one is unable to make while occupied with it. And that bluntness itself fits it to do harm: blacks and women are hardly likely to see through to what precisely is owed them while they are being accused of welcoming what is unjust.

NOTES

1. This essay is an expanded version of a talk given at the Conference on the Liberation of Female Persons, held

at North Carolina State University at Raleigh, on March 26–28, 1973, under a grant from the S & H Foundation. I am indebted to James Thomson and the members of the Society for Ethical and Legal Philosophy for criticism of an earlier draft.

2. To the best of my knowledge, the analogy between veterans' preference and the preferential hiring of blacks has been mentioned in print only by Edward T. Chase, in a Letter to the Editor, *Commentary,* February 1973.

3. Many people would reject this assumption, or perhaps accept it only selectively, for veterans of this or that particular war. I ignore this. What interests me is what follows if we make the assumption—as, of course, many other people do, more, it seems, than do not.

Critics

Robert Simon

Preferential Hiring

A Reply to Judith Jarvis Thomson

Judith Jarvis Thomson has recently defended preferential hiring of women and black persons in universities.[1] She restricts her defense of the assignment of preference to only those cases where candidates from preferred groups and their white male competitors are equally qualified, although she suggests that her argument can be extended to cover cases where the qualifications are unequal as well. The argument in question is compensatory; it is because of pervasive patterns of unjust discrimination against black persons and women that justice, or at least common decency, requires that amends be made.

While Thomson's analysis surely clarifies many of the issues at stake, I find it seriously incomplete. I will argue that even if her claim that compensation is due victims of social injustice is correct (as I think it is), it is questionable nevertheless whether preferential hiring is an acceptable method of distributing such compensation. This is so, even if, as Thomson argues, compensatory claims override the right of the white male applicant to equal consideration from the appointing officer. For implementation of preferential hiring policies may involve claims, perhaps even claims of right, other than the above right of the

white male applicant. In the case of the claims I have in mind, the best that can be said is that where preferential hiring is concerned, they are arbitrarily ignored. If so, and if such claims are themselves warranted, then preferential hiring, while *perhaps* not unjust, is open to far more serious question than Thomson acknowledges.

I

A familiar objection to special treatment for blacks and women is that, if such a practice is justified, other victims of injustice or misfortune ought to receive special treatment too. While arguing that virtually all women and black persons have been harmed, either directly or indirectly, by discrimination, Thomson acknowledges that in any particular case, a white male may have been victimized to a greater extent than have the blacks or women with which he is competing (pp. 381–382). However, she denies that other victims of injustice or misfortune ought automatically to have priority over blacks and women where distribution of compensation is concerned. Just as veterans receive preference with

Robert Simon, "Preferential Hiring: A Reply to Judith Jarvis Thomson," *Philosophy and Public Affairs* 3, no. 3 (Spring 1974): 312–320. Reprinted by permission of Princeton University Press.

respect to employment in the civil service, as payment for the service they have performed for society, so can blacks and women legitimately be given preference in university hiring, in payment of the debt owed them. And just as the former policy can justify hiring a veteran who in fact had an easy time of it over a non-veteran who made great sacrifices for the public good, so too can the latter policy justify hiring a relatively undeprived member of a preferred group over a more disadvantaged member of a non-preferred group.

But surely if the reason for giving a particular veteran preference is that he performed a service for his country, that same preference must be given to anyone who performed a similar service. Likewise, if the reason for giving preference to a black person or to a woman is that the recipient has been injured due to an unjust practice, then preference must be given to anyone who has been similarly injured. So, it appears, there can be no relevant *group* to which compensation ought to be made, other than that made up of and only of those who have been injured or victimized.[2] Although, as Thomson claims, all blacks and women may be members of that latter group, they deserve compensation *qua* victim and not *qua* black person or woman.

There are at least two possible replies that can be made to this sort of objection. First, it might be agreed that anyone injured in the same way as blacks or women ought to receive compensation. But then, "same way" is characterized so narrowly that it applies to no one except blacks and women. While there is nothing logically objectionable about such a reply, it may nevertheless be morally objectionable. For it implies that a nonblack male who has been terribly injured by a social injustice has less of a claim to compensation than a black or woman who has only been minimally injured. And this implication may be morally unacceptable.

A more plausible line of response may involve shifting our attention from compensation of individuals to collective compensation of groups.[3] Once this shift is made, it can be acknowledged that as individuals, some white males may have stronger compensatory claims than blacks or women. But as compensation is owed the group, it is group claims that must

be weighed, not individual ones. And surely, at the group level, the claims of black persons and women to compensation are among the strongest there are.

Suppose we grant that certain groups, including those specified by Thomson, are owed collective compensation. What should be noted is that the conclusion of concern here—that preferential hiring policies are acceptable instruments for compensating groups—does not directly follow. To derive such a conclusion validly, one would have to provide additional premises specifying the relation between collective compensation to groups and distribution of that compensation to individual members. For it does not follow from the fact that some group members are compensated that the group is compensated. Thus, if through a computer error, every member of the American Philosophical Association was asked to pay additional taxes, then if the government provided compensation for this error, it would not follow that it had compensated the Association. Rather, it would have compensated each member *qua* individual. So what is required, where preferential hiring is concerned, are plausible premises showing how the preferential award of jobs to group members counts as collective compensation for the group.

Thomson provides no such additional premises. Moreover, there is good reason to think that if any such premises were provided, they would count against preferential hiring as an instrument of collective compensation. This is because although compensation is owed to the group, preferential hiring policies award compensation to an arbitrarily selected segment of the group; namely, those who have the ability and qualifications to be seriously considered for the jobs available. Surely, it is far more plausible to think that collective compensation ought to be equally available to all group members, or at least to all kinds of group members.[4] The claim that although compensation is owed collectively to a group, only a special sort of group member is eligible to receive it, while perhaps not incoherent certainly ought to be rejected as arbitrary, at least in the absence of an argument to the contrary.

Accordingly, the proponent of preferential hiring faces the following dilemma. Either compensation is to be made on an individual basis, in which case the fact that one is black or a woman is irrelevant to whether one ought to receive special treatment, or it is made on a group basis, in which case it is far from clear that preferential hiring policies are acceptable compensatory instruments. Until this dilemma is resolved, assuming it can be resolved at all, the compensatory argument for preferential hiring is seriously incomplete at a crucial point.

II

Even if the above difficulty could be resolved, however, other problems remain. For example, once those entitled to compensatory benefits have been identified, questions arise concerning how satisfactorily preferential hiring policies honor such entitlements.

Consider, for example, a plausible principle of compensatory justice which might be called the Proportionality Principle (PP). According to the PP, the strength of one's compensatory claim, and the quantity of compensation one is entitled to is, *ceteris paribus,* proportional to the degree of injury suffered. A corollary of the PP is that equal injury gives rise to compensatory claims of equal strength. Thus, if *X* and *Y* were both injured to the same extent, and both deserve compensation for their injury, then, *ceteris paribus,* each has a compensatory claim of equal strength and each is entitled to equal compensation.

Now, it is extremely unlikely that a hiring program which gives preference to blacks and women will satisfy the PP because of the arbitrariness implicit in the search for candidates on the open market. Thus, three candidates, each members of previously victimized groups, may well wind up with highly disparate positions. One may secure employment in a prestigious department of a leading university while another may be hired by a university which hardly merits the name. The third might not be hired at all.

The point is that where the market place is used to distribute compensation, distribution will be by market principles, and hence only accidentally will be fitting in view of the injury suffered and compensation provided for others. While any compensation may be better than none, this would hardly

appear to be a satisfactory way of making amends to the victimized.

"Compensation according to ability" or "compensation according to marketability" surely are dubious principles of compensatory justice. On the contrary, those with the strongest compensatory claims should be compensated first (and most). Where compensatory claims are equal, but not everybody can actually be compensated, some fair method of distribution should be employed, e.g., a lottery. Preferential hiring policies, then, to the extent that they violate the PP, *arbitrarily* discriminate in favor of some victims of past injustice and against others. The basis on which compensation is awarded is independent of the basis on which it is owed, and so distribution is determined by application of principles which are irrelevant from the point of view of compensatory justice.

Now, perhaps this is not enough to show that the use of preferential hiring as a compensatory instrument is unjust, or even unjustified. But perhaps it is enough to show that the case for the justice or justification of such a policy has not yet been made. Surely, we can say, at the very least, that a policy which discriminates in the arbitrary fashion discussed above is not a particularly satisfactory compensatory mechanism. If so, the direction in which considerations of compensatory justice and common decency point may be far less apparent than Thomson suggests.

III

So far, I have considered arbitrariness in the distribution of compensatory benefits by preferential hiring policies. However, arbitrariness involved in the assessment of costs is also of concern.

Thus, it is sometimes argued that preferential hiring policies place the burden of providing compensation on young white males who are just entering the job market. This is held to be unfair, because, first, there is no special reason for placing the burden on that particular group and, second, because many members of that group are not responsible for the injury done to blacks and women. In response to the first point, Thomson acknowledges that it seems to her "in place to expect the occupants of comfortable professorial chairs to contribute in some way, to make some form of return to the young white male who bears the cost . . ." (p. 384). In response to the second point, Thomson concedes that few, if any, white male applicants to university positions individually have done any wrong to women or black persons. However, she continues, many have profited by the wrongs inflicted by others. So it is not unfitting that they be asked to make sacrifices now (p. 383).

However, it is far from clear, at least to me, that this reply is satisfactory. For even if the group which bears the cost is expanded to include full professors, why should that new group be singled out? The very same consideration that required the original expansion would seem to require a still wider one. Indeed, it would seem this point can be pressed until costs are assessed against society as a whole. This is exactly the position taken by Paul Taylor, who writes, "The obligation to offer such benefits to (the previously victimized) group . . . is an obligation that falls on society in general, not on any particular person. For it is the society in general that, through its established (discriminatory) social practice, brought upon itself the obligation."[5]

Perhaps, however, the claim that preferential hiring policies arbitrarily distribute burdens can be rebutted. For presumably the advocate of preferential hiring does not want to restrict such a practice to universities but rather would wish it to apply throughout society. If so, and *if* persons at the upper echelons are expected to share costs with young white male job applicants, then perhaps a case can be made that burdens are equitably distributed throughout society.

Even here, however, there are two points an opponent of preferential hiring can make. First, he can point out that burdens are not equitably distributed now. Consequently, to the extent that preferential policies are employed at present, then to that extent are burdens arbitrarily imposed now. Second, he can question the assumption that if someone gains from an unjust practice for which he is not responsible and even opposes, the gain is not really his and can be taken from him without injustice. This assumption is central to the compensatory argument for preferential

hiring since if it is unacceptable, no justification remains for requiring "innocent bystanders" to provide compensation.

If X benefits at the expense of Y because of the operation of an unjust social institution, then is the benefit which accrues to X really deserved by Y? It seems to me that normally the answer will be affirmative. But it also seems to me that there is a significant class of cases where an affirmative response *may* not be justified. Suppose X himself is the victim of a similarly unjust social practice so that Z benefits at his expense. In such circumstances, it is questionable whether X ought to compensate Y, especially if X played no personal role in the formation of the unjust institutions at issue. Perhaps *both* X and Y ought to receive (different degrees of) compensation from Z.

If this point is sound, it becomes questionable whether *all* members of nonpreferred groups are equally liable (or even liable at all) for provision of compensation. It is especially questionable in the case where the individual from the nonpreferred group has been unjustly victimized to a far greater extent than the individual from the preferred group. Hence, even if it were true that all members of nonpreferred groups have profited from discrimination against members of preferred groups, it does not automatically follow that all are equally liable for providing compensation. In so far as preferential hiring policies do not take this into account, they are open to the charge of arbitrariness in assessing the costs of compensation.

One more point seems to require mention here. If preferential hiring policies are expanded, as Thomson suggests, to cases where the candidates are not equally qualified, a further difficulty arises. To the extent that lowering quality lowers efficiency, members of victimized groups are likely to lose more than others. This may be particularly important in educational contexts. Students from such groups may have been exposed to poorer instruction than was made available to others. But they might have greater need for better instruction than, say, middle class students from affluent backgrounds.[6]

Suppose that members of previously discriminated against groups deserve special support in developing their capacities and talents. Then, it would seem that educational institutions charged with promoting such development have a corresponding obligation to develop those capacities and talents to the best of their ability. Presumably, this requires hiring the best available faculty and administration.

What we seem to have here is a conflict within the framework of compensatory justice itself. Even if preferential hiring is an acceptable method for distributing compensation, the compensation so distributed may decrease the beneficial effects of education. And this may adversely affect more members of the preferred groups than are helped by the preferential policy.[7]

IV

The argument of this paper is not directed against the view that victims of grave social injustice in America deserve compensation. On the contrary, a strong case can be made for providing such compensation.[8] Rather, I have tried to show that the case for using preferential hiring as a *means* of providing such compensation is incomplete at three crucial points:

1. It is not clear to whom compensation should be made, groups or individuals. If the former, it has not been shown that preferential hiring compensates the group. If the latter, it has not been shown why membership in a group (other than that composed of, and only of, the victimized) is relevant to determining who should be compensated.
2. It has not been shown that compensation should be awarded on grounds of marketability, grounds that certainly seem to be irrelevant from the compensatory point of view.
3. It has not been shown that arbitrariness and inequity are or can be avoided in distributing the costs of preferential hiring policies of the sort in question.

If these charges have force, then whether or not preferential hiring can be justified on other grounds, the compensatory argument for such a practice is far more doubtful than Thomson's article suggests.

NOTES

1. Judith Jarvis Thomson, "Preferential Hiring," *Philosophy & Public Affairs* 2, no. 4 (Summer 1973): 364–384. All further page references to this article will be made within the text.

2. This point also has been argued for recently by J. L. Cowen, "Inverse Discrimination," *Analysis* 33, no. 1 (1972): 10–12.

3. Such a position has been defended by Paul Taylor, in his "Reverse Discrimination and Compensatory Justice," *Analysis* 33, no. 4 (1973): 177–182.

4. Taylor would apparently agree, ibid.: 180.

5. Ibid.: 180. Parentheses are my own.

6. At the time these arguments were first formulated, I unfortunately did not have access to Charles King's article "A Problem Concerning Discrimination" (presented to a symposium on reverse discrimination at the Eastern Division Meetings of the American Philosophical Association in 1972) in which a similar point is made. King also argues, although along lines somewhat different from my own, that preferential hiring policies distribute compensatory benefits arbitrarily.

7. This will not apply as frequently as might be thought, however, if it is true that membership in a preferred group is itself an *educational* qualification. That this is so is sometimes argued on the grounds, for example, that women and black professors are necessary as "role models" for women and black students. Thomson, however, expresses doubts about arguments of this sort (pp. 365–369). More important, if such arguments were strong, it would seem that a case could be made for hiring black and women professors on grounds of merit. That is, they should be hired because they can do the job better than others, not (only) because they are owed compensation. In any case, however, my argument in the text would still apply to those instances in which the candidate from the preferred group was not as qualified (in the broad sense of "qualified" in which membership in the preferred group is one qualification) as the candidates from nonpreferred groups.

8. For a defense of the provision of monetary compensation or reparations, see Hugo Bedau, "Compensatory Justice and the Black Manifesto," *The Monist* 56, no. 1 (1972): 20–42.

16

Are Reparations for Slavery Wrong?

Horowitz and His Critics

From the beginning of its existence until the Civil War, the United States government permitted slavery to be practiced on its soil. When slavery was finally abolished, in 1865, the government continued to practice various forms of racial segregation and discrimination for many years after. Millions of Africans and African Americans suffered greatly during those years of slavery, segregation, and discrimination.

Virtually everyone now agrees that what the United States government did to Africans and African Americans during this period was terribly wrong. But this does not mean that everyone agrees about what should be done about it now. In particular, while some people believe that the United States now owes reparations to African Americans as a form of compensation for slavery and its aftermath, others believe that this call for reparations is unfounded and unjust. Indeed, putting things this mildly is a great understatement. The current debate over slave reparations is among the most heated and divisive issues in the current debate over race as a whole.

Nowhere is this fact move vividly illustrated than in the bitter controversy that surrounded the publication of David Horowitz's now (in)famous article "Ten Reasons Why Reparations for Blacks Is a Bad Idea for Blacks—and Racist, Too!" In 2001 Horowitz attempted to place that brief article as a paid advertisement in a number of college newspapers. Everywhere it was published, heated discussions followed. Some papers chose to run the ad, others chose not to. In either case, the editors' decisions were praised by some and bitterly criticized by others. In this chapter, we present Horowitz's article in its entirety, as it appeared in a number of campus newspapers, along with a piece written directly in response to it and another that responds to it indirectly.

Horowitz presents his case against slave reparations as a series of ten discrete and unconnected points. However, most of these points can be construed as parts of a larger, single argument, one that takes the form of a criticism of an argument from analogy (see Introduction) that Horowitz claims underpins the case for reparations. Horowitz rests the central case in favor of slave reparations on an analogy in which the relationship between the United States government and its present-day African American citizens is compared to the relationship between a perpetrator of some great injustice and the immediate victims of that injustice (e.g., between Germany and survivors of the Holocaust). In the latter case, most people will agree that it is fair and appropriate that the victims seek compensation from those who wronged them. And by using this analogy, the proponent of reparations hopes that people will come to accept the slave reparation claim as valid as well. Horowitz's "Ten Reasons" can then be largely understood as an attempt to undermine this analogy. This is most explicit in the case of reason 4, but applies as well to reasons 1–4 and reason 6, all of which, in one way or another, attempt to point to problems with the claim that the slave case is suitably analogous to other cases in which a claim of restitution is generally accepted. Reasons 8 and 9 can also be taken as an indirect attack on the analogy, since they argue for the claim that even if there had been a debt the debt has already been paid. Reasons 7 and 10 round out Horowitz's case against reparations by arguing that reparations would have negative consequences for blacks, in particular, and for Americans, in general.

If Horowitz's article is best understood as an extended criticism of the argument from analogy then Chrisman and Allen's response to it can best be thought of as an argument by process of elimination (see Introduction). One by one, the two authors go through Horowitz's ten reasons and attempt to eliminate each one. Like most arguments that proceed in this manner, Chrisman and Allen's argument is difficult to summarize. Readers are therefore encouraged to attend closely to the points raised under each of the authors' ten headings.

This chapter concludes with a short piece by Randall Robinson, author of *The Debt: What America Owes to Blacks,* and one of the most prominent proponents of reparations. In "America's Debt to Blacks," Robinson offers a brief restatement of the central argument of his book. Although the article and book were not written as responses to Horowitz's "Ten Reasons," the main point of Robinson's piece can nonetheless be understood in terms of Horowitz's position. Where Horowitz maintains that there is not a close enough connection between present-day African Americans and those who were directly responsible for the injustice of slavery, Robinson argues that the two sides are connected by compelling considerations. The present-day United States government is connected to that of the past because "the life and responsibilities of a nation are not limited to the life spans of its mortal constituents." And present-day African Americans are connected to those who were wronged in the past because each child begins "where its parents left off" and thus suffers when its predecessors suffer. Although the harms of slavery were originally inflicted by an earlier generation of Americans on an earlier generation of Africans, the debt that was generated by their wrongdoing is legitimately transferred to the present day because we inherit the debts that our government incurs, and African Americans have inherited the harms that their ancestors suffered.

QUESTIONS FOR CONSIDERATION

In thinking critically about the exchange between Horowitz and his critics, it is important to look broadly at all ten of the reasons Horowitz gives and all ten of the reasons Chrisman and Allen provide in response to him. At the same time, it is also important to focus more narrowly on the central question of whether or not the slave reparations case is suitably analogous to other cases in which claims of restitution are generally accepted.

- Is Horowitz correct in insisting that there are too many differences between the cases to allow the argument for reparations to succeed?
- Or is Robinson correct in maintaining that the apparent differences between the cases can be bridged?
- Would slave reparations unfairly punish the current generation of Americans, none of whom has ever owned a slave, for the sins of (some of) their predecessors?
- Or would reparations simply amount to the United States government's finally discharging an obligation it incurred long ago?
- Finally, readers should stop to consider a question that is not raised in Horowitz's article but that is nonetheless raised by the *existence* of that article. Did the newspapers that accepted Horowitz's advertisement do the right thing, or did those that refused to accept it do the right thing?

FURTHER READING

Boxill, Bernard. "A Lockean Argument for Black Reparations." *Journal of Ethics* 7, no. 1 (2003): 63–91.

Schedler, George. "Principles for Measuring the Damages of American Slavery." *Public Affairs Quarterly* 16, no. 4 (2002): 377–404.

David Horowitz | # Ten Reasons Why Reparations for Blacks Is a Bad Idea for Blacks— and Racist, Too!

1. There Is No Single Group Clearly Responsible for the Crime of Slavery

Black Africans and Arabs were responsible for enslaving the ancestors of African-Americans. There were 3,000 black slave-owners in the ante-bellum United States. Are reparations to be paid by their descendants too?

2. There Is No One Group That Benefited Exclusively from Its Fruits

The claim for reparations is premised on the false assumption that only whites have benefited from slavery. If slave labor created wealth for Americans, then obviously it has created wealth for black Americans as well, including the descendants of slaves. The GNP of black America is so large that it makes the African-American community the 10th most prosperous "nation" in the world. American blacks on average enjoy per capita incomes in the range of twenty to fifty times that of blacks living in any of the African nations from which they were kidnapped.

3. Only a Tiny Minority of White Americans Ever Owned Slaves, and Others Gave Their Lives to Free Them

Only a tiny minority of Americans ever owned slaves. This is true even for those who lived in the ante-bellum South where only one white in five was a

David Horowitz, "Ten Reasons Why Reparations for Blacks Is a Bad Idea for Blacks—and Racist, Too!" Originally posted on frontpagemag.com, January 3, 2001.

slaveholder. Why should their descendants owe a debt? What about the descendants of the 350,000 Union soldiers who died to free the slaves? They gave their lives. What possible moral principle would ask them to pay (through their descendants) again?

4. America Today Is a Multi-Ethnic Nation and Most Americans Have No Connection (direct or indirect) to Slavery

The two great waves of American immigration occurred after 1880 and then after 1960. What rationale would require Vietnamese boat people, Russian refuseniks, Iranian refugees, and Armenian victims of the Turkish persecution, Jews, Mexicans Greeks, or Polish, Hungarian, Cambodian and Korean victims of Communism, to pay reparations to American blacks?

5. The Historical Precedents Used to Justify the Reparations Claim Do Not Apply, and the Claim Itself Is Based on Race Not Injury

The historical precedents generally invoked to justify the reparations claim are payments to Jewish survivors of the Holocaust, Japanese-Americans and African-American victims of racial experiments in Tuskegee, or racial outrages in Rosewood and Oklahoma City. But in each case, the recipients of reparations were the direct victims of the injustice or their immediate families. This would be the only case of reparations to people who were not immediately affected and whose sole qualification to receive reparations would be racial. As has already been pointed out, during the slavery era, many blacks were free men or slave-owners themselves, yet the reparations claimants make no distinction between the roles blacks actually played in the injustice itself. Randall Robinson's book on reparations, *The Debt,* which is the manifesto of the reparations movement is pointedly sub-titled *"What America Owes to Blacks."* If this is not racism, what is?

6. The Reparations Argument Is Based on the Unfounded Claim That All African-American Descendants of Slaves Suffer from the Economic Consequences of Slavery and Discrimination

No evidence-based attempt has been made to prove that living individuals have been adversely affected by a slave system that was ended over 150 years ago. But there is plenty of evidence the hardships that occurred were hardships that individuals could and did overcome. The black middle-class in America is a prosperous community that is now larger in absolute terms than the black underclass. Does its existence not suggest that economic adversity is the result of failures of individual character rather than the lingering after-effects of racial discrimination and a slave system that ceased to exist well over a century ago? West Indian blacks in America are also descended from slaves but their average incomes are equivalent to the average incomes of whites (and nearly 25% higher than the average incomes of American born blacks). How is it that slavery adversely affected one large group of descendants but not the other? How can government be expected to decide an issue that is so subjective—and yet so critical—to the case?

7. The Reparations Claim Is One More Attempt to Turn African-Americans into Victims. It Sends a Damaging Message to the African-American Community

The renewed sense of grievance—which is what the claim for reparations will inevitably create—is neither a constructive nor a helpful message for black leaders to be sending to their communities and to others. To focus the social passions of African-Americans on what some Americans may have done to their ancestors fifty or a hundred and fifty years ago is to burden them with a crippling sense of victim-hood. How are the millions of refugees from tyranny and genocide who are now living in America going to receive these claims, moreover, except as demands for special treatment, an extravagant new handout that is only necessary because some blacks can't seem to locate the ladder of opportunity within reach of others—many less privileged than themselves?

8. Reparations to African Americans Have Already Been Paid

Since the passage of the Civil Rights Acts and the advent of the Great Society in 1965, trillions of dollars in transfer payments have been made to African-Americans in the form of welfare benefits and racial preferences (in contracts, job placements and educational admissions)—all under the rationale of redressing historic racial grievances. It is said that reparations are necessary to achieve a healing between African-Americans and other Americans. If trillion dollar restitutions and a wholesale rewriting of American law (in order to accommodate racial preferences) for African-Americans is not enough to achieve a "healing," what will?

9. What About the Debt Blacks Owe to America?

Slavery existed for thousands of years before the Atlantic slave trade was born, and in all societies. But in the thousand years of its existence, there never was an anti-slavery movement until white Christians—Englishmen and Americans—created one. If not for the anti-slavery attitudes and military power of white Englishmen and Americans, the slave trade would not have been brought to an end. If not for the sacrifices of white soldiers and a white American president who gave his life to sign the Emancipation Proclamation, blacks in America would still be slaves. If not for the dedication of Americans of all ethnicities and colors to a society based on the principle that all men are created equal, blacks in America would not enjoy the highest standard of living of blacks anywhere in the world, and indeed one of the highest standards of living of any people in the world. They would not enjoy the greatest freedoms and the most thoroughly protected individual rights anywhere. Where is the gratitude of black America and its leaders for those gifts?

10. The Reparations Claim Is a Separatist Idea That Sets African-Americans Against the Nation That Gave Them Freedom

Blacks were here before the *Mayflower*. Who is more American than the descendants of African slaves? For the African-American community to isolate itself even further from America is to embark on a course whose implications are troubling. Yet the African-American community has had a long-running flirtation with separatists, nationalists and the political left, who want African-Americans to be no part of America's social contract. African Americans should reject this temptation.

For all America's faults, African-Americans have an enormous stake in their country and its heritage. It is this heritage that is really under attack by the reparations movement. The reparations claim is one more assault on America, conducted by racial separatists and the political left. It is an attack not only on white Americans, but on all Americans—especially African-Americans.

America's African-American citizens are the richest and most privileged black people alive—a bounty that is a direct result of the heritage that is under assault. The American idea needs the support of its African-American citizens. But African-Americans also need the support of the American idea. For it is this idea that led to the principles and institutions that have set African-Americans—and all of us—free.

Critics

Robert Chrisman
Ernest Allen, Jr.

Ten Reasons

A Response to David Horowitz

David Horowitz's article, "Ten Reasons Why Reparations for Slavery Is a Bad Idea and Racist Too," recently achieved circulation in a handful of college newspapers throughout the United States as a paid advertisement sponsored by the Center for the Study of Popular Culture. While Horowitz's article pretends to address the issues of reparations, it is not about reparations at all. It is, rather, a well-heeled, coordinated attack on Black Americans which is calculated to elicit division and strife. Horowitz reportedly attempted to place his article in some 50 student newspapers at universities and colleges across the country, and was successful in purchasing space in such newspapers at Brown, Duke, Arizona, UC Berkeley, UC Davis, University of Chicago, and University of Wisconsin, paying an average of $700 per paper. His campaign has succeeded in fomenting outrage, dissension, and grief wherever it has appeared. Unfortunately, both its supporters and its foes too often have categorized the issue as one centering on "free speech." The sale and purchase of advertising space is not a matter of free speech, however, but involves an exchange of commodities. Professor Lewis Gordon of Brown University put it very well, saying that "what concerned me was that the ad was both hate speech and a solicitation for financial support to develop antiblack ad space. I was concerned that it would embolden white supremacists and antiblack racists." At a March 15 panel held at UC Berkeley, Horowitz also conceded that his paid advertisement did not constitute a free speech issue.

As one examines the text of Horowitz's article, it becomes apparent that it is not a reasoned essay addressed to the topic of reparations: it is, rather, a racist polemic against African Americans and Africans that is neither responsible nor informed, relying heavily upon sophistry and a Hitlerian "Big Lie" technique. To our knowledge, only one of Horowitz's ten "reasons" has been challenged by a black scholar as to source, accuracy, and validity. It is our intention here to briefly rebut his slanders in order to pave the way for an honest and forthright debate on reparations. In these efforts we focus not just on slavery, but also the legacy of slavery which continues to inform institutional as well as individual behavior in the U.S. to this day. Although we recognize that white America still owes a debt to the descendants of slaves, in addressing Horowitz's distortions of history we do not act as advocates for a specific form of reparations.

1. There Is No Single Group Clearly Responsible for the Crime of Slavery

Horowitz's first argument, relativist in structure, can only lead to two conclusions: (1) societies are not responsible for their actions, and (2) since "everyone" was responsible for slavery, no one was responsible. While diverse groups on different continents certainly participated in the trade, the principal responsibility for internationalization of that trade and the institutionalization of slavery in the so-called New World rests with European and American individuals and institutions. The transatlantic slave trade began with the importation of African slaves into Hispaniola by Spain in the early 1500s. Nationals of France, England, Portugal, and the

Robert Chrisman and Ernest Allen, Jr., "Ten Reasons: A Response to David Horowitz," *The Black Scholar* 31 (Summer 2001); 49–55. Reprinted by permission of the Black Scholar.

Netherlands, supported by their respective governments and powerful religious institutions, quickly entered the trade and extracted their pieces of silver as well. By conservative estimates, 14 million enslaved Africans survived the horror of the Middle Passage for the purpose of producing wealth for Europeans and Euro-Americans in the New World.

While there is some evidence of blacks owning slaves for profit purposes—most notably the creole caste in Louisiana—the numbers were small. As historian James Oakes noted, "By 1830 there were some 3,775 free black slaveholders across the South. . . . The evidence is overwhelming that the vast majority of black slaveholders were free men who purchased members of their families or who acted out of benevolence" (Oakes, 47–48).

2. There Is No Single Group That Benefited Exclusively from Slavery

Horowitz's second point, which is also a relativist one, seeks to dismiss the argument that white Americans benefited as a group from slavery, contending that the material benefits of slavery could not accrue in an exclusive way to a single group. But such sophistry evades the basic issue: who benefited primarily from slavery? Those who were responsible for the institutionalized enslavement of people of African descent also received the primary benefits from such actions. New England slave traders, merchants, bankers, and insurance companies all profited from the slave trade, which required a wide variety of commodities ranging from sails, chandlery, foodstuffs, and guns, to cloth goods and other items for trading purposes. Both prior to and after the American Revolution, slaveholding was a principal path for white upward mobility in the South. The white native-born as well as immigrant groups such as Germans, Scots-Irish, and the like participated. In 1860, cotton was the country's largest single export. As Eric Williams and C.L.R. James have demonstrated, the free labor provided by slavery was central to the growth of industry in western Europe and the United States; simultaneously, as Walter Rodney has argued, slavery depressed and destabilized the economies of African states. Slaveholders benefited primarily from the institution, of course, and generally in proportion to the number of slaves which they held. But the sharing of the proceeds of slave exploitation spilled across class lines within white communities as well.

As historian John Hope Franklin recently affirmed in a rebuttal to Horowitz's claims:

> All whites and no slaves benefited from American slavery. All blacks had no rights that they could claim as their own. All whites, including the vast majority who had no slaves, were not only encouraged but authorized to exercise dominion over all slaves, thereby adding strength to the system of control.
>
> If David Horowitz had read James D. DeBow's "The Interest in Slavery of the Southern Non-slaveholder," he would not have blundered into the fantasy of claiming that no single group benefited from slavery. Planters, did, of course. New York merchants did, of course. Even poor whites benefited from the legal advantage they enjoyed over all blacks as well as from the psychological advantage of having a group beneath them.

The context of the African-American argument for reparations is confined to the practice and consequences of slavery within the United States, from the colonial period on through final abolition and the aftermath, circa 1619–1865. Contrary to Horowitz's assertion, there is no record of institutionalized white enslavement in colonial America. Horowitz is confusing the indenture of white labor, which usually lasted seven years or so during the early colonial period, with enslavement. African slavery was expanded, in fact, to replace the inefficient and unenforceable white indenture system. (Smith)

Seeking to claim that African Americans, too, have benefited from slavery, Horowitz points to the relative prosperity of African Americans in comparison to their counterparts on the African continent. However, his argument that, "the GNP of black America makes the African-American community the 10th most prosperous "nation" in the world is based upon a false analogy. GNP is defined as "the total market value of all the goods and services produced by a nation during a specified period." Black Americans are not a nation and have no GNP.

Horowitz confuses disposable income and "consumer power" with the generation of wealth.

3. Only a Tiny Minority of White Americans Ever Owned Slaves, and Others Gave Their Lives to Free Them

Most white union troops were drafted into the union army in a war which the federal government initially defined as a "war to preserve the union." In large part because they feared that freed slaves would flee the South and "take their jobs" while they themselves were engaged in warfare with Confederate troops, recently drafted white conscripts in New York City and elsewhere rioted during the summer of 1863, taking a heavy toll on black civilian life and property. Too many instances can be cited where white northern troops plundered the personal property of slaves, appropriating their bedding, chickens, pigs, and foodstuffs as they swept through the South. On the other hand, it is certainly true that there also existed principled white commanders and troops who were committed abolitionists.

However, Horowitz's focus on what he mistakenly considers to be the overriding, benevolent aim of white union troops in the Civil War obscures the role that blacks themselves played in their own liberation. African Americans were initially forbidden by the Union to fight in the Civil War, and black leaders such as Frederick Douglass and Martin Delany demanded the right to fight for their freedom. When racist doctrine finally conceded to military necessity, blacks were recruited into the Union Army in 1862 at approximately half the pay of white soldiers—a situation which was partially rectified by an act of Congress in mid-1864. Some 170,000 blacks served in the Civil War, representing nearly one third of the free black population.

By 1860, four million blacks in the U.S. were enslaved; some 500,000 were nominally free. Because of slavery, racist laws, and racist policies, blacks were denied the chance to compete for the opportunities and resources of America that were available to native whites and immigrants: labor opportunities, free enterprise, and land. The promise of "forty acres and a mule" to former slaves was effectively nullified by the actions of President Andrew Johnson. And because the best land offered by the Homestead Act of 1862 and its subsequent revisions quickly fell under the sway of white homesteaders and speculators, most former slaves were unable to take advantage of its provisions.

4. Most Living Americans Have No Connection (Direct or Indirect) to Slavery

As Joseph Anderson, member of the National Council of African American Men, observed, "the arguments for reparations aren't made on the basis of whether every white person directly gained from slavery. The arguments are made on the basis that slavery was institutionalized and protected by law in the United States. As the government is an entity that survives generations, its debts and obligations survive the lifespan of any particular individuals. . . . Governments make restitution to victims as a group or class" (*San Francisco Chronicle,* March 26, 2001, p. A21).

Most Americans today were not alive during World War II. Yet reparations to Japanese Americans for their internment in concentration camps during the war was paid out of current government sources contributed to by contemporary Americans. Passage of time does not negate the responsibility of government in crimes against humanity. Similarly, German corporations are not the "same" corporations that supported the Holocaust; their personnel and policies today belong to generations removed from their earlier criminal behavior. Yet, these corporations are being successfully sued by Jews for their past actions. In the same vein, the U.S. government is not the same government as it was in the pre-Civil War era, yet its debts and obligations from the past are no less relevant today.

5. The Historical Precedents Used to Justify the Reparations Claim Do Not Apply, and the Claim Itself Is Based on Race Not Injury

As noted in our response to "Reason 4," the historical precedents for the reparations claims of African Americans are fully consistent with restitution accorded other historical groups for atrocities committed against them. Second, the injury in question—that of slavery—was inflicted upon a people designated as a race. The descendants of that people—still socially constructed as a race today—continue to suffer the institutional legacies of slavery some one hundred thirty-five years after its demise. To attempt to separate the issue of so-called race from that of injury in this instance is pure sophistry. For example, the criminal (in)justice system today largely continues to operate as it did under slavery—for the protection of white citizens against black "outsiders." Although no longer inscribed in law, this very attitude is implicit to processes of law enforcement, prosecution, and incarceration, guiding the behavior of police, prosecutors, judges, juries, wardens, and parole boards. Hence, African Americans continue to experience higher rates of incarceration than do whites charged with similar crimes, endure longer sentences for the same classes of crimes perpetrated by whites, and, compared to white inmates, receive far less consideration by parole boards when being considered for release.

Slavery was an institution sanctioned by the highest laws of the land with a degree of support from the Constitution itself. The institution of slavery established the idea and the practice that American democracy was "for whites only." There are many white Americans whose actions (or lack thereof) reveal such sentiments today—witness the response of the media and the general populace to the blatant disfranchisement of African Americans in Florida during the last presidential election. Would such complacency exist if African Americans were considered "real citizens"? And despite the dramatic successes of the Civil Rights movement of the 1950s and 60s, the majority of black Americans do not enjoy the same rights as white Americans in the economic sphere. (We continue this argument in the following section.)

6. The Reparations Argument Is Based on the Unfounded Claim That All African-American Descendants of Slaves Suffer from the Economic Consequences of Slavery and Discrimination

Most blacks suffered and continue to suffer the economic consequences of slavery and its aftermath. As of 1998, median white family income in the U.S. was $49,023; median black family income was $29,404, just 60% of white income. (2001 *New York Times Almanac,* p. 319) Further, the costs of living within the United States far exceed those of African nations. The present poverty level for an American family of four is $17,029. Twenty-three and three-fifths percent (23.6%) of all black families live below the poverty level.

When one examines net financial worth, which reflects, in part, the wealth handed down within families from generation to generation, the figures appear much starker. Recently, sociologists Melvin L. Oliver and Thomas M. Shapiro found that just a little over a decade ago, the net financial worth of white American families with zero or negative net financial worth stood at around 25%; that of Hispanic households at 54%; and that of black American households at almost 61%. (Oliver and Shapiro, p. 87) The inability to accrue net financial worth is also directly related to hiring practices in which black Americans are "last hired" when the economy experiences an upturn, and "first fired" when it falls on hard times.

And as historian John Hope Franklin remarked on the legacy of slavery for black education: "laws enacted by states forbade the teaching of blacks any means of acquiring knowledge-including the alphabet-which is the legacy of disadvantage of educational privatization and discrimination experienced by African Americans in 2001."

Horowitz's comparison of African Americans with Jamaicans is a false analogy, ignoring the different historical contexts of the two populations. The British government ended slavery in Jamaica and its other West Indian territories in 1836, paying West Indian slaveholders $20,000,000 pounds ($100,000,000 U.S. dollars) to free the slaves, and leaving the black Jamaicans, who comprised 90% of that island's population, relatively free. Though still facing racist obstacles, Jamaicans come to the U.S. as voluntary immigrants, with greater opportunity to weigh, choose, and develop their options.

7. The Reparations Claim Is One More Attempt to Turn African-Americans into Victims. It Sends a Damaging Message to the African-American Community

What is a victim? Black people have certainly been victimized, but acknowledgment of that fact is not a case of "playing the victim" but of seeking justice. There is no validity to Horowitz's comparison between black Americans and victims of oppressive regimes who have voluntary immigrated to these shores. Further, many members of those populations, such as Chileans and Salvadorans, direct their energies for redress toward the governments of their own oppressive nations—which is precisely what black Americans are doing. Horowitz's racism is expressed in his contemptuous characterization of reparations as "an extravagant new handout that is only necessary because some blacks can't seem to locate the ladder of opportunity within reach of others, many of whom are less privileged than themselves." What Horowitz fails to acknowledge is that racism continues as an ideology and a material force within the U.S., providing blacks with no ladder that reaches the top. The damage lies in the systematic treatment of black people in the U.S., not their claims against those who initiated this damage and their spiritual descendants who continue its perpetuation.

8. Reparations to African Americans Have Already Been Paid

The nearest the U.S. government came to full and permanent restitution of African Americans was the spontaneous redistribution of land brought about by General William Sherman's Field Order 15 in January, 1865, which empowered Union commanders to make land grants and give other material assistance to newly liberated blacks. But that order was rescinded by President Andrew Johnson later in the year. Efforts by Representative Thaddeus Stevens and other radical Republicans to provide the proverbial "40 acres and a mule" which would have carved up huge plantations of the defeated Confederacy into modest land grants for blacks and poor whites never got out of the House of Representatives. The debt has not been paid.

"Welfare benefits and racial preferences" are not reparations. The welfare system was set in place in the 1930s to alleviate the poverty of the Great Depression, and more whites than blacks received welfare. So-called "racial preferences" come not from benevolence but from lawsuits by blacks against white businesses, government agencies, and municipalities which practice racial discrimination.

9. What About the Debt Blacks Owe to America?

Horowitz's assertion that "in the thousand years of slavery's existence, there never was an anti-slavery movement until white Anglo-Saxon Christians created one" only demonstrates his ignorance concerning the formidable efforts of blacks to free themselves. Led by black Toussaint L'Ouverture, the Haitian revolution of 1793 overthrew the French slave system, created the first black republic in the world, and intensified the activities of black and white anti-slavery movements in the U.S. Slave insurrections and conspiracies such as those of Gabriel (1800), Denmark Vesey (1822), and Nat Turner (1831) were potent sources of black resistance; black abolitionists such as Harriet Tubman, Frederick Douglass, Richard Allen, Sojourner Truth, Martin Delany, David Walker, and Henry Highland Garnet waged an incessant struggle against slavery through agencies such as the press, notably Douglass's North Star and its variants, which ran from 1847 to 1863 (blacks, moreover, constituted some 75% of the subscribers to William Lloyd Garrison's Liberator newspaper in its first four years); the Underground Railroad, the Negro Convention Movement, local, state, and national anti-slavery societies, and the slave narrative. Black Americans were in no ways the passive recipients of freedom from anyone, whether viewed from the perspective of black participation in the abolitionist movement, the flight of slaves from plantations and farms during the Civil War, or the enlistment of black troops in the Union army.

The idea of black debt to U.S. society is a rehash of the Christian missionary argument of the 17th and 18th centuries: because Africans were considered heathens, it was therefore legitimate to enslave them and drag them in chains to a Christian nation. Following their partial conversion, their moral and material lot were improved, for which black folk should be eternally grateful. Slave ideologues John Calhoun and George Fitzhugh updated this idea in the 19th century, arguing that blacks were better off under slavery than whites in the North who received wages, due to the paternalism and benevolence of the plantation system which assured perpetual employment, shelter, and board. Please excuse the analogy, but if someone chops off your fingers and then hands them back to you, should you be "grateful" for having received your mangled fingers, or enraged that they were chopped off in the first place?

10. The Reparations Claim Is a Separatist Idea That Sets African-Americans Against the Nation That Gave Them Freedom

Again, Horowitz reverses matters. Blacks are already separated from white America in fundamental matters such as income, family wealth, housing, legal treatment, education, and political representation. Andrew Hacker, for example, has argued the case persuasively in his book *Two Nations.* To ignore such divisions, and then charge those who raise valid claims against society with promoting divisiveness, offers a classic example of "blaming the victim." And we have already refuted the spurious point that African Americans were the passive recipients of benevolent white individuals or institutions which "gave" them freedom.

Too many Americans tend to view history as "something that happened in the past," something that is "over and done," and thus has no bearing upon the present. Especially in the case of slavery, nothing could be further from the truth. As historian John Hope Franklin noted in his response to Horowitz:

> Most living Americans do have a connection with slavery. They have inherited the preferential advantage, if they are white, or the loathsome disadvantage, if they are black; and those positions are virtually as alive today as they were in the 19th century. The pattern of housing, the discrimination in employment, the resistance to equal opportunity in education, the racial, the inequities in the administration of justice, the low expectation of blacks in the discharge of duties assigned to them, the widespread belief that blacks have physical prowess but little intellectual capacities and the widespread opposition to affirmative action, as if that had not been enjoyed by whites for three centuries, all indicate that the vestiges of slavery are still with us.

> And as long as there are pro-slavery protagonists among us, hiding behind such absurdities as

"we are all in this together" or "it hurts me as much as it hurts you" or "slavery benefited you as much as it benefited me," we will suffer from the inability to confront the tragic legacies of slavery and deal with them in a forthright and constructive manner.

Most important, we must never fall victim to some scheme designed to create a controversy among potential allies in order to divide them and, at the same time, exploit them for its own special purpose.

BIBLIOGRAPHY

2001 New York Times Almanac (New York: Penguin Books, 2000).

Richard F. America. *Paying the Social Debt: What White America Owes Black America* (Westport, Conn.: Praeger, 1993).

J. D. B. DeBow. "The Interest in Slavery of the Southern Non-Slaveholder." In *Slavery Defended: The Views of the Old South,* ed. Eric L. McKitrick (Englewood Cliffs, NJ: Prentice-Hall, 1963), 169–77.

Ira Berlin, and others. *Slaves No More: Three Essays on Emancipation and the Civil War* (Cambridge [England]; New York: Cambridge University Press, 1992).

Dalton Conley. *Being Black, Living in the Red: Race, Wealth, and Social Policy in America* (Berkeley: University of California Press, 1999).

LaWanda Cox. "The Promise of Land for the Freedmen." *Mississippi Valley Historical Review* 45 (December 1958): 413–40.

Dudley Taylor Cornish. *The Sable Arm: Black Troops in the Union Army, 1861–1865* (1956; rpt. Lawrence, KS: University Press of Kansas, 1987).

Eric Foner. *Free Soil, Free Labor, Free Men: the Ideology of the Republican Party Before the Civil War* (New York: Oxford University Press, 1970).

John Hope Franklin, and Alfred A. Moss, Jr. *From Slavery to Freedom: A History of African Americans,* 7th ed. (New York: McGraw-Hill, 1994).

Andrew Hacker. *Two Nations: Black and White, Separate, Hostile, Unequal,* rev. ed. (New York: Ballantine Books, 1995).

James Oliver Horton and Lois E. Horton. *In Hope of Liberty: Culture, Community, and Protest Among Northern Free Blacks, 1700–1860* (New York: Oxford University Press, 1997).

James L. Huston. "Property Rights in Slavery and the Coming of the Civil War." *Journal of Southern History* 65 (1999): 249–86.

James Oakes. *The Ruling Race. A History of American Slaveholders* (New York: Vintage Books, 1983).

Melvin L. Oliver, and Thomas M. Shapiro. *Black Wealth/White Wealth: A New Perspective on Racial Inequality* (New York: Routledge, 1995).

Benjamin Quarles. *Black Abolitionists* (New York: Oxford University Press, 1969).

———. *The Negro in the Civil War* (Boston: Little, Brown, 1953).

Walter Rodney. *How Europe Underdeveloped Africa,* rev. ed. (Washington, D.C.: Howard University Press, 1981).

Jack Salzman, David Lionel Smith, and Cornel West, eds. *Encyclopedia of African-American Culture and His-tory,* 5 vols. (New York: Macmillan Library Reference USA: Simon & Schuster Macmillan; London: Simon & Schuster and Prentice Hall International, 1996).

Diana Jean Schemo. "An Ad Provokes Campus Protests and Pushes Limits of Expression." *New York Times,* 21 March 2001, pp. A1, A17.

Abbot Emerson Smith. *Colonists in Bondage; White Servitude and Convict Labor in America, 1607–1776* (Chapel Hill: Pub. for the Institute of Early American History and Culture at Williamsburg, Va., by the University of North Carolina Press, 1947).

Barbara L. Solow and Stanley L. Engerman, eds. *British Capitalism and Caribbean Slavery: The Legacy of Eric Williams* (Cambridge [Cambridgeshire]; New York: Cambridge University Press, 1987).

Eric Williams, *Capitalism & Slavery* (1944; rpt. New York: Russell & Russell, 1961).

Randall Robinson ┃ America's Debt to Blacks

Well before the birth of our country, Europe and the eventual United States perpetrated a heinous wrong against the peoples of Africa and sustained and benefited from the wrong through the continuing exploitation of Africa's human and material resources. America followed slavery with more than a hundred years of legal racial segregation and discrimination of one variety or another. It was only in 1965, after nearly 350 years of legal racial suppression, that the United States enacted the Voting Rights Act. Virtually simultaneously, however, it began to walk away from the social wreckage that centuries of white hegemony had wrought. Our country then began to rub itself with the memory-emptying salve of contemporaneousness. (If the wrong did not just occur, then it did not occur in a way that would render the living responsible.)

But when the black living suffer real and current consequences as a result of wrongs committed by a younger America, then contemporary America must shoulder responsibility for those wrongs until such wrongs have been adequately righted. The life and responsibilities of a nation are not limited to the life spans of its mortal constituents. Federal and state governments were active participants not only in slavery but also in the exclusion and dehumanization of blacks that continued legally up until the passage of key civil rights legislation in the sixties. Black calls for reparations began almost from the moment that slavery officially ended in 1865. However, although our calls far predate those of either the Japanese or the Jews, only the latter two communities have been responded to in a spirit of sober compassion and thoughtful humanity.

In response to our call, individual Americans need not feel defensive or under attack. No one holds any living person responsible for slavery or the later century-plus of legal relegation of blacks to substandard education, exclusion from home ownership via restrictive covenants and redlining, or any of the

Randall Robinson, "America's Debt to Blacks." Reprinted with permission from the March 13, 2000 issue of *The Nation.*

myriad mechanisms for pushing blacks to the back of the line. Nonetheless, we must all, as a nation, ponder the repercussions of those acts.

There are many ways to begin righting America's massive wrong. But resolving economic and social disparities so long in the making will require great resources (in the form of public initiatives, not personal checks) and decades of national fortitude. Habit is the enemy. Whites and blacks see each other the only way they can remember seeing each other— in a relationship of economic and social inequality. The system, which starts each child where its parents left off, is not fair. This is particularly the case for African-Americans, whose general economic starting points have been rearmost because of slavery and its aftermath. Slaves for two and a half centuries saw not just their freedom taken from them but their labor as well. Were it a line item in today's gross national product report, that value would undoubtedly run into billions of dollars.

America has made an art form by now of grinding its past deeds, no matter how despicable, into mere ephemera. And African-Americans, unfortunately, have accommodated this amnesia all too well. It would behoove African-Americans to remember that history forgets first those who forget themselves. To do what is necessary to accomplish anything approaching psychic and economic parity in the next half-century will require a fundamental shift in America's thinking. Before the country in general can be made to understand, African-Americans themselves must come to understand that this demand is not for charity. It is simply for what they are owed on a debt that is old but compellingly obvious and valid still. (Do not be fooled by individual examples of conspicuous black success. They have closed neither the economic nor the psychic gaps between blacks and whites, and are statistically insignificant.)

The blacks of Rosewood, Florida, and Greenwood, Oklahoma, have successfully brought their case for reparations to national attention. Indeed, in Oklahoma a biracial commission has just concluded that justice demands that reparations be paid to the victims of Oklahoma's Greenwood massacre. Congressman John Conyers has introduced HR 40, a bill "to examine the institution of slavery," subsequent "de jure and de facto discrimination against freed slaves and their descendants," the impact of these forces "on living African-Americans" and to make recommendations to Congress on "appropriate remedies." Passage of this bill is crucial; even the making of a well-reasoned case for broader national restitution will do wonders for the spirits of blacks.

This is a struggle that African-Americans cannot lose, for in the very making of it we will discover, if nothing else, ourselves. And it is a struggle that all Americans must support, as the important first step toward America's having any chance for a new beginning in which all its inhabitants are true co-owners of America's democratic ideals.

17

Is a White Musician Playing
the Blues Wrong?

Rudinow and His Critics

Is it wrong for a white person to sing the blues? This question may strike you as one of the strangest raised in this book. We do not normally think that the race you happen to be has any bearing on the moral permissibility of playing a particular kind of music. For example, it would probably strike you as very odd to ask whether it was morally permissible for a Korean woman to play Mendelssohn's Violin Concerto in E minor or for an Australian Aborigine to sing an American country-and-western song. What arguments could there be for the thesis that it is impermissible for white people to sing the blues?

There are at least two distinct arguments—the *proprietary argument* and the *experiential access argument*. The proprietary argument is based on the simple idea that somehow the blues, as a musical tradition, belongs to a certain cultural group, the African-American community, and that for someone outside that community to play the blues is thus impermissible appropriation of that musical form. We can reconstruct the argument as follows:

P1 The African American community owns the blues.
P2 To sing the blues is to appropriate the blues.
P3 A white man does not belong to the African-American community.
P4 It is always wrong to appropriate something that belongs to others.

C   It is wrong for a white man to sing the blues

Is the argument valid? Assuming the truth of the premises, would the conclusion also have to be true? It seems so. But are the premises true?

Rudinow raises several objections to the first premise—that the blues as a musical style is owned collectively by the African-American community. First, collective ownership by such a large and diverse group with rather ill-defined boundaries is problematic. And if the boundaries of the collective are ill-defined, is it obvious that no white man can ever be a member of that community? Second, the idea of ownership of a musical *style* is also problematic. Consider the second premise: Why is singing the blues a case of appropriating a tradition rather than, say, borrowing from it? Borrowing, particularly the borrowing of elements of a broadly defined style, is rife in the history of music. (No one thinks the worse of Beethoven for having borrowed and developed ideas from Mozart and Bach.) Finally, as for premise 4, ownership rights are not absolute or inalienable. They can be transferred or suspended or overridden by a variety of means and for a variety of reasons. So the fourth premise as stated is clearly false.

The second argument Rudinow considers is the experiential access argument. As stated by Rudinow, it is this:

P1   One cannot understand the blues unless one knows what it's like to live as an African American.

P2   One cannot know what it's like to live as an African American without being an African American.

P3   Singing the blues without understanding them is inauthentic.

P4   It is wrong to sing the blues inauthentically.

C   It is wrong for anyone who is not an African American to sing the blues.

The argument seems valid. Is it sound? Rudinow questions the truth of premise 2. Is the claim based on evidence or is it supposed to be just obvious? Rudinow claims that the premise presupposes a "myth of ethnic memory" according to which "mere membership in the ethnic group confers special access to the lived experience of ancestors and other former members." He claims that this ignores what is of universal human interest in the blues and that we cannot rule out the possibility that nonmembers of an ethnic group might be initiated into that group in ways that facilitate sufficient understanding.

In his critique of Rudinow's article, Paul Taylor claims that Rudinow has missed an essential element in performance: namely, the audience's response. According to Taylor, singing the blues is more than just producing musical sounds. It is an action on the part of performers intended to do much more—namely, "to bear witness to the racialized moral pain that the blues is about." If the performers are not members of the race that experienced this pain, then, Taylor maintains, they cannot successfully convey to this to an audience. Or they cannot really do this for those members of the audience who are what Taylor calls BBA adherents. A BBA adherent is someone who subscribes to the "Black Blues Authenticity Thesis"—that a white person cannot be an authentic performer of the blues. A BBA adherent will simply find the performance not to be a successful one, and so the performance will be (at least for that member of the audience) a failure. The blues, according to Taylor, is part of a "racial project," and membership of a race may well be relevant to whether or not one participates in such a project.

In his response to Taylor's criticism, Rudinow acknowledges that he did not allow for the possible significance of an audience consisting of BBA adherents as defined by Taylor. Rudinow claims that it is still an open question whether mere race is an essential feature for participating in the blues project or whether the blues is not more about more universal themes that do not exclude groups that have suffered gross discrimination. "It will not do simply to assert in a question-begging way that there is not anything crucially or universally human about the blues."

QUESTIONS FOR CONSIDERATION

• According to both Rudinow and Taylor this debate is about authenticity. The first question one might raise in connection with this exchange is a very basic one: Does this debate about the authenticity of whites singing the blues really involve *moral* permissibility? Suppose you play a Mozart sonata on the violin, and after the first few bars your violin teacher shouts, "Stop! You can't play it like that, with all that sliding and rubato. That's not authentic Mozart. That's totally wrong! You are playing it as though it were a romantic piece. It isn't. Mozart is a classical composer!" If your teacher is right, then you have clearly been playing the piece wrongly. Your playing has been inauthentic, and so in some sense *wrong*. But has your playing been *morally* wrong? You set out to play a classical piece, as it was intended to be played, and you are clearly failing to achieve that aesthetic goal. Isn't it this lack of authenticity aesthetically, rather than morally wrong? Failing to achieve an aesthetic goal, while definitely an aesthetic failing, is hardly a moral failing.

• Suppose the BBA thesis is correct, and there is a sense in which it is inauthentic for a white person to sing the blues. Doesn't that mean it is aesthetically impermissible, rather than morally impermissible?

• One response to this might be that the content of the blues is tragic human suffering on a vast scale, suffering that was inflicted largely as a result of highly immoral, entrenched racism. As such, singing the blues has a moral dimension to it that playing a Mozart sonata lacks. Is this part of what Taylor means by saying that singing the blues is a "racial project."

• In thinking about the proprietary argument you might ask what kinds of things can be owned and by whom. You can have intellectual property rights to a song you have composed, and a collective, such as Sony Corporation, can purchase those property rights from you. So a collective can take ownership of the song. But does that mean that you cannot sing that song? Or does it only mean that you cannot make money singing the song in public without the copyright holder's consent? Can a collective have similar kinds of property rights to a musical style? If so, can no one outside the collective write or sing songs in that style?

• In thinking about the experiential access argument you might focus on the truth of the second premise. Consider some analogous cases. How do novelists, for example, understand their characters even though they aren't those characters? Presumably they use imagination, empathy, and analogy. Are these tools we can all use in trying to come to know what it is like to live in a completely different community? Could a white singer, through the use of such tools, come to understand enough of what it is like to live as a black person in America to sing the blues with knowledge and feeling? If so, would his singing the blues be authentic after all?

FURTHER READING

Young, James O. "Should White Men Play the Blues?" *Journal of Value Inquiry* 28 (1994): 415–24.

Race, Ethnicity, Expressive Authenticity

Joel Rudinow

Can White People Sing the Blues?

The idea of a white blues singer seems an even more violent contradiction of terms than the idea of a middle class blues singer.

> Amiri Baraka (LeRoi Jones), *Blues People*

It is unlikely that [the blues] will survive through the imitations of the young white college copyists, the "urban blues singers," whose relation to the blues is that of the "trad" jazz band to the music of New Orleans: sterile and derivative. The bleak prospect is that the blues probably has no real future; that, folk music that it is, it served its purpose and flourished whilst it had meaning in the Negro community. At the end of the century it may well be seen as an important cultural phenomenon—and someone will commence a systematic study of it, too late.

> Paul Oliver, *Blues Off the Record*

Can white people sing the blues? Can white people play the blues? On the surface, these may seem to be silly questions. Why not? What is Mose Allison, if not a white blues singer? Surely the performances of guitarists Eric Clapton and Stevie Ray Vaughan and pianist Dr. John must count as playing the blues. But the question "Can white people sing (or play) the blues?" is much more persistent, elusive, and deep than such ready responses acknowledge. The above passage from Paul Oliver exemplifies a tradition of criticism which distinguishes between the performances of black and white blues musicians, preferring those of black musicians and refusing to recognize as genuine those of white musicians.[1] This tradition raises questions of race, ethnicity, and ex-

pressive authenticity which go to the heart of the contemporary debate over multi-culturalism, the canon, and the curriculum. I derive my title, and take my theme, from the late jazz critic Ralph J. Gleason, who raised the issue definitively, at least for white liberals in the late 1960s, saying:

> [T]he blues is black man's music, and whites diminish it at best or steal it at worst. In any case they have no moral right to use it.[2]

When I raise this issue in my Aesthetics classes, I find I must first get my students to appreciate it as a genuine and genuinely deep issue. They tend to dismiss it rather quickly by simple appeal to their own musical experience. They tend to think that the mere mention of the name "Stevie Ray Vaughan" settles it. It doesn't. Nevertheless, there's something in this naive response. It reflects the central dialectic of the issue—the difficulty of appreciating its depth and significance in the face of its apparent implications. In an age of renewed and heightened racial and cultural sensitivity such a critical stance seems paradoxically to be both progressive and reactionary, and to stand in need of both clarification and critique. It seems to embody, as well as any, the problematic of "political correctness." The stance taken, as in the case of Gleason and Oliver, by white critics and scholars seems progressive in that it unambiguously credits African-American culture as the authoritative source of the blues as musical genre and style, something the dominant culture has by and large systematically neglected. And yet it seems reac-

From Joel Rudinow, "Race, Ethnicity, Expressive Authenticity: Can White People Sing the Blues?" *Journal of Aesthetics and Art Criticism* 52, no. 1 (Winter 1994): 127–37. Some notes and some parts of the text have been deleted. Reprinted by permission of Blackwell Publishing Ltd.

tionary—indeed, prima facie racist—to restrict access to the blues as a medium of artistic expression. Check through the "blues" racks at your best local roots record store. There you'll find quite a few white recording artists among the many black recording artists. Mike Bloomfield, Paul Butterfield, Dr. John, Mark and Robben Ford, Nick Gravenites, John Hammond, Delbert McClinton, Charlie Musselwhite, Johnny Otis, Roy Rogers (not the cowboy), Stevie Ray Vaughan, Marcia Ball, Lou Ann Barton, Rory Block, Angela Strehli, and so on. This would appear to make the affirmative case. Add to this list the non-black sidemen in the backup bands of many recognized blues artists—Jesse Edwin Davis (in Taj Mahal's early bands), Tim Kaihatsu (the Japanese second guitarist in Robert Cray's touring band), Albert Gianquinto (James Cotton's piano player for many years), to name only a few—and the thesis that the blues is a musical idiom which knows no racial or ethnic barriers begins to look pretty well confirmed. In the face of such evidence, what could have prompted our question in the first place? Is there some crucial difference between John Lee Hooker's blues and John Hammond's? What sort of difference could it be? Do the notes sound different when played with black fingers? If Leontyne Price can sing opera, and Charlie Pride can sing country, why can't Bonnie Raitt sing the blues?

I. A "RACIST" ARGUMENT?

Part of appreciating the issue is rescuing it from a racist reading. Let us first get clear about what would make the negative position "racist." "Racism" is widely discussed and many would say even more widely practiced, but it is rarely defined or clarified conceptually. For present purposes I will consider as racist any doctrine or set of doctrines which presupposes that there are "races" whose members share genetically transmitted traits and characteristics not shared by members of other "races" and which makes moral distinctions or other (for example aesthetic) distinctions with moral implications, on this basis alone. Essentially racism seeks to establish a scientific, in this case biological, basis for differen-

tial treatment of human beings—a basis in the nature of things for discrimination.

Thus critiques of racism have attempted to establish that there is no genetic or biological (i.e., scientific) basis for *morally significant* classification of human beings into races, by arguing that those genetically determined gross morphological characteristics whereby individuals are assigned to racial categories (pigmentation, bone structure, and so on) are not morally significant and that those human characteristics which *are* or *can be* morally significant (intelligence, linguistic capability, and so on), though genetically determined, do not vary significantly with race. A more radical critique of racism would undercut the concept of "race" itself as an artificial and harmful construct without objective foundation in science, arguing in effect that there is no foundation in biology or genetics for *any* system of classification of humans by "race." This might be based on the observation that the degree of variation, with respect even to gross morphological characteristics, within a given "racial" group exceeds that between "typical" members of different groups, and on the generally accepted finding in genetics that the probability of any particular genetic difference occurring between two members of the same "racial" group is roughly the same as for any two human beings. We might do well to wonder whether, if either of these critiques has force, (and they both seem forceful to me), we can raise the issue of the authenticity of white blues musicians at all. Is there a way to enter into such a discussion without reifying "race" and investing it with moral significance? Doesn't the very question presuppose race as a morally significant human category with a verifiable basis of some sort?

Suppose we begin to answer this by distinguishing between race and ethnicity. Unlike race, let us say, which is supposed to be innate and in nature, ethnicity requires no genetic or biological foundation. Ethnicity is a matter of acknowledged common culture, based on shared items of cultural significance such as experience, language, religion, history, habitat, and the like. Ethnicity is essentially a socially conferred status—a matter of communal acceptance, recognition, and respect.

Thus the negative position may *seem* racist since it may appear that nothing other than race is available as a basis for what is evidently both an aesthetic and moral distinction between black and white blues artists and performances. The negative position would *be* racist if, for example, it held that white people were genetically incapable of producing the sounds essential to the blues. Is there a difference between John Lee Hooker's blues and John Hammond's blues? Well, certainly. There are many. The diction, phrasing, and intonation of each as vocalist, as well as their techniques of instrumental self-accompaniment are distinctive and immediately identifiable (which shows that whatever differences there are are relevant *aesthetically*). If someone proposed to explain these differences on the basis of the genetically inherited expressive capacities and limitations of members of different races, and then went on to argue for some form of differential assessment of performances or treatment of artists on this basis, that would qualify as a racist account.

However, the question raised by the negative position is not one of genetically transmissible expressive or musical capabilities and limitations, but rather one of "authenticity." Again, the negative position would *be* racist if it held that music made by white people, however much it may resemble blues and be intended as blues, isn't authentic blues *simply because it is made by people of the wrong race.* But nobody says this. Nor does any serious adherent of the negative position hold that white people are somehow *genetically* incapable of delivering an authentic blues performance. What makes one blues performance authentic and another inauthentic? The question of authenticity is really a matter of "credentials."

II. THE AUTHENTICITY QUESTION

Authenticity is a value—a species of the genus credibility. It's the kind of credibility that comes from having the appropriate relationship to an original source. Thus authenticity's most precise, formal, and fully institutionalized application in the artworld is to distinguish from the forgery a work "by the author's own hand." When we authenticate a work in this sense, what we want to know is whether or not the putative author is who he or she is represented to be. In this application the "authentic/inauthentic" distinction is dichotomous, the alternatives both mutually exclusive and exhaustive, and the appropriate relationship is one of identity.

More broadly, less precisely, but in an essentially similar way, "authenticity" is applicable to the artifacts and rituals which are a culture's "currency," conferring value on those "acceptably derived" from original sources. So, for example, an authentic restoration of a turn of the century Victorian house might be one reconstructed according to original plans and specifications and perhaps using only the tools, techniques, and building materials of the period. An authentic Cajun recipe might be one traceable to a source within the culture using ingredients traditionally available within the region. In such applications authenticity admits of degrees. A given piece of work may be more or less authentic than another. And the standards or criteria of authenticity admit of some flexibility of interpretation relative to purpose.

In the literature of musical aesthetics the authenticity question has been focused largely on the relation between performances and "the work"—or, because the work is conceived of as a composition, between performances and what the composer intended—and the criteria for authenticity have been understood in terms of accuracy or conformity with performance specifications which constitute the work. As applied to blues performances the authenticity question must be focused somewhat differently, for although we may speak of blues "compositions," what we thereby refer to consist of no more typically than a simple chord progression shared by many other such "compositions," with no definite key signature, no particular prescribed instrumentation, and a lyrical text which itself is open to *ad lib* interruption, interpretation, and elaboration in performance. As a musical genre, the blues is characterized by what we might call "compositional minimalism" and a complementary emphasis on expressive elements. The question of the authenticity of a given blues performance is thus one of stylistic and expressive authenticity, and our question becomes, "Is white blues 'acceptably enough derived' from the original sources of the blues to be stylistically authentic and authentically expressive within the style?" The negative position can now be understood as: white musicians cannot play the blues in an authentic way because they do not have the requisite relation or proximity to the original sources of the blues. No one has made the case for the negative position more provocatively, eloquently, profoundly, and forcefully than Amiri Baraka (LeRoi Jones). In what follows I will consider that case, which I believe consists of two interrelated arguments, which I will call the "Proprietary Argument" and the "Experiential Access Argument."[3]

III. THE PROPRIETARY ARGUMENT

The proprietary argument addresses the question of ownership. Who "owns" the blues? Who has legitimate authority to use the blues as an idiom, as a performance style, to interpret it, to draw from it and to contribute to it as a fund of artistic and cultural wealth, to profit from it? The originators and the major innovative elaborators of the blues were in fact members of the African-American community. Women and men like Ma Rainey, Bessie Smith, Charlie Patton, Robert Johnson, Muddy Waters, Howlin' Wolf, John Lee Hooker, T-Bone Walker, Professor Longhair, and so on. The question arises, to whom does this cultural and artistic heritage belong? Who are Robert Johnson's legitimate cultural and artistic heirs and conservators?

The proprietary argument says in effect that the blues as genre and style belongs to the African-American community and that when white people undertake to perform the blues they misappropriate the cultural heritage and intellectual property of African-Americans and of the African-American community—what Baraka refers to as "the Great Music Robbery."[4] Baraka describes a systematic and pervasive pattern throughout the history of black people in America—a pattern of cultural and artistic co-optation and misappropriation in which not just the blues, but every major black artistic innovation, after an initial period of condemnation and rejection as culturally inferior, eventually wins recognition for superior artistic significance and merit, only to be immediately appropriated by white imitators whose imitations are very profitably mass produced and

distributed, and accepted in the cultural mainstream as definitive, generally without due credit to their sources. Calling the blues "the basic national voice of the African-American people,"[5] he writes:

> . . . after each new wave of black innovation, i.e., New Orleans, big band, bebop, rhythm and blues, hard bop, new music, there was a commercial cooptation of the original music and an attempt to replace it with corporate dilution which mainly featured white players and was mainly intended for a white middle-class audience.[6]

This is not an aberrant or accidental phenomenon, nor is it benign. Rather it is part and parcel of a subtle and systematic form of institutionalized racism which reinforces a racist socioeconomic class structure.

> The problem for the Creators of Black Music, the African-American people, is that because they lack Self-Determination, i.e., political power and economic self-sufficiency, various peoples' borrowings and cooptation of the music can be disguised and the beneficiaries of such acts pretend they are creating out of the air.[7]

Let's consider a possible objection, or set of objections, to this argument. The crucial claim is the ownership claim: that the blues as genre and style belongs to the African-American community. How is this claim warranted? Part of the warrant is the factual claim that the originators and major innovative elaborators of the blues were members of the African-American community like Ma Rainey, Bessie Smith, Charlie Patton, Robert Johnson, Muddy Waters, Howlin' Wolf, John Lee Hooker, T-Bone Walker, Professor Longhair, and so on. There is an interpretive tradition which holds, contrary to this, that the blues is an oral folk form with an ancient and untraceable pre-history, but in spite of this let us take the factual claim as true. But what is the principle or set of principles which connects this factual claim with the ownership claim that the blues belongs to the African-American *community?*

The crucial assumption underlying this as a *critical* question—as the basis for a series of objections—is the modern notion of intellectual property as applied to the blues. On this assumption, an *individual* is understood to have certain rights regarding the products of his or her original creative work, including the right to control access to the work for the purposes of commercial exploitation, etc. So one could say that the musical literature of the blues rightly belongs to *certain members* of the African-American community like Ma Rainey, Bessie Smith, Charlie Patton, Robert Johnson, Muddy Waters, Howlin' Wolf, John Lee Hooker, T-Bone Walker, Professor Longhair, or their estates, legitimate heirs and assigns. But this list, even drawn up on the basis of a liberal reading of "legitimate heirs and assigns," even if *padded,* is not coextensive with "the African-American *community.*"

Moreover, these rights can be alienated voluntarily and involuntarily in various ways. They can be purchased, sold, exchanged, wagered, and so on. So for example the rights inherent in Robert Johnson's entire catalogue of recorded compositions now belong to something called King of Spades Music and the rights to the recordings of his performances of them belong to CBS Records, part of the Sony Corporation. In other words, on this assumption a number of individual and corporate ownership claims would seem to follow from the facts, but not the communal ownership claim central to Baraka's case.

Finally, the proprietary argument claims ownership of the blues as genre and style, so that musical and expressive elements as elusive as timbre, diction, vocal inflection, timing, rhythmic "feel," and their imitations become the subjects of dispute. For example, the rock group ZZ Top has obviously imitated or "borrowed from" elements of John Lee Hooker's distinctive style in several of their original compositions. For Baraka this constitutes misappropriation—just another instance of The Great Music Robbery. But where in the notion of music as intellectual property can one find precedent for this? If anything, the history of music provides ample precedent for accepting such borrowings as legitimate forms of tribute and trade in ideas. The modern notion of intellectual property as applied to music can be used to support ownership claims concerning compositions but not musical ideas as ephemeral and problematic for purposes of documentation as these "elements of style."

Arguably this series of objections does very little damage to the proprietary argument. First of all,

what the objection grants is important evidence in support of the proprietary argument. The modern notion of intellectual property, insofar as it is applicable to the blues, would seem to warrant at least an indictment of the American music establishment on the offense of Great Music Robbery, just as Baraka maintains. The means whereby the intellectual property rights inherent in the creative work of African-American blues musicians were alienated from the artists, later to turn up in various corporate portfolios at greatly appreciated value, were in many cases questionable, to say the least.

But more important, though it may not be entirely inappropriate to apply an eighteenth-century English legal concept of intellectual property to the blues— after all, the blues *is* modern American music—it's not entirely appropriate either. Approaching the blues via such a conceptual route entails treating the blues as a collection of compositions, discrete pieces of intellectual property, convenient as commodities to the economic apparatus of the twentieth-century American music and entertainment industries, whereas attention and sensitivity to the social context of the music, its production, presentation, and enjoyment disclose phenomena rather more in the nature of real-time event and communally shared experience, in which the roles of performer and audience are nowhere near as sharply delineated as would be suggested by the imposition of the notions of creative artist and consumer upon them.

> Stories, jokes, and music are all part of the blues performance. They flow together in small rooms filled with smoke and the smell of alcohol as couples talk, slow drag, and sing with the performer. . . . During blues sessions the audience frequently addresses the singer and forces him to respond to their comments through his music. . . . [T]he blues singer sometimes prevents fights by talking the blues with his audience and integrating their conversations between his blues verses. After he sings a verse, the musician continues instrumental accompaniment and develops a talk session. He may then sing another verse while participants remember rhymes and short jokes which they introduce at the next verse break. The singer always controls this talk through his instrumental accompaniment. . . . [This] shows the limitations of using blues records in the study of oral tradition, for studio conditions completely remove

the performeraudience dimension of blues. Listeners influence the length and structure of each blues performed and force the singer to integrate his song with their responses. . . . [W]hat I first saw as "interruptions" were, in fact, the heart of the blues performance.[8]

Thus the question of how to derive communal ownership claims from individual intellectual property rights needn't detain us. Indeed it arguably misleads attention from the real sources of the communal ownership claim, namely that the blues as genre and style originated as a communicative idiom and practice within the African-American community.

Finally, in insisting on a contrast between musical compositions as documentable items of intellectual property and relatively problematic ephemera of musical and expressive style, the objection begs a complex set of deeply intriguing questions concerning the ownership and regulation of musical "fragments" as commodified abstract ideas—which, ironically, rap music (particularly in its employment of the technology of digital sampling) has lately elevated to the status of a pressing legal issue. But even more to the point, far from being problematic ephemera, the elements of blues style, when understood within the context of the music's historical origins and the social context of its production, take on crucial semantic and syntactic significance.

On balance, the modern notion of intellectual property as applied to the blues seems little more than an elaborate red herring which in effect obscures crucial facts about the social circumstances of the music's production, appreciation, and indeed, *meaning.* This brings me to what I am calling the "experiential access argument."

IV. THE EXPERIENTIAL ACCESS ARGUMENT

Where the proprietary argument addresses the question of ownership, the experiential access argument addresses the questions of meaning and understanding as these bear centrally on issues of culture, its identity, evolution, and transmission. What is the significance of the blues? Who can legiti-mately claim to understand the blues? Or to speak authoritatively about the blues and its interpretation? Who can legitimately claim fluency in the blues as a musical idiolect? Or the authority to pass it on to the next generation? Who are the real bearers of the blues tradition?

The experiential access argument says in effect that one cannot understand the blues or authentically express oneself in the blues unless one knows what it's like to live as a black person in America, and one cannot know this without being one. To put it more elaborately, the meaning of the blues is deep, hidden, and accessible only to those with an adequate grasp of the historically unique experience of the African-American community. Members of other communities may take an interest in this experience and even empathize with it, but they have no direct access to the experience and therefore cannot fully comprehend or express it. Hence their attempts to master the blues or to express themselves in the idiom of the blues will of necessity tend to be relatively shallow and superficial, i.e., inauthentic. Jazz players have an expression, a motto of sorts: Fake it 'till you feel it— the point being that authentic expression is expression derived from felt emotion. The experiential access argument in effect posits the experience of living as a black person in America as a precondition of the felt emotion essential to authentic expression in the idiom of the blues. Delfeayo Marsalis, in the liner notes to Branford Marsalis's 1992 release *I Heard You Twice the First Time,* writes:

> Yes, one must pay serious dues in order to accurately translate the sorrow and heartache of the blues experience into musical terms. The great blues musician Charlie Parker once said, "If you don't live it, it won't come out of your horn."

And Baraka writes:

> Blues as an autonomous music had been in a sense inviolable. There was no clear way into it, i.e., its production, not its appreciation, except as concomitant with what seems to me to be the peculiar social, cultural, economic, and emotional experience of a black man in America. The idea of a white blues singer seems an even more violent contradiction of terms than the idea of a middle-class blues singer.

The materials of blues were not available to the white American, even though some strange circumstance might prompt him to look for them. It was as if these materials were secret and obscure, and blues a kind of ethno-historic rite as basic as blood.[9]

In the context of the kinds of questions raised here about culture, its identity, evolution, and transmission, the appeal to experience functions as a basis upon which to either establish or challenge authority, based on some such principle as this: Other things equal, the more directly one's knowledge claims are grounded in first hand experience, the more unassailable one's authority. Though there is room for debate about the centrality of experience as a ground of knowledge, as for example in current discussions of "feminist epistemology," such a principle as this one seems plausible and reasonable enough.

Nevertheless, stated baldly, and understood literally, the experiential access argument seems to invite the objection that it is either a priori or just dubious. The access that most contemporary black Americans have to the experience of slavery or sharecropping or life on the Mississippi delta during the twenties and thirties is every bit as remote, mediated, and indirect as that of any white would-be blues player. Does the argument subscribe to some "Myth of Ethnic Memory" whereby mere membership in the ethnic group confers special access to the lived experience of ancestors and other former members? It would be just as facile and fatuous for a Jewish-American baby boomer (such as myself) to take the position that only Jews can adequately comprehend the experience of the holocaust.

However the argument is susceptible of a more subtle and defensible reading, namely that the blues is essentially a cryptic language, a kind of secret code. Texts composed in this language typically have multiple layers of meaning, some relatively superficial, some deeper. To gain access to the deeper layers of meaning one must have the keys to the code. But the keys to the code presuppose extensive and detailed familiarity with the historically unique body of experience shared within and definitive of the African-American community and are therefore available only to the properly initiated.

There is a certain amount of theoretical and historical material, as well as textual material within the blues, available to support this argument. A general theoretical framework for understanding the development of cryptic devices and systems of communication under repressive circumstances can be found in the work of Leo Strauss. Strauss maintains that where control of the thought and communication of a subjugated population is attempted in order to maintain a political arrangement, even the most violent means of repression are inadequate to the task, for "it is a safe venture to tell the truth one knows to benevolent and trustworthy acquaintances, or . . . to reasonable friends."[10] The human spirit will continue to seek, recognize, and communicate the truth privately in defiance of even the most repressive regimes, which moreover cannot even prevent public communication of forbidden ideas, "for a man of independent thought can utter his views in public and remain unharmed, provided he moves with circumspection. He can even utter them in print without incurring any danger, provided he is capable of writing between the lines."[11] Unjust and repressive regimes thus naturally tend to engender covert communication strategies with "all the advantages of private communication without having its greatest disadvantage—that it reaches only the writer's acquaintances, [and] all the advantages of public communication without having its greatest disadvantage—capital punishment for the author."[12]

Evidence of the employment of such strategies within the African-American community is fairly well documented. For example, the evolution of "Black English," as well as a number of its salient characteristics, such as crucial ambiguity, understatement, irony, and inversion of meaning ("bad" means "good," and so on), may best be explained as the development of cryptic communicative strategies under repression.

Blacks clearly recognized that to master the language of whites was in effect to consent to be mastered by it through the white definitions of caste built into the semantic/social system. Inversion therefore becomes the defensive mechanism which enables blacks to fight linguistic, and thereby psychological, entrapment. . . . Words and phrases were given reverse meanings and functions changed. Whites, denied access to the semantic extensions of duality, connotations, and denotations that developed within black usage, could only interpret the same material according to its original singular meaning . . . enabling blacks to deceive and manipulate whites without penalty. This protective process, understood and shared by blacks, became a contest of matching wits . . . [and a] form of linguistic guerrilla warfare [which] protected the subordinated, permitted the masking and disguising of true feelings, allowed the subtle assertion of self, and promoted group solidarity.[13]

Ethnomusicologists, working independently and apparently absent any familiarity with Strauss's work in political philosophy or sociolinguistic studies of Black English, have arrived at strikingly similar conclusions regarding the origins, functions, and stylistic features of jazz and blues.

Lyrically the blues are rife with more or less covert allusions to the oppressive conditions of black life in America. If Jimmy Reed's "Big Boss Man"

(Big boss man, can't you hear me when I call [twice]
Well you ain't so big, you just tall, that's all)

is overt, it is merely extending a more covert tradition central to the blues. As Paul Oliver observes:

An appreciation of the part African-Americans have played in United States society and of the rights and other aspects of living that were denied them is of major assistance in understanding the blues. But there are barriers to appreciation presented by the manner of delivery, of speech, and of form, and [even] when these are overcome the full significance of the blues to the black audience still remains elusive. . . . Many black terms arose through the deliberate intention to conceal meaning. . . . [I]nnocuous words were often given secondary meanings which were closed to all but the initiated and by their use the singer could be more outspoken in the blues than might otherwise be prudent. Some of these became traditional terms recognized and used throughout the states by blacks, for whom the colored man was the "monkey," the white man the "baboon." With comparative immunity Dirty Red could sing:

Monkey and the baboon playing Seven-Up,
Monkey win the money, scared to pick it up.

The monkey stumbled, the baboon fell,
Monkey grabbed the money an' he run like hell![14]

Similarly, the blues are full of covert and even overt references, both musical and lyrical, to the esoterica of African religions whose practice on this continent was prohibited and systematically repressed. When Muddy Waters sings:

I got a black cat bone
I got a mojo too
I got John the conqueror root
I'm gonna mess wit' you

we understand very little unless we recognize the references to the conjures and charms of the Dahomean religion which migrated to the Americas under slavery as vodun or "voodoo." Similarly we lose whole realms of meaning in Robert Johnson's "Crossroads" if we miss the symbolic reference to the Yoruba deity Eshu-Elegbara. The prevalence of such references not only tends to confirm the Straussian hypothesis of a covert communicative strategy, but also begins to suggest what might be involved in a "proper initiation."

Having said all this, it nevertheless remains apparent that neither the proprietary argument nor the experiential access argument quite secures the thesis that white people can not sing (or play) authentic blues. The experiential access argument has undeniable moral force as a reminder of and warning against the offense of presumptive familiarity, but it distorts the blues in the process by obscuring what is crucially and universally *human* about its central themes. And it leaves open the possibility of the proper initiation of white people and other non-blacks, if not entirely into the African-American ethnic community, then at least in the use of the blues as an expressive idiom and so into the blues community. Obvious examples would include Johnny Otis and Dr. John. Given this, the force of the proprietary argument is also limited, since initiation into the blues community presumably carries with it legitimate access to the blues as a means of artistic expression.

This of course leaves the authenticity question still open on a case-by-case basis. Many white attempts at blues certainly come off as inauthentic, as no doubt do some black ones. However, if the authenticity question turns not on race but rather on ethnicity, which admits of initiation, and on the achievement and demonstration of genuine understanding and fluency, which are also communicable by other than genetic means, then it is hard to resist the conclusion that Professor Longhair's legitimate cultural and artistic heirs include Dr. John, and that Robert Johnson's legitimate cultural and artistic heirs include John Hammond. It is tempting to conclude on this basis that the answer to the question "Can white people sing (or play) the blues?" is: "Yes. Unless you're a racist." . . .

NOTES

1. For convenient reference, I'll call this the "negative position," and distinguish it from the "affirmative position" represented so far by the above "ready responses."

2. Ralph J. Gleason, "Can the White Man Sing the Blues?" *Jazz and Pop* (1968): 28–29.

3. See *Blues People* (New York: Quill, 1963) and *The Music: Reflections on Jazz and Blues* (New York: Morrow, 1987).

4. "The Great Music Robbery," in *The Music,* pp. 328–332.

5. "Blues, Poetry and the New Music," in *The Music,* p. 262.

6. "Jazz Writing: Survival in the Eighties," in *The Music,* p. 259.

7. "Where's the Music Going and Why?" in *The Music,* p. 179.

8. William Ferris, *Blues From the Delta* (New York: Doubleday Anchor, 1978), pp. 101–103.

9. *Blues People,* pp. 147–148.

10. Leo Strauss, *Persecution and the Art of Writing* (University of Chicago Press, 1952), pp. 23–24.

11. Ibid., p. 24.

12. Ibid., p. 25.

13. Grace Simms Holt, " 'Inversion' in Black Communication," in Thomas Kochman, ed., *Rappin' and Stylin' Out* (Urbana: University of Illinois Press, 1972), quoted in Richard Shusterman, *Pragmatist Aesthetics: Living Beauty, Rethinking Art* (Oxford: Blackwell, 1992), pp. 221–222.

14. Paul Oliver, *Blues Fell This Morning: Meaning in the Blues* (2nd ed., Cambridge University Press, 1990), pp. 265 ff.

Critics

. . . So Black and Blue

Paul Taylor

Response to Rudinow

Blues luminary Buddy Guy says of Eric Clapton, arguably the best living white bluesman, that "all I want to do is hear him play. Race, size, color, nothing matters when a guy's got it, and Eric's got it."[1] But Clapton himself says "I'm qualified to sing the blues because of what's happened to me; but I still don't think I'll ever do it as well as a black man."[2] Setting aside the possibility that the difference

between playing and singing the blues is relevant, these two statements juxtaposed reveal a tension that deserves further scrutiny. For Guy the blues is color-blind, while Clapton is convinced that his performances suffer somehow because he is white. Who is right?

Joel Rudinow has written about this tension in his article, "Race, Ethnicity, Expressive Authenticity:

Paul Christopher Taylor, " . . . So Black and Blue: Response to Rudinow," *Journal of Aesthetics and Art Criticism* 53, no. 3 (Summer 1995): 313–16. Some notes have been deleted. Reprinted by permission of Blackwell Publishing Ltd.

Can White People Sing the Blues?" He argues that we should prefer Guy's view to views like Clapton's because "the essence of the blues is a stance embodied in sound and poetry," a stance that one must, and therefore can, learn to assume, rather than a skill or entitlement conferred by race membership. But Rudinow misunderstands both the state of affairs toward which the "blues stance" is oriented as well as the way individual perspectives on the stance might find expression in statements like Clapton's. In this discussion I will argue that Rudinow's misunderstanding causes him to miss important nuances of the racialist discourse from which the claim emerges, and therefore to overlook a possible interpretation of the claim on which it becomes less objectionable.

First we have to summarize Rudinow's argument. He begins by clarifying his target, which I will call the Black Blues Authenticity Thesis, or "BBA" for short. Taking Amiri Baraka's formulations as the principal model, Rudinow argues that the BBA is the claim that "white blues" performances are unacceptably derived from the original sources of the blues, and so cannot count as authentic blues performances. Answers to the question of what counts as an acceptable derivation separate arguments for the BBA into two types. First is the proprietary argument, which holds that one can be a participant in an authentic blues performance only if one belongs to the community whose members stand in some sort of ownership relation to the blues idiom—the black community. Rudinow mentions some objections to this position, but dismisses the entire issue as "an elaborate red herring" and moves to the second type of argument: the experiential access argument. This route to the BBA "posits the experience of living as a black person in America as a precondition of the felt emotion essential to authentic expression in the idiom of the blues."

Rudinow raises three objections to the experiential access argument. He says first that the argument seems to require a "Myth of Ethnic Memory"—a clearly problematic commitment to the idea that "mere membership in the ethnic group confers special access to the lived experience of ancestors and other former members." The second problem is that reformulating the argument to avoid the memory myth—by interpreting the blues as a secret cultural

code that only the properly initiated can understand—obscures "what is crucially and universally *human* about [the] central themes" of the blues. Last, there is the point that the reformulated argument establishes the converse of the conclusion it is marshaled for: the possibility of authentic white performances in virtue of white initiation to the relevant cultural spaces.

Rudinow's counterarguments are appropriate to his characterization of the central issues; unfortunately, his characterization is inappropriately narrow. Very broadly speaking, the main difficulty with his approach is that he misunderstands the cultural forces acting to constitute the subject positions from which the BBA may be articulated, and so misconstrues the possible force and intent of the claim. Put another way: he paints much too simplistic a picture of the blues idiom as a racialized cultural space and of the subjectivities that occupy it. Appreciating this alternative way of viewing the central questions renders Rudinow's specific criticisms inapposite, because it replaces his attempts to set out and criticize the conceptual options in the abstract with the socially grounded project of understanding the subject positions from which the BBA emanates. Where Rudinow assumes that the BBA is an assertion about the capabilities or the moral status of the performer—either white performers are incapable of producing sounds that are essential components of authentic blues performances, or they ought not participate in the activity of attempting to produce such sounds—we can read the claim as a description of the perspective from which BBA-type claims are advanced. That is, the claim might be about certain *listeners* and only derivatively about performers.

An illuminating way to approach this point is through Dewey's theory of situations. Artworks for Dewey are experiences that art objects participate in and occasion, distinguished from other kinds of experiences principally in that they intensify and clarify certain features common to those experiences. Experience in general is made up of situations, or contextual wholes, within which events take on meanings in relation to their antecedents, consequences, and immediate qualities. The component events of situations are unified in the organism's consciousness by their collective provocation of a distinguishing feeling, much as the component events depicted in a film are unified for the viewer. Someone who sees an isolated scene from the middle of a film feels dislocated—wondering who the characters are and why they are doing what they arc doing—while someone who sees the scene in its proper place vis-à-vis the rest of the film experiences the scene as part of an unfolding whole, whose meaning is bound up with and provided by the rest of the film: situated events for Dewey are like the scene viewed in sequence.

With that apparatus in place, we can state the alternative approach. The BBA as a claim about capacity may be the following sort of claim about the listener: *Candidate blues performances in which white performers participate cannot work in the experience of the BBA-adherent listener in a way generating the feeling that marks blues performances proper.* Let us call this "BBA_1." Interpreted in this way the claim avoids what I will wager is the main intuitive worry about the BBA: that it is a claim about discernibility conditions for sound structures, so that if a "white" performance is indiscernible from a "black" one, as one that satisfies certain stylistic conventions would be, the BBA is falsified. On this Deweyan approach, even a performance that cannot be immediately identified as white may fail to produce the "authentic blues performance feeling": if the listener does not know the racial identity of the performer, her experience may be stunted so that the proper feeling does not emerge right away; and on discovering later that the performer was white, she cannot recruit the memory into present consciousness in a way that generates the proper quality.

This interpretation of the BBA as a claim about more or less subjective—not totally subjective, for reasons we shall encounter shortly—conditions for successful achievement of a certain kind of aesthetic experience links the capacity and moral status claims. The BBA as a claim about moral status starts with BBA_1 and adds the following: *The candidate performances fail because the blues is a racial project, and moral deference is owed to black contributions to the project.* Call this "BBA_2." This formulation borrows technical terms from sociologist Howard Winant[3] and Laurence Thomas.[4] Winant's concept of a racial project refers to a cultural space within which the meaning of race is articulated.

Thomas's moral deference is linked to what he calls bearing witness to the moral pain of another. To bear witness for another "is to have won her trust that one will tell her story with her voice, and not with one's own voice . . . that one will render salient what was salient for her in the way that it was salient for her."[5] Moral deference, then, is "the act of listening that is preliminary to bearing witness to another's moral pain, but without bearing witness to it."[6] If we read the blues idiom as a racial project that depicts the black race as a social category whose members are oppressed, insulted, and burdened with diminished life chances (but who still persevere and struggle—blues songs are tragic, not pathetic), then we can read the BBA_2 as the claim that *candidate blues performances in which whites participate fail because the BBA adherent is unconvinced that the performer can properly bear witness to the racialized moral pain that the blues is about.*

This brings us to another of Rudinow's worries and another of his oversights. He wonders how the blues can be about black experiences in any way that uniquely picks out black performers today, who are arguably as distant from the experiences of the black founders of the blues[7] as present-day whites are. The experiential divide problem iterates over a temporal gulf, blocking black performers' claims to authenticity in the same way that the racial gulf supposedly blocks the claims of whites. This is where he argues that the experiential access argument presupposes either a myth of racial memory or a conception of the blues as a code. Assuming that the "myth" is untenable, he moves immediately to the second, "more subtle and defensible reading."[8]

But this is much too fast. Talking about the idiom as a racial project has already taken us some distance toward complicating Rudinow's assumption: it may be that the blues is about what the contemporary and historical experiences of being African-American have in common—the experience of being, as Thomas says, a member of an oppressed and downwardly constituted social category, subject to racialized hostile misfortune. Or, as I have argued elsewhere,[9] about the response-dependent property of being perceived as black and the counterfactually specifiable susceptibility to certain forms of discrimination and insult that follows from it. In either case, there is no need to posit a myth of racial memory; fairly pedestrian sociological commonplaces will suffice. So it is not the case that, as Rudinow contends, membership in the ethnic group confers special access to the lived experience of ancestors and other former members; to the contrary, membership is *constituted*, at least in part, by such access—access forced upon contemporary blacks by the persistence of racial and racist conditions.

This confusion over the possibility of defining a black experience that unites Robert Cray and Robert Johnson is not really Rudinow's fault. He simply puts too much faith in Appiah's accounts of racialism and racism, which infect Rudinow's argument with their own problems. Rudinow also inherits from Appiah the last problem I shall discuss: an oversensitivity to the exclusivist rhetoric of racialist discourse. The fundamental worry behind Rudinow's complaints seems to be that BBA assertions lead to what Paul Gilroy calls ethnic absolutism, the granting of sanction to participate in the cultural practices of an ethnic group to all and only those who belong to the group.[10] And as we have seen Rudinow point out, such views obscure what is crucially and universally human about the blues.

But for the BBA-adherent sensibility I have been trying to sketch here, BBA assertions may be calculated to have precisely that effect, whether because attempts to universalize cultural practices in this country have all too often amounted to attempts to diminish and ignore the worth of the culture within which the practice began or because there is *not* anything crucially or universally human about the blues if the idiom is a racial project.[11] The BBA so understood need not be an immediate cause for concern, because the claim is not racist: on one level it is a shorthand statement of more or less subjective concerns or psychological facts. I say "more or less subjective" and "on one level" because concerns about entrepreneurial raids on cultural forms and the capacity to feel and understand the meanings that combine to produce "the blues feeling" are features of racialist discourses into which individuals are socialized. They are subjective only to the extent that they are appropriated by an individual mind from the common store of objective social meanings. Here the

subjective aspect of the BBA dovetails with a more objective character, which we can capture by saying that the BBA is shorthand also for statements about the currency of certain components of certain racialist discourses.

When Rudinow says that the essence of the blues is a stance embodied in sound and poetry, he fails to consider either who might be taking the stance—a racialized subject—or what the stance orients one toward—the blues as a racial project, rather than as a cultural practice of producing certain sound structures in fidelity to authenticating conventions. In addition, he does not see that defining race in terms of genetics is too strong and that replacing it with ethnicity by consent is too weak. So he does not see that "White people can't play the blues" can be analyzed as "I can't properly respond to candidate blues performances in which whites are the principal participants," that such a claim can advert to a nonconsensually undergone store of common black experiences to which whites do not have access, or that the claim may reveal much more about the speaker than about performers.

There is an important question to consider before I close. What if the racialized subject who assumes the blues stance is not real? What if the blues is essentially or significantly representational? Consider Mozart's "Musical Joke." While it appears to be the work of an incompetent, it is in reality the work of a master, constructed to *appear* to be the work of an incompetent. In cases where appearance diverges from reality in an artwork, we sometimes refer to an apparent or implied artist, whose fictional creative activity can account for the work's manifest features.[12] Suppose we complicate the analysis of blues performances by interpolating apparent black artists, whose experiences are represented by works in the idiom. The BBA then becomes an answer to the empirical question of whether whites can represent blacks or engage in activities of artistic production that eventuate in works that represent black experiences and/or perspectives. And generalizing the BBA stance has unfortunate outcomes—ruling out the casting of Denzel Washington as Hamlet, for example. Seen in this way, is not the BBA an appropriate target of Rudinow-style criticism?

I have space only to sketch a rather programmatic response. We have to remember the role of moral deference to racial projects. The blues is a racial project; *Hamlet* seems not to be. So one might argue that Hamlet's experiences are not of the sort that require moral deference. Rejecting Denzel Washington would be an expression of the ethnic absolutism that Rudinow fears; complaining that Johnny Winter frustrates one's emerging blues appreciation experience need not be, if what I have said above is right. Even if we need to postulate a fictional agent standing between the content of the blues and the real artist, the real artist's ability to create a representation that works properly in appreciative experience depends on whether she can be accepted as a witness to racialized moral pain. This fact blocks the analogy to *Hamlet* and the objection that results.

NOTES

1. Quoted in *The New York Times,* Sunday, October 2, 1994, sec. 2, p. 32.
2. Promotional spot, VH-1, October 19, 1994.
3. See Howard Winant, *Racial Conditions: Politics, Theory, Comparisons* (University of Minnesota Press, 1994), pp. 29–30.
4. From Laurence Thomas, "Moral Deference," *The Philosophical Forum* 24:1–3 (1992–93): 233–250.
5. Ibid., p. 245.
6. Ibid., p. 246.
7. Assuming with Rudinow and like him, for the sake of argument, the view that the roots of the blues can be definitively located in African-American culture.
8. Joel Rudinow, "Race, Ethnicity, Expressive Authenticity: Can White People Sing the Blues?" *The Journal of Aesthetics and Art Criticism* 52 (1994): 133.
9. Paul Taylor, "Racialism Without Metaphysical Difficulty; Racism Without Moral Error," *Proceedings of the 23rd Value Inquiry Conference,* forthcoming.
10. See Paul Gilroy's *Small Acts* (London: Snake Tail Press, 1993).
11. This, incidentally, is Baraka's point in *Blues People:* the idiom is a project through which we can track and understand the emergence of the African-American from the enslaved African. See the introduction to *Blues People.*
12. My discussion of this matter is greatly indebted to Robert Stecker, "Apparent, Implied, and Postulated Authors," *Philosophy And Literature* 11 (1987): 258–271.

Joel Rudinow | # Reply to Taylor

I quite like the pair of quotations Paul Taylor has used to capture and reframe the issue of the problematic authenticity of non-black blues, an issue which is presently making me a little dizzy. Taylor has me siding with Buddy Guy, who is American, black, with deep roots in the history of the blues, and unassailable credentials as a bluesman, and who expresses deep and unqualified appreciation for the blues performances of the white Englishman Eric Clapton. Taylor, in criticizing my defense of the thesis that white blues need not be disqualified as inauthentic, and in defending a version of what he calls the "Black Blues Authenticity Thesis" (BBA), evidently wants to side with Clapton (insofar as Clapton deprecates his own performances). As Cornel West observed in a related context, "contradictions, paradoxes, and ironies abound."[1]

Taylor interprets the "Black Blues Authenticity Thesis" (BBA) as a set of claims not about performers and performances but about audiences, audience members, and their experiences. But then what are we to make of Clapton's self-deprecation? On its face it appears to be a claim about his performances and about himself as a performer. Does Taylor think that Clapton has misunderstood or mischaracterized the central issues? By the same token, what are we to

From Joel Rudinow, "Reply to Taylor," *Journal of Aesthetics and Art Criticism* 53, no. 3 (Summer 1995): 316–18. Some notes and some parts of the text have been deleted. Reprinted by permission of Blackwell Publishing Ltd.

make of Buddy Guy's appreciation of Clapton's performances, in which Guy positions and orients himself as a listener?

If the BBA is really a claim about certain listeners, what does it say about those listeners? It seems to say that they are incapable of appreciating certain performances on account of the performer's race. Taylor's BBA₁ plainly says that for some listeners the racial identity of the performer is aesthetically relevant—relevant to an appreciation of the performance as music. I readily admit that it did not occur to me to consider such a view as a serious option. Indeed I said as much explicitly.

> [The BBA thesis] would *be* racist if it held that the music made by white people, however much it may resemble blues and be intended as blues, isn't authentic blues *simply because it is made by people of the wrong race.* But nobody says this.[2]

Apparently I was mistaken. Somebody does say this. Taylor's "BBA-adherent listener" says this. In fact, Taylor's "BBA-adherent listener" goes further: she must have verified the racial identity of the performer (presumably as black) as a precondition of the aesthetic experience of blues appreciation. Taylor's BBA-adherent listener is a "subjectivity"—a term of art, whose theoretical function is to reflect the degree to which we are each (according to Taylor's "social constructivist theory of persons") socially constituted. However much we may be "constituted *as* social beings" (i.e., in terms of our social roles and identities), and however much we may be so "constituted *by* society" (i.e., however much these very roles and identities are defined by forces reflecting the historical and current construction and distribution of power in society), I want to maintain that we are all—performers, audience members, theorists alike—still "persons," or less abstractly, "human beings." And to Taylor's "BBA-adherent listener" I would want to say, one human being to another, "Let's attend, shall we, to the music." By "attend to the music" I certainly do not mean merely as "sound structures satisfying certain stylistic conventions," as though the music played no organic role in the social life of the community.

Which community? Well, let us begin by supposing, with Taylor, that attending to the music in the case of the blues means recognizing it as a "racial project." But let us see also what that entails. According to Winant,

> The theoretical concept of racial projects is a key element of racial formation theory: A racial project is simultaneously an interpretation, representation, or explanation of racial dynamics and an effort to organize and distribute resources along particular racial lines.[3]

Racial formation theory is an attempt to account for the flexibility and resilience of race as a significant social category and of racism as a social and political state of affairs, and accordingly posits "race" as a fluid, transforming, historically determined concept. In that case, the blues must surely be *evolving* as a racial project, which leaves the question of the authenticity of white blues open. Suppose we recast the question this way: Is white blues (part of) the same racial project as black blues? For the moment, let us suppose not (with Taylor's BBA-adherent listener); but if not, other questions are open as well: Is the blues one racial project or many? Is contemporary black blues (part of) the same racial project as early delta blues? Arguably not, though it can also be argued that the blues is a single continuous evolving racial project. But either way the question of the authenticity of white blues remains open pending yet further argument. And the argument will have to do better than the mere suggestion that the blues might be about what contemporary and historical African-Americans have in common uniquely and to the exclusion of other downwardly constituted social groupings. It will not do simply to assert in a question-begging way that there is not anything crucially or universally human about the blues, nor simply to assume a particular racialized exclusivist delimitation of "the (true) blues community." . . .

NOTES

1. Cornel West, "Postmodern Culture," *Prophetic Reflections, Volume II: Notes on Race and Power in America* (Monroe, ME: Common Courage, 1993), p. 39.

2. Joel Rudinow, "Race, Ethnicity, Expressive Authenticity: Can White People Sing the Blues?," *The Journal of Aesthetics and Art Criticism* 52 (1994): 129.

3. Howard Winant, *Racial Conditions: Politics, Theory, Comparisons* (University of Minnesota Press, 1994), p. 24.

18

Is Racial Profiling Wrong?

Levin and His Critics

Police in the United States tend to stop young black males for questioning more often than they stop young white males. In the wake of the terrorist attacks of September 11, 2001, INS officials have taken a far more lively and active interest in young male Arabs from certain Middle Eastern countries than in, say, old white females visiting the United States from Scotland. These are both cases of racial profiling on the part of State officials—using racial characteristics to make decisions about whom to investigate. The question posed in this chapter is whether or not racial profiling is immoral.

In chapter 15 we have already seen that making discriminations on the basis of racial classification may not necessarily be morally illegitimate. At least, if preferential hiring is morally permissible then not all such race-based discrimination is morally wrong. In the featured article in this chapter, Michael Levin argues that racial profiling is a kind of discrimination on the basis of race that can be perfectly morally justified.

At first, Levin's argument seems quite straightforward, but as we read through the critical discussions that follow it we discover that it has a number of features that are not obvious at a first reading.

Levin's article and some of the rejoinders contain formulations of certain claims about race and crime that many readers may well find deeply offensive. Although it is sometimes very difficult to follow this advice, it is important not to be sidetracked by strong emotional reactions (positive or negative) to these claims. The point is to sort out the argumentation and to try to determine whether or not it is any good. If you strongly disagree with Levin's conclusion, then you have a very good reason to work out what is wrong with his argument.

Levin reports that the frequency of violent crimes committed by young black males is proportionately higher than the frequency of violent crimes committed by other groups. One of the key statistics he cites is that "approximately one black male in four is incarcerated at some time for the commission of a felony, while the incarceration rate for white males is between 2 and 3.5%." Suppose this is true. What follows? Levin considers the following case:

> Suppose, jogging alone after dark, you see a young black male ahead of you on the running track, not attired in a jogging outfit and displaying no other information-bearing trait. Based on the statistics given earlier you must set the likelihood of his being a felon at .25.

If Levin is right about this, how strong should your belief be that you are in imminent danger of being attacked? Not all felons attack all vulnerable people whenever they can get away with it. So, presumably, the probability that you will be attacked is less than 0.25. Levin sets it at 0.125 (i.e., he assumes that there is a fifty/fifty chance that in these circumstances a felon will attack you). This is greater than the standard level of statistical significance of 5 percent (0.05) (the level at which a factor is deemed to be relevant to some effect), and hence, Levin concludes, you are justified in concluding that you are at a significant risk of attack and you are morally justified in taking appropriate action, such as fleeing. On the other hand, if the other person were a white male, then the probability that he was a felon would drop to, say, 2.5 percent (0.025) and the probability that you will be attacked would drop to 1.25 percent (0.0125), which is well below the level of statistical significance of 5 percent (0.05). Consequently:

> A white (or black) encountering a young black male in isolated circumstances is more warranted in believing himself in danger, and in taking precautions, than when encountering a white in similar circumstances. . . . Epistemically, one is more justified in believing oneself in danger in the former case. . . . Morally, one is justified in . . . seeking to escape.

Let's summarize this conclusion in the following abbreviated form:

Racial profiling by an individual is morally justified.

Levin's first argument for racial profiling by individuals goes like this:

P1   25 percent of the adult black male population are convicted felons.
P2   2.5 percent of the adult white male population are convicted felons.
P3   The probability that a felon will attack you if he can get away with it is 50 percent.
P4   It is morally legitimate for an individual to use available information about potential criminal behavior to avoid being a victim of such behavior.

C   In the jogging case, racial profiling by an individual is morally justified.

In the more general argument to which Levin is adverting—of which this first argument is a particular instance—premises 1, 2, and 3 are all summarized in one general claim: Racial characteristics can carry information about potential criminal behavior.

P1   Racial characteristics can carry information about potential criminal behavior.
P2   It is morally legitimate for an individual to use available information about potential criminal behavior to avoid being a victim of such behavior.

C   Racial profiling by an individual can be morally justified.

The case for racial profiling by the State is an extension of this argument. The State regularly uses various kinds of information to target potential crimes and prevent them from happening. If a policeman sees that the backseat of a car is full of brand new radios and that there is a gun on the car's dashboard, then it is reasonable for him to use that information to infer that there is a good chance criminal activity has taken place, and to investigate the occupants of the vehicle. In light of this information, it is reasonably likely that the driver is involved in a crime and that, if he is not apprehended, he is likely to commit more such crimes. It is also quite possible that the man in the radio-filled car is innocent. The car's owner may deliver new radios ordered over the Web by customers who live in a dangerous neighborhood, and, for legal purposes of self-defense, he may possess a gun (with a gun permit). But even if all this is true, the policeman can still legitimately investigate.

According to Levin, the information carried by racial classification is just like the information carried by the presence of the radios and the gun. As a matter of statistics, both can indicate that a crime or potential crime requires investigating.

P1 Racial characteristics can carry information about potential criminal behavior.

P2 It is legitimate for the State to use available information about potential criminal behavior to preemptively investigate and detain individuals for questioning.

C Racial profiling by the State can be morally justified.

Levin considers quite a wide range of objections to his arguments and concludes that they are all wanting.

In "Statistical Badness," Laurence Thomas takes issue with Levin's claim that, in the jogger case you can legitimately conclude, on the basis of the approaching person's being a black male, that you have a 0.125 chance of being mugged. Thomas claims that there is a whole slew of information about the man that you can gather—from his dress, his demeanor, and so on—that might drastically reduce the likelihood that he is a felon with evil intent. Suppose he is wearing a tweed jacket and a tie? Doesn't that put him in a different category? After all, people in tweed jackets and ties (black or white) rarely mug lone joggers. Chana Cox, in her analysis, makes a closely related point, namely that even convicted felons do not attack lone joggers in anything like half of the encounters they have with them.

Louis Pojman comes to Levin's defense, pointing out several errors in Thomas's critique. He notes that part of Levin's example was that "the youth was *displaying no other information-bearing trait.*" So Levin is stipulating that all you can tell about the youth is that he is a young black male. You have no other information (e.g., that he is wearing a tweed coat and tie or a jogger's outfit) that would enable you to categorize him more precisely.

QUESTIONS FOR CONSIDERATION

Levin's critics concentrate on the plausibility of the first premise of his argument (that racial characteristics carry information relevant to the probability of the imminent commission of a violent crime) or on Levin's argument for that claim. But perhaps there is more to be said about Levin's second premise: It is morally legitimate for an individual or the State to use any available information about potential criminal behavior. Levin argues that the two cases are sufficiently alike. But are they? The first is a case of an individual and his right to avoid becoming the victim of a possible crime, by fleeing the scene. The second is the State's claimed right to investigate, detain, and interrogate people on the basis of information that they might commit a crime. These two cases might have to be treated very differently. Even if you have a right to flee anyone who you think, on the basis of limited information, might assault you, the State may not have the right to detain and interrogate people on the basis of the same information.

• If Levin's argument proceeds by an analogy here, then the analogy may seem to be a bad one. You are relatively powerless and defenseless. The State is neither. Your flight need not insult or injure anyone (although, of course, it might do so). Being detained by the police as a suspect inevitably could insult an innocent person. Are these differences important enough to undermine Levin's argument?

• Are there constraints on the type of information the State may use in preempting crime? Might the institutionalization of racial profiling have bad side effects? For example, might it alienate an entire category of people—those singled out on the basis of their skin color—thereby making them more likely, rather than less likely, to commit violations of the law? Might racial profiling by the State, therefore, drive up the very crime rate it is intended to diminish?

• What other differences are there between an individual and the State that might be relevant here? How might they be used to critique Levin's position?

FURTHER READINGS

Adler, Jonathan. "Crime Rates by Race and Causal Relevance: A Reply to Levin." *Journal of Social Philosophy* 24, no. 1 (1993): 176–84.

———. "More on Race and Crime: Levin's Reply." *Journal of Social Philosophy* 25, no. 2 (1994): 105–14.

Levin, Michael. "Reply to Adler, Cox, and Corlett." *Journal of Social Philosophy* 25, no. 1 (1994): 5–19.

———. "Reply to Adler's 'More on Race and Crime: Levin's Reply.'" *Journal of Social Philosophy* 25, no. 2 (1994): 115–18.

Michael Levin | Responses to Race Differences in Crime

I

It is widely agreed that young black males are significantly more likely to commit crimes against persons than are members of any other racially identified group. Approximately one black male in four is incarcerated at some time for the commission of a felony, while the incarceration rate for white males is between 2 and 3.5%.[1] Absolutely speaking, blacks commit most of the crime in the US, accounting for half of all arrests for assault and rape and two-thirds of arrests for robbery.[2] (Blacks are in fact proportionally more heavily represented in all categories of felony except those requiring access to large amounts of money, such as stock fraud.[3]) These figures parallel prevalence rates by race according to victims' reports,[4] so they do not represent bias in arrests. Some criminologists use the rule of thumb that a black male is ten times more likely than his white counterpart to be a criminal.[5]

While few people are familiar with these statistics, widespread intuitive a awareness of the reality they report creates the familiar contemporary phenomenon of fear of black crime. The present paper examines some of the philosophical issues about risk assessment and rights of risk avoidance raised by this phenomenon.

Black crime is obviously a problem for both blacks and whites, and most of my remarks will apply equally to black and white apprehension about it. Two considerations should be noted, however, which distinguish them. One is the ability of whites to flee black crime to an extent unavailable to blacks. Blacks, particularly young black males, cannot altogether avoid (other) young black males. It is therefore more pertinent to ask whether whites are entitled to flee black crime than it is to ask the same question of blacks. (Indeed, although black crime might no more threaten blacks than whites if the demographic distribution of the races were made random, such a distribution might—while reducing black exposure to black crime—inequitably increase white exposure.) The second factor is the asymmetry in interracial crime rates. It is commonly known that blacks are more likely than whites to be crime victims[6] and that their victimizers are more likely to be black than white: in 1987, for instance, 81.7% of aggravated assaults against blacks were committed by blacks, and 13.1% by whites.[7] However, more than 97% of white crime is committed against whites, while one-half to two-thirds of black crime is also committed against whites.[8] Since blacks are 12% of the population, 88% of the victims of black (and white) crime would be expected to be white if victim choice were random. Thus, whites attack blacks at about $\frac{1}{4}$ of the rate predicted by random choice, while blacks attack whites at more than $\frac{3}{5}$ of the predicted rate. Taking the ratio of these fractions as a measure of preference by race, black preference for white victims is at least 2.4 times that of white preference for black victims. Whether this figure indicates a greater propensity on the part of black criminals to seek white rather than black victims depends on questions of opportunity, but current residential patterns do not seem to present blacks with disproportionately many contacts with whites. The data are thus consistent with a greater preference for white victims on the part of black criminals, and to that extent warrant greater white than black apprehension about black crime.

It is for behavioral scientists to explain black crime, although I pass some methodological remarks below on some proposed explanations. What philos-

From Michael Levin "Responses to Race Differences in Crime," *Journal of Social Philosophy* 23, no. 1 (1992): 5–29. Some notes and some parts of the text have been deleted. Reprinted by permission of Blackwell Publishing Ltd.

ophy can do best is to assess the conflicting epistemic and, especially, moral intuitions such an issue is bound to produce. A system of a priori moral standards would be helpful, but I will not assume any here and I am inclined to doubt any exist.[9] I will confine myself to what I take to be the criteria of rational acceptability already implicit in our commitments on other issues, and noting the application of these criteria in a new, disputed case. (Such applications may of course react back on the initial judgments and commitments until reflection stabilizes at new judgments and commitments.) Indeed, this "our" might well be replaced by "your," with me trying to persuade *you* of something by showing *you* your commitment to it. Whether or not there is some less ad hominem role for reason in ethics is a meaningless question for you the persuadee, since you *endorse* your own standards. Deducing an individual judgment from principles will *convince* anyone already convinced of the principles, and likewise for extracting principles from antecedently accepted judgments. From within your own moral framework—the perspective you cannot help but take—a deduction from your actual standards is perceived as proof, and a showing of inconsistency with those standards is perceived as refutation. (In my view, moral philosophy can do no more than articulate extant value systems and moral argument is essentially ad hominem, but I can't defend these large theses here and I won't assume them [but see n. 9].)

To be as explicit as possible about ground rules, then, "justified" and its cognates as used here mean "justified modulo general principles and particular judgments I expect the reader to hold with some tenacity"—"ordinary standards," for short.

II

My central claim is that a white (or black) encountering a young black male in isolated circumstances is more warranted in believing himself in danger, and in taking precautions, than when encountering a white in similar circumstances. This differential warrant is both epistemic and moral. Epistemically, one is more justified in believing oneself in danger in the former case, and, absolutely speaking, in believing oneself in some danger in the former but not the latter case. Morally, one is justified in the former case in seeking to escape.

This section discusses the epistemic justification, the next one the moral justification.

The usual rule in statistical decision theory is to reject those hypotheses whose probability falls below .05. If you know that one in four Acme automobiles will break down in traffic, you cannot reject the hypothesis that the Acme you are stepping into will break down. There is a 25% chance it will. The failure of the hypothesis is "too remote to take seriously" only if fewer than 5 Acmes in 100 break down. Common sense is not quantitative, and is rarely called upon to evaluate statistical hypotheses, but it too recognizes fairly low credibility levels above which hypotheses become "likely enough" to be taken seriously. Note that the statistical rule (like common sense) distinguishes non-rejection from acceptance, which is demanded only of those hypotheses whose probability exceeds 95%.

There is nothing magic about .05. Textbook orthodoxy regards statistical hypotheses as never disproved, only shown to be less probable than some arbitrary confidence level—typically .05, but lower when rejection of truth is especially undesirable.[10] Nor does the pragmatist construal of acceptance as action as if a hypothesis were true, and non-rejection as allowance for its possibility when planning, select a natural confidence level. Perhaps the least arbitrary approach when forming expectations is pure Bayesianism, which incorporates a term for every hypothesis with non-zero probability. Rigorous Bayesianism also makes sense of eliminativism, at least about doxastic states. Eliminativism just sounds silly when taken to assert that nobody believes anything, but it is not silly when taken to assert that the binary notion of belief corresponds to nothing in the mind, being merely an abstraction from a Bayesian continuum of degrees of commitment. So there is something to be said for a revisionary theory of belief without confidence levels. Bear in mind, though, that rigorous Bayesianism preserves comparative acceptability judgments. As it should, it remains *more* reasonable to expect an Acme to break down than a Mercedes. Since most of the risk assessment issues raised by black crime are comparative, adopting Bayesianism would make little difference in the present context. In any case, Harman and Goldman have lately criticized Bayesianism on pragmatic, empirical and verific grounds,[11] so we may be stuck with confidence levels after all. In that case, .05 is as good as any.

This standard decision rule applies immediately to black crime. Suppose, jogging alone after dark, you see a young black male ahead of you on the running track, not attired in a jogging outfit and displaying no other information-bearing trait. Based on the statistics cited earlier, you must set the likelihood of his being a felon at .25. Of course, "felon" is a dispositional predicate, so the probability of his being prepared at that moment to attack you will generally be less than .25. At the same time, circumstances like the one described may raise the conditional probability of his attacking you if he is a felon above .5, in which case the "absolute" probability of danger is still a significant .125 or more. In any event felons are dangerous, so it is rational to take into account the possibility that you are in the presence of one, and irrational not to do so. On the other hand it would be rational to trust a white male under identical circumstances, since the probability of his being a felon is less than .05. Since whatever factors affect the probability of the black attacking you—the isolation, your vulnerability—presumably affect the probability of a white attacking you as well, it remains rational to be more fearful of the black than of the white. Assuming ordinary confidence levels, there will be many occasions on which it is noncomparatively rational to fear the black but not the white, but that conclusion is independent of the rank-ordering by danger.

To be sure, the odds are 3 out of 4 that the approaching black is not a felon. But you do not violate probabilities by acting as if he might be. The odds are 3 out of 4 that the beckoning Acme will hold up in traffic, but you do not violate probabilities by insuring access to other means of transportation. Confused expressions of this statistical intuition should be interpreted charitably. People may *say* "You can't trust Acmes," but what they probably mean is that sufficiently *many* Acmes break down to

warrant regarding any one of them with suspicion. By the same token, while (some) people may unthinkingly say "Most blacks are criminals," their aversive behavior reflects the correct probability assessment that a black is likely *enough* to be a criminal for blackness to signify danger.

The black in the park is definitely a felon or definitely not. Ideally, you would base your expectations about him on knowledge of which, just as your expectations about the Acme in front of you would ideally reflect complete knowledge of its characteristics. But you do not know. Relative to your state of knowledge, he is a typical member of a class one fourth of whose members are felons, and the probability to be assigned to a random member of that class being a felon is .25. So doing assumes some version of the principle of indifference, but under conditions which resist its abuse. This probability assignment does not asymmetrically partition the reference class of black males or humans generally, any more than the corresponding inference about Acmes asymmetrically partitions the class of Acmes or automobiles generally. The assignment does not illegitimately conjure knowledge from ignorance, since it does not say anyone *is* a felon. You are indeed reasoning under conditions of ignorance, but when reasoning under conditions of ignorance about the Acme, when it is known only to come from the Acme factory, common sense treats the car *as if* it were randomly chosen.[12] The assignment moves from an "objective" observed relative frequency to a "subjective" credal assessment, but frequencies standardly support subjective assessments despite what may be deep conceptual differences between them; once again, the move is unproblematic in the Acme case. Finally, the assignment obeys the constraints on information-seeking discussed in the post-Gettier literature. Two that might seem to impugn the snap credal decision in the park are: Seek more information when it is available, and, seek more information when judgment from current evidence would be immoral (as when current total evidence appears to condemn a friend). But such obligations may be overridden. Perhaps all Acmes that last 100 hours hold up for five years, but you may reasonably form a snap judgment about the Acme in front of you if you need a car *right now*, or if the salesman won't let you drive it for 100 hours unless you promise to buy expensive options. In general, you need not gather more information before deciding whether p if doing so costs more than error about p. The exemption in the park case would seem to be that you need not do A as a means to deciding whether p if the point of deciding whether p is to help reach a decision about doing A. Your park problem is whether to close the gap between yourself and the black male, but closing the gap is necessary for finding out more. So acting on present knowledge violates no informational constraints.

III

It is natural to treat the justification of private action separately from that of state action, and I do so in the present section. Ideally, discussions of state action should be flagged, in somewhat the way set theorists notationally distinguish theorems requiring the axiom of choice. Trusting such precautions are not necessary, I subsequently treat the two issues in the same breath to avoid stilted exposition.

Private Morality

Precautions against the anonymous black of the last section are also morally justified. Since flight from perceived danger is ordinarily permissible so long as it harms no innocent bystander, you are allowed to turn on your heels. Indeed, the perception of danger is not ordinarily required to be rational. Acrophobes who have wandered onto the observation deck of the Empire State Building are entitled to flee so long as they don't trample anyone on the way down. Anyway, as noted, the perception of danger in the running track case is rational.

It may be objected that, by possibly offending an innocent black, flight does risk harming an innocent. But this harm, should it occur, is (arguably) not imposed by you and is in any case outweighed by the right to safety. Certainly, flight did not cause the innocent black's chagrin in the sense of "cause" appropriate to blameworthiness. Responsibility for

harm is ordinarily borne by the author of the original wrong in the chain of events necessitating it, and the events necessitating flight were initiated by other black criminals. The innocent black wouldn't have been offended had you not run away, but you would not have run away were it not for those prior wrongful acts. You flee voluntarily more or less as Aristotle's storm-beset captain voluntarily jettisons his cargo. So responsibility for harm to the innocent black is most naturally assigned to other black criminals, not you. Indeed, the innocent black is epistemically obligated to realize that you are not judging him d*ere,* since you do not know anything about *him.* You are avoiding a statistical possibility he represents.

But even if *you* are responsible for insulting *him,* the expected moral cost incurred by continuing ahead exceeds the expected moral cost imposed by flight. As a first approximation, the expected moral cost of continuing is $.25\times$ the evil of assault, while the cost imposed by flight on the black ahead of you is $.75\times$ the evil of insult. (Insulting criminals is not an evil.) If assault is more than three times worse than insult, calculations of expected morality favor flight. This calculation overstates the expected evil of continuing ahead since, as noted earlier, a black convicted felon may not intend harm to you, but it *also* overstates the cost of flight, since an innocent black may not notice or care about your running away; he may even be understanding. Because the large moral difference between insult and assault is invariant, more refined estimates of the moral cost of flight and continuing ahead may also be expected to favor flight.

State Action

The right of individuals to use racial classification in preemptively seeking safety would seem to extend to the state.

The state's regular use of other information-bearing traits to prevent serious crime sets a precedent for state use of information supplied by race for the same purpose, in the same manner, and to the same extent. Consider, in particular, suspect profiles and search for probable cause. It is uncontroversial that customs agents may subject violin possessors to special scrutiny if possession of a violin suitable for hiding contraband is known to increase the probability that its possessor is a smuggler. A glimpse of a rifle and a stack of car radios on the back seat of an automobile similarly entitles the highway patrol to search it. The state may "discriminate" on the basis of such traits as possession of a violin and occupancy of a car with a stack of radios, i.e. it may calibrate its treatment of individuals on the basis of these traits even when they do not indicate specific wrongful acts. Indeed, the authorities charged with preventing and detecting crime are *obligated* to use relevant information in screening.

Race is an information-bearing trait. Knowledge of race redistributes probabilities about past and potential commission of crimes. So, unless countervailing considerations can be brought, the state is entitled to use race in screening. The New Jersey Highway Patrol, for instance, reportedly stops young black males in expensive new cars for drug searches. The reasoning behind the violin case covers this practice as well, if most drug couriers are young black males driving expensive cars, and few blacks not involved in drug trafficking or other illicit activity own expensive cars (as the low average income and high unemployment rates of young black males would suggest is the case). Given that the presence of a young black male in an expensive car is a better predictor of drug involvement than that of a young white male, ordinary standards sanction and possibly mandate searches of black males under circumstances in which searching white males would be impermissible. If the race of a driver affects the probability of finding drugs in his vehicle, agents of the state may stop vehicles on the basis of their drivers' skin color, just as state agents may search violin owners at airports if most violins at airports contain contraband and most smugglers use violins.

To repeat, these precedents create (modulo ordinary standards) a *presumption* favoring racial screening, rebuttable by some relevant difference between race and other information-bearing traits. A number of such proposed differences will be reviewed presently. Prior to that review, however, it is well to

reinforce the permissibility of racial screening by a systematic argument.

This argument begins with a reminder of what the state is *for*. All currently favored theories of the state assign provision of security as its raison d'etre. Lockeans base the state on protection of antecedent natural rights to property, which includes one's person; Hobbesians base the state on amoral interest in avoiding general war.[13] (Anarchists, who believe the state illegitimate, don't [vacuously] regard any state function as preceding security. Marxists, who expect the state to disappear, evidently regard state-enforced redistribution of property to its rightful owners as a temporary necessity.) Locke and Hobbes are both contractarians, deriving the state from an agreement between individuals to transfer their right of self-defense (Hobbes speaks of a "natural liberty") to some one enforcer. Now, part of that transferred right of self-defense is the use of information to gauge threats to oneself. Traces of this right can be discerned even in civil society, in the right of each individual to pre-empt clear and present dangers to himself. (If I see someone next to me draw a gun, I may disarm him.) Locke seems to accord each man in the state of nature the right to enforce the rights of another. On this view, although my right to use information in civil society does not extend to my entering a car if I see a stack of radios in the back seat, I presumably did have this right in the state of nature, since I had a right to act against perceived threats to anyone as well as myself. The state's right to pre-empt both non-specific threats (a man carrying burglar's tools) and threats to unknown targets (the burglar keeping his destination secret) does not emerge from or supervene upon individual rights. I myself am less confident of Locke's general executive right, and would prefer to derive the state's right by existentially generalizing over the individual rights it has received. Individual I_i can transfer only his right to pre-empt threats to I_i, but the state, having acquired the rights to pre-empt threats to $I_1, \ldots I_n$, takes upon itself the right to pre-empt threats to $I_1 \vee \ldots \vee I_n$, and thence threats whose target can be characterized only as "some I_i." However the state's right is derived, we *do* think the police may stop a car with a rifle on the back seat even if they cannot specify who the driver is threatening.

To be sure, the contractarian cannot argue that the state assumes an *obligation* to enforce individual rights by agreeing to do so. Individuals do not transfer their rights to the state by an agreement with *the state*, but by an agreement with each other to form a state. The effect, however, is much the same. The state acquires the rights of the individuals, with the understanding (between individuals) that this creature of their own will enforce those rights. Individuals acquire a right to have their rights enforced by the state, although this right is not against the state. (The salesman's promise that the vacuum cleaner will work gives me a right to a reliable vacuum cleaner, although it is not the vacuum cleaner that owes me proper functioning.) Moreover, since the state needs *agents* to achieve effective existence, these agents— the police—may literally be viewed as promising the rest of society to enforce their rights. So the state, as embodied in its agents, is *obligated* (because it has obligated itself) to provide security. Since what is obligatory is permissible, and the right to an end implies a right to otherwise permissible means, the state may use any otherwise permissible means to prevent attacks against individuals. Given the empirical salience of race in the commission of crime, attention to race is, absent some independent countervailing reason, permitted and indeed required by the state's protective function.

It is useful, in pursuing this argument, to follow theorists of the 14th Amendment in distinguishing two rationales for government classification of individuals corresponding to two "levels of scrutiny." (There is also an "intermediate" level of scrutiny, but as the philosophical questions are whether race can survive *any* scrutiny, or the *highest* degree of scrutiny, intermediate scrutiny may be ignored.) A classification is "benign" if, in the language of the Supreme Court's *Metro Broadcasting v FCC* (1990) decision, it "serve[s] important governmental objectives [and is]substantially related to the achievement of those objectives." "Benign" here does not mean "kindly"; it means "not intended to burden any individual or group on the basis of race." In fact, as in *Metro*—where the court permitted preferences for

blacks competing for broadcast licenses to serve the state's interest in "diversity in broadcasting"—the US Supreme Court has countenanced benign racial classifications. The argument from Locke and Hobbes is that if the state may identify individuals by race to enhance diversity, it surely may identify individuals by race for its more essential purpose of controlling aggression.

At the same time, however, the Court has held that race is a "suspect" category, that classification by race must be "strictly" scrutinized and permitted only when shown to be necessary for the achievement of a "compelling state interest." (The Court apparently resolves this inconsistency by construing as benign those racial classifications beneficial to blacks, and suspect those racial classifications burdensome to blacks; see below.) Insistence on this more stringent standard will not daunt Hobbes or Locke. Clearly, they say, protecting citizens from attack is a compelling state interest; it is in fact the state's primary function. Crime statistics strongly suggest that race-consciousness can reduce attack, and might well be *necessary* for its adequate control. In all-white states like Utah and Idaho, the rate of death by homicide is about 1 per 100,000, comparable to European rates. In predominantly black areas like Detroit and Washington, D.C., the rate of death by homicide exceeds 70 per 100,000. It is difficult to deny that a greater police readiness to stop and search groups of young black males would decrease the murder rate. Perhaps all crime could be prevented by race-neutrally stationing policemen every fifty feet, but short of turning society into an armed camp, the marked black propensity to violence may be controllable only by attention to factors extensionally equivalent to race.

The court has offered reasons for striking down virtually all race-based classifications burdensome to blacks; its chief reason, as expressed in *Korematsu*, another recent decision, is that such classifications may reflect "racial antagonism [rather than] pressing public necessity." This language suggests that, in the Court's view, such classifications *merely* express racial antagonism, and cannot serve any other purpose. This is at bottom an empirical claim about the motives behind such classifications and their possible uses; in fact, the claim about the malign motive behind racial classifications is in large measure an inference from their presumed inutility. The point of the crime statistics is precisely that special police attention to (say) groups of young black males is not a baseless expression of "racial antagonism." Stopping acts which, as a matter of objective fact young black males are more likely to commit, by perhaps an order of magnitude, is a "pressing public necessity" if anything is.

Mention of these recent Supreme Court decisions is apt to raise the point that the impermissibility of state racial screening has indeed become a "fixed point of moral intuition." As observed, the Court, a reasonable guide to contemporary standards, strictly scrutinizes and by this standard rejects many racial classifications. To be sure, not all stated racial classifications are deemed impermissible by this guide. There are laws (e.g. sec. 8a of the Small Business Administration Act) reserving funds for black-owned businesses and National Science Foundation Fellowships reserved for blacks, and, as also noted, the Supreme Court scrutinizes less closely, and permits, some racial classifications (in the preferential assignment of broadcast licenses to blacks in *Metro,* for instance). What appears to have become a fixed point is the impermissibility of classifications burdening blacks. If this appearance is accurate, then, in conjunction with the methodological resolve of Sec. I, it outweighs the analogies and arguments lately deployed.

Before looking more closely at this appearance, I'll reformulate it less tendentiously. Certainly, the Court prefers to term "benign" those classifications, like *Metro*'s, whose *purpose* is not burdening whites but some other end such as helping the disadvantaged or increasing diversity. But whatever the state's *purpose* when classifying by race (or classifying in any other way, for that matter), some individuals are better off and some worse off than they would have been had the state not so classified. Under some racial classifications permitted by the Court, for example those giving preference to blacks in the acquisition of broadcast companies in *Metro,* whites are worse off than they would have been had the classification been struck down. And here is the point of substance: the Court has *not* been as ready

to permit classifications under which blacks would be worse off than otherwise. It is this asymmetry I mean when I speak of the impermissibility of only those classifications burdening blacks. Those who accept the doctrine of "disparate impact"—that any practice which adversely affects blacks is, however intended, prima facie discriminatory—should have no trouble with this terminology.

The distinction registered, let me underscore some important differences between strict scrutiny for racial classifications burdening blacks and such paradigm fixed moral points as the wrongness of lying. First, strict scrutiny is new—less than three decades old—whereas lying seemed as wrong to the Greeks as it does to us. Thirty years is too little time to establish an intuition's fixity. Second, the paradigm fixed points as a class give hope of immediate subsumption under some one sweeping characteristic, such as "maximizing happiness" of "being driven by a universalizable maxim." Strict scrutiny for classifications burdening blacks lacks that same logical lucidity. A related point, or perhaps the same one differently expressed, is that the strict scrutiny rule is complex and asymmetrical in ways that paradigm fixed points are not. Lower levels of scrutiny are permitted for racial classifications benefitting blacks and burdening whites; the intuitive rule against lying recognizes exceptions, but not a large class of lies seemingly similar in principie to the lies it forbids. How can legal classifications burdening blacks be distinguished morally from symmetrical classifications exchanging "black" for "white"? There are reasons commonly cited, of course, but, ironically these reasons generate the deepest difference between strict scrutiny and paradigm fixed points. Unlike the imperative of honesty, the imperative of color-consciousness when and only when not burdensome to blacks is commonly based on a number of contingent and historically limited assumptions, among them: that the state seriously mistreated blacks in the past, that racial classifications burdening blacks reflect wrong and harmful "stereotypes," that such classifications can be motivated only by racial hostility. The wrongness of lying also has its empirical presuppositions, but such as are taken to be *self-evident* and *universal:* that lying destroys trust, that co-operation requires reliance on the words of others, that (a la Wittgenstein and Davidson) universal lying is impossible because the meanings of words are determined by their conditions of use. I am not now denying the factual presuppositions of strict scrutiny or their ability to support strict scrutiny itself, although I will later address "stereotypes," and I earlier suggested that crime statistics allow racial classifications burdening blacks to survive strict scrutiny. I am asserting, rather, that these factual presuppositions do *too much* work. The value of strict scrutiny is not *inherent,* as the value of truth-telling is, but a consequence of more fundamental values (no needless state burdens, no catering to hatred) presumed to apply to a particular sort of racial classification. Classifications burdensome to blacks are thought wrong because blacks were once enslaved, and (moral axiom) slavery is wrong; because such classifications indulge hatred, and the indulgence of hatred is self-evidently wrong and leads to further (self-evident) wrongs.[14] Color consciousness does not remain immediately and intuitively impermissible when the associated factual assumptions are relaxed, as they may easily be in imagination. Indeed, racial classifications burdening whites are thought more permissible precisely because the parallel factual assumptions are known to be untrue of whites. By contrast, it's more difficult to imagine lying not causing distrust or not destroying communication. The wrongness of lying is integral to the human condition, while the wrongness of racial classifications burdening blacks is not.

In any case, the "fixed point" objection is pertinent only if racial screening in fact is found to fail the Court's strict scrutiny test. At the time this is written, the Court is admittedly unlikely actually to permit measures like those under discussion. But times change. It is conceivable that at some point the Court might find black violence so threatening to public order, and its control so compelling a state interest, as to permit race-conscious measures while maintaining its doctrine that racial classifications are "suspect."

IV

The permissibility of private and especially state race-consciousness in seeking security will draw a number of objections, which I will consider in order of increasing intuitive force. But the burden of proof, as I have noted, rests on the objector. The statistical prevalence of black crime in conjunction with the rest of our ordinary moral beliefs may not force acceptance of race-consciousness, but the precedents cited together with the argument from the purpose of the state create a presumption favoring race-consciousness. Failure to rebut this presumption leaves race-consciousness permissible.

(1) Basing treatment on race is racist.

Much of the force of this objection depends on an ambiguity in "racism." If "racism" means *unjustified* race-consciousness, race-based differentiations need not be racist. In particular, race-based screening is not "racist" if justified by differential crime rates, and calling it "racist" in this sense simply begs the question. On the other hand, if—as it sometimes seems to—"racism" denotes any race-consciousness, racism is not automatically objectionable. Practices "racist" in *this* sense must be evaluated on their own merits. For those who favor them, affirmative action and the casting of white actors as Hamlet are unobjectionable forms of "racism," as the casting of female Ophelias is presumably an acceptable form of "sexism". Race-based screening is indeed "racist" in this sense, but must be evaluated on its merits.[15]

Of course, one might hold that in fact all forms of racism in this *second* sense are wrong, a claim both non-trivial and sweeping enough to bar racial screening. However, the moral objection it mounts to racial screening is not that it uses racial factors, but that all use of racial factors is wrong. Because this is the most penetrating and philosophically interesting objection, I am deferring it to last, as objection (5) below.

(2) Rights precede utility. Rights against screening by race override the possible benefits of screening.

This argument can easily beg the question, since the very issue at hand is the existence of a strong right against screening by race. But I won't press that point very hard at this stage, since the argument implicit in common sense for ordinary (and by extension racial) screening is not utilitarian at all, but "rights maximizing."[16] Maximum protection of rights permits local rights invasion which minimize invasion overall. Rights-maximizers admit the wrongness of detention without specific evidence of wrongdoing, but see such detention as most efficiently protecting citizens' net rights against aggression. Screening is not a matter of preferences vs. rights, but of rights vs. more rights. Criticizing racial screening for favoring *utility* is thus an ignoratio.

The distinction between rights- and preference-maximizing suffices to turn the present objection, but its contribution to the intrinsic plausibility of screening, and thereby racial screening, deserves to be noted. "Utilitarianism of rights," which is deontological in its fashion, takes the more attractive side of the rights-vs.-utility debate and withstands the counterexamples that blow away classical preference-maximizing utilitarianism. (Act-utilitarianism tells you to rescue ten strangers instead of your own child from a burning building; the implications of rule-utilitarianism are less clear. Aggression-minimizing allows you in no uncertain terms to ignore the strangers, since refusal to rescue is not aggression.)

Objection (2) might be modified to an endorsement of an absolute ban on rights violations as against any brand of maximizing. This again begs the question when applied to race, but, again, there are more illuminating replies which concede arguendo a right of indeterminate strength against racial screening. The maximizer might boldly adapt the utilitarian idea that ordinary morality really is maximizing but *appears* Kantian to get us to maximize successfully.[17] The maximizing character of morality is revealed (the maximizer continues) when maximizing is preferred to Kantianism in hard cases—such as probable cause detention. Or, the maximizer may reply more concessively that if ordinary morality is indeed Kantian, the pre-theoretical acceptability of screening shows such measures to be consistent with Kantianism. (The maximizer gladly leaves to the Kantian the job of reconciling Kantianism with screening.) And if screening is consistent with Kantianism, another argument is needed to show that *racial* screening is not.

In connection with the general case for "rights utilitarianism" against side-constraint Kantianism, it is instructive to recall the role of "minimizing" preemption in Nozick's rights-based derivation of the state.[18] A seeming absolutist about the obligation not to aggress, Nozick insists that the state is legitimate only if it can emerge from anarchy without aggression. He easily derives a dominant voluntary protective association, but he cannot get it to achieve an enforcement monopoly, the defining characteristic of the state, without its aggressively imposing its rules on "independents." To permit this imposition, Nozick cites, rather plausibly, the anxiety created in association members by the prospect of independents conducting affairs according to their own rules. This anxiety is deemed great enough to justify the association in imposing *its* rules on the independents, so long as it compensates ex-independents for this imposition by protecting them as well. Nozick's argument thus requires levels of merely potential aggression that justify limited preemptive aggression by the (proto)state, pretty much the principle I take to underlie extent screening practices. (State protection of the other rights of screening detainees realizes the compensation proviso.) Nozick's reluctant appeal to maximizing indicates the extent which maximizing intuitions permeate our conception of permissible state action.

Insofar as Objection (2) mounts a challenge to screening per se, it effectively concedes that racial screening is permissible if screening in general is. Not surprisingly, this Objection proves too sweeping. The impermissibility of race-based measures must rest on specifically racial factors, if on anything. An obvious one is:

(3) Slippery slope.

Once race-based screening is countenanced, where does use of racial criteria stop? Doesn't it grease the slope down to concentration camps?

Drawing the line on uses of race raises no issue of principle. Just as the use of race in screening is governed by general norms governing the traits to be used in screening, permissible uses of race are limited by the norms which govern the use of all classification.

I have already mentioned two principles that may be used to govern state classification, namely substantial relation to an important government objective, and service of a compelling state interest. These principles can be abused, but so can any principles. A bad will could interpret "reasonable" search and seizure to cover anything, yet, recognizing this danger, we permit wiretapping. The philosophical rights-utilitarian, certainly, has a clear standard: a race-conscious policy A is permissible if A maximizes *expected morality,* the sum over world-states W_i of the products $p(W_i)m(A/W_i)$, where $m(A/W)$ is the net respect for rights achieved by following A in W and $p(W)$ is the probability of W holding. Now, if objection (3) is an expression of the worry that the expected morality of race-based action is *always* suboptimal, always less than some race-blind alternative, it becomes a version of objection (5), the wrongness of any use of race whatever. So (3) is best interpreted as referring to possible misuses, particularly by the state, of racial classifications.

It is difficult to respond to the Hitler comparison, since mention of Hitler seems to paralyze thought. (Max Hocutt and George Graham call this ploy "argumentum ad Nazium."[19]) Nazis persecuted an inoffensive population, the Jews, for being too clever and for imagined anti-German conspiracies. The historical situation of blacks in the US is entirely dissimilar. It is a fact, not fantasy, that the murder rate in US cities has increased almost tenfold in the last half century as their black population has increased. Here are real innocent deaths, not hypothetical ones. Ordinary morality would demand that something be done about so large an increase if it were unrelated to race; it seems perverse to do nothing because it involves a factor reminiscent of something of concern to Hitler. Hitler's minions invented the multi-stage rocket— does this mean NASA should not use them?

To have any bite, objection (3) must explain without hyperbole why race is so amenable to abuse that, unlike abusable factors that are used, it must be ignored. The mos*t* familiar such explanation is the reinforcement of racial stereotypes by public or private use of racial factors. I now turn to that worry, but under the more general heading "race is special," which also permits discussion of a number of other important issues. In fact, so many topics arise that this objection merits its own section.

V

(4) Race differs from other screening criteria.
(4i) Causal irrelevance.

Standard probable causes, such as concealed rifles and stacks of car radios, are *causally relevant* to the commission of crime, while skin color is not. A stack of car radios, unlike race, carries information because it *results from* crime. (Car radios are *specific symptoms;* few crimes produce stacks of car radios in the back seat, but most stacks of car radios in the back seat are produced by crime.) The presence of a gun informatively correlates with the occurrence of a crime because both are effects of a common cause, criminal intent. Alternatively, a gun might be thought of as a factor likely to *cause* a crime. But race is not a characteristic cause of crime, or effect of crime, or co-effect with crime of some underlying cause. What is sometimes called the "unfairness" of race-based screening derives in part from this causal irrelevance.

This difference between race and many standard screening criteria is irrelevant to its informational value. Standard criteria are used because they carry information, *whatever* the source of this informativeness. *Why* they carry information is the separate issue of *why* they are criteria. To ask this is not to question, indeed it is to assume, that they are. Even though the rifle carries information due to its causal role, it is the information the rifle carries, not the reason that it carries information, that warrants a search when a rifle is noticed. Concealed weapons redistribute probabilities, and it is the redistributed probabilities that justify the state in stopping a man with a concealed weapon. Citing the causal relations between concealed weapons, criminal intent and crime is necessary to justify the revised probabilities, but it is the probabilities themselves, so long as they *are* justified, that warrant the search. By parity of reasoning, any factor which redistributes probabilities equally reliably is an equally legitimate probable cause. In general, A becomes a sign of B

when $p(B/A)$ is high enough. That $P(B/A)$ is often determined by causal relations between A and B fosters confusion between warrant and its (usual) causal basis. It is the magnitude of $p(B/A)$, *whatever* its basis, that warrants an inference from A to B, and would warrant the inference if it held in virtue of unexplained but projectable correlations.

Suppose Borsalinos become popular among drug couriers and almost no one else because most couriers come from the one city where Borsalinos are in fashion. Neither cause nor effect nor co-effect of drug trafficking, Borsalinos at an airport become a reliable sign of involvement in drug traffic. Now, even though it is *accidental* that most drug couriers wear Borsalinos—or "lucky," as the Aristotle of the *Categories* would say—the state would surely be justified in using Borsalinos as a basis for search. Of course, so doing would be irrational if the correlation between headwear and smuggling were expected to break down at any moment. The correlation between race and crime has held for decades, however, long enough to be considered projectable. It is difficult to imagine smugglers ignoring the conspicuousness of their Borsalinos for decades, but if they did the hat/crime correlation would also be projectable. (Strictly speaking, of course, it is the predicates "wears a Borsalino" and "is black" that are [or are not] projectable.)

(4ii) Race is a biological trait not chosen by its possessors.

People should not be penalized for what they cannot help. In this sense too race-based screening is unfair.

If screening is regarded as a punishment, the major premise is absurd. Were there a killer on the lose with a conspicuous, ineradicable birthmark, monitoring such men would be permissible even though birthmarks are not chosen. It would be absurd to forego knowledge that might turn up a murderer because the murderer can't help providing it. In fact, however, the use of identifying traits is not a penalty. (So we can keep the axiom that people shouldn't be penalized for what they can't help.) The killer will be penalized for murder, not possession of a birthmark. The involuntariness of the tip-off is irrelevant to the need to identify him; by the same token, the involuntariness of race has nothing to do with the propriety of race-based screening. If race cannot be used because it is biological, neither should birthmarks, eye color, or—if there is a genetic predisposition to obesity—weight.

Consider the use of age, typically 16, in licensing drivers. Not only is one's age not chosen and a denial of the right to drive arguably a state burden, but the age criterion produces injustice. There are individuals under 16 mature enough to drive and individuals over 16 who are not. But testing every adolescent for maturity is impossible, and traffic accidents (many of which involve rights-violations) must be minimized, so age is used as a reasonably accurate proxy for physical and psychological maturity. Protecting the innocent from reckless drivers is felt to offset the attendant injustice. To be sure, 15-year-olds eventually become 16-year-olds, but the unalterability of race does not destroy the analogy. There will be mature 15-year-olds who, dying before their 16th birthday, are never licensed. We regard an age proxy as proper despite the inevitability of such injustices. What is more, justice delayed is said to be justice denied, so the injustice of denying an able 15-year-old his license is not cancelled when he gets his license on his 16th birthday. That a biological condition may change is evidently irrelevant to the permissibility of imposing a burden on the basis of that condition before it changes. If mutability still seems crucial in the licensing case, it is well to re-emphasize the immutability of birthmarks and inherited obesity, which the state can use in classifying suspects.

It might be allowed that involuntary tests, including race, may be used to identify perpetrators of known acts, but not merely potential malefactors. That an act's ontological status should determine the traits to be used in identifying perpetrators seems quite ad hoc, but assume it so. This ontological feature of racial screening, as well as the immutability of race, is also found in the use of genetic predictors of aggression, should they be found, to track potential criminals from birth. Thought experiments involving such predictors might seem at first to decide against racial screening, since many people now say they would reject tracking. Yet it is very far from clear that tracking would be widely rejected were it actually, concretely available. Imagine genetic information on file but disregarded, while every year post-conviction tests showed that 10,000 murderers (committing about half the murders in the US annually) had the crime gene. Would tracking still be considered wrong if we could *see* the victims who would not have been murdered had potential criminals been tracked?[20] To intensify the problem, instead of supposing 50% of murders are committed by possessors of a crime gene, suppose that 50%, or 90%, of unsupervised possessors of the crime gene eventually commit murder. Would tracking *still* be considered impermissible because nobody chooses his genes? It seems to me likely that at some point the average person would endorse tracking, and even restrictions on the freedom of carriers. Intuitions about genetic tracking may thus prove to reinforce racial screening.

(4iiia) Racial screening will strengthen stereotypes and mistrust of blacks.

Indeed, since white suspicions are in considerable part responsible for black crime, racial screening unfairly hounds blacks for their reaction to being hounded.

Whether racial screening will cause rights violations comparable to those it prevents, and encourage private acts of injustice as whites become irrationally mistrustful of blacks, is an empirical issue which cannot be decided by quasi-a priori speculation. As my doubts about the incipiency of Nazism might suggest, I am somewhat skeptical about this prediction, and in fact there are reasons for skepticism which also bear on the second part of the objection. The stereotype of black criminality is indeed already strong, but there is no evidence that it depends significantly on any variable other than the black crime rate itself. This point is unnecessary for meeting objection (4iiia) if, as I go on to argue, racial screening is permissible even if it self-fulfillingly predicts black crime. (I eventually argue that the etiological question as a whole is virtually irrelevant.) Nonetheless, many people seem certain that black crime is caused by white attitudes and actions, so that burdening blacks for black crimi-nality impermissibly "burdens the victim." The self-fulfilling stereotype idea thus requires some discussion.

The most apparent shortcoming of this theory is methodological. It is not to be denied that many people privately view blacks as less intelligent, industrious and self-restrained than members of other groups, or that black educational and economic attainment, and obedience to law, conforms to this stereotype. Indeed, denying *either* point surrenders the self-fulfilling prophecy idea, by denying the prophecy or its fulfillment. As is widely recognized, however, the direction of the causal arrows between social phenomena is not self-evident, and in fact explaining stereotyped behavior by expectations quickly runs in a circle. Such an explanation renders inexplicable both the origin of stereotypes themselves and the assignment of particular stereotyped traits to particular groups. Group traits once *in place* may be supposed without circularity to be partly or wholly sustained by the expectations they confirm. But what starts the cycle? Whence the initial expectations? Positing a human propensity to stereotype, if it is just an aspect of the tendency to generalize experience, presupposes the stereotyped behavior. Stereotypes so construed are summaries of antecedently observed—perhaps misinterpreted but nonetheless observed—behavior. Including in the tendency to stereotype a need by the ingroup to ascribe disvalued traits to outgroups, the account favored by Sartre and Bettelheim, still fails to explain the ascription of *particular* traits to *particular* outgroups. If the array of outgroups is initially a *tabula rasa,* observation of which does not constrain ingroup ascriptions, these ascriptions must be supposed to be determined *arbitrarily.* Such a theory cannot explain why blacks are considered financially improvident and Jews canny, for instance, rather than vice-versa. And lacking an account of the choice of permutation among group/trait assignments we have no account of the origin of the feedback process, so no account of group traits *or* stereotypes. (It might also be noted that some racial stereotypes, such as Japanese efficiency and Jewish legal skill, are positive and do not obviously favor a need to feel superior.[21])

Reversing the causal arrow, by taking perceived group/trait correlations as independent variables and stereotypes as the dependent variables, explains stereotypes and leaves the cause of the correlations themselves an open question instead of a cul-de-sac. Such a "paradigm," in addition to permitting inquiry to continue[22] would be consistent with the kernel of empirical truth in most stereotypes.[23] And I think many critics of racial screening would, after some reflection, admit as much. However, as suggested earlier, the black behavior empirically validating stereotypes is itself often attributed to white misdeeds. To distinguish the idea that black crime is caused by the expectation thereof from the idea that black crime is caused by more general forms of racial thinking and acting, it is useful at this point to register objection (4iiib):

> *(4iiib) Even if stereotypes about black crime reflect rather than cause black criminal behavior, this behavior is a consequence of past racism.*

Other information-bearing traits like birthmarks and Borsalinos differ from race because their association with crime was not wrongfully caused. Anyone who would screen blacks on the basis of race resembles the Potter of the *Rubaiyat* "who threatens he will toss to Hell the luckless Pots he marr'd in making."

Indeed, since racism and poverty are often mentioned in the same breath as the "root causes" of black crime, it is also important to mention objection (4iiic):

> *(4iiic) Root causes.*

Society has a special responsibility to address the causes of black crime, not take it as a given to be handled by standard means.

(4iiic) can be treated in passing because it is an ignoratio. The legitimacy of racial screening and other race-conscious responses to black crime does not require their being the *best* or *only* legitimate responses. So long as race-conscious measures do not conflict with other legitimate measures, the existence of these other measures does not discredit race-consciousness. The root cause of arson may be depressed real estate values, but the urgency of buoying the real estate market does not forbid otherwise acceptable methods for foiling arson. Similarly, if poor education amplifies black crime, the need to improve schools has no bearing on what may be done

to control the present criminal tendencies which past poor education has, unfortunately, already produced. Indeed, the very deployment of (4iiic) is special pleading unless measures against crime associated with other ethnic groups (the Mafia, Chinese tongs, Jewish insider trading) are also to be assessed by their attention to root causes, a yardstick seldom applied. Deploying (4iiic) has the further disadvantage of opening the door to "root cause" hypotheses other than white racism, some of which, especially those involving genetic factors, are often deemed offensive. Since disconfirmation of the racism hypothesis would raise the probability of offensive alternatives, I note that inclusion of (4iiic) is a response to insistence on it by many readers.

Recurring to (4iiia-b), I view (4iiib) like (4iiia) as a non sequitur. Race-conscious state measures are permitted even if white racism has caused black crime. However, as with (4iiia), the empirical assumption behind (4iiib) is so often viewed as both obvious and morally dispositive that failure to discuss it might seem to ignore everything important. Once again, then, some remarks, primarily methodological, are in order.

Slavery, and subsequent public and private discrimination against blacks, certainly occurred. However, neither the direction nor even the existence of any causal relation between these actions, contemporary black crime and correlates like poverty immediately follows therefrom. In fact, two morally salient causal distinctions must be observed. The first separates the endogenous/exogenous question—whether the cause(s) of black crime lie(s) within or without the black population—from the fault question. The cause of wrongdoing need not itself be wrongdoing, much as our sense of fitness might prefer it so. Perhaps some environmental factor unrelated to past mistreatment differentially affects blacks. Perhaps some accidental, unintended and unsuspected, byproduct of past wrongs differentially produces black crime. In neither case would whites be responsible for the higher black crime rate—nobody would be—and restraints on race-consciousness imposed by such responsibility would fall away. (It would of course be imperative to remove the environmental factor.) Or, disproportionate black crime might be produced by some non-moral factor within the black population, such as genetically greater average aggressiveness.[24] Since people are not responsible for their genes, neither blacks nor whites would be to blame for black crime in that case either.[25]

The response of dismissing such possibilities as absurd in light of history necessitates the second distinction, between the thesis that white mistreatment has causally contributed to black crime and its correlates, and the thesis that white mistreatment is its sole cause. The causal relevance of state action or white mistreatment generally to some aspect of black crime (or socioeconomic attainment) does not imply that that mistreatment has caused all the discrepancy between black and white crime rates (or other behaviors). Black crime may resemble many social phenomena in being a vector sum; in statistical terms, the question bearing on (4iiib) is the "proportion of variance explained" by white misconduct. If race-conscious responses to crime are held to be illegitimate *because* black crime is the result of racism, such responses are illegitimate only *to the extent* that black crime is the result of racism. Race-conscious measures regain legitimacy with decreases in the proportion of variance white racism explains. The reasoning behind (4iiib) even seems to admit moral thresholds. If for instance white misdeeds account for 10% of the difference between black and white crime rates, white responsibility might be too slight to restrain race-conscious measures to any extent at all. So white causal contributions to black crime do not by themselves show race-consciousness to be just more of what originally caused black crime, or to "burden the victim" impermissibly.

It may again seem obvious that white misdeeds directly or indirectly explain all the variance in crime rates, but a number of writers have begun to question this hypothesis. First, black crime rates in other countries, including all-black countries, are comparable to those in the US.[26] White racism, while still perhaps a sufficient or INUS condition, is thus not necessary for the black crime rate. Second, however, black crime has increased since the passage of the Civil Rights Act in 1964 and the inception of affirmative action in 1965. The racism hypothesis predicts a decrease in black crime with more equitable treatment of blacks, and it is difficult to argue that white racism has increased in the US since 1965.[27] Indeed, most black crime is committed by black males under 25 who have never experienced Jim Crow and have been raised in a society in which preferences for blacks is public policy. The idea that blacks have had insufficient time to recover from slavery and Jim Crow predicts similar crime patterns and recovery times for similarly mistreated groups, but this prediction is also unsustained. One may insist on the uniqueness of the black experience in America, but the Jewish experience worldwide certainly looks comparable. In much of Europe Jews were legally confined to ghettos and forbidden to engage in certain trades. The accepted estimate of the number of Jews killed by the Nazis is 6,000,000; the highest estimate I have seen of the number of blacks lynched in the American South between 1900 and 1954 is 5,000. According to T.E. Reed,[28] at most 400,000 slaves were shipped to America during the slave trade, most of them during the 18th century. If one is assumed to have died for every two who survived, the resultant death rate remains three orders of magnitude smaller than that of the Holocaust.

Turn of the century Jewish immigrants fleeing European anti-Semitism lived in extreme poverty in New York, and Jewish crime of the period supports the poverty/oppression/crime link to some extent. However, while Jewish crime was then high relative to Jewish norms elsewhere, it was not, as is black crime, disproportional to the number of Jews in the overall population.[29] Moreover, Jewish crime was directed primarily against property rather than persons, as is black crime.[30] Finally, even the relative prevalence of Jewish crime subsided by World War II,[31] the period 1900–1939 being about equal in length to that between *Brown* (1954) and the present.

Positing ever more obscure forms of racism to explain away such data yields a theory vulnerable as a whole to the question Hume so devastatingly asks of theism in the *Dialogues:* Is the world as we would expect it to be if all we knew beforehand was that this theory were true? Does the world look as if blacks and whites are equally behaviorally restrained but for white racism? Additional assumptions may reconcile the racism theory with ubiquitously high black crime rates and increases in black crime upon passage of protective legislation, but the theory does not predict these phenomena. The theory becomes "conjecture piled atop hypothesis" without independent support.[32]

But race-conscious safety-seeking measures remain proper even if white racism, or stereotyping, or some combination of the two, is the cause of black crime. So much seems unarguable in the case of "private" safety-seeking. That the black male on the running track is more likely than a white to attack a jogger *because* of the jogger's suspicions, or because his father suffered discrimination, does not diminish the jogger's danger or his right to avoid it. This right might be challenged on grounds of the jogger's obligation to break the vicious cycle, a challenge arising from (4iiia) particularly. However, his obligation to weaken the cycle cannot be greater than his contribution to it, weighted by his chances of weakening it by running ahead, and this is less than the danger of continuing. So the jogger's flight remains "subjectively" permissible and probably objectively permissible as well. A more general obligation not to flee a danger by means which might sustain or increase it, on the other hand, seems not to exist. Even if the burning of fossil fuel has so poisoned my city's air that I must leave immediately or asphyxiate, most people would permit me to escape by car. Despite the appearance of involving a ban on the use of means to avoid evils caused by those very means, both principles actually derive what plausibility they enjoy from the general rule that flight must not injure the innocent. My automotive flight imposes some pollution on others, and my flight from the running path, we are supposing, to some slight extent sustains black crime. Yet the reflexive character of these acts does not enter into their evaluation, which consists entirely in balancing my right to safety against the harm I may impose. (In my own non-philosophical view, continuing to run toward the black man is the cowardly subordination of one's own instinct for survival to a heteronomous fear of violating taboos against "racism.")

State action raises facially additional issues, since the fleeing jogger does not interfere with the black,

while a police search does actively burden him. Yet this distinction does no work, since, as observed earlier, the state is usually understood to have acquired a right to use information to intervene preemptively from each individual's right or natural liberty to seek security. If some state intervention is permissible, (4iiia) and (4iiib) purport to show why it cannot be based on race. (4iiia) is the logically more compelling argument, in effect plausibly generalizing the rule against entrapment, namely: Do not punish a wrong caused by that very punitive act. The right to detain does not permit detaining someone for breaking a window in the room in which he is being held for breaking that window, since it is the state that has created the wrong on which it is basing detention. This is why acting on race-based suspicion seems wrong, on the self-fulfilling prophecy model. The cop on the beat is justifiably suspicious of black teenagers, but only because his suspicions dispose them to crime (by lowering their self-esteem or convincing them they have nothing to lose). But this objection loses its force when *specific* self-fulfillment is distinguished from *generic* self-fulfillment. Let us call an expectation-token E specifically self-fulfilling if E creates E-fulfilling conditions, whereas E is *generically* self-fulfilling if other tokens of E's type have created E-fulfilling conditions. The generalized rule against entrapment applies to specifically self-fulfilling suspicions but not to generically self-fulfilling ones. If this black's criminal propensity was not caused by this policeman's present suspicions of him, but only by past suspicions of blacks, possibly including him, this policeman's very suspicions are not responsible for the behavior which justifies them, and the policeman's acting on them does not impose a burden for a wrong created by the act of imposition. Perhaps those other suspicions should not have been harbored, but they *were* harbored and *have* had their effect on the black's character. These suspicions, we are assuming, have made him more likely to commit a crime. As an agent of the state the policeman is obligated to prevent those effects from manifesting themselves as criminal acts. The wrongness of the earlier suspicions bar the policeman from acting on his present ones only if he may never take preventive action in the light of *any* suspicions which are justified by (behavior produced by) some past wrong.

The response that the wrongs which cause black crime were not just any wrongs, but race-conscious wrongs, returns us to (4iiib): race-based measures are impermissible now because the purported need for them was created by past race-based injustice. But the character of those past causes, whatever they are, has turned out to be irrelevant so long as present race-based measures are not the specific causes of the behavior these measures are intended to prevent. Indeed, limited race-conscious screening is not even generically similar to the race-conscious measures said to have caused black crime. Stopping a group of black males because they are especially likely to be carrying guns is not slavery, lynching, separate drinking facilities or segregated schools. Such a measure does not resemble segregation in "reflecting racial antagonism," if this expression means that the measure exists *only* to express racial antagonism, without any further purpose. The crime statistics show such a measure to serve the independently justified purpose of controlling crime. To insist on an analogy between screening and segregation is simply to ignore the empirical fact that race predicts crime, and crime, to an even greater extent, predicts race.

Weakening (4iiib) to the impermissibility of race-based measures now because black crime was caused by *some* (perhaps distinct) unjust race-based measures, leaves it a non sequitur. Crime, like everything else, has causes, some of which are injustices, and the presence of a wrong in the causal chain leading to a crime does not normally constrain state action. It doesn't matter that I plan to steal your car because a swindle in 1950 impoverished my family, so long as my mental capacity is otherwise undiminished. It doesn't matter if the state abetted the swindle by finding the swindler innocent in a fixed trial. The state doesn't care *why* I plan to steal your car. (My theft might acquire some immunity if you had been the swindler and I meant to retaliate, but black criminals give no evidence of harboring retaliatory motives.) Our occasional tendency to think past wrongs mitigate their present effects may be due to a tendency to collapse causal chains—to think that when A causes B and B causes C it is really A that

causes C, with B a sort of epiphenomenal intermediary. This fallacy is particularly tempting when A and C are actions and B is the desire which caused C. Because my desire to steal was caused by wrongful action, we think, I am not the real criminal; the real criminal is the agent behind A. That this is sheer confusion is, I trust, obvious.

If in general the presence of wrongs in the causal history of behavior is irrelevant to state treatment of it, it is hard to see how the *racial* character of those wrongs can create relevance. The intuition that it does, the intuition behind (4iiib), is that race-consciousness is special because race-consciousness is what caused all the trouble in the first place. The countervailing intuition is: so what? Suppose the Holocaust turned many Jews into bank robbers. The police see a man with a Mogen David and a concentration-camp mark on his arm eyeing a bank vault. Should they disregard these factors in deciding whether to enhance surveillance because these factors and perhaps the crime being plotted were the result of anti-Semitism? Consider race-consciousness from the perspective of you, the social contractor in the street, attacked by a black male. Imagine a policeman arriving just too late to save you who confides: "I saw the black approach you and suspected he might attack, but I didn't intercede even to the minimal extent of showing myself to discourage him because my belief that he might attack was *race*-based. I would have felt no impulse to intercede had your attacker been white. But I shouldn't act on thoughts I shouldn't think, and I shouldn't think that way. I shouldn't think that way because your attacker's turn to crime was a result of his great-grandfather's enslavement, his father's inferior education and his own constricted opportunities, circumstances based on racial thinking. Doing *anything* because of his race is just the sort of thinking that caused him to attack you." If you retained your composure, you would surely note your personal innocence with respect to your attacker's history. You would insist that segregation was based on factual errors, while his suspicion of the black was based on empirical realities. In signing the social contract, you would continue, you created the office of policeman to prevent such attack. When he agreed to take this office, the constable assumed the enforcement of your right to self-defense and thereby obligated himself to protect you. You would admit to having limited his protective activities—no third degree, perhaps, no unreasonable invasion of privacy, no generalized entrapment. But the information that race predicts crime is untainted, because innocently acquired. Why couldn't the use it? Is it enough that use of that information bears a family resemblance to the thinking of segregationists?

VI

Even those who admit the irrelevance of the "root cause" issue may balk at the use of racial information because

(5) People should be treated as individuals, not as members of groups.

The alleged right of each person to be treated solely on the basis of his own traits rather than the category to which he belongs, particularly his racial category, is the fundamental objection.

I will eventually argue that Objection (5) rests on a confusion about "treating people as individuals," but let me first, dialectically, deny the objection to supporters of affirmative action. I take it as uncontroversial that affirmative action favors individual blacks (and women) solely on the basis of their race (and sex), without attention to the specifically demonstrated claims of any particular black or female beneficiaries. This is clear enough for the most familiar justification of affirmative action, the need to compensate or "remedy" blacks (and women) for the disabilities they now carry as a consequence of wrongs to themselves and their ancestors.[33] The presumption that a black favored over a better-qualified white has suffered from white misdeeds is applied to him not on the basis of his known individual circumstances and history, but on the racial group to which he belongs. Affirmative action entitlements to individuals are thus probability judgments based on empirical generalizations about classes, just as avoidance of an anonymous black is an implicit probability judgment about an individual based on empirical generalizations about classes. A black applying

for a job is deemed so *likely* to bear the burdens of discrimination, because a high but unspecified proportion of blacks do, that favoring him now "makes him whole." Even if, the replies to (4iiia–b) notwithstanding, it is insisted that every American black has been harmed by white racism, it must also be admitted, I think, that the extent of the harm cannot be exactly determined in any concrete case. It cannot be shown specifically, for instance, that the less-senior blacks promoted over Brian Weber in the *Weber* case would have been *senior to Brian Weber* had there been no racism. So preference for a particular black over a better-qualified white, since it cannot rest on a showing that that black would have been better qualified than that white absent racism, must rest on the statistical inference that that black *probably* suffered an injury as great as the difference in their qualifications.

Other arguments extant for affirmative action also involve classifying by race. If, for instance, more black role models are needed because there aren't as many inspiring blacks as there would have been absent discrimination, we have not advanced beyond the compensation argument. (Many role-model theorists seem not to realize this.) If on the other hand more black role models are needed because the presence of more blacks in different walks of life is not a requirement of justice but a good thing by some more general criterion, the question shifts to why it is good. "Diversity" might be considered good in itself, like pleasure or acting from universalizable maxims. Whatever the merits of such a view—as a justification of affirmative action it is circular, "diversity" being another name for what affirmative action seeks to achieve[34]—diversity as an end in itself self-evidently requires racial consciousness. Blacks become fungible if the end is proportionality per se, with no black being chosen because of any individual trait (except race). Or, one might justify "diversity" and derivatively affirmative action in terms of some values that blacks can distinctively contribute.[35] In that case, however, unless one is prepared to specify a desirable trait possessed by every black and no white, one must believe certain desirable traits more prevalent in the black population, so that preferring a black over a better-qualified white on the basis of his race is *likely* to inject that trait into a given situation.

By contrast, a racial classification may be justified, as in the *Metro* case, as helping the disadvantaged—which once again selects individuals because of presumed correlates of group membership rather than individual traits. (The Federal Communication Commission policy sanctioned in *Metro* did not extend preference to possibly disadvantaged white purchasers, or demand a showing by individual black purchasers that *they* had been disadvantaged.) On its face, the argument that preference-generated diversity will destroy stereotypes is a "distinctive black virtue" argument, since it takes all and only blacks to have the desirable characteristic of 'tending to contribute to the destruction of stereotypes.' But this property itself may involve appeal to a probabilistic assessment, the *likely* effect of a preferred black on stereotypes; more significantly, the thinking that is to be encouraged by affirmative action so justified—that blacks are more talented than might have been supposed—classifies individuals by race.[36]

It appears, then, that affirmative action however defended distributes benefits and burdens on the basis of group membership.[37] (This conclusion should not be surprising.) Proponents of affirmative action therefore cannot consistently deploy individualism—the principle that the distribution of benefits and burdens should never be based upon membership in racial groups—against racial screening, or anything else.[38]

In contrast, a proponent of racial classification in the service of individual security can consistently oppose affirmative action. He may claim that, because assaults are far worse than uncompensated discrimination, the expected morality of screening (the probabilistically weighted value of assaults prevented less the disvalue of detaining innocent blacks) exceeds the expected morality of affirmative action (the probabilistically weighted value of compensating discrimination-induced disabilities less the disvalue of penalizing innocent whites).[39] The burden imposed by affirmative action on possibly innocent whites is heavy, he may say, and the probability of a given white's actually having contributed to a given black's present position not clearly high. As noted, the harm of not compensating discriminatory injury

certainly seems less than the harm of an assault. But the harm of an assault is very great and the burden imposed on blacks by race-based measures to prevent it—the inconvenience of search—is lighter than the burden whites are made to bear by affirmative action. A great enough difference between the expected moralities of screening and affirmative action would justify endorsement of screening and rejection of affirmative action. After a time, affirmative action without screening may come to seem intuitively absurd. To be sure, the value of affirmative action can be raised above that of screening by suitable assumptions about the extent of discriminatory injury to blacks, the moral cost of not compensating it, and the harm to innocent blacks of screening. Nor would the screening proponent necessarily reject those assumptions. It is no part of his argument to call affirmative action *unjustified,* or to *deny* the remedial rationale for it. (Nor need he deny any of the other rationales, although he finds it strange that the state may use race-conscious measures thought to be related to subsidiary state goals like diversity, but not race-conscious measures more clearly related to the more fundamental state goal of security.) But even given empirical and normative assumptions favorable to affirmative action, the screening proponent regards it as hypocritical to advocate affirmative action while opposing race-based responses to crime *on the principle that individuals should always be treated solely as Individuals.* The advocate of racial screening, having accepted no such principle, can be accused of no comparable hypocrisy. He accepts race-based classifications rationally related to basic moral goods, chiefly prevention of aggression.

Now, I have been arguing thus far as if there is an acceptable principle of individualism, the only question being who has a right to it. There is in fact no such principle. People are and must always be judged by the classes to which they belong, the traits they share with others. What are called individual or intrinsic traits are simply traits which, given past experience with others possessing those traits, are known to have high predictive value. "Judging" an individual consists largely in anticipating his behavior and personality on the basis of observed correlations between traits he is known to have and further traits he may then be presumed to have. "Natural kind" traits, which seem a distinctively appropriate basis for judgment, are simply traits whose predictive value and role in quasi-laws has made reliance on them second nature.

Both proponents and opponents of race-based classification would probably agree in contrasting a student's high-school grades with his race as, respectively, an "individualistic" and a "group" criterion for college admission. Use of grades, especially, would be thought to illustrate judging a student "on his own merits." But why are grades an *intrinsic* trait, and a permissible basis of judgment? Simply because of the reliable correlation between high school grades and success in college. Simplifying greatly, there is a correlation coefficient of .5 between high school and college grade point averages; i.e. 75% of those with high school g.p.a.'s of 3.5 or above achieve the same g.p.a. in college.[40] College admissions officers favor an applicant with a 3.5 g.p.a. because most other applicants with that same g.p.a. have performed well. Admitting an applicant with high grades, then, is a probabilistic judgment based on the group to which he belongs. Grades are unlike race in reflecting effort and choice, and thus are susceptible of moral evaluation. So, we feel, students deserve what their grades, but not their race, earn them. But other expressions of effort and choice, such as a student's physique from years of body-building or his splendid collection of beer cans, play no role in admissions' deliberations because they do not predict academic performance.

It is in fact sheer error to look to voluntariness for a way of distinguishing individual from group traits. Many intuitively "individual" traits are acquired as involuntarily as group traits like race. A 5'4" 125-lb. freshman will be made waterboy rather than linebacker because of his size (as opposed to his race) and we would agree that the coach had judged him on an "individual" trait, his size. But size is largely beyond one's control. And here, too, the coach's basis for judgment is statistical: very few boys that size have ever succeeded as linebacker. There are exceptions, but that is the reasonable expectation—a conclusion

dovetailing with that of (4ii) about the irrelevance of the biological character of race.

VII

It would be tempting but misguided to dismiss the cluster of problems I have discussed as "racist." Some of them are significant enough to reach all of social philosophy. While I am fairly confident of the conclusions I've presented here, many problems remain to be explored. We need to determine the limits of race consciousness. If there are race differences in maturation rates[41] would it be permissible to treat blacks as adult offenders at an earlier age than whites? If reinforcement schedules strongly differentiate by race, would different average deterrent effects for the same punishment on the three main racial groups justify race-based punishment schedules? Is a presumed narrowness in the variance of responses to punishment the only reason punishments are not individually tailored *now?* The courts do have discretion in sentencing and in setting bail, with the likely effect on the individual an important determinant of the latter especially. Perhaps the idea of equal treatment under law does not mean that everyone should receive the same punishment for the same crime, but that everyone should receive an equally aversive punishment, a punishment with the same deterrent effect, for the same crime. These questions are as interesting as they are disturbing, and I would hope to see philosophers take them up.

I would also hope these discussions treat black crime for what it is—a difficult, many-sided dilemma like abortion, capital punishment or euthanasia. There is no need to falter in following the argument as if one has stepped onto holy ground.

NOTES

1. "The Black-on-Black Crime Plague," *US News and World Report,* Aug. 22, 1988, p. 54.

2. J. Philippe Rushton, "Race Differences in Behavior: A Review and Evolutionary Analysis," *Personality and Individual Differences* 9, 6 (1988), p. 1016; also see James Q. Wilson and R. J. Herrnstein, *Crime and Human Nature* (Basic Books, New York: 1985), pp. 461–66.

3. Rushton, loc. cit.

4. Rushton, 1016–17; also see Michael J. Hindelang, "Race and Involvement in Common Personal Crime," *American Sociological Review* 4 (February 1978), pp. 100–01.

5. "Marvin E. Wolfgang, a criminologist at the University of Pennsylvania, said that perceptions about who is more likely to commit a crime have some statistical basis. For four violent offenses—homicide, rape, robbery and aggravated assault—the crime rates for blacks are at least 10 times as high as they are by whites." Joseph Berger, *The New York Times News Service,* June 19, 1987.

6. Between 1979 and 1986, 44.3 out of 1,000 blacks, as opposed to 34.5 out of 1,000 whites, were victims of violent crime; *Black Victims,* Special Report, Bureau of Justice Statistics, United States Department of Justice, April 1990, Table 1.

7. National Crime Survey, Department of Justice, telephone interview, June 28, 1990.

8. In 1987, 50.2% of simple assaults by blacks had white victims (National Crime Survey); between 1979 and 1986, 2,416,696 of the 4,088,945 simple assaults committed by blacks were directed against whites (*Black Victims,* Tables 1, 16).

9. See my "Further Reflections on a Philosophical Problem," in Peter Suedfeld, ed., *Torture: Interdisciplinary Perspectives* (Westview, Washington, D.C.: 1990).

10. Thus R. L. Larsen and M. L. Marx: "*in many situations the beginning of reasonable doubt is taken as that critical value that is equalled or exceeded only 5% of the time* (when H_O [the null hypothesis] *is true*" (*Statistics* [Prentice-Hall, Englewood Cliffs, N.J.: 1990], p. 380). Also see e.g. William Feller, *An Introduction to Probability Theory and Its Applications,* vol I, 3rd ed. (Wiley, NY: 1968), p. 189; more typical in its *va sans dire* use of a confidence level of .95 is Dennis Aigner, *Principles of Statistical Decisions Making* (Macmillan, NY: 1968), chapters 5 and 6.

11. Harman stresses the unavailability of epistemic resources for the assignment of precise probabilities; see *Change of View* (MIT Press: Cambridge, Mass., 1986), pp. 22–26. Goldman cites experimental evidence of widespread de facto violations of the probability axioms, and discusses simple neurological models for transforming information into binary yes/no belief "decisions": see *Epistemology and Cognition* (Harvard University Press: Cambridge, Mass., 1986), pp. 90, 324–43. A judicious discussion of whether belief is analytically connected to behavior is F. Dretske, *Knowledge and the Flow of Information* (MIT Press: Cambridge, Mass., 1981), pp. 197ff.

12. To see why, consider arbitrary Acme A. If there are n Acmes, some subset of size $n/4$ are the defectives. There are $n!-(n-n/4)!$ such subsets if A is assumed to be in 25% of them. Assuming A to be in any other proportion of $n/4$-tuples of detective Acmes reduces the number of realizations of a 25% distribution of defective Acmes. So, if the distribution of defectives is known to be 25%, the "maximum entropy" distribution is more likely to be realized than any other. This is one approach to what Bayesians call the problem of "informationless priors." For a highly general discussion of this argument, see Roger Rosenkrantz, *Inference, Method and Decision* (Reidel, Dordrecht: 1977), Chapter 2.

13. The Hobbesian state aims at least at security, but is often thought to go farther. For a reconstruction of a libertarian Hobbes, and an attempt to explain why security is a special value, see Michael Levin, "A Hobbesian Minimal State," *Philosophy and Public Affairs* 11 (Fall 1982): 338–53; also J. Ronald Penock, "Correspondence," *Philosophy and Public Affairs* 13, 3 (Summer 1984): 255–62; Levin, "Reply to Pennock," ibid.: 263–67; Christopher Morris, "A Hobbesian Welfare State?," *Dialogue* 27 (1988): 653–63; David Schmidtz, "Contractarianism Without Foundations," *Philosophia* 19, 4 (December 1989): 461–70; Levin, "To the Lighthouse," ibid.: 471–74. Also see Gregory Kavka, *Hobbesian Moral and Political Philosophy* (Princeton, N.J.: Princeton University Press, 1986).

14. See Michael Levin, "Is Racial Discrimination Special?," *Journal of Value Inquiry,* 15 (1981): 225–32. The specialness of past racial discrimination is a theme that recurs in the Objections section of the present paper.

15. It is sometimes argued that "racism" must by definition disadvantage blacks. Since whites occupy a dominant position, race-conscious distinctions by or favoring blacks must therefore proceed from the good desire to create equality, while race-conscious distinctions burdening blacks must proceed from the bad desire to oppress. Whatever else may be said about this refinement of the second sense of "racism," it reinforces the point that the wrongness of race-consciousness depends upon its nature and purpose.

16. The phrase is Nozick's; he contrasts it with a Kantian morality of "side constraints" against doing wrong. See Robert Nozick, *Anarchy State and Utopia* (Basic Books, NY: 1975), pp. 28–33.

17. See "Further Reflections."

18. Op. cit., pp. 78–84, 110–113.

19. Max Hocutt, "Must Relativism Tolerate Evil?," *Philosophical Forum* 17 (Spring 1986): 188–200.

20. Cf. Roger Wertheimher's discussion of visible fetuses in "Understanding the Abortion Problem," in Marshall Cohen, Thomas Nagel and Thomas Scanlon, eds., *The Rights and Wrongs of Abortion* (Princeton University Press, Princeton, N.J.: 1974).

21. The self-fulfilling prophecy theory also fails to explain the cross-cultural robustness of stereotypes. 15th-century Arab slave-owners, with no prior direct or indirect contact with blacks, regarded them as highly sexed, highly rhythmic, and unintelligent. This perception cannot be explained by the servile status of the blacks with whom the Arabs were familiar, since Arabs stereotyped their Jewish slaves as very clever (as did the Romans); see Bernard Lewis, *Race And Slavery In The Middle East* (Oxford University Press: Oxford, 1990).

22. For a discussion of the idea that explanations should never limit further inquiry, see Michael Slote, *Reason and Scepticism* (Humanities, N.Y.: 1970), chapter II. A further methodological defect of the stereotype theory is the non-existence of any detailed, well-confirmed model of the transformation of perceived white mistrust into omnidirectional black aggression. Nor is it clear how such a model could be consistently constructed. Self-hate caused by disdain and mistreatment might explain black-on-black crime, but not black-on-white crime, while black resentment of whites does not easily explain black-on-black crime.

23. Of the theoretical works on prejudice known to me, only William Helmreich's *The Things They Say Behind Your Back* (Doubleday, N.Y.: 1982) attempts to gauge the empirical correctness of stereotypes. Helmreich examines 75 generalizations about Jews, blacks, Italians and other groups, and decides that one-third are true and "about half have a factual basis" (p. 244). Already considerably more than would be predicted by the psychological-needs theory, this number increases upon examination of Helmreich's examples. Many of Helmreich's assessments tend to treat wrongly caused group traits as not really there (calling to mind Russell's definition of a metaphysician as someone who says that something does not exist, and defines evil as the counterexamples). For instance, he discounts the stereotype of black oversensitivity by explaining this oversensitivity as a response to oppression. But a phenomenon cannot simultaneously be explained and denied, since the explanans of an explanation must be true and (at least on the DN model) entail the explanandum.

24. "Population P is genetically more prone to X than population Q" can be taken to mean "P is phenotypically more X than Q in any environment." The weaker definiens "P is phenotypically more X than Q in all likely environments" accommodates the possibility that there are some environments in which P is more X than Q and some in which P is less X. (Any theoretically satisfactory definition should include the proviso that phenotypic X was more adaptive in the environment in which P evolved than that in which Q evolved.) Block and Dworkin ("IQ, Heritability, and Inequality," in N. Block and G. Dworkin, eds., *The IQ Controversy* [Pantheon: New York, 1976]. pp. 479–85), like many authors, emphasize gene/environment interaction vis-a-vis race differences in intelligence, but cite no evidence of environments in which the norms of reaction for black and white genotypes yields similar phenotypes. The point of the well-formedness of both definitions and their rough extensional equivalence is that talk of genotypic differentiation is not impugned by the need for environmental mediation of genotypes.

It might be wondered how blacks can be more prone to aggression than whites, given that the most destructive wars have been waged by Europeans and Asians. One natural answer is a white advantage in organizational ability and technology. Although tribal conflict runs through African history, Africans were unable to form themselves into large armies with any regularity or develop weapons of mass destruction. The crime data is consistent with blacks being on average more *individually* aggressive than whites. Counterfactuals about what blacks would have done had they formed million-man armies runs into cotenability problems, since high levels of individual aggressiveness may impede cooperative enterprises.

25. The degree to which individual black criminals would then be responsible for their crimes is one aspect of the perennial determinism puzzle, which warrants four specific comments here. First, environmental causes are no more in the control of the agents affected than are genetic causes, so if genetic causation diminishes criminal responsibility, so does environmental causation. If genetic causation diminishes responsibility, so does any cause short of noumenal agency. Second, genetic factors diminish the responsibility of black criminals only if a genetic predisposition to race hatred diminishes the responsibility of bigots, an implication many will be reluctant to draw. Third, compatibilists such as the present author distinguish freedom to desire from freedom to act on one's possibly unfree desires. The consequent possibility of free action from desires not freely chosen reconciles genetic determination of high aggressiveness with responsibility for aggressive acts. However—and this fourth comment moves against the trend of the first three—the more refined compatibilism of Frankfort, Davidson, Sen, Davis and myself construes fully free action as action proceeding from desires the agent finds acceptable. (See my *Meta-*

physics and The Mind-Body Problem [Oxford University Press: Oxford, 1979], Chapter 7; also Lawrence Davis, *Philosophy of Action* [Prentice-Hall: Englewood Cliffs, N J.] for a graceful statement of this view.) Since aggressive emotions tend to preclude second-order reflection—indeed reflection of any sort—congenital aggression may well diminish freedom and responsibility.

26. See Rushton, and Herrnstein and Wilson.

27. This point is made in William Junius Wilson, *The Truly Disadvantaged* (University of Chicago Press: Chicago, 1987), pp. 11ff. Wilson explains relative black poverty in terms of the disappearance of manufacturing jobs, but he does not explain why blacks have not adapted to an economy more geared to service and information.

28. T. E. Reed, "Caucasian Genes in American Negroes," *Science* 165 (1969): 762–68.

29. "[A]t no time during the prewar period did Jews have more lawbreakers than their proportion of the population warranted. Rather, Jews were consistently underrepresented among those charged with committing felonies with, on occasion, half as many felony arrests as their numbers allowed. From a purely statistical perspective, Jews did not exceed admissible levels of criminal behavior." Jenna Weissman Joselit, *Our Gang: Jewish Crime and the New York Jewish Community, 1900–1940* (University of Indiana Press: Bloomington, 1983), p. 32.

30. "Close to 80 percent of all felony charges brought against Jews between 1900 and 1915 had to do with the commission of property crimes: burglary, larceny, arson, horse-poisoning, and receiving stolen goods. In contrast, only 12 percent of these arrests related to the commission of a violent crime, such as assault, murder, or rape." Ibid., p. 33.

31. "[F]or New York Jews, crime was a one-generation phenomenon, a social and economic consequence of the immigrant experience." Ibid., pp. 158–59.

32. Another popular explanation of black crime is low self-esteem caused by whites, but the boundary condition in this explanation appears to be a non-fact. In a survey of the literature as of 1966, Audrey Shuey found "at the preschool level there seems to be some evidence of awareness of color differences and a feeling of inferiority associated with dark skin, but at the grade school level and continuing through high school and college there is no consistent evidence of lower self esteem in Negroes; if there is a difference, it would appear to be more likely that Negroes have a *greater sense of personal worth,* rather than the reverse" (*The Testing of Negro Intelligence,* 2nd ed. [Social Science Press: NY, 1966], p. 512; ital. in original). A recent study of adolescent girls by Carol Gilligan indi-

cated, to its author's apparent surprise, that black adolescent females enjoy *higher* self-esteem than white adolescent females. (The survey has not been published at this writing; but see Suzanne Daley, "Little Girls Lose Their Self-Esteem on Way to Adolescence, Study Finds," *The New York Times,* Jan. 9, 1991.) The evidence for low black self-esteem most commonly cited (by, among others, the Supreme Court in *Brown v. Board of Education*) is the experimentally observed preference of American black children for white dolls in the United States. This experiment has been replicated in the all-black Dominican Republic, however, and the reply that racism has eroded the self-esteem even of blacks who have little contact with whites seems ad hoc. It should be remembered that self-esteem reflects one's idea of one's own abilities and, to a decreasing extent with a sharp gradient, those of one's immediate circle. But, as Nozick has perceptively remarked (op. cit., pp. 240–44), ability is comparative; to be good at something is to be better at it than most members of a reference group. Most blacks in racially mixed societies find themselves worse than average at most socially expected cognitive tasks, like reading. Cosmopolitan blacks elsewhere know that their societies have developed none of the technology developed by Europeans and Asians. (Whether good or evil, technology requires traits not displayed by black societies.) *If* contact with whites has lowered black self-esteem, this perceived disparity in achievement is the simplest explanation.

The cause of black crime, then, is likely to be endogenous, but explanations in terms of the values reinforced by black culture are circular. Perhaps young black males are socialized to defy authority, but why does black culture produce this particular value? Even if psychosocial explanation is autonomous in the sense that its characteristic predicates are not coextensive with any finite Boolean functions of biological predicates, as anti-reductivists claim, treating it as absolutely autonomous amounts to treating society or culture as an Unmoved Mover. Any non-circular account of culture, or a specific culture, must eventually appeal to noncultural, presumably biological factors. There is obviously no genetic proneness to commit crime, since crime is socially defined. What you get when you subtract the motion of a hand from an act of forgery is a legal norm. The well-formed empirical hypothesis is that blacks are genetically more prone than whites (see n. 24) to actions which in fact tend to be criminalized in societies with legal codes. Among such actions are those intended to cause physical injury. A readiness on the part of other members of the same social group to "punish" (i.e. negatively reinforce) such behavior is apparently found even in non-human primates (see L. Ellis, "Evolution and the Nonlegal Equivalent of Aggressive Behavior," *Aggressive Behavior* 12 [1987]; 57–71).

Genetic proneness requires a mediating physiological mechanism, and this may be found in the higher average level in black males of serum testosterone, a known facilitator of aggression: see R. Ross et al, "Serum Testosterone Levels in Healthy Young Black and White Men," *Journal of the National Cancer Institute* 76 (1986): 45–48; L. Ellis and H. Nyborg: "Racial Ethnic Variations in Male Testosterone Levels: A Probable Contributor to Group Differences in Health," *Steroids* 57 (February 1992): 1–4. There is some discrepancy between the Ross et al and Ellis-Nyborg estimates of the race difference, which Ellis and Nyborg attribute to age differences in the samples. It could of course be argued that higher black levels of serum testosterone is itself an effect of the stresses of racism, but, according to Ellis and Nyborg, "recent evidence has shown that black men exhibit biochemical responses to stress that are, on average distinct from white men" (Ellis and Nyborg). These differences in response readiness are themselves presumably non-social in origin.

33. "But the remedy is necessarily designed, as all remedies are, to restore the victims of discriminatory conduct to the position they would have occupied in the absence of such conduct," *Milliken v. Bradley* (1974). A clear statement of the compensation argument is George Sher, "Justifying Reverse Discrimination in Employment," *Philosophy and Public Affairs* 4 (Winter 1975). A very recent statement of the same argument is Sterling Harwood, "Fullenwider on Affirmative Action as Compensation," Abstract, *Proceedings of the American Philosophical Association* 64 (February 1991): 68.

34. See Lino Graglia, "The 'Remedy' Rationale For Permitting Otherwise Prohibited Discrimination: How the Court Overcame the Constitution and the 1964 Civil Rights Act," *Suffolk University Law Review* 22, 3 (Fall 1988), p. 581.

35. This maneuver triggers a series of awkward questions. It forces one to ask, first, whether there are any race differences, for, absent race differences, it is hard to see why one black/white ratio in a situation is better than another. But if there are race differences, is discrimination their cause? If these differences are not caused by discrimination—if they are endogenous to the black population—they may explain the very black attainment shortfall usually attributed to white racism and used to justify affirmative action in the first place. And where do these endogenous differences come from? "Culture," we saw, is circular. But if, to avoid calling these differences biological, we recur

to discrimination, we must explain how the psychological residue of racism—said to be low self-esteem, mistrust, aggrievement, poor academic attainment—can improve the university or workplace. Anyone basing affirmative action on "diversity" must answer these questions.

36. Appeal to the destruction of stereotypes is self-defeating without the assumption that less-qualified blacks will perform as well as better-qualified whites. This assumption is plausible if the usual selection criteria—grades, scores on standardized tests, and the like—are biased against blacks, but in fact these predictors are as valid for blacks as for whites; see Alexandra K. Wigdor and Wendel R. Garner, eds., *Ability Testing: Uses, Consequences and Controversies* (National Academy Press: Washington, D. C., 1982), vol. I, p. 77.

37. Ronald Dworkin's non-compensatory "utilitarian and ideal" rationale for preference (*Taking Rights Seriously* [Harvard University Press: Cambridge, Mass., 1977], pp. 223–39) parallels the reasoning of *Metro*-like decisions. Since Dworkin apparently cannot conceive a utilitarian basis for discriminating against blacks beyond the "external preferences" of whites for black frustration, he does not see the Pandora's box opened by utilitarian arguments for discriminating against whites. Suppose the presence of more than a threshold number of black children in a classroom impedes the intellectual development of white children. (There is some evidence for this: see Shuey, p. 120.) Here would be a utilitarian argument for school segregation appealing only to the "personal" preferences of white parents and children for academic success. Black males rape almost as many white females as they do black females, and (proportion of population held constant) rape white females twice as frequently as white males do. (Applying the rates given in *Black Victims* for single offender victimization [Table 16, part 1] to the aggregated number of victimizations [Table 1], black males rape 25,000 white females annually and 26,700 black females; the corresponding numbers for white males are 105,000 and 3,300. Applying the rates for multiple offender victimizations [Table 16, part 2] to any proportion of aggregate victimizations decreases white-on-white rape and increases black-on-white rape.) Given the opportunity for unplanned contact created by residence patterns, these figures indicate a pronounced preference by black rapists for white females. If separating black men from white women would sharply decrease the incidence of rape among white women without raising its incidence among black women correspondingly, the personal preference of white women to avoid rape would be utilitarian grounds for such separation.

38. Strictly speaking, the expected morality $e(A_i)$ of any affirmative action program A_i is $\Sigma_{jk}p(B_{jk})m(A_i/B_{jk})$, where $p(B_{jk})$ is the probability that black j has been damaged by discrimination to degree k. When B_{jk} is sufficiently near 0, $m(A_i/B_{jk})$ will fall below 0 because of the attendant injustice to whites.

39. A point made by Dworkin; see his "Why Bakke Has No Case," in R. Wasserstrom, ed. *Today's Moral Problems,* 3rd ed. (MacMillan: NY, 1985), pp. 141–42.

40. For more precise data, see Robert Linn, "Ability Testing: Individual Differences, Prediction, and Differential Prediction," in Wigdor and Garner, vol. II, pp. 335–88.

41. For evidence of a relatively accelerated black life cycle, see Rushton, pp. 1012–1013 and references therein.

Critics

Chana Berniker Cox | ## On Michael Levin's "Responses to Race Differences in Crime"

With Laurence Thomas, I find Michael Levin's "Responses to Race Differences in Crime"[1] unconscionable. Levin has, however, advanced arguments for his "preemptive racial screening" and, therefore, if we reject his conclusions, it is necessary to show either that his reasoning or his data is flawed. I have chosen to discuss two of the ways in which his reasoning can be attacked. My claim is that even if we accept Levin's statistics as *givens,* his arguments for racial screening at the individual level are weak, and his arguments justifying preemptive racial screening by the state are almost totally without merit.

I. THE INDIVIDUAL

Levin claims a person jogging alone at night seeing a young black male has a 12.5% probability of being attacked and therefore it is prudent (and morally acceptable) for that person to take evasive action to avoid the young black male. While I might agree that it would be both prudent and morally permissible to leave the jogging track, Levin's argument is seriously weakened because he has greatly overestimated the probabilities of attack, and because he has

not factored into consideration some of the indirect costs of self-protection.

(a) The Individual and the Probabilities

Levin claims the jogger's 12.5% percent chance of being attacked follows from the fact that 25% of all young black males are convicted felons. Because being a felon is a "dispositional state," Levin halves the probability of attack on any given night and so calculates the probability as 12.5%. This calculation of probability is much too high. Not every convicted felon is disposed to attack lone joggers, and even if the felon has been convicted of such attacks against lone pedestrians, there is no evidence that he has committed such crimes the many hundreds of times which would be necessary to justify the calculation of a 50% chance of attack on *any given* night. Or, to use Levin's own analogy, even if we know one in four Acme cars break down, we cannot assume that there is a 12.5% chance that any Acme will break down on a *particular trip,* although we would be irrational to not take into consideration the relative undependability of the Acme as one of the costs when purchasing a car.[2]

Chana Berniker Cox. "On Michael Levin's 'Responses to Race Differences in Crime,'" *Journal of Social Philosophy* 24, no. 1 (1993): 155–62. Reprinted by permission of Blackwell Publishing Ltd.

So too, our prudent jogger, considering the odds, might calculate the risk of being attacked by a black male as higher than the risk of being attacked by a white male and, *absent other knowledge,* might therefore choose to leave the jogging track, but the probability of such an attack on any given night is in fact quite small and very much below the reasonable 5% which Levin uses in his paper to calculate significance levels.[3]

(b) The Costs of Prudence

Not only does Levin overstate the probabilities, he understates the costs of evasive behavior. He claims to calculate the costs of insult to the black stranger and the assurance of safety to the jogger, but these are only the direct costs. Consider the analogous case of the female jogger who would be prudent to leave the track when she sees a male of any race. There is no question that such prudence can be empirically justified using Levin-type statistics. In opting for prudence, however, she has lost a great deal of personal freedom. In particular, she cannot ever jog at night. For their own protection we have counseled our daughters to be prudent and not to go walking at night, not be alone in rooms with men, not to wear tight clothing, etc. There is a world of "nots" here. All in the name of prudence. And over the course of human history the result has been a world where women are constrained by "nots" and men are free. By analogy, the cumulative effect of Levin's prudent jogger decisions would be to abandon all night use of jogging tracks to young black males—and then only to those males who already know themselves to be armed felons.

The cumulative effect of such "rational decision making" would almost certainly be Jim Crow laws. And these laws would be justified, no doubt, by an appeal to Levin's statistics. Levin claims that *his* screening would not be racist like the Jim Crow laws because his screening would not "exist *only* to express racial antagonisms, without any further purposes. The crime statistics show such a measure to serve the independently justified purpose of controlling crime."[4] It is disingenuous in the extreme to claim that the authors of the Jim Crow laws did not,

like Levin, base their thinking on some kernel of empirical information or that their laws were ever *only* an expression of racial antagonism which served no other purpose.

II. THE STATE

Even if we agree with Levin that an individual jogger has a moral right to use racial and/or gender classification in preemptively seeking safety, it does not follow that such rights extend to the state.

Levin advances a contractarian argument to "existentially generalize over individual rights."[5] He claims that the state acquires such rights because we, as individuals, cede our rights of self-protection to the state. Thus, states' rights represent the summing of individual rights. Not only is such an argument a fallacy of composition, it takes us well down the road to tyranny.

The state as a purely abstract entity does not exist. The enormous power of the state is wielded by individual human beings and many people (the founders of this nation among them) believed that there was a very great deal to fear from the power of the state and the potential abuse of that power. The Bill of Rights was included in the Constitution because the founders were unwilling to trust the state with unlimited power against the individual—even unlimited power to enforce domestic peace.

Michael Levin claims that "[a]ll men are created equal" is not an empirically true statement. He is clearly correct. All men are not created equally tall, equally clever, equally charming. But the truth Thomas Jefferson took to be "self-evident" was not an empirical truth. It was an assertion of what Jefferson took to be the fundamental ethical, religious, and legal principle of modern western civilization.

Nevertheless, our commitment to this "first principle" is also grounded in part, on historical considerations as empirical in nature as any Levin has advanced for racial screening. Having come from Europe, the founders of this nation understood that government "screening" on the basis of religion and national origin led to an increase, not a decrease, in civil unrest. They believed that security in the streets was a manageable problem, whereas civil war was not. And it is civil unrest, not crime in the streets, which most threatens Hobbes' state.

Therefore, the Constitution prohibited the state from discriminating on the basis of race or national origin and asserted that all citizens had the right to equal protection of the laws—interpreted procedurally, not necessarily substantively. Failure to specifically include race was, in large part, the cause of the most bloody war this nation has ever experienced. After that war, the Thirteenth, Fourteenth, and Fifteenth Amendments, were written to prohibit government at any level from discriminating on the basis of race. It is noteworthy for my argument that the Fourteenth Amendment rights of equal protection do not prohibit such discrimination by private individuals or corporations. It is discrimination by the state which is disallowed.

While the framers of the Fourteenth Amendment probably believed that the prohibiting of discrimination on the basis of race could be justified on utilitarian grounds and was certainly justifiable on universalist ethical and religious grounds,[6] they were not deluded about the empirical realities of their day. Even thirty years later Justice Harlan in his dissent in *Plessy v. Ferguson (1896),* the Jim Crow decision, seems to have personally believed that blacks were inferior and were bound to remain inferior. He also knew, however, that "[i]n view of the Constitution, in the eye of the law, there is in this country no superior, dominant ruling class of citizens. There is no caste here. Our Constitution is color-blind, and neither knows nor tolerates classes among citizens. In respect of civil rights, all citizens are equal before the law. . . . The law 'regards man as man.' " And he goes on to argue on historical grounds: "In my opinion, the judgment this day rendered will, in time, prove to be quite as pernicious as the decision made by this tribunal in the *Dred Scott Case.*"

(a) The Effectiveness of Preemptive Screening

Levin claims that such color-blindness is inconsistent with affirmative action laws. I would agree that Harlan's color-blindness is inconsistent with any quota-like affirmative action program. In fact, many proponents of affirmative action programs claim that such programs are consistent with the Fourteenth Amendment only because they are very temporary measures designed to redress a social injustice and therefore represent a *compelling state interest.* Unfortunately, as Thomas Sowell[7] seems to have shown, affirmative action programs tend not to be temporary, and, often, they do not succeed in their stated aims. Thus, if there is a compelling state interest, it may not be addressed by such affirmative action programs. Nevertheless, once the proponent of affirmative action has made such claims, Levin might legitimately counter that a compelling state interest to protect citizens against violent crime would override the provisions of the Fourteenth Amendment. To successfully make this claim, however, Levin must show first that there is an overriding state need and second that his preemptive screening would in fact be effective in meeting that need.

Even if we agree that there is such an overwhelming need to control crime, Levin has not demonstrated that his suggestion for preemptive screening by race would address that need. Other forms of screening would not only be entirely consistent with the letter and the spirit of the Fourteenth Amendment, but they would be more effective and less costly in controlling crime.

For example, Levin is asking us to screen *potential* malefactors when in fact the state has not made the truly massive commitment of funds and resources necessary to screen *actual* malefactors even when, as in the case of repeat violent sex offenders, the pattern of increasing violence has been very well established. In my home community, a multiple murderer of young boys was not apprehended because the police did not have a listing of convicted offenders in the area. That case led to a Washington State law which requires that convicted sex offenders register with the authorities in their home counties. Even that law is being challenged because many people believe that these offenders are no longer the business of the state after they have left the supervision of the penal authorities.

Apropos of which we know of one man who attacked a perfect stranger with a hammer and stabbed her many times, stuffed her body into her car, and went to the movies. Not only did our government not monitor this man's subsequent career, but this felon rose to the position of Executive Director of the congressional Democratic Steering and Policy Committee and Congressman Wright's (Speaker of the House of Representatives) right-hand man.[8] Is this the same government to which Levin intends to give wide-ranging preemptive powers? Surely it would be more cost effective and more just *"modulo ordinary standards"*[9] to begin by screening and tracking *known offenders.*

Not only would Levin's preemptive screening be far more costly, it is doubtful that it would yield benefits to the police in any way proportional to those costs. If, as Levin claims, it is valuable to target certain sets of individuals as "at-risk," it is possible and preferable, both on utilitarian and universalist grounds, to identify those characteristics which constitute "at-risk," and not simply use race or gender, in the language of *Garrett v. Board* (1991),[10] as "a proxy" for other predicates. Clearly, if the police have a description of a black male, approximately 21 years old, 5'10", weighing 170 pounds, and driving a Chevy Camaro, they are not now prohibited from stopping any person who fits that description.

De facto racial screening, insofar as it is constitutionally correct, is already in place. If police, like congressmen, were distributed geographically purely on the basis of population, Iowa would have a great many more police than it needed, and Chicago a great deal fewer. But, in fact, even without Levin's preemptive screening, police are not distributed on the basis of population. Nor are they distributed on the basis of race. One would hope they would be distributed purely in proportion to criminal behavior. Chicago should get its share whether or not the high-crime neighborhood is identified as black. If anything, it is likely to allocate less police to high-crime black areas. Assigning police using Levin's suggested racial screening would be counter-productive because it would result in our having far too many police in low crime black middle class neighborhoods.

In short, Levin is arguing that "young black male" is a proxy for "criminal." While he has estab-

lished a correlation, he has not established an identity. Again to use the language of *Garrett,* "While these statistics underscore a compelling need, they fall short of demonstrating that" Levin's preemptive screening would address that need or that the need could not be better and more efficiently addressed without such preemptive screening.

(b) Testosterone: A Genetic Fallacy

Finally, Levin claims that there is a genetic link between being black and being criminal. What of it? Such a genetic link does not, in itself, justify racial screening. There is a genetic link to alcoholism as well. Is Levin suggesting we tailor special laws to citizens of the United States who have such dispositional genes? Should we consider stiffer penalties to punish drunk drivers who happen to have been born with the suspect gene only because they are more disposed to drink? To do so is clearly unjust. "We say that we reprove or punish a man *because* he has broken a law."[11] and not because he has the disposition to do so. As a method of enforcing sobriety it is neither fair nor efficient.

In contrast, the Aztecs, who were very good at social control, solved their alcohol problem simply by killing anyone under a certain age who was found drunk in public. Only very old people were allowed to become intoxicated. As a method of social control, preemptive screening is not nearly as efficient as speedy and ruthless prosecution, and preemptively screening on the basis of merely *dispositional* characteristics raises profound questions about procedural justice. And if we were to screen by disposition, who would not be a legitimate target for investigation in cases of adultery and theft?

Levin claims that the black predisposition to crime may be caused by "unusually high levels of testosterone." Again, he may very well be right. I am fairly certain that most brutal assaults and virtually all rapes and wars have been committed by a minority who, viewed from my perspective have "unusually high levels of testosterone." As a member of the genetically determined majority blessed with relatively high estrogen levels, I could suggest all kinds of preemptive screening that would dramatically reduce

454

CHANA BERNIKER COX

violent crime. With modern methods of genetic counseling we could screen *in utero* to avoid the birth of 99% of such aggression-prone children. And, for those of us who balk at abortion, there are other methods. We've solved the problem for horses and for dairy herds, why not try it for humans? Or are we too squeamish, too weighted down by our quaint moral notions, to acknowledge the compelling state need to reduce the number of violent criminals?

If I were to seriously suggest such solutions to the crime problem my sons would accuse their mother of being a "feminazi." My sons would be right. I am not seriously suggesting aborting or castrating virtually all males. In the tradition of the ACLU, I am willing to concede that males are human beings even if they are violence-prone. I am also willing to concede that testosterone, like the sickle cell trait, probably has its uses—even apart from it's obvious uses. It is male aggressiveness that has gone out and conquered all kinds of worlds when any sensible woman would have stayed home and taken care of the kids. Someone has to worry about the perpetuation of the species when men are out doing their thing.

The difference between a Hitler and a Churchill was not their testosterone level. Just as the difference between Colin Powell and Saddam Hussein is not their testosterone level. The difference between young black male criminals and young black male school teachers, or ministers, is not their level of testosterone—it is a matter of character. There is a great deal to be said for male aggression in the service of good. As an avid Portland Trailblazer fan, I suspect that I share more values with Buck Williams and Terry Porter than I do with Michael Levin. And I'm certain that I would feel a great deal safer in a dark ally with either of those two young black men at my side.

(c) *Holy Ground*

Levin asks why race is different. History, a source of empirical information at least equal to some of Levin's statistical studies, has shown us that race, like religion and ethnicity, is different because it is extraordinarily amenable to abuse. Race is not just another way of classifying individuals like birthmarks or Borsalinos. In some societies the law man

dated the death of people born with "birth defects" such as harelips or epilepsy. However heinous such laws, they seldom resulted in wide-spread civil unrest. They were unjust but not fundamentally divisive. Laws discriminating on the basis of religion and race do cause civil war.

Race is not a predicate like "harelip" or "wearing a Borsalino," any more than opium is not just another habit-forming food like chocolate. When opium was made legal and made generally available in a part of China, over 90% of the population became opium addicts and as a result there was a bloody breakdown of society. It's too easy to become an opium addict. And it's too easy to hate other people because they differ from us with respect to race, religion, or ethnicity. It is too easy to think of other peoples as something less than human. Not only are such hatreds ethically wrong on universalist grounds, but they are also virulently dangerous. As much of this world sinks back into tribalism, we see just how bloody and how destructive of Hobbes' secure state such divisions can be.

We are a nation whose citizens come from many nations, of many religions, and all races. Laws discriminating against blacks, particularly if they are not perceived to be affirmative action laws rectifying past injustices, would threaten our existence as a nation.

As Justice Harlan writes in the *Plessy* dissent, "The destinies of the two races in this country are indissolubly linked together, and the interests of both require that the common government of all shall not permit the seeds of race hate to be planted under the sanction of law."

Like Justice Harlan, most people in this country know—even if Michael Levin does not—that we are indeed on holy ground.

NOTES

1. Michael Levin, "Responses to Race Differences in Crime," *Journal of Social Philosophy* XXIII, 1 (Spring 1991): pp. 5–29. All references to Levin will be to this essay.
2. Lack of dependability is only one of the costs of a car. A rational buyer might still choose the Acme if it was a great deal less expensive than a more dependable car like the Mercedes.

3. At times, Levin seems to interchange "significance levels" with what he calls "confidence levels." See p. 6.

4. Levin, p. 20.

5. Levin, p. 9.

6. *Exodus* XII, 49, also *Numbers* XV, 16.

7. Thomas Sowell, *Preferential Policies: An International Perspective* (New York: Morrow, 1991).

8. See *The Washington Post,* (May 4, 1989): p. B1, B8, B9.

9. Levin, p. 6.

10. In *Garrett v. Board of Education of Detroit (1991),* the Detroit Board of Education (the Defendants) argued unsuccessfully for the establishment of private all male black academies citing the very statistics which Levin claims as the empirical foundation of his arguments. The Plaintiffs were the ACLU and the NOW Legal Defense Fund. In the decision, Judge Woods argued that the use of "young black male" as a proxy for "at-risk" was not permissible under the law. Moreover, the academies would have served young black males who were not at-risk in the sense required and they would have excluded young black females who were at-risk. Unlike the situation in *Plessy v. Ferguson* (1896), here it is the local black community that is advocating for "separate but equal" and the "preemptive screening" of young black males. It is noteworthy that the NAACP Legal Defense & Educational Fund filed a statement for the Plaintiffs which included the following reasoning:

"First, we believe that the most dangerous aspect of the current proposals is the long-term effect that they may have by providing a new rationalization that could be seized by the majority community to justify racial separatism in the provision of public education, and perhaps ultimately other public good and services." ("Statement on Proposals for Separate Schools for African-American Male Pupils," p. 8.)

11. H. L. A. Hart, *The Concept of Law* (London: Oxford University Press, 1961), p. 11.

Laurence Thomas | # Statistical Badness*

If you know that one out of every four Acme cars is defective, then clearly: You really ought, from a rational perspective, to think twice about buying an Acme—certainly an Acme randomly chosen off of the dealer's lot. Of course, if turns out that you are friends with a dazzling mechanic, who first gives the car you chose a thorough going over and the car comes through in shining colors, then buying that particular Acme car suddenly becomes imminently more rational—perhaps even decisively so (given certain assumptions about price and so on.)

It is hardly irrational to buy an Acme that you actually know to be good, the general reputation of Acme cars notwithstanding. But, of course, if all that you have got to go on is the statistical information about the performance of Acme cars in general, then simply buying one off of the lot, without the blessings of a dazzling mechanic, is simply to act somewhat foolishly. This is so, even if after the fact it could be demonstrated that the Acme you would have purchased would have lasted you for years. (Suppose you remember the serial number on the car (for you have a keen memory for numbers); and two years later you run into a dazzling mechanic who happens to be driving that very car.)

Now, it has seemed to various individuals, Michael Levin among them, that this line of reasoning applies with equal force to fearing any *and all* black American male youths, given the statistics on crimes committed by them. If you are a white alone (with no real self-protection skills, as is true of most people) and you encounter a black jogging in the park, it would be rational for you to take flight and run on account of being afraid of the harm that you might suffer at the hands of the jogger. Hence, it is not racist for you to do so; for presumably a person does not act racist or sexist or whatever if rationality, and only that, is the explanation for her or his behav-

Laurence Thomas, "Statistical Badness," *Journal of Social Philosophy* 23, no. 1 (1992): 30–41. Reprinted by permission of Blackwell Publishing Ltd.

ior (though see the comment in the following paragraph). That the charge of racism does not obtain here is, obviously, what makes all of this particularly interesting. Given the usual assumptions, a white male running from another white male in a similar setting is presumably not being racist, whatever else is true. Silly?—Perhaps. Racist?—No.

Let me hasten to add here that I am well aware that the rationality of behavior is always relative to background assumptions. Normally, it is not rational for an adult to crawl as a means of moving through a hallway; but not so, if the hallway is full of smoke and the only means of escaping a fire. In times past, in an incredible display of *mauvaise foi,* some white owners of restaurants claimed that while they had no objection to serving blacks, doing so would be bad for business, since white customers would no longer patronize the restaurant. The white owners were quite right about serving blacks being bad for their business, given a racist society. Their claim constituted bad faith only because they were usually lying in saying that they, themselves, had no objections to serving blacks. Background assumptions can be morally suspect, as with the restaurant owners, or outright irrational, as is usually the case with fear of heights. The analogy—let us call it the black-car analogy—can have the force it is intended to have only if (Levin and others who would join him correctly hold that) whites are not irrational or morally suspect in their beliefs about black male youths. For the time being I want to grant that this is so.

Obviously, if the black-car analogy holds it is extremely powerful, indeed. For are you not a racist for taking flight and running even if harming you is the furthest thing from the black jogger's mind (that Acme car would actually have held up), and even though you did not take any extra steps to discern the intentions of the jogger. (Given the statistics on Acme cars, you need not consult a mechanic in order for it to be rational for you not to buy such a car.) In either case, your behavior conforms to the canons of rationality, in dealing with statistical cases.

In response, I can imagine some wanting to find fault with the statistics on crimes committed by black male youth. For instance, suppose either that

crimes committed by blacks are more likely to be reported than are crimes committed by whites, or that crimes committed by blacks are more likely to meet with a conviction, or that blacks are not as likely as whites to be charged with a lesser crime. The statistics, then, would be skewed against blacks in favor of whites. Others will no doubt suppose that, owing to the history of slavery and racism in America, a special burden falls upon white people, when it comes to discerning the intentions of blacks. More generally, one may vigorously object to the idea of treating people on the basis of the group to which they belong rather than as individuals. These approaches, especially the first, might very well meet with some success. However, I shall proceed in a different way. It is important to see what does and does not follow even if we proceed by conceding too much because, in truth, things are not as bad as they are made out to be. The more that can be conceded without having to accept the conclusion, the better.

Still, I shall challenge the thesis that the statistics about crimes committed by black male youth can be indiscriminately applied to all black male youths, as is maintained by those who put forth the black-car analogy. I shall also conclude (Section IV) with an example which turns the black-car analogy on its head. For there is a way in which it turns out to be perfectly rational for whites to avoid black male youth; but this is so, not because it is always next to impossible to discern, reasonably and safely, a good black from a bad black, but because, owing to past injustices, whites may very well have ASMI with respect to blacks—that is, acquired social monitoring inadequacy.

I

The black-car analogy breaks down precisely because human beings (including black people) are not cars, and conversely. Cars are not agents; nor, a fortiori, are cars social creatures. Cars have no stake in how they are perceived by people; nor, in particular, do cars do things that bear upon how people perceive them. Whether on the dealer's lot or the street, there are no actions which cars perform (qua agent) which bear upon how they are viewed by persons. Cars do not have themselves painted in hot pink in order to come across to humans as sexy, or in dark blue in order to come across as "cool." Nor do cars insist upon leather interior so that the wealthy will purchase them. Cars do not—because they cannot—posture at all. In the language of contemporary psychology, self-presentational behavior is not just something that cars refrain from doing, it is something that they absolutely cannot do.[1] Cars lack the capacity to either exhibit self-presentational behavior or to monitor it.

By contrast, self-presentational behavior is a part of the human condition, from the tribes in primitive societies to the Queen of England. Such behavior ranges over both attire and bodily language, including posture and acts of decorum. A person's overall self-presentational behavior usually reveals a great deal about the lifestyle to which she or he is accustomed. A person's self-presentational behavior on a specific occasion usually reveals a great deal about the kind of image that the person wants to project at the moment. The latter can be out of step with the former, as when an ordinary citizen of England is invited to be a guest at the Queen's table. And when, on a given occasion, a person's self-presentational behavior is out of character, this can often be detected, especially if a number of social activities must be performed during the occasion. Remember that an important part of self-presentational behavior is often referred to as comportment, a vague but yet ever so important notion. Two people in the finest of attire may comport themselves differently and revealingly. We suppose, and often correctly, that one is accustomed to be so attired and the other is not. Needless to say, if self-presentational behavior is a deep feature of the human condition, another such feature is that of social monitoring. A gesture, a pause, a moment of hesitation can all be so revealing precisely because human beings have considerable social monitoring skills which are often employed quite effortlessly and unreflectively. Naturally, some modes of self-presentation are culturally bound. (while visiting Paris, I once asked for "une baguette" in an admirable French accent. As I was leaving the bakery the woman asked

me what country I was from. Noticing that I was stunned, she remarked "You extended your hands to receive the change." Change is definitely returned on the counter in France! As I said, a slight gesture can be ever so revealing. Interestingly, an unobservant American with a minimal command of the French language might see the French manner of returning change as one more sign that they do not like Americans or of so-called French arrogance. I have hardly denied that the self-presentational behavior of individuals can be misread.)

Suppose, then, that one is walking alone in an isolated area and one encounters a black male youth—call him Lester—coming towards one. Lester is well attired, sporting a tweed coat and a tie. It is late spring, and one can see that this is what he is wearing. According to the black-car analogy, it is reasonable to cross the street or whatever out of fear of being harmed by Lester. This is so simply on account of the fact that he is a black male youth, and the statistics indicate that there is a high probability that a black male youth will harm one.

But surely this is way too fast. To put it mildly, very few white people—in fact, very few people of any group—can report having been robbed or otherwise harmed on the street by a black male youth sporting a tweed coat and tie. As of yet, anyway, it has not been a tactic on the part of black male youth to don traditional attire of respectability as a way of catching people, white or otherwise, off guard. If so, then the statistics do not apply to black male youth across the board, as proponents of the analogy would have us believe. Not only that, there are some rather visible indicators as to whether or not the statistics might apply to the black male youth approaching one. If, nothing else, if the black male youth is dressed like Lester, then it is probably no more likely that he will harm one than if he were white. The point here, of course, is not that only black male youths in tweed coats will refrain from harming individuals traveling alone, or that this attire is the only sort of reliable and visible indicator that a person could have that such a youth will not harm an individual walking alone. The point rather is that it would be unreasonable to fear that a Lester might harm one, notwithstanding the statistics about black male youth, since those statistics most certainly do not include people like him. Hence, it is false that the statistics can be applied indiscriminately to all black male youths.

I have focused on attire because it is one of the most important modes of self-presentational behavior in Western culture, and it is a very important dimension of social monitoring, especially among strangers. (Twenty years ago, foreigners could readily spot an American youth traveling: tennis shoes and jeans. These are the attire of a great many youth nowadays.) We have the saying that "The clothes make the person." If we have nothing else concrete to go on, how a person dresses makes all the difference in the world in terms of our initial thoughts about the person. One could insist that black people are the exception to this saying. But I take it to be obvious that such a move would be just so much nonsense. As I have remarked, very few people can report having been robbed or otherwise harmed on the street by a black male youth sporting a tweed coat. There is every good reason to believe that any such black youth has quite commendable moral and professional aspirations. A sports coat, after all, is markedly different in appearance from a jacket that is an outer-garment, certainly a black leather jacket of the sort that is often associated, rightly or wrongly, with gangs—the jackets that are commonly called motorcycle jackets.

It is already overkill to insist upon both a sports coat and tie. Surely a tie would suffice. For aside from weddings and funerals, a hoodlum, black or white, in a tie has got to be an extremely rare occurrence. But never mind that.

With typical social monitoring, it is quite normal to mark the difference between a white male stranger in a tweed coat and a white male stranger in gang-like garb, and to suppose that an isolated encounter with the former is less likely to be hostile than an isolated encounter with the latter. There is absolutely nothing about black males to suggest that a different judgment is warranted between either a black male in a tweed coat and a black male in gang-like garb or, for that matter, a black male in a tweed coat and a white male in gang-like garb. The latter point cannot be over emphasized. Only racism would have peo-

ple, black or white, fearing a black male youth in a tweed coat and tie more than a white male youth in boots and a black leather motorcycle jacket, given an isolated encounter with either, or fearing the tweed coat youth as much as they would fear a black with all the mannerisms and appearances of a hoodlum.

II

Let us allow that there is a class of black American male youths, call them black hoodlums, who are disposed to harm others, especially whites, and that, given the statistics, it would be rational to fear for one's safety if while walking alone one encountered a black hoodlum. What I should like to know is: How does it turn out that statistics about blacks male hoodlums apply indiscriminately to all black male youth? One answer is that it is absolutely impossible to distinguish, safely and with confidence, a decent black male youth from a black male hoodlum. But, of course, our story of Lester shows this to be patently false. In some cases, contrary to what is claimed by those who advance the black-car analogy, rudimentary social monitoring skills enable us to distinguish between the two, quite safely and confidently.

As an aside, or perhaps not, does it matter as well where one encounters a black American male youth? In the summer of 1990, an American woman traveling in Israel thought that a black American male, who walked from the guests rooms into the hotel lobby, was about to steal her pocketbook. There were no other blacks around. Was it rational for her to have had that thought? The black American called the woman on her behavior. She retorted that she had once been robbed by a black man in Harlem. He retorted that he had once been called a nigger in Harvard Yard (between Emerson Hall and Widener Library). Her response was: "I am not that kind of person." Well, consider: How many not-so-well-off people, black hoodlums or otherwise, take a holiday in Israel to relieve themselves of the monotony of poverty?

The example is less of an aside than one might have thought because it reveals the absurdity of indiscriminate generalizations, in the face of overwhelming evidence that the generalization does not hold, when it comes to imputing hostile intentions to human beings on account of their ethnicity. Why it is absurd to generalize indiscriminately is irrelevant. (I am the black American male about whom I have just written.)

If I dare say so, Michael Levin's example of a black jogger is quite revealing of rashness of thought on his part. For it is a black that one sees and takes to be a jogger—not simply a black youth running, a difference which makes all the difference in the world. It makes a difference regardless of the person's ethnicity, race, or gender. Anyone walking alone, in a somewhat isolated area, will want to determine just what is the concern of a person running towards him. The person's running will certainly be one very straightforward reason for having some concern. The observation that the person is a jogger provides a perfectly good explanation for the person's running. And notice that whether white or black, or female or male, a stranger who is running will be recognized as a jogger only if she or he is attired in a certain way: shorts, or a sweat suit, tennis shoes, and so on. No one is in the least bit inclined to suppose that a person in business attire or high-heels might be a jogger, regardless of the grace with which they manage to move. (So far, only the fictional character known as Wonder Woman is able gracefully to run in high-heels!) Recall the above remarks about self-presentational behavior. It is not simply a coincidence that no one in business attire or heels might be a jogger. The custom is that joggers wear attire suitable to that activity; and it holds regardless of race, ethnicity, or gender. What is more, jogging attire being what it is, most joggers are not likely to be carrying any assault weapons on their person; and the jarring of jogging being what it is, most joggers would probably not carry an assault weapon, because they would find it dangerous to themselves to do so, even if they could manage to conceal it. Most joggers have innocent intentions which is precisely why most of us feel a measure of relief when, upon hearing the running of someone behind us, we turn to discover that it is the running of a jogger.

Now, it could very well be that when a black youth is attired as a jogger he is nonetheless likely to act the part of a hoodlum, with a concealed weapon

and all. Once more, it could be a strategy to catch people off guard. But, as with a black youth wearing a tweed coat and tie, there is no evidence to support such a view about black youths who are joggers. This should not come as any surprise. Black joggers have not proven to be particularly adept at concealing potent weapons in socks and scanty jogging shorts; and the jarring of jogging is not race specific. Needless to say, it will not do to point to very isolated instances here, since by that line of reasoning there would be no category of people of whom all the world should not be afraid. Thus, once again, we can see that by the most rudimentary social monitoring skills, it is implausible to act as if a black jogger might harm one. As I have observed, then, Levin's example of the black jogger is quite revealing of rashness of thought. No doubt a different author would put the point less delicately.

Pulling the above remarks together in a more structured way, let me explicitly state the difference between a statistic that three out of four Acme cars do not hold up and a statistic that black hoodlums are likely to commit crimes. The first applies to all Acme cars; the second applies only to a particular group of black male youths. Regardless of the percentage of black hoodlums, it is rational to extend the statistic to all black youths only if black hoodlums cannot be reasonably and safely distinguished from other black youths, given a modicum of social monitoring skills and prevailing norms of self-presentational behavior.

To see that this is so, suppose that every so often Acme managers worked on the car assembly line, and that only the serial numbers of cars worked on by managers contain an "M." Suppose, further that, since everyone is especially careful when a manager is working on the line, these are especially durable cars, holding their own against the very best cars among other models in the same class. Now, if one has this information at one's disposal and one spots an Acme M-car in a dealer's showroom—imagine that all serial numbers are imprinted on the dashboard—it would be absurd to refrain from purchasing the car on the grounds that statistically three out of four, or four out of five, or nine out of ten Acme cars do not hold up well; for, ex hypothesi, if it's an

Acme M-car, then it will hold up extremely well; and this is precisely what one knows.

To be sure, there may be a thousand and one reasons why one would rather not own an Acme car, even if it's an M-car. Perhaps one wanted a model in a better class, say, a luxury car. Or, perhaps one's reputation for being a person of good taste will be sullied, Acme cars being what they are generally. And it is certainly possible that one's attitude here is, strictly speaking, irrational in the way that fear of flying is. But having a few quirks seems to be a part of the human condition. Just so, the general statistics simply cannot be justifiably invoked as a reason for not buying an Acme M-car, no more than the statistics about airplane accidents can be justifiably invoked as a reason for being afraid of flying. Mutatis mutandis, a statistic about black hoodlums who are disposed to harm others cannot be indiscriminately applied to all black youth when there are perfectly good reasons to believe that it does not apply to all such individuals, and a modicum of social monitoring skills enable us to distinguish, reasonably and safely, blacks who are hoodlums from those who are not.

Now, an irrational and negative attitude about a car model that one does not correct in light of the facts available to one is just that—an incorrect, irrational, and negative attitude towards a particular model of car. Not so with human beings. A mistaken, negative, and irrational attitude about a group of human beings that one does not correct in light of the facts readily available to one constitute a prejudice. What would make anyone think that a statistic specifically about black hoodlums could be justifiably extended to all black youth? Similarly, what would make anyone think that with regard to readily observable appearances and behavior it was next to impossible to distinguish between black youths who are hoodlums and those who are not, especially in a society which is as mindful of appearances as ours? The latter point cuts in two different directions. One is that we customarily and quite naturally make judgments about strangers on the basis of their appearances; the other is that it is silly to think that the attire of black youths who are not hoodlums will generally resemble that of black youths who are, just as it is equally silly for any black to treat any white

as if she or he might be a redneck, a paradigm example of a racist, on the grounds that generally it is rather difficult to distinguish on the basis of attire a redneck from a non-redneck. Most people think that they can readily spot a redneck.

III

It is well known that a statistic about, say, group Alpha of Gammas, claiming that they have property P, can be justifiably extended to all Gammas only if Alpha is representative of all Gammas. It is equally well known that one commits a statistical fallacy if one holds that P applies to all Gammas simply because the population of Alphas is so large that on any given chance encounter a Gamma is more likely to be an Alpha than a non-Alpha. For the truth that the population of Alphas is that large is formally compatible with the population of Gammas being divisible between Alphas and Betas, and that Betas, though few and far between, are readily distinguishable from Alphas.

Consider. Let Gamma stand for the class of Jews, Beta stand for the class of ultra-Orthodox Jews, and Alpha stand for the class of non-Orthodox Jews. The class of non-Orthodox Jews, Alpha, easily dwarfs the class of ultra-Orthodox Jews, Beta. This, however, leads to relatively little confusion as to who is and is not an ultra-Orthodox Jew—who is and is not an Alpha. Ultra-Orthodox Jews—Alphas—are recognizable at a glance; only the most obtuse of persons would have difficulty generally determining who, among Jews, is an ultra-Orthodox Jew, of distinguishing between Alphas and Betas within the class of Gammas. Suppose, then, to take a very silly example, that nine out of ten non-Orthodox Jews dine out six days a week in non-kosher restaurants. It would be very bad reasoning, indeed, to infer from that statistic that nine out of ten ultra-Orthodox Jews dine out six days a week in non-kosher restaurants, since that would surely be false.

So, as I have said, it is false as anything could be that if Alphas are Gammas, and it is true of most Gammas that they have the property P, then it follows, as a matter of logic or, at any rate, rational inference, that all Gammas have the property P, since there may be Betas of whom it is manifestly clear that they do not have the property P. And if it is manifestly clear that they do not have the property P, and if they can be reasonably and safely distinguished from those who do have P, then it cannot be rational to act as if they do have P just because most Gammas do.

When, in discussing a people, a person ignores well-known aspects of statistics while attributing negative behavioral traits to the people at large, one has to wonder about the innocence of the individual's motives. This is not to balk at rational inquiry, and thus at letting the factual chips fall where they may.[2] Rather the issue is about ignoring canons of reasoning, the ignoring of which in other domains would simply not be tolerated. Naturally, a canon of reasoning may itself be challenged, as classical two-valued logic has been challenged by, for instance, Alan Ross Anderson and Nuel D. Belnap.[3] But that is not what is being done by those who use statistics—the black-car analogy, in particular, to show that fear of any and all black youths is rationally justified. Quite the contrary, traditional techniques in statistics are being employed.

Consider an example in a related but different context. Time and time again, there are those who object to affirmative action solely on the grounds that an undesirable minority person might be hired. Whatever one thinks about affirmative action, this is a most peculiar kind of objection to a hiring practice. For there is no hiring practice known to humankind which precludes the possibility of hiring an undesirable person. By the line of reasoning of this objection, there would be no hiring at all. One can be opposed to affirmative action, and yet find this line of reasoning deplorable. What is intriguing, again, is that so many have found this line of reasoning against affirmative action incisive—people who are capable of detecting fallacies rather like a bloodhound is thought to be capable of detecting prey.

The fact that so many competent and able thinkers reason badly in a particular domain cries out for an explanation. This is especially so if the bad reasoning results in attitudes that are harmful to others, in particular, a group of people readily identifiable on the basis of their race, ethnicity, or gender. In the case at hand, the domain in question is black people. As a matter of logic, the explanation need not be racism. Perhaps the very idea of black people has certain mystical properties yet to be discovered which randomly interferes with the thinking of people who reason about blacks. Perhaps this is true when it comes to Jewish people as well, since some quite absurd reasoning about Jews tends to occur. Still, it must be acknowledged that as far as explanations go, racism is a very attractive candidate. For racism is not just a matter of having the belief that a people are inferior, but of having an invested interested in their being inferior.

Surely an objectionable bias is operating against a group Gamma: (i) when negative facts or statistics about Alpha, a sub-group of Gamma, are routinely generalized to all members of Gamma in ways that are obviously at odds with acceptable canons of reasoning, where the canons of reasoning are not themselves being challenged; or (ii) when, contrary to the facts of rudimentary social monitoring skills and prevailing norms of self-presentational behavior, it is denied that Alphas, of whom the negative facts or statistics hold true, can be reasonably and safely distinguished from Gammas who are not Alphas, and thus maintained that it is rational to act as if all Gammas are Alphas; or (iii) when assumptions of confidence which are routinely extended to persons who perform a specified set of tasks are not extended to members of Gamma who likewise perform the exact same tasks. A corollary of (iii) is this: An objectionable bias is operating against Gammas when a mistake made by virtually any member of Gamma counts more heavily against the judgment that Gamma is competent at the task at hand than do like mistakes made by others count against the judgment that they are competent. At the very least, racism is the propensity so to reason with respect to a race or an ethnicity.

Now, it is very much worth noting that in arguing that the black-car analogy fails, I have not argued that each and every black stranger encountered should be judged on an individual basis, where this is understood to mean that no relevant statistical information about the black stranger's intentions are to be employed. This view is no more plausible than is the view that each and every white stranger should be judged on an individual basis. Quite the contrary, what I have argued is that precisely what set of statistical information one employs is rightly a function of the self-presentational mode of the black stranger in question, where the focus has been upon appearances. It does not take the observational genius of an Erving Goffman to see that the facts do not support lumping blacks in jogger attire and blacks in tweed coats together with black hoodlums; accordingly, it has to be wrong to apply the statistics which hold for black hoodlums to either black joggers or blacks wearing tweed jackets. A different set of statistics apply to the former two; and those statistics warrant the conclusion that those blacks are very unlikely to harm one; for as I have noted, it simply has not been a strategy of black hoodlums to don jogging attire or tweed jackets in order to give the appearance of having innocent intentions. It has not by any means been shown that the statistics which hold for black hoodlums hold equally well for black joggers or blacks wearing tweed coats. Of course, things could change; and black hoodlums might very well see wearing suits as a wonderful way to disarm whites. But a view about how we should treat a group of people cannot be based upon a remote possibility. Black strangers should be treated on a group basis just as any other kind of stranger should be. The fallacy lies both in supposing that the only statistics about the behavior of blacks with respect to the intention to harm others, whites especially, which holds for all blacks are the statistics which hold for black hoodlums, and that blacks who are not hoodlums cannot be readily and easily distinguished from those who are, given rudimentary social monitoring skills.

I deny that all blacks, even at a distance, look alike, just as I deny that all whites from afar look alike.

Because I have not objected to treating blacks on a group basis, but only to treating them on the basis of one group, namely that of black hoodlums, the argument which I have presented is not vulnerable to a certain kind of dilemma, which goes something like this (Levin, Section VI):

P1　Affirmative action treats blacks on a group basis, not an individual basis.

P2　If it is wrong to treat blacks on a group basis, in one moral context, it is wrong to do so in another?

C3　Therefore, either affirmative action is unjustified or there is nothing wrong with responding to black strangers on a group basis.

I take it to be obvious that P2 is false, and thus the argument is unsound. Human beings are generally treated as a group in some instances, and on an individual basis in others. Although most people who do not steal treat human beings as a group, since the reasons for not stealing generally apply with equal force to all human beings, I dare say that most people treat close friends on an individual basis.

But even if P2 were true, rendering the argument sound, this argument opposing affirmative action would have no force against the argument which I have presented, since I allow that treating blacks as a group can be perfectly acceptable. What I have objected to is indiscriminately applying negative statistics and facts about a particular group of blacks to all groups of blacks—indeed, to applying any statistics and facts about one group of blacks to all blacks. And if the truth be told, even affirmative action distinguishes between groups of blacks. In universities and colleges, for instance, affirmative action has never meant indiscriminately hiring blacks off of the streets. Only blacks with certain qualifications are to be hired, a truth which holds even if it were true that blacks were being held up to a lower standard than whites; for a lower standard is not no standard at all.

IV

I should like to conclude with a number of remarks that I hope will serve to forestal misunderstanding. Along the way, I shall summarize various points.

It is not my view that treating strangers on the basis of some group is preferable to treating them as individuals. On the other hand, I realize that it is next to impossible not to invoke group categories when assessing strangers. What I have tried to show, however, is that even when we invoke group categories, things are far more complicated than defenders of the black-car analogy have allowed. Specifically, I have argued that the statistical reasoning which the analogy employs is so manifestly flawed that this creates a presumption of bias on the part of those employing the analogy. This is because even if we allow that there are black hoodlums, there is no reason whatsoever to believe either that all blacks are hoodlums or that at least some of the time, blacks who are not hoodlums cannot be reasonably and safely distinguished from those who are, given rudimentary social monitoring skills.

The last claim appealed to what I have called self-presentational behavior. Rather than rehearse those points, I should like to observe that although I focused upon attire for simplicity's sake, attire is but one of many salient features of self-presentational behavior, which human beings are quite adept at monitoring. Body language (a person's posture, gait, manner of gesticulation) is another. We are often able to determine the gender of a person simply on the basis of the manner in which the individual walks. The way in which a person comports himself is crucial to our assessment of him; and no black male youth dressed in a tweed jacket is likely to comport himself in a manner resembling a hoodlum. His gait is most unlikely to have the kind of readily recognizable swagger that is commonly associated with the "bad" black walk.[4] In fact, for any black male youth whose walk does not display this strut, whether in a tweed coat or not, the odds are very high that he is not a hoodlum.

My argument no doubt smacks of elitism. Joggers in immediately recognizable jogging outfits and wearers of sports coats are hardly the only black male youths who can be trusted not to harm others, especially white people. There are thousands upon thousands of black male youth who do not mean anyone any harm. But I have focused upon these two categories as a very swift and demonstrably clear way of securing the point that even if there are hordes of black hoodlums roaming the streets, it would be possible, with the most rudimentary of social monitoring skills, to recognize that some blacks are not black hoodlums and, therefore, that one has no reason to fear such blacks. But it is probably much closer to the truth that the average person has extensive social monitoring skills, as is evidenced by the fact that just about everyone is capable of instantly recognizing flirting behavior, for example; though such behavior is often very subtle in its display: a faint smile; a raised eyebrow. We are so adept at monitoring individuals on the basis of their self-presentational behavior, both attire and body language, that we generally do so easily and rather unreflectively.

Now, it is an unfortunate fact about life in America that (most) blacks are likely to be far more familiar with the non-verbal manner of whites than (most) whites are of blacks. For one thing, owing to the differential in power relations between blacks and whites, with the latter often having power over the former, thus generally making it in the interest of blacks to win favor with whites, it has been considerably more in the interest of blacks to grasp the non-verbal manner of whites than it has been for whites to grasp the non-verbal manner of blacks. Grasping the non-verbal behavior of whites has been very much in the self-interest of blacks. Obviously, this would be true of the interactions of any two groups of people with a substantial power differential between them, including women and men. It is true, for example, of interactions between children who have parents who abuse them. In general, whenever A is dependent upon B for A's well-being, where B is given to harmful behavior towards A, it will be far more in the interest of A—in fact, it will be a coping mechanism on A's part—to be sensitive to what might trigger hostile intentions on the part of B towards A, and to be deft at ways of diffusing B's hostile intentions towards A (whether A and B both range over individuals or both range over groups). Other things being equal, the more skillful an A is in this regard, the less harm A will suffer at the hands of B.[5] This is a particularly telling consideration against the black-car analogy. In the next two paragraphs, I shall illustrate this point with a very fanciful example.

Suppose that a group of five million well-off individuals with a very distinguishable phenotype, out of a population of 25 million, with yet a different very distinguishable phenotype, go into self-imposed isolation for twenty years, each unto her- or himself, never seeing a face for twenty years, with the results being that the five million become completely unable to read facial expressions generally. They cannot be counted upon even to see the difference between a frown and a smile, to say nothing of the difference between a look of concern or distress and a look of anger. A coy look of sexual interest is absolutely lost on them. This loss makes them easy prey for all sorts of social misfits. Clearly, it would be most rational for our former isolationists to avoid just about any meaningful public contact. What must be just as clear, however, is that the rationality of their avoiding public contact would have everything to do with their inadequacies and nothing to do with the shortcomings of Mary Q. Public as such. It is the former isolationists whose social monitoring skills are in need of serious augmentation. And if our former isolationists are beyond hope on this score, what most certainly does not follow is that Mary Q. Public can be held to blame because the poor social monitoring skills of our former isolationists make it next to impossible for them to read facial expressions. Mary Q. Public shoulders no blame even if things are somewhat awkward socially for our former isolationists because of their acquired social monitoring inadequacy (ASMI).

Because our former isolationists were easy prey for all sorts of social misfits, each adopted the strategy of having as little public contact as possible. Of course, while it would be nice if the public made things easy for our former isolationists by declaring isolationist time zones, during which times only isolationist were permitted to walk the streets, it is difficult to imagine that the public has an obligation to create such zones, let alone that the former isolationists have a right to having such zones created by the public. Nor, on account of their ASMI, would the former isolationists be justified in forcing the remaining public to adopt such time zone measures.

The significance of this fanciful example is obvious. Suppose that, owing to racism of the past, (most or a great many) whites have something like ASMI (acquired social monitoring inadequacy) with respect to blacks. This is not at all implausible; for it would seem that, in many cases, the number of social con-

tact hours that most whites have with blacks is far less than the number of hours that they watch blacks on television, which has certainly presented a very skewed view of blacks who are not well off.[6] Most people, black or otherwise, do not emulate the socioeconomic class of the Huxtables. At any rate, given ASMI with respect to blacks, it may very well be rational for whites to avoid any and all black male youth. But, contrary to what the black-car analogy would have us believe, the problem lies not with the behavior of black male youth, as such, but with a significant inadequacy on the part of whites. This, needless to say, turns the analogy on its head. For the rationality of not buying Acme cars is owing to the fact that serious defects in such cars is widespread—not the fact that some Acme cars have glaring defects but the average buyer is incompetent when it comes to recognizing them.

I realize that I have not shown that (most) whites have ASMI with respect to blacks. I have indicated, though, why the idea is not without considerable plausibility. That whites do have ASMI with respect to blacks is a point masterfully made by Ralph Ellison in his *Invisible Man* when he has the president of a black college scold the callow college student driver for showing the white visitors to the campus far too much. And if, as it seems, Booker T. Washington had every reason to believe that his contemporary whites would hear nothing of integrated schools, as W. E. B. DuBois called for, then it is the card of knowing-whites-better-than-they-know-blacks which he played with his brilliant hand metaphor in his Atlanta Exposition Address, when he declared that the races could be as united as the hand but as separate as the fingers. After all, the concession of separate but equal is better than no concession at all; for separate but equal is vastly superior to separate but unequal. And Washington spoke to an audience that had trouble conceding the first.[7]

In any case, I have said more than enough to make it clear that those, such as Michael Levin, who would advocate rounding up blacks, like so much cattle in the name of protecting defenseless whites from blacks, would do well to examine first whether they are in need of removing the beam from their own eye of social observation. And what a beam it must be if, in an isolated encounter, it is thought rational to fear a black male youth in a sports coat and tie or one jogging in sweat socks and running shorts just because he is black; for as I have shown, nothing else should warrant being afraid of such youth. To see black hoodlums for the undesirables that they are is, perhaps, all well and good. However, to write off all black male youth as black hoodlums is, without a very long and unobvious story, yet to be told, morally unconscionable.

NOTES

*This essay is a comment upon Michael Levin's paper, "Responses to Race Differences in Crime," *Journal of Social Philosophy* 23:1 pp. 5–29. All references to Levin, parenthetical or otherwise, will be to this essay by him. I am interested in making a general response to the line of reasoning represented by Levin rather than making a point-by-point, line-by-line rebuttal of Levin's claims.

1. See, e.g., Mark Snyder, "Self-Monitoring Processes," *Advances in Experimental Social Psychology* 12: 85–128.

2. Cf. Arthur A. Jenson's claim that blacks tend to score lover than whites on I.Q. tests. So much energy was spent denying the claim that people gave little thought to what followed or, in this case, did not follow if the claim were true. What did not follow, by any stretch of reasoning is that blacks should have less moral or social standing than whites, since the thesis that blacks on average score lower than whites on average is quite compatible with their being whites who score considerably lover than blacks. And it had not been suggested that whites with low I.Q. scores should have less moral and social standing than other whites. Taking Jenson's results at face value, no doubt there are all sorts of explanations for the difference which block the inference that blacks must be deemed intellectually inferior to whites. And these should certainly be aired. Still, it is of no small significance that a certain kind of conclusion is not forthcoming even if such explanations were not to be found. Jenson paper is "How Much Can We Boost I.Q. and Scholastic Achievement?," *Harvard Educational Review* 39: 1–123.

3. *Entailment: The Logic of Relevance and Necessity* (Princeton University Press, 1975).

4. Michael Argyle, an Englishman writes: "Some cultures have distinctive styles of bodily movement. For example, black Americans walk and move with energy and style, swing and swagger in a rhythmic manner, exhibiting their bodily competence and creativity. There is

an ancient stereotype that blacks have rhythm of dance, clapping, and music, though this is probably not innate." See his *Bodily Communication,* 2nd ed. (London: Metheun, 1988), p. 62. For all of his astuteness in observation, it probably did not occur to Argyle that his observations are about a particular kind of black American. The class of black Americans who does not fit the mold Argyle has in mind may very well be small. But a small class is not a nonexistent class. The class of whites who are among the true social elite is very small as well; yet, no one has any difficulty acknowledging its existence.

5. Most illuminatingly, Colin A. Ross has this to say about multiple personality disorder (MPD): "MPD is based not on defect but talent and ability. The patients have used their ability to dissociate to cope with overwhelming childhood trauma, which usually involves both physical and sexual abuse. MPD is a creative and highly effective strategy for preserving the integrity of the organism in the face of chronic catastrophic trauma. The problem with adult MPD is that, like any survival strategy gone wrong, it creates more problems than it solves" (p. 2). See his *Multiple Personality Disorder: Diagnosis, Clinical Features, and Treatment* (New York: John Wiley and Sons, 1989).

6. A person with whom I am very close observes with a certain amusement and wonderment that he watches the young boys, at the orthodox synagogue which he attends, mimicking his speaking gestures, much to the liking of their parents. The person is not sure that words can do justice to the symbolic significance of it all, stereotypes of blacks and Jews being what they are. Although ideologically Judaism is prior to race, the fact remains that these young Jewish boys are admiring a black male—not for his sports prowess or his entertainment fitness, but for his life as an intellectual. Few things will rival the positive impact that this will have upon their future interactions with other blacks.

7. Washington distinguished sharply between whites of extraordinary good will whose vision vas limited by racist ideology and whites whose vision was fueled by racist ideology I believe that, mutatis mutandis, this is a fundamental distinction that noways is often lost on groups who consider themselves oppressed. All oppressors are indiscriminately thrown in the latter camp. The distinction was drawn made by Frederic Douglass himself, a former slave who was a fearless and outspoken black critic of slavery. See *Narrative of the Life of Frederick Douglass: An Autobiography of an American Slave Written by Himself,* ed Benjamin Quarles (Harvard University Press, 1988). Needless to say, acting on the distinction requires that one has excellent social monitoring skills, as one cannot afford to be mistaken too often.

Race and Crime

Louis P. Pojman

A Response to Michael Levin and Laurence Thomas

As I write this essay, the National Institute of Health has just announced the cancellation of its funding for a scholarly conference on genetic causes of criminal behavior.[1] At the same time news reports of increased violence by blacks are a common occurrence. It was recently reported by the *New York Times* that on any given day in 1991 42% of black men in the District of Columbia were enmeshed in the criminal justice system (either in prison, on parole or out on bond). Blacks, representing about 12% of the population account for over 50% of violent crimes. In 1989 Jimmy the Greek was removed from CBS for suggesting that blacks had been bred as athletes and had superior musculature to whites, and Janet Morgan, a black teacher in Malverne, Long Island, was suspended without pay for discussing Jimmy the Greek's thesis in class.[2] Similarly in 1990 Andy Rooney was suspended from CBS's "60 Minutes" for his remarks that the "wrong people" were having children.

Race is a highly charged issue in today's society and discussing racism, racial violence, and affirmative action is more likely to raise one's blood pressure than one's level of understanding. Few philosophical journals will touch the subject, let alone face the problems involved head on. Yet it is precisely philosophers who should be on the cutting edge of such social concerns, sifting through the research, evaluating the epistemic claims, discussing the merits of these ideas dispassionately, and putting matters in their larger philosophical and moral perspective. If philosophers cannot discuss these matters rationally and in good faith, who will?

It is in the light of these larger issues that the exchange between Michael Levin and Laurence Thomas needs to be addressed. First of all, this journal has distinguished itself in taking on a topic which other philosophical journals and academic publishers have been too afraid to touch. The editor and reviewers of the *Journal of Social Philosophy* deserve our praise and admiration for publishing material on such a controversial subject. What then is the issue in this debate. It is whether race should be taken into consideration in evaluating people in certain situations where information about individuals is relevantly limited.

If I understand the debate in these essays, Levin is arguing that if we don't have supplementary information, then it is *sometimes* epistemologically and morally acceptable to engage in statistical racial screening. As far as I can see Thomas accepts this conclusion but accuses Levin of not recognizing the need for whites to overcome ASMI (acquired social monitoring inadequacy) in order to distinguish between black hoodlums and the majority of law-abiding black males.

While Thomas' point is well taken, it needs to be qualified, and does not affect Levin's basic argument. In cases where there is relevant information, we normally should use our social monitoring skills to distinguish varieties of self-presenting behavior. On the face of it, Thomas seems to be assuming that Levin wouldn't accept such a principle. Note here that Thomas misrepresents Levin's initial description. On page 7 Levin describes the case he's concerned with this way:

Suppose, jogging alone after dark, you see a young black male ahead of you on the running track, *not*

Louis P. Pojman, "Race and Crime: A Response to Michael Levin and Laurence Thomas," *Journal of Social Philosophy* 24, no. 1 (1993): 152–54. Reprinted by permission of Blackwell Publishing Ltd.

attired in a jogging outfit, and displaying no other information-bearing trait. Based on the statistics cited earlier, you must set the likelihood of his being a felon at .25 (my emphasis).

But here is how Thomas represents Levin:

Now, it could very well be that when a black youth is *attired as a jogger* he is nonetheless likely to act the part of a hoodlum, with a concealed weapon and all. Once more, it could be a strategy to catch people off guard. But, as with a black youth wearing a tweed coat and tie, there is no evidence to support such a view about black youths who are joggers. . . . As I have observed, then, Levin's example of the black jogger is quite revealing of rashness of thought. No doubt a different author would put the point less delicately (Thomas, p. 34 my emphasis).

But the rashness, alas, is not in Levin's account, but in Thomas' reading of Levin. Levin never says that the black male is a jogger and says specifically that he is *not attired in a jogging outfit.* Levin says that the youth was *displaying no other information-bearing trait.* Thomas has misread Levin and thus his criticism fails to engage the central argument. On p. 32 he accuses Levin of unqualifiedly "fearing any *and all* black American male youths," of claiming it is rational "to take flight and run on account of being afraid of the harm that you might suffer at the hands of a [black] jogger." On p. 32 he accuses Levin of arguing that it is rational to cross the street "out of fear of being harmed by Lester," a well-attired black male "sporting a tweed coat and a tie."

But all of this misses Levin's point, which is that when "no other information-bearing trait" is available, one is rationally and morally justified in reacting by doing a cost-benefit assessment of the situation and acting on it.

A variety of such situations come to mind. A woman, required to work overtime, is walking home on a poorly lit street in a high crime neighborhood. She sees a male (white or black) and runs away as fast as she can, perhaps hurting his feelings. A black visitor from New York is driving down a lonely Mississippi road (say it's 1960) and sees two pick-up trucks coming his way. Reminded of stories of blacks being accosted and harmed along such roads, he quickly turns the car and drives back to Memphis. In Detroit the school board has proposed all black

male high schools because of evidence that such youth will develop better in such a context. Affirmative Action hiring policies justify treating all blacks as deserving preferential treatment on the basis of the high probability that they have suffered disparate impact by belonging to an oppressed minority. Myrl Duncan writes in her defense of affirmative actions, "Because race was made a "morally relevant" factor for purposes of discriminating against a group, it must be "morally relevant" for purposes of compensation," and Jim Nickel similarly argues that affirmative action can be based solely on group membership for reasons of administrative convenience.[3]

Even Thomas' ASMI principle needs qualification. While we all need to improve our ability to distinguish between self-presenting behavior, we may nonculpably lack the opportunity. For example, a woman brought up in a sheltered environment may fail to understand male sex drives and be unable to distinguish men who are respectful from those who might rape her. Such a woman is in greater danger of being raped because she has a case of ASMI. But, surely, it's not her fault if she gets raped. She's the innocent victim. Likewise, with regard to whites being afraid of black males (or blacks being afraid of whites) the fault may not be the individual's, but that of those members of a race or gender who have caused a statistical probability to obtain. Hence, Thomas' claim that "the problem lies not with the behavior of black male youth, as such, but with a significant inadequacy on the part of whites" (p. 39) is not necessarily so. The principle of overcoming ASMI vis-à-vis a group is a prima facie, not an absolute, duty, which may be overridden for any number of reasons and from which a person may be excused. Normally it is far more evil for violence to be perpetrated on the innocent than for the innocent to fail to discern nonviolence.

NOTES

1. *New York Times* (front page), September 5, 1992.

2. Wayne King, "Jimmy the Greek Had Job Troubles. Now She Does," *New York Times,* December 19, 1989.

3. Myrl Duncan, "The Future of Affirmative Action: A Jurisprudential/Legal Critique" (Harvard Civil Rights-Civil Liberties Law Review 17, 1982).

PART 5

WHAT'S WRONG WITH COMMERCE?

Some forms of commercial exchange seem morally unproblematic. If I offered to sell you some carrots that I had grown in my backyard, for example, and if you freely agreed to the price that I asked for them, then virtually no one would find our transaction morally objectionable. Other cases of commercial exchange are clearly wrong. If I offered to sell you a thirty-year-old man whom I had raised in my backyard, virtually everyone would recognize this to be a moral abomination. Carrots are the kind of thing that are appropriately bought and sold on the open market, while human beings are not. But in between the relatively clear cases of selling food and selling slaves lies a variety of cases that are substantially more complicated and, as a result, substantially more controversial. Furthermore, even the selling of carrots can become somewhat problematic on closer examination. Suppose I have a slave, and my slave did all my gardening, including growing the carrots. Or suppose I know that carrots are selling down the road for a quarter of the price I am asking for mine. Or suppose that while both of us have plenty to eat, my next-door neighbors are starving. In these cases, the fact that we both willingly agree to the exchange may not be sufficient to render the transaction morally unproblematic.

Part 5 is devoted to an examination of such problems. The first two problems concern the buying and selling of stocks. What is the moral status of holding stock in companies that are, for whatever reason, morally objectionable (chapter 19). And what is the moral status of making use of insider knowledge when trading stocks (chapter 20)? We then focus on problems that arise from the application of market forces to three controversial cases of goods and services. Is it morally objectionable for people to sell their bodily organs on the open market (chapter 21)? Is it wrong for women to hire themselves out as surrogate mothers, carrying pregnancies to term in order to provide children for couples who are unable (or unwilling) to do so on their own (chapter 22)? In chapters 21 and 22, critics of a particular form of commercial exchange attempt to show that that exchange is parallel to (or, in one or two cases perhaps even identical to) the sale of human beings, while defenders of the exchange attempt to highlight the ways in which it resembles other commercial transactions that are generally viewed as unobjectionable. Finally, chapter 23 looks into a still more general moral problem that is generated by the wealth that commerce creates in the developed world. Is it wrong for us to spend so much of the money we earn from commercial transactions on ourselves given that there are millions of starving people in other parts of the world?

19

Is Failing to Divest from Immoral Companies Wrong?

Cahn and His Critics

Suppose a company in which you own stock has announced a new policy that you strongly believe to be immoral. For example, perhaps it has begun to produce and distribute violent pornography, or to provide abortions, or to perform research on animals, or to market clothing made from child labor. You then find yourself in a position in which you are profiting from the immoral conduct of others. What should you do?

Many people believe that, under such circumstances, it is wrong not to divest yourself of your holdings in that company. To refrain from doing so, they maintain, is to be complicit in the wrongdoings of the company. Indeed, one of the most common kinds of protest on college campuses for many years has been that in which students demand that their schools divest themselves of investments in a particular company or set of companies for just such reasons. In "A Puzzle Concerning Divestiture," Steven M. Cahn offers a startling argument against such "principled divestiture." His argument turns on the idea that if your owning the stock is itself immoral, then the act of selling it to a buyer amounts to helping the buyer do something immoral, which in turn would seem to be immoral itself. Cahn's argument can be unpacked as follows, where the assumption that holding stock in Corporation X is immoral is taken as a given:

P1   It is immoral to hold stock in Company X.

P2   If it is immoral to hold stock in Company X, then it is immoral to buy stock in Company X.

P3   If you divest yourself of your stock in Company X, then you assist someone else in buying stock in Company X.

P4   It is immoral to assist someone in doing something that is itself immoral.

C   It is immoral for you to divest yourself of your stock in Company X.

The upshot of Cahn's argument is that so-called principled divestment is in fact unprincipled.

Several philosophers have claimed to solve Cahn's puzzle. Three of their solutions are reproduced, in part, in the readings that follow Cahn's brief paper. Roger Shiner's response to Cahn's article focuses on what he claims to be an important ambiguity in Cahn's claim that by divesting oneself of tainted stock one "entangles" someone else in it. Shiner's claim is that once we understand more precisely what such a claim amounts to, we can see that the seller of the stock does not really "entangle" the buyer in wrongdoing in a way that warrants moral condemnation. Put in terms of the reconstruction of Cahn's argument, Shiner can be understood as objecting that there is a crucial *equivocation* over the use of the term *assist* in premises 3 and 4 (for more on equivocation objections, see the Introduction). In some sense of *assist,* Shiner concedes, it is true that the seller assists the buyer. If no one offers a stock for sale, for example, then the buyer cannot buy it. And in some sense of *assist,* he agrees, it is true that it is immoral to assist someone in doing something that is immoral. It is immoral, for example, deliberately to tempt or trap someone into committing an immoral act that they would otherwise have no desire to do, or to coerce someone into committing an immoral act that they would never freely choose to do. But, Shiner can be understood as arguing, the sense in which a seller assists a buyer in buying a stock is importantly different from the sense of assisting in which assisting someone in doing something immoral is itself immoral. If Shiner is correct, the result is that there is no one sense of "assisting" by which both P3 and P4 of Cahn's argument are true. And if this is so, then Cahn's argument is unsuccessful.

Kerry S. Walters raises a similar concern about Cahn's argument. Like Shiner, Walters can be understood as maintaining that the sense in which the seller assists the buyer in committing an immoral act is not sufficient to make the seller's act itself immoral. But rather than focusing on general claims about what kinds of assistance are sufficient to make an act of assisting a wrongdoing itself wrong, Walters instead tries to justify this claim by focusing on a more specific feature of the stockholder's predicament: the fact that the owner of the stock seems to have no further options beyond keeping the stock or divesting himself of it. Walters compares this person with one who can quit a job that has become morally objectionable only after he first helps to train a suitable replacement. He argues that given that such a person must either do the immoral work himself or prepare someone else to do it, it would be legitimate for him to quit the job, even knowing that this would involve "entangling" someone else in it. Therefore, Walters suggests, the same must go for the case of the stockholder. This may cast some doubt on premise 3.

Finally, Saul Smilansky also raises a problem with P3 of the argument. Cahn's argument against principled divestment turns in part on the assumption that divesting oneself of stock is either identical to or at least entails selling the stock to a buyer. But Cahn suggests two ways in which a person might be understood as divesting himself of stock without selling it: cases in which the stockholder either offers the stock for sale but finds no buyers or simply gives the stock up without selling it to anyone. If either or both of these cases are thought to be consistent with the notion of divestment in the sense that Cahn's puzzle is meant to argue against divestment, then they may prove to be counterexamples to P3.

QUESTIONS FOR CONSIDERATION

In considering the merits of Shiner's proposed solution to Cahn's puzzle, it may be helpful to focus on the question of how deeply "entangled" the buyer and seller in an exchange of stocks for money actually are.

• Shiner seems to be correct that the seller is not morally culpable for the buyer's wrongdoing in the same sense in which a person is wrong when he coerces another into committing a wrongful act. But is the seller more like an innocent bystander to the buyer's wrongdoing? (In this case we may well agree with Shiner's conclusion.) Or is the seller still deeply enough involved in the transaction for the buyer's wrongdoing to, in effect, rub off on the seller?

• In critically examining Walters's response to the puzzle, it may prove useful to think about the relevance (or lack thereof) of the stockholder's having only two options: to sell or retain the stock. Does the lack of an even better alternative suffice to make selling the stock the "principled" thing to do? Or would it be morally better to accept the taint of owning the stock oneself rather than shifting it to another, given that the taint will inevitably land somewhere?

• Finally, in thinking about Smilansky's reply to Cahn's argument, consider the motivations behind principled divestment and ask whether or not the examples that Smilansky proposes would be sufficient to satisfy those who demanded divestment while at the same time managing to escape the force of Cahn's argument. Would the mere act of offering to sell the stock, for example, be enough to remove the moral taint of continuing to own it if no one agreed to buy it? Or would the result simply be that one had attempted, but failed, to discontinue one's moral wrongdoing?

• What would the effect be of simply abandoning one's stock ownership without transferring it to anyone else? Would this count as a way of successfully eliminating the moral taint that went with the stock? Or would simply renouncing the stock have an effect on other people (other stockholders, perhaps, or other potential buyers or sellers) that would still amount to shifting the taint to others rather than making it go away?

FURTHER READINGS

Cahn, Steven M. "A Note on Divestiture." *Analysis* 49 (1989): 156–57 (a reply to Cohen, Walters, and Gordon and Sadowsky).

———. "Principled Divestiture and Moral Integrity." *Analysis* 51 (1991): 12 (a reply to Shiner).

Cohen, Daniel H. "A Reply to Steven M. Cahn." *Analysis* 48 (1988): 109–10.

Gordon, David and James Sadowsky. "Morally Principled Divestiture?" *Analysis* 49 (1989): 153–55.

Steven M. Cahn | # A Puzzle Concerning Divestiture

Suppose I hold 100 shares of stock in a company that has embarked on a policy I consider immoral. I therefore wish to divest myself of those 100 shares. In order for me to sell them, someone must buy them. But the buyer would be purchasing 100 shares of 'tainted' stock. And I would have abetted the buyer in this immoral course of action. Granted, the prospective buyer might not believe the stock "tainted," but that consideration would be irrelevant to me, since I am convinced that, knowingly or unknowingly, the buyer would be doing what is immoral. Surely I should not take any steps that would assist or encourage the buyer in such deplorable conduct. Nor should I try to release myself from a moral predicament by entangling someone else. How then is principled divestiture possible?

Critics

Roger A. Shiner | # The Divestiture Puzzle Dissolved

. . . There are two ways of looking at Seller's "moral predicament." The first concentrates on the state of Seller's soul, as it were, and regards Seller's soul as contaminated by association with the immoral company in which Seller holds shares. The second concentrates on the harm done—say, the economic support given to a corrupt regime—by the investment Seller had originally made. The "entangling" of Buyer which purportedly takes place when Seller sells Buyer the shares might refer to either of these considerations.

Let us take the first one first. The thought here is that by the act of selling Seller purifies Seller's soul at the cost of passing on the contamination to Buyer. A certain kind of paradigm of immorality is presupposed here, cases where initially innocent persons have their moral sensibilities gradually blunted to the point where they become willing partners in some nefarious enterprise, or else where they are forced to participate in such an enterprise by blackmail or other form of coercion. Such cases require some self-conscious intention to entangle on the part of the entangler and some ignorance or reluctance on the part of the entanglee if 'entangling' with the relevant negative connotations is to be properly applied. Although we can imagine a case where Buyer is coerced by Seller into purchasing the latter's shares, the ordinary case of selling shares on the open market is quite different. For one thing, the mechanics of the electronic stock exchange put increasingly in doubt that shares have the kind of identity-conditions which secure the claim that any given Buyer is buying the very particular shares that some given Seller is selling. If there is a very small

Steven M. Cahn, "A Puzzle Concerning Divestiture," *Analysis* 47, no. 3 (June 1987): 175–76. Reprinted by permission of Blackwell Publishing Ltd.

From Roger A. Shiner, "The Divestiture Puzzle Dissolved," *Analysis* 50, no. 3 (1990): 205–10. References and some parts of the text have been deleted. Reprinted by permission of Blackwell Publishing Ltd.

market in the shares, this may be possible; but if tens of thousands of shares are being regularly traded, it will not be possible. In the second place, Seller simply authorizes Broker to sell the shares; while Broker may know who Buyer is (though Broker may not, but sell only to another broker), Seller will not know. There are paradigms of harm being done to "unassignable individuals," in Jeremy Bentham's splendid phrase—pollution of a river or of the air. The pulp mill may culpably know that some people will be harmed by its discharges although it does not know which people. If one is prepared to regard Seller's selling shares when it may not be possible to identify who buys them, or when, even if it is possible, Seller will be ignorant of Buyer, as contamination of "unassignable individuals" comparable to a pulp mill discharging into a river, then I cannot confound that interpretation. But 'entangling' is already beginning to look like a tendentious description, and the distance of these cases from the paradigms of entangling is considerable. Third, as said, "entangling" presupposes innocence or reluctance on the part of the entanglee. It is extremely unlikely that the ordinary case of shares being purchased on an open market involves any such ignorance or reluctance.

In short, cases where Seller really does "entangle" Buyer and pass on the contamination of the soul, these are exceptional cases. What actually happens in the normal cases of a sale of shares would not support the description "entangling" at all.

The second way of interpreting "entangling" focusses on the harm done by the possession of the objectionable shares. Seller purportedly "entangles" Buyer by causing Buyer to do exactly the same harm as Seller was doing. . . . Cahn's puzzle require[s] that, if Seller is to be rightly described as "entangling," the causal connection from Seller to the harming investment remains unbroken by the act of selling the shares to Buyer. But it seems to me that this is simply not so. The voluntary purchase of the shares by Buyer on the open market is an intervening act which breaks the chain of causation from Seller to any harm done by the investment. Seller does *not* "cause" Buyer to buy the shares, so long as Buyer has acted voluntarily in buying them. . . .

Consider these two cases. (1) Vendor builds (it is indifferent whether the building is negligent, reckless, or intentional) a rickety porch on to a house. Vendor then sells the house directly to Purchaser, saying nothing when Purchaser fails to notice the condition of the porch. Shortly after, the porch collapses, injuring Lettercarrier. (2) Vendor builds the rickety porch as before, but commissions Realtor to sell the house. Purchaser purchases the house; Purchaser is merely a name on the contract to Vendor. Purchaser realizes the porch is rickety, but does nothing to fix it. Shortly after, the porch collapses, injuring Lettercarrier. In case (1), there is some plausibility to the claim that Vendor has "entangled" Purchaser in the situation which led to harm to Lettercarrier. There is very little plausibility to this claim in case (2). Given Purchaser's voluntary purchase of the house, and awareness of the state of the porch, there is no longer any causal responsibility on the part of Vendor for the harm to Lettercarrier—even though it is true that, but for Vendor building the rickety porch, the harm to Lettercarrier would not have occurred. The case of Buyer's purchase of Seller's shares on the open market is analogous to case (2), not case (1).

In short, if "entangling" is taken to refer to a causal connection between Seller and the harm Buyer is doing by investing in Armaments Manufacturer, then there is no such connection. Talk of "entangling" is not justified. . . .

Kerry S. Walters | Morally Acceptable Divestiture

. . . The following analogy sheds light on Cahn's puzzle. Suppose I'm employed by a firm that's embarked on a policy I consider immoral. I therefore wish to dissociate myself from the firm. This entails my resignation. Moreover, my employer assures me I will be replaced. But one of the conditions of my contract, which I freely accepted at the time of appointment and still see as morally binding, is as follows. If I give intent to resign, I may legitimately step aside only after the firm has found my replacement and I have cooperated in his on the job training for a stipulated length of time. As a condition of employment, my replacement presumably will be required to acquiesce to or at least not oppose the firm's objectionable policy. Consequently, my resignation "entangles" him in an immoral situation, and this is reprehensible. How then is principled resignation possible?[1]

Surely no one wants to suggest I'm duty bound not to tender my resignation merely because a third party will take my place. The ideal course of action, of course, might be for me to remain in the firm's employment and as an insider lobby against the immoral policy. That way no third party would become an accessory through my resignation. But such an action is supererogatory. If remaining goes against the grain, I may legitimately leave with no violation of duty if I conscientiously apprise my replacement of my negative evaluation of the firm. If he still willingly hires on, I can hardly be said to have "entangled" him. My resignation is a necessary condition for his replacing me, but not for his ethical appraisal of and subsequent response to the firm's immoral policy.

Similarly with divestiture. My ideal recourse might be to retain my stock, donate the dividends to charity and actively lobby for the reformation of corporate policy. True, I will remain a reluctant accessory in what I take to be an immoral situation, but at least I will avoid "entanglement" of a third party. But I am under no obligation to retain the stock. Doing so makes me an incredibly decent fellow. It shows I'm willing to sacrifice my peace of mind for the sake of others. But it is clearly supererogatory. If it too abuses my conscience or endurance, I may sell with no violation of duty, provided I conscientiously apprise the buyer of my reasons for divestiture. If he still willingly buys, either because he disagrees with my ethical reservations or agrees without giving a damn, I can hardly be said to have "entangled" him. My selling is a necessary condition for his purchase, but not for his ethical response.

Is this analysis merely a smokescreen for ethical buck-passing? I don't think so. I'm not claiming divestiture leaves me with spotless hands. I am, after all, retreating rather than redressing. But neither does it totally condemn me. Granted, divesting is a less than ideal recourse. But in light of the predicament's difficulty, it is morally acceptable. By morally acceptable I mean that course of action which falls within the bounds of ethical propriety without being fully virtuous. Given the complexity of certain ethical quandaries, it may be unlikely if not impossible to achieve a completely satisfying resolution. But this doesn't mean no resolution is possible. A careful examination may reveal courses of action which are acceptable although not what, in the best case scenario, one would desire. In short, shooting for moral acceptability is making the best of a bad situation. It may leave one with slightly soiled hands, but it may also be the best one can do under the circumstances.

Is, then, principled divestiture possible? If by "principled" one means fully virtuous and completely satisfying, probably not. Moreover I suspect no—or at least very few—actions are principled in

Kerry S. Walters, "Morally Acceptable Divestiture," *Analysis* 48 (1988): 216–18. Some parts of the text have been deleted. Reprinted by permission of Blackwell Publishing Ltd.

this strong sense. But if one more realistically takes "principled" to mean morally acceptable, then yes. Principled divestiture is possible.

NOTE

1. My colleague Chan Coulter has correctly pointed out that this analogy isn't perfect. If a shareholder wishes to sell, there is a logical entailment that he involve a buyer. If an employee wishes to resign, it is probable but not necessary that a replacement becomes involved. Still, I don't think the analogy fatally limps, since the employee wishing to resign here considers himself under an ethical obligation to wait out his replacement. That is, a morally necessary condition for his leaving is that his position be filled by a third party.

Saul Smilansky | The Point in Principled Divestiture

. . . Cahn's [argument] clearly depends on equating principled divestiture with the *selling* of stock. There is no reason, however, to equate the two. By putting the tainted stock on the market one does all one is required to do. If no one buys then one has not made a sale, and technically one still owns the stock. But one has done all one could to fulfill the moral requirement to divest oneself of the stock. If it happens that there is no demand for the stock (something which is not under the control of the person offering the stock), then we simply conclude that the stock happens to be worthless. If, however, someone does wish to buy the stock, then the person offering the stock does not, I maintain, acquire all of a sudden responsibility for the decision of the buyer. . . .

One could also be said to have divested oneself of morally tainted stock simply by giving it up, a process which clearly involves neither a seller nor a buyer. . . .

Saul Smilansky, "The Point in Principled Divestiture," *Public Affairs Quarterly* 7, no. 3 (1993): 257–60. Notes and some parts of the text have been deleted. Reprinted by permission of North American Philosophical Publications.

20

Is Insider Trading Wrong?

Werhane and Her Critics

Suppose George is on the Board of Directors of an apparently successful company, Hokey, the stocks of which are worth three dollars a share. George himself owns a million shares of the company's stock. At a board meeting, the directors are informed that the company is suddenly in real and unexpected financial trouble because of the probable failure of a number of big projects. The failure of these projects is not yet known outside the board of directors and the senior managers of the projects. The following day, George instructs his broker to sell his Hokey shares. He nets three million dollars. Some other insiders also start putting their shares up for sale, and within two weeks the share price has dropped to two dollars. When news of the Hokey failure becomes public, the share price drops to less than ten cents, and the company stops trading on the Stock Exchange.

Insider trading on the stock market is characterized as "the buying or selling of shares of stock on the basis of information known only to the trader or to a few persons." The case of George is a clear instance of it. The practice of insider trading recently achieved considerable prominence in the media with reported scandals involving famous individuals such as Martha Stewart and politically influential companies such as Enron and Harken. What exactly is insider trading and why is it widely considered not only worthy of government regulation but also, in some way, immoral? The case of George makes this widely held view plausible. Those who bought George's shares have collectively lost nearly three million dollars, whereas George is chuckling all the way to the bank. What is wrong with this is that George's gain has clearly been at the expense of those unwitting souls to whom he sold his shares. George knew full well that the value of those shares was going to plummet, and the unwitting buyers would not have bought the shares if they had known what George knew. So, the way in which George has exploited their ignorance seems patently unjust or unfair.

This is the gist of the George Will passage with which Werhane begins her article. It can be summarized as:

P1   The insider has information about the stock that the outsider lacks.

P2   Using privileged information to gain an advantage over those who lack that information is unfair.

P3   Unfair practices are immoral.

C   Insider trading is immoral.

Here is one kind of objection to the second premise of this unfairness argument. Those who object to insider trading are not against capitalism and free markets as such, and capitalism, by its very nature, embraces analogous inequalities or disparities in people's situations without characterizing them as unfair. The rich are better placed to make more money out of the stock market than the poor. Those willing to take risks are more likely to end up very rich (or very poor) than those who are risk averse. Those who have smart business ideas and business acumen are more likely to end up rich than those without. And, finally, the outcomes of free-market capitalism reflect these initial disparities. Some people get rich, and others remain or become poor. However, unless there is some other moral objection to capitalism itself, it is not unfair for people to make use of these initial disparities, and so these disparities are not really cases of unfairness in the moral sense. If a person takes a risk by investing his money in the stock market, then he deserves both whatever rewards he reaps and whatever losses he sustains. Having privileged information, as the insider does, is just one more disparity, and to use that information is perfectly morally permissible. There are other situations in which one gains a substantial advantage over others by virtue of possessing privileged information, and such gains are not considered unfair. For example people win Nobel Prizes for being the first to possess information that others do not possess (scientific theories and results), and no one considers that unfair.

Werhane briefly reports another kind of objection to the second premise of the unfairness argument, one made by Henry Manne. Manne argues that insider trading, far from being unfair to outsiders, is actually beneficial to outsiders. If insiders trade their shares on the basis of reliable information, then the price of the stock will more reliably reflect the actual value of the stock. When George sells his shares on the basis of his insider information that the company is in real trouble, the stock price begins to go down, eventually reaching its actual value—ten cents a share—once the information is made public. Since the company is in trouble, the stock price *should* go down. George's insider trading simply hastens that process by a few weeks. So, outsiders as a group are not really harmed by insider trading (remember that those who actually bought George's shares are a tiny proportion of all the outsiders who have been affected by George's actions). Of course, it is true that the insider gains (and some outsiders lose) by virtue of the insider's possessing and using the information first. But it is not clear that this in itself is unfair to outsiders.

Werhane retorts that Manne's objection ignores something fundamental about free markets: They rely on competition, and perfect competition "occurs only when both parties in the exchange are more or less on equal grounds." With insider trading, some have access to information that others do not have access to, and so "competition, which depends on the availability of equal advantage by all parties is precluded. . . . Pure competition, a supposed goal of the free market and an aim of most persons who defend insider trading, is more nearly obtained without insider trading."

In their response to Werhane, "Insider Trading Revisited," Martin and Peterson spring to Manne's defense, detailing ways in which insider trading brings benefits to outsiders by more rapidly aligning the market price of the share with its value. In a way, the insider who buys or sells on the basis of his information is a conduit for that information to reach the market earlier than it would otherwise, thereby putting outsiders in a better position overall. Consequently, insider trading makes the market more, not less, efficient: "The market can never be made less efficient by the inclusion of more information." Martin and Peterson go on to argue that Werhane has fundamentally misunderstood the nature of competition in a free market. The constraints on action in a free market are simply this: "all persons should be guaranteed the right to free and voluntary contract without fraud or coercion." That principle makes no apparent mention of refraining from using privileged information.

QUESTIONS FOR CONSIDERATION

• In the delightful children's novel *Matilda* (by Roald Dahl) Matilda's father is a second-hand car dealer who regularly sells cars he knows to be defective, but the defects are not immediately apparent to his customers. For example, he fills defective gearboxes with sand, so that the gearboxes sound fine while the car is being driven out of the dealership, but give out farther down the road. Unsuspecting customers thus end up having paid good money for cars that conk out sooner or later, usually sooner. Most people would judge Matilda's father's exploitation of his knowledge, and of his customers' ignorance, to be morally wrong. To what extent is George's use of insider information like that of Matilda's father? If the two are analogous, are they both unfair, or should we revise our judgment of Matilda's father and consider his practices to be entirely fair? Matilda's father seems to be practicing a form of fraud—portraying his goods as one kind of thing while knowing that they are something entirely different. But in selling what he knows will soon be practically worthless shares, isn't George doing something analogous? Will the market punish the two for their practices and put them out of business? Certainly in the case of the second-hand car dealer, word will soon get around about his cars, and he will probably go out of business. But George's offloading his Hokey shares is likely to be a one-time event, or at least a fairly rare one, so an unregulated market is not likely to punish him and put him out of business. Is this difference enough to undermine the analogy? Why and why not?

FURTHER READINGS

Ma, Y., and H. Sun. "Where Should the Line Be Drawn on Insider Trading Ethics?" *Journal of Business Ethics* 17, no. 1 (1998): 67–75.

Machan, T. "What is Morally Right with Insider Trading." *Public Affairs Quarterly* 10, no. 2 (1996): 135–42.

Snoeyenbos, M., and K. Smith. "Ma and Sun on Insider Trading." *Journal of Business Ethics* 28, no. 4 (2000): 361–63.

Werhane Patricia. "The Indefensibility of Insider Trading." *Journal of Business Ethics* 10, no. 9 (1991): 729–31.

Patricia H. Werhane | The Ethics of Insider Trading

> Insider trading is the reverse of speculation. It is reward without risk, wealth generated—and injury done to others—by an unfair advantage in information . . . [T]he core principle is clear: no one should profit from exploitation of important information not available to the public.[1]

Insider trading in the stock market is characterized as the buying or selling of shares of stock on the basis of information known only to the trader or to a few persons. In discussions of insider trading it is commonly assumed that the privileged information, if known to others, would affect their actions in the market as well, although in theory this need not be the case. The present guidelines of the Securities and Exchange Commission prohibit most forms of insider trading. Yet a number of economists and philosophers of late defend this kind of activity both as a viable and useful practice in a free market and as a practice that is not immoral. In response to these defenses I want to question the value of insider trading both from a moral and an economic point of view. I shall argue that insider trading both in its present illegal form and as a legalized market mechanism violates the privacy of concerned parties, destroys competition, and undermines the efficient and proper functioning of a free market, thereby bringing into question its own raison d'etre. It does so and therefore is economically inefficient for the very reason that it is immoral.

That insider trading as an illegal activity interferes with the free market is pretty obvious. It is like a game where there are a number of players each of whom represents a constituency. In this sort of game there are two sets of rules—one ostensive set and another, implicit set, functioning for some of the players. In this analogy some of the implicit rules are outlawed, yet the big players manage to keep them operative and actually often in control of the game. But not all the players know all the rules being played or at least they are ignorant of the most important ones, ones that determine the big wins and big losses. So not all the players realize what rules actually manipulate the outcome. Moreover, partly because some of the most important functioning rules are illegal, some players who do know the implicit rules and could participate do not. Thus not everyone in a position to do so plays the trading game the same way. The game, then, like the manipulated market that is the outcome, is unfair—unfair to some of the players and those they represent— unfair not only because some of the players are not privy to the most important rules, but also because these "special" rules are illegal so that they are adopted only by a few of even the privileged players.

But suppose that insider trading was decriminalized or not prohibited by SEC regulations. Then, one might argue, insider trading would not be unfair because anyone could engage in it without impunity. Although one would be trading on privileged knowledge, others, too, could trade on *their* privileged information. The market would function more efficiently since the best-informed and those most able to gain information would be allowed to exercise their fiscal capabilities. The market itself would regulate the alleged excesses of insider trading. I use the term "alleged" excesses because according to this line of reasoning, if the market is functioning properly, whatever gains or losses are created as a result of open competition are a natural outcome of that competition. They are not excesses at all, and eventually the market will adjust the so-called unfair gains of speculators.

There are several other defenses of insider trading. First, insider information, e.g., information about a

Patricia H. Werhane, "The Ethics of Insider Trading," *Journal of Business Ethics* 8, no. 11 (1989): 841–45. Reprinted by permission of Kluwer Academic Publishers.

merger, acquisition, new stock issue, layoffs, etc., information known only to a few, *should* be and remain private. That information is the property of those engaged in the activity in question, and they should have the right to regulate its dissemination. Second and conversely, even under ideal circumstances it is impossible either to disseminate information to all interested parties equally and fairly, or alternately, to preserve absolute secrecy. For example, in issuing a new stock or deciding on a stock split, a number of parties in the transaction from brokers to printers learn about that information in advance just because of their participation in making this activity a reality. And there are always shareholders and other interested parties who claim they did not receive information of such an activity or did not receive it at the same time as other shareholders even when the information was disseminated to everyone at the same time. Thus it is, at best, difficult to stop insider trading or to judge whether a certain kind of knowledge is "inside" or privileged. This is not a good reason to defend insider trading as economically or morally desirable, but it illustrates the difficulties of defining and controlling the phenomenon.

Third, those who become privy to inside information, even if they take advantage of that information before it becomes public, are trading on probabilities, not on certainties, since they are trading before the activity actually takes place. They are taking a gamble, and if they are wrong the market itself will "punish" them. It is even argued that brokers who do not use inside information for their clients' advantage are cheating their clients.

Finally, and more importantly, economists like Henry Manne argue that insider trading is beneficial to outsiders. Whether it is more beneficial than its absence is a question Manne admits he cannot answer. But Manne defends insider trading because, he argues, it reduces the factor of chance in trading both for insiders and outsiders. When shares are traded on information or probabilities rather than on rumor or whim, the market reflects more accurately the actual economic status of that company or set of companies. Because of insider trading, stock prices go up or down according to real, factual information.

Outsiders benefit from this because stock prices more closely represent the worth of their company than shares not affected by insider trading. Insider trading, then, actually improves the fairness of the market, according to this argument, by reflecting in stock prices the fiscal realities of affected corporations thereby benefitting all traders of the stocks.[2]

These arguments for insider trading are persuasive. Because outsiders are allegedly not harmed from privileged information not available to them and may indeed benefit from insider trading, and because the market punishes rash speculators, insider trading cannot be criticized as exploitation. In fact, it makes the market more efficient. Strong as these arguments are, however, there is something amiss with these claims. The error, I think, rests at least in part with the faulty view of how free markets work, a view which stems from a misinterpretation that derives from a misreading of Adam Smith and specifically a misreading of Smith's notions of self-interest and the Invisible Hand.

The misinterpretation is this. It is sometimes assumed that an unregulated free market, driven by competition and self interest, will function autonomously. The idea is that the free market works something like the law of gravity—autonomously and anonymously in what I would call a no-blooded fashion. The interrelationships created by free market activities based on self-interested competition are similar to the gravitational relationships between the planets and the sun: impersonal, automatic interactions determined by a number of factors including the distance and competitive self-interest of each of the market components. The free market functions, then, despite the selfish peculiarities of the players just as the planets circle the sun despite their best intentions to do otherwise. Given that picture of the free market, so-called insider trading, driven by self-interest but restrained by competitive forces, that is, the invisible hand, is merely one gravitational mechanism—a complication but not an oddity or an aberration in the market.

This is a crude and exaggerated picture of the market, but I think it accounts for talk about the market *as if* it functioned in this independent yet forceful way, and it accounts for defenses of unrestrained self-interested actions in the market place. It allows one to defend insider trading because of the positive market fall-out from this activity, and because the market allegedly will control the excesses of self-interested economic activities.

The difficulty with this analysis is not so much with the view of insider trading as a legitimate activity but rather with the picture of economic actors in a free market. Adam Smith himself, despite his 17th century Newtonian background, did not have such a mechanical view of a laissez-faire economy. Again and again in the *Wealth of Nations* Smith extols the virtues of unrestrained competition as being to the advantage of the producer and the consumer.[3] A system of perfect liberty he argues, creates a situation where "[t]he whole of the advantages and disadvantages of the different employments of labour and stock . . . be either perfectly equal or continually tending to equality."[4] Yet for Smith the greatest cause of inequalities of advantage is any restrictive policy or activity that deliberately gives privileges to certain kinds of businesses, trades, or professions.[5] The point is that Smith sees perfect liberty as the necessary condition for competition, but perfect competition occurs only both parties in the exchange are on more or less on equal grounds, whether it be competition for labor, jobs, consumers, or capital. This is not to imply that Smith favors equality of outcomes. Clearly he does not. But the market is most efficient and most fair when there is competition between equally matched parties.

Moreover, Smith's thesis was that the Invisible Hand works because, and only when, people operate with restrained self-interest, self-interest restrained by reason, moral sentiments, and sympathy, in Smith's case the reason, moral sentiments and sympathies of British gentlemen. To operate otherwise, that is, with unrestrained self-interest, where that self-interest causes harm to others would "violate the laws of justice"[6] or be a "violation of fair play,"[7] according to Smith. This interferes with free competition just as government regulation would because the character of competition, and thus the direction of the Invisible Hand, depends on the manner in which

actors exploit or control their own self-interests. The Invisible Hand, then, that "masterminds" the free market is not like an autonomous gravitational force. It depends on the good will, decency, self-restraint, and fair play of those parties engaging in market activities.[8] When self-interests get out of hand, Smith contends, they must be regulated by laws of justice.[9]

Similarly, the current market, albeit not Smith's ideal of laissez-faire, is affected by how people operate in the market place. It does not operate autonomously. Unrestrained activities of insider traders affect competition differently than Smithian exchanges which are more or less equal exchanges between self-interested but restrained parties. The term "insider trading" implies that some traders know more than others, that information affects their decision-making and would similarly affect the trading behavior of others should they become privy to that information. Because of this, the resulting market is different than one unaffected by insider trading. This, in itself, is not a good reason to question insider trading. Henry Manne, for example, recognizes the role of insider trading in influencing the market and finds that, on balance, this is beneficial.

Insider trading, however, is not merely a complication in the free market mechanism. Insider trading, whether it is legal or illegal, affects negatively the ideal of laissez-faire of *any* market, because it thwarts the very basis of the market: competition, just as "insider" rules affect the fairness of the trader even if that activity is not illegal and even if one could, in theory, obtain inside information oneself. This is because the same information, or equal information, is not available to everyone. So competition, which depends on the availability of equal advantage by all parties is precluded. Insider trading allows the insider to indulge in greed (even though she may not) and that, by eschewing stock prices, works against the very kind of market in which insider trading might be allowed to function.

If it is true, as Manne argues, that insider trading produces a more efficient stock market because stock prices as a result of insider trading better reflect the underlying economic conditions of those companies involved in the trade, he would also have to argue that competition does not always produce the best results in the marketplace. Conversely, if competition creates the most efficient market, insider trading cannot, because competition is "regulated" by insiders. While it is not clear whether outsiders benefit more from insider trading than without that activity, equal access to information would allow (although not determine) every trader to compete from an equal advantage. Thus pure competition, a supposed goal of the free market and an aim of most persons who defend insider trading, is more nearly obtained without insider trading.

Insider trading has other ethical problems, Insider trading does not protect the privacy of information it is supposed to protect. To illustrate, let us consider a case of a friendly merger between Company X and Company Y. Suppose this merger is in the planning stages and is not to be made public even to the shareholders for a number of months. There may be good or bad reasons for this secrecy, e.g., labor problems, price of shares of acquired company, management changes, unfriendly raiders, competition in certain markets, etc. By law, management and others privy to knowledge about the possible merger cannot trade shares of either company during the negotiating period. On the other hand, if that information is "leaked" to a trader (or if she finds out by some other means), then information that might affect the merger is now in the hands of persons not part of the negotiation. The alleged privacy of information, privacy supposedly protected by insider traders, is now in the hands of not disinterested parties. While they may keep this information a secret, they had no right to it in the first place. Moreover, their possession of the information has three possible negative effects.

First, they or their clients in fact may be interested parties to the merger, e.g., labor union leaders, stockholders in competing companies, etc., the very persons for whom the information makes a difference and therefore are the objects of Company X and Y's secrecy. Second, insider trading on privileged information gives unfair advantages to these traders. Even if outsiders benefit from insider trading, they are less likely to benefit as much nor as soon as insider traders for the very reason of their lack of proximity to the

activity. Insider traders can use information to their advantage in the market, an advantage neither the management of X or Y nor other traders can enjoy. Even if the use of such information in the market makes the market more efficient, this is unfair competition since those without this information will not gain as much as those who have such knowledge. Even if insider trading does contribute to market stabilization based on information, nevertheless, one has also to justify the fact that insider traders profit more on their knowledge than outsiders, when their information becomes an actuality simply by being "first" in the trading of the stock. Do insider traders deserve this added profit because their trading creates a more propitious market share knowledge for outsiders? That is a difficult position to defend, because allowing insider trading also allows for the very Boeskyian greed that is damaging in any market.

Third, while trading X and Y on inside information may bring their share prices to the value most closely reflecting their real price-earnings ratio, this is not always the case. Such trading may reflect undue optimism or pessimism about the possible outcome of the merger, an event that has not yet occurred. So the prices of X and Y may be overvalued or undervalued on the basis of a probability, or, because insider traders seldom have all the facts, on guesswork. In these cases insider trading deliberately creates more risk in the market since the stock prices or X and Y are manipulated for not altogether solid reasons. So market efficiency, the end which allegedly justifies insider trading is not guaranteed.

What Henry Manne's defenses of insider trading do show is what Adam Smith well knew, that the market is neither independent nor self-regulatory. What traders do in the market and how they behave affects the direction and kind of restraint the market will exert on other traders. The character of the market is a product of those who operate within it, as Manne has demonstrated in his defense of insider trading. Restrained self-interest creates an approximation of a self-regulatory market, because it is that that allows self-interested individuals and companies to function as competitively as possible. In the long run the market will operate more efficiently too, because it precludes aberrations such as those exhibited by Ivan Boesky's and David Levine's behavior, behavior that created market conditions favorable to no one except themselves and their clients.

NOTES

1. George Will, "Keep Your Eye on Guiliani," *Newsweek,* March 2, 1987, p. 84.

2. See Henry Manne, *Insider Trading and the Stock Market* (The Free Press, New York, 1966), especially Chapters X and XI.

3. Adam Smith, *The Wealth of Nations,* ed. R. A. Campbell and A. S. Skinner (Oxford University Press, Oxford, 1976), I.x.c, II.v.8–12

4. *Wealth of Nations,* I.x.a.1.

5. *Wealth of Nations,* I.x.c.

6. *Wealth of Nations,* IV.ix.51.

7. Adam Smith, *The Theory of Moral Sentiments,* ed. D. D. Raphael and A. L. Macfie (Oxford University Press, Oxford, 1976), II.ii.2.1.

8. See Andrew Skinner, *A System of Social Science* (Clarendon Press, Oxford, 1979), especially pp. 237ff.

9. See, for example, *The Wealth of Nations,* II.ii.94, IV, v.16.

Critics

Deryl W. Martin
Jeffrey H. Peterson | # Insider Trading Revisited

In a recent issue, Patricia H. Werhane argued that insider trading is an unethical practice leading to an inefficiently functioning market. The support for her contention relied on her perception that insider trading proponents misinterpret Adam Smith's notion of self-interest and the Invisible Hand. We submit for your consideration, instead, that her arguments involve gross inconsistencies and conclusions not necessarily implied by Smith's model, the resolution of which addresses the very boundaries of the definition of ethical behavior and morality.

Professor Werhane started with a quote from George Will which formed the tone and structure of not only the article in question, but also the general arguments to prohibit insider trading. Will's perception of three results of insider trading is absolutely incorrect on two counts and at least misleading on the other. The contention that inside traders do not take risk is inconsistent with the author's own explanation of her third negative effect of such trading, for she implicitly admits that they do take risk: ". . . insider trading *deliberately* creates more risk in the market . . ." (emphasis added). While the author apparently was referring to increased price volatility, as opposed to certainty of eventual outcome, this too by definition is a form of risk. As the paper correctly notes, however, the event that causes such trading has not yet and may never occur. If it is possible that insiders are incorrect in their judgment, then they indeed are taking a risk in its most resolute form. If the insider has perfect or certain information, a possibility that many find most repugnant in this whole process, then the notion that such trading increases price volatility is contrary to both economic theory and a plethora of empirical research. This does not imply that all inside trading is without risk, for insiders would trade earlier in the process as absolutely correct information becomes only more probable. At the point when information becomes certain, as detailed later, the firm's stockholders

Deryl W. Martin, "Insider Trading Revisited," *Journal of Business Ethics* (1991): 57–61. Notes have been deleted. Reprinted by permission of Kluwer Academic Publishers.

have the incentive to restrict insiders' behavior. As will be demonstrated, the fortunes of the stockholders require that they restrain their own employees' greed.

Second, the author readily admits that Manne's arguments for the beneficial effects of insider trading on market efficiency are convincing (p. 842). Often overlooked, however, is that this same process actually improves the returns to individual outsiders such that they are not harmed by it and instead receive true benefit from it. To see this, consider the incentive that an individual outsider has, for example, to sell her stock when information beneficial to the firm is forthcoming. All other factors equal and without insider trading, the stock price will fluctuate through time, perhaps not moving much either up or down until company officials make the good information public. As Manne suggests would occur with inside trading, the stock price would gradually rise through time to its equilibrium higher level. Under which scenario is it more likely that an outsider would sell her stock and thus not receive the financial benefit of the good news? The answer is obvious: a stock moving up will be held while a wallowing stock would be sold. Moreover, if the insider information proves incorrect and prices fall back to their previous level, some outsiders would have benefitted by selling at intermediately higher prices. Other outsiders who held the stock would be *no worse off* than they would have been under existing law. It is ironic that the person most at risk during this process is the insider herself. Thus, it is irrational to conclude that outsiders are harmed by the process, and equally irrational to use such arguments to prohibit insider trading on ethical grounds.

Finally, the implication of George Will's comment is that wealth is created only for the insider. As the foregoing paragraph demonstrates, this is misleading because wealth is indeed created, but for both insiders and outsiders. Insider trading accelerates the intertemporal realization of stock price changes, thus leading to quicker resolution of wealth transfers. This speed of market adjustment is the benefit which Manne primarily addressed.

The argument was also made that inside trading interferes with efficient market functioning. While it

may be true that insider trading does not always "bring their share prices to the value most closely reflecting their real price-earnings ratio" as the author suggests (p. 844), it is equally obvious that prohibiting insider trading *necessarily* prevents the true market price from being discovered. The market can never be made less efficient by the inclusion of more information.

Prohibiting insider trading on some vague notion of egalitarianism or equity implies that the insider receives *excess* benefits (above and beyond that to which she is entitled) simply by virtue of having access to information that others do not. If insider trading were legal, this viewpoint ignores the fact that the competitive labor market for executive services would adjust explicit compensation downward. For reasons given below, a firm should not hire executives and give them *carte blanche* to trade the firm's securities at will, but let us suppose they did. The firm could afford to pay the executive less salary precisely because the executive would take it! The lost salary could supposedly be made up by trading on inside information. In addition to outsiders, then, the other net beneficiary of such a system would be consumers in general because a lower price for the product or service would result.

Despite the above arguments, we cannot conclude that insider trading is totally without pitfalls. In acting on behalf of the stockholders, corporate executives and other insiders face a multitude of situations in which their own interests conflict with those of their constituents. The corporate arena is indeed fertile ground for unethical behavior. It is imperative to recognize though that the incentive structure is already in place to resolve such conflicts, if left to its own devices. For example, suppose a corporate insider is working in her office and hears an explosion, runs to the window, and sees the firm's largest production facility nextdoor ablaze. The unethical insider, if legal, might call her broker to short-sell the company stock, possibly even before calling the fire department! At the limit, the grossly unethical executive might even delay the second phone call or rationalize that someone else has already reported the incident and never make the call. Who is harmed by such activity? Of course, the firm's shareholders would be incensed and rightfully so. The collective shareholders of a firm can and should place limits on the trading (and other) activity of the firm's executives simply because it is in their economic best interest to do so. In this regard, Professor Werhane's description of how the firm's property right concerning the dissemination of inside information is violated (p. 844) only emphasizes the necessity of increased shareholder control of managerial behavior. In that scenario, corporate officials treated information, and its dissemination, as their domain instead of the property of the firm.

Often forgotten in such a scenario is that the shareholders have the incentive to restrict insider behavior for more than just the obvious reason, an oversight which pinpoints Professor Werhane's misinterpretation of Adam Smith. Shareholders of the firm must (and do) bear in mind that in addition to their immediate financial loss, public opinion may further compound their troubles over time. Much better than regulation, a free press will ferret out the miscreant's behavior, make it known, and thereby possibly create consumer boycotts of the firm, lawsuits, and the like. To the extent consumers find the executive's behavior unacceptable, the firm is commensurately pushed toward bankruptcy. In turn, the threat of bankruptcy serves to restrain managerial behavior. To this same extent, all stockholders of the firm, purely in their own self-interest, have the incentive to restrict insider behavior so as to maximize the present value of all the firm's future potential. That this incentive exists is obvious when the inside information becomes certain, as in the case above. One must remember though that what happens in the extreme, happens to some degree at some degree of the extreme. Given the litigiousness of our society, a not altogether bad characteristic, shareholders have the incentive to restrict executive behavior even when insiders receive only increasingly certain information.

This right of free and voluntary contracting between and among individuals and groups (as between shareholders and executives) *without fraud or coercion* is what Adam Smith envisioned in his use of the term "free market". The prescription by Smith that we must prohibit the "violation of fair play" pertains only to sanctions against outright fraud, and that the *government* should erect no barriers to entry for any business, that is, that "nobody can keep competitors out by force of law". Despite myriad legal restrictions and remedies concerning fraud, we have been unable to prevent the government from prohibiting the existence, much less the participation, of several business enterprises. As an example of the correct interpretation, Adam Smith would applaud the fact that until recently IBM had a virtual monopoly in the computer industry. The reason is simply because IBM was the most efficient producer, as determined by the marketplace, and was able to maintain that position without resorting to fraud or coercion.

Where then should society draw the line concerning what is ethical, what is not, what to allow, and what to prohibit? When economic arguments fail, should ethical concerns be sufficient to make a particular act illegal? The arguments surrounding the existing prohibition of insider trading have primarily centered on ethical pleadings by its proponents and economic defenses by its detractors. To be thorough, that is, to be ethical, we must examine the economics and ethics of prohibition itself. Professor Werhane has attempted the former. Her misinterpretation of Smith sheds light on the latter. In other words, and despite the fact that ethical behavior is a very subjective construct, we cannot exclude the possibility that *prohibiting* insider trading itself is patently unethical.

Information is an asset that has real economic value. Existing law renders that asset unmarketable, and prevents the information's owners (stockholders) from utilizing that resource. The value of that asset is lost forever, a deprivation from which no one benefits. The fact that information is private property is not altered by negligent stockholders squandering its value by permitting leaks. Again, the only rational conclusion concerning information leaks is that stockholders have failed to preserve the value of their own property. Being stupid or myopic is not illegal or unethical. Expropriating value from shareholders via prohibition, however, is both senseless and immoral.

In addition to voiding the firm's property right concerning information, disallowing insider trading essentially expropriates wealth from outsiders and gives it to shareholders. By force of law, shareholders are not held accountable for controlling agents acting on their behalf. Voiding their responsibility transfers wealth away from consumers, via higher prices for goods and services and increased taxes, and makes insiders the scapegoats when caught in the act. These higher prices translate into higher profits which ultimately accrue to stockholders. This effect is in addition to the reduced costs that stockholders "pay" because, by law, they do not have to exhaust time and assets monitoring their own agents.

Corporate executives also receive their share of this wealth transfer. As stated earlier, their salaries are higher because they cannot trade on inside information. Thus, a much larger portion (approaching 100%) of their total remuneration is risk-free. To the extent that higher corporate profitability also results, executives who are paid relative to performance receive greater remuneration via stock options and other incentive bonuses. So in addition to reducing the riskiness of their income and increasing their salaries to make up for lost trading profits, prohibition of insider trading increases some executives' compensation that much more. Consumers again are injured at least twice and perhaps thrice.

While these arguments seem economic in nature, they do point out the deeper ethical considerations inherent in not allowing insider trading. Legislators listening to ethical lobbies never discuss these hidden costs borne by outsiders, perhaps because they are unaware of them. These costs, however, are real, and contrary to Professor Werhane's interpretation of Adam Smith, the market indeed autonomously (not unlike the law of gravity) adjusts for their existence.

Considering these ideas, is it any wonder that stockholders and corporate executives alike remain quiet concerning existing laws on insider trading? It is not out of a sense of altruism or fear of reprisal that insiders accept prohibition. Instead, insiders tolerate existing law because they benefit from it. In sum, nothing could be more unethical, under the guise of "protecting" consumers, than outlawing insider trading while taking money from consumers' pockets and giving it to others. These are the ethics of prohibition.

As a matter for policy consideration, whether or not the economic arguments against prohibition are valid is an ultimately testable hypothesis. There is plenty of precedent for the Securities Exchange Commission to pick a sample of firms, permit insider trading, and examine the results. A test period of this sort would be a reasonable way to validate at least the economic aspects of this problem.

All the arguments from both sides concerning the insider trading issue (and many others) suggest that we should attempt to find that lowest common denominator of ethical behavior with which all civilized persons can agree—an admittedly difficult task. When properly interpreted, Adam Smith's ideas concerning the free market provide that common ground. In brief, the principle is that all persons should be guaranteed the right to free and voluntary contract without fraud or coercion. Such a system is ultimately ethical and will hold individuals and groups responsible for their actions. Once this point of commonality is reached, any attempt to structure society further must stop. As is sometimes the case, a clear-cut course of action may not be evident. If and when such situations arise, one overriding principle invariably becomes obvious: to err on the side of individual freedom can *never* be considered unethical. How distasteful and unethical it would be to capitulate on the explanation of the events occurring in Berlin, the Soviet Union, and other Eastern Block countries at this very moment.

21

Is Marketing Human Organs Wrong?

Chadwick and Her Critics

There is a huge demand for the vital organs of human beings, one that far exceeds the supply. The supply is largely voluntary: People who would like their organs or other bodily parts to be used by others (when they themselves are dead) have various ways of making such a donation. But organ donors are vastly outnumbered by those who need transplants in order to survive or to live functioning lives. One way to increase the supply of organs would be to allow people to sell them. There is widespread resistance to the idea of a free market in bodily parts. But is there anything *wrong* with such a market? What, if anything, is wrong with selling parts of your body?

In the featured article of this chapter, Ruth Chadwick traces the philosophical concern with this moral issue back to a lecture by the famous eighteenth-century philosopher Immanuel Kant. (Kant's ideas turn up in several places in this anthology. Chapter 8, on adultery, includes a succinct account of what is perhaps Kant's main contribution to ethical theory, the idea of the categorical imperative.) Kant, whose writings in ethics often contain a high level of abstraction, was also accustomed to giving highly readable lectures on issues in applied ethics. One of those lectures concerns duties to our own bodies. In *Lectures on Ethics,* Kant writes, "A human being is not entitled to sell his limbs for money, even if he were offered ten thousand thalers for a single finger." (It is somewhat puzzling that Kant should have been interested in the question of the permissibility of selling parts of one's own body, since, prior to the advent of transplant technology, there wasn't a huge demand for body parts.

Chadwick summarizes three slightly different arguments put forward by Kant for his conclusion, and arrives at the following claim: To sell parts of one's body is to do something that is intrinsically degrading to human beings. Chadwick finds defective Kant's various reasons for this. For example, Kant claims that "we can dispose of things which have no freedom but not of a being which has free will." But this principle does not itself entail that one cannot sell parts of one's body. I may be a being with free will, but my left kidney is not a being with free will!

Chadwick also reviews a recent development of Kant's line of reasoning put forward by Rom Harré. According to Harré, it is wrong to do anything to one's body that would destroy the body's organic integrity. If lopping off limbs (for money or pleasure) would destroy the body's organic integrity, then it would be impermissible. Harré's principle would rule out selling off one's vital organs while one was still alive, but it would not rule out, say, lopping off a gangrenous limb that was threatening to spread gangrene to the rest of the body (and eventually kill it). If I can dispose of my left kidney without harming the organic integrity of my body, then it would seem that Harré should not be opposed to that. Chadwick claims that Harré's position is defective because his main principle "assumes what is at issue, viz. that there are certain ways of treating the body which must be ruled out. Clearly more needs to be said."

Chadwick's own positive argument is also inspired by Kant's moral theory, and in particular, the idea that a rational being should be treated not as a mere means (as a resource for others), but rather as an end. The idea, then, is that to sell parts of one's body is to treat one's own body as a resource, or a means. And since we, as humans, are embodied creatures, to treat our bodies as mere means is to treat our*selves* as mere means, or as a resource. Chadwick's argument can be reconstructed as follows:

P1 To sell a part of one's body is to treat one's body as a mere means (a resource).
P2 To treat a body as a mere means is to treat the one embodied in it as a mere means.
P3 It is morally wrong to treat a person (a rational free being) as a mere means.
_____
C   It is morally wrong to sell a part of one's body.

Although this seems to be the core of Chadwick's argument, she buttresses it with a couple of closely related arguments.

> Now one undesirable consequence of the selling of our own bodies is that it contributes towards a society in which the bodies of persons are regarded as resources. The action of selling one's own body contributes to the prevailing ethos of everything being for sale, everything having a price. It reinforces the ethic of the market. The seller of bodily parts encourages the purchaser to think that everything is available, for a price. Kant's remark that the seller makes himself into a thing in the purchaser's eyes is expressing this insight.

According to Chadwick, this is among the central insights in Kant's essay: that selling parts of one's body makes of oneself a mere thing, a commodity, and that is what is degrading.

Tadd's article is a direct response to Chadwick's. He marshals a number of objections, but makes two central points. First, suppose we think it permissible, possibly even noble, for someone to *donate* one of his kidneys to another person, say, in order to save the recipient's life. Tadd effectively argues for the following principle: "If to sell a part of one's body is to treat one's body as a resource, a 'mere means,' then to donate a part of one's body is to treat one's body as a resource, a 'mere means.' " If you accept that principle, and if you agree that organ donation is permissible, then you have to reject one of the premises of Chadwick's argument. Suppose we accept the Kantian principle P3 (that rational persons should not be treated as mere means) and we accept the permissibility of organ donation. Then we are forced to accept either that selling parts of our bodies is not tantamount to treating our bodies as mere means, or that treating our bodies as mere means is not tantamount to treating our*selves* as mere means.

Tadd's second main point is that selling a part of one's body does not seem, in principle, different from selling one's labor. If selling one's labor is morally permissible, then so, too, is selling a part of one's body. Tadd goes on to suggest that the real problem with selling bodily parts is that it can lead to gross exploitation of the poor and oppressed. And he notes that this is also a problem with the market in labor.

Mark Nelson does not cite Chadwick's paper but he does marshal and discuss objections to the market in bodily parts, among them the *commodification objection,* which is expressed by Chadwick and which states that there are some things that should not be bought and sold, and human organs are among those.

QUESTIONS FOR CONSIDERATION

• In thinking about Chadwick's central argument, one should first try to clarify what it is to treat something as a "mere means." And what does it mean to treat a *person* as a "mere means"? Suppose you put a dollar in an ice cream vending machine in order to purchase an ice cream cone, but just as the machine is dispensing your ice cream cone, it starts to break down. It looks as if your ice cream cone will not make it down the chute, so you give the machine a shake. Much to your satisfaction, it releases your ice-cream cone and then conks out completely. You are relieved that your dollar was not wasted and that you have your ice-cream cone. The ice cream vending machine is a mere means for dispensing ice cream. It does not have any intrinsic worth, and if it conks out after dispensing your ice cream cone, it is a pity for those standing in line behind you, but the machine's fate is not in itself of any direct concern to you. Now suppose you give an ice cream vendor a dollar for an ice cream cone, and just as he is serving you the cone, he suffers what appears to be a serious heart attack. You quickly reach over and grab the ice cream cone before it falls on the ground along with the ailing vendor, and then walk off, licking your ice cream cone, relieved that your dollar was not wasted. You don't call an ambulance or take any further interest in the ice cream vendor's fate. That is, you treat the vendor as you treated the vending machine: simply as a means for acquiring ice cream. This would clearly be wrong.

• How does this idea apply to bodily parts? Is it wrong to treat bodily parts as mere means? Consider your eyes, for example. What are they good for? Well, they are good for seeing. Suppose your eyesight starts to decline and eventually your eyes do not enable you to see anything. Suppose now that you are offered a pair of artificial eyes as replacements, and the artificial eyes will enable you to see. Would it we wrong to accept the artificial replacements without hesitation? It doesn't seem so. But does that mean you are treating your old eyes simply as a means for seeing? Probably. But is this wrong? And if it is not wrong, then would it be wrong in general to treat parts of your body simply as things that perform various useful functions for you?

• Both Tadd and Nelson compare the donation of organs with the selling of organs. Can you think of any morally relevant difference between donating and selling that could be used to allow one but forbid the other? Are there other sorts of things (or services) that it is permissible to donate but not to sell? Are sexual favors an example? Between donating and selling we have exchanging. Suppose I have two defective kidneys and you have two healthy kidneys, and you have two defective lungs and I have two healthy lungs. I could survive with one of your kidneys, and you could survive with one of my lungs. Would it be wrong for us to exchange a lung for a kidney? If it is permissible for me to donate a lung to you, and for you to donate a kidney to me, is it not also permissible for us to exchange these organs? What could be wrong with exchanging if donating is permissible?

• Now suppose I need a kidney and you need a lung, but our blood types are incompatible. We join a cooperative of organ donors each of whom is prepared to donate bodily parts to others in the cooperative on the condition that he or she receives the bodily parts he or she needs from the cooperative. Isn't this just our private exchange writ large?

• Let us imagine that I am willing to join such a cooperative, but so far there is no one in the cooperative whose organs are compatible with mine. The cooperative considers changing its rules to allow people to join who are willing to pay a hundred thousand dollars if their organs turn out to be unsuitable. (The money will be used for flying other members of the cooperative to foreign countries for transplants.)

• Imagine, finally, that there are people who do not need organs but who may be willing to be part of the cooperative in case one day they happen to need organs. They are willing to donate healthy organs now, without any present need for organs in return, but only if they are appropriately compensated for the pain and possible danger of doing so,—say, with $100,000. If this final stage is permissible, then a market in bodily parts also seems morally permissible. Is this argument successful?

FURTHER READING

Morelli, Mario. "Commerce in Organs: A Kantian Critique." *Journal of Social Philosophy* 30, no. 2 (1999): 315–24.

Ruth F. Chadwick

The Market for Bodily Parts

Kant and Duties to Oneself

A penniless Italian awaiting trial for murder has offered to donate a kidney for transplant in exchange for a defence lawyer. Maurizio Bondini, aged 25, said in a letter to newspapers he could not afford counsel and believed a state-appointed lawyer could not defend him well enough. (*Guardian,* 11 January 1988)

The practice of selling one's organs for money is now a feature of contemporary life. Is there anything wrong in this? In particular, does the seller of the organ violate a moral duty to him or herself? In *Lectures on Ethics* Kant argues that we have duties towards our own bodies, and what he says gives rise to an argument that certain trends in modern medicine are wrong because the participants are not fulfilling these duties. In this paper I want to look at whether there is any sense in this notion of duties towards our own bodies, and its implications for medical ethics in the context of organ transplants.

A. DUTIES TO THE SELF

First, we must face the problem that traditionally the idea that there are duties to oneself has caused something of a problem in moral philosophy. Several arguments have been advanced which suggest that speaking of such duties makes no sense. We need to look at whether they can be answered, and in particular, whether Kant had an answer to them.

Some would say morality arises where the interests of different people conflict. The concept of morality would not be needed, on this view, in a

From Ruth F. Chadwick, "The Market for Bodily Parts: Kant and Dutieds to Oneself," *Journal of Applied Philosophy* 6 (1989): 129–39. Some notes and text have been deleted.

world inhabited by a solitary individual. It would never get off the ground. Morality is concerned with how people treat *each other*.

For example, according to one well-known view morality arises as a response to certain features of the human condition, viz. human beings have unlimited wants and demands, but exist in a situation not only where there are limited resources but also where they themselves have limited sympathies. These limitations make them liable to regard the demands of others as being of less importance than their own. Morality is a device designed to counteract the natural tendency of human beings to selfishness, the tendency to be moved more by their own needs than by those of others.[1]

Again, let us look at sociobiological explanations of morality. What has to be explained, according to the sociobiologists, is how it comes to be that human beings are apparently capable of altruism, which is defined in their theories as behaviour that as a matter of fact benefits individuals other than the agent. If what we have been told about the struggle for the survival of the fittest is true, why have all the altruists not died out?[2]

Both these views, in their different ways, take it as obvious that there is in general no deficiency in people's capacity to pursue their own interests, and no difficulty in understanding such a phenomenon. So there would be no *point* in speaking of a duty to ourselves. There would be a point in this only if it were necessary to exhort people to pursue their own good, but as it is they are doing so anyway.

If there *is* a problem it is one of failure to pursue enlightened, or long-term, as opposed to short-term self-interest. But if we say that we *ought* to pursue our long-term, as opposed to our short-term, self-interest, this "ought" is construed, by the critics of duties to oneself, as prudential rather than moral. It still falls outside the concept of morality.

Kant is quite clear that duty to oneself is not to be confused with prudence, saying in the *Lectures on Ethics* that "The basis of such obligation is not to be found in the advantages we reap from doing our duty towards ourselves."[3] Again, he says "In fact, the principle of self-regarding duties is a very different

one, which has no connexion with our well-being or earthly happiness."[4] On the contrary,

> Not favour but self-esteem should be the principle of our duties towards ourselves. This means that our actions must be in keeping with the worth of man.[5]

Kant's line of reasoning here is echoed and clarified in the *Groundwork of the Metaphysic of Morals*, where he argues that the content of our duty is determined by the categorical imperative. In its second formulation this states that we should always act so as to treat humanity, whether in our own person or in that of another, as an end, and never as a means only.[6] It is because human beings should be treated in a certain way, that we have obligations to ourselves *qua* human beings. His emphasis is thus on the preservation of human worth, and he depends on a notion of certain acts as intrinsically degrading. If we indulge in them we lose our worth.

This view, as we shall see, is open to the objection that there is widespread disagreement as to what counts as degrading.

However, there are alternative concepts of morality which can allow for duties to oneself. For example, any view which sees morality as concerned with the flourishing of human life in general (with the possibility of expanding to show concern for other species) should be able to account for moral obligations towards ourselves. For a view which says that the object or point of morality is to promote the flourishing of human beings (however this is interpreted) can surely include the promotion of one's own flourishing.

B. SELLING THE BODY

The main argument of Kant which we need to consider concerns the impermissibility of selling the body or any part of it, which has relevance for the current trend towards traffic in bodily parts.

Kant is *Lectures on Ethics* says:

> a human being is not entitled to sell his limbs for money, even if he were offered ten thousand thalers for a single finger.[7]

What are his arguments for this view? The first is as follows:

> (a) If he were so entitled, he could sell all his limbs.[8]

This seems to be an instance of a slippery slope argument. If I can sell one part of myself, I can sell the whole (which could result in slavery, if I sold myself all at once, or in death, if I sold myself in a succession of mutilations).

Let us follow Jonathan Glover's distinction between logical and empirical versions of this type of argument, and see how they work out.[9]

In *The Guardian*, 23 November 1984, there was an article entitled "Debtors sell their kidneys to pay loans." This article described how people in Japan were selling kidneys to avoid being subjected to violence from loan sharks who were anxious to recover what was owed to them.

Now it seems clear that if I have sold one kidney, thinking it justifiable so to do, that does not commit me, logically, to thinking it justifiable to sell the other. There is a very relevant difference between selling one kidney and selling two, viz., that I can survive with only one but not with none.

Whether any empirical research has been carried out on people who have surrendered one kidney I do not know, but from the psychological point of view, if I know that I have only one kidney left, it seems likely that that fact will make me more, rather than less, anxious over the fate of the other one.

So if I can sell one part of myself it does not at all follow that I can legitimately sell all of myself, or that I am likely to.

However, Kant has further considerations to adduce.

> (b) We can dispose of things which have no freedom but not of a being which has free will.[10]

The reason why it is wrong, according to Kant, to sell oneself, even a part of oneself, is that we are beings which have free will, and beings of this sort are not to be sold.

What exactly is the objection here? There are various possibilities.

(i) The objection might be that in selling myself I make it impossible to exercise my freedom in future. Thus one objection to the exercise of a free choice to sell oneself into slavery is that such a choice would close the door on future freedom of choice. But does selling a finger have the objectionable consequences that it leads to a loss of freedom? It is difficult to see how it could have such catastrophic consequences.

(ii) Kant elaborates upon his argument:

> A man who sells himself makes of himself a thing and, as he has jettisoned his person, it is open to anyone to deal with him as he pleases.[11]

In selling myself I make of myself a thing. Once I have placed myself in a position where I can be bought and sold then people can treat me as an object.

But does it follow from the selling of a finger that I can be treated in any way anyone happens to feel like treating me? Kant may be relying implicitly here on an argument, not merely that if I can sell a part I *can* sell the whole (shown to be implausible in (a) above), but that if I sell a part I *do* sell the whole. If so, this argument is equally implausible: the conclusion simply does not follow.

(iii) Kant seems ultimately, however, to invoke a notion of what is intrinsically degrading to human beings. What he seems to be saying is that human beings, having free will, are simply not the sorts of things that should be bought and sold, and if you offer any part of yourself for sale then you have made yourself into an object for other people's pleasure.

Kant unfortunately has not explained here why we should accept that to sell one's finger is intrinsically degrading. For example, is it any more degrading than selling one's labour in menial employment?

> (c) Kant has a further argument for the impermissibility of selling one's body.
> He says, in "Duties towards the body in respect of sexual impulse"

> Man cannot dispose over himself because he is not a thing; he is not his own property; to say that he is would be self-contradictory; for in so far as he is a

person he is a Subject in whom the ownership of things can be vested, and if he were his own property, he would be a thing over which he could have ownership. But a person cannot be a property and so cannot be a thing which can be owned, for it is impossible to be a person and a thing, the proprietor and the property. Accordingly a man is not at his own disposal. He is not entitled to sell a limb, not even one of his own teeth.[12]

The argument is that the would-be seller is involved in a contradiction. But Kant himself is not consistent in the use he makes of this type of argument. For in *The Doctrine of Virtue* at 417 he says that there is the following possible objection to duties to oneself:

If the obligating I is taken in the same sense as the obligated I, the concept of duty to oneself contains a contradiction. For the concept of duty contains the notion of being passively necessitated (I am obligated). But if the duty is a duty to myself, I conceive myself as obligating and so as actively necessitating . . . hence a contradiction.[13]

He goes on to assert that *nevertheless* man has duties to himself. It seems open to the would-be seller of a kidney to retort as follows: if a man can both owe and be owed a duty to himself, why cannot he be both owner and property?

The difference between the two cases must rest, not on the existence or non-existence of a contradiction, but elsewhere. Kant needs to find other reasons for saying that one is not "entitled" to sell a limb.

He claims that "a man is not at his own disposal." But this itself contradicts what he says elsewhere. He is prepared to admit that in some circumstances we do have rights of disposal over our own bodies. In the Lecture "Suicide," Kant says,

We may treat our body as we please, provided our motives are those of self-preservation. If, for instance, his foot is a hindrance to life, a man might have it amputated. To preserve his person he has the right of disposal over his body.[14]

But if I can have my foot amputated to save my life, why not sell my kidney to pacify the loan sharks from whom I am in fear for my life? After all, it may

be from motives of self-preservation that I feel the need to sell a part of myself.

For Kant, it seems, if the disposal amounts to a selling, it is ruled out, because of the arguments outlined above. But the arguments, as we have seen, do not provide the support he needs for his claims.

C. ROM HARRÉ:
THE ARGUMENT REVISED

In an article in *Cogito,* Rom Harré has attacked Kant's arguments and argued for an alternative way of looking at obligations towards the body. Harré proceeds to look at the similarities and differences between things and bodies. He starts from the premiss that in general the owner of a thing owns its parts and has rights of transfer of ownership. However, even in the case of things, such as works of art or classic cars, these rights are limited. In the case of such objects Harré argues that they are limited by the value of artistic integrity. However, when one tears out illuminations from a manuscript, Harré argues, one does not only an aesthetic but a moral wrong, partly because such an act deprives other persons of the possibility of seeing them.[15]

In the case of one's body, there is an organic, rather than an aesthetic value. If rights of disposal were not restricted then the organic value of the maintenance of life would be under threat. This is a moral point because the maintenance of life is necessary for the survival of persons.

So Harré suggests a tightened up version of Kant's argument.

If to be this person is to be embodied in this body then the maintenance of the body's organic integrity boils down to a defence of the person.[16]

However, if we are talking about the maintenance of life, then Kant's view, that one cannot dispose of even a finger, is too extreme, because such a disposal does not put the life of the person at risk. I take Harré here to mean that even if the disposal includes selling the finger, it need not be ruled out.

Harré adds the proviso that any disposal of a bodily part should lead to its being put to a "proper" use;

i.e. "a fate commensurate to the dignity and moral standing of the person from which it came."[17] So Harré, like Kant, seems ultimately to need some concept of what is intrinsically fitting to human beings.

One of the consequences of both Kant's and Harré's views appears to be that we do not have obligations to the body as such. For it turns out that we have obligations to the body only in order to serve the interests of the person whose body it is.

Harré would like to go further, for this account, he says, fails to meet the need for an account of the kind of talk that goes on in Fitness Clubs and magazines, where the body is spoken of as if it had moral claims in itself. Harré thinks that "the force of this talk seems to depend on the trick of personifying the body, on treating it as other than oneself, with its own moral qualities."[18] Harré wants to look at whether there is anything in this.

His suggestion is that there is one category of organic being to which we have accepted an obligation despite their non-personhood, and that is pets. He suggests that the human body is to be seen as a pet with a permanent live-in master or mistress.

Rather than solving anything, this account seems to introduce more difficulties. For one thing, it is not at all clear why I should regard my own body in the same way that I regard a distinct entity, a pet. The way in which we own our pets seems quite unlike our relationship to our own bodies. Harré's only argument in support of this account is that here we have a category of organic non-persons to whom we have obligations. But there must surely be different considerations pertaining to whether it is justifiable to sell a pet from those which arise in considering whether I can sell my own body. Harré's view fails to take into account the fact that a pet dog, for example, is a sentient being with a consciousness of its own. Further, as Harré himself admits, looking at the issue in this way does seem to involve a reintroduction of Cartesian dualism, the problem we mentioned in section A.2.

Harré also, however, does not want to be committed to saying that our obligations to our bodies reduce to our obligations to ourselves *qua* persons; he thinks this conclusion 'dull'. But in fact if we are forced to adopt that conclusion it is far from dull,

because there are still very difficult and interesting questions about how our obligations to ourselves as persons affect what we may do to our bodies.

Both Kant and Harré think that there are restrictions here: they both have two principles which are similar but different. Let us express Kant's first principle as follows:

It is necessary, but not a sufficient, condition of a right of disposal of a bodily part that it is done from the motive of self-preservation.

We may compare Harré's position, interpreting it in the following way:

It is a necessary, but not a sufficient, condition, of a right of disposal over a bodily part that it does not actually undercut the maintenance of the body's organic integrity.

These are not sufficient conditions because both Kant and Harré think that we have to add a proviso to the effect that there are certain modes of treatment of the body which are incompatible with the dignity of human beings. Though they share this second principle they come to different conclusions in practice, Harré thinking the selling of a tooth may be acceptable, Kant wanting to go further and rule even this out.

The first principle, the necessary condition that any disposal must be compatible with the preservation of life, will be too strong for anyone who wants to admit the possibility that suicide is justifiable in some circumstances, e.g. when there is no likelihood of future flourishing for a human being.[19]

The second principle is unhelpful because it leads Kant and Harré to different conclusions. There is little agreement on what is intrinsically degrading, and the principle assumes what is at issue, viz. that there are certain ways of treating the body which must be ruled out. Clearly more needs to be said.

D. DISPOSING OF BODILY PARTS

While Kant wants to rule out the selling of a bodily part, could he approve of the *donation* of a bodily part, e.g. the donation of a kidney to a sibling? His principle that any disposal must be carried out from the motive of self-preservation seems to exclude this possibility. But if we compare this with the first principles of Kant's moral philosophy, this is not what we would expect. If one may have a kidney removed in order to preserve one's own life, but not to preserve the life of another, this seems to introduce a partiality which is inimical to Kant's view of ethics.

There are two possible sources of difficulty here. First, it may be the case that Kant does not deal with this aspect of the issue because he is thinking only of how one may treat one's own body, and one's duties to it, and it alone. But second, he simply did not have the possibility of organ transplants to think about.

But having clarified that limitation, we still need to know whether there are good reasons, as he thought, for ruling out the selling of bodily parts.

Individual and Collective Ownership

A large part of the problem turns on the question of the sense in which one can be said to "own" one's body. Kant's view seems to be that this body is not "mine," it is me. But there is a sense in which it is clearly mine as opposed to anyone else's (ignoring, for present purposes, problems about personal identity), and even Kant recognises some rights of disposal, which as Harré points out usually go with the concept of ownership.

In the individualistic market-oriented society in which we live, ownership of the body may perhaps naturally be thought of in terms of rights to buy and sell. It is therefore not surprising that the idea of trafficking in bodily parts is becoming more common.

Some writers have suggested that we should, instead, think more in terms of collective ownership of bodies, at least after death.[20] For example, the proposal that there should be an "opting out" scheme for kidney donations, rather than an "opting in" scheme, rests on the assumption that we should presume that people's kidneys may be used to help others unless the "owner" registers an objection, rather than the other way round. This proposal has as yet not really caught on.[21]

Some people may fear the extension of this idea and the development of a society where schemes such as John Harris's "survival lottery" might become a reality.[22]

At one extreme we have an individualistic account that holds that we have complete rights of disposal over our own bodies, which includes the freedom to sell them. At the other we have a collectivist account which takes away our freedom to deny the use of our bodies by others when they are needed for the pursuit of social goals.

Although these two accounts seem to be at different extremes, they actually have a lot in common. That is, they both view the human body as a set of resources, to be exploited either by the individual "owner" or by the collective.

This may be because our concept of ownership, as Harré points out, is very much interpreted in terms of rights of transfer. We are so used to thinking in terms of the institution of private property that we think of ownership of our bodies in the same way. But this is a mistake, because there are clear differences between our bodies and possessions such as tables and chairs. If we abolished the institution of private property we should still, in some sense, own our bodies. If we recall Strawson's arguments in *Individuals,* in order to have a concept of myself as an individual person I have to be able to distinguish between my body and those of others.[23]

This body belongs to me *if* to anyone (for present purposes I shall ignore problems of personal identity and bodily transfer). So I may think that if anyone has the right to sell its parts, then I do. But that issue is not settled by saying it is mine, because that depends on seeing ownership of the body in terms of the institution of property, which it is not clear we should do.

So what is the way forward? Our bodies are, as Kant pointed out, the embodiment of persons. A significant thing about persons is that they have desires, feelings and interests. In general people do not like to be treated as objects. There is plenty of evidence for this, e.g. in women's attitudes to being regarded as sex objects. It is difficult if not impossible for people to flourish when they feel they are treated as just bodies or objects.[24]

For Kant, the realisation that one thinks that one should oneself be treated as an end, and not as a means, led via the application of universalisation to the conclusion that all rational beings should be treated as ends.

Now one undesirable consequence of the selling of our own bodies is that it contributes towards a society in which the bodies of persons are regarded as resources. The action of selling one's own body contributes to the prevailing ethos of everything being for sale, everything having a price. It reinforces the ethic of the market. The seller of bodily parts encourages the purchaser to think that everything is available, for a price. Kant's remark that the seller makes himself into a thing in the purchaser's eyes is expressing this insight. The potential effects on the purchaser may be as undesirable as the effects on the seller.

The above considerations provide reasons for the view that it is morally undesirable for people to sell their organs. But the following objections may be raised.

(1) What if someone actually wants to sell their organs? If the purchaser is acting in accordance with the seller's desire, how is the seller treated as an object? For the autonomous wish of the seller is surely then being respected. What of the person who is in that position where he or she feels there is no alternative, such as the accused in Italy or the debtor in Japan?

The answer to this is that what are really objectionable are the social conditions in which these sorts of situation arise. For it is not comfortably off people who sell their organs, engaging in an undertaking which involves non-negligible risk to health and life. It is people who find themselves in situations where they cannot flourish, and where the sale of an organ appears to be a way out. For the seller at the time it may be the lesser of two evils, but any such selling reinforces the social conditions in which people are forced by economic necessity into this type of transaction. This provides a reason for opposing it.

(2) It might be objected that any commercial transaction reinforces the market ethic and is therefore, on this argument, to be avoided. But not every transaction for buying and selling has as its object a person or part of a person, nor does it involve the threat to life and health mentioned above. (It might be said that some forms of selling one's body are difficult to dis-

tinguish from selling one's labour, and that needs to be worked out, but here I want to confine my attention to actually selling parts of one's body.)

(3) It might be suggested that there is a distinction to be made between the disposal of a renewable part of one's body, such as blood, and a non-renewable one, such as a kidney. Would selling renewable ones avoid the above difficulties?

This is too simple. Richard Titmuss, in his book *The Gift Relationship,* argued for voluntary blood donation rather than a system of paid donors, partly on health grounds, but also on the grounds that once the market ethic pervades that relationship it will have dire consequences for society's values as a whole. At the time he wrote he thought there was a correlation between the values of the voluntary blood donor system in Britain and those of the National Health Service. With the undermining of the latter in the late 1980s, and the consequent dangers of creeping commercialism, it is even more important to uphold donation as opposed to selling.[25]

E. CONCLUSIONS

It might be thought that the account I have given here gets away from the idea of duties to oneself, because I have spoken in terms of consequences for human society as a whole.

This is not, however, incompatible with the view that it makes sense to speak in terms of a duty to oneself. Whereas Kant has spoken of what is intrinsically degrading (as has Harré), I have spoken in terms of the conditions in which people can flourish. If I have a duty to promote the flourishing of human beings in general, then I have a duty to promote my own, as a member of the class of human beings.

Of course, the point that I am a *member* is significant. I am one person among others. My duty to promote my own flourishing will not always take priority, but on my view it at least makes sense to speak of a duty, other things being equal, not to sell my organs, if to sell would contribute to the diminishing likelihood of my own flourishing. What is it to flourish? It seems clear, at least, that you do not flourish if you feel undervalued and used by others. If to refuse to sell one's organs would help to avoid such an outcome, one has a duty, other things being equal, to do so.

That, however, is not the whole story. It is not simply a question of the duty of the individual, when deciding to sell or not to sell. We have to consider the social context in which such decisions are made. If we have a situation in which poor Third World people sell organs to the West, or where individuals in capitalist societies sell organs to extricate themselves from debt, we need to ask to what extent individuals are free to make a choice, and to what extent the values of the market are overriding other values, to the detriment of all.

Thus if contracts for the sale of organs are undesirable from a moral point of view, it may not be enough to suggest, for example, that they be unenforceable or illegal: the underlying economic forces and the values on which they rest need to be exposed and questioned, to see to what extent they provide the conditions in which people can flourish and act to promote their own flourishing.

NOTES

1. See, e.g., J. L. Mackie (1977) *Ethics: Inventing Right and Wrong* (Harmondsworth, Penguin), Ch. 5.

2. See Peter Singer (1981) *The Expanding Circle* (Oxford, Oxford University Press), esp. Ch. 1.

3. I. Kant (1963) *Lectures on Ethics* (translated by Louis Infield) (New York, Harper & Row), p. 121.

4. Ibid., p. 117.

5. Ibid., p. 124.

6. I. Kant (1948) *Groundwork of the Metaphysic of Morals* (translated by H. J. Paton as *The Moral Law*) (London, Hutchinson), p. 91.

7. Kant, *Lectures on Ethics,* p. 124.

8. Ibid.

9. Jonathan Glover (1977) *Causing Death and Saving Lives* (Harmondsworth, Penguin). Glover calls the argument he discusses the wedge argument.

10. Kant, *Lectures on Ethics,* p. 124.

11. Ibid.

12. Ibid., p. 165.

13. I. Kant (1964) *The Doctrine of Virtue* (Part II of The Metaphysic of Morals) (translated by Mary J. Gregor) (Philadelphia, PA, University of Pennsylvania Press), p. 79.

14. Kant, *Lectures on Ethics,* p. 149.

15. Rom Harre (1987) Body obligations, *Cogito,* 1, pp. 15–19.

16. Ibid., p. 16.

17. Ibid.

18. Ibid., p. 18.

19. To discuss suicide in detail would take us too far from our present concerns. Kant does of course have objections to suicide, e.g. that the suicide is involved in a self-contradiction, but I would argue that this argument is no more successful than the attempt to show that the position of the seller of bodily parts is self-contradictory.

20. Harré actually discusses the possibility of collective ownership of the bodies also of living people, in the context of surrogate motherhood.

21. R. A. Sells (1979) Let's not opt out: kidney donation and transplantation, *Journal of Medical Ethics,* 5.

22. John Harris (1975) The survival lottery, *Philosophy,* 50, pp. 81–87.

23. P. F. Strawson (1959) *Individuals* (London, Methuen), Ch. 3.

24. This argument is of course open to what might be called the 'contented slave' objection, that some people do not feel unhappy about what others might regard as exploitation, e.g. slavery, treating people as sex objects. But I shall not discuss that, or the standard 'false consciousness' reply, here.

25. Richard G. Titmuss (1970) *The Gift Relationship: from human blood to social policy* (London, Allen & Unwin).

Critics

G. V. Tadd

The Market for Bodily Parts

A Response to Ruth Chadwick

EXPLOITATION

Ruth Chadwick rightly blames adverse social conditions for the encouragement of the sale of bodily organs by the poor and needy.

She adds:

> it might be said that some forms of selling one's body are difficult to distinguish from selling one's labour ... [1]

It therefore seems reasonable to conclude that if relevant distinctions cannot be drawn between the two acts, then the recent legislation which professes to alleviate the exploitation of the poor, fails to attain this objective to any significant degree and furthermore risks the accusation that it represents little more than a "window dressing" exercise which merely discriminates against some forms of exploitation, whilst conveniently ignoring other, far more widespread forms.

It is acknowledged that if this anomaly is accepted, then this does not necessarily indicate that the Bill should not have been passed, but it does point to a need for a close scrutiny of the possible effects of this legislation.

Few would disagree that throughout the world there are countless numbers of workers who experience extreme privation and exploitation at the hands of their employers every day of their working lives. From the tin mines of Bolivia to the tea plantations of India, both adults and children can be found toiling, sometimes in the most appalling conditions, to earn in the space of a year, what a worker in a Western country would earn in a week.

The fact that these people, sometimes whole families, sell their labour under such adverse conditions is beyond dispute. In the developed world this circumstance has not only been known for many years but also to a large extent condoned.

In this situation it seems reasonable to question why there should be such a furore over the sale of bodily parts. Is it really so much worse a form of exploitation than others? Indeed, is there any fundamental moral difference between the two forms of exploitation? In what way might selling one's kidney be viewed as being substantially morally different from selling one's labour?

One claim that might be advanced, is that by dispensing with a kidney, one is faced with an increased risk from ill health, especially if renal disease should strike.

However, the working conditions that many Third World manual labourers have to suffer are equally detrimental to health. Sweat-shop conditions often prevail in these countries and legislation such as The Health and Safety at Work Act is non-existent. Moreover these adverse conditions have to be experienced from childhood to old age, not simply from the time that someone decides to dispense with an organ.

There is an additional factor also, in that these workers have no choice in the matter: they must either work or starve. It is not within their power to improve their working conditions. All they can do is to accept them.

By contrast, the paid organ donor does have some kind of choice, albeit a limited one. No matter what the pressures or the temptations that are put before him, he does have the opportunity to refuse the offer.

G. V. Tadd, "The Market for Bodily Parts: A Response to Ruth Chadwick," *Journal of Applied Philosophy* (1991): 95–102. Reprinted by permission of Blackwell Publishing Ltd.

In some countries the sale of blood for the Transfusion Services is sanctioned, as is the sale of hair for wig-making. These items, unlike kidneys, are capable of being replenished. It might be argued that they should be viewed as temporary loans or as a "hiring" of bodily parts rather than permanent donations and therefore be seen as being more morally acceptable.

The "hire" of one's labour might be similarly regarded, as it too might be seen as a temporary loan of muscle power and energy for a set period of each working day.

However the issue is one of possible exploitation, and it seems of little relevance whether one suffers exploitation on a temporary basis or on a permanent one. An individual who sold a kidney to raise money and then later found that a winning lottery ticket provided him with both the money and the opportunity to "recover" a kidney would be in the position of being able to modify a "permanent" disposal of a bodily organ to that of a temporary "loan." The morality of this situation would surely not depend on whether or not the loss was transient.

If exploitation is responsible, either for the permanent abuse of a body, or the disposal of any of its component parts, then it must be equally wrong if it compels individuals to suffer corporal abuse or disposal of bodily parts on a temporary basis.

It would thus seem that the hiring of labour and the "hiring" of bodily parts are both just as susceptible to being subject to coercive practices as the sale of bodily organs on a permanent basis.

MOTIVES FOR SELLING

The principle of payment for the use of bodily organs is not without precedent. For instance, medical students and other individuals are invited to act as volunteers for the testing of new drugs. The very necessity that human guinea pigs are required, points to the fact that uncertainty exists concerning the safety of these drugs on the human body. If it is accepted as reasonable for individuals to "loan" their bodies for the purpose of drug experiments and receive payment for the potential risks incurred, then why should not the same acceptance be extended to those wishing to sell or loan bodily organs?

It is acknowledged that some who volunteer do so from purely altruistic motives, but one cannot say that all are prompted by such reasons. It is sometimes claimed, that to deter needy, potential volunteers from being enticed by large amounts of money, only modest cash payments are made in such transactions.

However, the amount of money paid is surely irrelevant. If this is not the case then there is a danger of an absurd situation developing whereby the payment of a meagre financial sum to a poor peasant for a kidney might be considered less morally reprehensible than the payment of a generous sum.

The issue at stake rests not upon the size of the financial inducement but rather upon the autonomy of the individual. Drug experimentation is accepted in this country because it is needed and it is clear that the individuals participating are rational beings who have considered the risks entailed and have freely chosen to be party to the transaction.

In the same way, in North America some women receive financial compensation for the hire of their uterus for the purpose of commercial surrogacy arrangements. And whilst surrogacy on a commercial basis is prohibited in the UK, the Warnock committee did not envisage that private persons entering into surrogacy arrangements should be liable to criminal prosecution.[2]

It is clear that the Warnock committee were certainly troubled by fears of possible exploitation, if large sums of money were to be involved, as they undoubtedly would be in cases of commercial surrogacy.[3]

There seems to be something of an irony in the fact that so much discourse has centred on the possible exploitation of individuals for large sums of money, in areas such as surrogacy, drug testing and the sale of bodily parts, when in contrast there has been comparatively little concern displayed regarding the exploitation of the sale of the labour of millions of people for relatively small sums of money.

However it does seem a truism, that once money enters some types of transactions, that it somehow reduces the intrinsic value of the contract. Why is it that the disposal of an organ in the form of a gift is a valued concept but not its sale?

Not everyone operates solely for monetary gain. Family or public approval may be a preferable option as a reward to some individuals, rather than the mere acquisition of cash. It could be argued that *x* sells his kidney, and with the proceeds purchases a new car which provides him with a status symbol to gain public approbation. By contrast *y* gives his kidney freely, thereby receiving public commendation by a more direct route.

And suppose a man of reasonable affluence decided to sell an organ and give the proceeds of the sale to the poor and destitute? Does the mere fact of a cash transaction necessarily invalidate the noble intent? If instead of Kant we look to a contemporary of his, namely Hume, then it would appear not, as evidenced by his statement:

> . . . when we praise any actions, we regard only the motives that produced them . . . [4]

The fact that one receives payment for selling one's labour or for selling one's kidney is not necessarily a moral issue; what one does with the money conceivably might be.

Certainly, the deliberate enticement of a poor individual by a rich one, to part with a kidney in exchange for money to feed his children, must be viewed as an immoral act. But equally if an individual voluntarily wishes to sell a kidney and is not being exploited in the process, then it seems that to deny him this option unnecessarily restricts his autonomy.

SACRIFICE

It could be argued that a kidney transfer, regardless of whether one is paid or not, is an act of sacrifice. One might wish to question what sacrifice entails from a moral position. Aquinas for one, was clear that sacrifices if they were to be made, should be made to God alone. He wrote:

> And therefore as it is to God alone that we ought to offer the spiritual sacrifice, so it is to him alone that we ought to offer exterior sacrifices. [5]

However Aquinas went on to discuss different types of sacrifice and concluded:

> There is another class of outward sacrifices, in which the outward acts of other virtues besides reli-

gion are taken up for reverence of God: of which acts some fall under precept, and all are bound to them; others are works of supererogation, to which not all are bound. [6]

One might take the position that freely to donate a kidney could be seen as an act of supererogation and thus likely to be a rare occurrence. Chadwick admits that the proposal for an "opting out" scheme for kidney donations has "as yet not really caught on."

Therefore at a time when the demand for bodily organs for transplantation is high and the number of organs available is relatively few, it could be argued that financial inducements to part with bodily organs would not only make the best use of the technology available but also from a utilitarian perspective maximise the welfare of the greatest number of people.

Of course the word "sacrifice" has more than one meaning. Here, it is defined in the following manner:

> The surrender or destruction of something valued or desired for the sake of something having a higher claim. [7]

If one surrenders or sacrifices a kidney voluntarily it would presumably be for the sake of something having a higher claim, namely the possible salvation of a loved one.

Equally the surrender of a kidney in exchange for financial compensation could be seen as a sacrifice for the individual who, whilst valuing an intact healthy body, places an even higher worth on the acquisition of money, possibly for the purpose of helping his or her family. Providing both instances of sacrifice are free from coercive pressures, why should distinctions be drawn between them?

Some justification is required of why the legislation in question prohibits an autonomous decision to make a paid sacrifice, whilst it gives an individual the liberty to make an unpaid one.

BODY OWNERSHIP

As Chadwick pointed out, a possible reason for preventing the sale of bodily parts may lie in the belief that we are not the owners of our bodies and therefore are not in a position to effect a sale. [8] She discusses the concept of ownership of one's body at some length and is clearly not happy with Kant's assertion that:

> Man cannot dispose over himself because he is not a thing; he is not his own property; . . . [9]

She goes on to point out that we are conditioned to thinking of ownership of the body in the same way as we think of the institution of private property, at least in terms of rights of transfer. She continues by arguing that this is a mistake because there are clear differences between our bodies and material possessions such as furniture, and the issue is not settled by seeing ownership of the body in the same way as we view private possessions.

The charge that we are so conditioned is beyond dispute. Indeed, millions of women argue forcibly, when justifying a right to terminate a pregnancy, that their claim is based on the grounds that it is "their" body to do with as they wish. Furthermore, whilst arguments exist to oppose their view there can be no denying that they voice a commonly held belief.

Body ownership might entail more than mere property ownership, but this position is in need of more elaboration before one can dismiss completely the belief, commonly held by non-philosophical members of the public, that body ownership is closely linked with property rights. The evidence of everyday life indicates that people do perceive their bodies as properties belonging to themselves. For instance, accidents which entail loss of limbs or other physical disabilities, are subject to quite specific sums of money in litigation involving compensation claims.

There is little controversial, it would appear, in a cash payment's being made to an individual for the loss of a finger as a result of an industrial accident, or indeed for damage to internal organs caused by unnecessary and undue exposure to pollutants such as asbestos or radiation. In such cases there seems to be a "common consent," that for some purposes at least, the body should be viewed as a property. And just as in some circumstances one might sue for compensation for damage caused to personal possessions, one may also sue, in the same way, for damage caused to one's body.

If the position is taken that we are, at least in some respects, the owners of our bodies, and that that claim can justify abortion, it seems incongruous that as owners of our bodies, we do not have the right to sell them, or at least parts of them. For not only do people sell their bodies in the labour market, but tragically, some are also forced to sell them in prostitution.

Conversely if we are not in ownership of our own bodies then that must not only reduce the arguments in favour of abortion, it must also question why there is a need for a doctor to obtain informed consent before operating, if the body operated upon does not "belong" to the patient.

It may well be the case that what we currently classify as "things" is in need of further definition. For even amongst the classes of non-persons, that we categorise as objects, it is clear that we draw some quite sharp distinctions.

Animation imbues objects with a personification that is missing from objects that one might collect to furnish a sitting room. Some people will talk to living, breathing, plants in a belief that such discourse might encourage more rapid growth. It is doubtful if they engage in similar conversations with their settee! Cuddly toys such as teddy bears are often cherished long after childhood has passed because they appear to possess "personalities" which take them out of the realm of being mere objects.

Thus there are different degrees in which an object can manifest its characteristics, and it is possible that a human being should be viewed as both a person, and despite Kant's protestations, an object. Perhaps the mistake is to assume that it is an all-or-nothing situation, that either one has a self and is a person, or alternatively one is an object and therefore cannot be a person.

The claim that people do not like to be treated as objects needs to be viewed with some caution. Some women (and men too) set out deliberately to be regarded as sex objects. Some models and Hollywood stars might fall into this category. Many ordinary folk quite like the idea of being the object of someone's affection. Much seems to depend on the individual's perception of the desirability of the object that they are being treated as.

MARKET ETHICS

However a more serious objection to be made concerns Chadwick's assertion that:

> ... one undesirable consequence of the selling of our own bodies is that it contributes towards a society in which the bodies of persons are regarded as resources. The action of selling one's own body contributes to the prevailing ethos of everything being for sale, everything having a price. It reinforces the ethic of the market.[10]

Since the time that primitive man bartered a goodly hen for a sack of grain the market place has flourished. Indeed without the concept of trade the world as we know it could not exist. Whether we like it or not the ethic of the market is here to stay. That is not to say that market dealings should not be conducted in a fit and proper manner.

The sale of one's labour is particularly susceptible to the pull of market forces and one might question why, at a time when scarcity prevails, transactions in bodily parts should be considered immune from such forces.

Ruth Chadwick offers a possible reason when she points out:

> ... not every transaction for buying and selling has as its object a person or part of a person, nor does it involve the threat to life and health mentioned above.[11]

Clearly not every transaction does have as an object a person or part of a person. Equally, many do, and some quite definitely involve a threat to life and health. In order for society to function smoothly there is a need for some personnel to occupy hazardous positions. Firemen, policemen, miners, soldiers and deep sea divers are but a few examples. The purchase of their labour, from the pool available in the employment market, is as vital to the existence of modern day society, as the purchase of a kidney might be to a sick individual.

Furthermore, it could be argued, at least by a proponent of rights theory, that one has a right to treat one's body as one wishes. Many people continue to smoke, imbibe excessive alcohol and indulge in other habits injurious to their body, and do so in the belief that their body belongs to them and that they therefore have a justified entitlement to treat it, or mistreat it, as they choose.

Many believe that they have a right to sell their labour and some might well ask why the right to sell organs should be denied them, providing of course they are safeguarded by a right not to be exploited.

EXPLOITATION OF UNPAID DONORS

However, it is accepted that in real life there are likely to be very few individuals who would willingly sell their organs and be free from exploitation in the process. It would be wrong to assume that individuals who donate voluntarily are always necessarily free from exploitation. Beauchamp & Childress, in their book *Principles of Biomedical Ethics,* cite a case in which the father of a five-year-old girl who was suffering from progressive renal failure stated that he did not wish to donate a kidney to his daughter. They write:

> He admitted that he did not have the courage and that particularly in view of the uncertain prognosis, ... and the degree of suffering that his daughter had already sustained, he would prefer not to donate.[12]

No one can know how many other similar cases there may have been, for such instances are concealed by the veil of confidentiality. Conversely the cases whereby parents or relatives choose to donate organs are publicised, at least within the family. But what is not publicised is the degree of voluntariness inherent in that decision.

Parenthood is an esteemed condition. The popular image of it is that parental love is so great that if necessary one makes sacrifices for one's children, even the supreme sacrifice of life itself, if the occasion arises. That image might well be an appropriate one to hold. Nevertheless, it cannot be denied that some individuals feel they cannot live up to such noble standards and given a free choice might well choose to adopt a less generous attitude to their offspring.

It could be the case, however, that group, family and social pressure combine to prevent them doing as they would wish. It could be that the fear of feelings of guilt, if they refuse to donate, is a greater dread than the risk they incur in making a donation.

If they make a donation in these circumstances, is it really possible to say that it has been done so without elements of coercion? If not, then surely these "voluntary" donors are equally in need of some form of protection.

CONCLUSION

This paper takes the position that the legislation prohibiting the sale of bodily organs is to some extent flawed in the sense that it confuses two major issues. The first issue concerns itself with the autonomy of the individual, whilst the second deals with the concept of exploitation. Some linkage is bound to occur between these two concepts, but they are not necessarily totally interdependent.

If one considers a rational individual whose autonomy is in no way impaired, it is difficult to understand why he should be allowed to make a decision to donate his kidney to another, but not to sell it. Such a restriction not only intrudes upon the doctor/patient relationship, but more sinisterly places decisions concerning an individual's rights, in relation to the treatment of his own body, in the hands of the State, rather than in his own.

It is acknowledged that comparatively few individuals are likely to be affected by this circumstance, but that is no justification for riding roughshod over the rights of a minority group.

More seriously, the legislation has obscured the issue of informed consent and denied a public debate which could have focused on a much broader canvas, exploring possible causes of exploitation which may exist, in addition to financial ones.

The issue of exploitation adversely affects the lives of a great number of people. Undoubtedly, proponents of the legislation almost certainly recognise that other far more widespread practices of exploitation exist in the world, notably those concerned with the cheap labour market. Conceivably, they might argue that they cannot change the world overnight but at least, in passing the Bill, they are tackling some potential forms of exploitation.

There is a danger however that this Bill may generate perceptions that the UK is acting in a meaningful manner to prevent the corruption and exploitation of the Third World, when in actuality it represents little more than an easily made token gesture.

It is worth pointing out that even if it is found necessary to prevent the sale of bodily organs then this end could have been secured without the implementation of the Bill. It could have been made clear in ethical guidelines or Codes of Conduct that health professionals, found guilty of condoning such transactions, would be subject to the discipline of their Regulatory Bodies and be struck off their respective professional registers, with the subsequent loss of their livelihood.

The final and most telling criticism of the legislation is that it does absolutely nothing to bring about a fundamental change in the attitudes of those doctors and Health Service Personnel who were responsible for the purchasing of kidneys from individuals existing in poverty, in order to enhance the lifestyle of those living in comparative luxury.

Such is the rate of scientific progress, one cannot foresee what may become technologically possible in the forthcoming decades and the ethical issues which may result. Legislation by itself has a limited application for the resolution of ethical dilemmas.

What is likely to be more effective is the increased provision of moral education in the training of Health Care Professionals and a more stringent recognition by those Professionals of their own Codes of Conduct.

The case put forward here is that the legislation has obscured these issues and left society with the feeling that the matter has been satisfactorily dealt with when in fact major issues have been left unaddressed.

NOTES

1. R. F. Chadwick (1989) The market for bodily parts, *Journal of Applied Philosophy,* 6, pp. 129–40.

2. M. Warnock (1985) *A Question of Life* (Oxford, Blackwell), p. 47.

3. Ibid., p. 46.

4. D. Hume *Treatise of Human Nature,* Book 111, Part 11, opening of Section 1.

5. J. Rickaby (1896) *Aquinas Ethicus: the moral teaching of St Thomas,* Vol. 11, A Translation of the Principal Portions of the Second Part of the Summa Theolog ica (London, Burns & Oates), p. 134.

6. Ibid., p. 137.

7. *Oxford English Dictionary.*

8. Chadwick, op. cit., p. 132.

9. I. Kant (1930) *Lectures on Ethics* (London, Methuen), pp. 147–148.

10. Chadwick, op. cit., p. 137.

11. Ibid., p. 137.

12. T. Beauchamp & J. Childress (1983) *Principles of Biomedical Ethics,* 2nd edn (New York, Oxford University Press), p. 285.

Mark T. Nelson | # The Morality of a Free Market for Transplant Organs

INTRODUCTION: THE SHORTAGE OF TRANSPLANT ORGANS

If you are poor and have a kidney to spare, then Count Rainer Rene Adelmann von Adelmannsfelden has a deal for you: give this German businessman your kidney and he'll give you $45,000— and then he'll resell the kidney at a higher price to someone else in need of a transplant. Although the Count has lots of interested potential buyers and sellers, he also has lots of critics; "I'm doing good," he complains, "and people are acting as if I were just a cold-hearted brutal businessman."[1] *Is* there anything brutal about this arrangement? This is the question I shall pursue in this paper.

A few decades ago, this question would have been unthinkable; now it is not only thinkable, but pressing, because of recent medical advances, such as the development of cyclosporin, which have dramatically increased the success rates of transplant operations. The success rates for kidney and cornea transplants, for example, are now as high as 95%. As a result, there are now long lists of medically needy persons waiting for suitable transplant organs, on something like a first-come, first-served basis. The American Council on Organ Transplantation estimates that some 15,000 Americans are now waiting for new kidneys alone. The fact is there simply are not enough transplant organs to go around, and many persons die before their turn comes up, or else live under years of debilitating sickness and painful treatment.

REMEDIES FOR THE SHORTAGE

What can be done to make up for this shortage of transplant organs? Three possibilities suggest themselves. The first would be to increase voluntary donation, which typically involves educating the public about the need for donated transplant organs, and making donation easier. Following the Uniform Anatomical Gift act, a signed statement suffices to make one a donor, and in 43 states, a simple checkmark in the appropriate box on a driver's license suffices. Further, some states have enacted "required request" laws, requiring physicians to ask the families of newly deceased persons to donate organs from the body of the deceased. While it is still too early to predict the effects of all these efforts, the sad fact stands that, at present, less than 20% of the 25,000 healthy persons who die unexpectedly in the U.S. each year become donors.

A second possibility would be to compel "donation" via government policy. For instance some have suggested that the government require routine "organ harvesting" from neomorts, allowing the require-

From Mark T. Nelson, "The Morality of a Free Market for Transplant Organs," *Public Affairs Quarterly* (1991): 63–79. Some notes and some parts of the text have been deleted. Reprinted by permission of North American Philosophical Publications.

ment to be overridable by the next of kin. Yet, such a policy has seemed undesirable to many, on the grounds that we do not need more governmental coercion, especially on a subject as sensitive as the human body. Even a policy of overridable harvesting has seemed undesirable because it implies that the government has at least *prima facie* rights of disposal over the bodies of its citizens—an implication which few in a liberal state are willing to accept.

The third possibility is to open up a free market for transplant organs and let transplant organs be bought and sold like any other commodity. Since there is already a precedent in the buying and selling of blood (in the U.S., e.g.), economists such as Marvin Brams have suggested that the free market be extended to transplant organs as well.

> Where the linkage of personal concern between potential donors and donees is absent or weak, potential donors apparently have to be provided with incentives other than altruism, not an unusual situation in American society. A market system can provide these incentives. (Brams 1977, p. 6)

Brams' suggestion is based on the economic wisdom that we can usually increase the public supply of something if we increase the price for that thing, so we could increase the public supply of transplant organs by paying for them in a market. Of course, such a market would have to be carefully administered via hospitals, organ banks, and the law, but in *principle* it can work, argue its defenders, and would almost certainly result in more available organs.

In fact, in Brazil and West Germany there has in recent years been just such a market for transplant organs, sometimes advertised in the classified sections of newspapers. In Brazil, for instance, corneas have been advertised for as much as $40,000 and kidneys for as much as $30,000. For the poor or even the middle class, this sort of money is attractive. A single mother might well regard it as a way of financing her child's education—indeed, as a way of escaping poverty altogether. German transplant entrepreneur Rainer Scherer asks, "Which is better: for me to give a poor guy 20,000 marks or for him and his two healthy kidneys to be thrown onto the corpse cart after he starves?" (*Newsweek,* Dec. 5, 1988, p. 38)

Given the unattractiveness of donation and coercion, this free market solution seems especially attractive.

Attractive or not the market for transplant organs is illegal in the United States. In 1984, Congress passed the National Organ Transplantation Act which prohibits the sale of transplant organs; moreover, the medical establishment in America has rejected the idea as well. Any physician or hospital participating in the transplant of a bought organ would most likely be ostracized. Yet why should this be? Why should there not be a legal market for transplant organs, if that would increase the number of transplant organs available and save lives, all through non-coercive means?

Of course, it might be argued that a free market would not increase the supply of transplant organs. Similar arguments have been made by Titmus, e.g., against the sale of blood, and could be made against the sale of transplant organs as well. Such arguments are inconclusive at best in my view, but more importantly are beside the point of the present inquiry, since the moral problems with the sale of organs might still hold even if the supply of organs were increased. So let us assume for the sake of argument that economists such as Brams are right, and that a free market for transplant organs would result in a greater public supply of the needed organs. On this assumption, what *moral* objections might there be against such a free market? . . .

THE COMMODIFICATION OBJECTION

The noun "commodification" derives from the verb "commodify" which means "treat as a commodity," as something to be bought and sold. The "commodification objection," therefore, is the claim that a free market for transplant organs would make human organs a commodity, something to be bought and sold, and that this is intrinsically morally wrong. That is, apart from the horrible side effects of their sale and apart from distributional unfairness, there is something "plain, old wrong" about buying and selling certain kinds of thing, and that human organs are just that kind of thing.

Certainly, it seems clear that there are some things which it is wrong to buy or sell even apart from the side effects of their sale. For instance, most of us are convinced that it is wrong to buy or sell living persons, and that this is not wrong just because of the bad consequences it would have. Most of us suppose that buying and selling persons would still be wrong even if it had, on balance, better consequences than did not buying and selling persons. (Indeed, such a point is the basis of a frequently made criticism of utilitarian ethical theories.)

So, the question is: Horrible side effects and distributional unfairness aside, is there anything intrinsically morally wrong with the buying and selling of transplant organs? In considering this question I shall make the following assumptions: first, that it is morally permissible to buy and sell some kinds of thing, and for there to be free markets for these things, such as food, clothing, automobiles, and televisions; second, that it is morally permissible to *donate* transplant organs. These assumptions seem intuitively correct to me and to most persons in the West these days, though certainly not to everyone. Certain radical socialists may reject the legitimacy of free markets for *anything,* and certain religious groups, such as the Jehovah's Witnesses, perhaps, might reject the legitimacy of organ *donation.* Still, these assumptions seem at least reasonable, and I will make them for the purposes of the present inquiry. Having made these assumptions, I plan to examine a list of things which we commonly think ought not to be bought and sold, i.e., things for which there *ought* not to be a free market (whether or not there is a legal sanction against such a market). I shall try to uncover the moral reasons why these things should not be bought or sold, and see if these reasons apply in the case of transplant organs, entailing that transplant organs can be donated but not bought or sold.

THINGS FOR WHICH THERE OUGHT NOT TO BE A FREE MARKET

Things of this type include:

1. Another person's property
2. Persons

3. Sex
4. Pornography
5. Votes
6. Citizenship
7. Release for punishment
8. Release from draft
9 Academic grades
10. Certain weapons, such as hand grenades and silencers.

These are things which many of us believe should not be bought or sold on a free market. Some should not be bought or sold at all; others, perhaps, may be bought and sold, but only within such limits as would fail to be a free market. Not everyone will agree that all of these things should be on this list, but most will agree that most should be. In any event, my aim in listing them is to uncover a set of principles limiting the extent of the free market. The first such principle is:

1. Selling X is wrong if X does not belong to the seller.

This plausible principle explains why it is wrong for me to sell you some third person's car (let alone the Brooklyn Bridge), but does it explain why it would be wrong for me to sell you my kidney? It would explain this only if I didn't own my kidney, but most of us think that we *do* own our bodies, including our organs—if we've thought about it at all. Still, some thinkers might argue that it would be inaccurate to describe the relation of familiarity and control that we have over our bodies as one of ownership. Moreover, some religious thinkers might argue that we *don't* own our bodies, because God does, and that this is precisely what is wrong with the sale of organs.

Even if we do not own our organs, however, this principle does not answer in the present case. That is, it does not explain why is is wrong to sell but right to donate, since if we do not own our organs, we cannot rightly give them away either. Perhaps another principle will fare better. Another principle which suggests itself is:

2. Selling X is wrong if X has "dignity"

This explains why it is wrong to sell persons. While this idea has any number of sources, it finds a clear exponent in Kant, who argued that persons have a special status or property which he called dignity. Just what dignity is, on Kant's view, is not altogether clear, but whatever it is, it seems to accrue upon those features of ours which make us persons: self-consciousness, freedom, and rationality, for example. These characteristics endow me, for example, with a status which makes it wrong for me or anyone else to sell my person. Perhaps principle (2) will explain why it is wrong for me to sell my parts, too. But does principle (2), the dignity principle, apply here?

The dignity principle applies here only if our organs can properly be said to have dignity, and this is doubtful at best. For one thing, they don't (individually, at least) possess the characteristics such as self-consciousness, rationality, and freedom, which are supposed to be the necessary conditions for dignity. For another, it does not follow that since a person has dignity, each of his parts has dignity, too, any more than it follows from a person's weighing 200 lbs that each of his parts weights 200 lbs, too.

Yet, even if our organs did have dignity, principle (2) would not answer to the present case, either, since it would rule out the donation of organs as well. Dignity is incompatible with *ownership,* not just with sale. If a person has dignity it means I cannot *own* him: I can't sell him, and I can't make a gift of him either. If organs have dignity, then the same is true of them, too.

A third principle which might prohibit the sale of organs is:

3. Selling X is wrong when X involves degrading or physically harming some specific person.

This principle explains, at least in part, why it is wrong to sell sex and pornography. In the cases of child pornography or "snuff" films, children or other persons actually had to be harmed to make the pornography. In the case of more "ordinary" pornography, the models are (arguably) degraded, and in the case of prostitution, the prostitute himself or herself is degraded. Can principle (3) be extended to cover the sale of organs? Does the transfer of a transplant organ physically harm or degrade some specific person? Clearly, the removal of an organ does no physi-

cal harm to a posthumous source, and while risky, it is not necessarily harmful to a living source. Again, the transfer of an organ to a needy recipient is still somewhat risky, but is not necessarily a harm. Moreover, it is hard to see how the removal of an organ degrades its source or its recipient, where degrade means "treat as an inferior, or sully." Instead of degrading them, the transfer would, if anything, enhance the recipient and ennoble the donor.

More importantly, even if the transfer of an organ were physically harmful or degrading to some specific person in a way which made it wrong to sell a transplant organ, then presumably this would be enough to make donation wrong as well. In sum, principle (3), concerning the harm or degradation of specific persons won't do the trick either.

Perhaps, however, (3) is only a partial explanation of what is wrong with the sale of sex and pornography. Principle (3) focusses on harmful consequences to specific persons, but perhaps it is worth considering the general, social effects of such sales. That is, some might argue that prostitution is still wrong, even when it does not involve physical harm or degradation to either party, because it weakens certain crucially important institutions, notably marriage. It might be suggested, for instance, that marriage is built in part on sexual need, but that the commitment marriage requires is crucial for a stable society. Prostitution, then, is a way of getting sex without any commitment, which weakens the incentive for marriage, which in turn is bad for society overall. All of this suggests another principle prohibiting the sale of certain things:

4. Selling X is wrong if the sale of X weakens some crucially important social institution.

Not everyone will agree that (4) is plausible, that (4) adequately explains what is wrong with selling sex outside of marriage, that prostitution weakens marriage, or that marriage is a crucially important social institution. Yet, even if we do agree, the question remains, does (4) apply in the case of organ sales?

It seems unlikely that (4) does apply, since it seems unlikely that the sale of transplant organs weakens any crucially important institution. It is difficult even to think of a near equivalent to, say, marriage in this case. Monogamous organ swapping? The institution that first comes to mind is, perhaps, the medical profession, but it is hard to see how the sale of organs would weaken that institution. Indeed, if the aim of the medical profession is healing, and organ sales would increase the number of persons who are healed, then organ sales would presumably strengthen that institution.

Still, perhaps there is another crucially important institution (broadly speaking) which *would* be weakened by the sale of organs, namely the institution of altruism. Perhaps the sale of organs would tend to discourage altruistic donations in favor of self-interested sales. It is not at all obvious, however, that this would be the consequence of a market for transplant organs. Altruistic donation would still be possible in such a market; indeed, it would be endowed with greater significance, since it would involve foregoing financial rewards. Moreover, even if the organ market did discourage one kind of altruistic behavior, it might encourage a new kind of altruistic behavior: the altruism of a middle-class person selling an organ in order to give the proceeds to a needy cause.

Finally, it should be noted that, as far as altruism is concerned, (4) would apply to all sales. Everything which can be sold can also be given away altruistically, but this is not ordinarily taken to be a reason for prohibiting all sales whatsoever, so principle (4) would not explain why it was permissible to sell food and clothing but not organs. Apparently we need to look further.

Continuing our examination of prohibitions against the sale of sex, we find another promising principle. It might be suggested that selling sex is wrong because sex is an intimate thing, and that the selling of it is inconsonant with its intimacy. This would partly explain why selling sex outside of marriage is wrong (as in prostitution), but it would also explain why the sale of sex *inside* marriage is wrong as well. Let us consider then

5. Selling X is wrong if X is an "intimate" thing.

Principle (5) applies in the case of transplant organs only if there is something about organ transplantation which is intimate. Three possibilities suggest themselves: the organ, the personal relations between the source and the recipient of the organ, and the act of transfer. Are any of these things necessarily intimate in the relevant sense? Consider the organ itself first. It is no doubt true that I enjoy an especially close relation with my own liver, which makes it "intimate" in some way or other. Yet it is not enough that my liver and I are intimate in some way or other. If principle (5) is to be plausible and apply here, our organs need to be intimate in the same way that sex is intimate. But are they? Intimacy is a fairly vague notion, but whatever it means (in the relevant sense), it can only be predicated of activities or relations between conscious and mutually aware agents, or of certain aspects of things in relation to conscious and mutually aware agents. If this is so, then it would seem that my liver is not intimate in the relevant sense, and (5) does not apply to it specifically. But what about the relations between the organ source and recipient? In the case of posthumous transplants, this sort of intimate relation is no longer possible, but what about relations between living source and recipient? While the relations between some organ sources and some recipients—family members, say—are intimate in the relevant sense, surely not all such relations are. Indeed, many organ transfers are anonymous, and therefore could hardly be called intimate in the relevant sense, and principle (5) would not apply to them. Perhaps, however, it will be suggested that there is something intimate about the very transfer of an organ to a recipient from any source, living or dead, known or unknown. In the narrower sense of the term "intimate," there need be nothing intimate about a technical medical procedure, during most of which the patient is anaesthetized. But if we broaden the notion of intimacy to include such medical procedures, then principle (5) might well be too strong. On such a broadened notion of intimacy, principle (5) might well rule out the sale of many things which are intimate in some broad sense, including education, counselling, writing, and entertainment.

Another principle we might consider is:

6. Selling X is wrong if X is something that it is bad to want.

Principle (6) explains, in part perhaps, why it would be wrong to sell even pornographic *fiction* about sex with children. In such fiction, no actual person is harmed or degraded, but we are still inclined to think that the sale of such material is wrong. Of course, some might argue that what is wrong with such fiction is that it encourages the harming or degrading of actual persons, in that it encourages actual child molestation. Yet the evidence concerning causal relations between pornography generally and sex crimes is ambiguous, it seems, and even if such pornography did not tend to encourage such crimes, I expect that many of us would still think that there was something wrong with the sale of it. That is, according to (6), there are some things that it is simply morally bad to want, and that it is *eo ipso* wrong to pander to these bad wants by selling such things.

Perhaps most would agree with (6) that it would be bad for a free market to appeal to, and be driven by, exceedingly nasty and prurient interests, but does (6) apply in the case of transplant organs? That is, is the desire for a transplant organ itself a bad desire? Clearly such a desire (in cases of standard medical need) is not nasty or prurient, but notice, even if it were, it would presumably rule out organ donation as well. (Presumably, giving away child pornography is also wrong. Sale does not make its transfer appreciably worse.)

So far, many of the principles that we have examined have arisen out of considerations prohibiting the sale of sex or things involving sex. Perhaps we would do well to consider other prohibited sales. Another sort of thing whose sale is forbidden or at least limited, is certain types of weapons, for examples, hand grenades and silencers. While these things are legitimately sold, perhaps, by their manufacturers to government armies, no civilian has a legitimate interest in owning these things. Probably, the only civilians who really need silencers or hand grenades are criminals, and this suggests another principle:

7. Selling X is wrong if X will tend to be used only in violent, criminal activities.

This principle explains why we allow ordinary persons to buy deer rifles, but not hand grenades, or (in my opinion) silencers. Unfortunately, (7) is no help in the present case, since transplant organs manifestly do not tend to be used in violent criminal activities. Moreover, even if transplant organs, like silencers, did tend to be used only in violent, criminal activities, (7) would not answer to the present case. It would not answer to the present case because, again, it would not explain why it is wrong to sell organs but right to donate them. Presumably, no one would be happier about the open donation of silencers than about their sale, and under (7) the same would apply to organs as well.

A very different principle limiting the free market emerges from backward looking considerations of things like punishment. To consider one example, it seems that in previous centuries in India, wealthy people who had been convicted of crimes could buy exemptions from punishment. Specifically, wealthy people could pay some desperately poor person to take their places at the whipping post or on the gallows. The wealthy people avoided execution, and the poor proxies were able to leave their families better off. Even though such an arrangement was presumably voluntary, most of us would think it irremediably flawed. We think it so flawed because it distorts the connection between crime and punishment. When someone commits a crime, it is not enough that somebody someplace be punished. Rather, the criminal, and the criminal alone, should be punished, and only because he or she deserves it. Considerations such as these give rise to:

8. Selling X is wrong if X should be apportioned only on the basis of desert.

Principle (8) explains why it is wrong to buy and sell punishment and exemption from punishment as well as induction into national service, exemption from national service, grades, votes, and public office.

In each case, we think that persons should receive a certain harm or benefit only if they deserve it, and we are able to specify in each case what it takes to deserve it: in the case of punishment, it is guilt; in the case of exemption from punishment, innocence; in the case of national service, being a citizen; in the case of grades, academic achievement; in the case of a single vote, being a citizen; in the case of public office, being voted in or chosen by the appropriate parties. Doubtless, (8) has a firm intuitive hold on most of us, but does it apply to the sale of transplant organs?

Unlike punishment, organ transplantation is a new phenomenon, and our intuitions on the subject have not had comparable time to emerge and be resolved. It should not be surprising if we find that we have no clear intuitions on the apportioning of transplant organs comparable to those concerning the apportioning of punishment or votes. In fact it is hard even to say what the ground of desert should be in the case of transplant organs. Academic performance, guilt, innocence, being a citizen, and winning enough votes are obviously irrelevant, but notions like need and future productivity are unworkably vague. Once again, however, even if we could be sure that (8) was true and applied to transplant organs, it would be, as some of other principles have been, too strong. It would be too strong because it would rule out donation as well as sale. If something should be distributed on the basis of desert alone, it should not be sold, but it should not be given away willy-nilly, either. I cannot rightly sell good grades to students, but I also cannot just give them to whichever students I please; the students must deserve them. Similarly, if (8) applied to transplant organs we could not just give them to whomever we pleased; we would have to give them only to someone who deserved them on the basis of some specifiable merit. This probably would run contrary to the standard policy of kin donation in the case of kidneys, as there is no *a priori* reason to suppose that one's kin would tend to exhibit this merit more than anyone else. Principle (8), then, seems to fare little better than its predecessors.

Another principle which arises out of distributive concerns is:

> 9. Selling X is wrong if X may be sold by the poor to the rich on terms which are less favorable to the poor.

For some, this is another objection to prostitution, the idea being that the poor will be tempted to engage in it because of their plight, but in so doing will get the worse end of the deal. Indeed, just this objection has been levelled against organ sales in Brazil, so it is worth considering whether (9) answers to the present case. First, the principle would apply here only if the poor would in fact "get a bad deal" in such transactions. Presumably, "getting a bad deal" could amount to two things: not getting a fair price, or its being the case that *no* price is a fair price: that one is lured into giving up what is so vital that no one should ever give it up. If (9) assumes that one should *never* give up something as vital as an organ, then it is implausible when applied to posthumous transplants. Also, (9) would then rule out donations, if it is indeed true that organs should never be given up under any circumstances. On the other hand, if (9) allows that some price is a fair price, it doesn't rule out all sales. It rules only that needy would-be vendors get a good price. Finally, we should be reluctant to accept (9) at all, since it could apply to any commodity whatsoever. It is possible, for instance, for the needy to sell their labor to the wealthy on unfavorable terms, but most of us do not think that is a reason to prohibit the sale of labor. No doubt, radical Marxists will disagree, but one of the assumptions of the present inquiry *is* that a free market is an appropriate tool for distributing many kinds of things, including labor. Even principle (9) fails plausibly to rule out the buying and selling of transplant organs. With the failure of (9) it is perhaps time to draw our inquiry to a close.

DISCLAIMERS AND CONCLUSIONS

In closing, I will retrace the path our inquiry has followed. The question which prompted the inquiry was: Is there any good reason to allow the donation of transplant organs, and a free market for lots of things besides transplant organs, but not to allow for a (relatively) free market for transplant organs? Specifically, we asked whether there was anything intrinsically morally wrong with treating transplant organs as commodities. We looked at things commonly prohibited as commodities, we looked at the most plausible reasons for prohibiting them, and we tried to see whether such reasons would hold in the case of transplant organs, too.

Our results have been negative. Every principle which we have considered either fails to apply plausibly to transplant organs at all, or, if it applies, would rule out the donation of transplant organs or the selling of numerous accepted commodities. Of course, a few disclaimers are in order. First, I may have missed some relevant principle which would plausibly prohibit the buying and selling of transplant organs. It is possible that I have failed to list some indisputable non-commodity which is relevantly similar to such organs. It is equally possible that I missed some very good reason behind the non-commodities which I did list. Moreover, my strategy of argument via analogy has its limitations; it is possible that there is some true *sui generis* moral principle such as

10. Selling X is wrong if X is a human organ

which probably could not be discovered in this way.

Still, in the absence of further considerations, I think that the preceding discussion points to the conclusion that there is nothing intrinsically morally wrong with buying or selling human organs for implantation. Now, it does not follow from this that I think we should take steps to legalize a free market for organs. Not everything that is morally acceptable need be legal, and there may be insuperable practical and distributional problems with such a market, or with the move from the present regime to such a market. I leave these questions to other times and other thinkers.

NOTE

1. "Kidneys for Sale: The Issue in Tissue," *Newsweek,* Dec. 5, 1988, p. 38.

REFERENCE

Brams, Marvin. "Property Rights in the Human Body: Legalizing Markets for Transplantable Human Organs," paper presented to the Annual Conference of the Public Choice Society, March 1977.
———. "Markets for Organs to Reinforce Altruism," *Economic Affairs,* Nov. 1986, pp. 12–14.

22

Is Commercial Surrogate Motherhood Wrong?

Anderson and Her Critics

Commercial surrogate motherhood is the practice by which a woman is paid to undergo a pregnancy, bring the pregnancy to term, and deliver the resulting child to the party or parties who have contracted for her services. In "Is Women's Labor a Commodity?", Elizabeth S. Anderson argues that this practice is immoral, and should be illegal, on the grounds that it "constitutes an unconscionable commodification of children and of women's reproductive capacities."

Anderson's argument against commercial surrogate motherhood is a subtle one, and difficult to encapsulate fully in a brief introduction. One useful way to think about her strategy is to think of it in terms of an argument from inference to the best explanation (see Introduction). Anderson begins by assuming that the practice of slavery is wrong. A good explanation of the wrongness of slavery, she suggests, can be found in the distinction between what she calls two different "modes of valuation": We can value something purely for its usefulness to us or we can value and respect it, at least in part, for its own sake. People, we all agree, merit the latter form of respect; treating them as commodities to be bought and sold on the open market treats them as if they were of value only for their usefulness. To treat something as a commodity, on this account, is to allow the market to determine how it will be produced, exchanged, and enjoyed. And while this is (or at least may be) an appropriate way to distribute mere *things,* items that are of value only for their usefulness, it is an inappropriate way to govern the treatment of *persons,* beings who merit respect in their own right, independent of their usefulness to others.

If this account of commodification offers the best general explanation of our attitude toward cases in which we believe that the market is an inappropriate mechanism for determining how something should be done, the question then becomes what, if anything, does this imply about the case of commercial surrogate motherhood? Anderson offers two distinct arguments for the claim that it implies that the practice should be rejected. The first argument turns on the claim that commercial surrogate motherhood inappropriately treats the child who is produced as a commodity.

P1 Commercial surrogate motherhood commodifies the resulting child.

P2 Commodifying a child is unacceptable.

C Commercial surrogate motherhood is unacceptable.

In ordinary circumstances, after all, when a woman gives birth to a child, she has (at least partial) parental rights over that child (as well as parental obligations). That is, the child she gives birth to is *hers*. By means of the contract the woman signs in the case of commercial surrogacy, however, in exchange for a cash payment, she gives up any rights she would otherwise have to the child. This, on Anderson's account, amounts to the woman's selling the child to the party or parties with whom she has contracted. To sell a child is to treat it as a mere commodity; to treat it as a mere commodity is to treat it as if it were of value only for its usefulness to others. And since doing so fails to value the child in the way he or she should be valued, doing so is unacceptable.

Anderson's second argument builds from the same general account of commodification, but focuses instead on the value of the surrogate mother herself:

P1 Commercial surrogate motherhood commodifies the surrogate mother.

P2 Commodifying a surrogate mother is unacceptable.

C Commerical surrogate motherhood is unacceptable.

Under typical circumstances, Anderson argues, a pregnant woman is treated in a manner that fully respects her own perspective on her pregnancy—her desires, her emotions, her beliefs, and so forth. But in the case of a commercial surrogate mother, Anderson maintains, this is not so. How the pregnant woman is treated is determined by economic forces, by the terms of the contract the market has produced. The pregnant woman is treated not so much as a person, but rather as an incubation machine, a device for turning out a desired product. In this respect, Anderson maintains that the woman, like the child, is inappropriately treated as a mere commodity. And this provides a second reason to reject the practice of commercial surrogate motherhood.

Anderson's case against commercial surrogate motherhood rests on two claims: that the practice inappropriately commodifies something and that this fact suffices to warrant opposing and prohibiting the practice. A critic of Anderson's position may therefore respond in one of two ways: He can deny that the practice involves inappropriate commodification or he can maintain that the practice is an acceptable one even if it does involve such commodification.

In an excerpt from a longer piece, Richard J. Arneson largely pursues the first strategy. After raising a few general worries about Anderson's account of commodification in general, he responds to her claims about commodification of children and women. With respect to the former, Arneson argues that a market in surrogate motherhood does not entail that the children are being treated as mere property; he offers the example of pets as a case in point. Arneson claims that the market could be sufficiently regulated to prevent the child's interests from being ignored or discounted. With respect to the latter, Arneson offers a variety of responses to a number of Anderson's points; many of these responses revolve around the claim that the surrogate contract need not ignore or discount the pregnant woman's feelings or experiences because the contract regulates only how she behaves, not how she feels.

Finally, in an excerpt from a longer article, Alan Wertheimer primarily pursues the second strategy. In particular, he complains that Anderson does not put enough weight on the fact that surrogate motherhood contracts are entered into voluntarily. Acts that might be objectionable when done against a person's will may be acceptable when done with their consent, and Wertheimer suggests that commercial surrogate motherhood may be a case of this sort. In addition, he emphasizes the importance of distinguishing between the claim that an act commodifies someone and the claim that it *harms* someone. Being treated as a commodity might often be harmful, he maintains, but it need not always be. And if the woman who undergoes the pregnancy and the child who is born as a result are not harmed in the process (or if they are harmed but are also benefited in ways that outweigh these harms), then the practice of commercial surrogate motherhood might prove acceptable, even if it involves the sort of commodification that Anderson appeals to in arguing against it.

QUESTIONS FOR CONSIDERATION

In thinking critically about the exchange between Anderson and her critics, readers should consider both the question of whether commercial surrogate motherhood commodifies what should not be commodified and the question of whether, if it does, this provides a sufficient basis for opposing the practice.

• Does the practice, as Anderson maintains, treat the child and the woman as mere things to be used? Or, as both Arneson and Wertheimer suggest, can commercial surrogate motherhood be practiced in a manner that adequately respects both mother and child?

• If the practice does involve an inappropriate form of commodification, is this enough to warrant rejecting it, as Anderson's argument seems to require? Or, as Arneson maintains, might the practice have enough additional positive features to outweigh this fact?

• Finally, readers are encouraged to consider whether the critique of commercial surrogate motherhood presented by Anderson might work better in some cases than in others. Might there be some instances in which her critique really is sufficient and others in which it is not? If so, what sorts of cases ought to be permitted and what ought to be rejected?

FURTHER READING

Malm, Heidi. "Paid Surrogacy: Arguments and Responses." *Public Affairs Quarterly* 3 (1989): 57–66.
Tong, Rosemarie. "The Overdue Death of a Feminist Chameleon: Taking a Stand on Surrogacy Arrangements." *Journal of Social Philosophy* 21, nos. 2 and 3 (1990): 40–56.

Elizabeth S. Anderson | Is Women's Labor a Commodity?

In the past few years the practice of commercial surrogate motherhood has gained notoriety as a method for acquiring children. A commercial surrogate mother is anyone who is paid money to bear a child for other people and terminate her parental rights, so that the others may raise the child as exclusively their own. The growth of commercial surrogacy has raised with new urgency a class of concerns regarding the proper scope of the market. Some critics have objected to commercial surrogacy on the ground that it improperly treats children and women's reproductive capacities as commodities.[1] The prospect of reducing children to consumer durables and women to baby factories surely inspires revulsion. But are there good reasons behind the revulsion? And is this an accurate description of what commercial surrogacy implies? This article offers a theory about what things are properly regarded as commodities which supports the claim that commercial surrogacy constitutes an unconscionable commodification of children and of women's reproductive capacities.

WHAT IS A COMMODITY?

The modern market can be characterized in terms of the legal and social norms by which it governs the production, exchange, and enjoyment of commodities. To say that something is properly regarded as a commodity is to claim that the norms of the market are appropriate for regulating its production, exchange, and enjoyment. To the extent that moral principles or ethical ideals preclude the application of market norms to a good, we may say that the good is not a (proper) commodity.

Why should we object to the application of a market norm to the production or distribution of a good?

One reason may be that to produce or distribute the good in accordance with the norm is to *fail to value it in an appropriate way*. Consider, for example, a standard Kantian argument against slavery, or the commodification of persons. Slaves are treated in accordance with the market norm that owners may use commodities to satisfy their own interests without regard for the interests of the commodities themselves. To treat a person without regard for her interests is to fail to respect her. But slaves are persons who may not be merely used in this fashion, since as rational beings they possess a dignity which commands respect. In Kantian theory, the problem with slavery is that it treats beings worthy of *respect* as if they were worthy merely of *use*. "Respect" and "use" in this context denote what we may call different *modes of valuation*. We value things and persons in other ways than by respecting and using them. For example, love, admiration, honor, and appreciation constitute distinct modes of valuation. To value a thing or person in a distinctive way involves treating it in accordance with a particular set of norms. For example, courtesy expresses a mode of valuation we may call "civil respect," which differs from Kantian respect in that it calls for obedience to the rules of etiquette rather than to the categorical imperative.

Any ideal of human life includes a conception of how different things and persons should be valued. Let us reserve the term "use" to refer to the mode of valuation proper to commodities, which follows the market norm of treating things solely in accordance with the owner's nonmoral preferences. Then the Kantian argument against commodifying persons can be generalized to apply to many other cases. It can be argued that many objects which are worthy of a higher mode of valuation than use are not properly

From Elizabeth S. Anderson, "Is Women's Labor a Commodity?" *Philosophy and Public Affairs* 19, no. 1. (Winter 1990): 71–92. Some notes and some parts of the text have been deleted. Reprinted by permission of Princeton University Press.

regarded as mere commodities. Some current arguments against the colorization of classic black-and-white films take this form. Such films have been colorized by their owners in an attempt to enhance their market value by attracting audiences unused to black-and-white cinematography. But some opponents of the practice object that such treatment of the film classics fails to appreciate their aesthetic and historical value. True appreciation of these films would preclude this kind of crass commercial exploitation, which debases their aesthetic qualities in the name of profits. Here the argument rests on the claim that the goods in question are worthy of appreciation, not merely of use.

The ideals which specify how one should value certain things are supported by a conception of human flourishing. Our lives are enriched and elevated by cultivating and exercising the capacity to appreciate art. To fail to do so reflects poorly on ourselves. To fail to value things appropriately is to embody in one's life an inferior conception of human flourishing.

These considerations support a general account of the sorts of things which are appropriately regarded as commodities. Commodities are those things which are properly treated in accordance with the norms of the modern market. We can question the application of market norms to the production, distribution, and enjoyment of a good by appealing to ethical ideals which support arguments that the good should be valued in some other way than use. Arguments of the latter sort claim that to allow certain market norms to govern our treatment of a thing expresses a mode of valuation not worthy of it. If the thing is to be valued appropriately, its production, exchange, and enjoyment must be removed from market norms and embedded in a different set of social relationships.

THE CASE OF COMMERCIAL SURROGACY

Let us now consider the practice of commercial surrogate motherhood in the light of this theory of commodities. Surrogate motherhood as a commercial enterprise is based upon contracts involving three parties: the intended father, the broker, and the surrogate mother. The intended father agrees to pay a lawyer to find a suitable surrogate mother and make the requisite medical and legal arrangements for the conception and birth of the child, and for the transfer of legal custody to himself. The surrogate mother agrees to become impregnated with the intended father's sperm, to carry the resulting child to term, and to relinquish her parental rights to it, transferring custody to the father in return for a fee and medical expenses. Both she and her husband (if she has one) agree not to form a parent-child bond with her child and to do everything necessary to effect the transfer of the child to the intended father. At current market prices, the lawyer arranging the contract can expect to gross $15,000 from the contract, while the surrogate mother can expect a $10,000 fee. . . .

I shall argue that commercial surrogacy . . . represents an invasion of the market into a new sphere of conduct, that of specifically women's labor—that is, the labor of carrying children to term in pregnancy. When women's labor is treated as a commodity, the women who perform it are degraded. Furthermore, commercial surrogacy degrades children by reducing their status to that of commodities. Let us consider each of the goods of concern in surrogate motherhood—the child, and women's reproductive labor—to see how the commercialization of parenthood affects people's regard for them.

CHILDREN AS COMMODITIES

The most fundamental calling of parents to their children is to love them. Children are to be loved and cherished by their parents, not to be used or manipulated by them for merely personal advantage. Parental love can be understood as a passionate, unconditional commitment to nurture one's child, providing it with the care, affection, and guidance it needs to develop its capacities to maturity. This understanding of the way parents should value their children informs our interpretation of parental rights over their children. Parents' rights over their children are trusts, which they must always exercise for the sake of the child. This is not to deny that parents have their own aspirations in raising children. But the child's interests beyond subsistence are not definable independently of the flourishing of the family, which is the object of specifically parental aspirations. The proper exercise of parental rights includes those acts which promote their shared life as a family, which realize the shared interests of the parents and the child.

The norms of parental love carry implications for the ways other people should treat the relationship between parents and their children. If children are to be loved by their parents, then others should not attempt to compromise the integrity of parental love or work to suppress the emotions supporting the bond between parents and their children. If the rights to children should be understood as trusts, then if those rights are lost or relinquished, the duty of those in charge of transferring custody to others is to consult the best interests of the child.

Commercial surrogacy substitutes market norms for some of the norms of parental love. Most importantly, it requires us to understand parental rights no longer as trusts but as things more like property rights—that is, rights of use and disposal over the things owned. For in this practice the natural mother deliberately conceives a child with the intention of giving it up for material advantage. Her renunciation of parental responsibilities is not done for the child's sake, nor for the sake of fulfilling an interest she sabres with the child, but typically for her own sake (and possibly, if "altruism" is a motive, for the intended parents' sakes). She and the couple who pay her to give up her parental rights over her child thus treat her rights as a kind of property right. They thereby treat the child itself as a kind of commodity, which may be properly bought and sold.

Commercial surrogacy insinuates the norms of commerce into the parental relationship in other ways. Whereas parental love is not supposed to be conditioned upon the child having particular characteristics, consumer demand is properly responsive to the characteristics of commodities. So the surrogate industry provides opportunities to adoptive couples to specify the height, I.Q., race, and other attributes of the surrogate mother, in the expectation that these traits will be passed on to the child. Since no industry assigns agents to look after the "interests" of its commodities, no one represents the child's interests in the surrogate industry. The surrogate agency promotes the adoptive parents' interests and not the child's interests where matters of custody are concerned. Finally, as the agent of the adoptive parents, the broker has the task of policing the surrogate (natural) mother's relationship to her child, using persuasion, money, and the threat of a lawsuit to weaken and destroy whatever parental love she may develop for her child.

All of these substitutions of market norms for parental norms represent ways of treating children as commodities which are degrading to them. Degradation occurs when something is treated in accordance with a lower mode of valuation than is proper to it. We value things not just "more" or "less," but in qualitatively higher and lower ways. To love or respect someone is to value her in a higher way than one would if one merely used her. Children are properly loved by their parents and respected by others. Since children are valued as mere use-objects by the mother and the surrogate agency when they are sold to others, and by the adoptive parents when they seek to conform the child's genetic makeup to their own wishes, commercial surrogacy degrades children insofar as it treats them as commodities.

One might argue that since the child is most likely to enter a loving home, no harm comes to it from permitting the natural mother to treat it as property. So the purchase and sale of infants is unobjectionable, at least from the point of view of children's interests. But the sale of an infant has an expressive significance which this argument fails to recognize. By engaging in the transfer of children by sale, all of the parties to the surrogate contract express a set of attitudes toward children which undermine the norms of parental love. They all agree in treating the ties between a natural mother and her children as properly loosened by a monetary incentive. Would it be any wonder if a child born of a surrogacy agreement feared resale by parents who have such an attitude? And a child who knew how anxious her parents were that she have the "right" genetic makeup might fear that her parent's love was contingent upon her expression of these characteristics.

The unsold children of surrogate mothers are also harmed by commercial surrogacy. The children of some surrogate mothers have reported their fears that they may be sold like their half-brother or half-sister, and express a sense of loss at being deprived of a sibling. Furthermore, the widespread acceptance of commercial surrogacy would psychologically threaten all children. For it would change the way children are valued by people (parents and surrogate brokers)—from being loved by their parents and respected by others, to being sometimes used as objects of commercial profit-making.

Proponents of commercial surrogacy have denied that the surrogate industry engages in the sale of children. For it is impossible to sell to someone what is already his own, and the child is already the father's own natural offspring. The payment to the surrogate mother is not for her child, but for her services in carrying it to term. The claim that the parties to the surrogate contract treat children as commodities, however, is based on the way they treat the *mother's* rights over her child. It is irrelevant that the natural father also has some rights over the child; what he pays for is exclusive rights to it. He would not pay her for the "service" of carrying the child to term if she refused to relinquish her parental rights to it. That the mother regards only her labor and not her child as requiring compensation is also irrelevant. No one would argue that the baker does not treat his bread as property just because he sees the income from its sale as compensation for his labor and expenses and not for the bread itself, which he doesn't care to keep.

Defenders of commercial surrogacy have also claimed that it does not differ substantially from other already accepted parental practices. In the institutions of adoption and artificial insemination by donor (AID), it is claimed, we already grant parents the right to dispose of their children. But these practices differ in significant respects from commercial surrogacy. The purpose of adoption is to provide a means for placing children in families when their parents cannot or will not discharge their parental responsibilities. It is not a sphere for the existence of a supposed parental right to dispose of one's children for profit. Even AID does not sanction the sale of fully formed human beings. The semen donor sells only a product of his body, not his child, and does not initiate the act of conception.

Two developments might seem to undermine the claim that commercial surrogacy constitutes a degrading commerce in children. The first is technological: the prospect of transplanting a human embryo into the womb of a genetically unrelated woman. If commercial surrogacy used women only as gestational mothers and not as genetic mothers, and if it was thought that only genetic and not gestational parents could properly claim that a child was "theirs," then the child born of a surrogate mother would not be hers to sell in the first place. The second is a legal development: the establishment of the proposed "consent-intent" definition of parenthood. This would declare the legal parents of a child to be whoever consented to a procedure which leads to its birth, with the intent of assuming parental responsibilities for it. This rule would define away the problem of commerce in children by depriving the surrogate mother of any legal claim to her child at all, even if it was hers both genetically and gestationally.

There are good reasons, however, not to undermine the place of genetic and gestational ties in these ways. Consider first the place of genetic ties. By upholding a system of involuntary (genetic) ties of obligation among people, even when the adults among them prefer to divide their rights and obligations in other ways, we help to secure children's interests in having an assured place in the world, which is more firm than the wills of their parents. Unlike the consent-intent rule, the principle of respecting genetic ties does not make the obligation to care for those whom one has created (intentionally or not) contingent upon an arbitrary desire to do so. It thus provides children with a set of preexisting social sanctions which give them a more secure place in the world. The genetic principle also places children in a far wider network of associations and obligations than the consent-intent rule sanctions. It supports the roles of grandparents and other relatives in the nurturing of children, and provides children with a possible focus of stability and an additional source of claims to care if their parents cannot sustain a well-functioning household.

In the next section I will defend the claims of gestational ties to children. To deny these claims, as commercial surrogacy does, is to deny the significance of reproductive labor to the mother who undergoes it and thereby to dehumanize and degrade the mother herself. Commercial surrogacy would be a corrupt practice even if it did not involve commerce in children.

WOMEN'S LABOR AS A COMMODITY

Commercial surrogacy attempts to transform what is specifically women's labor—the work of bringing forth children into the world—into a commodity. It does so by replacing the parental norms which usually govern the practice of gestating children with the economic norms which govern ordinary production processes. The application of commercial norms to women's labor reduces the surrogate mothers from persons worthy of respect and consideration to objects of mere use.

Respect and consideration are two distinct modes of valuation whose norms are violated by the practices of the surrogate industry. To respect a person is to treat her in accordance with principles she rationally accepts—principles consistent with the protection of her autonomy and her rational interests. To treat a person with consideration is to respond with sensitivity to her and to her emotional relations with others, refraining from manipulating or denigrating these for one's own purposes. Given the understanding of respect as a dispassionate, impersonal regard for people's interests, a different ethical concept—consideration—is needed to capture the engaged and sensitive regard we should have for people's emotional relationships. The failure of consideration on the part of the other parties to the surrogacy contract explains the judgment that the contract is not simply disrespectful of the surrogate mother, but callous as well.

The application of economic norms to the sphere of women's labor violates women's claims to respect and consideration in three ways. First, by requiring the surrogate mother to repress whatever parental love she feels for the child, these norms convert women's labor into a form of alienated labor. Second, by manipulating and denying legitimacy to the surrogate mother's evolving perspective on her own pregnancy, the norms of the market degrade her. Third, by

taking advantage of the surrogate mother's noncommercial motivations without offering anything but what the norms of commerce demand in return, these norms leave her open to exploitation. The fact that these problems arise in the attempt to commercialize the labor of bearing children shows that women's labor is not properly regarded as a commodity.

The key to understanding these problems is the normal role of the emotions in noncommercialized pregnancies. Pregnancy is not simply a biological process but also a social practice. Many social expectations and considerations surround women's gestational labor, marking it off as an occasion for the parents to prepare themselves to welcome a new life into their family. For example, obstetricians use ultrasound not simply for diagnostic purposes but also to encourage maternal bonding with the fetus. We can all recognize that it is good, although by no means inevitable, for loving bonds to be established between the mother and her child during this period.

In contrast with these practices, the surrogate industry follows the putting-out system of manufacturing. It provides some of the raw materials of production (the father's sperm) to the surrogate mother, who then engages in production of the child. Although her labor is subject to periodic supervision by her doctors and by the surrogate agency, the agency does not have physical control over the product of her labor as firms using the factory system do. Hence, as in all putting-out systems, the surrogate industry faces the problem of extracting the final product from the mother. This problem is exacerbated by the fact that the social norms surrounding pregnancy are designed to encourage parental love for the child. The surrogate industry addresses this problem by requiring the mother to engage in a form of emotional labor. In the surrogate contract, she agrees not to form or to attempt to form a parent-child relationship with her offspring. Her labor is alienated, because she must divert it from the end which the social practices of pregnancy rightly promote—an emotional bond with her child. The surrogate contract thus replaces a norm of parenthood, that during pregnancy one create a loving attachment to one's child, with a norm of commercial production, that the producer shall not form any special emotional ties to her product.

The demand to deliberately alienate oneself from one's love for one's own child is a demand which can reasonably and decently be made of no one. Unless we were to remake pregnancy into a form of drudgery which is only performed for a wage, there is every reason to expect that many women who do sign a surrogate contract will, despite this fact, form a loving attachment to the child they bear. For this is what the social practices surrounding pregnancy encourage. Treating women's labor as just another kind of commercial production process violates the precious emotional ties which the mother may rightly and properly establish with her "product," the child, and thereby violates her claims to consideration. . . .

The treatment and interpretation of surrogate mothers' grief raises the deepest problems of degradation. Most surrogate mothers experience grief upon giving up their children—in 10 percent of cases, seriously enough to require therapy. Their grief is not compensated by the $10,000 fee they receive. Grief is not an intelligible response to a successful deal, but rather reflects the subject's judgment that she has suffered a grave and personal loss. Since not all cases of grief resolve themselves into cases of regret, it may be that some surrogate mothers do not regard their grief, in retrospect, as reflecting an authentic judgment on their part. But in the circumstances of emotional manipulation which pervade the surrogate industry, it is difficult to determine which interpretation of her grief more truly reflects the perspective of the surrogate mother. By insinuating a trivializing interpretation of her emotional responses to the prospect of losing her child, the surrogate agency may be able to manipulate her into accepting her fate without too much fuss, and may even succeed in substituting its interpretation of her emotions for her own. Since she has already signed a contract to perform emotional labor—to express or repress emotions which are dictated by the interests of the surrogate industry—this might not be a difficult task. A considerate treatment of the mothers' grief, on the other hand, would take the evaluative basis of their grief seriously.

Some defenders of commercial surrogacy demand that the provision for terminating the surrogate mother's parental rights in her child be legally enforceable, so that peace of mind for the adoptive parents can be secured. But the surrogate industry makes no corresponding provision for securing the peace of mind of the surrogate. She is expected to assume the risk of a transformation of her ethical and emotional perspective on herself and her child with the same impersonal detachment with which a futures trader assumes the risk of a fluctuation in the price of pork bellies. By applying the market norms of enforcing contracts to the surrogate mother's case, commercial surrogacy treats a moral transformation as if it were merely an economic change.

The manipulation of the surrogate mother's emotions which is inherent in the surrogate parenting contract also leaves women open to grave forms of exploitation. A kind of exploitation occurs when one party to a transaction is oriented toward the exchange of "gift" values, while the other party operates in accordance with the norms of the market exchange of commodities. Gift values, which include love, gratitude, and appreciation of others, cannot be bought or obtained through piecemeal calculations of individual advantage. Their exchange requires a repudiation of a self-interested attitude, a willingness to give gifts to others without demanding some specific equivalent good in return each time one gives. The surrogate mother often operates according to the norms of gift relationships. The surrogate agency, on the other hand, follows market norms. Its job is to get the best deal for its clients and itself, while leaving the surrogate mother to look after her own interests as best as she can. This situation puts the surrogate agencies in a position to manipulate the surrogate mothers' emotions to gain favorable terms for themselves. For example, agencies screen prospective surrogate mothers for submissiveness, and emphasize to them the importance of the motives of generosity and love. When applicants question some of the terms of the contract, the broker sometimes intimidates them by questioning their character and morality: if they were really generous and loving they would not be so solicitous about their own interests.

Some evidence supports the claim that most surrogate mothers are motivated by emotional needs and vulnerabilities which lead them to view their labor as a form of gift and not a purely commercial exchange. Only 1 percent of applicants to surrogate agencies would become surrogate mothers for money alone; the others have emotional as well as financial reasons for applying. One psychiatrist believes that most, if not all, of the 35 percent of applicants who had had a previous abortion or given up a child for adoption wanted to become surrogate mothers in order to resolve their guilty feelings or deal with their unresolved loss by going through a process of losing a child again. Women who feel that giving up another child is an effective way to punish themselves for past abortions, or a form of therapy for their emotional problems, are not likely to resist manipulation by surrogate brokers.

Many surrogate mothers see pregnancy as a way to feel "adequate," "appreciated," or "special." In other words, these women feel inadequate, unappreciated, or unadmired when they are not pregnant. Lacking the power to achieve some worthwhile status in their own right, they must subordinate themselves to others' definitions of their proper place (as baby factories) in order to get from them the appreciation they need to attain a sense of self-worth. But the sense of self-worth one can attain under such circumstances is precarious and ultimately self-defeating. For example, those who seek gratitude on the part of the adoptive parents and some opportunity to share the joys of seeing their children grow discover all too often that the adoptive parents want nothing to do with them. For while the surrogate mother sees in the arrangement some basis for establishing the personal ties she needs to sustain her emotionally, the adoptive couple sees it as an impersonal commercial contract, one of whose main advantages to them is that all ties between them and the surrogate are ended once the terms of the contract are fulfilled. To them, her presence is a threat to marital unity and a competing object for the child's affections.

These considerations should lead us to question the model of altruism which is held up to women by the surrogacy industry. It is a strange form of altruism which demands such radical self-effacement, alienation from those whom one benefits, and the subordination of one's body, health, and emotional life to the independently defined interests of others. Why should this model of "altruism" be held up to *women?* True altruism does not involve such subordination, but rather the autonomous and self-confident exercise of skill, talent, and judgment. (Consider the dedicated doctor.) The kind of altruism we see admired in surrogate mothers involves a lack of self-confidence, a feeling that one can be truly worthy only through self-effacement. This model of altruism, far from affirming the freedom and dignity of women, seems all too conveniently designed to keep their sense of self-worth hostage to the interests of a more privileged class.

The primary distortions which arise from treating women's labor as a commodity—the surrogate mother's alienation from loved ones, her degradation, and her exploitation—stem from a common source. This is the failure to acknowledge and treat appropriately the surrogate mother's emotional engagement with her labor. Her labor is alienated, because she must suppress her emotional ties with her own child, and may be manipulated into reinterpreting these ties in a trivializing way. She is degraded, because her independent ethical perspective is denied, or demoted to the status of a cash sum. She is exploited, because her emotional needs and vulnerabilities are not treated as characteristics which call for consideration, but as factors which may be manipulated to encourage her to make a grave self-sacrifice to the broker's and adoptive couple's advantage. These considerations provide strong grounds for sustaining the claims of women's labor to its "product," the child. The attempt to redefine parenthood so as to strip women of parental claims to the children they bear does violence to their emotional engagement with the project of bringing children into the world.

COMMERCIAL SURROGACY, FREEDOM, AND THE LAW

In the light of these ethical objections to commercial surrogacy, what position should the law take on the practice? At the very least, surrogate contracts should not be enforceable. Surrogate mothers should not be forced to relinquish their children if they have formed emotional bonds with them. Any other treatment of women's ties to the children they bear is degrading.

But I think these arguments support the stronger conclusion that commercial surrogate contracts should be illegal, and that surrogate agencies who arrange such contracts should be subject to criminal penalties. Commercial surrogacy constitutes a degrading and harmful traffic in children, violates the dignity of women, and subjects both children and women to a serious risk of exploitation.

NOTE

1. See, for example, Gena Corea, *The Mother Machine* (New York: Harper and Row, 1985), pp. 216, 219; Angela Holder, "Surrogate Motherhood: Babies for Fun and Profit," *Case and Comment* 90 (1985): 3–11: and Margaret Jane Radin, "Market Inalienability," *Harvard Law Review* 100 (June 1987): 1849–1937.

Critics

Richard J. Arneson | # Commodification and Commercial Surrogacy

Consider . . . Elizabeth Anderson's view that "to say that something is properly regarded as a commodity is to claim that the norms of the market are appropriate for regulating its production, exchange, and enjoyment."[1] Leaving aside the quibble that there are no "market norms" of enjoyment, I find this assertion ambiguous. It could mean that if something is a *proper commodity,* market norms *alone* are applicable to its production and exchange (call this the "strong sense"), or it could mean that if something is a proper commodity, market norms—perhaps along with other norms—are applicable to its production and exchange (call this the "weak sense"). I doubt that anything is a proper commodity in the strong sense. For instance, it is perfectly appropriate that strawberries are sold on a free and open market *and* properly appreciated for their color, taste, and other aesthetic qualities, some of which are reliably detectable only by strawberry cognoscenti. But from the fact that non-market norms are properly applicable to a type of good it does not follow that the good is not a proper commodity in the weak sense.

More important is the following: From the premise that from some reasonable standpoint the nature of a good is such that it should not be exchanged on the market it cannot be inferred that the state should remove the good from the sphere of market exchange. For it may be that from other equally reasonable standpoints the good is legitimately the object of market trading. The state cannot simply associate itself with one viewpoint shared by some citizens and denied by others. The state must be able to justify its policies by appeal to principles that offer a reasonable way of adjudicating among conflicting viewpoints in a diverse democracy.

In passing, I note that even if it were agreed that a good deserves to be treated in accordance with its worth and that such treatment is not guaranteed by permitting its exchange on the market, it still would not follow that the good should be made market-inalienable. The market may be the best that we can

From Richard J. Arneson, "Commodification and Commercial Surrogacy," *Philosophy and Public Affairs* 21, no. 2 (1992): 132–64. Some notes and some parts of the text have been deleted. Reprinted by permission of Princeton University Press.

do so far as ensuring appropriately respectful treatment is concerned.

Allowing a class of goods to be distributed by market exchange permits their sale by persons who do not truly appreciate the goods to persons who do not truly appreciate them either. But the existence of a market for a good does not guarantee unappreciative use. That depends on the tastes and resources of potential consumers and producers. Indeed, an unregulated market displays a tendency to place goods in the hands of those who truly appreciate them. I myself have little understanding or appreciation of Elvis Presley memorabilia, and the market effectively prevents unappreciative persons like me from retaining ownership of them. The market price is driven up by those who have the greatest appreciation of these relics. Of course, this tendency for ownership and appreciation to coincide when goods are freely exchangeable is quite weak, in that willingness to pay is limited by ability to pay. To evaluate the market on this score one must compare it with feasible institutional alternatives such as bureaucratic assignment. One must also evaluate nonmarket distribution mechanisms in the same way. The state may attempt to foster the widespread appreciation of great works of art by displaying them in public museums. This method of distribution allows tourists to degrade classic works of art by applying to them utterly inappropriate standards of interior decoration ("Honey, that Delacroix would look swell in our living room next to our pink sofa, against our velvet wallpaper"). This does not mean that it is deplorable for the state to exhibit great art in ways that permit its degradation. Public display at nominal cost to viewers with guards monitoring the viewers might be the best overall means for fostering widespread aesthetically sophisticated appreciation of the art.

In short, even if securing a particular mode of appropriate respect and valuation of a type of good is deemed to be of top priority, it might be that commodification of the good is the best means to this end. But in most cases, where citizens reasonably maintain quite divergent views about the nature of appropriate treatment of a type of good, the state should regulate the production and distribution of the good in a way that respects this diversity, and here tolerance of commodification is often, though not always, the best diversity-respecting mechanism. . . .

COMMERCIAL SURROGACY AND HARMS TO CHILDREN

One set of arguments against commercial surrogacy concerns harms and benefits to children who might be affected by the practice.

According to its detractors, commercial surrogacy substitutes market norms for norms of parental love. This same encroachment of market norms is threatened by proposals to relax the present constraints of adoption law so as to permit expanded market trading between childless couples who want a baby and women who are contemplating bringing a fetus to term and who might be induced to relinquish the child at birth for a price. These intrusions of the market into parental choice are sometimes called "baby-selling."

Notice first of all that the term *baby-selling* in this context is a misnomer. What those who advocate a market in surrogacy and adoption services propose is that the right and obligation to assume parental responsibility for the care of a particular child should be marketable. This may be a good or a bad idea but is not remotely a proposal for baby-selling.

This claim might be challenged by the observation that talk of buying and selling does presuppose that the object of exchange is private property, but this can be a matter of degree. After all, we do speak of "selling pets" even though there are legal and moral limits on what one may do to a pet one "owns." Pets are not privately owned in the same full sense that cars and toothbrushes are. But this observation does not establish the propriety of the label "baby-selling" for the practice of buying and selling parental rights and responsibilities. A parent does not in any sense own her child even if she acquires parental rights and responsibilities by purchase. For any entity, an owner with a property right in that entity has some (perhaps limited) legitimate freedom to dispose of it at will, according to her whim or pleasure, but parents do not have even limited rights to dispose of their children at will. The rights that parents have to control their children's behavior and to make major decisions affecting their lives while they are young are assigned to parents for the sake of their children's welfare and are supposed to be exercised for the good of their children. The point of parental rights is to enable parents to carry out their obligations to care for their children. These parental rights are not property rights, so buying and selling these rights does not equate with buying and selling a child.

Notice also that even the most extreme advocates of a greater role for markets advocate a very restricted market in the right to parent. After all, the normal presumption in favor of free trade does not apply in this case. Normally, if all parties voluntarily agree to an exchange of goods, the presumption is that all parties benefit from the exchange, so unless third parties are harmed, the sale should be permitted. But if the good being exchanged is the right and obligation to be the parent of a particular infant, that very infant cannot be a consenting party to the transaction, so there can be no presumption from the voluntary character of the transaction that it serves the interests of the infant. There is a prima facie case for free trade here only if the market is regulated in such a way as to ensure that the child who is indirectly the object of the transaction is not wrongfully harmed.

WOMEN'S LABOR

Aside from alleged harms to children and alleged harms to all of us that are supposed to flow from the commodification of childbearing, opponents of paid surrogacy point to the intrinsic indignity and perhaps indecency of the practice from the standpoint of the woman who is paid to bear children. Capron and Radin state that we should not permit women to become "paid breeding stock, like farm animals." They further observe, "The role of paid breeder is incompatible with a society in which individuals are valued for themselves and are aided in achieving a full sense of human well-being and potentiality."[2] Why think this? Hardly anyone, to my knowledge, believes that there is anything degrading about surrogacy when motivated by altruism or other friendly noncommercial aims. There is surely nothing wrong

with a woman volunteering to become a surrogate mother for her infertile sister, who will at birth by prior agreement become the child's mother. Nor is there anything necessarily undesirable or unfair in the acceptance of such offers. Why, then, is it wrong, or degrading, or intrinsically harmful to the surrogate, if she is paid for the service?

The answer sometimes offered is that women's labor—the labor of pregnancy and childbearing—is peculiarly intimate and personal, somewhat like making love. Hence performing women's labor for pay is degrading and alienating, so much so that it is reasonable to judge that the person who engages in commercial surrogacy is harming herself, whatever might be her own perspective on this engagement.

This line of argument against commercial surrogacy is matched by a parallel argument against legal tolerance of prostitution. Consider Elizabeth Anderson's views on the baseness of prostitution: "Sexuality as a specifically human, shared good cannot be achieved except through gift exchange; market motives cannot provide it. The failure of reciprocity implied in the sale of sexual services signifies not simply a failure to realize a good, but a degradation of the prostitute, whose sexuality is reduced to the status of a mere service to the customer: sexuality is equated with the lesser good of money."[3]

But, first of all, it is not clear why Anderson thinks that the distinction between freely given sex and prostitution warrants the judgment that prostitution is base and should be forbidden rather than the judgment that prostitution, though good, is less good than freely given sex. The same question would arise if the same claim were made about commercial surrogacy. One could accept what the quotation above asserts—except for the suitability of the label "degradation"—without accepting that the practice should be subject to either moral condemnation or legal prohibition.

One should recognize that the ideal of freely given sex is itself controversial, and, I claim, would remain controversial even after full rational deliberation with full information among the disputants. In a diverse democracy, citizens affirm many different and conflicting conceptions of the good in sexual matters. Given such deep-seated disagreement, an argument for the conclusion that society should adopt a posture of condemnation or prohibition toward some sexual practice must go beyond the appeal to one controversial ideal among others. Again, the same point holds with respect to a train of thought that concludes that commercial surrogacy should be banned.

The argument under review is that women's labor is noble labor and performance of noble labor for pay is degrading, so commercial surrogacy and other forms of paid women's labor should be banned. Besides the difficulties already canvassed, a further problem with this argument is that it does not identify women's labor as unique and in need of unique legal handling. Many kinds of work thought by many of us to be noble labor are nevertheless regarded as appropriately done for money, and no widely held norm in market societies denigrates the performance of noble labor for pay. One wonders why noble women's labor should be treated differently.

This is not to deny that some types of labor are partly insulated from the economic marketplace. By and large, religious sermons are not bought and sold on the market. Rather, a congregation customarily pays a minister who preaches for free to all who come to church at stated times. Churchgoers are expected to donate money to help defray the expenses of the church, but the nonmarket organization of religious services expresses the feelings of churchgoers that sacred matters should be kept somehow distinct from worldly affairs. The point to note here is that what sustains this partial separation of religious life and ordinary business affairs is the devotion of the faithful, not any legal prohibition.

In point of fact, from what we know of women who have volunteered to be commercial surrogates, many are not acting as purely self-interested profit-maximizers, but are moved by mixed motives, including empathy for the infertile couple they hope to help. One commercial surrogate explained her choice in these terms: "I'm not going to cure cancer or become Mother Theresa, but a baby is one thing I can sort of give back, something I can give to someone who couldn't have it any other way."[4] It strikes me that one has to be quite dogmatic to insist a priori that the personal experience of commercial surro-

gacy that this woman is describing must have been an instance of alienated, degrading labor.

Elizabeth Anderson argues interestingly for the position that I am claiming is dogmatic. She asserts that the commodification of women's labor—the labor of childbearing—violates women's claims to respect and consideration in three ways. First, permitting women's labor to be sold allows the exploitation of the potential surrogate's altruistic motives in seeking a surrogacy arrangement. The woman will be paid less by virtue of her partially altruistic motivation than she would be in its absence. Second, a surrogacy contract necessarily denies legitimacy to the pregnant woman's own evolving perspective on her pregnancy. Third, the contract turns women's labor into alienated labor by requiring the suppression of the feelings of parental love and attachment that the pregnant woman will predictably experience. Call these the failure of reciprocity, denial of perspective, and suppression of feeling problems.

Failure of Reciprocity

The claim is that the commercial surrogate's desire to help the commissioning couple puts her in a position of vulnerability to exploitation. That the potential commercial surrogate is likely to be poor and the commissioning couple well-to-do exacerbates the former's weak bargaining position.

But so long as there is no fraud or misrepresentation, I do not believe that the failure to reciprocate altruism is necessarily wrongful. If a surrogate mother expects lasting emotional ties to the commissioning couple and she is misled about the chances that long-term ties will develop, she is wronged. But it is reasonable to suppose that surrogacy contracts can be regulated to minimize the dangers of such wrong. (One might require that both parties to the contract engage legal counsel, or receive psychological counseling.) But the fact that someone is willing to accept a lower price for provision of a service because she altruistically cares about those who will benefit from the service does not tend to show that the purchase price is unjust. (Notice that if altruists and purely self-interested agents compete for trade, the altruists need not do worse than the egoists. If those who purchase babysitting services are willing to pay more for a babysitter who truly cares for babies [and provided the purchasers can reliably distinguish caring from noncaring babysitters], then the market will compensate caring babysitters more highly than egoistic babysitters.) At any rate, the failure of altruism issue at most raises a question about how to ensure fair pricing of surrogacy services. This concern might motivate setting a minimum price for the service or regulation of some other sort, but not prohibition.

Denial of Perspective

Any contract ties down the future and determines one's future behavior to some extent. That is what contracts are for. Signing a contract for future performance does not deny that one's views might change in the interim. Undergoing a change of one's perspective, however, does not change the terms of the contract. Our interest in having a device for providing mutual assurances of this sort is what motivates the institution of contract.

In this respect the problems that surrogacy contracts can engender are similar to the difficulties that any contract can cause. In particular, the idea that in case of a breach of contract for labor services, specific performance of the contracted-for labor should not be enforced perhaps applies with special force to surrogacy arrangements. There are two instances of changed views of the surrogate mother that raise special concerns. One is that surrogacy contracts might require amniocentesis and stipulate that the surrogate mother is to obtain an abortion if fetal abnormalities are revealed. I take it to be uncontroversial that courts should not require a surrogate to obtain an abortion against her will, regardless of contractual stipulation. For essentially the same reason, the surrogate mother should have the inalienable right to terminate the pregnancy by abortion against the wishes of the commissioning parties and against any contrary terms in the contract.

A second special concern is that the surrogate mother might change her mind during the pregnancy regarding her decision to turn over the baby to the commissioning couple. It is clearly desirable that the law clearly delineate rights and obligations for such scenarios, to minimize the occurrence of bitter lawsuits. The main alternatives appear to be to decide as a matter of public policy either (a) that whatever terms the parties have voluntarily agreed to will be enforced or (b) that the surrogate mother shall retain the right to keep custody of the child she bears until she relinquishes him physically to the commissioning couple after birth. The argument for (b) is that it is hard for a woman to predict how she will feel about relinquishing the child and that if she eventually wishes to retain custody it would be cruel to snatch the child from her arms.

The call between (a) and (b) seems to me close. Sometimes (b) is urged on grounds of consistency with adoption law, which in most jurisdictions does not regard as binding a prebirth agreement to give up a child for adoption. Adoption law forbids offering financial inducement to a pregnant woman or new mother to give up her baby for adoption, and also prohibits acceptance of such offers by parents. I suppose that if the assignment of the child to parents after birth in surrogacy arrangements is held to be legitimately determined by the terms of the contract, adoption law should probably be liberalized somewhat to bring it into alignment with surrogacy law.

Nonetheless, the situation of a pregnant woman considering whether to give up her child for adoption can be distinguished from the situation of a surrogate mother considering whether to breach the contract. First, we can agree that it would be painfully confusing for many prospective parents, who either have deliberately brought about a pregnancy or simply find themselves with a child in prospect, to be faced with a choice between keeping their child and relinquishing the child to others for money. Offering financial inducement to relinquish one's child in this way might sensibly be prohibited in order to prevent such painful confusion. Similarly, if after the onset of pregnancy a woman decides to relinquish custody of her child, she might sensibly be given the inalienable legal right to change her mind at least up to the point at which the child is born and she has physically relinquished it. The commercial surrogacy case is different because the commissioned child would not exist were it not for the contractual arrangement. The initial intention on the part of the surrogate mother is to assist in producing a child for whom others are to assume parental responsibility. Moreover, this child-creating intention has taken the form of a contractual promise. For the same reason, the commissioning couple has a greater legitimate stake in the outcome of a commercial surrogate pregnancy. The deliberate act of the commissioning couple has brought this child into existence. If they keep their part of the bargain and are not reasonably suspected to be unfit parents, they arguably should get custody of the child even if the surrogate has a change of heart, just as a change of heart on the part of the commissioning couple would not release them from their obligation to become the parents of the child born of the surrogacy arrangement. But on the other side there is the hardship to the surrogate. Perhaps the issue should be decided depending on whether the loss stemming from the lessened value of a voidable contract to commissioning couples plus the loss to couples who are disappointed when the surrogate reverses her decision are outweighed by the loss to the surrogates who would have to give up the children they have borne against their will if specific performance of surrogacy contracts is enforced.

Suppression of Feeling

To repeat: The contract does not require the surrogate mother to feel in certain ways, but rather to act

in certain ways. The contract might require the surrogate woman to act against her feelings in order to fulfill its terms. To this extent the labor of fulfilling the contract might turn out to be alienated labor. But in a liberal society (whether capitalist or socialist) alienated labor is not forbidden. Citizens should be left free to arrange their work lives in ways that trade off alienated labor against other benefits according to their own notions of acceptable compromises among diverse goals and values. . . .

NOTES

1. Elizabeth A. Anderson, "Is Women's Labor a Commodity?" *Philosophy & Public Affairs* 19, no. 1 (Winter 1990): 72. See also Elizabeth S. Anderson, "The Ethical Limitations of the Market," *Economics and Philosophy* 6 (1990): 179–205.

2. A. M. Capron and M. J. Radin, "Choosing Family Law over Contract Law as a Paradigm for Surrogate Motherhood," *Law, Medicine, and Health Care* 16 (1988): 36.

3. Anderson, "The Ethical Limitations of the Market," p. 188.

4. Barbara Kantrowitz, "Who Keeps Baby M?" *Newsweek,* 19 January 1987, pp. 44–49, as cited in Martha A. Field, *Surrogate Motherhood* (Cambridge, Mass.: Harvard University Press, 1988), p. 20.

Alan Wertheimer

Two Questions About Surrogacy and Exploitation

. . . Elizabeth Anderson says that "a kind of exploitation occurs when one party to a transaction is oriented toward the exchange of 'gift' values, while the other party operates in accordance with the norms of the market."[1] But *incommensurability,* as such, does not take us very far. First, to say that the values exchanged in a transaction are incommensurable does not establish that a market transaction is wrong, at

least not without further argument. The permissibility of market transactions does not require that the goods exchanged be commensurable on a single metric. It requires that the parties transact voluntarily and, perhaps, with a (reasonable) belief that the value received is at least as great as the value given. One can and (arguably) should be able to buy or sell a "priceless" painting without claiming that its value

From Alan Wertheimer, "Two Questions About Surrogacy and Exploitation," *Philosophy and Public Affairs* 21, no. 3. (Summer 1992): 211–39. Some notes and some parts of the text have been deleted. Reprinted by permission of Princeton University Press.

is "commensurate" with the money that is paid. Second, even if incommensurability provides a reason for thinking that a transaction is *wrong,* it does not entail that a party's interests are negatively affected by the transaction. So more will have to be said if incommensurability is going to support the claim that surrogacy is exploitative.

Incommensurability aside, it is widely thought that some goods and services are appropriately exchanged for money whereas others are not. On the one hand, automobiles, houses, books, television sets, and at least *some* forms of labor can legitimately be exchanged for money. By contrast, there are some things that should *not* be exchanged for money—citizenship, human beings, criminal justice, marriage rights, exemption from military service, and perhaps other forms of human labor (e.g., sexual and procreational labor). On this view, surrogacy is exploitative not because it comes too cheap, but because it *commodifies* that which should not be commodified.

If procreational labor should not be commodified, does it follow that surrogacy is harmful to the surrogate? It is not clear. It may have been wrong to commodify exemptions from military service during the Civil War, when citizens were allowed to pay $300 to purchase the services of a substitute, but it was hardly harmful to those who *bought* exemptions. And while the commodification of exemptions may have *caused* harm—by injury or death—to the substitutes, it is much less clear that the commodification of exemptions, as such, *constituted* a harm to them. And so we must ask whether the commodification of the surrogate's labor is (1) harmful, (2) harmful *because* it is wrong, or (3) wrong but not harmful (to the surrogate).

It may be thought that the commodification of the surrogate's labor is *psychologically* harmful to her, but the extent to which that is so is an empirical question, and little evidence has been adduced. We might say that the commodification of procreational labor is *objectively* harmful to the surrogate's interests, even if she does not feel harmed. This could occur in two ways.

First, as with nonmoral forms of objective harm, we might say that a woman has an interest in not being commodified, degraded, or treated merely as a means. But to say that a woman may be objectively harmed is one thing; to identify the nature of that harm is another. And it is not quite clear in what ways a woman is thought to be harmed by commodification or degradation, in the absence of the psychological connection.

Second, it might be claimed that a person can lose the respect of others or be degraded in *their* eyes, even if she does not lose *self*-respect or become degraded in her own eyes. So to the extent that a person has an interest in the way she is regarded by others, surrogacy may injure those interests. But that raises at least two points. First, it is not clear that surrogacy actually does have these effects. Second, to the extent that these effects stem solely from the way surrogacy is regarded by the society—as a matter of fact and without separate normative justification—it is not clear that it represents a basis for condemning the practice rather than a basis for condemning society's reaction. Although homosexuality was (or is) a basis for a loss of social respect, this provides no reason to condemn homosexuality.

In any case, even if commodification or degradation constituted objective harms to the surrogate, it cannot show that surrogacy is harmful to the surrogate, all things considered. Surrogacy would produce a *net* harm to the surrogate only if the degree of harm that resulted from commodification or degradation was *greater* than the benefits that she received *from* the compensation.

But there is a second way in which commodification or degradation might be regarded as harmful to the surrogate. It may constitute a *moral* harm, and this in one or both of two ways. First, we may harm someone by violating her *rights,* independent of any other physical, economic, or psychological harm. A trespasser harms the property owner by violating her rights to exclusive use of her property, even though there is no "ordinary" harm to her property. A man harms a woman by fondling her without her consent, even if the touching causes no physical pain or lasting psychological damage. If a woman has a right not to have her labor commodified, then surrogacy is harmful precisely because it is a violation of her rights. The problem here, of course, is that many acts that would constitute a violation of B's rights if done without B's consent are not rights violations if done with B's consent. It is no violation of a person's rights if her property is entered with her consent or if she is fondled with her consent. More generally, we do not treat a person *merely* as a means rather than an end-in-herself if we treat her in a certain way only if she consents to be treated in that way. Thus commodification is no obvious violation of this Kantian maxim if the commodification is consensual—absent some additional argument, for example, that the rights involved are inalienable or that consent given under objectionable background conditions is not sufficiently voluntary.

NOTE

1. Elizabeth S. Anderson, "Is Women's Labor a Commodity?" *Philosophy & Public Affairs* 19, no. 1 (Winter 1990): 71–92. For a critique of this view, see Richard J. Arneson, "Commodification and Commercial Surrogacy," *Philosophy & Public Affairs* 21, no. 2 (Spring 1992): 132–64.

23

Is Failing to Contribute
to Famine Relief Wrong?

Singer and His Critics

There are countries in the world where dying from famine is a commonplace. In affluent countries such as the United States, there are organizations that are dedicated to famine relief. These organizations can and do save thousands of lives. They could save more lives if we gave them more of our money.

Do you have a moral obligation to donate your money to famine-relief organizations, and if so, how much money should you donate? In the featured article of this section, Peter Singer raises this question and comes up with a startling answer: Most of us, perhaps all of us, fall seriously short of our moral obligations to the starving. Even if you have contributed from time to time to famine-relief organizations, even if you have contributed very substantial sums, doubtless you have also spent money on some of life's luxuries—a new CD, a night out at the movies, or a relatively expensive meal at a restaurant. If Singer's argument is sound, then by failing to spend that money on famine relief you have failed to do what you are morally obliged to do. You have acted wrongly, and seriously so.

Singer sets his argument out with two premises. The first is an obvious truth about the badness of suffering and death from starvation, and the second is a general principle about obligation. We call it the general principle. The conclusion that Singer draws is not as clear as one might wish, but what is clear is that he thinks we are all giving far less than we ought to give to famine relief.

P1 Dying from starvation is bad.
P2 If it is in one's power to prevent something bad from happening without sacrificing anything of comparable moral importance, we ought, morally, to do it.

C   I ought to give much than I do to famine relief.

This argument is not valid as it stands. The two premises could both be true while the conclusion is false. For example, nothing in the premises guarantees that I have anything to give to famine relief. Nor is it guaranteed by anything in the premises that by giving money to famine relief I won't be making a sacrifice that is comparable to dying from starvation. (Perhaps I will die from starvation if I give much more to famine relief than I already do.) To make the argument valid we need to make certain assumptions explicit: I can prevent someone's dying from starvation by giving money to famine-relief organizations, and by giving money to famine-relief organizations I would not be sacrificing anything that was comparable to the evil of death from starvation.

P1   Dying of starvation is bad.
P2   If it is in one's power to prevent something bad from happening without sacrificing anything of comparable moral importance, one ought, morally, to do it.
P3   I can prevent people's dying of starvation by giving more money to famine relief than I currently give.
P4   By giving more money to famine-relief organizations than I currently give I would not be sacrificing anything morally comparable to the evil of dying of starvation.

C   I ought, morally, to give more money to famine relief than I currently give.

This argument does seem to be valid. If the premises are all true, then so too is the conclusion. Are the premises all true? No one disputes premise 1. Premise 3 will be true provided that I have some money left over after I have catered to my own basic needs and that there are some reliable famine-relief agencies around, such as Oxfam. Premise 4 also seems true. I regard death from starvation as one of the worst things that could happen to me—much worse, say, than having to forego an expensive restaurant meal. And its badness does not depend on the fact that it is *I* who would die from starvation. Anyone else's death by starvation must be just as bad as mine. I would clearly regard foregoing an expensive restaurant meal as less bad than my dying from starvation. Since there is nothing morally special about me, my foregoing an expensive restaurant meal is not morally comparable to someone's dying from starvation. Furthermore, premise 4 is not only true as a matter of fact at the moment. It is true provided only that I won't die of starvation if I give some more money to famine relief. So the conclusion of the argument would seem to be that I have to keep giving to famine relief up to the point where I myself am threatened by death from starvation. That is a very radical conclusion indeed. Most people are loath to accept it, and few if anyone lives by it.

If premises 1, 3, and 4 are all true, then any good objection to Singer's argument will have to focus on premise 2, Singer's general principle. However, given that the principle, in conjunction with some apparently obvious facts, does appear to entail such sweeping consequences, consequences that no one is willing to accept or live by, why should one accept Singer's principle in the first place? What reasons can be cited in its favor?

In the Introduction we note that one way of reading Singer's argument is as an appeal to an analogy—an analogy between refraining from donating money to a famine relief and refraining from wading into a shallow pond to rescue a small child who will otherwise drown. Suppose that wading into the shallow pond to save the drowning child will cost you a certain amount in cleaning and replacing the clothes that will be ruined. Virtually everyone will agree that it would be morally wrong not to wade in and save the child, given that doing so will pose no risk of harm to the rescuer and will result only in a cost of $200. But then you could also save a starving child in Ethiopia by donating $200 to Oxfam. But if we agree that it would be wrong not to save the child in the shallow-pond case and that the shallow-pond case is morally analogous to the famine-relief case, then Singer's quite strong conclusion seems to follow: When people refrain from sending money to famine-relief efforts they behave in a manner that is seriously immoral. This analogical argument in defense of the moral obligation to contribute to such relief efforts can be represented as follows:

P1   Refraining from saving the child in the shallow pond is seriously morally wrong.
P2   Refraining from saving the child in the shallow pond is morally on a par with refraining from sending money to famine relief to prevent a child's death by starvation.

C   Refraining from sending money to famine relief is seriously morally wrong.

What is the relation between this two-premise analogical argument and the far-premise argument that preceded it? It is this: Singer's general principle is an attempt to spell out the morally relevant feature that the shallow-pond case and the starving-child case share, the feature that makes them morally on a par. (See the Introduction discussion of inference to the best explanation.) What would explain the judgment that it is wrong to refrain from saving the drowning child and judgments in other, similar cases where we think, intuitively, that one has an obligation to prevent something bad from happening when it is of little cost to oneself? These are cases in which one can prevent something very bad happening without sacrificing anything of comparable moral significance (indeed, as Singer points at in qualifying his general principle, anything of moral significance at all). So maybe that is what explains the moral obligation. Clearly this would explain the judgment in the shallow-pond case, as the following argument makes transparently clear.

P1   The death of the boy from drowning is a very bad thing.
P2   If it is in your power to prevent something bad from happening, without sacrificing anything of comparable moral importance, (or, at least, without sacrificing anything morally significant) you ought, morally, to do it.
P3   It is within your power to prevent the death of the boy from drowning by sacrificing clothes worth $200.
P4   The sacrifice of clothes worth $200 is not morally comparable with the death of the boy from drowning (or even morally significant).

C   You ought morally, to save the boy from drowning.

Singer's general principle, then, explains our moral judgment in the shallow-pond case and in closely related cases. It also delivers the analogous judgment in the starving-child case. What this highlights is that an argument from analogy can often be replaced with an argument to the best explanation.

We could begin a criticism of the analogical argument by spelling out differences between the cases that might make a moral difference. For example, you are near the boy in the pond, but you are far from the boy dying from starvation in Ethiopia. Or there are no other people standing around the pond to save the drowning boy, but there are lots of other people who could save the starving Ethiopian. Singer considers several such differences and argues that each of them is morally irrelevant. For example, how could distance alone make a moral difference to one's obligations? Each of these objections to the analogy, if justified, would also provide objections to the general principle Singer adopts. They point to extra conditions (such as spatial proximity) that would have to be satisfied for one to have the obligation to prevent the very bad thing from happening.

All three critical pieces attack Singer's general principle (which Arthur calls the "greater moral evil rule"). Arthur thinks there are obvious counterexamples to the principle. For example, suppose a stranger badly needs a kidney. He will die if he doesn't get one today. As it happens you still have two. What if you could survive on one kidney, albeit at an impaired level of well-being? The greater moral evil rule requires that you donate your kidney to the needy stranger. Or suppose that the same stranger also strongly desires your sexual favors and will be totally miserable unless you grant them to him. Suppose you could grant him those sexual favors without suffering the same kind of misery that denying them would cause him. The greater moral evil rule would appear to require you to grant him the sexual favors he so strongly desires, along with your "spare" kidney. But you are not morally obligated to give away either your kidney or your sexual favors to sickly, lusting strangers. Arthur concludes that Singer's general principle is false.

Arthur does more than point out the counterexamples to Singer's principle. He attempts to explain why the principle initially seems plausible, why it applies in the shallow-pond case, and why it fails in the starving-child case. The greater moral evil rule is what he calls a "prima facie moral principle." We do have to give some weight in our moral calculations to preventing evils, especially when there is no comparable cost to ourselves. But that something is an evil we could prevent is not the only morally relevant factor we can consider. There can be other factors to take into account. Arthur invokes the notion of an entitlement. You are entitled to keep your own kidneys, for example, whatever needs some sickly stranger might have, and you are entitled to withhold sexual favors from those to whom you do not wish to grant them. If one has an entitlement to something (one's own kidneys or choosing sexual partners) one is not obliged to sacrifice that entitlement, even if it means that someone else is going to suffer a great deal as a result.

How is this relevant to Singer's argument? The notion of property also involves an entitlement. Indeed, we tend to think that you don't have to give your kidneys away precisely because they are *yours;* you have a property right over parts of your own body. The reason you do not have to give away one of your kidneys to any stranger who needs one is that you don't have to give away your property to any stranger who would benefit by receiving it. A property right is merely a certain kind of entitlement. If you have this entitlement, then you cannot be obligated to give away all of your property to the point where you yourself are starving—even if there are some people whose starvation you could prevent by so doing.

One obvious difference between the drowning child and the starving child is that the former is *nearby* and the latter is *far away.* Is this difference morally relevant? Singer dismisses this idea rather swiftly. "I do not think I need to say much in defense of the refusal to take proximity and distance into account. The fact that a person is physically near to us . . . does not show that we *ought* to help him rather than another who happens to be further away." The greater moral evil rule reflects this judgment that spatial distance is morally irrelevant in that it makes no mention of physical proximity at all. Michael Slote attempts to explain why we sometimes feel, intuitively, that distance can make a moral difference. However, he derives this explanation from more fundamental considerations. Slote claims that the correct understanding of the nature and role of the virtue of *empathy* explains the intuitive notion that we have a more stringent responsibility to save the boy drowning in the shallow pond than we do to make comparable sacrifices to save people who we have been told are dying from starvation. Slote argues that a developed human empathy lies at the basis of moral action. Roughly speaking, an action is wrong if it reflects a deficiency of normal empathy. And it is permissible if it does not reflect a deficiency of normal empathy. To ignore the boy in the pond would be to exhibit a deficiency of normal human empathy, and would therefore be wrong. By contrast, consider the kind of empathic response that is appropriate when someone tells me that a child whom I do not know and with whom I have had no direct connection is drowning in a pond in a distant country. I know about the distant drowning child only by description, whereas I can *see* the nearby drowning boy with my own eyes. Slote seems to be right that it does not exhibit a deficiency in normal human empathy to say in the case of the distant drowning child, "Well, that's very unfortunate, but I can't spend all my time dwelling on incidents like that." So, according to Slote's virtue theory, it would be wrong to ignore the drowning boy that you can see, but not wrong to ignore the distant drowning boy.

QUESTIONS TO CONSIDER

• In thinking about this issue, first ask yourself what you think about the shallow-pond case. Do you agree with Singer that it would be morally wrong to walk away from the drowning boy if it would cost you, say, to replace the damaged clothing? What if it would cost you $100? $500? Construct some other possible cases in which you could prevent something very bad from happening to someone else at roughly equivalent costs. Suppose your next-door neighbor needs money to pay for a life-saving operation, money he doesn't have and that he cannot borrow. But you have more than enough in the bank. Is it your moral responsibility to pay $50 for your neighbor's operation? $100? $500?

• Would it make any difference if your neighbour happened to be on vacation, twelve thousand miles away, when the need for his operation arose?

• Suppose the stranger happens to be visiting your neighbor. Would the fact that he is a stranger (but right next door) make a difference?

• How does Slote account for the *apparent* moral significance of distance?

• Finally, is Arthur correct in arguing that Singer's general principle is unreasonably demanding? Or can Singer's principle, along with the shallow pond example, be interpreted in a less demanding way?

FURTHER READING

Kamm, F. M. "Faminine Ethics: The Problem of Distance in Morality," in *Singer and His Critics,* ed. Dale Jamieson (Oxford: Blackwell, 1999), pp. 162–208.

Otteson, James R. "Limits on Our Obligation to Give." *Public Affairs Quarterly* 14, no. 3 (2000): 183–203.

Peter Singer | Famine, Affluence, and Morality

As I write this, in November 1971, people are dying in East Bengal from lack of food, shelter, and medical care. The suffering and death that are occurring there now are not inevitable, not unavoidable in any fatalistic sense of the term. Constant poverty, a cyclone, and a civil war have turned at least nine million people into destitute refugees; nevertheless, it is not beyond the capacity of the richer nations to give enough assistance to reduce any further suffering to very small proportions. The decisions and actions of human beings can prevent this kind of suffering. Unfortunately, human beings have not made the necessary decisions. At the individual level, people have, with very few exceptions, not responded to the situation in any significant way. Generally speaking, people have not given large sums to relief funds; they have not written to their parliamentary representatives demanding increased government assistance; they have not demonstrated in the streets, held symbolic fasts, or done anything else directed toward providing the refugees with the means to satisfy their essential needs. At the government level, no government has given the sort of massive aid that would enable the refugees to survive for more than a few days. Britain, for instance, has given rather more than most countries. It has, to date, given £14,750,000. For comparative purposes, Britain's share of the nonrecoverable development costs of the Anglo-French Concorde project is already in excess of £275,000,000, and on present estimates will reach £440,000,000. The implication is that the British government values a supersonic transport more than thirty times as highly as it values the lives of the nine million refugees. Australia is another country which, on a per capita basis, is well up in the "aid to Bengal" table. Australia's aid, however, amounts to less than one-twelfth of the cost of Sydney's new opera house.

The total amount given, from all sources, now stands at about £65,000,000. The estimated cost of keeping the refugees alive for one year is £464,000,000. Most of the refugees have now been in the camps for more than six months. The World Bank has said that India needs a minimum of £300,000,000 in assistance from other countries before the end of the year. It seems obvious that assistance on this scale will not be forthcoming. India will be forced to choose between letting the refugees starve or diverting funds from her own development program, which will mean that more of her own people will starve in the future.[1]

These are the essential facts about the present situation in Bengal. So far as it concerns us here, there is nothing unique about this situation except its magnitude. The Bengal emergency is just the latest and most acute of a series of major emergencies in various parts of the world, arising both from natural and from man-made causes. There are also many parts of the world in which people die from malnutrition and lack of food independent of any special emergency. I take Bengal as my example only because it is the present concern, and because the size of the problem has ensured that it has been given adequate publicity. Neither individuals nor governments can claim to be unaware of what is happening there.

What are the moral implications of a situation like this? In what follows, I shall argue that the way people in relatively affluent countries react to a situation like that in Bengal cannot be justified; indeed, the whole way we look at moral issues—our moral conceptual scheme—needs to be altered, and with it, the way of life that has come to be taken for granted in our society.

In arguing for this conclusion I will not, of course, claim to be morally neutral. I shall, however, try to argue for the moral position that I take, so that

Peter Singer, "Famine, Affluence, and Morality," *Philosophy and Public Affairs* 1, no. 3 (Spring 1972): 229–43. Reprinted by permission of Princeton University Press.

anyone who accepts certain assumptions, to be made explicit, will, I hope, accept my conclusion.

I begin with the assumption that suffering and death from lack of food, shelter, and medical care are bad. I think most people will agree about this, although one may reach the same view by different routes. I shall not argue for this view. People can hold all sorts of eccentric positions, and perhaps from some of them it would not follow that death by starvation is in itself bad. It is difficult, perhaps impossible, to refute such positions, and so for brevity I will henceforth take this assumption as accepted. Those who disagree need read no further.

My next point is this: if it is in our power to prevent something bad from happening, without thereby sacrificing anything of comparable moral importance, we ought, morally, to do it. By "without sacrificing anything of comparable moral importance" I mean without causing anything else comparably bad to happen, or doing something that is wrong in itself, or failing to promote some moral good, comparable in significance to the bad thing that we can prevent. This principle seems almost as uncontroversial as the last one. It requires us only to prevent what is bad, and not to promote what is good, and it requires this of us only when we can do it without sacrificing anything that is, from the moral point of view, comparably important. I could even, as far as the application of my argument to the Bengal emergency is concerned, qualify the point so as to make it: if it is in our power to prevent something very bad from happening, without thereby sacrificing anything morally significant, we ought, morally, to do it. An application of this principle would be as follows: if I am walking past a shallow pond and see a child drowning in it, I ought to wade in and pull the child out. This will mean getting my clothes muddy, but this is insignificant, while the death of the child would presumably be a very bad thing.

The uncontroversial appearance of the principle just stated is deceptive. If it were acted upon, even in its qualified form, our lives, our society, and our world would be fundamentally changed. For the principle takes, firstly, no account of proximity or distance. It makes no moral difference whether the person I can help is a neighbor's child ten yards from me or a Bengali whose name I shall never know, ten thousand miles away. Secondly, the principle makes no distinction between cases in which I am the only person who could possibly do anything and cases in which I am just one among millions in the same position.

I do not think I need to say much in defense of the refusal to take proximity and distance into account. The fact that a person is physically near to us, so that we have personal contact with him, may make it more likely that we *shall* assist him, but this does not show that we *ought* to help him rather than another who happens to be further away. If we accept any principle of impartiality, universalizability, equality, or whatever, we cannot discriminate against someone merely because he is far away from us (or we are far away from him). Admittedly, it is possible that we are in a better position to judge what needs to be done to help a person near to us than one far away, and perhaps also to provide the assistance we judge to be necessary. If this were the case, it would be a reason for helping those near to us first. This may once have been a justification for being more concerned with the poor in one's own town than with famine victims in India. Unfortunately for those who like to keep their moral responsibilities limited, instant communication and swift transportation have changed the situation. From the moral point of view, the development of the world into a "global village" has made an important, though still unrecognized, difference to our moral situation. Expert observers and supervisors, sent out by famine relief organizations or permanently stationed in famine-prone areas, can direct our aid to a refugee in Bengal almost as effectively as we could get it to someone in our own block. There would seem, therefore, to be no possible justification for discriminating on geographical grounds.

There may be a greater need to defend the second implication of my principle—that the fact that there are millions of other people in the same position, in respect to the Bengali refugees, as I am, does not make the situation significantly different from a situation in which I am the only person who can prevent something very bad from occurring. Again, of course, I admit that there is a psychological difference between the cases; one feels less guilty about doing nothing if one can point to others, similarly placed, who have also done nothing. Yet this can make no real difference to our moral obligations.[2] Should I consider that I am less obliged to pull the drowning child out of the pond if on looking around I see other people, no further away than I am, who have also noticed the child but are doing nothing? One has only to ask this question to see the absurdity of the view that numbers lessen obligation. It is a view that is an ideal excuse for inactivity; unfortunately most of the major evils—poverty, overpopulation, pollution—are problems in which everyone is almost equally involved.

The view that numbers do make a difference can be made plausible if stated in this way: if everyone in circumstances like mine gave £5 to the Bengal Relief Fund, there would be enough to provide food, shelter, and medical care for the refugees; there is no reason why I should give more than anyone else in the same circumstances as I am; therefore I have no obligation to give more than £5. Each premise in this argument is true, and the argument looks sound. It may convince us, unless we notice that it is based on a hypothetical premise, although the conclusion is not stated hypothetically. The argument would be sound if the conclusion were: if everyone in circumstances like mine were to give £5, I would have no obligation to give more than £5. If the conclusion were so stated, however, it would be obvious that the argument has no bearing on a situation in which it is not the case that everyone else gives £5. This, of course, is the actual situation. It is more or less certain that not everyone in circumstances like mine will give £5. So there will not be enough to provide the needed food, shelter, and medical care. Therefore by giving more than £5 I will prevent more suffering than I would if I gave just £5.

It might be thought that this argument has an absurd consequence. Since the situation appears to be that very few people are likely to give substantial amounts, it follows that I and everyone else in similar circumstances ought to give as much as possible, that is, at least up to the point at which by giving more one would begin to cause serious suffering for oneself and one's dependents—perhaps even beyond this point to the point of marginal utility, at which by giving more one would cause oneself and one's dependents as much suffering as one would prevent in Bengal. If everyone does this, however, there will be more than can be used for the benefit of the refugees, and some of the sacrifice will have been unnecessary. Thus, if everyone does what he ought to do, the result will not be as good as it would be if everyone did a little less than he ought to do, or if only some do all that they ought to do.

The paradox here arises only if we assume that the actions in question—sending money to the relief funds—are performed more or less simultaneously, and are also unexpected. For if it is to be expected that everyone is going to contribute something, then clearly each is not obliged to give as much as he would have been obliged to had others not been giving too. And if everyone is not acting more or less simultaneously, then those giving later will know how much more is needed, and will have no obligation to give more than is necessary to reach this amount. To say this is not to deny the principle that people in the same circumstances have the same obligations, but to point out that the fact that others have given, or may be expected to give, is a relevant circumstance: those giving after it has become known that many others are giving and those giving before are not in the same circumstances. So the seemingly absurd consequence of the principle I have put forward can occur only if people are in error about the actual circumstances—that is, if they think they are giving when others are not, but in fact they are giving when others are. The result of everyone doing what he really ought to do cannot be worse than the result of everyone doing less than he ought to do, although the result of everyone doing what he reasonably believes he ought to do could be.

If my argument so far has been sound, neither our distance from a preventable evil nor the number of other people who, in respect to that evil, are in the same situation as we are, lessens our obligation to mitigate or prevent that evil. I shall therefore take as established the principle I asserted earlier. As I have already said, I need to assert it only in its qualified form: if it is in our power to prevent something very bad from happening, without thereby sacrificing anything else morally significant, we ought, morally, to do it.

The outcome of this argument is that our traditional moral categories are upset. The traditional distinction between duty and charity cannot be drawn, or at least, not in the place we normally draw it. Giving money to the Bengal Relief Fund is regarded as an act of charity in our society. The bodies which collect money are known as "charities." These organizations see themselves in this way—if you send them a check, you will be thanked for your "generosity." Because giving money is regarded as an act of charity, it is not thought that there is anything wrong with not giving. The charitable man may be praised, but the man who is not charitable is not condemned. People do not feel in any way ashamed or guilty about spending money on new clothes or a new car instead of giving it to famine relief. (Indeed, the alternative does not occur to them.) This way of looking at the matter cannot be justified. When we buy new clothes not to keep ourselves warm but to look "well-dressed" we are not providing for any important need. We would not be sacrificing anything significant if we were to continue to wear our old clothes, and give the money to famine relief. By doing so, we would be preventing another person from starving. It follows from what I have said earlier that we ought to give money away, rather than spend it on clothes which we do not need to keep us warm. To do so is not charitable, or generous. Nor is it the kind of act which philosophers and theologians have called "supererogatory"—an act which it would be good to do, but not wrong not to do. On the contrary, we ought to give the money away, and it is wrong not to do so.

I am not maintaining that there are no acts which are charitable, or that there are no acts which it would be good to do but not wrong not to do. It may be possible to redraw the distinction between duty and charity in some other place. All I am arguing here is that the present way of drawing the distinction, which makes it an act of charity for a man living at the level of affluence which most people in the "developed nations" enjoy to give money to save someone else from starvation, cannot be supported.

It is beyond the scope of my argument to consider whether the distinction should be redrawn or abolished altogether. There would be many other possible ways of drawing the distinction—for instance, one might decide that it is good to make other people as happy as possible, but not wrong not to do so.

Despite the limited nature of the revision in our moral conceptual scheme which I am proposing, the revision would, given the extent of both affluence and famine in the world today, have radical implications. These implications may lead to further objections, distinct from those I have already considered. I shall discuss two of these.

One objection to the position I have taken might be simply that it is too drastic a revision of our moral scheme. People do not ordinarily judge in the way I have suggested they should. Most people reserve their moral condemnation for those who violate some moral norm, such as the norm against taking another person's property. They do not condemn those who indulge in luxury instead of giving to famine relief. But given that I did not set out to present a morally neutral description of the way people make moral judgments, the way people do in fact judge has nothing to do with the validity of my conclusion. My conclusion follows from the principle which I advanced earlier, and unless that principle is rejected, or the arguments shown to be unsound, I think the conclusion must stand, however strange it appears.

It might, nevertheless, be interesting to consider why our society, and most other societies, do judge differently from the way I have suggested they should. In a well-known article, J. O. Urmson suggests that the imperatives of duty, which tell us what we must do, as distinct from what it would be good to do but not wrong not to do, function so as to prohibit behavior that is intolerable if men are to live together in society.[3] This may explain the origin and continued existence of the present division between acts of duty and acts of charity. Moral attitudes are shaped by the needs of society, and no doubt society needs people who will observe the rules that make social existence tolerable. From the point of view of a particular society, it is essential to prevent violations of norms against killing, stealing, and so on. It is quite inessential, however, to help people outside one's own society.

If this is an explanation of our common distinction between duty and supererogation, however, it is not a justification of it. The moral point of view requires us to look beyond the interests of our own society. Previously, as I have already mentioned, this may hardly have been feasible, but it is quite feasible now. From the moral point of view, the prevention of the starvation of millions of people outside our society must be considered at least as pressing as the upholding of property norms within our society.

It has been argued by some writers, among them Sidgwick and Urmson, that we need to have a basic moral code which is not too far beyond the capacities of the ordinary man, for otherwise there will be a general breakdown of compliance with the moral code. Crudely stated, this argument suggests that if we tell people that they ought to refrain from murder and give everything they do not really need to famine relief, they will do neither, whereas if we tell them that they ought to refrain from murder and that it is good to give to famine relief but not wrong not to do so, they will at least refrain from murder. The issue here is: Where should we drawn the line between conduct that is required and conduct that is good although not required, so as to get the best possible result? This would seem to be an empirical question, although a very difficult one. One objection to the Sidgwick-Urmson line of argument is that it takes insufficient account of the effect that moral standards can have on the decisions we make. Given a society in which a wealthy man who gives five percent of his income to famine relief is regarded as most generous, it is not surprising that a proposal that we all ought to give away half our incomes will be thought to be absurdly unrealistic. In a society which held that no man should have more than enough while others have less than they need, such a proposal might seem narrow-minded. What it is possible for a man to do and what he is likely to do are both, I think, very greatly influenced by what people around him are doing and expecting him to do. In

any case, the possibility that by spreading the idea that we ought to be doing very much more than we are to relieve famine we shall bring about a general breakdown of moral behavior seems remote. If the stakes are an end to widespread starvation, it is worth the risk. Finally, it should be emphasized that these considerations are relevant only to the issue of what we should require from others, and not to what we ourselves ought to do.

The second objection to my attack on the present distinction between duty and charity is one which has from time to time been made against utilitarianism. It follows from some forms of utilitarian theory that we all ought, morally, to be working full time to increase the balance of happiness over misery. The position I have taken here would not lead to this conclusion in all circumstances, for if there were no bad occurrences that we could prevent without sacrificing something of comparable moral importance, my argument would have no application. Given the present conditions in many parts of the world, however, it does follow from my argument that we ought, morally, to be working full time to relieve great suffering of the sort that occurs as a result of famine or other disasters. Of course, mitigating circumstances can be adduced—for instance, that if we wear ourselves out through overwork, we shall be less effective than we would otherwise have been. Nevertheless, when all considerations of this sort have been taken into account, the conclusion remains: we ought to be preventing as much suffering as we can without sacrificing something else of comparable moral importance. This conclusion is one which we may be reluctant to face. I cannot see, though, why it should be regarded as a criticism of the position for which I have argued, rather than a criticism of our ordinary standards of behavior. Since most people are self-interested to some degree, very few of us are likely to do everything that we ought to do. It would, however, hardly be honest to take this as evidence that it is not the case that we ought to do it.

It may still be thought that my conclusions are so wildly out of line with what everyone else thinks and has always thought that there must be something wrong with the argument somewhere. In order to show that my conclusions, while certainly contrary to contemporary Western moral standards, would not have seemed so extraordinary at other times and in other places, I would like to quote a passage from a writer not normally thought of as a way-out radical, Thomas Aquinas.

> Now, according to the natural order instituted by divine providence, material goods are provided for the satisfaction of human needs. Therefore the division and appropriation of property, which proceeds from human law, must not hinder the satisfaction of man's necessity from such goods. Equally, whatever a man has in superabundance is owed, of natural right, to the poor for their sustenance. So Ambrosius says, and it is also to be found in the *Decretum Gratiani:* "The bread which you withhold belongs to the hungry; the clothing you shut away, to the naked; and the money you bury in the earth is the redemption and freedom of the penniless."[4]

I now want to consider a number of points, more practical than philosophical, which are relevant to the application of the moral conclusion we have reached. These points challenge not the idea that we ought to be doing all we can to prevent starvation, but the idea that giving away a great deal of money is the best means to this end.

It is sometimes said that overseas aid should be a government responsibility, and that therefore one ought not to give to privately run charities. Giving privately, it is said, allows the government and the noncontributing members of society to escape their responsibilities.

This argument seems to assume that the more people there are who give to privately organized famine relief funds, the less likely it is that the government will take over full responsibility for such aid. This assumption is unsupported, and does not strike me as at all plausible. The opposite view—that if no one gives voluntarily, a government will assume that its citizens are uninterested in famine relief and would not wish to be forced into giving aid—seems more plausible. In any case, unless there were a definite probability that by refusing to give one would be helping to bring about massive government assistance, people who do refuse to make voluntary con-

tributions are refusing to prevent a certain amount of suffering without being able to point to any tangible beneficial consequence of their refusal. So the onus of showing how their refusal will bring about government action is on those who refuse to give.

I do not, of course, want to dispute the contention that governments of affluent nations should be giving many times the amount of genuine, no-strings-attached aid that they are giving now. I agree, too, that giving privately is not enough, and that we ought to be campaigning actively for entirely new standards for both public and private contributions to famine relief. Indeed, I would sympathize with someone who thought that campaigning was more important than giving oneself, although I doubt whether preaching what one does not practice would be very effective. Unfortunately, for many people the idea that "it's the government's responsibility" is a reason for not giving which does not appear to entail any political action either.

Another, more serious reason for not giving to famine relief funds is that until there is effective population control, relieving famine merely postpones starvation. If we save the Bengal refugees now, others, perhaps the children of these refugees, will face starvation in a few years' time. In support of this, one may cite the now well-known facts about the population explosion and the relatively limited scope for expanded production.

This point, like the previous one, is an argument against relieving suffering that is happening now, because of a belief about what might happen in the future; it is unlike the previous point in that very good evidence can be adduced in support of this belief about the future. I will not go into the evidence here. I accept that the earth cannot support indefinitely a population rising at the present rate. This certainly poses a problem for anyone who thinks it important to prevent famine. Again, however, one could accept the argument without drawing the conclusion that it absolves one from any obligation to do anything to prevent famine. The conclusion that should be drawn is that the best means of preventing famine, in the long run, is population control. It would then follow from the position reached earlier that one ought to be doing all one can to promote population control (unless one held that all forms of population control were wrong in themselves, or would have significantly bad consequences). Since there are organizations working specifically for population control, one would then support them rather than more orthodox methods of preventing famine.

A third point raised by the conclusion reached earlier relates to the question of just how much we all ought to be giving away. One possibility, which has already been mentioned, is that we ought to give until we reach the level of marginal utility—that is, the level at which, by giving more, I would cause as much suffering to myself or my dependents as I would relieve by my gift. This would mean, of course, that one would reduce oneself to very near the material circumstances of a Bengali refugee. It will be recalled that earlier I put forward both a strong and a moderate version of the principle of preventing bad occurrences. The strong version, which required us to prevent bad things from happening unless in doing so we would be sacrificing something of comparable moral significance, does seem to require reducing ourselves to the level of marginal utility. I should also say that the strong version seems to me to be the correct one. I proposed the more moderate version—that we should prevent bad occurrences unless, to do so, we had to sacrifice something morally significant—only in order to show that even on this surely undeniable principle a great change in our way of life is required. On the more moderate principle, it may not follow that we ought to reduce ourselves to the level of marginal utility, for one might hold that to reduce oneself and one's family to this level is to cause something significantly bad to happen. Whether this is so I shall not discuss, since, as I have said, I can see no good reason for holding the moderate version of the principle rather than the strong version. Even if we accepted the principle only in its moderate form, however, it should be clear that we would have to give away enough to ensure that the consumer society, dependent as it is on people spending on trivia rather than giving to famine relief, would slow down and perhaps disappear entirely. There are several reasons why this would be desirable in itself. The value

and necessity of economic growth are now being questioned not only by conservationists, but by economists as well.[5] There is no doubt, too, that the consumer society has had a distorting effect on the goals and purposes of its members. Yet looking at the matter purely from the point of view of overseas aid, there must be a limit to the extent to which we should deliberately slow down our economy; for it might be the case that if we gave away, say, forty percent of our Gross National Product, we would slow down the economy so much that in absolute terms we would be giving less than if we gave twenty-five percent of the much larger GNP that we would have if we limited our contribution to this smaller percentage.

I mention this only as an indication of the sort of factor that one would have to take into account in working out an ideal. Since Western societies generally consider one percent of the GNP an acceptable level for overseas aid, the matter is entirely academic. Nor does it affect the question of how much an individual should give in a society in which very few are giving substantial amounts.

It is sometimes said, though less often now than it used to be, that philosophers have no special role to play in public affairs, since most public issues depend primarily on an assessment of facts. On questions of fact, it is said, philosophers as such have no special expertise, and so it has been possible to engage in philosophy without committing oneself to any position on major public issues. No doubt there are some issues of social policy and foreign policy about which it can truly be said that a really expert assessment of the facts is required before taking sides or acting, but the issue of famine is surely not one of these. The facts about the existence of suffering are beyond dispute. Nor, I think, is it disputed that we can do something about it, either through orthodox methods of famine relief or through population control or both. This is therefore an issue on which philosophers are competent to take a position. The issue is one which faces everyone who has more money than he needs to support himself and his dependents, or who is in a position to take some sort of political action. These categories must include practically every teacher and student of philosophy in the universities of the Western world. If philosophy is to deal with matters that are relevant to both teachers and students, this is an issue that philosophers should discuss.

Discussion, though, is not enough. What is the point of relating philosophy to public (and personal) affairs if we do not take our conclusions seriously? In this instance, taking our conclusion seriously means acting upon it. The philosopher will not find it any easier than anyone else to alter his attitudes and way of life to the extent that, if I am right, is involved in doing everything that we ought to be doing. At the very least, though, one can make a start. The philosopher who does so will have to sacrifice some of the benefits of the consumer society, but he can find compensation in the satisfaction of a way of life in which theory and practice, if not yet in harmony, are at least coming together.

NOTES

1. There was also a third possibility: that India would go to war to enable the refugees to return to their lands.

Since I wrote this paper, India has taken this way out. The situation is no longer that described above, but this does not affect my argument, as the next paragraph indicates.

2. In view of the special sense philosophers often give to the term, I should say that I use "obligation" simply as the abstract noun derived from "ought," so that "I have an obligation to" means no more, and no less, than "I ought to." This usage is in accordance with the definition of "ought" given by the *Shorter Oxford English Dictionary:* "the general verb to express duty or obligation." I do not think any issue of substance hangs on the way the term is used; sentences in which I use "obligation" could all be rewritten, although somewhat clumsily, as sentences in which a clause containing "ought" replaces the term "obligation."

3. J. O. Urmson, "Saints and Heroes," in *Essays in Moral Philosophy,* ed. Abraham I. Melden (Seattle and London, 1958), p. 214. For a related but significantly different view see also Henry Sidgwick, *The Methods of Ethics,* 7th edn. (London, 1907), pp. 220–221, 492–493.

4. *Summa Theologica,* II-II, Question 66, Article 7, in *Aquinas, Selected Political Writings,* ed. A. P. d'Entreves, trans. J. G. Dawson (Oxford, 1948), p. 171.

5. See, for instance, John Kenneth Galbraith, *The New Industrial State* (Boston, 1967); and E. J. Mishan, *The Costs of Economic Growth* (London, 1967).

Critics

John Arthur

World Hunger and Moral Obligation

The Case Against Singer

INTRODUCTION

My guess is that everyone who reads these words is wealthy by comparison with the poorest millions of people on our planet. Not only do we have plenty of money for food, clothing, housing, and other necessities, but a fair amount is left over for far less important purchases like phonograph records, fancy clothes, trips, intoxicants, movies, and so on. And what's more we don't usually give a thought to whether or not we ought to spend our money on such luxuries rather than to give it to those who need it more; we just assume it's ours to do with as we please.

Originally published as "Famine Relief and the Ideal Moral Code," in *Applying Ethics,* ed. V. Barry (Belmont, Calif.: Wadsworth, 1981). Reprinted with the permission of the publisher.

Peter Singer, "Famine, Affluence, and Morality" argues that our assumption is wrong, that we should not buy luxuries when others are in severe need. But [is he] correct? . . .

He first argues that two general moral principles are widely accepted, and then that those principles imply an obligation to eliminate starvation.

The first principle is simply that "suffering and death from lack of food, shelter and medical care are bad." Some may be inclined to think that the mere existence of such an evil in itself places an obligation on others, but that is, of course, the problem which Singer addresses. I take it that he is not begging the question in this obvious way and will argue from the existence of evil to the obligation of others to eliminate it. But how, exactly, does he establish this? The second principle, he thinks, shows the connection, but it is here that controversy arises.

This principle, which I will call the greater moral evil rule, is as follows:

> If it is in our power to prevent something bad from happening, without thereby sacrificing anything of comparable moral importance, we ought, morally, to do it

In other words, people are entitled to keep their earnings only if there is no way for them to prevent a greater evil by giving them away. Providing others with food, clothing, and housing would generally be of more importance than buying luxuries, so the greater moral evil rule now requires substantial redistribution of wealth.

Certainly there are few, if any, of us who live by that rule, although that hardly shows we are *justified* in our way of life; we often fail to live up to our own standards. Why does Singer think our shared morality requires that we follow the greater moral evil rule? What arguments does he give for it?

He begins with an analogy. Suppose you came across a child drowning in a shallow pond. Certainly we feel it would be wrong not to help. Even if saving the child meant we must dirty our clothes, we would emphasize that those clothes are not of comparable significance to the child's life. The greater moral evil rule thus seems a natural way of capturing why we think it would be wrong not to help.

But the argument for the greater moral evil rule is not limited to Singer's claim that it explains our feelings about the drowning child or that it appears "uncontroversial." Moral equality also enters the picture. Besides the Jeffersonian idea that we share certain rights equally, most of us are also attracted to another type of equality, namely that like amounts of suffering (or happiness) are of equal significance, no matter who is experiencing them. I cannot reasonably say that, while my pain is no more severe than yours, I am somehow special and it's more important that mine be alleviated. Objectivity requires us to admit the opposite, that no one has a unique status which warrants such special pleading. So equality demands equal consideration of interests as well as respect for certain rights.

But if we fail to give to famine relief and instead purchase a new car when the old one will do, or buy fancy clothes for a friend when his or her old ones are perfectly good, are we not assuming that the relatively minor enjoyment we or our friends may get is as important as another person's life? And that a form of prejudice; we are acting as if people were not equal in the sense that their interests deserve equal consideration. We are giving special consideration to ourselves or to our group, rather like a racist does. Equal consideration of interests thus leads naturally to the greater moral evil rule.

RIGHTS AND DESERT

Equality, in the sense of giving equal consideration to equally serious needs, is part of our moral code. And so we are led, quite rightly I think, to the conclusion that we should prevent harm to others if in doing so we do not sacrifice anything of comparable moral importance. But there is also another side to the coin, one which Singer ignore[s]. . . . This can be expressed rather awkwardly by the notion of entitlements. These fall into two broad categories, rights and desert. A few examples will show what I mean.

All of us could help others by giving away or allowing others to use our bodies. While your life may be shortened by the loss of a kidney or less enjoyable if lived with only one eye, those costs are probably not comparable to the loss experienced by a person who will die without any kidney or who is totally blind. We can even imagine persons who will actually be harmed in some way by your not granting sexual favors to them. Perhaps the absence of a sexual partner would cause psychological harm or even rape. Now suppose that you can prevent this evil without sacrificing anything of comparable importance. Obviously such relations may not be pleasant, but according to the greater moral evil rule that is not enough; to be justified in refusing, you must show that the unpleasantness you would experience is of equal importance to the harm you are preventing. Otherwise, the rule says you must consent.

If anything is clear, however, it is that our code does not *require* such heroism; you are entitled to keep your second eye and kidney and not bestow sexual favors on anyone who may be harmed without them. The reason for this is often expressed in terms of rights; it's your body, you have a right to it, and that weighs against whatever duty you have to help. To sacrifice a kidney for a stranger is to do more than is required, it's heroic.

Moral rights are normally divided into two categories. Negative rights are rights of noninterference. The right to life, for example, is a right not to be killed. Property rights, the right to privacy, and the right to exercise religious freedom are also negative, requiring only that people leave others alone and not interfere.

Positive rights, however, are rights of recipience. By not putting their children up for adoption, parents give them various positive rights, including rights to be fed, clothed, and housed. If I agree to share in a business venture, my promise creates a right of recipience, so that when I back out of the deal, I've violated your right.

Negative rights also differ from positive in that the former are natural; the ones you have depend on what you are. If lower animals lack rights to life or liberty it is because there is a relevant difference between them and us. But the positive rights you may have are not natural; they arise because others have promised, agreed, or contracted to give you something.

Normally, then, a duty to help a stranger in need is not the result of a right he has. Such a right would be positive, and since no contract or promise was made,

no such right exists. An exception to this would be a lifeguard who contracts to watch out for someone's children. The parent whose child drowns would in this case be doubly wronged. First, the lifeguard should not have cruelly or thoughtlessly ignored the child's interests, and second, he ought not to have violated the rights of the parents that he helped. Here, unlike Singer's case, we can say there are rights at stake. Other bystanders also act wrongly by cruelly ignoring the child, but unlike the lifeguard they do not violate anybody's rights. Moral rights are one factor to be weighed, but we also have other obligations; I am not claiming that rights are all we need to consider. That view, like the greater moral evil rule, trades simplicity for accuracy. In fact, our code expects us to help people in need as well as to respect negative and positive rights. But we are also entitled to invoke our own rights as justification for not giving to distant strangers or when the cost to us is substantial, as when we give up an eye or kidney. . . .

Desert is a second form of entitlement. Suppose, for example, an industrious farmer manages through hard work to produce a surplus of food for the winter while a lazy neighbor spends his summer fishing. Must our industrious farmer ignore his hard work and give the surplus away because his neighbor or his family will suffer? What again seems clear is that we have more than one factor to weigh. Not only should we compare the consequences of his keeping it with his giving it away; we also should weigh the fact that one farmer deserves the food, he earned it through his hard work. Perhaps his deserving the product of his labor is outweighed by the greater need of his lazy neighbor, or perhaps it isn't, but being outweighed is in any case not the same as weighing nothing!

Desert can be negative, too. The fact that the Nazi war criminal did what he did means he deserves punishment, that we have a reason to send him to jail. Other considerations, for example the fact that nobody will be deterred by his suffering, or that he is old and harmless, may weigh against punishment and so we may let him go; but again that does not mean he doesn't still deserve to be punished.

Our moral code gives weight to both the greater moral evil principle and entitlements. The former emphasizes equality, claiming that from an objective point of view all comparable suffering, whoever its victim, is equally significant. It encourages us to take an impartial look at all the various effects of our actions; it is thus forward-looking. When we consider matters of entitlement, however, our attention is directed to the past. Whether we have rights to money, property, eyes, or whatever, depends on how we came to possess them. If they were acquired by theft rather than from birth or through gift exchange, then the right is suspect. Desert, like rights, is also backward-looking, emphasizing past effort or past transgressions which now warrant reward or punishment.

Our commonly shared morality thus requires that we ignore neither consequences nor entitlements, neither the future results of our action nor relevant events in the past. It encourages people to help others in need, especially when it's a friend or someone we are close to geographically, and when the cost is not significant. But it also gives weight to rights and desert, so that we are not usually obligated to give to strangers. . . .

But unless we are moral relativists, the mere fact that entitlements are an important part of our moral code does not in itself justify such a role. Singer . . . can perhaps best be seen as a moral reformer advocating the rejection of rules which provide for distribution according to rights and desert. Certainly the fact that in the past our moral code condemned suicide and racial mixing while condoning slavery should not convince us that a more enlightened moral code, one which we would want to support, would take such positions. Rules which define acceptable behavior are continually changing, and we must allow for the replacement of inferior ones.

Why should we not view entitlements as examples of inferior rules we are better off without? What could justify our practice of evaluating actions by looking backward to rights and desert instead of just to their consequences? One answer is that more fundamental values than rights and desert are at stake, namely fairness, justice, and respect. Failure to reward those who earn good grades or promotions is wrong because it's *unfair;* ignoring past guilt shows a lack of regard for *justice;* and failure to respect rights to life, privacy, or religious choice suggests a lack of *respect for other persons.*

Some people may be persuaded by those remarks, feeling that entitlements are now on an acceptably firm foundation. But an advocate of equality may well want to question why fairness, justice, and respect for persons should matter. But since it is no more obvious that preventing suffering matters than that fairness, respect, and justice do, we again seem to have reached an impasse. . . .

The lesson to be learned here is a general one: The moral code it is rational for us to support must be practical; it must actually work. This means, among other things, that it must be able to gain the support of almost everyone.

But the code must be practical in other respects as well. . . . [It] is wrong to ignore the possibilities of altruism, but it is also important that a code not assume people are more unselfish than they are. Rules that would work only for angels are not the ones it is rational to support for humans. Second, an ideal code cannot assume we are more objective than we are; we often tend to rationalize when our own interests are at stake, and a rational person will also keep that in mind when choosing a moral code. Finally, it is not rational to support a code which assumes we have perfect knowledge. We are often mistaken about the consequences of what we do, and a workable code must take that into account as well. . . .

It seems to me, then, that a reasonable code would require people to help when there is no substantial cost to themselves, that is, when what they are sacrificing would not mean *significant* reduction in their own or their families' level of happiness. Since most people's savings accounts and nearly everybody's second kidney are not insignificant, entitlements would in those cases outweigh another's need. But if what is at stake is trivial, as dirtying one's clothes would normally be, then an ideal moral code would not allow rights to override the greater evil that can be prevented. Despite our code's unclear and sometimes schizophrenic posture, it seems to me that these judgments are not that different from our current moral attitudes. We tend to blame people who waste money on trivia when they could help others in need, yet not to expect people to make large sacrifices to distant strangers. An ideal moral code thus might not be a great deal different from our own.

Michael Slote | Famine, Affluence, and Empathy

One of the greatest challenges to ordinary moral thinking and to recent moral theory has been the views and arguments advanced by Peter Singer in his classic paper, "Famine, Affluence, and Morality."[1] Philosophers have struggled with and in many cases attempted to refute Singer's conclusion that our moral obligation to relieve hunger or disease in distant parts of the world is just as great as, say, our obligation to save a child drowning in a shallow pool of water right in front of us. But although this debate continues to be very lively, virtue ethics has not joined in the fray. It has simply not taken up the main issue Singer's paper has been thought to raise, the issue of whether the making of substantial sacrifices in order to help those suffering in distant parts of the world is obligatory or (merely) supererogatory. In the present essay, however, I shall attempt to grapple with Singer's ideas from a virtue-ethical perspective. But I shall be making use, not of the tradition of Aristotelian virtue ethics that has occupied so prominent a place in the recent revival of virtue ethics, but of a form of virtue ethics that has its roots in eighteenth-century moral sentimentalism [as espoused by] Francis Hutcheson and David Hume. Let me now say a bit about recent developments within this alternative tradition of virtue ethics and then go on to discuss how such an approach might be able to offer us an answer to the questions Peter Singer raises.

Neither Hume nor Hutcheson focuses on "caring" about others as a motive: their discussions of morality made use, rather, of concepts like benevolence and sympathy. But the ethics of caring recently proposed and developed by Carol Gilligan, Nel Noddings, and others seems very clearly in the moral sentimentalist tradition and is naturally (and typically) also regarded as a form of virtue ethics, since it evaluates human actions by reference to how much

(of the inner motive of) caring they express or exhibit.[2] And I regard a virtue ethics of caring as the most promising (and interesting) form of present-day sentimentalism. Speaking very roughly, an ethics of caring holds that an act is morally (all) right if it doesn't exhibit a lack (or the opposite) of caring and wrong if it does. (Brushing your teeth may not evince caring, but the point is that it also doesn't evince, exhibit, or reflect a lack of caring concern about others.)

However, when Noddings originally wrote about caring, she had in mind the kind of caring for others that takes place, so to speak, in intimate or at least face-to-face relationships. Caring *about* the fate of (groups of) people one has merely *heard* about didn't come under the rubric of caring; and since morality does take in our relations with such distant and personally-unknown others, Noddings held that the ethics of caring represented only a limited—though important and previously neglected—part of morality. Others who came later, however, sought to show that caring about people who are distant from us can and should be taken within the purview of the caring approach to ethics (these others include Virginia Held and myself); and nowadays and in recent work Noddings seems to be convinced of the essential rightness of making such an expansionist move on behalf of the ethics of caring.

Therefore, when I speak of acts exhibiting a caring attitude or one inconsistent with caring, the caring I am speaking of includes attitudes toward distant and personally-unknown others, not just attitudes toward people we are acquainted with or love. The term "caring" is thus a placeholder for a description of an overall attitude/motivational state, one that takes in both one's concern for people one knows (intimately) and one's concern for distant

Michael Slote, "Famine, Affluence, and Empathy," is published here for the first time with permission of Michael Slote.

others and that embodies some sort of proportionality or balance between these concerns. An ethics of caring will hold that it is virtuous to be more concerned about near and dear than about strangers or those one knows about merely by description; but it will also insist that an ideally or virtuously caring individual will be substantially concerned about people who are distant from her (not to mention animals). The question of what constitutes an ideal or morally required proportionality or balance as between these concerns is a complex and difficult one, and our discussion in what follows will constitute an attempt at least partly to deal with it. Certainly, Singer seems to hold that we have as much reason to concern ourselves with distant others as with individuals we are personally intimate with; but there also something morally counterintuitive about this. The idea that we have special (or stronger) moral obligations to those who are near and/or dear to us is both familiar and ethically appealing at a common-sense level. But I hope now to show you how an ethics of caring, which has so far tended merely to *assume* such special obligations on the basis of the intuitive plausibility of such an assumption, can say something at least partly to justify it.

To do so, however, the ethics of caring needs to make use of some notions that play an important role in the thinking of Hume and other eighteenth-century figures, but that have been largely neglected by those seeking to develop a systematic ethics of caring. Hume (especially in his *A Treatise of Human Nature*) holds that our concern for others operates via a mechanism he calls "sympathy," but the notion he is working with (there) is actually closer to our contemporary term "empathy," and the difference or disparity may be partly accounted for by the fact that the latter term didn't enter English till the early twentieth century. So Hume doesn't have the terminology for distinguishing empathy from sympathy, but the phenomenon he calls sympathy seems much closer to what we mean by empathy than by sympathy.

Now these terms are not easy to define, but by "sympathy" I think we mean a kind of favorable attitude toward someone. One feels sympathy for someone in pain, for example, if one feels *for* them (or their pain), wishes they didn't have the pain, wants

their pain to end. By "empathy," on the other hand, we mean a state or process in which someone takes on the feelings of another: one empathizes for another who is in pain, if one "feels their pain" (as opposed to feeling *for* their pain). Obviously, a great deal more could be said about this distinction, but, given the prevalence of these notions in contemporary parlance, I hope the reader will readily follow what I shall be saying about empathy. Hume saw empathy/sympathy as a kind of *contagion* whereby the feelings of one person spread to (cause similar feelings in) another person, but in recent years there has been enormous interest in the subject of empathy on the part of social psychologists, and in that literature the "contagious" aspect of empathy is but one feature of the landscape. Numerous studies of the factors that affect empathy and of how empathy develops have been published, and various psychologists have also offered general accounts of the role empathy plays in human psychology and in human life. But one central aspect of that literature will most concern us here as I suggest a way of developing the ethics of caring further.

Recent work on empathy has to a substantial extent focused on the question whether the development of empathy is necessary to an individual's development of altruistic concern for others—this is called the "empathy-altruism hypothesis." Many (but by no means all) psychologists have seen recent work in the field as supporting the empathy-altruism hypothesis, and this literature is relevant to the present essay at least in part because it is possible to hold that caring works via empathy and that the contours of morally good caring can be specified in relation to how human empathy develops or can be made to develop. I believe that a virtue ethics of caring that grounds caring in human empathy as recently studied by psychologists can provide us with a way of answering Singer's arguments. But before appealing further to this interesting recent psychological literature, let me just briefly say how I came to realize the usefulness of appealing to (developed human) empathy in working out a sentimentalist virtue ethics of caring.

An ethics of caring can easily say that we have a greater obligation to help (born) fellow human beings than to help animals or fetuses, and such a comparative judgment has the kind of intuitive force or plausibility that a virtue ethics of caring might wish to rely on (though I assume that the intuition about born humans and fetuses will operate more weakly or will be undercut altogether in someone with a strong religious conviction that the fetus has an immortal soul). Some years ago, however, I was led in a different direction as a result of having my attention called to an article by Catholic thinker (and U.S. Circuit Court judge) John Noonan, in which (I was told) abortion is criticized, not for failing to respect the rights of the fetus, but for showing a lack of empathy for the fetus. I was absolutely galvanized by hearing about Noonan's article because (for one thing) it immediately occurred to me that the notion or phenomenon of empathy is a double-edged sword, and reading the article itself did nothing to disturb this conclusion. If we believe that empathy has moral force or relevance, then since it is in fact much easier for us to empathize with born humans (even neonates) than with a fetus, we can argue that it is for this reason morally worse to neglect or hurt a born human than to do the same to a fetus or embryo. And this conclusion might end up giving more sustenance to the pro-choice position than to the pro-life view of abortion.

Moreover, it almost as immediately occurred to me that a virtue ethics of caring, rather than rely on our intuitions about our stronger obligations to born humans than to embryos, fetuses, or animals, could explain the intuitions, the differential obligations, by incorporating the idea of empathy. (In thinking thus I was implicitly regarding the empathy-altruism hypothesis as at least somewhat plausible.) Instead of claiming that actions are right or wrong depending on whether they exhibit or reflect what intuition tells us is properly contoured and sufficiently deep caring, one can say that actions are wrong or right depending on whether or not they reflect or exhibit a deficiency of normally or fully empathic caring motivation. It would then, at least other things being equal, be morally worse to prefer a fetus or embryo to a born human being, because such a preference runs counter to the flow of developed human empathy or to caring motivation that is shaped by such

empathy. And similar points, arguably, could be made about our moral relations with lower animals.

I believe that the concept or phenomenon of empathy can also help us to formulate a virtue-ethical answer to the questions Singer raises in "Famine, Affluence, and Altruism" (and elsewhere). An ethics of caring expanded and reconfigured so as to hinge on the idea of *developed human empathy* gives us reason to hold, pace Singer, that a failure to save the life of a distant child by making, say, a small contribution to Oxfam is not morally as objectionable or bad as failing to save the life of a child who is drowning right in front of one. We shall see that such a sentimentalist ethics of empathic caring can also allow us to draw other important moral distinctions, and I shall then also speculate briefly on the prospects of such a theory as a general and systematic approach to morality and metaethics.

Recent moral philosophers have written a great deal on the question, raised by Singer's article, of how much we are obligated to spend of our own time, money, or other resources in order to save the lives of people who are personally unknown to us but whom we are in fact in a position to save. But this issue, as I have suggested, rests on the question of whether we are more obligated to help a child drowning before our very eyes than to help any given child who we know about only indirectly (as part of some labeled group rather than via personal acquaintance). As Singer points out in his article, the most *obvious* difference between the drowning child and a child we can save via contributions to Oxfam is one of spatial distance, and Singer himself hold that sheer distance simply cannot be morally relevant to our obligations to aid (or to how morally bad or objectionable it is *not* to aid). As a result, he concludes that we are just as obligated to give to Oxfam as to save the drowning child, and iterations of this argument lead him to the conclusion that most of us are morally obligated to make enormous sacrifices of our time, money, comfort, etc., in order to help distant (or nearby) others who are much worse off than we are.

However, in recent years Singer's quick dismissal of distance has come to be questioned on the basis of considerations that I want to examine here while, at the same time arguing that empathy in fact gives us a firmer basis than distance for distinguishing the strength of our obligations to the drowning child and our obligations to those we can only help (say) through organizations like Oxfam. Spatial distance and (decreasing) empathy do in fact correlate with one another across a wide range of cases, and that very fact may have helped to obscure the role empathy potentially has in explaining the sorts of distinctions people intuitively, or common-sensically, want to make with regard to the kinds of cases Singer mentions. But before saying anything further about the role of empathy here, it will be useful to say a bit more about the role sheer spatial distance might be thought to play in Singer-like cases.

Some of those who have lately considered the moral relevance of distance have regarded that issue as effectively involving two separate questions: first, whether we intuitively regard distance as making a difference to our obligations and, second, whether different intuitive reactions to third- or first-person cases involving distance would show anything important about (differences in) our actual obligations. In his book *Living High and Letting Die,* for example, Peter Unger considers both these issues and defends a negative answer to both of them.[3] He thinks that our superficial intuitions about cases may not ultimately carry much weight in moral theory of in determining where our obligations really lie. But he also holds that our differing moral intuitions about relevant cases don't track distance so much as (what he calls) salience and conspicuousness.

However, Frances Kamm disagrees with these views. She thinks that (a rather complicated notion of) distance *does* help to explain our differing intuitions about cases and also is relevant to our actual obligations in such cases.[4] Singer asks us to consider the difference between a situation where we can save a child from drowning at small cost to ourselves and one where we can save a distant child from starvation by making a small contribution to a famine relief organization, noting, but also deploring, our initial tendency to think that saving the child is morally more incumbent on us in the former situation than in the latter. But Kamm believes the factor of distance (or proximity) makes a relevant moral

difference in/between these two cases, and, in order to rule out other factors that might be thought to be determining our moral judgments in those cases (like whether others are in a position to help), she devises other examples that she believes bring out the intuitive and real moral force of the factor of distance (proximity).

Both Unger's book and Kamm's paper are rich and extremely complicated, and what I have to say here won't go into every nook and cranny of what they say. But I find it interesting and a bit surprising that neither one of them considers the moral importance of our empathic tendencies or capacities. For example, in denying the intuitive or actual moral relevance of distance, Unger comes up with a category of salience/conspicuousness (also with a category of the dramatic or exciting, but I will discuss that a bit later) that he does take to be relevant to our intuitive judgments, but never once considers how what one might easily take to be a related notion—what we can readily or immediately empathize with—might be relevant, or thought to be relevant, here. Similarly, Kamm considers and rejects what Unger says about salience or conspicuousness (she also talks about vividness) in favor of the idea that (complexly understood) distance is relevant to distinguishing between cases like the drowning child and starving examples mentioned earlier, but somehow the subject of empathy never comes up.[5]

But I believe the notion of empathy can help us sort out our intuitive reactions to the kinds of cases Singer, Unger, and Kamm describe better than the explanatory factors they mention, and let me say something about this now. In the familiar drowning examples, someone's danger or plight has a salience, conspicuousness, vividness, and *immediacy* (a term that, for reasons to be mentioned below, I prefer, but that Singer, Unger, and Kamm don't use) that engages normal human empathy (and consequently arouses sympathy and concern) in a way that similar dangers we merely know *about* do not. So if morality is a matter of empathy-based concern or caring for/about people, we can not only explain why a failure to help in the drowning case seems worse to us than a failure to give to famine relief, but also justify that ordinary moral intuition.

The idea that seeing or perceiving makes a difference in arousing or eliciting empathic and altruistic reactions is by no means, however, a new one. Hume makes this essential point (while using the term "sympathy") in the *Treatise;* and Hume also seems to hold that differences in what naturally or normally arouses sympathy/empathy affect the strength of our moral obligations and what virtue calls for.[6] Moreover, there are recent psychological studies of empathy that bear out Hume's earlier observations/speculations. Martin Hoffman's recent book, *Empathy and Moral Development: Implications for Caring and Justice,* usefully summarizes and reflects upon numerous psychological studies of the development of empathy and its role in creating or sustaining caring/concern for others, and one thing that both Hoffman and the previous studies emphasize is the difference that perceptual immediacy tends to make to the strength of empathic responses.[7] (However, Hoffman is more cautious than Hume is and I want to be about the moral implications of these psychological differences.)

In the light of the present moral emphasis on empathy, then, let's next consider what Kamm and Unger say about various cases. For example, in discussing the salience/conspicuousness that Unger invokes in explaining our (for him misguided) intuitions, Kamm distinguishes subjective and objective salience. Then, focusing on the former, she speaks of the science-fiction case of someone who can see a person suffering overseas with long-distance vision.[8] The suffering would then be salient, conspicuous, or vivid for the individual with the long-distance vision, but Kamm says that it is (intuitively) acceptable for that individual to "turn off" her long-distance vision (and pay no more attention to the fate of the person she has seen than to the fate of distant others she *hasn't* seen). But if she can turn it off, presumably she is also permitted simply to *turn away, avert her gaze;* and that is certainly what the view Kamm defends about the relevance of proximity implies.

However, I don't think this conclusion is in fact morally intuitive, and I believe considerations of empathy help to explain why. Turning away from someone we see (even if only at an extreme dis-

tance) seems *worse* than ignoring someone whom one knows about only by description; and assuming, for example, that one has the means instantly to deliver help either to someone whose danger or need one sees through long-distance vision or to someone whose danger or need one merely knows about, most of us, I think, would consider it inhumane to turn away from the person whose plight one saw and then (coldly) decide to give the aid to someone one merely knew about. What is inhumane here arguably has something to do with empathy, with a failure of empathic response to someone whose need one sees. The immediacy or vividness of such perceived need engages our (normal or fully developed) human empathy more deeply or forcefully than need known only by description, and so a morality that centers around empathy in the way(s) I have been suggesting can explain our moral reactions to Kamm's case here better than Kamm's appeal to (complexly contoured) distance and proximity does, and it is difficult to see how Kamm can use this example to argue successfully against the view that subjective salience or vividness is relevant to our moral intuitions.

Interestingly, Kamm does say that what we see at an overseas distance would exert "psychological pressure" on us to help. But she dismisses that pressure as somehow outside the bounds of our moral intuitions, because she thinks that we lack any intuition that tells us we have more obligation to the person we see than to someone we don't. If, however, and as I have just claimed, we do have such an intuition, then what she terms mere psychological pressure is in fact a moral intuition that her emphasis on distance fails to account for, but that a view based on empathy can.

Kamm then turns to an example of objective salience a la Unger. She imagines that the person with long-distance vision sees a group of people in trouble and that one of the people is wearing a clown-suit and is much more dramatically exhibiting his need for help than the others. Kamm holds that that should make no moral difference to whom one feels one should help, and she uses this example to argue for distance as opposed to objective salience. But a view emphasizing empathy can also (and perhaps more fully) account for our intuitions about this kind of case. The person in danger of drowning or starvation who is in a clown-suit and busy waving his arms or making histrionic gestures may be more visibly obtrusive; but such a person may seem to be faking fear or pain (hamming it up), whereas someone else who is quieter or less demonstrative may bear the marks of suffering or anxiety more genuinely than the person in the clown-suit and for that very reason more strongly engage our empathy. Such a case creates problems for an Ungerian objective-salience account of our moral intuitions, but not for a moral theory that is based in empathy; and I also believe the latter can account for differing intuitive reactions to variants on this kind of case better than a view that stresses distance.

Thus imagine that the person in the clown-suit isn't hamming it up. He and all the others are genuinely writhing in pain, but you notice him first because of his clown-suit and find yourself absolutely riveted on him. Assuming you can help only one of the people in the group, would we find it equally acceptable for you to turn away from the clown-suited man and decide that you might as well help *someone else* in the group, as for you to decide to help him? I think not. I think, again, we would find it lacking in or contrary to normally flowing human empathy, inhumane, for you to turn away from the man instead of helping him *in response to* your vivid recognition of his need. If his need has greater initial immediacy for you, then that, I think, is an intuitively good reason to go with the flow of empathy and help him out, given that one can only help one person in the group. But Kamm's account in terms of distance doesn't allow for this sort of reason. Let us, however, consider a further example.

Unger denies that there is any intuitive or real moral difference between cases where an accident victim one can help is nearby and visible to one and cases where the victim is at some distance and one learns about his plight via Morse code.[9] But Kamm thinks he is mistaken here about our intuitions and claims the difference is due to factors of distance;[10] and while I agree with Kamm that there is a significant difference between such cases, it seems to me

more plausible—or perhaps I should say more promising—to explain it in terms of empathy.[11]

We have illustrated the moral force of (considerations relating to) natural human empathy in terms of examples having to do with our moral relations with the fetus (and animals) and have gone on to discuss cases, familiar from the literature that has grown up around Peter Singer's work, that raise issues about our obligations to people whom we see or don't see, or who are near or far from us. The latter kinds of examples all involve dangers or emergencies of one kind or another, but we have yet to consider another sort of danger/emergency case that has often been discussed by philosophers, cases where the issue is not so much (or cannot so easily be imagined to be) spatial proximity or distance, but rather *temporal* proximity or distance.

I am thinking of the well-known example of miners trapped in a coal-mine (as a result, say, of a cave-in). We typically feel morally impelled to help the miners rather than (at that point) expend an equivalent amount of money to install safety devices in the mines that will save a greater number of lives in the long run. But some have disagreed. Charles Fried discusses this example in his *An Anatomy of Values* and claims that we/society should prefer to install the safety devices and let the miners die. (He gives his argument a rather barbaric twist by saying we should even be willing to convey this decision to the ill-fated miners face-to-face, if that is somehow possible.)[12]

This example, this choice, doesn't turn on a contrast between near and far or between what is perceived and what is not, because we can easily imagine that those who have to choose whom to save are at a distance from the mine and don't know or perceive either the trapped miners or those who might be in danger there in the future. We can well imagine, for example, that *we* are somehow empowered to make the choice, having heard or read reports of the mine cave-in, and I don't think the tendency to prefer saving the presently-trapped miners would then be explainable in terms of an empathy-derived preference for saving those whose dangers we are perceptually aware of rather than those whose dangers we merely know about.

Still, if we have to choose between the presently-trapped miners and those who will be in danger in the future, there is an immediacy to the danger the former are in that does, I think, engage our empathic/sympathetic juices in a way that the danger to the latter does not. Of course, there is also an immediacy to our previous examples of a child drowning and of a clown-suited person whose distress is (immediately) visible to us, but this immediacy, clearly, is perceptual and hinges on issues about the *spatial* distance that direct perception can accommodate. A rather different kind of immediacy is at issue in the miners example, an immediacy having more to do with the present-tense temporal character of the miners' danger—the fact that it is a "clear and present danger"—than with any spatial or spatially-correlated factors. But both kinds of immediacy appeal to our empathy in a way that situations not involving these forms of immediacy tend not to do. (The fact that the word "present" applies both to a time and to a mode of sensory contact seems very apt, given this common appeal to empathy.)

Thus we may not see or hear or personally know the miners who are now trapped, and, because they are thus known to us only as a class or by description, the empathic appeal of their plight—as compared with the plight of those who are going to be in danger later—is different from the empathic (moral) appeal of (dangers to) those we are perceptually aware of. But it is natural to think of both kinds of cases as involving some sort of immediacy, and that may be the best term for describing the (projected?) objective correlate, in certain kinds of situations, of our (subjective or psychological) tendency toward empathy. And the fact that we can use such correlated immediacy and empathy to explain our moral reactions not only in the cases discussed in the Singer literature, but also in the miners case gives further support to what was said above about Singer-type cases and to the general account of morality I have been sketching.[13]

If that account is correct, then what is morally wrong with installing safety devices (as Fried suggests) rather than helping miners who are in clear and present danger is that it exhibits (or reflects or expresses) a deficiency of normal(ly developed)

human empathy.[14] But by the same token someone who turns away from someone she sees in order to help someone she merely knows about (as in the kinds of examples Kamm and Unger talk about) will (other things being equal) also exhibit/demonstrate an underdeveloped capacity for empathy and a consequent coldness that we regard as morally questionable. And this sentimentalist (and virtue-ethical) way of approach moral issues also helps to explain why Singer is wrong to think that failures to save via organizations like Oxfam are in the same moral boat (so to speak) as a failure to save a child drowning right in front of one: the former simply doesn't exhibit as great a lack of (normal) human empathy as the latter does or would.

One implication of what I have been saying is that an ethics based on empathy yields a partialist, rather than an impartialist, understanding of morality. Fried's suggestions about what we should do in the miners case are ethically repugnant or worse, but it is not as if he is advocating a selfish or egoistic indifference to the miners. Rather, he is urging us to see them and everyone else, present or future, in terms of a strictly impartial concern for humans (or sentient beings) generally. If this seems morally inadequate, and if a virtue-ethical sentimentalist approach can make use of the idea of empathy to offer us a promising explanation of why it is inadequate, then we are given reason to see morality (and the world of our moral concern or caring) in a partialist way; and the same partialism likewise conflicts with and tells against the views Peter Singer defends. Indeed, Singer has claimed that partialism has never been given an adequate principled defense;[15] and whether or not this is true, the approach I am taking is intended as offering, or being on the way to offering, such a defense of partialism.

The observant reader may have noticed, however, that I have not so far explicitly argued that Singer is wrong to maintain that we are under a moral obligation to sacrifice a great deal of our time and/or money to help those less fortunate than ourselves. He reaches that conclusion via a lemma that we *have* questioned, namely, the idea that we are as obligated to help distant individuals we don't know as to save a child drowning right in front of us. But it is time for us now to be a little more explicit about the reasons why, on the present approach, we are not obligated to make enormous sacrifices of the kind Singer recommends, but can view such sacrifices, rather, as *supererogatorily* good or praiseworthy.

The social-psychological literature supports, on the whole, the idea that human beings have a substantial capacity for empathy and for altruistic concern(s) based on empathy. Hoffman in particular gives a fascinating and in many ways compelling account of how moral education can lead us in fact toward an empathic concern for (groups of) people we don't know very well or even at all (the people of Bangladesh, the homeless, victims of AIDS).[16] But Hoffman also makes it clear that (he thinks) there are limits to how much empathy for (disadvantaged) groups people can be led to develop. Self-interest (or egocentric desires, fears, hatred, etc.) can often strongly oppose or qualify what we may or might otherwise do out of empathy or empathic concern for others.[17] If so, then our general account will yield the conclusion that we are not morally obligated to sacrifice most of our time and money to help needy others, because a failure to do so doesn't evince an absence of normally or fully developed human empathy. In that case, if it would take someone with an unusually high degree of empathy and empathic concern—a degree of empathy and empathic concern beyond what most people can be led to develop—to be willing to make such a sacrifice, then such sacrifice will be morally supererogatory—morally praiseworthy and/or good but *not* (pace Singer) obligatory.[18]

But even if this is so, it may still be obligatory for individuals like ourselves to make some sort of substantial contribution toward the relief of hunger (or similarly worthy causes). Those who do not may be acting wrongly because they evince a degree of empathic concern that is *less* than what most people can be led to develop. (Hoffman and others say a great deal about how moral education can in fact induce empathy and caring for people we don't know personally.) At the very least, then, even if Singer exaggerates what morality demands of us, it may nonetheless be true that many of us should give

a good deal more for the relief of famine or disease around the world than we actually do.

However, in making use of a virtue-ethical moral sentimentalism based on empathic caring in order to argue against Singer's views, I have not considered certain well-known problems that any attempt to revive moral sentimentalism would have to face. Sentimentalism needs to be able to offer a plausible account of deontology (roughly, the moral distinction between doing and allowing, between killing and letting die), and this is something that it has, arguably, never successfully done. It also needs to explain how moral utterances or judgments can be grounded in sentiment rather than in rationality and rational concepts, and there is no doubt that this task represents a very difficult challenge to any attempt to revive moral sentimentalism. There are other difficulties too,[19] but let me at this point, and having noted these problems, simply say that I think that a contemporary sentimentalist ethics of caring is in fact up to tackling these challenges (something I attempt to do in a forthcoming book entitled *Moral Sentimentalism*). In any case, for present purposes it is enough, I think, to see that and how an ethics of empathic caring can offer us a substantive and intuitively plausible response to the ideas and arguments of Singer's classic paper.

NOTES

1. *Philosophy and Public Affairs* 1, 1972, pp. 229–43.
2. See, e.g., Carol Gilligan, *In a Different Voice: Psychological Theory and Women's Development*, Cambridge: Harvard University Press, 1982; and Nel Noddings, *Caring: A Feminine Approach to Ethics and Moral Education*, Berkeley: University of California Press, 1984. Noddings sees her approach as continuous with eighteenth-century sentimentalism; but the connection has also been frequently mentioned by others.
3. New York: Oxford University Press, 1996.
4. See her "Famine Ethics" in Dale Jamieson, ed., *Singer and His Critics*, Oxford: Basil Blackwell, 1999, pp. 162–208.
5. I don't think Kamm ignores empathy because she thinks it too *subjective*. Unger's salience, as she notes, has a subjective aspect, but can also be viewed in a more

objective way as what is or would be salient to a normal observer. But empathy also allows such a distinction, and the view I want to defend focuses on what calls forth (more or less) empathy (or empathy-involving concern) in a human being with a fully developed capacity for empathy.

6. On these points see the *Treatise,* ed., L. A. Selby-Bigge, Oxford: Clarendon Press, 1958, pp. 370, 439, 441, 483f., 488f., 518f.

7. New York: Cambridge University Press, 2000, pp. 209ff.

8. Pp. 182f.

9. Op. cit., esp. p. 36.

10. Op. cit., p. 184.

11. Unger in fact notes (p. 36) that such cases differ with respect to "experiential impact," a notion that ties in with empathy. But he doesn't pay much attention to impact, presumably because he (mistakenly) thinks that it makes no significant difference to our intuitions.

12. Cambridge: Harvard University Press, 1970, pp. 207–27 (esp. p. 226).

13. Interestingly, Hoffman, loc. cit., speaks of empathy as having a "here and now" bias, and the studies he cites make it very clear that our empathy flows more readily not only in regard to what is visible or perceived, but also in regard to what is current or contemporaneous.

14. Unger (op. cit., pp. 78f.) describes a case in which a meteor has fallen to earth and will explode with disastrous consequences in a densely populated area unless someone immediately steals an "Ejector" machine from its rightful owner and uses it to hurl the meteor to a deserted canyon. He thinks one is permitted to steal and operate the Ejector in such circumstances, but says that the "dramaticness" of the trouble involved here makes no difference to that permission. Yet this example involves just the sort of clear and present danger that we saw in the case of the trapped miners, and if empathy is relevant to morality, then dramaticness (or at least what makes for drama in the case Unger describes, namely, the clear and present danger) may in fact make a difference not only to our intuitions, but to (the strength of) our moral obligations.

15. See Singer's "A Response [to Critics]" in Dale Jamieson, ed., *Singer and His Critics,* Oxford: Basil Blackwell, 1999, p. 308.

16. Hoffman, op. cit., esp. Chapters 3 and 13.

17. See op. cit., esp. Chapters. 2, 8, and 13.

18. A virtue ethics based on empathy can point to the greater ease or naturalness of empathizing with those near and dear to us (with those we know and love) as a basis for arguing that we have especially strong moral reasons to be concerned with such people. But, for simplicity's sake, I am treating the issue of self-interest vs. concern for the unfortunate as if it didn't also involve issues about our obligations to near and dear. Note too that, if what I have been saying is on the right track, the issue of helping needy distant groups will arise (or will arise with greatest force) only when one is not facing any more *immediate* issue of need or danger.

19. For example, one might wonder whether our reliance on empathy would lead us to make *too many* moral distinctions. Thus if people of one race or gender are more empathically sensitive to those of the same race or gender, then the distinctions in our attitudes and behavior that empathy explains may, at least some of them, be morally invidious; and this would represent a serious problem for any attempt to explain morality systematically in terms of empathic caring. I offer a response to such worries in *Moral Sentimentalism.*

PART 6

WHAT'S WRONG WITH THE STATE?

Most of the readings contained in the previous parts of this book focus primarily on questions about individual behavior: about whether or not it is wrong for one individual to kill another, to enter into a commercial or sexual relationship with another, to marry another, and so on. This is as it should be. After all, most of the problems that moral philosophers are concerned with are about how individuals should and should not treat one another. But there is more to ethics than problems concerning individual behavior. Moral questions can be raised not just about how individuals behave, but also about how institutions behave. A few such questions are treated in some of the earlier parts of this book, such as in chapter 9, on sexual conduct codes. That chapter focuses on a particular kind of behavior engaged in by some colleges and universities and addresses the question of whether that behavior is morally justified.

The purpose of Part 6 is to focus in significantly more detail on one particular, and particularly powerful, institution: the State. Governments engage in at least three kinds of practices that raise worrisome moral questions: They forbid their citizens from engaging in certain forms of behavior. They require their citizens to engage in certain other forms of behavior. And they punish those citizens who violate these prohibitions and requirements. As with the other areas of applied ethics explored in this volume, some forms of State behavior generate relatively little moral controversy. Virtually everyone agrees that it is appropriate for a government to outlaw murder, for example, and virtually everyone agrees that it is wrong for a government to engage in genocide. But a wide range of cases lie between these extremes. We focus on a few such issues in Part 6.

We begin by considering whether a State may compel its citizens to pay taxes, as many governments do, as a means of redistributing the wealth among its people. We then move to an examination of two questions about what a State may do to those who violate its laws. Chapter 25 focuses on the lively debate over capital punishment in particular, while chapter 26 examines the more fundamental debate about whether or not the State has the right to punish at all. We conclude by considering two questions about what the State may permissibly forbid. Is it morally acceptable for a government to prohibit the use of tobacco (chapter 27)? And finally, would it be morally acceptable for a government to ban human cloning (chapter 28)?

24

Is Redistributive Taxation Wrong?

Nozick and His Critics

Modern nation states, without exception, redistribute people's incomes and assets, to a greater or lesser extent, via a system of taxation. Typically they take some money from the rich in order to benefit the poor. And sometimes they take some money from the poor and redistribute it to the rich. Even in the United States, where there is evidently enormous antipathy to taxation in any form—both on the part of individuals and on the part of vast and influential political organizations—redistributive taxation is alive and well. There are the obvious examples; programs such as Medicaid provide health care to those who cannot afford it, arguably taking money from the wealthy and giving it to the poor. But there are also less obvious examples, such as the system of U.S. farm subsidies, which provides billions of dollars each year to individual American farmers, many of whom are already in possession of vast capital wealth in the form of land holdings. Such redistributions take money from those who are, on average, less wealthy, and redistribute it among those who are considerably wealthier. Under what circumstances, if any, is it legitimate for the State to take a portion of one person's income or assets and give that to someone else in order to increase the latter's welfare.

In his provocative and influential book *Anarchy, State and Utopia,* Robert Nozick argues that *redistributive* taxation is unjust. (Note that he does not argue that *all* taxation is unjust.) If a person legitimately owns a good, Nozick argues, then he is entitled to keep it or dispose of it as he sees fit, and the State is not entitled to take it from him in order to increase someone else's welfare, even someone who is very much worse off. Nozick's argument (or arguments) can be reconstructed in a variety of ways. Here's one reconstruction:

We must first analyze what it takes to own something or how ownership comes about. There was a time when nobody owned anything. Now lots of people own lots of things. So somehow people can *acquire* a property right to something that was not previously owned. Furthermore, once something is owned, ownership can be transferred to others. Some ways of acquiring things not previously owned are legitimate, and some are not. Nozick calls the principles that govern the *acquisition* of previously unowned property principles of *justice in acquisition.* Ownership can be transferred in ways that are illegitimate (stealing it, for example) and others that are legitimate (buying it at a mutually agreed upon price, giving it away, etc.). The principles governing the legitimate *transfer* of ownership Nozick calls principles of *justice in transfer.* He then characterizes a class of theories of ownership that we will call *pure entitlement* theories. These are characterized by the following three principles:

Principle 1   A person who acquires a holding in accordance with the principle of justice in acquisition is entitled to that holding.

Principle 2   A person who acquires a holding in accordance with the principle of justice in transfer from someone else entitled to that holding is entitled to the holding.

Principle 3   No one is entitled to a holding except by repeated applications of 1 and 2.

Pure entitlement theories may differ over the exact formulation of the principles of justice in acquisition or over the exact formulation of the principles of justice in transfer, but given those principles, all entitlements are bestowed by repeated applications of legitimate acquisition and transfer.

Pure entitlement theories tell us what belongs to whom by virtue of the *history* of ownership of the holding. As such, a pure entitlement theory appears to place no constraint at all on the overall *pattern* of distribution of holdings that might result from a series of legitimate acquisitions and transfers. It is thus characteristic of pure entitlement theories that they do not require that holdings be distributed in any particular way. A pure entitlement theory may well be incompatible with what Nozick calls an *end-state principle.* One example of an end-state principle is the following version of extreme egalitarianism: The only legitimate distributions of holdings are those in which everyone owns holdings of the same value. Nozick introduces his Wilt Chamberlain argument to show that a pure entitlement theory is incompatible with end-state principles. Suppose we start off with a distribution of holdings that the egalitarian considers just. Suppose, for example, everyone starts off with holdings of equal value. (The egalitarian would think this was just.) Chamberlain, a gifted basketball player, agrees to play for a team, provided he can have some chunk of the gate takings—say, twenty-five cents per person—and the team agrees. We can imagine that there is a machine that allows people into the stadium when they place three dollars in one slot and an extra quarter in another, marked "For Wilt Chamberlain." This would seem to be a legitimate transfer, since everyone agrees to the price and every person in on the deal regards himself as better off at the end of it. A million people come to watch the games simply because Wilt is playing, and Wilt ends up richer than all the spectators. Question: Would a third party be justified in taking Wilt's earnings away and giving twenty-five cents back to every spectator, in order to restore the equal distribution? Apparently not.

We can construct an analogical argument against redistributive taxation using the Wilt Chamberlain example. Although it isn't obvious that this is the argument Nozick is endorsing, it is an argument that some have taken him to be endorsing.

P1   Wilt Chamberlain ends up with more holdings than others through voluntary exchanges of money for entertainment.

P2 It would be wrong for a third party to take Wilt's holdings from him in order to restore the wealth of those who are now poorer than he is because they attended his games.

P3 Redistributive taxation is morally on a par with a third party's taking Wilt's holdings in order to restore the wealth of those who arc now poorer than he is.

C Redistributive taxation is wrong.

Of course advocates of redistributive taxation do not think that the practice is morally on a par with seizing Wilt's new holdings and returning them to those who came to watch him. They would thus reject premise 3. But what exactly is the difference? Well, for one thing, hardly anyone argues that the State has a right to tax earnings at a rate of 100 percent, even over some large threshold. (There are exceptions: In the 2000 U.S. elections, Ralph Nader's Green Party platform argued that the maximum annual income should be $100,000, and that is equivalent to taxing all income over that amount at 100 percent rate of taxation.) However, most do claim that the State has a right to some proportion less than 100 percent, perhaps over some threshold. Furthermore, most advocates of redistributive taxation argue that it should be used to benefit those who are rather bad off. Not all those who watched Wilt's game are going to be bad off. But suppose there are some who cannot find work and who have children to feed and clothe and house. Isn't the State justified in taking *some* of Wilt's earnings to relieve the suffering of those children?

Nozick introduces a second argument to show that the State does not have a right to *any* portion of Wilt's earnings for redistributive purposes—not even to help the children of those who are destitute. Consider the case in which the State lays claims to *all* of the income Wilt makes from these games. Then the State is engaging in something tantamount to forced labor. Wilt is effectively obliged to work entirely for the sake of others; he does not own the fruits of his own labor. What entitles Wilt to the fruits of his own labor? One could treat this as a basic moral principle—in no need of further justification—but it isn't self-evident. There are at least two plausible ways of defending the principle that one is entitled to the fruits of one's own labor. Many philosophers have grounded this right in a deeper right—ownership of one's own person and body. To take the fruits of Wilt's own labor away from him is to force Wilt to labor on behalf of others, and that is to violate his deep right of self-ownership.

P1 For the State to appropriate some percentage of a person's earnings for redistribution to others is for the State to deprive a worker of that percentage of the fruits of his labor.

P2 To deprive a worker of some percentage of the fruits of his labor for redistribution to others is to violate the worker's right of self-ownership.

P3 It is morally wrong to violate anyone's right of self-ownership.

C Any redistributive tax is morally wrong.

Let us call this the *self-ownership* argument.

Another way to spell out what is wrong with forced labor employs an idea first made famous by the philosopher Immanuel Kant, that forcing one person to work for the welfare of another is treating a human being *merely as a means* to another's welfare. Redistributive taxation is thus wrong because it treats workers as mere means to the satisfaction of the desires of others.

P1   For the State to appropriate *n* percent of a person's earnings for redistributive purposes is for the State to force him to work for *n* percent of his working life for the sake of others.

P2   To force a person to work for the sake of others is to treat him merely as a means to another's welfare.

P3   It is morally wrong to treat any human being merely as a means to another's welfare for any length of time.

C   Any redistributive tax is morally wrong.

The third premise is a version of Kant's famous moral principle, the categorical imperative. We have outlined a different formulation of the Categorical Imperative in the chapter on adultery (see introduction to chapter 8), using the idea of *universalizability.* (That is, "Act only on that maxim by which you can at the same time will that it should become a universal law.") Whether these two principles are really formulations of one and the same idea is a highly disputed point. For the purposes of our discussion let us treat each principle on its own merits. The principle forbidding treating a person as a mere means to another's welfare does seem to have considerable merit. For example, it explains what is wrong with slavery. Being a slave is no doubt very unpleasant, but that is not the only thing that makes slavery wrong. We could imagine slaves who were happy with their lot—perhaps because they were moderately well treated or had been brainwashed into accepting their situation—but we would still condemn their bondage. The thing that makes any institution of slavery wrong is that it treats some human beings (the slaves) as mere means to the satisfaction of the desires of others (their masters). Forced labor is like slavery in that it treats humans as mere means.

In his contribution to the debate, Mark Michael critiques the self-ownership argument against redistributive taxation. He accepts the principle of self-ownership (premise 3) and agrees that, by virtue of self-ownership, a worker is entitled to the fruits of his own labor. However, he does not think that redistributive taxation is necessarily a case of taking from a worker the fruits of his labor. He disagrees, then, with premise 1. The key to his disagreement is his analysis of the notion of "fruits of labor." According to Michael, underlying premise 1 is a general principle that the fruits of one's labor encompass everything that is the *product* of one's labor. He then introduces a counterexample to this principle the case of the lucky cobbler. A rather mediocre cobbler makes rather mediocre shoes and he can earn a modest income only by selling the product of his labors. One day, as luck would have it, he finds a red pill that will render him a superb cobbler. He takes the pill and afterwards, by the same amount of effort, produces top-notch footware, enabling him to sell his products for a lot more money than before. Luck, rather than the cobbler's own efforts, makes the difference between his pre-pill income and his post-pill income. Michael claims that, since this difference in income is a matter of pure luck, not itself a product of the cobbler's labor, the extra income cannot be counted as the *fruits* of his labor. Only that income that comes to the cobbler by virtue of his own choices can be counted as the genuine fruits of his labor. Anything that comes to the cobbler by virtue of sheer luck does not count. The results of labor that can be attributed to luck "could therefore be expropriated by a redistributive tax without violating the principle of self-ownership".

Alan Goldman points out that we have an intuition about the holdings people are entitled to. Some of that intuition is encapsulated in Nozick's principles of acquisition and transfer. If someone is entitled to some holding, he is also entitled to give it freely to another—for example, to his children. And if he is free to give it to his children, surely his children are entitled to keep it. The right to give is hollow without a corresponding right to receive. However, we also have strong intuition about what holdings people are entitled to. According to Goldman, "people are not entitled to socially contingent advantages that they don't deserve," and "people often don't deserve the monetary advantages they are given, for example, by their parents as children." Suppose, for example, a tiny percentage of the population ends up *inheriting* almost all the wealth generated in society, while a vast number of the children of those with no accumulated wealth are starving. Are the fabulously wealthy few entitled to horde their wealth in such circumstances? Probably not. Why then, Goldman asks, should we accept the principles of the pure entitlement theory when those principles lead to conclusions we find unacceptable—for example, the right of a minority of undeserving inheritors of wealth to allow masses of poor to starve to death (for more on inheritance, see chapter 29).

Goldman also offers criticisms of the two arguments against redistributive taxation. One of his arguments against the forced-labor argument is very much like Michael's:

> . . . differences in earnings are generally not a function of effort expended or hours worked. They are more often an indirect reflection of the initial underserved advantages of that individual for obtaining that job. For this reason we can in no way equate redistributive taxation, which takes a portion of those extra earnings to provide for basic needs of those who lack such advantages, with making the individual work longer or harder for their benefit.

If a portion of one's income is the result of "initial undeserved advantages," then the first premise of the self-ownership argument is false. Taking some of that portion of a person's income to benefit another who does not have that advantage is not analogous to forcing the person to work for another.

Goldman marshals similar considerations against the first premise of the second argument. He argues that Kant's injunction not to use others as means must be applied to the economic system that enables people to earn income in the first place. Suppose that system enables some people with initial undeserved advantages to garner a large income while others without those advantages are unable to garner enough to sustain themselves. Then that system gives unfair advantages to some over others, and people can legitimately demand that redistributive taxation be used to moderate the worst outcomes of the rules of acquisition and transfer coupled with the initial undeserved advantages.

QUESTIONS TO CONSIDER

In thinking about these arguments, the following may be useful questions to consider.

• In discussing the principle of justice in acquisition, Nozick spends a good deal of time on the Lockean proviso. Locke, a seventeenth-century English philosopher, stipulated that one can legitimately acquire unowned resources *provided* one leaves "as much and as good" for others. Are there any resources of that sort left? Clearly, most of the *land* on the planet has now been appropriated. Most of the oil has been claimed by one body or another (States, corporations, individuals, and so on). What kinds of resources could satisfy the Lockean proviso? If the answer is "None," then does it follow that gross inequalities brought about by current acquisitions are unjust?

- Are there any resources that are effectively infinite so that the Lockean proviso always applies to them? Think of non-material items that people sometimes claim ownership over—things such as musical works (or the copyright of musical works), poems, novels, inventions, medical cures, philosophical ideas, and so on. Did Mozart leave "as much and as good" to other composers? Does each successive composer diminish the stock of unowned musical compositions or not? If he does, does that mean he has less of a property right in those works than did the first composers (who more nearly satisfied the Lockean proviso)?

- If you own a resource, are you entitled to dispose of it as you see fit, to give it away to whomever you choose, or to destroy it if you no longer want it, and so on? Suppose you make a lucky break in research on AIDS, discovering a cure for it. Are you entitled to horde all the revenue you could make on the patent of the cure? Are you entitled to destroy the stocks of the cure that you have made or your current knowledge of how to make it?

- Suppose someone gives you a famous artwork, say Picasso's *Guernica.* Are you, as the new owner, entitled to burn it in your fireplace to heat your living room?

- Suppose Bill Gates decides to buy the remains of the Amazon jungle. Is he entitled to burn it all down to make room for more cattle farms to supply McDonald's with beef for cheap hamburgers, even if it mean that the world might run out of sufficient oxygen? (Gates himself, we may imagine, will have built a machine to generate a constant supply of oxygen for himself.) If States made it illegal for Gates to burn down the Amazon jungle, in order that others might simply breathe, would that (according to the pure entitlement theory) be a violation of Gates's property rights? Would it be similar to redistributive taxation—taking something belonging to Gates (the jungle's power to generate oxygen) and distributing it among those who don't have enough oxygen to live? Would that be morally wrong?

FURTHER READING

Narveson, Jan. "Property Rights: Original Acquisition and Lockean Provisos." *Public Affairs Quarterly* 13, no. 3 (1999):205–27.

Skillen, Tony. "Active Citizenship as Political Obligation." *Radical Philosophy* no. 58 (1991):10–13.

Robert Nozick | # Distributive Justice

THE ENTITLEMENT THEORY

The subject of justice in holdings consists of three major topics. The first is the *original acquisition of holdings,* the appropriation of unheld things. This includes the issues of how unheld things may come to be held, the process, or processes, by which unheld things may come to be held, the things that may come to be held by these processes, the extent of what comes to be held by a particular process, and so on. We shall refer to the complicated truth about this topic, which we shall not formulate here, as the principle of justice in acquisition. The second topic concerns the *transfer of holdings* from one person to another. By what processes may a person transfer holdings to another? How may a person acquire a holding from another who holds it? Under this topic come general descriptions of voluntary exchange,

Excerpted from Robert Nozick, *Anarchy, State and Utopia* (New York: Basic Books, 1974). Reprinted by permission of Basic Books, a member of Perseus Books, L.L.C.

and gift and (on the other hand) fraud, as well as reference to particular conventional details fixed upon in a given society. The complicated truth about this subject (with placeholders for conventional details) we shall call the principle of justice in transfer. (And we shall suppose it also includes principles governing how a person may divest himself of a holding, passing it into an unheld state.)

If the world were wholly just, the following inductive definition would exhaustively cover the subject of justice in holdings.

1. A person who acquires a holding in accordance with the principle of justice in acquisition is entitled to that holding.
2. A person who acquires a holding in accordance with the principle of justice in transfer, from someone else entitled to the holding, is entitled to the holding.
3. No one is entitled to a holding except by (repeated) applications of 1 and 2.

The complete principle of distributive justice would say simply that a distribution is just if everyone is entitled to the holdings they possess under the distribution.

A distribution is just if it arises from another just distribution by legitimate means. The legitimate means of moving from one distribution to another are specified by the principle of justice in transfer. The legitimate first "moves" are specified by the principle of justice in acquisition. Whatever arises from a just situation by just steps is itself just. The means of change specified by the principle of justice in transfer preserve justice. As correct rules of inference are truth-preserving, and any conclusion deduced via repeated application of such rules from only true premises is itself true, so the means of transition from one situation to another specified by the principle of justice in transfer are justice-preserving, and any situation actually arising from repeated transitions in accordance with the principle from a just situation is itself just. The parallel between justice-preserving transformations and truth-preserving transformations illuminates where it fails as well as where it holds. That a conclusion could have been deduced by truth-preserving means from premises

that are true suffices to show its truth. That from a just situation a situation *could* have arisen via justice-preserving means does *not* suffice to show its justice. The fact that a thief's victims voluntarily *could* have presented him with gifts does not entitle the thief to his ill-gotten gains. Justice in holdings is historical; it depends upon what actually has happened. We shall return to this point later.

Not all actual situations are generated in accordance with the two principles of justice in holdings: the principle of justice in acquisition and the principle of justice in transfer. Some people steal from others, or defraud them, or enslave them, seizing their product and preventing them from living as they choose, or forcibly exclude others from competing in exchanges. None of these are permissible modes of transition from one situation to another. And some persons acquire holdings by means not sanctioned by the principle of justice in acquisition. The existence of past injustice (previous violations of the first two principles of justice in holdings) raises the third major topic under justice in holdings: the rectification of injustice in holdings. If past injustice has shaped present holdings in various ways, some identifiable and some not, what now, if anything, ought to be done to rectify these injustices? What obligations do the performers of injustice have toward those whose position is worse than it would have been had the injustice not been done? Or, than it would have been had compensation been paid promptly? How, if at all, do things change if the beneficiaries and those made worse off are not the direct parties in the act of injustice, but, for example, their descendants? Is an injustice done to someone whose holding was itself based upon an unrectified injustice? How far back must one go in wiping clean the historical slate of injustices? What may victims of injustice permissibly do in order to rectify the injustices being done to them, including the many injustices done by persons acting through their government? I do not know of a thorough or theoretically sophisticated treatment of such issues. . . .

The general outlines of the theory of justice in holdings are that the holdings of a person are just if he is entitled to them by the principles of justice in acquisition and transfer, or by the principle of rectification of injustice (as specified by the first two principles). If each person's holdings are just, then the total set (distribution) of holdings is just. To turn these general outlines into a specific theory we would have to specify the details of each of the three principles of justice in holdings: the principle of acquisition of holdings, the principle of transfer of holdings, and the principle of rectification of violations of the first two principles. I shall not attempt that task here. (Locke's principle of justice in acquisition is discussed below.)

HISTORICAL PRINCIPLES AND END-RESULT PRINCIPLES

The general outlines of the entitlement theory illuminate the nature and defects of other conceptions of distributive justice. The entitlement theory of justice in distribution is *historical;* whether a distribution is just depends upon how it came about. In contrast, *current time-slice principles* of justice hold that the justice of a distribution is determined by how things are distributed (who has what) as judged by some *structural* principle(s) of just distribution. A utilitarian who judges between any two distributions by seeing which has the greater sum of utility and, if the sums tie, applies some fixed equality criterion to choose the more equal distribution, would hold a current time-slice principle of justice. As would someone who had a fixed schedule of trade-offs between the sum of happiness and equality. According to a current time-slice principle, all that needs to be looked at, in judging the justice of a distribution, is who ends up with what; in comparing any two distributions one need look only at the matrix presenting the distributions. No further information need be fed into a principle of justice. It is a consequence of such principles of justice that any two structurally identical distributions are equally just. (Two distributions are structurally identical if they present the same profile, but perhaps have different persons occupying the particular slots. My having ten and your having five, and my having five and your having ten are structurally identical distributions.) Welfare economics is the theory of current time-slice principles of justice. The subject is conceived as operating on matrices

representing only current information about distribution. This, as well as some of the usual conditions (for example, the choice of distribution is invariant under relabeling of columns), guarantees that welfare economics will be a current time-slice theory, with all of its inadequacies.

Most persons do not accept current time-slice principles as constituting the whole story about distributive shares. They think it relevant in assessing the justice of a situation to consider not only the distribution it embodies, but also how that distribution came about. If some persons are in prison for murder or war crimes, we do not say that to assess the justice of the distribution in the society we must look only at what this person has, and that person has, and that person has, . . . at the current time. We think it relevant to ask whether someone did something so that he *deserved* to be punished, deserved to have a lower share. Most will agree to the relevance of further information with regard to punishments and penalties. Consider also desired things. One traditional socialist view is that workers are entitled to the product and full fruits of their labor; they have earned it; a distribution is unjust if it does not give the workers what they are entitled to. Such entitlements are based upon some past history. No socialist holding this view would find it comforting to be told that because the actual distribution *A* happens to coincide structurally with the one he desires *D, A* therefore is no less just than *D;* it differs only in that the "parasitic" owners of capital receive under *A* what the workers are entitled to under *D,* and the workers receive under *A* what the owners are entitled to under *D,* namely very little. This socialist rightly, in my view, holds onto the notions of earning, producing, entitlement, desert, and so forth, and he rejects current time-slice principles that look only to the structure of the resulting set of holdings. (The set of holdings resulting from what? Isn't it implausible that how holdings are produced and come to exist has no effect at all on who should hold what?) His mistake lies in his view of what entitlements arise out of what sorts of productive processes.

We construe the position we discuss too narrowly by speaking of *current* time-slice principles. Nothing is changed if structural principles operate upon a time sequence of current time-slice profiles and, for example, give someone more now to counterbalance the less he has had earlier. A utilitarian or an egalitarian or any mixture of the two over time will inherit the difficulties of his more myopic comrades. He is not helped by the fact that *some* of the information others consider relevant in assessing a distribution is reflected, unrecoverably, in past matrices. Henceforth, we shall refer to such unhistorical principles of distributive justice, including the current time-slice principles, as *end-result principles* or *end-state principles.*

In contrast to end-result principles of justice, *historical principles* of justice hold that past circumstances or actions of people can create differential entitlements or differential deserts to things. An injustice can be worked by moving from one distribution to another structurally identical one, for the second, in profile the same, may violate people's entitlements or deserts; it may not fit the actual history.

PATTERNING

The entitlement principles of justice in holdings that we have sketched are historical principles of justice. To better understand their precise character, we shall distinguish them from another subclass of the historical principles. Consider, as an example, the principle of distribution according to moral merit. This principle requires that total distributive shares vary directly with moral merit; no person should have a greater share than anyone whose moral merit is greater. (If moral merit could be not merely ordered but measured on an interval or ratio scale, stronger principles could be formulated.) Or consider the principle that results by substituting "usefulness to society" for "moral merit" in the previous principle. Or instead of "distribute according to moral merit," or "distribute according to usefulness to society," we might consider "distribute according to the weighted sum of moral merit, usefulness to society, and need," with the weights of the different dimensions equal. Let us call a principle of distribution *patterned* if it specifies that a distribution is to vary along with some natural dimension, weighted sum of natural dimensions, or lexicographic ordering of natural dimensions. And let us say a distribution is patterned if it accords with some patterned principle. (I speak of natural dimensions, admittedly without a general criterion for them, because for any set of holdings some artificial dimensions can be gimmicked up to vary along with the distribution of the set.) The principle of distribution in accordance with moral merit is a patterned historical principle, which specifies a patterned distribution. "Distribute according to I.Q." is a patterned principle that looks to information not contained in distributional matrices. It is not historical, however, in that it does not look to any past actions creating differential entitlements to evaluate a distribution; it requires only distributional matrices whose columns are labeled by I.Q. scores. The distribution in a society, however, may be composed of such simple patterned distributions, without itself being simply patterned. Different sectors may operate different patterns, or some combination of patterns may operate in different proportions across a society. A distribution composed in this manner, from a small number of patterned distributions, we also shall term "patterned." And we extend the use of "pattern" to include the overall designs put forth by combinations of end-state principles.

Almost every suggested principle of distributive justice is patterned: to each according to his moral merit, or needs, or marginal product, or how hard he tries, or the weighted sum of the foregoing, and so on. The principle of entitlement we have sketched is *not* patterned. . . . The set of holdings that results when some persons receive their marginal products, others win at gambling, others receive a share of their mate's income, others receive gifts from foundations, others receive interest on loans, others receive gifts from admirers, others receive returns on investment, others make for themselves much of what they have, others find things, and so on, will not be patterned. Heavy strands of patterns will run through it; significant portions of the variance in holdings will be accounted for by pattern-variables. If most people most of the time choose to transfer some of their entitlements to others only in exchange for something from them, then a large part of what many people hold will vary with what they held that others wanted. More details are provided by the theory of marginal

productivity. But gifts to relatives, charitable donations, bequests to children, and the like, are not best
conceived, in the first instance, in this manner. Ignoring the strands of pattern, let us suppose for the
moment that a distribution actually arrived at by the
operation of the principle of entitlement is random
with respect to any pattern. Though the resulting set
of holdings will be unpatterned, it will not be incom-
prehensible, for it can be seen as arising from the
operation of a small number of principles. These
principles specify how an initial distribution may
arise (the principle of acquisition of holdings) and
how distributions may be transformed into others
(the principle of transfer of holdings). The process
whereby the set of holdings is generated will be intelligible, though the set of holdings itself that results
from this process will be unpatterned. . . .

HOW LIBERTY UPSETS PATTERNS

It is not clear how those holding alternative conceptions of distributive justice can reject the entitlement
conception of justice in holdings. For suppose a distribution favored by one of these non-entitlement
conceptions is realized. Let us suppose it is your
favorite one and let us call this distribution D_1; perhaps everyone has an equal share, perhaps shares
vary in accordance with some dimension you trea-
sure. Now suppose that Wilt Chamberlain is greatly
in demand by basketball teams, being a great gate
attraction. (Also suppose contracts run only for a
year, with players being free agents.) He signs the
following sort of contract with a team: In each home
game, twenty-five cents from the price of each ticket
of admission goes to him. (We ignore the question of
whether he is "gouging" the owners, letting them
look out for themselves.) The season starts, and people cheerfully attend his team's games; they buy
their tickets, each time dropping a separate twenty-
five cents of their admission price into a special box
with Chamberlain's name on it. They are excited
about seeing him play; it is worth the total admission
price to them. Let us suppose that in one season one
million persons attend his home games, and Wilt
Chamberlain winds up with $250,000, a much larger
sum than the average income and larger even than

anyone else has. Is he entitled to this income? Is this
new distribution D_2, unjust? If so, why? There is *no*
question about whether each of the people was entitled to the control over the resources they held in D_1;
because that was the distribution (your favorite) that
(for the purposes of argument) we assumed was
acceptable. Each of these persons *chose* to give
twenty-five cents of their money to Chamberlain.
They could have spent it on going to the movies, or
on candy bars, or on copies of *Dissent* magazine, or
of *Montly Review*. But they all, at least one million
of them, converged on giving it to Wilt Chamberlain
in exchange for watching him play basketball. If D_1
was a just distribution, and people voluntarily
moved from it to D_2, transferring parts of their shares
they were given under D_1 (what was it for if not to
do something with?), isn't D_2 also just? If the people
were entitled to dispose of the resources to which
they were entitled (under D_1), didn't this include
their being entitled to give it to, or exchange it with,
Wilt Chamberlain? Can anyone else complain on
grounds of justice? Each other person already has his
legitimate share under D_1. Under D_1, there is nothing
that anyone has that anyone else has a claim of justice against. After someone transfers something to
Wilt Chamberlain, third parties *still* have their legitimate shares; *their* shares are not changed. By what
process could such a transfer among two persons
give rise to a legitimate claim of distributive justice
on a portion of what was transferred, by a third party
who had no claim of justice on any holding of the
others *before* the transfer? To cut off objections
irrelevant here, we might imagine the exchanges
occurring in a socialist society, after hours. . . .

The general point illustrated by the Wilt Chamberlain example and the example of the entrepreneur
in a socialist society is that no end-state principle or
distributional patterned principle of justice can be
continuously realized without continuous interference with people's lives. Any favored pattern would
be transformed into one unfavored by the principle,
by people choosing to act in various ways; for example, by people exchanging goods and services with
other people, or giving things to other people, things
the transferrers are entitled to under the favored distributional pattern. To maintain a pattern one must

either continually interfere to stop people from transferring resources as they wish to, or continually (or periodically) interfere to take from some persons resources that others for some reason chose to transfer to them. (But if some time limit is to be set on how long people may keep resources others voluntarily transfer to them, why let them keep these resources for *any* period of time? Why not have immediate confiscation?) It might be objected that all persons voluntarily will choose to refrain from actions which would upset the pattern. This presupposes unrealistically (1) that all will most want to maintain the pattern (are those who don't, to be "reeducated" or forced to undergo "self-criticism"?), (2) that each can gather enough information about his own actions and the ongoing activities of others to discover which of his actions will upset the pattern, and (3) that diverse and far-flung persons can coordinate their actions to dovetail into the pattern. Compare the manner in which the market is neutral among persons' desires, as it reflects and transmits widely scattered information via prices, and coordinates persons' activities.

REDISTRIBUTION AND PROPERTY RIGHTS

. . . Proponents of patterned principles of distributive justice focus upon criteria for determining who is to receive holdings; they consider the reasons for which someone should have something, and also the total picture of holdings. Whether or not it is better to give than to receive, proponents of patterned principles ignore giving altogether. In considering the distribution of goods, income, and so forth, their theories are theories of recipient justice; they completely ignore any right a person might have to give something to someone. Even in exchanges where each party is simultaneously giver and recipient, patterned principles of justice focus only upon the recipient role and its supposed rights. Thus discussions tend to focus on whether people (should) have a right to inherit, rather than on whether people (should) have a right to bequeath or on whether persons who have a right to hold also have a right to choose that others hold in their place. I lack a good

explanation of why the usual theories of distributive justice are so recipient oriented; ignoring givers and transferrers and their rights is of a piece with ignoring producers and their entitlements. But why is it *all* ignored?

Patterned principles of distributive justice necessitate *re*distributive activities. The likelihood is small that any actual freely-arrived-at set of holdings fits a given pattern; and the likelihood is nil that it will continue to fit the pattern as people exchange and give. From the point of view of an entitlement theory, redistribution is a serious matter indeed, involving, as it does, the violation of people's rights. (An exception is those takings that fall under the principle of the rectification of injustices.) From other points of view, also, it is serious.

Taxation of earnings from labor is on a par with forced labor.[1] Some persons find this claim obviously true: taking the earnings of *n* hours labor is like taking *n* hours from the person; it is like forcing the person to work *n* hours for another's purpose. Others find the claim absurd. But even these, *if* they object to forced labor, would oppose forcing unemployed hippies to work for the benefit of the needy. And they would also object to forcing each person to work five extra hours each week for the benefit of the needy. But a system that takes five hours' wages in taxes does not seem to them like one that forces someone to work five hours, since it offers the person forced a wider range of choice in activities than does taxation in kind with the particular labor specified. (But we can imagine a gradation of systems of forced labor, from one that specifies a particular activity, to one that gives a choice among two activities, to . . . ; and so on up.) Furthermore, people envisage a system with something like a proportional tax on everything above the amount necessary for basic needs. Some think this does not force someone to work extra hours, since there is no fixed number of extra hours he is forced to work, and since he can avoid the tax entirely by earning only enough to cover his basic needs. This is a very uncharacteristic view of forcing for those who *also* think people are forced to do something *whenever* the alternatives they face are considerably worse. However, *neither* view is correct. The fact that others intentionally intervene, in violation of a side constraint against aggression, to threaten force to limit the alternatives, in this case to paying taxes or (presumably the worse alternative) bare subsistence, makes the taxation system one of forced labor and distinguishes it from other cases of limited choices which are not forcings.

The man who chooses to work longer to gain an income more than sufficient for his basic needs prefers some extra goods or services to the leisure and activities he could perform during the possible nonworking hours; whereas the man who chooses not to work the extra time prefers the leisure activities to the extra goods or services he could acquire by working more. Given this, if it would be illegitimate for a tax system to seize some of a man's leisure (forced labor) for the purpose of serving the needy, how can it be legitimate for a tax system to seize some of a man's goods for that purpose? Why should we treat the man whose happiness requires certain material goods or services differently from the man whose preferences and desires make such goods unnecessary for his happiness? Why should the man who prefers seeing a movie (and who has to earn money for a ticket) be open to the required call to aid the needy, while the person who prefers looking at a sunset (and hence need earn no extra money) is not? Indeed, isn't it surprising that redistributionists choose to ignore the man whose pleasures are so easily attainable without extra labor, while adding yet another burden to the poor unfortunate who must work for his pleasures? If anything, one would have expected the reverse. Why is the person with the nonmaterial or nonconsumption desire allowed to proceed unimpeded to his most favored feasible alternative, whereas the man whose pleasures or desires involve material things and who must work for extra money (thereby serving whomever considers his activities valuable enough to pay him) is constrained in what he can realize? Perhaps there is no difference in principle. And perhaps some think the answer concerns merely administrative convenience. (These questions and issues will not disturb those who think that forced labor to serve the needy or to realize some favored end-state pattern is acceptable.) . . .

What sort of right over others does a legally institutionalized end-state pattern give one? The central core of the notion of a property right in X, relative to

which other parts of the notion are to be explained, is the right to determine what shall be done with X; the right to choose which of the constrained set of options concerning X shall be realized or attempted. The constraints are set by other principles or laws operating in the society; in our theory, by the Lockean rights people possess (under the minimal state). My property rights in my knife allow me to leave it where I will, but not in your chest. I may choose which of the acceptable options involving the knife is to be realized. This notion of property helps us to understand why earlier theorists spoke of people as having property in themselves and their labor. They viewed each person as having a right to decide what would become of himself and what he would do, and as having a right to reap the benefits of what he did.

When end-result principles of distributive justice are built into the legal structure of a society, they (as do most patterned principles) give each citizen an enforceable claim to some portion of the total social product; that is, to some portion of the sum total of the individually and jointly made products. This total product is produced by individuals laboring, using means of production others have saved to bring into existence, by people organizing production or creating means to produce new things or things in a new way. It is on this batch of individual activities that patterned distributional principles give each individual an enforceable claim. Each person has a claim to the activities and the products of other persons, independently of whether the other persons enter into particular relationships that give rise to these claims, and independently of whether they voluntarily take these claims upon themselves, in charity or in exchange for something.

Whether it is done through taxation on wages or on wages over a certain amount, or through seizure of profits, or through there being a big *social pot* so that it's not clear what's coming from where and what's going where, patterned principles of distributive justice involve appropriating the actions of other persons. Seizing the results of someone's labor is equivalent to seizing hours from him and directing him to carry on various activities. If people force you to do certain work, or unrewarded work, for a certain period of time, they decide what you are to do and what purposes your work is to serve apart from your decisions. This process whereby they take this decision from you makes them a *part-owner* of you; it gives them a property right in you. Just as having such partial control and power of decision, by right, over an animal or inanimate object would be to have a property right in it.

End-state and most patterned principles of distributive justice institute (partial) ownership by others of people and their actions and labor. These principles involve a shift from the classical liberals' notion of self-ownership to a notion of (partial) property rights in *other* people. . . .

LOCKE'S THEORY OF ACQUISITION

. . . [W]e must introduce an additional bit of complexity into the structure of the entitlement theory. This is best approached by considering Locke's attempt to specify a principle of justice in acquisition. Locke views property rights in an unowned object as originating through someone's mixing his labor with it. This gives rise to many questions. What are the boundaries of what labor is mixed with? If a private astronaut clears a place on Mars, has he mixed his labor with (so that he comes to own) the whole planet, the whole uninhabited universe, or just a particular plot? Which plot does an act bring under ownership? The minimal (possibly disconnected) area such that an act decreases entropy in that area, and not elsewhere? Can virgin land (for the purposes of ecological investigation by high-flying airplane) come under ownership by a Lockean process? Building a fence around a territory presumably would make one the owner of only the fence (and the land immediately underneath it).

Why does mixing one's labor with something make one the owner of it? Perhaps because one owns one's labor, and so one comes to own a previously unowned thing that becomes permeated with what one owns. Ownership seeps over into the rest. But why isn't mixing what I own with what I don't own a way of losing what I own rather than a way of gaining what I don't? If I own a can of tomato juice and spill it in the sea so that its molecules (made radioactive, so I can check this) mingle evenly throughout the sea, do I thereby come to own the sea, or have I foolishly dissipated my tomato juice? Perhaps the idea, instead, is

that laboring on something improves it and makes it more valuable; and anyone is entitled to own a thing whose value he has created. (Reinforcing this, perhaps, is the view that laboring is unpleasant. If some people made things effortlessly, as the cartoon characters in *The Yellow Submarine* trail flowers in their wake, would they have lesser claim to their own products whose making didn't *cost* them anything?) Ignore the fact that laboring on something may make it less valuable (spraying pink enamel paint on a piece of driftwood that you have found). Why should one's entitlement extend to the whole object rather than just to the *added value* one's labor has produced? . . . No workable or coherent value-added property scheme has yet been devised, and any such scheme presumably would fall to objections (similar to those) that fell the theory of Henry George.

It will be implausible to view improving an object as giving full ownership to it, if the stock of unowned objects that might be improved is limited. For an object's coming under one person's ownership changes the situation of all others. Whereas previously they were at liberty (in Hohfeld's sense) to use the object, they now no longer are. This change in the situation of others (by removing their liberty to act on a previously unowned object) need not worsen their situation. If I appropriate a grain of sand from Coney Island, no one else may now do as they will with *that* grain of sand. But there are plenty of other grains of sand left for them to do the same with. Or if not grains of sand, then other things. Alternatively, the things I do with the grain of sand I appropriate might improve the position of others, counterbalancing their loss of the liberty to use that grain. The crucial point is whether appropriation of an unowned object worsens the situation of others.

Locke's proviso that there be "enough and as good left in common for others" is meant to ensure that the situation of others is not worsened. (If this proviso is met is there any motivation for his further condition of nonwaste?) It is often said that this proviso once held but now no longer does. But there appears to be an argument for the conclusion that if the proviso no longer holds, then it cannot ever have held so as to yield permanent and inheritable property rights. Consider the first person Z for whom there is not enough and as good left to appropriate. The last person Y to appropriate left Z without his previous liberty to act on an object, and so worsened Z's situation. So Y's appropriation is not allowed under Locke's proviso. Therefore the next to last person X to appropriate left Y in a worse position, for X's act ended permissible appropriation. Therefore X's appropriation wasn't permissible. But then the appropriator two from last, W, ended permissible appropriation and so, since it worsened X's position, W's appropriation wasn't permissible. And so on back to the first person A to appropriate a permanent property right.

This argument, however, proceeds too quickly. Someone may be made worse off by another's appropriation in two ways: first, by losing the opportunity to improve his situation by a particular appropriation or any one; and second, by no longer being able to use freely (without appropriation) what he perviously could. A *stringent* requirement that another not be made worse off by an appropriation would exclude the first way if nothing else counterbalances the diminution in opportunity, as well as the second. A *weaker* requirement would exclude the second way, though not the first. With the weaker requirement, we cannot zip back so quickly from Z to A, as in the above argument; for though person Z can no longer *appropriate,* there may remain some for him to *use* as before. In this case Y's appropriation would not violate the weaker Lockean condition. (With less remaining that people are at liberty to use, users might face more inconvenience, crowding, and so on; in that way the situation of others might be worsened, unless appropriation stopped far short of such a point.) It is arguable that no one legitimately can complain if the weaker provision is satisfied. However, since this is less clear than in the case of the more stringent proviso, Locke may have intended this stringent proviso by "enough and as good" remaining, and perhaps he meant the non-waste condition to delay the end point from which the argument zips back.

THE PROVISO

Whether or not Locke's particular theory of appropriation can be spelled out so as to handle various difficulties, I assume that any adequate theory of justice in acquisition will contain a proviso similar to the weaker of the ones we have attributed to Locke. A process normally giving rise to a permanent bequeathable property right in a previously unowned thing will not do so if the position of others no longer at liberty to use the thing is thereby worsened. It is important to specify *this* particular mode of worsening the situation of others, for the proviso does not encompass other modes. It does not include the worsening due to more limited opportunities to appropriate (the first way above, corresponding to the more stringent condition), and it does not include how I "worsen" a seller's position if I appropriate materials to make some of what he is selling, and then enter into competition with him. Someone whose appropriation otherwise would violate the proviso still may appropriate provided he compensates the others so that their situation is not thereby worsened; unless he does compensate these others, his appropriation will violate the proviso of the principle of justice in acquisition and will be an illegitimate one. A theory of appropriation incorporating this Lockean proviso will handle correctly the cases (objections to the theory lacking the proviso) where someone appropriates the total supply of something necessary for life.

A theory which includes this proviso in its principle of justice in acquisition must also contain a more complex principle of justice in transfer. Some reflection of the proviso about appropriation constrains later actions. If my appropriating all of a certain substance violates the Lockean proviso, then so does my appropriating some and purchasing all the rest from others who obtained it without otherwise violating the Lockean proviso. If the proviso excludes someone's appropriating all the drinkable water in the world, it also excludes his purchasing it all. (More weakly, and messily, it may exclude his charging certain prices for some of his supply.) This proviso (almost?) never will come into effect; the more someone acquires of a scarce substance which others want, the higher the price of the rest will go, and the more difficult it will become for him to acquire it all. But still, we can imagine, at least, that something like this occurs: someone makes simultaneous secret bids to the separate owners of a substance, each of whom sells assuming he can easily purchase more from the other owners; or some natural catastrophe destroys all of the supply of something except that in one person's possession. The total supply could not be permissibly appropriated by one person at the beginning. His later acquisition of it all does not show that the original appropriation violated the proviso (even by a reverse argument similar to the one above that tried to zip back from *Z* to *A*). Rather, it is the combination of the original appropriation *plus* all the later transfers and actions that violates the Lockean proviso.

Each owner's title to his holding includes the historical shadow of the Lockean proviso on appropriation. This excludes his transferring it into an agglomeration that does violate the Lockean proviso and excludes his using it in a way, in coordination with others or independently of them, so as to violate the proviso by making the situation of others worse than their baseline situation. Once it is known that someone's ownership runs afoul of the Lockean proviso, there are stringent limits on what he may do with (what it is difficult any longer unreservedly to call) "his property." Thus a person may not appropriate the only water hole in a desert and charge what he will. Nor may he charge what he will if he possesses one, and unfortunately it happens that all the water holes in the desert dry up, except for his. This unfortunate circumstance, admittedly no fault of his, brings into operation the Lockean proviso and limits his property rights. Similarly, an owner's property right in the only island in an area does not allow him to order a castaway from a shipwreck off his island as a trespasser, for this would violate the Lockean proviso.

Notice that the theory does not say that owners do have these rights, but that the rights are overridden to avoid some catastrophe. (Overridden rights do not disappear; they leave a trace of a sort absent in the cases under discussion.) There is no such external (and *ad hoc?*) overriding. Considerations internal to the theory of property itself, to its theory of acquisition and appropriation, provide the means for handling such cases. The results, however, may be coextensive with some condition about catastrophe, since the baseline for comparison is so low as compared to the productiveness of a society with private appropriation that the question of the Lockean proviso being violated arises only in the case of catastrophe (or a desert-island situation).

The fact that someone owns the total supply of something necessary for others to stay alive does *not* entail that his (or anyone's) appropriation of anything left some people (immediately or later) in a situation worse than the baseline one. A medical researcher who synthesizes a new substance that effectively treats a certain disease and who refuses to sell except on his terms does not worsen the situation of others by depriving them of whatever he has appropriated. The others easily can possess the same materials he appropriated; the researcher's appropriation or purchase of chemicals didn't make those chemicals scarce in a way so as to violate the Lockean proviso. Nor would someone else's purchasing the total supply of the synthesized substance from the medical researcher. The fact that the medical researcher uses easily available chemicals to synthesize the drug no more violates the Lockean proviso than does the fact that the only surgeon able to perform a particular operation eats easily obtainable food in order to stay alive and to have the energy to work. This shows that the Lockean proviso is not an "end-state principle"; it focuses on a particular way that appropriative actions affect others, and not on the structure of the situation that results.

Intermediate between someone who takes all of the public supply and someone who makes the total supply out of easily obtainable substances is someone who appropriates the total supply of something in a way that does not deprive the others of it. For example, someone finds a new substance in an out-of-the-way place. He discovers that it effectively treats a certain disease and appropriates the total supply. He does not worsen the situation of others; if he did not stumble upon the substance no one else would have, and the others would remain without it. However, as time passes, the likelihood increases that others would have come across the substance; upon this fact might be based a limit to his property right in the substance so that others are not below their baseline position; for example, its bequest might be limited. The theme of someone worsening another's situation by depriving him of something he otherwise would possess may also illuminate the example of patents. An inventor's patent does not deprive others of an object which would not exist if not for the inventor. Yet patents would have this effect on others who independently invent the object. Therefore, these independent inventors, upon whom the burden of proving independent discovery may rest, should not be excluded from utilizing their own invention as they wish (including selling it to others). Furthermore, a known inventor drastically lessens the chances of actual independent invention. For persons who know of an invention usually will not try to reinvent it, and the notion of independent discovery here would be murky at best. Yet we may assume that in the absence of the original invention, sometime later someone else would have come up with it. This suggests placing a time limit on patents, as a rough rule of thumb to approximate how long it would have taken, in the absence of knowledge of the invention, for independent discovery.

I believe that the free operation of a market system will not actually run afoul of the Lockean pro-viso. . . . If this is correct, the proviso will not play a very important role in the activities of protective agencies and will not provide a significant opportunity for future state action. Indeed, were it not for the effects of previous *illegitimate* state action, people would not think the possibility of the proviso's being violated as of more interest than any other logical possibility. (Here I make an empirical historical claim; as does someone who disagrees with this.) This completes our indication of the complication in the entitlement theory introduced by the Lockean proviso.

NOTE

1. I am unsure as to whether the arguments I present below show that such taxation merely *is* forced labor; so that "is on a par with" means "is one kind of." Or alternatively, whether the arguments emphasize the great similarities between such taxation and forced labor, to show it is plausible and illuminating to view such taxation in the light of forced labor.

Critics

Alan H. Goldman | # The Entitlement Theory of Distributive Justice

According to Robert Nozick,[1] a social distribution is just if it is arrived at through legitimate acquisitions and transfers. Original acquisitions of property will be just if they violate no rights of others, e.g., if the goods are not already owned or claimed and if their appropriation does not leave others in a worse position (other than simply more limited opportunities to appropriate). Thereafter transfers are legitimate when voluntary. We are to measure the legitimacy of a distribution only according to how it came about, i.e., whether property to which owners were entitled was freely transferred or exchanged without violation of rights. Such historical principles are held incompatible in application with what Nozick appropriately terms *end-state principles,* principles that aim at some favored pattern of distribution like equality, maximization of average or mean utility, or the difference principle, since legitimate acquisitions

Alan H. Goldman, "The Entitlement Theory of Distributive Justice," *Journal of Philosophy* 73 (1976): 823–35. Reprinted by permission of the Journal of Philosophy.

and transfers are unlikely to result in any fixed pattern. If a fixed pattern were accidentally and momentarily achieved, it would immediately be upset by further free exchange, e.g., paying for entertainment when entertainers already have more than allowable under any likely end-state principle. What Nozick clearly has in mind as an embodiment of his just historical principles is the operation of free market exchange, without state controls (other than enforcement of contracts) or forced redistribution. All end-state principles imply that persons can have claims on others' property, but this contradicts the betterentrenched historical principles which imply that persons are entitled to what they acquire through free exchanges.

Why do our moral intuitions rebel at such unhindered operation of a free market economy as sole distributor of advantages? Have we come so far from it only through bureaucratic power-seeking or misguided good intentions? The deepest moral problem with such operation is that it allows or rather forces some to start in life with nothing but economic handicaps and prospects of misery and deprivation, through injustices done to their ancestors or perhaps simply through their stupidity. These factors may be impossible to separate in practice, but in any case we cannot see why children should be held responsible for the sins or omissions of their ancestors, or why they must remain almost inevitably locked within material and cultural deprivation because of their initial environments. Our intuition is that no system could be just which would allow this to an even greater extent than occurs in our present somewhat redistributive society; nor, as I will show, do Nozick's arguments force us from this initial reaction.

Let us analyze the sources of plausibility for the pure entitlement theory—why are certain individuals entitled to their holdings? We want to say first that persons are entitled to what they earn, that they are entitled to those rewards of their socially productive efforts which others are willing to pay. Second, we will admit that they are entitled to what they can freely appropriate even when this does not result in benefits to others, as long as their appropriation does not directly worsen the lot of others (this will have little application in an age when there is little

left to legitimately appropriate as opposed to trade for). Third, if persons are entitled to their holdings, they seem entitled to control their further distribution, to spend or give them as they like, e.g., on entertainment or to their children. It seems, finally, that the recipients must then be entitled to the assets if the givers were truly allowed to disburse them as they pleased. The right to give money to your children amounts to no right at all if the money may be confiscated as soon as it is in their hands.

On a deeper level we may ask further whether any more general principles justify these separate intuitions regarding entitlements. Do any moral features of free exchange and the market system which these modes of acquisition and transfer exemplify make that system prima facie morally preferable to alternatives? The principle that comes most readily to mind is maximizing freedom. Of course attempts at utilitarian justification have been made—we might view *The Wealth of Nations* as one—and we could conceive of arguments to the effect that totally free exchange satisfies the difference principle of Rawls. Empirical evidence seems to fall against such arguments, however, although the issue is still debated by economists and congressmen. Nozick would presumably dismiss such justifications for a different reason: he seems to think them inconsistent in that they call for patterns of distribution which must be upset by free exchange. But the principle of maximizing freedom is not an end-state principle that could be applied to current timeslice distributions of other goods in the way principles of welfare can be applied. It might seem rather to call for those historical rules of acquisition and transfer embodied in the unhindered exchange market. It certainly seems that what is morally noteworthy about free exchange is that it is free (not simply that each particular exchange tends to benefit both parties).

The justification of rules of entitlement themselves is relative to some more general conception of good or right which underlies them and, in application, to other moral rules embodying a system of values. It seems that, if principles of free acquisition and transfer are indeed to take precedence over all other claims on material property, it must be because we place a higher value on freedom than upon other goods like life (is this possible?), equality, or welfare, and because free exchange alone recognizes a maximum freedom of action for individuals. Nozick, however, objects to talk of maximization of any good as the goal of moral theory, and points out that his is not a maximization-of-freedom theory as utilitarianism is a maximization-of-welfare theory. We are not, for example, permitted to violate the rights of an individual in order to maximize the rights or freedom of others. Rather the underlying moral theory is Kantian in that it treats individuals as inviolable—we may never treat an individual without his consent as a means to the good of others or to any maximization of social good.

Thus the general principle from which Nozick's rules of transfer and acquisition must be seen to follow is the second formulation of Kant's categorical imperative. But if the principles of acquisition and transfer are meant to follow from the rule "Never treat another as a means without his consent," we want to examine more closely whether they do avoid such treatment as distinct from all alternatives. I admit at least the coherency of the distinction between maximizing freedoms or rights and prohibiting their violation in all cases. But it still seems that the Kantian prohibition is a way of expressing the absolute priority of the freedom of individuals over their welfare, for example. In any case we may raise questions at two levels: first, regarding the status of Nozick's principles of acquisition and transfer within the Kantian framework—do they fail to violate the Kantian injunction, and do all redistributive systems do so?; second, must we recognize the priority of individual freedom over all social goods expressed in Kant's principle? (I speak of the Kantian injunction as narrowly interpreted, but will argue that the spirit of Kant's injunction militates against the narrow interpretation Nozick gives it.) In deference to Nozick's refusal to remain too long on this level of moral theory, let us return for a moment to his specific entitlement principles, with these background questions in mind to be answered later.

As pointed out above, we want to say that (1) people are entitled to what they earn through socially productive efforts, and also that (2) they are entitled to spend their own earnings as they like. (Of course we can define "socially productive efforts" so as to build in end-state principles, but since this seems to violate the Kantian injunction and does not allow people to decide what they consider beneficial, I leave it for later.) (2) seems to follow from (1). It follows from (2) that (3) if these people desire to give away their earnings, then those to whom they are given must be entitled to them. The problem with this is that we also want to say that (4) people are not entitled to socially contingent advantages they don't deserve, and (5) people often don't deserve the monetary advantages they are given, for example, by their parents as children. (4) and (5) are clearly incompatible with (3). The fact that an individual has a moral right to what he acquires through effort and has the consequent right to do with those earnings what he wants does not seem to make it less morally arbitrary that one child starts off with all advantages and another with none. The right of the receiver here is totally dependent upon the right of the giver and cannot be independently claimed by him. If, as in traditional theories of distributive justice, we concentrate on the right of the receiver, that is, on (4) and (5), we are likely to limit the range of (3); whereas if, as Nozick does, we direct attention mainly to (1) and (2), we are likely to discount (4) and (5). We can use the first strategy to argue against Nozick that, since the right to give is correlative to the right to receive, it should not be construed more extensively than its counterpart. But of course he can simply reply that, given the correlation between giving and receiving, rights of receiving should not be construed as more limited than rights to give. Is there not some resolution or middle ground here?

First, we might discount the last reply by consideration of certain other analogous limitations on rights. Nozick himself admits that one's right to engage in a cooperative activity is limited by others' rights to do so. My right to hear different political views and thus various speakers on my campus is limited by the fact that some speakers I might want to hear are in jail and hence have no right to travel to speak. Insofar as giving is a relational or cooperative right, we might claim similarly that limitations generally take precedence over extensions from one participant to the other. Free exchanges are clearly to be limited by other rights—I cannot spend money to purchase nerve gas, since this violates others' rights to be free of unnecessary risk. Of course there is a question regarding gifts whether, in addition to not deserving their benefits, the recipients in this case violate others' rights in receiving them, and I will address that question shortly.

Even, however, if we refuse to allow the generalization regarding the precedence of limitations to this case and even if we continue to concentrate upon the right of the giver, i.e., the parent, that right does not seem to imply a right of the receiver to all future benefits accruing to his unequal start. We might, for example, allow the right to receive the total amount of money, but still claim the right to tax future interest or earnings on it for social benefits or remedial institutions. Since the receiver cannot claim his right to the money and its continued earning power with the same moral force as the giver can claim his right to bequeath the initial amount, the receiver cannot complain if later earnings are taxed. Furthermore, given that the receiver's future earning power in general, e.g., the job he gets, is also partially a function of his undeserved unequal start, we might tax in order to equalize somewhat that score as well. It might be objected in behalf of the *giver* that he meant to bequeath not only the capital, but the capital with its future earning power as well as the advantages it bestows, and that the capital is of far less use without these. It is doubtful, however, that a person earns the right to give more than the amount he earns, and in any case we would be taxing only a marginal amount of the future earnings. But the full answer to this awaits discussion of whether the rights of deprived children are violated by the unhindered operation of free transfer. We may admit a certain limitation on the right to give (and control future use) and yet argue that this results not only in a maximization of freedom, but in a satisfaction of Kant's injunction more sympathetic to its spirit.

We should first note an objection of Nozick to a point above, namely that, since future position and earning power are to a large extent determined by undeserved unequal starting position, we can tax these future rewards without legitimate complaint. He argues that attributing success to initial position

denigrates the degree of effort and autonomous choice involved, amounting to an overly deterministic and pessimistic view of human nature. In fact, however, the empirical evidence seems to support such a claim, if we compare the percentage of those who succeed starting with all advantages versus those who succeed starting with economic and cultural deprivation. (We have not yet justified taxing the latter.) Initial advantage constitutes neither a necessary nor a sufficient condition for future success (I assume a barometer for success), but I will stake this much of the argument on the belief that in our present society (and certainly in the society Nozick envisages) it comes statistically close to amounting to both. (In any case why should those with initial disadvantages have to work harder for success?) Second, those who do succeed could feel more certain of this as a reflection of effort or worth, within a system with remedial institutions to make competition more stiff and fair. Such a system, rather than lowering these persons' dignity and sense of achievement, would ensure that their accomplishments were recognized as such rather than regarded as the results of undeserved good fortune. It is true that those who do not succeed within a fair system may feel worse with the recognition that this is non-accidental. But there are other indicators of worth besides monetary success or even social productivity, and in any case we are after fairness, concerned with who is on top and who on bottom and why, not with minimizing the feelings of resentment of those who occupy the lower ranks.

Nozick has a further argument against redistributive taxation independent of these considerations regarding the giver-receiver relation, which will lead directly to our reassessment of the Kantian injunction in its relation to forced redistribution. He claims that such taxation is equivalent to forced labor—to take the results or earnings of someone's labor amounts to making him work a certain amount of time against his will purely for the benefit of others. This is to be equated with the doctrine that some persons (the beneficiaries of redistribution or the state) have property rights in others, and this seems clearly to violate the Kantian rights of those others not to be treated as means for the welfare of those who benefit. Nozick bolsters the argument further with examples of cases in which individuals have no right to make demands on the free activity of others even when their welfare depends upon such demands. Although Toscanini's orchestra members' welfare depended upon his continuing to conduct, they had no right to demand he not retire.

Once taxation is equated with forced labor, the argument seems to go through. But we must first question this equation more closely and, second, ask whether nonredistributive systems might not involve features plausibly construed as in violation of Kant's principle as well. There is certainly an initial distinction between what we usually picture as forced labor, e.g., chain gangs or Siberian work camps, and taxation even without consent. In the case of taxation a person is still free to work as long as he likes and at the job he chooses. He is simply required to contribute a percentage of earnings, presumably under a certain level of marginal utility to him, to those for whom it has a far greater marginal utility. Thus a demand on the conduct of Toscanini's life, for example, is far different from a demand on a marginal amount of his income.

Perhaps an equally damaging point is that differences in earnings are generally not a function of effort expended or hours worked. They are more often an indirect reflection of the initial undeserved advantages of that individual for obtaining that job. For this reason we can in no way equate redistributive taxation, which takes a portion of those extra earnings to provide for basic needs of those who lack such advantages, with making the individual work longer or harder for their benefit. Nor are the hours a person works very often a function of how much he wants to earn, so that if he doesn't earn as much as he needs in a given week he simply works longer to make up the difference. This may be true for those on the bottom of the economic scale whom redistribution benefits, but certainly almost never for those wealthy enough to lose through equitable social redistribution. Thus the equation of taxation for redistributive purposes with forced labor does not hold up in the face of all these disanalogies. And the claim that taxation involves using a *person* (as opposed to some of the money he acquires) as a means without his consent

and therefore violates the second formulation of the categorical imperative would require an extremely stretched interpretation of that principle.

The other assumed side of Nozick's position requires closer scrutiny as well, the question whether an economic system supported partly by those whose wages do not allow decent living, while others are maintained by that system in soft jobs for the acquisition of which they had initial advantages, does not more clearly violate a faithful rendering of the injunction against using persons as means. The ability and freedom to frame a meaningful life plan for oneself, which Nozick sees as underlying the demand to respect the autonomy of the individual, is denied to those who lack conditions that render such plans practicable. But for him this question does not arise, since he views the system of free exchange as based throughout on consent. Admittedly, the consent is often restricted—it may be a choice of working at a particular unpleasant low-paying job or starving. But Nozick points out that not all constraints on actions render them involuntary—the fact that I cannot choose to fly rather than walk to work does not render my choice of walking illusory. His criterion here is that restricted consent is not rendered involuntary unless those actions of others which constitute the restraints violate the rights of the person in question. My working as a professor when I would prefer to sing opera since other more competent baritones have been chosen for that profession still leaves my choice of profession voluntary (even if all other positions are taken?); my working as a professor under threats from avid students is not voluntary since my rights are violated in this case. But to use this criterion to justify a free market system in terms of consent is to beg the question of whether persons' rights are violated by that system.

The central question regarding the application of Kant's principle to the choice among rival social and economic systems is whether it violates the injunction against treating people as means to require or force certain individuals to help others in need by giving up some marginal amount of their earnings. It is clear that we do not violate the principle when we require that individuals not harm others or detract from their welfare in seeking their own satisfaction, and Nozick holds that the state violates no rights in enforcing this principle. Can the difference between the injunction not to harm others and the demand to help others in need be construed as so great that we violate the fundamental principle of morals in enforcing the second but follow it in enforcing the first? Nozick would presumably claim that the difference in the two cases is that, whereas it is moral to help others in need, no one can claim a right to be helped, and since people can claim rights to their property, we cannot enforce the demand to help in the name of justice—in fact to do so would be to violate the rights of property owners in treating them as means to others' welfare.

It is interesting to note in this context that Kant meant the second formulation of the categorical imperative to be equivalent to the first, the notion of acting under moral rules applied equally to all. It is also interesting that one of Kant's own examples of the application of the first principle involves the command to help others in need, under the claim that no one would will not to be helped when in need himself. A case could be made from this that a society with a set of rules of acquisition and transfer in which some are in need and not helped violates the first formulation of the principle in its rules and hence the second as well; that an economic system in which some prosper partly through the consumption and labor of those who, because of their initial positions (determined by the prior operation of the system), never have human needs filled, embodies rules that treat the latter individuals merely as means. This is equivalent to the claim that such a system embodies rules that could not be willed universally to apply in all conditions or could not be willed by anyone with the possibility of role switches (from a Rawlsian initial position).

It might be replied again that the first formulation of Kant's principle shows only that not helping others in need is immoral, not that the needy have a right to be helped or that this is a question of justice in which the state has a right to interfere. This much could be answered by pointing out that if, when attempting to will universally (playing the role of legislator in a "kingdom of ends"), we place ourselves in the position of someone in need, we undoubtedly not only

would want to be helped or to be answered favorably when begging for help, but would want to be able to demand help as a right so that the need for begging with its additional degradation would not arise. We would want not to await the beneficence of others as a hungry dog might do, but to be able to demand satisfaction of basic needs as a right of human beings in virtue of their worth or dignity. If the demand for satisfaction then becomes a right according to Kant's method of generating rules and if the state has the right to enforce rights or prevent their violation, then the state has the right of redistributive taxation, at least for this purpose.[2]

But Nozick has a further two-step argument to show that need does not create a right to the property of others. He first points out that we do not recognize such rights outside a mutual social context—one Robinson Crusoe who is faring very badly does not have a claim to the fruits of another's labor even when the other man is prospering; nor do we recognize claims of all people in the world in need upon our property. The second step consists in a challenge to stipulate what social cooperation adds to this picture in order to create the rights in question. I admit with Nozick that the difference does not lie in the fact that assets somehow become collective when a society is formed, nor in the fact that those on top benefit from social cooperation (since those on bottom are perhaps also better off than Robinson Crusoe). Part of the answer here is that, whereas in the case of Robinson Crusoe differences between their conditions are due to differences in natural assets or labor expended, in the social context of a relatively free market economy, differences are often due to unequal starts determined only by the prior operation of the conventional system itself. If the system had been set up differently, then the differences would not now exist to the same degree; therefore the system is responsible for lessening their effects somewhat.

A deeper answer can again be spelled out in Kantian terms in relation to what it means to enter a single moral community with others or to consider oneself part of such a community. Part of what this means is to recognize the common humanity of others and their moral equality. If this recognition is to be given content as well as form, it means that the rules one accepts within such a community must not only have equal application to all, but operate for the common good of all. This is expressed by Kant in the demand to place yourself in the position of another, i.e., under a different set of conditions, when attempting to will certain actions or rules, and by Rawls in his banning special advantages in the initial position from which rules are chosen. It means that there must be a presumption within the rules of an equality of conditions arising from common human needs, from which deviations must be justified. That this presumption operates on the level of moral intuition is clear from the fact that, although we feel uncomfortable if persons are treated differently or gain different benefits when no relevant difference between them has been found, we do not feel uncomfortable about treating people the same or giving them equal shares without finding a relevant sameness (other than a common humanity).

Nozick admits that before the operation of specific rules of entitlement or in the absence of satisfaction of those rules by the individuals in question there is a presumption of equal distributive shares of any good to be divided. Yet he claims that when such rules are in operation goods will generally be divided according to them, and equality becomes one type of end-state pattern incompatible with the operation of the rules. But if deviations from equality must be justified in the absence of such rules, it seems that this important presumption must have some consideration in the choice of rules themselves, must act as a constraint upon which principles are chosen. The rules must be justified not only in terms of the freedom to acquire and transfer (and how much of that freedom do those on the bottom have?) but insofar as they recognize a common humanity and consequent presumption of equality of conditions. The freedom to transfer must be weighed against the great inequalities created by it precisely in the name of the moral equality and autonomy of all individuals, so that they may be autonomous and capable of realistically framing meaningful life plans.

Nozick assumes in this last argument that his principles of entitlement apply in the Robinson Crusoe case or in a state of nature, and he cannot see why living in a society changes anything. My view is that no moral principles whatsoever would apply in a truly asocial context—in a real state of nature property would be seized when the opportunity arose, or rather it would make no sense to talk of property. Nozick has not succeeded in deriving a natural right to property, and admits difficulties in Locke's account. When such a right is determined within a social context by the choice of rules of acquisition and transfer, these will be relative to a balancing of moral values within the whole community. And if these are to be moral rules, they must be capable of being chosen by all from a position of equality, or capable of being willed by one who places himself in all possible conditions. These amount to the same constraints and are present in Kant's system, to which Nozick appeals, no less than in Rawls's, the target of his attack.

It might be replied one final time that I still have not done justice to the distinction between maximizing satisfaction of rights and absolutely prohibiting their violation, between an end-state moral system and a system with what Nozick terms "side constraints." Granted that a redistributive system will maximize satisfaction of Kant's principles, given that under it fewer will be in need and more will be able to formulate meaningful life plans, do *we* as members of a moral community or state have the right to interfere with the free activity (spending or saving) of some in order to realize this situation? Do we have a right to force it upon the wealthy? A negative answer would first of all assume that taxation is equivalent to treating others as means, which I questioned above. On a deeper level, I admitted above the intelligibility of the distinction between the two types of moral system, but not the rationality of accepting the "side constraint" type. To refuse to violate the absolute freedom of those who fail to recognize the rights of others arising from basic needs, is to press the distinction between positive and negative duties to an irrational point. It amounts here to a refusal to assume responsibility for an unjust state of affairs when the means to alter it are known. Finally, the abridgment of freedom involved in redistributive taxation is no more a violation of rights than is that involved in the prohibition against stealing, given that the right to the satisfaction of basic needs in an affluent society is as basic as the right to property.

One not inconsistent way in which considerations of equality or equity operate is through the operation of end-state principles in placing constraints on more specific rules of acquisition and transfer. Nozick sometimes writes, however, as if all end-state principles were incompatible with all rules of transfer or exchange which allow a reasonable degree of freedom in those activities. His reasoning here is that any distributive pattern that momentarily satisfied the end-state principle would be upset by any further free exchanges of money for services, for example, exchanges that would no longer leave the participants with the relative assets they had before. Nozick is guilty in this point of a straw-man fallacy, since no serious theory of justice, and certainly not Rawls's, demands a fixed pattern in final or current time-slice distributions, nor does any theory measure the justice of such distributions only according to their approximations to such patterns. If Rawls's difference principle were applied in this way to given patterns of held assets at a single time, it would be trivially equivalent to the demand for complete equality, since the maximization of each possible worst-off group at a single time would require making all equal (or, if we take the maximization of the actual worst-off group, the principle would demand switches whenever applied between worst off and best off at the extremes). It is clearly not meant to be applied in this way, but is intended for use at the level of designing basic institutions for society, when choosing rules of acquisition and transfer, for example, to guide future exchanges and property rights. According to its application at this level, extensive free exchange would undoubtedly be allowed (as it is under the most controlled economies), since such exchanges generally raise utility levels for both parties, worse as well as better off. Thus although basic institutions are to aim at a certain pattern in their design, the principles expressing this are self-defeating when applied to current time-slice distributions. The fact that principles are to apply to institutional design but not to results or instantiations of that design is similar to the familiar distinctions between rule and act utilitarian-

ism, rule and act egoism, etc. Considerations are applied at different levels not necessarily in virtue of some independently discoverable features of the levels (for which Nozick apparently seeks), but for the simpler reason that application at the more general level alone yields results in accord with moral intuitions against which the theory is to be tested.

To return to the relation of free exchange to end-state theories of distributive justice, none of the arguments I have put forward precludes the desirability of this universal institution as it operates within somewhat redistributive systems. No reasonable theory would prevent a person from spending money to see Wilt Chamberlain play basketball (Nozick's example), even though Wilt already has more money than his fans. I have not ruled out allowing a person to spend *all* his money on watching basketball, and am inclined to say that he deserves to starve if he should do so. I question only whether his children deserve to starve as well, whether we are not justified in requiring Chamberlain to give back a portion of his earnings beyond material needs and wants (no more would be required for truly redistributive purposes) to prevent such tragic occurrences.

To summarize: Nozick's principles of free acquisition and transfer rely upon his tacit claim that they alone accord with Kant's injunction to recognize the autonomy of individuals and not to use some as means to others' welfare; but he fails to show either that limited forced redistribution of wealth violates this injunction or that a system in which some prosper partly through the production and collective consumption of those in need does not. His equation of redistributive taxation with forced labor is artificial, and he fails to recognize the implications of entering into a moral community with others. The recognition of the moral equality of others generates a presumption of equality of conditions which constrains the choice of rules of transfer and exchange, and renders consistent and morally necessary in this choice the balancing of freedom with end-state goals like equality or social welfare. Brilliant and provocative philosophizing often occurs at the extremes in philosophical positions, for example, libertarian and egalitarian. It is the less spectacular and easier lot of some of us, having been provoked, to point out occasionally that truth or rightness lie somewhere between.

NOTES

1. *Anarchy, State, and Utopia* (New York: Basic Books, 1974).

2. Kant sees the duty to beneficence as imperfect, which means that (according to him) there is no duty to give specific amounts to specific individuals in need. I am not claiming here that Kant himself recognizes a right of individuals to have specific basic needs satisfied, but only that such a right can plausibly be generated from the Kantian moral point of view (furthermore, that this is more plausible than the attempt to generate an absolute right to property from that fundamental moral viewpoint).

Mark A. Michael | # Redistributive Taxation, Self-Ownership, and the Fruit of Labour

The leading idea of self-ownership is that persons have property rights to their bodies and powers. Three important moral claims concerning labour follow from this:

(P1) Persons may use their bodies in any non-harmful way they desire, including engaging in labour;

(P2) Persons may not be forced to work or lend their services or assistance to others; and

(P3) Persons may not be forced to give up or transfer any part of the fruit of their labour to others.[1]

In what follows I will use this metaphor of the fruit of labour to refer to that part of the product of one's labour which one may not be forced to give up according to the principle of self-ownership. This is admittedly imprecise; the purpose of this paper is to clarify exactly what this metaphor comes to.

Self-ownership has been the subject of much recent discussion, for it plays a central role in libertarian critiques of egalitarian and liberal principles of distributive justice. Nozick for example points out that a redistributive tax would be required to maintain any kind of egalitarian pattern of distribution in a society in which wages were not strictly controlled by the government. But such a tax appears to be a forced expropriation of the fruit of the labour of those subjected to the tax, and thereby it runs foul of (P3). And if libertarians are right in thinking that self-ownership is a core component of freedom, it follows that redistributive policies are incompatible with freedom so that, contrary to the claim of many egalitarians, a society becomes less rather than more free when it adopts egalitarian principles of distribution.[2] All this depends, of course, on what I will call the Incompatibility Thesis (IT hereafter), which says that taxation for the purpose of redistribution is inconsistent with self-ownership since it forces people to give up part of the fruit of their labour.

Nozick's argument applies to those cases in which the redistributive tax expropriates the fruit of one's labour. But might not some of the wages which a person receives as a result of her work represent more than the fruit of her labour, a condition we might think of as a person's being overpaid? Since self-ownership requires only that the fruit of a person's labour not be expropriated, and makes no claims about what may be done with any overpayment a person may receive as part of her wages, it appears that this excess could be expropriated as part

Mark A. Michael, "Redistributive Taxation, Self-Ownership and the Fruit of Labour," *Journal of Applied Philosophy* 14, no. 2 (1997): 137–46. Some notes have been deleted. Reprinted by permission of Blackwell Publishing Ltd.

of a redistributive tax without violating (P3). If overpayment is possible, then the IT is wrong; a redistributive tax would not violate self-ownership, as long as what was expropriated was the overpayment and not the fruit of the labour. So it is crucial to know whether and under what conditions it would be meaningful to claim that someone was overpaid in this specific sense, and this in turn depends on how the metaphor of the fruit of labour is cashed in. Both libertarians and their critics interpret the fruit of labour very broadly so that it includes all those changes and alterations in the world which are intentionally caused or brought about by a person's labour, which we will call here the results of that labour.

The libertarian idea is that self-ownership licenses a person's using his body in whatever non-harmful ways he chooses. In the typical labour arrangement a worker agrees to use his body to produce changes in raw materials or other goods owned by his employers. These alterations are all causally produced by a worker using his body in a non-harmful manner; they are the results of his labour and consequently the fruit of his labour. And inasmuch as he has a right to all these changes, since *ex hypothesi* they are the fruit of his labour, he has a right to whatever wages he can get in exchange for them. Thus as long as a person receives no more than the wages which were agreed upon, which would be very unlikely, one could not be overpaid. And then given the libertarian identification of the fruit of labour with all the results produced by one's labour, if either any of the results of that labour or any of one's wages are expropriated, then the fruit of that labour is expropriated and self-ownership is thereby violated.

But there are renderings of the idea of the fruit of labour according to which being overpaid could be a common occurrence. If the fruit of labour were to turn out to be a subset of the results, then, if a person were to receive a wage on the assumption that all the results belonged to her and could therefore be transferred by her to her employer, she would be overpaid. Part of the wage would be something to which she has no right, since she receives it in exchange for something that was not hers to sell in the first place, namely that subset of the changes which she brings

about through her labour but which we are supposing does not belong to her. So in order for Nozick's argument against redistributive taxation to work, there must be no possible rendering of the fruit of labour which is consistent with the original principle of self-ownership but which identifies it with some subset of the results rather than the full complement of results. But if a worker produces changes through the non-harmful use of her body, how could those not count as the fruit of her labour? The following story suggests one way.

One day in a fit of capriciousness God makes a little red pill which will significantly improve the quality of anyone's work who happens to find and take the pill. A mediocre cobbler who produces mediocre shoes and consequently who can command only a modest wage even in the best of times happens to find the pill. Thinking it a candy, he eats it, and the quality of his work improves immediately. Whereas before the cobbler bent most of the nails he was lucky enough to hit, he now hits nails dead centre. The cobbler's stitching of leather, which in the past could charitably be described as uneven and loose, becomes tight, regular, and even. This enables the cobbler to work much more quickly, as he no longer has to take as much time averting and correcting mistakes, and so he now produces more and higher quality shoes. There is a significant increase, both qualitative and quantitative, in the changes he is able to produce through his labour, so he finds himself able to negotiate a much higher wage on the basis of his improved output. But he also finds himself in a much higher tax bracket than what he was in prior to the accidental discovery of the pill. But when the tax bill comes, the cobbler is ready, for he has read Nozick and been converted to libertarianism. The cobbler argues that the tax, which will be used to achieve a more egalitarian distribution, will violate his self-ownership. Thus, anyone who values self-ownership should think it wrong to make him pay the tax bill.

We may agree that the cobbler's self-ownership should not be violated. And his additional output undoubtedly counts as part of the results of his labour, since the changes are brought about by *his* labour. Yet we may be skeptical about identifying those results of his labour which are attributable to his finding the pill with the fruit of his labour, since the ability to produce those additional results came about by luck rather than anything the cobbler did by choice. So our skepticism gives us a reason to think that the fruit of the cobbler's labour is to be identified with a subset of the results as opposed to them all. But which subset? Since it was simply good fortune to discover the pill, the natural suggestion here is that the fruit of labour is to be identified with that subset of the results which are somehow associated with the conscious choices and effort of the worker, as opposed to those results which come about by luck.

The trick of course is to explicate this distinction between luck and choice. This obviously is a complex task, but it need not be performed here. Our purposes here require something significantly more modest. It is necessary to show only that there is at least one reading of the fruit of labour which identifies it with some subset of the results rather than all the results, which is not wildly implausible, and which can serve as a competitor to the libertarian interpretation. We can do that by noting first that the cobbler story suggests that the libertarian interpretation does not fit all the facts. Not only is there nothing incoherent or bizarre in the hypothesis that the fruit of labour should be identified not with the full set of results but rather with that subset of the results which are due to one's choices rather than luck, but that hypothesis is one way of accounting for our intuitions about the cobbler story. Second, neither the intuition nor the hypothesis appears to be recalcitrant bits of data that can be rejected out of hand, for each conforms to the broader moral principle that social institutions should neither reward nor penalise people on the basis of occurrences that are beyond their control or due to luck, and that principle has a fairly secure place in moral theorising generally. And finally, even if at present we lack an algorithm which will give us a precise answer to the question of what percentage of the results of labour are due to luck, it is clear that for those persons with superior natural talents, some part of the results of their labour will be due to luck and so will not count as the fruit of their labour. These results could therefore be expropriated by a redistributive tax without violating the principle of self-ownership.

I think then that we must allow that there is nothing in principle which would bar us from constructing a coherent theory around the suggestion that we identify the fruit of labour with those results that are not due to luck. This theory then serves as a competitor to the libertarian interpretation of the fruit of labour, for it identifies the fruit of labour with something less than the full set of results. Since the fruit of labour need not be identified with the full set of results, then in the absence of further argument there is no reason to privilege the libertarian interpretation which makes this identification over the non-libertarian one. Of course libertarians will balk at any interpretation such as the one just proposed because it apparently reconciles self-ownership and redistributive tax policies and so the IT falls. But that cannot be a reason to think that there is something fundamentally misguided about this non-libertarian interpretation and hence to discard it. So under some initially plausible interpretation of the fruit of labour, namely the non-libertarian one, a redistributive tax will not be inconsistent with self-ownership, since the tax need not expropriate the fruit of one's labour, but rather may expropriate whatever was received in excess of the fruit of one's labour. Thus Nozick can no longer move straightaway from self-ownership to a rejection of redistributive taxation, and thereby argue that redistribution is necessarily inconsistent with freedom. For he must first show that his reading which identifies the fruit of labour with all the results is the superior one, since the above discussion shows clearly that it is not the only one.

How might a libertarian show that his reading of the fruit of labour is the most plausible one? Our initial concern was whether or not one could consistently maintain a commitment to both the principle of self-ownership and a policy of redistributive taxation. We have just seen that there is an initially plausible interpretation of the fruit of labour which appears to allow one to do just that. But while the non-libertarian interpretation is prima facie acceptable and seems to harmonise self-ownership and redistributive taxation, perhaps the non-libertarian interpretation is inconsistent with the other principles of self-ownership. The libertarian might then proceed in the following way. We have a clear and unambiguous account of two principles entailed by self-ownership, (P1) and (P2); it is the interpretation of (P3) that is up for grabs, because of the indeterminacy of the notion of the fruit of labour. Thus it may be possible to show that any reading of (P3) which identifies the fruit of labour with anything less than the complete set of results, an identification which is needed by the non-libertarian to enable him to harmonise redistributive taxation with self-ownership, will lead to situations either where one is forced to labour, which would make it inconsistent with (P2), or somehow involves forbidding people to engage in non-harmful activities with their bodies, which would be inconsistent with (P1). In either case the non-libertarian interpretation would have to be rejected by anyone who was simultaneously committed to self-ownership and then the IT would be re-established.

Some of Nozick's remarks suggest this strategy. He claims that a person's receiving anything less than all the results of her labour, whether as the result of the implementation of a redistributive tax or for any other reason, is tantamount to forcing her to labour. And inasmuch as forced labour is clearly a violation of (P2), any interpretation which identifies the fruit of labour with anything less than the full set of results and so allows for such an expropriation, as the non-libertarian interpretation does, would violate self-ownership. Regarding the issue of taxation Nozick says, "The fact that others intentionally intervene, in violation of a side constraint against aggression, to threaten force to limit the alternatives, in his case to paying taxes or (presumably the worse alternative) bare subsistence, makes the taxation system one of forced labour and distinguishes it from other cases of limited choices which are not forcings."[3] If Nozick is correct, then anyone committed to self-ownership will have no choice but to adopt the libertarian interpretation and identify the fruit of labour with the full set of results, since any other reading would conflict with (P2) and hence with self-ownership.

Nozick does not explain exactly how being forced to pay taxes amounts to a kind of forced labour, but we can reconstruct the details of the argument. If a person is forced to pay a tax and thereby give up some of her wages, she then has to work additional hours to recoup what was expropriated. Thus we might say that she was forced to labour for however many hours it takes to make up what was taken.[4] Or the argument might be that since people usually do not voluntarily engage in unpaid labour, and since taxation turns paid labour into unpaid labour, the person who is taxed must somehow have been forced to labour. Although this move from being forced to pay taxes to being forced to labour can be questioned, we should press on to what is clearly the central problem of the argument.[5] We first need to draw a distinction between holdings and property. The term 'holding' as I will use it here is normatively neutral and refers to whatever one has in one's possession; it does not entail that one has property rights to one's holdings. A burglar for example may have a holding without having property rights to it. In order to determine whether or not the expropriation of some holding is justified Nozick must apply his principle that 'the rights of others determine the constraints upon your actions,' and presumably this includes whatever constraints may be placed on the actions of the government.[6] A person has legitimate grounds for complaint when the government seizes his property, for he must work extra hours to replace whatever was expropriated. But when the government seizes a burglar's ill-gotten holdings surely the burglar cannot accuse the government of forcing her to labour because she must now spend additional time burgling in order to replace the seized holdings. Parallel considerations apply to taxation. Whether or not the expropriation of wages unjustifiably forces a person into extra labour to replace the expropriated income depends entirely on whether or not the income was something the person had a right to. So if Nozick wants to show that taxation amounts to forced labour, he must do more than point out that the government issues threats and thereby coerces people into surrendering the holdings which they obtained from their employers, that is, their income; he must also show that the government has done something that it has no right to do, and this is the case only if the person has a right to those holdings, or alternatively if they count as her property.

Now if that is correct, then any attempt to show that the expropriation of the results of one's labour amounts to forced labour must not assume that one has a right to all those results, since that would be circular. But the argument under consideration appears to do just that. Libertarians want to show that redistribution is inconsistent with self-ownership. But to do this they must show that any non-libertarian interpretation which identifies the fruit of labour with anything less than the full set of the results is inconsistent with self-ownership. Nozick introduced his claims about expropriation and forced labour to do just that. The argument appeared to be that the failure to identify the fruit of labour with the full set of results opens up the possibility that some of the results will be expropriated by a tax, and then one would be forced to labour, which clearly violates self-ownership. But Nozick can show that this is forced labour only if he has already shown that one has property rights to all the results of his labour. But he can't know or presuppose that, inasmuch as that is the very thing he is trying to establish by this argument. He could show that taking part of the results amounts to forced labour and so is inconsistent with self-ownership only if he had previously shown that one had a right to all those results. But since there is a plausible interpretation of the fruit of one's labour that does not entail that one has a right to all the results of one's labour, Nozick cannot assume that one has a right to all the results in his argument. He needs some independent argument for that. It is simply not true that a tax which expropriates the results would necessarily force one to labour, for what is expropriated might be one's holdings rather than one's property.

Perhaps any reading of the fruit of one's labour which fails to identify it with all the results will be inconsistent with (P1). In order to show this it would have to be the case that the expropriation of any of the results of a person's labour somehow prevents her from legitimately employing her powers in a non-harmful way. But this claim is extremely dubious. A person is not prevented from exercising her power to build a sand castle even though she is not allowed to keep as private property the sand castle

and the bit of beach on which it is built. More generally, the ability to exercise one's power to produce something does not seem to be impeded just because one is not allowed to keep as one's property whatever comes about as a causal product or result of the exercise of that power. Now it might be urged that being granted property rights to the results of one's labour is often what a person intends to do by her actions, so that acquiring property rights should be built into the description of the power which she wants to exercise. That is, when someone wants to exercise her power to split some logs, the real power she wants to exercise is the power to produce something that she can use as fuel for her fireplace. So if she is not allowed to keep the split logs as her property then the non-harmful exercise of her powers has been interfered with.

But consider the following case. Walker strolls across a plot of unowned land and he describes what he is doing as taking possession of unowned property. Not even libertarians will want to grant property rights to a plot of land simply because someone has walked across it. But Walker claims that if libertarians do not allow him to keep that land as his own property, they are not allowing him to engage in the non-harmful exercise of his powers, and so are violating his self-ownership. The correct response to Walker here is that while the failure to grant him ownership of the land prevents him from exercising his power to gain property by walking across it, we cannot infer that this prevents the legitimate or non-harmful exercise of his powers. Nozick's principle which was invoked in the earlier discussion of forced labour is also germane to this problem. Whether the exercise of some power is non-harmful and legitimate depends on the rights of ourselves and others. Any determination of whether or not the exercise of some power is legitimate will presuppose that we have already established exactly what sorts of actions one has a right to perform. Thus whether the failure to grant a person property rights to all the results of his labour interferes with the legitimate exercise of his powers and thereby violates his self-ownership depends on whether he has a right to those results. One cannot hold as a general principle that any taking of the results of his labour prevents a person from performing a legitimate, non-harmful action in the absence of a further argument which shows that he has a right to all those results. Once again the moral of the story is that we must first decide to which of the results of his labour a worker has a legitimate claim. Only after that has been established can we say that there has been a failure to allow a person to exercise his powers in a non-harmful way in those instances in which a worker is not allowed to keep as property whatever we have decided that he had a right to. But the argument cannot go in the other direction, since that would be circular. That is, it cannot be claimed that a person has property rights to a certain bit of stuff simply because not letting him have it will prevent him from exercising his powers in a non-harmful way. Otherwise, a burglar could claim that he has a right to his ill-gotten gain on the grounds that the failure to grant such a right would prevent him from exercising his burgling powers and skills. So the issue which must be addressed first is whether a person has a right to all the results of his labour. Consequently any description of the power that is being exercised which assumes anything about property rights will invite a charge of circularity.

The upshot of this discussion and the previous one concerning forced labour is that once we have determined what counts as the fruit of labour, we can then go on to say that self-ownership is violated whenever the fruit of labour is expropriated, since its expropriation will amount to a violation of both (P1) and (P2). But that cannot help us to determine what counts as the fruit of labour or whether the fruit of labour includes the entire set of the results of labour or some subset. And the libertarian needs a specific answer to that question to successfully defend the IT; she needs to show that the only plausible interpretation of the fruit of labour must be the one that identifies it with the complete set of results. So the only option left to the libertarian is to claim that the failure to identify the fruit of labour with the full set of results is directly contradictory to the core thesis of self-ownership. The claim "I own my body but not all the results of my labour" must turn out to be

a logical contradiction. If this is correct, then the claim that one owns all the results of one's labour is intrinsic to the concept of self-ownership, and then self-ownership would entail that the fruit of labour must be identified with the full set of results. One could only be said to truly own oneself where one also owned all the results of one's labour. Any theory which rejected this entailment could not by definition be a theory of self-ownership.

This specific claim about self-ownership presumably follows from a more general claim, namely that ownership of any object logically or conceptually entails ownership of all the changes or alterations that the object produces. Is this true? To begin with, it is worth noting that nowhere in Honore's classic discussion of property and ownership is there any mention of a person's right to whatever changes are produced by his property.[7] Honore does note that full liberal ownership entitles an owner to use an object in whatever non-harmful way he wants, and that he has a right to whatever income can be derived from allowing others to use his property. But it does not follow from either of these that one has a right to all the results that are produced by the things he owns. Rather, given that a person owns some machine, and given the determination of how much of what it produces is rightfully his, the right to income allows him to rent the machine and its ability to produce those results which it turns out that I own to others for income. So neither of these rights entails that an owner has property rights to everything which his property produces or which results from its use.

Perhaps Honore overlooked this component of property rights, so we should ask whether a case could be made for the claim that ownership of an object definitionally or conceptually entails ownership of those alterations that come about when that object is put to use. Consider the case of Taylor, who owns some highly automated equipment which turns bolts of cloth into finished shirts. On a normal day there is no need to replace the bolt of cloth, to oil or provide other maintenance for the machine; in a word, no labour is needed to produce the shirts. The introduction of this apparently superfluous detail will allow us to focus on the ownership of an object and to bracket off those complications which might arise based on questions about the ownership of whatever labour might otherwise be needed to keep the machine running. Suppose the machine can produce 1,000 shirts every day, and the government expropriates one of the shirts for redistributive purposes. Can the following set of claims be maintained consistently? (i) Taylor is the legitimate owner of all the raw material, i.e. he owns the bolt of cloth, the thread, etc., (ii) Taylor is the legitimate owner of the machinery and equipment, the energy used to keep the machine running, etc. and (iii) Taylor does not have a right to all the finished shirts, so the government does no wrong in its expropriation? Now it may be that iii) is mistaken. It may turn out, for example, that given (i), (ii) and some other premises, it could be shown that (iii) is false. But it does not appear to be *logically* inconsistent to hold claims (i)–(iii), and this shows that ownership of an object does not logically entail ownership of all the results brought about by the object. Another way to think about this is that from (i) and (ii) one cannot derive (iiia), "Taylor has a right to all the finished shirts." An additional premise that a person in fact does have a right to all the results that are produced by a machine she owns would be needed to arrive at (iiia). But this premise needs to be supported by some independent argument; it is not implicit in the concept of ownership. Thus the general principle that ownership of an object logically entails ownership of whatever it produces is false and cannot be invoked to support one of its instances, namely that ownership of one's body logically entails that one owns everything that one's body produces.

At this point a libertarian may, in a Wittgensteinian spirit, suggest that the discussion has been misguided from the start, since it has attempted to solve a pseudo-problem created by the conflation of a symbol with the reality which it was supposed to explicate. The fruit of labour, which was intended as nothing more than a metaphor, has been confused with the concept which this metaphor was supposed to explain, namely the results of labour. This has blinded us to the obvious truth that self-ownership, if it is about anything, is about the fact that one has a right to all the results of one's labour. Libertarians who have talked about the fruit of labour have always intended this as a metaphor for the complete set of the results of labour. Thus it is irrelevant whether or not there is only one plausible interpretation of the fruit of labour, since all the talk about the fruit of labour is metaphorical, nothing more. The claim that one has a right to all the results of one's labour is part and parcel of the notion of self-ownership.

It is undoubtedly true that libertarians who have tried to explicate and defend the concept of self-ownership have also generally assumed that a person has a right to all the results of her labour, since they have assumed that their interpretation of the fruit of labour is correct. But this paper suggests that there is no essential connection between self-ownership and the libertarian interpretation of the fruit of labour, so that self-ownership does not entail the principle that one has a right to all the results of one's labour. Libertarians have merely grafted the latter principle onto self-ownership proper. This has created the impression that self-ownership proper and this principle are somehow intrinsically related to one another. But this connection is nothing more than an appearance, based on the constant conjunction of self-ownership and the principle that one has a right to all the results of one's labour in the work of libertarian theorists. It is of course part of the libertarian programme to interpret the fruit of labour so that it incorporates the full set of results, and this interpretation is consistent with and perhaps follows from other things that libertarians believe. But that interpretation does not follow from self-ownership. When libertarians combine the principle that one has a right to all the results of one's labour, which depends on their interpretation of the fruit of one's labour, with self-ownership proper, they can and often do refer to the gerrymandered concept which results as self-ownership. But to simply incorporate two distinct principles, namely self-ownership and the principle that one has a right to all the results of one's labour, under one rubric is not the same as demonstrating that there is any kind of intrinsic or necessary relation between them. That is the thesis I have wanted to deny here. I have argued that self-ownership proper, which is an attractive thesis, neither logically nor conceptually entails that one has a right to the full set of the results of one's labour, since it neither logically nor conceptually entails the libertarian interpretation of the fruit of one's labour. It follows that the IT is false.[8]

We must conclude that one cannot derive any claim about how much of the results of one's labour one truly has a right to, or how much of the results count as the fruit of one's labour, from the principle of self-ownership proper. This might be understood as further support for the view advanced by some writers that the entire notion of self-ownership should be discarded because it is so hopelessly muddled that it fails to elucidate the relation between what a person produces by using his body in the act of labour and what a person has a right to as a consequence of that use. But self-ownership may yet serve an important function, and we should consider carefully whether we can really afford to jettison it. For first, as we have seen, after it has been determined that something does count as the fruit of one's labour, it will follow that its expropriation will be a violation of self-ownership and hence of one's freedom, and this provides a reason for objecting to the exploitation of workers. Second, self-ownership explains why, for example, we think it would be wrong to take an eye from a sighted person and use it to restore the sight of a blind person, were such an operation feasible. There may be other principles which will provide the same sort of safeguard against such practices, but self-ownership seems particularly well suited to this task.

NOTES

1. Robert Nozick's (1974) *Anarchy, State and Utopia* [*ASU* hereafter] (New York, Basic Books).

2. *ASU*, pp. 167–73.

3. *ASU*, p. 169.

4. This seems to be the point of the remarks in *ASU*, p. 170.

5. *ASU*, p. 169. He makes the claim that paying taxes is a kind of forced labour again on p. 172. This identification has significant rhetorical power, conjuring up images of slavery and other forms of enforced servitude. It is only in a footnote on p. 169 that he backs off the claim that taxation is a kind of forced labour, and suggests that it instead produces a situation which bears many similarities to forced labour. See Alan Ryan's remarks on the significant differences between taxation and forced labour in (1994) Self-ownership, autonomy, and property rights, *Social Philosophy and Policy*, 11, pp 255–6.

6. *ASU*, p. 29.

7. H. M. Honore (1961) "Ownership in A. G. Guest" (ed.) *Oxford Essays in Jurisprudence* (Oxford, Clarendon Press), 107–147.

8. Libertarians may ask, if the worker does not own all the results of his labour, who does? That is a fair enough question, but notice even if we fail to have a ready answer, that does not detract from the fact that we have no good reason to suppose that they are owned by the person who produced them. One plausible answer here is that no one owns them, so they can be used to satisfy the moral requirements of equality.

Is Capital Punishment Wrong?

van den Haag and His Critics

Critics of capital punishment have presented a wide variety of arguments against the State's practice of executing murderers. Capital punishment contains an unacceptable risk of mistakenly executing innocent people, they have maintained. It objectionably treats the murderer as a mere means to the end of reducing crime, they have added. And besides, they have asked, if what the murderer did in killing a human being is wrong, then shouldn't it follow that what the State does in killing the murderer is wrong as well? These arguments against capital punishment have grown in intensity and visibility over the last thirty years. And throughout this long period, Ernest van den Haag has stood resolute in attempting to rebut them. Van den Haag is by far the United States' most prominent defender of capital punishment. A small but representative sample of his work serves as the featured article for this chapter. It makes sense to read van den Haag if one wishes to find a clear, forceful statement in defense of capital punishment; it is less clear that it makes sense to read him before reading the works of his critics. Van den Haag's defense of capital punishment, it turns out, is largely a defense of the claim that capital punishment can be defended from the various objections that have been raised against it. Critics of capital punishment often develop their arguments against it specifically by trying to show how they are able to overcome defenses of capital punishment offered by van den Haag. That is, the debate about capital punishment is at least as much a case of van den Haag criticizing his critics as it is a case of his critics criticizing him. Therefore, in the one exception to our policy of focusing first on the featured article and then on the critical responses, we will begin here by summarizing the main arguments against capital punishment made by Jeffrey H. Reiman and Stephen Nathanson before turning to van den Haag's arguments against them. We suggest that readers examine the articles in the same order.

Reiman's argument against capital punishment begins by conceding one of the central claims made by its defenders: Morally speaking, the State has the right to execute people who commit murder. Reiman agrees with defenders of capital punishment that it is not unjust to execute a murderer, and that a murderer who is executed does, in fact, get what he deserves. But the fact that the State has the moral right to do something does not mean that it is morally unobjectionable for it to exercise that right. In the case of capital punishment, Reiman claims that there is a sound moral reason for the State *not* to exercise that right; doing so would be uncivilized. Reiman's argument for this claim turns largely on the important analogy he makes between murder on the one hand and rape and torture on the other. That is, even if the State has the right to rape rapists and torture torturers, Reiman asserts that it would be morally wrong for it to exercise that right. And, he argues, the features that make it wrong for the State to punish torture with torture—the extreme amount of suffering and subjugation involved in such a punishment—are present also and to a comparable degree, in the case of capital punishment. Reiman's argument can therefore be represented in terms of a simple two-premise argument from analogy (see the Introduction):

P1   It is immoral (although not unjust) to torture torturers.
P2   Torturing torturers is morally on a par with executing murderers.

C   It is immoral (although not unjust) to execute murderers.

If it would be wrong to torture torturers, that is it would also be wrong to execute murderers.

While Reiman's argument focuses on intrinsic features of capital punishment (features that it has regardless of the way that it happens to be carried out in any given society), Nathanson's argument against capital punishment is grounded in the claim that it has been and continues to be administered in an arbitrary manner. More specifically, Nathanson appeals to the claim that the death penalty has been used disproportionately against black and poor criminals: A poor black person who kills is more likely to receive a death sentence than is a wealthy white person who kills. And this fact, Nathanson claims, suffices to render the practice itself morally unacceptable. Like Reiman, Nathanson attempts to support his position by appealing to analogies. Suppose, for example, the State prohibited speeding, but then ticketed only those speeders who had beards and long hair. Or consider a teacher who tells his class that he will fail any student found guilty of plagiarism, but who then fails only the plagiarists he dislikes. In cases such as these, Nathanson argues, the imposition of punishment is unjust precisely because it is objectionably discriminatory. Even though the people who did receive punishment were guilty of the offense for which were punished, it is nonetheless the case that the justice of inflicting punishment on them is affected by the fact that others guilty of the same offense were spared comparable punishments for arbitrary reasons. It would be better, as Nathanson puts it, if the teacher failed none of the plagiarists than if he failed only the plagiarists he disliked. Put into the same two-premise structure used to represent Reiman's argument, Nathanson's central argument can be understood as follows:

P1   It is unjust to punish only bearded speeders (or only unlikable plagiarists).
P2   Capital punishment, as actually practiced, is morally on a par with punishing only the bearded speeders (or only the unlikable plagiarists).

C   Capital punishment, as actually practiced, is unjust.

It would be better for the State to execute no murderers, Nathanson concludes, than to execute them in a context in which such executions were arbitrarily distributed.

The defense of capital punishment that van den Haag offers in the Featured article aims to identify shortcomings in the arguments of Reiman and Nathanson. In the case of Reiman, van den Haag can be understood as directing three principal objections against the argument from analogy with torture. The first objection attacks the analogy itself: Torture, van den Haag maintains, is in and of itself repulsive, and this is why we do not engage in it, even if it is deserved. But death, in and of itself, is not repulsive, and so, on van den Haag's account, the analogy between torture and execution is unsuccessful. His second response to Reiman's argument is simply to bite the bullet: If the analogy is truly sustainable, he says, then it shows that we should sometimes torture torturers, not that we should never execute murderers. Finally, van den Haag raises a question about the theoretical basis underlying Reiman's analogy. Reiman's claim is that abolishing capital punishment is a further step in the "advancement" of civilization: Abolishing torture counts as some progress, while abolishing the death penalty would count as even more. But, van den Haag counters, why consider the direction that civilization is taking to be a good thing? What is the basis for saying that more civilization (in Reiman's sense of the term) is better than less? Readers should take note of a further consideration that van den Haag raises at the outset of his discussion of Reiman: Murderers are executed only because they voluntarily commit an act of murder knowing that their execution may be a consequence of this. This consideration, too, may help van den Haag in fending off Reiman's attack on capital punishment.

In defending capital punishment from Nathanson's argument, van den Haag can again be seen as arguing on multiple fronts. First, he challenges Nathanson's claim that black murderers are discriminated against. This, in effect, amounts to denying P2 of Nathanson's argument. Second, and more fundamentally, he argues that even if black murderers are discriminated against, this shows only that we should execute more white murderers, not that we should execute fewer black murderers. In particular, while Nathanson argues that it would be better to execute no murderers than to execute some arbitrarily, van den Haag maintains that it is better to ensure that at least some get the punishment they deserve than to ensure that none do. In this context, he explicitly responds to some of Nathanson's analogies by, in effect, denying P1 of Nathanson's argument. The punishment of the bearded speeders, for example, is not unjust; only the non-punishment of the non-bearded speeders is.

QUESTIONS FOR CONSIDERATION

• In considering the debate between van den Haag and Reiman, readers will find it helpful to focus on the merits of Reiman's analogy between torture and execution. Is Reiman right to think that the best account of the wrongness of the former also entails the wrongness of the latter? Or is van den Haag right to find torture distinctively repulsive?

• Is simply accepting the analogy and its implication a plausible strategy for the defender of capital punishment? Or must a clear difference between the two cases be identified in order to overcome the weight of Reiman's argument?

• Has Reiman said enough to justify the claim that an act's being uncivilized makes it wrong? Or can van den Haag support his suggestion that Reiman is simply begging the question (i.e., that he is covertly assuming what he needs to establish)?

• How much weight should be given to the fact that murderers commit their crimes voluntarily? Is this enough to justify what would otherwise be an objectionable form of subjugating them? Or is executing a person so horrible that we should refrain from carrying it out even if the person who committed the crime in question knew that he or she might receive the death penalty?

• In examining the exchange between van den Haag and Nathanson, readers should focus on the issue of distribution. Is the death penalty administered in as arbitrary a manner as are the punishments in Nathanson's various examples? If there are differences between Nathanson's cases and the death penalty, are they important enough differences to undermine his argument? Or is the distribution of executions still problematic enough to serve as a foundation for Nathanson's position?

- If Nathanson's analogies are close enough to be acceptable, do they in fact support his conclusion? Which, for example, is more unjust: the teacher who punishes none of the students who plagiarize or the teacher who punishes only the plagiarists he dislikes?

- Is Nathanson right to think that the injustice of the distribution of punishments can render some punishments of even the guilty unjust? Or is van den Haag right to insist that deserved punishments, even if arbitrarily meted out, are better than no punishments at all?

FURTHER READING

Baird, R. M., and S. E. Rosenbaum, eds. *Punishment and the Death Penalty: The Current Debate* Prometheus: Buffalo, 1995.

Conway, David. "Capital Punishment and Deterrence." *Philosophy and Public Affairs* 3 (1974): 431–43.

Ernest van den Haag | # Refuting Reiman and Nathanson

I shall consider Jeffrey Reiman's view of the punishment offenders deserve before turning to his moral scruples, alleged to justify lesser punishments, and to the discriminatory distribution of the death penalty which Stephen Nathanson stresses.

Reiman believes the death penalty is deserved by some murderers, but should never be imposed. Moral scruples should preclude it. If the punishment deserved according to the *lex talionis* is morally repugnant, we may impose less, provided the suffering imposed *in lieu* of what is deserved is proportional to the suffering inflicted on the crime victim. However, suffering exceeding that of his victim can never be deserved by the offender; to impose it would be "unjust for the same reasons that make punishment of the innocent unjust."[1]

MEASUREMENT

How do we know whether the punitive suffering to be imposed on the offender is less or "equal to that which he imposed on the victim" so as not to exceed what he deserves? Cardinal and interpersonal measurement of suffering would be required to find out. Although ordinal measurement is possible in some cases, the cardinal and interpersonal measurement required by Reiman's scheme is not. How many days must the kidnapper be confined, to suffer as much, but no more, than his victim? If he kept his victim three days, are three days of confinement correct? Or three hundred? Or one thousand? If he half-starved his victim, should we do as much to him, or, how do we commute starvation into additional time?

Punishment for kidnapping can be, within limits, of the same kind as the crime, although all we can actually do to conform to Reiman's prescription even here is to confine for a longer time the kidnapper who kept his victim for a longer time. We have no way of comparing the victim's suffering with the victimizer's, and to limit the latter accordingly. Execution too bears some similarity to the murderer's crime. But confinement? How do we make it com-

Ernest van den Haag, "Refuting Reiman and Nathanson," *Philosophy and Public Affairs* 14, no. 2. (Spring 1985): 165–76. Some notes have been deleted. Reprinted by permission of Princeton University Press.

mensurate with murder? What about the punishment for assault, burglary, or rape? How do we compare the pain suffered by the victims with the pain to be imposed on the offender by confinement, to make sure that the latter not exceed the former? There is no way of applying Reiman's criterion of desert. Fortunately, we don't need to.

ACTUAL DESERT

Even if, somehow, we knew that three days' confinement inflicts as much pain as his victim suffered on the kidnapper who kept his victim three days, we would feel that the kidnapper deserves much more punishment. That feeling would be appropriate. The offender imposed undeserved suffering on his victim. Why should society not impose undeserved (in Reiman's terminology) suffering on the offender? It would be undeserved only if one accepts Reiman's flawed view of retribution, for, in addition to whatever he deserves for what his victim suffered, the offender also deserves punishment for breaking the law, for imposing undeserved, unlawful suffering on someone. Retributionism of any kind cannot authorize less, despite Reiman's view that suffering imposed on the criminal is unjust when it exceeds the suffering of his victim.

Although occasionally he indicates awareness of the social harm caused by crime and even of the social function of punishment, Reiman treats crimes as though involving but a relationship between victim and offender implemented by judicial authorities. From this faulty premise he infers that retribution should not exceed the harm done to the victim, an idea derived from the *lex talionis*. But that primitive rule was meant to limit the revenge private parties could exact for what was regarded as private harm. The function of the rule was to guard against social disruption by unlimited and indefinitely extended vengeance.

Crimes are no longer regarded merely as private harms. Retribution for the suffering of the individual victims, however much deserved, is not punishment any more than restitution is. Punishment must vindicate the disrupted public order, the violated law, must punish for the social harm done. If my neigh-

bor is burglarized or robbed, he is harmed. But we all must take costly precautions, and we all feel and are threatened: crime harms society as it harms victims. Hence, punishment must, whenever possible, impose pain believed to exceed the pain suffered by the individual victim of crime. No less is deserved. Punishment must be determined by the total gravity of the crime, the social as well as the individual harm, and by the need to deter from the harmful crime. There are ordinal limits to deserved punishments, but cardinal upper limits are set only by harm, habit and sentiment—not by victim suffering.

Let me now turn to the moral scruples which should lead us to reduce punishment to less than what is deserved in some cases. I share some of Reiman's scruples: although he deserves it, I do not want to see the torturer tortured. Other scruples strike me as unjustified.

POVERTY AND CULPABILITY

Reiman believes "that the vast majority of murders in America are a predictable response to the frustrations and disabilities of impoverished social circumstances" which could be, but are not remedied because "others in America benefit," wherefore we have "no right to exact the full cost . . . from our murderers until we have done everything possible to rectify the conditions that produce their crimes." Murder here seems to become the punishment for the sins of the wealthy. According to Reiman, "the vast majority" of current murderers are not fully culpable, since part of the blame for their crimes must be placed on those who fail to "rectify the conditions that produce their crimes."

I grant that certain social conditions predictably produce crime more readily than others. Does it follow that those who commit crimes in criminogenic conditions are less responsible, or blameworthy, than they would be if they did not live in these conditions? Certainly not. Predictability does not reduce responsibility. Reiman remains responsible for his predictable argument. Culpability is reduced only when the criminal's ability to control his actions, or to realize that they are wrong, is abnormally impaired. If not, the social conditions in which the criminal lives have no bearing on his responsibility for his acts. Conditions, such as poverty, just or unjust, may increase the temptation to commit crimes. But poverty is neither a necessary nor a sufficient condition for crime, and thus certainly not a coercive one. If there is no compulsion, temptation is no excuse. The law is meant to restrain, and to hold responsible, those tempted to break it. It need not restrain those not tempted, and it cannot restrain those who are unable to control their actions.

Reiman's claim, that even "though criminals can control their actions, when crimes are predictable responses to unjust circumstances, then those who benefit from and do not remedy those conditions bear some responsibility for the crimes and thus the criminals cannot be held *wholly* responsible for them . . . " seems quite unjustified. Those responsible for unjust conditions must be blamed for them, but not for crimes that are "predictable responses to unjust circumstances," if the respondents could have avoided these crimes, as most people living in unjust conditions do.

If crimes are political, that is, address not otherwise remediable "unjust circumstances," they may be held to be morally, if not legally, excusable, on some occasions. But the criminal's moral, let alone legal, responsibility for a crime which he committed for personal gain and could have avoided, is not diminished merely because he lives in unjust circumstances, and his crime was a predictable response to them. Suppose the predictable response to unjust wealth were drunken driving, or rape. Would his wealth excuse the driver or the rapist? Why should poverty, if wealth would not?

Crime is produced by many circumstances, "just" and "unjust." The most just society may have no less crime than the least just (unless "just" is defined circularly as the absence of crime). Tracing crime to causal circumstances is useful and may help us to control it. Suggesting that they *eo ipso* are excuses confuses causality with nonresponsibility. *Tout comprendre ce n'est pas tout pardonner,* Mme. de Staël's followers to the contrary notwithstanding. Excuses require specific circumstances that diminish the actor's control over his actions.

Since "unjust circumstances" do not reduce the responsibility of criminals for their acts, I shall refrain from discussing whether Reiman's circumstances really are unjust, or merely unequal, and whether they do exist because someone benefits from them and could be eliminated if the alleged beneficiaries wished to eliminate them. I am not sure that unjust circumstances always can be remedied, without causing worse injustices. Nor do I share Reiman's confidence that we know what social justice is, or how to produce it.

CIVILIZATION

Reiman thinks that the death penalty is not civilized, because it involves the total subjugation of one person to others, as does slavery, or prostitution.

Whereas slavery usually is not voluntary, the murderer runs the risk of execution voluntarily: he could avoid it by not murdering. I find nothing uncivilized in imposing the risk of subjugation and death on those who decide to murder.

Nota bene: Persons who act with diminished capacity, during moments of passion, are usually convicted of manslaughter rather than murder. Even if convicted of murder, they are not sentenced to death; only if the court believes that the murderer did have a choice, and intended to murder, can he receive the death sentence.

Reiman refers to research finding a brutalization effect, such that executions lead to more homicides. The data are unpersuasive. Some researchers find an increase, some a decrease, of homicides immediately after an execution.[2] Either effect seem ephemeral, involving bunching, rather than changes in the annual homicide rate.

To argue more generally, as Reiman also does, that capital punishment is inconsistent with the advancement of civilization, is to rely on arbitrary definitions of "advancement" and "civilization" for a circular argument. If civilization actually had "advanced" in the direction Reiman, quoting Durkheim, thinks it has, why is that a reason for not preferring "advancement" in some other, perhaps opposite, direction? I cannot find the *moral* (normative) argument in Reiman's description.

DETERRENCE

The death penalty should be retained if abolition would endanger us, Reiman believes. But he does not believe that abolition would. He may be right. However, some of his arguments seem doubtful.

He thinks that whatever marginal deterrent effect capital punishment has, if it has any, is not needed, since life imprisonment provides all the deterrence needed. How can it be ascertained that punishment x deters "everyone who can be deterred" so that punishment x-plus would not deter additional persons? I can see no way to determine this, short of experiments we are unlikely to undertake. Reiman may fear life imprisonment as much, or more, than death. Couldn't someone else fear death more and be insufficiently deterred by life imprisonment?

I cannot prove conclusively that the death penalty deters more than life imprisonment, or that the added deterrence is needed. Reiman cannot prove conclusively that the added deterrence is not needed, or produced. I value the life of innocents more than the life of murderers. Indeed, I value the life of murderers negatively. Wherefore I prefer over- to underprotection. I grant this is a preference.

SELF-DEFENSE

Reiman also believes that murderers who are not deterred by the risk they run because their victims may defend themselves with guns will not be deterred by the risk of execution. This seems unrealistic. Murderers rarely run much risk from self-defense since they usually ambush unsuspecting victims.

TORTURE

On my reasoning, Reiman contends, torture should be used, since it may deter more than execution; or else, even if more deterrent than alternatives, the death penalty should be abolished as torture was: "either we must abolish the electric chair or reinstitute the rack," is his colorful phrase. But there is a difference. I do not oppose torture as undeserved or nondeterrent (although I doubt that the threat of the rack, or of anything adds deterrence to the threat of execution), but simply as repulsive. Death is not; nor is the death penalty. Perhaps repulsiveness is not enough to exclude the rack. If Reiman should convince me that the threat of the rack adds a great deal of deterrence to the threat of execution he might persuade me to overcome my revulsion and to favor the rack as well. It certainly can be deserved.

MORAL THEORY

In *The Death Penalty: A Debate*[3] I noted that only when punishments are based not on retribution alone, but also on deterrence, they rest on a theory, that is, on a correlation of recurrent facts to a prediction: punishment x will, *ceteris paribus,* reduce the rate of crime y by 10%, and x-plus will bring a reduction of 20%. Reiman censures me for using "theory" when I should have written "empirical theory." He is right. Further, deterrence does not morally justify any punishment, unless one has first accepted the moral desirability of reducing crime, and the tolerability of the costs. I should have pointed that out. Finally, I did not mean to deny that there are moral theories to justify retribution. They strike me as more dependent on feeling than empirical theories are. More to the point, unlike deterrence theory, justice theories are not meant to predict the effect of various punishments, and are not capable of determining, except ordinally, what these punishments should be, although they can help to justify the distribution of punishments.[4]

MODES OF EXECUTION

As Reiman stresses, the spectacle of execution is not pretty. Nor is surgery. Wherefore both should be attended only by the necessary personnel. I do not find Reiman's aesthetic or moral scruples sufficient to preclude execution or surgery. However, I share his view that lethal injections are particularly unpleasant, not so much because of the subjugation which disturbs him, but because of the veterinary air. (We put animals "to sleep" when sick or inconvenient.) In contrast, shooting strikes me as dignified; it is painless too and probably the best way of doing what is necessary.

LIFE IMPRISONMENT

Reiman proposes life imprisonment without parole instead of execution. Although less feared, and therefore likely to be less deterrent, actual lifelong imprisonment strikes me as more cruel than execution even if perceived as less harsh. Its comparative cruelty was stressed already by Cesare Bonesana, Marchese di Beccaria, and by many others since.

Life imprisonment also becomes undeserved over time. A person who committed a murder when twenty years old and is executed within five years—far too long and cruel a delay in my opinion—is, when executed, still the person who committed the murder for which he is punished. His identity changes little in five years. However, a person who committed a murder when he was twenty years old and is kept in prison when sixty years old, is no longer the same person who committed the crime for which he is still being punished. The sexagenarian is unlikely to have much in common with the twenty-year-old for whose act he is being punished; his legal identity no longer reflects reality. Personality and actual identity are not that continuous. In effect, we punish an innocent sexagenarian who does not deserve punishment, instead of a guilty twenty-year-old who did. This spectacle should offend our moral sensibilities more than the deserved execution of the twenty-year-old. Those who deserve the death penalty should be executed while they deserve it, not kept in prison when they no longer deserve any punishment.

DISCRIMINATION

Disagreeing with the Supreme Court, Stephen Nathanson believes that the death penalty still is distributed in an excessively capricious and discriminatory manner. He thinks capital punishment is "unjust" because poor blacks are more likely to be sentenced to death than wealthy whites. Further, blacks who murdered whites are more likely to be executed than those who murdered blacks. This last discrimination has been thrown into relief recently by authors who seem to be under the impression that they have revealed a new form of discrimination against black murderers. They have not. The practice invidiously discriminates against black victims of murder, who are not as fully, or as often, vindicated as white victims are. However, discrimination against a class of victims, although invidious enough, does not amount to discrimination against their victimizers. The discrimination against black victims, the lesser punishment given their murderers, actually favors black murderers, since most black victims are killed by black murderers. Stephen Nathanson and Jeffrey Reiman appear to think that they have captured additional discrimination against black defendants. They are wrong.

Neither the argument from discrimination against black victims, nor the argument from discrimination against black murderers, has any bearing on the guilt of black murderers, or on the punishment they deserve.

Invidious discrimination is never defensible. Yet I do not see wherein it, in Reiman's words, "would constitute a separate and powerful argument for abolition," or does make the death penalty "unjust" for those discriminatorily selected to suffer it, as Stephen Nathanson believes.[5] If we grant that some (even all) murderers of blacks, or, some (even all) white and rich murderers, escape the death penalty, how does that reduce the guilt of murderers of whites, or of black and poor murderers, so that they should be spared execution too? Guilt is personal. No murderer becomes less guilty, or less deserving of punishment, because another murderer was punished leniently, or escaped punishment altogether. We should try our best to bring every murderer to justice. But if one got away with murder wherein is that a reason to let anyone else get away? A group of murderers does not become less deserving of punishment because another equally guilty group is not punished, or punished less. We can punish only a very small proportion of all criminals. Unavoidably they are selected accidentally. We should reduce this accidentality as much as possible but we cannot eliminate it.

EQUAL INJUSTICE
AND UNEQUAL JUSTICE

Reiman and Nathanson appear to prefer equal injustice—letting all get away with murder if some do—to unequal justice: punishing some guilty offenders according to desert, even if others get away. Equal justice is best, but unattainable. Unequal justice is our lot in this world. It is the only justice we can ever have, for not all murderers can be apprehended or convicted, or sentenced equally in different courts. We should constantly try to bring every offender to justice. But meanwhile unequal justice is the only justice we have, and certainly better than equal injustice—giving no murderer the punishment his crime deserves.

MORE DISCRIMINATION

Nathanson insists that some arbitrary selections among those equally guilty are not "just." He thinks that selecting only bearded speeders for ticketing, allowing the cleanshaven to escape, is unjust. Yet the punishment of the bearded speeders is not unjust. The escape of the cleanshaven ones is. I never maintained that a discriminatory distribution is just— only that it is irrelevant to the guilt and deserved punishment of those actually guilty.

Nathanson further suggests that it is not just to spare some student plagiarizers punishment for (I suppose) irrelevant reasons, while punishing others. Again the distribution is discriminatory, i.e., unjust. But the punishment of the plagiarizers selected is not. (The non-punishment of the others is.) Nathanson thinks that giving a prize only to one of three deserving children (his own) is unjust. Not to the deserving child. Only to the others, just as it was unjust not to punish the others who deserved it, but not unjust to punish the deserving plagiarizers who were irrelevantly selected.

Nathanson taxes me with inconsistency because in a footnote I wrote that irrelevant discriminations are "not acceptable to our sense of justice." They are not. But I did not say that those who deserved the punishment received, or the reward, were unjustly treated, that is, did not deserve it and should not have received it. Rather those equally situated also should have received it, and the distribution was offensive because they did not. Whenever possible this inequality should be corrected, but certainly not by not distributing the punishment, or the reward at issue, or by not giving it to the deserving. Rather by giving it as

well to those who because of discrimination did not get it. (I might have done better to write in my footnote that discriminatory distributions offend our sense of *equal* justice. But neither the Constitution nor I favor replacing justice with equality.)

Nathanson quotes the late Justice Douglas suggesting that a law which deliberately prescribes execution only for the guilty poor, or which has that effect, would be unconstitutional. Perhaps. But the vice would be in exempting the guilty rich; the guilty poor would remain guilty, and deserving of prescribed punishment even if the guilty rich escape legally or otherwise.

Further on Nathanson points out that the inevitable capriciousness in the distribution of punishments (only a very small percentage of offenders are ever punished and the selection unavoidably is morally arbitrary) while no reason to abolish punishment in general, may still be an argument for abolishing capital punishment because of its unique severity, and because we could survive without. We can survive without many things, which is not reason for doing without, if one thinks, as I do, that we survive *better* with. As for the unique severity of the death penalty it is, of course, the reason for imposing it for uniquely heinous crimes. The guilt of those who committed them is not diminished, if they are selected by a lottery from among all those guilty of the crime.

Following Charles Black, Nathanson notes that those executed are not necessarily the worst murderers, since there is no way of selecting these. He is right. It seems quite sufficient, however, that those executed, though not the worst, are bad enough to deserve execution. That others who deserved it even more got away, does not make those executed insufficiently deserving.

Nathanson goes on to insist that "not every person who kills another is guilty of the same crime." True. Wherefore the law makes many distinctions, leaving only a small group of those guilty of homicide eligible for the death penalty. Further, capital punishment is not mandated. The court must decide in each case whether or not to impose it. To impose capital punishment, courts must find that the aggravating circumstances attending the murder outweigh the mitigating ones, both of which must be listed in the law. Nathanson is right in pointing out that the criteria listed in the law are not easy to apply. If they were, we would not need the judgment of the court. That judgment is not easy to make. It may seem too severe, or not severe enough, in some cases, as would mandated penalties. So what else is new?

NOTES

1. See Jeffrey H. Reiman, "Justice, Civilization, and the Death Penalty: Answering van den Haag," *Philosophy & Public Affairs* 14, no. 2: 128. Unless otherwise noted, all my quotations are taken from Reiman's article.

2. David P. Phillips, "The Deterrent Effect of Capital Punishment: New Evidence on an Old Controversy," *The American Journal of Sociology* (July 1980). For further discussion see loc. cit., July 1982. See also Lester, *Executions as a Deterrent to Homicides 44 Psychological Rep.* 562 (1979).

3. Ernest van den Haag and John P. Conrad (New York: Plenum Press, 1983).

4. See my *Punishing Criminals* (New York: Basic Books, 1975) which is superseded to some extent by the views expressed in my "Criminal Law as a Threat System 73, *Journal of Criminal Law and Criminology* 2 (1982)."

5. Stephen Nathanson, "Does It Matter if the Death Penalty Is Arbitrarily Administered?" *Philosophy & Public Affairs* 14, no. 2 (this issue). Unless otherwise noted, all further quotations are taken from Nathanson's article.

Critics

Jeffrey H. Reiman

Justice, Civilization, and the Death Penalty

Answering van den Haag

. . . I shall assume . . . that the retributivist principle is true.

The truth of the retributivist principle establishes the justice of the *lex talionis,* but, since it establishes this as a right of the victim rather than a duty, it does not settle the question of whether or to what extent the victim or the state should exercise this right and exact the *lex talionis*. This is a separate moral question because strict adherence to the *lex talionis* amounts to allowing criminals, even the most barbaric of them, to dictate our punishing behavior. It seems certain that there are at least some crimes, such as rape or torture, that we ought not try to match. And this is not merely a matter of imposing an alternative punishment that produces an equivalent amount of suffering, as, say, some number of years in prison that might "add up" to the harm caused by a rapist or a torturer. Even if no amount of time in prison would add up to the harm caused by a torturer, it still seems that we ought not torture him even if this were the only way of making him suffer as much as he has made his victim suffer. Or, consider someone who has committed several murders in cold blood. On the *lex talionis,* it would seem that such a criminal might justly be brought to within an inch of death and then revived (or to within a moment of execution and then re-

From Jeffrey H. Reiman, "Justice, Civilization, and the Death Penalty" *Philosophy and Public Affairs* 14, no. 2. (Spring 1985): 115–48. Some notes and some parts of the text have been deleted. Reprinted by permission of Princeton University Press.

prieved) as many times as he has killed (minus one), and then finally executed. But surely this is a degree of cruelty that would be monstrous.

Since the retributivist principle establishes the *lex talionis* as the victim's right, it might seem that the question of how far this right should be exercised is "up to the victim." And indeed, this would be the case in the state of nature. But once, for all the good reasons familiar to readers of John Locke, the state comes into existence, public punishment replaces private, and the victim's right to punish reposes in the state. With this, the decision as to how far to exercise this right goes to the state as well. To be sure, since (at least with respect to retributive punishment) the victim's right is the source of the state's right to punish, the state must exercise its right in ways that are faithful to the victim's right. Later, when I try to spell out the upper and lower limits of just punishment, these may be taken as indicating the range within which the state can punish and remain faithful to the victim's right.

I suspect that it will be widely agreed that the state ought not administer punishments of the sort described above even if required by the letter of the *lex talionis,* and thus, even granting the justice of *lex talionis,* there are occasions on which it is morally appropriate to diverge from its requirements. We must, of course, distinguish such morally based divergence from that which is based on practicality. Like any moral principle, the *lex talionis* is subject to "ought implies can." It will usually be impossible to do to an offender exactly what he has done—for example, his offense will normally have had an element of surprise that is not possible for a judicially imposed punishment, but this fact can hardly free him from having to bear the suffering he has imposed on another. Thus, for reasons of practicality, the *lex talionis* must necessarily be qualified to call for doing to the offender *as nearly as possible* what he has done to his victim. When, however, we refrain from raping rapists or torturing torturers, we do so for reasons of morality, not of practicality. And, given the justice of the *lex talionis,* these moral reasons cannot amount to claiming that it would be *unjust* to rape rapists or torture torturers. Rather the claim must be that, even though it would be just to

rape rapists and torture torturers, other moral considerations weigh against doing so.

On the other hand, when, for moral reasons, we refrain from exacting the *lex talionis,* and impose a less harsh alternative punishment, it may be said that we are not doing full justice to the criminal, but it cannot automatically be the case that we are doing an *injustice* to his victim. Otherwise we would have to say it was unjust to imprison our torturer rather than torturing him or to simply execute our multiple murderer rather than multiply "executing" him. Surely it is counterintuitive (and irrational to boot) to set the demands of justice so high that a society would have to choose between being barbaric or being unjust. This would effectively price justice out of the moral market.

The implication of this is that there is a range of just punishments that includes some that are just though they exact less than the full measure of the *lex talionis.* What are the top and bottom ends of this range? I think that both are indicated by the *retributivist principle.* The principle identifies the *lex talionis* as the offender's desert and since, on retributive grounds, punishment beyond what one deserves is unjust for the same reasons that make punishment of the innocent unjust, the *lex talionis* is the upper limit of the range of just punishments. On the other hand, if the retributivist principle is true, then denying that the offender deserves suffering equal to that which he imposed amounts to denying the equality and rationality of persons. From this it follows that we fall below the bottom end of the range of just punishments when we act in ways that are incompatible with the *lex talionis* at the top end. That is, we fall below the bottom end and commit an injustice to the victim when we treat the offender in a way that is no longer compatible with sincerely believing that he deserves to have done to him what he has done to his victim. Thus, the upper limit of the range of just punishments is the point after which more punishment is unjust to the offender, and the lower limit is the point after which less punishment is unjust to the victim. In this way, the range of just punishments remains faithful to the victim's right which is their source.

This way of understanding just punishment enables us to formulate proportional retributivism so that it is compatible with acknowledging the justice of the *lex talionis:* If we take the *lex talionis* as spelling out the offender's just deserts, and if other moral considerations require us to refrain from matching the injury caused by the offender while still allowing us to punish justly, then surely we impose just punishment if we impose the closest morally acceptable approximation to the *lex talionis.* Proportional retributivism, then, in requiring that the worst crime be punished by the society's worst punishment and so on, could be understood as translating the offender's just desert into its nearest equivalent in the society's table of morally acceptable punishments. Then the two versions of retributivism (*lex talionis* and proportional) are related in that the first states what just punishment would be if nothing but the offender's just desert mattered, and the second locates just punishment at the meeting point of the offender's just deserts and the society's moral scruples. And since this second version only modifies the requirements of the *lex talionis* in light of other moral considerations, it is compatible with believing that the *lex talionis* spells out the offender's just deserts, much in the way that modifying the obligations of promisers in light of other moral considerations is compatible with believing in the binding nature of promises.

Proportional retributivism so formulated preserves the point of retributivism and remains faithful to the victim's right which is its source. Since it punishes with the closest morally acceptable approximation to the *lex talionis,* it effectively says to the offender, you deserve the equivalent of what you did to your victim and you are getting less only to the degree that *our* moral scruples limit us from duplicating what you have done. Such punishment, then, affirms the equality of persons by respecting *as far as is morally permissible* the victim's right to impose suffering on the offender equal to what he received, and it affirms the rationality of the offender by treating him as authorizing others to do to him what he has done though they take him up on it only *as far as is morally permissible.* Needless to say, the alternative punishments must in some convincing way be comparable in gravity to the crimes which they punish, or else they will trivialize the harms those crimes caused

and be no longer compatible with sincerely believing that the offender deserves to have done to him what he has done to his victim and no longer capable of impressing upon the criminal his equality with the victim. If we punish rapists with a small fine or a brief prison term, we do an injustice to their victims, because this trivializes the suffering rapists have caused and thus is incompatible with believing that they deserve to have done to them something comparable to what they have done to their victims. If, on the other hand, instead of raping rapists we impose on them some grave penalty, say a substantial term of imprisonment, then we do no injustice even though we refrain from exacting the *lex talionis.*

To sum up, I take the *lex talionis* to be the top end of the range of just punishments. When, because we are simply unable to duplicate the criminal's offense, we modify the *lex talionis* to call for imposing on the offender as nearly as possible what he has done, we are still at this top end, applying the *lex talionis* subject to "ought implies can." When we do less than this, we still act justly as long as we punish in a way that is compatible with sincerely believing that the offender deserves the full measure of the *lex talionis,* but receives less for reasons that do not undermine this belief. If this is true, then it is not unjust to spare murderers as long as they can be punished in some other suitably grave way. I leave open the question of what such an alternative punishment might be, except to say that it need not be limited to such penalties as are currently imposed. For example, though rarely carried out in practice, a life sentence with no chance of parole might be a civilized equivalent of the death penalty—after all, people sentenced to life imprisonment have traditionally been regarded as "civilly dead."

It might be objected that no punishment short of death will serve the point of retributivism with respect to murderers because no punishment short of death is commensurate with the crime of murder since, while some number of years of imprisonment may add up to the amount of harm done by rapists or assaulters or torturers, no number of years will add up to the harm done to the victim of murder. But justified divergence from the *lex talionis* is not limited only to changing the form of punishment while maintaining equivalent severity. Otherwise, we would have to torture torturers rather than imprison them if they tortured more than could be made up for by years in prison (or by the years available to them to spend in prison, which might be few for elderly torturers), and we would have to subject multiple murderers to multiple "executions." If justice allows us to refrain from these penalties, then justice allows punishments that are not equal in suffering to their crimes. It seems to me that if the objector grants this much, then he must show that a punishment less than death is not merely incommensurate to the harm caused by murder, but so far out of proportion to that harm that it trivializes it and thus effectively denies the equality and rationality of persons. Now, I am vulnerable to the claim that a sentence of life in prison that allows parole after eight or ten years does indeed trivialize the harm of (premeditated, cold-blooded) murder. But I cannot see how a sentence that would require a murderer to spend his full natural life in prison, or even the lion's share of his adult life (say, the thirty years between age twenty and age fifty), can be regarded as anything less than extremely severe and thus no trivialization of the harm he has caused.

I take it then that the justice of the *lex talionis* implies that it is just to execute murderers, but not that it is unjust to spare them as long as they are systematically punished in some other suitably grave way. . . .

III.   CIVILIZATION, PAIN, AND JUSTICE

As I have already suggested, from the fact that something is justly deserved, it does not automatically follow that it should be done, since there may be other moral reasons for not doing it such that, all told, the weight of moral reasons swings the balance against proceeding. The same argument that I have given for the justice of the death penalty for murderers proves the justice of beating assaulters, raping rapists, and torturing torturers. Nonetheless, I believe, and suspect that most would agree, that it would not be right for us to beat assaulters, rape rapists, or torture torturers, *even though it were their just deserts*—and even

if this were the only way to make them suffer as much as they had made their victims suffer. Calling for the abolition of the death penalty, though it be just, then, amounts to urging that as a society we place execution in the same category of sanction as beating, raping, and torturing, and treat it as something it would also not be right for us to do to offenders, *even if it were their just deserts.*

To argue for placing execution in this category, I must show what would be gained therefrom; and to show that, I shall indicate what we gain from placing torture in this category and argue that a similar gain is to be had from doing the same with execution. I select torture because I think the reasons for placing it in this category are, due to the extremity of torture, most easily seen—but what I say here applies with appropriate modification to other severe physical punishments, such as beating and raping. First, and most evidently, placing torture in this category broadcasts the message that we as a society judge torturing so horrible a thing to do to a person that we refuse to do it even when it is deserved. Note that such a judgment does not commit us to an absolute prohibition on torturing. No matter how horrible we judge something to be, we may still be justified in doing it if it is necessary to prevent something even worse. Leaving this aside for the moment, what is gained by broadcasting the public judgment that torture is too horrible to inflict even if deserved?

I think the answer to this lies in what we understand as civilization. In *The Genealogy of Morals,* Nietzsche says that in early times "pain did not hurt as much as it does today."[1] The truth in this puzzling remark is that progress in civilization is characterized by a lower tolerance for one's own pain and that suffered by others. And this is appropriate, since, via growth in knowledge, civilization brings increased power to prevent or reduce pain and, via growth in the ability to communicate and interact with more and more people, civilization extends the circle of people with whom we empathize.[2] If civilization is characterized by lower tolerance for our own pain and that of others, then publicly refusing to do horrible things to our fellows both signals the level of our civilization *and, by our example, continues the work of civilizing.* And this gesture is all the more powerful if we refuse to do horrible things to those who deserve them. I contend then that the more things we are able to include in this category, the more civilized we are and the more civiliz*ing*. Thus we gain from including torture in this category, and if execution is especially horrible, we gain still more by including it.

Needless to say, the content, direction, and even the worth of civilization are hotly contested issues, and I shall not be able to win those contests in this brief space. At a minimum, however, I shall assume that civilization involves the taming of the natural environment and of the human animals in it, and that the overall trend in human history is toward increasing this taming, though the trend is by no means unbroken or without reverses. On these grounds, we can say that growth in civilization generally marks human history, that a reduction in the horrible things we tolerate doing to our fellows (even when they deserve them) is part of this growth, and that once the work of civilization is taken on consciously, it includes carrying forward and expanding this reduction.

This claim broadly corresponds to what Emile Durkheim identified, nearly a century ago, as "two laws which seem . . . to prevail in the evolution of the apparatus of punishment." The first, the law of quantitative change, Durkheim formulates as:

> The intensity of punishment is the greater the more closely societies approximate to a less developed type—and the more the central power assumes an absolute character.

And the second, which Durkheim refers to as the law of qualitative change, is:

> Deprivations of liberty, and of liberty alone, varying in time according to the seriousness of the crime, tend to become more and more the normal means of social control.[3]

Several things should be noted about these laws. First of all, they are not two separate laws. As Durkheim understands them, the second exemplifies the trend toward moderation of punishment referred to in the first.[4] Second, the first law really refers to two distinct trends, which usually coincide but do not always. That is, moderation of punishment accompanies *both* the movement from less to more advanced types of

society *and* the movement from more to less absolute rule. Normally these go hand in hand, but where they do not, the effect of one trend may offset the effect of the other. Thus, a primitive society without absolute rule may have milder punishments than an equally primitive but more absolutist society. This complication need not trouble us, since the claim I am making refers to the first trend, namely, that punishments tend to become milder as societies become more advanced; and that this is a trend in history is not refuted by the fact that it is accompanied by other trends and even occasionally offset by them. Moreover, I shall close this article with a suggestion about the relation between the intensity of punishment and the justice of society, which might broadly be thought of as corresponding to the second trend in Durkheim's first law. Finally, and most important for our purposes, is the fact that Durkheim's claim that punishment becomes less intense as societies become more advanced is a generalization that he supports with an impressive array of evidence from historical societies from pre-Christian times to the time in which he wrote—and this in turn supports my claim that the reduction in the horrible things we do to our fellows is in fact part of the advance of civilization.

Against this it might be argued that many things grow in history, some good, some bad, and some mixed, and thus the fact that there is some historical trend is not a sufficient reason to continue it. Thus, for example, history also brings growth in population, but we are not for that reason called upon to continue the work of civilization by continually increasing our population. What this suggests is that in order to identify something as part of the work of civilizing, we must show not only that it generally grows in history, but that its growth is, on some independent grounds, clearly an advance for the human species—that is, either an unmitigated gain or at least consistently a net gain. And this implies that even trends which we might generally regard as advances may in some cases bring losses with them, such that when they did it would not be appropriate for us to lend our efforts to continuing them. Of such trends we can say that they are advances in civilization except when their gains are outweighed by the losses they bring—and that we are only called upon to further these trends when their gains are *not* outweighed in this way. It is clear in this light that increasing population is a mixed blessing at best, bringing both gains and losses. Consequently, it is not always an advance in civilization that we should further, though at times it may be.

What can be said of reducing the horrible things that we do to our fellows even when deserved? First of all, given our vulnerability to pain, it seems clearly a gain. Is it however an unmitigated gain? That is, would such a reduction ever amount to a loss? It seems to me that there are two conditions under which it would be a loss, namely, if the reduction made our lives more dangerous, or if not doing what is justly deserved were a loss in itself. Let us leave aside the former, since, as I have already suggested and as I will soon indicate in greater detail, I accept that if some horrible punishment is necessary to deter equally or more horrible acts, then we may have to impose the punishment. Thus my claim is that reduction in the horrible things we do to our fellows is an advance in civilization *as long as our lives are not thereby made more dangerous,* and that it is only then that we are called upon to extend that reduction as part of the work of civilization. Assuming then, for the moment, that we suffer no increased danger by refraining from doing horrible things to our fellows when they justly deserve them, does such refraining to do what is justly deserved amount to a loss?

It seems to me that the answer to this must be that refraining to do what is justly deserved is only a loss where it amounts to doing an injustice. But such refraining to do what is just is not doing what is unjust, unless what we do instead falls below the bottom end of the range of just punishments. Otherwise, it would be unjust to refrain from torturing torturers, raping rapists, or beating assaulters. In short, I take it that if there is no injustice in refraining from torturing torturers, then there is no injustice in refraining to do horrible things to our fellows generally, when they deserve them, as long as what we do instead is compatible with believing that they do deserve them. And thus that if such refraining does not make our lives more dangerous, then it is no loss, and given our vulnerability to pain, it is a gain. Consequently, reduction in the horrible things we do to our fellows, when not necessary to our protection, is

an advance in civilization that we are called upon to continue once we consciously take upon ourselves the work of civilization.

To complete the argument, however, I must show that execution is horrible enough to warrant its inclusion alongside torture. Against this it will be said that execution is not especially horrible since it only hastens a fate that is inevitable for us. I think that this view overlooks important differences in the manner in which people reach their inevitable ends. I contend that execution is especially horrible, and it is so in a way similar to (though not identical with) the way in which torture is especially horrible. I believe we view torture as especially awful because of two of its features, which also characterize execution: intense pain and the spectacle of one human being completely subject to the power of another. This latter is separate from the issue of pain since it is something that offends us about unpainful things, such as slavery (even voluntarily entered) and prostitution (even voluntarily chosen as an occupation). Execution shares this separate feature, since killing a bound and defenseless human being enacts the total subjugation of that person to his fellows. I think, incidentally, that this accounts for the general uneasiness with which execution by lethal injection has been greeted. Rather than humanizing the event, it seems only to have purchased a possible reduction in physical pain at the price of increasing the spectacle of subjugation—with no net gain in the attractiveness of the death penalty. Indeed, its net effect may have been the reverse.

In addition to the spectacle of subjugation, execution, even by physically painless means, is also characterized by a special and intense psychological pain that distinguishes it from the loss of life that awaits us all. Interesting in this regard is the fact that although we are not terribly squeamish about the loss of life itself, allowing it in war, self-defense, as a necessary cost of progress, and so on, we are, as the extraordinary hesitance of our courts testifies, quite reluctant to execute. I think this is because execution involves the most psychologically painful features of deaths. We normally regard death from human causes as worse than death from natural causes, since a humanly caused shortening of life lacks the consolation of unavoidability. And we normally regard death whose coming is foreseen by its victim as worse than sudden death, because a foreseen death adds to the loss of life the terrible consciousness of that impending loss. As a humanly caused death whose advent is foreseen by its victim, an execution combines the worst of both.

Thus far, by analogy with torture, I have argued that execution should be avoided because of how horrible it is to the one executed. But there are reasons of another sort that follow from the analogy with torture. Torture is to be avoided not only because of what it says about *what* we are willing to do to our fellows, but also because of what it says about *us* who are willing to do it. To torture someone is an awful spectacle not only because of the intensity of pain imposed, but because of what is required to be able to impose such pain on one's fellows. The tortured body cringes, using its full exertion to escape the pain imposed upon it—it literally begs for relief with its muscles as it does with its cries. To torture someone is to demonstrate a capacity to resist this begging, and that in turn demonstrates a kind of hardheartedness that a society ought not parade.

And this is true not only of torture, but of all severe corporal punishment. Indeed, I think this constitutes part of the answer to the puzzling question of why we refrain from punishments like whipping, even when the alternative (some months in jail versus some lashes) seems more costly to the offender. Imprisonment is painful to be sure, but it is a reflective pain, one that comes with comparing what is to what might have been, and that can be temporarily ignored by thinking about other things. But physical pain has an urgency that holds body and mind in a fierce grip. Of physical pain, as Orwell's Winston Smith recognized, "you could only wish one thing: that it should stop."[5] Refraining from torture in particular and corporal punishment in general, we both refuse to put a fellow human being in this grip *and* refuse to show our ability to resist this wish. The death penalty is the last corporal punishment used officially in the modern world. And it is corporal not only because administered via the body, but because the pain of foreseen, humanly administered death strikes us with the urgency that characterizes intense physical pain, causing grown men to cry, faint, and lose control of their bodily functions. There is something to be gained by refusing to endorse the hardness of heart necessary to impose such a fate.

By placing execution alongside torture in the category of things we will not do to our fellow human beings even when they deserve them, we broadcast the message that totally subjugating a person to the power of others *and* confronting him with the advent of his own humanly administered demise is too horrible to be done by civilized human beings to their fellows even when they have earned it: too horrible to do, and too horrible to be capable of doing. And I contend that broadcasting this message loud and clear would in the long run contribute to the general detestation of murder and be, to the extent to which it worked itself into the hearts and minds of the populace, a deterrent. In short, refusing to execute murderers though they deserve it both reflects and continues the taming of the human species that we call civilization. Thus, I take it that the abolition of the death penalty, though it is a just punishment for murder, is part of the civilizing mission of modern states. . . .

NOTES

1. Friedrich Nietzsche, *The Birth of Tragedy and The Genealogy of Morals* (New York: Doubleday, 1956), pp. 199–200.

2. Van den Haag writes that our ancestors "were not as repulsed by physical pain as we are. The change has to do not with our greater smartness or moral superiority but with a new outlook pioneered by the French and American revolutions [namely, the assertion of human equality and with it 'universal identification'], and by such mundane things as the invention of anesthetics, which make pain much less of an everyday experience" (p. 215; cf. van den Haag's *Punishing Criminals* [New York: Basic Books, 1975], pp. 196–206).

3. Emile Durkheim, "Two Laws of Penal Evolution," *Economy and Society* 2 (1973):285 and 294; italics in the original. This essay was originally published in French in *Année Sociologique* 4 (1899–1900). Conrad, incidentally, quotes Durkheim's two laws (p. 39), but does not develop their implications for his side in the debate.

4. Durkheim writes that "of the two laws which we have established, the first contributes to an explanation of the second" (Durkheim, "Two Laws of Penal Evolution," p. 299).

5. George Orwell, *1984* (New York: New American Library, 1983; originally published in 1949), p. 197.

Stephen Nathanson | # Does It Matter If the Death Penalty Is Arbitrarily Administered?

I

In this article, I will examine the argument that capital punishment ought to be abolished because it has been and will continue to be imposed in an arbitrary manner.

This argument has been central to discussions of capital punishment since the Supreme Court ruling in the 1972 case *Furman v. Georgia.* In a 5-4 decision, the Court ruled that capital punishment as then administered was unconstitutional. Although the Court issued several opinions, the problem of arbitrariness is widely seen as having played a central role in the Court's thinking. As Charles Black, Jr., has put it,

> . . . The decisive ground of the 1972 Furman case anti-capital punishment ruling—the ground persuasive to the marginal justices needed for a majority—was that, out of a large number of persons "eligible" in law for the punishment of death, a few were selected as if at random, by no stated (or perhaps statable) criteria, while all the rest suffered the lesser penalty of imprisonment.[1]

Among those justices moved by the arbitrariness issue, some stressed the discriminatory aspects of capital punishment, the tendency of legally irrelevant factors like race and economic status to determine the severity of sentence, while others emphasized the "freakish" nature of the punishment, the fact that it is imposed on a miniscule percentage of murderers who are not obviously more deserving of death than others.

Although the Supreme Court approved new death penalty laws in *Gregg v. Georgia* (1976), the reasoning of *Furman* was not rejected. Rather, a majority of the Court determined that Georgia's new laws would make arbitrary imposition of the death penalty much less likely. By amending procedures and adding criteria which specify aggravating and mitigating circumstances, Georgia had succeeded in creating a system of "guilded discretion," which the Court accepted in the belief that it was not likely to yield arbitrary results.

The *Gregg* decision has prompted death penalty opponents to attempt to show that "guided discretion" is an illusion. This charge has been supported in various ways. Charles Black has supported it by analyzing both the legal process of decision making in capital cases and the legal criteria for determining who is to be executed. He has argued that, appearances to the contrary, there are no meaningful standards operating in the system. Attacking from an empirical angle, William Bowers and Glenn Pierce have tried to show that even after *Furman* and under new laws, factors like race and geographic location of the trial continue to play a large role and that the criteria which are supposed to guide judgment do not separate those sentenced into meaningfully distinct groups. Perhaps the most shocking conclusion of Bowers and Pierce concerns the large role played by the race of the killer and the victim, as the chances of execution are by far the greatest when blacks kill whites and least when whites kill blacks.[2]

The upshot of both these approaches is that "guided discretion" is not working and, perhaps, cannot work. If this is correct and if the argument from arbitrariness is accepted, then it would appear that a return from *Gregg* to *Furman* is required. That is, the

Stephen Nathanson, "Does It Matter If the Death Penalty Is Arbitrarily Administered?" *Philosophy and Public Affairs* 14, no. 2 (Spring 1985): 149–64. Some notes have been deleted. Reprinted by permission of Princeton University Press.

Court should once again condemn capital punishment as unconstitutional.

I have posed these issues in terms of the Supreme Court's deliberations. Nonetheless, for opponents of the death penalty, the freakishness of its imposition and the large role played by race and other irrelevant factors are a moral as well as a legal outrage. For them, there is a fundamental moral injustice in the practice of capital punishment and not just a departure from the highest legal and constitutional standards.

II

The argument from arbitrariness has not, however, been universally accepted, either as a moral or a constitutional argument. Ernest van den Haag, an articulate and longtime defender of the death penalty, has claimed that the Supreme Court was wrong to accept this argument in the first place and thus that the evidence of arbitrariness presented by Black, Bowers and Pierce and others is beside the point. In his words:

> . . . the abolitionist argument from capriciousness, or discretion, or discrimination, would be more persuasive if it were alleged that those selectively executed are not guilty. But the argument merely maintains that some other guilty but more favored persons, or groups, escape the death penalty. This is hardly sufficient for letting anyone else found guilty escape the penalty. On the contrary, that some guilty persons or groups elude it argues for extending the death penalty to them.[3]

Having attacked the appeal to arbitrariness, van den Haag goes on to spell out his own conception of the requirements of justice. He writes:

> Justice requires punishing the guilty—as many of the guilty as possible, even if only some can be punished—and sparing the innocent—as many of the innocent as possible, even if not all are spared. It would surely be wrong to treat everybody with equal injustice in preference to meting out justice at least to some. . . . [I]f the death penalty is morally just, *however discriminatorily applied to only some of the guilty,* it does remain just *in each case* in which it is applied [emphasis added].[4]

Distinguishing sharply between the demands of justice and the demands of equality, van den Haag claims that the justice of individual punishments depends on individual guilt alone and not on whether punishments are equally distributed among the class of guilty persons.

Van den Haag's distinction between the demands of justice and the demands of equality parallels the distinction drawn by Joel Feinberg between "noncomparative" and "comparative" justice.[5] Using Feinberg's terminology, we can express van den Haag's view by saying that he believes that the justice of a particular punishment is a *noncomparative* matter. It depends solely on what a person deserves and not on how others are treated. For van den Haag, then, evidence of arbitrariness and discrimination is irrelevant, so long as those who are executed are indeed guilty and deserve their punishment.

There is no denying the plausibility of van den Haag's case. In many instances, we believe it is legitimate to punish or reward deserving individuals, even though we know that equally deserving persons are unpunished or unrewarded. Consider two cases:

A. A driver is caught speeding, ticketed, and required to pay a fine. We know that the percentage of speeders who are actually punished is extremely small, yet we would probably regard it as a joke if the driver protested that he was being treated unjustly or if someone argued that no one should be fined for speeding unless all speeders were fined.

B. A person performs a heroic act and receives a substantial reward, in addition to the respect and admiration of his fellow citizens. Because he deserves the reward, we think it just that he receive it, even though many equally heroic persons are not treated similarly. That most heroes are unsung is no reason to avoid rewarding this particular heroic individual.

Both of these instances appear to support van den Haag's claim that we should do justice whenever we can in individual cases and that failure to do justice in all cases is no reason to withhold punishment or reward from individuals.

III

Is the argument from arbitrariness completely unfounded then? Should we accept van den Haag's claim that "unequal justice is justice still?"

In response to these questions, I shall argue that van den Haag's case is not as strong as it looks and that the argument from arbitrariness can be vindicated.

As a first step in achieving this, I would like to point out that there are in fact several different arguments from arbitrariness. While some of these arguments appeal to the random and freakish nature of the death penalty, others highlight the discriminatory effects of legally irrelevant factors. Each of these kinds of arbitrariness raises different sorts of moral and legal issues.

For example, though we may acknowledge the impossibility of ticketing all speeding drivers and still favor ticketing some, we will not find every way of determining which speeders are ticketed equally just. Consider the policy of ticketing only those who travel at extremely high speeds, as opposed to that of ticketing every tenth car. Compare these with the policy of giving tickets only to speeders with beards and long hair or to speeders whose cars bear bumper stickers expressing unpopular political views. While I shall not pursue this point in detail, I take it to be obvious that these different selection policies are not all equally just or acceptable.

A second difference between versions of the argument from arbitrariness depends on whether or not it is granted that we can accurately distinguish those who deserve to die from those who do not. As van den Haag presents the argument, it assumes that we are able to make this distinction. Then, the claim is made that from this class of people who deserve to die, only some are selected for execution. The choice of those specific persons from the general class of persons who deserve to die is held to be arbitrary.

Van den Haag neglects a related argument which has been forcefully defended by Charles Black. Black's argument is that the determination of *who* deserves to die—the first step—is itself arbitrary. So his claim is not merely that arbitrary factors determine who among the deserving will be executed. His

point is that the determination of who deserves to die is arbitrary. His main argument is that

> the official choices—by prosecutors, judges, juries, and governors—that divide those who are to die from those who are to live are on the whole not made, and cannot be made, under standards that are consistently meaningful and clear, but that they are often made, and in the foreseeable future will continue often to be made, under no standards at all or under pseudo-standards without discoverable meaning.[6]

According to Black, even the most conscientious officials could not make principled judgments about desert in these instances, because our laws do not contain clear principles for differentiating those who deserve to die from those who do not. While I shall not try to summarize Black's analysis of the failures of post-*Furman* capital punishment statutes, it is clear that if van den Haag were to meet this argument, he would have to provide his own analysis of these laws in order to show that they do provide clear and meaningful standards. Or, he would have to examine the actual disposition of cases under these laws to show that the results have not been arbitrary. Van den Haag does not attempt to do either of these things. This seems to result from a failure to distinguish (a) the claim that judgments concerning *who deserves to die* are arbitrarily made, from (b) the claim that judgments concerning *who among the deserving shall be executed* are arbitrarily made.

Van den Haag may simply assume that the system does a decent job of distinguishing those who deserve to die from those who do not, and his assumption gains a surface plausibility because of his tendency to oversimplify the nature of the judgments which need to be made. In contrast to Black, who stresses the complexity of the legal process and the complexity of the judgments facing participants in that process, van den Haag is content to say simply that "justice requires punishing the guilty . . . and sparing the innocent." This maxim makes it look as if officials and jurors need only divide people into two neat categories, and if we think of guilt and innocence as *factual* categories, it makes it look as if the only judgment necessary is whether a person did or did not kill another human being.

In fact, the problems are much more complicated than this. Not every person who kills another human being is guilty of the same crime. Some may have committed no crime at all, if their act is judged to be justifiable homicide. Among others, they may have committed first-degree murder, second-degree murder, or some form of manslaughter. Furthermore, even if we limit our attention to those who are convicted of first-degree murder, juries must consider aggravating and mitigating circumstances in order to judge whether someone is guilty enough to deserve the death penalty. It is clear, then, that simply knowing that someone is factually guilty of killing another person is far from sufficient for determining that he deserves to die, and if prosecutors, juries, and judges do not have criteria which enable them to classify those who are guilty in a just and rational way, then their judgments about who deserves to die will necessarily be arbitrary and unprincipled.

Once we appreciate the difficulty and complexity of the judgments which must be made about guilt and desert, it is easier to see how they might be influenced by racial characteristics and other irrelevant factors. The statistics compiled by Bowers and Pierce show that blacks killing whites have the greatest chance of being executed, while whites killing blacks have the least chance of execution. What these findings strongly suggest is that officials and jurors think that the killing of a white by a black is a more serious crime than the killing of a black by a white. Hence, they judge that blacks killing whites *deserve* a more serious punishment than whites killing blacks. Given the bluntness of our ordinary judgments about desert and the complexity of the choices facing jurors and officials, it may not be surprising either that people find it difficult to make the fine discriminations required by law or that such judgments are influenced by deep-seated racial or social attitudes.

Both legal analysis and empirical studies should undermine our confidence that the legal system sorts out those who deserve to die from those who do not in a nonarbitrary manner. If we cannot be confident that those who are executed in fact deserve to die, then we ought not to allow executions to take place at all.

Because van den Haag does not distinguish this argument from other versions of the argument from arbitrariness, he simply neglects it. His omission is serious because this argument is an independent, substantial argument against the death penalty. It can stand even if other versions of the argument from arbitrariness fall.

IV

I would like now to turn to the form of the argument which van den Haag explicitly deals with and to consider whether it is vulnerable to his criticisms. Let us assume that there is a class of people whom we know to be deserving of death. Let us further assume that only some of these people are executed and that the executions are arbitrary in the sense that those executed have not committed worse crimes than those not executed. This is the situation which Justice Stewart described in *Furman*. He wrote:

> These death sentences are cruel and unusual in the same way that being struck by lightning is cruel and unusual. For of all the people convicted of rapes and murders in 1967 and 1968, *many just as reprehensible as these,* the petitioners are among *a capriciously selected random handful* upon whom the sentence of death has in fact been imposed. (emphasis added)[7]

What is crucial here (and different from the argument previously discussed) is the assumption that we can judge the reprehensibility of both the petitioners and others convicted of similar crimes. Stewart does not deny that the petitioners deserve to die, but because other equally deserving people escape the death penalty for no legally respectable reasons, the executions of the petitioners, Stewart thought, would violate the Eighth and Fourteenth Amendments.

This is precisely the argument van den Haag rejected. We can sum up his reasons in the following rhetorical questions: How can it possibly be unjust to punish someone if he deserves the punishment? Why should it matter whether or not others equally deserving are punished?

I have already acknowledged the plausibility of van den Haag's case and offered the examples of the ticketed speeder and the rewarded hero as instances which seem to confirm his view. Nonetheless, I think that van den Haag is profoundly mistaken in thinking that the justice of a reward or punishment depends solely on whether the recipient deserves it.

Consider the following two cases which are structurally similar to A and B (given above) but which elicit different reactions:

C. I tell my class that anyone who plagiarizes will fail the course. Three students plagiarize papers, but only one receives a failing grade. The other two, in describing their motivation, win my sympathy, and I give them passing grades.
D. At my child's birthday party, I offer a prize to the child who can solve a particular puzzle. Three children, including my own, solve the puzzle. I cannot reward them all, so I give the prize to my own child.

In both cases, as in van den Haag's, only some of those deserving a reward or punishment receive it. Unlike cases A and B, however, C and D do not appear to be just, in spite of the fact that the persons rewarded or punished deserve what they get. In these cases, the justice of giving them what they deserve appears to be affected by the treatment of others.

About these cases I am inclined to say the following. The people involved have not been treated justly. It was unjust to fail the single plagiarizer and unjust to reward my child. It would have been better—because more just—to have failed no one than to have failed the single student. It would have been better to have given a prize to no one than to give the prize to my child alone.

The unfairness in both cases appears to result from the fact that the reasons for picking out those rewarded or punished are irrelevant and hence that the choice is arbitrary. If I have a stated policy of failing students who plagiarize, then it is unjust for me to pass students with whom I sympathize. Whether I am sympathetic or not is irrelevant, and I am treating the student whom I do fail unjustly because I am not acting simply on the basis of desert. Rather, I am acting on the basis of desert plus degree of sympathy. Likewise, in the case of the prize, it appears that I am preferring my own child in giving

out the reward, even though I announced that receipt of the award would depend only on success in solving the puzzle.

This may be made clearer by varying the plagiarism example. Suppose that in spite of my stated policy of failing anyone who plagiarizes, I am regularly lenient toward students who seem sufficiently repentant. Suppose further that I am regularly more lenient with attractive female students than with others. Or suppose that it is only redheads or wealthy students whom I fail. If such patterns develop, we can see that whether a student fails or not does not depend simply on being caught plagiarizing. Rather, part of the explanation of a particular student's being punished is that he or she is (or is not) an attractive female, redheaded or wealthy. In these instances, I think the plagiarizers who are punished have grounds for complaint, even though they were, by the announced standards, clearly guilty and deserving of punishment.

If this conclusion is correct, then doing justice is more complicated than van den Haag realizes. He asserts that it would be "wrong to treat everybody with equal injustice in preference to meting out justice at least to some." If my assessment of cases C and D is correct, however, it is better that everyone in those instances be treated "unjustly" than that only some get what they deserve. Whether one is treated justly or not depends on how others are treated and not solely on what one deserves.

In fact, van den Haag implicitly concedes this point in an interesting footnote to his essay. In considering the question of whether capital punishment is a superior deterrent, van den Haag mentions that one could test the deterrent power of the death penalty by allowing executions for murders committed on Monday, Wednesday, and Friday, while setting life imprisonment as the maximum penalty for murders committed on other days. In noting the obstacles facing such an experiment, he writes:

> . . . it is not acceptable to our sense of justice that *people guilty of the same crime would get different punishments* and that the difference would be made to depend deliberately on *a factor irrelevant to the nature of the crime* or of the criminal. (emphasis added)[8]

Given his earlier remarks about the argument from arbitrariness, this is a rather extraordinary comment, for van den Haag concedes that the justice of a punishment is not solely determined by what an individual deserves but is also a function of how equally deserving persons are treated in general.

In his case, what he finds offensive is that there is no difference between what the Monday, Wednesday, Friday murderers deserve and what the Tuesday, Thursday, Saturday, and Sunday murderers deserve. Yet the morally irrelevant factor of date is decisive in determining the severity of the punishment. Van den Haag (quite rightly) cannot swallow this.

Yet van den Haag's example is exactly parallel to the situation described by opponents of the death penalty. For, surely, the race of the criminal or victim, the economic or social status of the criminal or victim, the location of the crime or trial and other such factors are as irrelevant to the gravity of the crime and the appropriate severity of the punishment as is the day of the week on which the crime is committed. It would be as outrageous for the severity of the punishment to depend on these factors as it would be for it to depend on the day of the week on which the crime was committed.

In fact, it is more outrageous that death sentences depend on the former factors because a person can control the day of the week on which he murders in a way in which he cannot control his race or status. Moreover, we are committed to banishing the disabling effects of race and economic status from the law. Using the day of the week as a critical factor is at least not invidiously discriminatory, as it neither favors nor disfavors previously identifiable or disadvantaged groups.

In reply, one might contend that I have overlooked an important feature of van den Haag's example. He rejected the deterrence experiment not merely because the severity of punishment depended on irrelevant factors but also because the irrelevant factors were *deliberately* chosen as the basis of punishment. Perhaps it is the fact that irrelevant factors are deliberately chosen which makes van den Haag condemn the proposed experiment.

This is an important point. It certainly makes matters worse to decide deliberately to base life and death choices on irrelevant considerations. However, even if the decision is not deliberate, it remains a serious injustice if irrelevant considerations play this crucial role. Individuals might not even be aware of the influence of these factors. They might genuinely believe that their judgments are based entirely on relevant considerations. It might require painstaking research to discover the patterns underlying sentencing, but once they are known, citizens and policymakers must take them into consideration. Either the influence of irrelevant factors must be eradicated or, if we determine that this is impossible, we may have to alter our practices more radically.

This reasoning, of course, is just the reasoning identified with the *Furman* case. As Justice Douglas wrote:

> A law that stated that anyone making more than $50,000 would be exempt from the death penalty would plainly fall, as would a law that in terms said that blacks, those who never went beyond the fifth grade in school, those who make less than $3,000 a year, or those who were unpopular or unstable should be the only people executed. A law which in the overall view reaches the same result in practice has no more sanctity than a law which in terms provides the same.[9]

The problem, in Douglas's view, was that the system left life and death decisions to the "uncontrolled discretion of judges or juries," leading to the unintended but nonetheless real result that death sentences were based on factors which had nothing to do with the nature of the crime.

What I want to stress here is that the arbitrariness and discrimination need not be purposeful or deliberate. We might discover, as critics allege, that racial prejudice is so deeply rooted in our society that prosecutors, juries, and judges cannot free themselves from prejudice when determining how severe a punishment for a crime should be. Furthermore, we might conclude that these tendencies cannot be eradicated, especially when juries are called upon to make subtle and complex assessments of cases in the light of confusing, semi-technical criteria. Hence, although no one *decides* that race will be a factor, we may *predict* that it will be a factor, and this knowledge must be considered in evaluating policies and institutions.

If factors *as irrelevant as* the day of the crime determine whether people shall live or die and if the influence of these factors is ineradicable, then we must conclude that we cannot provide a just system of punishment and even those who are guilty and deserving of the most severe punishments (like the Monday killers in van den Haag's experiment) will have a legitimate complaint that they have been treated unjustly.

I conclude, then, that the treatment of *classes* of people is relevant to determining the justice of punishments for *individuals* and van den Haag is wrong to dismiss the second form of the argument from arbitrariness. That argument succeeds in showing that capital punishment is unjust and thus provides a powerful reason for abolishing it.

V

Supporters of the death penalty might concede that serious questions of justice are raised by the influence of arbitrary factors and still deny that this shows that capital punishment ought to be abolished. They could argue that some degree of arbitrariness is present throughout the system of legal punishment, that it is unreasonable to expect our institutions to be perfect, and that acceptance of the argument from arbitrariness would commit us to abolishing all punishment.

In fact, van den Haag makes just these points in his essay. He writes:

> The Constitution, though it enjoins us to minimize capriciousness, does not enjoin a standard of unattainable perfection or exclude penalties because that standard has not been attained. . . . I see no more merit in the attempt to persuade the courts to let all capital-crime defendants go free of capital punishment because some have wrongly escaped it than I see in an attempt to persuade the courts to let all burglars go because some have wrongly escaped imprisonment.[10]

It is an important feature of this objection that it could be made even by one who conceded the injustice of arbitrarily administered death sentences. Ra-

ther than agreeing that capital punishment should be abolished, however, this objection moves from the premise that the flaws revealed in capital punishment are shared by *all* punishments to the conclusion that we must either (a) reject all punishments (because of the influence of arbitrary factors on them) or (b) reject the idea that arbitrariness provides a sufficient ground for abolishing the death penalty.

Is there a way out of this dilemma for death penalty opponents?

I believe that there is. Opponents of the death penalty may continue to support other punishments, even though their administration also involves arbitrariness. This is not to suggest, of course, that we should be content with arbitrariness or discrimination in the imposition of any punishment.[11] Rather the point is to emphasize that the argument from arbitrariness counts against the death penalty with special force. There are two reasons for this.

First, death is a much more severe punishment than imprisonment. This is universally acknowledged by advocates and opponents of the death penalty alike. It is recognized in the law by the existence of special procedures for capital cases. Death obliterates the person, depriving him or her of life and thereby, among other things, depriving him or her of any further rights of legal appeal, should new facts be discovered or new understandings of the law be reached. In this connection, it is worth recalling that many people were executed and are now dead because they were tried and sentenced under the pre-*Furman* laws which allowed the "uncontrolled discretion of judges and juries."

Second, though death is the most severe punishment in our legal system, it appears to be unnecessary for protecting citizens, while punishments generally are thought to promote our safety and well-being. The contrast between death and other punishments can be brought out by asking two questions. What would happen if we abolished all punishments? And, what would happen if we abolished the death penalty?

Most of us believe that if all punishments were abolished, there would be social chaos, a Hobbesian war of all against all. To do away with punishment entirely would be to do away with the criminal law and the system of constraints which it supports.

Hence, even though the system is not a just one, we believe that we must live with it and strive to make it as fair as possible. On the other hand, if we abolish capital punishment, there is reason to believe that nothing will happen. There is simply no compelling evidence that capital punishment prevents murders better than long-term prison sentences. Indeed, some evidence even suggests that capital punishment increases the number of murders. While I cannot review the various empirical studies of these questions here, I think it can plausibly be asserted that the results of abolishing punishment generally would be disastrous, while the results of abolishing capital punishment are likely to be insignificant.[12]

I conclude then that the argument from arbitrariness has special force against the death penalty because of its extreme severity and its likely uselessness. The arbitrariness of other punishments may be outweighed by their necessity, but the same cannot be said for capital punishment.

VI

In closing, I would like to comment briefly on one other charge made by van den Haag, the charge that the argument from arbitrariness is a "sham" argument because it is not the real reason why people oppose the death penalty. Those who use this argument, van den Haag claims, would oppose capital punishment even if it were not arbitrarily imposed.

At one level, this charge is doubly fallacious. The suggestion of dishonesty introduced by the word "sham" makes the argument into an *ad hominem*. In addition, the charge suggests that there cannot be more than one reason in support of a view. There are many situations in which we offer arguments and yet would not change our view if the argument were refuted, not because the argument is a sham, but because we have additional grounds for what we believe.

Nonetheless, van den Haag's charge may indicate a special difficulty for the argument from arbitrariness, for the argument may well strike people as artificial and legalistic. Somehow, one may feel that it does not deal with the real issues—the wrongness of

killing, deterrence, and whether murderers deserve to die.

Part of the problem, I think, is that our ordinary moral thinking involves specific forms of conduct or general rules of personal behavior. The argument from arbitrariness deals with a feature of an *institution,* and thinking about institutions seems to raise difficulties for many people. Believing that an individual murderer deserves to die for a terrible crime, they infer that there ought to be capital punishment, without attending to all of the implications for other individuals which will follow from setting up this practice.

The problem is similar to one that John Stuart Mill highlighted in *On Liberty.* For many people, the fact that an act is wrong is taken to be sufficient ground for its being made illegal. Mill argued against the institutionalization of all moral judgments, and his argument still strikes many people as odd. If the act is wrong, they ask, shouldn't we do everything in our power to stop it? What they fail to appreciate, however, are all of the implications of institutionalizing such judgments.

Likewise, people ask, If so and so deserves to die, shouldn't we empower the state to execute him? The problem, however—or one of many problems—is that institutionalizing this judgment about desert yields a system which makes neither moral nor legal sense. Moreover, it perpetuates and exacerbates the liabilities and disadvantages which unjustly befall many of our fellow citizens. These are genuine and serious problems, and those who have raised them in the context of the capital punishment debate have both exposed troubling facts about the actual workings of the criminal law and illuminated the difficulties of acting justly. Most importantly, they have produced a powerful argument against authorizing the state to use death as a punishment for crime.

NOTES

1. *Capital Punishment: The Inevitability of Caprice and Mistake,* 2d ed. (New York: W. W. Norton & Co., 1981), p. 20.

2. Ibid., passim; W. Bowers and G. Pierce, "Arbitrariness and Discrimination under Post-*Furman* Capital

Statutes," *Crime & Delinquency* 26 (1980): 563–635. Reprinted in *The Death Penalty in America,* 3d ed., ed. Hugo Bedau (New York: Oxford University Press, 1982), pp. 206–24.

3. "The Collapse of the Case Against Capital Punishment," *National Review,* 31 March 1978: 397. A briefer version of this paper appeared in the *Criminal Law Bulletin* 14 (1978): 51–68 and is reprinted in Bedau, pp. 323–33.

4. Ibid.

5. "Noncomparative Justice," in *Rights, Justice, and the Bounds of Liberty: Essays in Social Philosophy* (Princeton, NJ: Princeton University Press, 1980); originally published in the *Philosophical Review* 83 (1974): 297–338.

6. Black, *Capital Punishment,* p. 29.

7. Reprinted in Bedau, pp. 263–64.

8. Van den Haag, "The Collapse of the Case Against Capital Punishment," p. 403, n. 12. (This important footnote does not appear in the shorter version of the paper.)

9. Reprinted in Bedau, pp. 255–56.

10. Van den Haag, "The Collapse of the Case Against Capital Punishment," p. 397.

11. For a discussion of the role of discrimination throughout the criminal justice system and recommendations for reform, see American Friends Service Committee, *Struggle for Justice* (New York: Hill and Wang, 1971).

12. In support of the superior deterrent power of the death penalty, van den Haag cites I. Ehrlich, "The Deterrent Effect of Capital Punishment: A Question of Life and Death," *American Economic Review* 65 (1975): 397–417. Two reviews of the evidence on deterrence, both of which criticize Ehrlich at length, are Hans Zeisel, "The Deterrent Effect of the Death Penalty: Facts v. Faith," and Lawrence Klein et al., "The Deterrent Effect of Capital Punishment: An Assessment of the Evidence." (Both of these articles appear in Bedau.) The thesis that executions increase the number of homicides is defended by W. Bowers and G. Pierce in "Deterrence or Brutalization: What is the Effect of Executions?," *Crime & Delinquency* 26 (1980): 453–84.

26

Is All Punishment Wrong?

Barnett and His Critics

When a government raises a sales tax or builds a highway or calls a person for jury duty, it acts in ways that predictably cause harm to some of its citizens. An increased tax will be costly to some businesses and some consumers; a new highway will cause headaches for those who live close by; and being on a jury will be time consuming and stressful for those who are drafted into serving. In all of these cases, of course, the State does not do what it does *in order to* harm some of its citizens. It does what it does in order to bring about a presumably legitimate end, while recognizing that some harm will fall upon some of its citizens in the process. The State builds roads in order to facilitate transportation, for example, not in order to give some of its citizens headaches; but building roads will cause headaches nonetheless.

There is one instance, however, in which the State does act with the explicit intention of causing harm to some of its own citizens: when it punishes people for breaking the law. When a criminal is thrown in jail, for example, he is put there *in order to* make him suffer for his wrongdoing. The harm to the criminal is not merely a foreseen byproduct of the act, in the way that the harm to people living near the highway is merely an unfortunate side effect of the road's being built. Rather, the harm to the criminal is precisely the point of the act of imprisoning him. The State punishes him to harm him.

This difference between punishment, on the one hand, and other government acts, on the other, renders the moral justification of punishment distinctly problematic. After all, most people would agree that, in general, it would be wrong for the State to intentionally harm some of its own citizens. Why, then, is it morally permissible for the State to intentionally harm some of its citizens merely because they have broken the law? This is the problem of punishment.

The problem of punishment has generated a large number of attempted solutions, most of which fall into two distinct camps: the *deterrence position* and the *retributivist position*. Put briefly, the deterrence position maintains that the State may punish people for breaking the law because doing so will presumably discourage others from breaking the law. The retributivist position maintains that the State may punish people for breaking the law because people who break the law deserve to be punished. In addition, a number of thinkers have argued that punishment can be justified as a form of rehabilitation, on the grounds that punishment is actually good for the person being punished. (Anyone whose parents ever told him "I'm doing this for your own good" will understand the core of this third position.) Philosophers who have written on the subject disagree sharply about just *how* the practice of punishment is justified, but virtually all of them agree that it is justified.

Randy Barnett does not accept that punishment can be justified. In "Restitution: A New Paradigm of Criminal Justice," Barnett argues that the State does not, in fact, have the right to punish people for breaking the law. When a person breaks the law, on Barnett's account, the State has the right to compel him to make restitution to his victims (where restitution means restoring them to the level of well-being they enjoyed prior to the offender's wrongful act), but that is all it may permissibly do. Barnett refers to this position as the theory of *pure restitution.*

This position, as Barnett recognizes, is a radical one. Virtually everyone agrees that restitution should be one part of the criminal justice system, but virtually no one other than Barnett thinks that it should be the only part. Barnett's argument for his extreme position can best be understood as consisting of two parts, each of which proceeds by means of process of elimination (see the Introduction). In the first part, Barnett considers the attempts that have been made to show that punishment is permissible and tries to show that all of them fail. Even though most people think that one of the three positions—deterrence, retributivist, or rehabilitationist—must be correct, Barnett attempts to establish that all of them have implications that most people will reject. In the second part of his argument, Barnett considers a variety of objections that can be raised directly against the theory of pure restitution itself. Here, he proceeds by process of elimination in a different way: attempting to eliminate the various objections that can be raised against his theory by showing that they all can be overcome. In short, Barnett first attempts to eliminate any reason for believing that punishment can be justified and then attempts to eliminate any reason for rejecting the rejection of punishment.

Since Barnett's argument depends on this two-pronged approach, it is vulnerable to two distinct kinds of criticism. First, a critic could attempt to provide a positive defense of punishment, trying to establish, for example, that Barnett's objections to the deterrence position or the retributivist position can be overcome, or providing still further defense of punishment. Second, a critic could attempt to identify an unacceptable implication of the theory of pure restitution, either by showing that Barnett fails to overcome satisfactorily one of the objections he considers or by raising objections Barnett does not consider.

In his brief reply to Barnett, Franklin G. Miller offers objections of both of these sorts. In response to Barnett's arguments against the justifications of punishment, Miller charges that Barnett neglects two further possibilities: the possibility of combining some of the justifications he does consider into a more powerful justification and the possibility of appealing to the condemnatory aspect of punishment, the respect to which the State uses punishment as a means of communicating its disapproval of the offender's behavior. In response to Barnett's attempt to fend off various objections to the pure restitution approach, Miller maintains that the exclusive focus on making restitution to victims leaves the approach unable to handle a variety of cases in which it is not clear just who the victim is or how he should be compensated, especially cases in which no particular individual is harmed or in which the offender attempted to cause harm or risked causing harm but did not, in fact, cause harm.

In two excerpts from a longer piece, Roger Pilon offers objections of both sorts to Barnett's position. With respect to Barnett's attempt to defend the theory of pure restitution against a variety of objections, Pilon considers cases involving wealthy individuals. He uses these cases to press the objection that restitution alone cannot address the guilty-mind component of criminal acts (that is, the component that distinguishes criminal acts from acts that merely warrant civil lawsuits). And with respect to Barnett's attempt to defeat the various defenses of punishment that have been proposed, Pilon defends a particular version of retributivism in which the offender has forfeited certain rights, which thereby renders him liable not merely to restitution but to punishment.

Finally, two quick points from a longer piece by Stanley S. Kleinberg round out the critical response to Barnett's proposal (readers interested in pursuing the debate still further should read the pieces by Pilon and Kleinberg in their entirety): First, even crimes that have clear individual victims, such as armed robbery, also victimize other members of society in a way that Barnett's proposal does not seem prepared to accommodate. Second, the system that Barnett envisions would seem to favor not only the wealthy (a point also noted by Pilon) but, perhaps even more disturbing, the professional criminal. The cumulative effect of the critical response to Barnett, then, is that many of his readers believe that he has failed to show that punishment is unjustified, and that he has failed to show that his proposed alternative is sufficiently appealing.

QUESTIONS FOR CONSIDERATION

In thinking about the exchange between Barnett and his critics, readers should focus on the two main sets of argument outlined here.

• Has Barnett succeeded in raising sufficient doubts about the justifiability of punishment or have his critics succeeded in making a satisfactory case in its defense?

• Can punishment be justified by one of the theories Barnett discusses or by one he neglects or by some combination of these? Or is Barnett correct to insist that, in the end, none of these considerations can justify the intentional harm of people in response to their having violated the law?

• Has Barnett succeeded in rendering his theory of restitution sufficiently attractive, or have his critics succeeded in demonstrating that it would have unacceptable implications?

FURTHER READINGS

Barnett, Randy. "The Justice of Restitution." In Jan Narveson, ed., *Moral Issues*. Toronto and New York: Oxford University Press, 1983, 140–53.

———. "Pursuing Justice in a Free Society: Part One—Power vs. Liberty." *Criminal Justice Ethics* 4, no. 2 (1985): 50–72.

Restitution

A New Paradigm of Criminal Justice

Randy E. Barnett

This paper will analyze the breakdown of our system of criminal justice in terms of what Thomas Kuhn would describe as a crisis of an old paradigm—punishment. I propose that this crisis could be solved by the adoption of a new paradigm of criminal justice—restitution. The approach will be mainly theoretical, though at various points in the discussion the practical implications of the rival paradigms will also be considered. A fundamental contention will be that many, if not most, of our system's ills stem from errors in the underlying paradigm. Any attempt to correct these symptomatic debilities without a reexamination of the theoretical underpinnings is doomed to frustration and failure. Kuhn's theories deal with the problems of science. What made his proposal so startling was its attempt to analogize scientific development to social and political development. Here, I will simply reverse the process by applying Kuhn's framework of scientific change to social, or in this case, legal development.[1]

In the criminal justice system we are witnessing the death throes of an old and cumbersome paradigm, one that has dominated Western thought for more than 900 years. While this paper presents what is hoped to be a viable, though radical alternative, much would be accomplished by simply prompting the reader to reexamine the assumptions underlying the present system. Only if we are willing to look at our old problems in a new light do we stand a chance of solving them. This is our only hope, and our greatest challenge.

THE CRISIS IN THE PARADIGM OF PUNISHMENT

"Political revolutions are inaugurated by a growing sense, often restricted to a segment of the political community, that existing institutions have ceased adequately to meet the problems posed by an environment they have in part created. . . . In both political and scientific development the sense of malfunction that can lead to crisis is prerequisite to revolution."[2] Kuhn's description of the preconditions for scientific and political revolutions could accurately describe the current state of the criminal law. However, simply to recognize the existence of a crisis is not enough. We must look for its causes. The Kuhnian methodology suggests that we critically examine the paradigm of punishment itself.

The problems which the paradigm of punishment is supposed to solve are many and varied. A whole literature on the philosophy of punishment has arisen in an effort to justify or reject the institution of punishment. For our purposes the following definition from the *Encyclopedia of Philosophy* should suffice: "Characteristically punishment is unpleasant. It is inflicted on an offender because of an offense he has committed; it is deliberately imposed,

Randy E. Barnett, "Restitution: A New Paradigm of Criminal Justice," *Ethics* 87, no. 4 (July 1977): 279–301. Some notes have been deleted. Reprinted by permission of University of Chicago Press.

not just the natural consequence of a person's action (like a hangover), and the unpleasantness is *essential* to it, not an accompaniment to some other treatment (like the pain of the dentist's drill)."[3]

Two types of arguments are commonly made in defense of punishment. The first is that punishment is an appropriate means to some justifiable end such as, for example, deterrence of crime. The second type of argument is that punishment is justified as an end in itself. On this view, whatever ill effects it might engender, punishment for its own sake is good.

The first type of argument might be called the *political* justification of punishment, for the end which justifies its use is one which a political order is presumably dedicated to serve: the maintenance of peaceful interactions between individuals and groups in a society. There are at least three ways that deliberate infliction of harm on an offender is said to be politically justified.

1. One motive for punishment, especially capital punishment and imprisonment, is the "intention to deprive offenders of the power of doing future mischief."[4] Although it is true that an offender cannot continue to harm society while incarcerated, a strategy of punishment based on disablement has several drawbacks.

Imprisonment is enormously expensive. This means that a double burden is placed on the innocent who must suffer the crime and, in addition, pay through taxation for the support of the offender and his family if they are forced onto welfare. Also, any benefit of imprisonment is temporary; eventually, most offenders will be released. If their outlook has not improved—and especially if it has worsened—the benefits of incarceration are obviously limited. Finally, when disablement is permanent, as with capital punishment or psychosurgery, it is this very permanence, in light of the possibility of error, which is frightening. For these reasons, "where disablement enters as an element into penal theories, it occupies, as a rule, a subordinate place and is looked upon as an object subsidiary to some other end which is regarded as paramount. . . ."[5]

2. Rehabilitiation of a criminal means a change in his mental *habitus* so that he will not offend again. It is unclear whether the so-called treatment model which views criminals as a doctor would view a patient is truly a "retributive" concept. Certainly it does not conform to the above definition characterizing punishment as deliberately and essentially unpleasant. It is an open question whether any end justifies the intentional, forceful manipulation of an individual's thought processes by anyone, much less the state. To say that an otherwise just system has incidentally rehabilitative effects which may be desirable is one thing, but it is quite another to argue that these effects themselves justify the system. The horrors to which such reasoning can lead are obvious from abundant examples in history and contemporary society.[6]

Rehabilitation as a reaction against the punishment paradigm will be considered below, but one aspect is particularly relevant to punishment as defined here. On this view, the visiting of unpleasantness itself will cause the offender to see the error of his ways; by having "justice" done him, the criminal will come to appreciate his error and will change his moral outlook. This end, best labeled "reformation," is speculative at best and counterfactual at worst. On the contrary, "it has been observed that, as a rule . . . ruthless punishments, far from mollifying men's ways, corrupt them and stir them to violence."[7]

3. The final justification to be treated here—deterrence—actually has two aspects. The first is the deterrent effect that past demonstrations of punishment have on the future conduct of others; the second is the effect that threats of future punishment have on the conduct of others. The distinction assumes importance when some advocates argue that future threats lose their deterrent effect when there is a lack of past demonstrations. Past punishment, then, serves as an educational tool. It is a substitute for or reinforcement of threats of future punishment.

As with the goals mentioned above, the empirical question of whether punishment has this effect is a disputed one.[8] I shall not attempt to resolve this question here, but will assume *arguendo* that punishment even as presently administered has some deterrent effect. It is the moral question which is disturbing. Can an argument from deterrence alone "justify" in any sense the infliction of pain on a criminal? It is particularly disquieting that the actual levying of punishment is done not for the criminal himself, but for the educational impact it will have on the community. The criminal act becomes the occasion of, but not the reason for, the punishment. In this way, the actual crime becomes little more than an excuse for punishing.

Surely this distorts the proper functioning of the judicial process. For if deterrence is the end it is unimportant whether the individual actually committed the crime. Since the public's perception of guilt is the prerequisite of the deterrent effect, all that is required for deterrence is that the individual is "proved" to have committed the crime. The actual occurrence would have no relevance except insofar as a truly guilty person is easier to prove guilty. The judicial process becomes, not a truth-seeking device, but solely a means to legitimate the use of force. To treat criminals as means to the ends of others in this way raises serious moral problems. This is not to argue that men may never use others as means but rather to question the use of force against the individual because of the effect such use will have on others. It was this that concerned del Vecchio when he stated that "the human person always bears in himself something sacred, and it is therefore not permissable to treat him merely as a means towards an end ouside of himself."[9]

Finally, deterrence as the ultimate justification of punishment cannot rationally limit its use. It "provides *no* guidance until we're told *how much* commission of it is to be deterred."[10] Since there are always some who commit crimes, one can always argue for more punishment. Robert Nozick points out that there must be criteria by which one decides how much deterrence may be inflicted.[11] One is forced therefore to employ "higher" principles to evaluate the legitimacy of punishment.

It is not my thesis that deterrence, reformation, and disablement are undesirable goals. On the con-

trary, any criminal justice system should be critically examined to see if it is having these and other beneficial effects. The view advanced here is simply that these utilitarian benefits must be incidental to a just system; they cannot, alone or in combination, justify a criminal justice system. Something more is needed. There is another more antiquated strain of punishment theory which seeks to address this problem. The *moral* justifications of punishment view punishment as an end in itself. This approach has taken many forms.[12] On this view, whatever ill or beneficial results it might have, punishment of lawbreakers is good for its own sake. This proposition can be analyzed on several levels.

The most basic question is the truth of the claim itself. Some have argued that "the alleged absolute justice of repaying evil with evil (maintained by Kant and many other writers) is really an empty sophism. If we go back to the Christian moralists, we find that an evil is to be put right only by doing good."[13] This question is beyond the scope of this treatment. The subject has been extensively dealt with by those more knowledgeable than I.[14] The more relevant question is what such a view of punishment as a good can be said to imply for a system of criminal justice. Even assuming that it would be good if, in the nature of things, the wicked got their "come-uppance," what behavior does this moral fact justify? Does it justify the victim authoring the punishment of his offender? Does it justify the same action by the victim's family, his friends, his neighbors, the state? If so what punishment should be imposed and who should decide?

It might be argued that the natural punishment for the violation of natural rights is the deserved hatred and scorn of the community, the resultant ostracism, and the existential hell of *being* an evil person. The question then is not whether we have the right to inflict some "harm" or unpleasantness on a morally contemptible person—surely, we do; the question is not whether such a punishment is "good"—arguably, it is. The issue is whether the "virtue of some punishment" justifies the *forceful* imposition of unpleasantness on a *rights violator* as distinguished from the morally imperfect. Any *moral* theory of punishment must recognize and deal with this distinction. Finally, it must be established that the state is the legitimate author of punishment, a proposition which further assumes the moral and legal legitimacy of the state. To raise these issues is not to resolve them, but it would seem that the burden of proof is on those seeking to justify the use of force against the individual. Suffice it to say that I am skeptical of finding any theory which justifies the deliberate, forceful imposition of punishment within or without a system of criminal justice.

The final consideration in dealing with punishment as an end in itself is the possibility that the current crisis in the criminal justice system is in fact a crisis of the paradigm of punishment. While this, if true, does not resolve the philosophical issues, it does cast doubt on the punishment paradigm's vitality as the motive force behind a system of criminal justice. Many advocates of punishment argue that its apparent practical failings exist because we are not punishing enough. All that is needed, they say, is a crackdown on criminals and those victims and witnesses who shun participation in the criminal justice system; the only problem with the paradigm of punishment is that we are not following it.[15] This response fails to consider *why* the system doggedly refuses to punish to the degree required to yield beneficial results and instead punishes in such a way as to yield harmful results. The answer may be that the paradigm of punishment is in eclipse, that the public lacks the requisite will to apply it in anything but the prevailing way.

Punishment, particularly state punishment is the descendant of the tradition which imparts religious and moral authority to the sovereign and, through him, the community. Such an authority is increasingly less credible in a secular world such as ours. Today there is an increasing desire to allow each individual to govern his own life as he sees fit provided he does not violate the rights of others. This desire is exemplified by current attitudes toward drug use, abortion, and pornography. Few argue that these things are good. It is only said that where there is no victim the state or community has no business meddling in the peaceful behavior of its citizens, however morally suspect it may be.[16]

Furthermore, if the paradigm of punishment is in a "crisis period" it is as much because of its practical drawbacks as the uncertainty of its moral status. The

infliction of suffering on a criminal tends to cause a general feeling of sympathy for him. There is no rational connection between a term of imprisonment and the harm caused the victim. Since the prison term is supposed to be unpleasant, at least a part of the public comes to see the criminal as a victim, and the lack of rationality also causes the offender to feel victimized. This reaction is magnified by the knowledge that most crimes go unpunished and that even if the offender is caught the judicial process is long, arduous, and far removed from the criminal act. While this is obvious to most, it is perhaps less obvious that the punishment paradigm is largely at fault. The slow, ponderous nature of our system of justice is largely due to a fear of an unjust infliction of punishment on the innocent (or even the guilty). The more awful the sanction, the more elaborate need be the safeguards. The more the system is perceived as arbitrary and unfair, the more incentive there is for defendants and their counsel to thwart the truth-finding process. Acquittal becomes desirable at all costs. As the punitive aspect of a sanction is diminished, so too would be the perceived need for procedural protections.

A system of punishment, furthermore, offers no incentive for the victim to involve himself in the criminal justice process other than to satisfy his feelings of duty or revenge. The victim stands to gain little if at all by the conviction and punishment of the person who caused his loss. This is true even of those systems discussed below which despense state compensation based on the victim's need. The system of justice itself imposes uncompensated costs by requiring a further loss of time and money by the victim and witnesses and by increasing the perceived risk of retaliation.

Finally, punishment which seeks to change an offender's moral outlook, or at least to scare him, can do nothing to provide him with the skills needed to survive in the outside world. In prison, he learns the advanced state of the criminal arts and vows not to repeat the mistake that led to his capture. The convict emerges better trained and highly motivated to continue a criminal career.

The crisis of the paradigm of punishment has at its roots the collapse of its twin pillars of support: its moral legitimacy and its practical efficacy. As Kaufmann concludes, "the faith in retributive justice is all but dead."[17]

ATTEMPTS TO SALVAGE THE PARADIGM OF PUNISHMENT

"All crises begin with the blurring of a paradigm and the consequent loosening of the rules for normal research."[18] And yet until a new paradigm is presented, authorities will cling to the old one, either ignoring the problem or salvaging the paradigm with ad hoc explanations and solutions. Why are paradigms never rejected outright? Why must there always be a new paradigm before the old one is abandoned? Kuhn does not explicitly discuss this, but R. A. Childs hypothesizes "that, as such, paradigms may serve the function of increasing man's sense of control over some aspect of reality, or some aspect of his own life. If this is so, then we would expect that a straightforward abandonment of a paradigm would threaten that sense of control."[19]

This psychological need for an explanation may in turn explain the many efforts to shore up the paradigm of punishment. The three attempts to be examined next have at their roots a perception of its fundamental errors, and at the same time they highlight three goals of any new paradigm of criminal justice.

1. Proportionate punishment. The king abandoned the composition system[20] for the system of punishment because punishment struck terror in the hearts of the people, and this served to inspire awe for the power of the king and state. But there was no rational connection between the seriousness of the crime and the gravity of the punishment and, therefore, no limit to the severity of punishment. Hideous tortures came to be employed: "But some of the men of the Enlightenment sought to counter the inhumanity of their Christian predecessors with appeals to reason. They thought that retributive justice had a mathematical quality and that murder called for capital punishment in much the same way in which two plus two equals four."[21]

The appeal to proportionality was one of the early attempts to come to grips with deficiencies in the paradigm of punishment. It was doomed to failure, for there is no objective standard by which punishments can be proportioned to fit the crime. Punishment is incommensurate with crime. This solution is purely ad hoc and intuitive. We shall, however, find the *goal* of proportionate sentencing useful in the formation of a new paradigm.

2. Rehabilitation. It was noted earlier that the infliction of punishment tends to focus attention on the plight of the criminal. Possibly for this reason, the next humanitarian trend was to explore the proper treatment of criminals. Punishment failed to reform the criminal, and this led observers to inquire how the situation might be improved. Some felt that the sole end of the penal system was rehabilitation, so attention was turned to modifying the criminal's behavior (an obviously manipulative end). Emphasis was placed on education, job training, and discipline.

Unfortunately, the paradigm of punishment and the political realities of penal administration have all but won out. There is simply no incentive for prison authorities to educate and train. Their job is essentially political. They are judged by their ability to keep the prisoners within the walls and to keep incidents of violence within the prison to a minimum; as a result, discipline is the main concern. Furthermore, since he is sentenced to a fixed number of years (less time off for good behavior—so-called good time), there is no institutional incentive for the prisoner to improve himself apart from sheer boredom. Productive labor in prison is virtually nonexistent, with only obsolete equipment, if any, available. Except perhaps for license plates and other state needs, the prisoners produce nothing of value; the prisons make no profit and the workers are paid, if at all, far below market wages. They are unable to support themselves or their families. The state, meaning the innocent taxpayer, supports the prisoner, and frequently the families as well via welfare.

Rehabilitation has been a long-time goal of the penal system, but the political nature of government-run prisons and the dominance of the paradigm of punishment has inevitably prevented its achievement. Prisons remain detention centers, all too temporarily preventing crime by physically confining the criminals.

3. Victim compensation. It is natural that the brutalities resulting from the paradigm of punishment

would get first attention from humanitarians and that the persons subjected to those practices would be next. Until recently, the victim of crime was the forgotten party. Within the last few years a whole new field has opened up called victimology.[22] With it has come a variety of proposals, justifications, and statutes.[23]

Certain features are common to virtually every compensation proposal: (a) Compensation for crimes would be dispensed by the state from tax revenue. (b) Compensation is "a matter of grace" rather than an assumption by the state of legal responsibility for the criminal loss suffered by the victim. (c) Most proposals allow for aid only on a "need" or "hardship" basis. (d) Most are limited to some sort of crime of violence or the threat of force or violence. (e) None questions the paradigm of punishment.

The goal of these proposals and statutes is laudable. The victim *is* the forgotten man of crime. But the means proposed is the same tired formula: welfare to those in "need." In short, the innocent taxpayer repays the innocent victim (if the victim can prove he "needs" help) while the guilty offender is subjected to the sanction of punishment with all its failings. Like proportionate punishment and rehabilitation, the goal of victim compensation is a recognition of very real problems in our criminal justice system, and at the same time it ignores the source of these problems: our conception of crime as an offense against the state whose proper sanction is punishment. Until a viable, new paradigm is presented, ad hoc solutions like the ones discussed here are all that can be hoped for. And it is a vain hope indeed, for they attack the symptoms while neglecting the causes of the problem. What is needed is a new paradigm.

OUTLINE OF A NEW PARADIGM

The idea of restitution is actually quite simple. It views crime as an offense by one individual against the rights of another. The victim has suffered a loss. Justice consists of the culpable offender making good the loss he has caused. It calls for a complete refocusing of our image of crime. Kuhn would call it a "shift of world-view." Where we once saw an offense against society, we now see an offense against an in-

dividual victim. In a way, it is a common sense view of crime. *The armed robber did not rob society; he robbed the victim.* His debt, therefore, is not to society; it is to the victim. There are really two types of restitution proposals: a system of "punitive" restitution and a "pure" restitutional system.

1. Punitive restitution. "Since rehabilitation was admitted to the aims of penal law two centuries ago, the number of penological aims has remained virtually constant. Restitution is waiting to come in."[24] Given this view, restitution should merely be added to the paradigm of punishment. Stephen Schafer outlines the proposal: "[Punitive] restitution, like punishment, must always be the subject of judicial consideration. Without exception it must be carried out by personal performance by the wrong-doer, and should even then be equally burdensome and just for all criminals, irrespective of their means, whether they be millionaires or labourers."[25]

There are many ways by which such a goal might be reached. The offender might be forced to compensate the victim by his own work, either in prison or out. If it came out of his pocket or from the sale of his property this would compensate the victim, but it would not be sufficiently unpleasant for the offender. Another proposal would be that the fines be proportionate to the earning power of the criminal. Thus, "A poor man would pay in days of work, a rich man by an equal number of days' income or salary."[26] Herbert Spencer made a proposal along similar lines in his excellent "Prison-Ethics," which is well worth examining.[27] Murray N. Rothbard and others have proposed a system of "double payments" in cases of criminal behavior.[28] While closer to pure restitution than other proposals, the "double damages" concept preserves a punitive aspect.

Punitive restitution is an attempt to gain the benefits of pure restitution, which will be considered shortly, while retaining the perceived advantages of the paradigm of punishment. Thus, the prisoner is still "sentenced" to some unpleasantness—prison labor or loss of X number of days' income. That the intention is to preserve the "hurt" is indicated by the hesitation to accept an out-of-pocket payment or sale of assets. This is considered too "easy" for the criminal and takes none of his time. The amount of payment is determined not by the *actual harm* but by the *ability of the offender to pay*. Of course, by retaining the paradigm of punishment this proposal involves many of the problems we raised earlier. In this sense it can be considered another attempt to salvage the old paradigm.

2. Pure restitution. "Recompense or restitution is scarcely a punishment as long as it is merely a matter of returning stolen goods or money.... The point is not that the offender deserves to suffer; it is rather that the offended party desires compensation."[29] This represents the complete overthrow of the paradigm of punishment. No longer would the deterrence, reformation, disablement, or rehabilitation of the criminal be the guiding principle of the judicial system. The attainment of these goals would be incidental to, and as a result of, reparations paid to the victim. No longer would the criminal deliberately be made to suffer for his mistake. Making good that mistake is all that would be required. What follows is a possible scenario of such a system.

When a crime occurred and a suspect was apprehended, a trial court would attempt to determine his guilt or innocence. If found guilty, the criminal would be sentenced to make restitution to the victim.[30] If a criminal is able to make restitution immediately, he may do so. This would discharge his liability. If he were unable to make restitution, but were found by the court to be trustworthy, he would be permitted to remain at his job (or find a new one) while paying restitution out of his future wages. This would entail a legal claim against future wages. Failure to pay could result in garnishment or a new type of confinement.

If it is found that the criminal is not trustworthy, or that he is unable to gain employment, he would be confined to an employment project.[31] This would be an industrial enterprise, preferably run by a private concern, which would produce actual goods or services. The level of security at each employment project would vary according to the behavior of the offenders. Since the costs would be lower, inmates at a lower-security project would receive higher wages. There is no reason why many workers could not be permitted to live with their families inside or outside the facility, depending, again, on the trust-

worthiness of the offender. Room and board would be deducted from the wages first, then a certain amount for restitution. Anything over that amount the worker could keep or apply toward further restitution, thus hastening his release. If a worker refused to work, he would be unable to pay for his maintenance, and therefore would not in principle be entitled to it. If he did not make restitution he could not be released. The exact arrangement which would best provide for high productivity, minimal security, and maximum incentive to work and repay the victim cannot be determined in advance. Experience is bound to yield some plans superior to others. In fact, the experimentation has already begun.[32]

While this might be the basic system, all sorts of refinements are conceivable, and certainly many more will be invented as needs arise. A few examples might be illuminating. With such a system of repayment, victim *crime insurance* would be more economically feasible than at present and highly desirable. The cost of awards would be offset by the insurance company's right to restitution in place of the victim (right of subrogation). The insurance company would be better suited to supervise the offender and mark his progress than would the victim. To obtain an earlier recovery, it could be expected to innovate so as to enable the worker to repay more quickly (and, as a result, be released that much sooner). The insurance companies might even underwrite the employment projects themselves as well as related industries which would employ the skilled worker after his release. Any successful effort on their part to reduce crime and recidivism would result in fewer claims and lower premiums. The benefit of this insurance scheme for the victim is immediate compensation, conditional on the victim's continued cooperation with the authorities for the arrest and conviction of the suspect. In addition, the centralization of victim claims would, arguably, lead to efficiencies which would permit the pooling of small claims against a common offender.

Another highly useful refinement would be *direct arbitration* between victim and criminal. This would serve as a sort of healthy substitute for plea bargaining. By allowing the guilty criminal to negotiate a reduced payment in return for a guily plea, the victim (or his insurance company) would be saved the risk of an adverse finding at trial and any possible additional expense that might result. This would also allow an indigent criminal to substitute personal services for monetary payments if all parties agreed.

Arbitration is argued for by John M. Greacen, deputy director of the National Institute for Law Enforcement and Criminal Justice. He sees the possible advantages of such reform as the " . . . development of more creative dispositions for most criminal cases; for criminal victims the increased use of restitution, the knowledge that their interests were considered in the criminal process; and an increased satisfaction with the outcome; increased awareness in the part of the offender that his crime was committed against another human being, and not against society in general; increased possibility that the criminal process will cause the offender to acknowledge responsibility for his acts."[33] Greacen notes several places where such a system has been tried with great success, most notably Tucson, Arizona, and Columbus, Ohio.[34]

Something analogous to the medieval Irish system of *sureties* might be employed as well.[35] Such a system would allow a concerned person, group, or company to make restitution (provided the offender agrees to this). The worker might then be released in the custody of the surety. If the surety had made restitution, the offender would owe restitution to the surety who might enforce the whole claim or show mercy. Of course, the more violent and unreliable the offender, the more serious and costly the offense, the less likely it would be that anyone would take the risk. But for first offenders, good workers, or others that charitable interests found deserving (or perhaps unjustly convicted) this would provide an avenue of respite.

RESTITUTION AND RIGHTS

These three possible refinements clearly illustrate the flexibility of a restitutional system. It may be less apparent that this flexibility is *inherent* to the restitutional paradigm. Restitution recognizes rights in the victim, and this is a principal source of its strength. The nature and limit of the victim's right to restitu-

tion at the same time defines the nature and limit of the criminal liability. In this way, the aggressive action of the criminal creates a *debt* to the victim. The recognition of rights and obligations make possible many innovative arrangements. Subrogation, arbitration, and suretyship are three examples mentioned above. They are possible because this right to compensation[36] is considered the property of the victim and can therefore be delegated, assigned, inherited, or bestowed. One could determine in advance who would acquire the right to any restitution which he himself might be unable to collect.

The natural owner of an unenforced death claim would be an insurance company that had insured the deceased. The suggestion has been made that a person might thus increase his personal safety by insuring with a company well known for tracking down those who injure its policy holders. In fact, the partial purpose of some insurance schemes might be to provide the funds with which to track down the malefactor. The insurance company, having paid the beneficiaries would "stand in their shoes." It would remain possible, of course, to simply assign or devise the right directly to the beneficiaries, but this would put the burden of enforcement on persons likely to be unsuited to the task.

If one accepts the Lockean trichotomy of property ownership,[37] that is, acquiring property via exchange, gifts, and *homesteading* (mixing one's labor with previously unowned land or objects), the possibility arises that upon a person's wrongful death, in the absence of any heirs or assignees, his right to compensation becomes unowned property. The right could then be claimed (homesteaded) by anyone willing to go to the trouble of catching and prosecuting the criminal. Firms might specialize in this sort of activity, or large insurance companies might make the effort as a kind of "loss leader" for public relations purposes.

This does, however, lead to a potentially serious problem with the restitutional paradigm: what exactly constitutes "restitution"? What is the *standard* by which compensation is to be made? Earlier we asserted that any such problem facing the restitutional paradigm faces civil damage suits as well. The method by which this problem is dealt with in civil cases could be applied to restitution cases. But while this is certainly true, it may be that this problem has not been adequately handled in civil damage suits either.

Restitution in cases of crimes against property is a manageable problem. Modern contract and tort doctrines of restitution are adequate. The difficulty lies in cases of personal injury or death. How can you put a price on life or limb, pain or suffering? Is not any attempt to do so of necessity arbitrary? It must be admitted that a fully satisfactory solution to this problem is lacking, but it should also be stressed that this dilemma, though serious, has little impact on the bulk of our case in favor of a restitutional paradigm. It is possible that no paradigm of criminal justice can solve every problem, yet the restitutional approach remains far superior to the paradigm of punishment or any other conceivable rival.

This difficulty arises because certain property is unique and irreplaceable. As a result, it is impossible to approximate a "market" or "exchange" value expressed in monetary terms. Just as there is no rational relationship between a wrongfully taken life and ten years in prison, there is little relationship between that same life and $20,000. Still, the nature of this possibly insoluble puzzle reveals a restitutional approach theoretically superior to punishment. For it must be acknowledged that a real, tangible loss *has* occurred. The problem is only one of incommensurability. Restitution provides *some* tangible, albeit inadequate, compensation for personal injury. Punishment provides none at all.[38]

It might be objected that to establish some "pay scale" for personal injury is not only somewhat arbitrary but also a disguised reimplementation of punishment. Unable to accept the inevitable consequences of restitutional punishment, the argument continues, I have retreated to a pseudorestitutional award. Such a criticism is unfair. The true test in this instance is one of primacy of intentions. Is the purpose of a system to compensate victims for their losses (and perhaps, as a consequence, punish the criminals), or is its purpose to punish the criminals (and perhaps, as a consequence, compensate the victims for their losses)? The true ends of a criminal justice system will determine its nature. In short, ar-

bitrariness *alone* does not imply a retributive motive. And while arbitrariness remains to some extent a problem for the restitutional paradigm, it is less of a problem for restitution than for punishment, since compensation has *some* rational relationship to damages and costs.

ADVANTAGES OF A RESTITUTIONAL SYSTEM

1. The first and most obvious advantage is the assistance provided to victims of crime. They may have suffered an emotional, physical, or financial loss. Restitution would not change the fact that a possibly traumatic crime has occurred (just as the award of damages does not undo tortious conduct). Restitution, however, would make the resulting loss easier to bear for both victims and their families. At the same time, restitution would avoid a major pitfall of victim compensation/welfare plans: Since it is the criminal who must pay, the possibility of collusion between victim and criminal to collect "damages" from the state would be all but eliminated.

2. The possibility of receiving compensation would encourage victims to report crimes and to appear at trial. This is particularly true if there were a crime insurance scheme which contractually committed the policyholder to testify as a condition for payment, thus rendering unnecessary oppressive and potentially tyrannical subpoenas and contempt citations. Even the actual reporting of the crime to police is likely to be a prerequisite for compensation. Such a requirement in auto theft insurance policies has made car thefts the most fully reported crime in the Unites States. Furthermore, insurance companies which paid the claim would have a strong incentive to see that the criminal was apprehended and convicted. Their pressure and assistance would make the proper functioning of law enforcement officials all the more likely.

3. Psychologist Albert Eglash has long argued that restitution would aid in the rehabilitation of criminals. "Restitution is something an inmate does, not something done for or to him. . . . Being reparative, restitution can alleviate guilt and anxiety, which can otherwise precipitate further offenses."[39]

Restitution, says Eglash, is an active effortful role on the part of the offender. It is socially constructive, thereby contributing to the offender's self-esteem. It is related to the offense and may thereby redirect the thoughts which motivated the offense. It is reparative, restorative, and may actually leave the situation better than it was before the crime, both for the criminal and victim.[40]

4. This is a genuinely "self-determinative" sentence.[41] The worker would know that the length of his confinement was in his own hands. The harder he worked, the faster he would make restitution. He would be the master of his fate and would have to face that responsibility. This would encourage useful, productive activity and instill a conception of reward for good behavior and hard work. Compare this with the current probationary system and "indeterminate sentencing" where the decision for release is made by the prison bureaucracy, based only (if fairly administered) on "good behavior"; that is, passive acquiescence to prison discipline. Also, the fact that the worker would be acquiring *marketable* skills rather than more skillful methods of crime should help to reduce the shocking rate of recidivism.

5. The savings to taxpayers would be enormous. No longer would the innocent taxpayer pay for the apprehension and internment of the guilty. The cost of arrest, trial, and internment would be borne by the criminal himself. In addition, since now-idle inmates would become productive workers (able, perhaps, to support their families), the entire economy would benefit from the increase in overall production.[42]

6. Crime would no longer pay. Criminals, particularly shrewd white-collar criminals, would know that they could not dispose of the proceeds of their crime and, if caught, simply serve time. They would have to make full restitution plus enforcement and legal costs, thereby greatly increasing the incentive to prosecute. While this would not eliminate such crime it would make it rougher on certain types of criminals, like bank and corporation officials, who harm many by their acts with a virtual assurance of lenient legal sanctions.[43] It might also encourage such criminals to keep the money around for a while so that, if caught, they could repay more easily. This would make a full recovery more likely.

A restitutional system of justice would benefit the victim, the criminal, and the taxpayer. The humanitarian goals of proportionate punishment, rehabilitation, and victim compensation are dealt with on a *fundamental* level making their achievement more likely. In short, the paradigm of restitution would benefit all but the entrenched penal bureaucracy and enhance justice at the same time. What then is there to stop us from overthrowing the paradigm of punishment and its penal system and putting in its place this more efficient, more humane, and more just system? The proponents of punishment and others have a few powerful counterarguments. It is to these we now turn.

OBJECTIONS TO RESTITUTION

1. Practical criticisms of restitution. It might be objected that "crimes disturb and offend not only those who are directly their victim, but also the whole social order."[44] Because of this, society, that is, individuals other than the victim, deserves some satisfaction from the offender. Restitution, it is argued, will not satisfy the lust for revenge felt by the victim or the "community's sense of justice." This criticism appears to be overdrawn. Today most members of the community are mere spectators of the criminal justice system, and this is largely true even of the victim.[45] One major reform being urged presently is more victim involvement in the criminal justice process.[46] The restitution proposal would necessitate this involvement. And while the public generally takes the view that officials should be tougher on criminals, with "tougher" taken by nearly everyone to mean more severe in punishing, one must view this "social fact" in light of the lack of a known alternative. The real test of public sympathies would be to see which sanction people would choose: incarceration of the criminal for a given number of years or the criminal's being compelled to make restitution to the victim: While the public's choice is not clearly predictable, neither can it be assumed that it would reject restitution.

This brings us to a second practical objection: that monetary sanctions are insufficient deterrents to crime. Again, this is something to be discovered, not something to be assumed. There are a number of reasons to believe that our *current* system of punishment does not adequately deter, and for the reasons discussed earlier an increase in the level of punishment is unlikely. In fact, many have argued that the deterrent value of sanctions has less to do with *severity* than with *certainty,*[47] and the preceding considerations indicate that law enforcement would be more certain under a restitutional system. In the final analysis, however, it is irrelevant to argue that more crimes may be committed if our proposal leaves the victim better off. It must be remembered: *Our goal is not the suppression of crime; it is doing justice to victims.*

A practical consideration which merits considerable future attention is the feasibility of the employment project proposal. A number of questions can be raised. At first blush, it seems naively optimistic to suppose that offenders will be able or willing to work at all, much less earn their keep and pay reparations as well. On the contrary, this argument continues, individuals turn to crime precisely because they lack the skills which the restitutional plan assumes they have. Even if these workers have the skills, but refuse to work, what could be done? Would not the use of force to compel compliance be tantamount to slavery? This criticism results in part from my attempt to sketch an "ideal" restitution system; that is, I have attempted to outline the type toward which every criminal justice system governed by the restitution paradigm should strive. This is not to say that every aspect of the hypothetical system would, upon implementation, function smoothly. Rather, such a system could only operate ideally once the paradigm had been fully accepted and substantially articulated.

With this in mind, one can advance several responses. First, the problem as usually posed assumes the offender to be highly irrational and possibly mentally unbalanced. There is no denying that some segment of the criminal population fits the former description.[48] What this approach neglects, however, is the possibility that many criminals are making rational choices within an irrational and unjust political system. Specifically I refer to the myriad laws and regulations which make it difficult for the unskilled or persons of transitory outlook[49] to find legal employment.[50] I refer also to the laws which deny

legality to the types of services which are in particular demand in economically impoverished communities.[51] Is it "irrational" to choose to steal or rob when one is virtually foreclosed from the legal opportunity to do otherwise? Another possibility is that the criminal chooses crime not because of foreclosure, but because he enjoys and obtains satisfaction from a criminal way of life.[52] Though morally repugnant, this is hardly irrational.

Furthermore, it no longer can be denied that contact with the current criminal justice system is itself especially damaging among juveniles.[53] The offenders who are hopelessly committed to criminal behavior are not usually the newcomers to crime but those who have had repeated exposure to the penal system. In Kuhn's words, "Existing institutions have ceased to meet the problems posed by an environment *they have in part created.*"[54] While a restitutionary system might not change these hard-core offenders, it could, by the early implementation of sanctions perceived by the criminal to be just, break the vicious circle which in large part accounts for their existence.

Finally, if offenders could not or would not make restitution, then the logical and just result of their refusal would be confinement until they could or would. Such an outcome would be entirely in their hands. While this "solution" does not suggest who should justly pay for this confinement, the problem is not unique to a restitutionary system. In this and other areas of possible difficulty we must seek guidance from existing pilot programs as well as from the burgeoning research in this area and in victimology in general.

2. *Distributionary criticisms of restitution.* There remains one criticism of restitution which is the most obvious and the most difficult with which to deal. Simply stated, it takes the following form: "Doesn't this mean that rich people will be able to commit crimes with impunity if they can afford it? Isn't this unfair?" The *practical* aspect of this objection is that whatever deterrent effect restitution payments may have, they will be less for those most able to pay. The *moral* aspect is that whatever retributive or penal effect restitution payments may have they will be less for those who are well off. Some concept of equality of justice underlies both considerations.

Critics of restitution fail to realize that the "cost" of crime will be quite high. In addition to compensation for pain and suffering, the criminal must pay for the cost of his apprehension, the cost of the trial, and the legal expenditures of *both* sides. This should make even an unscrupulous wealthy person think twice about committing a crime. The response to this is that we cannot have it both ways. If the fines would be high enough to bother the rich, then they would be so high that a project worker would have no chance of earning that much and would, therefore, have no incentive to work at all. If, on the other hand, you lower the price of crime by ignoring all its costs, you fail to deter the rich or fully compensate the victim.

This is where the option of arbitration and victim crime insurance becomes of practical importance. If the victim is uninsured, he is unlikely to recover for all costs of a very severe crime from a poor, unskilled criminal, since even in an employment project the criminal might be unable to earn enough. If he had no hope of earning his release, he would have little incentive to work very hard beyond paying for his own maintenance. The victim would end up with less than if he had "settled" the case for the lesser amount which a project worker could reasonably be expected to earn. If, however, the victim had full-coverage criminal insurance, he would recover his damages in full, and the insurance company would absorb any disparity between full compensation and maximal employment project worker's output. This cost would be reflected in premium prices, enabling the insurance company which settled cases at an amount which increased the recovery from the criminal to offer the lowest rates. Eventually a "maximum" feasible fine for project workers would be determined based on these considerations. The "rich," on the other hand, would naturally have to pay in full. This arrangement would solve the practical problem, but it should not be thought of as an imperative of the restitutional paradigm.

The same procedure of varying the payments according to ability to pay would answer the moral considerations as well (that the rich are not hurt enough) and this is the prime motive behind *punitive* restitution proposals. However, we reject the moral consideration outright. The paradigm of restitution calls not for the (equal) hurting of criminals, but for restitution to victims. Any appeal to "inadequate suffering" is a reversion to the paradigm of punishment, and by varying the sanction for crimes of the same magnitude according to the economic status of the offender it reveals its own inequity. *Equality of justice means equal treatment of victims.* It should not matter to the victim if his attacker was rich or poor. His plight is the same regardless. Any reduction of criminal liability because of reduced earning power would be for practical, not moral, reasons.

Equality of justice derives from the fact that the rights of men should be equally enforced and respected. Restitution recognizes a victim's right to compensation for damages from the party responsible. Equality of justice, therefore, calls for equal enforcement of each victim's right to restitution. *Even if necessary or expedient, any lessening of payment to the victim because of the qualities of the criminal is a violation of that victim's rights and an inequality of justice.* Any such expedient settlement is only a recognition that an imperfect world may make possible only imperfect justice. As a practical matter, a restitutional standard gives victims an enormous incentive to pursue wealthy criminals since they can afford quick, full compensation. Contrast this with the present system where the preference given the wealthy is so prevalent that most victims simply assume that nothing will be done.

The paradigm of restitution, to reiterate, is neither a panacea for crime nor a blueprint for utopia. Panaceas and utopias are not for humankind. We must live in a less than perfect world with less than perfect people. Restitution opens the possibility of an improved and more just society. The old paradigm of punishment, even reformed, simply cannot offer this promise.

OTHER CONSIDERATIONS

Space does not permit a full examination of other less fundamental implications of such a system. I shall briefly consider five.

1. Civil versus criminal liability. If one accepts a restitutionary standard of justice, what sense does it

make to distinguish between crime and tort, since both call for payment of damages? For most purposes I think the distinction collapses. Richard Epstein, in a series of brilliant articles, has articulated a theory of strict liability in tort.[55] His view is that since one party has caused another some harm and one of the parties must bear the loss, justice demands that it falls on the party who caused the harm. He argues that intention is only relevant as a "third-stage" argument; that notwithstanding some fault on the part of the plaintiff (a second-stage argument), the defendant intended the harm and is therefore liable.[56] With a restitutional system I see no reason why Epstein's theory of tort liability could not incorporate criminal liability into a single "system of corrective justice that looks to the conduct, broadly defined, of the parties to the case with a view toward the protection of individual liberty and private property."[57]

There would, at least initially, be some differences, however. The calculation of damages under the restitutionary paradigm which includes cost of apprehension, cost of trial, and legal costs of both parties would be higher than tort law allows. A further distinction would be the power of enforcers to confine unreliable offenders to employment projects.

2. Criminal responsibility and competency. Once a criminal sanction is based not on the offender's badness but on the nature and consequences of his acts, Thomas Szasz's proposal that the insanity plea be abolished makes a great deal of sense,[58] as does his argument that "all persons charged with offenses—except those grossly disabled—[are fit to stand trial and] should be tried."[59] On this view, Epstein's concept of fairness *as between the parties* is relevant. A restitution proceeding like a "lawsuit is always a comparative affair. The defendant's victory ensures the plaintiff's [or victim's] defeat. . . . Why should we prefer the injurer to his victim in a case where one may win and the other lose? . . . As a matter of fairness between the parties, the defendant should be required to treat the harms which he has inflicted upon another as though they were inflicted upon himself."[60]

3. Victimless crimes. The effect of restitutional standards on the legality of such crimes as prostitution, gambling, high interest loans, pornography,

and drug use is intriguing. There has been no violation of individual rights, and consequently no damages and, therefore, no liability. While some may see this as a drawback, I believe it is a striking advantage of the restitutional standard of justice. So-called victimless crimes would in principle cease to be crimes. As a consequence, criminal elements would be denied a lucrative monopoly, and the price of these services would be drastically reduced. Without this enormous income, organized crime would be far less able to afford the "cost" of its nefarious activities than it is today.

4. Legal positivism. What is true for victimless crimes is true for the philosophy of legal positivism. On the positivist view, whatever the state (following all the correct political procedures) says is law, is law; hence, whatever the state makes a crime is a crime. A restitutional standard would hold the state to enforcing individual rights through the recovery of individual damages.

5. Legal process. Because the sanction for crime would no longer be punitive, the criminal process could explore less formal procedures for dispute settlement. Also, the voice of the victim would be added to the deliberations. One possible reform might be a three-tiered verdict: guilty, not proven, and not guilty. If found "guilty," the offender would pay all the costs mentioned above. If the charges are "not proven," then neither party would pay the other. If found "not guilty," the defendant would be reimbursed by the enforcement agency for his costs and inconvenience. This new interpretation of "not guilty" would reward those defendants who, after putting on a defense, convinced the trier of fact that they were innocent.

These and many other fascinating implications of restitution deserve a more thorough examination. As any new paradigm becomes accepted, it experiences what Kuhn calls a period of "normal research," a period characterized by continuous expansion and perfection of the new paradigm as well as a testing of its limits. The experimentation with restitutionary justice will, however, differ from the trial and error of the recent past since we will be guided by the principle that the purpose of our legal system is not to harm the guilty but to help the innocent—a principle which will above all restore our belief that our over-riding commitment is to do justice.

NOTES

1. What immediately follows is a brief outline of Kuhn's theory. Those interested in the *defense* of that theory should refer to his book, *The Structure of Scientific Revolutions,* 2d ed., enl. (Chicago: University of Chicago Press, 1970). A paradigm is an achievement in a particular discipline which defines the legitimate problems and methods of research within that discipline. This achievement is sufficiently unprecedented to attract new adherents away from rival approaches while providing many unsolved questions for these new practitioners to solve. As the paradigm develops and matures, it reveals occasional inabilities to solve new problems and explain new data. As attempts are made to make the facts fit the paradigm, the theoretical apparatus gradually becomes bulky and awkward, like Ptolemaic astronomy. Dissatisfaction with the paradigm begins to grow. Why not simply discard the paradigm and find another which better fits the facts? Unfortunately, this is an arduous process. All the great authorities and teachers were raised with the current paradigm and see the world through it. All the texts and institutions are committed to it. Radical alternatives hold promise but are so untested as to make wary all but the bold. The establishment is loath to abandon its broad and intricate theory in favor of a new and largely unknown hypothesis. Gradually, however, as the authorities die off and the problems with the old paradigm increase, the "young turks" get a better hearing in both the journals and the classroom. In a remarkably rapid fashion, the old paradigm is discarded for the new. Anyone who still clings to it is now considered to be antiquated or eccentric and is simply read out of the profession. All research centers on the application of the new paradigm. Kuhn characterizes this overthrow of one paradigm by another as a revolution.

2. Ibid., p. 92.

3. Stanley I. Benn, "Punishment," in *The Encyclopedia of Philosophy,* ed. Paul Edwards (New York: Macmillan Publishing Co., 1967), 7:29 (emphasis added).

4. Heinrich Oppenheimer, *The Rationale of Punishment* (London: University of London Press, 1913), p. 255.

5. Ibid.

6. See Thomas Szasz, *Law, Liberty, and Psychiatry* (New York: Macmillan Co., 1963).

7. Giorgio del Vecchio, "The Struggle against Crime," in *The Philosophy of Punishment,* ed. H. B. Acton (London: Macmillan Co., 1969), p. 199.

8. See, e.g., Samuel Yochelson and Stanton E. Samenow, *The Criminal Personality,* vol. 1, *A Profile for Change* (New York: Jason Aronson, Inc., 1976), pp. 411–16.

9. Del Vecchio, p. 199.

10. Robert Nozick, *Anarchy, State, and Utopia* (New York: Basic Books, 1974), p. 61.

11. Ibid., pp. 59–63.

12. For a concise summary, see Oppenheimer, p. 31.

13. Del Vecchio, p. 198.

14. See, e.g., Walter Kaufmann, *Without Guilt and Justice* (New York: Peter H. Wyden, Inc., 1973), esp. chap. 2.

15. See, e.g., "Crime: A Case for More Punishment," *Business Week* (September 15, 1975), pp. 92–97.

16. This problem is examined, though not ultimately resolved, by Edwin M. Schur in his book *Crimes without Victims—Deviant Behavior and Public Policy, Abortion, Homosexuality, and Drug Addiction* (Englewood Cliffs, N.J.: Prentice-Hall, Inc., 1965).

17. Kaufmann, p. 46.

18. Kuhn, p. 82.

19. R. A. Childs, "Liberty and the Paradigm of Statism," in *The Libertarian Alternative,* ed. Tibor Machan (Chicago: Nelson-Hall Co., 1974), p. 505.

20. Composition was the medieval version of a restitutionary system. For a fascinating outline of how such a system operated and how it came to be supplanted by state-authored punishment, see Stephen Schafer, *Compensation and Restitution to Victims of Crime,* 2d ed., enl. (Montclair, N.J.: Patterson Smith Publishing Corp., 1970); Richard E. Laster, "Criminal Restitution: A Survey of Its Past History and an Analysis of Its Present Usefulness," *University of Richmond Law Review* 5 (1970): 71–80; L. T. Hobhouse, *Morals in Evolution* (London: Chapman & Hall, 1951).

21. Kaufmann, p. 45.

22. For a brief definition of "victimology," see Emilo C. Viano, "Victimology: The Study of the Victim," *Victimology* 1 (1976): 1–7. For an extensive collection of papers on various aspects of victimology, see Emilo C. Viano, ed., *Victims and Society* (Washington, D.C.: Visage Press, 1976).

23. For a discussion and list of symposiums, journal articles, and statutes concerning victim compensation, see Steven Schafer, pp. 139–57, and appendix; see also Joe Hudson and Burt Galaway, eds., *Considering the Victim: Readings in Restitution and Victim Compensation* (Springfield, Ill.: Charles C. Thomas, 1975), esp. pp. 361–436.

24. Gerhard O. W. Mueller, "Compensation for Victims of Crime: Thought before Action," *Minnesota Law Review* 50 (1965): 221.

25. Schafer, p. 127.

26. Ibid.

27. Herbert Spencer, "Prison-Ethics," in *Essays: Scientific, Political and Speculative* (New York: D. Appleton & Co., 1907), 3:152–91.

28. Murray N. Rothbard, *Libertarian Forum* 14, no. 1 (January 1972):7–8.

29. Kaufmann, p. 55.

30. The nature of judicial procedure best designed to carry out this task must be determined. For a brief discussion of some relevant considerations, see Laster, pp. 80–98; Burt Galaway and Joe Hudson, "Issues in the Correctional Implementation of Restitution to Victims of Crime," in *Considering the Victim,* pp. 351–60. Also to be dealt with is the proper standard of compensation. At least initially, the problem of how much payment constitutes restitution would be no different than similar considerations in tort law. This will be considered at greater length below.

31. Such a plan (with some significant differences) has been suggested by Kathleen J. Smith in *A Cure for Crime: The Case for the Self-determinate Prison Sentence* (London: Gerald, Duckworth & Co., 1965), pp. 13–29; see also Morris and Linda Tannehill, *The Market for Liberty* (Lansing, Mich.: Privately printed, 1970), pp. 44–108.

32. For a recent summary report, see Burt Galaway, "Restitution as an Integrative Punishment" (paper prepared for the Symposium on Crime and Punishment: Restitution, Retribution, and Law, Harvard Law School, March 1977).

33. John M. Greacen, "Arbitration: A Tool for Criminal Cases?" *Barrister* (Winter 1975), p. 53; see also Galaway and Hudson, pp. 352–55; "Conclusions and Recommendations, International Study Institute on Victimology, Bellagio, Italy, July 1–12, 1975," *Victimology* 1 (1976): 150–51; Ronald Goldfarb, *Jails: The Ultimate Ghetto* (Garden City, N.Y.: Anchor Press/Doubleday, 1976), p. 480.

34. Greacen, p. 53.

35. For a description of the Irish system, see Joseph R. Peden, "Property Rights in Medieval Ireland: Celtic Law versus Church and State" (paper presented at the Symposium on the Origins and Development of Property Rights, University of San Francisco, January 1973); for a theoretical discussion of a similar proposal, see Spencer, pp. 182–86.

36. Or, perhaps more accurately, the compensation itself.

37. For a brief explanation of this concept and several of its possible applications, see Murray N. Rothbard, "Justice and Property Rights," in *Property in a Humane Economy,* ed. Samuel L. Blumenfeld (La Salle, Ill.: Open Court Publishing Co., 1974), pp. 101–22.

38. That the "spiritual" satisfaction which punishment may or may not provide is to be recognized as a legitimate form of "compensation" is a claim retributionists must defend.

39. Albert Eglash, "Creative Restitution: Some Suggestions for Prison Rehabilitation Programs," *American Journal of Correction* 40 (November–December 1958): 20.

40. Ibid.; see also Eglash's "Creative Restitution: A Broader Meaning for an Old Term," *Journal of Criminal Law and Criminology* 48 (1958): 619–22; Burt Galaway and Joe Hudson, "Restitution and Rehabilitation—Some Central Issues," *Crime and Delinquency* 18 (1972): 403–10.

41. Smith, pp. 13–29.

42. An economist who favors restitution on efficiency grounds is Gary S. Becker, although he does not break with the paradigm of punishment. Those interested in a mathematical "cost-benefit" analysis should see his "Crime and Punishment," *Journal of Political Economy* 76 (1968): 169–217.

43. This point is also made by Minocher Jehangirji Sethna in his paper, "Treatment and Atonement for Crime," in *Victims and Society,* p. 538.

44. Del Vecchio, p. 198.

45. William F. McDonald, "Towards a Bicentennial Revolution in Criminal Justice: The Return of the Victim," *American Criminal Law Review* 13 (1976): 659; see also his paper "Notes on the Victim's Role in the Prosecutional and Dispositional Stages of the Criminal Justice Process" (paper presented at the Second International Symposium on Victimology, Boston, September 1976); Jack M. Kress, "The Role of the Victim at Sentencing" (paper presented at the Second International Symposium on Victimology, Boston, September 1976).

46. McDonald, pp. 669–73; Kress, pp. 11–15. Kress specifically analyzes restitution as a means for achieving victim involvement.

47. Yochelson and Samenow, pp. 453–57.

48. For a discussion rejecting the usefulness of the latter description, see Szasz, pp. 91–146; for a recent study verifying Szasz's thesis, see Yochelson and Samenow, esp. pp. 227–35.

49. Edward C. Banfield put forth his controversial theory of time horizon in his book *The Unheavenly City* (Boston: Little, Brown & Co., 1970) and amplified it in

The Unheavenly City Revisited (Boston: Little, Brown & Co., 1974), and most recently, "Present-orientedness and Crime" (paper prepared for the Symposium on Crime and Punishment: Restitution, Retribution, and Law, Harvard Law School, March 1977). For a critical, but favorable analysis of this approach, see Gerald P. O'Driscoll, Jr., "Professor Banfield on Time Horizon: What Has He Taught Us about Crime?" (paper prepared for the same symposium). A contrary, but ultimately compatible view is presented by Yochelson and Samenow, pp. 369–72.

50. For example, minimum wage laws, and so-called closed-shop union protectionist legislation.

51. For example, laws prohibiting gambling, prostitution, sale of drugs, "jitney" cab services, etc.

52. "It is not the environment that turns a man into a criminal. Rather it is a series of choices that he makes at a very early age. . . . [T]he criminal is not a victim of circumstances" (Yochelson and Samenow, pp. 247, 249). This is in essence the main conclusion of their research. (For a concise summary of their provocative book, see Joseph Boorkin, "The Criminal Personality," *Federal Bar Journal* 35 [1976]: 237–41.) In *The Criminal Personality,* vol. 2, *The Process of Change* (New York: Jason Aronson,

Inc., 1977) they relate and examine the methods they have employed to change the criminal thought pattern. Of course, such an approach can itself be subject to abuse.

53. See, e.g., Edwin M. Schur, *Radical Noninterventionism, Rethinking the Delinquency Problem* (Englewood Cliffs, N.J.: Prentice-Hall, Inc., 1973).

54. Kuhn, p. 92 (emphasis added).

55. Richard A. Epstein, "A Theory of Strict Liability in Tort," *Journal of Legal Studies* 2 (1973): 151–204.

56. Richard A. Epstein, "Intentional Harms," *Journal of Legal Studies* 3 (1975): 402–8; see also his article "Defenses and Subsequent Pleas in a System of Strict Liability," ibid., 3 (1974): 174–85.

57. Epstein, "Intentional Harms," p. 441.

58. Szasz, pp. 228–30.

59. Ibid., pp. 228–29. "The emphasis here is on gross disability: it should be readily apparent or easily explicable to a group of lay persons, like a jury" (p. 229). But even the qualification of gross disablement might be unjustified (see Yochelson and Samenow, pp. 227–35).

60. Epstein, p. 398. In his article "Crime and Tort: Old Wine in Old Bottles," he takes exactly this approach with the insanity defense in tort law.

Critics

Franklin G. Miller

Restitution and Punishment

A Reply to Barnett

Randy E. Barnett argues in a recent article, "Restitution: A New Paradigm of Criminal Justice,"[1] that traditional modes of punishment for criminal offenses should be abandoned. No longer should offenders be sentenced to prison or ordered to pay a fine to the state. Rather, they should be compelled to compensate their victims for the injuries or damages suffered as a result of the crime. In other words, Barnett proposes to substitute the "paradigm" of restitution for that of punishment.

Barnett rejects punishment on the grounds that none of the standard goals or reasons—deterrence, retribution, and rehabilitation—adequately justifies the practice of punishment. Against the rationale of deterrence, for example, he advances the familiar argument that a system devoted solely to deterrence would fail to be a system of criminal *justice*. For it would permit or require the "punishing" of the innocent if that would in fact deter crime. Barnett apparently believes that he can refute the paradigm of pun-

Franklin G. Miller, "Restitution and Punishment: A Reply to Barnett," *Ethics* 88 (1978): 358–60. Reprinted by permission of University of Chicago Press.

ishment by pointing out the grave difficulties involved in making deterrence, retribution, or rehabilitation the single overriding goal of a system of criminal justice. But this is mistaken. The argument rests on the dubious assumption that the institution of punishment can be justified, if at all, only by reference to a *single* fundamental rationale.[2] Barnett ignores the complexity of the problem of punishment. In performing a set of different though interconnected functions, a system of criminal justice should pursue a plurality of goals, none of which is allowed free reign. For instance, the goal of deterring crime must be coordinated with the imperative of just allocation of punishment. Although theories of pure deterrence or retribution or rehabilitation are unsatisfactory, a complex theory of punishment, combining deterrent, retributive, rehabilitative, *and* restitutive elements at appropriate points, might offer a satisfactory justification of punishment.

Barnett's argument against punishment is deficient not only because it fails to consider complex theories of punishment. It neglects an important aspect of punishment that bears upon its justification. The act of punishment constitutes symbolic condemnation of the offender for his offense. As such it serves to uphold and enforce collective moral norms violated by the criminal.[3] Before we choose to reject the paradigm of punishment in favor of the paradigm of restitution, we need to consider what might be lost as a result. Could a system of *pure* restitution preserve this condemnatory aspect of punishment? If not, is this something that we should be willing to give up? Even the civil law, dedicated to the purpose of compensating victims for harm intentionally or negligently caused by others, allows for *punitive* damages in some cases.

Barnett's theory of pure restitution raises some practical problems as well. Since the goal of a system of criminal justice should be to compensate victims of crimes rather than to punish offenders, the idea of crime as an offense against society has no place in Barnett's theory: "A restitutional standard would hold the state to enforcing individual rights through the recovery of individual damages."[4] A

variety of acts that our legal system regards as criminal could not be accounted for on the premise that the sole purpose of a system of criminal justice is to enforce *individual* rights by requiring restitution. Many crimes do not involve individual victims. Barnett considers it a virtue of his paradigm that "victimless" activities such as prostitution, pornography, gambling, and drug use would not be made criminal.

Fortunately there is no need to broach this difficult issue here, for there are less controversial crimes that cannot be easily adapted to Barnett's theory. (1) Cruelty to animals. Suppose a person, living in the country, delights in capturing wild deer and torturing them. Unless we are willing to consider deer as individual persons possessing legal rights, there can be no crime in this behavior under Barnett's restitutional paradigm. Moreover, to whom should restitution be paid? (2) Harm to public institutions. The criminal law prohibits tax evasion, bribery, obstruction of justice, and damage to public property. The rights of private persons are not necessarily violated by instances of such conduct. A system of restitution might provide for compensation payable to the state, but this would conflict with the individualistic focus of Barnett's paradigm. (3) Attempts. Attempted crimes may not cause any harm to particular individuals. For example, a terrorist is apprehended planting a bomb in the men's room of an office building. Whose individual rights has the terrorist violated? Restitution to the owner of the building merely for trespass would be far out of proportion to the gravity of the act. (4) Reckless driving and driving under the influence of alcohol. On what grounds could persons be prosecuted for such acts if no tangible harm is caused to others? What restitution would be appropriate? Other cases could be mentioned, but this list suffices to indicate the practical difficulties of Barnett's theory of restitution. If we do not wish to give up such crimes, then we cannot accept a paradigm of pure restitution.

Barnett makes a strong case for the merits of restitution. Punishment as practiced today does have serious defects, some of which might be remedied by provisions for restitution. It remains to be shown, however, that punishment should be abandoned in favor of a new paradigm of restitution.

NOTES

1. Randy E. Barnett, "Restitution: A New Paradigm of Criminal Justice," *Ethics* 87, no. 4 (1977): 279–301.

2. Cf. H. L. A. Hart, *Punishment and Responsibility* (New York: Oxford University Press, 1968), p. 3.

3. For the classical statement of this perspective see Émile Durkheim, *The Division of Labor in Society,* trans. George Simpson (New York: Free Press, 1964), chap. 2. See also Joel Feinberg, "The Expressive Function of Punishment," in *Doing and Deserving* (Princeton, N.J.: Princeton University Press, 1970), pp. 95–118.

4. Barnett, p. 301.

Roger Pilon

Criminal Remedies

Restitution, Punishment, or Both?

. . . To be sure, Barnett has correctly shifted our focus, for criminal acts of the kind under consideration do involve harms to victims—hence our first concern ought to be to make victims whole again. But is that all they involve? Are we really to treat, by way of remedy, my accidentally hitting you with my automobile and my intentionally hitting you with a club as acts of the same kind? Is the *mens rea* element to be allowed *no* place in the calculation? Even if we include in the compensation due the victim all that Barnett believes we should—special damages, including the costs of apprehension, trial, and legal fees for both sides, and general damages, including pain and suffering (p. 298)—there still remains a crucial element that these considerations do not touch. For thus far the compensation is identical with that ideally due the victim in a simple civil action.

Nowhere are these misgivings and this missing element brought out more sharply—if misleadingly, about which more in a moment—than in cases involving wealthy principals. Barnett considers and then elides but one of the variations, that of the wealthy criminal (p. 297). There is also the case of the wealthy victim and, perhaps of most interest, the case in which both the criminal and the victim are wealthy. However uncommon these three variations may be in the larger world of criminal activity (but perhaps they are not so uncommon), they are of interest because they bring clearly into focus the *mens rea* element omitted from Barnett's account, an element present in *all* criminal transactions but captured most poignantly here. What, really, does the wealthy criminal care about having to compensate his victim? Or the wealthy victim about receiving compensation? If a rich man rapes a rich woman, are we really to suppose that monetary damages will restore the status quo, will satisfy the claims of justice? A wealthy child molester will treat compensation simply as the price of pleasure! And what of the terrorist who murders, knowing that his wealthy backer will settle the account? The reduction of criminal wrongs to civil wrongs, in short, or at least

From Roger Pilon, "Criminal Remedies: Restitution, Punishment, or Both?" *Ethics* 88 (1978): 348–57. Notes and some parts of the text have been deleted. Reprinted by permission of University of Chicago Press.

the addressing of criminal wrongs with civil remedies, bespeaks an all too primitive view of what in fact is at issue in the matter of crime.

For all their heuristic value, however, we must not let examples such as these confuse the issue. It is not, as they may have suggested, that the requirement to compensate the victim does not make the criminal suffer if he is wealthy (as it seems to when he is not wealthy), for that would conflate the different purposes of punishment and compensation: thus, raising the compensation to fit the criminal will not only continue to miss the point but will produce this conflation as well. Rather, it is simply that the civil remedy by itself is altogether inadequate in the case of criminal acts. For the element missing from the mere tort but present in the criminal act is the guilty mind. The criminal has not simply harmed you. *He has affronted your dignity.* He has *intentionally* used you, against your will, for his own ends. He cannot simply pay damages as though his action were accidental or unintentional. How would this right the wrong? Using even Barnett's criterion for determining the obligation now owing, how would compensation make the victim whole again? For compensation does not reach the whole of what is involved—it does not reach the *mens rea* element. There is simply no amount of money that will rectify certain kinds of wrongs. The criminal act and the mere tort are of altogether different magnitudes; they are different categories of action, calling for different remedies.

Indeed, the criminal act calls not only for compensation but for punishment as well. . . .

We look at the original act to determine what form [. . .] the remedy should take. That act involved a violation of the victim's dignity; the criminal intentionally used the victim for his own ends, and against the victim's will. In so doing, the criminal alienated his own right against being similarly treated by the victim (or by anyone else acting on behalf of the victim), just as the tort-feasor alienates his right to that amount of his property necessary to right the wrongs he has caused. Notice that here, the problem of reflecting in the form of the remedy the mental character of the original act does not arise as it does in torts, for here we have an intentional wrong, capable of being mirrored in the remedy. The original act thus creates a right in the victim (or his surrogate) to use the criminal as he himself was used. Only so will the parties be treated as equals. For only so will the *character* of the original act be reflected in the remedy. Money damages simply do not do this. It is the *using* of one person by another—this affront to the victim's dignity or integrity—that must be captured in the criminal remedy. Thus the victim's treatment of the criminal is equal in character to the treatment he himself suffered. (Again, I leave open the question of what specifically constitutes equal treatment, just as I left open the criterion for measuring tort losses. These questions, especially the latter, involve a theory of value, which is beyond my present scope. . . .

Stanley S. Kleinberg | # Criminal Justice and Private Enterprise

. . . If we address ourselves only to crimes which undoubtedly have individual victims (e.g., a violent assault on a child in a public park) it is clear that the upset is not confined to the victim and his immediate family. Barnett is aware of this but treats community reaction as "lust for revenge" and thus not to be taken too seriously. But the upset is not identical with a vindictive desire to see the child's assailant suffer. What about the apprehension of parents of other children in the vicinity and the inconvenience

---

From Stanley S. Kleinberg, "Criminal Justice and Private Enterprise," *Ethics* 90 (1980): 270–82. Some notes and some parts of the text have been deleted. Reprinted by permission of University of Chicago Press.

caused by the fact that they can no longer safely allow their children to play in the park? Whether they have the right to expect the state to take action against the criminal, supposing that, for example, the child's parents do not wish to involve themselves in legal action, is not in my view a difficult moral issue. All that needs to be claimed against Barnett, however, is that criminals do offend against society, not just against their victims.[1] . . .

Apart from being wealthy, an additional source of advantage for a defendant would lie in being a professional criminal. Barnett says that crime would not pay, but clearly this only applies if the criminal is apprehended. A professional, I suggest, is confident of escaping detection in a certain proportion of his crimes. In case he should be apprehended, he would retain the gains of each crime until he judged that crime no longer to be under active investigation. If

his calculations go astray so that it looks as if he may face the possibility of being required to pay more than he has available, he can endeavor to commit some profitable crimes while awaiting trial. Alternatively, a fellow professional may be prepared to advance him the money in return for participation in some future crime. I conclude that in Barnett's system wealth and criminal professionalism, especially in combination, would confer a great advantage on any defendant. . . .

NOTE

1. There is not space to discuss Barnett's position on victimless crimes. It should be noted, however, that he appears to favor the legalization of all proscribed victimless acts, including unsuccessful criminal attempts and reckless conduct.

27

Is a Government Ban on Tobacco Wrong?

Goodin and His Critics

Most States pass laws to prevent activities that expose someone to a risk of significant harm to health or life or liberty—for example, laws against drinking and driving, or against the manufacture and sale of dangerous toys, or against the ownership and use of dangerous weapons. But many activities that expose people to comparable risks of harm are not outlawed—like drinking to excess, rock climbing, playing rugby, and smoking tobacco. The difference seems to be that the former activities pose a risk to others who are not engaging in them, whereas the latter pose a direct danger primarily to those who do engage in them. Some activities that pose a threat only to the participant may be outlawed for children, who cannot be assumed to know what they are getting into or to be freely consenting. But there is a strong presumption in the liberal political tradition that the State has no business passing *paternalistic laws*—laws that forbid knowledgeable and consenting adults from engaging in activities simply because those activities pose a significant risk of harm to the adult engaging in it. And this is presumably because we value *autonomy,* or *freedom.* The underlying idea is that it is the State's business to protect each person's sphere of freedom both from intrusions by the State itself and by others. Restricting a person's freedom in order to prevent him from harming himself is not permissible. Laws curtailing the freedom of children, who cannot be assumed to be engaging in the activity with full knowledge of the risks involved, may be justified. But comparable laws for adults are not.

In his famous essay *On Liberty*, the nineteenth-century philosopher John Stuart Mill gave expression to this view in what has become the most cited paragraph on this topic:

> The only purpose for which power can be rightfully exercised over any member of a civilised community, against his will, is to prevent harm to others. His own good, either physical or moral, is not a sufficient warrant. He cannot rightfully be compelled to do or forbear because it will be better for him to do so, because it will make him happier, because, in the opinions of others, to do so would be wise, or even right. These are good reasons for remonstrating with him,

or reasoning with him, or persuading him, or entreating him, but not for compelling him, or visiting him with any evil in case he do otherwise. . . . The only part of the conduct of any one, for which he is amenable to society, is that which concerns others. In the part which merely concerns himself, his independence is, of right, absolute. Over himself, over his own body and mind, the individual is sovereign.

Parents are sometimes justified in preventing their children from doing things that they know would harm the children. This is paternalism, but it is a justified paternalism. Mill's point is that the State cannot legitimately treat its adult members as a parent treats a child. We could call this *Mill's anti-paternalistic principle:* The State cannot legitimately forbid somebody from doing something *simply* on the grounds that in so doing he would run the risk of harming himself. The question in this chapter is whether anti-smoking laws violate Mill's anti-paternalistic principle.

Clearly some anti-smoking laws are motivated not by paternalism, but by the fact that smoking can be harmful to others. For example, in Boulder, Colorado, smoking is not permitted in any restaurant or bar, and such laws are justified by the risks that second-hand smoke poses to non-smokers. But not even in Boulder does the city council try to stop people from smoking in their own homes, even though smokers risk harm to themselves that is at least as great as the risk to which they expose non-smokers. One way of justifying this differential treatment is by appealing to the value we place on freedom. We might construct the following argument, which makes explicit the conditions under which Mill's anti-paternalistic principle applies (that is, the *knowledge condition* and the *voluntariness condition*).

P1 The State may not prevent a knowledgeable adult from voluntarily engaging in some activity on the grounds that it poses a risk of harm to himself but none to others (Mill's anti-paternalistic principle).

P2 Smoking in private is an activity that does not pose any risk to others.

P3 Adult smokers know the risks of smoking (*knowledge condition*).

P4 Adult smokers voluntarily engage in smoking (*voluntariness condition*).

C   The State may not prevent adult smokers from smoking in private.

The argument is valid; if the premises are accepted, then one must also accept the conclusion. In the extract from his book *No Smoking,* Robert Goodin agrees with Mill's anti-paternalistic principle, but argues that the State is nevertheless justified in heavily controlling the supply and consumption of tobacco by discouraging its use and even making it illegal. Goodin does this by challenging the truth of both the third and fourth premises of this argument.

Goodin claims that premise 3 is false. Despite the fact that reliable information about the risks of smoking is widely available, smokers irrationally underestimate those risks. Goodin argues that when it comes to smoking, smokers suffer from various cognitive defects. He also argues that the fourth premise is false. Nicotine is well known to be an addictive substance, and once a person is strongly addicted to a substance, it is not obvious that he is ingesting it "voluntarily." Addiction undercuts freedom. Goodin argues that nicotine addicts are not freely smoking. Hence the argument fails for two reasons.

This is not yet an argument *for* State intervention. If the harms of smoking were trivial, for example, then the fact that adult smokers were smoking in ignorance or were doing so not fully voluntarily, would not be grounds for the State to intervene. But Goodin espouses another principle: If the harms of an activity are "far reaching, potentially dangerous and irreversible," then, given that *either* the knowledge *or* the voluntariness conditions are violated, the State may intervene to discourage or prevent the activity. (Compare this with the State's requiring the use of seat belts, a law that is also presumably intended to stop people from exposing themselves to risks, and is presumably justified because people generally underestimate the risks involved. There is no doubt that people voluntarily refrain from putting on their seat belts, but there is a question about whether, when they do so, they know all the risks.)

Goodin's second kind of argument for State control of tobacco extends to a range of substances. Goodin claims that being addicted is, in and of itself, a very bad state for anyone to be in or to get into. Being addicted to something is *intrinsically* bad. The reason that being addicted is bad is that being free, or autonomous, is *good.* The point of Mill's principle is to protect people's autonomy or freedom, and the State must protect, not undermine, such autonomy. Now, if addiction compromises autonomy, then the State has a legitimate role in discouraging people from becoming addicted in the first place. And it can do this by controlling the supply and consumption of addictive substances such as nicotine, heroin, morphine and alcohol.

In his response to Goodin, Daniel Shapiro challenges Goodin's first argument for State intervention. First, he considers the information presented by Goodin to support the claim that smokers have severe cognitive defects when it comes to smoking and finds that information wanting. There are alternative interpretations of their behavior—for example, that smokers are less risk averse than non-smokers. Second, he considers Goodin's claim that nicotine is so addictive that, once hooked on it, a smoker cannot be said to be smoking voluntarily anymore. According to Shapiro, this claim is incompatible with the actual success rate for smokers who try to quit.

Goodin's second argument for State regulation takes as one of its main premises that addiction is intrinsically bad, whatever the particular nature of the addiction, because freedom is intrinsically good. This is certainly a widespread view. In his article "Addiction and the Value of Freedom," Graham Oddie investigates Goodin's third argument. He first gives an analysis of addiction and then goes on to ask what one has to assume about the value of freedom to justify the view that being addicted is *intrinsically* bad. Everyone concedes that being addicted to something that causes severe health problems (tobacco, for example) is bad for the addict. Its badness is dependent on the badness of the ill health that results. But that is not the claim behind Goodin's second argument. Rather, Goodin claims that being addicted is bad *in itself,* independently of any of the bad consequences a particular addiction might induce. Oddie presents two theses about the value of freedom that might deliver the result that being addicted is bad in itself. One delivers the result unproblematically but is highly implausible. The other delivers the result only given the extra assumption that being addicted is worse, in itself, than not being addicted. But this begs the question at issue. Oddie concludes that there is no good reason to hold that being addicted is bad in itself, and so Goodin's addiction argument fails.

This does not mean that the State should *not* control tobacco. Addiction to tobacco may be one of those bad addictions (bad not just by virtue of being additive, but because of the harms that its extensive consumption causes). But Goodin's second argument would establish not only State control of tobacco, but State banning of the use of all addictive substances, and more generally, all addictive activities.

QUESTIONS FOR CONSIDERATION

• Consider activities that pose a risk of harm to the person engaging in them, for example, not wearing a seat belt or motorcycle (or bike, or ski) helmet, drinking alcohol, smoking marijuana, injecting heroin, rock climbing, listening to loud rock music, skiing, playing rugby, viewing pornography. Some of these are the subjects of State regulation and others are not. Is there a principled difference between those that are and those that are not?

• Does Mill's principle entail that the State has no business regulating any of these? What should we say about the bad effects some of these activities have on third parties? (For example, those who do not wear seatbelts and are then involved in an accident are more likely to use up hospital beds that would otherwise be free. They also put their loved ones at risk of distress and unhappiness. Is this what legitimates a mandatory seat-belt law? If so, is there any reasonable analogy with smoking and rock climbing?)

• Under what circumstances is it legitimate for the State to regulate an addictive substance? What about addictive *activities* that are not substance related? For example, many hold that a large amount of exercise can be addictive for reasons that are physiologically connected to the addictiveness of substances—the production of pleasure-inducing endorphins in the brain. If exercising over many hours turn out to be addictive in this way, should the State regulate it?

• What do you think is the value of freedom? Is freedom valuable because free people more often get what they want? Or is freedom valuable? For reasons having nothing to do with the consequences of having it?

• If the satisfaction of desires is what is really valuable, then what about satisfying the addict's desires? Why should the addict's desires be singled out for special censure?

• Is Goodin's account of addiction—"being defined in terms of a desire to quit coupled with an inability to quit"—correct? Can someone who is addicted have no desire to quit? Would it nevertheless always be better if he did?

FURTHER READING

Gideon, Yaffe. "Recent Work on Addiction and Responsible Agency." *Philosophy and Public Affairs* 30, no. 2 (2001): 178–221.

Robert Goodin | No Smoking

The first and most obvious reason we may have for wanting to restrict smoking is to prevent harms that would be done to smokers themselves by their smoking. . . .

Of course, Mill and his followers would query whether "his own good, either physical or moral" is ever "sufficient warrant" for coercively interfering with a person's own behavior. But they would be the first to concede that it might be, if the behavior is not fully voluntary. If it is autonomy that we are trying to protect in opposing paternalistic legislation in general, then the same values that lead us to oppose such legislation in general will lead us to welcome it in those particular cases where what we are being protected from is something that would deprive us of the capacity for autonomous choice. Evidence of the addictiveness of nicotine, surveyed in section 2.2, suggests that even advocates of personal autonomy ought to favor smoking restrictions on those grounds. . . .

2.1 WHAT ARE THE RISKS?

Folk wisdom has long held tobacco smoking to be unhealthy. During the first outbreak of the smoking epidemic in the seventeenth century, the authorities tried to outlaw it on grounds of public health (Harrison 1986, p. 555). From the earliest days of our own century, cigarettes have been popularly known as "coffin nails," everyone's grandmother warned that they would stunt your growth, and so on.

Proper medical evidence scientifically supporting such suspicions began mushrooming in the 1950s and culminated in the justly famous reports of the Royal College of Physicians of 1962 and of the U.S. surgeon general two years later. The subsequent sci-

entific literature on smoking and health—now numbering over 50,000 studies (U.S. Department of Health and Human Services [DHHS] 1986, p. vii)—has merely served to reinforce those earlier fears. . . .

In a way, though, further reading is not really necessary. The basic findings are familiar enough already. Smoking leads to cancer (especially of the lung and respiratory tract, but also of the pancreas and bladder) and to cardiovascular diseases (particularly coronary heart disease, but also peripheral vascular disease) and is the major cause of chronic obstructive lung disease.

If the basic findings are familiar, the magnitude of the effects can still shock. To say that smoking is responsible for more than 350,000 deaths per year in the United States is to say that about 15 percent of all deaths in the United States are smoking-related (U.S. DHHS 1986, pp. vii, 5–6). Put in more personal terms, "about a quarter of the young men who smoke a pack a day or so of cigarettes are killed before their time by smoking"; and "on average . . . [they] have lost ten to fifteen years of life" (Peto 1980, p. 45).

Another way of putting the point is in terms of age-adjusted mortality rates. Of course, the older you are the more likely you are to die over the course of the next year. But factoring out age considerations, the point remains that at any given age smokers are 68 percent more likely to die over the course of the next year than are nonsmokers; and age-adjusted mortality rates for heavy smokers are about double that. In terms of such age-adjusted mortality rates, a moderate smoker's chances of dying from lung cancer are 10.8 times greater than a non-smoker's; of bronchitis or emphysema, 6.1 times greater; of cancer of the larynx, 5.4 times greater; or oral cancer, 4.1 times greater; of cancer of the esophagus, 3.4 times greater; of coronary artery disease or other heart diseases, 1.7 times greater; and so on down the list (U.S. DHEW 1964, p. 29). . . .

The evidence underlying these medical conclusions is largely epidemiological in character. They rest on analysis of statistical aggregates rather than on analysis of the aetiology of particular cases. What these studies show is simply that, in the population as a whole, smokers contract those various diseases many times more often than nonsmokers; and heavy smokers contract them much more often than light smokers. These differential rates of illness are much too large to be put down to mere chance. They seem to vary, in lagged fashion, with changes in the aggregate consumption of tobacco over time. And so on. . . .

Statistical purists and tobacco apologists will nonetheless insist that the case is still "not proven" because the findings are "merely statistical" (R. J. Reynolds 1986; Burch 1978; Eysenck 1980, 1986). It pays to consider carefully what other causal paths are being contemplated when they say that. In an early letter to the *British Medical Journal,* the distinguished statistician and geneticist, Sir Ronald Fisher, identified two alternative possibilities. One is that we have the causal arrow backward and that incipient cancer is what causes people to smoke rather than vice versa. So far as I can tell, nobody has taken this possibility sufficiently seriously to investigate it properly.

The other, more worrying possibility is multicolinearity. That is simply to say that there might be some common cause that leads both to smoking and to cancer, thus rendering any apparent connection between the two wholly spurious. The textbook example of multicolinearity is that the price of rum in Havana correlates tightly with the wages of Boston preachers—not because the holy men drink up all their extra wages, thus driving up the price of rum, but, rather, because changes in the state of the world economy drive up both prices and wages. Something similar may be going on in the link between smoking and cancer, Fisher fears.

There are, of course, a great many confounding factors involved in the relationship between smoking and lung cancer. Most of them (such as social class and workplace exposure to carcinogens) can be controlled statistically; and when they are, the relationship between smoking and cancer still remains significant. The most worrying possibilities are ones that are hard to control statistically. Primary among them is the possibility that an individual's genetic constitution causes both his smoking and his cancer, either directly or indirectly, through its influence on personality.

The best test of this "genetic constitutional hypothesis" would come through a comparison of smoking and lung cancer rates among monozygotic and dizygotic twins. The former share the same genetic constitution; the latter do not, but they do presumably share much the same environment as their fraternal twins. Early studies suggested that the former were indeed significantly more alike—both in their smoking behavior and in their cancer history—than the latter. That finding lent credence to the hypothesis that there is no direct link between people's smoking and their lung cancer but, rather, that there is some third factor (their genes) that causes both. Those early studies were beset by a number of methodological problems, however (U.S. DHEW 1964, p. 190; Slade et al. 1986–87). The findings of the latest and most thorough analysis of the most comprehensive collection of twin data—the Swedish Twin Register—"speak strongly against this [genetic] constitutional hypothesis" (Cederlof, Friberg, and Lundman 1977, p. 115). . . .

Certainly carcinogens merely "trigger" tumors in those who are genetically predisposed, so not everyone is necessarily at equal risk from smoking. There may even be both "genetic constitutional" and genuinely "causal" factors linking smoking and cancer (Burch 1978). Advocates of curbs on smoking can concede all that without cost. Their case goes through perfectly well, just so long as: a sufficiently large proportion of the population is genetically vulnerable; among them, smoking makes a sufficiently large contribution in causing their cancers; and there is no way, technically or politically, to target truly effective antismoking policies only at those who are genetically at risk. Given the likelihood of each (indeed, of all) of these conditions being satisfied, antismoking policies can nonetheless be defended as important contributions to public health.[1] . . .

2.2 DO SMOKERS VOLUNTARILY ACCEPT THE RISKS?

Given what we know of the health risks from smoking, we may well be tempted to "ban cigarette manufacturers from continuing to manufacture their product on the grounds that we are preventing them from causing illness to others in the same way that we prevent other manufacturers from releasing pollutants into the atmosphere, thereby causing danger to members of the community." That would be to move too quickly, though. For as Dworkin (1972/1983, p. 22) goes on to say, "The difference is . . . that in the former but not the latter case the harm is of such a nature that it could be avoided by those individuals affected, if they so chose. The incurring of the harm requires the active cooperation of the victim. It would be a mistake in theory and hypocritical in practice to assert that our interference in such cases is just like our interference in standard cases of protecting others from harm." . . .

Certainly there is, morally speaking, a world of difference between the harms that others inflict upon you and the harms that you inflict upon yourself. The question is simply whether, in the case of smoking, the active cooperation of the smoker really is such as to constitute voluntary acceptance of the consequent risks of illness and death. The question is decomposable into two further ones. The first, discussed in section 2.2.1, concerns the question of whether smokers know the risks. The second, discussed in section 2.2.2, concerns the question of whether, even if smoking in full knowledge of the risks, they could be said to "accept" the risks in a sense that is fully voluntary.

2.2.1 Do Smokers Know the Risks?

Here we are involved, essentially, with a question of "informed consent." People can be held to have consented only if they knew to what they were supposedly consenting. In the personalized context of medical encounters, this means that each and every person being treated is told, in terms he understands, by the attending physician what the risks of the treatment might be (Gorovitz 1982, chap. 3). For largely anonymous transactions in the market, such personalized standards are inappropriate. Instead, we are forced to infer consent from what people know or should have known (in the standard legal construct, what a "reasonable man" should have been expected to know) about the product. And in the anonymous world of the market, printed warnings necessarily take the place of face-to-face admonitions.

Cigarette manufacturers, in defending against product liability suits, have claimed on both these grounds that smokers should be construed as having consented to whatever risks that they have run. They claim, first, that any "reasonable" person should have known—and that the "ordinary consumer" did indeed know—that smoking was an "inherently dangerous" activity. Their interrogatories (pretrial questions put to the plaintiff before a case comes to trial) constantly seek to establish that plaintiffs had in their youth consorted with people calling cigarettes "coffin nails," and so on.

Of course, claiming that any reasonable person should have known smoking was unhealthy sits uneasily with the same corporations' claims—often in the very same litigation—that there is no evidence that smoking causes cancer, either in general or in the plaintiffs' particular cases. Caught in this inconsistency, one tobacco company recently withdrew any claims as to the plaintiff's negligence, lest it be required to answer interrogatories stating exactly what any "reasonable person" should have known about the dangers of its products.

Cigarette manufacturers have a fallback position here, though. They claim, second, that the printing of government-mandated health warnings on cigarette packets from 1966 onward has constituted further, explicit warning to users of the dangers of the products. The question, recall, is whether consumers were warned of the risks, not who warned them or why. So the fact that the health warnings were required by the Congress rather than printed voluntarily by manufacturers does nothing to undercut their value for this purpose. Indeed, according to the current run of court opinions, that might actually enhance the value of such warnings in deflecting tort liability suits.

Not only are those government health warnings printed on cigarette packets useful in defending companies against claims for harms that were inflicted at some time after 1966, when they first appeared, but tobacco company lawyers defending against product liability suits have even tried to use post-1966 behavior to infer "hypothetical consent" to risks before the warnings were given. As one company attorney argued in *Cipollone v. Liggett Group,* "because Rose Cipollone continued to smoke for at least 15 years while warnings were on every pack she bought, she would have smoked before January 1, 1966, even if the defendants had voluntarily warned her about possible health consequences" (quoted in Mintz 1988). Now, there may be certain circumstances in which hypothetical consent can be a convincing argument—some such logic must be what justifies the physician in cutting open the comatose patient in the emergency room, for example. This case does not seem to be among them, though. What we have here is more like an amateur boxer mugging you, on the grounds that since you belong to the same boxing club you obviously would have agreed to fight him if he had only asked. It takes actual, not merely hypothetical, consent to defend against a charge of assault and battery. Likewise, I would argue, in the case of the tobacco companies. That the companies should try to run the argument at all is indicative, however, of the hopes that they are pinning on printed warnings to relieve them of legal liability.

In the best of circumstances, warnings—whether from government or grandmother—will only get us so far. There are some risks of which smokers have historically never been warned by either government or grandmother. Among them are things like Buerger's disease, a circulatory condition induced in often quite young people by smoking, that can result in amputation of limbs.[1]

Furthermore, the warnings of both folk wisdom and cigarette packets, in the 1960s and 1970s at least, were desperately nonspecific. A more general question therefore arises: are all-purpose warnings that "X is hazardous to your health," without speci-

fying just how likely *X* is to cause just what sorts of harms, adequate warning to secure people's informed consent, at all? Certainly the psychological evidence suggests that an explicit, concrete message is a better spur to action than a vague, abstract one (Borgida and Nisbett 1977).

Problems of nonspecific warnings are not peculiar to cigarettes, of course. In principle, they might be as much of a problem with lawn mowers and insecticides. In practice, though, warnings there tend to be stated more strongly: they tend to say that certain bad things *will* happen to you if the product is misused (e.g., you will be poisoned), not just that they *may* (i.e., not just that the product "is dangerous to your health"); they mention death explicitly (often employing the conventional skull-and-crossbones symbol on the label); they suggest specific antidotes; and so on. All those factors make those warnings more successful at what warnings are supposed to do—convey a real sense of the seriousness of the hazard—than do the sorts of milquetoast warnings traditionally carried on cigarette packets.

There is a fair bit of evidence that smokers—especially young smokers—simply do not read what appears inside the surgeon general's boxed warning on cigarette packets and advertisements. One study, for example, monitored eye tracking of adolescents viewing tobacco advertisements and found that almost half of them did not cast eyes on the warning at all; when subsequently asked to identify, from the surgeon general's rotating list of warnings, which it was that appeared in the advertisement they had seen subjects did only slightly better than random. Warnings that are not—and perhaps are designed not to be—read cannot possibly be effective. The evidence suggests that tobacco health warnings fall largely into that category.

As important, cigarette manufacturers take back through their advertising what is given, inside the surgeon general's boxed notice, by way of warnings (White 1988, chap. 6). There are various examples. Admonitions that "smoking is dangerous to your health," when conjoined with pictures of people enjoying dangerous sports (white water rafting, and the like), perversely serve to make smoking more attractive. Warnings that "smoking by pregnant women may result in fetal injury, premature birth, and low birth weight," when conjoined with sexually provocative photos in magazines devoted to casual sex without procreation, again perversely undercut the health message. Perhaps most important of all, advertising that appeals to the rebelliousness of youth in general and young women and young blacks in particular (the "You've come a long way, baby" campaign, e.g.) constitutes a thinly veiled invitation for them to ignore the advice of authorities. Particularly striking, in this connection, was a 1983 billboard campaign in Britain employing the caption, "We're not allowed to tell you anything about Winston cigarettes, so here's a man blowing a raspberry" (Chapman 1986, p. 16). . . .

The point being made here is not that advertising bypasses consumers' capacity to reason, and somehow renders them unfree to choose intelligently whether or not to partake of the product. No one is saying that consumers of tobacco are brainwashed to quite that extent. The central point here is merely that the tobacco companies in effect are giving out— and, more important, consumers are receiving— conflicting information. The implicit health claims of the advertising imagery conflict with the explicit health warnings, and thus undercut any *volenti* or informed consent defense companies might try to mount on the basis of those warnings (Edell and Gisser 1985).

2.2.2 Is Acceptance of the Risks Fully Voluntary?

Obviously, people cannot voluntarily accept the health risks of smoking if they do not know what they are. Despite tobacco companies' best efforts, though, the great majority of people—smokers included—knows, in broad outline, what health risks smoking entails. In a 1978 Gallup poll, only 24 percent of even heavy smokers claimed that they were unaware of, or did not believe, the evidence that smoking is hazardous to health. That figure might somewhat overstate the extent of their acceptance of the statistics. There are various other false beliefs smokers sometimes employ to qualify their accept-

ance of those statistics and hence to rationalize their continued smoking (e.g., that the lethal dose is far in excess of what they smoke, however many that may be). Still, we can reasonably suppose that, in some sense or another, well over half of smokers know that what they are doing is unhealthy.

It is worth pausing, at this point, to consider just how we should handle that recalcitrant residual of smokers who deny the evidence. Having smoked thousands of packets containing increasingly stern warnings, and having been exposed to hundreds of column inches of newspaper reporting and several hours of broadcasting about smoking's hazards, they are presumably incorrigible in their false beliefs in this regard. Providing them with still more information is likely to prove pointless. People will say "if they are so bad for you as all that the government would ban cigarettes altogether." Or they will say "the government says that nearly everything is bad for you." Or they will find still some other way of rationalizing the practice.

Ordinarily it is not the business of public policy to prevent people from relying on false inferences from full information which would harm only themselves. Sometimes, however, it is. One such case comes when the false beliefs would lead to decisions that are "far-reaching, potentially dangerous, and irreversible"—as, for example, with people who believe that when they jump out of a tenth-story window they will float upward.

We are particularly inclined toward intervention when false beliefs with such disastrous results are traceable to familiar, well-understood forms of cognitive defect. There is something deeply offensive— morally, and perhaps legally as well—about the "intentional exploitation of a man's known weaknesses" in these ways.

One such familiar form of cognitive defect is "wishful thinking": smokers believing the practice is safe because they smoke, rather than smoking because they believe it to be safe. There is substantial evidence that smokers believe, groundlessly, that they are less vulnerable to smoking-related diseases (Leventhal, Glynn, and Fleming 1987, p. 3374). More surprising, and more directly to the "wishful thinking" point, is the evidence that smokers came to acquire those beliefs in their own invulnerability, and to "forget" what they previously knew about the dangers of smoking, *after* they took up the habit.

Another cognitive defect is the so-called anchoring fallacy (Kahneman, Slovic, and Tversky 1982). People smoke many times without any (immediately perceptible) bad effects. Naturally, people extrapolate from their own experience. They therefore conclude—quite reasonably, but quite wrongly—that smoking is safe, at least for them.

Yet another phenomenon, sometimes regarded as a cognitive defect, is "time discounting." Sometimes the ill effects of smoking would be felt almost immediately. Tonight's cigarette will make me short of breath when jogging tomorrow morning, for example. To ignore such effects, just on the grounds that they are in the future, is obviously absurd when the "future" in question is so close; it would imply a discount rate of 100 percent per hour, "compounding to an annual rate too large for my calculator," as Schelling (1980, p. 99) sneers. But most of the really serious consequences of smoking are some decades away for most of us. And since young smokers will not suffer the full effects of smoking-related diseases for some years to come, they may puff away happily now with little regard for the consequences, just so long as they attach relatively little importance to future pains relative to present pleasures in their utility functions. Economists, of course, are inclined to regard a "pure time preference" as a preference like any other, neither rational nor irrational. But reasons can be given for thinking that a lack of due regard for one's own future truly is a form of cognitive defect.

All of these cognitive defects point to relatively weak forms of irrationality, to be sure. In and of themselves, they might not be enough to justify interference with people's liberty, perhaps. When they lead people to take decisions that are far-reaching, potentially life-threatening, and irreversible, though, perhaps intervention would indeed be justifiable.

Interfering with people's choices in such cases is paternalistic, admittedly. But there are many differ-ent layers of paternalism. What is involved here is a relatively weak form of paternalism, one that works within the individual's own theory of the good and merely imposes upon him a better means of achieving what after all are only his own ends.[2] It is one thing to stop people who want to commit suicide from doing so, but quite another to stop people who want to live from acting in a way that they falsely believe to be safe. Smokers who deny the health risks fall into that latter, easier category.

The larger and harder question is how to deal with the great majority of smokers who, knowing the risks, continue smoking anyway. Of course, it might be said that they do not *really* know the risks. Although most acknowledge that smoking is "unhealthy," in some vague sense, few know exactly what chances they run of exactly what diseases. In one poll, 49 percent of smokers did not know that smoking causes most cases of lung cancer, 63 percent that it causes most cases of bronchitis, and 85 percent that it causes most cases of emphysema.

Overestimating badly the risks of dying in other more dramatic ways (such as car crashes, etc.), people badly underestimate the relative risks of dying in the more mundane ways associated with smoking. This allows them to rationalize further their smoking behavior as being "not all that dangerous," compared to other things that they are also doing.

Of course, logically it would be perfectly possible for people both to underestimate the extent of a risk and simultaneously to overreact to it. People might suppose the chances of snakebite are slight but live in mortal fear of it nonetheless. Psychologically, however, the reverse seems to happen. People's subjective probability estimates of an event's likelihood increase the more they dread it, and the more "psychologically available" the event therefore is to them (Kahneman, Slovic, and Tversky 1982). Smoking-related diseases, in contrast, tend to be "quiet killers" of which people have little direct or indirect experience, which tend to be underreported in newspapers (typically not even being mentioned in obituary notices) and which act on people one at a time rather than catastrophically killing many people at once. Smoking-related diseases being psychologically less available to people in these ways, they underestimate their frequency dramatically—by a factor of 8, in the case of lung cancer, according to one study (Slovic, Fischhoff, and Lichtenstein 1982, p. 469).[3] . . .

It may still be argued that, as long as people had the facts, they can and should be held responsible if they chose not to act upon them when they could have done so. It may be folly for utilitarian policy-makers to rely upon people's such imperfect responses to facts for purposes of constructing social welfare functions and framing public policies around them. But there is the separate matter of who ought to be blamed when some self-inflicted harm befalls people. There, arguably, responsibility ought to be on people's own shoulders. Arguably, we ought to stick to that judgment, even if people were "pressured" into smoking by the bullying of aggressive advertising or peer group pressure.

What crucially transforms the "voluntary acceptance" argument is evidence of the addictive nature of cigarette smoking. Of course, saying that smoking is addictive is not to say that all smokers are hooked and none can ever give it up. Clearly, many have done so. By the same token, though, "most narcotics users . . . never progress beyond occasional use, and of those who do, approximately 30 percent spontaneously remit" (U.S. DHHS 1988, p. v). Surprisingly enough, studies show that more than 70 percent of American servicemen addicted to heroin in Vietnam gave it up when returning to the United States (Robins 1973; Pollin 1984; Fingarette 1975, pp. 429–31). We nonetheless continue to regard heroin as an addictive drug. The test of addictiveness is not impossibility but rather difficulty of withdrawal.

There is a tendency, in discussing *volenti* or informed consent arguments, to draw too sharp a distinction between "voluntary" and "involuntary acts" and to put the dividing line at the wrong place, at that. The tendency is often to assume that any act that is in the least voluntary—that is in any respect at all, to any extent at all, within the control of the agents themselves—is to be considered fully voluntary for the purposes. If we want to claim that some sort of act was involuntary, we are standardly advised to look for evidence of "somnambulism" or "automatism" or

such like. Thus, U.S. Supreme Court justices wanting to argue for more humane treatment of addicts felt obliged to assert that "once [the defendant] had become an addict he was utterly powerless" to refrain from continuing to service his addiction (Fortas 1968, p. 567). That is an implausibly strong claim, given the above evidence.

There is no need to make such a strong claim, though, to vitiate arguments that the conduct was "voluntary" and the harm thus self-incurred. For purposes of excusing criminal conduct, we are prepared to count forms of "duress" that stop well short of rendering all alternative actions literally impossible. It is perfectly possible for bank tellers to let a robber break their arms instead of handing over the money; but no one expects them to do so. A credible threat of serious pain, or perhaps even very gross discomfort, is ordinarily regarded as more than sufficient to constitute duress of the sort that excuses responsibility for otherwise impermissible behavior.

So, too, I would argue should be the case with addiction-induced behavior. The issue is not whether it is literally impossible, but merely whether it is unreasonably costly, for addicts to resist their compulsive desires. If that desire is so strong that even someone with "'normal and reasonable' self-control" (Watson 1977, p. 331) would succumb to it, we have little compunction in saying that the addict's free will was sufficiently impaired that his apparent consent counts for naught.

This is arguably the case with nicotine addiction. To establish a substance as addictive, we require two sorts of evidence. The first is some sort of evidence of "physical need" for the substance among its users. That evidence is widely thought necessary to prove smoking is an addiction, rather than just a "habit" (U.S. DHEW 1964, chaps. 13–14), a psychological dependence, or a matter of mere sociological pressure (Daniels 1985, p. 159)—none of which would undercut, in a way that addictiveness does, claims that the risks of smoking are voluntarily incurred. That physical link has now been established, though. Particular receptors for the active ingredients of tobacco smoke have been discovered in the brain; the physiological sites and mechanisms by which nicotine acts on the brain have now been well mapped, and its tendency to generate compulsive, repetitive behavior in consequence has been well established. Such evidence—summarized in the surgeon general's 1988 report—has been one important factor in leading the World Health Organization ([WHO] 1978) and the American Psychiatric Association ([APA] 1987, sec. 305.1) to classify nicotine as a dependence-inducing drug. (Strictly speaking, the term "addiction" is out of favor in these circles, with "dependence" taking its place; in what follows, I shall continue using the more colloquial term in preference to the more technical one, though.)

None of that evidence proves that it would be literally impossible for smokers to resist the impulse to smoke. Through extraordinary acts of will, they might. Nor does any of that evidence prove that it is literally impossible for them to break their dependence altogether. Many have. Recall, however, that the issue is not one of impossibility but rather of how hard people should have to try before their will is said to be sufficiently impaired that their agreement does not count as genuine consent.

The evidence suggests that nicotine addicts have to try very hard indeed. This is the second crucial fact to establish in proving a substance addictive. Central among the WHO/APA criteria for diagnosing nicotine dependence is the requirement of evidence of "continuous use of tobacco for at least one month with . . . unsuccessful attempts to stop or significantly reduce the amount of tobacco use on a permanent basis" (APA 1987, sec. 305.1).

A vast majority of smokers do indeed find themselves in this position. The surgeon general reports the results of various studies showing that 90 percent of regular smokers have tried to quit (U.S. DHHS 1979, quoted in Pollin 1984). Another 1975 survey found that 84 percent of smokers had attempted to stop, but that only 36 percent of them had succeeded in maintaining their changed behavior for a whole year (Benfari, Ockene, and McIntyre 1982; see, further, Leventhal and Cleary 1980). Interestingly, graphs mapping the "relapse rate"—the percentage of ex-addicts that are back on the drug after a given period of time—are almost identical for nicotine and for heroin (Winsten 1986; U.S. DHHS 1988, p. 314 and chap. 5 more generally).

On the basis of all this evidence, the surgeon general has been led to three "major conclusions" contained in his 1988 report:

1. Cigarettes and other forms of tobacco are addicting.
2. Nicotine is the drug in tobacco that causes addiction.
3. The pharmacologic and behavioral processes that determine tobacco addiction are similar to those that determine addiction to drugs such as heroin and cocaine. [U.S. DHHS 1988, p. 9]

Evidence of smokers trying to stop and failing to do so is rightly regarded as central to the issue of addiction, philosophically as well as diagnostically. Some describe free will in terms of "second-order volitions"—desires about desires—controlling "first-order" ones (Frankfurt 1971). Others talk of free will in terms of a person's "evaluational structure" controlling his "motivational structure"—a person striving to obtain something if and only if he thinks it to be of value (Watson 1975; 1977). Addiction—the absence of free will—is thus a matter of first-order volitions winning out over second-order ones, and surface desires prevailing over the agent's own deeper values. In the case of smoking, trying to stop can be seen as a manifestation of one's second-order volitions, or one's deeper values, and failing to stop as evidence of the triumph of first-order surface desires over them. The same criteria the WHO and APA use to diagnose nicotine dependence also establish the impairment of the smoker's free will, philosophically.

For certain purposes, at least, even the courts now treat nicotine as addictive. Social security benefits are not payable to those claimants whose disabilities were voluntarily self-inflicted. But the courts have held that "smoking can be an involuntary act for some persons," and that those benefits may not therefore be routinely withheld from victims of smoking-related diseases on the grounds that they are suffering from voluntarily self-inflicted injuries.

Various other policy implications also follow from evidence of addictiveness, though. One might be that over-the-counter sales of cigarettes should be banned. If the product is truly addictive, then we have no more reason to respect a person's voluntary choice (however well-informed) to abandon his future volition to an addiction than we have for respecting a person's voluntary choice (however well-informed) to sell himself into slavery I am unsure how far to press this argument, since after all we do permit people to bind their future selves (through contracts, e.g.). But if it is the size of the stakes or the difficulty of breaking out of the bonds that makes the crucial difference, then acquiring a lethal and hard-to-break addiction is much more like a slavery contract than it is like an ordinary commercial commitment.

In any case, addictiveness thus defined makes it far easier to justify interventions that on the surface appear paternalistic. In some sense, they would then not be paternalistic at all. Where people "wish to stop smoking, but do not have the requisite willpower . . . we are not imposing a good on someone who rejects it. We are simply using coercion to enable people to carry out their own goals" (Dworkin 1972/1983, p. 32). . . .

The real force of the addiction findings, in the context of *volenti* or informed-consent arguments, though, is to undercut the claim that there is any *continuing* consent to the risks involved in smoking. There might have been consent in the very first instance—in smoking your first cigarette. But once you were hooked, you lost the capacity to consent in any meaningful sense on a continuing basis. As Hume says, to consent implies the possibility of doing otherwise; and addiction substantially deprives you of the capacity to do other than continue smoking. So once you have become addicted to nicotine, your subsequent smoking cannot be taken as indicating your consent to the risks.

The most that we can now say with confidence, therefore, is that "cigarette smoking, at least initially, is a voluntary activity," in the words of a leading court case in this area (Brown 1987, p. 627). If there is to be consent at all in this area, it can only be consent in the very first instance, that is, when you first began to smoke. That, in turn, seriously undercuts the extent to which cigarette manufacturers can rely upon *volenti* or informed-consent defenses in product liability litigation and its moral analogues.

It does so in two ways. The first arises from the fact that many of those now dying from tobacco-induced diseases started smoking well before warnings began appearing on packets in 1966 and were hooked by the time those warnings reached them. Their consent to the risks of smoking could only have been based on "common knowledge" and "folk wisdom." That is a short-term problem, though, since that cohort of smokers will eventually die off.

The second and more serious problem is a continuing problem in a way the first is not. A vast majority of smokers began smoking in their early to middle teens. Evidence suggests that "of those teenagers who smoke more than a single cigarette only 15 percent avoid becoming regular dependent smokers" (Russell 1974, p. 255). Studies show that, "of current smokers, about 60 percent began by the very young age of thirteen or fourteen" (Blasi and Monaghan 1986, p. 503), and the great majority—perhaps up to 95 percent—of regular adult smokers are thought to have been addicted before coming of age (Califano 1981, p. 183; Lewit, Coate, and Grossman 1981, p. 547, n. 8; Pollin 1984; Leventhal, Glynn, and Fleming 1987, p. 3373; Davis 1987, p. 730; U.S. DHHS 1988, p. 397).

The crux of the matter, then, is just this: being below the age of consent when they first began smoking, smokers were incapable of meaningfully consenting to the risks in the first instance. Being addicted by the time they reached the age of consent, they were incapable of consenting later, either. . . .

4.3 BAD HABITS AND ADDICTIONS

Many who oppose government regulation of smoking designed to protect smokers from themselves implicitly or explicitly treat it as nothing more than a bad habit. "Assumption of individual responsibility for one's own health" is, in these terms, far preferable to treating "sloth, gluttony, alcoholic overuse, reckless driving, sexual intemperance, and smoking" as "a national, not an individual responsibility" (Knowles 1977, p. 59).

In many ways, these writers have a point. Presumably it is perfectly true that we expect people to alter their own bad habits—or anyway not to complain when harms befall them in consequence of the practice of their own bad habits. After all, they could have altered their ways. Addictions are otherwise. They may, in the very first instance, have been self-induced. Once induced, however, they are not (easily) remediable thereafter, through any simple act of will. Indeed, that is one of the primary criteria used diagnostically to distinguish "drug dependence" from merely "habitual behaviors" (U.S. DHHS 1988, pp. 7–8).

Thus, the habit versus addiction issue can be cast as an issue about responsibility, but it comes out rather differently than "responsibility for self" theorists suppose. People may bear responsibility for their own bad habits and for whatever follows from them. They bear responsibility for having become addicted to drugs. Once addicted, though, they ought no longer be considered responsible for their addiction-driven actions. For that reason, the addiction evidence is crucial in making the case for governmental action on smoking in several respects.[4]

Some theorists—especially economists—might nonetheless resist these conclusions, insisting that the distinction between addictions and mere bad habits is meaningless. Essentially, there are three bases for grounding this distinction. Economists often remain unimpressed by all of them.

The first basis for the addiction-habit distinction has to do with the way in which, with addictive substances, the more you have consumed of them in the past the more you want to consume of them in the future. But that is merely to say that present preferences over those goods are a positive function of past consumption; and, put that way, there is nothing particularly unique about addictive as against all sorts of other goods.[5] One particularly blunt way of putting the point is to say that "there is, of course, a large degree of habituation in all consumption, in the sense that people seek to repeat activities they enjoy. How," economists ask, "is being 'habituated' to cigarettes any different from being habituated to chewing gum, ice cream, television, jogging, or swimming?" (Tollison and Wagner 1988, p. 39; see similarly Schwartz 1989). There is nothing wrong with habituation per se. Some habits are bad; others are good, in the sense that you are better off objectively as well as subjectively for having cultivated them. On that score, economists are absolutely right.

The second basis for a distinction between addiction and habit rests on essentially physiological evidence. Receptors in the brain have now been identified for the pharmacologically active substances in tobacco smoke; and partly on the basis of that discovery the American Psychiatric Association and the World Health Organization have deemed nicotine addictive. Yet, as economists are quick to add, there are presumably "pleasure centers" in the brain that are stimulated by ordinary consumption goods, too. Where, exactly, those centers are and how, exactly, consumption stimulates them we do not yet know in any detail. But there is no reason to believe that the neurochemical processes involved there are radically different than those involved in the relationship between nicotine and its receptors in the brain.

The third and most important basis for the addiction-habit distinction has to do with the addict's wanting to stop but being unable to do so. This is the central element in the APA/WHO diagnostic criteria used to class nicotine as addictive.

Economists critical of the habit-addiction distinction have a quick retort, here too. They say, "There are, of course, many overeaters who claim they want to lose weight but do not," also (Tollison and Wagner 1988, p. 39). They go on to say, "It is clear that many smokers say they would like to stop. . . . And it is equally clear that for most of them, the intensity of that wish is weak, as judged by the observation that they continue to smoke. Should we therefore say that the demand for cigarettes is somehow fraudulent? Perhaps, alternatively, it is the professed desire to stop smoking that is misleading" (Tollison and Wagner 1988, p. 39).

The central point in this economistic attempt to collapse the addiction-habit distinction is the claim that all temptations are resistable and all addictions curable, at a cost. To quote Tollison and Wagner (1988, p. 39) yet again: "We know that people can change their habits if they truly want to. . . . It surely makes less sense to say that those who do not lose weight are habituated to food . . . than to say that some people value losing weight more highly than others, and are thus willing to pay a higher price to overcome their eating "habit." And the same, they would say, is true of smoking: "There are many ex-smokers, so we know that people can stop smoking, just as they can stop overeating, if they are willing to pay the price—that is, if they value more highly the benefits they think they will derive from reducing their eating or from stopping their smoking than they value the continuation of their present eating or smoking practices" (Tollison and Wagner 1988, p. 39).

Thus, to the economist, the pain of withdrawal is just the cost that an addict has to pay for the good of a "clean" life. In that respect, it is formally analogous to the cost that anyone pays (also in terms of pain, or discomfort anyway) in breaking a bad habit. Neither, furthermore, is there any reason to suppose that the cost of breaking the one (breaking a weak addiction, e.g.) would necessarily always exceed that of breaking the other (breaking a long-standing, well-entrenched bad habit, e.g.). If people are not prepared to pay the price of stopping, then they surely must not mind smoking all that much after all. Or so the economist's logic would hold.

What this comes down to is an issue of whether addicts really are subjectively worse off smoking, or not. Their words may suggest that they are, but their actions suggest that they are not; and the latter is what counts most heavily in contemporary microeconomists' crassly behavioral concept of preference. There is no need to follow them in those conceptual rigidities, however. At least sometimes, what a person says is a better indicator of the true state of his mind than is what he does. Such would clearly be the case if he were physically restrained, in a way that rendered him simply unable to do what he said he wanted to do. We may well question the practical relevance of a preference for doing what he is unable to do. But we could hardly question, in those circumstances, that his true preference is to do as he says; and we would be quite wrong to infer from the fact that he does not do it that he does not really want to do it, after all. Similarly, if a person is physiologically restrained (by a drug dependence, defined inter alia in terms of the state of certain receptors in his brain), we might also say that he was simply unable to do what he truly wants to do, better revealed once again through his statements than through his actions.

If economists insist upon a more behavioral way of putting this point, we can employ a hypothetical-choice formulation: would the people involved have chosen otherwise, if they had it to do over again? If not, then their initial choice can unambiguously be said to have promoted their welfare; if so, it can unambiguously be said to have ill-served it. Where people plainly "regret" previous choices, and would choose differently next time, that is clear enough. In cases of addiction, matters are only a little more complicated. Once addicted, people would choose the same addictive good next time as last; but if given a chance to choose over whether or not to begin consuming the addictive substance in the first place, they would choose not to do so. (That is how "addiction" is here defined and how it is operationalized in the studies demonstrating the addictiveness of nicotine.) Stopping people from becoming addicts by stopping them from beginning to consume tobacco in the first place would thus be justified in terms of their own self-assessed welfare, defined in terms of their own (hypothetical) choices.

Of course, it is highly desirable that people should take charge of their own lives in both respects, breaking bad habits and addictions alike. Of necessity, that must be primarily a task for individuals themselves. But there are some things that governments can do to help—such as making practices people wish to abandon more expensive (through excise taxes) or restricting the number of hours or number of places in which they can engage in them. Such assistance can be justified on the grounds that, far from imposing paternalist policies on people, we are merely helping them enforce rules of their own choosing upon themselves. That rationale works equally well, whether it is a mere bad habit or an actual addiction that is involved.

Whether or not that argument is convincing in showing that smokers themselves would be subjectively better off if prevented from smoking, it is decisive in establishing another even stronger rationale for public policies against smoking. That has not so much to do with protecting present addicts from themselves as it has to do with preventing future addicts from becoming addicted. Addictions are unambiguously bad, from the point of view of the person addicted. Being defined in terms of a desire to quit coupled with an inability to quit, addictions necessarily would make the addict worse-off; and, on the evidence of section 2.2 above, a vast majority of those who do smoke will become addicted in this way. Once they are addicted, they face a high price to pay in overcoming the addiction, and we cannot be absolutely sure whether their health is worth that price to them. But we can be sure that those who are not yet addicted—just like those who already are— would much rather not have to face that choice. If they were to become addicted, they would almost certainly come to wish they had not. On the basis of that hypothetical choice that we can reasonably impute to people not yet addicted, we can justify public policies to prevent them from getting addicted.

The policy implications of a distinction between addictions and mere bad habits, couched in some such terms, are clear. Since habits are not necessarily bad, public policies discouraging them are not necessarily desirable (although it may of course be socially desirable to curtail the practice of those habits in public). Addictions, in contrast, are necessarily bad. Policies discouraging them are therefore always desirable. We might wish to show compassion toward present addicts. But clearly we should do what we can to prevent new addicts. . . .

NOTES

1. Strides are being made in identification of those at especially high risk of lung cancer and cardiac disease in consequence of smoking (Russell 1974, p. 257); but that, in itself, is not enough to undercut this case for a general antismoking campaign.

2. One of a person's ends—continued life—at least. Perhaps the person has other ends ("relaxation," or whatever) that are well served by smoking; and insofar as "people taking risks actually value the direct consequences associated with them . . . it is more difficult to intrude paternalistically" (Daniels 1985, pp. 158, 163). But assuming that smoking is not the only means to the other ends—not the only way to relax, etc.—the intrusion is only minimally difficult to justify.

3. Thus, health education campaigns have begun focusing on the risks of contracting Buerger's disease from smoking, the amputation of limbs being, like snakebites,

psychologically more accessible to people (especially teenagers, before they start to smoke) than rotting lungs.

4. Ranging from publicly sponsored smoking-cessation programs to restricting or banning the sale of tobacco (see, generally, U.S. DHHS 1988, esp. chap. 7).

5. One criterion—which even Stigler and Becker (1977) would recognize—is the tendency for an addict's tolerance to grow, the more of the substance he has taken. With ordinary goods (like olives, say) that are "acquired tastes," the more of the good you have consumed in the past the more pleasure you get out of each subsequent unit of consumption. With addictive substances (like heroin, say), this is not true: it takes increasingly large doses to produce the same subjective effects as before, thanks to increasing tolerance. This is a characteristic which nicotine dependence shares with all other addictions, however (Winsten 1986; U.S. DHHS 1988). That this phenomenon "tops out" sooner (at around twenty—or, given 50 percent underreporting of smoking behavior, perhaps thirty—cigarettes a day for most addicts) rather than later (as with heroin) is surely irrelevant for purposes of classifying a substance as addictive.

REFERENCES

American Psychiatric Association (APA). 1987. *Diagnostic and Statistical Manual of Mental Disorders*. 3d ed. Washington, D.C.: APA.

Benfari, Robert C.; Ockene, Judith K.; and McIntyre, Kevin M. 1982. Control of Cigarette-Smoking from a Psychological Perspective. *Annual Review of Public Health* 3:101–28.

Blasi, Vincent, and Monaghan, Henry Paul. 1986. The First Amendment and Cigarette Advertising. *Journal of the American Medical Association* 256:502–9.

Borgida, E., and Nisbett, R. E. 1977. The Differential Impact of Abstract vs. Concrete Information on Decisions. *Journal of Applied Social Psychology* 7:258–71.

Brown, John R. 1987. Opinion of the U.S. Court of Appeals. *Palmer v. Liggett Group, Inc.* 825 F.2d 620 (1st Cir. 1987).

Burch, P. R. J. 1978. Smoking and Lung Cancer: The Problem of Inferring Cause. *Journal of the Royal Statistical Society,* ser. A, 141:437–58.

Califano, Joseph A., Jr. 1981. *Governing America.* New York: Simon & Schuster.

Cederlof, R.; Friberg, L.; and Lundman, T. 1977. The Interactions of Smoking, Environment and Heredity and Their Implications for Disease Etiology, *Acta Medica Scandinavica,* vol. 612 (suppl. 1).

Chapman, Simon. 1986. *Great Expectorations: Advertising and the Tobacco Industry.* London: Comedia.

Daniels, Norman. 1985. *Just Health Care.* Cambridge: Cambridge University Press.

Davis, Ronald M. 1987. Current Trends in Cigarette Advertising and Marketing. *New England Journal of Medicine* 316:725–32.

Dworkin, Gerald. 1972. Paternalism. *Monist* 56, no. 1:64–84. Reprinted in Sartorius, ed., 1983, pp. 19–34.

Edell, Marc Z., and Gisser, Stewart M. 1985. *Cipollone v. Liggett Group, Inc.:* The Application of Theories of Liability in Current Cigarette Litigation. *New York State Journal of Medicine* 85, no. 7:318–21.

Eysenck, H. J. 1980. *The Causes and Effects of Smoking.* London: Maurice Temple Smith.

Eysenck, H. J. 1986. Smoking and Health. In Tollison, ed., 1986, pp. 17–88.

Fingarette, Herbert. 1975. Addiction and Criminal Responsibility. *Yale Law Journal* 84:413–44.

Fortas, Abe. 1968. Dissenting Opinion. *Powell v. Texas.* 392 US 514, 554–70.

Frankfurt, Harry G. 1971. Freedom of the Will and the Concept of a Person. *Journal of Philosophy* 68:5–20.

Gorovitz, Samuel. 1982. *Doctors' Dilemmas.* New York: Oxford University Press.

Harrison, Larry. 1986. Tobacco Battered and the Pipes Shattered: A Note on the Fate of the First British Campaign against Tobacco Smoking. *British Journal of Addiction* 81:553–58.

Kahneman, D.; Slovic, P.; and Tversky, A., eds. 1982. *Judgment under Uncertainty.* Cambridge: Cambridge University Press.

Knowles, John H. 1977. The Responsibility of the Individual. *Daedalus* 106, no. 1:57–80.

Leventhal, Howard; Glynn, Kathleen; and Fleming, Raymond. 1987. Is the Smoking Decision an "Informed Choice"? *Journal of the American Medical Association* 257:3373–76.

Lewit, E. M.; Coate, D.; and Grossman, M. 1981. The Effects of Government Regulation on Teenage Smoking. *Journal of Law and Economics* 24:545–69.

Mintz, Morton. 1988. Cigarette Trial Breaks New Ground. *Washington Post,* March 27, pp. H1, H8. Reprinted in *Washington Post National Weekly Edition,* April 11, pp. 20–21.

Peto, Richard. 1980. Possible Ways of Explaining to Ordinary People the Quantitative Dangers of Smoking. *Health Education Journal* 39:45–46.

Pollin, William. 1984. The Role of the Addictive Process as a Key Step in Causation of All Tobacco-related Diseases. *Journal of the American Medical Association* 252:2874.

R. J. Reynolds Tobacco Co. 1986. The Health Effects of Smoking. A Submission in the Case of *Browner v. R.J. Reynolds* (California Superior Court, County of Contra Costa). Reprinted in *Tobacco Products Litigation Reporter* 1, no. 4:5.45–56.

Robins, L. 1973. *A Follow-up of Vietnam Drug Users.* Interim Final Report, Special Actions Office for Drug Abuse Prevention. Washington, D.C.: Executive Office of the President.

Russell, M. A. H. 1974. Realistic Goals for Smoking and Health. *Lancet* 7851:254–58.

Schelling, Thomas C. 1980. The Intimate Contest for Self-Command. *Public Interest* 60:94–118. Reprinted in Schelling 1984a, pp. 57–82.

Slade, J.; Kopelowicz, A.; Hahn, A.; Gill, J.; Kabis, S.; and Vasen, A. 1986–87. An Analysis of R. J. Reynolds' Position Paper on the Health Effects of Smoking. *Tobacco Products Litigation Reporter* 1, no. 8:5.97–105; 1, no. 10:5.115–21; 2, no. 2:5.11–21.

Slovic, P.; Fischhoff, B.; and Lichtenstein, S. 1982. Fact vs. Fears: Understanding Perceived Risks. In Kahneman, Slovic, and Tversky, eds., 1982, pp. 463–89.

Stigler, George J., and Becker, Gary S. 1977. De Gustibus Non Est Disputandum. *American Economic Review* 67:76–90.

Tollison, Robert D., and Wagner, Richard E. 1988. *Smoking and the State: Social Costs, Rent Seeking, and Public Policy.* Lexington, Mass.: Lexington Books, D. C. Heath.

U.S. Department of Health, Education and Welfare (U.S. DHEW). 1964. *Smoking and Health.* Report of the Advisory Committee to the Surgeon General of the Public Health Service. Washington, D.C.: Government Printing Office.

U.S. Department of Health and Human Services. Surgeon General. 1979. *Smoking and Health.* Washington, D.C.: Government Printing Office.

U.S. DHHS. Surgeon General. 1986. *The Health Consequences of Involuntary Smoking.* Washington, D.C.: Government Printing Office.

U.S. DHHS. Surgeon General. 1988. *The Health Consequences of Smoking: Nicotine Addiction.* Washington, D.C.: Government Printing Office.

Watson, Gary. 1975. Free Agency. *Journal of Philosophy* 72:205–20.

Watson, Gary. 1977. Skepticism about Weakness of Will. *Philosophical Review* 86:316–39.

White, Larry C. 1988. *Merchants of Death: The American*

Tobacco Industry. New York: Beach Tree Books, William Morrow.

Winsten, Jay A., director. 1986. *Nicotine Dependency and Compulsive Tobacco Use.* A Research Status Report, Center for Health Communication, Harvard School of

Public Health. Reprinted in *Tobacco Product Liability Reporter* 1, no. 7.

WHO. 1978. *International Classification of Diseases.* 9th ed. Geneva: WHO.

WHO. 1986. *In Point of Fact,* no. 36. Geneva: WHO.

Critics

Daniel Shapiro	# Smoking Tobacco
	Irrationality, Addiction, and Paternalism

Smoking tobacco (henceforth, "smoking") is a very risky activity: between 18% to 36% of smokers die prematurely, and smokers on average lose three to seven years of life.[1] Nonsmokers also are seriously affected by smoking, by second-hand smoke, but my concern here is not with the harm that smokers do to others, but with the harm that they do to themselves, and whether laws that aim to prevent or strongly discourage the latter harm are justified in the case of adult smokers. It is generally difficult to justify paternalistic laws for sane adults, that is, laws which aim to prevent or strongly discourage those adults from harming themselves, particularly if their actions are voluntary and they know the risks involved. However, Robert E. Goodin argues in his provocative book *No Smoking*[2] that neither the voluntariness nor the knowledge condition applies to smokers and that accordingly paternalistic laws to prevent or strongly discourage adult smoking can be justified.[3]

First, he maintains that despite the information available about the risks of smoking, smokers falsely and irrationally underestimate the degree to which smoking can be harmful to themselves. Borrowing an argument made by Gerald Dworkin, Goodin says

that while it is ordinarily not the state's business to prevent people from relying on false and irrational inferences when decisions based on these inferences would harm only themselves, it may be the state's business when such inferences lead to decisions that are far-reaching, potentially dangerous and irreversible. The argument is that while paternalism is unjustified when one is imposing a conception of the good upon a person, it is not unjustified, or is a very weak form of paternalism, when one is simply imposing on someone a better means to achieve her ends. Smokers who deny that smoking is dangerous or do not genuinely appreciate the risks of smoking are not people with a different conception of the good than most of us, as the reason they continue to smoke is not due to their valuing health or continued life less than other people, but rather is due to their irrational and false beliefs about the harms of smoking. So a state policy which makes it harder for them to smoke is thus really a policy which is making it easier for them to each their own ends—health and continued life.[4]

Second, following a recent report by the Surgeon General[5] and the American Psychiatric Association, Goodin argues that smokers do not have a bad habit,

Daniel Shapiro, "Smoking Tobacco: Irrationality, Addiction, and Paternalism," *Public Affairs Quarterly,* 8, no. 2 (1994): 187–203. Reprinted by permission of North American Philosophical Publications.

but are addicts addicted to nicotine. Thus adult smokers do not voluntarily engage in their risky behavior, and laws which aim to prevent adult smoking cannot be condemned as objectionably paternalistic. Goodin uses this line of argument to suggest that we should consider banning over the-counter sales of cigarettes.[6]

I will call Goodin's first argument the irrationality argument and the second argument the addiction argument. My specific aim is to show that they both fail, and my general aim is to show that only under very limited conditions could arguments of this type succeed. Section I concerns the irrationality argument, and section II concerns the addiction argument.

I. IRRATIONALITY, SMOKING, AND PATERNALISM

I have three aims in this section. First, I shall discuss whether it is true that smokers falsely and irrationally underestimate the risks of smoking.[7] Second, shall discuss whether *if* the kind of irrationality described by Goodin existed, such irrationality would justify paternalist measures to prevent or strongly discourage smoking. And third, I shall discuss under what conditions, if any, the irrationality argument could justify paternalist intervention.

Are Smokers Irrational?

Goodin's claim that smokers falsely and irrationally underestimate the risks of smoking rests on two kinds of evidence. First, he cites a 1981 survey that shows that smokers do not know or deny that smoking causes most cases of lung cancer, emphysema and bronchitis.[8] Second, he argues that smokers engage in various sorts of reasoning errors, the two most important of which are wishful thinking (believing that they won't be vulnerable to smoking-related diseases), and the anchoring fallacy (reasoning that since they have smoked many times without any ill effect that therefore smoking is safe, at least for them).[9]

The survey that Goodin cites, however, does not reveal smokers' assessment of the relevant risks. The beliefs that are most relevant are not beliefs about the percentage of lung cancer or other diseases caused by smoking, but beliefs about the percentage of smokers that die from those diseases. Surveys taken by the economist W. Kip Viscusi show that smokers as well as nonsmokers *overestimate* the risk of smokers dying from lung cancer. The most recent data from the Surgeon General suggests that smokers face a 5 to 12 percentage chance of dying from lung cancer, while the population at large believe it to be 43 percent, and smokers believe it is 37 percent.[10] (The same overestimation occurs with the overall mortality rate from smoking, though the degree of error here is somewhat smaller.)[11] This overestimation can be explained by recent work of psychologists, which shows that people tend to underestimate hidden risks, and overestimate publicized ones.[12] That smoking can cause lung cancer is very highly publicized, far more than other risks, yet such publicity rarely, if ever, provides information about the degree of risk, so it's not surprising that people think that the risk of smokers dying from lung cancer is quite high. Goodin is aware that people overestimate highly publicized risks, but he argues that deaths from lung cancers are not highly publicized; e.g., they are not featured prominently in news reports, and they tend to occur to people one-by-one rather than catastrophically killing a lot of people at one time—which explains why in one survey the frequency of lung cancer deaths was grossly underestimated.[13] However, people's beliefs about the riskiness of an activity is not revealed by their beliefs concerning how many people prematurely die from it, but from their beliefs about the percentage of people that are harmed by it. So the fact that information about the former is not highly publicized and that people accordingly underestimate it is beside the point.

So smokers do not falsely underestimate the risks of smoking.[14] But do they, as Goodin suggested, irrationally assume that the risks won't apply to them or are they instead simply less risk averse than nonsmokers? The evidence is mixed. Viscusi presents evidence which shows that smokers are less risk averse than nonsmokers: the former are more willing to work in riskier jobs, as measured by how much money they would need to feel compensated by a greater chance of accidents on the job.[15] On the other hand, while some of the surveys that Goodin cites as evidence that smokers irrationally assume the risks won't apply to them can be dismissed on the ground that these were surveys of adolescent smokers—as the concern here is with adults—there does remain one survey which presents evidence of this irrationality in adult smokers.[16] However, the fallacies of wishful thinking and anchoring are common to humans in general, not just smokers.[17] Unless there is evidence that smokers engage in these fallacies far more than nonsmokers, the evidence that smokers are less risk-averse remains as a better explanation of smokers' behavior than does the claim that smokers irrationally believe that they are invulnerable.

Goodin's Irrationality Argument

Goodin's claim that smokers falsely and irrationally underestimate the risks of smoking has been badly damaged. But it's worth considering whether if his claim was true the irrationality argument would justify taking measures to prevent or strongly discourage the harms that adult smokers incur. However, before discussing the irrationality argument, let us note one way in which it needs to be changed. The argument says that we are justified in preventing someone from making decisions based on false and irrational beliefs when these beliefs would lead to decisions that are far-reaching, potentially dangerous, and irreversible. However, a decision to smoke (or continue smoking) is not *irreversible,* since, as I shall discuss in section II, significant numbers quit. So that the irrationality argument applies to smoking, I suggest a reinterpretation whereby the argument refers not only to irreversible decisions, but to decisions that are difficult to reverse. Notice that addiction is one, but not the only, reason decisions could be difficult to reverse. Thus my reinterpretation makes the irrationality argument separate from the issue of addiction, which is at it should be. If to apply the irrationality argument we had to first establish a finding of addiction, then the irrationality argu-

ment would be parasitic on the addiction argument. However, while Goodin does indicate that the addiction argument is more important than the irrationality argument,[18] he does not believe that the latter is dependent upon the former.

With this reinterpretation out of the way, let us examine whether the argument succeeds. At first glance, it seems plausible: if smokers place the same value on continued life and health as the rest of us, and if they falsely believe that smoking is not that detrimental to those ends, then preventing or discouraging them from smoking can be viewed as merely enabling them to better achieve their ends, rather than imposing ends or a conception of the good upon them. However, smoking is a very important means to a *variety* of ends. Smokers smoke to relax, to concentrate, to handle anxiety, stress and difficult interpersonal situations, as a way of taking a break during the day, as a social lubricant, as a substitute for putting food in their mouths—the list could be extended.[19] *Why* smoking is so important to smokers' lives is an interesting question (I will address it to some extent in section II), but for now the issue is simply *that* it is important. This means that it is false that preventing or discouraging smoking simply enables the smoker to better achieve her ends of increased life and health. If concentrating and smoking are linked, or smoking and relaxing are linked, or smoking and handling anxiety and stress are linked, etc., then preventing or discouraging smoking doesn't just involve preventing or discouraging a potentially life and health-threatening activity, but involves preventing or discouraging other values or activities, such as relaxing, concentrating, etc.

At one point Goodin recognizes this problem, and replies that since smoking is not the *only* means to other ends, legislation which aims at preventing or discouraging smoking is an intrusion which is only minimally difficult to justify.[20] All this response shows, however, is that preventing someone from smoking does not make it *impossible* for her to concentrate, relax, etc., without smoking; but since it would make it *difficult* for her to achieve a variety to ends, it's hard to see how Goodin can say that such a policy is only minimally difficult to justify. We certainly have moved a long way from the original claim, which was that preventing smoking *merely* enabled a person to achieve her ends of continued life and health. Another problem with the reply is that the most plausible explanation or reason why the state would adopt a policy that makes it easier for some people to achieve some ends (in this case, continued life and health) and harder to achieve others (relaxation, concentration, reduction of stress and anxiety, etc.) is that the former are ranked as more important by the state. Now differences between people's conception of the good often depend heavily on how one *ranks* various values, as opposed to merely being disagreements about which values should be in the ranking. Thus one can claim that when the state ranks continued life and health as more important than concentrating, relaxing, etc., it is not imposing a conception of the good upon smokers only if there is good evidence that smokers have the same ranking. But such evidence is lacking, for on the assumption that smokers underestimate the risks of smoking, they are not directly aware that there is a conflict, as things stand now, between the way in which they achieve relaxation, concentration, etc., and their continued life and health.

Another defect of the irrationality argument is that it does not recognize that an explanation for someone's false and irrational beliefs about the risks of a certain activity could be her epistemic attitudes and values, which are certainly part of one's conception of the good life. The way in which I assess and am open to evidence, the value I place on discovering the truth, the degree to which I desire to hold coherent beliefs—all of these are to some degree a function of the kind of person I want to be, of the kind of life I want to lead. If, despite the voluminous evidence of the risks of smoking, some smokers underestimate the risks of smoking (as we've seen, most don't, but right now we are discussing the hypothetical question), a plausible explanation for this could be that they have a very skeptical (or hostile) attitude towards scientific evidence and inquiry, or perhaps they view themselves as "lucky" persons who can defy the odds, or perhaps they take perverse pride in doing what everyone else considers irrational. These are the sort of considerations that indicate that one wishes to be a certain kind of person or that one wishes to lead a certain kind of life. For

these kinds of smokers, the irrationality argument fails. When the irrationality that smokers manifest is due to epistemic values that are an important part of their conception of the good, then it will be untrue that making it more difficult for irrational smokers to smoke simply makes it easier for them to achieve their ends.

Of course, it could be that the smokers who falsely and irrationally underestimate the risks of smoking do so not because of a certain self-conception but because they engage in the kind of reasoning errors to which humans are prone, such as the wishful thinking and anchoring fallacy noted earlier. My point is that Goodin assumes that faulty inferences about risks is simply a cognitive mistake, and does not recognize that some forms of irrationality can be important components of the kind of life one wishes to lead.

Why the Irrationality Argument Fails

We can now generalize the arguments made in this section and see under what conditions the irrationality argument can succeed. Succeed, in this context, means: the argument justifies paternalistic laws which aim to prevent or strongly discourage sane adults from engaging in activities the risks of which they systematically underestimate, on the grounds that such laws merely enable them to achieve important ends, e.g., health or continued life, that they do not realize, due to their underestimation of the risk, are placed in serious jeopardy by that activity.

First, the activity the law aims to prevent or strongly discourage must not be one which is a central or important means to a variety of ends or valued activities. If it is such a means, then it is false that preventing or discouraging people from engaging in that activity merely enables them to achieve the ends that they do not realize are in serious jeopardy by engaging in that activity, e.g., health or continued life. For such prevention or discouragement will also make it more difficult for them to achieve the ends or valued activities with which the risky activity is linked.

Second, it must be true that the reason for the underestimation of the risks of the activity has nothing to do with epistemic attitudes and values that are an important part of one's conception of the good or a desire to be a certain kind of person. If the reason for the underestimation of the risk is due to those factors, then preventing or discouraging a person from engaging in the risky activity will involve imposing a conception of the good upon that person rather than merely helping her to achieve her ends.

Third, the decision to engage in the activity must be one which is difficult to reverse, for if it was not difficult, then it wouldn't matter that much, as far as the person's well-being is concerned, whether or not she underestimated the risks of the activity.

Fourth, the argument must be independent of the question of addiction, for if one is addicted to the activity, then one could justify laws preventing adults from engaging in the activity without using the irrationality argument.

Now the problem is this: the first two conditions work against the third condition. If the activity is not central to a variety of ends and one's underestimation of the risk has nothing to do with epistemic attitudes or values which are central to one's life, then the decision to engage in the activity is not difficult to reverse. What would make the activity difficult to reverse is that it is linked with other activities or ends which the person values, or that it is central to the kind of person one wishes to be or the life one wants to lead, or that one is addicted. But all of these requirements have been ruled out, given the third and fourth conditions listed above. Thus it is doubtful that there are any conditions under which the irrationality argument could succeed.

II. ADDICTION, SMOKING, AND PATERNALISM

The failure of the irrationality argument seems to have no bearing on the addiction argument.[21] Even if smokers do not falsely and irrationally underestimate the risks of smoking, if they are addicted, then they do not voluntarily assume those risks, in which case paternalistic measures to stop or strongly discourage adult smokers from harming themselves would not appear to be objectionable. I shall first discuss Goodin's addiction argument, show why it fails, and then show that the conditions under which

the addiction argument can succeed in justifying paternalist intervention for sane adults are very limited indeed.

Goodin's Addiction Argument

By saying that smokers are addicted, Goodin means that after smoking for a while, the desire to do so is so strong that someone with normal and reasonable self-control would succumb to the desire.[22] Accordingly, we should "have little compunction in saying that the addict's free will was sufficiently impaired that his apparent consent counts for naught."[23] Goodin says two pieces of evidence show that (almost) all smokers are addicted. First, there is a physical need to continue smoking: "the physiological sites and mechanisms by which nicotine acts on the brain have now been well mapped, and its tendency to generate compulsive, repetitive behavior in consequence has been well established."[24] Such evidence, says Goodin, is necessary in order to show that smoking is an addiction, not merely a bad habit, a psychological dependency or a matter of mere sociological pressure, "none of which would undercut, in a way that addictiveness does, claims that the risks of smoking are voluntarily incurred."[25] Second, there is much evidence that smokers have to try very hard to stop smoking: Goodin cites a 1979 Department of Health and Human Services study that shows that 90% of regular smokers have tried to quit, as well as a 1975 survey that showed that 84% of smokers have attempted to stop, but only 36% of them have succeeded in maintaining their changed behavior for a whole year.

Thus Goodin's view is that the physiological (or neurophysiological) effects of smoking make withdrawal from nicotine extremely difficult to do; though a person can resist the compulsive desires that cigarette smoking induces, this involves "extraordinary acts of will"[26] that a person with a normal and reasonable amount of self-control will be unable to muster.

No doubt many smokers find it hard to quit. However, Goodin exaggerates the difficulty by using outdated information. As of a few years ago, almost half of adult smokers had successfully quit,[27] and according to the American Cancer Society, over 90% of those have done so on their own without professional treatment.[28] This throws some doubt on Goodin's claim that it takes extraordinary acts of will to resist the desire to smoke, since resisting that desire seems to be close to an ordinary occurrence for many smokers at some point in their lives. But I will not press this point, as my main concern in this section isn't with the level of difficulty of giving up smoking but with refuting Goodin's claim that this difficulty is due to the neurophysiological effects of nicotine.

Before doing that, one modification in Goodin's concept of addiction is necessary. Goodin maintained that to establish that one is addicted to X, one must show that it is difficult to give up X, *and* that one physically needs to continue X. I agree that the difficulty of giving up X is not *sufficient* to establish that one is addicted to X. It could be difficult to give up something for reasons which have nothing to do with addiction or whether one acts voluntarily. E.g., activities or habits which are central or important to one's life can be difficult to give up, yet were we to say that therefore these activities or habits are addictions or that we are compelled to continue these activities or habits, much of what we do would not be considered voluntary. However, the something else that in addition to the difficulty of giving up X is required to establish that X is an addiction, does not have to be a physical need to continue to do X or evidence of neurophysiological compulsion. Goodin's point in saying that there is a physical need to smoke is to undercut the claim that smokers voluntarily continue to smoke, since one doesn't voluntarily come to physically need something. However, a need does not have to be *physical* in order to undercut a claim of voluntariness: under some circumstances, psychological or other needs could do so as well. If the key element is nonvoluntariness, it seems completely arbitrary to focus just on physical needs.

I suspect the reason Goodin focused on physical needs and ignored psychological needs is that the former don't seem to be the sort of things for which one could ever be held responsible, while this is untrue for at least some kind of psychological needs. This suggests that Goodin's account of the concept of addiction should be modified so that the two key elements are the difficulty in quitting a certain activity because one needs it and the lack of responsibility for needing it. On this revised account, the neurophysiological evidence that Goodin cites would not be *necessary* to establish that one is addicted or that one does not voluntarily engage in or assume the risks of a certain activity, but would be *one kind,* perhaps the best kind, of evidence that shows that one does not voluntarily engage in the activity. In my discussion of Goodin's argument in what follows, it should be kept in mind that the relevance of the issue of the physical or physiological effects of nicotine concerns the larger issue of smokers' responsibility for their behavior.

Why Goodin's Addiction Argument Fails

The success of Goodin's addiction argument requires, first, that the physical or physiological effects of nicotine must actually *explain,* or play a large role in explaining, why many smokers find it difficult to quit, and, second, that this explanation be compatible with the fact that in the last thirty years an increasing percentage of smokers have quit. I shall concentrate mainly on the former, and say a few words about the latter.

Goodin believes that it is obvious that the physiological effects of nicotine explain the difficulty in quitting: recall his statement that it has been "well established" that the sites and mechanisms in the brain for nicotine tend to "generate compulsive, repetitive behavior *in consequence.*" Goodin is referring here to studies summarized in the Surgeon General's 1988 report on nicotine addiction and in the American Psychiatric Association's account of "tobacco dependence disorder." However, if these studies show that the physical need to continue to smoke or the physiological effects of nicotine explain the difficulty in quitting, then the difference between successful and unsuccessful quitters should be due in large part to differences in strength of those needs or effects. But these studies do not show that. What they do show[29] is that smokers who quit smoking in a treatment program have a relapse rate similar to heroin addicts in treatment programs, that smoking produces tolerance, and that quitting smoking produces withdrawal symptoms. The relapse rate of smokers in treatment programs is irrelevant, since smokers in treatment programs are a rather atypical group—as mentioned earlier, over 90% of smokers quit on their own. Nor does tolerance to nicotine explain the difficulty of quitting. Tolerance means that smokers must increase their intake until they achieve the effect that they want, and while this explains why smokers smoke every day to achieve the effect they want—the effects of nicotine are partly lost during sleep—it does not show why smokers would find it difficult to stop wanting to achieve this effect.

This leaves us with the existence of withdrawal symptoms after stopping smoking—the more common ones are cravings for tobacco, impairment of concentration, irritability, anxiety and restlessness, sleep and gastrointestinal disturbances[30]—as the way to establish the explanatory link that Goodin requires. But for withdrawal symptoms to establish that link, two conditions must hold: (1) their severity after initial attempts to quit must provide good evidence of the degree of one's physical need to smoke, and (2) there must be a clear connection between the difficulty in quitting and severity of withdrawal symptoms. However, both (1) and (2) are false. As for (1), both the American Psychiatric Association and the Surgeon General's report admit that the problems smokers face after initial attempts to quit are not a reliable indicator of physical dependence on nicotine.[31] The problem is fairly obvious: the terms listed as withdrawal symptoms are almost all psychological in nature, or have a psychological component. So, for example, if smoker A suffers from more severe anxiety than smoker B after they both quit smoking, this could be explained by A having a greater physical need to smoke/being subject to greater neurophysiological compulsion than B or by A having more problems than B in handling anxiety provoking situations without nicotine (i.e., A is more anxious than B.) Only the former fits the model of nicotine addiction, but to support the former we need independent evidence that A and B were equally anxious without the use of nicotine. As for (2), studies which compare successful and unsuccessful quitters do not show any significant correlation[32] be-

tween success in quitting and the severity of withdrawal problems or symptoms: withdrawal symptoms usually disappear by the end of a few weeks, but many smokers who relapse after quitting do so after that time period.[33] Furthermore, there is no correlation between success in quitting and the years one smoked or between success in quitting and whether one is a heavy or light smoker.[34]

Notice also that the inability of the nicotine dependence model to explain the success and failure of quitting means that Goodin has no suitable way of explaining the increasing percentage of quitters in the last thirty years. During that time publicity about the risks of smoking has increased, as have the costs of smoking, both monetary (increased excise taxes) and nonmonetary (increased unpopularity of smoking, restrictions on smoking in enclosed areas, etc.), while presumably the physiological effects of nicotine have remained the same. Now decisions that the risks or costs of an activity make that activity no longer worthwhile are the type of decisions for which we generally hold people responsible. Goodin is thus logically committed to arguing that whatever contributory role these decisions played in increasing the percentage of quitters, it was not sufficient to hold those smokers who didn't quit responsible for their continuing to smoke.[35] That is, he must argue that while increasing the costs of and information concerning smoking made it somewhat less difficult to resist the compulsive-nicotine induced desire to smoke than would otherwise be the case, these desires are still difficult enough to resist so that smokers who still smoke cannot be said to do so voluntarily. However, that argument must fail since the claim that it is difficult to stop smoking because of the desires induced by nicotine has already been refuted.

Although I have refuted Goodin's addiction argument, unless I can provide a plausible account of why it is difficult to stop smoking, the suspicion may remain that smokers do not voluntarily continue to smoke or assume the risks of smoking. A point made last section, that smoking is a means to or part of a *variety* of ends, suggests an alterative explanation.

Smokers smoke to relax, to concentrate, to handle anxiety, stress and difficult interpersonal situations, as a way of taking a break during the day, as a social lubricant, etc. Smoking is thus linked with a lot of different situations, moods and emotional states. Furthermore, smoking is well *integrated* into smokers' lives. Though most smokers smoke on a fairly continual basis,[36] smokers aren't, for the most part, prevented from carrying out normal life activities: rather, they weave smoking into those activities. This is partly for social reasons—despite the increasing unpopularity of smoking, one can still use nicotine in more situations than other drugs (e.g., there are no legal prohibitions on smoking and driving or on smoking while walking on public streets)—and perhaps partly for pharmacological reasons—the effects of nicotine are mild and subtle enough that it can be used nondisruptively in many situations. Now because smoking is so well-integrated into smokers' lives, it will be difficult to give up: no central change in people's lives is easily achieved. Since concentrating and smoking are linked, or smoking and relaxing are linked, or smoking and handling stress are linked, etc., then giving up smoking doesn't just involve giving up an unhealthy activity, but involves either giving up relaxing, concentrating, etc., which of course almost no one will do, or learning how to concentrate, handle stress, etc., in a new way, and that is something that may be difficult for many people. In light of this, it would seem to be safe to predict that those who will be more successful at quitting will a) have or develop the skills or strategies to handle stress, anxiety, etc., without nicotine, and/or b) have greater self-confidence that they can handle a major life change such as learning how to concentrate, relax, etc., without the use of tobacco. And this is just what has been found. Concerning (a), there is significant evidence that successful quitters employ a wide variety of strategies for coping with the temptation or urge to smoke. Concerning (b) a recent longitudinal study of people who made New Years' resolutions to quit smoking found that the only characteristic that separated successful quitters (after 2 years) from those that did not succeed was that the former expressed, at the beginning of the period when they had given up smoking, a stronger desire to quit smoking and were more likely to believe that quitting would not be that difficult, which bespeaks a greater self-confidence; while some earlier studies found that successful

quitters are more likely to be "internally motivated," that is, believe that their own effort rather than fate, luck or things beyond their control will bring them rewards, and still others found them to be more "secure," both of which again point roughly in the same direction of confidence in one's abilities to bring about a major life-change.[37]

This information would seem to wreck the addiction argument. If whether one quits smoking depends largely not on neurophysiology but on psychological characteristics, character traits, etc.,[38] then the claim that smokers do not voluntarily incur the risks of smoking can only succeed at the very large price of viewing such character traits, characteristics, etc., as something one is not responsible for or something that is not voluntarily incurred. This is a very large price in general, because to make such a move would mean most of what we do we are not responsible for or is not voluntary. It would be a large price for Goodin in particular, since such a move would make bad habits, psychological dependencies and the like undercut claims of voluntariness, something Goodin explicitly rejects.

Why It's Difficult for the Addiction Argument to Succeed

Unlike the irrationality argument, there is no in principle reason why an addiction argument cannot succeed. The problem with the addiction argument is not logical or conceptual, it is empirical: the conditions required for this argument to succeed turn out to be exacting.

The addiction argument is supposed to overcome the strong presumption against paternalist laws for sane adults. This means, first, that one must show not just that the harmful activity in question is difficult to give up but that a clear majority have this difficulty. If only some find it difficult to quit, and thus only some could be construed as addicts, then given the presumption against paternalist laws, it will be very difficult to justify such laws unless the law could somehow prevent or strongly discourage addicts without thereby discouraging or preventing the non-addicts. Second, the presumption against paternalism means that the evidence one uses to show that a clear majority of people are not responsible for their continuing to engage in the activity must avoid implying that people aren't responsible for bad habits, their character flaws and the like, for then much of what we do will be nonvoluntary and accordingly the scope for legitimate paternalist intervention would threaten to become enormous. Third, addiction arguments must explain changes, if any, in the number of people who have quit. If those numbers have increased (as they have in the case of smoking) then to maintain the nonresponsibility criterion one is forced to argue either that the changes were caused by factors one is not responsible for, or that these are due to factors one is responsible for, but that these played a minor role in explaining the increasing quit ratio.

To put matters another way, an addiction argument is most likely to succeed if the majority of people that try to quit, fail, and their failure is relatively invariant to differences in character traits, psychological characteristics, assessment of risks, beliefs about the benefits versus the costs of the risky activity, etc. If this invariance held, then adults who engaged in the risky activity would virtually be trapped, for even if they recognized the risks and costs of the activity, no longer thought the benefits of the activity outweighed the costs or risks, and were the kind of people who could make major life changes, this would turn out to make little difference in helping them to quit. Thus addiction would be a kind of slavery, as it sometimes is analogized to be. But smoking isn't even remotely like this. About half of smokers who try to quit succeed, and their quitting is indeed significantly dependent on the factors just mentioned, and not on matters for which they could not be held responsible for, such as their neurophysiological reactions to nicotine or whether they can summon extraordinary acts of will.

The failure of smoking to fit the requirements of a successful addiction argument indicates the difficulty with addiction arguments. Smoking is a unique legal activity: in no other case do so many people (25% of the population) throughout much of their lives engage in an activity which produces such dramatic self-regarding harms (smoking is the leading cause of preventable death.)[39] If addiction argu-

ments can't succeed in the case of smoking, they are unlikely to succeed with other legal activities: if those have higher quit rates and produce less severe harms, then addiction arguments can't get off the ground. The issues are more complicated in the case of *illegal* activities which harm the participants, such as the use of illegal drugs, for while most users of these drugs are not addicts, and thus the addiction argument doesn't seem to apply,[40] one would need to know the extent of addiction were these drugs legalized, and that is something I cannot discuss here. My own view is that the evidence shows that legalization would bring at most a modest increase in addiction. If I'm right about this, then the addiction argument cannot justify paternalist intervention to stop or strongly discourage adult drug use. This does not mean that there *couldn't* be drug use or a risky activity which fits the requirements of an addiction argument—i.e., an activity which produced such an overwhelming need or desire to continue that most people could only resist using heroic or extraordinary measures. It's just that it's very unlikely that there is such an activity at present. Nor does it mean that addiction, in the sense defined in this paper, does not exist. To say that addiction arguments fail is not to deny that some sane adults are addicted to certain harmful activities, but to deny that this justifies paternalist laws which aim to prevent people from engaging in those activities.

III. CONCLUSION

My arguments imply that we should reject any smoking regulation whose purported justification would very likely depend upon the addiction and/or irrationality arguments. Many *present* smoking regulations do not fall into this category. Laws regulating smoking in confined places invoke harm-to-other, not harm-to-self arguments. Warning labels are justified by the principle that one's right to choose to engage in risky activities is conditioned on these being informed choices—though given the public's overestimation of the risks of smoking, there's a strong case for revising the warning label so as to yield more accurate information. Even regulations that aim to decrease the amount of tobacco consumption could, perhaps, be defended on grounds other than the irrationality and addiction arguments—one might argue, for example, that tobacco taxes are justified on the grounds of discouraging *minors* from smoking. However, regulations which prohibit or aim at preventing smoking altogether are a different matter: to support them, one would almost certainly rely on irrationality and/or addiction arguments. In the future such regulations may be seriously considered; indeed, Goodin's proposal to ban over-the-counter sale of cigarettes can be viewed as a step in this direction. The failure of his arguments, and the general problems with the addiction and irrationality argument, strongly suggests we should not take this step.[41]

NOTES

1. W. Kip Viscusi, *Smoking: Making the Risky Decision,* (New York: Oxford University Press, 1992), p. 70 and p. 80. Except where noted, all statistics in this paper concern the United States.

2. Robert E. Goodin, *No Smoking: The Ethical Issues* (Chicago: University of Chicago Press, 1989). Henceforth called NS.

3. Henceforth, all references to smoking, smokers, etc., exclude minors.

4. NS, pp. 21–4.

5. United States Department of Health and Human Services, A report of the Surgeon General, *The Health Consequences of Smoking: Nicotine Addiction* (Washington, DC: Government Printing Office, 1988).

6. NS, pp. 25–9.

7. Ibid., pp. 21–4.

8. NS, p. 23. The survey is: The U.S. Federal Trade Commission, Matthew Mayers, Chairman *Staff Report on Cigarette Advertising Investigation* (Washington, DC: Government Printing Office, 1981). Goodin also mentions a survey of British smokers: Alan Marsh, "Smoking and Illness: What Smokers Really Believe," *Health Trends,* 17 (1985), pp. 7–12. This presents some special problems which I discuss in note 14.

9. Ibid., pp. 21–2. On the issue of invulnerability, Goodin cites H.M. Alexander, R. Calcott, and A. J. Dobson, "Cigarette and Drug Use in Children. IV: Factors Associated with Changes in Smoking Behavior," *International Journal of Epidemiology,* vol. 12 (1983), pp. 59–65, and Howard Leventhal, Kathleen Glynn, and Raymond Fleming, "Is the Smoking Decision an 'Informed

Choice'?" *Journal of the American Medical Association,* vol. 257 (1987), pp. 3373–376. The study by Alan Marsh, "Smoking and Illness" could also be taken to provide evidence about invulnerability; see note 14. Goodin does not actually cite any studies that show that smokers engage in the anchoring fallacy; he instead cites Daniel Kahneman, Paul Slovic and Amos Tversky, eds., *Judgment Under Uncertainty* (Cambridge: Cambridge University Press, 1982), where it is argued that this is a common reasoning error. Goodin also says that smokers discount the future to an irrational extent, but I leave this aside, since the question of how much concern rationality requires one to have for one's future self is quite controversial.

10. Viscusi, *Smoking: Making the Risky Decision,* pp. 68–9.

11. Ibid., pp. 77–8.

12. See Paul Slovic, Baruch Fischhoff, and Sarah Lichtenstein, "Facts and Fears: Understanding Perceived Risk," in *Judgment Under Uncertainty,* pp. 463–87.

13. NS, pp. 23–4. The survey he cites comes from ibid., p. 469.

14. One possible exception to this claim is the survey by Alan Marsh, "Smoking and Illness" pp. 7–8, which found that 33% of all smokers denied that smoking brought about any increased liability to lung cancer. This seems incompatible with the Viscusi results. However, Marsh also found, p. 9, that when smokers were asked *if* they did get lung cancer (or heart disease or bronchitis) how likely it would be due to smoking, 85% implicated smoking at least to some extent. Marsh notes that this inconsistent data probably means that smokers are aware that they are gambling but deny that anything bad will happen to them. Thus Marsh's data provides some evidence about smokers' belief in invulnerability, rather than an underestimation of the relevant risks of smoking.

15. Viscusi, *Smoking,* pp. 112–13.

16. See note 14. The survey which includes adults in Alan Marsh, "Smoking and Illness."

17. Slovic et al., "Facts and Fears," in *Judgments Under Uncertainty,* pp. 468–72.

18. NS, p. 25 can be read this way.

19. For a thorough list of reasons why people smoke, see J. Alan Best and A. Ralph Hakstian "A Situation-Specific Model for Smoking Behavior," *Addictive Behaviors* vol. 3 (1978) pp. 79–92.

20. NS, p. 23, footnote 20.

21. However, if those addicted to engaging in a very risky activity *thereby,* because of cognitive dissonance, come to irrationally and falsely underestimate the risks, then, by *modus tollens,* the failure of the irrationality argument would undermine the addiction argument. To avoid

this easy refutation of the addiction argument, I shall assume that addicts need not irrationally and falsely underestimate the relevant risks.

22. Goodin at times gives a different account of addiction, whereby it is understood in terms of it being "unreasonably costly for addicts to resist their compulsive desires" (p. 25). This is clearly a mistake. First, voluntariness should not be analyzed in terms of the unreasonable costs of resisting a desire. If someone offers me one hundred times the market price for an item I want very much to sell, it would be unreasonably costly for me to resist my desire to sell that item, but this hardly shows that I didn't voluntarily sell it. Second, it's doubtful Goodin could even hope to show that smokers are addicted on this analysis. Probably the best and least controversial way of showing that the costs of giving up an activity are unreasonable is to show that the costs grossly outweigh the net expected benefits (that is, the net benefits that are expected once the activity is given up). It will be difficult to argue, however, that the costs of giving up smoking grossly outweigh the benefits, for even if the costs of giving up smoking are considerable, so are the benefits: a statistically significantly lowered probability of getting cancer, emphysema, heart disease, etc.

23. NS, pp. 25–6.

24. Ibid., p. 27.

25. Ibid., p. 26.

26. Ibid.

27. United States Department of Health and Human Services, A report of the Surgeon General (Executive Summary), *Reducing the Health Consequences of Smoking: 25 Years of Progress* (Washington DC: Government Printing Office, 1989) pp. i and 11. 44.7% of all adult smokers have successfully quit. Since a small fraction of smokers don't try to quit, about half of smokers that have tried to quit have succeeded.

28. Cited in G. Alan Marlatt, S. Curry, and J. R. Gordon, "A Longitudinal Analysis of Unaided Smoking Cessation," *Journal of Consulting and Clinical Psychology,* vol. 56 (1988), pp. 715–20.

29. For a good summary, see Jay Winsten, director of Center for Health Communication at Harvard Medical School *Research Status Report: Nicotine Dependency and Compulsive Tobacco Use,* reprinted in *Tobacco Product Liability Reporter,* vol. 1 (1986), pp. 5.91–5.95.

30. Ibid.

31. U.S. Department of Health and Human Services, *Nicotine Addiction,* pp. 149, 200, 202, 296.

32. Some studies of *smokers who enter treatment clinics* have shown a correlation between the severity of withdrawal symptoms and the difficulty of quitting. But as already noted, this is a very atypical group, and in any event, other studies of this group have shown no correlation between the severity of withdrawal symptoms and success in quitting. Far more significant is a study by Stanley Schacter that looked at unaided smoking cessation in two complete and self-contained communities (the Psychology Department in Columbia University in 1977 and the entrepreneurial community in Amagansett, Long Island in 1980) and found no correlation whatsoever between the difficulty of withdrawal and success in quitting. See "Recidivism and Self-Cure of Smoking and Obesity," *American Psychologist,* vol. 37 (1982) pp. 436–44. Some studies on smokers in treatment programs are P. Zeidenberg, J. H. Jaffe, M. Kanzler, M. D. Levitt, J. J. Langone, and H. V. Vunakis, "Nicotine: Cotinine Levels in Blood During Cessation of Smoking," *Comprehensive Psychiatry,* vol. 18 (January–February 1977) pp. 93–101; O. Pomerleau, D. Adkins and M. Pertschuk, "Predictors of Outcome and Recidivism in Smoking Cessation Treatment," *Addictive Behaviors,* vol. 3 (1978) pp. 65–70; S. M. Hall, R. I. Herning, J. T. Jones, N. L. Benowitz and P. Jacob III, "Blood Cotinine Levels as Indicators of Smoking Treatment Outcome," *Clinical Pharmacology and Therapeutics,* vol. 35 (June 1984) pp. 810–14; and R. C. Gunn, "Reactions to Withdrawal Symptoms and Success in Smoking Cessation Clinics," *Addictive Behaviors,* vol. 11 (1986) pp. 49–53.

33. On withdrawal symptoms see Winstein, *Nicotine Dependency and Compulsive Tobacco Use* p. 5.92; on relapse time, see Howard Leventhal and Paul D. Cleary, "The Smoking Problem: A Review of the Research and Theory in Behavioral Risk Modification," *Psychological Bulletin,* vol. 88 (1980) p. 390 and Marlatt et al., "Unaided Smoking Cessation," pp. 715–20.

34. U. S. Department of Health and Human Services, *Nicotine Addiction,* p. 521 and Schacter, "Self-Cure of Smoking and Obesity," p. 439.

35. NS, pp. 29, 53, 99, notices that these factors made it easier to quit, but does not notice that he is committed to arguing that their role is not a major one.

36. Less than 10% of smokers are occasional users (i.e., smoke less than 5 cigarettes a day.) 1988 Surgeon General's Report, *Nicotine Addiction,* pp. 253–4.

37. On smokers being more "secure," see Robert C. Benfari, Judith K. Ockene, and Kevin M. McIntyre "Control of Cigarette Smoking From a Psychological Perspective" *Annual Review of Public Health,* vol. 3 (1982) p. 117. On smokers being "internally motivated," see The U. S. Department of Health and Human Services, a report of The Surgeon General *Smoking and Health* (Washington, DC, The Government Printing Office, 1979), chapter

18, p. 9. The information on coping skills comes from the longitudinal study by Marlatt et al., "Unaided Smoking Cessation," pp. 715–20. Corroboration of Marlatt's findings can be found in Alan Marsh, "Smoking: Habit or Choice?," *Population Trends,* vol. 20 (1984), p. 18.

38. The explanation I have offered does not *ignore* the neurophysiological evidence. As noted earlier, it may be that part of the reason smoking is so easy to integrate into people's lives is because the effects of nicotine on the brain are such that smoking does not impair one's ability to do a variety of everyday activities.

39. U.S. Department of Human Health Services, *Nicotine Addiction,* pp. iii and 566 respectively. Only a small fraction of deaths caused by smoking fall on nonsmokers.

40. Most users of cocaine and heroin—the drugs popularly believed to be the most addictive—do not do so on a continual basis. See Michael Gazzaniga, "The Opium of the People: Crack in Perspective," in *Drug Legalization: For and Against* eds. Rod L. Evans and Irwin M. Berent, (La Salle, IL: Open Court Publishing, 1992), pp. 232–46, Arnold S. Trebach, *The Heroin Solution* (New Haven, CT: Yale University Press, 1982), pp. 3–4, and John Kaplan, *The Hardest Drug* (Chicago: University of Chicago Press, 1983), pp. 32–4.

41. I would like to thank the philosophy department of West Virginia University for their comments on an earlier (October 1990) and different version of this paper. I would also like to thank Michael Gorr, Richard Montgomery and Mark C. Wicclair for written comments on an earlier version.

Graham Oddie | Addiction and the Value of Freedom

It is widely held that being addicted is a bad thing. Obviously there are circumstances in which the consequences of particular forms of addiction will be of low overall value. It may even be that such circumstances are fairly typical. But the opponents of the use of (for example) addictive substances generally cite the possibility of addiction *itself* as one of the main reasons against use. It is not only against recreational uses of addictive substances that this argument is wielded, but also against their use in the treatment of chronic and acute pain. An important philosophical task here is to clarify the nature of addiction with a view to determining the disvalues of addiction, and to determine, in particular, whether addiction possesses a disvalue *in itself*—that is, whether addiction possesses an *intrinsic* disvalue. If the answer to this question is *no* then being addictive is not itself an argument against use, and each case of addiction will have to be assessed on its merits.

I begin with some cases which highlight the role of the presumption against addiction both in medical practice and in policy decisions. I then give a fairly detailed account of the various conceptual features of addiction which form the basis of the ensuing arguments. I argue that these features generate a *prima facie* argument against addiction—I call it *the argument from bad cases.* But the strength of the argument varies considerably according to the circumstances surrounding particular addictions, and in a clear sense the disvalue of addiction which arises from the possibility of bad cases is *not* intrinsic. Then I turn to the question of whether or not addiction might also possess intrinsic disvalue. I show that any argument for the thesis of the intrinsic disvalue of addiction will turn on the loss of freedom, autonomy, or self-control, which addiction involves—and then I show why such arguments must fail. If this is right then we need to take a hard look at a whole range of

From Graham Oddie, "Addiction and the Value of Freedom," *Bioethics* 7, no. 5 (1993): 373–401. Some notes and some parts of the text have been deleted.

attitudes and practices connected with addiction and addictive substances.

I. THREE CASES

Case 1

Ms A is a 76 year old, retired school teacher who lives on her own. She has advanced osteoporosis with collapsed vertebrae and severe pain in her back and neck. She has taken a variety of pain medication over time, but is no longer able to take aspirin or other non-steroidal anti-inflammatory drugs because of gastric bleeding. Her GP would like to prescribe morphine but is warned against doing so by a colleague who has been investigated on a charge of inappropriate prescribing of narcotics. Further, in consulting the medical literature the GP is made aware that caution is advised in opioid prescribing, especially in the elderly, since long-term effects of opioids, including the risk of addiction, are not fully understood.

Case 2

Mr B, a 50 year old male with three dependents, has diabetes mellitus and a three-year history of pain related to diabetic neuropathy. He has been treated with a variety of analgesics without adequate pain control. The pain has become worse over the last 12 months and made it impossible for Mr B to continue in his job as a petrol pump attendant so that he is now receiving a sickness benefit. During this time he was referred to a Pain Clinic and was prescribed an opioid drug for a trial of six weeks. He experienced considerable relief from pain and was able to return to his job on a casual basis. He wants to be able to continue on the opioid drug, and to return to full-time paid employment, but neither his GP nor the specialists at the Pain Clinic are willing to prescribe further opioid medication for him, citing the risk of addiction as their main concern. (There is no history of drug abuse, no evidence of inappropriate drug use during the six week trial, and no suggestion of significant psychological problems.) . . .

Case 3

A nicotine inhaler is a device which enables a person to take nicotine directly into the bloodstream via the lungs, thereby closely reproducing many of the effects which smokers desire. Unlike a nicotine patch, which gradually releases the nicotine into the bloodstream, the inhaler delivers a quick burst of the substance to the brain. However, since the nicotine comes without smoke, tar and harmful carcinogens, it has none of the usual harmful side-effects of smoking. Health professionals in Britain advise against the device being made publicly available. The reason?—it might encourage addiction to nicotine.

These three cases, which are by no means unusual, illustrate a commonly held assumption about addiction—an assumption which not only drives medical decisions in the treatment of chronic and acute pain, but influences many policies governing the availability and handling of addictive substances. This assumption is that something's being addictive is a strong reason, often an overriding one, against its availability and use.

In the first two cases becoming addicted was considered, by the health professionals concerned, to be such a harm in itself that they judged it better for their patients to suffer distressing physiological conditions, together with serious side-effects (like unemployment), rather than allow them to run any risk of them becoming addicted.[1]

[The] practitioners (as in case 1) may well have been responding not to their considered judgement on the cases, so much as to the legal situation. We happen to live in a society in which the taking of addictive substances is tightly constrained by law, and practitioners are subject to heavy legal and professional penalties if they are deemed to have transgressed that law. But this only demonstrates that the law has come to embody the strong presumption against addiction.

Of course neither the law, nor the rest of us, are terribly consistent about addiction. Some addictive substances (like alcohol and tobacco) are readily available in western countries for recreational purposes, while others are not. But even in our thinking about these the presumption against becoming addicted operates selectively, sometimes with seemingly bizarre results, as in the fourth case. The upshot of the decision on the nicotine inhaler is that while nicotine can be traded and consumed provided it comes traditionally packaged with a host of carcinogens and other substances which are harmful to users and bystanders alike, it is not available in a form in which the only possible undesirable effect is that it is addictive. The reason, I conjecture, is that the nicotine inhaler, unlike the cigarette, sharply focuses our attention on the main motive people have for consuming nicotine (sating their addictive desires) and the presumption against addiction then gains ready application. I suspect people would have a similar reaction to the marketing of a small device which enabled people to take alcohol intravenously.

In this article I am not mainly concerned about the availability of addictive substances in general, although the analysis of addiction and the associated arguments are quite general and important implications can be readily drawn. However, I am concerned about the effect which the presumption against addiction has on the treatment of pain by health professionals. That "the treatment of severe pain in hospitalized patients is regularly and systematically inadequate"[2] is now well documented.[3] That children suffer particularly badly in this respect seems an unfair twist to the situation.[4] That this systematic undertreatment is driven by the strong presumption against addiction seems undeniable.[5] If the presumption against addiction is not generally justified then an excess of needless preventable suffering has been sanctioned, and continues daily to be sanctioned, by the medical profession.

II. ADDICTION: AN ANALYSIS

Much of the literature on addiction is sceptical about the possibility of giving a unified and coherent treatment of the concept. I am not so pessimistic. Firstly, many of the studies on addiction begin with an interest specifically in drug addiction, and import into the study special features of particular forms of drug

taking which are no part of addiction, or even of drug addiction itself (for example, tolerance). Secondly, the fact that the concept has grey edges does not mean that no explication can be successful. To be successful an explication need only give us the right judgements in the *clear-cut* cases. An explication which is successful in those cases is entitled to legislate for the unclear cases. Lastly, there is now a generally accepted criterion of *dependence* which is on the right tracks, but which is not quite fully adequate as an analysis of addiction.

We will begin with the standard account of dependence, endorsed by the World Health Organisation and the American Psychiatric Association. According to this account, a person is dependent upon something to the extent that s/he wants to give it up, tries to give it up, but tends to fail to do so. (And by extension a substance is classified addictive if that is the standard experience amongst most of its users.) This account (which we will dub the WHO/APA account) certainly helps to distinguish addictions from a host of habits (provided we grant that habits can be broken relatively easily). But the WHO/APA account as it stands is too narrow—and if it is amended in an obvious way it is too wide.

To see that it is too narrow, suppose that there is substance, call it *soma,* which a chemist accidentally manufactures in her laboratory. For some reason she consumes it, it has very pleasant effects, but it is also addictive, and she duly becomes addicted to it. She can make as much of it for herself as she wants, and she does so. She never gives a sample to anybody else, nobody else ever consumes it, and she continues to want to take it, and does so, for the rest of her life. The chemist was (by assumption) addicted to soma, but soma does not possess the WHO/APA property, since nobody who took it (the chemist is the only one) ever actually wanted to stop taking it, and so nobody ever found it difficult or impossible to stop taking it. And since nobody else ever took soma, there are no experiences which are typical of soma-takers. Hence the substance is not, according to the WHO/APA account, addictive.

Of course, the chemist *would have* found it difficult or impossible to stop taking soma *if* she had wanted to. It is this *conditional* feature, rather than the unconditional WHO/APA feature, which undergirds her addiction. The fact that she never wanted to is neither here nor there.

Unfortunately it is not sufficient to modify the definition quite generally along these conditional lines. Suppose we do so amend it, and say that for a person to be addicted to something is tantamount to the following: *if* that person were to want to give it up and tried to do so, she *would* (tend to) backslide. This captures the chemist's soma addiction, but it catches too much besides. On this account it would transpire that most people would be addicted to eating, drinking, and breathing. And, by extension, food, water and air would all be addictive substances.

In what follows I will give a more accurate account of the concept of addiction, one which will explain where the WHO/APA definition gets it right, while correcting it where it goes wrong.

Substance addiction assumes a high profile in our thinking about addiction—perhaps because of the importance of drug addiction in law, and the relative ease with which addictive substances can be legally controlled—and this might easily mislead one into thinking that the objects of addiction are invariably substances. But, firstly, there can be addictions which do not involve material substances, or involve them only indirectly—like addiction to violence, or to exercise or (if advertised treatments to it are genuine) to relationships. Only if all addictions are grounded in physiological dependence on a substance will they all involve material substances, and even if that is true *in fact* it is no part of the *concept* of addiction. One can easily conceive of addictions which are not substance-related. Secondly even substance addiction is more fruitfully thought of as directed towards an *activity* rather than simply towards a substance. The substance addict does not just want the *substance*. Give him the substance in an impenetrable steel cask and he will be disappointed. What the addict wants is for there to be an appropriate *interaction* between himself and the substance.

What this suggests is that addiction is primarily directed to special kinds of states of affairs, or processes: namely, to *activities* in which the addict himself plays a prominent role.

Clearly addiction to an activity—like taking cocaine, drinking coffee or exercising—involves a disposition for the person to desire that s/he engage in the activity. I maintain that the addiction *is* this disposition. The desires produced by the addiction are not the addiction itself. Call the desires so triggered by the addiction *addictive desires*. The addictive desires need not plague the addict constantly (although they may), but will typically be triggered by characteristic circumstances. (To speak here from experience, a mild addiction to coffee usually triggers desire for coffee drinking only at certain times of the day.)

An addiction is a disposition to trigger desires, but not all such dispositions are addictions. We have to distinguish addictions from a host of other dispositions to desire, and in particular from some dispositions which share many features in common with addiction.

Firstly there are the basic "natural" dispositions to desire food, water, air, sex and other fundamental goods, and (typically) these dispositions are not addictions. They are natural to the extent that they are constitutive of human nature. But they are not distinguished from addictions simply by virtue of being natural. For some of these natural dispositions can *become* addictions, and it is not at all illuminating to characterise the transition as that from a "natural" to an "unnatural" condition.

Secondly there are a host of dispositions to desire which are "unnatural" or perhaps "non-natural" in the sense that they are not constitutive of human nature in general, and these may also either be, or not be, addictions. A person who has a standing disposition to desire listening to Mozart whenever a well-known exponent of Mozart's music is in town, would not necessarily be judged to be addicted to listening to Mozart. Similarly, a person who has a disposition to desire to floss his teeth at bedtime is not necessarily addicted to bedtime flossings. Neither disposition is "natural" in the strict sense (they are not constitutive of human nature) and so the addictive/non-addictive distinction does not coincide with the natural/non-natural distinction.

Clearly the addictive disposition and the associated addictive desires have to have a certain character. Three features of addiction are particularly important for our purposes.

Firstly, both the disposition and the addictive desires it generates must have a certain *resilience:* they are difficult to dislodge. It is important to note that resilience, of both desires and dispositions, is a matter of a degree. But being addicted is also a matter of degree, and I submit that the degree of addiction will be some appropriate function of the degrees of resilience of disposition and resulting desires. What exactly does resilience amount to?

Take the resilience of the disposition first. The resilience of the disposition is part of what distinguishes an addiction from a mere habit. To the extent that a habit is not an addiction it is within the power of the habit-bearer to break it, or override it, should circumstances *require* it. Smoking may be a habit, but if it is an addiction it is not merely a habit. This feature explains why it sounds distinctly odd to say: "I am addicted to smoking, but the addiction is one it is easy for me to throw off. I could cease being an addict at any moment I choose."

But it is not just the disposition which is resilient. An important feature of addictions is that the addictive desires are also resilient in an important sense. It is difficult for the addict to dislodge an addictive desire without the desire being fulfilled. Other desires, like that to floss teeth at bedtime, or to have a large gin and tonic, may be strong without being the products of an addiction. So what does this difficulty involve?

The resilience at issue involves an important normative component. A desire is resilient to the extent that the strength of the desire is *insufficiently sensitive* to considerations of the person's overall interests or of overall value. The resilience of a desire clearly admits of degrees. At one extreme a desire which is not resilient (in this sense) is one which the desirer is capable of overriding *if that is what is required.* The more severe the addiction the more resilient are the addictive desires, the more difficult it is for the desirer to dislodge them or override them when required to do so. At the other extreme, when resilience is *complete,* the desire cannot be voluntarily dislodged without its first being fulfilled, even when fulfilment of the desire is not in the person's best interests, or in the interests of overall value, and

the person knows it. Typically the resilience of addictive desires will not be complete. Only in the most intransigent cases of addiction will the addictive desires have that kind of grip on the desirer. But in cases of severe addiction the addictive desires will have a high degree of resilience.

The resilience of addictive desires is what underlies the addict's sense of loss of control. It connects addiction with weakness of the will, and that seems right. Weakness of the will occurs just when a person does not act in accordance with his own best, all-things-considered, judgement (however that is to be analysed). In many of those circumstances in which an addictive desire is stronger than its fulfilment warrants, to act in accordance with the desire will be to display weakness of will.

Resilience of addictive desires is one feature which distinguishes a natural disposition, like the disposition to want to breathe, from an addiction. One reason it is inappropriate to say that one is addicted to breathing is that rarely is fulfilment of the desire to breathe against a person's own best interests.

Resilience of the addictive desires also distinguishes addiction from other resilient dispositions to desire. Contrast an alcoholic's desire for a gin and tonic with a strong desire on the part of a non-alcoholic for the same thing. The alcoholic's and the non-alcoholic's desire might be equally strong. What distinguishes the alcoholic is that he is less likely to be able to act on overriding factors. For example, suppose his child requires medical attention and the delay involved in his having the drink may put the child's health at some risk. The non-alcoholic will typically be able to forego satisfying even a strong desire for a gin and tonic for the child's sake. The strength of his desire can be moderated by other considerations of value. But suppose that the risk to his child's health would not move the desirer to forego his drink. Suppose he (perhaps reluctantly) acknowledges the greater claim of the child, but nevertheless feels driven to have the gin and tonic. In this case his desire is resilient, and so at least bears the marks of addiction. . . .

The third important feature of addictive desires turns on the familiar distinction between desire fulfilment and desire satisfaction. A desire for a state is *fulfilled* if the state desired actually comes about. The desire is *satisfied* if, upon its fulfilment (or belief in its fulfilment), the person feels a characteristic subjective sense of relief at release from the desire. A desire can be fulfilled without being satisfied (like the desire that one's friends mourn one's death); or satisfied without being fulfilled (like the desire that one achieve something significant).

A salient feature of addictive desires is that lack of fulfilment ensures lack of satisfaction. Of course, this lack of satisfaction must be something relatively unpleasant for the addict: relative, that is, to satisfaction of the desire. I will call this property of addictive desires—that lack of fulfilment ensures relative dissatisfaction—the *dissatisfaction* property. . . .

Thus an addiction is a resilient disposition to form resilient desires with the dissatisfaction property. Particular desires other than those that spring from addiction can, of course, be both resilient and have the dissatisfaction property. What is characteristic of addictive desires is that they are brought about by a resilient disposition to generate such desires in a certain range of circumstances.

It is worth noting that all three properties are involved in, and jointly entail, a familiar feature of addiction: withdrawal. Intuitively, someone would not be addicted if withdrawal were not an unpleasant and difficult affair. To withdraw the addict must resist the addictive desires. But, by the resilience of the addictive desires, to resist individual addictive desires will be difficult and, by the dissatisfaction property, unpleasant. Further, by the resilience of the disposition itself, to dislodge the disposition will itself be difficult and hence will tend to take time. These features of withdrawal explain in turn why people who are addicted tend to backslide when they try to withdraw. Hence the account delivers as a consequence the core of truth in the WHO/APA account of dependence.

III. THE ARGUMENT FROM BAD CASES

It should now be evident that there is a rational kernel to the presumption against addiction. By becoming addicted one becomes more or less bound to a disposition to generate desires. *That,* however, is a common enough phenomenon and far from objectionable in itself. By developing a keen interest in one's own career, in music, knowledge, art, sport, a love affair, or in any number of human projects, one may well be binding oneself to such a disposition. What separates addiction from these more common (and presumably acceptable) dispositions are the two properties of resilience and dissatisfaction.

Because of resilience, the addictive desires will be hard to resist even when their fulfilment is not in the addict's best interests. This is because the strength of an addictive desire can be well out of proportion to the importance of its fulfilment. And because of dissatisfaction, if *either* the addict can and does choose to deny an addictive desire, *or* the addictive desire is thwarted by external circumstances, the addict will suffer.

So we have two sorts of *bad cases* for the addict. The first kind of bad case is that in which it is possible for the addictive desires to be fulfilled, but in which it is not the best thing (either for the addict, or perhaps for the world) for the addictive desires to be so fulfilled. When the resilience of the addictive desires becomes complete, and the addict is in a position to fulfil the desire, then she simply has *no choice* but to keep in step with the addiction, even when that is not in her own best interests. But if the addiction is not complete, the addict can overcome the addictive desire only at the cost of dissatisfaction. So by becoming addicted a person may well be engineering for her future self situations in which she cannot win. Either she will be bound to the addiction even when it is not in her own best interests to act on the addictive desires; or, even if she is not so bound, resisting the addictive desire will carry with it dissatisfaction.

The second kind of bad case is that in which external circumstances deny the fulfilment of the addictive desire. Then, of course, the addict will again suffer dissatisfaction.

Thus there is a prima facie case against voluntarily becoming addicted based on conceptual features of addiction: that it generates the possibility of bad cases. Bad cases arise from the fact that denying the addictive desires will be difficult and unpleasant, together with the fact that denying them may be either necessitated by circumstances beyond the addict's control, or in the addict's own best interests.

That is the down-side of addiction in general. But how good is the argument from bad cases? Its strength will clearly depend on local features. More precisely, it will depend on just how likely, and how bad, bad cases are likely to be. In other words, it will depend on how likely it is that the fulfilment of addictive desires will conflict with one's best interests or with overall value, how likely it is that circumstances will make fulfilment impossible, and how much disvalue attaches to lack of fulfilment.

Consider three fairly unproblematic cases: becoming addicted to coffee; becoming addicted to heroin when one would otherwise have a long future and good prospects; becoming addicted to morphine in the last year of a terminal illness.

Many of us elect to become addicted to coffee. Drinking coffee has its modest pleasures, and an addiction to coffee may enhance the pleasure of drinking it. The supply of the substance is fairly well assured, and it is cheap—so to keep feeding the addiction one does not have to forego a lot of other important options. Coffee addicts are usually aware that there might well be a point at which continuing to drink coffee will not be in their own best interests, because of the likelihood of kidney damage, headaches and so forth. But, if the coffee addict is forced to forgo consumption by lack of supply, or chooses to forgo because of countervailing disvalues, the dissatisfaction is not usually so great that it cannot be handled. Withdrawal from caffeine addiction is uncomfortable, but not disastrous. So, not unreasonably, many of us judge the pleasures to be gained from caffeine addiction to be worth the risk. The coffee addict may well be engineering bad cases for his future self, but the risk is small and the disvalues whichever way he chooses in a bad case will not usually be so great.

Heroin addiction, at least for a youngster with otherwise good prospects, is quite a different matter, at least under current conditions. While the pleasures of heroin are much greater than those of coffee, the dissatisfaction which results from the addictive desires being thwarted are much greater. The diffi-

culty of withdrawing from the addiction is considerable. Further, it is an expensive addiction, and so, for all but the very wealthy, the addict must forgo lots of other opportunities to assuage the addictive desires. And because it is both illegal and expensive, the supply is by no means assured, the quality of the substance is difficult to guarantee, and there are obvious risks involved in procuring it. In contemplating activities likely to produce heroin addiction a young person with an otherwise promising future would probably be well advised to turn the offer down. By becoming addicted he will almost certainly be engineering for himself some very bad cases.

Now consider a person with a painful terminal illness, with rather a long time to die: say, one year. To manage the pain effectively large doses of morphine are necesary, and the regularity and sizes of these doses will certainly engender an addiction. Suppose the person does want to live through this final year; that he finds the prospect of enduring the pain of the illness worse than the disvalues of being constantly on morphine; that he will be in a position to monitor and handle the dosages himself eliminating the possibility that he will be dependent on the judgement of others about his need for relief; and that he lives in a stable and fairly wealthy society in which the supply of the drug is well assured for the duration of the illness. Given these conditions he is unlikely to face any future bad cases. It will almost certainly be in his interests throughout his terminal illness to keep taking whatever dosages of morphine are necessary to make the pain tolerable and to assuage his addictive desires. The balance here clearly goes in favour of becoming addicted.

The upshot of this sample of cases is straightforward. The argument from bad cases against addiction can be strong or weak depending on particular circumstances. It depends ultimately on whether addiction is likely to generate bad cases, and just how great the disvalues in such cases will be. In the coffee example the argument is very weak; the bad cases are not so terribly problematic, and not terribly likely. In the morphine example, the argument has no force at all: bad cases are very unlikely, even if the disvalues in such cases may be considerable. In the heroin example the argument carries considerable force: bad cases are both highly likely, given the addict's circumstances, and will involve considerable disvalues. It all depends on the addiction at issue and the circumstances which surround it. The disvalues are thus in a clear sense extrinsic.

IV. FREEDOM AND ADDICTION

Those who largely agree with my analysis of the concept of addiction may still find the foregoing analysis of the values and disvalues of addiction shallow and even question begging. By weighing the consequences of addiction in particular cases I could be accused of assuming that being addicted is not *itself* a disvalue to be weighed in the balance. I have assumed, in other words, that addiction is not itself a morally relevant feature.

Indeed the prima facie argument against addiction in the case of heroin is strong, according to this analysis, partly *because* of the current law against it. It is this law which is largely responsible for the fact that supply is precarious, expensive and dangerous. So according to my analysis heroin addiction is likely to be a bad choice at least partly *because* it is currently illegal. But according to the opponents of the addiction the rationale should presumably be the other way around. It is supposed to be illegal because, heroin being an addictive substance, it is bad to use it.

To counter this line the opponent of addiction will have to maintain that addiction possesses an intrinsic disvalue, that this intrinsic disvalue is considerable, and that in many cases it can be relied upon to outweigh whatever benefits an addiction is supposed to yield.

It is not easy to find explicit advocates of the view that addiction has an intrinsic disvalue. It is clear to me from the literature that that is the most plausible suppressed premise in many of the arguments (where arguments occur at all). But non-philosophers tend not to make a clear distinction between intrinsic and extrinsic disvalue, and philosophers tend to be rather wary of making unequivocal claims about what is of intrinsic value. However, I am grateful to Robert Goodin for as clear and unequivocal statement as one

could hope for: "The policy implications for a distinction between addictions and mere bad habits are clear. . . . Since habits are not necessarily bad, public policies discouraging them are not necessarily desirable. *Addictions, in contrast, are necessarily bad. Policies discouraging them are therefore always desirable.*"[6]

What argument could there be that addiction is necessarily bad, that it possesses an intrinsic disvalue, a cost additional to whatever consequential costs becoming addicted might have in a particular circumstance? What have been characterised here as the consequential costs of addiction are closely tied to the essential nature of addiction: the resilience and dissatisfaction properties which make withdrawal difficult and unpleasant. But these costs arise only in bad cases: that is, if the fulfilment of the addictive desires is prevented by external circumstances, or non-fulfilment is in the addict's best interests. If these are consequential disvalues then any intrinsic disvalue attaching to addiction cannot turn *simply* on the likelihood of bad cases.

Goodin doesn't just define an addiction as a harmful habit. He has an argument to support the claim that addiction is necessarily bad, and the argument is valid (the conclusion follows from the assumptions). But unfortunately one of the assumptions is the WHO/APA account of dependence/addiction, which I have shown independently to be inadequate: "Addictions are unambiguously bad, from the point of view of the person addicted. Being defined in terms of a desire to quit coupled with an inability to quit, addictions necessarily would make the addict worse off."[7] Goodin's argument is thus essentially connected with bad cases. He assumes that the addict will always have to face bad cases, because (by the WHO/APA account) the addict is someone who wants to deny some of his addictive desires, but (because he is addicted) finds himself unable to do so. However, as pointed out in section 2, the assumption that an addict will invariably want, at some stage, to quit is unjustified. That is no part of the notion of addiction. And if the addict never wants to quit, and he faces no problem of supply, then he may never face a bad case, and so may never be worse off.

What, apart from bad cases, could support the intrinsic disvalue of addiction? The answer here is fairly obvious: the disvalue must turn on the addict's loss of freedom. A resilient disposition to generate resilient desires will limit a person's freedom: the greater the resilience the more severe the limitation. In the extreme case a complete addict will simply have no choice but to follow the dictates of his addictive desires. Suppose, what is entirely plausible, that freedom has an intrinsic value. Since addiction is *necessarily* in conflict with freedom, it is necessarily in conflict with something of intrinsic value. But that is just what it is for something to possess intrinsic disvalue.

V. A BARE DIFFERENCE ARGUMENT

One way of determining whether or not a certain feature possesses intrinsic value or disvalue is the method of bare difference. Construct two situations which are alike in all respects *except* the feature in question, and then ask whether there is any *value* difference between the two situations. In order to determine whether or not addiction has a disvalue in itself we have to construct two situations in which the only difference is that addiction occurs in one and not in the other.

Suppose that a person, say Ernie, has a chronic medical problem for which there are two different but equally effective remedies: drug A and drug B. Neither remedy yields a permanent cure, but a daily dose of either would make the problem entirely manageable. There is only one difference between the two remedies: drug A (A for addiction) is highly addictive, while drug B is not addictive at all. In order to ensure bare difference, taking drug A must, in the circumstances, have no bad or good consequences for Ernie which are not also associated with taking drug B.

But herein lies a real difficulty for bare difference. As we have seen, withdrawal from addiction necessarily involves relative disvalues. If Ernie became A-addicted failing to take the drug would not only involve the return of his ailment (as would failing to take drug B if that were the treatment he opted for), but it would also involve the relative dissatisfaction of denying an addictive desire. That is an *extra* disvalue not involved in the B-treatment.

What this means is that to ensure bare difference we must build into the story that if Ernie chooses drug A there will be absolutely no chance that he will have to face withdrawal. We must stipulate that the supply of A is completely assured, and that there are no hassles or anxieties associated with treatment A that are not also associated with treatment B.

Provided we build all these factors into the story the argument from bad cases against becoming addicted does not work against drug A, for the story guarantees that Ernie will not face bad cases. The consequences of Ernie's opting for drug A are thus identical to his opting for drug B—apart from the addiction itself, and whatever is directly and necessarily involved in A-addiction. What *is* necessarily involved is a certain loss of freedom.

Two questions arise. Firstly, is there, intuitively, any residual value-difference between the two treatments provided all these conditions are met? Secondly, if the answer to the first question is *yes,* is the value-difference explained by Ernie's loss of freedom consequent upon treatment A?

I suspect that answers to the first question will vary somewhat. On the one hand there really doesn't seem to be much, if anything, to choose between the two treatments. But many people may be inclined to have a preference for treatment B. And a preference for treatment B would suggest that addiction in itself is deemed to possess intrinsic disvalue. However, this does not follow directly, for there may be another rational explanation for the preference. It may be that the judgement that treatment A is less satisfactory than treatment B stems from an unwillingness to accept the very stringent conditions of the story: namely, that there really is *no chance* that, once A-addicted, Ernie will ever have to face withdrawal. After all, how can I, or Ernie, be *sure* about that?

The answer is that *I* can be sure (even if Ernie cannot) because I am the story teller. From my God-like vantage point I simply stipulate it. It's *my* story. However, it would be very unrealistic to suppose that *Ernie,* if he is anything like us, can be sure about that—since none of us has a God's-eye view of the situations in which we find ourselves. And given even a very modest subjective uncertainty about the continued supply of A it would be rational for Ernie to prefer B. A non-zero probability that the supply of A will dry up yields a non-zero probability that Ernie will face bad cases. No matter how small the probability, that will be enough to tip the balance of *expected* value in favour of treatment B. This still holds if the same subjective uncertainty attaches to the possibility of the supply of drug B drying up. This is because, by the resilience and dissatisfaction properties, the possibility of the supply of drug A drying up is worse than the possibility of the supply of drug B drying up.

So Ernie, by virtue of limited knowledge, is justified in *regarding* treatment B as more valuable than treatment A. But this does not show that treatment B *is* more valuable. For Ernie's subjective ranking of the two treatments is based on what we (from our God's-eye view) know to be *false* information: namely that there is some small chance the supply of A will dry up.

What this shows is that for agents, such as ourselves, who have limited knowledge of the future the argument from bad cases will always have to be weighed in deciding what it *seems* best to do. There will always be some subjective probability that, once addicted, a bad case will turn up. But that is only on the side of *estimated* value, not on the side of actual value. (Even in actual cases this will not necessarily be a decisive factor in our estimates of value, because the probability of a bad case might be quite small.)

In Ernie's case, then, the possibility that treatment A is *objectively* worse than treatment B must turn on some feature other than that of the possibility of bad cases. The only difference between the two situations, as I will show, involves a certain loss of freedom.

How is Ernie's freedom impaired by A-addiction? Let us suppose that A is *powerfully* addictive. By tak-

ing A *once* Ernie will be completely hooked: he will acquire a *completely* resilient disposition to desire a daily dose (the disposition cannot be thrown off); the addictive desires themselves will also be completely resilient (Ernie will not be able to forego satisfying them whenever it is possible to do so); and it would be extremely unpleasant for Ernie if the desires are denied by external circumstances (dissatisfaction upon non-fulfilment is high). So, once addicted Ernie will be incapable of choosing to kick the addiction or forego the addictive desires. However, to ensure bare difference, no *other* choices of Ernie's will be impaired because, by assumption, we want to rule out other consequential effects. What is the structure of Ernie's choice situation in the two cases?

With treatment A Ernie becomes and remains addicted to A. In particular he cannot choose to revert to the non-addictive state. Consequently he cannot, for example, switch treatments and be just as well off. With treatment B, we may suppose, Ernie has more choice. He could halt the treatment, and then either suffer the ailment, or switch to the alternative treatment. So in case of treatment B Ernie definitely has some extra choices which are denied to him on treatment A. The intuition that even in the case of bare difference his freedom is impaired is born out. But the question remains whether this particular *kind* of freedom is intrinsically valuable.

Let us strengthen the story a little in a way which should not affect the judgement on the value-ranking of the two treatments. Suppose that Ernie's ailment is an incredibly painful one, so that faced with an apparent choice between continuing with the pain on the one hand, and having one or other of the treatments on the other, Ernie cannot do anything but to opt for some treatment or other. He really has no choice between being treated and not being treated. Given this, treatment A will still involve relative loss of freedom. Once hooked on A Ernie *cannot* switch to B. But treatment B does not limit his freedom in this way. If he is taking treatment B he can give it up—but only, by assumption, to switch to A. So as far as choices affected by the two treatments go Ernie's future choice-structure looks like this:

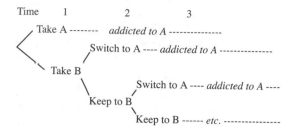

Abstracting from the particular details of the case what this amounts to is the following:

So Ernie's fundamental choice (remember bare difference) is between becoming addicted on the one hand, and remaining unaddicted with the opportunity to so choose again at a later date.

VI. THE VALUE OF FREEDOM: THE STRONG THESIS

In this section I will consider what I call the *strong* thesis about the value of freedom: that intrinsic value attaches merely to the *having* of genuine choices *regardless of whether there are any value differences between those choices*. Assume the strong thesis of the value of freedom. Then at each decision node in the above tree, where Ernie faces the choice between addiction (A_i) and remaining non-addicted (B_i), the latter choice will be more valuable than the former. This is because opting for addiction involves a loss of future choice, whereas opting for non-addiction does not. The strong thesis thus tells us that having the choice (in this case between addiction and non-addiction) is valuable even if there is no *other* value difference between addiction and non-addiction.

The strong thesis thus yields the required intrinsic disvalue of addiction: but at a cost. For the strong thesis is unattractive. According to the strong thesis it would be more valuable to be able to choose from a range of ten different brands of toothpaste than from a certain subset of that range, say five different brands, *even if there are no value-differences between the brands*. While one might think such choice instrumentally valuable (say, through the effect of competition on quality or price of the end products) it is hard to see why one would consider it intrinsically valuable.

Or again, suppose you go into a travel agent because you have seen advertised a Pacific Island holiday of which you would like to take advantage. When you ask to book for the holiday the travel agent replies:

"We can do better than merely booking you. We can offer you a choice between two different Pacific Island holidays: you can either go to the Pacific Island we advertised, or you can go to another Pacific Island."

"What is the difference between them? What do they each offer?" you ask.

"No real difference at all!" the agent replies, and continues: "In fact we can *guarantee* that they are equally valuable because, although they are distinct islands, they are almost completely indistinguishable. One is the *mirror image* of the other. Apart from that inversion you would never know you were on one rather than the other. But aren't you lucky to have the choice?"

Pehaps these stories and arguments will not change the opinion of a devotee of the intrinsic value of sheer choice. But such a devotee would have to admit that the value involved, even if positive, must be rather small. As such it would hardly be sufficient to swamp the other, instrumental, values and disvalues. For example, suppose that in order to have the choice between a Pacific Island Holiday and its mirror image Island Holiday you had to deal with a slightly boorish and unpleasant travel agent. Would it not be better to deal with the agency which, while it offers only the one island holiday, nevertheless has pleasant and helpful staff?

VII. THE VALUE OF FREEDOM: THE WEAK THESIS

The examples in section VI undermine the strong thesis of the value of freedom and motivate consideration of a (logically) weaker thesis. What we value in freedom, what it is about being free that makes us significant and valuable beings, is not merely that we have choices which differ in their *content*. Rather, what we value is that our choices make a *value-difference*: that our choices differ in their *value*. The more significantly they differ in their value, the more significant the value of the choice itself. According to this more plausible view of the value of freedom it is not just the sheer number of choices that is valuable. Rather, it is being able to choose between options which differ in value. We don't just value making a *difference* to the world, or to our lives, we value making a *value*-difference. Call this the weak thesis of the value of freedom

Consider Ernie again in the last scenario of section 5. Can we apply the weak thesis of the value of freedom to generate the postulated intrinsic disvalue of addiction? Consider again Ernie's choice situation. By the bare difference postulate A_1 and B_1 differ only over what choices they leave Ernie in the future. A_1 leaves Ernie no choice at all: B_1 leaves Ernie with a choice between A_2 and B_2. So by the weak principle B_1 will be more valuable than A_1 if and only if there is a value-difference between A_2 and B_2. But the *only* difference between A_2 and B_2 is that between being addicted and not being addicted. Hence, *the weak principle delivers the desired result only on the assumption that there is a value difference between being addicted and not being addicted.* The argument thus begs the very question at issue. . . .

Note that there is nothing special about this particular scenario which guarantees the argument will be question-begging. The same conclusion applies equally to *any* case in which the only difference between becoming addicted and remaining unaddicted is that the former does not, and the latter does, allow the person future choices between becoming addicted and remaining unaddicted. In any such case any argument for the intrinsic disvalue of addiction which appeals to the weak principle of the value of freedom will have to beg the question by assuming that there is such an intrinsic value-difference. This is in no way a criticism of the weak thesis of freedom's intrinsic value. Indeed, it is a thesis which I myself endorse, along with other theses of the value of autonomy. . . .

VIII. REVIEWING THE CASES

It will be instructive to review the cases I began with in the light of the above discussion. But before doing so let me briefly summarize the main results of this analysis. An addiction is a resilient disposition to generate resilient desires with the dissatisfaction property. That an activity is addictive is the basis of a prima facie argument against indulging in it—an argument from bad cases. But the strength of this argument depends on how likely, and how bad, bad cases are likely to be. Any argument for an additional intrinsic disvalue to addiction, a disvalue which could substantially alter the balance against possible consequential benefits, will have to invoke the value of freedom. But then it will either appeal to an implausibly strong thesis of freedom's value; or, if it settles for a more attractive (and, in my view, *true*) thesis, it will have to beg the question at issue. I conclude that there is no intrinsic disvalue to addiction, and each case of possible addiction will have to be examined for consequential values and disvalues before deciding what should be done.

With regard to the first two cases much of the medical literature suggests, other things being equal, that the risk of becoming addicted to narcotics through their use in the treatment of pain is surprisingly small.[8] However, the *risk* of such treatment could still be large, and hence worthy of taking seriously, if being addicted were a sufficiently bad thing. For the size of a risk is a function not just the *probability* of a bad outcome, but the *badness* of that outcome: a small chance of a very bad outcome may generate a risk worth noting. But quite apart from the magnitude of the chance of becoming addicted, what I have shown is that *the chance of becoming addicted by itself does not constitute a reason for preferring one course of action to another.* Rather, we have to examine the *nature* of the addiction, in particular the likelihood and severity of the bad cases it could generate. In many cases this is enough to substantially shift the burden of proof, *especially* if we place a value on rational autonomy.

Case 1

In itself becoming addicted to the morphine is not bad for Ms A. Provided the health professionals she employs are reliable and trustworthy, she can clearly be confident of keeping up the supply for as long as is required. . . . The known effects of long-term addiction to morphine would appear to be much less undesirable than the effects of her condition. Given that there are no other relevant and unstated factors to the case, and given the presumed value of rational autonomy, Ms A should have the known advantages and disadvantages of prolonged morphine use explained to her and then given the choice.

Case 2

Very similar remarks apply to Mr B's condition. The use of the morphine enabled him to lead a satisfying life. Even if he did become addicted to morphine, the known long-term effects of this seem much less undesirable than the effects of his condition. . . .

Case 3

Whatever one's views of the disvalue of addiction, the nicotine inhaler is clearly far preferable to cigarettes as a means of delivering nicotine to the body. Since both contain nicotine they are equally addictive, but cigarette smoke harbours all manner of additional disvalues. Particularly important here are the disvalues which smoking involves for the surrounding non-smokers—from the moral point of view the inhaler is far superior to the cigarette. But even prudentially it would be wise for a nicotine addict to choose the inhaler. It seems that any defensible justification for restricting the availability of the inhaler while cigarettes continue to be freely available, must be to do with the *indirect* conse-

quences of its availability. That is to say, to make the inhaler available would be to concede that a substance's being highly addictive (as nicotine is) is not a good reason, in itself, for constraining its availability—and that might encourage people to think that they should have the choice concerning the consumption of *other* addictive substances. And, of course, they might be right about that.

NOTES

1. For an insightful account, by a medical practitioner, of the inter-relations between pain, pain treatment, and concomitant suffering, see Cassel 1982.
2. See Angell 1982.
3. Marks and Sachar 1973 in a much cited study concluded that undertreatment was the *characteristic* treatment. Morgan and Pleet 1983 concluded that ten years later there had been "minimal evidence of improvement and patients with severe pain are still markedly undertreated."
4. For example, see Beyer, De Good, Ashley, and Russell 1983.
5. Consider, for example the following passage in Melzack 1990, p. 19: "Morphine is the safest, most effective analgesic (painkiller) known for constant severe pain, but it is also addictive for some people. *Consequently* it is typically meted out sparingly, if it is given at all." The italics are mine, but the point is clear. It is because of the risk of addiction that it is not used. Or again, in Bakalar and Grinspoon 1984 "The most important justification for strict legal and social control on drugs is dependency or addiction . . . it provides the best reason for saying that the drug user is not free, and that anyone exposed to the drug may lose personal freedom." (p. 35).
6. Goodin 1989, p. 100 (my emphasis).
7. Goodin 1989, p. 99.
8. See Robins, Davis and Nurco 1974, Porter and Hershel 1980, Morgan and Pleet 1983, and Melzack 1990.

REFERENCES

American Psychiatric Association. *Diagnostic and Statistical Manual of Mental Disorders.* (3rd edition), Washington DC: American Psychiatric Association, 1987.

Angell, M. "The quality of mercy." *The New England Journal of Medicine* 306 (2), 1982, pp. 98–99.

Bakalar, J.B. and Grinspoon, L. *Drug Control in a Free Society.* Cambridge: Cambridge University Press, 1984.

Beyer, J.E., De Good, D.E. Ashley, L.C. and Russell, G.A. "Patterns of post-operative analgesic use with adults and children following cardiac surgery." *Pain* (17), 1982, pp. 71–81.

Cassel, E.J. "The nature of suffering and the goals of medicine." *The New England Journal of Medicine,* 306 (11), 1982, pp. 639–645.

Goodin, R.E. *No Smoking: The Ethical Issues,* Chicago: The University of Chicago Press, 1989.

Marks, R.M. and Sachar, E.J. "Undertreatment of medical inpatients with narcotic analgesics." *Annals of Internal Medicine,* 78(2), 1973, pp. 173–181.

Melzack, R. "The tragedy of needless pain," *Scientific American,* 262 (2), Feb. 1990, pp. 19–25.

Morgan, J.P. and Pleet, D.L. "Opiophobia in the United States: the undertreatment of severe pain," in Morgan, J.P. and Kagan, D.V. (eds) *Society and Medication: Conflicting Signals for Prescribers and Patients,* D.C. Heath and Company, 1983.

Porter, J. and Herschel, J. "Drug addiction rare in patients treated with narcotics." *New England Journal of Medicine,* 10, Jan 1980, p. 123.

Robins, L.N., Davis, D.H., and Nurco, D.N. "How permanent was Vietnam drug addiction?" *American Journal of Public Health Supplement,* 96, Dec. 1974, pp. 38–43.

World Health Organisation, *International Classification of Diseases.* (9th edition), Geneva: World Health Organisation, 1978.

28

Is a Government Ban
on Human Cloning Wrong?

Kass and His Critics

The cloning of an animal is the production of a new animal, from an original, that is genetically identical to the original. Cloning experiments have been carried out in recent years on a variety of nonhuman species, with mixed and widely publicized results. As a consequence, there has been an increasingly heated debate over the moral status of attempting to clone human beings.

Leon R. Kass, the chair of President George W. Bush's Bioethics Advisory Council, is perhaps the most prominent and influential opponent of human cloning. In the article excerpted in this chapter, which was originally published in the *New Republic* in 2001, Kass focuses on cloning for reproductive purposes (as opposed to therapeutic purposes) and presents four distinct arguments in defense of the claim that such cloning is immoral and should be illegal. The *unethical experimentation argument* begins with the fact that cloning of non-human animals has often resulted in deformed or stillborn offspring. The argument maintains that since cloning a human being is very likely to produce similar results, it should be rejected as a form of unethical experimentation on the resulting human beings. Kass's second argument raises the following question: What would it be like for a person to be the result of a successful cloning procedure? In what might be called the *identity (or individuality) argument*, Kass maintains that reproductive cloning would result in significant psychological harm to the cloned offspring, and that this counts as a second and distinct objection to the procedure. Kass presses this concern by focusing both on the effects cloning would have on parent-child relationships and on the effects it would have on the self-identity of the child himself. In what could then be called the *manufacturing babies argument*, Kass next objects that cloning amounts to replacing reproduction with manufacturing, in a way that would artificially elevate a parent even further over his or her offspring and dehumanize the resulting child. And in what we call the *parental experience argument*, Kass concludes by adding that cloning would prevent parents from enjoying part of what is most unique and valuable about the parenting experience, that is, the way in which it involves opening oneself up to the unknown.

Not every defender of cloning has responded directly to Kass. And not every response to Kass has responded to each of his arguments. However, the literature in defense of the moral acceptability of cloning, as a whole, does try to grapple with the objections to cloning that Kass most prominently represents. And at least some of these arguments are addressed in the critical responses that follow Kass's article. For example, although David Elliott does not refer to Kass by name, the selection from Elliott's article on cloning can readily be construed as a rebuttal to Kass's manufacturing babies argument. Elliott argues that cloning need not be construed as manufacturing children in Kass's sense, and that even if it is so construed, the same is true of many non-cloning forms of reproduction that are commonly taken to be morally acceptable. And although David Hershenov cites some of Kass's other writings in his response to the anti-cloning position, much of what Hershenov writes can be taken as an attempted rebuttal to the identity (or individuality) argument that Kass presents in the excerpt reprinted here. In particular, Hershenov accuses Kass of the philosophical sin of overgeneralization: Even though cloning would be objectionable for some of the reasons Kass cites in some cases, other cases lack those features. Hershenov attempts to find a general principle for distinguishing the objectionable instances of cloning from acceptable ones.

QUESTIONS FOR CONSIDERATION

In thinking critically about Kass's case for a federal ban on reproductive cloning, readers should begin by focusing on those of his arguments to which Elliott and Hershenov can most readily be understood as responding.

• In what sense does cloning involve "manufacturing" a human being? Is it a strong enough sense to warrant Kass's opposition to cloning? Or is Elliott right in thinking that we find such "manufacturing" acceptable in other contexts?

• What are the sources of Kass's concerns about what it would be like for a person to be the result of a successful cloning procedure? Is Kass right to picture these features as essential features of cloning? Or is Hershenov right to think that they would pose problems only in some cases of cloning but not in others?

• It is also important to think critically about points raised by Kass that neither author offers a direct response to. Is Kass right, for example, to think that the risks of producing stillborn or deformed children are great enough to justify opposing the attempt to clone human beings? Or is society entitled to undertake such risks in pursuit of scientific progress? Is it better to produce no clone at all than to produce one that has significant birth defects? Why or why not? If a clone were born with a birth defect, would he have a legitimate complaint against the people who created him? Would he have been wronged by being created? Would he have been harmed?

• Finally, readers should keep in mind that Kass is claiming not only that reproductive cloning is wrong, but also that the federal government should prohibit it. Do Kass's arguments entitle him to this second claim? Or is there room to agree with Kass that cloning is wrong but to maintain that it should be legally permitted nonetheless?

FURTHER READING

Glannon, Walter. "The Ethics of Human Cloning." *Public Affairs Quarterly* 12, no. 3 (1998): 287–305.

Leon R. Kass | # Preventing a Brave New World

II

What is cloning? Cloning, or asexual reproduction, is the production of individuals who are genetically identical to an already existing individual. The procedure's name is fancy—"somatic cell nuclear transfer"—but its concept is simple. Take a mature but unfertilized egg; remove or deactivate its nucleus; introduce a nucleus obtained from a specialized (somatic) cell of an adult organism. Once the egg begins to divide, transfer the little embryo to a woman's uterus to initiate a pregnancy. Since almost all the hereditary material of a cell is contained within its nucleus, the re-nucleated egg and the individual into which it develops are genetically identical to the organism that was the source of the transferred nucleus.

An unlimited number of genetically identical individuals—the group, as well as each of its members, is called "a clone"—could be produced by nuclear transfer. In principle, any person, male or female, newborn or adult, could be cloned, and in any quantity; and because stored cells can outlive their sources, one may even clone the dead. Since cloning requires no personal involvement on the part of the person whose genetic material is used, it could easily be used to reduce living or deceased persons without their consent—a threat to reproductive freedom that has received relatively little attention.

Some possible misconceptions need to be avoided. Cloning is not Xeroxing: the clone of Bill Clinton, though his genetic double, would enter the world hairless, toothless, and peeing in his diapers, like any other human infant. But neither is cloning just like natural twinning: the cloned twin will be identical to an older, existing adult; and it will arise not by chance but by deliberate design; and its entire genetic makeup will be pre-selected by its parents and/or scientists. Moreover, the success rate of cloning, at least at first, will probably not be very high: the Scots transferred two hundred seventy-seven adult nuclei into sheep eggs, implanted twenty-nine clonal embryos, and achieved the birth of only one live lamb clone.

For this reason, among others, it is unlikely that, at least for now, the practice would be very popular; and there is little immediate worry of mass-scale production of multicopies. Still, for the tens of thousands of people who sustain more than three hundred assisted-reproduction clinics in the United States and already avail themselves of in vitro fertilization and other techniques, cloning would be an option with virtually no added fuss. Panos Zavos, the Kentucky reproduction specialist who has announced his plans to clone a child, claims that he has already received thousands of e-mailed requests from people eager to clone, despite the known risks of failure and damaged offspring. Should commercial interests develop in "nucleus-banking," as they have in sperm-banking and egg-harvesting; should famous athletes or other celebrities decide to market their DNA the way they now market their autographs and nearly everything else; should techniques of embryo and germline genetic testing and manipulation arrive as anticipated, increasing the use of laboratory assistance in order to obtain "better" babies—should all this come to pass, cloning, if it is permitted, could become more than a marginal practice simply on the basis of free reproductive choice.

What are we to think about this prospect? Nothing good. Indeed, most people are repelled by nearly all aspects of human cloning: the possibility of mass production of human beings, with large clones of look-alikes, compromised in their individuality; the

From Leon Kass, "Preventing a Brave New World," *The New Republic,* May 21, 2001. Some parts of the text have been deleted.

idea of father-son or mother-daughter "twins"; the bizarre prospect of a woman bearing and rearing a genetic copy of herself, her spouse, or even her deceased father or mother; the grotesqueness of conceiving a child as an exact "replacement" for another who has died; the utilitarian creation of embryonic duplicates of oneself, to be frozen away or created when needed to provide homologous tissues or organs for transplantation; the narcissism of those who would clone themselves, and the arrogance of others who think they know who deserves to be cloned; the Frankensteinian hubris to create a human life and increasingly to control its destiny; men playing at being God. Almost no one finds any of the suggested reasons for human cloning compelling, and almost everyone anticipates its possible misuses and abuses. And the popular belief that human cloning cannot be prevented makes the prospect all the more revolting.

Revulsion is not an argument; and some of yesterday's repugnances are today calmly accepted— not always for the better. In some crucial cases, however, repugnance is the emotional expression of deep wisdom, beyond reason's power completely to articulate it. Can anyone really give an argument fully adequate to the horror that is father-daughter incest (even with consent), or bestiality, or the mutilation of a corpse, or the eating of human flesh, or the rape or murder of another human being? Would anybody's failure to give full rational justification for his revulsion at those practices make that revulsion ethically suspect?

I suggest that our repugnance at human cloning belongs in this category. We are repelled by the prospect of cloning human beings not because of the strangeness or the novelty of the undertaking, but because we intuit and we feel, immediately and without argument, the violation of things that we rightfully hold dear. We sense that cloning represents a profound defilement of our given nature as procreative beings, and of the social relations built on this natural ground. We also sense that cloning is a radical form of child abuse. In this age in which everything is held to be permissible so long as it is freely done, and in which our bodies are regarded as mere instruments of our autonomous rational will, repugnance may be the only voice left that speaks up to defend the central core of our humanity. Shallow are the souls that have forgotten how to shudder.

III

Yet repugnance need not stand naked before the bar of reason. The wisdom of our horror at human cloning can be at least partially articulated, even if this is finally one of those instances about which the heart has its reasons that reason cannot entirely know. I offer four objections to human cloning: that it constitutes unethical experimentation; that it threatens identity and individuality; that it turns procreation into manufacture (especially when understood as the harbinger of manipulations to come); and that it means despotism over children and perversion of parenthood. Please note: I speak only about so-called reproductive cloning, not about the creation of cloned embryos for research. The objections that may be raised against creating (or using) embryos for research are entirely independent of whether the research embryos are produced by cloning. What is radically distinct and radically new is reproductive cloning.

Any attempt to clone a human being would constitute an unethical experiment upon the resulting child-to-be. In all the animal experiments, fewer than two to three percent of all cloning attempts succeeded. Not only are there fetal deaths and stillborn infants, but many of the so-called "successes" are in fact failures. As has only recently become clear, there is a very high incidence of major disabilities and deformities in cloned animals that attain live birth. Cloned cows often have heart and lung problems; cloned mice later develop pathological obesity; other live-born cloned animals fail to reach normal developmental milestones.

The problem, scientists suggest, may lie in the fact that an egg with a new somatic nucleus must reprogram itself in a matter of minutes or hours (whereas the nucleus of an unaltered egg has been prepared over months and years). There is thus a greatly increased likelihood of error in translating the genetic instructions, leading to developmental defects some of which will show themselves only much later. (Note also that these induced abnormalities may also affect the stem cells that scientists hope to harvest from cloned embryos. Lousy embryos, lousy stem cells.) Nearly all scientists now agree that attempts to clone human beings carry massive risks of producing unhealthy, abnormal, and malformed children. What are we to do with them? Shall we just discard the ones that fall short of expectations? Considered opinion is today nearly unanimous, even among scientists: attempts at human cloning are irresponsible and unethical. We cannot ethically even get to know whether or not human cloning is feasible.

If it were successful, cloning would create serious issues of identity and individuality. The clone may experience concerns about his distinctive identity not only because he will be, in genotype and in appearance, identical to another human being, but because he may also be twin to the person who is his "father" or his "mother"—if one can still call them that. Unaccountably, people treat as innocent the homey case of intrafamilial cloning—the cloning of husband or wife (or single mother). They forget about the unique dangers of mixing the twin relation with the parent-child relation. (For this situation, the relation of contemporaneous twins is no precedent; yet even this less problematic situation teaches us how difficult it is to wrest independence from the being for whom one has the most powerful affinity.) Virtually no parent is going to be able to treat a clone of himself or herself as one treats a child generated by the lottery of sex. What will happen when the adolescent clone of Mommy becomes the spitting image of the woman with whom Daddy once fell in love? In case of divorce, will Mommy still love the clone of Daddy, even though she can no longer stand the sight of Daddy himself?

Most people think about cloning from the point of view of adults choosing to clone. Almost nobody thinks about what it would be like to be the cloned child. Surely his or her new life would constantly be scrutinized in relation to that of the older version. Even in the absence of unusual parental expectations for the clone—say, to live the same life, only without its errors—the child is likely to be ever a curiosity, ever a potential source of déjà vu. Unlike "normal"

identical twins, a cloned individual—copied from whomever—will be saddled with a genotype that has already lived. He will not be fully a surprise to the world: people are likely always to compare his doings in life with those of his alter ego, especially if he is a clone of someone gifted or famous. True, his nurture and his circumstance will be different; genotype is not exactly destiny. But one must also expect parental efforts to shape this new life after the original—or at least to view the child with the original version always firmly in mind. For why else did they clone from the star basketball player, the mathematician, or the beauty queen—or even dear old Dad—in the first place?

Human cloning would also represent a giant step toward the transformation of begetting into making, of procreation into manufacture (literally, "handmade"), a process that has already begun with in vitro fertilization and genetic testing of embryos. With cloning, not only is the process in hand, but the total genetic blueprint of the cloned individual is selected and determined by the human artisans. To be sure, subsequent development is still according to natural processes; and the resulting children will be recognizably human. But we would be taking a major step into making man himself simply another one of the man-made things.

How does begetting differ from making? In natural procreation, human beings come together to give existence to another being that is formed exactly as we were, by what we are—living, hence perishable, hence aspiringly erotic, hence procreative human beings. But in clonal reproduction, and in the more advanced forms of manufacture to which it will lead, we give existence to a being not by what we are but by what we intend and design.

Let me be clear. The problem is not the mere intervention of technique, and the point is not that "nature knows best." The problem is that any child whose being, character, and capacities exist owing to human design does not stand on the same plane as its makers. As with any product of our making, no matter how excellent, the artificer stands above it, not as an equal but as a superior, transcending it by his will and creative prowess. In human cloning, scientists and prospective "parents" adopt a technocratic attitude toward human children: human children become their artifacts. Such an arrangement is profoundly dehumanizing, no matter how good the product.

Procreation dehumanized into manufacture is further degraded by commodification, a virtually inescapable result of allowing baby-making to proceed under the banner of commerce. Genetic and reproductive biotechnology companies are already growth industries, but they will soon go into commercial orbit now that the Human Genome Project has been completed. "Human eggs for sale" is already a big business, masquerading under the pretense of "donation." Newspaper advertisements on elite college campuses offer up to $50,000 for an egg "donor" tall enough to play women's basketball and with SAT scores high enough for admission to Stanford; and to nobody's surprise, at such prices there are many young coeds eager to help shoppers obtain the finest babies money can buy. (The egg and womb-renting entrepreneurs shamelessly proceed on the ancient, disgusting, misogynist premise that most women will give you access to their bodies, if the price is right.) Even before the capacity for human cloning is perfected, established companies will have invested in the harvesting of eggs from ovaries obtained at autopsy or through ovarian surgery, practiced embryonic genetic alteration, and initiated the stockpiling of prospective donor tissues. Through the rental of surrogate-womb services, and through the buying and selling of tissues and embryos priced according to the merit of the donor, the commodification of nascent human life will be unstoppable.

Finally, the practice of human cloning by nuclear transfer—like other anticipated forms of genetically engineering the next generation—would enshrine and aggravate a profound misunderstanding of the meaning of having children and of the parent-child relationship. When a couple normally chooses to procreate, the partners are saying yes to the emergence of new life in its novelty—are saying yes not only to having a child, but also to having whatever child this child turns out to be. In accepting our finitude, in opening ourselves to our replacement, we tacitly confess the limits of our control.

Embracing the future by procreating means precisely that we are relinquishing our grip in the very activity of taking up our own share in what we hope will be the immortality of human life and the human species. This means that our children are not our children: they are not our property, they are not our possessions. Neither are they supposed to live our lives for us, or to live anyone's life but their own. Their genetic distinctiveness and independence are the natural foreshadowing of the deep truth that they have their own, never-before-enacted life to live. Though sprung from a past, they take an uncharted course into the future.

Much mischief is already done by parents who try to live vicariously through their children. Children are sometimes compelled to fulfill the broken dreams of unhappy parents. But whereas most parents normally have hopes for their children, cloning parents will have expectations. In cloning, such overbearing parents will have taken at the start a decisive step that contradicts the entire meaning of the open and forward-looking nature of parent-child relations. The child is given a genotype that has already lived, with full expectation that this blueprint of a past life ought to be controlling the life that is to come. A wanted child now means a child who exists precisely to fulfill parental wants. Like all the more precise eugenic manipulations that will follow in its wake, cloning is thus inherently despotic, for it seeks to make one's children after one's own image (or an image of one's choosing) and their future according to one's will.

Is this hyperbolic? Consider concretely the new realities of responsibility and guilt in the households of the cloned. No longer only the sins of the parents, but also the genetic choices of the parents, will be visited on the children—and beyond the third and fourth generation; and everyone will know who is responsible. No parent will be able to blame nature or the lottery of sex for an unhappy adolescent's big nose, dull wit, musical ineptitude, nervous disposition, or anything else that he hates about himself. Fairly or not, children will hold their cloners responsible for everything, for nature as well as for nurture. And parents, especially the better ones, will be limitlessly liable to guilt. Only the truly despotic souls will sleep the sleep of the innocent. . . .

David B. Elliott | # Uniqueness, Individuality, and Human Cloning

THE MANUFACTURING OBJECTION

When you think about it, cloning a human would be a very simple, and yet enormously efficient way to select for an individual with certain biological features. The other way to do this would be to engage in genetic alchemy—gene therapy as it is now (perhaps euphemistically) called—and try to change that individual's genome. But this technology is nascent, uncertain, risky, complicated, enormously expensive, and to date, not terribly successful. This fact alone seems to be why certain forms of mammalian cloning in domestic animal husbandry have been largely favoured over biotechnology that involves manipulating genomes. You simply find the cow that you like, and then go about producing "copies" of it. Human cloning would seem directly to involve these same 'manufacturing' or selection opportunities. Indeed, someone might suggest that these capacities are built right into the decision to clone. It is inherently a decision to produce an individual of a certain type, with certain features that we hope are based in his or her genome. This is how Jeremy Rifkin, a popular biotechnology critic, sees the matter. As he puts it: "It's a horrendous crime to make a Xerox of someone . . . [because] you're putting a human into a genetic straitjacket. For the first time, we've taken the principles of industrial design—quality control and predictability—and applied them to a human being." The moral idea here seems to be that in manufacturing people, we devalue them; we treat them as objects to be designed rather than as potential subjects or agents capable of their own making.

There are several familiar problems with this familiar line of argument. First, let us assume that the decision to clone is inherently a manufacturing choice (I will question this assumption in a moment). The problem is that these sorts of choices seem to typify so many choices that people make which, even if they are not conscious choices of this sort, at least have the effect of shaping or selecting the traits of their child. The process, for example, of selecting a partner where children could arrive in the future, while it surely is not (and I would hope it never should be) *merely* a decision to select the traits of one's children, it does in part present an opportunity for just this sort of selection. Additionally, if we really do believe that 'manufacturing' choices are morally objectionable, then it becomes difficult to imagine why people seeking to adopt a child should have to be consulted about the adoption of any particular child once they have expressed a general interest in adoption. The same might hold for a woman seeking to have a child through artificial insemination by donor. It seems rather strong to hold that her moral qualities as a future parent are seriously diminished by any interest in the general features of the donor, or that she would be an ideal parent if she were to accept sperm only if she could know nothing at all about the physical appearance, family medical history, etc., of its donor.

Furthermore, even if it were just false that people really do make many choices that have the effect of trait selection prior to the birth of their children, they certainly do go to considerable trouble to see that their children develop certain traits after they are born. All of this "manufacturing" seems appropriate, however, given certain standard moral assumptions—e.g., when it is at least not harmful to the child, when it does not severely restrict her opportu-

From David Elliott, "Uniqueness, Individuality, and Human Cloning," *Journal of Applied Philosophy* 15, no. 3 (1998): 217–30. Notes and some parts of the text have been deleted. Reprinted by permission of Blackwell Publishing, Ltd.

nities to become an autonomous, self-affirming individual or when it is in her interest to have (or avoid) certain characteristics (say, a debilitating disease). The same could be said about pre-conception selection decisions. Many of these decisions could indeed be frivolous, selfish, and so on. But many of them might be capable of moral defence by showing how they might be important for cultivating the capacities and opportunities for a person's self-development.

What tends to upset many of us about manufacturing decisions, I suspect, is not really that *some* of them might occur in ordinary choices about having a child, but rather that *too many* of them might be present. What might be objectionable, then, is the total quantity of the same sort of choice. Too many manufacturing choices, it might be suggested, push us to the point where we would be treating a (potential) child as an object of his or her parent's desires and goals, rather than a person in his or her own right. Furthermore, being able to determine a person's traits to a very considerable extent might raise concerns about whether that parent is capable of valuing or loving a child unconditionally, or loving him for the person that he might become through self-development. It could also raise questions about whether the potential person would be able adequately to develop her own sense of self and personal agency. In this regard, Joseph Fletcher, another early bioethicist, surely overstated his response to the manufacturing argument when he enthusiastically *celebrates* our potential to manufacture people. "Man," he writes, "is a maker and a selecter [sic] and a designer, and the more rationally contrived and deliberate anything is, the more human it is." Fletcher even goes so far as to claim that laboratory reproduction is "radically human compared to conception by ordinary heterosexual intercourse" because the manufacturing is willed, chosen, purposed, controlled; it is a matter of "choice, and not chance."

Whatever merit there might be in responding to the manufacturing objection by arguing either that manufacturing is a standard decision most parents make or that it is not itself morally objectionable, let us for the moment set both of these suggestions aside. There is another consideration that is, I would suggest, even more decisive. The decision to clone is not *inherently* a choice to manufacture a particular individual in a certain way, even though this consequence may be foreseeable. It can simply be a choice to have a child of one's own in the only way possible. The familiar examples standardly offered in the literature as morally defensible reasons to clone illustrate this point. These examples can usually be classified under two main categories: (1) the prevention (by bypassing) of infertility and (2) the avoidance of genetic disease. Given either one or both of these situations, some cloning technique may be the only way that some people might be able to have children of their own. In these cases, however, the decision to have a child could be only that of having a child of one's own; it need not be a detailed manufacturing decision—a point which seems particularly true with respect to bypassing infertility. This is just the sort of outlook that we might arguably suggest is the ideal outlook that couples having children through sexual reproduction should have. Cloning, of course, does come with biological foreknowledge; one would have a fairly good idea of what the child's genome would be, and all that this entails. But, again, simply because there is foreknowledge that a duplication of one's genome will be the outcome of one's decision to have a child, it simply does not follow that the decision to have a child involves or entails a determination to have a child for these reasons. Imagine an analogy with a couple where infertility and genetic disease is not a known consideration, but who may know in advance (say due to some established medical condition) that all of their offspring will be female. It is not obvious that their choice to have a child should be regarded as an instance of sex-selection. If this is right, then there is simply no reason to regard all instances of cloning as instances of manufacturing humans. Other more general, recognizable, and morally defensible motivations, I would suggest, can be present.

An Argument for Limited Human Cloning

David B. Hershenov

I believe a rather useful principle can be found for distinguishing legitimate from illegitimate cases of cloning. After surveying the different types of cases, I will present this principle as a guideline for legislative and institutional policy.

My hope is that this guideline will be received by most of the opponents of cloning as a welcome compromise because it rules out the more repugnant cases while allowing the few that are more appealing. We do not have to accept Leon Kass's claim that "the only safe trench we can dig across the slippery slope . . . is to insist upon the inviolable distinction between animal and human cloning."

. . . If a person clones himself, the clone is actually his younger identical win. Many of the opponents of cloning are repulsed by the prospect of children being created and raised by siblings rather than their true genetic parents. The bioethicist James Nelson imagines clones seeking out their genetic parents and pursuing a child-parent relationship despite the fact that the child's origins are the result of their older siblings' doing and not the parents who perhaps didn't want any more children. It would be very unfair to place the genetic parent in such a situation. And it would be awful for the cloned child who seeks out but is not welcomed by such a parent.

Along similar lines, Leon Kass writes of how cloning will disrupt traditional roles and duties:

> In the case of self-cloning, the "offspring" is, in addition, one's twin; and so the dreaded result of incest—to be parent of one's sibling—is here brought about deliberately, albeit without any acts of coitus. Moreover, all other relationships will be confounded. What will father, grandfather, aunt, cousin, sister mean? Who will bear what ties and what burdens? What sort of social identity will someone have with one whole side—"father's" or "mother's"—necessarily excluded? It is no answer to say that our society, with its high incidence of divorce, remarriage, adoption, extramarital childbearing and the rest, already confounds lineage and confuses kinship and responsibility for children (and everyone else), unless one also wants to argue that this is, for children, a preferable state of affairs.

Kass also expresses the fear that asexual reproduction will give rise to an increase in the number of single parents as people raise their own clones. Kass complains:

> In the case of cloning, however there is but one "parent." The usually sad situation of the "single parent child" is here deliberately planned, and with a vengeance. . . . asexual reproduction, which produces single parent offspring, is a radical departure from the natural human way.

There is also the worry that the cloned child shall be the responsibility of an older sibling who will lack the devotion to the well-being of the child that parents normally have. Just because those who cloned themselves are genetically identical to their younger siblings, it would be a mistake to think that this means that they will care as much about the clones as most parents do for their children. Siblings have not historically been molded by the same evolutionary pressures as their parents, so they are not endowed with the concern and affection for each other that their parents innately possess toward them.

With a little imagination, the reader could add to this list of unsavory cloning scenarios. . . . I will

From David B. Hershenov, "An Argument for Limited Human Cloning," *Public Affairs Quarterly* 14, no. 3 (July 2000): 245–258. Notes and some parts of the text have been deleted. Reprinted by permission of North American Philosophical Publications.

mention four types of scenarios in which cloning is an appealing option. The first, which I also find the most compelling of the set, would involve couples who have become "infertile as couples" through menopause or abnormality, who then lose their only child—or perhaps all their children. Not only is it extremely distressing for parents to have their children precede them to the grave, but to have the family lineage cease just adds to the pain. I imagine that the number of parents who lose all their children prior to the birth of any grandchildren is not insignificant. And of course, in times of war or epidemic, this number would sadly escalate. And even if in normal times the numbers are not large, the suffering of those few in such predicaments warrant a sympathetic societal response. However, if such infertile parents were allowed to clone their lost child, this would lessen their grief. And if the child had yet to reach what was deemed a mature age, his consent would not be required. But if the deceased child had reached such an age, then perhaps his consent would have to have been acquired through some process analogous to that for organ donation. Where there is not a record of the mature child's view on his posthumous cloning by his parents, maybe the default position should be the parents can choose to clone their deceased child. In any event, the details need not be worked out here.

Less likely to occur than the premature death of an only child, but still compelling, would be a case where an ill child needs a bone marrow transplant. I am just going to assume that the reader would not think it wrong for the parents to conceive another child through normal sexual procreation in order to save the afflicted one, as long as the parents would also love and cherish this additional child. Now suppose that the parents were infertile because of advanced age or some form of abnormality, such that cloning the ill child would in the absence of an available donor be their only recourse. And even if the couple is fertile, the chances of a genetic tissue match makes cloning the preferable option.

Cloning also appears as a sympathetic solution to a third scenario. This involves parents who are at a high risk for passing on a deadly or debilitating disease. Imagine that before they become aware

of this, they conceived a child who fortunately wins the genetic lottery, beating the odds by being born healthy. Another possibility is that they are likely to pass on a disease like hemophilia to male offprsing and thus would like to clone their only daughter. Should this family be condemned to a Chinese-style communist one-child family? This hardly seems fair. Most Americans desire, even feel entitled to, at least a two-child family. Cloning would permit the family plagued by unwelcome genes to still reach an acceptable sized family.

There is a fourth scenario, which is basically a combination of the first and third. This would involve a couple who, after having one child, lose the capacity to produce viable eggs or sperm, yet wants to enlarge their family. Allowing them to clone their only child will enable them to have another child to whom they are *both* genetically related—which would not be the case with a gamete donor or adoption.

I hope that the reader is sympathetic to the plight of those in the four types of cases just surveyed. What is it that these cases have in common that the earlier repugnant cases lacked? The four positive cases all mirror normal procreation. That is, *a new child is being deliberately created and brought into the world by the decision of two willing partners (the parents), from each of whom the child gets half of his or her DNA.* Both normal sexual procreation and the advocated form of cloning meet this criterion. The four types of cases of preferred cloning differ from normal sexual procreation only in that the parents make the decision to *reuse* the DNA they earlier decided to fuse in order to create the first child. But none of the repugnant cases involves the cloning decision being made by the parents of the clone or, if they do have a say in the matter, the practice is distasteful for adults other than the genetic parents of the being cloned are taking possession of the clone, perhaps because they purchased the genetic material from which the clone emerges. What also distinguishes the two categories of cloning is that the favored form involves infertility or, at least, the inability to have healthy babies. We are sympathetic to those who want to do what the vast majority of other couples do: combine their genetic material with a loved one and create a new life.

So our short survey suggests some necessary conditions for cloning. (1) people should not be allowed to clone themselves; (2) people should not take possession of the "product" of a cloning process unless they are the genetic parents of the clone; (3) the genetic parents of the clone should themselves be unable or just unlikely to conceive a healthy child; (4) and both genetic parents should freely enter into the discussion to initiate the cloning process. Combining these necessary conditions, we can formulate the promised principle as the following: *A clone may be created only by a pair of people who, unable to conceive together a healthy offspring in any other way, freely decide to create and rear a child that will receive half of his (or her) genetic material from each of them.*

This principle would make the pair who initiate the cloning the parents of the resulting clone and not older siblings of the clone. Such a "pro-family" and "pro-parent" form of cloning, which relieves the distress of infertility, is probably the only feasible form of cloning given the present political environment. It is this principle that allows us to build a barrier on the slippery slope of cloning. Others might want to avoid the slippery slope by never approaching the cloning hill, but I think they do this without having an argument against the cases of cloning that elicit our sympathy. Their only argument against the relief cloning provides in such cases is that permitting cloning there increases the likelihood of the occurrence of the unattractive cases surveyed above. But I believe it is better to have a well-delineated and principled line upon which to base our policies even if this takes us somewhat down the feared slope—provided that we avoid those areas that are *inherently* wrong, i.e., morally flawed even if we slide no further. The recommended principle does just that. All the distasteful cases fail to involve the genetic parents of the clone freely initiating the process and taking possession of the resulting clone when there is no other safe way for them to have more healthy children. In fact, many of the cases mentioned do not even involve the consent of the clone's parents since the decision is being made by

their children to clone themselves and take control of their resulting sibling(s). Not only could people be made into parents without their choosing to become so, but they may not even be aware that they have become parents.

II

So we have seen what property all the distasteful cases lack. But this does not rule out that many of the disagreeable attributes of the repugnant cases are shared by our three more attractive types of scenarios. Fortunately, this is not the case—or, at least, the distasteful features in question are not shared to the same extent by the endorsed types of cases. So we will be able to disarm the opponents of cloning by pointing out to them that their general objections to cloning either do not apply to the cases of cloning championed in this essay, or do so only to a much lesser degree than they envisioned.

Many of the opponents of cloning, such as Kass, are repulsed by the prospect of children being created and raised by siblings rather than genetic parents. We have mentioned the fears of the bioethicist James Nelson who imagines clones seeking out their genetic parents and pursuing a child-parent relationship despite the fact that the child's origins are the result of his or her older sibling's doing and not the parents who perhaps did not want any more children. But given the necessary conditions for cloning that I put forth, these objections are not telling. The only clones made are by infertile parents, or more accurately, those who cannot have healthy children through sexual reproduction. Thus traditional family roles, loyalties, and obligations remain the same.

Nor do we need to share Kass's fear of asexual reproduction giving rise to an increase in the number of single parents as people raise their own clones. We can avoid this because the advocated principle stipulates that only the genetic parents of the possible clone can make the cloning decision. Since people would not be allowed to clone themselves, no child will be raised by a single parent except in the case of an untimely death. And not allowing a person to decide by him- or herself to clone themselves avoids not only the distasteful cases of narcissistic and arrogant cloning surveyed, but frees us from the worry that the cloned child shall be the responsibility of an older sibling who will lack the devotion to the well-being of the child that parents normally have. . . .

PART 7

WHAT ELSE IS WRONG?

The central goal of this book has been to provide an introduction to the study of applied ethics by means of a detailed examination of the philosophical exchange that takes place between applied ethicists and their critics. For this reason, the readings in the first six parts of the book have focused primarily on articles that tackle widely discussed problems and that have drawn direct critical responses from members of the philosophical community. But not every worthwhile work in applied ethics discusses such standard topics and not every valuable contribution to the philosophical literature elicits a direct rebuttal. Part 7 concludes this anthology by providing a sample of some of the interesting and provocative work that applied ethicists have produced on some less familiar and less widely discussed questions.

In chapter 29, D. W. Haslett challenges the widely accepted practice of inheritance, by which parents can leave their wealth to their children. In chapter 30, Walter Block defends the equally startling proposal that blackmail should not be illegal. David Lewis asks what would justify our practice of effectively punishing people for their bad luck in chapter 31. The difference between a murder and an attempted murder is often a matter of chance, but we punish those who commit murder more severely than we do those who attempt to murder. Lewis argues that this is just, although his argument for it is a highly surprising one. In chapter 32, Lawrence C. Becker maintains that people who are capable of doing productive labor have a moral obligation to do so, even if they can afford not to. Finally, in chapter 33, Selmer Bringsjord uses a form of argument that closely resembles Lewis's argument in chapter 32 to argue that it is not wrong to make copies of copyrighted material (including, if you like, of this very book).

Each of these chapters consists of a single, self-contained, reading, with no critical-response pieces or suggested further reading provided. It is hoped that the brief introductions that precede each article, along with the practice that readers will have gained from study of the previous parts of this book, will enable readers to engage the material critically and fruitfully.

29

Is Inheriting Wealth Wrong?

The right to own and amass private property is an essential component of capitalism. Suppose you own something, say $100 in cash or a CD collection of the complete works of Mozart. If it's your property, isn't it also yours to dispose of however you see fit, and in particular yours to give away? If it isn't yours to give away, then in what sense is it yours in the first place? (See chapter 24 on redistributive taxation.) And if you are entitled to give it to whomever you choose, then isn't the person you choose to give it to also entitled to receive it? In particular, are you not entitled to make provision to gift your goods to whomever you choose when you die? So, the right to private property seems to entail the right to give your property away, and the right to give it away is no right at all unless the recipient has the corresponding right to receive it. This is a simple argument to show that capitalism requires the right to bequeath and inherit. (Call these *inheritance rights*.)

In "Is Inheritance Justified," D. W. Haslett argues that not only does capitalism not entail inheritance rights, but it also is incompatible with such rights. According to Haslett, the basic ideals of capitalism require that inheritance rights be abolished. Haslett begins the article noting the distinction between wealth and income. Your wealth is the property you have accumulated, whereas your income is what you add to it year by year. There are vast inequalities in income in the United States. Quite a few people earn the minimum wage (around five dollars an hour) while a tiny proportion of the population, such as the CEOs of pharmaceutical companies, count their annual incomes in the hundreds of millions of dollars. What's not so widely appreciated is the even vaster inequality in wealth. Haslett quotes figures from a 1983 survey; for example, "the top one or two percent of American families own from around 20 to 30 percent . . . the top fifth owns almost 80% of the wealth." Twenty years later, the inequality in wealth has become even more pronounced. According to Edward N. Wolff, in "Recent Trends in Wealth Ownership, 1983–1998," April 2000 (available at *www.levy.org/docs/wrkpap/papers/300.html*), by 1998 the wealthiest one percent in the U.S. owned more than 38 percent of the total wealth. Suppose one thought that equality was a good thing, and inequality a bad thing. Then it would be good to reduce or eliminate these large inequalities. What role does inheritance play in generating this inequality—the concentration of the vast proportion of the country's (and world's) wealth in the hands of a tiny fraction of the population? Estimates vary, but as much as 67 percent of the wealth of the ultra-rich is acquired through inheritance. Abolishing the ability to inherit wealth would thus go some way to equalizing the distribution of wealth.

A simple argument for abolishing inheritance rights as suggested by the data Haslett would be reconstructed as follows:

P1   Inheritance rights are a major contributor to vast inequalities in wealth.
P2   Inequalities in wealth are a bad thing.
_____
C   It would be better if there were not inheritance rights.

Whether or not this argument is valid (is it?), it is not the argument put forward by Haslett. He does think that vast inequalities in the distribution of wealth are a bad thing, but he does not start from that assumption in his main argument. Capitalism, by legitimizing the competition for resources, not only tolerates inequalities in wealth but also promotes such inequalities. Thus any argument that starts from the assumption that inequality is bad in and of itself, and that it should be abolished or minimized, is not going to make much headway among those who accept that capitalism is basically a good way to organize our economic institutions. Rather, Haslett argues that capitalism embraces basic ideals that themselves require that we abandon inheritance rights.

Haslett focuses on three ideals that help justify capitalism because they appear to be worthy ideals and capitalism appears to implement them better than do its rivals. They are: (1) the distribution of wealth according to productivity; (2) equal opportunity; and (3) freedom.

The point of an economic system is to produce goods and services. One of the strengths of capitalism is that it does not *force* people to work to produce goods and services. Rather, it *entices* them into doing so, by promising that more productivity will earn them a bigger share of income and wealth. But inheritance undermines that enticement, by rewarding very unproductive people with large quantities of wealth, which then generates large incomes that are also unrelated to productivity.

Haslett's first argument can be characterized as follows:

P1   Capitalism requires that wealth and income be distributed according to productivity and that practices that undermine the distribution of goods according to productivity be abolished.
P2   Inheritance rights grossly undermine the distribution of goods according to productivity.
_____
C   Capitalism requires that inheritance rights be abolished.

Another virtue of capitalism is that it embodies an ideal of equal opportunity. The degree of social mobility in a capitalist economy is much greater, for example, than the degree of mobility in a feudal economy. In a feudal economy, a serf's position in society is fixed at birth, and no matter how talented or energetic he is, he has virtually no opportunity to exercise his talents and energy to improve his lot. In a capitalist society, there is a far greater degree of equality of opportunity, though it is still grossly deficient in this respect. To the extent that wealth endows one with opportunities, gross inequalities in wealth entail that some people begin life with far greater opportunities than others. The children of the very poor have very few opportunities compared with the children of the very wealthy.

Haslett's second argument can be summarized thus:

P1 The more equal the opportunities people have, the more efficiently capitalism operates.

P2 Inheritance rights grossly distort equality of opportunity.

C The perfect implementation of capitalism requires the abolition of inheritance rights.

Finally, one of the most frequently cited arguments for capitalism is that it maximizes freedom. Under a capitalist system, people are free to exchange goods and services to mutual advantage without fear of constant government intervention. Haslett argues that the abolition of inheritance rights would require a small loss in freedom compared with huge compensating gains in freedom that would vastly outweigh the losses. The rest of Haslett's article is devoted to the details of the abolition of inheritance rights. Any such abolition would have far-reaching effects.

QUESTIONS FOR CONSIDERATION

• As we have reconstructed these arguments, each of them makes a claim about capitalism (for example, that it requires equality of opportunity), and a claim about inheritance rights (for example, that they undermine equality of opportunity). Are the claims about capitalism plausible? Are the corresponding claims about inheritance rights plausible? Do the conclusions follow from the premises cited?

• Haslett does not lay his arguments out in the way we have done here. Are ours the most plausible reconstructions of his arguments? Can you think of other ways of representing his arguments?

• Haslett claims that if inheritance rights were abolished, people would not lose the motivation to acquire wealth. What evidence does he present for this claim? Is it good evidence?

D. W. Haslett | # Is Inheritance Justified?

Old ways die hard. A social practice may be taken for granted for centuries before humanity finally comes to realize it cannot be justified. Take, for example, slavery. Another example is the inheritance of political power. For many centuries, throughout most of the world, the suggestion that political power should be determined by democratic vote rather than heredity would have been met with scorn; today we realize just how unjustified determining political power by heredity really is.

Although we no longer believe in the inheritance of political power, most of us still believe in the inheritance of wealth, of *economic* power. But might not the inheritance of economic power be equally unjustified? This is the question to be examined here. Inheritance involves property rights; so another way

From D. W. Haslett, "Is Inheritance Justified?" *Philosophy and Public Affairs* 15, (1986): 122–55. Some notes and some parts of the text have been deleted. Reprinted by permission of Princeton University Press.

of putting this question is: Should property rights incorporate the practice of inheritance as it exists today?

I shall not address the question of whether individuals may justifiably continue to take advantage of this practice as long as it exists, by continuing to bequeath and inherit property. (As far as I am concerned, they may.) I address only the justifiability of the practice (or institution) itself. Finally, in asking whether the practice of inheritance is justified, I focus specifically upon whether it is justified in the *United States, today.* Any conclusions I reach, however, will be applicable, no doubt, beyond this limited frame of reference, one chosen mainly for convenience. And, for convenience also, I shall be using the word "inheritance" throughout to refer to any large amount one is *given* (as opposed to *earns,* or *wins*), whether it be, technically, a bequest, or a gift.

This investigation is divided into three sections. Section I presents some facts about wealth distribution and inheritance in the United States today, facts that provide a useful background for the discussion which follows. Many people support inheritance because they believe it to be essential to capitalism. In Section II I try to show that, far from being essential, inheritance is actually *inconsistent* with capitalism. Or, to be more exact, I try to show that it is inconsistent with fundamental values that underlie capitalism. For those, such as myself, who share these values, its inconsistency with them is prima facie reason for abolishing inheritance. But prima facie reasons for doing something can be overridden if the objections to doing it are strong enough. So, in Section III, I examine what I take to be the most important objections to abolishing inheritance. I conclude that the practice of inheritance, as it exists today, should indeed be abolished.

I. BACKGROUND INFORMATION

Family income in the United States today is not distributed very evenly. The top fifth of American families receives 57.3 percent of all family income, while the bottom fifth receives only 7.2 percent.[1]

But, for obvious reasons, a family's financial well-being does not depend upon its income nearly as much as it does upon its wealth, just as the strength of an army does not depend upon how many people joined it during the year as much as it does upon how many people are in it altogether. So if we really want to know how unevenly economic well-being is distributed in the United States today, we must look at the distribution not of income, but of wealth.

Although—quite surprisingly—the government does not regularly collect information on the distribution of wealth, it has occasionally done so. The results are startling. One to two percent of American families own from around 20 to 30 percent of the (net) family wealth in the United States; 5 to 10 percent own from around 40 to 60 percent.[2] The top fifth owns almost 80 percent of the wealth, while the bottom fifth owns only 0.2 percent.[3] So while the top fifth has, as we saw, about eight times the income of the bottom fifth, it has about 400 times the wealth. Whether deliberately or not, by regularly gathering monumental amounts of information on the distribution of income, but not on the distribution of wealth, the government succeeds in directing attention away from how enormously unequal the distribution of wealth is, and directing it instead upon the less unequal distribution of income. But two things are clear: wealth is distributed far more unequally in the United States today than is income, and this inequality in the distribution of wealth is enormous. These are the first two things to keep in mind throughout our discussion of inheritance.

The next thing to keep in mind is that, although estate and gift taxes in the United States are supposed to redistribute wealth, and thereby lessen this inequality, they do not do so. Before 1981 estates were taxed, on an average, at a rate of only 0.2 percent—0.8 percent for estates over $500,000—hardly an amount sufficient to cause any significant redistribution of wealth.[4] And, incredibly, the Economic Recovery Act of 1981 *lowered* estate and gift taxes.

Of course the top rate at which estates and gifts are *allegedly* taxed is far greater than the 0.2 percent rate, on the average, at which they are *really* taxed. Prior to 1981, the top rate was 70 percent, which in 1981 was lowered to 50 percent. Because of this relatively high top rate, the average person is led to believe that estate and gift taxes succeed in breaking up the huge financial empires of the very rich, thereby distributing wealth more evenly. What the average person fails to realize is that what the government takes with one hand, through high nominal rates, it gives back with the other hand, through loopholes in the law. Lester Thurow writes, ". . . it is hard to understand why we go through the fiction of legislating high nominal rates and then nullifying them with generous loopholes—unless someone is to be fooled. The most obvious purpose of high nominal rates and low effective rates is to use the high nominal rates as a smoke-screen to hide the transfer of wealth from generation to generation."[5] I do not know if the government deliberately intends the law on estate and gift taxation to be deceptive but, due to the complications, exceptions, and qualifications built into this law, it *is* deceptive and, more seriously still, it is ineffective as a means of distributing wealth more evenly. Indeed, as George Cooper shows, estate and gift taxes can, with the help of a good attorney, be avoided so easily they amount to little more than "voluntary" taxes.[6] As such, it is not surprising that, contrary to popular opinion, these taxes do virtually nothing to reduce the vast inequality in the distribution of wealth that exists today.

Once we know that estate and gift taxes do virtually nothing to reduce this vast inequality, what I am about to say next should come as no surprise. This vast inequality in the distribution of wealth is (according to the best estimates) due at least as much to inheritance as to any other factor. Once again, because of the surprising lack of information about these matters, the extent to which this inequality is due to inheritance is not known exactly. One estimate, based upon a series of articles appearing in *Fortune* magazine, is that 50 percent of the large fortunes in the United States were derived basically from inheritance.[7] But by far the most careful and thorough study of this matter to date is that of John A. Brittain.[8] Brittain shows that the estimate based upon the *Fortune* articles actually is too low;[9] that a more accurate estimate of the amount contributed by inheritance to the wealth of "ultra-rich" males is 67 percent.[10] In any case, it is clear that, in the United States today, inheritance plays a large role indeed in perpetuating a vastly unequal distribution of wealth.

This is the final thing to keep in mind throughout the discussion which follows.

II. INHERITANCE AND CAPITALISM

Capitalism (roughly speaking) is an economic system where (1) what to produce, and in what quantities, is determined essentially by supply and demand—that is, by people's "dollar votes"—rather than by central planning, and (2) capital goods are, for the most part, privately owned. In the minds of many today, capitalism goes hand in hand with the practice of inheritance; capitalism without inheritance, they would say, is absurd. But, if I am right, the exact opposite is closer to the truth. Since, as I shall try to show in this section, the practice of inheritance is incompatible with basic values or ideals that underlie capitalism, what is absurd, if anything, is capitalism *with* inheritance.

Before proceeding, however, let me say a few brief words about ideals, or values, in general. Ideals, or values (and I use these terms interchangeably here) serve to delineate what is good; what, consequently, is to be striven for, and to be striven for even though in no way capable of ever being achieved fully. Take, for example, the ideal of the medical profession that everyone be in a state of perfect health. Ideals can be either absolute or prima facie. Absolute ideals admit of no compromise; they are to be realized as fully as possible no matter what the cost. Prima facie ideals do admit of compromise; they are to be realized only to the extent that they do not conflict with, for example, more fundamental ideals. None of the ideals to be discussed here are absolute; all are merely prima facie. Finally, political values or ideals such as the ones we shall be considering, are, in my view, related to political morality, roughly, as follows. Political morality places an obligation upon a government to do what is in the general welfare, subject to being constrained by rights that people have against the government. Values or ideals, delineating, as they do, what is to be striven for, serve as general guides to what is in the general welfare. Accordingly, any governmental policy that is contrary to legitimate ideals is, other things being equal, unjustified. But if the contravened ideals are only prima facie, then the policy contrary to them can be shown to be justified after all, by showing that other things are not equal; by showing, in other words, that the policy, although contrary to these ideals, is required for other, more weighty reasons. But if it cannot be shown that the policy is required for other more weighty reasons, then we must conclude that the policy is indeed unjustified.

I do not try to show here that the ideals underlying capitalism are worthy of support; I only try to show that inheritance is contrary to these ideals. And if it is, then from this it follows that, *if* these ideals are worthy of support (as, incidentally, I think they are), then we have prima facie reason for concluding that inheritance is unjustified. What then are these ideals? For an answer, we can do no better than turn to one of capitalism's most eloquent and uncompromising defenders: Milton Friedman.

Distribution According to Productivity

The point of any economic system is, of course, to produce goods and services. But, as Friedman tells us, society cannot very well *compel* people to be productive and, even if it could, out of respect for personal freedom, probably it should not do so. Therefore, he concludes, in order to get people to be productive, society needs instead to *entice* them to produce, and the most effective way of enticing people to produce is to distribute income and wealth according to productivity. Thus we arrive at the first ideal underlying capitalism: "To each according to what he and the instruments he owns produces."[11]

Obviously, inheritance contravenes this ideal. For certain purposes, this ideal would require further interpretation; we would need to know more about what was meant by "productivity." For our purposes, no further clarification is necessary. According to *any* reasonable interpretation of "productivity," the wealth people get through inheritance has nothing to do with their productivity. And one need not be an adherent of this ideal of distribution to be moved by the apparent injustice of one person working eight hours a day all his life at a miserable job, and accumulating nothing, while another person does little more all his life than enjoy his parents' wealth, and inherits a fortune.

Equal Opportunity

But for people to be productive it is necessary not just that they be *motivated* to be productive, but that they have the *opportunity* to be productive. This brings us to the second ideal underlying capitalism: equal opportunity—that is, equal opportunity for all to pursue, successfully, the occupation of their choice.[12] According to capitalist ethic, it is OK if, in the economic game, there are winners and losers, provided everyone has an "equal start." As Friedman puts it, the ideal of equality compatible with capitalism is not equality of outcome, which would *discourage* people from realizing their full productive potential, but equality of opportunity, which *encourages* people to do so.[13]

Naturally this ideal, like the others we are considering, neither could, nor should, be realized fully; to do so would require, among other things, no less than abolishing the family and engaging in extensive genetic engineering.[14] But the fact that this ideal cannot and should not be realized fully in no way detracts from its importance. Not only is equal opportunity itself an elementary requirement of justice but, significantly, progress in realizing this ideal could bring with it progress in at least two other crucial areas as well: those of productivity and income distribution. First, the closer we come to equal opportunity for all, the more people there will be who, as a result of increased opportunity, will come to realize their productive potential. And, of course, the more people there are who come to realize their productive potential, the greater overall productivity will be. Second, the closer we come to equal opportunity for all, the more people there will be with an excellent opportunity to become something other than an ordinary worker, to become a professional or an entrepreneur of sorts. And the more people there are with an excellent opportunity to become something other than an ordinary worker, the more people there will be who in fact become something other than an ordinary worker or, in other words, the less people there will be available for doing ordinary work. As elementary economic theory tells us, with a decrease in the supply of something comes an increase in the demand for it, and with an increase in the demand for it comes an increase in the price paid for it. An increase in the price paid for it would, in this case, mean an increase in the income of the ordinary worker vis-à-vis that of the professional and the entrepreneur, which, surely, would be a step in the direction of income being distributed more justly.

And here I mean "more justly" even according to the ideals of capitalism itself. As we have seen, the capitalist ideal of distributive justice is "to each according to his or her productivity." But, under capitalism, we can say a person's income from some occupation reflects his or her productivity only to the extent there are no unnecessary limitations upon people's opportunity to pursue, successfully, this occupation—and by "unnecessary limitations" I mean ones that either *cannot* or (because doing so would cause more harm than good) *should not* be removed. According to the law of supply and demand, the more limited the supply of people in some occupation, then (assuming a healthy demand to begin with) the higher will be the income of those pursuing the occupation. Now if the limited supply of people in some high-paying occupation is the consequence of a "natural" scarcity—a scarcity that is not the result of unnecessary limitations upon opportunity, but is the result instead of few people having the inborn capacity to pursue this occupation, or of few people freely choosing to do so—then (it is fair to say) the high pay does reflect productivity. Willingness or capacity to do what few people are willing or have the capacity to do *is* socially valuable, and those who in fact do it *are* therefore making an unusually valuable contribution; they are, in other words, being highly productive. But if, on the other hand, the limited supply of people in some high-paying occupation is the result of unnecessary limitations upon people's opportunity to pursue that occupation, then the scarcity is an "artificial" one, and the high pay can by no means be said to reflect productivity. The remedy is to remove these limitations; in other words, to increase equality of opportu-

tunity. To what extent the relative scarcity of professionals and entrepreneurs in capitalist countries today is due to natural scarcity, and to what extent to artificial scarcity, no one really knows. I strongly suspect, however, that a dramatic increase in equality of opportunity will reveal that the scarcity is far more artificial than most professionals and entrepreneurs today care to think—*far* more artificial.

If my suspicions are correct, a dramatic increase in equality of opportunity not only would be desirable for its own sake (since equal opportunity is itself an elementary requirement of justice) but would also be desirable for the sake of greater productivity, a more equal distribution of income, *and* fuller realization of the ideal of distribution according to productivity. Indeed, a dramatic increase in equality of opportunity would, I suspect, do more to meet the objections that many throughout the world today have against American capitalism than could anything else.[15]

That inheritance violates the (crucial) second ideal of capitalism, equal opportunity, is, once again, obvious. Wealth *is* opportunity, and inheritance distributes it very unevenly indeed. Wealth is opportunity for realizing one's potential, for a career, for success, for income. There are few, if any, desirable occupations that great wealth does not, in one way or another, increase—sometimes dramatically—one's chances of being able to pursue, and to pursue successfully. And to the extent that one's success is to be measured in terms of one's income, nothing else, neither intelligence, nor education, nor skills, provides a more secure opportunity for "success" than does wealth. Say one inherits a million dollars. All one then need do is purchase long-term bonds yielding a guaranteed interest of ten percent and (presto!) one has a yearly income of $100,000, an income far greater than anyone who toils eight hours a day in a factory will probably ever have. If working in the factory pays, relatively, so little, then why, it might be asked, do not all these workers become big-time investors themselves? The answer is that they are, their entire lives, barred from doing so by a lack of initial capital which others, through inheritance, are simply handed. With inheritance, the old adage is only too true: "The rich get richer, and the poor get poorer." Without inheritance, the vast fortunes in America today, these enormous concentrations of economic power, would be broken up, allowing wealth, and therefore opportunity, to become distributed far more evenly.[16]

Freedom

But so far I have not mentioned what many, including no doubt Friedman himself, consider to be the most important ideal underlying capitalism: that of liberty or, in other words, freedom. This ideal, however, takes different forms. One form it takes for Friedman is that of being able to engage in economic transactions free from governmental or other types of human coercion. The rationale for this conception of freedom—let us call it freedom in the "narrow" sense—is clear. As Friedman explains it, assuming only that people are informed about what is good for them, this form of freedom guarantees that " . . . no exchange will take place unless both parties benefit from it."[17] If at least the parties themselves benefit from the transaction, and it does not harm anyone, then, it is fair to say, the transaction has been socially valuable. So people with freedom of exchange will, in doing what is in their own best interests, generally be doing what is socially valuable as well. In other words, with this form of freedom, the fabled "invisible hand" actually works.

All of this is a great oversimplification. For one thing, a transaction that benefits both parties may have side effects, such as pollution, which harm others and, therefore, the transaction may not be socially valuable after all. So freedom, in the narrow sense, should certainly not be absolute. But the fact that freedom, in this sense, should not be absolute does not prevent it from serving as a useful ideal.

Next, those, such as Friedman, who oppose governmental coercion in the realm of economic exchanges often oppose governmental coercion of another sort as well: paternalism. In other words, they oppose governmental coercion designed to force us to do what is, supposedly, in our own best interests. Examples of governmental paternalism would be a law prohibiting the drinking of alcoholic beverages, on the grounds that doing so is unhealthy, or a law requiring everyone to wear seat belts. But, provided that it does not significantly affect freedom of exchange (that is, freedom in the narrow sense), paternalism has little to do with capitalism; therefore, "antipaternalistic" freedom does not, it seems to me, deserve to be included among the ideals that underlie capitalism. More to the point, neither inheritance, nor its abolishment (at least not for the reasons put forth here), could be correctly viewed as paternalistic anyway. So we need not give this conception of freedom further consideration here.

There are others whose conception of freedom is that of not being subject to any governmental coercion (or other forms of human coercion) for any purposes whatsoever—a conception sometimes referred to as "negative" freedom. It is true that governmental (or other) coercion for purposes of enforcing the abolition of inheritance violates this ideal, but then, of course, so does any such coercion for purposes of *maintaining* inheritance. So this "anticoercion" ideal, just like the antipaternalistic ideal, neither supports nor opposes the practice of inheritance, and therefore this conception of freedom need not concern us further here either.

A very popular variation of the anticoercion conception of freedom is one where freedom is, once again, the absence of all governmental (or other human) coercion, *except for any coercion necessary for enforcing our fundamental rights.* Prominent among our fundamental rights, most of those who espouse such a conception of freedom will tell us, is our right to property. So whether this conception of freedom supports the practice of inheritance depends entirely upon whether our "right to property" should be viewed as incorporating the practice of inheritance. But whether our right to property should be viewed as incorporating the practice of inheritance is just another way of stating the very point at issue in this investigation. Consequently, this popular conception of freedom cannot be used here in support of the practice of inheritance without begging the question.

But there is still another conception of freedom espoused by many: that which we might call freedom in the "broad" sense. According to this conception of freedom, to be free means to have the ability, or the opportunity, to do what one wants. For example, according to this conception of freedom, rich people arc, other things being equal, freer than poor people, since their wealth provides them with opportunities to do things that the poor can only dream about.

I think it is clear that when Friedman, and most other *conservative* defenders of capitalism, speak about the importance of freedom, they have something like what I have labelled the "narrow" sense in mind, along with perhaps one of the senses of freedom we have dismissed as irrelevant to our investigation. Those who, on the other hand, espouse freedom in the broad sense are often opponents of capitalism, and they use the broad sense of freedom to try to show how capitalism, with the vast inequalities of wealth to which it gives rise, is actually inconsistent with freedom. But those who espouse the broad sense of freedom need not be opponents of capitalism since, arguably, capitalism, or some modified version of it, provides even the less well off with more wealth and opportunities than does any other system and, accordingly, may be quite compatible with freedom in the broad sense after all. Indeed, it is, I think, freedom in the broad sense that is espoused by most *liberal* defenders of capitalism, those who, although they believe in the free market, are more sympathetic to governmental aid for the poor than are conservatives. Therefore, I include freedom in the broad sense among the ideals that underlie capitalism even though this ideal is not supported by all defenders of capitalism, and is, in fact, supported by many of its foes.

Let us now see whether inheritance and freedom are inconsistent. Consider, first, freedom in the narrow sense. Although inheritance may not be inconsistent with this ideal, neither is the *abolishment* of inheritance. This ideal forbids governmental interference with free exchanges between people; it does not necessarily forbid governmental interference with *gifts* or *bequests* (which, of course, are not *exchanges*). Remember, Friedman's rationale for this ideal is, as we saw, that free exchange promotes the "invisible hand;" that is, it promotes the healthy functioning of supply and demand, which is at the

very heart of capitalism. Supply and demand hardly require gifts, as opposed to exchanges, in order to function well.

If anything, gifts and bequests, and the enormous concentrations of economic power resulting from them, hinder the healthy functioning of supply and demand. First of all, gifts and bequests, and the enormous concentrations of economic power resulting from them, create such great differences in people's "dollar votes" that the economy's demand curves do not accurately reflect the needs of the population as a whole, but are distorted in favor of the "votes" of the rich. And inheritance hinders the healthy functioning of supply and demand even more, perhaps, by interfering with supply. As we have seen, inheritance (which, as I am using the term, encompasses large gifts) is responsible for some starting out in life with a vast advantage over others; it is, in other words, a major source of unequal opportunity. As we have also seen, the further we are from equal opportunity, the less people there will be who come to realize their productive potential. And, of course, the less people there are who come to realize their productive potential, the less overall productivity there will be or, in other words, the less healthy will be the economy's *supply* curves. So, while inheritance may not be *literally* inconsistent with freedom in the narrow sense, it does, by hindering indirectly both supply and demand, appear to be inconsistent with the "spirit" of this ideal.

To this it might be replied that *abolishing* inheritance would be even more inconsistent with the "spirit" of this ideal, since inheritance is necessary for promoting savings and investment and thus capital growth, or for maintaining people's incentives to work hard, things which, for the healthy functioning of supply and demand, are absolutely essential. We shall see in Section III, however, that this reply is not convincing.

All conservatives are suspicious of concentrating great economic power in the hands of government. And if the Soviet Union is any indication, these suspicions are well founded. Some conservatives are suspicious of concentrating great economic power in the hands of corporations. On the whole, these suspicions are well founded also; with the proviso that, because of economies of scale, certain of these concentrations are a necessary evil. No conservative, as far as I know, is suspicious of concentrating great economic power—*via* private fortunes—in the hands of individuals. Perhaps it is time for conservative thinking to become more consistent: the truth is, I suggest, that all great concentrations of economic power are suspicious, whether emanating from government, corporations, *or* individuals.

So we may conclude that, at best, inheritance receives no support from freedom in the narrow sense. But it remains for us to consider whether inheritance receives any support from the other relevant ideal of freedom, an ideal many, including myself, would consider to be the more fundamental of the two: freedom in the broad sense—being able to do, or having the opportunity to do, what one wants. So we must now ask whether, everything considered, there is more overall opportunity throughout the country for people to do what they want with inheritance, or without it.

On the one hand, without inheritance people are no longer free to leave their fortunes to whomever they want and, of course, those who otherwise would have received these fortunes are, without them, less free to do what they want also.

But to offset these losses in freedom are at least the following gains in freedom. First, as is well known, wealth has, generally speaking, a diminishing marginal utility. What this means is that, generally speaking, the more wealth one already has, the less urgent are the needs which any given increment of wealth will go to satisfy and, therefore, the less utility the additional wealth will have for one. This, in turn, means that the more evenly wealth is distributed, the more overall utility it will have.[18] And since we may assume that, generally speaking, the more utility some amount of wealth has for someone, the more freedom in the broad sense it allows that person to enjoy, we may conclude that the more evenly wealth is distributed, the more overall freedom to which it will give rise. Now assuming that abolishing inheritance would not lessen *overall* wealth (an assumption I shall try to show in Section III to be warranted), and that it would indeed distribute wealth more evenly, it follows that, by abolish-

ing inheritance, there would be some gain in freedom in the broad sense attributable to the diminishing marginal utility of wealth. Next, abolishing inheritance would also increase freedom by increasing equality of opportunity. Certainly those who do not start life having inherited significant funds (through either gift or bequest) start life, relative to those who do, with what amounts to a significant handicap. Abolishing inheritance, and thereby starting everyone at a more equal level, would obviously leave those who otherwise would have suffered this handicap (which would be the great majority of people) more free in the broad sense.

I, for one, believe these gains in freedom—that is, those attributable to the diminishing marginal utility of wealth and more equality of opportunity—would *more* than offset the loss in freedom resulting from the inability to give one's fortune to whom one wants. Abolishing inheritance is, I suggest, analogous to abolishing discrimination against blacks in restaurants and other commercial establishments. By abolishing discrimination, the owners of these establishments lose the freedom to choose the skin color of the people they do business with, but the gain in freedom for blacks is obviously greater and more significant than this loss. Likewise, by abolishing inheritance the gain in freedom for the poor is greater and more significant than the loss in freedom for the rich. So to the list of ideals that inheritance is inconsistent with, we can, if I am right, add freedom in the broad sense.

To recapitulate: three ideals that underlie capitalism are "distribution according to productivity," "equal opportunity," and "freedom," the latter being, for our purposes, subject to either a narrow or a broad interpretation. I do not claim these are the *only* ideals that may be said to underlie capitalism; I do claim, however, that they are among the most important. Inheritance is inconsistent with both "distribution according to productivity," and "equal opportunity." Perhaps it is not, strictly speaking, inconsistent with the ideal of freedom in the narrow sense, but neither is the abolishment of inheritance. On the other hand, it probably *is* inconsistent with what many would take to be the more fundamental of the two relevant ideals of freedom: freedom in the broad sense. Since these are among the most important ideals that underlie capitalism, I conclude that inheritance not only is not essential to capitalism, but is probably inconsistent with it.[19]

For those who, like myself, are inclined to support these ideals, the inconsistency of inheritance with them creates a strong presumption that inheritance is unjustified. But only a *presumption,* for none of these ideals are absolute. There may, therefore, be objections to the abolishment of inheritance that are strong enough to override its inconsistency with these ideals (or to show that my conclusion about its inconsistency with the ideal of freedom to be premature). So, before we can make any final judgment about the justifiability of inheritance, we must examine the most significant of these objections.

III. OBJECTIONS

In order to examine properly the objections to abolishing inheritance, we should have a definite proposal for abolishing inheritance before us, so that we know to what, exactly, these objections are meant to apply. I shall begin, therefore, by setting out a proposal that incorporates the main features I think any law abolishing inheritance should incorporate.

First, my proposal for abolishing inheritance includes the abolishment of all large gifts as well—gifts of the sort, that is, which might serve as alternatives to bequests. Obviously, if such gifts were not abolished as well, any law abolishing inheritance could be avoided all too easily.

Of course we would not want to abolish along with these large gifts such harmless gifts as ordinary birthday and Christmas presents. This, however, raises the problem of where to draw the line. I do not know the best solution to this problem. The amount that current law allows a person to give each year tax free ($10,000) is too large a figure at which to draw the line for purposes of a law abolishing inheritance. We might experiment with drawing the line, in part at least, by means of the distinction between, on the one hand, consumer goods that can be expected to be, within ten years, either consumed or worth less than half their current value and, on the other hand, all other goods. We can be more lenient in allowing gifts of goods falling within the former category since, as they are consumed or quickly lose their value, they cannot, themselves, become part of a large, unearned fortune. The same can be said about gifts of services. But we need not pursue these technicalities further here. The general point is simply that, so as to avoid an obvious loophole, gifts (other than ordinary birthday presents, etc.) are to be abolished along with bequests.

Next, according to my proposal, a person's estate would pass to the government, to be used for the general welfare. If, however, the government were to take over people's property upon their death then, obviously, after just a few generations the government would own virtually everything—which would certainly not be very compatible with capitalism. Since this proposal for abolishing inheritance *is* supposed to be compatible with capitalism, it must therefore include a requirement that the government sell on the open market, to the highest bidder, any real property, including any shares in a corporation, that it receives from anyone's estate, and that it do so within a certain period of time, within, say, one year from the decedent's death. This requirement is, however, to be subject to one qualification: any person specified by the decedent in his will shall be given a chance to *buy* any property specified by the decedent in his will before it is put on the market (a qualification designed to alleviate slightly the family heirloom/business/farm problem discussed below). The price to be paid by this person shall be whatever the property is worth (as determined by governmental appraisers, subject to appeal) and any credit terms shall be rather lenient (perhaps 10 percent down, with the balance, plus interest, due over the next 30 years).

Finally, the abolishment of inheritance proposed here is to be subject to three important exceptions. First, there shall be no limitations at all upon the amount a person can leave to his or her spouse. A marriage, it seems to me, should be viewed as a joint venture in which both members, whether or not one stays home tending to children while the other earns money, have an *equally* important role to play; and neither, therefore, should be deprived of enjoying fully any of the material rewards of this venture by having them taken away at the spouse's death. And unlimited inheritance between spouses eliminates one serious objection to abolishing inheritance: namely, that it is not right for a person suddenly to be deprived, not only of his or her spouse, but also of most of the wealth upon which he or she has come to depend—especially in those cases where the spouse has, for the sake of the marriage, given up, once and for all, any realistic prospects of a career.

The second exception to be built into this proposal is one for children who are orphaned, and any other people who have been genuinely dependent upon the decedent, such as any who are mentally incompetent, or too elderly to have any significant earning power of their own. A person shall be able to leave funds (perhaps in the form of a trust) sufficient to take care of such dependents. These funds should be used only for the dependent's living expenses, which would include any educational or institutional expenses no matter how much. They should not, of course, be used to provide children with a "nest egg" of the sort others are prohibited from leaving their children. And at a certain age, say twenty-one (if the child's formal education has been completed), or upon removal of whatever disability has caused dependency, the funds should cease. This exception eliminates another objection to abolishing inheritance—the objection that it would leave orphaned children, and other dependents, without the support they needed.[20]

The third and final exception to be built into this proposal is one for charitable organizations—ones created not for purposes of making a profit, but for charitable, religious, scientific, or educational purposes. And, in order to prevent these organizations from eventually controlling the economy, they must, generally, be under the same constraint as is the government with respect to any real property they are given, such as an operating factory: they must, generally, sell it on the open market within a year.

A limit of some sort could be placed upon the amount a person would be entitled to give to charitable organizations; I am inclined, however, to oppose any limit. Allowing unlimited contributions would, to be sure, weaken one of the advantages of abolishing inheritance, that of providing government with a major, new source of revenue, one that would serve to lessen the burden of income taxes. For rather than allowing their estates to pass to the government, most people would probably choose to leave their estates to charitable organizations. But even if they did, the advantage of lessening our tax burden would not be lost, for if vast amounts were given to charitable organizations, these organizations could be expected to fund much of the welfare, medical research, scholarships for the poor, aid to education, and so on, that must (or should) now be funded by the government, thereby lessening our tax burden not by increasing governmental revenues, but by decreasing governmental expenses. And charitable organizations would become, even more than they are today, a healthy counterbalance to the power of government in these areas.

Among the objections to abolishing inheritance is that it would serve to dry up charitable giving and, indeed, leave our charitable instincts, which are among our most noble, with no (monetary) ways of being expressed. But with the unlimited exception for charitable giving built into this proposal for abolishing inheritance, charitable giving, far from drying up, would actually increase, and increase significantly. Thus the effect of this proposal upon charitable giving, far from providing an argument against abolishing inheritance, actually provides an argument in *favor* of it.

(1) With a specific proposal now before us, let us begin our survey of objections to abolishing inheritance with the one that is weakest: the objection that abolishing inheritance would be a violation of property rights. The trouble with this objection is, quite simply, that it begs the question. Property rights are not normally viewed as being unqualified, nor certainly should they be. On the contrary, property rights normally are, and certainly should be, viewed as having built into them a number of qualifications or exceptions: an exception for taxes, an exception for uses which pose a danger of injury to others, an exception for eminent domain, and so on. As pointed out at the very beginning, the purpose of our investigation is precisely to determine whether we should recognize still another exception to property rights—an exception in the form of abolishing inher-

itance—or whether, instead, property rights should incorporate the practice of inheritance. Obviously we cannot determine this simply by slamming our fists on the table and insisting that property rights *do* allow inheritance, that abolishing inheritance *would* be a violation of property rights. The only way to determine whether property rights should incorporate the practice of inheritance is the way we are proceeding here, the hard way: by patiently examining, one by one, the various pros and cons of abolishing inheritance and then, in light of this examination, making as accurate an overall assessment as we can.

And lest my opponent claim this to be merely an appeal to utilitarian considerations and hence (in his view) illegitimate, let me hasten to point out that the "pros and cons" of which I speak need not be limited merely to utilitarian considerations. Considerations of right (other than the very one in question), of obligation, of (nonutilitarian) value, or of anything else, would all be welcome additions to the debate, as far as I am concerned. The only thing not welcome is a demand that we merely accept my opponent's view of property rights without question.

(2) Let us turn next to the reason Milton Friedman supports inheritance, and does so in spite of the fact that, as we have seen, it is incompatible with the values he himself says underlie capitalism.[21] And, incidentally, Friedman is not alone in finding this particular objection to abolishing inheritance convincing; others who do include Robert Nozick, and F. A. Hayek.[22] The argument upon which this objection is based proceeds somewhat as follows. Inheritance of property ("material" inheritance) is not the only source of unequal opportunity. Some people, for example, gain an unearned advantage over the rest of us by inheriting from their parents a beautiful singing voice, or keen intelligence, or striking good looks ("biological" inheritance). If we allow people to enjoy unearned advantages from biological inheritance, so the argument goes, it is only fair that we allow people to enjoy unearned advantages from material inheritance as well. We are told, in effect, that if we continue to allow one kind of unearned advantage to exist, we are, in all fairness, committed to allowing all other kinds of unearned advantages to continue to exist also.

The fallacy in this way of arguing should be apparent. One might just as well insist that racial discrimination is justified by arguing that, because we allow unearned advantages resulting from biological inheritance to continue to exist, we are, in all fairness, therefore committed to allowing unearned advantages resulting from racial discrimination to continue to exist also. To be sure, we do "allow" unearned advantages resulting from biological inheritance to continue to exist because, first of all, we cannot eliminate them and, second, even if we could, we would not want to since the costs of doing so would outweigh the benefits. Unearned advantages resulting from material inheritance, on the other hand, can be eliminated. Perhaps the costs of doing so outweigh the benefits here as well. But, once again, we can determine whether this is so only the hard way: by a careful and patient investigation into what the pros and cons actually are. We must not be dissuaded from this task by the above quick, but fallacious argument with which Friedman and others tempt us.

(3) Let us turn now to some objections of a more practical nature. The first of these is that, regardless of whether abolishing inheritance is justified or not, the simple truth is that Americans are solidly against doing so; therefore our discussion is a waste of time. The reply, of course, is that, unless popular opinions are sometimes challenged, how, after all, can we ever make any progress? What if, for example, just because the public was against it, no one in the South a century ago had been willing to consider whether abolishing slavery was justified? If abolishing inheritance really is justified, chances are the public will eventually *come* to favor it, but the first order of business, clearly, is to decide if it really is justified. . . .

(4) We turn next to what is, I suppose, the most common objection to abolishing inheritance: the objection that, if people were not allowed to leave their wealth to their children, they would lose their incentive to continue working hard, and national productivity would therefore fall. In spite of the popularity of this objection, all the available evidence seems to indicate the contrary. For example, people who do not intend to have children, and therefore are obviously not motivated by the desire to leave their children a fortune, do not seem to work any less hard

than anyone else. And evidence of a more technical nature leads to the same conclusion: people, typically, do not need to be motivated by a desire to leave their children (or someone else) great wealth in order to be motivated to work hard.[23]

Common sense tells us the same thing. The prospect of being able to leave one's fortune to one's children is, no doubt, for some people one factor motivating them to be productive. But even for these people, this is only *one* factor; there are usually other factors motivating them as well, and motivating them to such an extent that, even if inheritance were abolished, their productivity would be unaffected. Take, for example, professional athletes. If inheritance were abolished, would they try any less hard to win? I doubt it. For one thing, abolishing inheritance would not, in any way, affect the amount of money they would be able to earn for use during their lives. So they would still have the prospect of a large income to motivate them. But there is something else which motivates them to do their best that is, I think, even more important, and is not dependent on money: the desire to win or, in other words, to achieve that which entitles them to the respect of their colleagues, the general public, and themselves. Because of the desire to win, amateur athletes compete just as fiercely as professionals. Abolishing inheritance would in no way affect this reason for doing one's best either. Athletes would still have the prospect of winning to motivate them. Businessmen, doctors, lawyers, engineers, artists, researchers—in general, those who contribute most to society—are not, with respect to what in the most general sense motivates them, really very different from professional athletes. Without inheritance, these people would still be motivated by the prospect of a sizable income for themselves and, probably even more so, by the prospect of "winning"; that is, by the prospect of achieving, or continuing to achieve, that which entitles them to the respect of their colleagues, the general public, and themselves.

But even if abolishing inheritance did lessen incentive by leaving people with no motivation to accumulate for their children, it would, in another respect, *increase* incentive. This can be illustrated by the often used race analogy. Consider two different hundred-meter races between Jones and Smith where, in the first race, Jones is given a fifty-meter head start while, in the second race, they start even. In which of these races will each be most likely to run his fastest? The answer, of course, is race two. In race one, Jones will figure that even if he does not run his fastest, he will win, while Smith will figure that even if he does run his fastest, he will lose; so very likely neither will run his fastest. What is true in this example is probably true in the "game of life" as well: the more equal people's starting points, the more incentive they will have to try hard. Since abolishing inheritance would do much to equalize people's starting points, it should, in this way, increase people's incentives. And this increase, attributable to more equality of opportunity, would, I should think, more than make up for any decrease in incentive attributable to having no one to leave one's fortune to—if, indeed, there *were* any such decrease.[24]

(5) We come now to the most technical and, potentially, the most serious objection to abolishing inheritance: the objection that this would cause a substantial decrease in savings and investment, thus causing a serious reduction in capital which, in turn, would erode our standard of living.[25] Abolishing inheritance, it is said, would reduce savings for two reasons. First, by breaking up large fortunes, it would reduce the number of people whose wealth far exceeded their capacity to consume, and who, therefore, were able to sink vast amounts into savings and investment. Without these vast amounts going into savings and investment, it is argued, overall savings and investment, and thus capital, would go down. Secondly, it is said that, not only would abolishing inheritance reduce people's *capacity* to save by breaking up large fortunes, it would also reduce people's *incentive* to save. Although, as we have seen, abolishing inheritance probably would not significantly affect people's incentive to produce, their incentive to save might well be affected. If people could not leave their wealth to their children, then rather than leave it to charity, or to the government, they might well decide to consume it instead. In short: abolishing inheritance would shift people's

consumption-savings pattern more in the direction of consumption.

These points, although probably well taken, should not be exaggerated. Abolishing inheritance would distribute wealth more evenly, the relatively few enormous fortunes of today being replaced, in part, by a larger number of moderate fortunes. Thus any slack in investment attributable to a decrease in the *size* of the fortunes of those with enough to invest substantial amounts would, to some extent, be taken up by an increase in the *number* of people with fortunes large enough for them to invest substantial amounts. And people's *motives* to save and invest would certainly not evaporate altogether with the abolishment of inheritance. People would, of course, still want to hold something back for a "rainy day." People would still want to save for their retirement (and no one knows for how many years one will need to be covered). Investments would still remain attractive aside from the savings motive; they combine the excitement of a gamble with the satisfaction of doing what is socially useful. And many people, especially the more wealthy, would still want to save for charitable purposes; to have a scholarship or perhaps a university building named after them, to support medical research, or even to establish a charitable foundation to carry on with some project in which they deeply believe. Another point to keep in mind is that most corporate investment—and corporate investment constitutes a large percent of total investment—is generated by corporate income. Given the separation between ownership and management in large corporations today, it is unlikely that management would be influenced by the abolishment of inheritance to reduce the percentage of corporate income used for the replacement of capital and new investment. Indeed, if private funding became increasingly scarce, funding from corporate income might well take up some of the slack. In short, no one really knows for sure exactly how abolishing inheritance would affect savings and investment, but the effect might turn out to be far less than some critics think. . . . But it, is now time to turn to some objections that *are* warranted. The only question is how serious these objections are.

(6) First, there is the objection about administrative costs. As we saw, in order to prevent the government and charitable organizations from eventually owning virtually everything, they would be required to sell to the highest bidder all real property, including shares in corporations, that passed to them from people's estates. Administering these sales would be a major and costly burden. Yet even today, *with* inheritance, much of the property from most estates where there is no surviving spouse is put up for sale. But these sales are conducted privately by the heirs of the estates, the administrative burden thus being shared by many, rather than falling upon the government. Of course if inheritance were abolished, not all of the burden of selling property from people's estates would fall upon the government either; numerous charitable organizations would, together, shoulder much, if not most, of the burden. And the decedents themselves can be expected to have sold more of their property sometime before their death than they would have were inheritance allowed. But the government would probably still have a sizable amount of property to dispose of. This administrative burden, along with the additional burden of administering any subsidies for investments that might become necessary, qualifies as a genuine disadvantage of abolishing inheritance.

(7) Finally, abolishing inheritance might be objected to on the grounds that it deprives people of property that clearly would have more value for them than for others. Take, for example, precious family heirlooms. Although their monetary value for those within and outside the family is the same, for those within the family they have, in addition to their monetary value, a sentimental value as well. Abolishing inheritance, it might be argued, would deprive families of these precious heirlooms, allowing them to pass to others for whom they have far less value. But, more serious yet, consider the son or daughter who has taken over the family business or farm, and who has neither the training nor desire to pursue any other occupation. Again, for such a person the business or farm can be expected to have value far above the mere monetary value it has for others; indeed, he or she may have built a whole life around it. Yet

abolishing inheritance would take the business or farm away from this person and allow it to pass to someone for whom it had far less value.

The family heirloom problem seems less serious than that of the family business or farm. According to the proposal for abolishing inheritance we are considering, if the decedent had provided for it in his will, family members would have a chance to buy any family heirlooms before they went on the open market and, except for the most expensive heirlooms, they would normally have the means to do so. If the decedent had provided for it, a son or daughter would be given the same chance to buy a family business or farm. But even with the rather liberal credit terms built into this proposal for sales to those specified by the decedent (10 percent down, and 30 years to pay the rest) probably most sons and daughters would not be in a strong enough financial position to take advantage of this opportunity.

Yet it is important to realize that even the family business/farm problem is, today, rather limited in scope. There was a period in American history when disrupting occupational continuity from parent to child by abolishing inheritance would have had grave consequences for the nation as a whole. Higher education, and other occupational training, were not readily available for most people; more often than not, children learned their occupation from their parents so as to carry on with the family business or farm after their parents died. To disrupt this continuity by abolishing inheritance, thereby depriving vast numbers of people of the only job for which they were adequately prepared, might well have been a national economic disaster. Inheritance, in those days, might well have been one of society's main devices for achieving continuity from one generation to the next in the production of goods and services.

But those days have long since passed—and, incidentally, I see little reason for trying to resurrect them. Today higher education and other forms of occupational training *are* readily available; people are far more mobile than before; children do not, for the most part, follow in the exact footsteps of their parents anymore; and continuity from one generation to the next in the production of goods and ser-

vices is now achieved instead largely through the separation of ownership from management that is found in today's large corporations. Disrupting occupational continuity from parent to child by abolishing inheritance might have serious consequences for the limited number of children who would like to carry on from their parents, but the number is indeed limited. . . .

It is time now to take stock of where we stand. In the previous section we found that inheritance is inconsistent with the ideal of distribution according to productivity, with the ideal of equal opportunity, and probably with the ideal of freedom in the broad sense. Thus we began this section with a presumption against inheritance being justified. But this was only a presumption; it could be overridden if we succeeded in finding objections to abolishing inheritance that were strong enough to outweigh this presumption. In this section we have been examining the most common and most serious potential objections. Most of them, however, turned out, upon closer scrutiny, to be unfounded. The two objections that did, in part at least, survive our scrutiny were the one concerning administrative costs, and the one concerning family heirlooms, businesses, and farms. It remains only to ask whether these objections are strong enough to tip the balance back in favor of inheritance.

It is impossible to determine exactly how great the administrative costs of abolishing inheritance would be. This, as we saw, depended on the extent to which government would have to be involved in the sale of property from estates, and the extent to which it would have to subsidize investments, two matters that we cannot know in advance. There was some reason to believe that administrative costs might not be extensive. But even if they were extensive, they would have to be far more so than it is reasonable to believe they ever would be to override the presumption against inheritance. For this presumption involves considerations of justice and freedom against which mere administrative costs should have, I would think, relatively little weight.

But what about the second objection to abolishing inheritance: that it would deprive families of family heirlooms and, more seriously, family businesses and farms? In weighing the importance of this objection we need to keep in mind the main rationale behind it: by abolishing inheritance, we prevent people within the decedent's family from getting what would have been of far more value to them (for sentimental reasons, etc.) than to those who do get it.[26] No doubt abolishing inheritance *would* redistribute wealth so that some of its value would, in this way, be lost. But to offset this loss would be a very significant *gain* in the value to which this wealth, upon being redistributed, would give rise; a gain attributable, as we saw in Section II, to the diminishing marginal utility of wealth; to the fact that, other things being equal, the more evenly wealth is distributed, the greater its overall utility, or value. Indeed, this gain would, I should think, *more* than offset any loss attributable to family businesses and farms going to those to whom they have less value—especially since, as we saw, any such loss would be far less serious than it would have been during an earlier period in American history.

So we must conclude, I think, that the family heirloom/business/farm objection and the administrative cost objection are not, neither by themselves nor combined, weighty enough to override our initial presumption against inheritance. And even these two genuine disadvantages of abolishing inheritance could, to a large extent, be avoided by a certain tempting compromise proposal according to which gifts and bequests would not be abolished, or even taxed, but instead a limit would be placed upon the amount in gifts and bequests any one person could receive in a lifetime. In other words, this proposal calls for the establishment of a *lifetime accessions quota*.[27] The key to this proposal would, of course, be the figure at which this quota was put. Any set figure, say $50,000, would, due to changes in the value of the dollar, soon become outmoded. So, rather than some set figure, it might be wiser to choose a figure that, according to some predetermined formula, would adjust itself automatically to changing conditions over the years. I would tentatively suggest a figure equivalent in amount to the average dollar value (rounded off to the nearest ten thousand) of all the estates of all Americans who, at age twenty-one or over, died during the five years previous to the year in which the quota is to

be applicable. This figure would, I think, make the quota modest enough so as not to compromise unduly the advantages that could be achieved by abolishing inheritance altogether (Immense concentrations of economic power would still be broken up, wealth, and therefore opportunity, would still be distributed more evenly, etc.). Yet, on the other hand, this quota would be large enough so as to avoid, for the most part, the administrative costs of abolishing inheritance. Relatively few people would have estates larger than, say, five times the average, and since most people would know at least five eligible people to whom they would want to leave their wealth (children, grandchildren, nephews, nieces, close friends, loyal employees, and the like), relatively few estates would therefore require any more from the government than an appraisal of assets, something which the government already does under current estate and gift tax law anyway. And many people would have a motive for saving and investment they would not have if inheritance were abolished—this motive being that of leaving wealth to these individuals. Finally, this quota would be large enough to significantly alleviate the family heirloom/business/farm problem as well.

One final point: if, through either abolishing inheritance altogether or establishing a *modest* quota, family members could not inherit or buy a valuable business or farm upon the owner's death, then it might be bought, jointly, by the employees of the business or farm instead. A large number of employees, by splitting the financial burden among themselves, could perhaps afford to purchase a valuable business or farm while a small number of family members could not—especially in view of the fact that, whatever profits had previously gone to the decedent would, if the employees purchased his interest, now go to them, thus increasing their salaries to the point where they might well be able to handle the monthly payments. Furthermore, the government could, and I think should, encourage joint purchases by employees with "supportive legislation" designed to make such purchases easier by granting employees very favorable purchasing terms. (In return for these favorable terms the government could require that all *future,* full-time employees be required to purchase an equal share as well, so that the establishment would then never have "second class citizens.") As joint owners, workers would have some control over their own destiny; they would periodically elect management; they would share in profits and losses; they would, in short, enjoy what may be referred to as "workers' democracy." This democracy would not, of course, be a "direct," but rather a "representative" one, where the elected managers—normally highly trained, and highly paid, professionals—would be in full charge of everyday affairs (just as in a political democracy), yet answerable, ultimately, to the workers. I am inclined to think most workers' democracies would be highly desirable. The potential gains from such arrangements are considerable: they include a decrease in worker alienation, an increase in the tolerability of working conditions, and a greater share for workers in the profits from their own work.[28] In general, the gains to be realized in going from a "totalitarian" business establishment to a workers' democracy parallel those in going from a totalitarian *state* to a *political* democracy. If either abolishing inheritance altogether or establishing a modest quota, combined with the right kind of supportive legislation, did succeed in creating a gradual, and voluntary, evolution toward workers' democracies, this would, I suggest, be a significant bonus.[29]

Throughout the world today, capitalism is on the defensive. Its many enemies point to the extreme inequalities of wealth it generates, to the shameless inequalities of opportunity, and they ask if such a system deserves to survive. Frankly, I am not sure it does. Yet it is a system with virtues as striking as its deficiencies: it is extraordinarily productive, and it generates important freedoms.[30] A system with so much going for it is worth trying to remedy from within. This will, I think, require major changes, not the least of which will be to unburden capitalism of an outmoded practice of inheritance.

NOTES

1. Lester C. Thurow, "Tax Wealth, Not Income," *New York Times Magazine,* 11 April 1976, p. 33.

2. The latest governmental study of the distribution of wealth, carried out in 1983, estimates the amount of net wealth held by the top 2 percent to be 28 percent, and that held by the top 10 percent to be 57 percent. R. Avery, G. Elliehausen, G. Canner, and T. Gustafson, "Survey of Consumer Finances, 1983: Second Report," *Federal Reserve Bulletin* 70 (December 1984): 865.

3. Thurow, "Tax Wealth, Not Income," p. 33.

4. Lester C. Thurow, *The Impact of Taxes on the American Economy* (New York: Praeger Publishers, 1971), p. 127.

5. Thurow, "Tax Wealth, Not Income," pp. 100–101.

6. George A. Cooper, *A Voluntary Tax? New Perspectives on Sophisticated Estate Tax Avoidance* (Washington, D.C.: Brookings Institution, 1979).

7. Richard A. Smith, "The Fifty-Million Dollar Man," *Fortune* (November 1957); Arthur M. Louis, "America's Centimillionaires," *Fortune* (May 1968); and Arthur M. Louis, "The New Rich of the Seventies," *Fortune* (September 1973).

8. John A. Brittain, *Inheritance and the Inequality of National Wealth* (Washington, D.C.: Brookings Institution, 1978).

9. Ibid., pp. 14–16.

10. Ibid., p. 99.

11. Milton Friedman, *Capitalism & Freedom* (Chicago: University of Chicago Press, 1962), pp. 161–162.

12. For a useful analysis of the concept of "equal opportunity," see Douglas Rae, *Equalities* (Cambridge, MA: Harvard University Press, 1981), ch. 4. Using Rae's terminology, the ideal of equal opportunity being discussed here is "means-regarding," rather than "prospect-regarding."

In spite of the usefulness of Rae's analysis, it is, I think, mistaken in one crucial respect. According to Rae, means-regarding equal opportunity receives whatever ideological, or moral, credibility it has only by being confused with prospect-regarding equal opportunity (pp. 67, 73). If what I say below about the value of (means-regarding) equal opportunity is correct, this is a serious mistake.

13. Milton & Rose Friedman, *Freedom to Choose* (New York: Harcourt Brace Jovanovich, 1979), pp. 131–40. Friedman also talks favorably of another ideal of equality, which he calls "equality before God." But equality before God turns out to be a restatement of the ideal of liberty, which is discussed below.

14. See, for example, Bernard Williams, "The Idea of Equality," *Philosophy, Politics and Society,* ser. 2, ed. Peter Laslett and W. G. Runciman (Oxford: Basil Blackwell, 1962).

15. I say this fully aware of the criticism of equal

opportunity, and meritocracy in general, made by Michael Young in *The Rise of Meritocracy* (Harmondsworth, England: Penguin Books, 1961). The problem with these criticisms is that they are based upon taking equal opportunity (along with productivity) to be, not merely a prima facie value as it should be, but absolute. Any legitimate prima facie value can easily be reduced to absurdity if it is wrongly viewed as being absolute.

16. Although abolishing inheritance would, I should think, do more to increase equal opportunity than any single other (feasible) reform, it is by no means the only reform that is needed for this purpose. If we are serious about achieving significantly more equality of opportunity within a capitalistic framework—and I think we certainly should be—we should combine inheritance reform with, among other things, the following two additional reforms: a program that guarantees access to higher education for all who are qualified, and a program to bring about equal access to medical care for all. This latter reform would remove the financial obstacle preventing children of the very poor from receiving prompt and reliable medical care; prompt and reliable medical care is, in turn, necessary for preventing their medical needs from progressing to the point where they have suffered irreversible damage that could handicap them for the rest of their lives. One way of achieving equal access to medical care for all is through a program of "socialized" medicine, but this is not the only way.

17. Friedman, *Capitalism & Freedom,* p. 13.

18. The more evenly wealth is distributed, the more overall utility it will have since any wealth that "goes" from the rich to the poor, thereby making the distribution more even, will (given the diminishing marginal utility of wealth) have more utility for these poor than it would have had for the rich, thus increasing overall utility.

19. Inheritance is, no doubt, equally inconsistent with the ideals that underlie socialism, but we need not pursue this matter here.

20. Society must not, of course, forget about orphans, and other dependents, of the relatively poor either; they should be adequately provided for somehow by the state. Yet it might be prohibitively expensive for the state to care for orphans of the poor at the level of luxury at which this exception to the abolishment of inheritance would allow orphans of the rich to be cared for, thus raising a question of fairness. But if we accept the proposition that (since we do not want to abolish the family) it is justified for the children of the rich to live in more luxury than those of the poor while their parents are alive, then it is reasonable for us to allow this higher standard to continue even if these

parents happen to die. It is usually traumatic enough for a child to have to adapt to the death of both parents without, at the same time, having to adapt to an altogether different standard of living as well.

21. Friedman, *Capitalism & Freedom,* pp. 163–64; and *Freedom to Choose,* p. 136.

22. Robert Nozick, *Anarchy, State, and Utopia* (New York: Basic Books, 1974), pp. 237–38; F. A. Hayek, *The Constitution of Liberty* (Chicago: University of Chicago Press, 1960), pp. 90–91. Cf. John Rawls, *A Theory of Justice* (Cambridge, MA: Harvard University Press, 1971), p. 278.

23. See, for example, D. C. McClelland, *The Achieving Society* (Princeton: Van Nostrand, 1961), pp. 234–35; and Seymour Fiekowsky, *On the Economic Effects of Death Taxation in the United States* (unpublished doctoral dissertation, Harvard University, 1959), pp. 370–71.

24. Gordon Tullock claims that a better way to redistribute income and wealth than abolishing inheritance would be a direct tax on either income or wealth. See Tullock, "Inheritance Justified," *The Journal of Law and Economics* (October 1971). But, if I am right, abolishing inheritance would not, in general, decrease people's incentive to be productive (on the contrary, it would probably increase incentive); whereas the same cannot be said of Tullock's method of still greater income taxes, or of a substantial tax upon wealth. In any case, Tullock fails to realize that by no means is redistribution the only, or even the main, goal of abolishing inheritance; another goal, for example, is greater equality of opportunity (i.e., "starting places" that are more equal). Any tax upon income or wealth which still permitted vast sums to be inherited from various sources would not be as successful as abolishing inheritance, or as a modest quota (see below), in accomplishing *this* goal.

25. Gordon Tullock says that, for economists, this has been, traditionally, the "principle" objection to abolishing inheritance (yet it is not an objection Tullock himself makes). Although it is what he calls the principle objection, he says the point has not been made as strongly in the literature as one might expect. Ibid., p. 465, n. 1. Nevertheless, Tullock goes on to say, it is discussed in G. E. Hoover, "The Economic Effects of Inheritance Taxes," *American Economic Review* 17 (1927): 38–49; and Alvin H. Johnson, "Public Capitalization of the Inheritance Tax," *Journal of Political Economy* 22 (1914): 160–80.

26. In the case of family farms, there is a further rationale: by preventing people from inheriting them, the farms will, in being sold, be fragmented into a number of small, inefficient units. The problem of fragmentation, however, does not appear to be very serious; if significant

fragmentation did occur, and did prove to be inefficient, it could easily be remedied by some sort of legislation requiring that any farms sold by the government in settling a person's estate be (normally) sold only as a whole, and requiring (perhaps) that any resale within a period of, say, five years also be only as a whole.

27. A quota would be far superior to a lifetime accessions *tax:* it is, first of all, simpler—a not insignificant advantage!—but, even more importantly, a quota would indeed place a ceiling, as a tax would not, upon how much any one person could receive from all sources—the lack of any definite ceiling being perhaps the most insidious loophole of all.

28. For more on the potential gains, see David Schweickart, *Capitalism or Worker Control?* (New York: Praeger, 1980).

29. Ronald Chester believes that any reform in inheritance law that would greatly reduce the vast inequalities of opportunity attributable to inheritance today might provide yet another bonus. Chester writes that "numerous observes, including J. B. Mays (who is British) and Americans such as E. H. Sutherland and Daniel Bell believe that preaching equal opportunity without its fulfillment has made American social structure powerfully criminogenic." Chester, *Inheritance, Wealth and Society* (Bloomington: Indiana University Press, 1982), p. 161. So greatly reducing these vast inequalities of opportunity may, he argues, pave the way toward significant reductions in property crime.

30. On the relationship between capitalism and certain freedoms see, for example, Friedman, *Capitalism & Freedom,* especially chap. 1.

30

Is Criminalizing Blackmail Wrong?

Suppose I come across some information that proves that you are cheating on your spouse. And suppose I come across this information in a manner that is perfectly legal. I do not, for example, break into your house or wiretap your telephone or beat a confession out of your lover. I simply see you kissing your lover in a public park that I have every right to be in or come across a photograph of the two of you in bed that you carelessly dropped by the curb of a motel parking lot.

Now, if I were to ask you to give me $5,000, I might be guilty of being pushy, but my behavior, in and of itself, would be perfectly legal. Similarly, if I were to tell your spouse about your adulterous affair, I might be guilty of being a malicious gossip or of butting into your business, but I certainly would not be breaking the law. There is no law against such gossip. But suppose I combine these two perfectly legal acts and announce that I will gossip about your secret affair unless you provide me with $5,000. If you give me the money, I won't tell. If you don't give me the money, I will. Suddenly, I have done something illegal: I have blackmailed you.

A number of philosophers and legal theorists have pointed out this puzzling feature of blackmail—how two legal rights, when combined, become a legal wrong. Put in terms of the example outlined here, what has come to be called the *paradox of blackmail* can be put as follows:

P1 I should have the legal right to tell your spouse your secret or not, as I choose.
P2 You should have the legal right to give me $5,000 or not give me $5,000 as you choose.
P3 My act of blackmailing you is the act of choosing to tell your spouse your secret if and only if you choose not to give me $5,000.

C I should have the legal right to blackmail you.

Virtually every writer who has addressed this argument has treated it as a paradox, taking the argument's conclusion to be plainly unacceptable. The question has not been "should we accept the argument's surprising conclusion?" but rather "where does the argument go wrong?" A number of proposed answers to this question have been treated as possible "solutions" to the "problem" posed by the existence of blackmail laws.

In "The Crime of Blackmail: A Libertarian Critique," Walter Block turns this approach to the paradox of blackmail on its head. Rather than viewing the argument against laws against blackmail as a problem in need of a solution, Block maintains that it is simply a good argument against laws against blackmail. Presenting a concise argument in the form of a process of elimination (see the Introduction), Block considers the various responses that have been offered to the paradox of blackmail and argues that none of them is successful. The result is that the State should simply decriminalize blackmail.

QUESTIONS FOR CONSIDERATION

• Since Block's argument depends on the merits of his replies to a variety of arguments against blackmail, critics of his piece are left with two options. First, one can ask whether Block has satisfactorily addressed all of the arguments he considers. For example, many people argue that it is right that blackmail is criminalized because it involves an element of coercion. Block counters this approach by emphasizing that the blackmailer is only threatening to do what he would independently have a legal right to do. Is Block correct in maintaining that this makes blackmail crucially different from other, clearly illegal, acts of coercion, such as robbing someone at gunpoint? Or does blackmail still have enough in common with such acts to account for its criminalization?

• Can laws against blackmail be shown to be just as a means of preventing exploitation or protecting privacy or promoting the social good?

• Are there further reasons for banning blackmail beyond those Block has addressed? If such reasons are identified, this should not be taken as a decisive objection to Block's position. One will still need to consider how Block might reply to those reasons, based on the kinds of arguments he presents here. But, in thinking about the various ways in which laws against blackmail might be justified, readers are encouraged not to allow a critic of such laws to fully determine which set of reasons should be considered.

Walter Block	# The Crime of Blackmail: A Libertarian Critique

There is something deeply paradoxical about laws that criminalize blackmail. How is it that, as Glanville Williams put it, "two things that taken separately are moral and legal whites together make a moral and legal black"?[1] For the crime of blackmail involves the criminalization of two otherwise legal acts when they occur in combination—for example, the threat to disclose damaging information about another, and the offer to refrain from disclosing it for some valuable consideration. Were Alfred to (threaten to) disclose damaging information concerning Bill's extramarital affairs, no offense recognized by law would be involved (even if there were something distasteful about such gossip); were Alfred to ask Bill for $5000, again there would be no contravention of any proper law (even if it displayed a degree of chutzpah). But were Alfred to threaten Bill that he would disclose information concerning Bill's extramarital affairs unless Bill paid him $5000, his two-part act would—under current laws-constitute the crime of blackmail. Why should the conjunction of such otherwise legal acts have an entirely different legal status?

Walter Block, "The Crime of Blackmail: A Libertarian Critique," *Criminal Justice Ethics* 18, no. 2 (Summer/Fall 1999): 3–10. Reprinted by permission of Criminal Justice

The paradox is heightened when we consider the reverse situation. Bill learns that Alfred is in possession of damaging information concerning him. He socks Alfred out, and offers him $5000 to keep silent. If Alfred accepts Bill's offer, and subsequently keeps mum, he should not be held to have blackmailed Bill. Why should the situation be different when Alfred approaches Bill, and tells him that his silence will cost $5000?

This is the heart of the libertarian critique of blackmail laws, and in this essay I propose to defend that critique against a number of arguments that have been advanced to justify them. Although my critique of such laws depends ultimately on my belief that criminal prohibitions are justified only when some material threat is posed to another (by means of force, fraud, or theft), my arguments here will show that various attempts to avoid or account for the paradox do not succeed, even on their own terms. Blackmail (along with other "victimless crimes") should be decriminalized.[2,3]

SOME DEFINITIONAL PRELIMINARIES

Although standard instances of blackmail involve a threat to disclose damaging information if some monetary payment is not made, the range of possibilities is somewhat wider. Leo Katz, for example, suggests as alternative threats:

> Pay me $10,000—or I will: cause some really bad blood at the next faculty meeting, . . . seduce your fiancé, . . . persuade your son that it is his patriotic duty to volunteer for combat in Vietnam, . . . give your high-spirited, risk-addicted 19-year-old daughter a motorcycle for Christmas, hasten our father's death by leaving the Catholic church.[4]

Demands as well as threats may vary: usually it is for money, but it could also be for sexual favors or some other valued consideration. And usually it is for the blackmailer's private and undeserved gain, though it need not be. Imagine, writes Eric Mack,

> that you can deter a factory owner from (safely) burning his plant to the ground (and thus thoroughly

eliminating many employment opportunities) for the sake of destructive glee only by threatening to reveal his secrets. Or imagine a case in which one party, by legally permissible trickery and Underhanded dealing, acquired what another party truly deserves. Wouldn't it be perfectly moral for the morally deserving party to blackmail the first party into transferring that valued good—especially if what was threatened was precisely the [revelation] of the trickery and underhandedness?[5]

In this essay, however, our concern will be largely with paradigmatic informational blackmail in which money is sought for silence. Blackmail should not be confused with extortion. In the latter, a threat to do something that would otherwise be illegal is made in demanding something from another: If Charles threatens to break David's knees or burn down his house if David does not give him $5000, Charles is guilty of extortion, not blackmail. Extortion is properly considered illegal.

IS THERE REALLY A PARADOX OF BLACKMAIL?

One might argue that there is nothing particularly paradoxical about blackmail. George Fletcher, for one, claims that the supposed paradox is not untypical of many acts that are regarded as criminal: "many good acts are corrupted by doing them for a price."[6] Fletcher instances bribery, prostitution, and payment for confessing to a crime. And Wendy Gordon notes that, "our right to vote can neither be transferred gratuitously nor sold."[7]

But are these plausible counter instances? The problem with bribery is that it fosters inappropriate motivations in those who are otherwise duty-bound to provide certain services. Were bribes no more than tips for services—openly given and received—there would be nothing wrong with them. What makes bribery problematic is not the conjunction of service and money, but the fact that money given secretly becomes an incentive to forgo duty and/or to do it only when more is giver than one is contractually obliged to accept. Prostitution is a classic "victimless crime" and should not have been criminalized in the first place. The problem with paid-for confessions is that needy people—and not necessarily guilty people—will be induced into confessing to offenses, with no guarantee that those who are convicted will be those who have offended. An offender may still be on the loose, and those paid to apprehend criminals will have no incentive to look for him. As for the right to vote, it could have been otherwise. The only reason that political votes (unlike votes in publicly traded corporations) cannot be sold is that a majority has agreed not to commodify them.

BLACKMAIL AND OTHER COMMERCIAL TRANSACTIONS

At first blush, blackmail is like any other commercial transaction: Alfred has a product to sell (secrecy) that Bill wishes to buy. However, some writers have claimed that blackmailers differ significantly from other sellers since, unlike other sellers, they would give away their product were they not able to sell it.[8] Perhaps so, perhaps not![9] In any case it is not easy to see any significance to the difference. For other sellers, perhaps, the product to be sold represents all investment on their part, and therefore something they would be unlikely to give away, whereas the incriminating information that the blackmailer possesses is much more likely to have been gained without significant investment.

May be the difference lies in motivation, Wendy Gordon suggests that blackmail should be outlawed because "the blackmailer acquires information *for the sole purpose of obtaining money or advantage from the victim, and . . . , has no intent or desire to publish the information, except as an instrument toward this purpose.*"[10] But why should the blackmailer's intent be of any interest to the law unless the conduct in question has independently infringed another's rights? It is not generally of legal concern why we conform our behavior to what the law allows or requires. Intent only becomes an issue once the law is broken. But since Alfred's disclosure of Bill's infidelities does not constitute conduct of a kind the law would ordinarily prohibit, it should not be of any legal interest to know why Alfred may or may not choose to disclose the information he has about Bill.[11]

Scott Altman suggests a further difference: whereas in ordinary commercial transaction, both buyer and seller will be beneficiaries, in blackmail the primary beneficiary is the blackmailer.[12] But why should the person who buys silence not also be seen as benefiting from the transaction? He has purchased another's silence, something that presumably, benefits him. It is true that, antecedent to the blackmailer's approach, the blackmailee was not seeking to purchase the silence of others, but that was because he believed that his secret was safe, and did not need to be secured through purchase.

BLACKMAIL AND COERCION

Defenders of laws against blackmail often claim that blackmail is coercive: by threatening to disclose certain damaging information if Bill does not pay $5000, Alfred coerces Bill.[13] Or so it is said. However, the idea of coercion cannot clearly be extended to such cases. In paradigm cases, Alfred coerces Bill into parting with $5000 if he tackles Bill and steals his wallet containing $5000, or if he puts a gun to Bill's head and threatens to pull the trigger should Bill refuse to hand over $5000. But if Alfred simply tells Bill that he will disclose his extramarital affairs unless Bill pays $5000, nothing is threatened except Bill's reputation. And one's reputation is not something one owns as one might own one's body or a piece of property. Reputation is a form of social recognition to which one does not have a right as one might have a right to one's property.[14] Should Alfred spread the information without making any claim for money, he will have done nothing illegal. Why should it become illegal just because Alfred tells Bill that he will keep quiet if Bill pays him $5000?

Perhaps the argument from coercion can be expressed as follows: The blackmailer's act is coercive because he proposes to reveal information that he is obligated not to disclose.[15] But this will not do either. Even if Alfred were obligated not to reveal the information, it would still not show the threat to reveal it to be blackmail; rather, it would be a coercive threat, for example, extortion. It would indeed be legally wrong for Alfred to reveal what he told Bill in confidence, but the threat to disclose it unless Bill pays Alfred to keep quiet would be a legal wrong not because it is blackmail, but because it breached Alfred's contractual obligation to Bill. But if there is no obligation for Bill to keep the damaging information to himself, then and only then would there be no coercion involved in making it known, Should Alfred accidentally find out about Bill's extramarital affairs, he is under no obligation at all regarding its disclosure.[16] Why, then, should his informing Bill that he will reveal what Bill has been up to be coercive?

Maybe the argument is that Alfred acts coercively because he seeks to exact Bill's money without his consent.[17] Although no literal gun is being pointed at Bill's head, something else is—serious damage to his life, reputation, job prospects, or whatever—should he refuse to pay. This account, of course, would not work with cases in which Bill, on hearing that Alfred possesses (and is likely to reveal) the information, seeks him out to offer him "hush money, but perhaps the supporter of blackmail laws may not mind cutting these cases adrift from the scope of such legislation. Once again, however, we need to remind ourselves of the disanalogy with the gunman. Absent monetary considerations, if the gunman pulls the trigger a legally significant wrong is done to his victim, whereas, if Alfred spills the beans on Bill's philandering no crime is committed.

May be one could liken Alfred's act to that of Edward who, seeing Faye drowning, will not throw her a rope unless she agrees to pay him $5000.[18] This is surely exploitative of Faye's situation, but is it coercive? Were Edward to have pushed Faye into the water in the first place, there would indeed be an argument for saying that the demand for $5000 was coercive; but *ex hypothesi* he did not, and so, given that he does not violate a legal obligation in not throwing a rope to her, it is hardly coercive for him to demand something for his assistance.[19] Bill's follies, likewise, are his own doing, and not the result of a "set up" by Alfred, and if Alfred has come into possession of information that could be Bill's undoing, may he not offer to withhold it on his own terms?

BLACKMAIL AND EXPLOITATION

Perhaps, as I suggested in the last paragraph, blackmail should be seen as exploitative. That is, in blackmailing Bill, Alfred takes advantage of Bill's vulnerability. If so, should this justify its legal proscription?

Note, first of all, that the notion of exploitation is none-too-clear; it is, for example, used by Marxist writers to characterize ordinary capitalist labor relations: in making a profit, employers of labor are said to return to their employees less than the full value of their labor. Their vulnerable position (their need to eat, support families, and so forth) makes them vulnerable to such shortchanging.

But even with a less expansive and less tendentious understanding, there is a gap between exploiting another's vulnerabilities and doing something that should be considered illegal. If George exploits Harold's generosity to get a loan, or Ivan exploits John's poor management of a rival business or even John's sudden and debilitating illness to gain a larger share of the market or to put John out of business, neither George nor Ivan have done anything illegal, however opportunistic they may have been. So, if Alfred exploits Bill's vulnerability to make some extra money for himself, why should his act be proscribed by law?

BLACKMAIL AND PRIVACY

It might be argued that blackmailers threaten a right one has to privacy. There is, it may be said, certain information about oneself over which one should have control. It is "one's own business," and not the business of others. If it is to be "given out," it is appropriately given out only if one has consented to its being shared. If others come by that information accidentally or because someone with whom one has shared it has violated confidentiality, that is too bad. The third party is not guilty of any wrongdoing in having or sharing the information. However, if the third party, realizing that one wanted to keep the information to oneself, now chooses to use it as leverage for self-enrichment then that person is violating the privacy rights of another no less improperly than the person who taps one's telephone or bugs one's house or looks in one's personal files.

But there are significant differences between these various cases. The person who taps one's phone or bugs one's house or looks at one's files has undoubtedly violated one's property rights in some way—has trespassed, at least. Even private detectives are limited in what they may be permitted to do to obtain

Information. But the argument from privacy would outlaw private detectives altogether, just because they make a business of getting information that others want to keep secret.[20] The blackmailer need not violate any so-called privacy rights[21] to obtain his information: a sharp eye, an open ear, and a little advantageous positioning may be all that is necessary. Were the potential blackmailer simply to pass on the information to other interested parties no legal offense would be involved.[22] Why should that change if the blackmailer seeks to take advantage of what he knows by seeking cash for silence?

REPEAT BLACKMAIL

Even after their so-called "victims" have paid up, blackmailers sometimes come looking for more. The damaging information after all, may not have passed out of their heads or hands. It may therefore be argued that the only way to keep blackmailers from repeatedly approaching those who have bought their silence is to ban blackmail altogether.[23]

But repeated attempts at blackmail maybe prevented much more easily if blackmail is decriminalized. All that is required is that blackmailers sign a contract with the blackmailee that stipulates the blackmailers' permanent silence in return for a payment of $X. Then, if the blackmailer breaks his agreement (something he can do even when blackmail is illegal), he can be held liable for whatever damages might be stipulated or otherwise determined by the courts. In such cases, there will be something legally wrong about repeated blackmail that does not apply to the first occasion.

What is more, to outlaw blackmail in the first instance because blackmail demands may be repeated in the future is not to punish someone for a past crime done but for a (potential) future crime— hardly what we have in mind when we speak of criminal justice. If this were allowed to be a general legal principle, moreover, we would have to entrench in the law the concept of preventive detention, for all members of groups statistically over represented in the criminal category.

In any case, the argument from repeated blackmail would hold in only a limited number of cases— those in which there was some likelihood that a fur-

ther approach would be made or that the agreement would be breached. It would hardly provide a general argument against blackmail.

THE CONSEQUENCES OF BLACKMAIL

Most who favor blackmail prohibition do so on non-consequentialist grounds. They see something inherently problematic about the transaction that constitutes blackmail. Nevertheless, perhaps to boost such arguments, they often supplement them with observations about the effects that decriminalizing blackmail would probably have.

Richard Epstein, for example, suggests that were blackmail to be legalized, it would encourage the formation of corporations such as his hypothetical "Blackmail, Inc.," an organization devoted to ferreting out embarrassing (or worse) information on people and then blackmailing them to have it kept quiet.[24] Assuming the profitability of such an enterprise, a blackmailee might find himself the target of numerous independent approaches and, to meet the financial obligations incurred by this, might be led (or even encouraged) into committing crimes to pay for his chronic secrecy need.

But are such fears well founded? Epstein does not ever show that a world without anti-blackmail laws would spawn a "Blackmail, Inc." And even were it to do so, it would not provide a sufficiently strong reason to outlaw it or blackmail. The tastelessness or unseemliness of a social institution is not a sufficient reason to ban it or enterprises that exploit it. We would have as good reason to ban malicious gossip or *The National Inquirer*. And the social pressure that might lead a person into committing crimes to pay for secrecy would not differ substantially from the social pressure to "be somebody" or "impress others," motivations that may be just as likely to lead people to commit crimes.[25]

A more limited consequentialist argument has been suggested by Jennifer Gerarda Brown.[26] She suggests that were blackmail in cases of incriminating information legalized, there would likely be a reduction of crime. The criminally inclined would face the real possibility that they would have to "split" the profits of their criminality or otherwise pay to cover up their crimes, and such "costs" would constitute a significant deterrent to criminal activity. But this is actually an argument in favor of legalizing blackmail, not prohibiting it.

BUYING SILENCE

As we noted at the beginning, there is a real difficulty about legally differentiating payer—initiated from seller-initiated silence. If Bill learns that Alfred possesses damaging information that he might be inclined to disclose to others, and offers Alfred $5000 to keep quiet, it is hard to argue that Alfred has either coerced or exploited Bill, or that the transaction should be outlawed.

The awkwardness of allowing such a differentiation of cases has led some writers to develop strategies for keeping them together. Thus Scott Altman has claimed:

> Evidentiary and definitional problems with payer initiation can undermine any power it has to separate coercive from non-coercive transactions. Some bargains appear payer-initiated because the payer initially suggests the deal. But the payer might only learn of the other party's intent to reveal the embarrassing information after that party discloses this intent in order to elicit an offer or payment. Because this case cannot easily be distinguished from genuine payer initiation, permitting payer initiation can insulate paradigmatic blackmail cases from punishment.[27]

Similar arguments used to be employed against all forms of euthanasia, lest it should become a cloak for murder. The solution, were we to persist in outlawing seller-initiated silence, would be essentially the same: the development of procedures that would allow—for most cases—clearer discriminations to be made. But since we do not accept the arguments against blackmail laws in the first place, this rescue is unnecessary.

BLACKMAIL AND VICTIMIZATION

Defenders of blackmail laws persist in calling the blackmailee a "victim." Once seen as such, blackmailers are easily tarred with wrongdoing. Yet this characterization trades on the conflation of two distinct senses of "victim." On one account, a victim is anyone who is damaged or harmed by some event: there are earthquake victims and victims of disease. Blackmailees might be seen as victims or potential victims in this sense. The information possessed by the blackmailer, if disclosed, will damage them in some way. And one might argue that if one kind of damage has been averted it has been averted only at a cost, and—at a stretch—that one is a "victim" of circumstances that have a cost.

But the term "victim" may also be used in a more restricted sense—as when we speak of someone being victimized. Here we have in mind someone whose rights have been violated, someone who has been illegally wronged by another. Is the person who is blackmailed a "victim" in this second sense? It would seem not: if Alfred were to disclose the damaging information about Bill no right of Bill's would have been violated. That he should refrain from doing what he had a right to do in exchange for some monetary consideration does not change the matter.[28]

Those who persist in speaking of blackmailees as "victims" can mean "victim" only in the first sense. Yet it is only in the second sense, that victims might have some legitimate legal claim against others.

HARD CASES

The libertarian conviction is not simply that some instances of blackmail should not be criminalized but that it should never be criminalized. The libertarian therefore needs to confront some hard cases.

(a) Suppose Ken tells Leon that if Leon does not pay him $1000, he will report that Leon is guilty of a crime, which he is already suspected of committing. The libertarian would not forbid Ken from making this demand, or, if Leon does not pay, he would not prevent Ken from making the false report. Ken has free speech rights, including the right to speak falsely about another. True, the police-and courts-may subsequently accept Ken's word about Leon, so that Leon is unjustly punished, but if they do that, that injustice is on them for failing thoroughly to investigate Ken's report. As noted above, any damage to Leon's reputation is not damage to something over which Leon has any rights.[29]

While the foregoing is perfectly compatible with libertarian theorizing, it will strike many as repugnant. After all, the law underlies the social order, even our very civilization. If one may with impunity place a spoke in the wheel of justice in this manner, it bespeaks ill of the libertarian philosophy. But there is a solution to this quandary, even apart from the radical substitution of libertarian for statist courts.[30] And that is to pay or "tie up" witnesses so that they are contractually obligated to tell the truth upon pain of contract violation. One of the great injustices of our present court system is that witnesses are in effected drafted into testifying, and, so, for that matter, are jurors. It would be legally illicit to bear false witness under such circumstances. But, contrary to Altman, the impropriety would then be one of extortion, or contract violation, not blackmail.

(b) What if Michael learns that Nicholas has embezzled $1 million from his company, but suggests to Nicholas that for a payment of $56,000 he will not report it? Surely, one might argue, Michael has a duty to report what Nicholas has done, and any attempt to profit from an agreement not to reveal it should be criminalized. Although some libertarians might balk at cases of this kind, it is certainly open to others—myself included—to argue that whatever moral duty might be claimed to report the crimes of another (and not to profit from them), nevertheless there is no basis for legally requiring that the crimes of another should be reported. Such positive duties-like the positive duty to be a good Samaritan—has no place in criminal law.

CONCLUSION

Blackmail laws are often taken for granted. Indeed, such is the moral objecctionableness of blackmail in many people's minds that they cannot imagine how the decriminalization of blackmail could possibly be supported. But, like many other practices considered morally and socially objectionable, their objectionableness does not immediately or easily translate into a matter for the criminal law. It has been my contention that this is true of blackmail. As the paradox of blackmail should have alerted us, there's indeed something deeply problematic about crimi-

nalizing an act that conjoins two other acts that, in themselves, are not criminal.

NOTES

1. Williams, *Blackmail* [1954] *Crim. L. Rev.* 79, at 163 (1954). It was Williams who originally spoke of "the paradox of blackmail." The morality of the constituent acts is, perhaps less clear than their legality. But my concern here is with the justification of blackmail's criminalization not with its morality per se.

2. Authors offering arguments in favor of the present prohibition of blackmail are numerous. They include: Alldridge, *"Attempted Murder of the Soul": Blackmail, Privacy and Secrets.* 13 *Oxford J. Legal Stud.* 363 (1993); Altman, *A Patchwork Theory of Blackmail,* 141 *U. Pa. L. Rev.* 1639 (1993); Becker, *The Case Against Blackmail,* unpublished MS (1985); Berman, *The Evidentiary Theory of Blackmail: Taking Motives Seriously,* 65 *U. Chi. L. Rev.* 795 (1998); Boyle, *A Theory of Law and Information. Copyright, Spleens, Blackmail, and Insider Trading,* 80 *Calif. L. Rev.* 1413 (1992); Brown, *Blackmail as Private Justice,* 141 *U. Pa. L. Rev.* 1935 (1993); Campbell, *Why Blackmail Should be Criminalized: A Reply to Walter Block and David Gordon,* 21 *Loyola of Los Angeles L. Rev.* 883 (1933); Campbell, *The Anomalies of Blackmail,* 55 Legal Q. Rev. 382(1939); Coase, *The 1987 McCorkle Lecture: Blackmail,* 74 Va. L. Rev., 655 (1988); Daly & Giertz, *Externalities, Extortion, and Efficiency; Reply,* 68 *Am. Econ. Rev.* 736 (1978); DeLong, *Blackmailers, Bribe Takers, and the Second Paradox,* 141 *U. Pa. L. Rev.* 1663 (1993); Ellsberg, *The Theory and Practice of Blackmail,* in *Barganing: Formal Theory of Negotiation* 343 (O.R. Young, ed. 1975); Epstein, *Blackmail, Inc.,* 50 *U. Chi. L. Rev.,* 553 (1983); Evans, *Why Blackmail Should be Banned,* 65 Phil. 89 (1990); Feinberg, *The Paradox of Blackmail,* 1 Ratio Juris 83 (1988); J. Feinberg, *Harmless Wrongdoing* (1990); Fletcher, *Blackmail. The Paradigmatic Case,* 141 *U. Pa. L. Rev.* 1617 (1993); C. Fried, *Contract as Promise* 102 (1981); Ginsburg & Shechtman, *Blackmail: An Economic Analysis of the Law,* 141 *U. Pa. L. Rev.* 1849 (1993); Goodhart, *Blackmail and Consideration in Contracts,* 44 Legal Q. Rev. 436 (1928), repr. in A.L. Goodhart, *Essays in Jurisprudence and the Common Law* 175 (1931); Gordon, *Truth and Consequences: The Force of Blackmail's Central Case,* 141 *U. Pa. L. Rev.* 1741 (1993); Gory, *Nozick's Argument Against Blackmail,* 58 *Personalist* 187 (1977); Gorr, *Liberalism and the Paradox of Blackmail,* 21 *Phil. & Pub. Aff.* 43 (1992);

Haksar, Coercive Proposals, 4 *Pol. Theory,* 65 (1976); Hale, *Bargaining, Duress, and Economic Liberty,* 43 *Colum. L. Rev.* 603 (1943); Hale, *Coercion and Distribution in a Supposedly Non-Coercive State,* 38 *Pol. Sci. Q.* 470 (1923); Hardin, *Blackmailing for Mutual Good* 141 *U. Pa. L. Rev.* 1787 (1993); M. Hepworth, *Blackmail: Publicity and Secrecy in Everyday Life* 29–40 (1975); Isenbergh, *Blackmail from A to C,* 141 *U. Pa. L. Rev.* 1905 (1993); Jandoo & Harland, *Legally Aided Blackmail,* 27 *New L. J.* 402 (1984); Katz, *Blackmail and Other Forms of Arm Twisting,* 141 *U. Pa. L. Rev.* 1567 (1993); Katz & Lindgren, *Instead of a Preface,* 141 *U. Pa. L. Rev.* 1565 (1993); Landes & Posner, The Private Enforcement of Law, 4 *J. Legal Stud.* 1 (1975); Lindgren, *Unraveling the Paradox of Blackmail,* 84 *Colum. L. Rev.* 670 (1984) Lindgren, *More Blackmail Ink; a Critique of "Blackmail Inc.,"* Epstein's Theory of Blackmail 16 *Colum. L. Rev.* 909 (1984) Lindgren, *In Defense of Keeping Blackmail a Crime: Responding to Block and Gordon,* 20 *Loyola of Los Angeles L. Rev.* 35 (1986); Lindgren, *Blackmail: On Waste, Morals and Ronald Coase* 36 *U.C.L.A. L. Rev.* 597 (1989); Lindgren, *Kept in the Dark; Owen's View of Blackmail,* 21 *Conn. L. Rev.* 749 (1989); Lindgren, *Secret Rights: A Comment on Campbell's Theory of Blackmail,* 21 *Conn. L. Rev.* 407 (1989); Lindgren, *Blackmail: An Afterword,* 141 *U. Pa. L. Rev.* 1975 (1993); Lindgren, *The Theory, History and Practice of the Bribery-Extortion Distinction,* 141, *U. Pa. L. Rev.* 1695 (1993); Lyons, *Welcome Threats and Coercive Offers,* 50 *Phil.* 425 (1975); Murphy, Blackmail: A Preliminary Inquiry, 63 *Monist* 156 (1980); R. Nozick, *Anarchy, State, and Utopia* (1974); Owens, *Should Blackmail be Banned?,* 63 *Phil.* 501 (1979); R.A. Posner, *Economic Analysis of Law* (4th ed. 1992); Posner, *Blackmail, Privacy and Freedom of Contract,* 141 *U. Pa. L. Rev.* 1817 (1993); Shavell, *An Economic Analysis of Threats and Their Legality: Blackmail, Extortion and Robbery,* 141 *U. Pa L. Rev.* 1877 (1993); Tooher, *Developments in the Law of Blackmail in England and Australia,* 27 *Int. & Comp. L. Q.,* 337 (1978); Waldron, *Blackmail as Complicity,* unpublished MS (1992); Williams, Blackmail, supra n.1; Winder, *The Development of Blackmail,* 5 *Modern L. Rev.* 21 (1941).

3. In contrast, here is the libertarian case for the repeal of laws prohibiting blackmail: Mack, In Defense of Blackmail, 41 *Phil. Stud.* 273 (1982); M.N. Rothbard, *The Ethics of Liberty* (1998); M.N. Rothbard, *Man, Economy and State* 443 n. 49 (1993); Block, *The Blackmailer as Hero, The Libertarian Forum* 1 (Dec. 1972); W. Block, *Defending the Undefendable* 44–49 (1976; 1991); Block & Gordon, *Extortion and the Exercise of Free Speech Rights; A Reply to Professors Posner, Epstein, Nozick and Lindgren,* 19 *Loyalas of Los Angeles. Rev.* 37 (1985); Block, Trading Money for Silence, 8 *U. Hawaii L. Rev.* 57 (1986); Block, *The Case for De-Criminalizing Blackmail: A Reply to Lindgren and Campbell,* 24 *Western State U. L. Rev.* 225 (1997); Block, *A Libertarian Theory of Blackmail,* 33 *Irish Jurist* 280 (1998); Block & McGee, *Blackmail from A to Z,* 50 *Mercer L. Rev.* 569 (1999); Block, *Towards a Libertarian Theory of Blackmail, J. Libertarian Stud.* (forthcoming); Block & McGee, *Blackmail As a Victimless Crime,* 31 *Bracton L. J.* 24 (1999); Block, Kinsella, & Hoppe, *The Second Paradox of Blackmail, Q, J. Bus. Ethics,* (forthcoming); Block, *Let's Legalize Blackmail, Seton Hall L. Rev* (forthcoming); Block, *Blackmailing For Mutual Good Vermont L. Rev.* (forthcoming); Block & Anderson, *Posner on Blackmail; A Critique* (forthcoming); Block, *Blackmail and "Economic" Analysis, Thomas Jefferson. Rev.* (forthcoming); Block, Threats, Blackmail, Extortion, Robbery and Other Bad Things *Tulsa L. Rev.* (forthcoming); Block, *Blackmail is Private Justice, U. Brit. Colum. L. Rev.* (forthcoming).

4. Katz, *Blackmail and Other Forms of Arm Twisting,* supra n. 2, at 1567–68. Sometimes the threat may take the form of an offer—though of a form that Hillel Steiner refers to as a "throffer"—in which failure to take it up is associated with threatened consequences. See Steiner, *Individual Liberty,* 75 *ARISTOTELIAN SOC'Y PROC.* 33, at 39 (1974–75).

5. Mack, *In Defense of Blackmail,* supra n. 3, at 277. To counter the response that these are cases in which the blackmailees are being blackmailed only into not doing something, Mack suggests that the factory owner might be blackmailed into donating money for Cambodian relief (278).

6. Fletcher, *Blackmail; The Paradigmatic Case,* supra n. 2.

7. Gordon, *Truth and Consequences,* supra n. 2, at 1744.

8. See Altman, *A Patchwork Theory of Blackmail,* supra n. 2, at 1640.

9. Restaurants and supermarkets often donate "day old" food to the poor.

10. Gordon, *Truth and Consequences,* supra n. 2, at 1746. Mack's counterexamples (supra n. 5) cast some doubt on the generality of this claim.

11. In actual fact, a blackmailer's motives might be much more complicated. Although taking monetary advantage of a situation may well be one consideration, moral umbrage might also figure, along with, say, a more remote desire to obtain money to pay for a sick child's

operation. Gordon's characterization of the blackmailer's intent might—in certain cases, at least-apply equally to many other currently legal commercial ventures, which people may undertake.

12. Altman, *A Patchwork Theory of Blackmail*, supra n. 2, at 1641.

13. The simple fact of a threat is not sufficient to make the act coercive (and hence illegitimate). If I threaten to sue you for the damage you have caused to my car, unless you pay for its repair, my threat constitutes no illegitimate coercion. Should it be argued that some threats one has a right to make (as in the latter case) whereas others one has no right to make (as in blackmail), the libertarian will reply that this begs the question: Why should Alfred not threaten to reveal Bill's extra-marital affairs unless some payment is made?

14. Should it be objected that the destruction of reputation by means of disclosure of information about one does constitute a violation of rights (as is sometimes allowed by laws against libel and defamation), the libertarian will respond that the question is begged. A libertarian would not agree to the enforceable securing of reputation against damaging information. On this see W. Block, *Defending the Undefendable*, supra n. 3, at 59–62; M. Rothbard, *Ethics of Liberty*, supra n. 3, at 121–22.

15. For this argument, see Altman, *A Patchwork Theory of Blackmail*, supra n. 2, at 1642, fn. 11. For a rejoinder, see Block & McGee, *Blackmail as a Victimless Crime* supra n. 3, text at note 23.

16. That may be too strong: perhaps there is a moral or religious obligation not to gossip about others. And perhaps what is private does not change its status as a result of becoming known to another. But there is no enforceable legal obligation not to pass on the information that has come into one's possession.

17. Katz, *Blackmail and Other Forms of Arm-Twisting*, supra n. 2, at 1599.

18. See Altman, *A Patchwork Theory of Blackmail*, supra n. 2, at 1643.

19. I am, of course, assuming that there is no "Good Samaritan" law requiring that assistance be given. Were there such a law, a libertarian would of course oppose it.

20. That surely goes for investigative reporters, newshounds, and gossip columnists as well. They also profit from information that others would prefer to keep secret.

21. Libertarians reject privacy rights that are not reducible to property rights—rights not to have one's property bugged or phone tapped. See M. Rothbard, *The Ethics of Liberty*, supra n. 2, at 121–22.

22. Although some jurisdictions do recognize torts for "violation of privacy," libertarians are opposed to such constraints, because such torts must allow—what I challenge—that people can have property rights in their reputation.

23. See e.g., Fletcher, *Blackmail: The Paradigmatic Case*, supra n. 2, at 1623, 1627. See also Altman, *A Patchwork Theory of Blackmail*, supra n. 2, at 1648. Fletcher sees the possibility of the blackmailer's coming back for more as constituting a permanent domination of the blackmailer over the blackmailee. But that is only if no contract is made between the blackmailer and blackmailee forbidding any further claims.

24. Richard Epstein, *Blackmail, Inc.*, supra n. 2.

25. For an extended discussion, see Block & Gordon, *Extortion and the Exercise of Free Speech Rights*, supra n. 3.

26. Brown, *Blackmail as Private Justice*, supra n. 2.

27. Altman, *A Patchwork Theory of Blackmail*, supra n. 2, at 1649.

28. Indeed, one might be inclined to argue that the blackmailer displays a kind of decency toward the blackmailee by offering him a way out of his predicament (the blackmailer's opportunity to damage the potential blackmailee by disclosing—as he has a right to do—the information he has on him). The gossip provides no such injury-averting option. See Block & Gordon, *Blackmail, Extortion and Free Speech*, supra n. 3, at 39: "In contrast to the gossip, who tells the secret without even affording the victim the opportunity of purchasing silence, the blackmailer can be seen as a benefactor."

29. See W. Block, *Defending the Undefendable*, supra n. 3, at 59–62; also, M. Rothbard, *The Ethics of Liberty* supra n. 3, at 126–27.

30. On this see M. Rothbard, *For a New Liberty* (1973)

31

Is Punishing People for Bad Luck Wrong?

Consider two cases of wrongdoing that do not differ in any way at all except for what comes about entirely as a matter of chance. For example, suppose two people (call them Dee and Dum), each equally skilled with firearms, set out with the wicked intention to shoot and kill someone, simply for the fun of it. Each takes aim at his victim, exposing his victim to exactly the same risk of death. But while Dee strikes his mark, at the last moment a random gust of wind diverts Dum's bullet. Dee's victim dies; Dum's escapes unscathed. Because of bad luck, Dee is convicted of murder and sentenced to a horrible death in the electric chair. Dum is convicted only of *attempted* murder and gets off with a couple of years in prison. Is it wrong that Dee should be punished so severely by comparison with Dum, when the difference between the two situations is entirely due to chance? In other words, should we punish people for the contribution that dumb luck plays in the outcome of their actions? David Lewis addresses this problem in his contribution to this chapter.

Lewis begins by showing why our current practice of punishing the successful criminal more severely than the unsuccessful, where the difference in success is just a matter of luck, seems unjustified according to all the main theories of punishment. For example, suppose punishment is a matter of dishing out *just deserts*. Maybe the wicked deserve to be punished. But Dum and Dee are equally wicked, and so on these grounds they deserve the same punishment. Suppose those who knowingly expose others to a risk of harm deserve to be punished. Dum and Dee expose their victims to exactly the same risk of harm. Suppose the point of punishment is to deter others. But deterring murder is exactly the same as deterring attempts at murder. We can just as easily deter murder by penalizing those who attempt it as by penalizing those who succeed. Suppose the point of punishment (either by detention, death, or deportation) is to keep known offenders off the streets. Then since we have the same reason to suspect that Dum will offend again as to suspect that Dee will do so, it would be profitable to prevent both from roaming the streets. Therefore, we have reason to treat them the same. (In fact, although Lewis does not point this out, we surely have *more* reason to lock up Dum than to lock up Dee. After all, the guy Dee wanted to dispatch is gone, whereas Dum's target is still out there!)

One might argue that what Dee did was worse than what Dum did. Dee *murdered* his victim. Dum merely exposed his intended victim to a risk of death. Each violated his victim's right not to be exposed to the risk of death, but in addition Dee violated his victim's right not to be *killed,* whereas Dum didn't. Hence we are justified in punishing Dee more severely than Dum. Lewis has two replies to this: "We punish the *doer* not the *deed.*" And what Dum and Dee *did* was, in fact, the *same.* Dee's *performance* was (in some sense) exactly the same as Dum's *performance.* The different ways in which events unfolded after each made his respective contribution was purely a matter of chance. We can describe Dee's performance as an act of murder, while we can describe Dum's performance as an act of attempted murder. But these different descriptions refer to the very same kind of performance.

Lewis concludes from his survey that current theories of punishment cannot explain the differential treatment. The structure of the argument implicit here is the following:

P1   All plausible justifications for penal institutions entail that it isn't permissible for Dee (our successful murderer) and Dum (our unsuccessful would-be murderer) to suffer different penalties.

P2   According to our current penal practices, successful murderers should suffer more severe penalties than unsuccessful would-be murderers.

C   Our current penal practices are not plausibly justified.

The argument is valid, and the second premise seems to be true, so if one denies the conclusion one must deny premise 1. The rest of Lewis's article is effectively an attack on premise 1 of this argument.

Lewis outlines an interesting and novel institution of punishment—one we do not appear to employ and that does not appear to treat the successful criminal more harshly than his barely different unsuccessful counterpart. He calls it the *penal lottery.* Suppose we grant that subjecting a victim to a hundred-percent risk of a some harm should be punished by subjecting the perpetrator to some appropriate punishment—the *appropriate* punishment for a crime that inflicts a harm on someone with a hundred-percent likelihood. If you subscribe to the *jus talionis* (i.e., an eye for an eye), then the appropriate punishment has to be *identical* to the harm done or the quantity of harm done. So, for example, the appropriate punishment for subjecting someone to a hundred-percent risk of death would be death. Let's assume this eye-for-an-eye principle is valid. (Nothing substantive hangs on this assumption.) What is the appropriate punishment if a criminal subjects his victim to risk of some harm where the risk is less than a hundred percent say, eighty-percent? According to the penal lottery, we should punish him by subjecting him to an 80 percent risk of the appropriate punishment had he been successful. So, someone who subjects his victim to an 80 percent risk of being killed, regardless of whether he was successful or not will, if convicted, be punished by being subjected to an 80 percent risk of being killed. He might be led to the electric chair and forced to participate in a lottery with an 80 percent risk of losing. He may have to choose one straw from a set of ten, eight of which are short. If he draws a short straw, he is strapped in and the current is switched on. If he draws a long straw, he walks free.

The penal lottery has a number of obvious virtues. First, there is a clear sense in which it treats the successful criminal and his barely different unsuccessful counterpart alike. Dum and Dee will face exactly the same lottery. Second, it seems to satisfy the principle of *proportionality*—that the punishment fit the crime. The criminal faces exactly the same risk of comparable harm to which he exposed his victim. Lewis goes on to argue that the penal lottery is not obviously unjust. He then argues, somewhat surprisingly, that if the penal lottery is just, then so are our current practices.

Lewis's ingenious argument has the following structure. He starts with the penal lottery case—calling it Case 1 in a sequence of six cases. Then he amends Case 1 slightly, calling it Case 2. In Case 2 the lottery that will seal the criminal's fate if he is convicted is held in advance of the trial and of the verdict, and the results of the drawing of straws are kept secret. A state official—known as the "Public Drawer"—draws lots in the criminal's stead and holds onto them in case they are needed. If the criminal is convicted, then the public drawer announces the results. However, since it is not known in advance of the court's determination which particular risk of death the criminal exposed his victim to, the public drawer will have to run a number of different lotteries: one for a risk of nine out of ten, another for a risk of eight out of ten, and so on. When the court announces its verdict—say, 80 percent risk of death—then the Public Drawer takes out the sealed envelope with "80 percent" written on it and reveals the result of the eighty-percent lottery. If he drew a short straw in that lottery, the convicted criminal dies. If he drew a long straw, the convicted criminal goes free.

If Case 1 is just, then Case 2 is also just, because the difference in the *timing* of the lottery cannot make any morally significant difference. What's important for justice is not when the lottery is held, but that the lottery exposes the criminal to the very same risk of death as that to which he exposed his victim.

Lewis carries on in this way, making small (or not so small) changes to the way in which the penal lottery is conducted, and he claims that none of these changes undermines the justice of the institution, provided that the previously considered institution is just. Lewis's final case, Case 6, corresponds to our current practice. The argument goes as follows:

P1 Case 1 (the penal lottery) is just.
P2 If Case 1 is just, then Case 2 is just.
P3 If Case 2 is just, then Case 3 is just.
P4 If Case 3 is just, then Case 4 is just.
P5 If Case 4 is just, then Case 5 is just.
P6 If Case 5 is just, then Case 6 (our current practice) is just.

———

C   Our current practice is just.

In Case 2, the results of the various lotteries are kept secret until it is determined what risk the criminal exposed his victim to. Case 3 is merely Case 2 without the secrecy. The result of all the lotteries is made public in advance. Making that information public in advance cannot change the justice of imposing the penalty.

In some cases, however, advance notice of the lottery results might drain the courtroom enterprise of the drama—for example, if all the draws come out negative. To remove this defect, we could assign a minimum prison sentence in such a case. This is Lewis's Case 4.

To determine which lottery envelope to open, the court will need to ascertain two things: first what actually happened, and second, what risk was imposed on the victim. This is a difficult. We could simplify the task of determining the risk by finding out what happened and then running a perfect *reenactment* of the event. In a perfect reenactment, the victim's actor will run the same risk of death as the original victim. We can then use the reenactment *itself* as a lottery that determines the criminal's fate (if found guilty). If the acting victim dies, then so too does the criminal. If not, not. However, if we ran the reenactment lottery in advance, we would have to run a series of reenactments (one for each of the possible ways the criminal might have committed the crime).

Case 5 would be difficult and costly to run (because of all those actors' fees!). Case 6 removes this serious defect by replacing various reenactments of the crime with the *enactment* of the crime. We take the *original crime* to be *its own perfect reenactment,* and let that stand as the lottery that determines whether the criminal will face the electric chair or not. If the criminal is found guilty, then he is sentenced to die, if in the original lottery (the crime itself) his victim died. Otherwise he gets the modest sentence (as in Case 4). This is Case 6. It is cheaper and more accurate than Case 5 because we don't need to find out exactly how the crime was committed. We only have to determine that the criminal intended to harm his victim. We don't have work out the risk. We don't have to stage any reenactments at all. The criminal's fate is decided by a lottery that imposes on him *exactly* the same risk of death as his victim faced *in whatever sense or senses of risk might be relevant.*

Case 6 is virtually identical to our current practice. The only difference is in what it is we think we are doing. (We don't think of the practice as a penal lottery, with the original crime serving as a lottery.) The only defect with our current practice is that it sows confusion, because we tend to think that the successful criminal deserves a worse punishment than the unsuccessful, when in fact we simply collapse two lotteries into one—the first lottery, to which the victim is subjected by the criminal, and the second lottery, in which the criminal faces a lottery just like the one to which he subjected his victim.

QUESTIONS TO CONSIDER

We have here an argument that relies on the repeated application of a single, simple rule of inference *modus ponens:*

A

If A then B

B

It is thus clearly valid, and any attack on Lewis's argument will have to attack one of the six premises. Probably the most controversial premise is the first. Is the penal lottery a just way to determine the fate of a convicted criminal? That depends on what makes for just punishment, so here one can use Lewis's tactic and run through the various justifications.

• Would the penal lottery be as successful as a deterrent? (The successful murderer may not suffer very much even if found guilty. But what about unsuccessful would-be murderers?)

• Would the penal lottery adequately serve the expressive function of punishment?

• What about getting potential criminals off the streets? Clearly it would release some successful murderers onto the streets sooner than otherwise, but would it put away other potential criminals who would otherwise be released.

• Now consider whether or not the convicted criminal gets what he *deserves.* Here the key question is the following: Is a *risk* of a harm (or a *chance* at good) worth the same as some proportion of that harm (or of that good)? Is (for example) a one-in-ten chance of winning $1,000,000 really worth $100,000?

• What is the maximum amount you would pay to have a one-in-ten chance of winning $1,000,000? Whatever it is, it is almost certainly less than $100,000. Conversely, how much would you pay to avoid a risk of a one-in-ten chance of losing $1,000,000? (Although this sounds strange, we do all pay to avoid being involved in lotteries that subject us to a certain risk of loss or harm. That is precisely what insurance is all about.) Clearly $100,000 is probably too much, but $100 is probably too little. But there must be some amount you would be willing to pay, say, $20,000. If that is the sum you would put up, that means you judge a one-in-ten risk of losing $1,000,000 to be worth the loss of $20,000. So it seems that we do think that the risk of loss is itself a harm we are willing to pay to avoid.

• In setting up the initial problem, Lewis employs an argument by process of elimination (see the Introduction). He assumes that if neither the deterrence theory the expressive theory the defense theory, nor the desert theory can explain differential treatment of criminals, then it must be unjust. But does Lewis consider every theory of our penal institutions?

• One theory Lewis does not consider is the *restitution theory* (see chapter 26). Suppose one viable justification for (something like) our penal institutions is the theory of restitution: that criminals should restore to their victims what they have wrongly taken from them. A surprising range of penal practices can be rationalized using this model. Even incarceration may be so justified, because incarceration may be the best way of restoring security to the indirect victims of a crime. If the purpose of the criminal justice system were to make criminals restore to their victims what they had taken away, would we be justified in punishing successful criminals more severely than unsuccessful ones? Suppose Joe and Jason both try to steal $1000 from Jane. Joe succeeds, and Jason doesn't. What would constitute appropriate restitution in both cases, and would we demand more from Joe than from Jason?

David Lewis | # The Punishment That Leaves Something to Chance

I

We are accustomed to punish criminal attempts much more severely if they succeed than if they fail. We are also accustomed to wonder why. It is hard to find any rationale for our leniency toward the unsuccessful. Leniency toward aborted attempts, or mere preparation, might be easier to understand. (And whether easy or hard, it is not my present topic.) But what sense can we make of leniency toward a completed attempt—one that puts a victim at risk of harm, and fails only by luck to do actual harm?

Dee takes a shot at his enemy, and so does Dum. They both want to kill; they both try, and we may suppose they try equally hard. Both act out of malice, without any shred of justification or excuse. Both give us reason to fear that they might be ready to kill in the future. The only difference is that Dee hits and Dum misses. So Dee has killed, he is guilty of murder, and we put him to death.[1] Dum has not killed, he is guilty only of attempted murder, and he gets a short prison sentence.

Why? Dee and Dum were equally wicked in their desires. They were equally uninhibited in pursuing their wicked desires. Insofar as the wicked deserve to be punished, they deserve it equally. Their conduct was equally dangerous: they inflicted equal risks of death on their respective victims. Insofar as those who act dangerously deserve to be punished, again they deserve it equally. Maybe Dee's act was worse than Dum's act, just because of Dee's success; but it is not the act that suffers punishment, it is the agent. Likewise, if we want to express our abhorrence of wickedness or of dangerous conduct, either exemplar of what we abhor is fit to star in the drama of crime and punishment. Further, Dee and Dum have equally engaged in conduct we want to prevent by deterrence. For we prevent successful attempts by preventing

From David Lewis, "The Punishment That Leaves Something to Chance," *Philosophy and Public Affairs* 18, no. 1 (Winter 1989): 53–67. Some notes and some parts of the text have been deleted. Reprinted by permission of Princeton University Press.

attempts generally. We cannot deter success separately from deterring attempts, since attempters make no separate choice about whether to succeed. Further, Dee and Dum have equally shown us that we might all be safer if we defended ourselves against them; and one function of punishment (at any rate if it is death, imprisonment, or transportation) is to get dangerous criminals off the streets before they do more harm. So how does their different luck in hitting or missing make any difference to considerations of desert, expression, deterrence, or defense? How can it be just, on any credible theory of just punishment, to punish them differently? . . .

II

In what follows, I shall propose a new rationale. *I do not say that it works.* I do say that the new rationale works better than the old ones. It makes at least a prima facie case that our peculiar practice is just, and I do not see any decisive rebuttal. All the same, I think that the prima facie case is probably not good enough, and probably there is no adequate justification for punishing attempts more severely when they succeed.

Our present practice amounts to a disguised form of *penal lottery*—a punishment that leaves something to chance. Seen thus, it *does* in some sense punish all attempts alike, regardless of success. It is no less just, and no more just, than an undisguised penal lottery would be. Probably any penal lottery is seriously unjust, but it is none too easy to explain why.

By a penal lottery, I mean a system of punishment in which the convicted criminal is subjected to a risk of punitive harm. If he wins the lottery, he escapes the harm. If he loses, he does not. A pure penal lottery is one in which the winners suffer no harm at all; an impure penal lottery is one in which winners and losers alike suffer some harm, but the losers suffer more harm. It is a mixture: part of the punishment is certain harm, part is the penal lottery.

An overt penal lottery is one in which the punishment is announced explicitly as a risk—there might be ways of dramatizing the fact, such as a drawing of

straws on the steps of the gallows. A covert penal lottery is one in which the punishment is not announced as a risk, but it is common knowledge that it brings risk with it. (A covert lottery must presumably be impure.)

A historical example of an overt penal lottery is the decimation of a regiment as punishment for mutiny. Each soldier is punished for his part in the mutiny by a one-in-ten risk of being put to death. It is a fairly pure penal lottery, but not entirely pure: the terror of waiting to see who must die is part of the punishment, and this part falls with certainty on all the mutineers alike. . . .

V

. . . I shall introduce the differences between an overt penal lottery and our present practice one at a time, by running through a sequence of cases. I claim that at no step is there any significant difference of justice between one case and the next. Such differences as there are will be practical advantages only, and will come out much in favor of our present practice.

Case 1 is the overt penal lottery as we have imagined it already, with one added stipulation, as follows. We will proportion the punishment to the heartedness of the attempt, as measured by the risk of death[2] the criminal knowingly and wrongfully inflicted on the victim. We will do this by sentencing the criminal to a risk equal to the one he inflicted on the victim. If the criminal subjected his victim to an 80 percent risk of death, he shall draw his straw from a bundle of eight short and two long; whereas if he halfheartedly subjected the victim to a mere 40 percent risk, he shall draw from four short and six long; and in this way his punishment shall fit his crime. Therefore the court's task is not limited to ascertaining whether the defendant did knowingly and wrongfully subject the victim to a risk of death; also the court must ascertain how much of a risk it was.

Case 2 is like Case 1, except that we skip the dramatic ceremony on the steps of the gallows and draw straws ahead of time. In fact, we have the drawing even before the trial. It is not the defendant himself who draws, but the Public Drawer. The Drawer is sworn to secrecy; he reveals the outcome only when and if the defendant has been found guilty and sentenced to the lottery. If the defendant is acquitted and the drawing turns out to have been idle, no harm done. Since it is not known ahead of time whether the sentence will be eight and two, four and six, or what, the Drawer must make not one but many drawings ahead of time. He reveals the one, if any, that turns out to be called for.

Case 3 is like Case 2, except without the secrecy. The Drawer announces at once whether the defendant will win or lose in case he is found guilty and sentenced. (Or rather, whether he will win or lose if he is sentenced to eight and two, whether he will win or lose if he is sentenced to four and six, and so on.) This means that the suspense in the courtroom is higher on some occasions than others. But that need not matter, provided that the court can stick conscientiously to the task of ascertaining whether the defendant did knowingly and wrongfully subject the victim to risk, and if so how much risk. It is by declaring that a criminal deserves the lottery that the court expresses society's abhorrence of the crime. So the court's task is still worth doing, even when it is a foregone conclusion that the defendant will win the lottery if sentenced (as might happen if he had won all the alternative draws). But the trial may seem idle, and the expression of abhorrence may fall flat, when it is known all along that, come what may, the defendant will never face the lottery and lose.

Case 4 is like Case 3, except that we make the penal lottery less pure. Losers of the penal lottery get death, as before; winners get a short prison sentence. Therefore it is certain that every criminal who is sentenced to the lottery will suffer at least some penal harm. Thus we make sure that the trial and the sentence will be taken seriously even when it is a foregone conclusion that the defendant, if sentenced, will win the lottery.

Case 1 also was significantly impure. If the draw is held at the last minute, on the very steps of the gallows, then every criminal who is sentenced to face the lottery must spend a period of time—days? weeks? years?—in fear and trembling, and imprisoned, waiting to learn whether he will win or lose.

This period of terror is a certain harm that falls on winners and losers alike. Case 2 very nearly eliminates the impurity, since there is no reason why the Drawer should not reveal the outcome very soon after the criminal is sentenced. Case 3 eliminates it entirely. (In every case, a defendant must spend a period in fear as he waits to learn whether he will be convicted. But this harm cannot count as penal, because it falls equally on the guilty and the innocent, on those who will be convicted and those who will be acquitted.) Case 4 restores impurity, to whatever extent we see fit, but in a different form.

Case 5 is like Case 4, except that the straws are replaced by a different chance device for determining the outcome of the lottery. The Public Drawer conducts an exact reenactment of the crime. If the victim in the reenactment dies, then the criminal loses the lottery. If it is a good reenactment, the risk to the original victim equals the risk to the new victim in the reenactment, which in turn equals the risk that the criminal will lose the lottery; and so, as desired, we punish a risk by an equal risk.

If the outcome of the lottery is to be settled before the trial, as in Cases 2, 3, and 4, then it will be necessary for the Drawer to conduct not just one but several reenactments. He will entertain all reasonable alternative hypotheses about exactly how the crime might have happened—exactly what the defendant might have done by way of knowingly and wrongfully inflicting risk on the victim. He will conduct one reenactment for each hypothesis. The court's task changes. If the court finds the defendant guilty of knowingly and wrongfully inflicting a risk of death, it is no longer required also to measure the amount of risk. Nobody need ever figure out whether it was 80 percent, 40 percent, or what. Instead, the court is required to ascertain which hypothesis about exactly how the crime happened is correct. Thereby the court chooses which of all the hypothetical reenactments is the one that determines whether the criminal wins or loses his lottery. If the court finds that the criminal took careful aim, then the chosen reenactment will be one in which the criminal's stand-in also took careful aim, whereas if the court finds that the criminal halfheartedly fired in the victim's general direction, the chosen reenactment will be one in which the stand-in did likewise. So the criminal will be more likely to lose his lottery in the first case than in the second.

The drawbacks of a lottery by reenactment are plain to see. Soon we shall find the remedy. But first, let us look at the advantages of a lottery by reenactment over a lottery by drawing straws. We have already noted that with straws, the court had to measure how much risk the criminal inflicted, whereas with reenactments, the court has only to ascertain exactly how the crime happened. Both tasks look well-nigh impossible. But the second must be easier, because the first task consists of the second plus more besides. The only way for the court to measure the risk would be to ascertain just what happened, and then find out just how much risk results from such happenings.

Another advantage of reenactments over straws appears when we try to be more careful about what we mean by "amount of risk." Is it (1) an "objective chance"? Or is it (2) a reasonable degree of belief for a hypothetical observer who knows the situation in as much minute detail as feasible instruments could permit? Or is it (3) a reasonable degree of belief for someone who knows just as much about the details of the situation as the criminal did? Or is it (4) the criminal's actual degree of belief, however unreasonable that might have been? It would be nice not to have to decide. But if we want to match the criminal's risk in a lottery by straws to the victim's risk, then we must decide. Not so for a lottery by reenactment. If the reenactment is perfect, we automatically match the amount of risk in all four senses. Even if the reenactment is imperfect, at least we can assure ourselves of match in senses (3) and (4). It may or may not be feasible to get assured match in senses (1) and (2), depending on the details of what happened. (If it turns out that the criminal left a bomb hooked up to a quantum randomizer, it will be comparatively easy. If he committed his crime in a more commonplace way, it will be much harder.) But whenever it is hard to get assured match in senses (1) and (2), it will be harder still to measure the risk and get assured match in a lottery by straws. So however the crime happened, and whatever sense of match we want, we do at least as well by reenactment as by straws, and sometimes we do better.

Case 6 is like Case 5, except that enactment replaces *re*enactment. We use the original crime, so to speak, as its own perfect reenactment. If the criminal is sentenced to face the lottery, then if his victim dies, he loses his lottery and he dies too, whereas if the victim lives, the criminal wins, and he gets only the short prison sentence. It does not matter when the lottery takes place, provided only that it is not settled so soon that the criminal may know its outcome before he decides whether to commit his crime.

The advantages are many: we need no Drawer to do the work; we need not find volunteers to be the stand-in victims in all the hypothetical reenactments; the "reenactment" is automatically perfect, matching the risk in all four senses; we spare the court the difficult task of ascertaining exactly how the crime happened. If we want to give a risk for a risk, and if we want to match risks in any but a very approximate and uncertain fashion, the lottery by enactment is not only the easy way, it is the only remotely feasible way.

The drawback is confusion. When a criminal is sentenced to face the lottery by straws, nobody will think him more guilty or more wicked just because his straw is short. And when a criminal is sentenced to face the lottery by reenactment, nobody will think him more guilty just because the stand-in victim dies.[3] But if he is sentenced to the lottery by enactment, then one and the same event plays a double role: if his victim dies, that death is at once the main harm done by his crime and also the way of losing his lottery. If we are not careful, we are apt to misunderstand. We may think that the successful attempter suffers a worse fate because he is more guilty when he does a worse harm, rather than because he loses his lottery. But it is not so: his success is irrelevant to his guilt, his wickedness, his desert, and his sentence to face the lottery—exactly as the shortness of his straw would have been, had he been sentenced to the lottery by straws.

VI

I submit that our present practice is exactly Case 6: punishment for attempts regardless of success, a penal lottery by enactment, impurity to help us take the affair seriously even when the lottery is won, and the inevitable confusion. We may not understand our practice as a penal lottery—confused as we are, we have trouble understanding it at all—but, so understood, it does make a good deal of sense. It is another question whether it is really just. Most likely it isn't, but I don't understand why not.

NOTES

1. I do not wish to enter the debate about whether the traditional death penalty is ever justified. If you think not, substitute throughout whatever you think is the correct maximum penalty; my argument will go through almost without change.

2. I note a complication once and for all, but I shall ignore it in what follows. The relevant risk is not really the victim's risk of death, but rather the risk of being killed— that is, of dying a death which is caused, perhaps probabilistically, and in the appropriate insensitive fashion, by the criminal's act. Likewise for the criminal's risk in the penal lottery. (On probabilistic and insensitive causation, see my *Philosophical Papers,* vol. II [New York: Oxford University Press, 1986], pp. 175–88.)

3. If it were known that the victim's risk was fifty-fifty, or if we did not care about matching risks, we could just as well reverse the lottery by enactment: the criminal loses if the victim lives, wins if the victim dies. Certainly nobody will think the criminal is more guilty if the victim *lives.*

32

Is Refusing to Work Wrong?

Suppose you suddenly and unexpectedly inherited an enormous amount of money, an amount so large that it would easily enable you to spend the rest of your life in comfort without ever doing a day's worth of productive labor. One question you might ask yourself under such circumstances would be whether living such a life would make you happy. After all, many people would find a life without productive labor (the life, for example, of the ski bum or beach bum) to be unsatisfying. But let us suppose that your answer to this first question is "*yes*": You would be perfectly happy spending the rest of your life living off your lucky windfall inheritance and you have absolutely no desire to engage in any form of productive labor, either in the context of a paid job or in a volunteer setting, despite the fact that you are fully capable of doing such work. If this is the case, then a second, distinctly moral question arises: Would there be anything wrong with your choosing to live such a life? Most people are inclined to say that there would not be anything morally wrong with your choice. It might be better if you engaged in some productive tasks, they might concede, but your declining to do so would not be in any positive way immoral. The life of leisure, such people emphasize, does nothing to harm anyone or to violate anyone's rights, and so. On this popular account, there is nothing morally wrong about avoiding productive labor.

The thesis of Lawrence C. Becker's provocative article, "The Obligation to Work" is that this commonsense view is mistaken. Becker argues that if you are capable of doing productive labor, then you have a moral obligation to do so, and that the person who refrains from doing so is, in his word, a "parasite." And although Becker recognizes that the claim he wishes to defend is an unpopular one, he attempts to defend it by showing that it follows from other beliefs that most people are likely to share. More specifically, Becker attempts to argue for his position by means of an argument from inference to the best explanation (see section 4.3 in the Introduction). In a variety of contexts, Becker argues, people will agree that if one person voluntarily benefits a second person, then the second person incurs a moral obligation to benefit the first. Most people, for example, agree that it would be wrong for you not to assist friends or parents who have benefited you in the past. Becker maintains that the best explanation of our assessment of such cases is that we are committed to a more general principle of what he calls *proportionate reciprocity,* a principle on which a person who benefits from the voluntary acts of another incurs a moral obligation to benefit the other person in a manner and amount that is at least roughly equivalent to the benefit he has received. But if this is correct, Becker argues, then you have incurred a moral obligation to work. As a person who lives in a complex market society, Becker maintains, you have benefited from (and continue to benefit from) the fact that others do productive work. If this empirical claim about your life in a complex market society is correct, then the result of conjoining it with the general principle of proportionate reciprocity is that you have incurred a moral obligation to benefit those whose labor has benefited you.

To say that you have an obligation to benefit such people in some way or another is not the same as saying that you have an obligation to do productive labor in particular. But Becker attempts to move from the former claim to the latter by arguing that, in general, obligations of proportionate reciprocity require us to confer benefits in the same way that the benefits we receive were conferred. By claiming that the kinds of considerations that sometimes justify our repaying our benefactors in other ways do not arise in the context of the benefits we have received from the productive labor of others. Sometimes, for example, it is more efficient to pay for a benefit of one kind by conferring a benefit of a different kind, and sometimes doing so is fair. But Becker maintains that these considerations do not arise in the case of productive labor. The result is an argument against the morality of avoiding work that can be represented as follows:

P1 If A benefits from B's actions, then A incurs a moral obligation of reciprocity to benefit B.

P2 You have benefited from, and continue to benefit from, the fact that others do productive work.

C1 You have incurred a moral obligation of proportionate reciprocity to benefit those from whose productive work you have benefited.

P3 If you have incurred a moral obligation of proportionate reciprocity to benefit those from whose productive work you have benefited, then you have incurred a moral obligation to do productive work.

_____

C2 You have incurred a moral obligation to do productive work.

P1 of the argument, which represents the principle of proportionate reciprocity, is meant to be justified on the grounds that it does the best job of accounting for our judgments about such cases as helping our friends and parents. P2 is meant to be a simple empirical truth about life in a complex market society. And P3 is grounded in Becker's claim that the kinds of considerations that sometimes justify paying back one kind of benefit with a different kind do not apply in the case of productive labor.

QUESTIONS FOR CONSIDERATION

If all three premises of Becker's argument are accepted, his conclusion must be accepted as well. A critical evaluation of his argument should therefore attempt to raise questions about at least one of these premises.

• Since P1 rests on an argument from inference to the best explanation, for example, you might consider whether Becker's principle of proportionate reciprocity really does provide the most satisfying account of the reactions we have to the particular cases he cites. Could there be some other reason we have obligations to our friends and parents in such cases? If so, is Becker guilty of overgeneralizing from these cases? (see chapter 11 for some further ideas along these lines).

• Becker admits that in at least some contexts it is permissible to repay one kind of benefit for another. For example, you benefit from the fact that others serve in the military, but this does not mean that you must do so also. You can instead do your fair share to support the military through your payment of taxes. Because of this, you could consider whether Becker is too quick to insist on the truth of P3. Even if you owe a debt to the society that has provided so much to you, couldn't it be enough simply to donate some of your inheritance to charities and continue to live a life of unproductive leisure? Becker thinks he has an adequate reply to this objection, but you should think about whether you find it convincing.

• Finally, even ski bums end up benefiting some of those who do productive labor. After all, if you choose to live the life of the ski bum, you will be giving lots of money to ski companies, to waiters in fancy restaurants and lodges, and so on. As long as you compensate those who benefit you by paying for the goods and services you receive from them, shouldn't that count as discharging your obligation of proportionate reciprocity?

• Again, Becker claims that the answer to this question is "No." While you should make sure you understand Becker's reason for saying this, you should also make sure that you do not simply accept his assertion uncritically.

Lawrence C. Becker | # The Obligation to Work

Many of the putative obligations of citizenship are nonvoluntary. The obligation to obey the law applies to children well before the law itself declares them capable of making enforceable, voluntary agreements. And every existing state enforces obligations on adults who never consented to those obligations—or even to any second-level procedure (such as majority rule or judicial review) which they imagined might produce such obligations. (I am not thinking here of the sweeping tacit agreements one might attribute to good-spirited, thoughtful, civic-minded people. I am thinking instead of the more meager agreements we must be content with in the case of mean-spirited, shortsighted, resolute free riders. At least for them, it is true that many putative citizenship obligations are nonvoluntary.) My purpose here is to explore one such putative obligation: the obligation to do socially useful work. It is an interesting case because people who agree that work is a good thing differ sharply over whether it is a social obligation,[1] and people who agree that it is an obligation differ sharply and vehemently over whether

the obligation to work should be enforced by law. I shall argue that work *is* a social obligation. . . .

A GENERAL SOCIAL OBLIGATION TO WORK

The questions I want to explore are, first, whether a general citizenship obligation to work can be justified and, second, whether such an obligation, once justified, ought to be enforced by law. These are uncomfortable questions for most citizens of the United States. Here, of course, there is no constitutional duty to work. In fact, the U.S. Constitution does not specifically enumerate a citizen's duties at all. It enumerates the powers of state and federal governments, powers which logically entail the existence of liabilities of the form: "If the state makes a law . . . then citizens have the duty to. . . ." And, of course, the rights granted to citizens clearly imply corresponding duties in everyone to respect those rights. But the only obligations explicitly mentioned in the Constitution are those on governments and governmental

From Lawrence C. Becker, "The Obligation to Work," *Ethics* 91 (1980): 35–49. Some notes and some parts of the text have been deleted. Reprinted by permission of University of Chicago Press.

officials. Furthermore, anything like the USSR's parasite law is politically unthinkable here.

On the other hand, a "work ethic" has considerable power. Some opponents of welfare argue vigorously that work requirements should be made a condition for receipt of the benefits; and even opponents of such strings on welfare do not argue that people should not work if they are able.

Nonetheless, people who are brought up, politically, on the liberal theory of justice are likely to find the parasite laws deeply offensive. One source of offense is the actual implementation of the laws in the Soviet Union: the regime of labor camps, the paternalistic methods of enforcement, and the occasional abuse of the laws to get at political dissidents. Another source is the conviction that work obligations should not be made a matter of law at all. So far, the general Western antipathy to these laws (which I certainly share) seems unremarkable.

But another source of offense is clearly regrettable: the unreflective bias against certain citizenship obligations—work being among them—that liberalism tends to produce. Liberalism teaches that there is something natural, fundamental, and inescapable about people's right to liberty. Consequently, the duty to respect others' liberties (though derivative) is equally natural and inescapable. But an obligation to work for the benefit of others is seen as artificial rather than natural and as something which—if it can ever be justified at all—must be subordinate to the demands of liberty.

This is a simple non sequitur. It must be granted that nonvoluntary obligations to pay taxes and to do socially useful work are artificial, that is, that their moral basis lies in the ongoing human artifacts known as social institutions rather than in an imaginary state of nature. But it does not follow that their justification is any more difficult than the justification of the (equal) right to liberty or that they must be subordinate to liberty.

The Reciprocity Argument

I wish to argue that there is at least one nonvoluntary social obligation, namely, reciprocity: the obligation to make a proportional return of good for a good received. In outline, the argument runs as follows.

No one is self-made. Whatever good there is in our lives is, in part, a product of the acts of others. Moreover, it is also the product of others' fulfilling their putative social obligations: obligations of restraint (such as are found in the criminal laws against murder and theft), of care (as found in the law of negligence), of effort ("trying" to help), or of contribution (paying taxes).

All the standard theories of justice support a requirement (obligation) of reciprocity, that is, a proportional return of good for good. (Returning bad for bad is a more complex problem and may be ignored here.) Such a practice has obvious social utility and would be adopted by utilitarians either as a rule or as part of a "role." A society in which people returned good for good seems likely to be preferred by rational contractors to one which differed only in the respect that reciprocity was not observed. And the concept of reciprocity seems embedded in natural rights theory as well, for example, in the reciprocal relationship between rights and obligations. (When I respect your right to liberty, you must respect mine. When I invade your right, you may invade mine to protect yours.)

Fulfilling the requirement of reciprocity sometimes involves meeting the demands of one's benefactors because sometimes only that will count as a "fitting and proportional" return of good for good. (Think of a friend asking for a favor in return for past good deeds: "No, I don't want the money back. What I need is the use of your car for the day.") Citizenship obligations may be thought of as the institutionalized demands of our benefactors for reciprocity. Thus, an important class of nonvoluntary social obligations is justified.

Now, of course, there are severe limits to the obligations which can be so established. In particular, the requirement here is only that we return good for *good* and then only in proportion to the good received. Thus, we need not reciprocate for malicious acts which accidentally produce good (unless it is by being ineptly malicious in return). And we need not reciprocate for the "good" done by speculators in reciprocity—people who shower us with unwanted benefits to put us in their debt. At least, to the extent that such speculation is a bad thing, we need not return good for it. The requirement of reciprocity is not strong enough to justify Christian charity. In short, although there are interesting complications left to be explored, the reciprocity argument, as I shall call it, is a promising avenue for the justification of nonvoluntary citizenship obligations. For the sake of the argument to follow, I shall simply assume that it is sound.

The question then becomes whether it is possible to derive a general work obligation from the requirement of reciprocity. By a "general" obligation, I mean a nonvoluntary obligation which applies "generally" or "equally" across the whole class of members of society. And in one sense of 'equal obligation' this is obviously impossible. Obligations must be scaled to competence, ability, and benefits. People differ widely along those three dimensions, so widely that it is obvious that it would be impossible to justify any proposal to require the same work from everyone. (Similarly, it would be unreasonable to require everyone to pay the same dollar amount of taxes.)

But I shall use another sense of equal obligation here, one which makes it clear that a work obligation could in principle apply equally to all members of society. I shall say that work obligations are equal if, after they are scaled to competence, ability, and benefits, they apply to everyone. Thus, all members of a society may be said to be equally obligated to work even though the quality and quantity of required work varies widely from member to member.

The question now is whether there is any reason to conclude that people do have a social obligation to work. Here, two things can be shown: first, that the form of a justification is easily available, but that, second, whether the form can be filled in and applied to a given society depends on contingent truths about that society. As a result, it is not possible to show, from purely conceptual considerations alone, that an equal obligation to work exists. The best one can do is to establish a presumption in favor of it.

The form of a justification is not difficult to see, once the requirement of reciprocity is granted. Each of us is the product, in part, of the work done by others, work which creates an environment in which whatever happiness we have is possible. It is true that we did not ask to be born; we did not (at least at first) intentionally make demands on others; we did not

invite the nourishment they gave and continue to give us. But it is also true that most of our benefactors had no part in bringing us into their midst. Yet their work continues to benefit us, whether they like it or not.

I have assumed that reciprocity is required for the good provided to us by the restraint, care, efforts, and contributions of others. Reciprocity requires the return of benefits which are fitting and proportional to the ones received. When the benefits we receive come from the work others do—rather than just from their restraint or carefulness—a purely passive response from us (i.e., restraint or care) may not be fitting or proportional to the benefits we have received. Work may have to be reciprocated by work. This is one source of a general social obligation to work, which can, in principle, be institutionalized as a citizenship obligation.

Here is another source: Each of us is a burden on others. Our mere existence diminishes natural resources; we pollute; we consume the time and energy of those who have to deal with us. We are a net burden on others if we do not make an offsetting contribution to their welfare. Now, it is a fact that some people do make an effort to offset these burdens and succeed in offsetting them. Reciprocity to them is as much in order as it is for people who produce "positive" good for us. And reciprocity here may also require a contribution produced by effort.

Obligations based on the reciprocity argument are in principle directed only to one's benefactors, a set of people which need not be coextensive with society, or the nation, or the family as a whole. Yet social obligations, as defined at the outset, are those whose beneficiaries "of record" are all the members of the group. So how is it that the reciprocity argument can create a social obligation?

There are two ways. For one thing, some goods are not partitionable; they are public goods—goods which, if they are available at all, are equally available to everyone. If the requirement of reciprocity yields an obligation to produce or contribute to the production of a public good, then it has yielded what is in effect a social obligation. But more importantly, reciprocity may require compliance with the demands of one's benefactors, demands institutionalized as membership obligations designed by one's benefactors to benefit all members. Hence, reciprocity may yield social obligations directly, as well as obligations which are merely inescapably social ones "in effect."

Showing how an equal work obligation might be justified does not take us very far, however. What we want to know is whether such a social obligation is justified—here and now. More generally, we want to know when work is the form of reciprocity which can be required of us. One obvious answer is that when reciprocity is required, and when work is the only way reciprocity can be given, then work is required. But when is that the case? When is it that nothing but work will do? Here, a purely conceptual analysis fails to yield detailed guidance, because so much depends on empirical findings about existing social conditions. But a few things of interest can be said. For one thing, the justifiability of producing various social goods is a logically prior question. It may have been evident to the Soviets that in order to achieve the goals of rapid industrialization, a stable socialist economy, and an improved standard of living for all, work would have to be made a citizenship obligation. But the logically prior question is whether it is justifiable to require people to contribute to producing those social goods.

Second, after the social goals are decided, one needs to know whether work from everyone is needed or just needed from a subset of the population. If it is just the latter, then the general work obligation could at most be a conditional one, similar to the obligation to serve in the military. If more workers are needed (due to a lack of volunteers or a temporary crisis), then a work obligation may be imposed.

Finally, before a general work obligation is imposed, the question of acceptable substitutes for work must be carefully considered. Even if a given quantity of political party activity is a social necessity, and even if an obligation to produce such activity falls equally on all citizens, it does not quite follow that the obligation must actually be to work in party politics. Money contributions might be an acceptable substitute. Some of the relevant concerns here are simply about efficiency: Can the job be done if some people offer only substitutes for work? Can the job be done well if they offer substitutes? Will

there be a net loss of social good if they do so? And so on.

But there are questions of fairness and fittingness here too. Just as it is inappropriate (unfitting) to make a cash payment in place of returning a friend's dinner invitation, so too it may sometimes be unfitting to buy one's way out of socially useful work. And it may even be unfair, as when the wealthy were once permitted to buy their way out of the draft, effectively shifting the risks of war inequitably onto the poor.

Beyond these very general remarks, however, I cannot deduce any further guidance on when a social obligation to work is justifiable. To get conclusions about specific obligations, specific social conditions will have to be considered in detail. It seems reasonable, however, to assume that a general obligation to do socially useful work is justifiable in the case of contemporary, "developed" societies. So much work is required to keep them going, and we all profit so much from the work of others in these societies, that it certainly seems reasonable to put the burden of proof on people who claim that they themselves (or any others they mention) have no obligation to work. People who are able to work, and do not work, are parasites, however unattractive and emotionally loaded that label is. People in this society all live, in part, off the labor of others. And there is a chronic oversupply of jobs which need to be done to sustain and improve the quality of life for us all. (I am not speaking here of simply income-producing jobs.) So reciprocity in the form of work seems not only appropriate but necessary in our present circumstances. At least, it seems reasonable to adopt a rebuttable presumption in favor of the obligation to work. . . .

NOTE

1. By "obligation" I mean an act that is required, as opposed to one that is merely good or permitted. A "social" obligation is a requirement whose beneficiaries are all the members of the group which imposes the obligation: Alternatively, social obligations are requirements whose fulfillment produces (or contributes to) a public good—a good like clean air which, if available at all, is equally available to all.

33

Is Copying This Book Wrong?

As digital technology becomes more and more powerful, the moral problems associated with copying become more acute, as is illustrated by the recent legal wrangles over the downloading of music and film files from the Internet. There are quite strict laws governing the copying of such works, but what we are interested in here is the moral question. Would it be immoral for you to make a complete photocopy of this book? Selmer Bringsjord argues that it would not. He uses the example of copying a rented video, not with a view to selling it but to playing it back at some later stage. His argument, like Lewis's argument in chapter 31 involves a sequence of possible situations, each of which is held to differ only insignificantly from its predecessor. The first situation in Bringsjord's sequence is one that most of us judge to be permissible. At each stage, the new situation is constructed in such a way that it does not differ from its predecessor in any *morally* significant way. The last item in the sequence is the situation in which you use a mechanical device to copy a videotape and play it back at some later time.

Bringsjord uses a somewhat forbidding notational apparatus in setting up his argument, but in fact the argument is really very simple. We start with a familiar case (Case 1): Someone rents a video, watches it, returns it, but from time to time thinks about it, remembers scenes, and so on, for her own enjoyment. Case 1 is clearly morally permissible. Through a series of cases (Case 2, 3, and so on), Bringsjord gradually improves the person's memory and allows her to share her memories with others. By the time we get to Case 8, she is endowed with a perfect visual and auditory memory and extraordinary communicative abilities so that she can induce in her friends' minds accurate simulations of the movie. Case 9 involves using a brain scanner to extract her faithful memories and project them (somewhat fuzzily) onto a screen, again for her friends' consumption and enjoyment. Bringsjord then perfects the scanning and projecting equipment so that, by Case 12, our heroine provides us with a VHS recorder and projector. At no stage, Bringsjord argues, do we introduce anything that would be morally significant enough to make the difference between judging the behavior morally permissible and morally impermissible. What Bringsjord's argument exploits is the fact that the brain is both a recording device and a transmitting device—although for the purposes of faithfully copying and transmitting copyrighted content it is not a particularly reliable one. So he improves the brain, step by step, forcing us to imagine someone with a brain that is a perfect recording device. He then adds a little mechanical aid that enables the possessor of that brain to record and transmit the content more efficiently to a more publicly accessible medium than speech allows.

No one would disagree with the validity of the argument (which, like Lewis's in chapter 31, is a series of simple conditionals). Nor would anyone dispute the first premise of the argument (i.e., that Case 1 is morally permissible). Hence any disagreement with the conclusion will have to take issue with one of the intermediate premises of the form:

If Case n is morally permissible, then Case n + 1 is also morally permissible.

Which step or steps take us across the threshold from the morally permissible to the morally impermissible? Bringsjord considers various possibilities and rejects them.

There is, however, another kind of objection to this form of argumentation. Philosophers are very familiar with what is called the *sorites* paradox. Take a concept like *short.* Some adults are short (those under three feet tall, for example) and some are not (those over six feet tall). Now, if a person is short, then someone else who is barely taller but who looks exactly the same height must also be short. (How could the difference between someone who is short and someone who is tall be something that a normal observer wouldn't even *notice?*) So a difference in height of, say, one eighth of an inch, will not make the difference between someone who is short and someone who isn't. But now we can show that *everyone is short!* Take the three-foot-tall guy (Case 1). No one will dispute the premise that the guy in Case 1 is short. The guy in Case 2 is three feet and one eighth of an inch. If the guy in Case 1 is short, then the guy in Case 2 is also short (since that one-eighth of an inch clearly cannot make the difference between being short and being not-short). But if we repeat this again and again, we will be able to conclude (after two hundred eighty-eight steps) that the six-foot-tall guy is also short. And that's plainly false.

Philosophers are genuinely puzzled about sorites paradoxes. Should we say that there is a *precise* point (say, four feet seven and five-eighths of an inch) such that everyone under that is short, and everyone who is at least that is not short? This seems weird because our concept of *short* is simply not that precise. Most of us might be unclear about what to say about the guy who is four feet seven and five-eighths of an inch, but it is unlikely we will say "He's obviously not short, but the guy who is four feet seven and a half *is* obviously short." And since the concept of *short* is *our* concept, it cannot be completely opaque to us where the cutoff is. Bringsjord replies that the concept of *short* generates a genuine paradox because we both already *know* that the conclusion is false and cannot point to the false conditional in the argument. However, his argument does not produce a genuine paradox because we do not *know* that the conclusion is false. That's precisely what is at issue. So there is no paradox.

QUESTIONS FOR DISCUSSION

What is interesting about Bringsjord's argument is not so much the individual steps (to some of which you might object) or even the conclusion. Rather it is the argumentative method. We might call it the *method of tiny increments.*

• We are wondering about the permissibility of practice Z. We start with a practice that we all agree is permissible, say A. Then we describe a series of very small changes—from A to B, from B to C, and so on. None of these changes *by itself* seems to be morally weighty enough to take us out of the realm of permissibility. Finally we make the last incremental step, from Y to Z, and conclude that Z is also permissible. But is this argumentative strategy sound?

• Consider an analogy. We know that there can be two patches of color, A and B, such that no one looking at them side by side would say that they were different. They *look* exactly the same when they are compared directly. We can also have another pair, B and C, which also look exactly the same when placed side by side. However, when we place A and C side by side there is a small discernible difference in their color. That is to say, a sequence of step-wise indiscernible differences can add up to a discernible difference. Could this be the same with our moral judgments, our judgments about what seems morally permissible? A might *look* to be morally on a par with B, and B might likewise *look* to be morally on a par with C. But is that any guarantee that A and C are morally on a par? No. And it is no guarantee even that they will not look to be morally on a par.

• Here is a moral example. Suppose Joe does something deliberately and knowingly and without Jim's consent that will shorten Jim's life expectancy by one thousandth of one second. Is this morally impermissible? Surely not. Since we cannot discern differences in the length of life that are that small, surely Joe's actions can't matter, morally. By the same token, *if* it would not be wrong of Joe to shorten Jim's life expectancy by some period of time, say *t seconds,* it would not be wrong of Joe to shorten Jim's life expectancy by *t + 1/1000 seconds.* Now we can put the initial premise together with all the relevant conditionals and conclude that it is not wrong for Joe to shorten Jim's life expectancy by one hundred years. And that's false, because you can only shorten someone's life expectancy by that large amount by doing something that would kill him now. And Joe's killing Jim now might well be morally impermissible.

• We are thus led to the conclusion that there is something wrong with the argumentative method of tiny increments. And yet, what exactly is it? On that question, we will leave you hanging.

Selmer Bringsjord | # In Defense of Copying

There rages a brouhaha revolving around the question: Is it morally permissible to copy rented movies (or books, articles for students, computer software, and so on)? I think the answer to this question is "Yes," and in order to defend this opinion I'll present a deductive argument for the schema

T   *Ceteris paribus,* it is morally permissible for s to copy [. . .], without permission, and without payment, for her use and the use of others, as long as s does not sell [. . .] and [. . .] is in public circulation

where [. . .] may be filled in with such expressions as "rented video movies," "computer software," "paintings," "books," and so on.

Here's the plan I follow. In section II present an argument schema A for T; how one fills in A depends on how one fills in [. . .]. In II, I fill in [. . .] with 'rented video movies' and present twelve thought experiments which yield an instance of A which shows the "movie instance" of T to be true. It will become transparent that the argument schema A can be filled in successfully for [. . .] set to the other expressions I've mentioned. Finally, in Section III, I rebut some objections against my case for T.

Selmer Bringsjord, "In Defense of Copying," *Public Affairs Quarterly,* 3 (1989): 1–9. Notes have been deleted. Reprinted by permission of North American Philosophical Publications.

I. THE ARGUMENT SCHEMA

Let $A_1, A_2, A_3, \ldots, A_{n+1}$ denote $n + 1$ moral agents, not necessarily distinct. Then the argument schema A runs as follows:

(1) A_1's actions in case (=thought-experiment) 1 are morally permissible.

(2) If A_1's actions in case 1 are morally permissible, then A_2's actions in case 2 are morally permissible.

(3) If A_2's actions in case 2 are morally permissible, then A_3's actions in case 3 are morally permissible.

.

.

.

(n) If A_n's actions in case n are morally permissible, then A_{n+1}'s actions in case n + 1 are morally permissible.

Therefore:

(n + 1) A_{n+1}'s actions in case n + 1 are morally permissible.

Now once n is fixed to some natural number, the resultant argument is formally valid by successive applications of *hypothetical syllogism,* and one application of *modus ponens.* The length of an instance of A is determined by how many cases one chooses to devise; this choice is in turn determined by how "fine grained" one wants to be with regard to copying [. . .]. The intuitive notion of "fine grained" will be clarified ostensively below.

II. THE THOUGHT EXPERIMENTS

Now here's an instance of T with its corresponding instance of A. Set [. . .] = 'rented video movies,' $n = 12$. The twelve cases are as follows.

Case 1. A_1 rents a video movie *m,* watches it on her VCR, and then A_1 returns *m.* A_1 liked *m,* and so in the future she sometimes thinks about the scenes, dialogue, and so on, in *m* for her own enjoyment.

Case 2. A_2 has a very good memory. Like A_1, she rents a movie *m,* watches it on her VCR, and returns it. A_2 liked *m,* and so in the future she sometimes thinks about the scenes, dialogue, and so on, in *m* for her own enjoyment. Because A_2, has a good memory, she is sometimes able to make the scenes in *m* quite vivid in her mind.

Case 3. A_3 has an *extraordinary* memory. She behaves just like A_2, except that because A_3 has an extraordinary memory, she sometimes is able to make the scenes in *m utterly* vivid in her mind.

Case 4. A_4, a genius of some sort, is blessed with what you might call a superhuman visual and auditory memory. Like A_3, she rents a movie *m,* watches it, and then returns it. The viewing of *m* affected A_4 deeply: she loved the movie. And so in the future she sometimes employs her special gift when thinking about the scenes and dialogue in *m.* Because A_4 has a memory like the one she has, she is able to run the scenes of *m* by her "mind's eye" exactly as they ran past her eyes when *m* ran on her VCR.

Case 5. A_5 has the superhuman memory of A_4, but is also blessed with excellent verbal fluency. She behaves like A_4, except that in addition to running *m* by her mind's eye exactly as it ran past her eyes when running on her VCR, she is able to, in good part, express verbally what is going on in the movie as she recollects it.

Case 6. A_6 is like A_5, but has *astonishing* verbal fluency. And so she is able not only to run the scenes of *m* by her mind's eye exactly as they ran past her actual eyes and at the same time express what's happening in *m,* but she can express to an astonishingly high degree what is going on in the movie as she recollects it. She can also repeat dialogue in *m* verbatim, with an inflection that mirrors that of the actors.

Case 7. The agent here, A_7, acts just like A_6, except that she visualizes and describes *m* in "real time": if *m* was two hours long, it takes her two hours to visualize and describe *m.*

Case 8. The agent here, A_8, acts just like A_7, except that she entertains her friends for the length of *m* by visualizing and describing it for them so that they can get the gist and, even picture, in their own minds of some of the images of *m.*

Case 9. Agent A_9 acts just like A_8, except that she entertains her friends by creating and using a remarkable machine, *D*, which scans the mental imagery and auditory memories in her brain and projects them onto a screen for her enjoyment and for the enjoyment of her friends. *D* isn't fine-tuned: the screen shows a series of events which, though *somewhat* like what you see when you watch *m*, is a bit vague, choppy, and out of focus.

Case 10. A_{10} behaves like A_9, except that she has perfected the brain scanning and projecting device *D*.

Case 11. This case involves two agents: B_1 and A_1. B_1 behaves just about like A_{10}, except that rather than using *D*, she attaches *D* firmly to her head, and then takes a drug which renders her semiconscious, but which leaves her in a state which allows another person to operate her visual system and *D*. B_1 has given permission to a friend, A_{11}, to do the following while B_1 is "asleep." A_{11} can rent *m*, run it on her VCR while B_1 is "watching" it, return *m*, and then later flip on the device *D* hooked up to B_1 in order to run, for her and her friends, what is now fairly called a copy of *m*. A_{11} does exactly what she's been given permission to do.

Case 12. this case, like its predecessor, involves two agents: B_2 and A_{12}. B_2 behaves similarly to B_1, except that what she does is give A_{12}, a great inventor and scientist, permission to build a portable self-contained device D' modeled on the composite device which is B_2's brain and *D*. A_{12} builds D' and it works perfectly. A_{12} rents *m*, uses D' to make a copy of *m*, returns *m*, and views the copy of *m* in the future with friends.

Denote the instance of *A* to which cases 1 through 12 give rise by "A^{movie}." And let *T* with [...]= "rented video movies" be T^{movie}. I think A^{movie} is a sound argument for T^{movie}. Clearly, this argument is formally valid, and, I would say, just as clearly, premise (1) is true. Each of the material conditionals encapsulates, of course, the contention that the change from case n to case n + 1 isn't such as to make a moral difference; and so each conditional is in some sense a challenge to those who think A^{movie} unsound: find a morally significant distinction between A_i's actions in case i and A_{i+1}'s actions in case i + 1.

Before considering objections, let me point out that it does not require much ingenuity to follow this recipe so as to fashion a series of cases which support *T* with [...] set to "computer software," "books," "paintings," and so on.

III. OBJECTIONS

The first type of objection consists in the claim that there is a faulty transition, that is, that one of the aforementioned challenges can be met. Some of the software creators I know have gone feverishly out of their way to try to find a morally significant difference between two successive cases. I think this line of attack is unpromising, however. For what happened in my debates with software creators is that the instance of *A* in question, to their dismay, ballooned to as many as 30 cases. And in light of this, or rather in light of the apparently limitless expansion of *A*, I'm inclined to think that for every reasonable assignment to [...] there is an instance of *A* with n set to a natural number large enough to yield a sufficiently fine-grained proof of the instance of *T* in question.

The rather rhetorical previous paragraph can, to some degree, be focused if we consider a specific objection regarding a faulty transition: "The transition I find problematic is that between Case 11 and Case 12—a transition from a brain to a mechanical recording device. At this transition it becomes clear that the argument depends on the brain being treated as a machine all along—as just a naturally occurring recording device. On this implicit but crucial assumption, memorizing isn't merely analogous to copying, it's the *same* as copying. But the moral equivalence between copying and remembering is precisely what's at issue, and so to tacitly assume equivalence is to beg the question."

There are (at least) *three* promising routes one can take in rebutting this objection. In the *first route* one "expands" the transition in question. It's possible to do so in a way that requires as much imagination as the original sequence Case 1–Case 12. Though I believe such an expansion surmounts the objection under consideration, it requires too much space to present here. And anyway, I suspect that my opponent would still insist that there's a transition where a mechanical device is substituted for the brain—a transition she will find problematic.

The *second route* is to confront the objection head on, by claiming that it's plausible, on independent grounds, that the brain *is*, in *some* sense, a copying device. If the justification for this claim comes from somewhere outside A^{movie}, then the argument wouldn't be question-begging. Is there independent support for the claim that the brain is in some sense a copying device? If it's true that the brain represents reality in some principled way, then I think so. In some quarters of Artificial Intelligence (AI), for example, what agents believe (know, remember, hope for, . . .) are thought to be formulas in some formal language Σ which includes first-order logic. Visual information grasped by the agent, in this scheme, would be expressed in Σ; and so, then, would our movie m. Now this particular scheme may seem just an idealization, but something like it is, I think, taken very seriously in AI, psychology, and the philosophy of mind. To rebut the charge of circularity, I could let this idealization undergird my thought experiments.

The *third route* is different from, but arises out of, the second. In it one works out some of the details in the idealization alluded to in the second route, and then claims that this idealization doesn't imply that the brain is "a naturally occurring recording device," but rather that it implies something much more *subtle* about the brain. This route seems pretty powerful to me, largely because I see the "just a" in "just a naturally occurring copying device" as a gloss. For the debate to continue down route three, it will be necessary for my opponent to get somewhat more precise about "x is a copying device." As things stand, I should think there are permissible construals of this locution that leave my argument intact. The point here can to some extent be made by way of a little thought experiment: Suppose that I have a computer program P, hooked up to sensors, capable of taking in movies (books, paintings, computer code, . . .) and representing them in Σ; and suppose P, when queried in English, can translate these queries into Σ, reason,

and supply replies first in Σ, and then in English (all of this in such a way that the creators of P like to say that their program *understands*). Would we want to say that P is *copying* the movies (books . . .) and the queries? The answer isn't clear. And I submit that things are similarly unclear when we ask about what the brain is doing on an explicit version of the idealization I've sketched above. But then the charge of circularity against A^{movie} is inconclusive.

Attacks on A^{movie} which aim at transitions seem unpromising. I think a more formidable type of objection involves an appeal to paradoxes like the Short Man.

The paradox of the Short Man, "PSM" for short, is familiar: You start with a man, say, one inch in height. Such a man, surely, is short. Adding one billionth of an inch (or one trillionth, or one zillionth, . . .) to the height of any short man still leaves you with a short man—this too seems true. But these two facts, with the aid of either mathematical induction or successive application of natural deduction rules, entail, say, that a man 500 feet in height is short, which is surely absurd.

How does PSM figure in an objection to A? The objection is that my argument is just like that used in PSM. And since the argument in PSM is unsound, so is mine. Unfortunately, this is a very weak objection. Here's why.

What makes PSM a paradox, indeed what makes a paradox in general, is that the argument involved is formally valid and has apparently obviously true premises, yet the conclusion is absurd. So to say that argument A^{movie} is of the same type as that employed in PSM implies that A^{movie} is formally valid and has what appears to be obviously true premises. But to say this is to come very close to conceding that A^{movie} is sound! In fact the only thing in the way of accepting the argument now would seem to be the absurdity of the conclusion. But clearly, the conclusion in A^{movie} isn't absurd, since, among other reasons, there are a number of rational people who affirm it. It's hard to see how this appeal to PSM has any force.

There is, however, another objection to A involving PSM, one I've encountered in conversation, and I think it's more sophisticated than its predecessor.

It's simply this. What PSM shows is that, although it seems incredible from an intuitive standpoint, and although no one knows where it falls, there just *is* an absolute cut-off between short and non-short. And A^{movie} can be handled the same way: although it seems hard to believe, and although it can't be located, there just *is* a transition which is crucial—a transition in which you go from moral permissibility to moral *im*permissibility.

What can be said in response to this objection? Two things, both, I think, cogent. One, this way of handling PSM is almost universally regarded to be unpalatable. Two, this way of handling PSM would be the way to go only because *not* to go it would mean swallowing an utterly absurd proposition, namely that a man 500 feet in height is a short man. But accepting the conclusion of A^{movie} is not to do something irrational at all; it just may be that A is part of a recipe for showing that copying things for personal use is morally permissible. Keeping an open mind about the moral permissibility of copying should be easier than keeping an open mind about whether or not a 500 foot man is short.

The final objection against A based on PSM runs as follows. What PSM shows us is that some concepts, indeed many concepts, are just too vague to figure in arguments like that used to generate PSM.

When we try to use these vague concepts as if they *aren't* vague, we get into trouble, trouble like PSM. Now what A shows, my opponent here maintains, is that the concept of moral permissibility is *also too* vague to be used in the way that I want to use it. PSM shows that you can capitalize on the vagueness of "short" to generate the consequence that a man 500 feet in height is short. A shows that you can capitalize on the vagueness of "morally permissible" to generate the consequence that copying *a la T* is morally permissible.

This final objection, unsurprisingly, is no more powerful than its predecessor. Let me essentially repeat myself: It may very well be that "short" should not be used as it is in the argument which generates PSM. If so, what tells us this is that by so using "short" we arrive at an utter absurdity. But what tells us that we can't employ "morally permissible" in the way A employs it? Surely one thing which *doesn't* tell us we can't so employ it is the absurdity of the conclusion. After all, the conclusion *isn't* absurd. To say that it is is just to beg the question against the proponent of A and T.

I conclude that T, in light of A, is true. At the very least I think I've shown that T deserves to be taken seriously, which is something many people just don't do.